MW01251007

The Developing Child

Understanding

Children

and Parenting

GLENCOE

The Program

Student text

We have met your requests to:

- retain the popular ages-and-stages approach
- increase the family orientation
- emphasize parenting skills and work-and-family issues
- address teen parenting issues
- strengthen observing and participating components
- emphasize school-to-work skills and competencies
- provide performance assessment activities...

and the seventh edition of **Developing Child** *is bigger and better than ever!*

Teacher's Wraparound Edition

Guide students through the text with extensive lesson plans and a multitude of activities that help you teach, reinforce, and expand your students' learning.

Student Workbook

Study guides and activity sheets reinforce learning and application of content. The *Teacher's Annotated Workbook* provides convenient answers.

Testmaker Software

A totally flexible bank of computerized test items provides you with a quick tool for assessing students' progress.

Teacher's Classroom Resources

Hundreds of activities, handouts, worksheets, and visuals help you serve the widely diverse students in today's child development classes.

Student Text

DEVELOPING CHILD:

Understanding Children and Parenting

has been revised and expanded to include the topics you asked for, and reorganized into Units, Chapters, and short lesson-sized Sections.

Sections open with objectives and vocabulary, and they close with a review that helps students check their own mastery of content.

Essential information is highlighted in specially-designed features.

Building Self-Esteem

feature boxes present a variety of tips for your students to apply to children.

Parenting in Action

dialogues help students make the connection between theory and practical application.

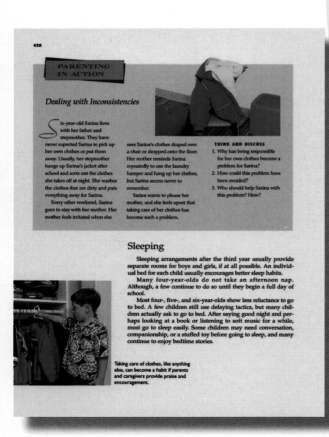

Ask the Expert

feature boxes give answers to real-life questions and dilemmas.

Positive Parenting Skills

offer your students concrete ways to interact with children.

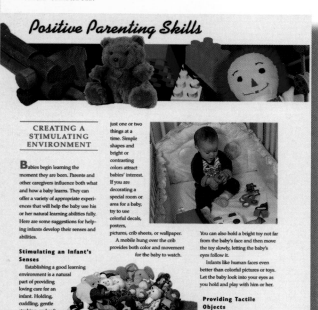

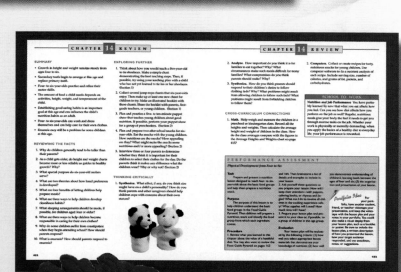

Chapter reviews

include review, exploration, critical thinking, cross-curricular connections, performance assessment, and a special school-to-work feature.

Cultural Exchange

features give your students a broader perspective and appreciation of child care practices around the world.

Cultural Exchange

A COMMUNITY OF FAMILIES

Many parents worry about how the emotional and social development of their children will be affected by having multiple caregivers. Reassurance comes from research that suggests the number of caregivers is not as important as the stability and responsiveness of those caregivers. A study of children raised in an Israeli kibbutz, for example, supports this idea. In the kibbutz, young children are raised communally by several caregivers. The children stay in residential nurseries and see their parents only a few hours a day or even just on the weekends. These children show normal, healthy development, both emotionally and socially, as long as the caregivers are sensitive and responsive.

The Effects of Substitute Child Care

Professionals in all areas of child care and development agree that emotional and intellectual development are directly influenced by a child's environment and experiences, beginning at birth. These professionals consider parents a child's best source of love and learning.

Many child development specialists advise that a parent should stay home to provide child care for as long as possible. For many parents, however, the longest possible options for staying home may not extend more than a few weeks beyond the child's birth. Extended maternity or paternity leave is not an option for many working parents. Does this mean that parents must choose between having an income to pay household bills and giving their child a good start in life?

Fortunately, parents do not usually have to make this kind of choice. Long-term studies find that good substitute care has no adverse effects on children's intellectual and emotional development. The key, of course, is finding good substitute care. Parents must spend time, care, and effort selecting a substitute caregiver for their child. The best caregiver is someone who enjoys the child and spends time playing with him or her. In a group facility, there should be a warm, caring atmosphere and enough staff to provide each child with individual attention.

Whether a child is cared for in a private home or in a child care center, parents may choose to drop in periodically to check the facility and its care.

Teacher's Wraparound Edition

Lesson Plans

Extensive lesson plans organize all components and provide discussion starters, motivators, vocabulary builders, and cross-curricular connections.

Activities for observing/participating with children, critical thinking, and journal writing provide you with multiple options for teaching.

Additional Teaching Support

- **"More About"** boxes are extra tidbits you can use to add sparkle and build enthusiasm as you teach.

- **"Healthy Families/Healthy Children"** boxes help you teach about family wellness issues and safety.

- **"Observing and Participating"** boxes help you guide students' observation, participation, and portfolio activities.

- **"Teen Parenting"** boxes give you additional help in teaching pregnant or parenting teens.

- Other boxes provide you with multiple options for teaching **Ages-and-Stages**, **Cooperative Learning** activities, **Classroom Management** ideas, and **Performance Assessment** strategies.

Using the Teaching Features

Specially-designed boxes such as *Developing a Portfolio, School-to-Work,* and *Technology Option* provide guidance for using the teaching feature. Answers to all review questions are also provided.

Teacher's Classroom Resources

Developed specifically to ease your preparation time, the *Teacher's Classroom Resources* provides you with ready-to-use teaching materials in booklet format. These resources will save you hours of preparation time.

- **Observing and Participating with Children** - activities and observation guides.

- **Creative Activities for Children** - exercises and games.

- **Teen Parenting** - teaching tips, activities, and handouts.

- **Cooperative Learning** - teaching strategies and activities.

- Glencoe also provides you with **Reproducible Lesson Plans** and a complete **Testing Program.**

- **Performance Assessment** - activities and strategies. New in the 7th edition!

- A packet of **Full-Color Transparencies** completes the program.

For more information, contact your nearest regional office or call 1-800-334-7344.

Northeast Region
Glencoe/McGraw-Hill
15 Trafalgar Square #201
Nashua, NH 03063-1968
603-880-4701 • 800-424-3451
Fax: 603-595-0204
(CT, MA, ME, NH, NY,RI, VT)

Mid-Atlantic Region
Glencoe/McGraw-Hill
P.O. Box 458
Hightstown, NJ 08520-0458
609-426-5560 • 800-553-7515
Fax: 609-426-7063
(DC, DE, MD, NJ, PA)

Atlantic-Southeast Region
Glencoe/McGraw-Hill
Brookside Park
One Harbison Way, Suite 101
Columbia, SC 29212
803-732-2365 • 800-731-2365
Fax: 803-732-4582
(KY, NC, SC, VA, WV)

Southeast Region
Glencoe/McGraw-Hill
6510 Jimmy Carter Blvd.
Norcross, GA 30071
770-446-7493 • 800-982-3992
Fax: 770-446-2356
(AL, FL, GA, TN)

Mid-America Region
Glencoe/McGraw-Hill
936 Eastwind Drive
Westerville, OH 43081
614-890-1111 • 800-848-1567
Fax: 614-899-4905
(IN, MI, OH)

Great Lakes Region
Glencoe/McGraw-Hill
846 East Algonquin Road
Schaumburg, IL 60173
708-397-8448 • 800-762-4876
Fax: 708-397-9472
(IL, MN, WI)

Mid-Continent Region
Glencoe/McGraw-Hill
846 East Algonquin Rd.
Schaumburg, IL 60173
708-397-8448 • 800-762-4876
Fax: 708-397-9472
(IA, KS, MO, ND, NE, SD)

Southwest Region
Glencoe/McGraw-Hill
320 Westway Place, Suite 550
Arlington, TX 76018
817-784-2113 • 800-828-5096
Fax: 817-784-2116
(AR, LA, MS, NM, OK)

Texas Region
Glencoe/McGraw-Hill
320 Westway Place, Suite 550
Arlington, TX 76018
817-784-2100 • 800-828-5096
Fax: 817-784-2116
(TX)

Western Region
Glencoe/McGraw-Hill
709 E. Riverpark Lane
Suite 150 • Boise, ID 83706
208-368-0300 • 800-452-6126
Fax: 208-368-0303
(AK, AZ, CO, ID, MT, NV, OR, UT, WA, WY)

California Region
Glencoe/McGraw-Hill
15319 Chatsworth Street
P.O. Box 9609
Mission Hills, CA 91346
818-898-1391 • 800-423-9534
Fax: 818-365-5489
(CA, HI)

Glencoe Catholic School Region
Glencoe/McGraw-Hill
25 Crescent St., 1st Floor
Stamford, CT 06906
203-964-9109 • 800-551-8766
Fax: 203-967-3108

Canada
McGraw-Hill Ryerson Ltd.
300 Water Street
Whitby, Ontario
Canada L1N 9B6
905-430-5000 • 800-565-5758
Fax: 905-430-5020

International
McGraw-Hill, Inc.
International Group
1221 Avenue of the Americas
28th Floor
New York, NY 10020
212-512-3641
Fax: 212-512-2186

DoDDS and Pacific Territories
McGraw-Hill School
Publishing Company
1221 Avenue of the Americas
13th Floor
New York, NY 10020
212-512-6128
Fax: 212-512-6050

Program Components

Textbook	
Student Edition	0-02-647730-0
Teacher's Wraparound Edition	0-02-647731-9
Workbook	
Student Workbook	0-02-647732-7
Teacher's Annotated Edition*	0-02-647738-6
Teacher's Classroom Resources Box	0-02-647733-5
ABCNews Interactive Bar Code Correlation*	0-02-642706-0
Linking Home, School, and Community*	0-02-642845-8
Dealing with Sensitive Issues*	0-02-642798-2
Observing and Participating with Children*	0-02-647734-3
Creative Activities for Children*	0-02-647739-4
Teen Parenting*	0-02-647740-8
Cooperative Learning Activities*	0-02-647741-6
Extension Activities*	0-02-647742-4
Enrichment Activities*	0-02-647743-2
Reteaching Activities*	0-02-647744-0
Reproducible Lesson Plans*	0-02-647745-9
Performance Assessment Activities*	0-02-647749-1
Testing Program*	0-02-647746-7
*Color Transparency Binder**	0-02-647747-5
Testmakers	
Macintosh	0-02-647735-1
Apple	0-02-647737-8
IBM	0-02-647736-X

*These components are included in the *Teacher's Classroom Resources*

GLENCOE
McGraw-Hill

Teacher's Wraparound Edition

The Developing Child

Understanding Children and Parenting

Seventh Edition

GLENCOE
McGraw-Hill

New York, New York   Columbus, Ohio   Mission Hills, California   Peoria, Illinois

Contributors to the Teacher's Wraparound Edition

Carol Alford
Teacher and Department Chairperson
Consumer and Family Studies
Fort Collins High School
Fort Collins, Colorado

Anna Sue Couch, Ed.D.
Associate Professor and Program Director
    for Home Economics Education
Texas Tech University
Lubbock, Texas

Linda R. Glosson, Ph.D.
Home Economics Teacher
Wylie High School
Wylie, Texas

Brenda Barrington Mendiola
Home Economics Teacher
Irion County Schools
Mertzon, Texas

Connie R. Sasse, C.H.E.
Home Economics Writer
Shawnee, Kansas

Deborah Ross Stone
Assistant Professor of Home Economics
University of Central Arkansas
Conway, Arkansas

Glencoe/McGraw-Hill

A Division of The McGraw-Hill Companies

Copyright © 1997 by Glencoe/McGraw-Hill. All rights reserved. Except as permitted under the United States Copyright Act, no part of this publication may be reproduced or distributed in any form or by any means, or stored in a database or retrieval system, without prior written permission of the publisher.

Send all inquiries to:
Glencoe/McGraw-Hill
3008 W. Willow Knolls Drive
Peoria, Illinois 61614-1083

ISBN 0-02-647730-0 (Student Text)
ISBN 0-02-647731-9 (Teacher's Wraparound Edition)

Printed in the United States of America.

2 3 4 5 6 7 8 9 10 VH 02 01 00 99 98 97

Contents

TEACHING WITH *THE DEVELOPING CHILD*

Welcome to the seventh edition of *The Developing Child*. This text is an established and preferred one in child development and parenting classes; however, this comprehensive revision with its easy-to-use format, integrated features, and practical reinforcement and applications makes this program better than ever. Now this popular program has been further enhanced by the addition of the Teacher's Classroom Resources. This new component not only provides additional teaching support, but enables teachers to select those areas that are of greatest concern to child care and child development teachers—cooperative learning, observation and participation skills, teen parenting, and more. The Teacher's Classroom Resources joins a family of components that together provide a total package for teaching and learning.

The Developing Child is based on several assumptions:
- That learning about child development increases self-understanding.
- That parenting and child care skills depend on knowledge of child growth and development coupled with appropriate attitudes and skills.
- That much of the same knowledge and many of the same attitudes and skills are needed by both parents and child care workers.

The Developing Child is designed to bring child development and parenting concepts alive for students. Basic information is presented in depth, yet clearly and concisely. Concepts are combined with practical application to ensure that knowledge gained can be put to use. The text encourages learning because of its outstanding visual appeal, its warm and readable writing style, and its use of concrete examples.

After introducing students to the importance of studying children and parenting, the text focuses on development from conception through age six. Development includes not only physical maturation, but also an understanding of how emotional, social, and intellectual development are fostered and hin-dered. Throughout, the interrelationship of all areas of development is stressed. This developmental approach is interwoven with application to parenting and child care situations.

The components of *The Developing Child* program are completely integrated for easy use. They include:

- **Student Text.** This 619-page book introduces students to child development, parenting decisions and skills, and career opportunities working with children.

- **Teacher's Wraparound Edition.** This revised component provides complete lesson plans, teaching suggestions, supplemental information, cross-references, and more—conveniently "wrapped" around every page of the student text.

- **Teacher's Classroom Resources.** This component contains separate supplemental booklets that include reproducible lesson plans; reteaching, enrichment, and extension activities; cooperative learning activities; special focused booklets on Teen Parenting, Creative Activities with Children, and Observation and Participation Activities; and a complete reproducible testing program, and much more.

- **Student Workbook.** The activity sheets in this component help maximize students' learning.

- **Testmaker Software.** This computer program helps you vary and personalize tests quickly and easily.

- **Color Transparency Set.** Ready-to-use color transparencies provide effective ways to introduce topics, reinforce concepts, and spark discussion.

On the following pages, you will find more information about each of these components as well as suggestions for using them effectively. We hope that both you and your students enjoy discovering what *The Developing Child* has to offer.

USING THE STUDENT TEXT

The Developing Child Student Text provides an appealing format for introducing students to child development, parenting, and child care concepts. The written presentation is supplemented by realistic photographs which spark discussion and help maintain interest. The organization of the text, its special features, and the visual presentation combine to make this book a positive learning experience for students.

Organization of the Text

The text is divided into six units. Each unit brings together chapters which have a common theme.

- **Unit 1: Children, Parenting, and You** introduces students to the subject of child development and helps them appreciate its relevance to their lives. The unit provides perspective on the importance of childhood, the influence of the family on a child's development, the responsibilities of those who care for children, and the challenges of teen parenthood.
- **Unit 2: Pregnancy and Birth** helps students understand the beginnings of human life—pregnancy and birth. The three chapters explore the many changes that take place from the time of conception through the baby's birth and first days at home.
- **Unit 3: The Baby's First Year** focuses on the first year of a baby's life and highlights the major physical, social, and intellectual developmental advances made by the time a child reaches his or her first birthday.
- **Unit 4: The Child from One to Three** focuses on the development of one-, two-, and three-year-olds. Students understand the important milestones in physical growth during these years as well as the general social and intellectual patterns.
- **Unit 5: The Child from Four to Six** examines the development of children during the preschool and early school years. Development of self-care habits, understanding moral decisions, and the child's individual learning needs are discussed in the unit.
- **Unit 6: Special Areas of Study** expands on important topics relevant to children of all ages and to people who contemplate a career in the child-care related fields. These include health and safety, challenging situations for children, child observation and participation skills, and career options.

Each unit consists of two to four chapters focusing on specific major topics. Each chapter is further divided into individual sections. These sections break the chapters into shorter reading segments and divide the concept load into manageable pieces.

Written Text

Like the book as a whole, individual sections are clearly organized. Distinctive headings divide the body of the sections into major topics and subtopics.

The text is interesting and readable. Topics are clearly explained. Specific examples are used to clarify information. Cross-references direct students to related information in other chapters.

Vocabulary development, which begins on the section opening pages with "Terms to Learn," is carried through the body of the chapter. When first used in the chapter, vocabulary terms appear in **boldface type**. A clear definition is given in italics, as well as examples or further explanation when needed. (All vocabulary terms are included in the Glossary and Glosario at the end of the book.)

Elements of Each Chapter

Each chapter of the text includes a number of carefully designed features to enhance student interest and learning.

Chapter Opening

The first two pages of each chapter are designed to motivate students, orient them to the chapter content, and set the stage for learning. A two-page chapter opening provides a photograph and opening set of questions which tie in with the theme of the chapter.

Parenting in Action

Each chapter includes one or more Parenting in Action features. These provide case studies chosen to relate theory to real life. Each Parenting in Action is an independent feature that reinforces the concepts of the chapter and is followed by questions for thought and discussion. (Suggested answers are provided in the Teacher's Wraparound Edition.)

Ask the Experts

This regular chapter feature has a question-and-answer format. A specific question, pertinent to the child care issues in the chapter, is posed to one of the six professional experts profiled in **Meet the Experts**.

The expert then provides his or her viewpoint and recommendations. The feature familiarizes students with resources available to parents and caregivers, and it introduces students to a range of child-care career opportunities.

Illustrations, Captions, and Charts

Hundreds of large, full-color photographs and drawings bring the text information to life. These do more than add interest—they are *illustrations that teach*. They serve to instruct, to reinforce text learning, to heighten students' awareness, and to improve their observation skills. The captions are also utilized as teaching tools. Many ask questions to help students review facts, apply text concepts, and develop critical thinking skills. Throughout the text, colorful charts highlight key points.

Chapter Review Page

Each chapter ends with a two-page, comprehensive review which includes:

* **Summary**—A short recap of important chapter concepts.
* **Reviewing the Facts**—Questions to check students' recall of facts from the chapter. (Answers are provided in the Teacher's Wraparound Edition.)
* **Exploring Further**—Discussion and activities to reinforce and extend learning.
* **Thinking Critically**—Three or four activities designed to encourage higher level thinking skills.
* **Cross-Curriculum Connections**—Two or three interdisciplinary activities.
* **School to Work**—Practical advice about future job and career opportunities.
* **Performance Assessment**—An activity that demonstrates mastery of the chapter's content in a nontest situation.

Section Features

Each section of the text serves as a self-contained lesson to maximize student learning. Within each section you will find the following fundamental elements.

Section Opening

Student Objectives are listed under the heading Objectives. The clearly stated objectives set learning goals to focus students' reading. Terms to Learn introduces the section's important vocabulary. These terms are further reinforced by other vocabulary development features in the text and supplements.

Building Self-Esteem reinforces positive methods of interacting with children that foster a good self-concept. Short paragraphs are displayed alongside the text addressing such topics as the value of saying "no" and encouraging sibling friendships.

Health Tips/Safety Tips stress the importance of taking proper precautions to prevent childhood accidents and illnesses. These tips run alongside appropriate text material as integral, not optional, reading.

Cultural Exchange develops students' perspective of child care practices throughout the world. They stress the similarities between practices of the United States as compared to other countries, but also illustrate diversity and uniqueness.

Section Review is located at the end of each section and is divided into Check Your Understanding questions, which reinforce main ideas and check students' comprehension, Discuss and Discover, and Observing & Participating, which helps them apply what they have learned. Answers to the review questions are supplied in the Teacher's Wraparound Edition.

Other Text Features

In addition to the chapter and section elements just described, special text features are designed to promote interest and foster in-depth learning.

Meet the Experts

Six professionals representing a variety of fields related to child development are profiled on this two-page spread following the Table of Contents. (See pages 12-13 in the Student Text). The text includes information about their career training and personal accomplishments that distinguish them in their respective fields. Later, each expert is re-introduced as the student reads the **Ask the Expert** feature included in each chapter.

Unit Opening Pages

Each unit is introduced with a two-page color photograph, a list of chapters in the unit, and an opening poem. The poem serves as a motivational feature for students and teachers.

Positive Parenting Skills

Twelve illustrated photo essays, called Positive Parenting Skills, provide practical, interesting ways to help students become more confident and effective as caregivers. The photo essays present ideas for spending "quality time" with children as well as suggestions for guiding behavior in a positive way.

The Positive Parenting Skills are presented as a culminating feature at the end of the chapters in Units 2, 3, 4, and 5. They are designed for flexible use. For example, you may want to use a particular photo essay as part of the study of a chapter. Another alternative is to use a group of Positive Parenting Skills as a mini-lesson after completing the study of a unit. Specific suggestions for using each photo essay are provided in the Teacher's Wraparound Edition.

Performance Assessment

This special section, appearing on each chapter review, brings an added dimension to *The Developing Child*. The activities suggest opportunities for stu-dents to show what they have learned. Unlike tradi-tional testing, students' work will more closely reflect how the information is used in the real world. The activities encourage students to apply their knowl-edge for various types of projects and for diverse audiences.

Glossary and Glosario (Spanish)

The Glossary, beginning on page 588, defines all the chapter vocabulary terms. Pronunciation guides are included for difficult terms. Students can use the glossary to quickly review their understanding of new terms. The Glosario begins on page 597.

THE TEACHER'S WRAPAROUND EDITION

The book you now hold in your hands is the Teacher's Wraparound Edition. It provides greatly expanded teaching support in a convenient, easy-to-use format.

The Teacher's Wraparound Edition allows you to follow along page by page with the student text. Material from the student text pages is reproduced in a slightly smaller size to allow more room for teaching material, which fills the side and bottom margins of your page.

This teaching material follows a consistent, easy-to-use pattern. Note that the complete lesson cycle—*Focus, Teach, Assess,* and *Close*—is contained within each section. As you cover the pages of the student text in class, the teaching suggestions are right in the margins where you need them.

The teaching material in the Teacher's Wraparound Edition is correlated to the other components of *The Developing Child* program. Suggestions are made for appropriate places to use other program resources. Of course, you always have the option of using these resources at any other point or not at all.

The Teacher's Wraparound Edition provides you with support material in three general categories.

- **Lesson Plans.** The "core" of the Teacher's Wraparound Edition, this material provides you with complete suggestions for *introducing* each unit and chapter, *teaching* the chapter content, and *completing* each segment of study. In addition, special self-contained lesson plans are provided for the text's photo essay features, Positive Parenting Skills.

- **Bottom Column Annotations.** Boxes at the bottom of the page give you additional information related to the content of the student text. These supplement the core lesson plan by focusing on various areas of interest. The categories are: Teen Parenting, Cooperative Learning, Classroom Management, Observing and Participating, Healthy Families/ Healthy Children, More About, Section Review Answers, and Performance Assessment. Each category is color-coded for quick reference.

- **Teaching Aids.** A number of additional features save you time and help make the Teacher's Wraparound Edition easy to use. These include unit, chapter, and section overviews, resource lists, bulletin board suggestions, cross-references, and answers to review questions. The Teacher's Wraparound Edition provides a wealth of material. From this, choose what best fits your classroom situation, the needs of your students, and your community's viewpoints. You will probably find more than enough suitable material for each section, allowing you to adapt your lesson plans according to class dynamics, current events and trends, or simply for the sake of variety, if desired.

Following is a more detailed explanation of what you will find on typical pages of the Teacher's Wraparound Edition and suggestions for using this material effectively.

Unit Opening Pages

In the student text, each unit begins with an illustrated two-page opener, emphasizing the interaction between caregiver and child. In the Teacher's Wraparound Edition, you will find several helpful features in the side margins of these pages.

Left Column

- **Unit Resources.** This list refers you to the special supplementary materials available in the Teacher's Classroom Resources that are provided for the unit as a whole.

- **Unit Overview.** The left column provides a capsule description of each chapter in the unit. This unit overview helps you see the scope of the unit at a glance, find the topics you are looking for, and plan how much time to spend on each chapter.

- **Unit Objectives.** This itemized list presents concise statements of the topics discussed in each chapter. The statements serve as specific goals for lesson planning.

- **Bulletin Board Suggestions.** In the left bottom margin of unit opening pages, you will find descriptions of simple but creative bulletin boards that can help you introduce topics and motivate students. You may wish to have students participate in creating the displays.

Right Column

- **Introducing the Unit.** Here you will find suggestions for making the transition to each unit and motivating your students.

- **Assess.** After the chapters in the unit have been studied, refer back to these suggestions for review and evaluation. An additional Extension activity provides one final opportunity to strengthen the unit objectives.

- **Using the Poem.** In the right bottom column, suggestions for examination of the unit poem provide a language-related activity that stimulates creative thinking. The bulletin board and the poem make excellent springboards for discussion.

Teaching the Chapter

The twenty chapters of *The Developing Child* are arranged in an ages-and-stages progression. The material on the opening pages sets the framework for the sections within the chapter, while the review activities complete the scope of the chapter's contents. Each chapter builds on the previous ones and prepares students for the chapters to follow.

Chapter Opening Pages

On the opening pages of each chapter, you will find the following material in the Teacher's Wraparound Edition.

Left Column

- **Chapter Resources.** This list shows you at a glance what supplementary materials in the Teacher's Classroom Resources, Student Workbook, and other program components are correlated with the chapter.

- **Chapter Overview.** This gives a broad overview of the subject that is covered in the chapter, then summarizes the content of each section.

- **Classroom Management.** Each bottom column on this page of the chapter opening is titled Resources Beyond the Classroom and highlights local, state, or national organizations that can provide resources appropriate to the content of the chapter. Whenever possible, the address and phone number of the organization is provided.

Right Column

- **Chapter Objectives.** This itemized list of objectives clearly outlines the focus of each section within the chapter. The specific goals help guide your lesson planning.

- **Introducing the Chapter.** This heading offers activities that mark the beginning of the lesson plan materials for the chapter. The activities are designed to lay a good foundation for chapter study. One of

the items refers to a discussion of the photo found on the student text page.

- **Healthy Families/Healthy Children.** The chapter also opens with this bottom column annotation written to highlight the significance of family interactions on the growth and development of a child. Individual topics are called out in the sub-head.

Chapter Review Pages

Each chapter's lesson plan concludes with *Assess* and *Close*, found in the margin of the Chapter Review page. (See pages 34-35 for an example.) This chapter wrap-up includes:

- **Checking Comprehension.** Directions for using the Reviewing the Facts questions are given.

- **Chapter Review Answers.** These are answers to the factual recall questions from the Chapter Review page.

- **Evaluate.** Suggestions given here include activities from the Chapter Review page, the Chapter Text, and the Testmaker Software.

- **Extension.** One or more ideas for activities to help you extend your lessons.

- **Close.** A final classroom exercise, designed to summarize one principle concept presented in the chapter.

After the Close exercise, one of three boxed features—**Technology Option, School to Work, Developing a Portfolio**—expands on either the School to Work feature or the Performance Assessment activity on the Chapter Review page.

Teaching the Section

Within each chapter, the core lesson plan material for each section appears in the side columns and follows a sequence of four distinct parts to enhance the effectiveness of your teaching. It begins at the top of the first page of each section and continues until the section ends. (You may wish to refer to pages 18-23 for an example of the features described below.)

- **Focus.** This initial category helps you fix students' attention on the lesson material. In the category you will find the following:
  Section Resources. Included in the list are related resources found in the Teacher's Classroom Resources (TCR) and Student Workbook.
  Section Overview. Under this heading are one or more paragraphs that summarize the content of the section.

Motivator. These teaching suggestions will help you generate student interest in the topics about to be studied. Additional motivators can be used as desired. Students need not have read any section materials beforehand. Use the motivator as creative ways to "warm up" your students and prepare them for learning.

Using Terms to Learn. These teaching suggestions are linked to the list of "Terms to Learn" on the student text page. By following these suggestions, you can help your students become familiar with the terms introduced in the section. In addition, as students take a closer look at one or more of the terms listed, they will be developing lifelong vocabulary skills. Emphasis is placed on analyzing unfamiliar terms using clues such as root words, prefixes and suffixes, compound words, and comparison with familiar terms.

- **Teach.** This second, and most extensive, of the lesson plan sequence presents numerous and varied activities that correlate to the text on the same page where they appear. The *Teach* sequence is itself divided into two categories: Guided Practice and Independent Practice. A sampling of the Guided Practice activities are explained below:

Promoting Discussion. This section of the lesson plan helps you expand the lesson with more in-depth discussion. It suggests ways for you to:
- Open discussion with specific topics or questions.
- Use illustrations and captions as teaching tools.
- Emphasize key points.
- Give further explanation where needed.
- Help students review previous learning.
- Use transparencies and handouts found in the Teacher's Classroom Resources.

Critical Thinking. These activities in the lesson plan provide suggested activities to reinforce and extend student learning. A variety of activities are suggested, including in-class work and outside assignments for individual students, small groups, and the class as a whole. These activities are designed to be suitable for a wide range of student ability levels. They help students use critical thinking skills to analyze, compare and contrast, and evaluate the text content and related issues.

Making Connections. Many of these activities reinforce not only the subject of the lesson, but also academic and life skills. The heading is followed by a label to indicate the major skills that are reinforced. The skills identified include:
- Language Arts (Reading, Writing, and Literature)
- Math
- Science (including Physics, Physiology, and Zoology)
- Social Studies
- Management
- Art/Music/Drama/Design
- Careers
- Health and Nutrition
- Speech

Family Focus. Although child care is often studied as a one-to-one interaction between caregiver and child, in reality, this interaction more often takes place within a broader family environment. The Family Focus activities acknowledge this fact through discussion, explanation, case studies, and activities that help students think about such issues as these:
- How can children be helped to feel that they are valuable members of the family?
- What is the importance of sibling relationships?
- How can family members work together to solve problems?

Students will find these learning experiences applicable not only to the study of child development and parenting, but also to their own experiences as family members.

Using Management Skills. Activities included under this heading are designed to encourage an awareness of consumer issues and decisions facing parents and caregivers. Usually they are asked to survey retail products for the purpose of making a budget or to research safety standards included in the manufacturing of items related to children.

Practicing Decision Making. Because child care demands some of the most important decisions a person will ever have to make, these activities simulate situations where assorted factors are involved in the making of a decision. Students have the chance to practice their critical thinking skills as well as applying their common sense, then discuss the options available and weigh the decisions of others. This practice is a preliminary "dry run" at the real-life events that they may encounter in their lives. It also gives them the opportunity to appreciate the complexities of making decisions.

Cooperative Learning. Activities suggested under this heading are designed to encourage collaborative efforts by having students working in pairs or small groups. Special attention is paid to the nature of these activities, so that the students can assume some degree of responsibility and have an opportunity to share their results, either within the group or in the form of a group presentation to the class.

The second category of *Teach* is Independent Practice and is designed to encourage efforts by students that are more self-guided and individual. Most of these activities can be assigned as homework or as independent classroom assignments. Examples of Independent Practice activities are:

Journal Writing. The essence of this activity is designed to further students' written reflections in a journal. As the course progresses, the reflections allow for a review of growth and understanding.
Student Workbook. Refers you to the specific title in the Student Workbook designated to the section.
Extension. These activities expand students' understanding of the lesson by giving them opportunities to explore content in greater depth.

- **Assess.** The third section of the basic lesson plan provides ways for you to meet special student needs.
Checking Comprehension directs you to assign the Check Your Understanding questions at the end of the section, and that the answers are given at the bottom of the page.
Evaluate reminds you of the additional section test available in the TCR.
Reteaching activities are suitable for any situation in which students need additional guidance or practice to master the chapter concepts.
Enrichment activities are suitable for students who would benefit from independent study or more challenging content.
Extension recommends an additional activity that draws from areas outside the classroom or the content of the sections, such as a guest speaker to share knowledge of a particular topic or a field trip to reinforce the subject matter.

- **Close.** This final part of the lesson plan characteristically offers a short exercise designed to be used in the closing moments of class discussion. It may direct students to complete a sentence and discuss their responses, or it will guide you in creating a sense of closure to the material in the section.

Special Features

On pages that present a special feature such as Safety Tips, Health Tip, Cultural Exchange, or Building Self-Esteem, an accompanying text in the Teacher's Wraparound Edition helps you extend the concept into a brief discussion of relevant points. The content or activity is visually set off from other lesson plan material by a box or heading that mirrors the heading style used in the student text.

Bottom Column Annotations

At the bottom of most pages in your Teacher's Wraparound Edition, you will find one or more helpful features, including More About details, Classroom Management tips, Cooperative Learning activities, and cross-references.

More About

The orange boxes tell you More About the topics discussed on the student text page. The information provided here has several possible uses.
- Share the information with your students (when appropriate) to spark interest, generate discussion, or extend the lesson.
- Draw upon the information as a resource for answering student questions.
- Use the information to enhance your own understanding of the subject or to guide you toward further research.

Observing and Participating

Observation and participation are two of the most valuable tools for the study of child development and parenting. This blue box in the bottom column in the Teacher's Wraparound Edition suggests simple observation activities that can help bring the text content alive for students. Before assigning students any of these bottom column activities or the Observing and Participating activities found on the section review pages, be sure they understand the basic principles of observation and participation. Important points to stress include objectivity, appropriate behavior, and confidentiality.

Many of the Observing and Participating activities would be ideal for use with an in-class child care laboratory. However, the activities can be used in a variety of settings. When choosing activities, consider the type of setting that would be most appropriate for each situation. Possible out-of-class sites include playgrounds, parks, neighborhoods where children play, shopping centers, supermarkets, and the homes of family members or friends.

If you feel that students may not have access to an appropriate site or to children of the appropriate age, there are several possible solutions. You may wish to set up a prearranged observation for the class as a whole. For example, you could invite parents to bring their children to class or arrange for the class to visit a child care center. Another approach is to ask for volunteers for each activity rather than assigning the activity to all class members. If you choose a variety of activities throughout the course, each student should eventually be able to take part in one.

When assigning observation and participation activities, include guidelines for how students are to record their findings. Do you want a formal written record or an informal oral report? Have sample reports available to serve as models for your students.

To further develop these important skills, use the Observing and Participating booklet found in the TCR.

Teen Parenting

Teen parenting has become a major concern in today's society—and especially for you as a teacher. You must deal with teen parenting not only as a topic to be discussed in your course, but also, perhaps, as a reality for some or all of your students.

In response to these needs, *The Developing Child* Teacher's Wraparound Edition includes special brown Teen Parenting boxes. Whether some, all, or none of your students are themselves teen parents, you will find useful ideas among the teaching suggestions given in these boxes.

The philosophy of the Teen Parenting boxes is defined by two goals:
* To discourage additional teen pregnancies.
* To help teens who are already parents, or who are pregnant, develop the skills and self-confidence they need to be good parents.

The Teen Parenting boxes help you work toward these goals using a variety of approaches. For example, many of the boxes give supplemental information about teen pregnancy and parenting that can be shared with students. Through class discussion, students are encouraged to think critically about the consequences of teen pregnancy. Questions and case studies help students put themselves in the place of teen parents. Recurring themes include maturity and responsible decision making.

As you use the Teen Parenting boxes, remember to be sensitive to individual students. Choose those boxes which are appropriate in your specific classroom situation.

Healthy Families/Healthy Children

These light teal boxes highlight important health and safety considerations relevant to the text material. In particular, the emphasis is placed on preventative health and safety measures that are designed to foster positive growth and development. Different run-in heads identify the focus of the material in any one box. The scope of the material in these boxes may include the following:
* How does the family environment influence development?
* How do the different stages of development that children go through influence the family as a whole?
* What are some effects of differing family structures and lifestyles?

Classroom Management

Both seasoned and new teachers recognize the importance of maintaining an efficient, stimulating environment for learning. This grape box offers a wide range of ideas from suggestions for bulletin board displays to outside resources that will, in some cases, supply you with print material to use in conjunction with the chapter contents.

Two topic-specific Classroom Management boxes are worth noting; you may find it helpful to locate and review these boxes as you plan your course. On the left bottom of each chapter opening page is a box that identifies an organization that serves as a resource for material particular to the issues in the chapter. At the end of most chapters, another box focuses on learning strategies, created with the child development class in mind.

Cooperative Learning

Suggested activities in the Cooperative Learning boxes create a structured, natural environment where students are encouraged to work together for the purpose of a predetermined project or goal. This format draws more heavily on interpersonal skills than does the traditional classroom lecture pattern. However, the purpose of collaborative learning activities is not to replace traditional methods, rather, it is to provide an alternative learning environment where students contribute freely and responsible to a small group.

To help you understand and implement cooperative learning practices, the green boxes provide a mixture of both theoretical information and practical activities. The theoretical information explains such concepts as how to evaluate for healthy group dynamics, establishing a sense of community, delegating responsibility, how to handle dysfunctional groups, using journals, setting goals, encouraging cognitive development, even the psychology of arranging a classroom. The second type of Cooperative Learning box offers suggestions for group activities based on the content of the student text.

To help you generate a solid foundation for collaborative learning in your classroom, consult the Cooperative Learning booklet provided in the TCR.

See How They Grow

As previously stated, the organization of *The Developing Child* is an ages-and-stages blueprint. Thus, the See How They Grow box is a natural extension of that pattern as it presents significant material about the physical, social, and intellectual characteristics of children as they grow and develop. Also included are observations about the changing dynamics of the family which are a normal consequence of the child's growth. These red boxes help you remind the students of the never ending, and always fascinating, process of growth and development.

Section Review Answers

As explained earlier, each text chapter is broken into two or more sections followed by Section Review questions. Suggested answers to these questions are conveniently located at the bottom of the page. Look for the cream boxes (color-coordinated with the questions in the text).

Performance Assessment

Designed to accompany the Performance Assessment activity on the Chapter Review page, these pale blue boxes offer additional suggestions to help you implement the activity in your classroom. Remember that your ultimate goal when assigning these activities is to help students actively participate in meaningful learning.

Teaching Positive Parenting Skills

The lesson plans accompanying the Positive Parenting Skills photo essays follow a different pattern from the section lesson plans. This is because the photo essays are themselves distinct from the chapter and section material. Each photo essay is treated as a self-contained "mini-lesson." The Positive Parenting Skills lesson plans include the sections listed below, as well as others used in the Teach sequence of each section. (See pages 150-151 for an example.)

- **Motivator.** Suggestions are given for beginning the "mini-lesson" with a motivational activity, either before or after student reading.

- **Promoting Discussion.** Suggestions, in the form of questions, are offered to incorporate the photo essay individually into the study of a particular chapter, tying it in with related material.

- **Critical Thinking.** Several suggestions are given for examination of appropriate points made in the photo essay. Emphasis is given to higher level thinking skills combined with a general knowledge and experience.

- **Using the Photograph.** This gives suggestions for analyzing the photos and discussing the accompanying text.

- **Practicing Parenting Skills.** Most of the Positive Parenting Skills lesson plans include this activity, which allows students to apply their learning in a real-life situation. Here you will find activities that tie in with the subject of the photo essay to reinforce and extend student learning. Included are suggestions for using related materials as well as a variety of other activities.

- **Close.** The lesson plan for the photo essay concludes with a suggestion for helping students think about what they have learned.

USING OTHER PROGRAM COMPONENTS

Student Workbook

The Developing Child Student Workbook provides creative and varied activity sheets to enhance student learning. For each chapter, a study guide of fill-in and short-answer questions is provided to guide students' reading and review. Additional activity sheets reinforce section content and vocabulary, extend students' learning, and strengthen basic skills such as reading, writing, math, critical thinking, and problem solving.

The activity sheets in the Student Workbook can be used at the points suggested in the Teacher's Wraparound Edition or whenever you choose. They can be used in many ways: as in-class work, homework, pretests, post tests, review activities, reteaching activities, or extra credit assignments.

The perforated pages can be detached and turned in for grading. Answers are found in the Student Workbook Teacher's Annotated Edition.

The Student Workbook is designed as a consumable item. Therefore, it may not be reproduced in part or whole. Such reproduction is a violation of copyright law.

Teacher's Classroom Resources

The Developing Child Teacher's Classroom Resources (TCR) is a resource for reference materials for your own use and reproducible masters for classroom use. Its diversity enables you to select the most appropriate activities to meet the needs of your students and curriculum emphasis. The file includes the following supplemental booklets:

- **Reteaching Activities.** Activities in this booklet are presented in the format of concept mapping. The purpose of Reteaching exercises is to offer another method of review to those students who have not completely grasped the principle ideas in each section. Concept mapping stimulates understanding through visual patterns of association, similar to the technique of clustering.

- **Enrichment Activities.** For students who have successfully completed the section quiz, the activities found in this booklet challenge them to build on the concepts presented in each section. The activities encourage critical thinking skills as well as practical decision making.

- **Cooperative Learning Activities.** As an alternative to classroom instruction, cooperative learning activities give students the opportunity to help each other learn and increase their own interpersonal skills. It develops such skills as speaking and listening, social interactions, critical thinking, and making judgements. Finally, it enhances self-esteem as the success of a group's work is linked to the success of individual students within the group. Above all, students who are reluctant to participate openly in class are often more comfortable and contribute more in the intimate setting of a small group. The benefits of collaborative efforts extends beyond the student to you, the teacher, as well. You have the opportunity to observe students, both as individuals and as a team member, and you have the chance to confer with smaller groups than the traditional class structure allows.

  The Cooperative Learning activities in the TCR were developed to supplement the content of each chapter. The introductory material supplies rationale for incorporating cooperative learning techniques in the classroom and offers methodology and practical guidelines. The activities found in the Cooperative Learning booklet give you ideas for setting up students in teams or in pairs, with each student being responsible for each other's learning as well as his or her own. Also included are tips for student conferences and an up-to-date bibliography of suggested readings.

- **Extension Activities.** These activities are written for students who are inspired to learn more about people, ideas, and events associated with the chapter contents. The focus of each activity takes the student beyond the scope of the textbook contents and offers possible topics for research projects and self-guided study. This booklet is a perfect resource for extra credit projects.

- **Observing and Participating with Children.** This booklet in the TCR reinforces the significance of active learning stressed throughout the student text and the lesson plans. The activities offer students another opportunity to concentrate on individual people, whether they be children or adults, who provide a practical balance to the theoretical concepts learned in the text. Through keen observation and active participation, your students receive guided experience that prepares them for the role of caregiver. The activities can be used in conjunction with the Observing and Participating suggestions found on each section review page.

- **Teen Parenting.** If your class includes teen parents, you will find a supplementary Teen Parenting booklet in the TCR that addresses their specific needs. Suggestions are given for activities to help teen parents interact with their children and build parenting skills. In addition, students are encouraged to discuss common problems, share possible solutions, and identify personal and community resources that can help them. Topics of discussion include stress, conflicting feelings, health and nutritional concerns, decisions about the future, living in a three-generation household, and more—the specific challenges that teen parents face. By sharing their experiences and ideas with the class, teen parents can help each other while at the same time educating class members who are not parents. This booklet can be used in conjunction with the Teen Parenting boxes in the Teacher's Wraparound Edition.

- **Creative Activities for Children.** To encourage children's creative expression, the TCR includes a booklet devised specifically to encourage the natural curiosity of children. The booklet's 36 activities are divided into four sections: Art Activities; Games, Thinking, and Senses Activities; Science and Nature Activities; and Drama and Music Activities. Each activities lists necessary materials, recommended ages, and step-by-step instructions.

- **Color Transparencies.** The TCR also includes a set of 44 ready-to-use, overhead, color transparencies with suggestions for use. (See the description that follows.)

- **Testing Program.** The Teacher's Classroom Resources includes a complete set of section quizzes, and chapter and unit tests in a reproducible format.

Color Transparency Set

The Developing Child program includes a set of 44 ready-to-use, full-color transparencies with accompanying teaching suggestions.

The photos, drawings, diagrams, and charts on the transparencies are effective tools for focusing students' attention and increasing comprehension. They can be used to introduce topics, reinforce concepts, stimulate discussion, and sharpen critical thinking skills. Specific discussion suggestions are provided to help you make the most effective use of each transparency.

Testmaker Software

Also available for *The Developing Child* is a Testmaker Software program. The Testmaker allows you to draw upon a test bank of hundreds of objective questions. The program allows you to prepare and print out tests quickly and easily. You may choose the questions you want or allow the program to randomly select questions for you. You may also add questions of your own making to the test bank. At your direction, the program will scramble test questions to instantly create multiple versions of the same test. It will also print an answer key to accompany each test. The Testmaker is "user friendly" and comes with clearly written documentation.

The editors of *The Developing Child* have attempted to address contemporary educational trends in the subject field of child care and development. Making yourself familiar with the organizational design and individual features of this text will help you maximize class time and course content while incorporating current ideas and approaches to teaching. To help you generate a strategy to your teaching curriculum that is tailored to your needs and those of your students, Suggested Course Outlines and a Scope and Sequence Chart are presented on the following pages.

Course Planning

The responsibility for overall course planning varies from school to school. Some teachers—especially in the large districts—are expected to teach from predetermined outlines. Other teachers may need to plan their own course outlines or may be free to adapt existing outlines to their own needs.

The chart on these two pages suggests some ways classes might be structured using *The Developing Child*. Included are plans for a nine-week parenting course and nine-, eighteen-, and thirty-six-week courses combining child development and parenting. These outlines can easily be adapted to meet your particular needs.

Another aid to planning is the Scope and Sequence Chart on pages TM-20 through TM-27. This chart shows how major themes are woven throughout *The Developing Child*. You will find it useful for planning your course themes, and correlating *The Developing Child* to your curriculum.

Suggested Course Outlines

	Parenting Class	Child Development/Parenting Class		
Chapter	9-Week Class (Days Spent)	9-Week Class (Days Spent)	18-Week Class (Days Spent)	36-Week Class (Days Spent)
1. Growing with Children	2	2	2	4
2. Living in Families	3	2	3	6
3. Effective Parenting Skills	4	2	5	10
4. Teen Pregnancy and Parenthood	2	1	3	5
5. Prenatal Development	2	4	6	12
6. Preparing for Birth	2	2	6	12
7. The Baby's Arrival	3	3	5	10
8. Physical Development During the First Year	5	4	5	10
9. Emotional and Social Development During the First Year	4	4	5	10
10. Intellectual Development During the First Year	3	4	5	10
11. Physical Development from One to Three		4	5	10
12. Emotional and Social Development from One to Three	4	3	5	10
13. Intellectual Development from One to Three		3	5	10
14. Physical Development from Four to Six			5	9

| Chapter | Parenting Class | | Child Development/Parenting Class | |
	9-Week Class (Days Spent)	9-Week Class (Days Spent)	18-Week Class (Days Spent)	36-Week Class (Days Spent)
15. Emotional and Social Development from Four to Six	3		5	9
16. Intellectual Development from Four to Six			4	8
17. Health and Safety	4	4	5	8
18. Special Challenges for Children	2	2	4	10
19. Caring for Children	1		4	10
20. Careers Relating to Children	1	1	3	7
	45 days/ 9 weeks	45 days/ 9 weeks	90 days/ 18 weeks	180 days/ 36 weeks

SCOPE AND SEQUENCE

	Chapter 1 Growing with Children	Chapter 2 Living in Families
EFFECTIVE PARENTING	• Parental love and affection (2)	• Importance of families (1)
RESPONSIBILITY AND READINESS	• Understanding the responsibilities of children and parenthood (1)	• Considerations of parenthood (2) • Adjustments of parenthood (2) • Rewards of parenthood (2)
CHILD CARE SKILLS	• Importance of developing child care skills (1)	
CHILD OBSERVATION AND PARTICIPATION	• Guidelines for observing children (2)	
HEALTH, SAFETY, AND NUTRITION	• Improvements in nutrition (1)	• Characteristics of healthy families (1)
DECISION MAKING, MANAGEMENT, AND CRITICAL THINKING		• Parenthood decisions (2) • Management skills of parents (2)
CONSUMER INFORMATION		• Financial considerations of parenthood (2)
DEVELOPMENTAL STAGES AND INFLUENCES	• Characteristics of development (2) • The importance of play (2) • Heredity vs. environment (2)	
FAMILY AND PERSONAL RELATIONSHIPS		• Types of families (1) • Family life cycle (1) • Trends affecting families (1) • Adoption and foster care (1)
SOCIETY AND COMMUNITY		
CAREERS	• Career preparation (1)	

Chapter 3 Effective Parenting Skills	Chapter 4 Teen Pregnancy and Parenthood	Chapter 5 Prenatal and Birth
• Nurturing (1) • Communicating effectively (1) • Guiding behavior (2) • Consistency (2)		• Proper medical care during pregnancy (1) • Building positive attitudes (PP)
• Parenting resources (1)	• Sexual responsibility (1)	• Preventing birth defects (3) • Avoiding harmful substances (4)
• Providing physical care (2) • Nurturing (2) • Guiding (2) • Encouraging appropriate behavior (2) • Setting appropriate limits (2) • Handling conflicts (2)		
• Health and safety of child care centers (3) • Latchkey children (3)	• Avoiding pregnancy (1) • Stress and teen pregnancy (1)	• Conception (1) • Nutrition during pregnancy (1) • Exercise during pregnancy (1) • Emotional health during pregnancy (1) • Influence of heredity (2) • Infertility (2) • Birth defects (3) • Genetic counseling (3) • Prenatal tests (3) • Risk of teenage pregnancy (3) • Substance abuse (4) • STDs and AIDS (4)
• Problems of overparenting (1) • Guidance techniques (2) • Offering choices to children (2) • Evaluating substitute child care (3)	• Defining *sexuality* (1) • Values (1) • Decision-making process (1) • Decisions about sexual activity (1) • Parenthood alternatives (2) • Consequences of teen parenthood (2)	• Options for infertility (2) • Genetic counseling (3) • Avoiding harmful substances (4)
• Parenting resources (1) • Comparison of child care centers (3)		• Prenatal testing (3)
		• Stages of prenatal development (1) • Inherited traits (2) • Sex determination (2) • Multiple births (2) • Causes of birth defects (3)
	• Parent and friends as resources (2)	• Adoption (2) • Impact of birth defects on families (3)
• Offering parenting courses (1)	• Counseling resources (2)	

	Chapter 6 Preparing for Birth	Chapter 7 The Baby's Arrival
EFFECTIVE PARENTING		• Bonding and attachment (2, PP) • Needs of the parents (2) • Providing care (3)
RESPONSIBILITY AND READINESS	• Personal care during pregnancy (1) • Financial preparation for parenthood (2) • Emotional preparation for parenthood (2)	• Providing for the newborn's needs (3)
CHILD CARE SKILLS		• Care for premature babies (2) • Adjusting to care routines (3)
CHILD OBSERVATION AND PARTICIPATION		• Apgar scale (2) • Observing the newborn's reflexes (3) • Understanding the newborn's needs (3)
HEALTH, SAFETY, AND NUTRITION	• Signs of pregnancy (1) • Prenatal examinations (1) • Discomforts of pregnancy (1) • Nutrition during pregnancy (1) • Exercise during pregnancy (1) • Emotional health during pregnancy (1)	• Stages of labor (1) • Delivery procedures (1) • Cesarean birth (1) • Postnatal care of mother (2) • Premature babies (2) • Newborn health care (3) • Sudden infant death syndrome (SIDS) (3)
DECISION MAKING, MANAGEMENT, AND CRITICAL THINKING	• Establishing a budget (2) • Employment and child care (2) • Balancing roles (2) • Breast- versus bottle-feeding (2) • Childbirth choices (3) • Selecting a birth attendant (3)	• Medication during pregnancy and delivery (1) • Length of hospital stay (2)
CONSUMER INFORMATION	• Maternity clothes (1) • Basic baby supplies (2) • Evaluating a crib for safety (PP) • Health insurance coverage (2) • Setting a budget (2) • Alternative birth centers (3)	• Rooming in (2) • Birth certificate (2)
DEVELOPMENTAL STAGES AND INFLUENCES		• Physical changes at birth (2) • Reflex patterns of newborn (3) • Early temperament (3)
FAMILY AND PERSONAL RELATIONSHIPS	• Preparing family members for newborn (2) • Effect of parental employment on children (2)	• Parent-child bonding (2, PP) • Family support during "baby blues" (2) • Influence of parent and child on one another (2) • Promoting family unity with rooming in (2)
SOCIETY AND COMMUNITY	• Family leave policies (2) • Childbirth classes (3)	• SIDS Alliance (3)
CAREERS	• Obstetrician (3) • Family doctor (3) • Licensed midwife (3)	• Pediatrician (3)

Chapter 8 Physical Development During the First Year	Chapter 9 Emotional and Social Development During the First Year	Chapter 10 Intellectual Development During the First Year
• Providing positive mealtime experiences (2) • Establishing healthful eating habits (2) • Encouraging self-feeding (2)	• Consistency (1) • Developing a trust (1)	• Promoting intellectual development (2) • Providing a stimulating environment (2) • Encouraging safe exploration (2)
• Responsibility to provide physical care (2, 3) • Dependence of infant on caregiver (2, 3)		• Relationship between responsive care and intellectual development (2) • Responsibility for baby's safety (2)
• Handling of baby (2) • Bottle-feeding and burping (2) • Introducing new foods (2) • Encouraging self-feeding (2) • Bathing, diapering, and dressing a baby (3) • Preparing baby for sleep (3)	• Comforting a crying baby (1) • Understanding a baby's personality and needs (2)	• Selecting age-appropriate toys (2) • Communicating with baby (2)
		• Games for baby (2, PP)
• Signs of hearing loss (1) • Primary teeth (1) • Avoiding injury to baby (1) • Nutrition for infants (2) • Cradle cap (3) • Bathtime safety procedures (3) • Diaper rash (3) • Diaper sanitation (3)	• Failure to thrive (2)	• Benefits of rocking (1) • Toy safety (2)
• Establishing consistent routine (2) • Choosing safe and healthful foods (2) • Types of diapers (3) • Handling bedtime problems (3)		
• Selecting clothing for babies (3) • Determining clothing size (3)		• Selecting developmentally appropriate toys (2)
• Patterns of growth and development (1) • Hand-eye coordination (1) • Depth perception (1) • Sensory perception (1) • Auditory perception (1) • Motor skills development (1) • Teething (1)	• Building trust in infancy (1, PP) • Emotions in infancy (1) • How emotions develop (1) • Signs of social development (2) • Stranger anxiety (2) • Influences on personality (2) • Developing self-concept (2)	• Understanding the learning process (1) • Piaget's stages of development (1) • Heredity versus environment (2) • Importance of play (1) • Language development (2)
• Influence of family stresses on introducing new foods (2) • Quality time with baby (PP)	• Attachment to caregiver (1) • Emotional climate of home (1) • Learning through relations with others (2) • Need for human interaction (2) • Stranger anxiety (2)	• Need for human interaction (2) • Parents as playmates (2) • Communicating with baby (2)
• La Leche League (2) • Women, Infants, and Children Program (2)		• Learning environment beyond the home (2)
• Audiologist (1)	• Parenting consultant (1)	

	Chapter 11 Physical Development From One to Three	Chapter 12 Emotional and Social Development From One to Three
EFFECTIVE PARENTING	• Understanding developmentally appropriate (1) • Encouraging self-help skills (2) • Developing language skills (2) • Promoting healthy eating habits (2)	• Evaluation emotional adjustment (1) • Teaching self-control (1) • Encouraging companionship (2) • Promoting a positive self-concept (2) • Respecting individual differences (3) • Encouraging independence (3, PP)
RESPONSIBILITY AND READINESS	• Select nutritious foods for children (2) • Importance of early tooth care (1) • Responsibility for toddler's safety (2)	• Responding to temper tantrums (1) • Controlling one's own anger and fear (1) • Being a positive role model (1)
CHILD CARE SKILLS	• Mealtime tips (2) • Bathtime and bedtime routines (2) • Self-dressing skills (2) • Toilet training (2)	• Handling anger, fears, jealousy (1) • Effective discipline (3) • Using time-outs (3) • Coping with temper tantrums (1)
CHILD OBSERVATION AND PARTICIPATION		
HEALTH, SAFETY, AND NUTRITION	• Meal planning (2) • Prevention of tooth decay (1) • Childproofing the home (2, PP) • Water safety (2)	• Discipline necessary for safety (3) • Allowing safe exploration (3)
DECISION MAKING, MANAGEMENT, AND CRITICAL THINKING	• Preparing appealing meals (2) • Handling bedtime fears (2)	• Anticipating and minimizing toddler's frustrations (1) • Evaluating emotional adjustments (1)
CONSUMER INFORMATION	• Choosing foods for toddlers (2) • Self-help clothing features (2) • Fibers and fabrics for children's clothes (2) • Stretching the clothing budget (2)	
DEVELOPMENTAL STAGES AND INFLUENCES	• Growth patterns (1) • Proportion and posture (1) • Heredity and tooth quality (1) • Large and small motor skills (1)	• Negativism (1) • Push for independence (1) • Parallel play (2) • Cooperative play (2) • Separation anxiety (2)
FAMILY AND PERSONAL RELATIONSHIPS	• Socialization at family meals (2)	• Parent and child relationship (1) • Sibling rivalry (1) • Socialization (2) • Developing friendships (2) • Promoting positive self-concept (2)
SOCIETY AND COMMUNITY	• American Dental Association (1)	
CAREERS		

Chapter 13 Intellectual Development from One to Three	Chapter 14 Physical Development from Four to Six	Chapter 15 Emotional and Social Development from Four to Six
• Fostering creativity and imagination (1) • Stimulating learning environment (1) • Parents as teachers (1) • Guiding learning (2)	• Encouraging self-care practices (1) • Encouraging motor skills development (1) • Monitoring television viewing (PP)	• Promoting moral development (2) • Developing social acceptance (2) • Minimizing jealousy (1) • Positive guidance (PP)
	• Teaching nutrition to children (2) • Encouraging self-help skills (2)	• Setting an example of self-control (1) • Guidelines for moral development (2)
• Selecting toys (2)	• Providing nutritious snacks (2) • Teaching good nutrition (2) • Packing nutritious lunches (2) • Establishing grooming routines (2) • Bedtime routines (2)	• Handling fears (1) • Helping children cope with stress (1)
• Nutrition and intellectual development (1) • Providing safe exploration (1) • Toy safety (2) • Speech disabilities (3)	• Permanent teeth (1) • Thumb sucking (1) • Effect of diet on health (2) • Weight problems (2) • Enuresis (2)	• Children and stress (1)
• Teaching decision making (1) • Encouraging problem-solving abilities (1)	• Making good food choices (2)	
• Selecting safe toys (2) • Age-appropriate toys (2)	• Selected children's clothes (2) • Clothing care (2)	
• Influence of heredity and environment on intelligence (2) • Methods of learning (1) • Concept development (1) • Intellectual processes (1) • Speech development (2)	• Hand-eye coordination (1) • Dexterity (1) • Motor skill development (1) • Hand preference (1)	• Advantages and disadvantages of competition (1) • Emotional patterns (1) • Personality and behavior (2) • Socialization and starting school (2) • Moral development (2)
• Talking to children (2) • Spending time with children (2) • Reading to children (2, PP)		• Sibling rivalry (1) • Family traditions (1) • Developing friendships (1) • Competition (1) • Influence of peers and teachers (2)
• Food and Drug Administration (2) • Consumer Product Safety Commission (2)		• Community ethnic resources (2)
• Speech therapist (2)		

	Chapter 16 Intellectual Development from Four to Six	Chapter 17 Health and Safety
EFFECTIVE PARENTING	• Providing quality time with children (1) • Promoting exploratory activities (1) • Developing appreciation for art, music, and reading (1) • Helping children adjust to school (2)	• Providing a safe environment (1) • Providing health care (2) • Caring for a sick child (3)
RESPONSIBILITY AND READINESS	• Responsibility to provide learning opportunities (1)	• Responsibility for child's health and safety (1) • Emergency preparedness (2)
CHILD CARE SKILLS	• Teaching through everyday learning activities (1) • Reading to children (1) • Art activities (1) • Finger plays (1) • Meeting needs of gifted children (2)	• Accident prevention (1) • Teaching rules of safety (1) • Handling emergencies (2) • First aid procedures (2) • Caring for a sick child (3)
CHILD OBSERVATION AND PARTICIPATION		
HEALTH, SAFETY, AND NUTRITION	• Medical testing before entering school (2) • Learning disabilities (2)	• Safety guidelines (1) • Infant mortality (1) • Health care (1) • Immunizations (1) • Allergies (1) • First aid (2) • Rescue techniques (2) • Common childhood illnesses (3)
DECISION MAKING, MANAGEMENT, AND CRITICAL THINKING	• Spending quality time (1) • Disadvantages of IQ tests (1)	• Childproofing the home (1) • Fire prevention (1) • Crime prevention (1)
CONSUMER INFORMATION	• Guidelines for selecting children's books (1)	• Nontoxic play materials (1) • Awareness of common household poisons (1)
DEVELOPMENTAL STAGES AND INFLUENCES	• Signs of preoperational thinking (1) • Benefits of recreational activities (1) • Dramatic play (1) • Entering school (2) • Make-believe play (PP)	• Matching safety measures to child's developmental stage (1)
FAMILY AND PERSONAL RELATIONSHIPS	• Sharing household responsibilities (1) • Interacting with gifted children (2) • Effect of family environment on speech development (2)	• Dealing with strangers (1) • Entertaining a sick child (3) • Providing support during hospital stay (3) • Effect of child's illness on family (3)
SOCIETY AND COMMUNITY	• Measuring intelligence (1) • Special education classes (2)	• Medical advances (1) • Infant mortality rate (1) • American Red Cross (1) • Poison Control Center (1)
CAREERS		

Chapter 18 Special Challenges for Children	Chapter 19 Caring for Children	Chapter 20 Careers Relating to Children
• Helping children with special needs (1) • Breaking the cycle of abuse (2) • Helping children cope with stress (3) • Explaining separation and divorce (3) • Dealing with death (3) • Adjusting to a move (3)		
• Helping abusive parents gain self-control (2) • Effect of caregivers' attitudes on child's ability to cope (3)	• Being a good role model (1) • Promoting positive behavior (3) • Using positive reinforcement (3)	• Preparing for a career (1) • Traits of successful workers (1)
• Bathing and feeding the handicapped child (1)	• Responsibilities of babysitting (1)	• Importance of developing child care skills (1)
	• Observation skills (2) • Types of observation records (2) • Promoting positive behavior (3) • Dealing with inappropriate behavior (3)	
• Types of disabilities (1) • Adapting home for physical disabilities (1) • Recognizing signs of emotional disturbance (2) • Child abuse and neglect (3)	• Health care routines (3) • Safety guidelines (3)	• Child-related health careers (2)
• Seeking help for emotional disturbances (2)	• Planning appropriate activities (3) • Writing learning activity plans (3) • Making effective schedules (3)	• Aptitude tests (1) • Career planning (1) • Educational goals (1) • Employer responsibilities (1) • Management skills on the job (1) • Entrepreneurship (1)
		• Financial aid for education (1)
	• Developmental checklist (2) • Types of learning centers (3)	
• Acceptance of children with disabilities (1) • Challenges of raising child with disabilities (1) • Family stresses (3)	• Confidentiality (2)	• Influence of parents on career planning (1)
• Crisis nurseries (2) • Mental Health Association (2) • National Committee for the Prevention of Child Abuse (2) • Social service and child welfare agency (2)		• Trend toward more frequent career changes (1) • Volunteer experience (1) • Scholarships and loans (1) • Demand for child care workers (2)
	• Child care centers work experience (2)	• Career exploration (1) • Child-related careers (2) • Educational requirements (2) • Employment outlook (2)

USING COMMUNITY RESOURCES

National Council on the Aging
409 3rd St., S.W., Suite 200
Washington, DC 20024
(202) 479-1200

Al-Anon, Alateen Group Headquarters
P.O. Box 862 Midtown Station
New York, NY 10018-0862
(212) 302-7240

American Academy of Pediatrics
P.O. Box 927
141 Northwest Point Road
Elk Grove Village, IL 60007
(847) 228-5005

American Academy of Pediatric Dentistry
211 E. Chicago Avenue, Suite 700
Chicago, IL 60611
(312) 337-2169
http:\\aapd.org

American Automobile Association
Traffic Engineering - Safety Department
8111 Gatehouse Road
Falls Church, VA 22047
(703) 222-6000

American Cancer Society
1599 Clifton Road
Atlanta, GA 30329
(404) 841-0700

American College of Obstetrics and Gynecologists,
   Resource Center
409 12th St., S.W.
Washington, DC 20024
(202) 638-5577

American Dietetic Association
216 W. Jackson Blvd.
Chicago, IL 60606
(312) 899-0040

American Heart Association
7272 Greenville Avenue
Dallas, TX 75231
(214) 373-6300
http:\\www.amhrt.org

American Institute of Nutrition
9650 Rockville Pike
Bethesda, MD 20814
(301) 530-7050
http:\\www.nutrition.org\nutrition\

American Insurance Association, Engineering and
   Safety Service
85 John Street
New York, NY 10038
(212) 669-0400

American Lung Association
1740 Broadway
New York, NY 10019
(212) 315-8700

American Medical Association
515 North State Street
Chicago, IL 60610
(312) 464-5000
http:\\www.ama-assn.org

American Optometric Association
243 North Lindbergh
St. Louis, MO 63141
(314) 991-4100

American Society of Safety Engineers
1800 E. Oakton Street
Des Plains, IL 60018-2187
(847) 699-2929

American Society for Psychoprophylaxis in Obstetrics
   (Lamaze)
1200 19th St., N.W., Suite 300
Washington, DC 20036-2422
(202) 857-1128
(800) 368-4404
http:\\www.lamazechildbirth.com\

Association for Childhood Education International
11501 Georgia Ave., Suite 315
Wheaton, MD 20902
(301) 942-2443
http:\\www.udel.edu\educ\acei\

Association for Children and Adults with Learning
   Disabilities
4156 Library Road
Pittsburgh, PA 15234
(412) 341-1515

Asthma and Allergy Foundation of America
1125 15th St., Suite 502
Washington, DC 20005
(202) 466-7643

Autism Society of America
7910 Woodmont Ave., Suite 650
Bethesda, MD 20814
(301) 565-0433

Child Care Information Service/ National Association for
the Education of Young Children
1509 16th St., N.W.
Washington, DC 20036
(800) 424-2460

Children's Defense Fund
25 E St., N.W.
Washington, DC 20001
(202) 628-8787
cdf@tmn.com

Council on Environmental Quality
722 Jackson Place, N.W.
Washington, DC 20503
(202) 395-5750

Disabled Sports USA
451 Hungerford Dr., Suite 100
Rockville, MD 20850
(202) 393-7505

Educational Resource Information Center (ERIC)
Early Childhood Education
University of Illinois
805 W. Pennsylvania Avenue
Urbana, IL 61801
(217) 333-1386
http://ericir.sunsite.syr.edu/

Family Services
11700 Westlake Park Drive
Milwaukee, WI 53224
(414) 359-1040

Food and Drug Administration
5600 Fishers Lane
Rockville, MD 20857
(301) 594-6740

International Food Information Council (IFIC)
1100 Connecticut Ave., N.W., Suite 430
Washington, DC 20036
(202) 296-6540

International Childbirth Association Education
Association
P.O. Box 20048
Minneapolis, MN 55420
(612) 854-8660
icea c/o metrix@notes.wordcom.com

Juvenile Diabetes Foundation International
432 Park Avenue South
New York, NY 10016
(212) 889-7575

Juvenile Products Manufacturers Association
236 Route 38 West, Suite 100
Moorestown, NJ 08057
(609) 231-8500

La Leche International
9616 Minneapolis Avenue
Franklin Park, IL 60131
(847) 455-8317
(800) LA-LECHE

March of Dimes Birth Defects Foundation
1275 Mamaroneck Avenue
White Plains, NY 10605
(914) 428-7100

The Michigan Childcare Clearinghouse
201 N. Washington Square
Lansing, MI 48913
(800) 377-2097

National Association of Child-Bearing Centers
3123 Gottschall Rd.
Perkiomenville, PA 18074
(215) 234-8068
birthctr@midwives.org

National Autism Hotline
P.O. Box 507
Huntington, WV 25710
(304) 525-8014

National Committee for the Prevention of Child Abuse
332 So. Michigan Avenue, Suite 1600
Chicago, IL 60604
(312) 663-3520

National Council on Patient Information and Education
666 11th Street N.W., Suite 810
Washington, DC 20001
(202) 347-6711

National Congress of Parents and Teachers, Alcohol
Education Program
330 N. Wabash Ave., Suite 2100
Chicago, IL 60611-3690
(312) 670-6782

National Down Syndrome Society
666 Broadway
New York, NY 10012
(212) 460-9330

National Easter Seal Society
230 W. Monroe, Suite 1800
Chicago, IL 60606
(312) 726-6200

National Foundation for Wheelchair Tennis
4000 Macarthur Boulevard, Suite 420E
Newport Beach, CA 92660
(714) 259-1531

National Institute of Allergy and Infectious Diseases,
 Information Office
9000 Rockville Pike
Bethesda, MD 29892
(301) 496-5717

National Institute of Child Health and Human
 Development
Research on Mothers and Children
6100 Executive Blvd., Rm. 4B05K
Rockville, MD 20852
(301) 496-4000

National Mental Health Association
1025 Prince Street
Arlington, VA 22314
(703) 684-7722

National Safety Council
1121 Spring Lake Drive
Itasca, IL 60143-3201
(708) 285-1121

Parents Magazine
685 Third Avenue
New York, NY 10017
(212) 878-8700

Planned Parenthood Federation of America, Inc.
810 Seventh Avenue
New York, NY 10019
(212) 541-7800

Reader's Digest
Reprint Editor
Reader's Digest Road
Pleasantville, NY 10570
(914) 238-1000

The Skin Cancer Foundation
245 5th Ave,. Suite 2402
New York, NY 10016
(212) 725-5176
(800) 754-6490

USDA Food and Nutrition Service
National Agricultural Library
Information Center 304
10301 Baltimore Boulevard
Beltsville, MD 20705
(301) 504-5719

The Developing Child

Understanding Children and Parenting

The Developing Child

Understanding Children and Parenting

Seventh Edition

Holly E. Brisbane

GLENCOE
McGraw-Hill

New York, New York   Columbus, Ohio   Mission Hills, California   Peoria, Illinois

CONTRIBUTORS

Carol Alford
Teacher and Department Chairperson
Consumer and Family Studies
Fort Collins High School
Fort Collins, Colorado

Arlene Fulton
Child Development Specialist
Oklahoma Cooperative Extension Service
Stillwater, Oklahoma

REVIEWERS

Dr. Ethan Bergman
Nutrition Consultant/Professor
Central Washington University
Ellensburg, Washington

Marcia Britton-Wheeler
Department Chairperson, Home Economics
Julian High School
Chicago, Illinois

Pat Brodeen
Teen Parent Coordinator
San Antonio, Texas

Sue Chang
Home Economics Teacher
Mandarin High School
Jacksonville, Florida

Laurie Kanyer
Family Life Specialist
Yakima Valley Memorial Hospital
Yakima, Washington

Judy Lee
Director
Yakima Valley Community College Childcare Center
Yakima, Washington

Darlene Montz
Early Childhood Consultant
Yakima, Washington

Linda Murray
Family Life Instructor
Yakima Valley Community College
Yakima, Washington

Nancy Horn
Home Economics Teacher
Fresno High School
Fresno, California

Gail Park Fast
Certified Childbirth Educator
Yakima, Washington

Mary Patrick
Coordinator of Home Economics and Family Life
Yakima Valley Community College
Yakima, Washington

Mary Richmond
Home Economics Teacher
San Luis Obispo High School
San Luis Obispo, California

Judy Solomon-Marks
Child Development Instructor
Los Angeles Unified School District

Dr. Allen G. South
Gynecologist/Obstetrician
Yakima, Washington

Nancy South
Site Coordinator for Early Childhood Center
Yakima, Washington

Glencoe/McGraw-Hill

A Division of The McGraw-Hill Companies

Copyright © 1997, 1994 by Glencoe/McGraw-Hill. Previous copyrights 1988, 1985, 1980, 1971, 1965 by Holly Brisbane. All rights reserved. Except as permitted under the United States Copyright Act, no part of this publication may be reproduced or distributed in any form or by any means, or stored in a database or retrieval system, without prior written permission from the publisher.

Send all inquiries to:
Glencoe/McGraw-Hill
3008 West Willow Knolls Drive
Peoria, Illinois 61614-1083

ISBN: 0-02-647730-0 (Student Text)
ISBN: 0-02-647731-9 (Teacher's Wraparound Edition)

Printed in the United States of America.

2 3 4 5 6 7 8 9 10   VH/VH   02 01 00 99 98 97

CONTENTS

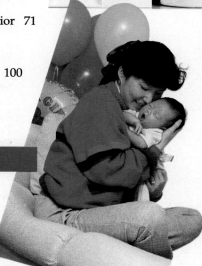

UNIT 3   THE BABY'S FIRST YEAR   224

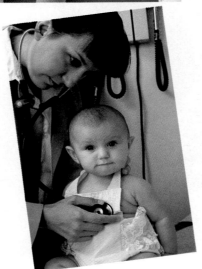

FEATURES

Parenting in Action

Positive Parenting Skills

Asa Hilliard
UNIVERSITY PROFESSOR OF URBAN STUDIES

Asa Hilliard is a Fuller E. Callaway Professor of Urban Education at Georgia State University and was instrumental in setting program requirements and standards of professional training for the Head Start Program.

He earned an Ed.D in Educational Psychology from the University of Denver where he also taught in the College of Education and in the Philosophy Colloquium for the Centennial Scholars Honors Program.

Dr. Hilliard feels that students will learn ways of professional thinking by first having as much experience as possible with children, and he urges students to "have faith in your ability to think and learn." He challenges professional educators to seek a greater balance between unstructured play and programmed instruction.

Jackie Mault
DIRECTOR OF SPECIAL SERVICES

Jackie Mault brings to her profession a background rich in diverse experiences. She has worked in childhood education administration, with a State Department of Education, the public school at the community level, and as a consultant.

In her position as Director of Special Services, she develops and manages programs for children from birth through high school. Currently, the rural community of Toppenish, Washington, challenges her talents. Dr. Mault urges people to "continue to meet the demands of the changing families and work within the communities for quality, comprehensive care." She feels that students should keep all options open and pursue career paths that are fulfilling and reality-based.

She received her doctorate from the University of Oregon, and in her spare time, teaches college-level classes at Heritage College in Toppenish.

Pat Brodeen
TEEN PARENT COORDINATOR

Pat Brodeen has been a teacher at Theodore Roosevelt High School in San Antonio, Texas for the past 22 years. She received both her bachelor and master of science degrees in Home Economics from Texas Tech University, specializing in Child Development and Family Studies.

Six years ago, Ms. Brodeen became one of the first teachers of the School Age Parenting class for teen parents at Roosevelt High School. She finds her greatest reward in watching a teen develop into a responsible parent. Her concern is for the teenage parent caught in the dilemma of being both a child and a parent. She advises teen parents to "stay in school if you want to avoid a lifetime of dependency."

When not involved with school, Ms. Brodeen finds time for her husband, four adult daughters, and an adolescent son.

Dr. Van D Stone
PEDIATRICIAN

Dr. Stone is a practicing pediatrician in Tupelo, Mississippi, and Chief of Pediatrics at Baptist Medical Center in Little Rock, Arkansas. He received his medical degree at Mississippi Medical School in Jackson, Mississippi, and his pediatric training at Arkansas Children's Hospital.

Over the last twenty years he has seen a substantial change in the area of children's nutrition and is pleased that "parents of all ages are open to new ideas and methods of quality care." Many of his patients' mothers are teens whose mothers participate in raising their grandchildren. He finds that these younger grandmothers are familiar with current trends in child care, and he values the wisdom of their experience.

In spite of his many obligations, including his own four children, Dr. Stone enjoys taking time to play with his young patients.

Jean Illsley Clarke
AUTHOR AND PARENTING WORKSHOP FACILITATOR

Jean Illsley Clarke is the director of J.I. Consultants in Minneapolis, where she designs and directs workshops in self-esteem, parenting, and group dynamics. Her emphasis is on observation and group activities, which she believes are vital to self-improvement. International studies have convinced her that people have much to learn from observing the customs and habits of other cultures. She stresses that "all human needs are the same; how we meet those needs will vary from one group to another."

Jean Clarke received an Honorary Doctorate of Human Service from Sierra University in Costa Mesa, California. Much of her background in child-rearing came from teaching and on-site research abroad.

Her publication credits include several books, magazine and journal articles, as well as videotapes and a local television show. Currently, she is co-author of a new book called *Help! For Parents of School-Age Children and Teenagers.*

Linda Espinosa
DIRECTOR OF PRIMARY EDUCATION

Linda Espinosa is Director of Primary Education for the Redwood City School District, and Treasurer of the National Association of Education for Young Children. She received her doctorate in Educational Design and Implementation from the University of Chicago where she studied multiple influences on child education, such as early experiences, geography, and culture.

While an undergraduate in college, Dr. Espinosa ignored warnings that a career in child education was pointless. She urges students to "follow your passion in whatever field you choose. Talented people are too often discouraged from professions where their energy is needed."

In a recent contribution to *Developmentally Appropriate Curriculum and Assessment Guidelines,* Dr. Espinosa examines the process of the changing school system and suggests ways to develop programs that can serve as models for other schools.

INTRODUCE

UNIT I RESOURCES

Teacher's Classroom Resources
- Unit 1 Test
- Testmaker Software
- Color Transparency 1

UNIT OVERVIEW

Unit 1 introduces students to the subject of child development and helps them appreciate its relevance to their lives.

In Chapter 1, students examine their own relationships with children and consider the importance of childhood as a time for essential development. Chapter 2 guides students in discussing the importance of family units and explains how couples can decide whether to become parents.

Chapter 3 helps students identify and discuss parenting skills. Students learn about effective techniques of guiding children and examine the options available for substitute child care.

In Chapter 4, students examine issues relating to teen pregnancy and parenthood. They learn about the decision-making process and making choices about sexual activity and pregnancy.

UNIT OBJECTIVES

After completing Unit 1, students will be able to:

- Discuss the importance of childhood and explain the benefits of studying child development.

- Describe the importance of families and identify issues couples should consider before deciding on parenthood.

- Discuss parenting skills, including providing discipline and selecting substitute child care.

- Explain how teens can make decisions about sexual activity and pregnancy.

CLASSROOM MANAGEMENT

Bulletin Board Suggestions

"Development Is Influenced By ..." Print the words *heredity, family, friends, classmates, television, neighbors, clubs*, and *religion* on pieces of colored construction paper. Clip magazine pictures representing each influence on development. Display each picture above its corresponding word.

"Score with Effective Parenting Skills!" Cut basketballs out of construction paper, and label each with a parenting skill: love, discipline, time, mutual respect, open communication, positive reinforcement, etc. Place a basketball net at one end of the board. Arrange the balls as though they were falling into the net one after another

UNIT 1

Children, Parenting, and You

CHILDREN LEARN WHAT THEY LIVE

If children live with criticism, They learn to condemn.

If children live with hostility, They learn to fight.

If children live with ridicule, They learn to be shy.

If children live with shame, They learn to feel guilty.

If children live with tolerance, They learn to be patient.

If children live with encouragement, They learn confidence.

If children live with praise, They learn to appreciate.

If children live with firmness, They learn justice.

If children live with security, They learn to like themselves.

If children live with acceptance and friendship,

They learn to find love in the world.

Dorothy Law Nolte

INTRODUCING THE UNIT

- Display photographs of infants and children; include children from various backgrounds and, if possible, from various cultures around the world. Stimulate discussion by posing questions such as these: What do all these children have in common? What makes each individual child unique? How can learning about the growth and development of all children help you understand and care for an individual child?

Conclude the discussion by telling students that in Unit 1, they will learn more about childhood and children, and about the context for children—families and parents.

- Ask one of the students to read the poem "Children Learn What They Live" to the rest of the class. Ask: Who can be responsible for helping children learn to value themselves and other people? Why should everyone be concerned about how children live and what children learn?

ASSESS

EVALUATE

Use the reproducible Unit 1 Test in the TCR, or construct your own test using the Testmaker Software.

EXTENSION

Invite several older adults to visit the class; if possible, invite a few of their children, grandchildren, and/or great-grandchildren to accompany them. Ask the visitors to share their memories of childhood and to discuss their understanding of the importance of family life. Encourage students to ask questions.

MORE ABOUT

Using the Poem

Dorothy Law Nolte's poem "Children Learn What They Live" reflects today's growing recognition of the important role that parents, caregivers, and family members play in shaping a child's self-esteem. Remind students that if a child's positive self-esteem is not firmly planted by the time the child reaches high school, he or she may have difficulty forming positive adult relationships. Ask for a student volunteer to read aloud the poem; then have students use it as a source of inspiration to have each student create a poem, story, or piece of art that reflects his or her individual thoughts and attitudes about children. Have the students share their creations in small groups or, if time allows, with the entire class.

INTRODUCE

CHAPTER OVERVIEW

Chapter 1 introduces students to the field of child development and helps them begin the process of learning about infants and young children.

In Section 1, students examine the experiences they have already had with young children and their attitudes from those experiences. They read about the specific benefits they can expect from studying children—an understanding of children, of self, and of options for the future.

In Section 2, students consider childhood as a unique stage in life. They also discover that this concept of childhood is relatively new; current attitudes toward children in our society date back only to the beginning of the twentieth century.

Then students examine the growth of child study; they read about the pioneers of child development scholarship and consider the study and research yet to be completed in the field.

In exploring child development, students examine the characteristics of all development. They go on to consider the importance of play to children, and they examine some basic guidelines for observing children at play. Finally, students discuss the major influences of heredity and environment on the development of children.

CLASSROOM MANAGEMENT

Resources Beyond the Classroom

In Chapter 1, students will evaluate their attitudes toward children and identify the benefits of studying children. They will realize that their relationships with young children depend on their own interest and knowledge. This realization may motivate students to extend their awareness of children and child-related issues. To learn more about children in their particular state and to learn how their elected officials vote on children's issues, students may call the Children's Defense Fund (CDF). Upon request, this organization can send brochures such as *An Opinion Maker's Guide to Children*, a fact sheet providing information of individual voting records, and CDF's annual *State of American's Children* report. To request this information, call CDF's toll-free line: 1-800-CDF-1200.

Growing with Children

SECTION **1** Children and You

SECTION **2** Childhood: A Time for Development

THINK ABOUT

Try to remember the last time you were around children. Maybe you were babysitting, attending a family gathering with cousins, or at a store where other customers brought children. How did you respond to the children? How did they respond to you? Now think about how learning more about child development will improve your relationship with children.

ASK YOURSELF

The photo on the opposite page shows a teen brushing the hair of a young girl. What might the child and the teen be thinking? What might they say to each other? Besides learning to keep the child's hair clean and healthy, how does this experience help the teen learn how to relate to young children? How does the experience teach the child to relate to the teen? How do both people benefit by spending time together?

NOW TRY THIS

Make a list of people who were important to you in your childhood. Next to each name, briefly describe the person and why he or she is memorable to you. Identify the personal qualities and values you now have that were influenced by these people. Now think of yourself as a role model to children. What qualities do you feel you best demonstrate to them? How would you like to influence the children in your life?

17

CHAPTER OBJECTIVES

After completing Chapter 1, students will be able to:

• Identify and discuss the various ways in which they can benefit from studying children.

• Explain how the concept of childhood has changed and discuss the characteristics of development.

INTRODUCING THE CHAPTER

• Tape record a young infant crying vigorously for at least five minutes. As students enter the classroom, play the tape loudly and display a life-sized baby doll. Ask volunteer students to use the doll and demonstrate what they would do for a baby who continues to cry as long and as loudly as the child on the tape. Ask: How confident do you feel caring for either a crying infant or an energetic four-year-old? How does this level of confidence affect your ability to be successful when caring for children?

Tell students that in this chapter they will begin to learn about children and how they can be cared for successfully.

• Use the photo on the opposite page and the three features on this page — Think About, Ask Yourself, and Now Try This — to begin a discussion about growing with children.

HEALTHY FAMILIES/HEALTHY CHILDREN

The Family Foundation

Ask students whether they have heard the statement, "The best thing you can do for your child is to love his mother." After students have discussed their interpretation of the statement, explain that the statement could also read, "The best thing you can do for your child is love his father." Then have students reflect on how the two statements are related to the child. Tell students that a solid foundation for raising a child involves a healthy relationship between the child's parents. Healthy spouses complement each other. They share power, equality, and leadership in their relationship. A strong, loving bond between parents flows to the children and instills a sense of security, trust, and high self-esteem.

SECTION 1
Children and You
Pages 18-23

FOCUS

SECTION 1 RESOURCES

Teacher's Classroom Resources
- Enrichment 1
- Reteaching 1
- Section 1 Quiz

Student Workbook
- Thinking about Children

SECTION OVERVIEW

Students begin Section 1 by examining their own current relationships with children of various ages. They go on to examine the ways in which studying child development will help them understand children and themselves, and think about their own futures.

MOTIVATOR

Ask students this question: What do you have in common with all other human beings? As they respond, list their suggestions on the chalkboard. If necessary, elicit the fact that all humans begin life as infants and pass through childhood.

Then ask: How do you think studying children will help you understand yourself? Again, encourage a variety of ideas, and note these ideas on the board. Explain to students that as they read this opening section, they will learn more about what child development is and how such a study will affect them.

USING TERMS TO LEARN

Let students pronounce both the vocabulary terms, and have volunteers define the terms as they now understand them. Remind students that they will learn specific definitions as they study Section 1. If necessary, help students recognize the relationship between the noun *behavior* and the verb *behave,* and between the noun *development* and the verb *develop.*

SECTION 1   Children and You

TERMS TO LEARN

behavior
child development

OBJECTIVES

- Evaluate your attitude toward children.
- Identify benefits of studying children.

Understanding how children fit into your life—both now and in the future—can help you understand yourself. You can begin by exploring your attitudes towards children. By doing so, you will discover that parenting skills are needed by almost everyone who comes in contact with children, whether they are parents or not. This understanding can also help you make meaningful plans for your future.

Children in Your Life

How would you describe your relationships with the children in your life today? Do you like children? Do you talk with and enjoy children of all ages? Do you know what to do when you are caring for children of different ages? Just as important—do children like you?

Think about these questions seriously. Your honest answers tell a great deal about you—the person you are today, the child you once were, and the adult you will become. After you have studied child development, you will have a better understanding of these questions and the meaning of your answers.

Perhaps children seem just naturally to enjoy being with you. In that case, you probably enjoy children and feel comfortable with them. On the other hand, perhaps children seem a little uncomfortable around you—and you feel uncomfortable with them. People vary a great deal in the way they feel and act toward children.

Your relationship with young children—brothers, sisters, friends, or babysitting charges—depends on your interest in children. It also depends on your knowledge of their changing stages and needs, and on your skill in applying that knowledge.

OBSERVING AND PARTICIPATING

Volunteering

If students are interested in a career in helping children, suggest that they try volunteering. It is a good way to learn more about children, discover new places in the community, and find out whether a career related to children will suit their needs.

To find a volunteer job, students should consult their community's volunteer placement and referral service. This is a central organization that registers volunteers and refers them to organizations that need help. These community placement and referral centers are usually called something like the County Involvement Council, Governor's Volunteer Program, United Way, Volunteer Action Center, Volunteer Bureau, or Volunteers in Action. After students contact the referral center, someone will interview them and try to place them in a position with an agency that needs their help.

As a young child, do you remember how much fun it was when older children and teens spent time with you? Now you are on the other side of that relationship. The more you understand children, the more you will enjoy being with them.

Why Study Children?

Learning about children is important in more ways than you may realize. Learning about children and their development can improve your understanding both of children and of yourself. It can also help you think about your future in relation to parenthood and career choices.

Understanding Children

As you study children, you will read about them, observe them, talk with them, play with them, and help them. In the process, your understanding of children will grow in many ways.

- **You will more fully appreciate all characteristics of human development.** **Child development** is *the study of how children grow in different ways—physically, mentally, emotionally, and socially.* As you discover the variety and complexity of growth, you will begin to understand why children remain dependent on their parents for such a long time. You will learn why they need affection in order to grow emotionally. You will also understand why they need the guidance and support of older people.

- **Your powers of observation will improve.** Books cannot teach everything you need to learn about children. Children are all around you, perhaps even in your own home. With some background and interest, you can increase your knowledge of children every day.

SEE HOW THEY GROW

The Study of Child Development
Students may be surprised to learn that child development is a relatively recent discipline. The study of child development had its beginnings in the 1920s, as specialists in various disciplines first came together to study the child as a whole person. Prior to this, society was relatively unconcerned with childhood as a phenomenon. Pioneer child development centers were located at the Merrill-Palmer School in Detroit and at the universities of California, Cornell, Georgia, Iowa, Minnesota, McGill, and Toronto. Specialists in anthropology, education, medicine, nutrition, nursing, physiology, psychology, social work, and sociology worked together to educate themselves and each other in the common problems of the developing child.

TEACH
Pages 18-23

- Children in Your Life
- Why Study Children?

GUIDED PRACTICE
Promoting Discussion
Encourage students to share and discuss some of their own experiences with children. How do you spend time with children? What have you learned from your experiences with children? What do you find hard to understand in children and their behavior? What would you like to know about children?

Critical Thinking
Let students share their ideas in response to these questions: Why do you think some people seem to get along especially well with children? To what extent is the ability to work well with children a natural talent? To what extent do you think it is a learned skill?

Using the Photograph
Have students describe and discuss the people in the photograph on this page. Then ask questions such as these: Do you take opportunities now to spend time with children? How do young children benefit from spending time with you? How do you benefit from spending time with them?

Critical Thinking
Encourage students to share their responses to this question: Why is it important to understand not just how children act, feel, and think, but also why they act, feel, and think as they do?

Cooperative Learning
Let students work in small groups to identify five situations in which a specific behavior is appropriate for a child of one age but not for a child of another age.
Have the members of each group share their ideas with the rest of the class. Then help students discuss how they decided which behaviors were or were not appropriate.

PARENTING
IN ACTION

Promoting Discussion

Before students begin reading this selection, guide them in a brief discussion of their own experiences with and ideas about caring for young children. You may ask these questions: Have you done any babysitting? How do you feel about babysitting? What do you think it takes to be a good babysitter? Why? Have you ever hired a babysitter? If so, what do you look for in a babysitter? Have you ever taken any babysitter training classes? What do these classes usually teach? How important is it for babysitters to have that information? What else do you think babysitters need to know? Why? How is being a babysitter like being a parent? How is it different?

Let students read "Caring for Children" independently.

Thinking Critically

Encourage students to share their reactions to Jim and his friends. How does Jim's part-time job taking care of little children affect your opinion of him? Why? Would his job seem different if he took care of only his five-year-old nephew? Why or why not? What do you think of Chris's response to Jim's job? Why? What do you think of Sue's response? Why? Why do you imagine Jim's sister asked him to take care of her children? What other options do you think she probably had? Did she make the best choice?

Answers to Think and Discuss

1. Jim has fun, feels helpful, earns money, and gains experience that will help him plan his future. Encourage a variety of responses.

2. Encourage students to present and support various opinions.

3. Encourage students to present and support various opinions.

PARENTING
IN ACTION

Caring for Children

Jim, who is 16, babysits three afternoons a week for his sister's two children, a kindergarten-age son named Kyle and an infant daughter named Kelly. One day, Jim mentioned his job to his friends Chris and Sue.

"Babysitting? How boring!" Chris responded. "My kid brother is a pest. How can you stand two little kids?"

Sue had a different reaction. "You take care of two children on your own? That's a lot of responsibility. Aren't you nervous—especially with a tiny baby?"

"It's not so bad," Jim told them. "My nephew reminds me of myself when I was his age. We have a lot of fun playing with his toy cars. As for Kelly—my sister leaves me plenty of instructions. If I didn't help out, my sister wouldn't be able to keep her part-time job. It's a way for me to earn extra money, too. Besides, I may decide to be a father someday—and I'm thinking about being a teacher or a doctor. This is a pretty good way to see if I'm cut out for working with children."

THINK AND DISCUSS

1. How does Jim benefit from his babysitting job? Which benefits do you think are most important to him? Which would be most important to you?

2. Do you assume that Jim has a natural ability for working with children? Why or why not? What has Jim done to learn about children?

3. What disadvantages do Jim's friends see in his babysitting job? What other disadvantages might there be?

• **You will begin to see why children act, feel, and think as they do.** Have you ever misinterpreted or been confused by something that a child said or did? That's normal. It can be difficult to understand children, especially before they learn to talk. Yet there is predictable, appropriate **behavior**—*a way of acting or responding*—for every stage of life. For example, when a two-year-old tries and fails to pull a tricycle up a flight of stairs, an angry outburst is predictable behavior. That same behavior from a frustrated ten-year-old, however, would not be considered appropriate.

• **You will be able to apply your learning to everyday life.** Simply studying child development is not enough; you need to apply your knowledge to real situations. For example, you may have a four-year-old sister who grabs your softball

---

OBSERVING AND PARTICIPATING

Volunteer Opportunities

With today's emphasis on social responsibility, more and more students are participating in volunteer activities. This not only helps them contribute and learn, but also is becoming an increasingly important factor in obtaining jobs and college placement.

Another way to find out about volunteer opportunities is to call various agencies. Inter-

ested students can call to see whether the organization needs volunteers their age and with their abilities. They might call the hospital, park or recreation department, library, museum, school guidance or volunteer placement office, religious organization, or any group, club, or association that interests them. Newspapers and radio and television stations often announce volunteer openings in the community.

glove at every opportunity. Your response to her actions may change when you understand her motivation: Younger children naturally admire those who are older, and they like to imitate the people they admire. With this understanding in mind, you may be able to accept your sister's actions as complimentary, rather than simply annoying.

- **You will learn practical techniques of caring for children.** Children respond favorably to people who care for them with confidence. Knowing how to bathe a baby, how to select and prepare a nutritious meal for a toddler, and how to encourage a three-year-old to settle down for a nap will give you that confidence. It will also bring you considerable satisfaction.

- **You will discover that children are fun.** The more time you spend with children, the more you can appreciate how delightful they are. In their innocence, humor, and generous affection, you will find much that is fascinating and rewarding.

Understanding Yourself

As you learn to understand children better, you will also come to know yourself better. You will learn more about what makes you the person you are.

You may think of yourself as a different person from the child you were a decade ago. It's true that you have grown and changed in many ways. However, no one changes entirely. The young man or woman you are right now has developed from the child you once were and will continue to develop into your adult self. Experience, education, and life's situations help you mature. Still, the self you have already developed will always be a part of you.

You may want to ask family members or older friends what you were like as a young child. Maybe they will recall that you were "a typical kid"—close to average development. Perhaps, though, they will describe you as "a quiet child" or "amazingly independent" or "constantly active." How closely do those descriptions of your young self correspond to the personality you have today? The similarities may surprise you!

As you study child development, you will discover that all children are similar in some ways. You will also find that every child has characteristics that are unique. In addition, you will see that development continues throughout life. All these insights can help you understand yourself.

Your own childhood has influenced your life today. What do you remember about your childhood? What do others recall about you?

GUIDED PRACTICE (continued)

Using the Photograph
Encourage students to describe the scene in the photograph and to share their responses to the questions below it.

Family Focus
Have students find out about their own characteristics as babies. Which have stayed the same? Which have changed? How do your parents, guardians, or other older family members think your characteristics have affected the family?

INDEPENDENT PRACTICE

Journal Writing
Ask students to write journal entries exploring their own ideas and opinions about the relationships between childhood and parenthood. Encourage them to respond to questions such as these: Is a happy childhood good preparation for parenthood? Can a person who has had an unhappy childhood become a good parent? If so, how? If not, why not?

Student Workbook
Have students complete "Thinking about Children" in the Student Workbook.

Extension
Let students work independently or in small groups to complete one or more of these extension activities:

- Collect photographs of yourself as a child. Select photos that show activities that are still meaningful to you today. Display your photos, and discuss them as evidence of the continuity of personality.

- Imagine that you are preparing to spend an afternoon with a five-year-old child (or with a young child of another specific age). What activities would you plan? Why? Write your ideas up as a schedule. Then share and discuss your schedule with classmates.

COOPERATIVE LEARNING

Evaluation
Current research suggests that positive interdependence and individual accountability are among the most important barometers of group success. When conducting an assessment of a group's collaborative performance skills, ask yourself the following questions to help you focus on these invaluable criteria:

- Do members of the groups appear to be "reaching out" to each other?

- Could any group members be fairly classified as "freeloaders"?

- Do any members of the group appear directionless or unaccounted for?

- Do group members work hard at maintaining self-discipline and at resolving conflicts?

Issues and Advice

1. According to Dr. Hilliard, what should a person develop in order to feel comfortable with children? (*Personal abilities and confidence.*)

2. Who should a person observe when learning more about children and child care? (*Teachers, child care workers, and parents.*)

3. What should be observed regarding these people? (*Possibilities are: how they talk and listen, their expressions, physical contact, and methods of reinforcement and/or discipline.*)

4. Why are successful parents, caregivers, and teachers important to someone who cares about children? (*They serve as models of action and attitudes which in turn guide others to be good models to children.*)

Thinking Like an Expert

Dr. Hilliard's observations and comments regarding the value of role models give students the opportunity to think about the people they admire. Ask students to write in their journals for a few minutes about this topic: Who are your role models? What characteristics do they have that make them commendable examples to you? After students have written and thought about these people, begin a general discussion about the relative merits of having role models. Encourage students to think about all areas of life that are touched by influential people.

Now ask them to think about parents, caregivers, and teachers who stand out as exemplary. What qualities make them unique? How do they guide your behavior with children? In what way(s) would you modify their actions and attitudes to develop your personal style of caregiving?

ASK THE EXPERTS

Making a Difference in a Child's Life

Q. **What can I do to make a difference in a child's life?**

A. You're off to a good start in making a positive difference to children—you are interested, and you are concerned about learning how to help children. Even your attitude in itself is a contribution to a child with whom you spend time.

I think what you need now is a chance to watch others work with children; you also need many comfortable experiences that will help you develop your own abilities and confidence.

Probably the best way to learn about interacting with children is to watch parents and teachers who work successfully with young children. Take time to observe these experienced people carefully. How do they talk to children? How do they listen? How do they use words, facial expressions, and physical contact to encourage and support children? How do they use positive reinforcement to guide children's behavior?

After your observation, think about how each teacher or parent approached the children. Which of these approaches will you feel comfortable using when you interact with children?

Remember, when you observe successful parents and teachers, you are looking at models. As you learn more and more about children and about successful approaches and attitudes, you will develop your own personal style of interacting successfully with young children.

It's also important to remember that, just as teachers and parents serve as your models, you serve as a model for young children. Young children will observe—and try out for themselves—the words, attitudes, and actions that you demonstrate.

Dr. Asa Hilliard
Fuller E. Callaway Professor
of Urban Education at
Georgia State University

Thinking About Your Future

Your increased understanding of children will be valuable not only now, but throughout your lifetime. Today, it may simply help you understand your family or the children in your neighborhood. You may also want to use your knowledge and skills, working as a babysitter, a teacher's aide, or a playground

CLASSROOM MANAGEMENT

Interest Inventories

In 1948, B. R. Forer developed what was probably the first interest inventory. He believed that preferences for occupations were expressions of personality. His inventory assessed how a person's responses to questions about vocational interests and activities expressed aspects of personality. Studies by later researchers in this field have shown that interest scales are related to people's values, academic achievement, liberalism, adventurousness, and other personal characteristics. Students are often confronted with a perplexing array of educational and vocational opportunities. Since these choices are often being made at a relatively young age, any input students have to help them make informed choices will help improve their contentment and success later. Encourage students to visit a school counselor and complete an interest inventory survey.

supervisor. In the future, your understanding of children may help you become successful as a parent or as a worker in a career related to child care.

Studying children at this point in your life can help you make decisions about your future career. For example, a high school student was planning to be a nurse at the beginning of a child study course, but by the end of the course had decided to go into teaching. The reason? "Now that I understand them better, I like kids more than I used to. I want to work with a group of children."

A classmate expressed a different reaction: "I thought I wanted to be a teacher, but now I'm not so sure. I didn't have any idea how much responsibility was involved!"

Learning about child development can also help you think about parenthood and prepare for its responsibilities. "It's made me more aware that having a child is really a lifetime commitment," one student commented. Another said, "I have the feeling I could handle anything now. I'm going to adopt about six children."

One instructor of a child study class stated, "Parenthood is the most important occupation most of us are ever engaged in. Whatever this course may or may not accomplish in helping these students make a choice of occupation, I know it will help them be better parents."

SECTION 1 REVIEW

CHECK YOUR UNDERSTANDING

1. List the three main benefits of studying children.
2. What is child development?
3. What is behavior?
4. List two benefits of learning practical techniques of caring for children.
5. During which stages of life does development continue?
6. How can studying child development help students plan their future?

DISCUSS AND DISCOVER

1. Do you agree that parenthood is one of the most important occupations anyone may have? Why or why not? What particular aspects of parenting make it difficult? What do you think makes it rewarding?

Observing & Participating

Take care of one or two young children for part of a day. Notice how you feel about the children. How confident are you at the beginning of your time with them? As the time together passes, do you feel more comfortable and confident—or less? Also, notice how the children respond to you. How do their responses affect your feelings about your abilities?

SECTION 1 REVIEW

1. Your understanding of children will grow; you will come to know yourself better; you will develop skills that will be valuable throughout your lifetime.
2. The study of how children grow in different ways—physically, mentally, emotionally, and socially.
3. A way of acting or responding.
4. You will understand children and get along with them better.
5. Development continues throughout one's lifetime.
6. It may help students make decisions about parenthood as well as about careers that involve working with children.

ASSESS

CHECKING COMPREHENSION

Assign students to write their responses to the Check Your Understanding questions in the Section 1 Review. Answers to the questions are given at the bottom of this page.

EVALUATE

Have students complete the Chapter 1, Section 1 quiz in the TCR.

Reteaching

1. Have students complete Reteaching 1 in the TCR.
2. Working with small groups, ask students to relate some of their own experiences in working with or caring for children. How can studying child development now help in similar situations in the future? How else can learning about child development help you?

Enrichment

1. Challenge students to complete Enrichment 1 in the TCR.
2. Have students write short essays on the responsibilities and rewards of parenthood. Why do people become parents? What commitments do they make when they have children? What benefits can parents expect to receive? Encourage students to share their essays with the rest of the class. Then save their work so that students can reconsider their views at the end of this course.

Extension

Invite graduates of this course to speak to the class about what they learned in the course, allowing a question-and-answer discussion.

CLOSE

Go around the room, letting each student pose a question he or she hopes to be able to answer by the end of this course. Ask a student to record the questions to keep for later use.

FOCUS

SECTION 2 RESOURCES

Teacher's Classroom Resources

- Enrichment 2
- Reteaching 2
- Section 2 Quiz

Student Workbook

- Countdown to Children and Childhood
- Describing Development
- Observation Practice

SECTION OVERVIEW

In Section 2, students consider that until recently childhood did not have the separate identity it has now, and compare conditions of childhood in the past and the present. They read about the establishment of child development as a field of study.

Next, they consider characteristics of development and examine the importance of play in it. They discuss the balance of heredity and environment.

MOTIVATOR

Write on the chalkboard: "Taylor is like a child." First, tell students to assume that the statement is intended as a criticism. Ask them to suggest specific traits and behaviors that might have led someone to make the statement about an adult. Then, assume that the statement is intended as a compliment. Ask the same question.

Finally, help students generalize about the differences between childhood and adulthood on the basis of their responses to the statement on the board.

USING TERMS TO LEARN

Help students read and discuss the vocabulary words. Ask them to share the science-related definition of environment, then relate to it in the context of child development.

Childhood: A Time for Development

OBJECTIVES

- Compare childhood in the past and in the present.
- Give examples of progress in understanding how and why children develop as they do.
- Describe five characteristics of development.
- Explain influences on development.

TERMS TO LEARN

environment
formula
heredity
nutrition
sequence

What does *childhood* mean to you? Do you picture a baby taking a few stumbling steps? A four-year-old playing on a swing? A classroom of fifth-graders? What makes children different from adults?

What Is Childhood?

However you respond to the questions above, you probably think of childhood as a period of life separate from adulthood. During this separate period, development occurs very rapidly. Human beings begin childhood almost completely dependent on adults for every need. By the time childhood ends, most people have become mature and ready for independence.

You would probably also agree that children have special needs as they grow and learn. Imagine you were preparing to spend a day with a five-year-old. You would not plan the same activities you would plan for spending the day with someone your own age, and you wouldn't expect to talk about the same things you discuss with people your own age. You wouldn't expect the five-year-old to think, feel, or behave exactly as you do.

We now consider childhood a distinct period of life, and many people have made a special study of this period. They have devoted time and effort to finding out more about how children develop, what their special needs are, and how those needs can best be met. Many important concepts have emerged from this kind of study; perhaps the most important is that

OBSERVING AND PARTICIPATING

Thoughts About Childhood

Have students observe children at play and share personal opinions related to the following quotations:

"Childhood is a blissful time of play and fantasizing, of uninhibited sensual delight."

Clare Booth Luce

". . . in all of our efforts to provide 'advantages' we have actually produced the busiest, most competitive, *highly pressured and over-organized generation of youngsters in our history—and possibly the unhappiest. We seem [determined to eliminate] much of childhood."*

Eda J. LeShan

In what ways was the play truly blissful? In what ways was the play competitive and structured? Which seemed the dominant mode?

childhood has a significant influence on later life. Those who study children and human development believe that every child has a right to a happy, healthy, loving childhood.

However, childhood has not always been considered a separate, important stage of life. In fact, childhood—as we know it—is a fairly recent "discovery."

Childhood: Past and Present

Before the beginning of the twentieth century, few people in Western civilization believed that there was anything unusual or important about the early years of life. During the Middle Ages and the centuries that followed, European adults were almost totally unaware of the special needs of children. They did not recognize the importance of providing children with sunshine, wholesome food, protection, loving care, and a variety of learning experiences.

Artworks created in these earlier centuries reflect society's attitude toward children. In paintings and statues, children appeared as miniature adults. They had the proportions, expressions, and clothing of grown-ups.

During the colonial period in America, people still believed that children differed from adults only in size, experience, and abilities. Children were dressed, fed, and doctored just as adults were.

These ideas persisted into the nineteenth century. An example is Louisa May Alcott's famous novel, *Little Women*. The book's central character, Jo, is constantly in trouble because she acts like the exuberant child she is rather than the little lady that girls of her time were expected to be.

Some of the differences between childhood in the past and childhood in the present are the result of changing attitudes toward children. Others are the result of advances in technology.

Work

In the past, children were expected to work hard at an early age. In American pioneer families, children were expected to take care of many farming and household tasks. During the Industrial Revolution, many children worked as laborers in factories.

Today, most children in our society are not thrown into the world of adult work so abruptly. The "job" of young children is simply to grow, learn, and play. Children assume responsibility gradually by helping with household tasks and, later, by taking part-time jobs.

What adjectives do you think of when you see the children in this picture? Is that how you would describe childhood?

TEACH

Pages 24-33

- What Is Childhood?
- Childhood: Past and Present
- The Growth of Child Study
- Characteristics of Development
- The Importance of Play
- Influences on Development
- Children and You

GUIDED PRACTICE

Promoting Discussion

Encourage students to share their own ideas about childhood as a separate stage of life. When do you think childhood ends? Does it end at the same time for all people in all parts of the world? Why or why not? Which stage of life follows childhood? How are the two stages different? In the full expanse of human life, how important is childhood? Why?

Using the Photograph

Let students describe and discuss the children in the photograph on this page. How do you think their experience of childhood is similar to yours? How do you think it might be different?

Promoting Discussion

Help students consider how different their childhoods might have been if they had been expected, from an early age, to work hard for long hours to earn a wage. How would your lives be different now? What would you have gained by assuming an early share of adult responsibility? What would you have lost?

Critical Thinking

Ask students to share and discuss their responses to these questions: Why do you think parents allowed their children to work long hours in unsafe environments? What choices did most parents have? Do you think their limited choices affected their feelings for their children? If so, how? If not, why not?

MORE ABOUT

Childhood of the Past

Because the English were the first to settle widely in North America, their ideas about the treatment of children set the pattern for colonial America. The puritanical Calvinists who settled in New England believed that children were wicked and born filled with evil. It was the responsibility of the parents to eradicate that innate evil with harsh discipline. Children who disobeyed were considered under the influence of the Devil and were appropriately punished, often severely. Parents were expected to develop obedience, honesty, industry, and piety in their children. Stubbornness and falsehood were considered special sins of childhood, and children were punished to correct their sins. It certainly was not a pleasant time to be a child; unfortunately, many of these attitudes persisted for a long time.

GUIDED PRACTICE (continued)

Cooperative Learning

Have students work in groups to consider the following situation from earlier times: Sarah was apprenticed to a seamstress when she was eight years old. She sewed by candlelight from 6 a.m. until 6 p.m. six days a week. She was served no breakfast; bread and cheese for lunch; and meat, bread, and vegetables for dinner. She lived with the seamstress and saw her own family only on Sundays.

Let group members compare and discuss responses to this question: What are the implications of this lifestyle for Sarah?

Using the Photograph

Let students describe the early baby bottles in the photo on this page. How—and why—have baby bottles changed?

Making Connections: Art

Have students examine painting reproductions in art history books or other sources. Ask them to find and share examples of the clothing worn by children and adults in earlier centuries. For example, Goya's The Family of Charles IV shows children dressed as adults in 1800.

Family Focus

Let students work in groups to plan skits illustrating their perceptions of family life under the circumstances described in the text. Have each group present its skit to the rest of the class.

Making Connections: Writing

Ask students to write short stories or brief essays, presenting their own concepts of an ideal childhood. Give students an opportunity to share their writing with the rest of the class.

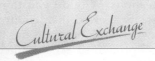

Cultural Exchange

Colors and designs for infant clothes have progressed far beyond the traditional pink and blue. Some designers have even created fashion lines uniquely for babies!

Would you recognize these objects as early baby bottles? They date back to around the turn of the century. Why do you think they are shaped so unusually?

Cultural Exchange

WHY PINK AND BLUE?

The custom of dressing boys in blue and girls in pink has its origin in the idea of protecting newborns from evil spirits. Blue, as the color of the heavens, was especially potent in frightening away demons, hence it was allotted to the most important child, the boy. Girls were thought so little of in early centuries that there was no point in giving them a particular color; pink was probably a later attempt to balance the color scheme. A European legend is much prettier. Baby boys were found under cabbages, which were somewhat blue in color. A baby girl was born in the heart of a pink rose.

Health and Nutrition

Before the beginning of the twentieth century, parents could not hope to raise every child born to them. Diseases such as diphtheria, typhoid fever, and smallpox caused the deaths of children in almost every family. Today, in the United States and other developed countries, these and many other diseases have been controlled by medical advances, personal cleanliness, and strict public health regulations.

In the past, babies either thrived on breast-feeding, or they died. Today, of course, breast-feeding still provides an infant with complete **nutrition**—*a balance of all the food substances needed for health and growth.* Parents also have the option of bottle-feeding a baby with commercially prepared **formula**, which is *a mixture of milk or milk substitutes and added nutrients.* Infant formulas are safe and scientifically balanced for nutrition. Special formulas are available for infants with digestive problems or other special health needs. Older babies now usually eat strained, unseasoned foods, made either commercially or at home, rather than the adult table food served to babies in the past.

Dress

Until the seventeenth century, children were dressed as small adults. Around that time, special clothing styles began to develop for children, though these styles did not encourage activity and play. Even early in the twentieth century, all children wore dresses for the first years of life.

Preschool boys and girls were dressed alike until the early part of the twentieth century. Then styles began to change, and sex differences were reinforced by the style and color of clothes worn from infancy on.

Today, young children now usually wear clothing that is suitable in both style and color for either boys or girls. Modern children wear practical, washable, lightweight garments designed to provide freedom of movement and maximum comfort.

Parental Love

Although childhood in the past was different in many ways from what we know today, one thing has not changed—the love of parents for their children. History is filled with stories that include striking examples of parental love.

Despite their genuine affection, parents in the past had little awareness of the special needs of children. They did not know how to encourage the best physical, emotional, social, or intellectual development. This kind of knowledge is fairly recent.

HEALTHY FAMILIES/HEALTHY CHILDREN

Childhood Diseases

Diphtheria, typhoid fever, and smallpox were dreaded diseases that killed many children, as well as adults, in the past. Diphtheria is a contagious disease that causes the formation of false membranes in the throat and other air passages. This condition results in high fever, breathing problems, and weakness. Typhoid fever is a highly infectious disease spread by contaminated food or water. Its symptoms are red rashes, high fever, bronchitis, and intestinal hemorrhaging. Smallpox is a highly infectious viral disease. It first causes chills, high fever, headache, and backache. Later, widespread pimples erupt, which blister, produce pus, and form pockmarks. Fortunately, modern medicinal advances in inoculation have all but eradicated these diseases.

The Growth of Child Study

Attitudes toward children have changed. Our society now attaches great importance to understanding and guiding children. The fact that you are studying and learning about children is one indication of this change in attitude.

Over the past several generations, interest in studying children and their behavior has grown remarkably. For the first time, researchers and scholars have been able to study child growth and development scientifically. Several pioneering scholars have made basic contributions to our understanding and appreciation of children and childhood.

- Alfred Binet, a French psychologist, developed a series of tests to measure intellectual processes.
- Jean Piaget, a Swiss psychologist, theorized that intelligence develops in stages that are related to age. According to Piaget's theories, the new mental abilities at each stage determine the limits of what a child can learn during that period.
- Sigmund Freud, an Austrian physician, developed the theory that the emotional experiences of childhood have a lasting effect on the personality of an adult.
- In the United States, theorists including Arnold Gesell and Erik Erikson have explored child development in terms of social and emotional growth.

Much remains to be learned about children. However, with the help of scientific research, the superstitions and misunderstandings of the past are being replaced by sound knowledge.

Today there are many resources available to help parents in the study of children.

OBSERVING AND PARTICIPATING

Keen Observation

Like most scientific innovations, most of the early research in child development was a result of keen observation. The inquisitive researcher saw a common behavior or action from a different perspective, asked appropriate questions about it, observed it more, tested its limits, and arrived at some logical generalization about the behavior or action. Although research today may be more sophisticated in design and measurement techniques, because of the inherent difficulties of using children for research, most child development research still relies on accurate observations and the ability to draw conclusions from these observations.

GUIDED PRACTICE (continued)

Making Connections: Health
Point out to students that the lives of children in earlier times would be considered unhealthy and unsafe by today's standards. Many children died in infancy and childhood, and the practice of medicine was very different. Have students investigate early medical practices and compare them with those used today. Let them share their findings in brief oral reports.

Critical Thinking
Explain that in the past, children learned about the world of work by participating in it. Ask students how children today learn about work and the responsibilities that go along with it.

Promoting Discussion
Help students identify and discuss well-known examples of parental love.

Cooperative Learning
Let students work in groups to collect pictures that show examples of parental love. Have group members plan an appealing display and then show their collected pictures to the rest of the class. Help all students discuss their responses to these questions: Is physical affection the only way for parents to show their love? Is it the best way? What else can parents do to show their children their love?

Making Connections: Reading
Have interested students read a biography of one of the early pioneers in the study of child development; ask these students to present brief oral reports summarizing their reading to the rest of the class.

Using the Photograph
Encourage students to describe and discuss the scene shown in the photo at the bottom of this page.
How can parents benefit from these resources? What other resources can help parents?

Promoting Discussion

Guide students in considering the contributions individual scholars have made to our understanding of child development. What do you think motivated the research and study these people undertook? Do you believe they were aware of the significance of their work? Why or why not?

Critical Thinking

Encourage students to share their responses to these questions: Are parents today more or less likely to raise their children as they themselves were raised? Why?

Cooperative Learning

Let students work in groups to consider examples of the sequence of development. Have group members select two different skills; then, for each skill, have them write up a sequence of earlier skills on which the final skill is based.

Promoting Discussion

Discuss with students the relationship between the individual rate of development and the safety of a child. Some children at age three may be able to use playground equipment independently, while others may not be physically developed enough and may need assistance and careful watching. Ask students to give other examples of how developmental rate is related to the safety of the child.

Family Focus

Point out to students that the ages of children in a family can have a major effect on the family. Then guide them in discussing how the rapid pace of development in childhood causes changes in family life. For example, a family with an infant who needs feeding every four hours may find lack of sleep causes irritability that interferes with good family relationships. What other examples can students relate?

Information about children and their needs has become not only more complete but also more readily available. In the past, older family members were almost the only source of information and advice about child care and development. Today, people without the help of nearby relatives can find books, articles, and radio and television programs on the subject of child development.

All these resources can give you valuable knowledge about children. Still, the best way to understand human development is to study and observe it for yourself.

Characteristics of Development

The study of childhood has led to an understanding of some basic facts about human development. You may be able to recognize examples of these characteristics of development in your own life and in the lives of other people you know.

- **Development is similar for everyone.** Children all over the world go through the same stages of development in approximately the same order. For example, all babies lift their head before they can lift their body, and all stand before they can walk.

- **Development builds on earlier learning.** The skills a child learns at age two build directly on those he or she mastered at age one. After learning to walk, a child will soon be able to run. Before learning to speak in sentences, a child must learn to say single words. Thus, development follows an orderly **sequence**, *a step-by-step pattern*.

- **Development proceeds at an individual rate.** Although all children follow a similar pattern of development, each child is an individual. The style and rate of growth differ from one child to another.

- **The different areas of development are interrelated.** In studying children, it is convenient to focus on one area of development at a time. However, it is important to remember that, as a child grows, many kinds of changes are taking place at once. A child does not, for example, develop physically one week and emotionally the next week. All areas of development—physical, intellectual, social, and emotional—interact continually.

- **Development is continuous throughout life.** It does not stop at a certain age. Sometimes development is rapid; at other times, it is much slower. We all continue to develop in many ways throughout our lives.

MORE ABOUT

Development

Development refers to the changes over time in the structure, thought, or behavior of a person as caused by both biological and environmental influences. Usually, these changes are progressive and cumulative, and they result in increasing body size, increasing complexity of activity, and increasing integration of organization and function. Some development, such as prenatal growth,

is primarily biological, while other development, such as emotional growth, depends mainly on the environment. Most development, however, cannot be so neatly categorized as either biological or environmental, because it involves the interaction of both elements. Consequently, it is important for students to realize the complexity of the factors governing development so that they can accurately analyze them.

All children follow a similar step-by-step pattern of development, yet each child is unique in many ways. Can you see how physical, intellectual, emotional, and social development influence one another?

The Importance of Play

One of the most effective ways to learn about children and their development is to observe them and interact with them in their most natural setting—the world of play. Play makes an essential contribution to a child's development. Consider all the ways that play benefits children:

- **Physically.** Activities such as running, climbing, jumping rope, and riding a tricycle help the large muscles of the back, arms, and legs develop. Strength and balance improve as a result. Activities such as putting puzzles together, finger painting, and stringing beads help develop control of the small muscles.

- **Intellectually.** A toy or game does not have to be "educational" to promote intellectual development. Simple play activities, such as singing nursery rhymes, stacking blocks, and sorting through a box of buttons, provide experiences in gathering, organizing, and using information about the world.

OBSERVING AND PARTICIPATING

Children at Play

Working with children and observing them leads to greater understanding of development. As students observe children playing, have them notice the following:

- Physical and motor development—growth patterns, hand-eye coordination, manipulative skills, and body control.

- Intellectual development—formation of concepts, problem solving, and learning through the senses.

- Socialization—getting along with others, feelings about group activities, and adjustment to routines and limitations.

- Emotional development—feelings about self and others; attitudes and behaviors which express one's feelings about how things are.

GUIDED PRACTICE (continued)

Using the Photograph

Encourage students to describe and discuss the scene in the photo on this page. What evidence of physical development do you see? Of emotional development? Of social development? How have they influenced one another?

Promoting Discussion

Show students photographs of various kinds of playground equipment and of various toys. (Instead, you might simply ask students to suggest different kinds of equipment and toys; list their suggestions on the chalkboard.) Encourage students to describe how children play with or on each. How does that play promote physical development and intellectual development?

Critical Thinking

Let students share and discuss their responses to these questions: Do you think children are playing when they watch television? If so, how does this kind of play compare with other forms of play? If not, why not? How might watching television affect the physical, intellectual, emotional, and social development of a young child? Why? What are the implications of your opinion?

Cooperative Learning

Have students work in groups. Each group should pick a skill they would like to encourage and develop in a child. It could be academic, athletic, musical, or another type of skill. Have students identify activities and experiences that could promote this skill in the child. At what point might excess encouragement turn off the child?

Making Connections: Social Studies

Let interested students research the kinds of toys popular among young children in other cultures. How are they similar to toys familiar in this country? How are they different? Ask students to summarize their findings for the rest of the class.

GUIDED PRACTICE (continued)

Cooperative Learning

Let students work in small groups to develop lists of at least ten locations where they could observe children. What types of activities could be observed in each of these places? Then have the groups share their lists, and ask the class to develop a complete listing of local sites for observing young children.

Promoting Discussion

Encourage students to discuss their ideas about recording observations. Why is it important to write observations down? Why is it important to record observations objectively? What problems can subjective observations create? Why?

Cooperative Learning

Show students a short video of children at play. Then let the students work in groups to write an objective observation of the children or of one of the children in the video. Encourage group members to work together to keep judgments, opinions, and feelings out of their recorded observation.

Promoting Discussion

Guide students in considering the importance of confidentiality. Why is it important to keep information about a child confidential? Who might be hurt when you fail to keep information confidential? How could they be hurt?

Using the Photograph

Let students discuss the children in the photograph on page 31. How does this illustrate environmental influences on development? How might heredity also influence a child's appreciation of music?

- **Emotionally.** Play can help children work through life's challenges and problems. For example, acting out the role of a parent, a fire fighter, or a jungle explorer can diminish the frustrations of being a small person in a big world.

- **Socially.** As children grow, they progress from playing alone to playing beside one another. Gradually, they learn to play together and to get along with others—sharing and taking turns. Leadership, friendly competition, and cooperation are some of the valuable social skills that children learn through play.

Guidelines for Observing Children at Play

Direct experiences with young children will enhance your understanding of child growth and development. Here are some guidelines to help you observe young children.

- **Choose a time and a place.** The setting in which you observe children may vary. Some of your observations may be made informally; for example, you might watch children playing at a park. Other observations will be more formal; you might observe in a preschool classroom, in a family child care home, or in a private home, for example. For a formal observation, phone ahead and set up a scheduled time for your observation. Once you arrive, observe from a position that will not interfere with children's routine or play activities.

- **Record what you observe.** Writing down what you observe helps you recognize patterns of behavior, rates of growth, and stages of development. It also helps you identify individual differences in children. When you record your observations, the effects of environment and of other people on each child also become more apparent.

    In recording your observation, use action words to identify children's behavior and development. Here's an example: *Curtis took off the fire fighter's hat and handed it to Jane, saying, "You can have the dumb old hat." He turned and walked away from the housekeeping area toward the blocks.*

    During observations, look at children objectively—seeing them as they are—rather than subjectively. In other words, try to avoid being influenced by who you think the child is or what you think the child should be doing.

    On each set of observation records, include the following basic information: the title of the observation, your name, the date and time of the observation, the names and ages of the children observed, the number of children present, the number of adults working with the children, and the type of

OBSERVING AND PARTICIPATING

Recording Observations

Remind students that the quality of an observation depends on their ability to be objective. It depends on accurate recordings of what is actually going on. Following are various methods of recording observations:

- Anecdotal records are written descriptions of one episode in the child's life.

- Diary-type records record development over a period of time. The descriptions include what the child is doing in many situations.

- Time samples are used to study specific kinds of development during a limited time period and in a given setting.

- Event samples record a certain type of behavior, such as cooperative play or quarreling.

situation you are observing (such as a private preschool or a kindergarten in a public school, for example). Also include notes about any other relevant information, such as *during a field trip* or *on the outdoor play yard*.

- **Watch how children interact with other children and with adults.** As you observe, ask yourself questions such as these: With which other children does this child interact? How does the child communicate with other children? Under what circumstances does the child approach an adult? How does the child ask an adult for help? Does the child use words or gestures?

- **Keep observation information confidential.** Any information you gather about a child—whether from your own observations or from discussions you have overheard or participated in—should be shared only with your child development teacher or with the child's parents. Talking about a child's behavior, attitudes, or abilities with anyone else is inappropriate.

Each of these four children has a different personality. What might you record on an observation sheet about each?

Influences on Development

As you observe children in play, you will see that each child is a unique individual. Why and how does each child develop as a unique individual? Aspects of the child's development are influenced by various factors, beginning even before birth and continuing throughout his or her life.

Being encouraged to appreciate music is an example of an environmental influence.

OBSERVING AND PARTICIPATING

Confidentiality

Remind students that everyone has the right to privacy. Therefore, they should respect the privacy of the children they work with. As observers in a preschool setting, students should remember the importance of maintaining a professional demeanor and should treat all observation information as confidential. They should not leave observation records in public view or share them with others. Instead, observation records should be reserved for purposes of study and discussed in view of the total situation.

Students should also be aware of the damaging effects associated with labeling children. If a particular child has been categorized with phrases such as "attention-deficient disorder" or "has weak ego control," students should not misinterpret these labels. Labels, which can be self-fulfilling, may cause observers to treat the child in a way that makes the description come true.

GUIDED PRACTICE (continued)

Using the Photograph

Encourage students to describe the scene in the photograph on the top of page 32. Then let them share and discuss their own experiences having fun with children.

Critical Thinking

Explain that students in child development or parenting classes are often exposed to concepts and care techniques that contradict the practices in their homes. Ask students how they can take advantage of knowing more than one way of handling children. How might they be able to experiment to discover which seems most effective with children?

Family Focus

Point out that for young children, the family is the most important environmental influence. Ask students to describe ways that families influence the development of children.

Promoting Discussion

Help students develop a list of personal characteristics (such as red hair, a quick temper, skill at baseball, and an interest in music). Let one of the students record the list on the chalkboard. Then go over the list item by item. Which characteristics are inherited? Which are likely to be learned from the environment? Which seem to represent a combination of factors from heredity and environment?

Promoting Discussion

Focus students' attention on this sentence on page 33: "Bring your resources—all your resources—to enrich your study [of children]." What are the resources they can bring to the study of children? How can they best use those resources? How can they expect to benefit if they bring those resources to the study of children?

INDEPENDENT PRACTICE

Journal Writing

Pose a series of questions such as these: How do people learn about human development? What have I, at this point in my life, already learned about human development? What have I learned from talking with other people? From observing other people? From observing myself? What have I learned from reading books and articles, from listening to radio shows, and from watching television programs? What is the best way for me to learn about human development? Why? Is that the best approach for everyone? Why or why not? Ask students to explore their responses to some or all of these questions in their journals.

Student Workbook

Distribute and have students complete activity sheets "Countdown to Children and Childhood," "Describing Development," and "Observation Practice" in the Student Workbook.

Extension

Let students work independently or in small groups to complete one or more of these extension activities:

- Review books you have already read (or skim books you have not yet read), looking for passages that describe conditions of child workers during the 1700s and 1800s. For example, Chimney Sweeps by James Cross Giblin contains moving accounts of the hardships of children living and working under harsh conditions without parents. Select one passage to read aloud to the rest of the class.

- Examine a recent copy of the Reader's Guide to Periodical Literature (or use a library's computer program to search for magazine articles), looking for entries listed under "Children." What specific topics are included under that general heading? What kind of articles in what different magazines are listed under each specific topic? Record your findings, and compare them with those made by other students.

Having fun with children is one of the best rewards of learning about and understanding their development.

One important influence on development is **heredity**, *the passing on of characteristics that are physically inherited from previous generations*. Another important influence on development is **environment**, *the people, places, and things that surround and influence an individual*. Scientists and philosophers have debated for centuries whether heredity or environment has the stronger influence. Today, most agree that the two work together.

Consider how heredity and environment have helped shape your development. From your parents and past generations, you inherited your own physical characteristics out of millions of possibilities. When you were born, you became part of a family whose relationships are unique. Directly or indirectly, your family passed on certain attitudes and certain ways of doing things. These behaviors reflect your family's personal and religious or moral values; they also reflect the customs of the society in which you live.

Eventually, every individual chooses to join many groups outside the family. These groups may include friends, classmates, coworkers, neighbors, social clubs, religious and personal organizations, and many others. Each group exerts some influence on its members' thoughts and actions. You are also influenced by the type of community you live in, what you read, what you see on television, your personal experiences, and countless other forces.

HEALTHY FAMILIES/HEALTHY CHILDREN

Heredity and Environment

The influences of heredity and environment are often not easy to separate. For example, a parent and child may both be overweight. Is the tendency toward obesity inherited, or is the weight problem a result of dietary patterns and habits learned in the family? In general, heredity sets the physical limits, while environment determines how far toward the limits the person will go. Students should be aware of the correlational-causational fallacy. Simply because things go up, go down, or act inversely together does not always indicate that one factor directly causes the other. In fact, a third factor may be the causing factor.

This is not to say that you copy the attitudes and actions of everyone you come in contact with. In fact, sometimes you may try to do just the opposite! Because you are an individual, you always react to outside influences in your own unique way. Still, you are constantly being shaped by people and experiences.

The same is true for every child. During infancy and early childhood, outside forces have an especially strong influence on development. That is why caring for children is such an important responsibility—and such a challenging opportunity.

Children and You

You are in an excellent position to study children—close to adulthood, yet not so removed from childhood that you cannot remember it clearly. Bring your resources—all your resources—to enrich your study. Become involved personally, and you will find the study of children enjoyable and rewarding.

As you learn, you will find some of your opinions challenged, others reinforced. You will discover answers to questions that have puzzled you. You will also raise questions to which there are no answers yet. Perhaps someday you will help find the answers to some of those questions.

SECTION 2 REVIEW

CHECK YOUR UNDERSTANDING

1. How were children regarded during the colonial period in America?

2. What is nutrition?

3. What is formula?

4. List three factors that have resulted in the control of many dangerous diseases.

5. What theory did Jean Piaget contribute to child development studies?

6. List five characteristics of development.

7. Explain the difference between heredity and environment.

DISCUSS AND DISCOVER

1. Discuss your ideas about this statement from the chapter: "The job of young children is simply to grow, learn, and play." In what sense are these activities a job for young children? What do children contribute by performing this job? What do they get in return? Should adults help children in this job? If so, how? If not, why not?

Observing & Participating

Visit a child care center or a public place, such as a playground, where you can observe three or more children of the same age. Describe how they play—alone, beside each other, or together. Besides age, how are the children alike? How are they different? What conclusions can you make about the physical, emotional, social, and intellectual characteristics of this age group?

SECTION 2 REVIEW

1. They were considered small adults, differing only in size, experience, and abilities.

2. A balance of all the food substances needed for health and growth.

3. A liquid food for baby that consists of a mixture of milk and milk substitutes and added nutrients.

4. Medical advances, personal cleanliness, and public health regulations.

5. Intelligence develops in stages related to age. Mental abilities at each stage determine what the child is capable of doing during that period.

6. Development is similar for everyone, builds on earlier learning, proceeds at an individual rate, is interrelated, and is continuous.

7. Heredity refers to characteristics that are physically inherited from past generations. Environment refers to the influence of the people, places, and things that surround a person.

ASSESS

CHECKING COMPREHENSION

Assign students to write their responses to the Check Your Understanding questions in the Section 2 Review. Answers to the questions are given at the bottom of this page.

EVALUATE

Have students complete the Chapter 1, Section 2 quiz in the TCR.

Reteaching

1. Have students complete Reteaching 2 in the TCR.

2. Guide small groups of students in reviewing the influences of both heredity and environment on the development of children. Working in twos, have students make a poster with a picture of a child in the center. Around the picture, have them draw or place pictures of environmental influences on the child.

Enrichment

1. Challenge students to complete Enrichment 2 in the TCR.

2. Have students select a popular book or magazine articles about child development. Ask them to read and evaluate their selections, and present brief reports to the class summarizing the information and the point of view they found in the works.

Extension

Many of Charles Dickens' novels portray the lives of children during the nineteenth century. Show students a movie based on one of these novels, and ask them to pay particular attention to the experiences of the children. Afterwards, guide them in discussing what they have learned about the lives of children and childhood.

CLOSE

Ask students to complete this statement, orally or in writing: Childhood is a time of ...

ASSESS

CHECKING COMPREHENSION

Use the Summary and the Reviewing the Facts questions to help students go over the most important ideas presented in Chapter 1; encourage students to ask questions and add details, as appropriate.

CHAPTER 1 REVIEW

1. Can help them understand themselves, the children they once were, and the adults they will become.

2. Any four: appreciate more fully all characteristics of human development; improve powers of observation; begin to see why children act, feel, and think as they do; apply learning to everyday life; learn practical techniques of caring for children; discover that children are fun.

3. Do I want to be a parent? Do I want to work in a career related to child care?

4. About 100 years ago.

5. Took care of many farming and household tasks.

6. Medical advances, personal cleanliness, and public health regulations.

7. French psychologist; developed a series of tests to measure intellectual processes.

8. Theory that the emotional experiences of childhood have a lasting effect on the personality of an adult.

9. A step-by-step pattern.

10. Promotes physical development, intellectual development, emotional development, and social development.

11. An objective observation records things as they are; a subjective observation is influenced by feelings and opinions.

12. The passing on of characteristics that are physically inherited from previous generations; the people, places, and things that surround and influence an individual.

CHAPTER 1 REVIEW

SUMMARY

- Your relationship with young children depends on your interest and your knowledge.
- Study, observation, and practical experience help you understand children.
- Understanding children will help you better understand yourself.
- Your knowledge about children and your experiences with them can help you think about parenthood and about career choices.
- Childhood today is different from childhood in the past. The differences result largely from changes in attitude and advances in health care and nutrition.
- The study of child growth and development is a recent science.
- Development always follows an orderly sequence, but it proceeds at individual rates.
- All aspects of development are interrelated, and development is continuous.
- A variety of hereditary and environmental influences affect development.

REVIEWING THE FACTS

1. What can students learn from thinking seriously about their relationships with young children?

2. List four ways in which your understanding of children will grow as you study child development.

3. List two questions about your own future that studying child development can help you consider.

4. About how long ago did most people in Western civilization begin to regard childhood as a separate, important stage of life?

5. What responsibilities did children in American pioneer families have?

6. What are epidemics? How common are they in the United States now?

7. Who was Alfred Binet? What did he contribute to our understanding of children?

8. What theory did Sigmund Freud develop?

9. What is a sequence?

10. List four benefits of play for children.

11. What is the difference between an objective and a subjective observation?

12. Define these terms: *heredity, environment.*

EXPLORING FURTHER

1. Every day for one week, check a local newspaper for articles about children and parenting. Read and save all the articles you find. At the end of a week, bring to class the two articles you consider most interesting; share and discuss them with your classmates. (Section 1)

2. Think about your own concept of childhood. Using magazines, photographs, and your own artwork as sources, collect pictures and use them to create a collage that communicates your concept. Share and discuss your collage with a group of classmates. (Section 2)

3. Bring to class an article of clothing that you wore as a baby or a photograph of yourself as a baby. Discuss the particular outfit you wore, comparing it with the outfits worn by others, both boys and girls. For whom was your outfit suitable? What kinds of activities did it encourage? Would you expect a baby today to wear a similar outfit? (Section 2)

THINKING CRITICALLY

1. **Synthesize.** Discuss your response to the following statement: "Only students who already are parents, who plan to become parents, or who want careers in child-related fields should study child development." Do you agree or disagree? Why?

2. **Compare and contrast.** Why do you think parents allowed their children to work long hours as factory laborers during the Industrial Revolution? How do you think those parents felt about their children? About their children's work? Why don't American parents send their children to work in factories today? Do you think the fact that children no longer work in factories means that parents are better today than they were 200 years ago? Why or why not?

CLASSROOM MANAGEMENT

Community Resource People

The child development class offers many opportunities to use outside people as resources. As these people visit your classroom, they will gain a better understanding of the scope and content of your program. Invite parents, local businesspeople, and community leaders to serve as guest speakers, panel discussion participants, authorities for certain content areas (health and nutrition, prenatal care, child care, parenting, etc.), experts via real-life experiences, such as being the parent of an adopted or special-needs child.

Contact the resource people well in advance. The initial contact may be made through a personal visit, telephone call, or letter. After agreement has been reached about an appropriate date, time, and place, send a letter of confirmation. A thank-you note is appropriate after the speaker has been to the class. A student or student committee may assume this task.

3. **Analyze.** How do you think your heredity has affected your development? How do you think your environment has affected your development? What examples can you cite—in yourself, your family, or your friends—of the interacting influences of heredity and environment? Which do you consider more influential on the development of young children, heredity or environment? Why?

CROSS-CURRICULUM CONNECTIONS

1. **Art.** Examine one or more art books, and select a painting or sculpture that depicts at least one child. When was the artwork created? What attitudes toward children does it portray? Share and discuss your findings with the rest of your class.

2. **Reading.** Read *Little Women* by Louisa May Alcott. As you read, identify specific incidents that reflect nineteenth-century attitudes toward children, parents, and families. With a group of classmates, compare and discuss your ideas.

SCHOOL TO WORK

Researching Careers Learning about child development is a step toward becoming a positive parent. However, this class could help shape your career plans as well. Physical therapy, pediatric medicine, children's book illustrator, teacher, occupational therapy, and child care worker are only a few of the many careers related to children. Why not talk to your school counselor or interview a child-care professional to learn more about possible career paths for you?

PERFORMANCE ASSESSMENT

Growing with Children

Task
Use what you learned about a child's physical, emotional and social, and intellectual development to create a time line that highlights your personal growth.

Purpose
The purpose of your time line will be to create a visual documentation of your own growth and development.

Procedure
1. Use a pencil to sketch a time line that shows each year of your life.
2. Brainstorm a list of developmental achievements such as the following: stand alone, walk, ride a bicycle, talk, attend school, read, print name, and have a best friend.

3. Ask a family member to help you remember or do your best to recall your age when you achieved each of the stages on your list. As you reflect, add any other significant events, such as ate solid foods or learned to swim, to your list.
4. Draw your final time line and insert the events in the appropriate places to show your age at the time of each achievement. Be prepared to explain how each stage of development builds upon an earlier one, and how developmental stages are interrelated.
5. Choose an age or stage on your time line, such as toddler, preschool, or early childhood. Identify appropriate activities that you think would encourage physical, social and emotional, and intellectual development for that stage.

Evaluation
Your time line will be evaluated for organization and clarity of presentation. Content should be clear, concise, and accurately identify appropriate activities for the stage you have selected. Your time line should be neat and visually appealing.

Portfolio Idea
Make a version of your time line that focuses on your teen years. Explain how your activities and interests contribute to your physical, social and emotional, and intellectual development.

EVALUATE

Use the reproducible Chapter 1 Test in the TCR, or construct your own test using the Test-maker Software.

EXTENSION

Invite a panel of young parents to speak with the class. If possible, include teen parents and both married and unmarried parents in the panel. Ask panel members to share their responses to these questions: How has an understanding of child development helped you as a parent? How has it helped you in other aspects of your life? How have you learned about child development? What do you wish you had known about child development before you became a parent? Why?

CLOSE

Ask each student to complete the following sentence:
Learning about child development will help me ...

DEVELOPING A PORTFOLIO

Purpose A portfolio is a collection of samples of a person's work, carefully selected and refined in order to show skills and knowledge. The samples are assembled in a binder, folder, or other container that allows for simple, attractive presentation.

Portfolios are presented to potential employers to increase chances of being chosen for a job. They may also be used for admission to a college, university, or training program. In all cases, a portfolio is designed to reflect relevant skills and knowledge.

PERFORMANCE ASSESSMENT

Personal Time Lines
To help students begin, work with the class on a master list of developmental stages to include on their time lines. Then discuss appropriate activities for each stage of development. Make sure students understand that there is only an approximate age for each stage of development. Any students unable to get assistance from home should be encouraged to do their best at recalling or estimating these stages.

If students have the opportunity to compare and contrast their time lines, they will see how each person is unique, but all are similar in many ways. This activity helps students become acquainted and comfortable with giving and receiving feedback from each other.

INTRODUCE

CHAPTER OVERVIEW

Chapter 2 presents insights into the basic societal unit, the family. As they study this chapter, students learn more about the family groups in which they are growing up and about the family groups they may hope to establish.

In Section 1, students begin by defining the family as a group of people who care about each other and are committed to each other—a definition broad enough to encompass the many different forms of family groups familiar in our society today. Then students examine the four main kinds of family groups—nuclear, extended, single-parent, and blended.

They continue by examining the family life cycle and discussing modern societal trends that affect family systems, the need for healthy families, and specific approaches that can help strengthen the family.

In Section 2, students focus on one aspect of family life: parenthood. They discuss the many kinds of changes that parenthood brings with it—new responsibilities, changes in lifestyle, emotional adjustments, and changes in relationships. They also consider the special rewards and benefits of parenthood. Then students examine the process of making decisions about parenthood and identify five basic factors to be taken into account during this process.

CLASSROOM MANAGEMENT

Resources Beyond the Classroom

Since teens are generally less prepared for the responsibilities of parenthood and need to realistically assess both the rewards and demands of parenting, Planned Parenthood has many local education centers where representatives are often willing to speak to groups. They will distribute appropriate literature, including a wide array of information about prospective parents'

choices, parenting, adoption, etc. For further information, either call your local chapter or, the national office, or write to:

Planned Parenthood Federation
of America, Inc.
810 Seventh Avenue
New York, NY 10019
(212) 541-7800

Living in Families

SECTION 1	Understanding Families
SECTION 2	Considerations of Parenthood

CHAPTER OBJECTIVES

After completing Chapter 2, students will be able to

- Discuss various kinds of families and explain how all kinds of families can be strengthened.
- Describe the changes that parenthood brings and identify the questions people should ask themselves before they choose to become parents.

INTRODUCING THE CHAPTER

- Write the word *family* on the board. Ask students simply to read the word and jot down the first ten words or phrases that come to mind in response. After students have written their lists, encourage volunteers to read their responses aloud. Discuss the similarities and differences. Explain to students that as they study Chapter 2 they will learn more about families and how they function.
- Use the photo on the opposite page and the three features on this page—Think About, Ask Yourself, and Now Try This—to begin a discussion about living in families.

THINK ABOUT

The strength of an individual family depends on a few major factors—a sense of commitment, time spent together, strong communication and coping skills, an appreciation for each other, and shared beliefs. Think about the relationships you have with other family members. How many of these factors are present? Which ones need improvement?

ASK YOURSELF

Study the expressions on the two people in the photo on the opposite page. How can you tell that they enjoy each other's company? How is their relationship strengthened by the time they spend together? Assuming the adult and child are related, how can the man use this moment to assure the child of her importance in the family unit?

NOW TRY THIS

Think about an event in your life that included family members. What was the focus of the gathering—a holiday, birthday, religious observance, family reunion, or other celebration? How did family members help make the gathering fun and memorable? What traditions, if any, were associated with the event? How did this event emphasize the importance of families?

HEALTHY FAMILIES/HEALTHY CHILDREN

Family Communication

Virginia Satir said, "I see communication as a huge umbrella that covers and affects all that goes on between human beings. Once a human being has arrived on this earth, communication is the largest simple factor determining what kinds of relationships he makes with others and what happens to him in the world about him."

Dolores Curran, in her study of healthy families, found that the number one trait of a healthy family was that the healthy family communicates and listens. Without communication, family members don't know one another. When one doesn't know another, it is difficult to really care about the other. It is when we share our intimacies that we grow closer to each other. Sharing intimacies involves communicating one's feelings, thoughts, beliefs, values, desires, goals, and fears.

FOCUS

SECTION 1 RESOURCES

Teacher's Classroom Resources
- Enrichment 3
- Reteaching 3
- Section 1 Quiz

Student Workbook
Family Focus

SECTION OVERVIEW

Students begin Section 1 by examining a definition of family broad enough to encompass various family groups in society today, then consider four main kinds of family groups.

Students then learn about the family life cycle and discuss societal trends that affect modern family systems. They consider the need for healthy families and examine ways in which families can be strengthened.

MOTIVATOR

List familiar television programs that feature families on the chalkboard. Then ask students to discuss the TV families. Who are the family members? How are they related to one another? How do they seem to get along? How similar to—or different from—your own family do these TV families seem to be? Do you think they are realistic? Idealized? Exaggerated? Why?

Tell students that the first section will help them understand real families and how they function.

USING TERMS TO LEARN

Help students pronounce and discuss all ten vocabulary items. Guide students in recognizing the relationships between adopt and adoption, commit and commitment, extend and extended.

Understanding Families

OBJECTIVES

- Explain the importance of the family.
- Identify various types of families
- Identify stages in the family life cycle.
- Explain how social trends affect the family.
- Explain ways to strengthen the family.

TERMS TO LEARN

adoption
blended family
commitment
coping skills
extended family
family
family life cycle
foster child
nuclear family
single-parent family

When you think about the word, *family*, what comes to mind—your own family at home? A friend's family? A family you see on a favorite TV program? There are many different groups of people that function as families.

The Importance of Families

A **family** is *a group of two or more people who care about each other and are committed to each other*. Usually, the members of a family live together, and in most families, the members are related by marriage, by birth, or by adoption.

People seem to have a need for families. Perhaps you've heard someone say—or have even said yourself—something like this: "We've known him for years—he's like family." "You know I care about you—you're like family to me." "I know I can always count on her—she's like part of my family."

Why does family seem to matter so much? A family is every child's first connection to the world. As a child gets older, family provides a safe environment from which to explore—and to which he or she can return.

All the members benefit from a family. The family provides an important sense of belonging for every member. Within a family, each individual has the opportunity to love and to be loved, to care and to be cared for, to help others and to receive help.

COOPERATIVE LEARNING

Beyond Journals

Personal journals are commonplace in today's classroom. You may wish to expand the concept of journal writing into the realm of cooperative learning by having the class as a whole maintain a Group Status Log. Housed in either a looseleaf folder or spiral notebook and placed in a prominent location in the classroom, the log can be a repository for thoughts, reactions, comments, and suggestions with respect to the experience of cooperative learning. Encourage individuals and groups to develop the habit of adding to the log following the completion of a group activity and to consult it prior to embarking on new ones.

A strong family foundation is one of the best gifts for a child. The family is the child's first connection to the world and it provides each individual with the opportunity to love and to be loved.

Types of Families

Family groups take many different forms. As you probably know from experience, family groups may vary widely in size and structure. A family may include a single parent and several children, or two parents and one child, or two married or committed adults with no children. Some people form their own unique family groups. For example, two or more single adults may live together as a family, helping each other meet the individual and group needs of all the family members.

In spite of these many variations, there are four main kinds of family groups: the nuclear family, the extended family, the single-parent family, and the blended family.

The Nuclear Family

A **nuclear family** is *a family group with two generations—a father and mother and at least one child—sharing the same household.* There are, of course, many variations among nuclear families, depending at least in part on the occupation of the parents and on the number and ages of the children. In some nuclear fami-

MORE ABOUT

The Family System

Every family is made up of individuals who interact with each other and, together, form a separate whole—the family itself. For this reason, a family can be thought of as a system—just as the national government or the human body is a system of interacting parts.

The following statements can be applied to the family system:

• All the parts of a system are interdependent and interrelated. In a family, this means that every family member depends on the other family members. It also means that actions and emotions of each member affects the other members.

• The system itself tries to maintain a balance and to keep functioning. If one family member stops fulfilling a specific function, other members will try to take over that function.

• The system has certain needs. Families need services of various government agencies.

TEACH

Pages 38-48

• The Importance of Families
• Types of Families
• The Family Life Cycle
• Trends Affecting Family Systems
• The Need for Healthy Families
• How Can Families Be Strengthened?

GUIDED PRACTICE

Promoting Discussion

Help students consider and discuss the definition of family presented on page 38. How many different kinds of family units are included in this definition? What qualities are emphasized by this definition? Do you agree with this definition? Why or why not?

Cooperative Learning

Let students work in groups to discuss the ways in which various family members benefit from belonging to a family. How do you benefit from being part of your own family group? How do you contribute to your family? What advantages do other family members derive from being part of your family group?

Using the Photograph

Encourage students to describe the family group in the photograph at the top of this page. Which type of family do they form? How do you imagine each member benefits from being part of this family?

Promoting Discussion

Have students identify the numbers and ages of family members in various nuclear families with which they are familiar. Help them note the variety within this type of family group. How do variations in family size and in the age of family members affect the experiences of the family?

GUIDED PRACTICE (continued)

Promoting Discussion

Encourage students to discuss their responses to these questions: Why do you think some nuclear families include only one child? Why do you think other parents have four or more children? What do you think motivates parents who adopt children? Who take foster children into their families? If you were ready to start a family, would you choose to have biological children, adopted children, or foster children? Why?

Making Connections: Reading

Have interested students research the procedures and costs of adopting an infant. Do these differ from the procedures and costs of adopting an older child? If so, how? Let students share their findings with the rest of the class.

Cooperative Learning

Let students work in small groups; ask the members of each group to imagine themselves as a family unit trying to decide whether to take in a foster child. Have them use the six steps of the decision-making process to reach their decision. (These are the six steps: identify the decision to be made; identify the alternatives; consider the consequences of each alternative; choose the best alternative; act on the decision; evaluate the decision.) Then let the members of each group share their decision with the rest of the class.

BUILDING SELF-ESTEEM

Parents and caregivers who are open with a child about adoption reap even greater rewards than they realize. Honesty helps build trust; trust is vital to a healthy family relationship.

BUILDING SELF-ESTEEM

Telling the Truth about Adoption

An adopted child can be expected to ask why his or her biological parents "gave me away." Parents should avoid saying that the biological parents did not want the child. A simple "I don't know, honey, but I'm glad it worked out this way," accompanied by a hug, is much better. This helps avoid the feeling of rejection that some adopted children have. Showing adopted children that they are loved and wanted helps them realize that they truly belong in the family—and that they will not be given up again. Children need to understand that it is often difficult, but necessary and unselfish, for birth parents to give up a child.

lies, one parent works outside the home to provide family income. The other parent stays home to care for the children and to keep the household functioning. In other nuclear families, both parents work outside the home. The number of dual-earner nuclear families has grown rapidly in recent decades and has contributed to an ever-increasing need for quality child care.

Although the majority of nuclear families include only the parents' biological children, some nuclear families include adopted children and/or foster children.

Attitudes toward **adoption**, *the legal process in which people obtain the permanent right to raise a child who is not biologically their own*, have undergone some important changes in recent decades. In the past, children were always matched as closely as possible to their adoptive parents, with special consideration given to their race, ethnic and religious background, and physical characteristics.

Now, the emphasis of adoption is on finding good homes for children who need them. Matching the characteristics of parents and adoptive children is no longer considered especially important. Older children, disabled children, children from other countries, and children of mixed races are adopted much more frequently than in the past.

Some families choose to care for a **foster child**, *a child whose parents or other close family members are unable to care for him or her*. In these cases, foster parents assume temporary legal responsibility for the child.

Although family groups may vary widely in size and structure, healthy families show appreciation and commitment to one another and share quality time together.

MORE ABOUT

Foster Parenting

Despite its impermanent nature, foster parenting can be a rewarding and enriching experience for both the adult and the child. However, not everyone can become a foster parent. Most states have strict rules about the types of families that can become foster families. The number and ages of children already in the family, the health and careers of the family members, and the family's current living arrangements are usually considered. Additionally, the situation is often monitored by state regulatory agencies. Foster families usually receive a small amount of money each month to assist in providing for the foster child's basic needs, but the real motivation should be the satisfaction of providing a caring environment to a child in need.

The important consideration in any family is not how its members are related, but whether they are able to provide each other with love, care, and support.

The Extended Family

An **extended family** is *a family group that includes relatives other than parents and children within a single household.* A woman raises her two grandsons. An elderly man lives with his daughter, his son-in-law, and his granddaughter.

The term *extended family* sometimes also refers to additional relatives outside the household—the cousins, aunts, uncles, grandparents, and great-grandparents who don't live with a young person but who can be important sources of emotional support and guidance.

The Single-Parent Family

A **single-parent family** is *a family group that consists of one parent and one or more children sharing a household.* The parent in this type of family may be either a mother or a father. That parent may be raising children alone because he or she has never married or because he or she has been left alone after a divorce or death.

Single parenting puts many demands on the parent. He or she has a great deal of responsibility, little free time, and no spouse with whom to share problems. Many single parents find support in a network of friends and relatives who feel involved both with the parent and with the child or children in the family. Some communities have organizations for single parents, which provide emotional support and social opportunities.

BUILDING SELF-ESTEEM

Positive Role Models

One special concern that faces single parents is every child's need to develop positive relationships with adults of both genders. A child needs a close and meaningful relationship with a caring adult who is the opposite gender of the single parent. The parent's adult friends and relatives can often provide a positive example of male or female behavior and relationships. In addition, some single parents, especially those in big cities, can turn to programs such as Big Brothers, Big Sisters, or scouts for help.

GUIDED PRACTICE (continued)

Using the Photograph
Encourage students to describe the family scene in the photo at the top of this page. What do you imagine each pictured member contributes to this family? How do you think each family member benefits?

PROMOTING DISCUSSION

Let students share their ideas in response to these questions: How do you think living in a nuclear family compares with living in an extended family? What are the advantages of each living situation? What might the disadvantages be? What special benefits might a single parent find in living with an extended family? What additional challenges might an extended family face if it includes a blended family?

MAKING CONNECTIONS: READING

Have students read at least three recent newspaper stories or magazine articles about the rate of births to single mothers. What current trends are explained in these stories and articles? Do you see these trends reflected in your own community? Let students share their findings and conclusions with the rest of the class.

Promoting Discussion
Encourage students to share their own ideas about sources of support for single parents. Why is adult support important for parents? What do you consider the best sources of support for single parents? Why?

OBSERVING AND PARTICIPATING

Celebrating Individual Differences
A child's caregivers may include grandparents, aunts, uncles, and other relatives. Today, extended family members are more likely to be geographically separated than in the past. However, this does not mean that the extended family has disappeared entirely as a factor in raising children. The increase in diversity of cultural traditions, the impact of economic stresses, and

other factors influence whether households include extended family members. Additionally, through the increase in the frequency of remarriage of a parent, many children gain additional extended family members, such as stepparents and stepgrandparents.

BUILDING SELF-ESTEEM

Have students identify resources in their communities that provide children of single-parent homes with exposure to adults of both genders. What other activities would provide role models for these children?

GUIDED PRACTICE (continued)

Promoting Discussion

Let students share and discuss their own feelings about blended families. Who can especially benefit by becoming part of a blended family? Why? What special problems do members of blended families sometimes face? Why? How do you think they can best resolve those problems?

Critical Thinking

Ask students to share their opinions about stepparenting. Is being a stepparent necessarily different from being a parent? If so, how? If not, under what circumstances are the two roles the same? What special challenges do most stepparents face? How do you think they should meet and overcome those challenges?

Making Connections: Literature

Ask interested students to examine the depiction of stepparents in folklore and fairy tales. Let these students summarize their findings for the class. Then guide all students in discussing responses to these questions: How do you think these views of stepparents affect children? How do you think they affect parents? Do you think children today should continue to hear these tales? Why or why not?

Making Connections: Zoology

Have interested students research and report on family life among various species of animals. Which species, for example, mate for life? Which are polygamous? Which raise their young together? Which teach their young systematically? Which live in extended families? How do the young of various species develop life skills and learn to interact? After students have reported their findings, let the entire class consider which species seem to follow patterns of family life similar to those of humans.

The Blended Family

A **blended family** is *a family group that consists of a married couple and at least one child from a parent's previous relationship.* Like other types of families, blended families can involve many variations.

In the first few months or years, the members of a blended family may experience problems in establishing a new family unit. Everyone has to learn about a new person while living with him or her. Accommodations and compromises may be necessary on many different levels.

Stepparenting brings many challenges. However, when all family members work together to overcome problems, the results can be rewarding for everyone. Both stepchildren and stepparents can benefit from the new perspectives and resources that are brought to the family.

The Family Life Cycle

There are many differences between families, but there are similarities, too. Each family group goes through the **family life cycle**—*a series of stages in a predictable order*—though, of course, the timing and duration of these stages may vary widely from family to family. The chart on page 43 gives an overview of the stages through which families develop.

Every family is made up of individuals who interact with each other, and together form a separate whole—the family itself. Healthy families work together to accomplish tasks.

MORE ABOUT

Blended Families

Stepfathers in newly formed blended families tend to have a low level of involvement with stepchildren; they are often uncertain about how much discipline or affection to show stepchildren. As the blended family becomes established, his involvement increases. In fact, college students report a greater attachment to stepfathers than to noncustodial fathers.

The addition of a stepfather often improves functioning in a mother-headed family. The standard of living in mother-headed families may increase with remarriage. Having a stable and intimate relationship may increase the self-esteem of the remarried mother and benefit her children. Children whose noncustodial parent has lost touch may find a stepfather provides support and companionship.

THE FAMILY LIFE CYCLE

As you study the chart, think about the special challenges and rewards that may be associated with each stage in the family life cycle. Also consider how adults who never marry, who marry but do not have children, who divorce, or who divorce and remarry may experience their own special versions of the family life cycle.

BEGINNING STAGE

A couple works to establish a home and a marriage relationship.

CHILDBEARING STAGE

The couple prepares and adjusts to parenthood.

CHILD-REARING STAGE

As children grow, the parents work to meet their children's changing needs and help them develop independence.

LAUNCHING STAGE

Children gradually leave home to support themselves. Parents help their children adapt to life on their own.

EMPTY-NEST STAGE

After the last child has left home, the couple renews their relationship and adjusts to the change in their parenting role.

RETIREMENT STAGE

The couple adjusts to the aging process. They may develop new interests or renew old ones.

VARIATIONS IN THE FAMILY LIFE CYCLE

Any of the following situations may change the pattern of the family life cycle or the characteristics of each stage:

* Single adulthood
* Single parenthood
* Divorce
* Remarriage
* Couples without children
* Adult children who move back in with parents

Trends Affecting Family Systems

Families of every type and in every stage of the family life cycle are affected by social trends. As the number of individuals in various societal groups change, the entire society experiences shifts that affect the family system. For example, as more women become active in the work force, society faces a growing need for

MORE ABOUT

The Family Life Cycle

The amount of time a particular family spends in each stage of the family life cycle varies. The beginning stage of the life cycle used to be short, since most couples had children soon after marriage. However, some couples today may wait until they are in their thirties before having children. The number and spacing of children determines the length of the childbearing and child-rearing stages. Timing of the earlier stages determines how soon families enter and complete the launching stage. Couples who had children in their thirties will have a shorter empty-nest stage than those who had children at younger ages.

GUIDED PRACTICE (continued)

Using the Chart
Guide students in studying and discussing the chart The Family Life Cycle. What are the major events during each stage in the family life cycle? What is the significance of the beginning stage? How do you think couples adjust when they skip that stage and enter immediately into the childbearing stage? What special challenges do you think employed parents face during the child-rearing stage? What special challenges do you think parents who do not work outside the home face during the launching stage? What challenges and rewards do you think couples can expect during the empty-nest stage? Which couples probably get the most enjoyment out of the retirement stage? Which of the stages in the family life cycle appeals most to you? Why?

Critical Thinking
Let each student select one of the situations that may change the pattern of the family life cycle (single adulthood, single parenthood, divorce, remarriage, couples without children) and write a revised family life cycle for a person in that situation.

Promoting Discussion
Ask students to share their ideas about the family life cycle. Who should know about the stages of the cycle? Why? How should information about these stages be used by family members—as a guide to behavior, as an aide to expectations, or in some other way? Why?

Making Connections: Current Events
Have interested students read about the increasing number of people who are spending an increasing number of years in the retirement stage. How are these increases affecting the society as a whole? How are they affecting demands made on health care services? On government programs? Let these students share and discuss their findings with the rest of the class.

GUIDED PRACTICE (continued)

Promoting Discussion

Let students share their feelings about changing family roles. Why are these roles changing? Who do you think benefits when mothers are employed? How do they benefit? Who do you think benefits when one parent stays home to raise the children and run the household? How do they benefit? Who do you think benefits when parents have choices about their family roles?

Critical Thinking

Encourage students to share and discuss their responses to these questions: Do you believe that most people are more accepting of men's moving into women's traditional family roles or of women's moving into men's traditional family roles? Why do you think that? What do you think accounts for this attitude?

Promoting Discussion

Have students share their ideas about the impact of the mobile society on family life. What evidence of this mobility have you seen or experienced? What effects do you think it has?

Making Connections: Current Events

Ask students to find and read news stories that relate to family values. Who is supporting "family values"? What do those individuals or groups mean by the term? What programs or laws are being associated with family values? Do you believe those programs or laws will really benefit families? If so, how? If not, why not? Give students an opportunity to share and discuss what they have read.

Cultural Exchange

FAMILIES—PRESERVING CULTURAL HERITAGE

All families, whether consciously or not, pass down to successive generations the essence of their culture in the form of values, behavior, foods, language, customs, and traditions. Immigrant families are often faced with the challenge to preserve their values and belief systems while assimilating into mainstream society. As cultures adapt and modify, so does the concept of a traditional family pattern. This process is call *enculturation.*

The best way to influence children is to recognize the inherent strengths within all families. Sharing stories of past experiences, discussing feelings, and exploring traditions are the first steps to preserving your cultural heritage. Think about what your culture has to offer, and what you have learned from others. What unique qualities will you pass on to your descendants?

facilities and individuals that provide quality child care. Another current trend is the rising population of older citizens. Some current trends create additional stresses on family systems; other trends may encourage family unity. Other examples of trends in society are: changing family roles, mobility, and awareness of family values.

Changing Family Roles

Not long ago, each member of a family group had a clearly defined role to play. Traditionally, a husband cared for the family by earning money; a wife cared for the family by raising children and running the household. Children attended school and anticipated assuming the same family roles they saw their parents filling. Each family member knew what was expected.

In recent decades, family roles have become much less clearly defined. Increasing numbers of families are headed by single parents or by two employed parents. Adults in these families may face particular stresses in arranging quality care for their children, in setting aside time to spend with their children, and in scheduling time for their own needs and activities.

Mobile Society

A hundred years ago, it was not unusual for an adult to die in the same home where he or she had been born. Today, most adults no longer live in the same community—much less the same home—they were born in. Our society has become very mobile; individuals and families move often.

Because of these frequent moves, families often lack close, supportive connections with friends and relatives. Family groups need to rely more on their own members and on long-distance relationships with members of their extended families and their familylike friends.

Awareness of Family Values

In recent years, the importance of the family unit has gained increasing recognition. The term *family values* is heard around the country. Many people feel strongly that government institutions should offer encouragement and support to families. They believe that laws and programs should help ensure that all children, elderly, disabled, and sick individuals are able to experience the best quality of life possible. They also believe in providing affordable and accessible health care for all families.

Cultural Exchange

Encourage students to discuss cultural differences found in their communities. Possibilities are: street names, ethnic restaurants, family-owned businesses, festivals, and landmarks.

HEALTHY FAMILIES/HEALTHY CHILDREN

Changing Roles

There was a time when male and female roles were clearly defined and most people knew what was expected of their gender. Males were to be aggressive, strong, assertive, athletic, and self-reliant. Females were to be nurturing, caring, gentle, warm, and empathetic. If one failed to fit the mold, he or she was viewed unfavorably or rejected. Today, androgynists promote the idea that all individuals will be more productive, healthy, and happy if they possess androgynous characteristics—a balance of traditionally masculine (andro) traits and traditionally feminine (gyny) traits. As husbands, fathers, and employees, males are more effective if they can be caring, warm, and empathetic as well as self-reliant, strong, and assertive. The reverse is true of females as they play their roles of wife, mother, and employee.

ASK THE EXPERTS

Employers and Families

Q. **What are employers doing to meet the changing needs of American families?**

A. You're right to notice that the needs of American families are changing. For a number of different reasons, more and more parents are working outside the home. More than 80 percent of mothers with children under age 18 are employed. In addition, the number of single-parent families is on the rise. These changes have caused gradual revisions in work policies, making many businesses more "family friendly."

"Family friendly" policies are still in the developing stages. It is estimated that from 10 to 25 percent of all companies in the United States provide some kind of support for employees' families. In most cases, this support may involve more flexible working hours or cafeteria-type health benefits. It may also involve before-tax support for child care costs.

A few progressive companies go beyond these basic family-support policies. For example, some employers provide on-site child care centers or educational scholarship opportunities. The numbers are still small, but there is a growing trend for companies to support the needs of families.

As employees ask for—and make use of—new policies, employers respond by providing increasing support for all family members.

Linda Espinosa

Linda Espinosa
Director of Primary
Education for the Redwood
City School District in
California

The Need for Healthy Families

Every healthy family system fulfills certain functions. A family provides each member with protection, economic support, emotional support, a sense of identity and acceptance, and opportunities for personal development. By functioning in these ways, the family benefits not only its own family members but also other individuals and families, as well as the larger community in which the family lives.

COOPERATIVE LEARNING

Shared Domestic Responsibilities
According to a survey conducted by the Association of Home Appliance Manufacturers and *Forecast for the Home Economist* magazine, most teenagers in today's home economics classes think housework should be shared by both sexes. A majority of the males and females surveyed felt that food shopping, meal preparation, dish washing, housecleaning, and laundry should be shared. Females were in favor of shared household tasks in larger percentages than males. (You may want to have students conduct a similar survey in your school, adding child care to the list.)

ASK THE EXPERTS

Issues and Advice

1. According to Dr. Espinosa, what percent of mothers with children under the age of eighteen are employed? (*80 percent.*)
2. What percent of companies in the United States provide some type of support for families of employees? (*10 to 25 percent.*)
3. Give examples of support given to employees. (*Flexible working hours, health benefits, and before-tax support for child care.*)
4. Give an example of progressive support. (*Possibilities are: on-site child care centers and educational scholarship opportunities.*)

Thinking Like an Expert

Our country's recent presidential election saw the rise of family issues as a political attention-getter. As child care and parental leave become increasingly necessary, new reforms are expected from the current administration. Have students offer their impressions of events in the news about family issues. Ask them to describe changes they may be aware of in their own families that have come about in the last few years. Possibilities are: more flexible working hours, the length of maternity leave or leave to care for an ill family member, health care benefits, on-site child care, or improved support for substitute child care.

As a class project, have students cut articles from newspaper and magazines that address the developments in the work place that affect the family. Display the articles on a poster or a bulletin board with an appropriate title. For discussion, ask: What concerns are at the center of any controversy surrounding the issues? What resolutions do they have to offer? Can they speculate about major changes that are yet to come?

GUIDED PRACTICE (continued)

Critical Thinking

Remind students that people learn a great deal by example, especially during childhood. Then let them share their responses to these questions: Do you believe that it is necessary to grow up in a strong family in order to establish and participate in a strong, healthy family of your own? Why or why not?

Promoting Discussion

Let students share their own ideas about commitment. To whom or what—besides family—can people be committed? What are the benefits of commitment? What happens when an individual makes unwise commitments? When an individual makes too many commitments?

Using the Photograph

Let students describe the activities of the child in the photo on this page. How is this child making a contribution to his family? How do you think his parents or other family members have helped him participate in family life this way? What evidence of commitment do you see in this photo? Do you think you also observe evidence of time together?

Promoting Discussion

Ask students to share their ideas about spending time together. How do you enjoy spending time with your family? How have your preferences—and your family's activities—changed over the years? What problems often arise in families where children participate in many extracurricular activities? How can those activities be integrated into family time?

Cooperative Learning

Let students work in groups to brainstorm a list of ways to improve listening skills. Then have each group share its list with the rest of the class. How can better listening improve a family's communication?

Children of all ages make important contributions to the family.

Each family serves another vitally important function: It assumes responsibility for the socialization of children. Within the family setting, young children begin to learn about acceptable behavior: What kind of language is appropriate? How should a young child speak to adults? To other children? How should anger and frustration be expressed? What are the appropriate ways to express affection? These and many similar questions are first answered by a child's family—usually not through words and explanations, but through daily examples and modeling desirable behavior.

As children grow and come into contact with influences outside the family, their families continue to guide their behavior and direct their learning. Parents and other responsible family members explain guidelines and discuss the reasons for particular kinds of behavior. They also reinforce each child's appropriate behavior and correct inappropriate behavior.

How Can Families Be Strengthened?

Because families serve such important functions in society, they should be supported and encouraged. Family members themselves can assume major responsibility for strengthening their own family.

Recognizing the characteristics of strong, fully functioning families can help people in all situations understand how to help strengthen their own families. The first step in strengthening one's own family is knowing what to look for in a healthy family. Next, the family members can identify the strengths of their own family. Finally, they can strive to improve the areas that need strengthening.

Members of strong families show commitment to the family, make a point of spending time together, communicate openly with one another, show appreciation for one another, share beliefs and traditions, and use coping skills effectively.

Commitment

A **commitment** is *a pledge or promise of loyalty*. In a healthy family, each member of the family group feels a commitment to the family as a unit and to the other family members. A commitment to family is reflected in polite and respectful behavior toward one another, in friendly support, and in consideration.

For busy adults and teenagers, commitment to family is reflected in decisions to spend time with other family members. A parent who consistently thinks, "Oh well, the kids are old enough to get their own dinner tonight—I'll just stay at the office and keep working," does not display a commitment to

---

HEALTHY FAMILIES/HEALTHY CHILDREN

Parents as Leaders

Parents are the leaders in their families and consequently, have certain responsibilities. As leaders, they guide and influence the family group. Good leaders listen empathetically to the concerns, problems, and ideas of those in the group and give appropriate feedback. Furthermore, they help the group define and reach its goals. In helping accomplish group goals, leaders organize the activities and work of the group and help the group make decisions. Leaders also help solve conflicts among group members, participate in activities with other group members, and manage the group's resources. Parents who are good leaders perform these and other leadership tasks for their families.

family. On the other hand, a high school student who says, "Thanks—I'd love to go along, but my family's expecting me. We always have dinner together and watch a video on Thursday," is showing a strong commitment to family.

Time Together

Healthy families plan time to spend together. As the family members grow and change, the activities they do together change. A family with young children might set aside a weekend afternoon to spend in the park. A family with teenagers might decide to spend one Saturday each month on a sports outing—skiing in the winter and biking in the summer, for example.

Time spent together should not be limited to recreation and entertainment. Family members can spend time together shopping for groceries, reading aloud, taking a walk, refinishing furniture—or doing almost anything that interests and involves everyone. For many families, eating meals together provides an important opportunity for sharing time and discussing interests, problems, successes, and concerns.

Communication

Open communication is essential in any strong family system. Family members of all ages should show their interest and involvement by talking and listening to each other.

When family members talk openly, they can't possibly agree all the time. Learning to express and work through differences of opinion can help family members feel close and secure. Family members can be encouraged to recognize, express, and react to a full range of emotions—anger, fear, joy, anxiety, love, elation—in a strong family with active communication skills.

Appreciation

Individuals in strong, healthy families like each other—and say so. They affirm each other, and they speak and act affectionately to each other. Each family member is appreciated for who he or she is, not for what he or she looks like, has, or does. Individuals do not make the mistake of remaining silent when there is an opportunity to praise another family member.

Shared Beliefs

Strong families usually share a clear set of beliefs and traditions. These beliefs may—or may not—be based on the teachings and practice of organized religion. Whatever their basis, shared beliefs provide a sense of commitment and an essential frame of reference for making decisions.

INDEPENDENT PRACTICE

Journal Writing

Ask students to write journal entries describing an "ideal family," either the family in which they wish they had been raised or the family they hope to establish as their own.

Student Workbook

Distribute "Family Focus" in the Student Workbook and have students share their answers with the class.

Extension

Let students work independently or in small groups to complete one or more of these extension activities:

• Find out about the requirements and the procedures for becoming a foster parent in your state. Summarize your findings in a chart to be posted in your classroom.

• Read three or more news stories or magazine articles about large family reunions. What brings family members together? How do they feel they benefit from these associations? What problems are there in organizing and having these large gatherings? How do families deal with these problems? Summarize your findings in a short oral report.

• Read about the two main forms of adoption: open and closed. What are the differences? What are the advantages of each form of adoption for the adopted child? For the birth parents? For the adoptive parents? Write a short report about these forms of adoption.

• Read a book that advocates either traditional family roles or nontraditional family roles. Write a book report summarizing the content of the work and describing your reaction to the opinions and details presented.

OBSERVING AND PARTICIPATING

Communicating with Children

Use these guidelines to praise children:

• Look directly at the child.

• Move close to the child.

• Smile so that your facial expression reinforces the words you say.

• Vary the nice things you say to the child. Doing so shows that you care.

• Praise behavior, not the child; praise the child for what he or she has done, not what he or she is.

• Be physically affectionate. Touch the child on the shoulder or provide a big hug along with your words of praise.

• Deliver the praise immediately after the desired behavior occurs.

ASSESS

CHECKING COMPREHENSION

Assign students to write their responses to the Check Your Understanding questions in the Section 1 Review. Answers to the questions are given at the bottom of this page.

EVALUATE

Have students complete the Chapter 2, Section 1 quiz in the TCR.

Reteaching

1. Have students complete Reteaching 3 in the TCR.
2. Have students work with partners to plan and make family posters. In the center of the poster, have students write the definition of family, then draw or glue pictures of various kinds of family groups around it.

Enrichment

1. Challenge students to complete Enrichment 3 in the TCR.
2. Have students research and report on family life in other cultures or at other times. You might suggest that students select as topics family life within traditional native cultures or within ancient cultures.

Extension

Organize a panel of speakers to talk with the class about their own family experiences. Include on the panel individuals living in nuclear families, extended families, single-parent families, and blended families. Encourage the panelists to discuss the special benefits and the challenges involved in family life for them. Also encourage them to discuss their own efforts to strengthen their families. You may also want to schedule time during which students can ask the panelists questions.

CLOSE

Go around the class, and ask each student to complete the following sentence:

In a healthy family, family members ...

Often, shared beliefs involve rituals and traditions that further unite family members. Family members may attend weekly services together, for example, or they may participate together in volunteer activities on a regular basis. They may also have special holiday celebrations or family gatherings. Each of these enhances the family's sense of kinship and roots.

Coping Skills

Every family has to deal with stresses and problems; strong families confront those difficulties openly and use **coping skills**, *techniques that help people solve a problem or adapt to a situation.*

Members of a healthy family begin by recognizing that having problems or difficulties is not a sign of weakness. Instead of ignoring problems, they develop skills in identifying potentially serious problems and attacking them early. Members of a healthy family do not become unduly concerned or stressed by unpleasant events. When family members try to solve problems, they consider several options, and they make sure that everyone involved has a chance to contribute. They further recognize that not all problems can be solved within the family, so they seek and accept help from support systems and from professional sources. As these families find solutions, they experience satisfaction and become healthier, ready to face and solve the next problem that may arise.

SECTION   1   REVIEW

CHECK YOUR UNDERSTANDING

1. Name three ways that the family benefits its members.
2. What is the difference between a foster child and an adopted child?
3. What are the stages in the family life cycle?
4. How has the trend toward a mobile society affected families?
5. What five things does a healthy family system provide for each family member?
6. How does a family assume responsibility for the socialization of children?
7. How do shared rituals and traditions help family members feel united?
8. What are coping skills?

DISCUSS AND DISCOVER

1. In your opinion, what makes members of the extended family important to children who live in nuclear families, single-parent families, or blended families? How can extended family members help parents? How can they help children? What role should grandparents and other extended family members assume in the lives of young children? What problems might they face in trying to assume that role?

Observing & Participating

Introduce your own family group to an activity that could become a family tradition. Discuss your own interest in the activity, and encourage other family members to discuss their opinions and ideas. In class, discuss the value of family traditions.

SECTION   1   REVIEW

1. Gives to each a sense of belonging, love, and care, and allows them to give the same to others.
2. Foster care is temporary custody and adoptive care is permanent custody.
3. Beginning, childbearing, child-rearing, launching, empty-nest, and retirement stages.
4. Loss of close connections with friends and relatives, causing them to rely on each other more.
5. Gives protection, economic and emotional support, a sense of identity and acceptance, and a chance for personal development.
6. By daily showing what is acceptable behavior.
7. They give a sense of commitment and a framework for making decisions.
8. Techniques that help people solve a problem or adapt to a situation.

Considerations of Parenthood

OBJECTIVES

- Discuss the changes that parenthood brings.
- List questions couples should consider before deciding on parenthood.

Family groups take many different forms and come in many different sizes. Many adults choose to expand their family group by having children. However, the decision to become a parent should not be taken lightly. Parenthood brings many changes, and there are several important questions to consider before one decides whether or not to become a parent.

Parenthood Brings Changes

Any person who becomes a mother or father of a biological or an adopted child enters into **parenthood**, *the state of being a parent*. Having a child brings dramatic and long-lasting changes to every parent's life. Some of these changes involve joy and deep satisfaction. Other changes can be difficult to deal with, especially when parents are unprepared for them.

New Responsibilities

Raising a child is more than just a day-to-day assignment. It is a lifelong commitment. A child's needs for physical care, financial support, love, and guidance continue until adulthood. Being a parent means having a constant concern for the present and future welfare of another human being. Once they become parents, people are no longer able to consider only their own wants and needs when making choices and planning for the future.

For first-time parents, these new responsibilities can seem overwhelming. Good management is the key to fulfilling these responsibilities. New parents need to manage their time, money, energy, knowledge, and skills in meeting their responsibilities. They also may call on family, friends, and community resources for help and support.

TERMS TO LEARN

parenthood

HEALTHY FAMILIES/HEALTHY CHILDREN

Balancing Work and Family

Many prospective parents must decide whether to give up an outside job to stay at home. This decision is just one example of the need to balance various roles.

Anyone who has a career really has two jobs—the work done for the employer and the work of managing the home. Successful people find ways to get both jobs done. At the same time, they realize the importance of other aspects of their lives, such as health and well-being, relationships with friends and family, and personal growth. Parenthood adds yet another dimension to this balancing act.

Trying to balance so many different roles and needs can be stressful. One key to success is the ability to set priorities. Another is the realization that no one can achieve perfection. When reasonable goals and standards are set, multiple roles can bring multiple rewards.

FOCUS

SECTION 2 RESOURCES

Teacher's Classroom Resources
- Enrichment 4
- Reteaching 4
- Section 2 Quiz

Student Workbook
- Find the Keys to Good Parenting

SECTION OVERVIEW

Students begin Section 2 by examining and discussing the various changes that come with parenthood. They also discuss the special satisfactions and rewards that parents enjoy.

Students consider the process involved in deciding whether or not to become parents and examine five central considerations related to parenthood—emotional maturity, desire for parenthood, health considerations, management skills, and financial considerations.

MOTIVATOR

Encourage students to share their current ideas about parenthood. What makes a person a parent? Who has parents? Who needs parents? Why? What does being a parent really involve? What are the most rewarding aspects of parenthood? The difficult challenges? Encourage students to express and support various opinions and beliefs.

USING TERMS TO LEARN

Let students read the vocabulary word introduced in this section, and have volunteers offer their own definitions of parenthood. Be sure students recognize the root word parent and the suffix hood. You may have students identify words that end with that same suffix

- Parenthood Brings Changes
- Making Decisions About Parenthood

GUIDED PRACTICE

Promoting Discussion

Encourage students to share their responses to these questions: Do you think you have a realistic understanding of parenthood? Do you think most teens do? What might prevent many teens from understanding what parenthood involves? How important do you think it is for teens to know the realities and the rewards of parenthood? Why?

Using the Photograph

Encourage students to describe the parent and child in the photo on this page. How is this mother taking care of her child? How do you think she feels about her responsibility to care for him at this stage in his life? How much longer will she be responsible for him? How will her responsibilities toward him change?

Using Management Skills

Let students work with partners to act out the roles of couples planning for the lifestyle changes of first-time parenthood. They might discuss issues such as careers, household tasks, and infant care.

Making Connections: Math

Have students use this information to discover how much time a new parent might spend feeding an infant: Suppose the newborn baby is fed every three hours, and each feeding lasts an average of 45 minutes. How much time is spent feeding the baby each day? Each week? (8 x .75 hours = 6 hours/day; 7 x 6 hours = 42 hours/week.)

A big part of being a parent is accepting responsibility for the child's welfare— not just a few days or weeks, but for many years.

Changes in Lifestyle

New parents face important adjustments in their day-to-day living. Caring for a child—especially a newborn baby—takes a surprising amount of time and energy. A newborn must be fed every few hours around the clock, in addition to being diapered, bathed, played with, and comforted. When you add laundry and other household chores, it's not hard to see why new parents feel they have no time for themselves.

With a child of any age, parents are faced with limits on their personal freedom. This is an especially difficult adjustment for new parents. Suddenly, it's not so easy to go anywhere on the spur of the moment.

Emotional Adjustments

Parenthood, with its changes in lifestyle and new responsibilities, requires a number of emotional adjustments. Going through so many changes at once is stressful in itself. It takes time for new parents to sort through their conflicting feelings and grow accustomed to their new role.

Most new parents are happy, proud, and excited. However, most also experience a variety of more difficult and confusing feelings. Common reactions include the following:

- Anxiety about the baby and how to care for him or her.
- Fear of not being a good parent.

TEEN PARENTING

Resolving Conflicts

Being a teenager and being a parent by itself can be a difficult experience. In addition, teens who have become parents often face unique conflicts when living in three-generation households. Trying to satisfy two roles, as parent and child, can be confusing to the teen parent as well as the rest of the family. Often complicating this role confusion is the necessity of the grand-

mother filling the role of caregiver/parent to the grandchild. Cassie says about her own mother, "She won't let me be the mother, and she never agrees with anything I do." Ask students why these conflicts occur. How can they be resolved? Specifically, how is adjustment and compromise achieved? Who is responsible? What advantages are there for teen parents who live at home?

- Frustration at the loss of personal freedom and the addition of new responsibilities.
- Loneliness and isolation from spending most of the time at home with the baby.
- Doubts about the decision to become a parent.
- Worry over financial matters.
- Jealousy of the baby and the attention he or she gets.
- Depression related to exhaustion or to the physical changes of pregnancy and birth.

Each new parent's attitude and individual situation affect his or her ability to handle these emotional adjustments. The adjustments, of course, are easier for parents who are prepared for these reactions and who understand that they are normal. With the patience and support of family members and friends, most new parents eventually resolve their conflicting feelings. They are able to get over the rough spots and enjoy the positive aspects of parenthood.

Changes in Relationships

When a child is born or adopted, the parents have the unique experience of getting to know a new family member. At the same time, the parents are likely to experience changes in the way they interact with each other, with other family members, and with friends. This is especially true for first-time parents.

There's no doubt that the birth of a baby can be a wonderful time for new parents. However, it can also cause problems between them. New parents are likely to be physically exhausted and under emotional stress. Suddenly, they are faced with new roles, new worries, and a baby who demands a great deal of time and energy. All these can put a strain on the parents' relationship.

Parents who are anxious or frustrated sometimes take out their feelings on their spouse. Without patience and understanding on both sides of the relationship, tempers may flare. A marriage may also suffer when one or both partners are so involved with child care that they neglect each other. Money problems are another source of conflict. Many new parents need more living space at a time when expenses for doctors, baby items, and child care are already adding up.

The couples who adjust most easily during the early, difficult time are those who plan carefully. They read books and articles on parenting and child care. They talk to family members or friends who have been through the experience. Many take parenting or child care classes before or after the baby's arrival.

Like the relationship between new parents, the parents' relationships with family and friends also undergo changes. New parents usually find they have little time or freedom for the

It's natural for a new parent to feel a bit left out if the baby gets all the attention. What could this couple do to solve the problem?

MORE ABOUT

Parents and Partners
In addition to learning what to expect from parenthood, what can a couple do to avoid problems in the relationship? Here are some suggestions:

- Talk issues over ahead of time, such as budgets and philosophies of child rearing. Then they are unlikely to become problems later.
- Decide how to share parenting and household tasks. How doesn't matter, if the division is fair.
- Make time for each other. Take a break from responsibilities and share some time.
- Relax, keep a sense of humor, and remember, no new parents feel confident. This perspective can keep minor tensions from becoming major sources of conflict.

GUIDED PRACTICE (continued)

Cooperative Learning
Have students work in groups to make a list of suggestions for dealing with the emotional adjustments of parenthood. Ask a recorder from each group to write the suggestions on the board. Example: To lessen anxiety, become better prepared by taking a parenting or child care class.

Making Connections: Reading
Have students find and read current magazine articles or books on time management and/or on dealing with stress. Ask them to write short summaries of the information in the articles or books. How could new parents benefit from that information?

Critical Thinking
Encourage students to share and discuss their responses to these questions: In what situations do you think having a child is likely to improve a couple's relationship and strengthen their marriage? In what situations do you think having a child is more likely to cause marital problems for a couple? Do you think it is possible for a couple's relationship to be unaffected by their having a child? Why or why not?

Using the Photograph
Have students describe the family scene in the photo on this page. How does each family member appear to feel? Why? In your opinion, who is responsible for the father's sense of being left out? If this style of functioning as a family continues, what implications might it have for the couple's relationship? How do you think it might affect their child? If you could give this couple advice, what would you say?

Promoting Discussion
Let students share their responses to this question: How has increased mobility in our society affected support systems for new parents?

GUIDED PRACTICE (continued)

Promoting Discussion

Guide students in considering the advantages of having a child's grandparents nearby. How does having regular contact with a grandparent benefit a child? How do grandparents benefit from spending time with a grandchild? How can this proximity affect the relationship between the child's parents and the child's grandparents?

Critical Thinking

Ask students to explain their ideas in response to this question: Why do parenting styles frequently change from generation to generation?

Cooperative Learning

Let students work in groups to discuss what the arrival of a new baby often means to older siblings. Encourage them to share their responses to questions such as these: How are family members affected by the birth of a baby? What can adult family members do to minimize problems when a new baby arrives?

Promoting Discussion

Encourage students to respond to these questions: What do you consider the most important rewards of parenthood? Why? Do you think some parents expect unrealistic kinds of satisfaction from parenting? What can or should those people do to adjust their expectations? Why is it important for parents to have realistic expectations?

Making Connections: Writing

Discuss with students the fact that many people considering parenthood never look beyond the first few years of a child's life. What would these people consider if they looked ahead to raising a teenager? Have students assume the point of view of a parent, and ask them to write an essay describing the rewards and frustrations of being the parent of a teenager.

The birth of a new brother or sister can bring happiness, love, and fun. At the same time, it alters the relationships within the family.

social life they once enjoyed. They may also feel they have less in common with some of their friends than before. New friendships may develop with other parents who can understand and share their experiences.

A new child brings new roles to extended family members— grandparent, aunt, uncle, cousin, perhaps sister or brother. Like the child's parents, these other family members may have to adjust to their new roles. For example, a couple may feel that the well-meaning advice offered by the baby's grandparents is a criticism of their own ability to care for the child. They may resent what they see as interference in their decisions. Meanwhile, the grandparents may feel hurt that their offers of advice are rejected. Sometimes the situation is the opposite. Grandparents may feel overburdened if a child's parents expect them to provide more help than they can manage.

On the positive side, many new parents feel that having a child brings them closer to their own parents. For the first time, they truly understand what being a parent is like. Grandparents and other relatives can share their experiences with the new parents and give help, advice, and support.

When there are already children in the family, the arrival of a new baby can bring on jealousy and misbehavior. Parents and other close family members need to be understanding and provide special attention and love.

The Rewards of Parenthood

In spite of all the adjustments and problems involved, parenthood can bring many joys. Nothing is quite like a baby's first smile or a hug from a three-year-old. Parents discover special feelings of happiness, pride, and love that are different from anything they have felt before.

Raising children can give parents a great sense of accomplishment. They may also find that having children can enrich an already strong marriage. By helping their children discover the world, they can see it with new eyes themselves.

Making Decisions About Parenthood

Deciding whether or not to become a parent is one of the most important decisions most people ever make. Those who are thinking about parenthood should get as clear a picture of it as possible before they make a decision. They should also take a realistic look at themselves. The decision of whether to have children—and when to have them—may depend on these five considerations: emotional maturity, desire for parenthood, health, management skills, and finances.

CLASSROOM MANAGEMENT

Cross-Reference

At this point, you may want to introduce the students to the steps of the decision-making process, which appear on pages 96 and 97, in Chapter 4. The six steps of the decision-making process include:

1. Identify the decision to be made.

2. Identify the alternatives.

3. Consider the consequences of each alternative.

4. Choose the best alternative.

5. Act on the decision.

6. Evaluate the decision.

Remind students that the same steps can be applied to many issues, including whether or not to become sexually involved or to become a parent.

Parenthood is a major step. When a couple fully understands the responsibilities involved as well as their own feelings and motivations, they will be better able to make a wise decision.

Emotional Maturity

Being a parent, like being an adult, involves more than physical maturity. It requires emotional maturity as well. That means being responsible enough to put someone else's needs before your own. It means being secure enough to devote your full attention to an infant without expecting to receive attention in return. It also means being able to hold your temper when you find that a toddler has dumped all the dirt out of the plants on the window sill.

Age is no guarantee of emotional maturity. However, most people do become better able to handle situations like these as they grow older. Prospective parents should take an honest look at their emotional maturity. Are their expectations of parenthood realistic? Are they equipped to handle the pressures and responsibilities involved? If they have any doubts, they should decide to postpone parenthood.

Desire for Parenthood

"Do I really want to be a parent?" This question can be difficult to answer. Just as important, and often just as difficult, is this question: "Why do I want a child now?"

Not all reasons for wanting children indicate real preparation for parenthood. Think about the reasons shown in the chart on page 54.

MORE ABOUT

Planning a Family

How many children to have has long been considered a personal decision. Reasons for having or not having children may come from a person's early home experiences, or they may be influenced by religious beliefs or other values. For instance, recently, many people have become aware that the world's resources are limited. It appears that if world population continues to grow at its present rate, everyone will be in serious trouble. As a result, many young parents are following the suggestions of a group called Zero Population Growth and having no more than two children. In this way, they will replace only themselves in the world's population.

GUIDED PRACTICE (continued)

Promoting Discussion
Ask students to describe the process they think most parents use when they choose parenthood. How does that process differ for couples who choose not to become parents? What problems arise when one member of a couple wants children and the other does not?

What approaches would you suggest for resolving this kind of conflict?

Using the Photograph
Let students discuss what they see happening in the photo at the top of this page. What can make accepting the responsibilities of parenthood difficult? What can happen if parents fail to accept their responsibilities? Why?

Critical Thinking
Encourage students to share their ideas in response to these questions: What do you think is involved in being emotionally mature? Why do most people become more emotionally mature as they get older? Do you think all adults are emotionally mature? Why or why not?

Cooperative Learning
Let students work in small groups to develop a list of personal characteristics parents need (such as patience and flexibility). Then have the groups share and compare their lists.

Using the Chart
Go over Why Parenthood?, the chart at the top of page 54, with the class. How familiar are the reasons on the chart? Why is each reason on the chart sound or unsound? Which do you think are the most common motivators for parenthood? Why? Do you think there is one "right reason" or one "best reason" for choosing parenthood? If so, what is it? If not, why not?

INDEPENDENT PRACTICE

Journal Writing

Ask students to consider their responses to these questions: Why should parenthood be a choice? Why do some people feel they have no choice about becoming parents? What are the possible consequences for parents who feel they have no choice about parenthood? What are the possible consequences for the children they have? Have students write journal entries exploring their opinions and ideas in response to these questions.

Student Workbook

Distribute "Find the Keys to Good Parenting" in the Student Workbook.

Extension

Let students work independently or in small groups to complete one or more of these extension activities:

• Research current statistics to find the average cost of raising a child to the age of 18. Be sure you know what is included in the figures you find. What else would you want to provide for a child? How much would that increase the cost of raising a child? Share your findings and your reactions with the rest of the class.

• Research approaches to parenting in another culture. Summarize your findings in a brief oral report. Then ask your classmates to discuss why parenting styles differ from one part of the world to another.

• Develop a list of agencies, organizations, and programs in your community that can help parents understand and fulfill the responsibilities of parenthood. Plan and prepare a flier or brochure that presents the list in an interesting format; if possible, make your flier or brochure available to local parents.

WHY PARENTHOOD?

UNSOUND REASONS	SOUND REASONS
• Our marriage is in trouble. Maybe this will solve our problems.	• Having children will add depth to our relationship, which is already strong.
• A baby is someone who will love me and belong to me.	• I want to give a baby my care and love.
• I feel like I'm nobody. Being a parent will make me somebody.	• I feel good about myself. I believe that parenthood will be a meaningful and rewarding experience.
• I want someone who will take care of me when I'm old.	• I want to experience the special bond between parent and child that lasts for a lifetime.
• Our parents want grandchildren.	• I love children, and I want to be a parent.

Prospective parents should try to understand their own desires and doubts as clearly as possible. Only in this way can they be sure of their decision.

Health Considerations

The health of prospective parents is an important consideration, particularly before pregnancy. It is best for both prospective parents to go to the doctor for a checkup. If either has a medical problem, it could affect the health of the baby or their ability to care for the child.

The age of the prospective mother should also be considered. If she is under seventeen or over thirty-five, pregnancy is riskier for both the mother and the baby.

Parents must be willing to do without things they might enjoy in order to devote time, energy, and other resources to the child's needs.

MORE ABOUT

Delayed Parenthood

At one end of the age scale, there are more teen pregnancies than in earlier times. At the other end, more couples are delaying childbearing until their thirties or forties so that they can complete their education or establish careers before starting families. In fact, particularly among college-educated couples, delaying childbearing has increased in popularity. You may want to have your students discuss both the advantages and disadvantages of the two extremes. They may speculate on the social conditions that have given rise to the phenomena.

Management Skills

Because parenting is such a complex task, it requires good management skills. Parents must evaluate their family's needs and wants, decide on the family's goals, then find resources they can use to reach those goals. Successful parents consider their options and make sound decisions. Finally, they evaluate this management process by deciding whether their decisions have helped the family progress toward its goals.

Financial Considerations

The expenses that raising a child add to a family budget can be surprisingly large. Before deciding on parenthood, couples should take a careful look at the costs involved over the years ahead. They may need to make some changes in their way of life and set aside some savings.

New parents need skill in money management. Expenses increase, and if one parent stays home with the baby, income drops. A personal checking account can help parents control and keep track of their expenses. If they find they need a loan, parents must know how to shop for the loan, apply for it, and plan for and manage its repayment. These are all skills that parents should acquire before they have children.

SECTION 2 REVIEW

CHECK YOUR UNDERSTANDING

1. List three responsibilities that parents must face.

2. How does parenthood typically change a couple's lifestyle?

3. List four emotional reactions common among new parents.

4. What are the five factors a couple should consider as they decide whether to have children?

5. List two unsound reasons for choosing to become a parent.

6. What money management skills are parents likely to need?

DISCUSS AND DISCOVER

1. With a group of classmates, take turns acting out various situations in which parents express their feelings about having a new child. Identify the specific emotions being expressed, and discuss the probable reasons for those emotions.

Observing & Participating

Observe a first-time parent caring for a young baby during a period of two hours or more. Briefly describe the demands made by the baby. Then explain how the parent responds to those demands. Does the parent attempt to accomplish anything else during this period? If so, with what success? If not, why not? What emotional responses does the parent seem to have to the infant and to the responsibilities involved in caring for the infant?

SECTION 2 REVIEW

1. Providing physical care, nurturing, and guidance.

2. Answers will vary, but may include more responsibility; changes to personal freedom; stress in managing work and family; adjusting to changing roles.

3. Answers will vary, but may include anxiety, fear of not being a good parent, frustration at losing personal freedom, loneliness and isola-tion, worry over financial matters, jealousy of the baby, depression.

4. Emotional maturity, desire for parenthood, health, management skills, and finances.

5. Any two: Shaky marriage, wanting someone to love, low self-esteem, desire to be grandparents.

6. Knowing how to use a checking account, apply for a loan, and establish a budget.

ASSESS

CHECKING COMPREHENSION

Assign students to write their responses to the Check Your Understanding questions in the Section 2 Review. Answers to the questions are given at the bottom of this page.

EVALUATE

Have students complete the Chapter 2, Section 2 quiz in the TCR.

Reteaching

1. Have students complete Reteaching 4 in the TCR.

2. Work with small groups of students to review the implications of parenthood, discussing the differences between being a parent and being a child care worker. Each group should make a chart showing similarities and differences between parents and child care workers.

Enrichment

1. Challenge students to complete TCR Enrichment 4.

2. Have students develop a 60-second spot for radio on the rewards of parenthood and encouraging couples to plan ahead before having children. Have students tape their radio spots; then play them back for the class.

Extension

Invite the parent of an infant to bring the baby to class. Ask the parent to show what items had to be brought along (diapers, bottles, etc.) and explain why each item is necessary. How long does it take to get ready to go out with the baby? How is the timing of an outing affected by the baby's schedule? Encourage questions.

CLOSE

Let each student complete the following statement, either orally or in writing:

You aren't ready to become a parent until …

CHECKING COMPREHENSION

Use the Summary and the Reviewing the Facts questions to help students go over the most important ideas presented in Chapter 2; encourage students to ask questions and add details, as appropriate.

1. A group of two or more people who care about each other and are committed to each other.

2. A family group that includes relatives other than parents and children within a single household.

3. A family group that consists of a married couple and at least one child from a parent's previous relationship.

4. Help the child feel secure, loved, and wanted; help the child understand that it is often difficult, but necessary and unselfish, for birth parents to give a child up.

5. Roles have become less clearly defined.

6. Examples will vary. Possible example: A teen turns down an invitation from friends to go home for the family's weekly evening together.

7. Almost anything that interests and involves all family members. Students may suggest various specific activities.

8. All emotions.

9. Parents often have less time to spend with friends; they may also find they have less in common with friends who aren't parents.

10. Parenting is a complex task.

SUMMARY

- All members of a family benefit from the family and have responsibilities to the family.

- There are many kinds of family groups; the most common are the nuclear family, the extended family, the single-parent family, and the blended family.

- Families are affected by societal trends, including changing family roles, greater mobility, and an awareness of family values.

- In healthy families, family members show commitment to the family, spend time together, use good communication skills, show appreciation for each other, share traditions, and have good coping skills.

- Parenthood brings new responsibilities, changes in lifestyle, emotional adjustments, changes in relationships, and special rewards.

- Before deciding to have children, prospective parents should evaluate their own emotional maturity, desire for parenthood, health, management skills, and financial readiness.

REVIEWING THE FACTS

1. What is a family?

2. What is an extended family?

3. What is a blended family?

4. How should parents respond to an adopted child's interest in his or her biological parents?

5. How have family roles changed in recent decades?

6. Briefly describe a situation in which family members demonstrate their commitment to the family.

7. What can families do to spend time together?

8. In a healthy family, which emotions can be acceptably expressed?

9. What effect does parenthood often have on a couple's relationships with friends?

10. Why do parents need management skills?

EXPLORING FURTHER

1. Collect newspaper and magazine articles about family members who show their support and consideration for one another. Discuss these articles with your classmates, noting the variety of family groups represented. Then use your articles as part of a bulletin board display about healthy families. (Section 1)

2. Make a list of local sites, events, and outings appropriate for families that include teenagers. Work with classmates to plan, make, and display posters advertising two or three of your choices. Include in your posters some information about the importance of spending time together with family members. (Section 1)

3. With a group of classmates, develop a list of specific questions prospective parents can use in deciding whether they are ready to have children. Organize your questions into the five categories of consideration: emotional maturity, desire for parenthood, health, management skills, and finances. Then design and prepare an attractive handout entitled "Am I Ready for Parenthood?" Share your handout with interested students and, if appropriate, with others in your community. (Section 2)

4. Survey five parents to find out how old they were when their first child was born. Looking back, do they think they were too young, too old, or about the right age. Combine and discuss the survey results in class. (Section 2)

THINKING CRITICALLY

1. **Analyze.** Why is it important to understand the characteristics of a healthy family? How do you think you and other students should use those characteristics to evaluate the families in which you were raised? What should be the purpose of your evaluation? Why do you consider that an appropriate purpose?

2. **Analyze.** The adoption of older children can present special challenges for parents and other family members. What potential problems do you think may be associated with the adoption of older children? What might cause those problems? How do you think adoptive parents should deal with those problems? Why?

CLASSROOM MANAGEMENT

Community Visibility

Planning learning activities that extend class content into the home and community is one way to make your program more visible to the outside community. Another way is featuring a child care service during back-to-school nights or other evening school-sponsored activities. Yet another alternative is to provide a Parent's Day Out Center in your classroom one morning or afternoon per week for approximately a month. Have your students select and lead games and provide age-appropriate activities for young children. By promoting such visible activities, you not only will be providing a necessary service, but also will be educating the public on the diverse value of your program. When the need to request funding comes up, this public outreach may be an influencing factor.

3. **Synthesize.** Why is it important to make decisions about parenthood before pregnancy begins? What effects do you think an unplanned pregnancy can have on a married couple? On an unmarried couple? Do you think there is one best way for couples to respond to an unplanned pregnancy? If so, what is it? If not, why not?

CROSS-CURRICULUM CONNECTIONS

1. **Math.** With a group of classmates, survey a selected portion of your school population. Collect information about the kind of family group in which students are living in now and the kind of family group they hope to live in as adults. Then plan and draw a graph or chart that summarizes the information you have gathered.

2. **Writing.** Plan and write a skit or a short story about parents' adjusting to life with a new baby.

SCHOOL TO WORK

Identifying Abilities and Aptitudes A good way to start thinking about career goals is to consider your interests and abilities. What are your hobbies? How do you spend your spare time? What subjects do you like the most in school? Do you prefer to work with people, things, or information? Your responses to these questions might guide you toward a career. You can also talk to your school counselor about taking an aptitude test to measure your natural ability to learn certain skills. The more you know about yourself, the better your chances of finding a rewarding career.

PERFORMANCE ASSESSMENT

Living in Families

Task
Create a resource file identifying books, magazines, audiotapes, and other resources that provide information and offer advice to families.

Purpose
Family members often find they need help adjusting to the various stages of the family life cycle. They may use print, media, or community resources to help them gain greater knowledge or understanding of the stage. You will analyze and evaluate resources, then select 10-15 of them for a resource list. Each item will include a brief description.

Procedure
1. Begin by locating source materials. Books and magazines on parenting and family issues are a logical place to start, but don't overlook videotapes, hot lines, and organizations that serve the needs of parents.
2. For each resource, begin an index card or separate sheet of paper for

notes. Later, your notes will be neatly copied to clean index cards. Include all pertinent bibliographical data, including name or title, publishing information, if appropriate, as well as information about how a person can locate the resource.
3. Review each entry carefully and keep notes about what you find. Use the following guidelines for evaluation and develop more of your own: What specific area(s) of family life does the resource address (i.e., prenatal, infants, toddlers, adolescence, and so on)? Who is the author of the material? Does this person have reliable credentials? How easy or difficult is the resource to locate and use?
4. You might develop your own rating system for the resources using a scale of 1 to 5 or award a number of stars based on how valuable you feel the resource to be. If you judge any resources to be of poor quality or useless, don't exclude them from your file. This information is as valuable as identifying worthwhile resources.

5. Neatly copy your information onto new index cards that will become part of your permanent resource file.

Evaluation
Your resource file should demonstrate that you have carefully reviewed and evaluated the assigned number of resources. Evaluation of a good resource file should indicate that you understand the needs of a healthy family. You will also be assessed on presentation of material and correctness of bibliographic form.

Portfolio Idea Your finished resource file will be useful outside the classroom in your personal life and, perhaps, your career. Keep this in mind as you adapt it for your portfolio. You may want to add additional comments regarding your entries as you use them or add new entries as you learn about them.

Use the reproducible Chapter 2 Test in the TCR, or construct your own test using the Testmaker Software.

EXTENSION

Help a group of volunteers plan and present a series of skits showing incidents in family life. After each skit, guide students in discussing the family portrayed. Who were the family members? How did they benefit from family life? How did they contribute to their family? What might be done to strengthen the family unit? How are the parents adjusting to and accepting their role as parents and family leaders? What specific suggestions would be relevant to the family's parents?

CLOSE

Ask students to write short answers (ranging in length from a sentence to a paragraph) to this question:
Why are families important?

SCHOOL TO WORK

SCANS Competencies In 1990, the Secretary's Commission on Achieving Necessary Skills (SCANS) began an examination of the demands of the workplace. The commission identified five competencies—resources, interpersonal skills, information, systems, and technology—which, in conjunction with three foundation skills—basic skills, such as reading, writing, and math, thinking skills, and personal qualities—lie at the foundation of job performance. The School to Work features located on each chapter review page are designed to focus on these necessary skills.

PERFORMANCE ASSESSMENT

Family Resource File
Bring examples of resources that students might use, including books, magazines, and videotapes. Review the elements of bibliography (e.g., title, author, table of contents, copyright information) and have students practice writing this information in correct form. You might present this lesson together with your school librarian or a Language Arts teacher. If practical, take

the class to a library where they can practice additional research skills. As an alternative to having each student identifying 10-15 resources, make each one responsible for one resource to be added to a classroom file.

You might suggest that students compile a *Parenting Resource Book*. Encourage students to use their computer expertise to make the resource book look professional.

INTRODUCE

CHAPTER OVERVIEW

Chapter 3 guides students in examining the skills involved in parenting and in considering the choices many parents make as they evaluate substitute care for their children.

In Section 1, students consider the difference between parenthood and parenting; they recognize that parenting is a process engaged in by all who care for children, helping them grow and learn. Students examine parenting skills and identify steps people can take to improve them.

Section 2 leads students in a consideration of discipline, the task of helping children learn to behave in acceptable ways. Providing effective discipline is an essential parenting skill; students read about the most effective methods of encouraging appropriate behavior and of dealing with inappropriate behavior. They discuss important benefits of consistency, and the kinds of problems caused by poor discipline

In the final section, students identify the circumstances that lead many parents to seek substitute care for their children, and examine types of substitute care, both home-based and center-based. They discuss questions parents should ask and standards of evaluation parents should use as they consider and select substitute child care.

CLASSROOM MANAGEMENT

Resources Beyond the Classroom

In today's society, the absence of the traditionally relied upon family support structure often makes it difficult for teenage parents to remain in school. They are often pressured by the conflict of school and the demands of the child. Because of the critical importance of a complete education for the family's long-term success, teen parents need to make informed choices about substitute care. Furthermore, to pursue their education without significant worry, they need to feel reassured about the quality of the care they have chosen.

For local referrals of accredited child care programs, they can call the Child Care Information Service/National Association for the Education of Young Children, in Washington, D.C., toll-free at (800)-424-2460.

Effective Parenting Skills

SECTION 1	What Is Parenting?
SECTION 2	Guiding Children's Behavior
SECTION 3	Providing Substitute Care

THINK ABOUT

Because more people realize that parenting skills are crucial to the health of a family, more teens are taking child development classes such as this one. As a result, their understanding of the ages and stages of child development makes them better able to handle the ups and downs of parenting and child care. Also, when parents need to find substitute care, their knowledge of parenting skills helps them make wiser decisions about who will care for their children.

ASK YOURSELF

Look at the photo on the opposite page. If the woman in the photo is the boy's mother, how does she show her love for her son? What parenting skills does she demonstrate? If the woman is a child care provider, would you be comfortable leaving your child in her care? Why or why not? Besides an environment that appears to be clean and healthy, how does she show her awareness of a child's basic needs?

NOW TRY THIS

Think about how you would respond to this statement: Parenting is a lifelong process because. . . . Share your responses with two or three other students and, together, decide on the best three. Choose a spokesperson to present your findings to the rest of the class. Compare your final statements with others presented.

59

CHAPTER OBJECTIVES

After completing Chapter 3, students will be able to:

- Define *parenting* and discuss what parenting skills are and how they can be acquired.
- Identify and discuss effective methods for guiding the behavior of young children.
- Discuss the need for substitute care and identify the options available to those who need child care.

INTRODUCING THE CHAPTER

- Write the following on the board: Wanted—Perfect Parents. Ask students to work together to brainstorm qualities, characteristics, and other requirements that describe perfect parents. Record their suggestions on the board. Then have students work in small groups to write and illustrate advertisements for perfect parents, using the suggestions on the board. Provide time for students from each group to share and discuss their ads.
- Use the photo on the opposite page and the three features on this page—Think About, Ask Yourself, and Now Try This—to begin a discussion about effective parenting skills.

Childhood Reflections

"We parents must have a crucial foundation upon which we base our lives in order to give it to our children. In my opinion, it is the most valuable treasure we can pass on to our offspring."

Ross Campbell, M.D.

HEALTHY FAMILIES/HEALTHY CHILDREN

Healthy Family Attitudes

According to psychiatrist David Palframan, family fun is essential for child development and family attitudes. Healthy families take time to enjoy togetherness in daily activities—mealtime, household tasks, and bedtime. These activities offer time to talk, tease, and resolve issues in nonhostile ways.

Healthy families encourage individual recreation. They also respect personal pursuits. Healthy families know the importance of relaxing together, and they celebrate and vacation together. They cultivate recreation that everyone enjoys and, when necessary, compromise for individual preferences.

FOCUS

SECTION I RESOURCES

Teacher's Classroom Resources
- Enrichment 5
- Reteaching 5
- Section 1 Quiz

Student Workbook
- Parenting in Action

SECTION OVERVIEW

In this first section of Chapter 3, students examine and discuss the process of parenting—caring for children and helping them grow and learn. They examine the skills involved in parenting and evaluate the methods by which people learn parenting skills. Students also read about the importance of understanding child development and of providing encouragement, love, and support for all children. In the last part of this section, students discuss the importance of communicating clearly with children and consider techniques for achieving good communication.

MOTIVATOR

Write on the chalkboard: What do parents do? Encourage a variety of responses; record students' ideas by writing phrases on the board, around the question. Then help students discuss and evaluate their ideas. What are the most important responsibilities parents undertake? How do parents meet children's needs? Tell students they will learn more about parenting and parenting skills in Section 1.

USING TERMS TO LEARN

Let students pronounce and discuss their understanding of the two vocabulary words. Help students recognize the verb deprive in deprivation and parent in parenting. Let students use parent as a noun and as a verb.

SECTION 1 — What Is Parenting?

TERMS TO LEARN

deprivation
parenting

OBJECTIVES

- Describe how parents and other caregivers can encourage a child's development.
- Explain the importance of giving children love and support.
- List techniques for communicating positively with children.

Many people spend large parts of their lives caring for children. They become parents of their own children, or they care for other parents' children—as teachers, child care workers, doctors, psychologists, or workers in other fields. All these people need parenting skills. These are skills that, unfortunately, no one is born with—but that, fortunately, everyone can learn.

Parenting: A Learning Process

Unlike parenthood, which is simply a state or condition, **parenting** is a process—*the process of caring for children and helping them grow and learn.*

Parenting is a complicated task. It requires an understanding of a child's needs in all areas, and it requires the family leadership to meet those needs. It involves providing physical care, encouragement, love, support, and guidance. All these should be provided with the goal of helping each child develop to his or her fullest capacity.

How do people qualify to undertake all these tasks? No one has to pass a test to become a parent. There isn't even one right method of parenting. To care for children well, however, a person needs many different parenting skills.

It takes time and practice to develop parenting skills. In addition, the skills a parent or caregiver needs change as children grow up. Infants' needs are different from those of preschoolers or teens. Parents continue to need to adapt their parenting skills at each stage of a child's development. For these reasons, effective caregivers continue to develop parenting skills all their

---

OBSERVING AND PARTICIPATING

Developing Observational Skills

Just as roles of parents differ from one family to another, so do approaches to parenting. For example, in one family the parents may set specific rules for their children. In another, the parents and children may work together to establish guidelines for behavior. Parenting styles can be classified as authoritarian, permissive, and democratic. Although most people are not likely to fit into exact categories, the categories give you a general understanding of the attitudes toward guidance. Observe parents interacting with their children and categorize the type of parenting style you observe.

Parenting begins with physical care, but it does not end there. Love, encouragement, and positive guidance are just as important.

lives. These are some of the steps they take to expand and improve their parenting skills:

- They ask the advice of friends and family members.
- They read books and magazine articles about parenting.
- They observe other parents and children.
- They attend parenting classes.
- They gain experience with children.

Today there is a trend toward more formal training in parenting for those with children of all ages. Parents can take courses in hospitals, at schools, through community organizations, or from private instructors. Many communities have a variety of options for parents who want to learn more about children.

Most of the groups that offer parenting courses do so because they are interested in the healthy growth and development of children. They work to ensure that parents respect the rights of children and know how to nurture, discipline, and guide children in ways that respect these rights.

An important aspect of developing parenting skills is learning to nurture children. A parent or other caregiver nurtures a child by providing encouragement and enriching experiences. Nurturing also involves showing love, support, concern, and understanding.

Parenting courses, offered through hospitals, schools, and community organizations, enable people to learn more about child development and parenting skills.

MORE ABOUT

Children's Rights

One trend in society today is a concern for the rights of children. This trend is shown in many ways. One example is the concern for child abuse, including sexual abuse. Children have a right to grow up free of the fear of physical or emotional abuse. Concern for children's rights is shown in the legal system, through which some children have even successfully sued their parents. Some states allow children in contested divorce and custody cases to have their own representatives to be sure that the children's rights are considered and respected in whatever decision is made. Parent training programs, based on the premise that children are entitled to healthy growth and development in all areas of life, are another part of the trend toward concern for children's rights.

TEACH

Pages 60-66

- **Parenting: A Learning Process**
- **Understanding Children**
- **Providing Enrichment and Encouragement**
- **Providing Love and Support**
- **Communicating Positively**

GUIDED PRACTICE

Promoting Discussion

Ask students to identify the jobs they could be hired to do if they had no training or experience. How much responsibility is involved in such jobs? How much responsibility is involved in parenting children? Do you think that parents need training? If so, where and how should they get it? Should training actually be required before a person can become a parent? Why or why not?

Critical Thinking

Let students share their own opinions about the sources listed for improving parenting skills. Which do you consider most reliable? Why? Which—if any— might be unreliable? Why? Is there one "best" source for learning about parenting skills?

Using the Photograph

Guide students in discussing the photograph at the top of this page. What parenting skills do you think this woman is using? How do you imagine she acquired those skills? How will her parenting skills need to change as the child grows and matures?

Critical Thinking

Encourage students to share their responses to these questions: How can learning more about children make parents more accepting of their own children? Why is this acceptance important to children?

ASK THE EXPERTS

Issues and Advice

1. How does Ms. Clarke suggest people learn about effective parenting skills? (*By observing parents and caregivers who have contented, well-adjusted children.*)

2. What in particular should be observed? (*Possibilities are: how the person responds in words and actions; how the person responds emotionally to the child; how the person and the family have fun together.*)

3. What other resources or models for effective parenting are available? (*Encourage a variety of answers including books, magazines, audio- and videotapes, support groups, and an examination of one's childhood experiences.*)

4. According to Ms. Clarke, how long does it take to learn about effective parenting? (*A lifetime.*)

Thinking Like an Expert

Ask students to name the major changes that have taken place in families over the past two generations. (To encourage their thinking, ask them to remember stories they have heard from their parents and grandparents.) Ask: What are the differences in family size? Divorce rates? Number of single-parent families? Economic conditions? How different is the role of a parent now than in these past generations? What information is available now that was not known in the past? What influences are stronger now than before?

Next ask students to consider how powerful the medium of television is, or is not, in shaping the contemporary role of the parent. Ask them to describe programs that accurately portray modern family situations and offer positive examples of effective parenting.

Learning About Parenting Skills

Q. Where can I go to learn more about effective parenting?

A. You'll be glad to know that there are many different resources for learning effective parenting skills.

You can learn a lot about effective parenting by watching the parents of young children whom you consider healthy and contented, alert, and responsive. When you have the opportunity to observe such a family, notice how the parent responds to the child's words and actions, respects the child as an individual, and shows the child love and care. Notice how the parent comforts a sad child and offers protection and information to a frightened child. Notice, too, how the parent helps an angry child express and deal with his or her emotions. Notice how family members have

fun together, and watch as the parent helps a child celebrate being happy.

Another good way to learn about effective parenting is to discuss the topic with the parent of a child you admire. Ask that parent to tell you about his or her approach to parenting. You might also ask grandparents—yours or someone else's—to explain how parenting is different today from the parenting practices they remember.

If you enjoy reading, you can get ideas about parenting from books, pamphlets, and magazines. Audiotapes and videotapes can also be good resources. Libraries and schools often loan tapes, as

well as books and pamphlets, on many aspects of parenting.

You can also learn a lot about parenting by examining your own childhood. List the things adults did that were helpful for you as a child. Think about how you can do those things to help your own child, in your own way. Then list the things adults did that were not helpful. Consider how you can do things differently, without going too far in the opposite direction.

Learning about parenting is exciting, and it is an undertaking that can last a lifetime.

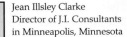

Jean Illsley Clarke
Director of J.I. Consultants
in Minneapolis, Minnesota

OBSERVING AND PARTICIPATING

Learning Through Participation

Often, young adults are confident that they will take a different course in parenting their children than was taken with them, but are at a loss to know how to proceed. Practicing effective communication techniques and new methods of expressing emotions gives a person alternatives. Later, when they have children to care for and are involved in typical situations

that stress all people, they can have a reserve of improved techniques to use. Have students practice new skills by suggesting to them a typical circumstance that creates tension in a family, such as a tantrum or a child's showing resistance to instruction. Ask students to suggest as many ways as possible to handle the situation, including ways that are less admirable. Discuss the relative merits of each technique.

Understanding Children

Have you ever heard an adult tell a child, "Act your age"? Children usually *do* act their age. The trouble is, parents and other caregivers often do not understand what to expect from children. Learning about children's capabilities, interests, and needs at various ages is an essential first step in helping children develop.

Parents and other caregivers need to have realistic expectations. Giving a preschooler a puzzle that is too difficult will frustrate and discourage the child. An understanding parent or caregiver can help guide the child toward a more suitable activity.

Parents and caregivers who have learned about the various stages all children go through are better able to handle the difficult or unsettling stages when they occur. For example, Liz was bewildered at first because her nine-month-old daughter suddenly began crying whenever a stranger approached. As the crying episodes continued, Liz became more and more impatient with the baby. Then she learned from her own mother that all babies go through a stage of stranger anxiety—a development that indicates babies can distinguish new, strange people from their familiar caregivers. From then on, Liz looked on her daughter's outbursts as a sign of healthy development rather than as a problem.

In addition to recognizing normal patterns of development, parents and other caregivers should learn to understand and respect the differences between children. Some learn to walk earlier than others. Some children need more encouragement to make friends. The more time parents spend interacting with and observing their children, the better they will be able to meet each child's individual needs.

Providing Enrichment and Encouragement

Part of a parent's job is to teach children. Parents are children's first teachers. Children naturally learn by exploring their world, trying new things, and imitating others. Nurturing parents give children the freedom they need in order to learn. They provide positive examples, encouragement, and enriching experiences.

As much as possible, caregivers should eliminate barriers that might prevent children from discovering things on their own. For an infant or a toddler, this means putting away breakable objects, covering up electrical outlets, locking up poisons, and so on. For a preschooler, it might mean letting the child dig for worms without worrying about dirty hands and clothes.

GUIDED PRACTICE (continued)

Promoting Discussion

Help students consider the example of Liz and her nine-month-old daughter presented on this page. How did Liz find out what caused her baby's crying? How else could she have found out about stranger anxiety? What might have happened if Liz had not learned about the reasons for her daughter's crying? If you were Liz's friend, do you think you would recommend that she seek some formal training in parenting skills? Why or why not?

Critical Thinking

Let students share and discuss their responses to these questions: Why do children go through difficult stages as they develop? What are some specific examples of these stages? What challenges to parenting skills do these difficult stages pose? Why? Do you think "easy" stages also pose special challenges? If so, what are they?

Cooperative Learning

Let groups of students work together to plan dialogues that illustrate how caregivers can provide encouragement, enriching experiences, love, and support for children. Have members of each group read their dialogues to the rest of the class. Ask other students to identify the aspects of nurturing illustrated in each dialogue.

Promoting Discussion

Ask students to consider barriers to learning. What physical barriers to learning exist in many homes? What psychological barriers may exist? Which are easier for children to overcome? Why? Which are easier for parents to eliminate? Why?

OBSERVING AND PARTICIPATING

Developing Observational Skills

Use the following guidelines to discuss methods of observing children and understanding their development:

- Observe only a few children at a time rather than a large group.

- To avoid their suspicion or mutual interest, appear to be merely looking on, even disinterested, not observant.

- Be objective and complete in your written report or summary of the observation. For example, if you report that a child was angry but did not have a tantrum, you imply that a tantrum was expected.

- When analyzing observed behavior, be aware of the principles of growth and development and apply them to the specific age and stage of the child, or children, you have observed.

GUIDED PRACTICE (continued)

Using the Photograph

Encourage students to describe the child in the photograph on this page. What is she doing? How does she appear to be responding to the activity? How might a caregiver stifle the creativity and learning that this activity provides? Why is it important for caregivers to eliminate barriers to learning?

Promoting Discussion

Present the following family situation to the class: Dana's father has been ill and unable to work for over a year. Her mother was laid off from her job and cannot find another. The family has very little money and cannot make ends meet. Dana's family has pulled together during these trying times, and Dana feels loved and secure, despite her parents' unemployment and financial problems.

Encourage students to discuss the situation. Is Dana deprived? If so, in what way? If not, why not? What do you think Dana probably has that most overprotected children probably lack?

Critical Thinking

Let students share their ideas in response to questions such as these: What do you think motivates parents to be overprotective or overattentive? What does this approach to parenting often indicate about a parent? What are the implications of this approach for the children who are overprotected or who receive too much attention? Why? What kinds of guidance do you think might help overprotective or overattentive parents?

Cooperative Learning

Have students work in small groups to discuss and agree on specific examples of effective communication with an infant, a two-year-old, and a six-year-old. Then let group members demonstrate their examples for the rest of the class, and encourage the observing students to evaluate and offer constructive criticism, as appropriate.

Give children plenty of opportunity for exploratory play. That may mean letting a child get her hands and clothes dirty. The activities that provide the most learning, creativity, and fun are often the messiest.

Enrichment can be provided through everyday objects and experiences. Parents and others who hold and talk to an infant, play with the baby, and give him or her safe objects to look at and handle are stimulating the infant's growth and development. Caregivers can turn daily routines into learning experiences for a child of any age. In a supermarket, for example, a parent can help a three-year-old name objects and colors, smell a ripe pineapple, and learn about how onions grow. A parent might let an older child steer the cart, find certain products, and count change.

Parents should not push children to try activities they are not yet ready for. On the other hand, parents should not hold children back just because they are afraid a child might fail. Trying and failing are part of learning about life. A child's efforts should be acknowledged and praised. Mistakes should be met with understanding and patience. These responses encourage children to try again, no matter what the outcome.

When Children Are Deprived

Unfortunately, some children grow up with parents who have not learned parenting skills and who do not encourage learning. By the time they are four years old, these children are measurably behind others in development. They suffer from **deprivation**, *the lack of a healthy, nurturing environment.*

MORE ABOUT

Deprivation

Children who are deprived tend to have too little: too little space, too little food and clothing, too little love and support, too little medical care, too little information about themselves and their world, too little curiosity, too little self-esteem, and too little to play with and read. Some of this does relate to poverty, such as inadequate space, food, and medical care. True deprivation, however, involves much more. Some parents do not have the knowledge, ability, or desire to provide for their children. They may lack knowledge about children and their development. They may not stimulate the child and may even be uninterested in the child's growth and development. The result can be deprivation, a problem that is more than just a physical one. It includes intellectual, emotional, and social difficulties for the child as well.

The words *deprivation* and *poverty* are sometimes mistakenly used to mean the same thing. Children who are deprived may come from families who are wealthy or poor—or anywhere between. To avoid depriving their children, parents need not money, but the know-how, the concern, and the willingness to make time for teaching.

Fortunately, the effects of deprivation are not irreversible. Development that has been delayed by deprivation can be improved once a child's environment is enriched.

Providing Love and Support

In many ways, nurturing is the same as loving. Love is the sum of the caring and positive things we do for the benefit of others. Children need love just as much as they need food to eat and a place to sleep.

Parents can show children their love in many different ways. Hugs, kisses, and smiles are clear indicators of a parent's love. Listening patiently and attentively is another effective way to show love. This lets children know that parents respect their feelings and are concerned about their ideas and interests. Parents can also show love and support by giving time and attention—helping a child fix a broken toy or discussing ways to get along better with a playmate, for example.

Some parents have difficulty showing affection for their children. They may be embarrassed or feel that displays of affection will make their children "too soft." Without a loving parent's recognition of their accomplishments, however, children feel insecure and worthless. They may resort to inappropriate behavior just to get attention. It is difficult for such children to form healthy relationships because they have never learned how to give and receive love.

Overparenting

Some parents become overprotective and overattentive. They tend to shower the child with too much attention, too many toys, and too many treats. Such a parent makes excuses for the child's inappropriate behavior and tries to shield the child from difficult or unpleasant experiences.

An overprotective parent forgets that children learn from trial and error and that mistakes are an essential part of the growth process. A child who has been overparented continues to seek out adult help. He or she lacks the initiative to try out new things independently. Because parents have always made choices for them, such children may have difficulty making decisions on their own.

BUILDING SELF-ESTEEM

Parental Love: The Greatest Gift of all

Think back to your childhood. What do you remember best about your parents and family life? For many people, "it's the little things" that mean the most. Going on camping trips, baking holiday cookies, riding bikes, watching a favorite television program, and participating in other daily rituals. These people feel that spending time together and sharing in the little things in life have been some of the most memorable and enriching family experiences.

Some parents worry, however, that they don't have enough money to give their children the "finer" things in life, a special trip, money for clothes, or a new car. Instead, all parents need to remember that the greatest gift for children can't be wrapped in a package or tied with a bow. It's the love that comes from a warm, nurturing, and caring parent—truly the greatest gift anyone can give to his or her child.

GUIDED PRACTICE (continued)

BUILDING SELF-ESTEEM

Have students read "Parental Love: The Greatest Gift of All" and discuss the activities they have enjoyed doing with their family. Ask: Do you agree that spending quality time with family members is the greatest gift? Why or why not?

INDEPENDENT PRACTICE

Journal Writing

Ask students to write journal entries about their own goals for themselves as parents (should they decide to become parents). Pose questions such as these to stimulate students' thinking: How do you want to treat your children? What do you hope to do to provide enrichment and encouragement, love and support for your children? Do you worry about whether your children might be deprived? Overparented? What can you do to avoid those problems? Have students pose other questions.

Student Workbook

Distribute "Parenting in Action" in the Student Workbook. Have students complete the activity sheets.

Extension

Let students work independently or in small groups to complete one or both of these extension activities:

- Arrange to tutor a child in a nearby elementary school. Keep a log of the communication techniques you use in getting to know the child, in keeping the child's attention, and in helping the child with his or her work. Share your experiences with the rest of the class.

- Select and read a book about homeless families, such as *Homeless Children* by Karen O'Connor. Discuss the book, focusing on the kinds of deprivation homeless children are likely to face.

OBSERVING AND PARTICIPATING

Learning Through Participation

Using these guidelines for building confidence and self-esteem, have students suggest real-life situations that demonstrate how they can be successful:

- Help a child set reasonable goals that will not result in frustration.
- Identify honorable role models.

- Maintain an atmosphere of respect and love in spite of disagreement and anger.
- Encourage a child to complete a goal and follow through with his or her plans.
- Emphasize unconditional love.
- Teach a child that mistakes are an opportunity to learn.

ASSESS

CHECKING COMPREHENSION

Ask students to write their answers to the Check Your Understanding questions in the Section 1 Review. Answers are given at the bottom of this page.

EVALUATE

Have students complete the Chapter 3, Section 1 quiz in the TCR.

Reteaching

1. Working with small groups, have students suggest ways in which parents and children show their love for each other. Then ask students why it is important for parents to show children their love. What do children gain? What factors can make it difficult for some parents to express their love for their children? What do children lose in these circumstances?

2. Have students complete Reteaching 5 in the TCR.

Enrichment

1. Have students plan and write short stories about family situations in which the children are either deprived or overprotected. Encourage students to plan their story plots around problems arising from deprivation or overprotection. Give students an opportunity to share their completed stories with the rest of the class.

2. Challenge students to complete Enrichment 5 in the TCR.

Extension

Invite a psychologist or family counselor to visit the class and discuss the importance of positive communication between children and parents.

CLOSE

Let students review the ads for perfect parents they composed as an opening activity for this chapter (page 59). Then ask students to suggest changes they would now make in those ads. Why do those changes seem appropriate?

Communicating Positively

Good communication is an important part of the relationship between children and caregivers. Being a good listener is one way to show children that you respect them. The way you talk to children is equally important. Children are most responsive when you speak in kind, respectful tones and use simple language.

Techniques for good communication depend somewhat on a child's age, but include:

- Get on the child's level. Sit or kneel so that you are eye-to-eye with the child.
- Be simple. Use words the child can understand.
- Be clear. Think in terms of the child's point of view.
- Be positive and polite. Hearing a constant series of "don'ts" is discouraging. Try saying, "Please shut the door quietly."
- Give praise and love. Everyone needs to hear good things about themselves, but especially young children. Remember, a smile or hug often says more than words.

Using good communication skills has many benefits. It can help you avoid conflict and misunderstanding. When communication is based on mutual respect and love, children learn to value their own thoughts and ideas. They also learn to respect other people's opinions. Open, trusting communication is the foundation for a good lifelong relationship between parent and child.

SECTION 1 REVIEW

CHECK YOUR UNDERSTANDING

1. What is the difference between parenting and parenthood?
2. List four steps caregivers can take to expand and improve their parenting skills.
3. How does a parent or other caregiver nurture a child?
4. What is deprivation?
5. Why is it important for parents to show affection for their children?
6. What is overparenting? What negative effects can overparenting have on children?
7. List five guidelines to follow when communicating with young children.

DISCUSS AND DISCOVER

1. Do you know anyone who seems to be a "natural parent"? If so, what makes you consider that person such a good parent? What do you consider the most important influence on an individual's parenting skills? Why?

Observing & Participating

Observe adults and children in a public place, such as a park, a playground, or a shopping mall. Notice instances in which caregivers encourage a child's natural curiosity. How often do you see this encouragement happening? How successful does it appear to be? Describe other situations in which caregivers provide enrichment through everyday objects and experiences.

SECTION 1 REVIEW

1. Only certain people are parents: parenting is a process for helping a child grow and learn.
2. Ask advice of family and friends; read about parenting; observe parents; attend parenting classes; gain experience with children.
3. By providing encouraging and enriching experiences.
4. The lack of a healthy, nurturing environment.
5. Without affection, it is difficult for them to form healthy relationships.
6. Overparenting is when parents are overprotective and overattentive. Children have difficulty making decisions on their own.
7. Use simple language; speak in a respectful tone; get on eye level; give praise and love; be positive and polite.

Guiding Children's Behavior

OBJECTIVES

- Discuss effective techniques for encouraging appropriate behavior.
- Explain how and why to set limits.
- Discuss effective ways of dealing with misbehavior.

One of the most challenging aspects of a parent's job is **discipline**, *the task of helping children learn to behave in acceptable ways*. The term *discipline*, when understood in this way, means the same as the term *guidance*—both refer to directing children toward acceptable forms of behavior.

Understanding Discipline

Some people think of discipline only in terms of punishment. Actually, punishment is just a small part of effective guidance. It should be used only when necessary and only in specific ways, as you will learn. Furthermore, discipline does not mean "making children behave." Children cannot be forced to act according to adult standards. However, when caregivers combine firmness with understanding, children can learn to control their actions.

This learning process is a very important part of a child's development. It relates to the child's emotional and social development. Effective guidance helps children learn to get along with others and to deal with their own feelings in acceptable ways. It promotes security and a positive feeling about self.

Guidance is also part of moral development. Very young children understand right and wrong only in terms of being praised or scolded. Gradually, children begin to understand *why* certain actions are right or wrong. They develop a **conscience**, *an inner sense of what is right*.

The ultimate goal of discipline is to help children achieve **self-discipline**, *the ability to control one's own behavior*. Effective guidance helps children learn, to direct their own behavior in a responsible way. In the process, children learn how to make decisions, and take responsibility for their actions. Discipline is important to the child's task of gaining independence.

TERMS TO LEARN

conscience
discipline
negative reinforcement
positive reinforcement
self-discipline
time-out

OBSERVING AND PARTICIPATING

Celebrating Individual Differences

Many parents and caregivers are concerned with finding the right balance point in discipline. Some may wonder whether they are being too strict in their approach to discipline. Others may ask themselves whether they are being too permissive.

Is there an answer? In reality, no one approach to parenting is right for all parents and children in all situations. Most parents are neither extremely strict nor extremely permissive. They use an approach that lies somewhere between, but the exact balance point varies from family to family. As you observe children and their parents, you may see evidence of these different approaches to discipline.

SECTION 2
Guiding Children's Behavior
Pages 67-79

FOCUS

SECTION 2 RESOURCES

Teacher's Classroom Resources
- Enrichment 6
- Reteaching 6
- Section 2 Quiz

Student Workbook
- Giving Guidance

SECTION OVERVIEW

Section 2 treats one of the central issues of parenting: discipline. Students clarify their understanding of discipline as the task of helping children learn to behave in acceptable ways, the ultimate goal of their achieving self-discipline.

Students examine discipline practices that are effective in encouraging appropriate behavior and distinguish between intentional and unintentional misbehavior. They read about effective means of dealing with inappropriate behavior. They discuss poor disciplinary measures, and they conclude by considering the importance of consistency in guiding the behavior of young children.

MOTIVATOR

Write the word discipline on the chalkboard; ask students to jot down at least six words or phrases the word brings to mind. Then let volunteers read their lists aloud, and encourage students to discuss their various ideas about and responses to discipline.

USING TERMS TO LEARN

Guide students in pronouncing and discussing all six vocabulary words introduced. Have students use dictionaries to check the derivation of discipline, which comes from a Latin word meaning "teaching." How does this help clarify the meaning?

TEACH

Pages 67-79

- **Understanding Discipline**
- **Encouraging Appropriate Behavior**
- **Setting Limits**
- **Dealing with Inappropriate Behavior**
- **Handling Conflict**
- **Consistency**

GUIDED PRACTICE

Promoting Discussion

Guide students in discussing the definition of discipline presented on page 67. How does this definition differ from your previous understanding of the word? How does it affect your feelings about discipline? How do you think keeping the goal of self-discipline in mind might affect a parent's or caregiver's choice of discipline techniques?

Using the Photograph

Encourage students to describe the actions of the child in the photo at top of this page. What might have motivated her to put her clothes away? How do you think she feels about accomplishing this task? How is she being guided toward self-discipline?

Promoting Discussion

Let students explain and discuss the importance of setting a good example in disciplining children. How can children's inclination to imitate others serve as a positive factor in guiding behavior? When and how can it present special problems for parents? For teachers? For other caregivers?

Using the Photograph

Have students describe the behavior of the child in the photo at the bottom of this page. Why is it important not only to tell children what is expected but also to show them? Why is it easier for children to follow rules when they understand what is expected?

Self-discipline develops gradually. It shows whenever a child behaves appropriately without having to be told how by a caregiver.

Matthew needs to be shown—not just told—that a real dog should be handled more gently than a stuffed toy.

These are three keys to effective discipline:

- Encouraging appropriate behavior.
- Setting and enforcing limits.
- Dealing with inappropriate behavior in effective ways.

Encouraging Appropriate Behavior

Put yourself in the place of a young child. Suppose no one ever explains what kind of behavior is expected or praises you for doing the right thing. Every so often, you are punished for something. Perhaps it is for talking too loudly in a movie theater one day and for pulling someone's hair the next day. How are you likely to respond? A child cannot learn anything constructive from that kind of situation. A child would have no way of understanding what kinds of behavior are considered wrong and what kinds of behavior are expected instead.

Discipline that is practiced only after a child has done something wrong has little chance of success. To be effective, discipline should begin with encouraging appropriate behavior through examples, explanations, praise, and choices.

Setting a Good Example

Children are great imitators. Children learn best by being shown what to do rather than by just being told. For instance, parents who want their child to talk politely to others should set a good example by talking politely themselves to all the people they have contact with.

The desire to imitate applies to all the examples set for children—not just the good examples. For example, five-year-old Mark notices that his parents and his older sister all tell occasional lies to their friends. Is it any wonder that Mark rebels when his parents remind him, "Always tell the truth"?

Telling What Is Expected

Children need to be told what is expected of them in ways they can understand. At first, it is not necessary to explain the reasons for expected behavior. For a one-year-old, the instruction "Pat the doggy," combined with a demonstration of gentle handling, is enough.

Around the age of three, children begin to understand simple reasoning. Then this might be a more helpful direction: "It hurts the dog when you pull his tail. If you want to play with him, you will have to be gentle." Understanding why the behavior is necessary makes it easier for children this age and older to follow the rules.

MORE ABOUT

Positive Reinforcement

Positive reinforcement is a way of disciplining children that supports desirable behavior and ignores behavior that is unwanted. The idea behind positive reinforcement is that children want praise, attention, or rewards. If certain behavior is praised or rewarded, they will repeat that behavior. Criticism and punishment can reinforce undesirable behavior because they are a kind of attention. To some children even this type of attention may be better than none.

Everyone needs and responds to praise. Children, like adults, need to know when they have done things well. This is called giving positive feedback. If caregivers want a child to repeat good behavior, they have to praise that behavior.

Praising Appropriate Behavior

Giving praise is an excellent way to provide encouragement. Praise helps children feel good about themselves. It also makes them want to continue the desired behavior. Praise is an example of what researchers call **positive reinforcement**, *a response that encourages a particular behavior.* When children associate their actions with a reward, such as attention and praise, they are likely to repeat those actions.

These guidelines can help you offer children effective, encouraging praise:

- **Be specific.** Focus on what the child is doing appropriately. For example, you might say, "You remembered to brush your teeth, didn't you? I'm proud of you!"

- **Be sincere and positive.** Children are quick to sense when praise is false or halfhearted. A mumbled "That's nice" or "You didn't mess up too much this time" can't be genuinely encouraging.

- **Give the praise as soon as possible.** A compliment given for something done the previous day has little meaning for a child. When praise is given soon after the desired behavior, the child is able to associate the two.

- **Tailor the praise to the needs of the child.** For example, many children need encouraging praise when they manage to sit quietly and listen to stories. However, a child who also remains silent during a sing-along doesn't need praise for being quiet during the story time. Observing children can help caregivers know which behaviors need to be encouraged.

All children need to hear positive things about themselves. Make your praise specific and sincere.

CLASSROOM MANAGEMENT

Resources Beyond the Classroom

The National Association for the Education of Young Children (NAEYC), the largest professional organization of early childhood educators, has developed pamphlets that presents its guidelines for developmentally-appropriate practices. Written for a range of adults from parents to child care administrators, the statements of procedures apply specifically to children between the ages of 2 1/2 and 4 years old. The content is unique in that it describes both appropriate and, for comparison, inappropriate practices. A nominal fee (50 cents) is charged for each five pamphlets in the series. Write or call:

National Association for the Education of Young Children; 1834 Connecticut Avenue, N.W., Washington, DC 20009, 800-424-2460

GUIDED PRACTICE (continued)

Promoting Discussion
Let students share their own ideas about positive reinforcement. Why is this an effective discipline technique to use with young children? Do you think it would be effective in modifying the behavior of teens and adults? Why or why not?

Cooperative Learning
Discuss with the class the idea that parents and other caregivers may find it difficult at first to respond to appropriate behavior and to avoid responding to inappropriate behavior. It is important to remember, however, that by routinely acknowledging good behavior, parents and other caregivers can usually reduce the frequency of inappropriate behavior, as well as the energy and attention that is expended on these episodes.

Then let students form groups, and have the members of each group work together to devise systems for rewarding routine appropriate behavior. (One example is a chart on which stickers or stars can be placed to acknowledge specific appropriate actions.) Give members of each group an opportunity to share their ideas with the rest of the class.

Promoting Discussion
Ask students to suggest specific behaviors the parent of a four-year-old might notice and reinforce with praise.

Critical Thinking
Ask students whether they think food should be used as a form of praise in response to children's behavior. Why or why not?

Using the Photograph
Encourage students to describe the interaction between mother and baby shown in the photo on this page. What do you think the mother might be saying? How is the baby responding? Why?

GUIDED PRACTICE (continued)

Promoting Discussion

Let students share their own opinions about offering choices to young children. How do you think choices help children behave in acceptable ways? What challenges do parents and other caregivers face in offering children choices? How can artificial choices undermine the effectiveness of this technique? Do you think parents and teachers should offer teens choices related to their behavior and attitudes? Why or why not? Do you think offering choices might be an effective management tool in the workplace? Why or why not?

Practicing Decision Making

Let students discuss these situations and suggest choices that a parent or other caregiver might offer to encourage appropriate behavior.

- A three-year-old is throwing food onto the floor.
- A six-year-old is throwing food at a sibling.
- A five-year-old wants to splash through deep puddles.
- A two-year-old refuses to get into the bathtub.
- A five-year-old refuses to turn the television off.
- A six-year-old wants to stay up late to visit with out-of-town guests.
- A five-year-old does not want to help set the table.
- A three-year-old refuses to leave the park.

Promoting Discussion

Ask students to reread the description of the interaction between Alex and his mother on page 59. What specific steps did the mother use to guide Alex's learning? With what results?

Using the Photograph

Encourage students to describe and discuss the scene in the photo on this page. What choice do you think the children were offered? Why?

Offering Choices

As children become more mature, they should be allowed to make some decisions about their behavior. This helps them learn that they are responsible for their own actions. It also minimizes feelings of frustration. A parent or other caregiver, rather than making demands, can offer the child a choice and respect the child's decision.

For example, three-year-old Gavin sometimes hits his younger sister. To encourage appropriate behavior, his parent might say, "You seem to be angry with Sonya. I know sometimes she wants to play with the same toy you do, and that makes you angry. I cannot allow you to hurt her. Would you like to choose one of your toys she can play with, or would you like me to sit down and build a house with both of you?"

A caregiver should offer only alternatives that are readily available and should make sure the child's choice is carried out. Whatever choice the child makes, it must be honored. If it is not, the child will lose trust in the parent.

When examples, simple instructions, praise, and choices are combined, efforts to improve the child's behavior are likely to succeed.

Being told that you can't do somethng isn't quite so bad if you can choose what to do instead.

COOPERATIVE LEARNING

The Accessible Classroom

Although the matter is often overlooked, the physical organization of the classroom can have a dramatic impact on the success of any cooperative enterprise. Organize your room so that it is economically sound. Give some attention to physical layout—to such matters as general traffic flow and location of resources. The computer and other tools with which students are expected and encouraged to have hands-on contact should be situated so as to accommodate as large a student group as possible (e.g., not shoved up against a wall or in a corner with limited access). See to it, moreover, that there are distinct areas where certain activities always take place (e.g., a "conference corner," a research "bullpen").

**PARENTING
IN ACTION**

PARENTING IN ACTION

Encouraging Appropriate Behavior

Becky was frustrated because her four-year-old son Jamal never put his toys away. Sometimes Becky put them away herself. Most of the time, however, she was too busy to worry about the toys, and they were simply left out. When friends or relatives came by, Becky was embarrassed by the mess. Her scoldings upset Jamal but did little to solve the problem.

Finally, Becky tried a new approach. One evening before bathtime, she sat down with Jamal as he played. She explained, "Jamal, if you pick up your toys after you've finished playing with them, they won't become lost or broken. I'll help you put the toys away and show you where they go. Should we start with the blocks or the train set?"

Though he was reluctant at first, Jamal soon became interested in this new game.

When they were finished, Becky said, "Thank you for putting your toys away. You did a good job."

This scene was repeated on the following evenings. Jamal was more than willing to please his mother once he had been shown how. After a few weeks, he was able to put the toys away all by himself. Occasional reminders were all he needed.

Becky also found that handling the situation this way reduced her own frustration. Although the house was indeed much neater now, she no longer got upset if things were not perfectly orderly at all times. Both she and Jamal were happier.

THINK AND DISCUSS

1. What did Jamal learn from Becky's earlier approach to the problem of his toys?

What new techniques did she use to encourage him to put his toys away?

2. What might have happened if Becky had started putting Jamal's toys away on her own? What might have happened if she had insisted that Jamal put his toys away without her help?

3. How did this solution benefit Jamal? How did it benefit Becky?

Setting Limits

Setting limits is another way to guide children toward appropriate, safe behavior. The term *limits* may refer to physical restrictions, such as preventing a child from crossing the street. Another kind of limit is a rule of behavior: "We don't hit other people."

PARENTING IN ACTION

Promoting Discussion
Introduce this selection by asking students to describe the scene shown in the drawing. What problem do you think the scene suggests? If, as a parent, you were faced with it, how would you feel? What approaches to the problem would you consider? What approach do you believe would be most effective? Why?

After discussion, let students read the selection.

Thinking Critically
Encourage students to share their initial responses to Becky and Jamal's situation. How serious was their problem? Why did the problem develop, and how could it be avoided? What if Becky had not changed her approach?

Answers to Think and Discuss
1. He learned it was usually not important to put toys away, and when it was important, his mother would do it. In trying a new approach, Becky explained why it was necessary to put toys away; and set a good example by working with him. She gave him a choice, and praised his accomplishment.

2. Jamal might not have learned any responsibility for his own belongings. He would have been overwhelmed and given up.

3. Jamal began learning to take care of his own belongings; gained the satisfaction of doing the job; and had better access to his toys that were kept in order. Becky felt less frustrated and less concerned about the appearance of the home; and had the satisfaction of establishing good habits in Jamal.

OBSERVING AND PARTICIPATING

Celebrating Individual Differences
Although setting limits is a constructive and necessary child-raising behavior, how limits are set and enforced varies from family to family. Limits are not absolutes. One family's limits may be totally inappropriate for another family. Limits must take into account the personality of the child. Children who are active, curious, and high-strung will require limits different from those for children who are calm, placid, and sedentary. Additionally, the personality of the parents affects how limits are set. Parents who are highly organized and live a structured life will set limits that are different from those of parents who live more spontaneously. Consequently, productive limits are those produced through an interaction of both children's and parents' personalities and needs.

GUIDED PRACTICE (continued)

Family Focus

Point out that setting limits can be difficult in some families. Ask students to think about what can happen in certain family structures. What happens when parents set different limits? Could divorce make this more likely to happen? How? Might stepparents sometimes feel insecure about what limits to set? Why? Why might a single parent have problems in setting limits? How can communication help people in all these situations?

Using the Photograph

Let students describe the actions of the child in the photo at the top of this page. What limits do you think this child is following? How do you think this child's limits have changed over the past months? Over the past years?

Cooperative Learning

Have students work in groups to list the basic limits needed for each of these age categories:

- Under two years old.
- Two and three years old.
- Four and five years old.
- Six and seven years old.

Encourage group members to discuss and agree on the number of limits they will include for each age category, as well as any specific limits they consider appropriate. Then let group members discuss their responses to these questions: How should the limits be communicated to the child? How do you know when to change a child's limits? How could a parent or other caregiver use positive reinforcement with limits?

Making Connections: Reading

Have students look through parenting magazines for articles or columns written by psychologists. Ask each student to find two good ideas about guiding children's behavior and to share those ideas with the rest of the class.

As children grow older they need fewer restrictions, especially when they show they will follow rules.

"Yes, you may ride the bike, but you must wear this helmet." Setting limits for activities helps create conditions that are right and safe for the child.

What Should the Limits Be?

In deciding on specific limits, parents and other caregivers often follow this general guideline: Limits should keep children from hurting themselves, other people, or property. The specific limits that a parent or other caregiver sets will depend on the individual child. Children will respect and follow limits if they are few and reasonable. When setting limits, parents and other caregivers should keep these questions in mind:

- Does the limit allow the child to learn, explore, and grow? Too much restriction hinders development.
- Is the limit fair and appropriate for the child's age? A toddler might be restricted to a fenced-in yard. By school age, the same child may be permitted to walk to school alone and to visit a friend who lives down the street.
- Does the limit benefit the child, or is it merely for adults' convenience? Restrictions should not be placed on behavior simply because that kind of behavior interferes with an adult's orderly routine.

Making Limits Clear

Limits should be simple and briefly stated—for example, "We walk inside the house. Running is done outside." Be prepared to repeat the limits or rules several times. Young children do not realize that the same rule applies to different situations.

The most useful limits are those that a child can succeed in following. For example, restricting three-year-old Julie to splash-

---

SEE HOW THEY GROW

Moral Conscience

In general, intellectual development accompanies the development of a conscience. As children mature intellectually, they are better able to understand the expectations of others and can see the reasons for certain restrictions and standards. With intellectual development comes the ability to generalize principles and apply them to many situations as well as the ability to understand abstract concepts, such as truth, equality, and justice. A child's relationship with the parents is another component in the development of conscience. Children who strongly identify with parents tend to have more highly developed consciences. Cultural values, as transmitted by parents to children, are still another influence on the development of a conscience.

ing her sister "just a little" during pool playtime is not a useful limit. A three-year-old doesn't yet have the experience to know what "just a little" splashing is. More than likely, "a little" will soon become what an adult considers "a lot" without Julie's ever recognizing any difference. A better limit in this case would be "no splashing." A three-year-old can understand what that means and can succeed in complying with that limit.

Limits should be presented to the child in a calm, direct tone of voice that indicates the limit is real and to be respected. When introducing a limit, it is best to follow these steps:

- **Be understanding of the child's desires.** "I know you think it's fun to draw on the wall."

- **Set the limit, and explain it.** "You may not draw on the wall. We use paper to draw on."

- **Acknowledge the child's feelings.** "I know you may not be happy with this, but sometimes I must make rules."

- **Give alternatives.** "You may draw on this piece of paper, or you may play with your blocks. Which would you like to do?"

Once established and explained, limits should be firmly and consistently enforced. Children respect their parents more if they know their parents stick to the rules. Parents who give in teach their children that they do not mean what they say.

When you explain limits to a child, use language that is simple and clear. Although you should be firm, avoid scolding or belittling the child.

MORE ABOUT

Setting Limits

An early researcher in child behavior was interested in exploring the concept of whether or not children needed limits. A group of children was accustomed to playing in a yard surrounded by a chain link fence. The researcher removed the fence, thinking that the children would experience more freedom in their play. However, the children huddled together in the center of the yard. Few ventured to the edge of the yard, and none tried to wander away. On the basis of experiments such as this, researchers have concluded that children find security within defined limits.

GUIDED PRACTICE (continued)

Critical Thinking

Encourage students to share and discuss their own ideas about setting limits. Do you believe that setting and enforcing limits is an effective way for parents to show their love for their children? Why or why not? Do you believe that a parent who does not set and enforce limits might be motivated by something other than a lack of concern for the child? If so, what might that be?

Using the Photograph

Let students describe the situation in the photo at the bottom of this page. What kinds of limits might be involved? Why is the language used in explaining limits so important? What role does the adult's tone of voice play?

Practicing Decision Making

Let students consider the following situations, each involving a four-year-old child. What limits should be set? How should those limits be communicated to the child?

- Robert will be attending his friend's birthday party at the zoo.
- Melissa is going to a public swimming pool with her older sister.
- Jarrod is going to finger-paint at the kitchen table.
- Zelda is going with a friend and the friend's babysitter to play in a park.

Making Connections: Writing

Ask students to recall situations in which limits were not set for young children or in which limits were set but not enforced. What were the results for the parent or caregiver? For the child or children? Have students write essays or short stories about these situations.

GUIDED PRACTICE (continued)

Promoting Discussion

Ask students to suggest examples of intentional and unintentional misbehavior. How does a child's age affect the determination about certain kinds of behavior?

Critical Thinking

Point out to students that a child whose inappropriate behavior is pointed out often responds by saying, "I forgot" or "I didn't mean to." Let students discuss the implications of such a response. What has the child learned about unintentional misbehavior? What do you think a parent or caregiver should do to determine whether the behavior was intentional? What assumptions—if any—should the parent or caregiver make? Why?

Promoting Discussion

Let students identify and discuss the differences between positive and negative reinforcement. How are they likely to affect children? How are they likely to affect the relationship between a parent or caregiver and a child?

Using the Photograph

Have students discuss the behavior of the child in the photo on this page. If you were the child's parent or caregiver, how would you respond? Why?

Promoting Discussion

Point out that many parents who otherwise avoid physical punishment tend to use those forms of punishment when children act in unsafe ways. For example, children may be spanked if they run into the street or have their hands slapped if they reach for a hot burner or an electrical outlet. Have students list at least ten household safety hazards for young children. Then guide them in discussing how positive discipline and guidance can be used to teach children about safety.

Dealing with Inappropriate Behavior

No matter how much adults do to encourage appropriate behavior, all children misbehave sometimes. Parents and other caregivers must deal with this misbehavior appropriately and effectively.

One thing that determines how a caregiver should respond to misbehavior is the child's age. A one-year-old who bites another child can be told, "No! Don't bite," but the child should not be expected to understand the meaning of his or her action. Behavior at this age can best be controlled by distraction. On the other hand, a four-year-old is capable of understanding that biting is unacceptable behavior and can be expected to control any urges to bite another person.

These are the questions a caregiver should ask when responding to a child's misbehavior:

- Does the child understand that the behavior is wrong?
- Was the behavior intentional (done on purpose), or was it simply beyond the child's control?

Unintentional Misbehavior

With children of any age, misbehavior is sometimes unintentional. For example, a three-year-old may cry or whine if forced to wait a long time for food at a restaurant. This is a natural reaction to being hungry, not deliberate misbehavior. A young child simply does not have the patience of an adult in that situation. Similarly, a child may drop a glass of milk that is too heavy, or accidentally break a vase that should have been put out of reach. These examples of misbehavior, because they are unintentional, should not be punished.

Misbehavior is also unintentional if the child had no way of knowing it was wrong. For example, while playing in the park, Tyler picked a flower and brought it to his father. Tyler's father did not get angry with him or scold him. Instead, Tyler's father explained that the flowers in the park were for everyone to look at and enjoy, not to pick. Since this limit had never been presented to him before, Tyler was not deliberately misbehaving.

Using Punishment Effectively

When children deliberately do something that they know is wrong, some form of punishment may be necessary. Punishment is **negative reinforcement**, *a response that tends to discourage a particular behavior from being repeated*. Punishing should never take the place of encouraging appropriate behavior and setting clear limits. When used with good judgment, however, punishment can be a part of positive and effective discipline.

To this child, a cat's tail looks like a convenient handle to grab. Would this be intentional or unintentional misbehavior?

HEALTHY FAMILIES/HEALTHY CHILDREN

Punishment and Negative Reinforcement

In psychological terms, there is a difference between punishment and negative reinforcement. Negative reinforcement refers to painful stimulation for failure to perform an action, such as when a child is not allowed to go out and play because the toys were not picked up. This dif-

fers from punishment, which is painful stimulation for performing an action, as when a child is denied dessert for deliberately spilling milk on the floor. Neither punishment nor negative reinforcement is as effective as positive reinforcement in encouraging desired behaviors in children.

Being careless near traffic is an example of misbehavior that can be dangerous. In this situation, letting the child suffer the natural consequences is not an appropriate means of discipline.

The first time a child breaks a rule, the parent or caregiver may choose to give a warning rather than punishment. Even a child who usually has good self-control occasionally makes mistakes. Mistakes are especially likely under unusual circumstances, such as the excitement of a birthday party.

Punishment should be in proportion to the seriousness of the misbehavior. A relatively minor offense, such as forgetting to put away a bicycle one time, does not deserve a severe punishment. In this case, it might be fair for the child to have to give up using the bicycle for a day—but not for a whole week.

Reasonable punishment will not cause a child to resent his or her parents—as long as the parent has established a positive, mutual relationship of love and respect with the child. The parent should also be careful to make clear that he or she disapproves of the child's behavior but continues to approve of the child as a person. Children must be assured that their parents love them and want to help them learn how to behave properly.

Following are some useful techniques for dealing with inappropriate behavior. These techniques can be used in many situations.

- **Natural consequences.** Sometimes it is punishment enough for a child to suffer the consequences, or natural results, of

MORE ABOUT

Natural Consequences
   The secret of successfully using natural consequences is in the way this technique is applied. Caregivers should not use natural consequences as a threat in anger. At that point, the consequences have ceased to be "natural" and have become punishment. However, if natural consequences are used in a nonpunitive, matter-of-fact way, children are quick to see their justice and usually accept them without resentment. This type of natural consequence use provides children with valuable, objective real-life experience. Additionally, it allows children a certain degree of control over either accepting or rejecting the consequence.

GUIDED PRACTICE (continued)

Cooperative Learning
   Let students work in groups to consider and discuss the following situation: Your child has gotten into the bathroom cabinet and is drawing on the mirror with a tube of lipstick.
   Ask group members to agree on the best response to the situation. Then have two students from each group act their solution out for the rest of the class. After all the groups have presented their solutions, encourage a discussion and evaluation of the various options.

Promoting Discussion
   Ask students why children need to understand that parents can disapprove of their behavior and still love them at the same time. How can this be communicated to children?

Critical Thinking
   Point out to students that children with serious behavior problems may be using their behavior to communicate their special concerns and anxieties. For example, Stuart continually "acts up" to get attention. What do you think his parents should conclude about Stuart and his behavior? Why? How could Stuart be helped? What messages might be conveyed by a child who lies frequently? By a child who is unusually defensive—often saying, for example, "I didn't do it" or "It's not my fault"?

Promoting Discussion
   Let students review the communication skills identified on page 66. How can these skills help parents handle the conflict and anger often associated with discipline?

Family Focus

Remind students that when disciplinary methods are ineffective, families suffer. The problems they have when children are young are often compounded as the children grow older. Ask students why parents must set and enforce reasonable limits and deal with behavior when children are very young. What can happen if parents fail to set and enforce limits?

Let students consider this example: Parker was always told what not to do—"Don't touch this. Don't do that"—but he soon learned that his parents never followed through when he did touch this and did do that. As a teenager, Parker now does as he pleases, and his parents wonder why. How could Parker's parents have prevented this problem? How do you think they should handle it now?

Critical Thinking

Ask students to consider these situations:

- Whenever five-year-old Jenny is frustrated or has trouble doing something—buttoning a shirt, cutting her meat, or making her bed—a parent steps in to help. In most cases, the parent ends up completing Jenny's task for her.

- Whenever four-year-old Ryan has an argument with his older brother or with a neighborhood playmate, one of his parents steps in and punishes the offender.

Then let students share and discuss their responses to these questions: What is each child learning? Why? What do you think motivates the child's parents to behave this way? What do you think Jenny's parents should do? If her parents do not change their response, what will the long-term effects be? What should Ryan's parents do? What could be the consequences of their continuing to act as they do now?

his or her own misbehavior. For example, although her grandmother has called her twice to come to dinner, Sandra does not respond. Sandra's grandmother does not ask the other family members to wait any longer, nor does she save seconds of mashed potatoes for the child. Instead, her grandmother lets Sandra eat by herself when she does finally come to the table. Next time, Sandra will be more likely to come when called.

- **Loss of privileges.** In some cases, the natural consequences of a child's actions are not appropriate to use as punishment. For example, suppose a five-year-old keeps running into the street while playing. The natural consequences of that behavior are likely to be serious injuries. A good way to deal with this situation might be to give a warning that if the child runs into the street again, there will be no more outdoor play that day. This type of punishment is most effective for children five or older. The privilege that is taken away should always be related to the misbehavior so that the child associates the two.

For older children, "time-out" might mean going to a quiet place to think about what happened and why what they did was wrong.

OBSERVING AND PARTICIPATING

Celebrating Individual Differences

Although consistent discipline is seldom easy for any parent or caregiver, it can be especially difficult for parents of aggressive children (see Chapter 7, page 201, for a description of the aggressive child). The more irregular and non-adaptive aggressive children are, the more they need calm, consistent treatment from parents. It is not always easy for parents to remain patient with a child who creates disturbances several times a day. Establishing firm limits, ignoring tantrums, and maintaining a sense of humor can help parents be consistent in dealing with children who are difficult to discipline.

- **Ignoring.** Sometimes a young child misbehaves simply to get attention. As long as the behavior is not harmful, the best response may be to ignore the child until the behavior stops. Any other reaction will give the desired attention and make it more likely that the behavior will be repeated.

- **Time-out.** Another way to respond to misbehavior is to use a **time-out,** *a short period of time during which the child sits away from the presence of others or from the center of activity.* The purpose is to give the child time to calm down and regain self-control. The time-out period might last a specific number of minutes—perhaps one for each year of the child's age—or the caregiver might say, "You may return to playing with the others when you are ready to do so without hitting." This type of time-out reinforces the idea that the child must learn to control his or her own behavior.

Issues Concerning Discipline

Some discipline methods continue to be debated. One example is spanking. Some child care experts feel that spanking should be avoided. They point out that spanking does not help children learn desirable behavior and may teach them that hitting is acceptable. Other experts believe that in certain situations, appropriate use of spanking can produce effective results without causing harm to the child.

Whatever their views on spanking, most experts would agree on two points. First, caregivers should never use spanking as a way to vent anger or frustration. This creates a risk of losing control and sets a poor example for handling emotions. Second, in most situations, there are many effective, positive guidance techniques that can be used as alternatives to spanking.

Poor Disciplinary Measures

Well-meaning parents and caregivers sometimes use disciplinary methods that are poor choices. These methods are less effective than others in the long run. Some may even be harmful. Parents and caregivers who follow the positive discipline techniques already described in this chapter should find there is little or no need to use the measures listed below.

- **Bribing.** Bribing a child with a special treat if he or she stops misbehaving can backfire. Instead of learning self-control, the child learns to expect external rewards for good behavior. The child may even misbehave on purpose, knowing that a treat is likely to be offered.

GUIDED PRACTICE (continued)

Promoting Discussion
Ask students to suggest specific situations in which it would be inappropriate to use the natural consequences technique for dealing with misbehavior. What makes natural consequences inappropriate in each of those cases? What other measures would be more effective? Why?

Using the Photograph
Let students describe the child in the photo on page 76. What is he doing? Why? Should time-out be used for a two-year-old? Why or why not? At what age would this technique lose its effectiveness? Why?

Critical Thinking
Point out that, once they become parents, many people who grew up in families where poor disciplinary measures were common find themselves using these same techniques with their own children. Ask students whether they think this cycle can be broken. If so, how? What are the rewards to the family if the cycle is broken? What is the effect on society if the cycle continues?

Promoting Discussion
Ask students why it is important for children to discuss conflict and express anger. What positive results can occur from communicating openly about conflict? What problems can arise when conflict and anger are ignored?

Critical Thinking
Explain to students that parents often respond with anger when their children are angry. How do you think parents should handle these feelings of anger?

Promoting Discussion
Let students share their ideas in response to this question: How can parents who rely on other caregivers ensure that discipline will be consistent?

MORE ABOUT

Time-Outs
Discuss these guidelines for using time-outs:
- Use them for very negative behavior; if overused, they lose effectiveness.
- Tell the child what you don't like about behavior to distinguish between behavior and self.
- Keep time-outs short; most children forget why they have misbehaved after ten minutes.
- After time-out is over, give the child another chance without humiliation or resentment.
- If a child resists or has a temper tantrum, wait until it stops; then continue the time-out, but do not mention the tantrum.
- If a child will not stay in a quiet area, put away toys, turn off the television, and walk away until the time-out period is over.

INDEPENDENT PRACTICE

Journal Writing

Ask students to write journal entries exploring their own ideas and feelings about spanking. Encourage students to respond to some or all of these questions as they write: How do you think spanking affects a child? How do you think it affects the child's parent? How does it affect their relationship? Under what circumstances, if any, do you think it is acceptable to spank? How can the risks of spanking be minimized? Why do you think some parents who intend not to spank their children end up spanking anyway?

Student Workbook

Distribute and have students complete "Giving Guidance" in the Student Workbook.

Extension

Let students work independently or in small groups to complete one or more of these extension activities:

•Select another culture or another period in history; read about approaches to discipline in that culture or period. Write a brief report summarizing your findings.

•Visit a child care center, and talk with the care providers there. What are the center's guidelines for disciplining children? How do providers encourage appropriate behavior and discourage inappropriate behavior? Summarize your findings in a short oral report.

•Read a popular parenting book that presents guidelines for discipline. Then plan and present a short oral book report.

•Design a magazine advertisement that promotes consistency in dealing with children. Post your ad in the classroom, and encourage other students to discuss and evaluate it.

• **Making children promise to behave.** In the process of learning to control their behavior, children will naturally make mistakes. When a promise has been made, the child may feel forced to lie about misbehavior rather than disappoint someone he or she loves.

• **Shouting or yelling.** When a child misbehaves, it is natural for the caregiver to feel anger and disappointment. These feelings should be expressed, but in a calm, reasonable tone of voice. A loud, harsh voice can frighten a young child. Older children often learn to "tune out" yelling.

• **Shaming or belittling.** Parents and caregivers should not ridicule a child's mistakes or use responses such as "If this keeps up, you'll never amount to anything." Doing so can harm the child's self-confidence.

• **Threatening to withhold love.** Parents should never use statements such as "I won't love you anymore if you don't stop hitting your brother." Threats such as these create a fear of being rejected and abandoned.

Handling Conflict

Discipline can create conflict between parents and children. Children may feel angry when they can't get their way. Parents must be prepared to deal with this anger. They should not make the child feel guilty about his or her anger; everyone in a family must remember that anger is a normal emotion.

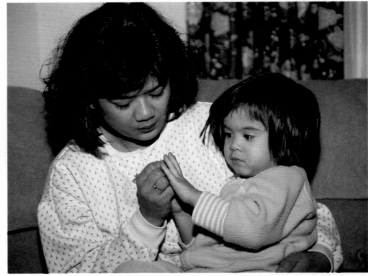

Parent-child chats about acceptable behavior can be a time to reinforce both consistent discipline and loving reassurance.

MORE ABOUT

Disciplinary Measures

• In late 1996, the American Academy of Pediatrics released a special report summarizing the findings of a conference devoted to reviewing the research on spanking. The report states, "Given a relatively 'healthy' family life in a supportive environment, spanking in and of itself is not detrimental to a child or predictive of later problems."

• Clinical evidence shows that children who experience inconsistent parenting and excessive punishment suffer anxiety and insecurity.

• Research carried out in schools and with parents and children has shown that verbalizations of more than three sentences by adults are rewarding to children. Therefore, too much talk over a specific misbehavior can actually be rewarding to the misbehaving child.

Instead of encouraging guilt, parents should give children an opportunity to discuss the conflict and to express their anger. It may help to discuss the misbehavior and the punishment some time after the incident. In this discussion, the parent can help the child understand why he or she misbehaved. The parent can also explain what the child should have done instead and can offer reassurance and encouragement.

Consistency

Being consistent is the key to guiding children's behavior. Consistency helps children learn the limits of behavior. It helps them know what is expected of them and what responses to expect from their parents.

Children lose trust and confidence in a parent or caregiver who constantly changes limits or fails to enforce limits in a consistent manner. If a parent or caregiver laughs at a child's behavior one day and punishes the same behavior the next day, the child will feel confused and insecure. When more than one person cares for a child, they should agree in advance on limits and on methods of enforcing those limits. If caregivers do not agree, children learn to use the inconsistency to their advantage.

Parents should allow the child to express his or her feelings about a situation. They should then agree on any discipline needed.

SECTION 2 REVIEW

CHECK YOUR UNDERSTANDING

1. What is discipline?
2. What is the ultimate goal of discipline? What does that involve?
3. List three keys to effective discipline.
4. List four guidelines for praising a child's good behavior.
5. List three questions parents should ask themselves as they choose specific limits for children.
6. List two questions parents should ask themselves before responding to a child's misbehavior.
7. Why should spanking not be done in anger?

DISCUSS AND DISCOVER

1. Do you think it is possible to raise a child without using any form of punishment? Why or why not? If you think punishment is necessary, which form do you consider most effective? Why? How and when do you think that kind of punishment should be used?
2. How does the discipline of parents and caregivers help a child develop self-discipline? What effect can punishment have on the development of self-discipline? Why?

Observing & Participating

Take care of a five- or six-year-old for an afternoon. Discuss discipline and limits both with the child's parents and, when appropriate, with the child. Describe those limits that the child is expected to observe. How does the child seem to respond to these limits? How easy—or difficult—is it to explain and enforce those limits?

SECTION 2 REVIEW

1. Helping children learn to behave in acceptable ways.
2. Help children learn self-discipline, or the ability to control one's own behavior. Effective guidance.
3. Through examples, explanations, and praise.
4. Encouraging appropriate behavior, setting and enforcing limits, and dealing with inappropriate behavior in effective ways.
5. Be understanding of the children's desires; set the limits and explain them; acknowledge the children's feelings; give alternatives.
6. Does the child understand that the behavior is inappropriate? Was the behavior intentional, or was it beyond the child's control?
7. Spanking in anger sets a poor example for dealing with emotions. Students may also say it creates a risk of losing control.

ASSESS

CHECKING COMPREHENSION

Ask students to write their answers to the Check Your Understanding questions in the Section 2 Review. Answers are given at the bottom of this page.

EVALUATE

Have students complete the Chapter 3, Section 2 TCR quiz.

Reteaching

1. Display pictures of children who are behaving inappropriately. Help students identify and discuss the problems. Ask them to suggest how to deal effectively with each situation.
2. Distribute and have students complete Reteaching 6 in the TCR.

Enrichment

1. Have students use psychology books to find out more about shame and guilt. How are these feelings used to control behavior? What are the uses of these feelings? What are the dangers in promoting shame and guilt in children? How do feelings of shame and guilt affect the lives of adults? Ask students to write brief reports.
2. Challenge students to complete Enrichment 6 in the TCR.

Extension

Invite a child psychologist to class to discuss setting and enforcing limits for children. In preparation for the visit, have students write specific examples of ways in which children test limits. If possible, ask them to describe situations they have observed or experienced. Present these descriptions to the speaker, and ask him or her to explain how caregivers might respond to each situation.

CLOSE

Ask each student to complete the following sentence: When they discipline their children, parents should ...

FOCUS

SECTION 3 RESOURCES

Teacher's Classroom Resources
- Enrichment 7
- Reteaching 7
- Section 3 Quiz

Student Workbook
- Child Care Vocabulary

SECTION OVERVIEW

In Section 3, students learn about substitute care for infants and children. They begin by examining the reasons that so many parents need part-time or full-time care for their children, then students examine the choices these parents have, including various forms of home-based and center-based care.

Next, students consider the questions parents should ask in evaluating substitute care for their children. The section concludes by presenting information about the effects of substitute child care.

MOTIVATOR

Encourage students to discuss their responses to these questions: When you imagine yourself as a parent, do you see yourself and your spouse as assuming full-time responsibility for the care of your child? Do you think your expectations are realistic? What do you already know about the options available to parents who need to have their children cared for, either part-time or full-time?

USING TERMS TO LEARN

Have students read all ten vocabulary terms. Encourage students to share their understanding of each term. Help students recognize the two shorter words in the compound word latchkey.

Providing Substitute Care

OBJECTIVES

- Explain the need for substitute care.
- Describe the types of substitute care available.

TERMS TO LEARN

child care aide
child care center
family child care
Head Start
latchkey children
Montessori preschool
nanny
parent cooperative
play group
preschool

One of the responsibilities of parents is providing quality substitute care when they must be away from their children. In some families, substitute care is needed only occasionally. However, an increasing number of parents depend on others to care for their children on a regular basis.

The Need for Substitute Care

There are several reasons for the trend toward placing children in substitute care:

- Many children live in one-parent homes, and the single parent typically has a full-time job. In this situation, the parent usually needs full-time or at least part-time substitute child care.

- In many two-parent families, both parents work away from home. Unless the parents have different work schedules, the children usually need substitute care.

- Some parents who do provide full-time care for their own children at home feel that their children can benefit from the social aspects of a preschool. In such situations, the young child usually attends a child care facility two or three times a week.

Types of Substitute Care

Parents who are faced with finding substitute care must choose wisely from the many types of child care services available. All provide the child with physical care and a place to play. Some also include planned activities to encourage the child's

80

HEALTHY FAMILIES/HEALTHY CHILDREN

Balancing Work and Family

"How can I raise children and have a career too?" In the past, women usually chose one alternative or the other. Today more and more people believe that both men and women can combine the responsibilities of parenthood with those of a career. Ask your students to think critically about careers and parenthood by responding to the following:

- Why do many women today want and need careers?

- Is homemaking a career?

- Do you think a career can be successfully combined with parenthood? What factors should be considered when making this decision?

physical, emotional, social, and intellectual development. A few also provide health and social services for the child and, in some cases, for the family as well.

Child care services are provided in two general settings. Some services are offered in a home. Others are provided in a child care center. Within these two basic categories, each type of care has its own advantages and disadvantages. Finding the best type of care for the individual child is extremely important for the child's future and for the parents' peace of mind.

Home-Based Care

Many young children receive substitute care in their own home or in another family's home. Care in a home setting may be easier for a child to get used to because the surroundings are familiar. Home-based care may also be more readily available and convenient for parents. Usually, it involves a smaller group of children than center-based care. This makes it an especially good choice for infants and other children who need a great deal of individual attention. There are three main types of home-based care:

The growing need for quality substitute child care has revived the nineteenth-century tradition of the nanny. The nanny lives with the family and is trained in all aspects of child development and child care.

TEACH

Pages 80-89

- **The Need for Substitute Care**
- **Types of Substitute Care**
- **Choosing Substitute Care**
- **The Effects of Substitute Child Care**

GUIDED PRACTICE

Promoting Discussion

Encourage students to share and discuss their own ideas about substitute care. Why do some people believe that substitute care should not be used on a regular basis? What disadvantages are these people likely to identify? Why do others support regular use of substitute care for children? What advantages do they probably consider important? How do you think an individual's opinion about the regular use of substitute child care is affected by his or her economic status? Why? By his or her education? Why? By his or her employment status and career goals? Why? Do you believe there is one "right" answer to the question of whether to use substitute care? If not, why not? If so, what is that answer?

Making Connections: Math

Have students find current statistics on working women, single parents, dual-career families, and on the numbers of children now living in each kind of family. Ask students to compile their findings in graph form to show what changes have occurred over the past ten years.

Using the Photograph

Encourage students to describe the people shown in the photo on this page. What are the nanny's responsibilities toward these two children? What kind of relationship does she appear to have with them? What other responsibilities do you think the nanny has? What do you imagine are the most rewarding aspects of her job? The least rewarding?

MORE ABOUT

Substitute Child Care

- Millions of preschool children are now cared for in substitute child care. One expert estimates that about two-thirds of all children between the ages of three and five spend part of their days in substitute care.

- The U.S. Civil Rights Commission says that the lack of child care or inadequate child care is one of the barriers to equal employment opportunity for women. Many women would like to work if they could find and afford adequate child care. This is especially true for mothers who are young, unmarried, and poor.

- In a survey of working women, 29 percent of clerical, service, factory, and plant workers said child care was a major problem. The figure rose to 36 percent among professional, managerial, and technical workers.

GUIDED PRACTICE (continued)

Promoting Discussion

Let students share their ideas in response to these questions: What special problems are faced by parents who work at night or during other nontraditional hours? What kinds of child care arrangements are likely to be most effective for them? Why?

Critical Thinking

Ask students to share their ideas about grandparents as substitute caregivers. What are the advantages of having a child's grandparent provide substitute care? What are the disadvantages? Do you think grandparents have an obligation to provide regular care for their grandchildren? Why or why not? Do you think grandparents have an obligation to provide occasional care (babysitting)? Why or why not?

Promoting Discussion

Have students identify the advantages and disadvantages of having a professional nanny.

Making Connections: Research

Encourage students to investigate the requirements for becoming a nanny. Have students contact agencies that provide professional training to obtain information on the course curriculum, supervised work experiences, length of training, costs involved, and placement service.

Using the Photograph

Let students describe the family child care setting shown in the photo on this page. What are the particular advantages of this kind of substitute care? For whom is it likely to be most beneficial?

Cooperative Learning

Assign groups of students to work together to plan a play group. Have the group members decide on the basic rules, the general format, the daily routine, the number of children, and the objectives of their play group.

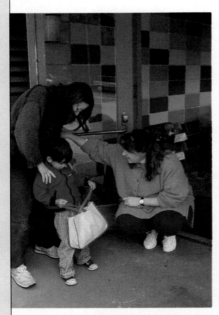

Quality family child care programs are licensed. They must meet minimum health and safety requirements and are limited to the number of children they can accept.

• **Care in the child's own home.** Many parents prefer to have their child cared for by someone who comes to their own home. Almost all parents make use of this type of care at least occasionally, as for an evening out. Many parents also use it on a regular basis. In-home care is especially convenient. However, it can be costly, and it does not usually provide an opportunity for playing with other children outside the family.

The caregiver may be a member of the child's extended family, a friend, or a babysitter. A less common alternative is to employ a live-in child care provider. Although a live-in arrangement is relatively expensive, it has the advantage of making reliable care available at almost any time of day or night.

The need for quality substitute care has revived the nineteenth-century tradition of the **nanny**, *a specially trained person employed to provide live-in child care services.* Many modern nannies have completed a course of academic study in all areas of child development and care. They may have also completed a period of supervised on-the-job training. Among those who can afford their services, nannies are in high demand.

• **Family child care.** For some young children, parents choose **family child care**, *a child care arrangement in which a small number of children are cared for in the caregiver's home.* Family child care combines the familiarity of a home setting with opportunities for social play and learning. Since the group size is small, all the children can be given individual attention. The cost of family child care is usually less than for care in the child's own home.

• **Play groups.** A **play group** is *a child care arrangement in which a group of parents take turns caring for each other's children in their own homes.* A play group is similar to family child care, but it involves a number of different homes and caregivers. The children are usually brought to the home of the parent who is providing care. Most play groups involve no fees. This type of substitute care is often a good choice for parents who do not work full-time.

Quality home-based care includes a daily routine of quiet and active times. Both planned activities and informal play are included. Caregivers should participate with the children in some of their activities. At other times, the caregivers should supervise as the children play by themselves. In no care setting should the children simply be placed in front of a television set or left without supervision.

MORE ABOUT

Licensing for Child Care Centers

Some experts feel that the two most important questions to ask of any substitute caregivers are: What is the ratio of adults to children? What training and experience do the caregivers have? In addition to these questions and those shown on the Checklist for Evaluation Quality Care (page 87), parents should be aware of their states' licensing requirements, which may differ dramatically from one state to another. Since state requirements can be minimal, possession of a current license is not in itself a guarantee of quality care. Remember, standards are only as good as their enforcement.

Center-Based Care

Many communities have facilities in which a staff of several adults care for one or more groups of children. These child care centers vary widely in their hours of operation; in the size, training, and experience of the staff; in the ages of children accepted; in the activities, equipment, and play areas provided; and in fees charged.

Some child care centers are businesses run for profit. Others charge fees to cover expenses but do not try to make a profit. Still others are funded by the city, state, or federal government. Care at government-funded centers may be offered free or at a reduced cost to those who qualify.

Child care centers must meet minimum health and safety requirements in order to be licensed. The license also limits the number of children a center may accept, depending on space, facilities, and the size of the staff.

These are the most common types of center-based child care:

- **Child care centers.** A **child care center** is *a facility designed primarily to provide care for children of working parents.* A variety of activities is typically offered at a child care center. Some centers may emphasize specific learning activities, while others may allow more time for informal play. Usually, there is a daily routine with time set aside for indoor and outdoor play, meals, and naps. Most child care centers are designed for children aged two years and older. Some centers provide care for infants.

Center-based care allows children to have social interaction and learning experiences under the guidance of a trained adult.

- **Preschools.** A **preschool** is *a child care center that provides educational programs, usually for children aged three to five.* A preschool typically offers activities designed to enrich the child's development in all areas. For example, there may be games to help children improve motor skills, language skills, and social skills. Art, music, and science activities may be a regular part of the program. The staff usually includes one or more teachers and a number of aides. (A **child care aide** is *an assistant to the person in charge of a child care program.*)

Usually, a preschool operates half-day sessions two or more days a week. Some centers combine nursery school and a child care program as a convenience for working parents.

- **Parent cooperatives.** A **parent cooperative** is *a child care facility in which part of the supervision is provided by the parents of enrolled children, who take turns donating their services.* While they are helping supervise the children, the parents are guided by a preschool teacher or other qualified caregiver who organizes the program. A parent cooperative offers several important advantages. Working at the center helps

---

HEALTHY FAMILIES/HEALTHY CHILDREN

Center-Based Care

Regular substitute care will not take sick children, and often there are no relatives available to help. Usually, parents cannot stay home from work to care for the children. In the last few years, a growing number of child care services have begun to accept sick children. Many of the sponsors of these programs are hospitals that offer sick-child care on the pediatric ward. Most hospitals do not make money on sick-child care. However, the programs use vacant pediatric beds, provide work for hospital employees, and create goodwill that hospitals hope will lead to later use of their facilities by families. Also, more agencies are sending trained, bonded personnel to care for the sick child at home. It is more expensive, but is popular with those who can afford it.

GUIDED PRACTICE (continued)

Critical Thinking
Ask students to compare the advantages and disadvantages of home-based care and center-based care. Who are the parents for whom home-based care is likely to seem the better choice? Why? For whom is center-based likely to be the better choice? Why?

Promoting Discussion
Explain that most children become ill with unusual frequency during the first year in which they have daily contact with other children—typically, during the first year they spend in a child care center or at school. Discuss with students how parents can take preventive measures and cope with the problems these illnesses bring.

Critical Thinking
Let students share their ideas about nonprofit child care centers and for-profit child care centers. What important differences would you expect to find between the two kinds of centers? What similarities would you expect?

Promoting Discussion
Ask students how center-based care for an infant would differ from home-based care. What are some important considerations when choosing infant day care?

Making Connections: Reading
Ask students to read about preschool programs that are linked to retirement homes or senior citizen programs. How does this kind of arrangement benefit the children? The seniors? Who else might benefit? How? Let students share their findings with the rest of the class.

Using the Photograph
Encourage students to describe the preschool setting shown in the photo on this page. How does the physically disabled child appear to be interacting with the other children in the program? What are the advantages of a program that includes children with special needs?

GUIDED PRACTICE (continued)

Using the Photographs

Encourage students to describe and discuss the children shown in the photos on this page. What kinds of programs are they participating in? What are the differences between those two kinds of programs? How do you think the children are benefitting from these preschool programs?

Making Connections: Current Events

Let interested students research the current levels of funding and support for Head Start programs. What kinds of attention is Head Start getting from members of Congress? From the administration? From the press? Ask students to share their findings.

Family Focus

Discuss with students their responses to these questions: What effect do you think placing a child in full-time substitute care has on the family? Are there both positive and negative effects? How can families deal with the negative effects?

Making Connections: Research

Have students find out which types of child care facilities must be licensed in your state. What health and safety requirements must be met? What are other requirements for licensing? Does licensing ensure high-quality care? Could licensing requirements be a problem for some home-based care programs? If so, what is the effect on the availability of child care? Let students share and discuss the results of their research.

Promoting Discussion

Ask students to recall instances they have read or heard about in which the health or safety of children was impaired in a child care center. Point out that when these situations happen, they receive special attention from the media. Discuss what precautions parents should take to prevent such occurrences. What recourses do parents of an injured child have?

The federal government began the Head Start program in the 1960s. It continues in operation today, offering lower-income families a program to enhance the development of their children.

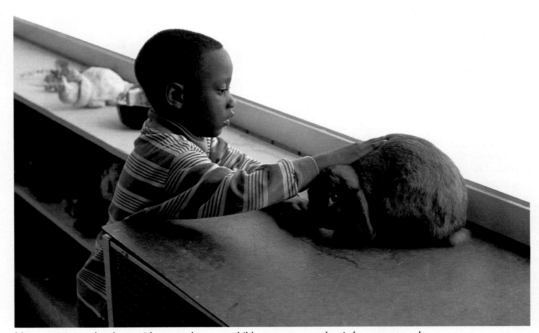

Montessori preschools provide an exploratory child care program that is less structured.

MORE ABOUT

Head Start Programs

In 1965, the Head Start program was instituted as part of the Community Action Program developed by the Office of Economic Opportunity. The program was designed to provide comprehensive activities intended to promote the physical, social, emotional, and intellectual growth of disadvantaged pre-school children and

their families. Guidelines for the program were flexible enough to allow for variations according to the profile of the local community and its needs. Between 1970 and 1974, the program was expanded to include related programs that extended the benefits of Head Start to other family members.

parents understand their child's development. In addition, a parent cooperative provides relatively inexpensive care. However, this type of care is rarely suitable for a parent who works full-time.

- **Head Start centers.** In the 1960s, the federal government began **Head Start**, *a program of locally operated child care facilities designed to help lower-income and disadvantaged children function effectively at home, in school, and in the community.* Most Head Start centers serve three- to five-year-olds.

   Head Start offers a variety of activities that enhance development. In addition, it offers meals that provide one-third to one-half of a child's daily nutritional needs. Head Start also provides health care and social services, such as counseling, for both parents and children. Parents are expected to become actively involved in the Head Start program.

- **Montessori preschools.** Some child care centers provide a specialized program that is different from the traditional preschool. An example is the **Montessori preschool**, *an educational facility for three- to six-year-olds that provides special learning materials which children are free to explore on their own.* This type of program is named for Dr. Maria Montessori, the founder of the methods used. In a Montessori classroom, the children are encouraged to explore the materials and to move from one activity to another as they wish.

Care for Older Children

Infants, toddlers, and preschoolers are not the only children who need substitute care. Many school-aged children also need care. They may have a gap of several hours between the time school lets out and the time parents arrive home from work.

Some children do not receive substitute care during these after-school hours. Often this is because affordable care is not available. It is estimated that our country now has at least two million **latchkey children**, *children who are unsupervised from the time they come home from school until their parents return from work.* If their parents leave for work early, these children may also be alone before school.

Child care experts advise against leaving children without adult supervision before the teen years. An increasing number of school, community groups, and nonprofit agencies are arranging activities to fill the parenting gap for latchkey children. These programs include supervised recreation, such as games, films, and art projects. Children may also do homework, read, or rest. Some programs provide before-school supervision, including breakfast.

OBSERVING AND PARTICIPATING

Observing Montessori Preschools

Montessori preschools emphasize the use of a carefully prepared environment to encourage children to make independent decisions. They teach children to take responsibility for their own learning and allow them to move at their own individual pace. By doing this children can develop educational/approaches and behavior appropriate to their individual personalities and learning styles. A wide variety of sensory materials for learning are found in Montessori schools. Have students visit a Montessori classroom and report back to the class on the classroom environment and sensory materials used in the program.

GUIDED PRACTICE (continued)

Making Connections: Research
   Have interested students survey local businesses about provision for child care. How many provide on-site care for the children of employees? How many help employees find substitute care for their children? How many help pay for substitute care? Ask students to summarize their findings for the rest of the class.

Cooperative Learning
   Let students work in groups to plan and prepare charts that summarize the advantages and disadvantages of various types of child care. Display each group's chart, and encourage students to compare and discuss them.

Making Connections: Research
   Ask students to survey local child care services to determine what options are available for parents of disabled children. Which programs are specifically for children with disabilities? Which programs mainstream disabled children into groups composed mainly of children without disabilities? At what age do disabled children qualify for each program? What are the costs of these programs? Let students share and discuss their findings.

Promoting Discussion
   Encourage students to discuss the likely attitudes of older children toward caregivers. How, for example, would a ten-year-old feel about going to a care center after school each day? How would that child's attitude probably be affected by the care arrangements made for his or her friends?

Making Connections: Research
   Have students research local programs that provide care for school-aged children between the end of the school day and the time parents arrive home from work. Ask students to contact schools, community groups, and nonprofit agencies to compile a list of available activities and programs.

GUIDED PRACTICE (continued)

Promoting Discussion

Ask students why active involvement by parents in a child care program is important in helping ensure quality care. What else can parents do to improve the quality of child care service?

Critical Thinking

Let students share and discuss their responses to these questions: What special problems do most single parents face in finding quality child care? What options do single parents have in making child care arrangements?

Promoting Discussion

Guide students in discussing the importance of taking a child along on visits to child care facilities. What kinds of reactions would you expect from a four-year-old? A two-year-old? Do you think parents considering child care for their infant should take the baby along to visit various care sites? Why or why not?

Making Connections: Writing

Have students create newspaper advertisements for child care services. Let them decide on the type of program they will advertise and the special features their program will provide. Then allow time for students to share and discuss their completed ads. Which are parents most likely to respond to? Why?

Did You Know?

According to a survey by American Baby, 35 percent of husbands change diapers as often as their wives, and 81 percent say they are assuming a larger role in child care than their fathers did.

Choosing Substitute Care

Which type of child care is best for an individual child? There are no easy answers. Parents must consider many factors. The types of care available locally, the costs, the convenience, and the particular needs of the child will all influence the decision.

It is essential that the parents visit each home or child care center they are considering. The child should be taken along on these visits, because the child's happiness and well-being are among the most important considerations. As they evaluate each care facility, parents might use the checklist on page 87 as a guide.

Once the parents have chosen a child care facility, they should drop by unexpectedly from time to time. These visits can help make the parent confident that the care is and remains as it was promised. After the child has attended the program for two or three weeks, the parent can ask the child how he or she feels about it. The child's happiness is the most dependable indicator of quality in child care.

Most children enjoy a quality preschool environment that promotes healthy social interaction. In what other ways do these children benefit from this outdoor environment?

MORE ABOUT

Latchkey Children

• According to a 1987 Census Bureau study, about 2,065,000 children—or 7.2 percent of all children ages five to thirteen—are left to care for themselves after school.

• The census bureau projects that 9.3 percent of children under the age of six are either alone or cared for by siblings.

• Some studies have found that latchkey children score lower than others on social adjustment and academic achievement; however, the differences are not large. Latchkey children seem to be more fearful than those who have adult supervision, but they also are better informed about how to keep themselves safe.

CHECKLIST FOR EVALUATING QUALITY CARE

THE CAREGIVER

* How many children are there for each caregiver?
* Do the caregivers seem to have time for each child?
* What type of training or experience has the caregiver had?
* Is the caregiver warm and loving toward the children? Calm and patient?
* Does the caregiver provide and direct activities well?
* Does the caregiver participate with the children frequently and respond to their questions?
* Do you agree with the caregiver's child-rearing attitudes and with the methods of discipline used?
* Does the caregiver seem to understand and respond to children's individual needs?
* Does the caregiver regularly take time to talk with parents about their children?

THE PROGRAM AND FACILITIES

* Where do the children eat, sleep, and play? Are the areas safe, comfortable, and sanitary?
* What kinds of social and learning opportunities are provided?
* Are books, toys, and large-play equipment available?
* Are children encouraged to participate in a variety of activities?
* Is there enough indoor and outdoor space for the children to play without crowding?
* If meals or snacks are provided, are they nutritious?
* Are the rules and routines reasonable? Are they easy for children to understand?
* What arrangements will be made if the caregiver is away or ill? What arrangements are made for children who are ill?

OVERALL IMPRESSIONS

* Do the children seem to be involved and happy?
* If you were a child, would you like to spend time there?

MORE ABOUT

Substitute Care

* Because quality child care is such an important issue for parents, some employers provide child care assistance as part of their benefit packages. Some employers keep a listing of nearby home-based and community-based facilities to help parents locate care. Others may pay for child care or allow employees to pay for child care with before-tax dollars. A few large employers operate child care centers that are in the same building where parents work or are nearby. Some employees are able to work at home or have flexible hours to help meet their child care needs.

GUIDED PRACTICE (continued)

Using the Chart

Guide students in reading and discussing the chart on this page. Why should parents ask each question? What special efforts might parents have to make to find the answers to these questions? What problems could arise if parents fail to find accurate answers to the questions? Which three questions do you consider most important? Why?

Practicing Decision Making

Ask students to consider the following situation: Joni has taken a full-time job and needs substitute care for her three-year-old son, Sam. She has heard about a young woman who lives nearby and cares for children in her home. Joni has already spoken to this woman on the phone, to arrange a visit. Joni thinks that the woman sounds friendly and understanding and that the cost is reasonable. She has also discovered the home is only six blocks away from her own apartment. As she walks into the house, Joni notices several children watching a game show on TV and sipping soft drinks. A glance around the small yard shows that there is no outdoor play equipment.

Let students discuss their reactions to this situation. What are the advantages of this child care situation for Joni and Sam? What are the disadvantages? If you were in Joni's situation, what would you do? Why?

Cooperative Learning

Let groups of students work together to write detailed descriptions of imaginary child care services. Then have each group pass its description to another group. Ask group members to use the Checklist for Evaluating Quality Care to rate the imaginary service presented in the description they have been given.

Cultural Exchange

Have students read "A Community of Families" and discuss how communal arrangements such as the Kibbutz, would counteract some of the challenges facing children and families in our country today.

INDEPENDENT PRACTICE

Journal Writing

Ask students to write journal entries exploring their own ideas about federally funded child care programs. Let students begin by discussing their responses to questions such as these: What advantages are associated with federally funded programs? What disadvantages? Whom should they serve? Why? Who should be expected to support child care programs? Why? Then have students explain their own opinions in their journals.

Student Workbook

Have students complete "Child Care Vocabulary" in the Student Workbook.

Extension

Let students work independently or in small groups to complete one or more of these:

- Investigate early psychological research done on maternal deprivation. How was this research used to convince new mothers that substitute care was harmful to children? Was this conclusion warranted by the research? Summarize findings and opinions in an oral report.

- Read about options for substitute child care in another country (such as Russia, Israel, or China). Discuss the advantages and disadvantages of each program.

- Read about recent research into the impact of substitute care on children's growth and development. Write a short report.

Cultural Exchange

A COMMUNITY OF FAMILIES

Many parents worry about how the emotional and social development of their children will be affected by having multiple caregivers. Reassurance comes from research that suggests the number of caregivers is not as important as the stability and responsiveness of those caregivers. A study of children raised in an Israeli kibbutz, for example, supports this idea. In the kibbutz, young children are raised communally by several caregivers. The children stay in residential nurseries and see their parents only a few hours a day or even just on the weekends. These children show normal, healthy development, both emotionally and socially, as long as the caregivers are sensitive and responsive.

The Effects of Substitute Child Care

Professionals in all areas of child care and development agree that emotional and intellectual development are directly influenced by a child's environment and experiences, beginning at birth. These professionals consider parents a child's best source of love and learning.

Many child development specialists advise that a parent should stay home to provide child care for as long as possible. For many parents, however, the longest possible options for staying home may not extend more than a few weeks beyond the child's birth. Extended maternity or paternity leave is not an option for many working parents. Does this mean that parents must choose between having an income to pay household bills and giving their child a good start in life?

Fortunately, parents do not usually have to make this kind of choice. Long-term studies find that good substitute care has no adverse effects on children's intellectual and emotional development. The key, of course, is finding good substitute care. Parents must spend time, care, and effort selecting a substitute caregiver for their child. The best caregiver is someone who enjoys the child and spends time playing with him or her. In a group facility, there should be a warm, caring atmosphere and enough staff to provide each child with individual attention.

Whether a child is cared for in a private home or in a child care center, parents may choose to drop in periodically to check the facility and its care.

TEEN PARENTING

Sharing Home Responsibilities

A teen mother who lives at home and depends on the support of her family should be encouraged to design a contract that outlines her responsibilities and helps solve tensions that might arise. Some issues to address in the contract are:

- **Housecleaning.** Who takes care of the baby's clutter, as well as bathrooms and living areas?

- **Meals.** What is the feeding schedule, who prepares the food and cleans up?

- **Discipline.** Who has primary responsibility for the decisions made about the baby and how is support to be provided?

- **Social activities.** Is a curfew for the baby's mother in effect? What arrangements are acceptable for visits from the baby's father?

Quality child care programs recognize the need they are filling and the influence they have on the physical and emotional development of children. Parents can improve the quality of child care by making their particular needs and wants known. Active involvement helps parents and other concerned individuals ensure that their expectations for quality child care are being met.

Child care centers often provide children with opportunities they might not otherwise have. Children can take part in a variety of planned learning activities. Some child care centers encourage parent participation.

SECTION 3 REVIEW

CHECK YOUR UNDERSTANDING

1. List three reasons for the trend toward placing children in substitute care.

2. What is a nanny?

3. How is family child care different from a play group? How are the the two kinds of care similar?

4. List one advantage and one disadvantage of a parent cooperative.

5. Who are latchkey children? What special needs do they have?

6. List four factors that influence a parent's decision about child care.

7. List four questions parents should try to answer during a visit to a child care facility they are considering.

DISCUSS AND DISCOVER

1. Working with a group of other students, gather information about child care facilities in your community. Organize your information into listings of home-based care facilities and center-based care facilities. Include the address and phone number of each facility, as well as basic information about ages of children they accept and hours of operation. Make your listings available to interested parents.

Observing & Participating

Visit a substitute care facility and observe how the caregivers provide for the growth and development of the children. Speculate about why parents would choose this facility and what factors might influence their choices. What other factors might families need to consider when making decisions about substitute care?

SECTION 3 REVIEW

1. Single-parent has a full-time job; in two-parent families, both parents work; parents want their children to have the social aspects of a preschool.

2. A specially trained person employed to provide live-in child care services.

3. Family child care is when a small number of children are cared for in the caregiver's home. Play group is when groups of parents take turns caring for each other's children.

4. Advantages: helps parents understand their child's development and provides relatively inexpensive care. Disadvantage: Rarely suitable for parent who works full-time.

5. Children who are unsupervised after school until parents return from work.

6. Types available, costs, convenience, and individual needs of the child.

7. Answers vary, and include those on page 87.

ASSESS

CHECKING COMPREHENSION

Ask students to write their answers to the Check Your Understanding questions in the Section 3 Review. Answers to questions are given below.

EVALUATE

Have students complete the Chapter 3, Section 3 TCR quiz.

Reteaching

1. Write the name of each type of home-based and center-based care on an index card. On separate cards, write brief descriptions of these types of care. Let students match the name of each type of care with the appropriate description and identify it as either home- or center-based. Discuss advantages of each type of substitute child care.

2. Distribute and have students complete Reteaching 7 in the TCR.

Enrichment

1. Have students read about the history of Head Start. When, why, and how did Head Start begin? How has it developed? What future does it appear to have? Ask students to orally summarize their findings.

2. Challenge students to complete TCR Enrichment 7.

Extension

Invite representatives from several substitute care facilities to class to speak on local options in child care. Have the panel members discuss the types of services available, the hours of operation, the ages of the children served, the cost of services, and the daily routine of activities. Students may prepare questions in advance.

CLOSE

Give each student an opportunity to identify the type of substitute care he or she prefers and to explain briefly the reasons for that preference.

Use the Summary and the Reviewing the Facts questions to help students go over the most important ideas presented in Chapter 3.

CHAPTER **3** REVIEW

1. Hospitals, schools, community organizations, private courses.

2. They need to have realistic expectations.

3. With understanding and patience; to encourage children to keep trying.

4. Punishment (negative reinforcement intended to discourage inappropriate behavior) may be used as one part of discipline (the task of helping children learn to behave in acceptable ways).

5. Inner sense of what is right.

6. Children imitate others; they learn best by being shown what to do.

7. Positive reinforcement is a response that encourages a particular behavior; praise is one example. Negative reinforcement is a response that tends to discourage a particular behavior from being repeated; temporary loss of a privilege is one example.

8. Choices help children learn they are responsible for their own actions; they also help minimize frustration.

9. Any four: bribing; making children promise to behave; shouting or yelling; shaming; threatening to withhold love.

10. A play group is a form of home-based care in which parents take turns caring for each other's children; a parent cooperative is a form of center-based care in which parents provide part of the supervision.

11. Good substitute care has no adverse effects on intellectual and emotional development.

CHAPTER **3** REVIEW

SUMMARY

- Acquiring parenting skills is a lifelong learning process.
- Caregivers who understand children and their individual differences are better able to promote healthy development.
- Children need encouragement, enriching experiences, love, and support.
- Good behavior should be encouraged through examples, simple explanations, praise, and reasonable choices.
- Children want and need reasonable limits on their behavior.
- A child's misbehavior should be handled calmly in a manner appropriate to the situation.
- Many different types of substitute child care, both home-based and center-based, are available.

REVIEWING THE FACTS

1. List four places where formal training in parenting is often offered.

2. Why should parents and other caregivers learn about the various stages all children go through?

3. How should parents and other caregivers respond to a child's mistakes? Why?

4. How are discipline and punishment related? What are the differences between the two?

5. What is a conscience?

6. Why is it so important for parents and other caregivers to set a good example for children?

7. What is positive reinforcement? What is negative reinforcement? Give an example of each.

8. List two reasons for allowing children to make decisions about their own behavior.

9. List four methods of discipline that should be avoided because they are poor choices.

10. What is the difference between a play group and a parent cooperative?

11. What do long-term studies show about the effects of substitute care on the development of children?

90

EXPLORING FURTHER

1. Find out about parenting classes offered in your community. Note when and where the classes are offered. Also find out who is welcome in the classes and what fee, if any, is charged. Then make fliers or posters to share the information you have gathered. (Section 1)

2. Read a magazine article that deals with disciplining children. What definition of discipline is stated or implied in the article? What approaches are recommended? Why? What do you think of the attitudes expressed in the article.? Discuss your ideas with classmates. (Section 2)

3. Working with a group of classmates, prepare and administer a questionnaire to gather data about the use of substitute child care in your community. Decide what kinds of information you want, and plan questions to elicit that kind of information. Finally, summarize the information in a graph or chart, and post that summary in your classroom. (Section 3)

4. Gather information about a Head Start program in your area. When was it established? Whom does it serve? How is it regarded by the families whose children attend it? How is it regarded by teachers at the elementary school the program graduates attend? Prepare and present a short oral report of the information you have gathered. (Section 3)

THINKING CRITICALLY

1. **Evaluate.** What might cause a parent to have trouble expressing love for his or her own child? How do you think a parent should try to deal with this difficulty? Do you think the parent should focus on the source of his or her own problem or focus on changing his or her behavior? Why? Some parents who have difficulty showing affection say, "It's all right— the kids know I love them, no matter what I say or do." Do you agree? Why or why not?

2. **Compare.** React to this statement: "It doesn't really matter what kind of discipline parents use, as long as they teach their children how to behave." Compare your response with your classmates.

CLASSROOM MANAGEMENT

Planning Field Trips

Field trip opportunities are available in most communities. Child care facilities, recreational facilities, and department stores welcome visits by students. Field trips outside the school usually involve detailed planning to obtain permission from school administrators and parents and to arrange transportation. For field trips that are longer than one class period, there may be additional planning involved to determine the cost of the trip, set departure and arrival times, obtain additional chaperones, and make provisions for meals, if necessary. Check with your school administration about securing the proper release forms required by your school district.

3. **Analyze.** Discuss and defend your ideas in response to these questions: Do you believe children really want parents and other caregivers to set limits? If so, at what age do you believe people no longer want limits imposed by others? If not, why do you think parents and other caregivers continue to set limits?

CROSS-CURRICULUM CONNECTIONS

1. **Science.** Research B. F. Skinner's classic studies on operant conditioning. Write a brief report on these studies, noting particularly how they relate to effective discipline techniques.

2. **Speaking.** Read *The Montessori Method* by Maria Montessori, or read a summary of Montessori's educational theories. Then visit a Montessori preschool, and observe the children and teachers. Prepare and present an oral report, discussing the concepts of Montessori preschools and the application of those concepts in the school you visited.

SCHOOL TO WORK

Your Personality If you prefer to spend time with people rather than alone, you might be attracted to a career such as teaching. That's because your personality makes you comfortable among people and you value social situations. Here's an exercise to help you learn more about how personality affects your choice of careers. Make a list of words that describe you. You could also make another list that describes what you are *not*. Now talk to successful people in a profession that appeals to you and find out if you share personality characteristics. What do your findings tell you about your future in that field?

PERFORMANCE ASSESSMENT

Effective Parenting Skills

Task

Prepare a multimedia lesson that focuses on one parenting skill learned in this chapter. Present the lesson to your class as if they were prospective parents in a parenting workshop.

Purpose

Your lesson should be an informative, instructional, and inspirational presentation of a selected parenting skill intended to interest all people who consider parenthood.

Procedure

1. Brainstorm a list of the parenting skills you learned about in this chapter. Select one for your lesson.
2. Think first about the information you want to provide. Jot down notes and specifics that are relevant.
3. Then determine what you want to say and how you will say it. You may want to give a demonstration and include a poster or chart. You may use music, dance, photographs, videotape, drawings, or any other acceptable media to relay your message. Be creative.
4. Include in the content of your presentation a way for parents to evaluate whether they are remembering or effectively practicing your parenting tool. It could be in the form of a question or helpful hint that could be placed in a location that is seen every day, such as a bathroom mirror or refrigerator door.
5. Prepare your final multimedia lesson. If necessary, rehearse for family members or friends.

Evaluation

The following criteria will be used to evaluate your multimedia lesson on parenting skills. Content: Did you select a parenting skill you learned about in this chapter? Was your content accurately presented? Did you include a helpful tool for parents to assess their own effectiveness with this parenting skill? Presentation: Was your presentation clear and understandable? Was it interesting? Was it effective?

Portfolio Idea

The format of your lesson will determine how you will store it in your portfolio. Include any components that will fit in your portfolio with a clearly written explanation of the objective. You could also use a photograph display. Your portfolio adaptation should include the objective of your lesson, the lesson plan itself, a summary of your preparation, and teacher or peer response. Remember to label every item carefully.

PERFORMANCE ASSESSMENT

Multimedia Lesson

To generate peer interaction, have students work in pairs to reflect on what they've learned and to help each other list parenting skills. You might also pair highly motivated students with students who need help getting started or those acquiring English. If they work on their lesson presentation in pairs, remember to have each student make an individual representation for the portfolio. If you own or can borrow special equipment such as audio- or videotape equipment, bring it to class and set aside time for students to use it. See the Technology Options box on this page for more ideas.

EVALUATE

Use the reproducible Chapter 3 Test in the TCR, or construct your own test using the Testmaker Software.

EXTENSION

Have students work in pairs or small groups, discussing what they have learned about parenting. Ask each pair or group to create a questionnaire that could be used by parents to evaluate their own skills and determine areas in which they need to improve.

CLOSE

Give each student an opportunity to complete the following statement:

"Parenting skills can help me …"

TECHNOLOGY OPTION

VCR Encourage students who have access to videocassette recorders to tape interviews or demonstrations to use in their Performance Assessment activity on this page. For example, they could tape a family meeting to demonstrate communication skills or a parent disciplining a child. Students might tape "Before" and "After" versions of the same parenting skill, the first showing a parent's reaction before he or she learned about child development, the second showing an improved response to the situation.

Computers Students could use word processing programs or graphic programs to create work sheets for the audience. Work sheets might include important information about the topic as well as space for the audience members to write notes during the presentation. The lesson presenter could include a post-lesson evaluation form to receive feedback about the success of the lesson.

INTRODUCE

CHAPTER OVERVIEW

Chapter 4 addresses the issue of teen sexuality and provides sexually active students with a model for intelligently deciding on a course of action in the event of an unwanted pregnancy.

Section 1 introduces the subject of teen sexuality and factors that have an impact on a teen's decision on whether to have sex.

Section 2 covers sources of help pregnant teens can turn to and explores the consequences of teen parenthood.

CHAPTER OBJECTIVES

After completing Chapter 4, students will be able to:

- Discuss what sexuality does—and does not—involve.
- Explain the relationship between values and sexuality.
- List the steps in the decision-making process.
- Discuss how teens can approach decisions about sexual activity.
- Explain how pregnancy can be prevented.
- Describe the decisions that pregnant teens must make.
- List possible sources of help available to pregnant teens.
- Discuss the alternatives available to pregnant teens.
- Describe the consequences of teen parenthood.

CLASSROOM MANAGEMENT

Resources Beyond the Classroom

Teenagers who are considering or who have chosen to become parents need to fully acquaint themselves with the realities of teen parenting in order to be successful. Teen parents face more difficulties which tend to be unique to them and complicate an already demanding role. For more information on the particular burdens of teen parenting as well as referrals to local support groups (or how to begin one in their area), interested teenage parents can write:

National Organization of Adolescent
Pregnancy and Parenting, Inc.
P.O. Box 2365
Reston, VA 22090

Teen Pregnancy and Parenthood

SECTION 1   Making Responsible Decisions

SECTION 2   Realities of Teen Pregnancy and Parenting

THINK ABOUT

Every day you make decisions—some major, some minor; some simple, some complex; some easy, some difficult. While the minor, simple, and easy decisions seldom cause you to worry, the more serious ones, especially those involving sexual activity, need careful consideration. Did you ever think that making a decision involves a process? Learning about the decision-making process and practicing it often will give you the skill to handle the serious decisions that confront you. Equally important is your awareness that all decisions have consequences that should be considered before a decision is made.

ASK YOURSELF

Study the photo on the opposite page that shows a teen girl deep in thought.

Her thoughts and concerns might be similar to yours—about friends, relationships, family, school, or career. Suppose she were faced with decisions about sexual activity. What might be going through her mind? What decisions would she face? How would her decisions affect her future? Who could she turn to for worthwhile advice?

NOW TRY THIS

Make a list of all the decisions you have already made today. Cross out those decisions that seem insignificant, such as what toothpaste to use when you brushed your teeth or which sweater to wear to school. Now look at the remaining decisions. Next to each one, identify one consequence, either positive or negative, that will be a result of the decision you made.

93

INTRODUCING THE CHAPTER

• Have three students role-play a situation in which a teenage daughter tells her parents that she is pregnant. After the role play, have every student fold a sheet of paper into three vertical columns, using the following three headings: Child, Mother, and Father. Under each heading, students should list words describing the reactions and emotions they observed in each character. Explain that in this chapter students will learn about the realities and responsibilities of pregnancy and parenting.

• Use the photo on the opposite page and the three features on this page—Think About, Ask Yourself, and Now Try This—to begin a discussion about teen pregnancy and parenthood.

CHAPTER PROJECT

Have students simulate a TV talk show on the subject of teenage pregnancy and parenthood. One class member is to function as moderator and three others as experts on the following topics: sex among teens, the problems faced by teen parents, and the health risks—including AIDS—that today face anyone engaging in sexual intercourse. The rest of the class is to function as the studio audience. Before beginning the activity, all students should be encouraged to gather information on one or more of the areas for discussion. Each student in the studio audience is to frame at least three good questions.

HEALTHY FAMILIES/HEALTHY CHILDREN

The Myth of Healthy Families

Healthy families are not trouble-free families as myth would lead one to believe. Nor have families of the past operated only as healthy families. The reality is that families of the past also had marital discord, unwed motherhood, angry or schizophrenic children, and other sorts of problems. However, families of the past were taught to hide their problems. Today's healthy families expect problems and consider them a part of family life. They work together to face the problem or crisis head-on, use a variety of problem-solving techniques, and have the ability to see something positive from every situation, now matter how challenging.

FOCUS

SECTION 1 RESOURCES

Teacher's Classroom Resources
- Enrichment 8
- Reteaching 8
- Section 1 Quiz

Student Workbook
- Understanding Sexuality

SECTION OVERVIEW

In Section 1, students learn about the factors, such as peer pressure and personal values, that have an influence on a teen's decision to engage in or refrain from sexual activity. Students are also provided with a six-step problem-solving model that can be used for evaluating the consequences of having sex.

MOTIVATOR

Ask students to volunteer decisions, both big and small, that they have been faced with lately. To start students thinking, you may wish to share a recent decision of your own (e.g., whether or not to buy a particular car, what to serve for dinner) and the process you used in arriving at a decision. Ask: What is common to all decision making? How did you go about choosing in each case you named?

USING TERMS TO LEARN

Before they read the chapter, ask students to fold a sheet of paper into two columns. Then have them list in one column all the terms in "Terms to Learn" that they believe relate to the topic of sex, and in the second column, all other terms. After they have read the chapter, ask students to review and, where necessary, revise their lists.

TERMS TO LEARN

abstinence
consequences
contraception
hormones
peer pressure
sexuality
values

SECTION 1

Making Responsible Decisions

OBJECTIVES

- Discuss what sexuality does—and does not—involve.
- Explain the relationship between values and sexuality.
- List the steps in the decision-making process.
- Discuss how teens can approach decisions about sexual activity.
- Explain how pregnancy can be prevented.

Teenagers have to make many decisions. Some decisions seem very important; a teen may devote a lot of time and energy to selecting the "right" choice. Other decisions may seem insignificant and go almost unnoticed, such as which clothes to wear or what movie to see. However, the kinds of decisions that will have an important impact on the rest of a teenager's life and on the lives of other people should be carefully considered.

Teen Sexuality

Many decisions a teenager makes relate in some way to his or her **sexuality**—*a person's concept of himself or herself as a male or a female*. Sexuality involves much more than physical maturity or the ability to be sexually active. Sexuality involves a person's regard for himself or herself, as well as that person's sense of responsibility and understanding of other people. Thus physical, intellectual, emotional, and social development are all aspects of sexuality.

Individuals express their sexuality in various ways. They show their maleness or femaleness in the way they walk, talk, move, dress, dream, and laugh.

Teenagers are in the process of establishing their own sexual identity—that is, they are developing their own sense of them-

---

MORE ABOUT

Pressures from the Opposite Sex

Remind students that not all teens have sex. Real love and caring means getting to know someone and respecting that person's limits and rights. Read aloud the following lines:

- Everyone's doing it.
- I'll break up with you if you don't.

- If you really love me, you'll do it.
- It will make you a real man or a real woman.
- You won't get pregnant. It will be safe.

Explain that if a teen is being pressured to have sex, one of the lines above may be used. Stress to students that even protected sex can result in pregnancy or a sexually transmitted disease.

selves as male or female individuals. This process is influenced by a number of powerful factors. Teens undergo dramatic physical changes, many of which are part of achieving sexual maturity. At the same time, changing **hormones**, *body chemicals*, often cause mood swings or emotional ups and downs. Learning about these processes can help teens cope better with their physical and emotional changes. These changes usually cause social changes. Teens often find themselves attracted to new friends, pressured by peers, or involved in new kinds of interactions with family members.

A teenager adjusting to these changes makes daily decisions about how to behave and how to interact with other people. Many of these decisions reflect the teen's self-esteem or attitude toward himself or herself; at the same time, these decisions help establish that teen's understanding and expression of his or her sexuality.

During this crucial period, teens face many kinds of pressure relating to sexuality and sexual activity. This pressure comes from the media—television, radio, music, movies, and commercials—that often imply sexual activity is necessary for mature sexuality. Teens also face **peer pressure**, *the influence of people one's own age*. Teens may pressure one another to engage in an activity that is inappropriate or not in keeping with an individual's values. "Everyone is doing it—what's wrong with you?" they may ask or imply.

In the face of these pressures and confusion, it is essential for teens to understand that sexual intercourse and other forms of sexual activity are not a necessary part of sexuality.

Values and Sexuality

Any decision a person makes may reflect that person's **values**, *the principles a person considers important and uses to guide his or her life*. All people have values; familiar examples include trust, self-respect, respect for others, commitment, and loyalty.

During the early years, a person's values are shaped by his or her family. For example, a parent who values honesty passes this value on by example and is likely to discuss the importance of honesty with a child. A child's values are also influenced by other caregivers, by teachers and others at school, by friends, and often by organizations, such as religious groups or community clubs.

During adolescence, teens may question the values of their parents, of other family members, and of society. This questioning and evaluating is part of the process by which teens decide what they believe and what values they want to uphold during the rest of their lives. In other words, it is part of becoming mature and establishing identity.

The teen years should be a time of enjoyment. How can an early pregnancy affect the teen years?

TEACH

Pages 94-99

• Teen Sexuality
• Using the Decision-Making Process
• Decisions About Sexual Activity
• Avoiding Pregnancy

GUIDED PRACTICE

Promoting Discussion

Have students discuss the factors that lead some teenagers to engage in sex, including physical and emotional desires. Have students map strategies for handling these pressures and desires while avoiding pregnancy and STDs.

Critical Thinking

Have students brainstorm other ways, besides the one noted in the text, in which peer pressure can affect teens, both positively and negatively. It can lead teens to take unnecessary risks, such as driving too fast; teens can inspire each other to take constructive action, such as cleaning up a community dump.

Using the Photograph

Direct students' attention to the photo on this page. Ask: How would you describe the emotional state of the teens in this picture? What effect would an unwanted pregnancy have on this emotional state? What are some of the other risks that go along with giving in to pressure to have sex?

Using Management Skills

Have several volunteers individually conduct interviews with teens outside the class in an effort to learn which values are most important to them. Afterwards, students should compile a master list of the values most cited. Use this list as a starting point for a class discussion of how yielding to sexual pressure affects values. How, for example, might bending to pressure affect a young person who most values self-respect?

MORE ABOUT

Peer Counseling

Many schools have set up peer counselors, students who receive formal training that provides them with skills in leading discussions, facilitating groups, and communicating. Peer counseling is a counseling technique that many communities and schools are using effectively with teens. Many teens find someone their own age a much more comfortable resource than an adult. Furthermore, other teens can more readily empathize with teen problems. The programs are supervised by an adult coordinator. Have students find out whether there are peer counseling opportunities in their school or community.

GUIDED PRACTICE (continued)

Critical Thinking

Have students discuss the contention of some teenagers that sexual activity, far from detracting from their self-esteem, actually enhances it (e.g., by making a male teen feel more like a "man"). Ask students whether they can identify the logical fallacy in this line of reasoning. ("Using" another person to achieve a goal is self-demeaning.)

Making Connections:
Social Studies

Have students research periods of history in which women were branded as social outcasts for engaging in sex before marriage. Have students determine other aspects of the moral climate and code of such times. Conclude with a discussion of the positive and negative effects of strict codes of sexual behavior.

Practicing Decision Making

Have students review the six steps in the decision-making process. Then divide the class into groups of three or four students, and have each group brainstorm three situations in which a problem is to be solved. Have groups share their situations. Conclude by having each group select a situation devised by another group and apply the problem-solving model to it to reach a solution.

HEALTH TIP

Although most everyday problems can by solved without resorting to an elaborate model such as the one presented here, students should never underestimate the usefulness of breaking down a problem into its component steps.

Every day, teens are bombarded by media and peer pressure, which can make them confused about values and goals.

A teen's values influence the way he or she thinks about and responds to questions that relate to sexuality: Who am I? What does it mean to be a male or a female? Is sexual activity an essential part of my being a man or a woman? What are some of the possible consequences of sexual activity? Who may be affected by my sexual activity? What responsibilities am I willing to accept for the effects of my sexual activity?

Using the Decision-Making Process

Some say the teen years are the best years of your life. However, teenagers face decisions that may have long-lasting effects on their lives as teens and even as adults. Some of these decisions relate directly to sexuality and to sexual activity. Every teen who has sexual intercourse—even the teen who says, "Well, it just seemed like the thing to do," or "I don't know quite how; it just happened"—has made a decision. Decisions about sexual activity are too important to make casually. These decisions deserve careful consideration, because they can have **consequences** —*the results that come from a decision*—that will last throughout life.

All decisions have consequences for the person who makes the decision; many also have consequences for other people. Thinking about and analyzing the possible consequences is an essential part of making responsible decisions.

Making a decision should be a process, not a single, impulsive act. Understanding and using the six basic steps in the decision-making process can help people of all ages make responsible decisions.

1. **Identify the decision to be made.** The first step in the decision-making process is to recognize that a decision needs to be made and to identify exactly what that decision is.

2. **Identify the alternatives.** The second step involves identifying all the possible choices. Sometimes there may be only two options; sometimes there may be many. Often, one of the options is to avoid doing anything. It is important to remember, however, that doing nothing is itself a decision that has specific consequences.

3. **Consider the consequences of each alternative.** What results is each possible choice likely to have? What are the positive consequences of each option? What are the negative consequences? Are there differences between the short-term consequences and the long-term consequences? If so, what are those differences? Thoroughly examining the responses to these questions is the third step in the decision-making process.

MORE ABOUT

Values

Examining values makes it easier to understand yourself and the world around you. Some examples of values are honesty, family, religion, freedom, knowledge, health, respect for others, and respect for the environment. It is important for students to recognize that there is no one absolute value system. We all develop our own value system from our parents, friends, and the society we live in. We should try to respect values that differ from ours. This difference occurs frequently in a multicultural society. Have students discuss what influenced their values, and how values may vary from one culture to another.

Avoiding Pregnancy

Abstinence, *avoiding or abstaining from sexual intercourse*, is a choice that everyone can make. It is the only completely reliable means of protecting oneself from pregnancy and STDs.

Those who choose to be sexually active and choose not to use any protection are taking risks. Health officials advise individuals who decide to be sexually active to use **contraceptives**, *devices or methods that prevent pregnancy*. When used correctly and consistently, contraceptives such as condoms, oral contraceptives ("the pill"), sponges, foams, and diaphragms can dramatically reduce the risk of pregnancy. In addition, condoms can decrease the risk of transmitting STDs.

SECTION 1 REVIEW

CHECK YOUR UNDERSTANDING

1. Define the term *sexuality*.
2. What are values?
3. List the six steps in the decision-making process.
4. When teens are making decisions about sexual activity, with whom should they discuss their alternatives and the consequences of those alternatives?
5. List three possible health consequences of having sexual intercourse.
6. What are hormones?
7. What is the only completely reliable method of preventing pregnancy?

DISCUSS AND DISCOVER

1. How can teens in your community learn more about sexual activity, contraceptives, and the prevention of STDs? With a group of classmates, compile a list of classes, hot lines, clinics, and other sources of information and assistance. Publish your list in a brochure, a poster, or another convenient format.

2. List five specific values that you consider important in your own life. Then discuss your list with a group of classmates. How are the lists alike? How and why are they different? How do you think the values you listed were formed and became important to you?

Observing & Participating

Identify two decisions that you currently face—one that deals with an everyday issue and one that is more serious or complex. Then list the six steps of the decision-making process on pages 96-97. Using the list, write responses to each step for the everyday decision and again for the more serious one. If possible, arrive at acceptable decisions. Finally, write a brief analysis of how this process helps you think more clearly and rationally about each situation.

SECTION 1 REVIEW

1. A person's concept of himself or herself as male or female.
2. The principles a person considers important and uses to guide his or her life.
3. Refer to the list of steps presented on pages 96 and 97.
4. Parents, friends, trusted adults, partner.
5. Pregnancy; risk of infection with an STD, possible consequence of HIV, the virus that causes AIDS.
6. Body chemicals.
7. Abstinence, abstaining from sexual intercourse.

ASSESS

CHECKING COMPREHENSION

Assign students to write their responses to the Check Your Understanding questions in the Section 1 Review. Answers to the questions are given below.

EVALUATE

Have students complete the Chapter 4, Section 1 quiz in the TCR.

Reteaching

1. Ask students to restate the six steps in the decision-making model in their own words. Students are then to give examples of two problems: one that would require this process and one that could be solved without using such an elaborate model.
2. Assign Reteaching 8 in the TCR and have students complete the activity and review their responses.

Enrichment

1. Review with students the decision-making scenario in the teacher's side column on page 97 involving Carlos and Mindy. Have students imagine that Carlos has yielded to his own fears of being "found out" and has threatened to leave Mindy unless she agrees to have sex with him. Have students use the decision-making process to determine Mindy's options.
2. Assign Enrichment 8 in the TCR.

Extension

Have students learn more about HIV, the virus that causes AIDS. Have them determine, in particular, ways in which this virus can be contracted and the number of people infected each year.

CLOSE

Have students create original posters that express the sentiment of this new version of an old maxim: "Abstinence makes the heart grow fonder."

FOCUS

SECTION 2 RESOURCES

Teacher's Classroom Resources
- Enrichment 9
- Reteaching 9
- Section 2 Quiz

Student Workbook
- Teen Parenting and Parenthood

SECTION OVERVIEW

In Section 2, students learn about individuals and agencies they can turn to for support and counseling in the event of an unwanted pregnancy; and are provided with a list of alternatives to teen marriage. It concludes with a discussion of consequences of teen parenthood.

MOTIVATOR

Propose this case: teens who are a sexually active couple discover that they are about to become parents. Encourage students to make an exhaustive list of decisions that face the couple. This chapter will discuss options available to teen parents-to-be, and the challenges and struggles of teen parenthood.

HEALTH TIP

The best advice for any teen is to abstain from sexual activity. Some ignore such advice and engage in sexual intercourse anyway. These teens should know the facts about conception, which include the following:

- A female can get pregnant if she has intercourse during her menstrual period.

- A female can get pregnant the first time she has intercourse.

- Pregnancy can occur even if the couple has intercourse standing up.

SECTION 2   Realities of Teen Pregnancy and Parenting

OBJECTIVES

- Describe the decisions that pregnant teens must make.
- List possible sources of help available to pregnant teens.
- Discuss the alternatives available to pregnant teens.
- Describe the consequences of teen parenthood.

Every year in the United States, about one out of nine girls between the ages of fifteen and nineteen becomes pregnant. Each girl's pregnancy is a consequence of decisions she and a sexual partner made. Each pregnancy also raises a number of decisions that the teen—and, if possible, her partner and her parents or other family members—must make.

Identifying the Decision

Unless a teen has planned and hoped to become pregnant, she may have trouble believing and acknowledging the symptoms of pregnancy. A girl who fears she might be pregnant may try to ignore the symptoms. This kind of avoidance, though completely understandable, makes it impossible for the girl to begin responding to the question: How will I deal with this pregnancy?

Teens who are sexually active should be aware of the early signs of pregnancy. (They are discussed in Chapter 6.) As difficult as this may be, a teen who suspects she might be pregnant should discuss her concerns with someone she feels close to—her boyfriend, a parent or other family member, a trusted friend, or a special teacher or counselor. She should also see a physician, who can tell her definitely whether or not she is pregnant.

Once her pregnancy has been confirmed, a teen can begin the process of deciding what to do. In order to make a responsible decision, she will have to consider all her alternatives; she will

---

TEEN PARENTING

Drop-Outs

Half of all teen mothers drop out of school before or after their babies are born. In Texas in 1987, for example, pregnancy and marriage were the most common reasons students dropped out of school. As a result, of Texas parents with children under the age of six, 40 percent of mothers and 30 percent of fathers have not finished high school. Because this trend can trigger a cycle, it is important for teens to have adequate support systems to encourage them to remain in school. Have your students discuss why students drop out of school, and specifically, what could be done to lower the drop-out rate.

also have to think about the consequences of each alternative. Pregnant teens are faced with important, difficult decisions. Fortunately, they do not have to go through the decision-making process alone.

Sources of Help

As she works through the decision-making process, a teenage girl may be helped by many different people, including the father-to-be, her parents, a member of the clergy, a member of the school staff, and a family planning counselor.

- **Fathers-to-Be.** Whenever possible, the partner of a pregnant teenager should be an active participant in decisions made about the pregnancy. The father of the unborn baby has rights and responsibilities, just as the mother does. No matter what decision is finally reached, the pregnancy will have a long-lasting effect on his life. He will have to face the consequences of the decision, no matter which alternative is finally chosen.

- **Parents.** Most pregnant teens are reluctant to discuss their situation with their parents. Parents are often hurt or angry when they first learn of the pregnancy. However, the teens' own parents are often uniquely able to help them think through the meaning and implications of pregnancy and parenthood. The emotional support that the parents of a teenage girl and her partner offer can be critical in helping the teens through the stresses of reaching a decision and living with its consequences.

Parents are often the best source of help, reassurance, and comfort when a teen finds out she is pregnant.

TEACH
Pages 100-109

- Identifying the Decision
- Considering the Alternatives
- Consequences of Teen Parenthood

GUIDED PRACTICE

Promoting Discussion

1. Ask students to review the early signs of pregnancy discussed in Chapter 6. Have students brainstorm a range of likely emotional responses a teenager who experiences one of these signs might have. (Volunteers in your class who have experienced pregnancy firsthand can, of course, recall and share their own responses.)

2. Have students review the list of individuals a teen could turn to in the event of an unwanted pregnancy. Have students discuss the advantages and disadvantages in contacting each of these sources of help (Responses might include the comfort afforded by someone close or the reduced embarrassment of dealing with a disinterested professional.) Can students think of any other groups or individuals they would add to this list?

Critical Thinking

Have students share with classmates career goals and other long-term ambitions. Ask: What effect would unexpectedly becoming a parent have on such plans and dreams?

Using the Photograph

Have students look at the photo on this page and read the accompanying caption. Ask: What is going on in this picture? How does the parent seem to be responding to her daughter? What visual clues can students find to support their assumptions?

MORE ABOUT

Teenage Pregnancy

Over 1 million American teens become pregnant each year; about 600,000 give birth. This rate is double that of 25 years ago. Of every 100 teenage females, 10 will get pregnant and 6 will give birth to babies before age 20. This rate for teenage pregnancy is twice that of European countries.

Pregnancy during adolescence has special risks.

Before the age of 20, a young female is still growing. Her pelvis may not be large enough for the passage of a full-grown fetus. Her growing body may not be ready for the physical stress of pregnancy. Since her own nutritional needs are high, she may not eat enough nutrients for herself and her baby. Teenage mothers are more likely than any other age groups to have low-birth-weight babies that have a high mortality, or death, rate.

Cooperative Learning

Have pairs of students take turns role-playing a conversation between a teenage father-to-be and one of the sources of help mentioned on the previous and current pages. In preparing their dramatizations, pairs should agree on specific details of the scenario (e.g., whether the pregnancy was intentional or not, the relationship between the father- and mother-to-be, the father's intentions with respect to the child).

Cooperative Learning

Have the class work jointly to prepare a booklet titled "Teens in Trouble." The booklet should detail steps a teen living in their own community can take in the event of an unplanned pregnancy. It should include specific names of school personnel, members of the clergy, and agencies that can offer support and other forms of help. Students should be urged to photocopy the booklet and advertise its availability to other students in the school.

Using Management Skills

Have small groups of volunteers interview representatives of family planning agencies to determine the training of such professionals and other preparation needed for the job. Have researchers share their findings with the class in the form of an oral report.

Childhood Reflections

"If you want children to improve, let them overhear the nice things you say about them to others."

Dr. Haim Ginott

Each year about 20,000 unwed teenage girls decide to give their babies up for adoption. These girls decide that adoption will be the most beneficial situation for themselves and for their children.

- **Clergy.** Teens who feel uncomfortable talking with their parents may be able to discuss the pregnancy with a minister, priest, or rabbi. A member of the clergy is usually able to help teens think through their readiness for pregnancy and parenthood. In many cases, he or she can also help teens discuss the pregnancy with their own parents. Frequently, the clergy member can serve as a source of support for both the teenagers and for their parents.

- **School Personnel.** School personnel can be another source of support for pregnant teens and their partners. A teacher, counselor, or nurse can offer advice and assistance when teens feel frightened or confused. Although rules in schools do vary, conversations with school personnel can generally be kept confidential, unless a teen's life or health is in danger.

- **Family Planning Counselors.** Nonprofit and privately funded agencies, as well as public agencies such as county departments of social services, have trained counselors. These counselors help individuals and couples consider all the options in making decisions about unplanned pregnancies. They can also help teens connect with other agencies that provide financial and medical assistance during the pregnancy, or baby clothes, food supplies, and furniture when the baby arrives. Many adoption agencies also provide such services, even when one or both parents are uncertain about giving up their child for adoption or foster care.

COOPERATIVE LEARNING

Empowerment by Participation

Cooperative learning encourages students to use their cognitive faculties in the planning and execution of assignments. You can enhance this learning experience by challenging more able students to devise their own cooperative learning exercises. This strategy is best used with pairs of students and should be limited to explo-rations where the interest level is sure to be high (e.g., developing a board game that uses or extends concepts covered in the section or chapter). After students have established the rules and parameters of their activity and submitted the same for your inspection, permit them to assign the activity to other groups.

Considering the Alternatives

A pregnant teenager should carefully consider her alternatives. She can become a single parent. She can marry and, with her husband, become a parent. She can continue the pregnancy but give the baby up for adoption, or she can terminate the pregnancy. However, some teens may have strong, clear values that eliminate at least one of these alternatives.

Single Parenthood

Having a tiny baby to cuddle and love can seem very attractive. In fact, it can be rewarding to care for someone who is helpless and dependent. However, caring for a newborn is a huge responsibility, and becoming a parent is a lifetime commitment. Anyone who is considering becoming a parent, either alone or with a spouse, should carefully consider the responsibilities, challenges, and rewards of parenthood. (See Chapter 2.)

Single parents face special parenting challenges because they must assume complete responsibility for raising their children, as well as for household chores, financial obligations, and decision making. All these responsibilities can be draining—especially for an adolescent. Burnout or depression may become a problem for many single teen parents.

Many teenage parents have to juggle school, a job, housework, and child care. They become overwhelmed by the emotional and financial costs of being a parent along with the natural demands a baby makes.

TEEN PARENTING

Teens as Single Parents

Teen parents are often single parents. Even if teenage parents marry, they often end up as single parents later in life because many teen marriages do not last. Discuss with students what factors teens might consider in deciding whether or not to marry if a pregnancy occurs. What would be the advantages of marriage? The disadvantages? What happens to a mother who does not have the support, financial or otherwise, of the father? How do fathers feel when excluded from parenting? Are teen single parents at a greater disadvantage than older single parents? Why?

GUIDED PRACTICE (continued)

Practicing Decision Making

Present the following scenario to students: Holly, who is 18, has just discovered that she and her boyfriend, Mark, are going to have a baby. Mark, also 18, has made it clear he wants no part of the child—or Holly. Have students evaluate each of the following possible options:

- Holly attempts to force Mark to accept legal responsibility for the child.
- Holly tries to persuade Mark to marry her.
- Holly decides to raise the child by herself. Have students develop arguments indicating the course of action that is best not only for Holly's own emotional and physical well-being but for that of the child as well.

Critical Thinking

On the chalkboard, write the words baby and puppy. Have students make a list of similarities between child care and pet care. Ask: In what ways might this list be misleading to people who are considering having a baby because babies are so cuddly and helpless?

Promoting Discussion

Have students review the information in Chapter 2 on the responsibilities, challenges, and rewards of parenthood. Have them discuss which of these aspects of parenthood looms largest for a teenager. Make sure students support their assumptions with relevant observations and facts.

Using the Photograph

Ask students to discuss what is happening in the photo on this page. Ask: What might the young woman's facial expression suggest about the price of baby carriages and strollers? What are some of the other purchases parents-to-be have to consider making?

GUIDED PRACTICE (continued)

Critical Thinking

Have students write a fictionalized journal entry from the point of view of a single teenage mother. Compositions should address the responsibilities, including difficulties and limitations, of single parenthood.

Have students reread the bulleted list of statistics and observations about teen marriages on this page. Ask students to consider which of these disadvantages also pertain to single parenthood. Ask: Which statistic strikes you as the most sobering? Why?

Making Connections: Social Studies

Have interested students research laws pertaining to paternity in each of the 50 states. For each state, researchers should determine, among other things, the rights and responsibilities of an unmarried father and how paternity is legally established when there is some question. Allow time for students to discuss their findings in class.

Promoting Discussion

Invite a school nurse or community health worker to share with students some of the reasons for the current high rates of both planned and unplanned teenage pregnancies. Have the speaker discuss the services available to teens who want to avoid pregnancy and be tested for pregnancy. Urge students to frame questions of their own for the guest speaker.

Teens who are considering single parenthood should be as realistic as possible. How much help—emotional and financial—can the teen mother expect from the baby's father? From her own parents and other family members? A teen who is considering single parenthood must be especially careful to avoid romanticizing her situation. A teenage partner who was not interested in marriage during her pregnancy is unlikely to change his mind once the baby is born, for example. Parents, counselors, and other adults can help teens develop realistic expectations for their own situations as single parents.

Marriage

For many pregnant teens, marriage and parenthood are appealing alternatives. It is important to recognize, however, that teens who marry because of a pregnancy face many difficulties. Statistics show that early marriages have the following results:

- Divorce rates for females who marry between the ages of fourteen and seventeen are twice as high as the divorce rates for females who marry at age eighteen or nineteen; they are three times as high as the divorce rates for females who marry between the ages of twenty and twenty-four.
- About 80 percent of teens who marry because of a pregnancy divorce within six years.
- Teens who marry are likely to have low incomes and little education; both these factors are associated with increased likelihood of divorce.
- In many teen marriages, neither partner completes high school; couples without high school diplomas are more likely to divorce than couples in which both partners have college degrees.

The prospect of getting married may seem exciting, but married teens face many problems. As the early excitement wears off, and as the strains of responsibility set in, many teen marriages deteriorate. In addition, it is not unusual for married teens to feel socially isolated. They no longer fit in with their single friends, but their interests and activities are not the same as those of most other married couples.

Teens who marry because of a pregnancy face an additional problem. They have to adjust to parenthood while they are still adjusting to marriage.

TEEN PARENTING

Financial Support

Teenage fathers can be required to pay child support even when they do not marry the mother of their child. If the father does not voluntarily admit paternity, he may be ordered to take a blood test to see if he is the child's father. No matter what his age or financial status, he can be ordered to pay support for his child. Federal law allows child support to be taken out of an employee's wages.

A Wisconsin state law, passed in 1985, makes the parents of teenage mothers and fathers responsible for supporting their grandchildren until the teens reach age eighteen. Grandparents who fail to comply with the law could be facing as much as $10,000 in fines and up to two years in prison. The law is designed to make sure the baby's basic needs are met and to encourage parents of teens to get involved in pregnancy prevention.

ASK THE EXPERTS

Managing the Stress of Teen Parenting

Q. I am a teen mom with a four-month-old son. Sometimes I just feel completely overwhelmed—can you help me help myself?

A. Of course you feel overwhelmed—having a child has added a lot of stress to your life. You can make your life—and your baby's life—easier and more enjoyable by learning techniques for managing stress.

I know you feel you already have too much to do, but you'll handle stress better when you find time to take good care of yourself. Here are some specific things you should try to do:

- **Exercise every day.** Even taking a short walk will help keep you physically healthy. It will also encourage good emotional health.
- **Eat a balanced diet.** Every time you skip a meal or grab a cola and some chips instead of a

sandwich and some fruit, you're undermining your health and making yourself more vulnerable to stress.

- **Take time every day to relax.** Try to learn some relaxation techniques, including deep, slow breathing.

You'll be more comfortable handling stress if you have a network of supportive friends. Make an effort to establish friendships with other mothers your age, as well as with teens and adults who understand your responsibilities and support you in your efforts to be a good parent. When you feel tense and angry—or simply overwhelmed—make contact with a friend you can count on.

Keep a positive attitude. That's an important part of

handling stress, but it can be hard to do on your own. Don't hesitate to let your friends help you keep your spirits up.

Another important part of managing stress is making plans for the future. Ask a counselor or teacher to help you explore your employment options. Perhaps there's a special class or program that will help prepare you for an interesting job. If you need more advice or more details than your current school can offer, contact a local community college or a public vocational school.

Pat Brodeen

Pat Brodeen
Teacher and Teen Parent Coordinator
at Theodore Roosevelt High School in
San Antonio, Texas

TEEN PARENTING

Support Groups

Building a strong support system is perhaps one of the most important strategies for managing stress. The supportive people may include family, friends, a church leader, a teacher, or employers. A strong support system might include several of

these people. A community support group can give teen parents a chance to socialize with others who are going through the same experiences. Ask students to research support groups for teen parents. If none exist, discuss the possibility of starting one.

GUIDED PRACTICE (continued)

ASK THE EXPERTS

Issues and Advice

1. What are examples of ways for a teen mother to take care of herself? (*Possibilities are: daily exercise; eat a balanced diet; relax.*)

2. Why are friends important to a teen parent? (*They understand problems; they listen and support; they provide an outlet for emotional tension.*)

3. Why is it important for a teen parent to make plans for the future? (*It provides for economic security.*)

4. Who, or what, can assist a teen parent in making future plans? (*Teachers, counselors, programs that offer job training, local community colleges, and vocational schools.*)

Thinking Like an Expert

Have three small groups of students each research one of three suggestions described in the Ask the Experts feature for controlling stress—regular exercise, eating a balanced diet, and relaxation. A fourth group can investigate other stress management techniques, including laughing, learning to budget time, and rechanneling negative energy into positive energy. Each group should present its findings to the class.

Also, ask students to learn about the phenomenon of positive stress. In particular, students should determine how experts define this form of stress, what relationship it has to negative stress, and what remarkable feats have been accomplished in the name of positive stress (e.g., a frail mother lifting a ten-ton truck to free her trapped baby). Information on the topic should be shared in a class forum.

GUIDED PRACTICE (continued)

Critical Thinking

Divide the class into two groups and have them debate the following statement: "A good parent is one who knows the importance of spending brief periods of time away from his or her baby every now and then."

Using Management Skills

Have interested students arrange to interview parents of an adopted child to learn about the adoption procedures in their own community. Students should focus on learning about the screening process a couple must undergo before they are considered as candidates for adoptive parenthood, whether a couple has any say in the age or gender of the child they will receive, and how long it takes, on the average, before the couple become parents. Have students share their findings with classmates in the form of an oral presentation.

Promoting Discussion

Have students explore and discuss the key issues in the ongoing debate on whether or not abortion should be legal. Ask: What role do religious and moral beliefs play in people's views on this volatile subject? What role do civil liberties and the United States Constitution play?

Cooperative Learning

Assign a group of volunteers to investigate the laws governing abortion in your state. Students should determine the circumstances under which a mother is eligible for abortion. Some students may also wish to learn about the penalties for illegally aborting a fetus.

Cultural Exchange

EDUCATION: A KEY TO SURVIVAL

Teen parents who drop out of school are more likely to commit themselves and their children to a lifetime of economic dependency. The commitment to children often leads to an abandonment of educational goals. Without a high school diploma, teens have little hope for rising above minimum wage level. With the added financial responsibilities of children, minimum wage just isn't enough. Also, the divorce rate is higher for couples who are in the poverty range and have little education.

Fortunately, most cultural groups offer examples of men and women who educate themselves and break out of the poverty cycle. They are models to teens who want to ensure a better future. Teen parents improve the long-term opportunities for themselves and their children if they stay in school.

Adoption

Another alternative for pregnant teens to consider is adoption. Adoption involves the termination of all rights and responsibilities for both the biological mother and the biological father; another family takes on all the rights and responsibilities of raising the child. Many teens who choose adoption feel they are giving their child an opportunity for more care, guidance, and love than they can provide at this stage of their lives.

It is important for teen parents who place their child for adoption to choose a reputable adoption agency or program. Adoption should involve professionals who carefully screen prospective parents and prepare them for a new baby. Many agencies also offer biological parents counseling and health care. Some agencies also give the biological mother an opportunity to select prospective adoptive parents from a pool of applicants. Teens can find reputable adoption agencies by requesting information from their county department of human services, from a member of the clergy, from a school official, or from a health department official.

Pregnancy Termination

A pregnant woman will sometimes experience a spontaneous abortion, commonly called a miscarriage. An intentional or induced abortion is a medical procedure. To be safe, it must be performed by a fully trained doctor.

Few issues are as controversial and emotional as legal abortion. Abortion remains an extremely troubling issue; some people are strongly opposed to it. Abortion should never be considered a method of birth control. One reason is that no matter how a person stands on the issue, abortion is emotionally traumatic. The decision and turmoil can be avoided by practicing abstinence and preventing pregnancy in the first place.

Consequences of Teen Parenthood

Some pregnant teens decide to raise their children, either as single parents or with a marriage partner. It is important for teens considering these alternatives to examine thoroughly the consequences of parenthood.

The teenage years are a time of choices and changes. They are a time of learning to be responsible for self, of developing a style for interacting with others. Teens are involved in an important process—getting to know and understand themselves, planning

TEEN PARENTING

Adoption as an Alternative

In the past, adoption was a much more common alternative for pregnant teens than it is today. Explore with your students the sensitive and yet important issues surrounding this situation. Ask them why teens today often keep their babies to raise themselves. What social changes support and discourage this trend? What are the pros and cons for both mother and baby of doing this? The lists of couples who are waiting to adopt are very long today. Why is this? Should this be a factor in how we view a teen's decision of whether or not to keep the baby?

Although teen fathers may not marry the mother of their child, they can be required to pay child support. What are some of the other challenges partners in a teenage marriage must confront that older couples do not face?

what they want to do with their lives, and taking advantage of educational opportunities. In almost every case, teen parenting interferes with this important process.

Teens who become parents find they have fewer options available to them. They also have to face health risks, financial difficulties, changes in educational plans, and emotional and social stresses.

Early Pregnancy—Fewer Choices

Teens who are raising children have important and demanding responsibilities. Caring for a baby or young child takes time—time that other teens may be spending studying, participating in school or community events, playing sports, or just hanging out.

Teen mothers and fathers often find that they are too busy taking care of children or working to attend school. Plans to complete high school or to go on to college may have to be postponed or even abandoned.

Many teens drop out of school when they recognize that they are pregnant. Other teen mothers and fathers drop out soon after the baby is born. Of the teen mothers who leave school, nearly half never return to complete their education. This lack of educa-

MORE ABOUT

Teen Fathers

Much of the information about teen parents focuses on teen mothers, but most teen fathers are at least initially interested in their children. Only about 10 percent marry, but many fathers continue to date the mothers during their children's early years. At first, most young fathers see or talk to the mother and baby daily or weekly, if allowed. Such contact often drops off in a year or

so. The young men become overwhelmed by the financial demands on them, so teen fathers and their funds often disappear from their children's lives. Many teenage pregnancy projects now include teenage fathers to keep them involved with their children and supportive of the mothers. Evidence shows that the majority of teen fathers who complete a program become responsible and caring parents.

GUIDED PRACTICE (continued)

Critical Thinking
Have students try the following experiment with the cooperation of a parent or other adult in the home. For a three-day period, the student is to imagine him- or herself to be the parent of a newborn baby. To help foster this illusion, the parent or other adult is to set off an alarm clock at thirty-minute intervals, and the student—at the sound of the bell—is to drop what he or she is doing and spend the next ten minutes on housework (e.g., washing dishes, doing laundry). Have students who try the experiment, talk to the class about how "parenthood" affected their routine.

Making Connections: Social Studies
Have interested students research other times and cultures in which teen parenthood was the norm. Students should be instructed to seek out other cultural differences and factors that might explain why teen parenthood was encouraged. Have students report their findings.

Using Management Skills
Have pairs of students check supermarket bulletin boards and newspaper ads for baby furniture (both new and used). Ask them to research the availability and cost of housing in your community. Have each pair of students report on how they would cover such expenses if they suddenly discovered they were to be parents.

Did You Know?

Teen fathers tend to have lower incomes, less education, and more children than men who wait until their twenties to have children. Most teen fathers had little meaningful contact with their own fathers and have little idea of what it means to be a father.

GUIDED PRACTICE (continued)

GUIDED PRACTICE (continued)

Making Connections: Literature

Have a group of volunteers familiarize themselves with and dramatize Act I, scene 3, from Shakespeare's *Romeo and Juliet*. In the scene, Juliet, who is rapidly approaching the "advanced" age of fourteen without having borne children, is pressured by her mother to marry. After the dramatization, have students discuss how parental values have changed since Shakespeare's time and what factors might explain the changes.

INDEPENDENT PRACTICE

Journal Writing

Have students imagine they have just received a letter from an out-of-state friend announcing his or her intentions to "go all the way" with a date. Students are to write back to their friend detailing some of the possible consequences of his or her intended actions.

Student Workbook

Have students complete "Teen Parenting and Parenthood" in the Student Workbook.

Extension

Let students work independently or in small groups to complete one or more of these extensions activities:

• Investigate the phenomenon of child support in marriages that fail. In particular, determine whether fathers alone pay child support and how courts fix the amount to be paid.

• List typical daily activities in a teen's life, such as club meetings and afterschool jobs. Discuss how you would balance these activities with having to care for a baby.

tion makes finding a job difficult; it is not unusual for a teen mother to be unable to support herself and her child.

In response to these problems, some schools now have special parenting classes for teen parents. Some even provide in-school child care programs, where children receive care while parents attend classes.

Social and athletic options are similarly restricted by parenthood. A teen parent who is able to continue in school or return to school rarely has the opportunity to join a school sports team, sing with the school choir, or participate in after-school clubs. Being a responsible parent means spending time with an infant or child—time that cannot be spent in the activities most teens enjoy.

Health Risks

Pregnancy during the teen years presents special health risks for both the teen mother and her baby. Before the age of twenty, a young woman is still growing. Her body may not be ready for the stresses of pregnancy. Because her own nutritional needs are high, she may be unable to provide the nutrients her developing baby needs.

Teen mothers are more likely than mothers in other age groups to suffer from toxemia and from iron deficiency. They are more susceptible to urinary tract infections, and they are more likely to have prolonged labor.

The baby of a teenage mother also faces special health risks. Babies born to teen mothers are more likely to die before their first birthday, more likely to be premature, and more likely to have low birth weight. Both prematurity and low birth weight have been linked to other problems, including epilepsy, birth defects, blindness, and learning deficiencies.

Financial Problems

The cost of having a child does not end with the bills for medical care during pregnancy and for the baby's delivery. The financial responsibilities of raising a child typically last 18 years or more, until the child becomes independent and begins to support himself or herself. For teens, undertaking these major, long-term financial obligations can be especially overwhelming.

Often, teens leave school in order to work or care for a baby, so their educational preparation for work is limited. Without an education, it is difficult to find a good job. Teen parents who are able to find jobs also face the task of finding—and paying for—dependable child care.

For many adolescent parents, the financial responsibilities of childbirth and child rearing become overwhelming. The stress of

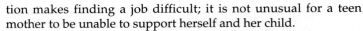

TEEN PARENTING

Repeated Pregnancy

Repeat pregnancy is a frequent occurrence with teen parents. A first pregnancy is difficult enough for a teen, but a second one compounds the problems faced. Discuss with your students the problems of a second teen pregnancy. Ask them to speculate on why repeat pregnancies occur. If you have pregnant or parenting teens in your class, help them find the information they need in order to avoid this situation.

dealing with these obligations may strain the teen parent's relationship with his or her spouse or other family members, or even with the baby.

Emotional and Social Stresses

Adolescence is a period of changes and choices. Adding the responsibilities of parenthood to adolescence can be very stressful. Teen parents must make emotional adjustments as they learn to accommodate the needs and interests of their babies. At the same time, they must deal with their own emotional responses to pregnancy and parenthood and, in many cases, a new marriage. Social stresses result from adjustments in relationships with parents, other family members, friends, classmates, and others in the community.

Most people want to provide the best possible care, attention, love, food, clothing, safety, and protection for their children. They want to give their children the best opportunities to grow and thrive in the best environment. When a child is planned, expected, and wanted, these goals are more easily achieved.

SECTION 2 REVIEW

CHECK YOUR UNDERSTANDING

1. List four sources of help to which a teenage girl might turn when she suspects she is pregnant.

2. What special challenges do single teen parents face?

3. List three statistics about teen marriages. What is the implication of these statistics?

4. What additional problem must teens who marry because of a pregnancy face?

5. What rights and responsibilities do biological parents give up when they allow another family to adopt their child?

6. How do the responsibilities of raising a child limit the opportunities for teen parents?

7. What are the special health risks that the baby of a teenage mother faces?

DISCUSS AND DISCOVER

1. What rights and responsibilities do you believe a teenager has when his sexual partner becomes pregnant? How—if at all—does the role of the father-to-be differ from that of the mother-to-be? If you believe there are differences, what accounts for those differences?

2. How would you respond if your 17-year-old sister told you—in confidence—that she was pregnant? What advice would you give her? What practical kinds of help would you offer? How would your response change if your sister were 15 years old? If she were 13?

Observing & Participating

With a group of classmates, find out about family planning counselors at private and public agencies in your community. Describe which of these agencies you would recommend to a pregnant teen. Explain why.

SECTION 2 REVIEW

1. Any four: parents, fathers-to-be, clergy, school personnel, family planning counselors.

2. They assume complete responsibility for raising their children, responsibilities of household chores, financial obligations, and decision making.

3. See statistics on page 104. These statistics imply that teen parents are likely to get divorced.

4. Adjusting to marriage and parenthood at one time.

5. Adoption terminates all rights and responsibilities of both the biological mother and father.

6. Caring for a baby takes time away from teen activities.

7. A teenage mother is still growing and may not supply nutrients for the developing baby. Babies born to teens are more likely to die, be premature, or have low birth weights.

ASSESS

CHECKING COMPREHENSION

Assign students to write their responses to the Check Your Understanding questions in the Section 2 Review. Answers to the questions are given at the bottom of this page.

EVALUATE

Have students complete the Chapter 4, Section 2 quiz in the TCR.

Reteaching

1. Have students write six sentences summarizing the section content—two on sources of help for a pregnant teenager, two on the alternatives available to a teenager in this situation, and two on the consequences of teen parenthood.

2. Assign Reteaching 9 in the TCR and have students complete the activity and review their responses.

Enrichment

1. Provide students with several examples of political cartoons, and familiarize them with the symbolism used. Ask students to create political cartoons of their own addressing one of the issues covered in this section.

2. Assign Enrichment 9 in the TCR.

Extension

Have students research the lifestyle in Japan, where in recent years, the incidence of stress-related illness his risen. Have students determine the causes for this increase.

CLOSE

Have students work jointly on the contents of a poster titled "The Ten Most Important Things a Teen Should Know About Pregnancy and Parenting."

Use the Summary and the Reviewing the Facts questions to help students go over the most important ideas presented in Chapter 4; encourage students to ask questions and add details, as appropriate.

CHAPTER 4 REVIEW

1. Physical, hormonal, and social.

2. The media and peers.

3. With questions, challenges, distrust, and suspicion.

4. The results that come from a decision.

5. Evaluate the decision; it improves decision-making skills and leads to more responsible decisions in the future.

6. Before making the decision; it allows time to think about the decision and its consequences.

7. Avoiding or abstaining from sexual intercourse.

8. Devices or methods that prevent pregnancies.

9. Possibilities are: she may be unaware of the pregnancy or in denial of it; she may not have support at home; she may fear rejection from family or friends.

10. He or she can help the teen think through the decisions, act as a liaison between the teen and her parents, and can serve as a source of support for the teen and family.

11. Mother is more likely to suffer from toxemia and iron deficiency, more susceptible to urinary tract infections, and likely to have long labor. A higher infant mortality rate; higher rate of premature birth; babies are more likely to have a low birth weight.

12. A teen might want to care for someone who is helpless; the responsibilities and stress of raising a child as well as the serious economic and emotional demands.

CHAPTER 4 REVIEW

SUMMARY

- Sexuality is a person's concept of himself or herself as a male or a female.

- Responsible decisions, including decisions about sexual activity, can best be made using a six-step process.

- The possible consequences of sexual intercourse include pregnancy, transmission of STDs, and infection with the virus that causes AIDS.

- Alternatives for pregnancy include single parenthood, marriage, adoption, and termination of the pregnancy.

- The consequences of teen parenthood include fewer educational and recreational options, health risks to both mother and baby, financial problems, and emotional and social stresses.

REVIEWING THE FACTS

1. List three kinds of changes to which teens have to adjust.

2. What are two sources of pressure on teens to engage in sexual activity?

3. During the teen years, how do many people regard the values with which they were raised? Why?

4. What are consequences?

5. What is the sixth step in the decision-making process? Why is it important?

6. When should teens consider the consequences of sexual intercourse? Why?

7. What is abstinence?

8. What are contraceptives? List three different kinds of contraceptives.

9. What often makes it difficult for a teen to begin the decision-making process about how to handle an unplanned pregnancy?

10. How might a member of the clergy be able to help pregnant teens?

11. What special health risks do pregnant teens face?

12. Why does becoming a single parent seem attractive to many teens? What are the major difficulties in single teen parenthood?

EXPLORING FURTHER

1. Select one form of media—television, radio, music, movies, or commercials. Analyze the way sexuality and male and female roles are portrayed in this media form. What does the media imply about sexual activity? What does it imply about male and female roles? Do you think some people prefer the days when sex roles were more rigidly defined? Explain. (Section 1)

2. With a partner, plan a skit showing one of these situations: a teenage girl tells her boyfriend she is pregnant; a teenage boy tells his parent he is going to be a father; a teenage girl tells her parent she is going to be a mother; a teen tells a friend he or she is going to become a parent. Together, act your skit out for the rest of the class. (Section 2)

3. With a group of classmates, gather information about the pregnancy rate among teens in your school, your school district, your town, or your county. How many teen pregnancies are reported in that population? Which alternative do most teens choose in response to pregnancy? What are the implications of your findings? (Section 2)

4. Interview students and adults who have strong opinions about adoption. Listen carefully to their ideas, and try to understand both points of view. Then discuss your interviews with classmates. (Section 2)

THINKING CRITICALLY

1. **Analyze.** How do you think teens can benefit from discussing the alternatives and consequences of sexual activity with their peers? What qualities would you want in peers with whom you seriously discuss those alternatives and consequences? Why would you look for those qualities? What do you consider the particular benefits of discussing the alternatives and consequences with adults? With which adults would you be comfortable discussing these aspects of sexual activity? Why?

2. **Evaluate.** Discuss your ideas about this statement from the text: "If two people can't talk about the possible consequences of having sexual intercourse together, they aren't ready for that

CLASSROOM MANAGEMENT

Problem Solving

Although the word problem has a negative connotation, many challenges in life are examples of positional problems. Where do I go for dinner? What career plans do I pursue? Solving problems involves a complex process of knowing, thinking, and understanding, but the skills are often unnurtured. The capacity to make critical judgments and come to a conclusion about a problem often results from the ability to:

- Know visual, verbal and nonverbal cues and behavior.

- Be aware of the feelings of others and have respect for them, empathize.

- Understand and verbalize feelings.

- Infer from information, however incomplete.

- Question another's logic or methods.

level of involvement." Rephrase the statement in your own words. Do you agree or disagree with the statement? Why? Do you think there are any exceptions? If so, what are those exceptions?

3. **Analyze.** In recent years, increasing numbers of pregnant teens have chosen single parenthood. What do you consider the significance of this trend? What does it imply about the needs and interests of teenage girls? Of teenage boys? What do you think the trend means for the babies of teen parents?

CROSS-CURRICULUM CONNECTIONS

1. **Health.** Read about the symptoms, the transmission, the methods of prevention, and the current available treatments for a specific STD. Share your findings with the rest of the class, either in a brief oral report or in a clear, complete chart.

2. **Reading.** Read at least two magazine articles about the experiences of pregnant teens or of teen parents. With a group of classmates, share and discuss your reactions to the articles.

SCHOOL TO WORK

Setting Career Goals Even while in high school you can establish a plan to guide short- and long-term decisions about future career plans. Consider your career goal. Then write out your responses to the following questions. What courses can I take to help me train for that career? What education or training beyond high school is necessary? Where can I get this education or training? What financial resources are available? What part-time work will help me prepare for my career? Turn your responses into a series of small goals or a planning guide that helps you make progress toward your ultimate goal.

PERFORMANCE ASSESSMENT

Teen Pregnancy and Parenthood

Task

Design a public service announcement (PSA) that calls attention to the responsibilities and realities of teen parenthood.

Purpose

Your purpose is to inform your peers or other teens about the responsibilities and realities of teen parenthood. Your format will be either a design for a billboard or a script to be read on the radio.

Procedure

1. Determine the message you want to convey to peers about teen parenthood. Use what you read in the

chapter to encourage teens to make responsible decisions.
2. Think about advertisements you see and hear. Remember your goal is to promote your message. Then establish a catchy slogan or phrase that conveys your message.
3. Select details you want to feature in your billboard or radio script. Where appropriate, support your message with facts and statistics.
4. Make a rough draft or outline of your information. Ask a peer or classmate to evaluate whether your message is clear and effective.
5. Make any final changes in content or design and complete your PSA.

Evaluation

Your PSA will be evaluated on its content, visual or aural appeal, and the appropriateness of its message.

 Portfolio Idea Your billboard design or radio script for a PSA is already in a format that fits easily into your portfolio. If you have ideas about ways you would amend or redesign your PSA, make a note of those ideas. Don't overlook peer responses as well. You can always revise your work at a later date.

111

EVALUATE

Use the reproducible Chapter 4 Test in the TCR, or construct your own test using the Test-maker Software.

EXTENSION

If your school has a nurse on the staff, invite him or her to speak to the class about school policies and regulations regarding teen pregnancies and STDs.

CLOSE

Ask each student to write and complete the following sentence:
Teens are/are not doing themselves a favor if they think that ...

DEVELOPING A PORTFOLIO

Providing Models If possible, have several portfolio models available to students. In this way, they can better visualize what is expected of them; and be sure to have a range within these models that includes both high-end and low-end examples. Show them how former students have adapted such items as mobiles, collages, videotapes, and photo essays to fit into the portfolio. Stress the importance of writing name, date, and objective or assignment on each piece of work that goes into the portfolio.

PERFORMANCE ASSESSMENT

Public Service Announcements

In preparation for this assignment, ask students to describe any PSAs they see on billboards, TV, or hear over the radio. Encourage them to characterize the features that attract them to these PSAs. Are they visually appealing? Do the messages have impact? Make sure stu-

dents set a clear objective about the message they want to convey. Some students might be motivated to use one format for their PSA, then translate it to the other format suggested. For example, if a student writes an effective radio script, ask her or him to modify that same message for a billboard design.

INTRODUCE

UNIT 2 RESOURCES

Teacher's Classroom Resources
- Unit 2 Test
- Testmaker Software
- Color Transparency 10

UNIT OVERVIEW

Unit 2 helps students understand the beginnings of human life—pregnancy and birth.

In Chapter 5, students learn about the three stages of pregnancy and examine the process by which characteristics are passed on at conception. They also read about birth defects and the problems that substances such as alcohol and other drugs can cause in a pregnancy.

Chapter 6 describes how parents can best prepare for the birth of a baby. Students discuss the importance of prenatal checkups, good nutrition, rest, and exercise. They also examine decisions expectant parents should make about their financial plans and about the delivery of their baby.

The final chapter of Unit 2 describes the arrival of a baby. Students learn about the three stages of labor and about the appearance typical of a newborn. They also read about the events and procedures common during the postnatal period, and they discuss the care that newborn babies require.

UNIT OBJECTIVES

After completing Unit 2, students will be able to:

- Describe the normal development of babies before birth and identify hazards that can interfere with normal development.
- Discuss preparations parents-to-be should make, including caring for the mother's health and planning for the baby's delivery.
- Describe the process by which a baby is born and discuss the kinds of care a newborn requires.

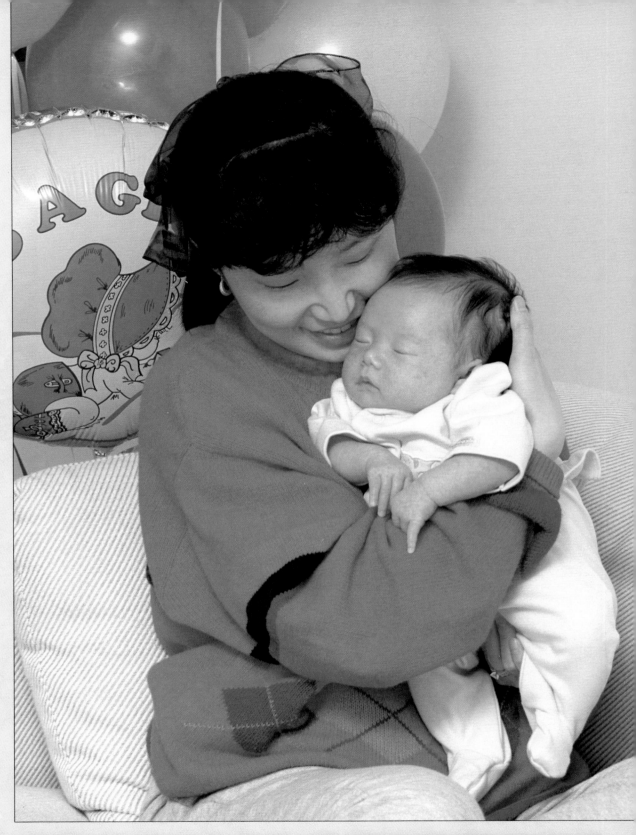

CLASSROOM MANAGEMENT

Bulletin Board Suggestion

Help! These Things Hurt Me! Cut the title *Help!* out of red construction paper, using large letters. Cut the subtitle out of another color, using smaller letters. Mount a large photo of a crying baby in the upper right corner of the bulletin board. Clip magazine illustrations of women smoking; drinking coffee, soft drinks containing caffeine, and alcoholic beverages; eating junk food; taking pills; and using drugs. Arrange the illustrations randomly on the board after mounting them on construction paper of different colors. (Note: Since drugs taken by a male can affect his offspring, you may also wish to convey this in the display.)

U N I T   2

Pregnancy and Birth

SOME THINGS DON'T MAKE
ANY SENSE AT ALL

My mom says I'm her sugarplum.
My mom says I'm her lamb.
My mom says I'm completely perfect
Just the way I am.
My mom says I'm a super-special terrific little guy.
My mom just had another baby.
Why?

Judith Viorst

MORE ABOUT

Using the Poem
Although the birth of a baby is an opportunity to celebrate new life, older children in the family might feel confused, even rejected. Have students notice the words of affection used by the speaker in the poem above. Can they imagine the hurt that an older child feels when he or she hears these same words repeated to the new baby? What is real about the child's feeling of jealousy? What is imagined? What possible ways, both positive and negative, can the parents deal with sibling rivalry that would have an impact on the emotional environment of the home? Ask students to volunteer their own experiences with the arrival of a new baby in the family.

INTRODUCING THE UNIT

• Show students a large photograph of a healthy newborn infant, if possible, one taken right after birth. Encourage students to describe and discuss the newborn. In what ways is this baby like your image of a typical baby? How is this newborn different from that image? How and where has this baby been developing? Who has cared for the baby during the important period before birth? What do you think those people have done to help care for the baby? Who will be responsible for the baby now? What will they be expected to do?

After a brief discussion, tell students that as they study Unit 2, they will learn more about the amazing growth and development that prepare a baby for birth.

• Let students read and share their responses to the poem "Some Things Don't Make Sense at All." From whose point of view is the poem written? Do you imagine that many siblings feel this way when a new baby is born? Why?

ASSESS

EVALUATE
Use the reproducible Unit 2 Test in the TCR, or construct your own test using the Testmaker Software.

EXTENSION
Invite a panel of pregnant women to discuss their experiences during pregnancy. How have they felt physically? Emotionally? What preparations are they making for delivery? For care during the first few weeks after the baby's birth? If possible, include in the panel women who are only two or three months pregnant as well as women who are nearing the end of pregnancy.

INTRODUCE

CHAPTER OVERVIEW

Chapter 5 introduces students to the complex and fascinating process by which life begins.

In Section 1, students gain an overview of the 40 weeks of pregnancy. They review the process of conception, the beginning of every pregnancy and the specific developments that take place during pregnancy — the zygote, the embryo, and the fetus periods. During each period, important changes take place for the developing baby and within the body of the expectant mother.

Section 2 covers conception more carefully, exploring the process by which inherited characteristics are passed from one generation to the next. Students learn how the sex of a developing baby is determined and read about the reasons for multiple births. They study the special problems faced by infertile couples and consider the options available in dealing with infertility.

Section 3 presents students with information about birth defects — what they are, what can cause them, and how they can be detected and prevented.

In the final section of Chapter 5, students learn about environmental hazards that can interfere with healthy prenatal development: alcohol and other drugs, X rays, rubella, and sexually transmitted diseases. The potentially devastating effects (continued next page)

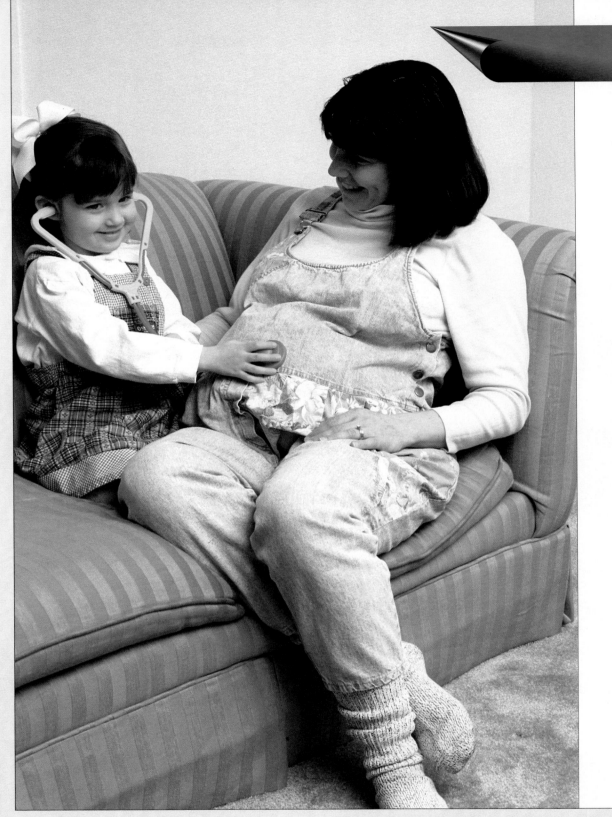

CLASSROOM MANAGEMENT

Resources Beyond the Classroom

The March of Dimes supports health service programs and professional and public education as well as research at the local and national levels. Research is conducted through four allied programs: basic laboratory-oriented research into the causes of birth defects; studies of the means of preventing and treating birth defects in humans; starter grants to promising young scientists; and investigations into the social and behavioral effects of low birth weight in early childhood with summer stipends to enable medical students to work with senior scientists. The March of Dimes provides excellent resource materials on birth defects. Contact your local chapter or write to:

March of Dimes
1275 Mamaroneck Avenue
White Plains, NY 10605

Prenatal Development

THINK ABOUT

The nine months before a baby is born is a time of important development both for baby and parents. The fetus develops in response to its unique genetic package and the environment provided by the mother. Each stage of fetal growth has effects on the mother, and while these effects are predictable, each woman experiences them individually, if at all. Overall, the general health of an expectant mother, good prenatal care, and her choice of a healthy life-style are critical to a baby's healthy development.

ASK YOURSELF

Study the photo on the opposite page and imagine a conversation between the pregnant woman and the child. What would each be saying? How is the woman helping the girl understand prenatal development? If the woman is the girl's mother, how does this exchange encourage a bond between the girl and her new brother or sister?

NOW TRY THIS

Write a list of factors that you think might have an effect on a baby while it is in the womb. Remember to think of factors related to environment, nutrition, and heredity. Next to each factor, identify one positive life-style choice that a mother can make to ensure healthy prenatal development for her child. Volunteer to explain the choices you list.

115

of these hazards and ways expectant mothers can protect the health of their developing babies is discussed.

CHAPTER OBJECTIVES

After completing Chapter 5, students will be able to:

- Describe prenatal development during each of the three stages of pregnancy.
- Explain how personal characteristics are inherited, describe how multiple births occur, and discuss the options available to infertile couples.
- Discuss birth defects, including how they are caused, diagnosed, and prevented.
- Identify the dangers posed by exposure to alcohol, drugs, and other environmental hazards during pregnancy.

INTRODUCING THE CHAPTER

- Display photographs of various individuals from different stages of life, including infancy, childhood, adolescence, early adulthood, middle age, and old age. Ask: How did each person begin life? How did each grow? What happened to each individual before birth? How might the course of his or her development before birth have affected each individual's life? Encourage students to share and discuss answers to these questions.

  Tell students that in Chapter 5 they will learn more about how prenatal development can affect a person's life after birth.

- Use the photo on the opposite page and the three features on this page—Think About, Ask Yourself, and Now Try This—to begin a discussion about prenatal development.

HEALTHY FAMILIES/HEALTHY CHILDREN

Building Healthy Families

Most of us want to be the best we can be—in our relationships, in our jobs, and as parents. If the question, "When does a person begin to prepare for the role of a parent?" is posed to young adults who are not yet parents, a variety of responses are possible. Although a likely answer is, "When we decided we wanted children," probably the most insightful response is, "I've been preparing all my life." Every experience adds one more piece to the puzzle of life, and when we learn to acknowledge the value of both positive and negative events, we equip ourselves to understand the complex responsibilities of parenting. Ask your students to volunteer their insights in response to the question above.

SECTION 1 RESOURCES

Teacher's Classroom Resources

- Enrichment 10
- Reteaching 10
- Section 1 Quiz

Student Workbook

- Stages of Prenatal Development

SECTION OVERVIEW

Section 1 gives students a basic understanding of prenatal development — the preparation that takes place during the 40 weeks of pregnancy.

Students explore prenatal development and the process of conception. They discuss the specific growth and development, in both baby and mother, during the periods of the zygote, the embryo, and the fetus.

MOTIVATOR

Display, one at a time, several photographs or drawings showing the zygote, the embryo, and the fetus within the uterus. Begin with the earliest stage of pregnancy, and ask students to identify, as completely as they can, the content of the picture. If students cannot recognize a subject, show them each later stage of prenatal development. Encourage students to describe and discuss the sequence of development shown in the pictures.

USING TERMS TO LEARN

Guide students in reading and discussing all 11 vocabulary terms. Then focus on the word *prenatal*, and ask students to identify the prefix *pre*, meaning "before," and the root *natal*, meaning "of or relating to birth." What other words do they know that begin with the prefix *pre*?

SECTION 1

TERMS TO LEARN

amniotic fluid
conception
embryo
fetus
ovum
placenta
prenatal
sperm
umbilical cord
uterus
zygote

Forty Weeks of Preparation

OBJECTIVES

- Name the three stages of pregnancy.
- Describe the prenatal development during each of the three stages of pregnancy.

During pregnancy, a single cell grows and develops into a human being capable of independent existence. This amazing process takes place over a period of 40 weeks (or about nine months).

Prenatal Development

Prenatal development is the development of a baby *during the period before birth.* Prenatal development is usually considered in three stages: the period of the zygote, the period of the embryo, and the period of the fetus. The chart on pages 118-119 shows how the unborn baby develops during these three periods. It also shows corresponding physical changes in the mother.

Conception

Once each month, an **ovum**—*a female cell or egg*—is released by one of a woman's ovaries. The egg moves through the Fallopian tube to the **uterus,** or womb, *the organ in a woman's body in which a baby develops during pregnancy.* This short journey takes about two or three days. It is only in the Fallopian tube that fertilization can take place.

When the egg reaches the uterus, it usually disintegrates and is flushed away with the menstrual flow. However, if the egg meets and is fertilized in the Fallopian tube by a **sperm**, or *male cell*, **conception**—*the union of an ovum and a sperm, resulting in the beginning of pregnancy*—takes place. This union is called a zygote.

COOPERATIVE LEARNING

The Benefits of Cooperative Interaction

The benefits of cooperative interaction are not confined to the students alone. The approach also yields dividends to the teacher. First, he or she is provided with a rare opportunity to observe and assess students, both as individuals and as members of a group. In addition, the approach provides the teacher with a chance to meet and confer with smaller groups of students than more traditional classroom design affords. The teacher is thereby able to tailor his or her resources and time to that group's specific needs.

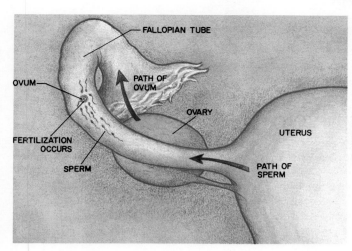

Conception—the beginning of pregnancy—occurs when an ovum is fertilized. The ovum is about the size of the dot over a printed letter i.

Period of the Zygote

The first stage in the development of a human baby is called the period of the **zygote**, or *fertilized egg*. It lasts approximately two weeks.

When the fertilized egg reaches the uterus, it attaches itself to the thickened lining of the uterus and begins to grow. Since the lining is needed to nourish the fertilized egg, it cannot be shed in menstruation as usual. Therefore, menstruation does not take place. The woman's menstrual periods stop and will not begin again until after the baby is born.

The thickened lining of the uterus provides both a soft, warm bed and food for the fertilized egg. It grows by a process called cell division. This single, complete cell divides and becomes two. Two cells become four and so on, until there is a mass of cells. In spite of the remarkable growth during this period, at the end of two weeks, the zygote is still only the size of a pinhead.

The embryo has made its home by attaching itself to the inner lining of the uterus. The uterus is about 3 inches long at this stage. The embryo is still smaller than a grain of rice.

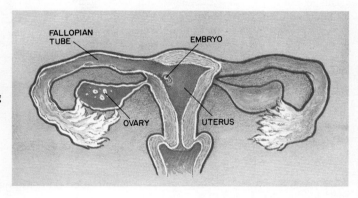

SEE HOW THEY GROW

Fertilization

Fertilization occurs about two hours after a sperm enters the vagina. After one sperm penetrates the egg, a change in the outer layer of the egg prevents additional sperm from entering. After fertilization, it takes about three to five days for the fertilized egg, which is also called a zygote, to reach the uterus. Another five-day period is needed for the egg to become implanted on the uterine wall. When implantation is complete, the egg produces hormones that give the signal to stop the menstrual period. Occasionally, implantation takes place in some other location, such as the Fallopian tube. This is called an ectopic pregnancy, and most often ends naturally in a miscarriage (see page 131). Sometimes these must be ended by medical procedures because of complications and risks to the mother.

(see page 131)

TEACH

Pages 116-123

- **Prenatal Development**
- **Conception**
- **Period of the Zygote**
- **Period of the Embryo**
- **Period of the Fetus**

GUIDED PRACTICE

Promoting Discussion

Encourage students to review what they already know about the beginning of prenatal development, conception. When and how does conception take place? Why is it important to understand this process? How can a couple improve their chances of conception? What can couples do to avoid conception? Which methods of preventing conception are most effective? Why?

Using the Drawing

Have students explain the process of conception using the drawing at the top of this page. Ask students to point out the paths of the ovum and sperm during conception. Where does fertilization occur? Where does implantation of the fertilized egg take place?

Cooperative Learning

Have small groups of students work together to plan and draw posters explaining the process of conception. The following terms should be labeled: *ovum, uterus, Fallopian tube,* and *sperm.* Have students draw arrows to indicate the path of fertilization.

Using the Drawing

Guide students in discussing the drawing at the bottom of this page. To what familiar object — other than a grain of rice — can you compare the size of the embryo at this stage? How big is the uterus? What will happen to the uterus as the embryo grows? What makes these changes possible?

GUIDED PRACTICE (continued)

Using the Chart
Guide students in reading the chart and discussing its contents. How rapidly does prenatal development progress? How does that compare with the rate of growth and development after birth?

Promoting Discussion
Remind students that some infants are born before prenatal development is complete. Ask them to predict the development that must take place before an infant can survive outside the uterus. Discuss the predictions; then ask students to verify or correct them as they continue reading.

Critical Thinking
Ask students to identify factors that might interfere with prenatal development by referring to the chart and not the developmental stages affected. They may be able to name some environmental hazards that are discussed later.

Making Connections: Physiology
Let interested students read about the immune system. What organs are essential to this system? How does each of those organs function? When and how does each develop? What risks are faced by an infant born before this system has developed fully? Have students share written reports with the class.

Family Focus
Once a pregnant mother feels the fetus moving substantially, she may wish to allow other members of the family to share the experience. Father and siblings may feel the movement of the fetus within the uterus by placing a hand on the mother's abdomen. As the fetus becomes larger, the movement of an arm or leg can even be seen across the abdomen. Have any students shared this experience with someone? How might such sharing be helpful to family members?

PRENATAL DEVELOPMENT MONTH BY MONTH

Keep in mind that growth patterns and reactions are individual. Not all babies develop at exactly the same rate, nor does every pregnant woman experience all of the effects described here.

	PRENATAL DEVELOPMENT	EFFECTS ON MOTHER
During the First Month	• Cell multiplication begins. • The fertilized egg attaches itself to the lining of the uterus. • Internal organs and the circulatory system begin to form. The heart begins to beat. • By the end of the month, small bumps indicate the beginning of arms and legs.	• Missed menstrual period. • Other signs of pregnancy may not yet be noticeable.
During the Second Month	• At five weeks, the embryo is only about ¼ inch (6 mm) long. • Face, eyes, ears, and limbs take shape. • Bones begin to form. • Internal organs continue to develop.	• Breasts begin to swell. • Pressure on bladder from enlarging uterus results in need to urinate more frequently. • Possible nausea ("morning sickness"). • Fatigue is common.
During the Third Month	• As this month begins, the fetus is about 1 inch (25 mm) long. • Nostrils, mouth, lips, teeth buds, and eyelids form. • Fingers and toes are almost complete. • All organs are present, although immature.	• Breasts become firmer and fuller and may ache. • Nausea, fatigue, and frequent urination may continue. • Abdomen becomes slightly larger. The uterus has grown to about the size of an orange. • Weight gain totals 2-4 pounds (0.9-1.8 kg).
During the Fourth Month	• At the beginning of this month, the fetus is about 3 inches (76 mm) long and weighs about 1 ounce (28 g). • The fetus can suck its thumb, swallow, hiccup, and move around. • Facial features become clearer.	• Size change continues slowly. • Most discomforts of early pregnancy are usually gone by this time. • Appetite increases.

(Continued on next page)

TEEN PARENTING

Meeting Special Needs
School age parents usually have distinct special needs in addition to those of the average student. Foremost, teen parents need to feel accepted and worthwhile. They usually need activities to build self-esteem because they do feel "different," left out, or inferior to other students. These students also need guidance in making good decisions for themselves and their babies that will affect the rest of their lives. Some teen mothers may need assistance finding good medical care, proper food, and housing. They need to learn good parenting and employability skills. It's difficult being a teenager, but especially difficult to be a teenage parent.

PRENATAL DEVELOPMENT MONTH BY MONTH

	PRENATAL DEVELOPMENT	EFFECTS ON MOTHER
During the Fifth Month	• As this month begins, the fetus is about 6 ½-7 inches (16-18 cm) long and weighs about 4-5 ounces (113-142 g). • Hair, eyelashes, and eyebrows appear. • Teeth continue to develop. • Organs are maturing. • The fetus becomes more active.	• Enlarged abdomen becomes apparent. • Slight fetal movements are felt. • Fetal heartbeat may be heard through a stethoscope. • Increased size may begin to affect posture.
During the Sixth Month	• The fetus is now about 8-10 inches (21-25 cm) long and weighs about 8-12 ounces (227-340 g). • Fat is being deposited under the skin, but the fetus still appears wrinkled. • Breathing movements begin.	• Fetal movements are now sensed as strong kicks, thumps, and bumps. Some may be visible. • Weight gain by the beginning of this month may total 10-12 pounds (4.5-5.4 kg).
During the Seventh Month	• The fetus is about 10-12 inches long and weighs about 1½-2 pounds (680-907 g). • Periods of fetal activity are followed by periods of rest and quiet.	• Increased size may begin to affect posture.
During the Eighth Month	• Weight gain continues rapidly. The fetus is about 14-16 inches (36-41 cm) long and weighs about 2 ½-3 pounds (1.0-1.4 kg). • The fetus may react to loud noises with a reflex jerking action. • In most cases, the fetus moves into a head-down position.	• There may be discomfort as size increases. Backache, leg cramps, shortness of breath, and fatigue are common. • Fetal kicks continue to be felt; they may disturb the mother's rest. • At the beginning of this month, weight gain totals about 18-20 pounds (8.2-9.1 kg).
During the Ninth Month 	• At the beginning of the final month, the fetus is about 17-18 inches (43-46 cm) long and weighs about 5-6 pounds (2.3-2.7 kg). Weight gain continues until the week before birth. • Skin becomes smooth as fat deposits continue. • Fetal movements decrease as the fetus has less room to move around. • The fetus acquires disease-fighting antibodies from the mother's blood. • The fetus descends into the pelvis, ready for birth.	• "Lightening" is felt as the fetus drops into the pelvis. Breathing becomes easier. • Other discomforts of late pregnancy may continue. • A total weight gain of 24-30 pounds (10.9-13.6 kg) is typical. The uterus is the size of a small watermelon by the time of birth. • False labor pains may be experienced.

OBSERVING AND PARTICIPATING

Developing Observational Skills

Instruct each student to interview at least one pregnant woman and observe whether the effects of the pregnancy on her are the same as those listed on this chart. (If possible, have students interview as many women as possible who are at different stages of pregnancy.) Ask students to find out whether the woman's symptoms were similar to or different from those on the chart. If the woman has been pregnant before, encourage your students to discover how this pregnancy compares with any previous ones. Have the students write a summary of the interview and comment about the use of this chart as a guideline for understanding the stages of pregnancy.

GUIDED PRACTICE (continued)

Making Connections: Health

Have interested students research recent developments in caring for infants born before prenatal development is complete. How has technology affected the survival rate of premature infants? What problems do many premature infants face, despite such great improvements in technology? Ask students to share and discuss their findings with the rest of the class.

Cooperative Learning

Let students work in groups to collect objects that represent the size of the embryo and fetus at each stage of development shown in the chart. Then have each group display its collected objects and describe the growth represented by each.

Making Connections: Nutrition

Ask interested students to research the importance of nutrition during pregnancy. How can deficiencies of specific nutrients affect the health of the pregnant mother? How can they affect the development of an unborn baby at various stages of pregnancy? Let students summarize their findings in a chart to be posted in the classroom.

Promoting Discussion

Ask students to generalize about the development that takes place during the last two months of pregnancy. Then ask: What special attention, care, and support might be required by an infant born after only seven months of pregnancy?

Making Connections: Math

Have students use information from the chart to prepare graphs showing the length and weight of the embryo and fetus during each of the nine months of development. Ask students to identify the stage during development when the majority of growth occurs.

GUIDED PRACTICE (continued)

Promoting Discussion

Ask students to consider the role played by the umbilical cord in nurturing the embryo and fetus. If the umbilical cord were pinched or the free flow of fluid obstructed in some way, how might the developing fetus be affected?

Making Connections: Physiology

Have students conduct research into the placenta. How does it permit growth and development in an unborn baby, who can neither eat nor breathe? How is the functioning of the placenta related to metabolic processes? Which steps in metabolism do not take place before birth? Let students share their findings with the rest of the class.

Promoting Discussion

Ask students how the sensation of being underwater, as in a swimming pool, might be compared to the protection amniotic fluid provides the embryo and fetus. What other comparisons might help clarify the role of the amniotic fluid?

Cooperative Learning

Divide students into three groups. Have the members of each group work together to research and write a report on one stage of prenatal development. Instruct groups to include information on the length of the stage, changes in length and weight, important terms, and development that occurs.

Promoting Discussion

Encourage students to discuss their ideas about the three stages of pregnancy. Which do you think would be most difficult for the mother-to-be? Which would be easiest? Which events and developments would be especially exciting for the mother? How might the father be involved in each state? How would other family members and friends probably be affected?

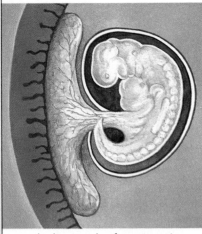

At three weeks after conception, the embryo is surrounded by a sac of amniotic fluid (shown in dark gray). Between the amniotic sac and the uterine lining is the membrane that will soon develop into the placenta. The heart is the largest organ so far and has already begun to beat.

Period of the Embryo

The second stage of pregnancy is the period of the embryo. The **embryo** is *the developing cluster of cells in the uterus during about the third through eighth weeks of pregnancy.* In the course of this period, an amazing change occurs as the mass of embryonic cells develops into all the major organ systems of the human body.

Throughout this stage, the embryo grows rapidly. It becomes firmly attached to the inner lining of the uterus. By the end of this stage, the **placenta**, *the tissue that connects the sacs around the unborn baby to the mother's uterus,* has developed. The **umbilical cord**, *a long tube that connects the placenta to the unborn baby,* has also developed. Nourishment and oxygen from the mother's bloodstream are carried from the placenta to the developing baby through the umbilical cord.

The umbilical cord is uniquely formed to supply nourishment to the baby and to take waste products away from the baby. The cord contains three blood vessels. It is usually stiff and firm, like a garden hose filled with water. Usually, it is not flexible enough to loop around the fetus, although this may occur in rare cases. Only after the baby is born does the umbilical cord become limp and ropelike.

The growing embryo is soon surrounded by a bag of liquid called **amniotic fluid**, *a special fluid that surrounds and protects the developing baby during pregnancy.* The amniotic fluid acts as a cushion to protect the embryo, even through minor bumps or falls of the mother. The baby remains within this sac of liquid until just before birth.

Period of the Fetus

The third and last stage of pregnancy begins about the eighth or ninth week and lasts until birth. This stage is called the fetal period, or the period of the **fetus**, *the unborn baby from about the eighth or ninth week of pregnancy until birth.*

By the beginning of this period, the embryo has developed the beginnings of all organs and body parts. The cells are now recognizable as a developing human. Arms, legs, and even fingers and toes have developed. Facial features are also forming. All the internal organs are present, but they are not ready to function yet. They continue to develop in the remaining months of pregnancy.

Sometime during the fourth or fifth month, the kicks and other movements of the fetus touch the wall of the uterus. These fluttering movements are faint and infrequent at first. Gradually, they become stronger and more frequent. This sensation of feel-

MORE ABOUT

Amniotic Fluid

The amniotic sac is sometimes called the "bag of waters." The amount of fluid it contains increases rapidly after fertilization, reaching about 1/4 cup (60 mL) at 12 weeks and about 1 2/3 cups (400 mL) at midpregnancy. The maximum is about 4 cups (1L) at 36 to 38 weeks. The vol- ume then decreases as the time of birth nears. After about 5 months of development, the fetus is able to swallow amniotic fluid. It is thought that this process helps provide the fetus with nutrients. Too little or too much amniotic fluid is a factor that can increase the chance of a breech birth.

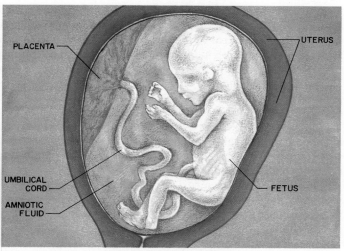

By the fourth month, the fetus looks more like a baby. The eyelids will remain shut until about the sixth month.

ing life, sometimes called quickening, tells the mother that she does, indeed, carry a live child within her. Actually, the baby has been very active long before this time.

Her doctor usually asks the expectant woman when she first felt life. Knowing this helps the doctor estimate the baby's fetal age and project a more accurate delivery date. The fetus's heartbeat can usually be heard before movement is felt.

As the fetus grows, so does the volume of the surrounding fluid. The uterus expands, too, and the woman's abdomen grows. Just before delivery, the amniotic fluid decreases as the baby becomes more active and swallows it. As the fetus grows, it no longer has the room to stretch out. The developing baby curls up in what is called the fetal position.

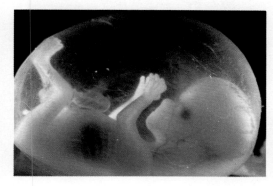

The fetus floats comfortably within the amniotic sac. After brief active periods, the fetus spends long hours resting. The same will be true of the baby after birth.

SEE HOW THEY GROW

Fetus Development

At about the fifth month, the fetus weighs only 8 ounces (227 g). At full term, however, it may weigh as much as 7 to 9 pounds (3 to 4 kg). At five months the fetus is covered with a fine, downy hair, called lanugo. By the ninth month, lanugo may be present only on the shoulders and arms. During the ninth month, hundreds of pints of blood are pumped through the fetus each day. At any one time, however, the fetus has only about 1 cup (240 mL) of blood in its system. Also during the ninth month, the fetus may have hairs as long as 1 inch (2.5 cm), even longer. The eyes are usually slate colored, with the final color not yet discernible.

GUIDED PRACTICE (continued)

Critical Thinking
Ask students why it is important for the expectant mother to be aware of when she feels life (quickening).

Using the Drawings
Have students compare the drawings on page 120 and on this page. How does the three-week-old embryo compare with the four-month-old fetus? What further changes will take place before the fetus is ready for birth?

Family Focus
A pregnant woman has emotional as well as physical effects from pregnancy. Sometimes she may feel sad, and other times, very happy. Although most of these mood swings are normal, it is usually a good idea to talk with someone about such feelings. Teen parents often face special circumstances that can affect them emotionally. Ask students to think about the emotions of a teen parent. Have them make a list of emotions that a teen parent might feel and then note the likely reasons for these emotions. Guide students in discussing healthy outlets for these emotions and in suggesting both formal and informal sources of support for teens experiencing these emotions.

Using the Photograph
Encourage students to discuss their responses to the photograph at the bottom of the page. What kinds of activities can the fetus engage in? Do you believe the fetus "enjoys" these activities? Why or why not?

Critical Thinking
Ask students to explain why the cry of a fetus is soundless. What would the fetus need in order to make sounds as it cried?

INDEPENDENT PRACTICE

Journal Writing

Ask students to write journal entries describing their own feelings about understanding the stages of prenatal development. Pose questions such as these to spark the students' thinking: To whom is an understanding of prenatal development important? Why? What can those people gain from understanding the growth and development of a baby before birth? When should they learn about prenatal development? Why is that the best time? To whom is such information irrelevant? Why?

Student Workbook

Distribute "Stages of Prenatal Development" in the Student Workbook.

Extension

Let students work independently or in small groups to complete one or more of these extension activities:

• Interview several expectant parents, or read magazine articles about the experiences of expectant parents: How do parents "communicate" with their baby before birth? When do they begin communicating? Is there a difference between the approaches mothers and fathers are likely to take toward communicating with their unborn child? If so, what is that difference. Report your findings to the rest of the class, and discuss your reactions.

• Interview an obstetrician or an obstetric nurse practitioner. Ask about his or her experiences in monitoring the stages of prenatal development. Then discuss the results of the interview with the rest of your class.

• Investigate and report on recent research into the senses and behavior of the unborn baby, such as hearing, tasting, seeing, coughing, sneezing, and yawning. Include in your report a description of techniques used in determining prenatal behavior.

By the seventh month, most fetal development has already taken place. The fetus is capable of living outside the womb, but not without a great deal of medical help. Now the fetus's main task is to get ready for independent life outside the womb. In these remaining months, the major organs become ready to function without the assistance of the mother's body. The fetus also gains weight rapidly. Fat deposits, which will help the baby maintain body heat after birth, are added under the skin. Gradually, the fetus, which had been thin and wrinkled, takes on the smoother, rounder appearance of a baby. During these final weeks of pregnancy, the fetus also stores nutrients and builds immunity to diseases and infections.

The fetus can do a surprising number of things—suck its thumb, cough, sneeze, yawn, kick, and hiccup. A baby can even cry before birth. In almost all cases, the crying is soundless.

Sometime during the ninth month of pregnancy, the baby's weight seems to shift down and the mother feels noticeably more comfortable in her upper abdomen. Lightening has occurred. This means that the baby has dropped into the birth canal. Birth is not far off. With a first baby, lightening may take place several days—or even weeks—before labor begins. If the mother has given birth before, lightening may occur just before the beginning of labor. Sometimes lightening is accompanied by slight abdominal pains, which first-time mothers may mistake for the beginning of labor.

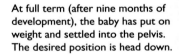

At full term (after nine months of development), the baby has put on weight and settled into the pelvis. The desired position is head down.

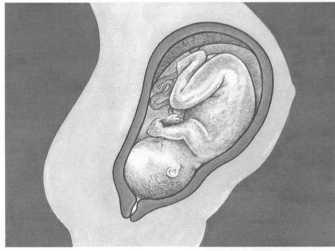

OBSERVING AND PARTICIPATING

Developing Observational Skills

Point out to students the growth in the skin of the mother's abdomen, which appears to be stretched to capacity by the ninth month. If a pregnant woman gains weight rapidly, the skin will retain stretch marks after the baby is born and the uterus contracts. Tell students that the abdominal muscles are stretched, too, and that both skin and muscles are capable of remarkable stretching—and contracting. The muscles of the uterus and abdomen can be stretched up to 60 times their original size during pregnancy, yet they return to nearly their original size within a month or so after pregnancy.

At this point in the pregnancy, the fetus is usually upside down, with the head nestled in the pelvis. This is the easiest and safest position for birth. The baby is less active than in previous weeks, because there is so little space in which to move.

The skin of the mother's abdomen appears stretched to capacity. The abdominal muscles are stretched, too. Both are capable of remarkable stretching—and contracting. The muscles of the uterus and abdomen can be stretched up to 60 times their original size during pregnancy, yet they return to nearly their original size within a month or so after the birth.

The nine months of pregnancy bring many changes, both in the pregnant woman and the developing baby. For family members, the signs are clearly evident and their anticipation of a new family member is usually greeted with enthusiasm. After about 40 weeks of preparation, the baby is ready to be born.

SECTION 1 REVIEW

CHECK YOUR UNDERSTANDING

1. What is conception? Where does it take place?
2. During what period of pregnancy do the placenta and umbilical cord develop? Why are they important to the developing baby?
3. What is amniotic fluid? Why is it important to the developing baby?
4. What is a fetus?
5. What is quickening? When does it usually first occur?
6. What are the most important changes that take place in a fetus during the last two months of pregnancy?
7. What is lightening? When does it usually occur?

DISCUSS AND DISCOVER

1. What emotional changes do women experience during pregnancy? Read about these changes, or discuss them with women who are or have been pregnant. Do all women experience the same emotional changes? How do you think a woman's emotional responses to pregnancy vary according to her situation? How do you think a woman's age, marital situation, and economic situation affect her emotions during pregnancy?

Observing & Participating

Talk to pregnant females about the physical and emotional changes they have experienced since conception. Record their responses. Identify those changes that all the women share and those that are unique to each woman. Speculate about how you think a woman's emotional responses to pregnancy might vary according to her individual circumstances. How do you think a woman's age, marital status, and economic situation affect her emotions during pregnancy?

SECTION 1 REVIEW

1. The union of an ovum and a sperm, resulting in pregnancy. In the Fallopian tube.
2. During the period of the embryo. They provide nourishment and oxygen to the developing baby.
3. A special fluid that surrounds and protects the developing baby during pregnancy. Acts as a cushion to protect the embryo and fetus.
4. An unborn baby from about the eighth or ninth week of pregnancy until birth.
6. The sensation of feeling life; during the fourth or fifth month of pregnancy.
7. The dropping of an unborn baby into the birth canal; several hours to several weeks before the beginning of labor.

ASSESS

CHECKING COMPREHENSION

Assign students to write their responses to the Check Your Understanding questions in the Section 1 Review. Answers are given below.

EVALUATE

Have students complete the Chapter 5, Section 1 quiz in the TCR.

Reteaching

1. Have students complete Reteaching 10 in the TCR.
2. Duplicate the chart on pages 118-119, and cut apart the sections to create a matching game. Have pairs or small groups to match the sections correctly. Review and discuss the development during each month of pregnancy.

Enrichment

1. Challenge students to complete TCR Enrichment 10.
2. Have students investigate recent research into the effects of prenatal care on prenatal development. How are approaches and attitudes toward prenatal care changing? What specific recommendations are being revised and/or reconsidered? How, and why?

Extension

Invite an expectant mother in her ninth month of pregnancy to class to describe her experiences to the class. When did quickening occur? How do the movements feel? What steps has she taken to protect her baby's health? How have her activities changed in the final months of pregnancy? How does ninth month baby activity compare with that of earlier months? Encourage questions.

CLOSE

Give each student an opportunity to share what he or she finds most interesting about prenatal development.

FOCUS

SECTION 2 RESOURCES

Teacher's Classroom Resources
- Enrichment 11
- Reteaching 11
- Section 2 Quiz

Student Workbook
- Heredity in the Works

SECTION OVERVIEW

As they read Section 2, students gain a more thorough understanding of the process and results of conception. They examine the "genetic package," exploring the interaction of dominant and recessive genes in the passing on of inherited characteristics. They discuss sex determination, and explore the causes of multiple births. Finally, students learn about infertility and options available to infertile couples.

MOTIVATOR

Invite interested students to share photographs of themselves and other family members; you may also want to share some of your own. Discuss the photos of each family. What physical characteristics do various family members have in common? What are the most striking physical differences between members of the same family? How do you account for these similarities and differences? Section 2 presents how traits are passed from one generation to the next.

USING TERMS TO LEARN

Guide students in reading and discussing the vocabulary terms introduced in Section 2. You may want to help students recognize the prefix *in*, meaning "not," in the word *infertility*.

SECTION 2

A Closer Look at Conception

TERMS TO LEARN

chromosomes
dominant
genes
infertility
recessive
surrogate

OBJECTIVES

- Describe how personal characteristics are inherited.
- Explain how multiple births occur.
- Discuss possible solutions for infertility.

Pregnancy is the 40-week period of preparation that begins with conception, when the sperm and egg meet to form a new life. In that meeting of sperm and egg, many of the baby's future characteristics are determined.

The Genetic Package

Every individual inherits characteristics from previous generations. Inherited characteristics include such traits as these:

- Physical build.
- Skin color.
- Hair texture and color.
- Color and shape of the eyes.
- Shape and size of ears, hands, and feet.
- Blood type.
- Some medical conditions.

Heredity—the passing on of these and other characteristics—has been observed since ancient times. However, only in the last century has science begun to understand how heredity works.

At the moment of conception, every human baby receives a total of 46 **chromosomes**, *tiny threadlike particles in the nucleus of every cell that carry hereditary characteristics*. The father's sperm provides 23 of these chromosomes; the other 23 come from the mother's ovum. Each chromosome contains thousands of **genes**, *the units that determine inherited characteristics*. Genes make up chromosomes as beads make up a necklace. These genes determine all the characteristics—from facial features to coloring to physical size—that each of us inherits.

OBSERVING AND PARTICIPATING

Celebrating Individual Differences

Early Greek philosophers believed that blood was the basic element of heredity. Terms such as *blood relative* and *bloodline* reflect this idea. Have students volunteer their observations about physical characteristics in their own families that have been passed down from one generation to another. Today, geneticists know that basic men-

tal ability and special aptitudes, such as a good singing voice, are also inherited. Ask your students to think about specific people who have the same talent as one or both of their parents. How could they explain this talent in terms of genetics? To what degree is a talent the result of environmental influences, not heredity?

Hair color is an example of a characteristic that is genetically determined. Each of these parents contributed one recessive gene for red hair to their son. As a result the child's hair is redder than that of either parent.

For every inherited characteristic, an individual receives two copies of a gene—one from the mother and one from the father. When both copies are the same—for example, both for blue eyes—the child is certain to have that characteristic. However, an individual who receives two different genes for a given characteristic—such as one gene for blue eyes and one gene for brown eyes—will have the trait dictated by the **dominant,** or *stronger*, gene. In this example, the gene for brown eyes is dominant and the gene for blue eyes is **recessive**, or *weaker*; the child will have brown eyes. These terms refer only to the relationship of the gene copies to each other. Blue eyes are not weaker than brown eyes.

A person with brown eyes may carry a recessive gene for blue eyes. If this is true of both parents, each of their children has one chance in four of having blue eyes. What would happen if only one parent carried the recessive gene?

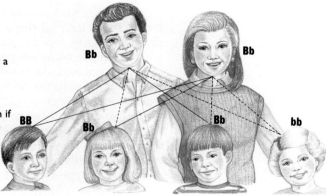

MORE ABOUT

Genetics
People have bred and cross-bred plants and animals for hundreds of years, but only in the twentieth century has genetic engineering emerged as a science. Researchers seek to improve the quality of plants and animals by selecting only those which exhibit desirable traits and by controlling the breeding process to ensure offspring that maintain desired types. Thus, even a recessive gene can become dominant if genetically engineered. Some examples of this process are hybrid varieties of fruits and vegetables such as corn, tomatoes, and wheat. Additionally, animals are selected and cross-bred to produce particular strains that resist disease, produce a high yield of milk or meat, or are exceptionally strong and virile.

TEACH

Pages 124-129
- **The Genetic Package**
- **Sex Determination**
- **Multiple Births**
- **Infertility**

GUIDED PRACTICE

Promoting Discussion
Encourage students to share and discuss their own experiences with inherited characteristics. In your own family, or in other families you know, what instances of unusual physical resemblance have you noticed? What instances of unusual physical differences?

Using the Photograph
Encourage students to describe the family in the picture at the top of this page. What physical traits has the son inherited from his parents? Discuss the characteristic of red hair color as the recessive trait carried by the parents. What were the sons chances of having red hair?

Making Connections: Math
Have students gather information about the following recessive traits within the class: blue eyes, straight hair, blond or red hair, and second toes that are longer than big toes. Tally on the chalkboard the number of students having each recessive trait. Then have students calculate the percentage of those in the class who have each recessive trait.

Using the Drawing
As students study the drawing at the bottom of this page, ask them to explain why each child in this family has one chance in four of having blue eyes. In a family with two blue-eyed parents, what would be the chances of a child's having brown eyes? Why?

GUIDED PRACTICE (continued)

Promoting Discussion

Encourage students to consider how differences in genetic packaging may affect siblings. For example, one sibling may be taller, more intelligent, or better coordinated than another; one may have a more attractive combination of physical features. How can siblings be affected by thoughtless remarks such as, "Your sister always earns A's in math. What's wrong with you?" or "Why can't you throw straight like your brother?" How might an understanding of heredity discourage such remarks?

Critical Thinking

Why do multiple-birth infants commonly have lower birth weights than single-birth infants? The babies in one set of quints ranged in weight from 1 pound 12 ounces (794 g) to 2 pounds 3 (992 g) ounces at birth.

Promoting Discussion

Consider the effects of having a twin. What are the emotional, social, and physical advantages and disadvantages of twins? Do they change for fraternal rather than identical twins?

Family Focus

Discuss how families must adjust to multiple births of more than two. Multiple-birth infants often have greater physical risks than full-term infants. How might such a birth affect family resources? Family relationships? How could problem-solving skills help parents and others deal with this kind of situation?

Childhood Reflections

"How can I judge them or tell them apart? Child of my body and child of my heart?"

Lois Duncan, "Song of a Mother"

Heredity explains why brothers and sisters often resemble each other. It also explains why they can look quite different. Of the father's 46 chromosomes, only half go into the sperm cell—one from each of his 23 pairs. Which chromosome from each pair is used? This is a matter of chance. The same is true of the mother's egg cell. Thus each sperm or egg cell contains a different combination of chromosomes and of genes. The uniting of each sperm and egg creates a unique individual.

At conception, the fertilized egg inherits all the physical traits its parents can ever give it. Though it is less than one-fourth the size of a pinhead, the fertilized egg has its own complete genetic blueprint. This may include its father's brown eyes; its mother's dimples; a grandfather's tall, lean build; and a grandmother's clear, sweet singing voice. These traits—and many, many others—are determined by the particular combinations of genes brought together at conception.

Sex Determination

The sex of a child is also determined at the moment of conception. It is determined by the special chromosomes that come in two types, X and Y. Each ovum from the female contains an X chromosome. Each male sperm contains either an X chromosome or a Y chromosome. If the sperm that fertilizes the ovum carries an X chromosome, an XX combination results and the child is a girl. If the sperm carries a Y chromosome, an XY combination results and the child is a boy.

Multiple Births

As you know, a fertilized egg starts growing by dividing into two cells. These cells continue to divide until there are millions of cells.

Sometimes the growing mass of cells splits apart soon after fertilization. Each of these two clumps of cells continues to divide and grow into a separate embryo. This is the process by which identical twins are produced. Identical twins are always the same sex and always have very similar characteristics, because the two babies have developed from one zygote. Why the zygote splits apart is still a mystery of nature.

Unlike identical twins, fraternal twins develop when two eggs are released at the same time and each is fertilized by a different sperm. They grow side by side in the uterus. Fraternal twins can be either the same sex or opposite sexes. They are no more alike in appearance than any other brothers and sisters.

OBSERVING AND PARTICIPATING

Developing Observational Skills

An old superstition claims that if a baby says "mama" first, the next child born to the family will be a girl. Likewise, if a baby first says "dada," a boy will follow. Parents today have access to more practical methods that claim to influence the gender of a child. Ask your students to investigate self-help books and techniques, and then report on the methods recommended.

Encourage your students to evaluate the procedures and speculate about the probability of success. If possible, have them find parents who tried one or more of these methods and can attest to its reliability. For comparison, some students might investigate how the superstition mentioned above came to be and whether it has any legitimate basis.

Identical twins share the same genetic pattern. That is why their appearance is so similar. Since a child's sex is determined by the genes, identical twins are always the same sex.

In multiple births of more than two, the babies may be identical or fraternal or a combination of identical and fraternal. Triplets, for example, are identical if the single zygote splits into three parts, each of which continues to develop independently. They are fraternal if three separate ova are fertilized by three different sperm. If the triplets develop from two zygotes, one of which splits apart, there are two identical babies and one fraternal baby.

Multiple births of more than two are usually quite rare, but births of twins are not that rare. In the United States, one birth in approximately 87 is a twin birth. (Identical twins occur only one-fourth as frequently as fraternal twins.)

Infertility

Not all couples who want to have children are able to conceive. A couple's **infertility,** or *inability to conceive children,* may have many causes. Many couples seek medical advice when they suspect they are infertile, typically after a year of trying without success to conceive. A doctor usually makes a fertility analysis, a detailed physical study of both the man and the woman. The analysis includes taking medical histories and giving both partners thorough physical examinations.

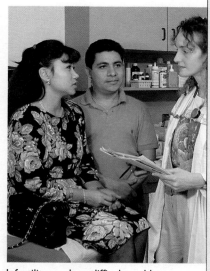

Infertility can be a difficult problem for couples who want to have children. They may decide to undergo a fertility analysis. In many cases, the doctor is able to determine the cause of the infertility and suggest a course of treatment.

MORE ABOUT

Infertility

In the United States about 10 million people, or one in six couples, are unable to conceive or successfully complete a pregnancy. More than one-half of normal couples can achieve a pregnancy within a three-month period. Ninety percent can be successful within one year. Infertility is usually diagnosed if a woman has not become pregnant during one year of unprotected intercourse. *Secondary infertility* describes a condition where a couple has difficulty conceiving a second child. This form of infertility is attributed to additional stress, a woman's irregular period after the previous birth, and a decline of sexual activity resulting from the increased energy required to care for a child.

GUIDED PRACTICE (continued)

Promoting Discussion

Let students share their responses to questions such as these: What specific objections do you think people might have to artificial insemination? To in vitro fertilization? To ovum transfer? To surrogate motherhood? Do you personally object to any of these procedures? If so, which and why? If not, why not?

Practicing Decision Making

As students consider the various options for infertile couples, encourage them to describe and discuss the differences between the available options. Stress that tests and treatment for infertility problems, as well as the use of available options, can be both time-consuming and costly. Have students debate the pros and cons of options for infertile couples. Remind them to include moral and legal questions in the debate.

Critical Thinking

Ask students to suggest what they consider the best legal resolution for each of the following situations. In each case, an infertile couple has selected a surrogate mother, who has been artificially inseminated with sperm from the husband. A contract has been drawn up. The couple has agreed to pay for the expenses of pregnancy and to deliver a further sum to the surrogate mother; she, in turn, has agreed to relinquish the baby to the couple immediately after birth.

• The surrogate mother has a miscarriage during the fourth month of pregnancy.

• The baby is born with a severe birth defect, and the couple does not want the baby.

• As soon as the baby is born, the surrogate mother decides she wants to keep and raise the baby.

GUIDED PRACTICE (continued)

Cultural Exchange

More information about international adoption agencies and services can be found in Are Those Kids Yours? by Cheri Register (1990, The Free Press, New York).

INDEPENDENT PRACTICE

Journal Writing

Let students write journal entries about their opinions and reactions to adoption, artificial insemination, in vitro fertilization, ovum transfer, or surrogate motherhood. Encourage them to relate their topic to their own lives, both past and future, and how it might affect children who are born and/or raised as a result of the option.

Student Workbook

Distribute "Heredity in the Works" in the Student Workbook and have students review key concepts.

Extension

Let students work alone or in groups to complete one or more of these activities:

• Read research about identical twins raised apart. Why is this research done? What methods are used to gather information and what conclusions can be drawn from it? Share your findings with the class.

• Plan and draw a poster illustrating the cell division of identical, fraternal, and Siamese twins.

• Imagine you are in a position to interview women interested in becoming surrogate mothers. List the five most important questions you would ask each potential surrogate about her medical health; then five questions about her emotional health.

Cultural Exchange

INTERNATIONAL ADOPTIONS

American families wishing to adopt a child will often explore international adoptions. One reason is the more liberal adoption policies of some foreign countries, another is the speed in which the adoption can be processed. Still other families want to share their homes and lives with someone in great need. As with all adoptions, families follow a procedure. First a reputable agency is contacted and a search is made for a suitable match for the family. Next, arrangements must be made for the release of the child and his or her entry into the United States.

International adoptions have been highly successful for many American families. Today, American parents have become interested in helping their adopted children to understand and think about the country and people that are a part of their heritage. Maintaining a link with their background has helped young people appreciate their past as well as their present way of life.

Often, the fertility analysis reveals that the man, the woman, or both have physical problems that prevent pregnancy. Surgery or medication may solve the problem. For example, the woman's ovaries may not be releasing an egg each month. In this case, the doctor may prescribe fertility drugs, compounds that stimulate a woman's ovaries to release eggs. Fertility drugs, however, have several drawbacks, as do all drugs. Some women who take them are troubled by serious side effects, such as lung problems, abdominal pain, nausea, diarrhea, or dizziness. Also, it can be difficult to determine how much of a fertility drug an individual woman should be given. If she takes too little, there will be no pregnancy. If she takes too much, there may be multiple births. Two or three—or even eight or more—eggs may be released and fertilized at one time. The uterus was not designed to carry so many babies, and they have little chance of survival.

Males also account for a large percentage of infertility problems. Drugs can often be used to assure a man is making enough healthy sperm for conception to occur.

Despite the problems associated with infertility treatment, it is estimated that half of all couples who would otherwise have been childless are able to conceive after medical treatment.

People who are unable to have children often feel, that they aren't normal, that they are less masculine or feminine than others, or that they are alone in facing this situation. Medical and counseling support are usually very important.

Options for Infertile Couples

A couple who cannot conceive a child themselves may consider several other options.

• **Adoption.** Couples who cannot become parents biologically may choose to adopt. Adoption can be a means of providing a loving home for one or more children who would not otherwise have one.

• **Artificial insemination.** This is the process of injecting sperm into a woman's uterus with a special needle. A doctor does this during the woman's fertile period. The sperm may be from the woman's husband or from another male, usually unknown to the couple, called a donor. Donor sperm is sometimes used by couples in which the man has a history of inherited disorders.

• **In vitro fertilization.** A woman whose damaged Fallopian tubes prevent pregnancy may have a doctor remove a mature egg from her ovary. The egg is placed in a small glass dish containing a special solution, to which her husband's sperm are added. If fertilization takes place, the doctor then

---

MORE ABOUT

Infertility Drugs and Multiple Births

Drugs are often successfully used to combat infertility, with one side effect that is almost as phenomenal as the problem itself—multiple births. Because infertility is sometimes a result of infrequent or irregular ovulation, infertility drugs are designed to stimulate the pituitary gland to produce necessary hormones, which, in turn, trigger ovulation. However, the drugs often overstimulate the ovaries, resulting in a release of more than one egg. To counteract this situation, the male partner might be given a hormone injection that suppresses sperm count. Parents faced with the possibility of having twins, triplets, quadruplets, or even quintuplets say that those prospects are better than being childless!

inserts the zygote into the woman's uterus. There, the zygote may attach itself to the lining of the uterus, and a normal pregnancy can proceed.

- **Ovum transfer.** This procedure is sometimes called adoptive pregnancy. An egg obtained from a female donor is fertilized by the man's sperm with in vitro fertilization and then implanted in the uterus of an infertile woman. Ovum transfer is sometimes used by women who lack working ovaries or who have a history of inherited disorders.

- **Surrogate mother.** A **surrogate**, or *substitute*, mother is a woman who carries and delivers a baby for another couple. In some cases, the surrogate carries a couple's fertilized egg, which is removed from the biological mother because she is unable to carry a pregnancy to term. Other surrogates are artificially inseminated with sperm from the husband of an infertile woman. Such options are usually managed through legal arrangements or according to various state laws.

As technology continues to advance, there may soon be other options available. However, the alternatives that science makes possible are not always considered acceptable by everyone. Procedures such as ovum transfer and surrogate motherhood are controversial. They raise many philosophical questions that society has not had to face before.

SECTION 2 REVIEW

CHECK YOUR UNDERSTANDING

1. List at least five traits that an individual inherits from previous generations.
2. What is a chromosome?
3. How many chromosomes does each person have? How many genes does each chromosome contain?
4. What is the difference between a dominant gene and a recessive gene?
5. How is the sex of a baby determined?
6. Explain the difference between identical twins and fraternal twins.
7. What is infertility? List three options for infertile couples who want to have children.

DISCUSS AND DISCOVER

1. Discuss the physical traits you think you inherited from previous generations of your family. If possible, make a display of photographs, showing you and various other family members from whom you think you inherited certain traits.

Observing & Participating

Take time to observe the behavior and physical characteristics of twins you see in public places or any twins you know. Are they identical twins or fraternal twins? In what ways are the twins in each pair alike? How are they different? If you are acquainted or friendly with any twins, describe how the personalities of the two differ. How are their personalities alike?

SECTION 2 REVIEW

1. Five answers may be: build; color of skin, eyes, and hair; size and shape of ears, hands, and feet; blood type; medical conditions; and other responses.
2. A tiny threadlike particle in the nucleus of every cell that carries hereditary characteristics.
3. 46 chromosomes; thousands of genes.
4. A dominant gene is the stronger of the two.
5. By the Y or X chromosome in the male sperm; Y for boys and X for girls.
6. Identical twins result from one zygote; fraternal twins develop when two eggs released at the same time are fertilized by two sperms.
7. Inability to conceive children. Any three: adoption; artificial insemination; in vitro fertilization; ovum transfer; surrogate motherhood.

ASSESS

CHECKING COMPREHENSION

Assign students to write their responses to the Check Your Understanding questions in the Section 2 Review. Answers are given below.

EVALUATE

Have students complete Chapter 5, Section 2 quiz in TCR.

Reteaching

1. Have students complete Reteaching 11 in the TCR.
2. Work with small groups of students to identify and discuss examples of inherited family traits. Then ask these general questions: What physical features can be inherited? What mental abilities? What special aptitudes?

Enrichment

1. Challenge students to complete Enrichment 11 in the TCR.
2. Have students interview a social worker or a representative from an adoption agency to discuss the legal, financial, social and psychological aspects of adoption. What are the current attitudes toward adoption? How have those attitudes changed in recent years?

Extension

Invite an obstetrician specializing in infertility to visit the class and discuss treatment for infertile couples. Ask the physician to deal specifically with options, medical and personal concerns, and costs involved. Encourage questions.

CLOSE

Engage students in a brief discussion of the importance of understanding how characteristics are inherited. What makes this topic important to children, both biological and adopted, within a family? What makes it important to biological parents? To adoptive parents?

FOCUS

SECTION 3 RESOURCES

Teacher's Classroom Resources
- Enrichment 12
- Reteaching 12
- Section 3 Quiz

Student Workbook
- Understanding Birth Defects

SECTION OVERVIEW

In Section 3, students learn about problems that cause birth defects and implications of those defects for the new baby and the family. They read about the most common defects, the role of genetic counselors, and about specific prenatal tests that can be used to diagnose some birth defects during pregnancy.

MOTIVATOR

Read aloud to the class a brief selection from a book, either nonfiction or fiction, that deals with birth defects. Two books by Helen Keller, *The Story of My Life* and *Midstream: My Later Life*, provide many appropriate passages. Encourage students to share their responses to the selection, then guide them in discussing what they already know about birth defects — their seriousness, their causes, their detection, and their prevention.

USING TERMS TO LEARN

Have students read and briefly discuss all seven vocabulary terms. You may want to point out the prefix *pre* in *premature* and remind students of that same prefix in *prenatal*. You might have students explore the meaning of the prefix *ultra* and how that prefix helps clarify the definition of *ultrasound*?

SECTION 3

TERMS TO LEARN

amniocentesis
birth defect
chorionic villi sampling
miscarriage
premature
stillbirth
ultrasound

Problems in Prenatal Development

OBJECTIVES

- Name and describe specific types of birth defects.
- Discuss the causes of birth defects.
- Describe how birth defects can be diagnosed and prevented.

Will the baby be all right? This is a major concern for nearly all parents-to-be. Fortunately, most babies develop normally and are born healthy. For a variety of reasons, however, prenatal development does not always proceed normally.

Birth Defects

Premature babies are *born before their development is complete.* This usually means that the pregnancy was less than 36 weeks. These babies have not had time to gain weight, as weight gain usually takes place during the last month of pregnancy, so they often weigh less than 5 ½ pounds (2.5 kg). (A full-term baby usually weighs between 7 and 8 pounds [3.2 and 3.6 kg]). Babies can also weigh less than 5 ½ pounds (2.5 kg) even though they were born on time. These babies are said to be low birth weight babies. Premature babies and low birth weight babies must be given special care. Their small size and incomplete development make them vulnerable to infection, lung ailments, and other problems.

Prematurity is one example of a **birth defect**—*an abnormality, present at birth, that affects the structure or function of the body.* Strictly speaking, almost everyone is born with some type of imperfection. Most, such as birthmarks, are relatively minor. However, some babies are born with more serious kinds of problems, referred to generally as birth defects. In any pregnancy, no matter what the situation, there is a chance the baby will have a birth defect.

MORE ABOUT

Prematurity

The outlook for premature babies improves with each week of pregnancy. Not long ago, babies born before 34 weeks, gestation time were unlikely to survive. Today, babies at 25 weeks of gestation are coming through in good shape. More premature babies survive now because of the availability of neonatal intensive care, which was developed in the 1960s and continues to make tremendous strides in caring for critically ill newborns. Drugs commonly used to prevent a premature birth are effective only if administered before the membrane has ruptured and before the cervix has dilated to 3 centimeters. Emphasis, however, continues to be placed on prevention.

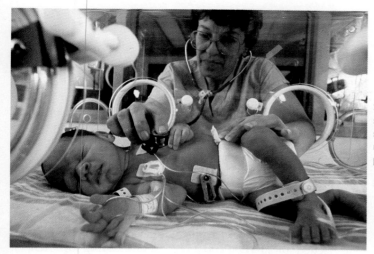

Sometimes a baby is born with a serious health problem. Medical science is constantly working to find not only better ways of treating these problems, but ways to prevent them.

Types of Birth Defects

There are hundreds of kinds of birth defects, with widely differing symptoms and effects. Most, however, are quite rare.

Some birth defects affect the shape or size of the body or of certain parts of the body. For instance, a child may be born with a misshapen foot or an extra or a missing finger. Other birth defects involve a part or system of the body that does not function properly. Blindness, deafness, and mental retardation are examples.

Not all birth defects are apparent at birth. Sometimes the abnormality does not cause problems until months—or even years—have passed.

Birth defects vary widely in their severity. Some are mild or can be readily corrected. Others result in severe lifelong disabilities or even death.

In some cases, if prenatal development is not proceeding normally, a **miscarriage**—*the natural ending of a pregnancy before the embryo or fetus could possibly survive*—occurs. A **stillbirth** is *the natural ending of a pregnancy after 20 weeks.* Usually, these losses happen by accident and are not the fault of either the father or the mother.

As soon as they find out they are pregnant, most couples start making plans for their baby. Thus, when they lose that pregnancy, either by miscarriage or by stillbirth, for most, it is the same as losing a child who had been born. They go through stages of grief, as does anyone who has had a family member die. There are special services and support groups for people who have had a pregnancy loss.

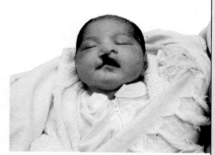

Prenatal development is a complex process. When something interferes with it, a birth defect may result. The development of this baby's lip was not completed the way it should have been.

MORE ABOUT

Miscarriage

About 20 percent of all pregnancies end because of a maternal or fetal defect. This process is called a miscarriage or a spontaneous abortion. Possible causes include abnormal implantation of the placenta; chromosomal abnormalities; abnormalities in fetal development; and maternal factors, such as infections or nutritional deficiencies. Some women mistakenly feel that they miscarry because they are physically active. No evidence supports this observation, although doctors recommend that once a woman miscarries, she should get adequate rest and exercise moderately. Above all, pregnant women should not smoke, drink alcohol, or take any drugs not prescribed by a doctor.

TEACH
Pages 130-141
- Birth Defects
- Types of Birth Defects
- Causes of Birth Defects
- Prevention and Diagnosis of Birth Defects

GUIDED PRACTICE
Promoting Discussion

Encourage students to share and discuss what they already know, either through direct experience or through talking with others, about various birth defects. With what specific birth defects are you familiar? How has each birth defect affected the life of that person? Of that person's family members? Of friends?

Critical Thinking

Ask students why premature babies have a greater risk of serious health problems or death compared with full-term babies. What effects might a premature baby have on the parents and family members?

Using the Photograph

Encourage students to describe the situation shown in the photograph at the top of this page. What is your response to this baby's condition? How do you imagine the baby's parents would respond? Why?

Promoting Discussion

What is a miscarriage and what factors are involved? What adjustments will a couple have to make after a miscarriage? How does a stillbirth differ from a miscarriage? Do you think the effects of a stillbirth are different ? If so, how? If not, why not?

Critical Thinking

Ask students to share their ideas about miscarriage. Given the fact that a miscarriage is an indication that prenatal development is not proceeding normally, how do you think a woman should respond to the first signs of a possible miscarriage? Why? To what lengths should she go to avert a miscarriage? Why?

GUIDED PRACTICE (continued)

Practicing Decision Making

A pregnant woman should identify and minimize environmental hazards during pregnancy. The optimal development of the baby is dependent upon nourishment and oxygen provided by the mother. What specific decisions need to be made by a pregnant woman who has not yet established healthy eating habits? Who has been exposed to dangerous infections? Who drinks alcohol regularly? Who drinks alcohol occasionally? Who smokes cigarettes? Who takes prescription drugs? Who takes street drugs? Who may be exposed to radiation?

Why are these decisions so important? Who can be affected by them? Who is responsible for making them? Who—if anyone—is responsible for helping the mother make such decisions?

Cooperative Learning

Let students work in small groups to explore answers to these questions: Why is it important for a pregnant woman not to smoke during pregnancy? How can smoking affect fetal development? Then have group members work together to investigate recent research in this area and write a summary of their findings.

HEALTH TIP

During the first three months of pregnancy, women should not use hot tubs or saunas. At least one study has shown that intense heat increases the odds of a baby's developing spinal cord defects, such as spina bifida. In fact, using a hot tub just twice during the first trimester of a pregnancy triples the risk.

HEALTH TIP

We do not know a "safe level" for possible harmful substances. The best course is to avoid all these substances during pregnancy. Since most women don't realize they are pregnant until the embryo is formed, the ideal is to plan a pregnancy and avoid all possibly harmful substances before becoming pregnant.

Causes of Birth Defects

Just as the types of birth defects differ, so do the causes of birth defects. Some are inherited from one or both parents. Others are caused by factors in the environment. Researchers believe that most birth defects result from a combination of environment and heredity. However, the exact causes of many birth defects are not yet fully understood. Some seem to happen totally by chance—not caused by any environmental exposure, and not inherited.

Environmental Causes

As you have learned, prenatal development takes place very rapidly. In just a few weeks, a baby develops all the bodily systems needed for survival and a normal life. During this prenatal period, the developing baby is completely dependent on the mother's body for nourishment and oxygen.

Many choices the mother makes—as well as many conditions of which the mother may be unaware—can affect the development of her baby. These are some of the environmental factors that can influence the development of a baby:

- The nutritional balance of the mother's diet.
- Any diseases or infections the mother has during pregnancy.
- Harmful substances, such as alcohol, tobacco smoke, and drugs, including some medicines that would ordinarily benefit the mother.
- Exposure to outside hazards such as radiation, especially early in pregnancy.

People once thought that the placenta was a barrier that protected the baby from many dangerous substances. However, we now know this is untrue.

Everything a pregnant woman takes into her body—pills, injections, food, tobacco smoke, coffee, and alcohol—may affect her unborn child. The placenta may act as a partial barrier, and certain substances may have difficulty crossing to the child. It is now clear, however, that most substances reach the embryo or fetus. If the concentration of any substance in the mother's blood is high enough, some will surely leak across the placenta and reach the fetus.

As you can see, how the mother takes care of herself during pregnancy is crucial. An important part of taking care of herself is seeking medical care. A woman should see a doctor as soon as she suspects she is pregnant, and she should follow the doctor's advice to stay healthy.

MORE ABOUT

Rh Incompatibility

Rh incompatibility is related to the Rh factor—an inherited substance present in most people. Someone whose blood contains this factor is called Rh-positive; someone lacking it is called Rh-negative. The presence or absence of this factor makes no difference in a person's health. It causes problems only if an Rh-positive male and an Rh-negative female have more than one child. The first child is seldom affected because few blood cells pass from the baby to the mother during pregnancy. The mother's body produces enough antibodies to destroy the foreign blood cells. In subsequent pregnancies, these antibodies cross the placenta to attack and destroy the baby's blood cells.

Hereditary Causes

Everyone has five or six imperfect recessive genes among the thousands that make up his or her personal blueprint. A single copy of these genes will have no effect on the development of the person with the gene or of a baby to whom it is passed on. However, if each parent passes on the same defective recessive gene, the baby will then have two copies of this gene and therefore will not have a normal gene for the trait determined by this gene. Depending on how important this trait is, there may be a high risk of a birth defect.

Normal genes are usually dominant over defective genes, which are most often recessive. A recessive gene usually produces an effect only when transmitted by both parents. Very often parents do not learn that they carry recessive genes for a particular defect until they have a child born with that defect. If both parents have a recessive gene for the same disorder, *each* of their children has one chance in four of developing that disorder.

Not all hereditary defects are passed on this way. For example, some inherited conditions affect only males. Hemophilia, a condition that prevents the blood from clotting, and color blindness are such conditions. Other defects and conditions are passed straight through families from one affected person to some of their children and grandchildren.

Interaction of Heredity and Environment

Most birth defects are believed to result from a combination of heredity and environment. For example, sometimes the structure of the heart is defective at birth. Such a defect is usually the result of two factors working together. First, there was an inherited tendency for a heart defect. Second, the defect was triggered by some factor in the environment, such as a drug or a virus. If only one of these conditions had been met, the heart would probably have been normal. This type of interaction between heredity and environment is probably the cause for cleft lip, cleft palate, and spina bifida.

Errors in Chromosomes

A few types of birth defects are linked to a problem with the affected baby's chromosomes. For example, there may be too many—or too few—chromosomes in each cell of the body. Although this type of defect involves genetic material, it is not the same as a hereditary defect. The child does not inherit the defect from the parents. Researchers are still working to understand why chromosomal errors occur.

A positive, encouraging approach can help children with Down syndrome make the most of their abilities.

GUIDED PRACTICE (continued)

Using the Photograph

Let students describe the child and teacher shown in the photograph on this page. What do they appear to be doing? How does the child seem to be responding? Why? What do you think parents and other caregivers can do to help foster self-confidence in a child with a serious birth defect?

Making Connections: Science

Have students prepare posters to illustrate how birth defects can be inherited. Instruct them to include illustrations showing how recessive and dominant genes are received by children from parents who are carriers of a defect.

Making Connections: History

Have interested students read about birth defects within royal families or among other historical figures. One example that students might want to research is hemophilia in the son of Russia's Czar Nicholas II. Rasputin's ability to relieve the boy's suffering gave him tremendous influence over Empress Alexandra and, in turn, over the ruling family. What relationships can be identified between the crown prince's hemophilia, Rasputin's influence, and the causes of the Russian Revolution? Let students research answers to these or similar questions and report their findings to the rest of the class.

Promoting Discussion

Ask students to share their ideas about how parents may respond to the birth of a baby with a birth defect. Are parents' reactions likely to differ according to the cause of the defect? For example, might parents have more difficulty accepting a birth defect caused by the mother's exposure to environmental hazards than a birth defect with hereditary causes? Why or why not?

HEALTHY FAMILIES/HEALTHY CHILDREN

Health and Safety

A blood test is routinely given at the beginning of pregnancy to determine whether the mother's blood is Rh-negative or Rh-positive. If the mother tests Rh-negative, the father's blood is also checked. Rh incompatibility produces no symptoms in the mother; however, the threat to the welfare of babies in subsequent pregnancies is substantial. Fortunately, prevention is now possible. A vaccine can be given to the Rh-negative woman after her first pregnancy with an Rh-positive child. The vaccine prevents the Rh antibodies from forming in her bloodstream. She can then safely give birth to another Rh-positive child.

1. Who is the first source of help for parents of special-needs children? *(The child's pediatrician or the family's general physician.)*

2. Besides instructional programs, what other services are found in public schools? *(Possibilities are physical, speech, language, and occupational therapy; counseling; and transportation.)*

3. What resources are available for families of special-needs children? *(Extended families and support programs connected with hospitals, the department of social services, and state and local health departments.)*

Thinking Like an Expert

Put students into small groups and ask them to imagine they are the parents of a newborn with a physical handicap. Ask each group to select a specific handicap or assign a different one to each group. Next, ask them to brainstorm how they would accommodate the newborn and provide for his or her particular needs. Remind them to consider emotional support for themselves and their families. Have them think ahead to the child's infant and toddler years and speculate about the resources available to them and their child. As an alternative, have the groups do the same exercise with a child who has a mental or emotional handicap.

ASK THE EXPERTS

Sources of Support for Special-Needs Children

Q. **Where can the parents of young children with special needs go for help and support?**

A. Special-needs children require extra medical attention; most also require other kinds of professional help in dealing with particular physical, social, or educational problems. In addition, parents and other family members usually benefit from support in coping with the stresses related to their responsibilities.

The first source of help usually is the child's pediatrician or the family's general physician. Physicians are able to refer babies and young children to medical specialists. More and more, physicians are also able to refer families to other helpful resources within the community.

In many communities across the country, the public school has become an important source of assistance. Services may include center- or school-based preschool classes and home-based instruction. Speech/language therapy, physical therapy, occupational therapy, counseling, and transportation may be available as well. Many programs emphasize providing parents with the skills to help their developing child.

Some public schools may also provide assessment and support for children from birth to age three.

For emotional support, many parents turn to their own extended families or specific support programs, often affiliated with a local hospital, the department of social services, or the local, county, or state health department.

Jacqueline F Mault

Jackie Mault
Director of Special Services
for the Toppenish School
District in Toppenish,
Washington

The most common type of chromosomal error is called Down syndrome. One child in every 650 births has this condition. The risk increases as the mother gets older. A child with Down syndrome has an extra chromosome 21, as shown in the photograph on page 137. Because each chromosome carries hundreds of genes, the defect can interfere with development in many ways.

HEALTHY FAMILIES/HEALTHY CHILDREN

Health and Safety

Why do only males have hemophilia? It is an example of *sex-linked inheritance*. The gene for hemophilia is carried on the X chromosome that determines the sex of the child. Females have XX sex chromosomes and males have XY. A female who has one normal sex chromosome (X) and one carrying the hemophilia gene (x) does not actually suffer from hemophilia. If she passes on the affected chromosome to her son, he will have the disease (xY). What if a male with hemophilia (xY) marries an (XX) female and they have a daughter? He passes the affected gene to his daughter, who becomes a carrier (xX), and the process continues. In rare cases, a daughter of a male hemophiliac (xY) who marries a female carrier (xX) could have the disease (xx).

SELECTED BIRTH DEFECTS

CEREBRAL PALSY

* **Description:** Cerebral palsy is a general term for a variety of motor system disorders. The symptoms can include lack of coordination, stiffness, jerkiness, difficulty in speech, and paralysis.
* **Causes:** Cerebral palsy results from brain damage before, during, or shortly after birth. The causes of the brain damage vary.
* **Detection:** The symptoms usually become recognizable sometime during the first year of life.
* **Treatment:** The brain damage associated with cerebral palsy is irreversible. However, physical therapy, speech therapy, occupational therapy, surgery, and medication can minimize the disabilities in many cases.

CLEFT LIP AND/OR CLEFT PALATE

* **Description:** A gap in the upper lip and/or palate causes problems with eating, swallowing, speech, and appearance.
* **Causes:** Often the cause is unknown; it may be hereditary and/or environmental.
* **Detection:** Both cleft lip and cleft palate are apparent at birth.
* **Treatment:** Surgery can correct the gap and eliminate the problems associated with it.

CYSTIC FIBROSIS

* **Description:** Cystic fibrosis is a functional defect that involves the respiratory and digestive systems. Many of those affected die before reaching adulthood.
* **Cause:** This is a hereditary condition, carried on a recessive gene. An affected child has two copies of the defective gene, one from each parent.
* **Detection:** Tests can identify carriers of the gene and can diagnose an affected child or fetus.
* **Treatment:** There is no known cure for cystic fibrosis. Those affected can be helped by special diets, lung exercises, and treatment of any complications.

DOWN SYNDROME

* **Description:** Down syndrome is a group of associated defects that may include mental retardation, delayed development, heart defects, and other characteristics.
* **Cause:** Down syndrome is caused by a chromosomal error. For reasons not yet understood, there is an extra chromosome 21.
* **Detection:** The syndrome is detected by an analysis of the chromosomes. Amniocentesis or chorionic villi sampling can detect the syndrome in a fetus.
* **Treatment:** Those affected benefit from special therapy and schooling and, in some cases, from corrective surgery.

MUSCULAR DYSTROPHY

* **Description:** There are many different types of muscular dystrophy; all involve a progressive weakness and shrinking of the muscles. The most common form begins between the ages of two and six.
* **Causes:** Most types of muscular dystrophy are hereditary. The most common form is transmitted by female carriers of the gene but affects only males.
* **Detection:** The disease is apparent at its onset. Genetic counseling can identify carriers.
* **Treatment:** There is no known cure. Physical therapy can minimize the disabilities.

MORE ABOUT

In Utero Surgery

Fetal medicine is said to have its beginnings in the early 1960s, when medical researchers developed a way to treat Rh incompatibility with an intrauterine blood transfusion. More recently, doctors are specially trained to detect and treat a variety of fetal diseases that would otherwise mean death to the fetus or result in birth defects.

At the University of California at San Francisco, Dr. Michael Harrison and his colleagues have successfully performed operations on human fetuses who were diagnosed as suffering from a kidney disease called hydronephrosis. Although risks involved with fetal surgery remain high, advanced technology and drug research promise that more tiny patients will be cured before birth.

GUIDED PRACTICE (continued)

Using the Chart
Guide students in studying and discussing the information presented in Selected Birth Defects. With which birth defects are you familiar? What do you already know about those birth defects? What range of disabilities seems to result from any one kind of birth defect? How might the range of disabilities affect a family's response to diagnosis of a birth defect?

Critical Thinking
Ask students to describe the emotional and financial strains that an entire family may experience when one of the family members has a birth defect. Are there ever benefits for a family when a child has a birth defect? If so, what are they? How can families be encouraged to recognize them?

Using the Photograph
Ask students to describe the photograph shown on page 137. Explain that this kind of chart, showing matched pairs of chromosomes, is called a karyotype. Let students point out the genetic defect resulting in Down syndrome.

Family Focus
Present the following situation to students: Todd is thirteen and enjoys activities with his friends at school. Although he occasionally goes to a friend's house, he never invites anyone to his home. Six years ago, his little brother Jimmy was born. Todd does not like to tell people about Jimmy, nor does he want anyone to meet him. Jimmy was born with Down syndrome.
Ask students to explain why Todd might feel the way he does. Is Todd winning or losing in this situation? Why? Is Jimmy winning or losing? Why? What would you do if you were in Todd's situation? Why, and how? What do you think other members of Todd's family might do to help?

Cooperative Learning

Let students work in groups to select and research one of the birth defects presented in the chart on page 135 and this page. Ask each group to prepare a short report, including information on the causes, diagnosis, and treatment of the defect, as well as the impact on family members in relation to their finances, emotions, time, and energy.

Making Connections: Math

Ask students to assume that an average of ten infants are born each day in a single hospital. Using statistical probability (see page 134), calculate the number of infants likely to be born with Down syndrome at that hospital every year. What factors might affect the actual number of babies born with Down syndrome there?

Family Focus

Discuss the emotional, social, and financial effects for a family in these situations:

- A child born after seven months of pregnancy is hospitalized for nine weeks, mostly in a special intensive care unit. There are two other children in the family, ages two and six.

- A single mother with little education and only a part-time, minimum wage job gives birth to a daughter with cystic fibrosis.

- A young couple's first child is diagnosed with cerebral palsy. The couple had wanted a large family.

Promoting Discussion

Ask students to organize birth defects according to these categories as a review:

- Genetically inherited defects.

- Environmentally caused defects.

- Defects detected by chorionic villi sampling or amniocentesis.

- Defects that can be detected immediately after birth.

- Defects caused by carriers that can be detected in prospective parents.

SELECTED BIRTH DEFECTS (cont'd.)

PKU

- **Description:** PKU is a condition in which the body is unable to process and use a specific protein. Mental retardation can result.
- **Cause:** This is a hereditary condition, carried on a recessive gene. An affected child has two copies of the defective gene, one from each parent.
- **Detection:** Newborns are tested for PKU, as required by law in all states.
- **Treatment:** There is no known cure for PKU. If it is diagnosed early, a special diet can reduce or prevent brain damage.

SICKLE-CELL ANEMIA

- **Description:** Malformed red blood cells interfere with the supply of oxygen to all parts of the body. The symptoms include tiredness, lack of appetite, and pain. Sickle-cell anemia can lead to early death.
- **Cause:** This is a hereditary condition, carried on a recessive gene. An affected child has two copies of the defective gene, one from each parent.
- **Detection:** Sickle-cell anemia can be detected by blood tests. Amniocentesis or chorionic villi sampling can identify anemia in a fetus. Genetic counseling can identify carriers.
- **Treatment:** There is no known cure for sickle-cell anemia. Medication can treat the symptoms.

SPINA BIFIDA AND/OR HYDROCEPHALUS

- **Description:** Spina bifida is a condition in which an incompletely formed spinal cord causes partial paralysis. Spina bifida often occurs with hydrocephalus, a condition in which an excess of fluid surrounds the brain, which can lead to brain damage.
- **Causes:** Both hereditary and environmental factors may cause these conditions.
- **Detection:** Both conditions are apparent at birth. A combination of tests of the mother's blood, amniocentesis, and ultrasound can reveal suspected cases in a fetus.
- **Treatment:** Any paralysis or brain damage associated with these conditions is permanent. Corrective surgery, physical therapy, and special schooling can minimize disabilities. Hydrocephalus can often be controlled by an operation performed shortly after birth.

TAY-SACHS DISEASE

- **Description:** Babies born with Tay-Sachs disease lack a specific chemical in their blood, resulting in an inability to process and use fats. Tay-Sachs leads to severe brain damage and to death, usually by the age of two or three.
- **Cause:** This is a hereditary condition, carried on a recessive gene. An affected child has two copies of the defective gene, one from each parent.
- **Detection:** Blood tests can identify carriers and can test for the disorder in a newborn. Amniocentesis or chorionic villi sampling can identify Tay-Sachs disease in a fetus.
- **Treatment:** There is no known cure or treatment for this disease.

HEALTHY FAMILIES/HEALTHY CHILDREN

Health and Safety

Occasionally, babies are born with certain birth defects of the brain and spinal cord, called neural tube defects. One of these is anencephaly, an abnormal development of the brain and head. Another is spina bifida, a defect of the spinal column. When such defects are present, a large amount of alpha-fetoprotein (AFP) is produced by the fetus. This substance passes into the amniotic fluid and then to the mother's blood. The AFP test, a simple blood test taken at 15 to 22 weeks, can be used to measure the amount of alpha-fetoprotein in the mother's blood. A high level indicates a 4 to 10 percent chance that a neural tube defect exists. With further testing (ultrasound and amniocentesis), more accurate results can be obtained.

Prevention and Diagnosis of Birth Defects

In the past, little could be done to improve the chances of having a healthy baby. Today, organizations like the National Foundation/March of Dimes fund ongoing research into the cause, prevention, and treatment of all types of birth defects. Some causes of birth defects, such as infections, drugs, and alcohol, can be controlled. Although most birth defects cannot yet be prevented, tests can sometimes determine the probability that specific defects will develop. Advances in the detection of defects before birth make early treatment possible.

It is difficult for a child born with a serious medical problem to lead a normal life. The rest of the child's family is necessarily affected by the emotional and financial strain the defect causes. Responsible couples do everything they can to minimize the possibility of birth defects.

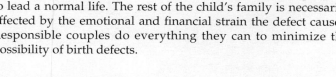

Genetic Counseling

Some hereditary or chromosomal defects can be predicted by genetic counseling. This service combines a knowledge of heredity and birth defects with laboratory tests. It tells parents in advance the statistical odds that their children will have certain diseases or defects. The couple can then use this information to plan their pregnancy. Genetic counseling does not tell people what to do; it only explains the options and risks. Most people who seek genetic counseling do so because they are aware of a specific possible problem.

Although genetic counseling may be provided by family doctors, it is best provided by a genetic specialist. Genetic counselors are individuals specifically trained to understand genetic disorders. They have good communication skills, so they

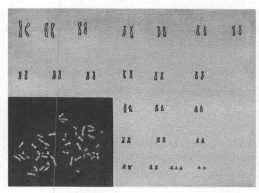

Some genetic defects can be identified by making a photograph of chromosomes from the person's tissues. In the case of Down syndrome, there are three, rather than two of chromosome 21 (bottom row).

CLASSROOM MANAGEMENT

Cross-Reference
For more information about careers relating to pregnancy and child care, see Chapter 20, pages 570-587. Also, encourage students to read the profiles of the professionals who contributed to the Ask the Experts features in each chapter. These appear on "Meet the Experts," pages 12-13.

GUIDED PRACTICE (continued)

Practicing Decision Making
Present the following situation to the class: Alex and Gina were married three years ago. They have been looking forward to raising a family with two or three children. Through genetic counseling, they have learned that there is a chance that any child born to them could have a rare disorder that results in death to the child, usually within the first five years of life.

Ask students to discuss their responses to Alex and Gina's situation: What decision do they have to make? If you were in their position, what would you do? Why? What special problems might develop if Alex and Gina disagree about these decisions? How could Alex and Gina resolve those problems?

Making Connections: Writing
Have students assume the viewpoint of a newborn infant and write a brief story about the care he or she received during pregnancy. Ask students to emphasize any environmental hazards that were encountered or avoided during development and the importance of prenatal care. Have students exchange the stories they have written and provide feedback to the writers.

Practicing Decision Making
Ask students to weigh a pregnant woman's options in the following situation: Her doctor suspects that, unless corrective surgery is performed on the fetus in the uterus, the woman's baby will be born with a serious birth defect. However, in order to make a definite diagnosis of the baby's condition, the doctor must perform a test that carries a relatively high risk of miscarriage. Encourage students to discuss the pros and cons of the woman's options. What decision would you make? Why?

GUIDED PRACTICE (continued)

Promoting Discussion

Ask students how genetic counseling can be helpful to people. What group of potential parents is most likely to seek such services? Why?

Using the Photograph

Encourage students to describe and discuss the family shown in the photograph on this page. What kind of birth defect does the oldest child in the family appear to have? How has it affected his physical abilities? How might it affect his confidence and his self-concept? How might it affect the lives of the other members of his family? On the basis of this picture, what do you think the parents in this family are doing to help all three of their children deal successfully with the son's birth defect?

Promoting Discussion

Ask students to share their ideas about the usefulness of support groups for families with members who have birth defects. Who could benefit from such support groups? How? Are there people for whom such groups might be inappropriate? If so, who and why? Are you aware of any such support groups in the local community? What populations do they serve, and with what success?

Critical Thinking

Help students review the options for infertile couples discussed in Section 2. Ask students to consider the relevance of these options to couples with a family history of hereditary birth defects. How might such a history affect decisions about adoption, sperm donors, ovum transfer, and surrogate motherhood?

Promoting Discussion

Ask students to consider the groups of people likely to use genetic counseling and prenatal testing. Do you think teen parents often use these services? Why or why not? Do you believe they should be encouraged to? Why or why not?

Raising a child who has a serious birth defect involves many challenges. Parents are faced with the drain on their finances, emotions, time, and energy. At the same time, family members should treat the child as normally as possible. They need to help the child gain confidence and overcome feelings of being "different."

can explain the situation to the family, and help family members deal with the emotional and financial impact of their specific situation. Genetic doctors are usually specialists either in recognizing and diagnosing genetic conditions or in performing specialized prenatal care. The most specialized testing is done at major medical centers in large cities, but most states have regional services so that genetic counseling is readily available close to home for families throughout the United States.

A genetic counselor begins by obtaining a complete family medical history from the patients. The patients could be a couple who are concerned about their chances of having a child with a serious birth defect or a couple who, because they already have a child with a problem, want more information. Both the husband and the wife are asked for information relating to diseases and causes of death of all their close relatives. They are also questioned about events during this pregnancy and during any previous pregnancies, and they are asked for other relevant information.

The patients—and, in some cases, other family members—may be given thorough physical examinations. If necessary, special laboratory tests are also performed.

MORE ABOUT

Genetic Counseling

Counseling for genetic disorders is not limited to before or during pregnancy. Infants who show signs of any developmental delay, or of mental retardation, or who are born with a birth defect such as cleft palate, spina bifida, heart defect, or Down syndrome can benefit from genetic counseling. Additionally, people who might choose to seek advise from a counselor are those who have a history of miscarriages or stillborn infants; couples who are concerned with birth defects common to their ethnic groups; couples who are close relatives; and couples who feel they have been exposed to drugs, radiation, chemicals, infections, and medications that might have harmful effects on a baby.

When all the questionnaires and tests are completed, the counselor is usually able to tell the couple whether genetic problems are present. The couple may also be told their mathematical chances of having a child with a serious birth defect. The genetic counselor explains the findings and describes alternative courses of action. The genetic counselor does not tell the family which course of action to take. That is always a personal decision for the family.

Prenatal Tests

If a woman is already pregnant and she or her doctor suspects that a birth defect may be likely, special prenatal tests can be given. These tests determine whether specific birth defects are present. No tests will tell whether a baby will be normal. Some tests may alert the physician to a condition in the baby that must be treated before or immediately after birth. Blood testing to estimate the risk for some defects is common. Although it will not be possible in the foreseeable future to test for all birth defects, new methods of prenatal diagnosis are constantly being developed. Three of the most useful diagnostic procedures are ultrasound, amniocentesis, and chorionic villi sampling.

- **Ultrasound** is *a technique of using sound waves to make a video image of an unborn baby to check for specific health problems.* It can show whether the fetus is developing on schedule. Certain defects, especially those involving the skeleton and other organs, can also be detected by ultrasound.

  Researchers are still studying possible risks of ultrasound. For this reason, most experts advise that ultrasound be used only as part of necessary medical tests. When it is used in

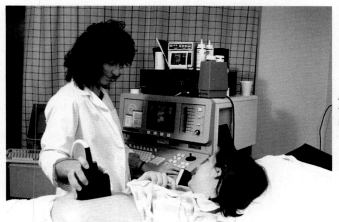

An ultrasound scan produces a picture of the fetus that can give the doctor information about its development.

HEALTHY FAMILIES/HEALTHY CHILDREN

Health and Safety
Researchers predict increased use of MRI (magnetic resonance imaging) scans to supplement ultrasound in detecting problems during pregnancy. MRI gives clearer pictures than ultrasound without the risk of X rays.

GUIDED PRACTICE (continued)

Using the Photograph
Let students describe the scene in the photograph at the bottom of this page. Help them discuss the risks involved in the procedure and the most common reasons for performing it. Point out that the high-frequency sound waves used in ultrasound are much like the sonar used by ships.

Promoting Discussion
Encourage students to describe and discuss any ultrasound experiences they may have had or heard about. What did the ultrasound show? How did seeing the unborn baby affect the baby's parents?
If possible, show students an ultrasound picture of an unborn baby; let them identify the features of the developing fetus. Then ask: What do you think are advantages and disadvantages of ultrasound as a diagnostic technique?

Making Connections: Physics
Have interested students read more about how ultrasound works, and its most common uses. Present their findings to the class.

Critical Thinking
Since amniocentesis can determine the sex of an unborn baby, have students participate in a debate discussing the pros and cons of knowing the sex of a baby ahead of time.

Promoting Discussion
Ask students to share responses to these questions: Under what circumstances would doctors be likely to recommend chorionic villi sampling over amniocentesis? Amniocentesis rather than chorionic villi sampling? Why?

Critical Thinking
Tell students that some people feel technology has "gone too far" in developing the ability to diagnose and treat the fetus. Ask students to identify the specific factors they think contribute to this point of view. Do you agree or disagree with that point of view? Why?

INDEPENDENT PRACTICE

Journal Writing

Ask students to assume they are the parents of a baby, recently born with one or more serious birth defects. In their journals, have students write a letter to a family member or friend, explaining the birth defect, their reactions to it, their hopes, their fears, and their specific intentions.

Student Workbook

Have students complete "Understanding Birth Defects" in the Student Workbook.

Extension

Let students work independently or in small groups to complete one or more of these extension activities:

- Research and write a brief report on incompatibility problems with blood types — A, B, and O. Compare these incompatibility problems with Rh factor incompatibility, and discuss possible complications that can arise with different combinations of blood types.

- Read about Rhogam, the drug given to an Rh-negative woman after her first pregnancy with an Rh-positive child. Discuss the advantages, possible side effects, and mechanism of action of the drug.

- Investigate and report on recent research into birth defects (other than Down syndrome) that are linked to a problem with the baby's chromosomes. These could include Trisomy 13, Trisomy 18, Turner syndrome, and Kleinfelter syndrome.

- Interview the parents of a child with Down syndrome, or read at least one magazine article about such parents. How does raising a child with Down syndrome affect the family's finances? Emotional health? Time and energy available for one another? What special approaches do the parents have for meeting the challenges of raising a child with Down syndrome? What special rewards do they feel they enjoy? Write a brief summary of your conclusions.

Amniocentesis can detect a number of rare genetic defects. It is performed in the fourth month of pregnancy or later, but only if they suspect a problem.

this way, ultrasound often provides additional information that can be reassuring or helpful to both the parents-to-be and the physician. It can help verify the baby's due date. In addition, ultrasound may reveal the sex of the developing baby or the presence of twins.

- **Amniocentesis** is *the process of withdrawing a sample of the amniotic fluid surrounding an unborn baby with a special needle and testing that fluid for indications of specific birth defects or other health problems.* The doctor withdrawing the fluid uses an ultrasound image as a guide when inserting the needle. Some of the cells from the fetus are contained within the sample of amniotic fluid. These cells are tested for evidence of birth defects.

  The most common use of amniocentesis is as a test for Down syndrome when the expectant mother is over age 35. Because the procedure involves some risks, including the possibility of miscarriage, it is performed only when there is a valid medical reason. It is always the woman's decision whether or not to have genetic amniocentesis.

- **Chorionic villi sampling** is *the process of testing for specific birth defects by sampling small amounts of the tissue from the membrane that encases the fetus.* Guided by an ultrasound image, a doctor inserts a catheter, or small tube, through the vagina into the uterus. There, samples of the villi—fingers of tissue that protrude from the chorion, the membrane encasing the fetus—are snipped or suctioned off for analysis.

  Chorionic villi sampling is used to test for the same disorders as amniocentesis, but the sampling can be done earlier in a pregnancy. Unfortunately, the risks that chorionic villi sampling will cause miscarriage or birth defects are much greater than the risks involved in amniocentesis. It is performed only after careful consideration of the medical reasons and risks. It is always the woman's decision whether or not to have chorionic villi sampling.

More than 100 kinds of birth defects can now be diagnosed prenatally. In some cases, the problem can be treated before the baby is born. For example, the first child of a Boston woman died at three months of age from a hereditary condition. During her second pregnancy, the woman underwent amniocentesis. The test results indicated that this child also had the condition. A biochemical defect would cause mental retardation in the developing child. Vitamin therapy was administered to the mother, and thus through the placenta to the fetus, to correct the problem, and the baby was normal at birth.

MORE ABOUT

Prenatal Testing

As commonly agreed, the risk of having a baby with some disability increases with a woman's age. More research shows that the increased age of the father also plays a significant role in determining the baby's health. Sperm, like the egg, is changed by time. Although utero tests may reveal an abnormality, many genetic counselors feel that these should be administered with caution. Recent statistics show that 90 percent of all prenatal tests reveal no danger of abnormality. Additionally, results that are not reliable and inconclusive cause needless anxiety. Couples who discover that their baby has an untreatable disease may find themselves thinking about terminating the pregnancy.

Several other methods of prenatal diagnosis are now in the experimental stages. These may someday provide more accurate information at earlier stages of development. For example, it has become possible to view the fetus directly through a special instrument, obtain samples of fetal blood and tissue, and even perform surgery on an unborn child. The testing is currently quite dangerous. Further breakthroughs may make these procedures safe enough for widespread use.

Currently in common use are some blood test screenings to estimate the risk for certain birth defects. The information from these blood tests can be helpful to a woman and her doctor when deciding whether there is a valid medical reason to perform one of the diagnostic procedures described above.

SECTION 3 REVIEW

CHECK YOUR UNDERSTANDING

1. What is a birth defect? List three kinds of birth defects.

2. Under what circumstances is a baby considered premature? What special problems does a premature baby face?

3. What is a miscarriage?

4. What is the cause of Down syndrome? What is one factor that increases the risk of Down syndrome?

5. What is the purpose of genetic counseling?

6. What is the purpose of ultrasound testing during pregnancy? What kinds of defects can be detected by an ultrasound?

7. What is the difference between amniocentesis and chorionic villi sampling? What risks are involved in each procedure?

DISCUSS AND DISCOVER

1. Read about the rate of premature births in your community or in your state. Then investigate programs designed to help mothers have healthy, full-term pregnancies. Work with other students to make posters or fliers promoting these programs.

2. What stresses do you think are involved in adjusting to life with a healthy new baby? How do those stresses compare with the stresses involved in adjusting to life with a baby who has a serious birth defect? How do you imagine the birth defect affects the baby's parents? Siblings? Grandparents?

3. Why do you think some couples might have trouble deciding whether or not to seek genetic counseling? What are the advantages of using genetic counselors? Are there any disadvantages? If so, what are they? Do you think a genetic counselor would—or should—tell a couple whether or not they should have children? Why?

Observing & Participating

Visit a class or care center for children with severe birth defects. Describe the kinds of problems each child deals with. Explain how the children and the caregivers cope with those problems. What special skills is each child learning? Why? What techniques are used by caregivers to teach these skills?

SECTION 3 REVIEW

1. A birth abnormality that affects the structure or function of the body. Examples: blindness, deafness, mental retardation, etc.

2. Pregnancy of less than 36 weeks. Small size, incomplete development, vulnerability to infection, lung ailments, and other problems.

3. The natural ending of a pregnancy before the embryo or fetus could possibly survive.

4. Chromosomal error; mother's age increases risk.

5. Explaining options and risks of pregnancy.

6. To check for health problems and fetal development; skeletal and organ defects.

7. Chorionic villi sampling can be done much earlier, but can involve a much higher risk of miscarriage or birth defects.

ASSESS

CHECKING COMPREHENSION

Assign students to write their responses to the Check Your Understanding questions in the Section 3 Review. Answers are given below.

EVALUATE

Have students complete Chapter 5, Section 3 TCR quiz.

Reteaching

1. Have students complete Reteaching 12 in the TCR.

2. Work with groups of students to discuss the work of genetic counselors. What kinds of problems and solutions to them can they identify? What problem is a genetic counselor unable to identify? Why? If possible, have a genetics counselor discuss his or her work briefly with the group.

Enrichment

1. Challenge students to complete Enrichment 13 in the TCR.

2. Have students read about the current findings on benefits and risks of specific prenatal tests. What new tests are being developed and what benefits and risks will they have? What advantages will they have over existing prenatal tests? Let students summarize their findings for the class.

Extension

Invite a neonatologist to visit the class, or arrange for the class to tour the neonatalogy intensive care unit of a local hospital. Ask the neonatologist to describe the hospital's intensive care of premature infants, including financial costs, emotional stress on family members, average length of stay in the hospital, and procedures used.

CLOSE

Ask each student to complete the following sentence, either orally or in writing:
    Birth defects affect . . .

SECTION 4 RESOURCES

Teacher's Classroom Resources

• Enrichment 13

• Reteaching 13

• Section 4 Quiz

Student Workbook

• Help This Unborn Child

SECTION OVERVIEW

In this final section of the chapter, students explore the potential effects of alcohol, other drugs, X rays, rubella, and sexually transmitted diseases on the growth and development of the embryo or fetus. They discuss how teens can avoid these hazards.

MOTIVATOR

Present this situation to the class: A young married woman is in generally good health. She smokes about a pack of cigarettes per day, and has a cocktail and a glass or two of wine with dinner three times a week. About once a month she drinks five or six mixed drinks at a party. Two weeks ago, she tried some cocaine at another party. Today, she learned that she is six weeks pregnant.

Discuss this woman's situation. What risks does her unborn baby face due to her actions?

USING TERMS TO LEARN

Go over the two vocabulary terms with the class. Have volunteers offer informal definitions of the words *effects* and *syndrome*, or let one of the students check the definitions in a dictionary. Which of the two is likely to be the more serious condition?

Avoiding Environmental Hazards

TERMS TO LEARN

fetal alcohol effects
fetal alcohol syndrome

OBJECTIVES

• Identify the hazards that alcohol and other drugs pose to prenatal development.

• Discuss other environmental hazards that should be avoided during pregnancy.

In *every* pregnancy, the mother-to-be is responsible for taking the most important step in increasing the chances of having a healthy baby: She must take care of herself and keep herself safe and healthy. One important part of good prenatal care is understanding the harmful effects of environmental hazards such as alcohol and other drugs, smoking, X rays, and infections.

Alcohol

Though many people still avoid realizing this fact, alcohol is a drug—and it can be a dangerous one. Ever since ancient times, writers have commented on the poor mental and physical health of children born to alcoholic women. Modern medicine has confirmed these observations. Women who drink alcohol during pregnancy often bear children with a variety of birth defects, some of which can be fatal.

A woman who drinks during pregnancy risks having a child with **fetal alcohol syndrome,** *a condition of physical deformities and cognitive problems resulting from a mother's consumption of alcohol during pregnancy.* Almost all babies born with fetal alcohol syndrome are mentally retarded. This is because alcohol interferes with tissue growth and development, and brain tissue is most easily injured by this interference. Many childern born with fetal alcohol syndrome also have other problems, such as slow growth, poor coordination, behavior problems, heart defects, and facial disfigurement.

COOPERATIVE LEARNING

Evaluating Environmental Hazards

On the chalkboard, write the following environmental hazards: alcohol, drug abuse, caffeine, tobacco, X rays, rubella, and STDS. Ask students to copy the hazards on a sheet of paper and arrange their individual lists in an order from most harmful to least harmful. Then put the students into small groups to compare rankings.

Each group is to discuss their findings and agree on a single list that reflects how the group would rank the hazards. Next, have a volunteer from each group write the list on the board. Have students discuss the similarities and differences between the groups' final order. Encourage students to speculate about why one hazard might be more serious than another.

Children whose mothers drink less alcohol during pregnancy may suffer from **fetal alcohol effects**, *a less severe condition involving some, but not all, of the symptoms of fetal alcohol syndrome.* There is no safe amount of alcohol that a woman can drink during pregnancy without taking the chance of causing harm to her unborn child.

The degree of damage to the child is usually directly related to the amount of alcohol the mother consumed during pregnancy. It may also be affected by the stage of the pregnancy during which she drank and by the presence of other drugs in her system. Because the damage is done before birth, there is no cure for fetal alcohol syndrome or fetal alcohol effects.

Although fetal alcohol syndrome and fetal alcohol effects can't be cured, they can be prevented. Doctors do not yet know just how much alcohol presents a danger to the developing baby. For this reason, most health professionals recommend that pregnant women safeguard the health of their babies by avoiding alcohol altogether when they plan a pregnancy, as well as during pregnancy.

Other Drugs

Many doctors believe that drugs taken during pregnancy are among the major causes of birth defects linked to environmental factors. The drugs of which pregnant women should be especially aware include the following:

- Alcohol, as you have just read.
- Medicines that doctors prescribe.
- Over-the-counter remedies such as aspirin, cold medicines, nose drops, and vitamins.
- Chemicals such as caffeine, found in some foods and beverages, and nicotine, found in tobacco.
- Illegal drugs such as heroin, LSD, marijuana, crack, and other forms of cocaine.
- Inhalants—fumes that are inhaled into the lungs.

Prescription and Over-the-Counter Drugs

Every pregnant woman should remember that there is no such thing as a completely safe drug. Even over-the-counter drugs, such as aspirin, cold remedies, and antihistamines, can be dangerous for the unborn child. One extreme example is thalidomide, which was considered a safe drug for relieving the symptoms of morning sickness in pregnant women during the late 1950s. Thalidomide caused severe birth defects in more than 5,000 infants before its effects were discovered.

Over 62,000 nonprescription drugs and other environmental hazards carry warning labels for pregnant and nursing women.

TEACH

Pages 141-149

- Alcohol
- Other Drugs
- X Rays
- Rubella
- Sexually Transmitted Diseases (STDs)

GUIDED PRACTICE

Promoting Discussion

Pour and display two 8-ounce (240 mL) glasses of water. Explain that recent studies have shown that a woman who drinks as few as one or two mixed alcoholic drinks — the equivalent to the amount shown in the two glasses — increases her baby's risks of prematurity and low birth weight. What are the implications of these studies for all pregnant women?

Making Connections: Writing

Have students write newspaper editorials explaining why teens should abide by laws that prevent their use of alcohol. Remind students to support their arguments with facts, details, and statistics.

Promoting Discussion

Encourage students to share their ideas about possible relationships between drinking and unplanned pregnancies. Do you think drinking alcohol increases the possibility of unplanned pregnancy? If so, how? Why might a baby in an unplanned pregnancy run an increased risk of suffering from fetal alcohol syndrome or fetal alcohol effects?

Using the Photograph

Refer students to the photo on this page. Discuss the harmful effects of prescription medicines, over-the-counter medications, and vitamins. Should a mother ever take medications during pregnancy?

SEE HOW THEY GROW

The Effects of Antibiotics

Antibiotics are prescribed by a physician to fight infections. These drugs can cross the placenta quickly. Some are used to treat the unborn baby. Others, if not used correctly, may damage it. The baby's permanent teeth may be discolored. Bone growth may be affected. Even the baby's liver function may be disturbed. Any medication taken by a pregnant woman has the potential to cross the placenta, reach the embryo or fetus, and cause problems. For this reason, no medication should be taken by a woman during pregnancy unless a physician has been consulted. If a prescription is to be written, the physician should always be informed when a woman thinks or knows that she is pregnant. This will allow the physician to prescribe a different medication, if necessary, or suggest another method of treatment.

GUIDED PRACTICE (continued)

Practicing Decision Making

Present this situation to the class: For over a week, Karla has had bad chest congestion. Her doctor writes a prescription for her. Before she leaves the doctor's office, Karla remembers her period was to start a few days ago. There is a chance she is pregnant.

What should Karla do. Why?

Cooperative Learning

Teen health habits now and in the future will have an effect on the next generation. Ask students for examples showing why this is true. What impact does this have on our country? Divide students into groups. Ask them to write a pledge they could follow to help preserve the health of the next generation.

Critical Thinking

Many widely used substances were already on the market before the government's FDA began regulating substance use. Would the FDA permit such substances as tobacco, alcoholic and caffeine beverages, if they were being introduced for the first time? Encourage students to use what they know of current laws and effects of these substances on a developing fetus to answer.

HEALTH TIP

Drugs can effect the fetus right up until the time of delivery. Drugs used to relieve pain of delivery, for example, will depress the respiration of both the mother and the newborn. Most drugs have not been tested for safety to the fetus because testing would be dangerous to the fetus.

HEALTH TIP

It is almost always impossible to predict the effect that any particular dose of a specific medication will have on a developing baby. For this reason, a woman who even suspects she may be pregnant—or who intends to become pregnant—should avoid medicines and other drugs altogether.

Medicines or infections that reach the fetus through the third month of pregnancy will have their most devastating effect. Any drug a pregnant woman takes reduces the flow of nutrition-bearing blood to the baby. During these months, the body systems, organs, arms, and legs are being formed, so the chances of malformation are greatest during this period. Brain development is also at a critical period, and mental retardation can be caused.

In the last six months of pregnancy, harmful substances that reach the fetus usually cause slow growth, infections, or abnormal bleeding at birth. Drugs taken just before delivery will still be in the baby's body at birth and may cause serious problems.

Doctors advise strict limits on the use of medications during pregnancy. A pregnant woman should not take any medicines—even aspirin or vitamins—unless they are specifically prescribed by her physician.

Drugs that are necessary in managing serious conditions, such as diabetes and high blood pressure, can be taken under a doctor's direction. However, a pregnant woman should be encouraged to give up medications for complaints like headaches and hay fever; avoiding such medications can be a worthwhile contribution to the normal development of her baby. In fact, any woman who is likely to become pregnant would be wise to avoid taking unnecessary drugs. Usually, a woman does not know she is pregnant until several weeks after conception has taken place.

An expectant mother should not take any medication unless it is prescribed or recommended by a doctor who knows of the pregnancy. Even vitamin supplements can pose a risk to the unborn baby unless taken under a doctor's advice.

HEALTHY FAMILIES/HEALTHY CHILDREN

Health and Safety

Even aspirin has been found to cause problems in pregnancy. In early pregnancy, an occasional aspirin should not be harmful. Frequent use in late pregnancy, however, can be harmful. The baby's blood-clotting mechanism can be disrupted, and the same problem can occur for the mother at delivery. Also, the normal onset of labor may be delayed by heavy aspirin use, and bleeding before and after delivery might be excessive.

Decisions Affecting the Unborn

Five-year-old Susan and her four-year-old sister Emily are playing together in their quiet backyard. Emily runs to hide behind a tree. Her movements, however, are slower than those of other four-year-olds. Susan tries to chase Emily. However, instead of running directly to the tree, she stumbles past it.

The girls' mother, Char, sits on a lawn chair and watches them sadly. She recognizes that both her daughters have below-average intelligence, little strength, and, at times, no muscle control. She also sees that, although both girls are quite pretty, slight irregularities in their facial features indicate abnormalities.

For Char, the worst part of her daughters' problems is the knowledge that she herself is the cause of those problems. Char married when she was eighteen.

Since her husband was serving in the army, the couple had to move from one military base to another. Char found it difficult to make new friends, knowing that in a few months she would have to start all over again somewhere else. She began drinking to relieve her loneliness and boredom. Char continued drinking throughout her two pregnancies.

Susan's ailments did not become apparent until after Emily was born. Several months later, the specialists gave the verdict: Both the girls had defects resulting from their mother's drinking during pregnancy.

Char explains, "I'd do anything for my girls. Of course I would have quit drinking—if only someone had told me!" Char did stop drinking, but the change came too late for Susan and Emily.

THINK AND DISCUSS

1. Why did Char drink during her pregnancies? Why do you imagine no doctor discussed the problem with her? Why do you think her husband and other family members might have avoided discussing it?
2. What could Char have done to overcome her loneliness and boredom instead of drinking?
3. What do you think Char can do now to help her family?
4. Where would you go if you had a drinking problem? What—if anything—would you say to a friend who had a drinking problem?

Caffeine

Of all the compounds that have been investigated as possible causes of birth defects, none has been so completely taken for granted as caffeine. Caffeine is widely found in beverages such as coffee, tea, cocoa, and many soft drinks, as well as in some foods and many medications. Because it is so common, caffeine

HEALTHY FAMILIES/HEALTHY CHILDREN

Health and Safety

Alcohol use by the pregnant mother is the third leading cause of birth defects and mental retardation. Drinking alcohol at any time during pregnancy may be harmful to the unborn child. The use of alcohol can result in a variety of fetal abnormalities. The defects seem to be related to the degree of alcohol consumption by the mother. Current research suggests that consumption of two alcoholic drinks per day or binge drinking early in pregnancy can be associated with birth defects in infants. Smaller amounts can also cause problems, such as prematurity and low birth weight.

PARENTING IN ACTION

Promoting Discussion

As an introduction to this Parenting in Action selection, ask students to imagine themselves at a party where most of the guests are drinking alcohol. They see a friend who graduated from high school last year, drinking wine and smoking a cigarette. After greetings, she asks with a big smile, "Have you heard the news? I'm going to be a mom. I'm nearly three months pregnant." What would students think of her news? What would they say to her?

Let students then read "Decisions Affecting the Unborn" independently.

Critical Thinking

Discuss Char's situation: Who is responsible for Char's drinking during pregnancy? Why? Who has to deal with the consequences of her drinking? How? What do you think Char and her husband should do now to help their daughters?

Answers to Think and Discuss

1. She drank to relieve loneliness and boredom. Encourage students to present a variety of ideas about possible reasons her doctor, husband, and other family members avoided discussing her drinking.
2. Encourage a variety of ideas; be sure students recognize that Char could have found other activities, including volunteer work, and that she might have joined support groups.
3. Encourage a variety of responses; students should note that, to help her daughters, Char must recognize that her daughters do have physical and developmental problems.
4. Encourage a variety of responses.

GUIDED PRACTICE (continued)

Making Connections: Health

Encourage interested students to read about recent research into the health threats posed by cigarette smoke, both to smokers and to those who live and work with smokers. How and by whom is research being conducted? How are the results of the research being shared with the public? What steps has the tobacco industry taken to restrict research and to limit publication of findings? Have these students share their findings with the rest of the class.

Critical Thinking

Ask students to compare street drugs, prescription drugs, and over-the-counter drugs. What risks does each kind of drug pose to unborn babies? Which kind of drug is likely to affect the highest number of unborn babies? Why?

Promoting Discussion

Ask students to identify local professionals, clinics, and groups that help people deal with or avoid addictive behaviors. Guide them in discussing the benefits of professional counseling in coping with abuse of environmental hazards. Why is it often difficult for an individual to give up abuse of drugs without the help of trained professionals and support groups?

Cooperative Learning

Remind students that each year, thousands of babies are born severely and irreversibly affected by their mothers' addiction to alcohol or cocaine. Let students work in small groups to discuss the implications of this fact. What legal, medical, and societal strategies might reduce the numbers of babies born with such afflictions? Encourage the members of each group to share their ideas with the rest of the class.

is often not considered a drug. However, pregnant women—and those likely to become pregnant—should be cautious. Women who take in moderate amounts of caffeine probably don't need to worry about birth defects. It is known, however, that feeding large doses of caffeine to pregnant mice and rabbits causes birth defects in their offspring. Doctors usually advise women to be cautious about drinking coffee, tea, and cola during pregnancy.

Tobacco

The nicotine in cigarettes is also a drug—and a potentially dangerous one. The more a mother smokes, the smaller her baby is likely to be. This is important because the weight of the newborn is a critical factor in the ability to survive. Heavy smoking is also believed to cause premature birth. Doctors advise smokers that they should try to stop smoking before becoming pregnant. If they cannot quit smoking, they should at least cut down during pregnancy.

Illegal Drugs

Increases in the use of cocaine, marijuana, and other "street drugs" have presented physicians with new problems in preventing birth defects.

A mother who is addicted to drugs at the time of delivery usually passes her addiction on to her baby. Immediately after birth, these addicted infants must go through a period of withdrawal—painful illness resulting from the body's dependence on drugs. Some addicted babies even die as a result of severe withdrawal symptoms. For the babies who survive withdrawal, the future is uncertain. Experts are concerned that the long-range effects of this prenatal addiction may be serious, possibly affecting a child's learning ability and behavior. Many of these children seem unorganized; they are able to follow only very simple directions and are often unable to understand school classes.

Little is known about the specific effects of such drugs as marijuana, cocaine, barbiturates, and amphetamines on a developing fetus. However, considering the fact that even over-the-counter medications are cause for concern, you can see the potential danger of these drugs. Cocaine is known to cause miscarriage, stillbirth, prematurity, and birth defects. Similar results are suggested in studies on marijuana. While this kind of research continues, the best advice is to avoid taking *any* drugs before or during pregnancy.

MORE ABOUT

Smoking

Research shows that a baby's birth weight is reduced by about 1/4 pound (115 g) for every pack of cigarettes smoked daily by the mother during pregnancy. Passive smoking (inhaling others' smoke) has a similar effect. The usual dividing line between normal and low birth weight is 5 1/2 pounds (2.5 kg). When babies weigh under 4 pounds 6 ounces (2 kg), there is a risk of critical illness involving breathing, heart action, body temperature, and blood sugar. Without treatment, brain damage or death may result.

X Rays

X rays present another potential danger to the unborn baby. Radiation from X rays or other sources can cause birth defects. A pregnant woman who is in an accident or who is sick should inform medical personnel of her pregnancy. They can then take special precautions if X rays are necessary. For the same reason, she should also be sure her dentist or orthodontist is aware of her pregnancy. It is also important to avoid unnecessary X rays before pregnancy. Both men and women should request abdominal shielding during routine X rays.

Rubella

The terrible effect of certain infections on unborn children was highlighted by the epidemic of rubella (sometimes called German measles) that swept the country several decades ago. Thousands of unborn babies were affected when their mothers came down with German measles during pregnancy. Although most of the women had few or even no symptoms of illness, the effects on the developing babies were devastating. Because of their mothers' infection with rubella, babies were born with deafness, blindness, heart disease, and/or mental retardation.

A vaccine for rubella is now available, and millions of children have been vaccinated. The vaccine may be dangerous, however, for women who are pregnant or who become pregnant shortly after receiving it. A woman who is unsure whether she has been vaccinated can check her health records. If records are unavailable, she can consult a doctor, who will be able to determine her immunity with a simple blood test. Every woman should be sure she is immune to rubella before she considers pregnancy.

Sexually Transmitted Diseases (STDs)

Like rubella, sexually transmitted diseases, or STDs, are infections that can have dreadful effects on unborn babies. All the following are sexually transmitted diseases:

- Syphilis.
- Gonorrhea.
- Genital herpes.
- AIDS (acquired immune deficiency syndrome).

HEALTHY FAMILIES/HEALTHY CHILDREN

Health and Safety

Premature births are a primary factor in long-term health problems. Fortunately, mothers can help prevent the chance of premature delivery by following these guidelines: Plan regular rest periods to avoid high physical stress levels. If emotional stress is a problem, seek professional help. Avoid long periods of standing or strenuous housework. Stop smoking completely, and do not consume any alcohol. Do not use drugs unless prescribed by a doctor who knows that you are pregnant. See a doctor immediately if you are exposed to any contagious disease. Monitor weight gain carefully; notify your doctor if you have sudden and extreme changes in weight.

GUIDED PRACTICE (continued)

Critical Thinking

Ask students to consider the dangers of exposure to X rays. Do these dangers justify disqualifying women of child-bearing age from jobs that involve X rays? Why or why not?

Promoting Discussion

Encourage students to discuss the impact of rubella on prenatal development. Point out that 50 percent of babies whose mothers have rubella during the first four weeks of pregnancy will have at least one major birth defect. Ask students to consider the significance of this statistic. Who is responsible for avoiding such birth defects? How could rubella be eradicated? Who should assume responsibility for eradicating the disease? Why?

Cooperative Learning

Divide students into four groups, and ask the members of each group to work together in researching one of the following sexually transmitted diseases: syphilis, gonorrhea, genital herpes, AIDS. Have the group members write a short report about the disease, explaining its causes, detection, physical complications, and treatment. Then have the members of each group present the information to the rest of the class, and guide students in discussing the effects of these STDs on prenatal development.

Making Connections: Health

Have students read at least one newspaper, magazine, or journal article about babies with AIDS. What special problems do these babies face? What kinds of medical treatment do they have to undergo? What kind of future do they have? How are they often treated by their parents? Who often assumes the care of these AIDS babies. Ask students to share and discuss their findings with the rest of the class.

INDEPENDENT PRACTICE

Journal Writing

Have students write journal entries discussing their ideas about sexually transmitted diseases. What should teens know about STDs? Why? When and where should they learn about STDs? Is an understanding of these diseases important for people who are not planning on becoming pregnant? For people who have only one sexual partner? For people who are not sexually active?

Student Workbook

Have students complete "Help This Unborn Child" in the Student Workbook.

Extension

Let students work alone or in small groups to complete one or more of these:

- Read about current research into the causes and effects of fetal alcohol syndrome and fetal alcohol effects. Write a summary

- Read about Prohibition and its effects on politics in the United States. Why did Prohibition gain support? When and why did it fail? What were the major concerns about the consumption of alcohol during that period? How have those concerns changed? What groups might argue in favor of a new prohibition now? Why? Discuss your findings with the class.

- Plan, write, and illustrate a pamphlet discussing the hazards of drug use during pregnancy. Include information on the dangers posed by one or more of the following, when used during pregnancy: alcohol, prescription medicines, over-the-counter remedies, caffeine, nicotine, illegal drugs. Make copies of your pamphlet, and distribute them to other students.

- Conduct research into a specific drug, such as thalidomide, that has a harmful effect on fetal development. Prepare and present an oral report summarizing your findings.

- Group B streptococcus.
- Chlamydia.

These and other sexually transmitted diseases can affect prenatal development or be passed on from an infected mother to the developing baby. They can result in serious illness, deformity, or even death.

It is possible for a person to be infected with a sexually transmitted disease without realizing it. For this reason, special measures are often taken to protect unborn babies against the effects of sexually transmitted diseases. Most doctors routinely test pregnant women for syphilis. Such tests are required by law in many states. In addition, doctors usually treat the eyes of newborns with a solution to kill gonorrhea germs that could otherwise cause blindness. The laws of many states make this kind of treatment mandatory.

Drugs and treatment can cure syphilis and gonorrhea and can relieve the symptoms of herpes in adults. Untreated, these diseases can affect the heart, brain, reproductive system, and spinal cord, and can eventually lead to death. No drug can cure the damage to the newborn that results from a delay in diagnosis and treatment. Any pregnant woman who suspects she could have a sexually transmitted disease should discuss the condition frankly with her doctor.

AIDS, a viral infection that attacks the immune system, is a particularly dangerous sexually transmitted disease. There is no cure, and AIDS is invariably fatal. Like other STDs, it can be spread by unprotected sexual intercourse. In addition, individu-

AIDS is a deadly disease with no known cure. Health organizations have developed educational campaigns to inform the public about the realities of AIDS and other sexually transmitted diseases.

COOPERATIVE LEARNING

Research and Presentation

Divide students into small groups and assign each group to research one of the six sexually transmitted diseases listed at the bottom of page 147. Instruct each group to acquire as much information as possible and prepare a display for the class. Encourage them to make charts, diagrams, illustrations, and any other form of visual material to help make the presentation meaningful. After all groups have completed their research and visual displays, select a class period to have them present their findings. Discuss how teenagers can be further educated about STDs. If possible, include the school nurse as part of the discussion.

als can be infected with AIDS by sharing infected needles or through contact with infected blood. A fetus can be infected with AIDS by the mother. The AIDS virus may lie hidden in a person for many years before causing symptoms, so there is no way to tell whether someone is infected just by looking at him or her. If a woman who has AIDS gives birth to a child, there is a 20 to 50 percent chance that her baby will also develop AIDS and die.

Not all infections in a pregnant woman pose a threat to the developing baby. However, a pregnant woman should tell her doctor about any illness, no matter how mild it may seem.

Genetic Counseling

Genetic counselors can provide information and answer questions for women who have been exposed to any of the above substances or diseases. A genetic counselor can provide information in response to questions such as these: What is the chance that this substance or disease will cause a problem? Is there any special care needed during pregnancy? Should any special tests be considered?

SECTION 4 REVIEW

CHECK YOUR UNDERSTANDING

1. What causes fetal alcohol syndrome? List three kinds of problems associated with fetal alcohol syndrome.

2. During what period of pregnancy are the harmful effects of medications on a fetus most severe? Why?

3. List two problems that can be caused by smoking during pregnancy.

4. How might a pregnant woman be exposed to radiation? What effect can radiation have on a developing baby?

5. List three problems that may result for the developing baby if a pregnant woman is infected with rubella.

6. List four sexually transmitted diseases.

DISCUSS AND DISCOVER

1. The use of alcohol can result in a variety of fetal abnormalities. The defects seem to be related to the degree of alcohol consumption by the mother. What suggestions would you give to someone who has a drinking problem and is pregnant?

2. It is reported that passive smoking (inhaling others' smoke) has an effect on the unborn child similar to the effect of actually smoking cigarettes. What should a pregnant woman do to protect herself and her developing baby from these harmful effects?

Observing & Participating

Poll a group of peers to find out which over-the-counter medications are taken regularly. Which of these medications is considered safe to take during pregnancy? Why? Describe the specific risks that might be involved when taking these medications during pregnancy.

SECTION 4 REVIEW

1. A mother's consumption of alcohol during pregnancy. Any three: mental retardation, slow growth, poor coordination, behavior problems, heart defects, facial disfigurement.

2. The first three months of pregnancy; body systems, organs, arms, and legs are being formed, and brain development is at a critical period.

3. Low birth weight and premature birth.

4. Through medical or dental X rays; can cause birth defects.

5. Any three: deafness, blindness, heart disease, mental retardation.

6. Any four: syphilis, gonorrhea, genital herpes, AIDS, group B streptococcus, chlamydia.

ASSESS

CHECKING COMPREHENSION

Assign students to write their responses to the Check Your Understanding questions in the Section 4 Review. Answers are given below.

EVALUATE

Have students complete the Chapter 5, Section 4 TCR quiz.

Reteaching

1. Have students who need additional practice complete Reteaching 13 in the TCR.

2. In the center of a bulletin board, mount an illustration of a fetus. Write the names of these hazards at the top of separate pieces of construction paper: alcohol, drug abuse, caffeine, tobacco, X rays, rubella, STDs. Arrange them around the fetus. Guide students in reviewing the danger each substance poses to a developing baby. Have a student record the facts on the papers.

Enrichment

1. Challenge students to complete Enrichment 13 in the TCR.

2. Have students use several different sources to gather information about HIV and AIDS among teens. At what rate is this disease spreading among American teens? What can and should be done by whom to stop the spread of AIDS? Why is prevention in teens important? Hold a class discussion.

Extension

Invite a representative from Alcoholics Anonymous to discuss alcohol dependency. Discuss services available, techniques used, and the advantages of using a support group to overcome alcohol addiction.

CLOSE

Have students respond to: What should parents do to protect their unborn babies?

Positive Parenting Skills

Positive Parenting Skills

MOTIVATOR

Ask students to name "positive" feelings (e.g., happiness, joy, or elation). Ask them how these feelings are a result of a person's ability to take responsibility for good health.

Promoting Discussion

1. How does a parent's positive attitude influence a child's life?
2. How do people care for their emotional well-being?
3. What is social health?

Critical Thinking

The Positive Parenting Feature suggests that a person's attitude is a combination of physical, emotional, and social factors. How can a young adult learn to distinguish the outward signs or characteristics of each factor? Are we more likely to ignore any one factor in favor of another? What are some symptoms of a person who has not developed positive attitudes?

Family Focus

Invite to class a mother and a father who would be willing to openly discuss their experience as parents. Encourage them to reveal what adjustments they felt had to be made in their lifestyles to accommodate their child.

Practicing Decision Making

Ask students to discuss this situation: Close friends recently became parents but are finding it hard to adjust to the financial demands of parenting. They fought violently over how to spend their income tax return. The husband wanted them to take a weekend ski trip; the wife wanted to buy a new television for their den. Now they are not speaking to each other or helping each other with the daily care of the infant. How would you advise the couple?

BUILDING POSITIVE ATTITUDES

Whenever you spend time with a young child you have the opportunity to help that child feel good about himself or herself. As you continue to study child development, and as you gain experience observing and participating with young children, you will learn many specific techniques to use in guiding children toward positive attitudes. However, you should also keep in mind the importance of your own attitudes and your own self-esteem.

In order to develop positive feelings

in children, you need positive feelings about yourself. These positive feelings are possible only if you assume responsibility for your own good health.

How can maintaining your own good health help you take better care of children? When you feel healthy, you enjoy life—and the people around you. Young children respond to that enjoyment with positive attitudes of their own; your good attitude can help children enjoy you, their environment, and—most important—themselves.

Physical Health

An essential aspect of maintaining good health is taking care of your physical well-being. Here are some reminders about keeping yourself physically healthy:

- **Eat a balanced diet.** Include a variety of nutritious foods in your diet.

- **Get regular exercise.** Choose sports and other activities that you enjoy, either on your own or as part of a team or other group.

- **Get plenty of sleep.** Remember that eight hours per night is a minimum requirement for most teens.

- **Learn safety rules**—and remember to follow them.

- **Take care of your health and your appearance.** Shower or bathe regularly, keep your hair and nails clean and neat, and brush and floss your teeth daily.

- **Avoid harmful substances.** Harmful substances include tobacco, alcohol, and drugs.

HEALTHY FAMILIES/HEALTHY CHILDREN

Health and Safety

Pregnant or not, many teenagers do not eat right. Consequently, teens are more likely to have premature babies whose low birth weight is responsible for a multitude of problems, including mental retardation. If teenagers are reluctant to change their diets for the sake of themselves and their babies, they are likely to continue their poor eating habits after giving birth, which sets a bad example for infants. Encourage students to keep an account of their food intake for a period of time, and then compare the results with a chart that shows the recommended daily allowance of food (page 164).

Emotional Health

Another essential aspect of maintaining good health is caring for your emotional well-being. Every individual has emotional needs, including the need to give and receive love, the need to experience a sense of belonging, and the need to feel worthwhile. You can foster good emotional health by recognizing your own emotional needs and seeking out situations, activities, and relationships that meet those needs.

In addition, every individual experiences a wide range of emotions. Part of maintaining emotional health is recognizing and accepting all your emotions, and finding safe and appropriate outlets for expressing those emotions.

Social Health

A third essential aspect of maintaining good health is assuming responsibility for your own social well-being. You probably think of your social life as involving your friends—and they can make an important contribution to your social health. Your relationships with family members, neighbors, teachers, and others with whom you come in daily contact are also important to your social health. If you enjoy most of these relationships and feel both supportive of and supported by the people around you, you are developing your own social good health.

You can foster good social health by playing an active part in your community—perhaps by volunteering at a local recycling center or at a shelter or even in a child care center.

Remember that as you care for yourself, you are also preparing yourself to help care for others.

MORE ABOUT

Expectant Fathers
Fathers once were assigned a benign, often detached role in the childbearing process; today, they are encouraged to participate as fully as possible. Unfortunately, many find that their fears and anxieties are not considered as valid as those of the mothers. Many are uncomfortable with the birth process and are reluctant to be present. Some are overwhelmed with the increased responsibility that comes with being a parent. Still others are suddenly aware of the possibility of birth defects or, worse yet, the death of a spouse or the baby during childbirth. As men expand their involvement in childbirth, so will an understanding of their fears and needs.

Journal Writing
Ask the students to write a story from the viewpoint of a parent who has just been informed that his or her child was born with a serious birth defect. The child will probably never fully recover and will have to have extensive medical treatment for the next two years. Financial resources have already been strained and the extended family is unable to offer much help. Ask them to consider how they will care for the child and what means are available for financial, physical, and emotional support.

Enrichment
Pregnant teens who are eligible can receive recommended foods from the WIC (Women Infant and Children) program. Have students research the telephone number and the procedure for acquiring information from your local or state health department.

Cooperative Learning
Have students find a partner and practice measuring their heart rates both while at rest and after a brief exercise period. Have them take the pulse rate of their partner at the wrist or the neck for ten seconds, then multiply by 6 to get the heartbeats per minute. Then after a brief period of exercise, which can be running in place or doing jumping jacks, take the pulse again and compare the results. Remind them that a pregnant woman should keep her heart rate at less than 140 beats per minute. How much exercise is required to achieve that rate?

Extension
Have students research the current statistics on divorce rates, number of teen parents, number of single-parent families, and the leading causes of emotional stress in the family.

CLOSE

Have students discuss past and present experiences that have shaped their attitudes and helped prepare them for their future role as a parent.

Use the Summary and the Reviewing the Facts questions to help students go over the most important ideas presented in Chapter 5. Encourage questions.

CHAPTER 5 REVIEW

1. Development of a baby during the period before birth. Periods of the zygote, embryo, and fetus.

2. Ovum and sperm.

3. The organ in a woman's body in which a baby develops during pregnancy.

4. From the placenta via the umbilical cord.

5. Any four: suck its thumb, cough, sneeze, yawn, kick, hiccup, cry.

6. 46 chromosomes; 23 from father's sperm and 23 from mother's ovum.

7. Three separate ova, released at the same time, are fertilized by three different sperm.

8. Both are a natural ending of a pregnancy; miscarriage occurs before embryo or fetus could possibly survive; stillbirth after at least 20 weeks.

9. Nutritional balance of mother's diet; diseases or infections mother has during pregnancy; harmful substances, such as alcohol, tobacco smoke, and drugs, including some medicines; exposure to outside hazards, such as radiation.

10. Ultrasound, amniocentesis, chorionic villi sampling.

11. Drinking alcohol during pregnancy can cause birth defects, including fetal alcohol syndrome and fetal alcohol effects.

12. Street drugs can cause miscarriage, stillbirth, prematurity, birth defects; babies may be born addicted and have to undergo withdrawal, which can be fatal. All drugs reduce the flow of nutrition-bearing blood to the developing baby.

CHAPTER 5 REVIEW

SUMMARY

- Prenatal development begins with conception. It progresses through three stages: the period of the zygote, the period of the embryo, and the period of the fetus.

- Chromosomes carry the genes that determine all inherited characteristics.

- Infertility problems can sometimes be solved through treatment; if treatment is unsuccessful, couples can consider other options.

- Birth defects have a variety of causes.

- Genetic counseling and prenatal tests can predict some birth defects.

- To minimize risks to her unborn baby, a pregnant woman should avoid environmental hazards such as alcohol, other drugs, and tobacco.

REVIEWING THE FACTS

1. What is prenatal development? In what three stages does it take place?

2. Which two cells are necessary for conception?

3. What is a uterus?

4. How do unborn babies receive their nourishment?

5. List at least four things a fetus can do.

6. How many chromosomes does each human have? What are the two sources of those chromosomes?

7. Briefly describe how fraternal triplets develop.

8. What is the difference between a miscarriage and a stillbirth?

9. List four kinds of environmental factors that can influence the development of a baby.

10. List three prenatal tests that can be used to test for birth defects.

11. Why should a woman avoid alcohol during pregnancy?

12. What are the potential dangers of street drugs to an unborn child? Why should all drugs—including over-the-counter and prescription drugs—be avoided during pregnancy?

EXPLORING FURTHER

1. Investigate one local agency or office through which babies or children can be adopted. How can adults qualify to adopt? Are the qualifications for adopting a newborn different from those for adopting an older child? What fees should adoptive parents expect to pay? What other costs may be involved in the adoption? Share and discuss your findings with other students in your class. (Section 2)

2. Gather pamphlets and other resource materials on birth defects from the March of Dimes or from another organization. Read and discuss the materials. Then make them available to pregnant women, perhaps by giving them to a prenatal clinic. (Section 3)

3. With a partner or a small group, plan and act out a skit about teens being offered alcohol or other illegal drugs. In your skit, demonstrate effective ways to say "no" to drugs. Perform your skit for your classmates. (Section 4)

4. Prepare three hot drinks that a pregnant woman could enjoy in place of coffee. Be sure that none of your drinks contains any caffeine. Serve the drinks to classmates, and ask them to share their reactions. (Section 4)

THINKING CRITICALLY

1. **Analyze.** How do you think a woman is affected by the physical changes that take place during pregnancy? How do you imagine most husbands react to these changes? What effects might her husband's responses have on a woman's emotions during pregnancy? On her physical well-being?

2. **Analyze.** How do you think infertility affects a couple? What effects might a diagnosis of infertility have on the relationship between husband and wife? On their relationships with other family members and friends? Why?

3. **Evaluate.** What do you consider valid reasons for prenatal testing? Why? Do you think some women undergo prenatal tests for inappropriate reasons? If so, what are those reasons? What

---

HEALTHY FAMILIES/HEALTHY CHILDREN

Health and Safety

With the growing number of tests currently available, how does a woman know which are valuable and which are not? Here are three questions to ask:

1. What risk is involved? It is imperative that the test pose no harmful effects. Those tests requiring a blood or urine sample are convenient to administer and safe for both baby and mother.

2. What information will be provided from the test? If test results are not reliable, or if it takes an unusually long time to get results, a woman might opt to avoid the test.

3. How will the information from the test affect the course of treatment? If a test supplies interesting, but not useful, information, perhaps it should be avoided.

questions do you think prospective parents should ask themselves before prenatal testing? After they get the results of prenatal tests?

4. **Analyze.** What effects do illegal drugs have on unborn babies? Why, given these effects, do some mothers continue to use drugs such as cocaine and heroin during pregnancy? What, if anything, do you think should be done to help these women? What, if anything, do you think should be done to punish them?

CROSS-CURRICULUM CONNECTIONS

1. **Science.** Research recent developments in the use of fertility drugs. How has the safety of these drugs been improved? What advantages and disadvantages are associated with the use of fertility drugs? Summarize your findings for the rest of the class.

2. **Reading.** Read *The Broken Chord* by Michael Dorris. Summarize the book for your classmates, and discuss your reactions to it.

SCHOOL TO WORK

Finding Job Openings Whether you are looking for a part-time job as part of your career planning or to save money for personal expenses, locating a job is less complicated if you know where to look. Your school counselor may have a job placement center. Do your family or friends know any job leads? Employment agencies, newspaper advertisements, and government offices may have listings of available jobs. One more tactic is to call companies that interest you and ask the personnel director if there are any job openings that match your qualifications. The more leads you have, the better your chances of finding a position.

PERFORMANCE ASSESSMENT

Prenatal Development

Task

Imagine that you are an unborn infant during the fetal period and you wish to communicate with your mother. Write a letter or a script as if you were talking to her from the womb. Use what you have learned to tell her how you feel she is providing for your prenatal development.

Purpose

Although you will be addressing an imaginary pregnant mother, your purpose will be to inform potential parents about the effects of environment and behavior on an unborn baby.

Procedure

1. Draft an outline of ideas you want to include in your letter or script. Think about your sensory perceptions during this stage: What can you hear? Feel? Imagine to see or smell?

2. Focus on either a specific situation or a pattern of behavior. Perhaps your mother attends a party where others are smoking. Maybe your mother does not exercise or works on her feet all day. Don't overlook positive situations, such as when your mother has an ultrasound scan, where she can see you.

3. Use a personal tone of voice to write your letter or script. Demonstrate that you know how environment, nutrition, and behavior influences prenatal development.

4. Proofread your letter or script to correct content, spelling, and grammar. If you wrote a letter, use correct letter form and fold it into an envelope. If you wrote a script, give it a title and identify your characters.

Evaluation

Your letter or script will be evaluated on your knowledge of content and the originality and presentation of information. Both should conform to correct standards of spelling, punctuation, and grammar.

Portfolio Idea

For your portfolio, use a recorder to tape your letter or script. With a vocal recording you can add inflection and tone to your written work. If you want, you may use music or background sounds to embellish your recorded reading. Be sure to begin the tape by stating your name, the lesson name, and the date. Then save both the written letter or script and your recorded message in your portfolio for later review. Make sure each item is labelled properly and stored safely.

153

PERFORMANCE ASSESSMENT

Prenatal Letter or Script

If necessary, review the formal parts of a letter with students. Remind them that they may use an informal tone. When students are finished, encourage volunteers to read their letters or scripts to the class. If applicable, let them role-play as they perform. If classroom equipment is available, you may want to offer class time for students to record their letters or scripts for their portfolios if recording equipment is not available to them outside the classroom.

EVALUATE

Use the reproducible Chapter 5 Test, or construct your own test using the Testmaker Software.

EXTENSION

Invite several parents to visit the class and discuss their own experiences with students. If possible, include parents of young children born with birth defects. Ask all the parents to share their own feelings and ideas about the importance of prenatal care and safety. In addition, ask parents of children with birth defects to explain how they have met the challenges of their children's disabilities. Then give interested students an opportunity to ask questions.

CLOSE

Ask each student to write and complete the following sentence:

I think every expectant parent should …

DEVELOPING A PORTFOLIO

Storage Students who have the responsibility of storing their portfolios themselves should be cautioned to do so with care. A safe, consistent location is best. If you store portfolios in a classroom, space management is critical, especially if you have a large number of students. Security is also an issue. If each student has a large, expandable folder, or one with pockets, you could keep them in storage boxes or empty computer paper boxes. As work samples are completed, have students place them in their working portfolios. Each item should be dated and marked with identification.

CHAPTER OVERVIEW

In Section 1, students learn about the preparations pregnant mothers make to assure the health of their developing baby, including all physical and emotional health of the mother. They become familiar with the first signs of pregnancy, and discuss the importance of consulting a doctor for confirmation of pregnancy and to begin the routine checkups that are an essential part of prenatal care. Students read about the normal discomforts of pregnancy and about other symptoms that may indicate serious complications during pregnancy.

In Section 2, students consider some of the decisions expectant parents make and some of the responsibilities they begin to assume. Students discuss parents' decisions about child care, about preparing themselves and any other children for the new baby and about methods of feeding the new baby. Students also consider the basic supplies parents need to provide for a new baby, and discuss how planning and budgeting can help parents meet the expenses of having a baby.

Section 3 presents information about the childbirth choices parents make. Students learn what prepared childbirth is and explore parents' options in choosing childbirth attendants and settings.

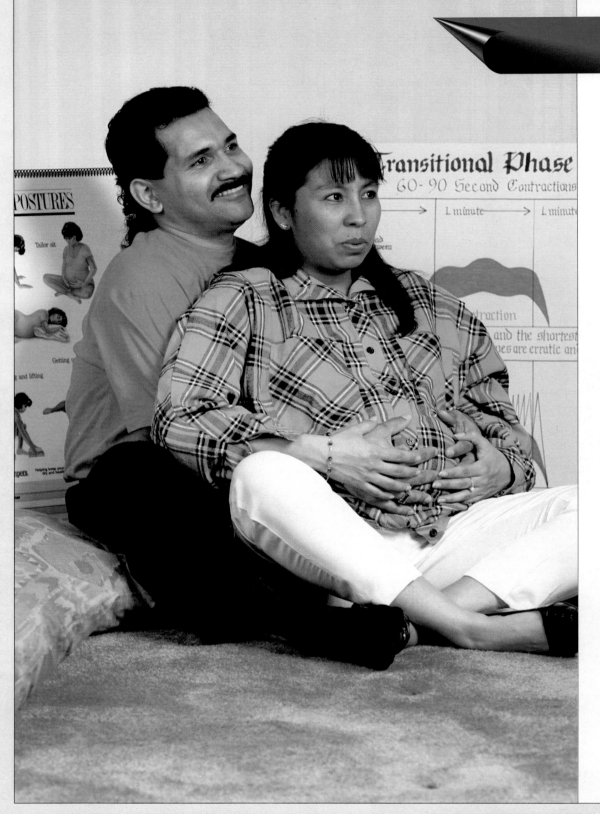

CLASSROOM MANAGEMENT

Resources Beyond the Classroom

Many new parents are shopping for baby furniture, accessories, and toys for the very first time. While this should be an exciting preparatory adventure for them, it is also important that they realize that thousands of infants and young children are injured or even die each year while using unsafe products. To inform them about safety issues and research that affects their choice of products for their infants, have your students write to the United States Consumer Product Safety Commission, a regulatory agency that develops and enforces federal safety standards:

U.S. Consumer Product Safety Commission
Washington, DC 20207

Preparing for Birth

SECTION 1	A Healthy Pregnancy
SECTION 2	Getting Ready for the New Arrival
SECTION 3	Childbirth Choices

THINK ABOUT

After conception, the mother's body nourishes and accommodates the growing fetus. Think about how her food choices affect the quality of nutrients available to her baby. Equally important are regular checkups with a physician or medical provider, sensible exercise, and her choice to avoid alcohol, tobacco, and other drugs. At the same time, the baby does its part by developing from a tiny fertilized egg to a complex human being. Together, the mother and baby form a special team!

ASK YOURSELF

Refer to the photo on the opposite page. The couple are practicing breathing and relaxation techniques during a childbirth class. How do these techniques help the woman be better prepared to manage the birth process? How is the man like a coach on an athletic team? Why is his role important? How does his participation contribute to the woman's confidence?

NOW TRY THIS

Imagine that you are about to become a parent. What changes would you make in your life-style to prepare for the role? Why? How would these changes affect your health? The health of your child? Write a letter to your imaginary child telling him or her about the decisions you will make to prepare for a healthy birth.

155

CHAPTER OBJECTIVES

After completing Chapter 6, students will be able to:

- Explain how women can care for their own health and for the health of their developing baby during pregnancy.
- Discuss the preparations that expectant parents should make before the arrival of their baby.
- Describe the options expectant parents have in deciding where and how their baby will be delivered.

INTRODUCING THE CHAPTER

- Read each of the following statements one at a time. Ask students to indicate whether they agree, disagree, or are not sure. Take time to discuss students' opinions as they respond to each statement.
  — As long as a woman feels healthy, she does not need to see a doctor until the last months of pregnancy.
  — A woman who has a poor diet before or during pregnancy may reduce her baby's intelligence.
  — During pregnancy, it is best to avoid physical activities, such as tennis, bicycling, and swimming.
  — A woman's physical and emotional stress during pregnancy can affect the developing baby.
  — Discussions about child rearing and child care should be postponed until after a baby is born.
- Use the photo on the opposite page and the three features on this page—Think About, Ask Yourself, and Now Try This— to begin a discussion about preparing for birth.

HEALTHY FAMILIES/HEALTHY CHILDREN

Building Healthy Families

Nine months of pregnancy can be a busy time for parents, especially if this baby is their first. No matter how prepared or mature they might be, the magnitude of the role of parenting is difficult to grasp. Much attention is paid to the development of the fetus and the health of the mother, but more and more, the role of the father is changing dramatically. Today's fathers are just as curious about the stages of fetal development, and they are anxious to be actively involved with the birth. They want to know whether they can be a spouse and a parent who meets the needs of this new family. Yet, who are their role models? How can they be nurturing and involved when they might not have observed this type of parenting in their own fathers?

FOCUS

SECTION OVERVIEW

As they read Section 1, students learn what expectant mothers can do to maintain their own good health and to help their unborn babies grow and develop. Students begin by learning about the early signs of pregnancy and by discussing the importance of medical care throughout pregnancy. Then they explore approaches to good nutrition, emotional health, and personal care during pregnancy.

MOTIVATOR

Show students photographs of two pregnant women, one who does not yet look pregnant and the other who is clearly ready to deliver soon. Ask students what they imagine the two women are doing to prepare for the birth of their babies. How would their preparations be similar? How would they be different? What might each be doing to assure her own health and the health of her developing baby?

USING TERMS TO LEARN

Have volunteers read aloud all three terms, and encourage students to share their understanding of their definitions. You may want to point out the relationship between *obstetrician and obstetrics*, "a branch of medicine that deals with childbirth and with treating women in connection with childbirth." *Obstetrics* comes from a Latin word meaning "midwife."

SECTION 1   A Healthy Pregnancy

TERMS TO LEARN

anemia

obstetrician

pregnancy test

OBJECTIVES

• List the early signs of pregnancy.

• Explain the importance of early and regular medical care during pregnancy.

• Explain the importance of nutrition during pregnancy.

• Give recommendations for a pregnant woman's diet, activities, and personal care.

Pregnancy is a time of change and preparation. As the baby grows and develops within the uterus, the mother-to-be undergoes many physical changes. During this time, the pregnant woman's most important responsibility is to stay in good health.

Early Signs of Pregnancy

How does a woman know that she is pregnant? There are no immediate signals that conception has occurred. However, within several weeks of conception, a woman will probably recognize one or more of these early signs of pregnancy:

• Usually, a missed period is the first indication of pregnancy. This sign is particularly reliable for women who have regular menstrual cycles.
• The woman may have a mild ache or feeling of fullness in her lower abdomen.
• She may have a sense of fatigue, be drowsy, or occasionally feel faint.
• She may need to urinate more frequently than usual.
• She may have discomfort or tenderness in her breasts.
• She may have periods of nausea, especially early in the day.

Any of these physical symptoms can be caused by something other than pregnancy. A woman who notices one—or even several—of these early signs should not conclude that she definitely is pregnant. Rather, she should have a **pregnancy test**, *a test to determine whether or not a woman is going to have a baby.*

COOPERATIVE LEARNING

Group Dynamics

Consider varying the size and makeup of cooperative learning groups from one activity to the next. Doing so not only heightens student interest in a given assignment by introducing the element of variety but also yields a broader range of student interaction. This latter dividend can be particularly useful to you in assessing individual performance. Remember, too, that different grouping strategies

serve different needs. For example, assigning a pair of less able students to work together on a reteaching activity helps both students better master lesson objectives and key concepts while, simultaneously, promoting self-esteem.

Unusual sleepiness, when combined with other signs, can be a clue that a woman might be pregnant. She should confirm the suspicion with a visit to the doctor for a pregnancy test.

Medical Care During Pregnancy

As soon as a woman suspects she is pregnant, she should consult a doctor. She may begin by visiting her own general physician. Many women prefer to see an **obstetrician,** *a doctor who specializes in pregnancy and birth.*

The pregnant woman and her doctor will have an important relationship over the next nine months. The woman will make regular office visits for checkups, and she should discuss any questions or problems openly with her doctor. The doctor who monitors her pregnancy will also assist in the birth of her baby. For these reasons, it is important for an expectant mother to select a doctor she likes and trusts.

Once a woman's pregnancy has been confirmed, her doctor usually performs a thorough examination which includes the following:

- Blood pressure, pulse, respiration, and initial weight are recorded.
- Pelvic measurements are taken to determine whether the birth passageway is wide enough to allow a normal-sized baby to be born without difficulty.
- An analysis of urine checks the condition of the kidneys, which carry a heavier burden during pregnancy.
- A blood test provides valuable information about the woman's health. For example, it tells whether there is a tendency toward **anemia,** *a condition caused by lack of iron, which results in poor appetite, tiredness, and weakness.* The blood test is also used to identify the woman's blood type in case a transfusion is necessary.

SAFETY TIP

For a completely reliable pregnancy test, a woman who suspects she is pregnant, should consult a doctor, who can use laboratory tests of her blood or urine to determine whether or not she is pregnant. Simplified versions of these tests are available for home use, but pregnancy should always be verified by a physician.

SEE HOW THEY GROW

Pregnancy Testing
Remind students that even before a pregnancy test shows positive, the fetus has begun to grow (review page 117). The commonly used urine tests for pregnancy are generally accurate at two to six weeks after conception and are used after a missed period. Pregnancy can be detected within days of conception with a sensitive blood hormone test (which measures human chorionic gonadotrophin). This test is accurate well before the first missed period. Home pregnancy tests are less sensitive and may show a negative result even though conception has occurred.

TEACH
Pages 156-168
- Early Signs of Pregnancy
- Medical Care During Pregnancy
- Nutrition During Pregnancy
- Personal Care and Activities
- Emotional Health During Pregnancy

GUIDED PRACTICE

Promoting Discussion
Ask students if it is possible for a woman to be pregnant and not know it. Is it possible for a woman to think she is pregnant when she is not? What are the implications of this?

Cooperative Learning
Let students work in groups to discuss home pregnancy tests, examining a sample one if possible. Ask then to consider responses to these questions: What are advantages and disadvantages of home pregnancy tests? Why is a test at a doctor's office also necessary?

Promoting Discussion
Ask students to explain why a woman should consult a doctor if she suspects she is pregnant. What information in Chapter 5 supports this recommendation? What risks does a woman run when she postpones or resists having an initial prenatal checkup?

Using the Photograph
Encourage students to describe the woman in the photograph on this page. What is she doing and for what reason? What other physical conditions could cause this sleepiness? How do you think being aware of her pregnancy affects this woman's response to her unusual sleepiness?

SAFETY TIP

Home pregnancy tests are not accurate until six or seven weeks after the last menstrual period. Recording the date that the test was taken and the date the last menstrual period began will help accurately determine the gestation age of the fetus.

GUIDED PRACTICE (continued)

Using the Photograph

Have students describe what is happening in the photograph on this page. Why is this an important part of a routine visit to the physician? What else can this woman expect to do during a regular prenatal checkup?

Critical Thinking

Have students examine a sample health record form used by obstetricians. Why does a doctor need the information recorded on the form?

Practicing Decision Making

Present this situation to the class: When Surina began to suspect she was pregnant, she called for an appointment with the obstetrician who had delivered her sister's baby. To her surprise, the first appointment she could get was in two months.

Ask students whether it is safe for Surina to wait two months for her first appointment. How might the delay affect her health and that of the baby? What do you think Surina should do? Why?

Promoting Discussion

Ask students to consider the meaning of a due date. How many babies are delivered exactly on their due date? What attitude should expectant parents have toward the date? What might expectant parents say when others ask, "When will your baby be born?"

Making Connections: Math

Andrea's last menstrual period started May 4th. How can you calculate the approximate due date of her baby?

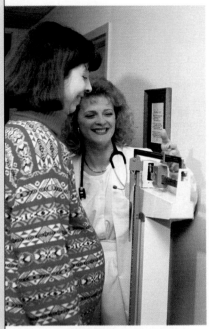

Regular medical checkups are an important part of prenatal care. Checking the baby's heartbeat and recording weight gain are routine parts of each visit.

- A history of past illnesses and operations is recorded. These may reveal conditions that require special treatment or observation.

Doctors usually schedule regular checkups for pregnant women. The examinations during these office visits may seem fairly routine. They are important, however, in monitoring the development of the baby and in making sure that the woman remains healthy. Typically, an expectant mother has a checkup once a month until the sixth or seventh month of pregnancy. Then most doctors schedule two visits a month until the ninth month, when the pregnant woman has a checkup once a week.

When will the baby be born? This is one of the first questions a prospective mother asks her doctor. To answer this question, the doctor makes a simple calculation, based on the date on which the woman's last menstrual period began. The doctor adds nine months and one week to that date to find the approximate date on which the baby will be born.

Discomforts of Pregnancy

Pregnancy is a condition, not an illness. Many women go through pregnancy without any problems or complications. In fact, some women find pregnancy a time in which they feel particularly healthy. Other women may be mildly affected by some of the common discomforts listed here. Although these discomforts usually do not indicate serious problems, a woman who experiences any of these symptoms should discuss them with her doctor.

- Nausea is the most common complaint among pregnant women. It is commonly called morning sickness, although some women experience it in the evening and others feel it all day long. Snacking on soda crackers and eating smaller, more frequent meals can help relieve nausea for many women. Fortunately, nausea rarely lasts beyond the fourth month of pregnancy. A woman who suffers severe and prolonged nausea should contact her doctor.
- Sleepiness is a fairly common symptom during early pregnancy. Unusual fatigue results in part from hormonal changes in the woman's body. Because pregnancy affects every system and organ in the body, some women feel unusually tired throughout pregnancy. For many women, fatigue decreases during the middle months of the pregnancy but may recur during the final months.
- Pregnant women often suffer from heartburn, a digestive disturbance not associated with the heart. A woman with heartburn should ask her doctor about the safest source of relief.

Childhood Reflections

"We believe in the Great Hoop: the Great Circle of Life; everything comes back to where it started. We believe this. That is the Indian way."

Matthew King

HEALTHY FAMILIES/HEALTHY CHILDREN

Building Healthy Families

Although a woman might be preoccupied with the physical discomforts of pregnancy, the emotional discomforts are equally strong. Women often feel ambivalent and contradictory feelings about the prospects of having the baby. Some are overwhelmed by the importance and demands of the years ahead. Some are suddenly aware of their own inadequate training and background. A sense of grieving is not uncommon as the woman shifts into a new phase of her life and realizes that the arrival of a new baby, even if it is not her first, will require new adjustments. It's natural to feel a full range of emotions, but what is important is that the mother realize that her emotions are in reaction to the circumstances, not a reflection of her love and commitment to the baby.

- In the late months of pregnancy, a woman may feel short of breath. This is caused by pressure on the lungs from the growing uterus.
- Some pregnant women develop varicose (swollen) veins from pressure on the blood vessels in their legs. A woman with varicose veins should rest with her legs and feet elevated whenever possible. She may also find elasticized stockings and certain exercises helpful.
- It is not unusual for pregnant women to suffer muscle cramps in their legs. These cramps can be relieved by rest and gentle stretching. A diet rich in calcium may prevent these cramps.
- During the last months of pregnancy, many women experience lower back pain. For back comfort throughout the pregnancy, pregnant women should wear low-heeled shoes and be sure to bend their knees when lifting. Certain exercises can help relieve backache.

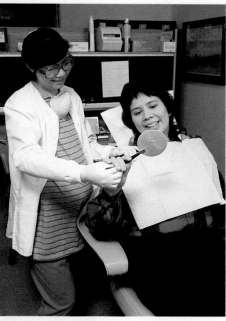

If no unusual problems develop, a woman can keep up her normal activities during pregnancy. Balancing work, rest, and recreation will help her feel her best.

MORE ABOUT

Varicose veins

Varicose veins are enlarged veins with walls that have thinned and stretched. Their causes include:

- Poor return of blood from the legs during pregnancy because of pressure on the blood vessels.
- The increased volume of blood during pregnancy.
- The hormone progesterone, which is produced during pregnancy and which relaxes the walls of the blood vessels.

Suggestions for avoiding varicose veins include:

- Avoid prolonged standing.
- Elevate legs for five minutes each hour.
- Avoid tight clothing.
- Wear support hose, putting them on before getting out of bed in the morning.

GUIDED PRACTICE (continued)

Promoting Discussion

Remind students that because the monthly visits to the doctor during pregnancy may seem routine, many women may feel that they are not important. Encourage students to discuss why these visits are so important. How could they be especially helpful to a woman who is suffering from some of the discomforts of pregnancy? Would you recommend that a woman who is experiencing no discomforts and no other problems skip one or two prenatal checkups? Why or why not?

Cooperative Learning

Let students work in small groups to consider the various discomforts common among pregnant women. What might each indicate? How is a pregnant woman likely to react to these discomforts? Would a pregnant teen have the same reaction? Why or why not? What advice would you give to a pregnant teen who was having difficulty handling these discomforts? Hold a class discussion.

Family Focus

In some ways, pregnancy is a very personal experience for a woman. Guide students in discussing the extent to which family members and friends can or should become involved in a pregnancy. What responsibility should the expectant mother take for including the expectant father in the experiences of pregnancy? Why? What responsibility for that participation should the expectant father undertake? Why? Which other family members might want to be actively involved in a woman's pregnancy? What could they do to feel and be more involved? What are the benefits of increasing family involvement in pregnancy? What are the disadvantages, if any?

Using the Photograph

Encourage students to discuss the pregnant women shown in the photos at the bottom of this page. Which normal activities can a woman continue during pregnancy? What types of activities might it be better to avoid?

ASK THE EXPERTS

Issues and Advice

1. What are possible sources for myths about pregnancy? (*Individual experiences, cultural beliefs or expectations.*)

2. Under what circumstances will a baby be harmed by what a mother eats? (*If she does not eat a balanced, nutritious diet.*)

3. What is the reason a woman may have problems with her teeth during pregnancy? (*Hormonal changes may cause gum inflammations.*)

4. Who is the best source of information about pregnancy concerns? (*A physician or a care provider.*)

5. What additional resources are available? (*Books, health professionals, nutritionists, teachers, librarians.*)

Thinking Like an Expert

Despite the abundance of information readily available to just about everyone, misconceptions about pregnancy, childbirth, and child rearing abound. The myths are sometimes grounded in fact, as shown in the feature on this page, but often they are based on lack of knowledge. Ask students to speculate about the possible sources of the myths. Can they contribute any other myths? Why would pregnant women be inclined to believe a myth without verifying its legitimacy? What dangers do myths present? How do doctors and health professionals counteract their influence?

Ask interested students to conduct a survey of mothers and fathers representing a range of ages asking parents whether they were aware of any myths about pregnancy, childbirth, or child rearing. If so, how were they influenced and would they repeat them to a younger generation? Have students report their findings.

ASK THE EXPERTS

The Myths of Pregnancy

Q. How can I unravel the myths associated with pregnancy?

A. I'm glad you realize that not everything you hear about pregnancy is true. Some of the stories you hear reflect the particular experiences of individual women. Other stories pass down cultural beliefs or expectations. Still other stories actually do give information or reliable advice about pregnancy.

Have you ever heard these tales about pregnancy?

• If a pregnant woman sleeps too much, the baby will stick to her backbone.

• A car ride on a bumpy road will end a woman's pregnancy.

• A pregnant woman who sees something frightening will have a baby with an ugly birthmark.

• If a pregnant woman lifts her arms above her head, the umbilical cord may strangle her baby.

All these stories are completely false. Normal activities cannot affect the baby's safety. Nor will what the mother sees or eats affect the baby's safety or appearance—as long as the mother has a nutritious, balanced diet.

Some age-old adages about pregnancy are at least partially true. Maybe you've heard people say this:

• A woman loses a tooth for every baby she has.

This is another pregnancy story that's untrue, but it does have a clear basis. A pregnant woman may lose some calcium from her bones (not her teeth) if her daily diet does not provide enough calcium for the baby's development. In addition, a woman may have problems with her teeth during pregnancy because hormonal changes sometimes cause gum inflammations; these changes make oral hygiene especially important.

A pregnant woman has an excellent source of information—her physician or other care provider. During her regular checkups, she should discuss her questions and concerns openly with that person. Books written by doctors, nutritionists, or other health professionals are also good sources of information about pregnancy. You can also rely on teachers or librarians to help you find and evaluate information.

Pat Brodeen

Pat Brodeen
Teacher and Teen Parent Coordinator at Theodore Roosevelt High School in San Antonio, Texas.

MORE ABOUT

Myths of Pregnancy

In addition to the above-mentioned myths, people have believed certain myths about breast-feeding, for example, that some women are unable to produce enough milk for their babies. On the contrary, the amount of milk produced by a woman's mammary glands is based on the amount demanded by an infant. If a woman feeds her baby on a regular basis and until the baby is satisfied, the body will seldom be unable to furnish enough. Along the same lines, the size of a woman's breasts are no indication of her ability to adequately feed her baby. Mother's milk comes from glandular tissue in the breasts, not from the fatty tissue that shapes the breasts.

Possible Complications

A few women experience more serious complications during pregnancy. A pregnant woman who has any of the following symptoms should report them to her doctor immediately:

- Vaginal bleeding.
- Unusual weight gain.
- Excessive thirst.
- Reduced or painful urination.
- Severe abdominal pain.
- Persistent headaches.
- Severe vomiting.
- Fever.
- Swelling of face, hands, or ankles.
- Blurred vision or dizziness.
- Prolonged backache.
- Increased vaginal mucus.

Nutrition During Pregnancy

Good nutrition is the single most important factor in prenatal care. By eating a balanced diet, a pregnant woman helps her baby develop properly. She also helps maintain her own health.

Doctors once thought that a developing baby took whatever it needed from the mother's body. We now know that this is not true. The fetus may take certain nutrients, such as calcium, from the mother's system. However, the mother is responsible for providing, through a healthy diet, almost all the nutrients the baby needs, as well as all the nutrients her own body needs.

Because of the importance of the mother's diet to prenatal development, any woman who might become pregnant should establish healthy eating habits before conception.

A well-balanced diet is important both before and during pregnancy. A variety of nutritious foods should be eaten daily.

GUIDED PRACTICE (continued)

Cooperative Learning
Let groups of students work together to investigate the symptoms of complications during pregnancy. Have the members of each group select a specific symptom and find answers to questions such as these: What might cause that symptom? What underlying problem could the symptom indicate? What other conditions, unrelated to pregnancy, might cause the same or similar symptoms? Why is it important for a pregnant woman to discuss the symptom with her health care provider? Then have the members of each group report their findings to the rest of the class.

Promoting Discussion
Ask students why it is important to know the difference between the symptoms of possible complications during pregnancy (listed on this page) and the routine discomforts of pregnancy (discussed on pages 158 and 159).

Cooperative Learning
Have students work in groups to review and discuss the discomforts of a normal pregnancy and the symptoms that may indicate serious complications during pregnancy. Ask the group members to prepare a separate index card for each discomfort and each symptom. Then have group members place all the index cards face down on a table or desk and take turns selecting a card and telling whether the symptom on the card is a normal discomfort or an indication of a possible serious problem.

Promoting Discussion
Ask students to explain why good nutrition during pregnancy is important to the health of the developing baby. Then ask how good nutrition before the beginning of pregnancy can contribute to the health of a baby.

HEALTHY FAMILIES/HEALTHY CHILDREN

Health and Safety
Nutritious snacks can contribute to a more healthful diet. For a pregnant woman, making the most of calories consumed is especially important. Some good ideas for snacks are:

- Apple wedges with peanut butter.
- Celery sticks stuffed with cheese.
- Nuts and raisins.
- Popcorn with limited butter and salt.
- Cheese and crackers.
- Milkshakes made with fresh fruit.
- Carrot sticks with yogurt dip.
- Mini pizzas.
- Banana slices dipped in a mixture of peanut butter and honey.

Promoting Discussion

Ask students to identify foods that are good sources of iron. What are some ways these foods could be included in the diet? Why is iron, always important in a woman's diet, especially important during pregnancy? How does this iron affect the health of a baby during the first few months of life?

Making Connections: Writing

Have students create and draw a cartoon character to represent each nutrient; then have them write a job description for each of their nutrient cartoon characters.

Practicing Decision Making

Explain to students that during the first three months of pregnancy, women need only about 150 additional calories a day. Have students use a nutrient/calorie chart to choose foods of about 150 calories that would be nutritious additions to a pregnant woman's daily diet.

Using Management Skills

Ask students to survey the produce department of a grocery store and list all the fruits and vegetables available. Provide students with a chart that lists the vitamins and minerals in fruits and vegetables. Which of the available fruits and vegetables would be especially good for pregnant women? Why?

Critical Thinking

Remind students that although a pregnant woman and her developing baby can both benefit from a diet rich in vitamins, she should not take vitamin supplements unless they have been recommended or prescribed by the doctor. Why do you think this is so? What risks could vitamin supplements pose? In which circumstances do you think a doctor is most likely to prescribe vitamin supplements? Why?

Cooperative Learning

Have students work in small groups to plan and prepare posters on this theme: Nutrients for a Healthy Pregnancy.

The Role of Nutrients

A healthy diet contains all the food nutrients: protein, vitamins, minerals, fats, and carbohydrates. Each nutrient performs very special functions and forms an essential part of a healthy diet.

- **Protein.** This nutrient can be obtained from meat, fish, poultry, eggs, milk, cheese, and beans. Protein is vital for the growth of the baby. It also helps keeps the mother's body in good repair. Because of the added needs of the growing fetus, a woman should have additional protein during pregnancy. A diet lacking in protein is generally lacking in other nutrients, too.

- **Vitamins.** Vitamins promote general good health, protect against infection and disease, and regulate body processes. A woman needs more vitamins during pregnancy. If her diet is lacking in vitamins, there is an increased risk that her baby will be born with birth defects.

  A woman needs additional vitamin A during pregnancy to assure proper development of her baby's eyes. She also needs extra B vitamins to assure healthy fetal development. B vitamins release the energy in foods, build the nervous system, keep the digestive system working well, and promote healthy skin.

  A woman should also increase her intake of vitamin C during pregnancy. It helps build healthy teeth and gums, and helps make the material that holds body cells together. She also needs additional vitamin D, which aids in the development of strong bones and teeth.

  Vitamin-rich foods are usually those that are also rich in other nutrients. Fresh fruits and vegetables, whole-grain breads and cereal products, and fortified milk are especially rich sources of vitamins.

- **Minerals.** These nutrients are needed for sturdy bones and teeth, healthy blood, and the regulation of daily elimination. Many different foods are rich in minerals. If a pregnant woman needs mineral supplements, her doctor will prescribe them.

  Pregnant women have a particular need for iron. Iron helps prevent anemia in the mother. It also helps the developing fetus build its own blood supply. In addition, extra iron is stored in the baby's liver to be used for several months after birth, during the period when the baby's diet lacks iron. Meat is a good source of iron, especially organ meats such as liver and kidney. Other sources include beans, peas, spinach, raisins, and dates.

  Calcium and phosphorous are other minerals especially important during pregnancy. They help build the baby's

An expectant mother should drink plenty of milk. The calcium and phosphorus in milk help keep teeth and bones strong, both for the mother and for her unborn baby.

MORE ABOUT

Salt Intake

For years, pregnant women were told to avoid salt during pregnancy. Salt was assumed to promote fluid retention and swelling, which were considered problems. Moderate fluid retention is now known to be necessary for an adequate volume of blood and amniotic fluid. Abnormal fluid retention during pregnancy is caused by kidney and liver impairment rather than too much salt. Adequate salt intake during pregnancy helps maintain the proper fluid balance.

bones and teeth. The mother's body also has a greater need for calcium and phosphorous during pregnancy. Milk supplies much of the calcium and phosphorous a pregnant woman needs.

- **Carbohydrates and fats.** These nutrients are necessary for heat and energy. Good sources are fruits, vegetables, whole-grain breads and cereal products, and vegetable oils. However, too much fat and sugar are not part of a healthy diet.

The Food Guide Pyramid

Planning a daily diet that provides all the food nutrients can be quite simple. Everyone can eat a well-balanced diet by choosing foods from the basic food groups in the Food Guide Pyramid. The Food Guide Pyramid recommends various amounts from each group for children and adults, with special recommendations for pregnant women.

- **Milk, Yogurt, and Cheese Group.** A pregnant woman should drink four to five glasses of vitamin D fortified milk each day. She may choose whole milk, low-fat milk, skim milk, or buttermilk, depending on her own preferences, her particular need for calories, and her desire to limit fat. She may also substitute cheese, yogurt, and ice cream for some of the milk.

- **Meat, Poultry, Fish, Dry Beans, Eggs, and Nuts Group.** The foods in this group include all types of meat, poultry, and fish and seafood, as well as eggs, nuts, dry beans and peas, and lentils. A pregnant woman should eat three or more servings from this group every day, and she should include both fish and liver in her diet at least once a week.

- **Vegetable Group.** A pregnant woman should eat three to five servings of vegetables every day. At least one of these servings should be a deep yellow or dark green, leafy vegetable. She should also try to include vegetables high in vitamin C, such as cabbage, in her diet on a regular basis.

- **Fruit Group.** Two, three, or four servings of fruit should be included in the daily diet of a pregnant woman. One or more of these servings should be a fruit high in vitamin C, such as citrus fruit, berries, and melons.

- **Bread, Cereal, Rice, and Pasta Group.** A pregnant woman should eat six to eleven servings of these grain products every day. These may include whole-grain or enriched breads, cereals, and other grain products, such as rice, macaroni, and noodles.

OBSERVING AND PARTICIPATING

Developing Observational Skills

Pregnant women should eat nutritious foods and avoid foods that contain too much sugar. Most processed foods contain sugar, even those that don't taste sweet. Synonyms for *sugar* include *fructose, sucrose, maltose, dextrose, honey, corn syrup,* *corn sweetener, dextrin,* and *sorghum.* Since ingredients are listed on food labels in the order of greatest to least quantity, reading the labels can help pregnant women avoid foods that contain a large proportion of sugar.

GUIDED PRACTICE (continued)

Using the Photograph

Let students describe the scene in the photograph on page 162. What is the woman buying? Why? How will her choice affect her health? How will it affect the health of her developing baby?

Making Connections: Health

Ask interested students to research the causes, effects, and prevalence of lactose intolerance. What food choices should a pregnant woman make if she suffers from lactose intolerance? Have these students report their findings to the rest of the class.

Promoting Discussion

Ask the students to suggest favorite foods, and list their suggestions on the board. Then guide students in identifying the pyramid food group in which each belongs. How much of this food should a woman eat during pregnancy? What other foods — in the same group or in another group — might represent healthier choices?

Cooperative Learning

Ask students to work in groups to plan and evaluate daily menus for meals and snacks. Have each group member plan and write out a complete menu. Then have group members work together to evaluate each menu. Does it meet the Food Guide Pyramid recommendations for pregnant women? If not, what changes should be made?

Then let each group select one of its menus to share with the rest of the class.

Critical Thinking

Have students consider and share their responses to these questions: Does eating nutritiously cost more than not eating well? How can a pregnant woman who has a strictly limited food budget make the best choices for her diet? What specific recommendations would you make? Why?

Using Management Skills

Have students survey the vitamin supplements available in a drug or grocery store. Do any of the supplement packages present specific information about pregnancy? Which brand would you choose for a pregnant woman whose doctor has told her to take a vitamin supplement? Why?

Making Connections: Health

Discuss with students how nutrients interact in the body. For example, vitamin C affects how the body uses iron. The body can absorb up to three times as much iron if vitamin C is present in the same meal with a food that is high in iron. This is especially important if a woman suffers from anemia during pregnancy. Calcium and phosphorus are absorbed better by the body when they are eaten together in equal amounts. Vitamin D helps calcium and phosphorus be deposited in the bones. Why is it important for a pregnant woman to have this kind of information? What can or should be done to make such information more widely available to women during pregnancy?

Promoting Discussion

Explain to students that pregnant women who are overweight, underweight, diabetic, or vegetarian need special help in planning for good nutrition. What kinds of help do they need? What sources of help would you suggest?

Critical Thinking

Have students explain why feeding a baby a nutritious diet after birth cannot make up for poor nutrition during pregnancy.

Making Connections: Math

Let students select a specific fast-food restaurant. Ask them to use the menu to plan two nutritious meals for a pregnant woman. Have them calculate the cost and, if possible, the calories and fat content. Did they find it difficult to make nutritious choices?

Food Guide Pyramid
A Guide to Daily Food Choices

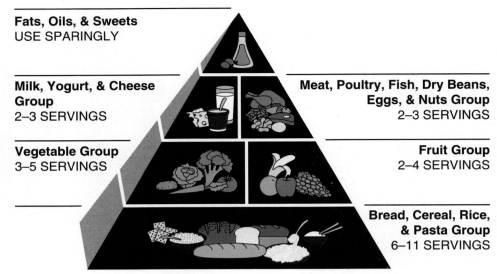

The Food Guide Pyramid shows the number of servings of each group that a person needs each day. Women who are pregnant or breast-feeding, teenagers, and young adults to age 24 need 3 servings of the milk group.

- **Fats, Oils, and Sweets Group.** The foods in this group, such as margarine and sugar, are generally high in calories and low in nutrition. They are not considered part of a healthy diet and should be used sparingly.

If a woman breast-feeds her baby, her need for extra nutrients continues after the birth. The chart above shows the Food Guide Pyramid's recommended amounts for different age groups, for pregnant women, and for nursing mothers.

There are other important dietary recommendations for pregnant women. They should drink six to eight glasses of water daily. They should also avoid rich and fried foods, which are often hard to digest and usually provide few nutrients.

Teenage Diets

In order to have a healthy baby, a woman herself must be healthy. Her diet throughout her life plays an important role in establishing her health—and the health of any babies she will have. A crash nutrition program during pregnancy, or even just before pregnancy, cannot make up for years of poor eating habits. For this reason, the diet of teenage girls is especially

---

MORE ABOUT

The Food Guide Pyramid

Following are quantities in each food group that equal one serving:

Bread and Cereal 1 slice of bread; 1/2 cup (113 g) cooked cereal, rice, or pasta; 1 ounce (28 g) cereal.

Vegetables 1/2 cup (113 g) raw or cooked vegetables; 1 cup (227 g) leafy raw vegetables; 1/4 cup (60 mL) vegetable juice.

Fruits 1 medium whole fruit or melon wedge;

1/2 cup (113 g) canned fruit; 1/4 cup (57 g) dried fruit; 3/4 cup (180 mL) fruit juice.

Milk, Cheese 1 cup (240 mL) milk or yogurt; 1 1/2 ounces (43 g) ripened cheese; 2 ounces (57 g) processed cheese.

Meat, Poultry, Fish 2 1/2 to 3 ounces (71 to 85 g) cooked lean meat, poultry, or fish; 1 1/2 cups (340 g) cooked dry beans; 3 eggs; 6 tablespoons (90 mL) peanut butter.

important. Teenagers should try to cut back on low-nutrition snacks and eat balanced meals, following the recommendations from the Food Guide Pyramid.

Improving Eating Habits

A woman who is pregnant, or who wants to become pregnant, should consider her eating habits carefully. How does her current diet compare with the recommendations of the Food Guide Pyramid? Then she should decide what changes are necessary to improve her chances of having a healthy baby.

In most cases, just a few changes can make a great difference. A woman who does not like milk, for example, can choose foods made with milk, such as yogurt, cottage cheese, or creamed soups. She may want to get some of her calcium from other foods, such as broccoli, kale, sardines, and tofu.

Protein is an especially important nutrient during pregnancy. Meat, poultry, and eggs are high in protein and other nutrients. Dried beans and peas are also good protein sources, especially when eaten in combination with enriched breads, grains, and seeds.

Weight Gain During Pregnancy

A woman usually gains about 24 to 30 pounds (10.9 to 13.6 kg) during her pregnancy. This gain is not due solely to the baby, who typically weighs 7 to 8 pounds (3.2 to 3.6 kg) at birth. The chart below shows how added weight is usually distributed.

DISTRIBUTION OF WEIGHT GAIN DURING PREGNANCY

	Pounds	Kilograms
Weight of average baby at birth	7-8	3.2-3.6
Placenta	1-2	0.45-0.9
Amniotic fluid	1½-2	0.7-0.9
Increased size of uterus and supporting muscles	2	0.9
Increase in breast tissue	1	0.45
Increase in blood volume	1½-3	0.7-1.4
Increase in fat stores	5	2.3
Increase in body fluids	5-7	2.3-3.2
Total	24-30	11.0-13.65

TEEN PARENTING

Diet and Nutrition

Because teenagers are still growing, they need more of some nutrients than adults do. This is especially true of pregnant teenagers, who must provide for their own nutrient needs as well as those of the baby. To fill these needs, a pregnant teen may need more protein, calcium, and vitamin C than the recommendations for pregnant women. Have students plan a day's menu that provides additional amounts of these three nutrients.

GUIDED PRACTICE (continued)

Cooperative Learning
Have students work in groups to develop a day's menu for a pregnant woman who is a vegetarian. Group members should be sure their menu fulfills the recommendations of the Food Guide Pyramid.

Making Connections: Writing
Ask students to consider the guidance they think pregnant teens need in improving their eating habits. What specific information would most help a pregnant teen? What information would best motivate her to improve her eating habits? Then have students plan and write a public service announcement, to be played on a popular radio station, communicating that information to pregnant teens.

Using the Chart
Guide students in reading the chart and in considering the many factors that contribute to weight gain during pregnancy. What is the importance of each factor?

Promoting Discussion
Ask students why they think the risk of fetal death and premature birth increases when a pregnant woman gains less than 20 pounds (9.1 kg).

Making Connections: Math
Have students work in groups to make a pie chart showing the components of weight gain during pregnancy.

Critical Thinking
Point out that some women might look at the chart, Distribution of Weight Gain During Pregnancy, and think that if they gained just 5 pounds (2.3 kg) less, they could avoid the 5-pound (2.3-kg) increase in fat stores. What is wrong with that reasoning? What would you say to a woman who planned to restrict her weight gain in that way?

GUIDED PRACTICE (continued)

Promoting Discussion

Guide students in discussing the possible effects of pregnancy on a woman's career. What kinds of work might a woman need to give up during pregnancy? Why? What special challenges might a working woman face in maintaining a nutritious diet or in obtaining adequate rest? How might such factors as nausea, fatigue, and the need to wear maternity clothing affect her image and her on-the-job performance? How might pregnancy affect a woman's chance of being hired for a new job, in spite of any pertinent legislation?

Using the Photograph

Let students describe the activity of the woman in the photograph on this page. Under what circumstances is physical activity like this good for a pregnant woman? When could it be harmful to her? Why should a pregnant woman check with her doctor or health care advisor before starting a new exercise program?

Promoting Discussion

Let students share their ideas to these questions: If a woman travels during the later part of her pregnancy, what information should she obtain in advance about the places she plans to visit or pass through? Why? How might she obtain that information?

Family Focus

Family discussion can often help lessen worries and fears about pregnancy and parenting. Have students create and perform skits depicting the following situations:

- Husband and wife discussing the wife's depression, even though she is happy about the upcoming baby.

- Pregnant woman and her mother discussing the woman's concerns over the health of the baby.

- Pregnant woman talking to a friend about whether her husband will find her attractive during pregnancy.

- Husband and wife discussing how they will meet their bills for the pregnancy and birth.

Gaining at least 20 pounds (9.1 kg) is an essential part of ensuring a healthy baby. There is an increased risk of fetal death among pregnant women who gain less than that amount. Also, mothers who gain less than 20 pounds (9.1 kg) during their pregnancy are twice as likely to give birth prematurely.

Many doctors recommend that a woman gain no more than 30 pounds (13.6 kg) during a pregnancy. However, it is never a good idea for an expectant mother to restrict her intake of nutritious foods. Pregnancy is not the time to go on a weight-loss diet. Moderate exercise and a diet that excludes sugary, fatty foods can help a woman keep her weight gain within the recommended levels.

Personal Care and Activities

In addition to practicing good nutrition, an expectant mother should take good care of herself in other ways. She should avoid alcohol, tobacco, and all drugs or medications. She should also make a point of getting plenty of rest and of exercising regularly but moderately.

- **Rest.** The need for rest varies from individual to individual. To maintain a feeling of well-being, a pregnant woman should get ample rest. Because schedules often prevent naps during the day, frequent breaks may be very refreshing. It is important for a pregnant woman to take such breaks or naps and to get plenty of sleep each night.

Regular exercise can help a pregnant woman stay fit and feeling well. As long as she is careful not to tire herself out, she can continue most of the physical activities she enjoys.

MORE ABOUT

Maternal Nutrition

Women who are underweight are sometimes malnourished, especially if they are strict dieters. According to the American College of Obstetricians and Gynecologists, a woman is likely to be malnourished if she is pregnant under 16 years of age; smokes, drinks, or abuses drugs; is a food-fad-

dist; is anemic; is poor; or has had three or more pregnancies within two years. Although overweight women generally have a sufficient store of nutrients for themselves and the child, their added weight makes them more apt to suffer pregnancy complications.

- **Exercise.** Moderate exercise can help keep an expectant mother in good physical condition. It can also maintain appropriate weight gain and make the pregnancy more comfortable.

  Many doctors recommend exercise such as walking, swimming, or biking during pregnancy. Special programs of prenatal aerobics are offered in some communities. Hobbies such as tennis and golf can also be continued. However, pregnancy is not a time to begin any strenuous new activities.

- **Hygiene.** Daily baths or showers are especially important during pregnancy. The skin helps maintain correct body temperature and eliminate waste, so it should be kept clean. Just before bed is a good time for a bath or shower, because the warm water encourages relaxation and sleep.

- **Other activities.** A pregnant woman usually maintains the same work routines she had before pregnancy. If she works outside the home, she can continue to do so as long as she wants, unless her doctor advises differently. She can also continue to do daily household activities.

The most important point for a woman to remember is that her lifestyle should not change radically during pregnancy. Moderation may be necessary in some circumstances, but on the whole, she should continue her life as before.

Maternity Clothes

By about the fourth or fifth month of pregnancy, a woman usually needs special clothing. Attractive maternity clothes need not be expensive, but they must be comfortable. They should be loose enough to allow for freedom of movement and for good circulation. For her own health and the health of her developing baby, a pregnant woman should always avoid wearing tight clothing.

Simple garments are the best choices in maternity wear. An expectant mother should consider how each garment will fit in the last month of pregnancy. Cotton knit fabrics stretch to allow room for the growing baby. Skirts and pants may include a stretch panel for comfort.

Comfortable, low-heeled shoes with good support are recommended throughout pregnancy. A pregnant woman should avoid wearing high heels. They throw the body out of balance and increase the risk of falling.

By shopping carefully, an expectant mother can put together a basic wardrobe of mix-and-match items that will see her through many different occasions.

HEALTHY FAMILIES/HEALTHY CHILDREN

Health and Safety

The following guidelines will help the pregnant woman avoid injury and get the most benefit from exercising:

- Exercise daily.
- Use smooth movements; avoid jerking or bouncing.
- Exercise on a firm surface.

- Breathe continuously while doing an exercise; holding the breath increases pressure on the pelvic floor and stomach muscles and can cause dizziness.
- Do not continue exercise that is painful.
- Begin with a few repetitions of easy exercises; then increase the number and difficulty.

INDEPENDENT PRACTICE

Journal Writing

Ask students to think about their current lifestyle — their daily activities, their habits, the kinds of food they eat, and the amount of exercise and rest they get. Then ask them to consider the lifestyle they would have if they were following the suggestions in this section for a healthy pregnancy. What changes would be necessary? How would they feel about making those changes? Why? Have students respond by writing journal entries about caring for a developing baby during pregnancy.

Student Workbook

Have students complete "Find the File That Fits" in the Student Workbook.

Extension

Let students work independently or in small groups to complete one or more of these extension activities:

- In the past, pregnancy was often considered an illness, and women were encouraged to withdraw from their normal activities. Research attitudes toward pregnancy in the past or in other countries. Then make up diary entries for a week from the point of view of a pregnant woman in another time or country.

- Read about the process of enrichment. What foods are usually enriched? What is added to them? How does this affect their nutritional value? Then write a short report summarizing your findings.

- Medical professionals often consider pregnancy in terms of three trimesters. Conduct research to find answers to these questions: Which part of a pregnancy is included in each trimester? What are the advantages and disadvantages of considering pregnancy in these stages? Share your findings with the rest of the class.

- Plan an exercise program for a pregnant woman who is physically fit and was very active before she became pregnant. Share your planned program with classmates.

ASSESS

CHECKING COMPREHENSION

Assign students to write their responses to the Check Your Understanding questions in the Section 1 Review. Answers to the questions are given below.

EVALUATE

Have students complete the Chapter 6, Section 1 TCR quiz.

Reteaching

Working with small groups, help students discuss this situation: Maria and her husband want to start a family. For several months, Maria has been hoping for indications of pregnancy. What signs should she look for? When she notices those signs, what should she do? Why? Should Maria be making any lifestyle changes now? If so, what?

Enrichment

Have students research various relaxation exercises and select the exercises most suitable for pregnant woman to compile a booklet. The booklet should be illustrated and include the importance of relaxation during pregnancy. If possible, have the booklet duplicated and distributed to pregnant women.

Extension

Invite three pregnant women to a panel discussion about how to ensure healthy pregnancies. Prepare questions ahead.

BUILDING SELF-ESTEEM

Pregnant women can experience nearly constant fatigue. Care should be taken to get ample rest because fatigue enhances stress and negative emotions such as anxiety and fear.

CLOSE

Ask students to identify the single most important advice pregnant women should follow to ensure a healthy pregnancy.

BUILDING SELF-ESTEEM

Emotional Support During Pregnancy

*T*oo much stress or too many emotional upsets are not healthy for anyone. An expectant mother should talk over any upsetting problems or situations with members of her support team, including her partner, friends, nurse, childbirth educator, or physician. She should turn to professionals for assistance with prolonged feelings of anxiety, depression, or stress.

Emotional Health During Pregnancy

Pregnancy is a time of emotional adjustments for both the expectant mother and the prospective father. It is normal for both parents-to-be to have some concerns about the baby's arrival. Talking over their concerns with each other and with family members can be reassuring.

Many of the mother's emotional changes may be related to her own physical changes. Pregnancy causes hormonal changes, and these may result in mood swings. A pregnant woman may shift unexpectedly from happiness to distress—and then back again, for no apparent reason. It is natural for even the most even-tempered woman to feel upset and worried at times during her pregnancy. It is important for the couple to discuss these emotional swings, to share their feelings, and to make plans for stress reduction.

In general, however, a pregnant woman who takes good physical care of herself—especially by exercising moderately and relaxing often—is helping assure her mental and emotional health, as well as her physical health and the health of her developing baby.

SECTION 1 REVIEW

CHECK YOUR UNDERSTANDING

1. List three early signs of pregnancy.
2. What is the most reliable way for a woman to determine whether she is pregnant?
3. List two discomforts pregnant women sometimes have. List two symptoms that may indicate serious complications during pregnancy.
4. What are the basic food nutrients? Which of these does a woman need during pregnancy?
5. Why does a woman need extra iron during pregnancy? Which foods are good sources of iron?
6. Why is weight gain important during pregnancy? What is the recommended weight gain?

DISCUSS AND DISCOVER

1. Do you think an unmarried teenager faces any special problems in having a healthy pregnancy? If so, what are those problems? How would you recommend that she cope with them? If not, why not?

Observing & Participating

Over the course of a week, take time to observe pregnant women in public places, such as malls, parks, and grocery stores. Notice the kinds of activities these pregnant women undertake. Describe how each woman's pregnancy appears to affect her activities. If possible, interview one or more women to discover what adjustments she has made in personal care and activities.

SECTION 1 REVIEW

1. Any three: missed period; mild ache or feeling of fullness in lower abdomen; fatigue; need to urinate frequently; tenderness in breasts; periods of nausea.
2. Be tested by a physician.
3. Any two: nausea; sleepiness; heartburn; shortness of breath; varicose veins; leg cramps; lower back pain. Any two: vaginal bleeding; unusual weight gain; thirst, urination, abdominal pain, headaches, swelling, and vomiting; fever; blurred vision or dizziness; prolonged backache; increased vaginal mucus.
4. Protein, vitamins, minerals, carbohydrates and fats; all.
5. Helps prevent anemia in mother and helps fetus build its own blood supply; organ meats, beans, peas, spinach, raisins, dates.
6. Failing to gain at least 20 pounds increases risk of fetal death and prematurity; 24 to 30 pounds.

Getting Ready for the New Arrival

OBJECTIVES

- Describe how parents-to-be can plan for a baby's care.
- Discuss the purchases and other preparations parents-to-be should make.
- Give examples of how to estimate and reduce the expenses of having a baby.

The nine months of pregnancy provide parents-to-be with an opportunity to consider and adjust to the changes that are taking place in their lives. During this time, the expectant parents should make plans and decisions as they prepare for the arrival of a new family member.

TERMS TO LEARN

budget
fixed expenses
flexible expenses
formula
maternity leave
paternity leave
postnatal period

Roles, Responsibilities, and Decisions

During pregnancy, every couple must decide how they will meet the responsibilities of child care. They need to consider many factors—each partner's goals, skills, schedule, and personal characteristics, as well as the financial needs of the family.

In many families, both parents work outside the home. For these couples, decisions about arrangements for child care are especially important.

Many new mothers who work outside the home take a **maternity leave**, *time off from a job allowing a woman to give birth, recuperate, and care for her new baby.* A woman's employer may offer leave ranging from a few weeks to several months. During her leave, a new mother is able to care for her baby full-time before returning to her job. Some employers offer **paternity leave**, *time off from a job allowing a father to care for his new baby.* These leave arrangements allow parents to spend time with their baby during the important early stages of development.

MORE ABOUT

Maternity Leave Benefits
The size of the company a woman works for, the location of the company, and the type of job a woman has all affect her maternity leave benefits. Women who hold white-collar jobs in large firms receive the most substantial benefits during maternity leave. Women who live in states that mandate short-term disability leave (which covers pregnancy) also receive more benefits than those who live in states without such laws.

SECTION 2
Getting Ready for the New Arrival
Pages 169-181

FOCUS

SECTION 2 RESOURCES

Teacher's Classroom Resources
- Enrichment 15
- Reteaching 15
- Section 2 Quiz

Student Workbook
- Budgeting for Baby

SECTION OVERVIEW

In Section 2, students consider the many decisions and the preparation that expectant parents make during pregnancy and examine the choices that parents-to-be must make regarding care for the new baby, child-rearing practices, and preparation of other children in the family. They also read about parents' options for feeding the new baby, consider clothing and equipment needs, furnishings for the baby's room, and the process of planning to reduce and meet the expenses involved in having and caring for a child.

MOTIVATOR

Ask student volunteers to role-play this situation: A married woman has just learned that she is pregnant, and she hurries home to tell her husband the news. They are both taken by surprise; they begin to discuss the decisions and arrangements they must make in preparation for the baby's arrival. At the close of the role-playing, encourage the rest of the class to respond and to share other ideas. Then have students read Section 2 for further ideas about the preparations expectant parents make.

USING TERMS TO LEARN

Discuss the seven terms introduced in Section 2. Point out the prefix *post*, meaning "after," in *postnatal*. How do the meanings of the prefixes pre and post clarify the words *prenatal* and *postnatal*.

TEACH

Pages 169-173

- **Roles, Responsibilities, and Decisions**
- **Preparing for Parenthood**
- **Other Children in the Family**
- **Decisions About Feeding**

GUIDED PRACTICE

Promoting Discussion

Help students consider the importance of decisions parents make about their own employment. How do these decisions directly affect a baby's life and development? How do they affect the parents' sense of security and happiness? How do those effects influence the baby's early experiences?

Using the Photograph

Encourage students to describe the scene in the photograph on this page. Then ask questions such as these: Why has the mother traditionally stayed home with children? How and why has this traditional practice changed? Do you think most couples would prefer to have one parent at home full-time? Why or why not? What would the advantages and disadvantages be?

Cooperative Learning

Let students work in groups to discuss factors that couples should take into account when deciding on answers to these questions: Should one parent quit work to care for a new baby? If so, which parent? Ask the members of each group to agree on and list the five most important factors; then ask the members of each group to share their list with the rest of the class.

IT'S MORE THAN A NAME

The imagery and beauty of Native American names is a treasure worth preserving. Traditionally, Hopi newborns are given a name in a ritual that begins before dawn twenty days after birth. With all relatives assembled, the grandmother washes the baby then rubs the head four times with a perfectly formed ear of corn. The same rite is performed on the baby's paternal aunts who each suggest a name based on the father's clan. As dawn approaches, the grandmother chooses a name, then takes the infant outside where they both pay homage to the rising sun. A grand feast follows.

Later, when the child has reached the age of initiation, another name is added to symbolize a new birth. Today, babies are often given Christian names and the father's last name.

If their finances permit it, a couple may decide that one parent will stay home to care for the child on a long-term basis. In most of these situations, the mother is the one who becomes the primary caregiver. Some couples reverse the traditional roles either temporarily or permanently. The father stays home to care for the house and children, and the mother becomes the primary wage earner.

Regardless of who is primarily responsible for daily care tasks, every parent should know the basics of child care. This allows the parents to share the work—and the special joys—of providing routine care for their baby.

In many families, neither parent stays home to care for the baby after the first few months. A couple may decide that both must work to provide enough income for the family; a couple may decide that both want the satisfactions of employment outside the home; a single parent may discover that he or she must work outside the home to support the family. Whatever the reasons for this decision, parents are then faced with another decision: Who will take care of the baby? Some parents can arrange to work at different times, so that they can take turns caring for the baby. Other parents arrange to have a relative or other caregiver stay with the baby, either in the baby's home or in another home. Other parents choose to take their baby to an infant care center. Parents need to consider all their options carefully.

Some parents must find someone to care for the baby while they return to work. Infant care centers are one option. It is best to consider this decision early so that any necessary arrangements can be made in advance.

Cultural Exchange

Ask students to discover the source and/or significance of their names as well as any tradition or ritual associated with them.

CLASSROOM MANAGEMENT

Cross-Reference
More about substitute child care is found in Chapter 19, pages 540-569.

Preparing for Parenthood

Most parents-to-be wonder whether they will be able to take good care of their child. Considering all the different ideas about children and parenting they have probably heard, it is not surprising that expectant parents are concerned. Even the most confident mothers and fathers worry about doing the right thing.

A couple should discuss their ideas about parenting methods with each other before the baby is born. For example, they might share their ideas about questions such as these: What attitudes and approaches to discipline do we want to use? What part will organized religion play in our children's lives? How will we share the responsibilities for earning money and for caring for our children? What goals and aspirations do we have for our children? Of course, parents cannot plan what they will do in every possible situation. As they become experienced in parenting, some of their ideas may change. However, by agreeing ahead of time on general philosophies of raising children, parents can reduce conflict later on.

Preparing for parenthood also involves anticipating changes in the other roles parents fill. Parents may be spouses, family members, workers, students, volunteers, and citizens. As they undertake new responsibilities in caring for children, parents may find they have less time and energy available for their other responsibilities. Couples should discuss their concerns and problems about these roles with each other and with friends or family members. They should also strive to use good management practices in balancing their roles.

Other Children in the Family

Many parents are aware that a new baby will require some adjustments for the other children in the family. The reactions of an older child to a new sibling depend largely on how well prepared the child was before the arrival of the newborn. During pregnancy, parents should include the older child in discussions about the pregnancy and about plans for the baby. Giving the older child opportunities to help get the room ready will make the child feel involved.

Parents should be prepared for a wide range of attitudes toward the new baby. It is normal for the older child to respond with feelings of jealousy and confusion, as well as excitement and love. These feelings will come and go as the baby grows and changes. Many parents find that open communication and acceptance of each child's feelings will help foster a positive relationship between siblings.

OBSERVING AND PARTICIPATING

Learning Through Participation

Although unheard of not long ago, more families are allowing older children to attend the birth of a new baby. Some parents want to eliminate the separation from the mother that childbirth usually entails. Some parents want children to experience the joy of the birth process, and others want the children to share in the early bonding with the new baby. A decision to allow children at the birth depends on the ages, wishes, and personalities of the children as well as the parents' ability to be comfortable with children present during the childbirth process. Obviously, children have to be well prepared for their participation.

GUIDED PRACTICE (continued)

Practicing Decision Making

Present the following situation to the class: Renee loves her job in fashion sales. She will miss it if she does not return after the baby is born. However, she and Harry do not like the idea of leaving their baby all day with someone else. Harry cannot easily quit his construction job since he makes more money than Renee does. Still, if Renee does not work, finances will be tight. Renee is afraid that she will not be content at home all the time, especially if there isn't money for occasional extras.

Ask students to explain what they think Renee and Harry should do. Why?

Critical Thinking

Encourage students to share their ideas in response to this question: When is the best time for a couple to discuss their ideas about parenting? Ask students to rank the following times from most to least preferable:

- When planning a pregnancy.
- During pregnancy.
- Before marriage.
- On a case-by-case basis, as issues arise.

Promoting Discussion

While waiting for the baby to be born, what can expectant parents do to learn more about children and parenting? What can they do that will help them balance parenthood with the many other roles they fill?

Making Connections: Psychology

Have pairs of students work together to plan and perform a skit showing how parenting methods of a mother and father might differ. What effect would this lack of agreement have on the couple? The child? How can the situations in the skits be resolved?

Making Connections: Reading

Have students find, read, and evaluate children's books that help siblings adjust to a new baby in the family. (Examples are *The New Baby* by Fred Rogers and *Daddy's New Baby* by Judith Vigna.)

GUIDED PRACTICE (continued)

Promoting Discussion

Let students share their responses to these questions: Why do most medical experts recommend breast-feeding? What are the advantages of breast-feeding for the baby?

Using Management Skills

Have students compute the cost of ten 8-ounce (240-mL) bottles of different types of formula. Include homemade, powdered, concentrated, and ready-to-use. What factors besides cost must be considered in deciding which to use? Which would they recommend using?

Practicing Decision-Making

Present the following situation to the class: Carla and Wayne do not agree on whether their baby should be breast-fed or bottle-fed. Wayne wants Carla to breast-feed because he feels the baby will be healthier. Carla plans to return to work soon after the baby's birth; she feels it is not worth the effort to breast-feed for only six weeks.

Ask students to identify the source of Wayne and Carla's disagreement. Is one of them "right"? If so, which one? Why? How do you think Wayne and Carla can resolve their differences?

INDEPENDENT PRACTICE

Journal Writing

Ask students to write journal entries expressing their own feelings about feeding infants. Which feeding method would you prefer for your own children someday, breast- or bottle-feeding? Is your choice clear, or does it depend on other factors, such as your age and your work when you have a child? Explain the facts and the emotions that underlie your opinion.

Student Workbook

Have students complete "Budgeting for Baby" in the Student Workbook.

Many hospitals offer special programs for young children who will soon be welcoming home a new baby brother or sister. This helps the youngsters understand and feel part of what is happening.

Feeding is a time for establishing close bonds with baby. Whether breast-feeding or bottle-feeding, allow plenty of time in a relaxed, unhurried atmosphere.

Decisions About Feeding

Will the new baby be breast-fed or bottle-fed? This is one of the significant decisions parents make before the arrival of the baby. Many parents discuss their ideas and reach a decision during pregnancy.

When choosing a method for feeding their baby, parents should be aware that experts consider breast-feeding the best source of nutrition for human infants. On the basis of research that proves the benefits of breast milk for the baby, medical experts recommend breast-feeding whenever possible, for as long as possible.

Breast-feeding has many advantages. Breast milk is best suited to the nutritional needs of a baby. It also provides immunity against many diseases. In addition, experts feel that the physical closeness of breast-feeding helps create a special bond between mother and child. Parents who decide to bottle-feed their baby can achieve this same closeness, too, by holding the baby close and providing caring attention during every feeding.

Bottle-feeding with formula is a convenient alternative to breast-feeding. **Formula**, *a mixture of milk or milk substitute, water, and nutrients*, provides nearly the same nutrition as breast milk. It may be mixed at home or purchased in a variety of convenient forms. Powdered, concentrated, and ready-to-use formulas are available.

The decision to breast-feed or bottle-feed is a personal one. It will depend on the mother's anatomy, schedule, and lifestyle.

MORE ABOUT

Breast Milk

Most of the calories in human milk are provided by fat, which helps the infant's digestion. Human milk contains a greater percentage of lactose (milk sugar) than cow's milk. Lactose is easily metabolized and helps the infant absorb calcium. Whey is the primary protein in human milk, and casein is the primary protein in cow's milk. Whey is more easily digested by the infant than is casein. Milk varies in composition even within a feeding. The foremilk is the first milk released and is about one-third of the volume of milk in the feeding. The hindmilk, or remaining two-thirds of the milk, contains more fat and protein than the foremilk.

Many mothers successfully breast-feed for certain feedings and supplement with bottles at other feedings. However parents decide to feed their baby, they should remember that the baby responds to the feeling and care that accompany each feeding.

The chart below lists some of the pros and cons of both feeding methods.

COMPARING BREAST-FEEDING AND BOTTLE-FEEDING

BREAST-FEEDING

ADVANTAGES

* Creates a bond through physical closeness with the mother.
* Provides some natural immunity against diseases.
* Speeds the return of the mother's uterus to normal size.
* Causes fewer digestive upsets.
* Is conveniently available at all times.
* Reduces baby's risks of allergies.

DISADVANTAGES

* Prevents father from participating in feeding.
* Limits medications the mother can safely take.
* May be painful for some mothers.
* May be difficult because of work schedule.
* May become difficult if anxiety or illness interferes with production of milk.

BOTTLE-FEEDING

ADVANTAGES

* Allows father to participate in feeding.
* Allows mother to have a more flexible schedule.
* Permits baby to be fed by anyone, anywhere.

DISADVANTAGES

* Can be expensive.
* Involves greater chance of allergies.
* Involves risk that baby may not be given close physical contact during feeding.

HEALTHY FAMILIES/HEALTHY CHILDREN

Health and Safety

When a nursing mother smokes, the nicotine from the cigarette stays in breast milk for up to eight hours. Some studies have shown that smoking increases nausea, colic, and diarrhea in babies. Heavy smoking tends to reduce milk production. Women who smoke breast-feed less than women who don't.

INDEPENDENT PRACTICE (continued)

Extension
Have students read at least two magazine articles that advise parents on how and when to feed newborns. Ask students to write brief summaries of the articles and then to compare and discuss them.

ASSESS

CHECKING COMPREHENSION
Ask students to identify and discuss various child care options expectant parents should consider.

EVALUATE
Have students list two things parents can do to help older siblings prepare for a new baby.

Reteaching
Working with small groups, help students review some of the practical preparations parents need to make before the birth of a baby. Then ask each student to list at least six questions expectant parents should ask—and answer—about their own roles and responsibilities as new parents.

Enrichment
Ask students to investigate federal or state laws on parental leave. Are the laws different for maternity and paternity leave? Have students prepare and present brief oral reports summarizing their findings.

Extension
Invite a lactation specialist to speak to the class about breast-feeding. If a specialist is not available, you might have students write to La Leche International for information; the mailing address is 9616 Minneapolis Avenue, Franklin Park, IL 60131.

CLOSE

Go around the class, asking each student to identify a decision expectant parents need to make during pregnancy.

GUIDED PRACTICE

Promoting Discussion

Encourage students to share their own ideas about acquiring basic supplies for a new baby. Why do many expectant parents spend more than they need to on such items as baby clothes, cribs, and strollers? Does this extra spending make sense? How can it be avoided?

Practicing Decision Making

Have students determine specific low-cost ways to solve the following problem: Trina and Juan live in a small two-room apartment, which has very little storage space. When Trina bought some cans of formula and clothes for the baby they expect, there was no place to put them, so she left them in boxes on the floor in the corner of the living area. They have not yet bought a crib because they cannot figure out where to put it. Trina and Juan cannot afford to move, but they don't know where they are going to put the baby's food, clothing, equipment, and toys.

Critical Thinking

Have students work in groups to suggest how a baby's room could be adapted for a parent in a wheelchair. Have the members of each group report their conclusions to the class.

SAFETY TIP

Ask students to find out whether local hospitals require or provide infant car seats when a newborn leaves the hospital.

SAFETY TIP

Automobile accidents are the leading cause of death among young children; a secure safety restraint is the best protection a baby or child can have against injury or death in a car accident. These facts make an infant car seat a necessity for any baby who rides in a car. Beginning with the ride home from the hospital or birthing center, an infant should be buckled into an appropriate car seat every time he or she is taken out in a car.

Clothing and Equipment Needs

Basic supplies for a baby include clothing, bedding, feeding equipment, bathing supplies, and travel equipment. Wise parents begin with only a minimum number of the basic items that the baby will need at birth. The family may receive some of these items—as well as later necessities—as gifts or as loans.

As a rule, the most appreciated baby gifts are practical items. Family members and friends who plan to buy baby gifts should be encouraged to ask the parents about their particular needs. In many cases, a dozen extra diapers or a simple sleeper will be more welcome than a fancy outfit.

The chart on pages 175-176 shows basic needs for a typical baby. This list merely suggests possibilities. Expectant parents may get specific suggestions from a doctor or from family and friends. Advice is also given at the hospital and at classes for new parents.

Baby's Room

Every baby needs a special place to sleep. If it is available, a separate room for the newborn is best. During the first six months, most babies sleep for 15 to 18 hours every day.

Of course, many families cannot provide a new baby with his or her own room. Parents should remember that love and pleasant conditions are more important than a spacious home. If the baby cannot have a separate room, a quiet corner of a room can be made into the baby's special place. A room divider can be used to provide the baby—and other family members—with a sense of privacy.

Adequate and convenient storage in the baby's room makes daily routines easier. Clothing and supplies can be kept in many types of storage areas—closets, drawers, stacking cubes, or shelves, for example.

CLASSROOM MANAGEMENT

Cross-Reference

Refer students to the Positive Parenting Skills feature of this chapter (pages 188-189) for a more thorough treatment of guidelines for the selection of infant equipment.

BASIC BABY SUPPLIES

DIAPERING NEEDS

+ Disposable diapers. (Quantity depends on whether they will be for regular use or occasional use.)
+ 3-4 dozen cloth diapers (if chosen for regular use).
+ Diaper pins (for cloth diapers).
+ 4-6 waterproof pants (for cloth diapers).
+ 6-10 washcloths.
+ Diaper-rash ointment.
+ Covered diaper pail.
+ Clothes basket or hamper.

CLOTHING

+ 6-8 undershirts.
+ 4-6 one-piece footed sleepers.
+ 4-6 gowns.
+ 6 cotton receiving blankets.
+ 1 warm outer wrapping blanket.
+ 1 sweater and cap set.
+ 1-2 sun hats or bonnets.
+ 1 dress-up outfit (optional).
+ Coat (optional).
+ Mittens (optional).

FEEDING EQUIPMENT

+ 6-8 large bottles (8-ounce or 237-mL) if the baby is bottle-fed.
+ 2-3 large bottles (8-ounce or 237-mL) if the baby is breast-fed.
+ Breast pump and pads.
+ Plastic bottles for storing breast milk.
+ 2-4 small bottles (4-ounce or 118-mL) for water and juice.
+ Nipples (the same number as bottles, plus a few extra).
+ Bottle caps (the same number as bottles).
+ Bottle and nipple brush.
+ Saucepan for hot water to warm bottle (optional).
+ Bibs.
+ High chair.

(Continued on next page)

HEALTHY FAMILIES/HEALTHY CHILDREN

First Aid Supplies for Babies

Elaborate first aid supplies are not needed for babies. However, keep a separate stock that is easy to reach and kept locked. This supply might include:

• Assorted adhesive bandages
• Sterile gauze
• Adhesive tape
• Nonaspirin pain and fever reducer
• Antiseptic liquid to disinfect caregiver's hands
• A large, laundered hankerchief, sealed in a plastic bag, to cover serious wounds
• Scissors
• A soothing lotion for sunburn or rashes
• Insect sting reliever
• Infant thermometer
• Squared-end tweezers and needles for splinters, including matches for sterilizing

---

GUIDED PRACTICE (continued)

Using the Chart
Guide students in reading and discussing the Basic Baby Supplies chart on this page and the next page. Let volunteers describe and explain the uses of each suggested item.

Making Connections: Science
Ask interested students to research the environmental effects of the use of disposable diapers. What problems do these diapers pose? How have the manufacturers of disposable diapers tried to deal with those problems? With what success? Is the use of disposable diapers increasing or decreasing? Why? Have students share their findings with the rest of the class.

Making Connections: Writing
Thousand of infants and children are injured each year while using unsafe products. It is the responsibility of parents to see that children's furniture, clothing, and toys are properly made and used. The U.S. Consumer Product Safety Commission is a regulatory agency that develops and enforces federal safety standards. Have students write the CPSC, Washington, DC 20207, for information on safety issues for infants.

Using Management Skills
Explain to students that full-term healthy babies usually double their weight in the first five months. Newborn clothing is generally wearable up to 13 to 14 pounds (5.9 to 6.4 kg). If a baby weighs 7 pounds (3.2 kg) at birth, how long would the baby probably be able to wear newborn-sized clothing?

Making Connections: Math
Tell students that a newborn baby typically uses 350 disposable diapers in the first month. Have students investigate to find out how much the diapers would cost for one month. Assume that the baby continues to use 350 diapers per month and is toilet trained at age three. Calculate the approximate total cost of disposable diapers for one child.

Promoting Discussion

Ask students how each of the items listed under Bathing and Other Supplies is used. Why are special nail scissors needed? When and how should a baby's nails be cut? Why does a baby need a special comb and brush set? What kind of thermometer should be used? When and how might parents need to take an infant's temperature?

Using Management Skills

Have students investigate what makes a car seat safe. Then ask them to price and evaluate at least three different car seats. If they were parents, would they purchase any of the three? Why?

Cooperative Learning

Have students work in small groups to make a floor plan or drawing showing their concept of an ideal nursery. What type of furniture and equipment would it have? How would it be decorated? Allow the members of each group to share their plans with the rest of the class.

Using Management Skills

Explain that some items of baby furniture serve two purposes, such as a crib that converts to a changing table. Have students investigate the costs of such furniture and the pieces each would replace. Are the dual-purpose pieces of furniture cheaper than the combined cost of the other two? Would the dual-purpose pieces be a good buy? Why?

Promoting Discussion

Let students explain what a bassinet is. Do you consider a bassinet a luxury or a necessity? Why?

Critical Thinking

Ask students to identify the factors that make having a first baby more expensive than having a second or third. What particular expenses are involved in having a second or third child?

Cooperative Learning

Let students work in groups to list specific sources for inexpensive or secondhand baby supplies.

BASIC BABY SUPPLIES (cont'd.)

BEDDING/BEDROOM

* 4 fitted crib sheets.
* Waterproof mattress cover.
* 2-4 absorbent pads.
* 2 lightweight blankets or spreads.
* 1 heavier crib blanket.
* Bumper pad (fits around inside of crib just above mattress; keeps baby's arms and legs in, drafts out).
* Storage space, such as a chest of drawers.
* Wastebasket.

BATHING AND OTHER SUPPLIES

* Baby bathtub or other container.
* Mild, pure soap.
* Baby shampoo.
* Several soft washcloths.
* 2 soft cotton bath towels.
* Cotton balls.
* Baby oil and baby lotion.
* Blunt-tipped nail scissors.
* Baby comb and brush set.
* Thermometer.

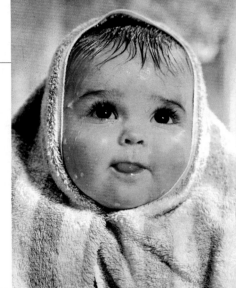

TRAVEL EQUIPMENT

* Car seat (safety approved).
* Tote bag for carrying supplies.
* Stroller, carriage, or infant carrier (optional).

The baby's first bed does not need to be a crib, or even a bassinet. A clothes basket, long and wide enough to allow the baby to stretch out, will do nicely. With slight padding to protect against rough sides, and extra padding on the bottom to function as a firm "mattress," the basket can serve as a good, inexpensive portable bed. See Positive Parenting Skills "Safety Guidelines for Baby Equipment" on pages 188-189.

CLASSROOM MANAGEMENT

Resources Beyond the Classroom

Thousands of infants and children are injured each year while using unsafe products. It is the responsibility of parents to see that children's furniture, clothing, and toys are properly made and used. The U.S. Consumer Product Safety Commission is a regulatory agency that develops and enforces federal safety standards. Have students survey brands of toys, clothing, and furniture to find safety labels. Ask them to list instructions included on garments and warnings about possible misuse of furniture. What standards are set for toy manufacturers?

Basic Supplies: The Diaper–Changing Area

Parents need to plan a place where the baby can be changed and dressed. Special changing tables are available for this use. However, any surface that is a convenient height and that is padded with blankets can serve the same purpose. The top of a chest of drawers can be used as a changing table if it is the correct height and size. A crib with adjustable mattress height also works well. Whatever changing area is used, all caregivers must never leave the baby unattended on it. They should pay constant attention to protect the baby from a fall and possible injuries.

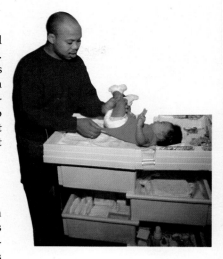

Secondhand Equipment

Baby supplies and equipment need not be new, even for a first baby. Many parents-to-be are able to reduce their expenses significantly by borrowing major items or by buying secondhand items. Relatives and friends often share needed supplies among themselves. Expectant parents can frequently find bargains at neighborhood yard sales, rummage sales, and secondhand clothing stores. Cribs, bedding, and baby clothes are all available secondhand for only a fraction of the cost when new. These items may show little wear, because babies outgrow things quickly.

Everything that is borrowed or purchased secondhand should be thoroughly washed, even though it may appear clean. Special caution should be taken with equipment. Secondhand or borrowed cribs, playpens, car seats, and other items should meet current safety standards.

Estimating Expenses

The financial aspects of having a baby are a concern for most parents. The costs do not end with the hospital bill for birth, or even with the first few years. They continue until the child can live independently. A couple who understands all the costs involved can plan early to meet the expenses of having a child.

The expenses of having a baby begin with the pregnant woman's first appointment with a physician. Many doctors charge a lump sum that covers prenatal care, delivery, and the **postnatal period**—that is, *the time after the baby's birth.*

The hospitalization fee is another major expense of birth. Costs for a hospital stay vary, but they usually depend on the type of delivery the mother has, the medical needs of the baby, and the length of time the mother and baby stay in the hospital. Extra charges are often made for laboratory tests, medicine, and supplies. Expectant parents can check with local hospitals for current rates and policies.

OBSERVING AND PARTICIPATING

Learning Through Participation

• Encourage students to use these guidelines when changing a baby's diaper.

• Place all needed items for changing the baby in a bucket or box that is easy to carry so that the baby can be changed easily in any location.

• Wear a pair of clean rubber gloves if the baby is wet and slippery.

• Do not place toiletries on an overhead shelf; they could accidentally fall on the baby.

• Use S-hooks and shower curtain rings to attach toys, pacifiers, and other items to the changing table or shelves. (Be sure the hooks and rings are not small enough to be swallowed.)

• Use a plastic doll to practice bathing and changing the baby so that you know everything is within reach.

GUIDED PRACTICE (continued)

Using Management Skills
Point out to students that although used baby furniture can be a big money saver, it needs to be evaluated carefully for safety. For example, older cribs may have slats that are too widely spaced. An old high chair may have legs that do not form a stable base, and an old infant seat may not have a skid-proof base. The paint on some older furniture and toys may contain lead. Ask students what other hazards used baby furniture might have.

Suggest to students that when a piece of baby equipment or furniture has been assembled for the first time, it should be tested by placing a 10-pound (4.5-kg) sack of potatoes or pet food where the baby will lie. What are the advantages of this kind of testing?

Promoting Discussion
Ask students whether they think most people consider the financial impact of having a child. Why is it difficult for most prospective parents to think beyond pregnancy and the first few years of a child's life? What problems might arise as a result of this limited thinking?

Using Management Skills
Have students investigate the standard charges for routine delivery in local hospitals. Are the costs the same? If not, by how much do they vary? Encourage students to share their findings and to discuss their reactions to the costs of hospital deliveries.

Promoting Discussion
Ask students why, when they are budgeting for a new baby, parents should be careful not to restrict medical expenses. Be sure students recognize that babies need regular well-baby care, immunizations, vitamins, and other health-related expenditures. Skimping on these expenses for a newborn may mean health problems and even greater expenses later in the child's life.

GUIDED PRACTICE (continued)

Using the Photograph

Let students describe and discuss the scene in the photograph on this page. How can prospective parents find out about their insurance coverage? Why is it important for them to investigate the specifics of their coverage for pregnancy and birth?

Promoting Discussion

Encourage students to share and discuss responses to the question: Why do most states have laws that require health insurance policies to include newborns?

Cooperative Learning

Have groups of students work together, using newspapers and other advertisements, to find sales on baby clothes and equipment. Ask group members to list the items on sale and the amount of money that could be saved by purchasing those items at sale prices.

Using Management Skills

Have students make a list of items they purchased the past week. Which expenditures represent fixed and which represent flexible expenses? How could you most easily reduce your expenses if you needed to do so?

Cooperative Learning

Have students work in groups to develop lists of some of the future needs a baby might have. How many of these needs are major expenses? How do you think most families meet these needs?

Practicing Decision Making

Provide students with a case study of a couple, giving information about their current income and expenses. Have students work in groups, making decisions about expenditures during pregnancy and birth, and making a budget to reflect how the couple will meet these expenses.

Making Connections: Management

Have students investigate costs for premature babies and those born with complications that require surgery or long hospital stays. How do families handle these catastrophic costs? Have students write a report on their findings.

Because costs change so rapidly and are not the same in all parts of the country, it is difficult to estimate the cost of having a baby. In addition to doctor and hospital fees, parents should consider these costs:

- Maternity clothes.
- The clothing, equipment, and supplies listed on pages 175-176, as well as any other items the parents want to provide.
- Formula and baby foods.
- Medical care for the baby.
- Furnishings for the baby's room.
- Child care services, if needed.

In addition, parents should recognize that, with another family member, they may need larger living quarters. They must also consider the costs of raising the child in the years ahead. Food, clothing, medical care, and education will all be major expenses during the many years in which the child needs to be supported. Parents should have a clear idea of the total expenses involved and of how they will manage those expenses.

Reducing Expenses

As parents plan for the birth of a baby, they should consider ways in which they can reduce the expenses involved in raising a child. Many parents are able to reduce or even eliminate certain expenses by having good health and hospitalization insurance and by shopping carefully.

The medical costs of pregnancy and birth are high. Expectant parents should make sure they have adequate health insurance and find out exactly what is covered.

TEEN PARENTING

Financial Assistance

Teens who become pregnant often find themselves unable to support their families financially. When this happens, they may turn to the state for help. The cost to taxpayers can be enormous. For example, according to a recent article, it costs the state of Oklahoma $144 million a year to assist teen parents.

Health Insurance Coverage

Health insurance can enable parents to meet the major expenses involved in the birth of a baby. Newly married couples should immediately make certain that they are covered by a good health insurance plan. If they already have insurance, they should review the hospital and medical coverage to see what it includes. Couples should review and, if necessary, improve their insurance coverage before they begin a pregnancy. It is also a good idea for couples to find out whether their insurance company will pay hospital bills directly or reimburse the parents after they have paid the hospital.

Some large hospitals have free or special-rate clinics to help those without insurance who are unable to pay the full fees. Social workers are often able to help expectant parents with budgeting problems and financial arrangements.

Careful Shopping

With nine months' advance notice, expectant parents have plenty of time to comparison shop on the items they need. Every few months, most stores and mail-order catalogs have special sales. The same item may be sold at three different prices in three different stores.

Cost comparisons are also useful when choosing between alternatives. For example, the costs of diapering an infant vary, depending on whether the family uses disposable diapers, a diaper service, or cloth diapers washed at home. Each method has advantages and disadvantages that must be weighed against the differences in cost.

When buying items for the baby, it pays to shop carefully. Both cost and quality are important considerations. Reading consumer magazines and comparison shopping can help expectant parents find out what features to look for.

MORE ABOUT

Health Insurance

One aspect of planning for a family involves careful scrutiny of available health insurance. Most companies will not allow policyholders to add additional family members or conditions to their policies once a female member is determined to be pregnant, and many require that a policyholder be covered for a specific period before they will cover pregnancy. Therefore, couples are wise to study their insurance benefits carefully before the woman becomes pregnant. Always know what the delivering doctor's fees are, and know what the cost of contingency procedures, such as a cesarean delivery, will be. There may be limits to the amounts covered under emergency situations.

INDEPENDENT PRACTICE

Journal Writing
Write this statement on the chalkboard:
Babies cost too much! Ask students to record their reactions as journal entries; remind them to express their feelings and opinions and to support those feelings with facts and details.

Student Workbook
Have students complete "Budgeting for Baby" in the Student Workbook.

Extension
Let students work independently or in small groups to complete one or more of these extension activities:
- Write a complete list of the expenses involved in pregnancy, birth, and early infancy. Then discuss the list with classmates. Are these costs easily affordable for a young couple just starting out? What can be done to help make the expenses more manageable?
- Survey the infant department of a clothing store. What garments are available? How many are for only one sex or the other? How many could be used for either sex? Write a list of criteria expectant parents could use in selecting basic garments for their baby.
- Attend a garage, yard, or rummage sale, and locate secondhand baby supplies and equipment. Note the quality, condition, and prices of the items, and compare them with those of new items. Which secondhand items would you choose to buy? Why? How much money would you save? Discuss your decisions with a group of classmates.
- Read about basic health insurance policies, especially as they relate to pregnancy and birth. Note the definitions of specific insurance-related terms, such as deductible. Summarize your findings in a short oral report.

PARENTING IN ACTION

Promoting Discussion

Have students read and discuss the title, "Paying for Prenatal Care." How much does prenatal care cost? Who pays these costs? Who might have trouble paying for private prenatal care? What options do they have? How important is medical care during pregnancy and for whom? Who should undertake responsibility for finding and paying for good prenatal care? For finding sources of free care?

Encourage students to discuss prenatal care experiences they have had or have heard about. What takes place during routine prenatal checkups? What kinds of problems can be identified and solved or averted? How do these checkups help women whose pregnancies are trouble-free?

Then have students read the selection.

Thinking Critically

Discuss the situation presented in this Parenting in Action selection. What influenced the decision that Julie and Steve made? Might they have made a different decision if they discussed plans with friends and/or family members? What options would they have had if vaginal bleeding was during the third month or persistent headaches during the sixth month? How would they have felt about their limited options?

Answers to Think and Discuss

1. They could have contacted a physician when Julie first suspected she was pregnant—or planning to be.

2. No; by postponing medical care, they risked Julie's health and the healthy development of their unborn baby.

3. Encourage a variety of specific responses; they placed the health of both at risk.

PARENTING IN ACTION

Paying for Prenatal Care

Julie and Steve were both pleased when they realized that Julie was pregnant with their first child. They wanted to take good care of their baby, but they also wanted to save money. Julie was in good health, and she came from a large, healthy family, so she did not anticipate any problems with her pregnancy. The couple decided that they should save the cost of monthly checkups by consulting a doctor only toward the end of her pregnancy.

Julie and Steve were in for a real surprise. When, in the seventh month of her pregnancy, Julie tried to make an appointment, she learned that all the doctors in their community charged a lump sum for pregnancy care. The fee was the same, whether it covered nine months or nine days.

THINK AND DISCUSS

1. How could Julie and Steve have avoided the unpleasant surprise they received?

2. Even if Julie and Steve had been able to save money by postponing medical care, would it have been a wise choice? Why or why not?

3. How could Julie and Steve's decision have affected Julie's health? How could it have affected the health of their unborn baby?

Making a Budget

Do you keep a personal budget? A **budget** is *a spending plan.* Its purpose is to help people set financial goals and work toward those goals in steps. Everyone can benefit from this kind of spending plan. Expectant parents find a budget especially useful as they plan for the added expenses of having and raising a baby.

In preparing a budget, parents-to-be should begin by considering where their money currently goes. **Fixed expenses** are *the costs of items that cannot be changed, such as rent, mortgage payments, taxes, insurance payments, and loan payments.* **Flexible expenses** are *costs for items over which people have some control and which can be cut back if necessary.* Usually, this category includes food, household maintenance, recreation, clothing, and similar expenses.

MORE ABOUT

Making a Budget

Some women may not be able to afford the kinds of food they need for themselves and their babies. A doctor or someone in a health center usually knows about community agencies that provide help. For example, the WIC Program (Special Supplemental Food Program for Women, Infants, and Children) is available in many cities and counties. Food is provided to qualified women and their children. Food stamps are another possibility for women who need help.

Next, expectant parents should get an idea of the added expenses they will soon face. How much of their medical expenses will be covered by insurance? Which items will they need to buy rather than borrow? Another important consideration is whether there will be any income lost if one of the parents plans to take time off from a paying job.

Once they have a clear idea of their new expenses, the parents can plan how to meet them. The expenses involved in having a baby must be budgeted like any other expenses. The couple has to recognize that the additional money spent on having a baby must be subtracted from another part of their budget. Often, flexible expenses have to be cut back.

Parents who have set aside some savings will find it easier to meet the early, large expenses of having a baby. Although, it is often difficult to set aside money for the future, having a budget can make this process easier. It is a good idea for the prospective parents to include a regular savings plan in their new budget. Even a few dollars set aside each month can help pay for the baby's future needs.

SECTION 2 REVIEW

CHECK YOUR UNDERSTANDING

1. Why is it important for the family that parents have either maternity leave or paternity leave? What is the difference between the two?

2. What can parents do to help prepare other children for the arrival of a new sibling?

3. List three questions that parents-to-be should ask themselves when deciding whether to breast-feed or bottle-feed their child.

4. List three ways that parents can reduce expenses when outfitting the nursery.

5. What is a budget?

6. What is the difference between a fixed expense and a flexible expense? Give two examples of each kind of expense.

DISCUSS AND DISCOVER

1. What factors do you think influence a mother's choice to breast-feed or bottle-feed her baby? Which of these factors is probably most important for teen mothers? Why?

2. Check to see whether your state has a law requiring family health insurance policies to include coverage of newborn infants. If so, when was it passed? If not, what efforts have been made to pass such a law? Share and discuss your findings with other students.

Observing & Participating

Visit a retail store that sells baby equipment, such as cribs, strollers, car seats, or high chairs. Choose one item and study its basic construction. Notice any accessories that come with it. Evaluate the safety of the item. If you were a parent, would you purchase the equipment you evaluated? Why or why not?

SECTION 2 REVIEW

1. Allows parents to spend time with their baby during the important early stages of development.

2. Discuss the pregnancy and plans for the baby; help child feel involved in preparations; accept child's full range of feelings about new baby.

3. Sample questions: How do both parents feel about the physical involvement of breast-feeding? What involvement does father want in feeding baby? How much flexibility in schedule does mother

need? (Other questions are also acceptable.)

4. Buy secondhand equipment; borrow equipment; comparison shop.

5. A spending plan.

6. A fixed expense is a cost that cannot be changed. Possible examples: rent, loan payments. A flexible expense is the cost of an item over which people have some control and which can be cut back if necessary. Possible examples: food, clothing.

ASSESS

CHECKING COMPREHENSION

Assign students to write their responses to the Check Your Understanding questions in the Section 2 Review. Answers to the questions are given at the bottom of this page.

EVALUATE

Have students complete the Chapter 6, Section 2 quiz in the TCR.

Reteaching

Working with small groups, help students develop a basic budget for a young married couple. Which fixed expenses are part of the budget? Which flexible expenses are part of the budget? Then guide students in identifying additional expenses the couple would incur during a pregnancy and in the first year of a baby's life.

Enrichment

Have students write a detailed plan for decorating a baby's room, spending only $50. What items will you buy? Where will you buy them? How much do they cost? What items will you make? Where will you buy the supplies? How much will they cost? Encourage students to compare and discuss their completed plans.

Extension

Invite two mothers to speak to the class. One should be a full-time homemaker and the other should have a full-time job outside the home. Ask the two mothers to discuss how they reached the child care decisions they made and what the consequences of their decisions have been.

CLOSE

Let each student answer these questions, either orally or in writing:

In order to save money, what familiar piece of baby equipment would you do without? What would you use instead?

FOCUS

SECTION 3 RESOURCES

Teacher's Classroom Resources
- Enrichment 16
- Reteaching 16
- Section 3 Quiz

Student Workbook
- It's Your Decision

SECTION OVERVIEW

An important part of preparing for a baby is making choices about childbirth. In Section 3, students learn about approaches to prepared childbirth and consider parents' options in selecting a birth attendant. Students also learn about parents' options in selecting a setting for the birth of their baby.

MOTIVATOR

Guide students in discussing what they know about trends in childbirth during the past century. Where and how were most babies delivered 100 years ago? Who usually assisted with the delivery? Where were most babies delivered 50 years ago? Who usually assisted? Where did the baby's father typically wait for news of the arrival? What childbirth practices have become popular in recent decades? How are these "new" practices similar to those used 100 years ago?

At the close of this discussion, explain to students that as they study Section 3, they will learn more about childbirth techniques and options.

USING TERMS TO LEARN

With the class, go over all six vocabulary terms introduced in Section 3. To help students understand the term *midwife*, you may want to point out that it comes from two Old English words meaning "with or accompanying" (*mid*) and "woman" (*wife*).

TERMS TO LEARN

alternative birth center
delivery
labor
lay midwife
nurse-midwife
prepared childbirth

SECTION 3 Childbirth Choices

OBJECTIVES

- Discuss the childbirth choices available to most parents.
- Describe how parents can make decisions and prepare for childbirth.

Not many years ago, birth practices in all hospitals were very similar. Today, there are many options from which to choose. Expectant parents must make arrangements for someone to deliver the baby. They should also decide on a place for the birth and on the methods or procedures they prefer.

What Is Prepared Childbirth?

Prepared childbirth, sometimes called natural childbirth, is *a method of giving birth in which pain is reduced through the elimination of fear and the use of special conditioning exercises.* Though a woman's body knows instinctively how to give birth, most women find childbirth education classes helpful in preparing them for this event. There are many different types of prepared childbirth classes, including Bradley and Lamaze methods. In recent years, however, there has been a blending of these styles, so that most classes offer similar information.

During a childbirth preparation course, class members learn what happens during **labor**—*the process by which the baby gradually moves out of the uterus into the vagina to be born*—and **delivery**—*the birth itself.* Class members see films of childbirth and receive reading material. Typically, they also take a tour of a hospital maternity department.

Much of the class time is spent learning skills to cope with the discomforts of labor, such as relaxation techniques and patterned breathing. The father, or anyone else the mother chooses to serve as a partner or childbirth coach, learns along with the mother. She depends on her partner for emotional support and guidance in practicing the exercises. The partner is also prepared to be an active participant throughout the labor and delivery.

OBSERVING AND PARTICIPATING

Birth Methods

Today there are as many as 20 birth methods and approaches available. Lamaze, Bradley, and Leboyer are common ones. These questions should be asked when choosing a class:

- Who sponsors the class?
- How large is the class?
- What are the instructor's qualifications?

- What is the cost and length of the class?
- Will the class include discussion, information, and rehearsal?
- Will the class address feelings as well as techniques?
- Will the father and/or a friend be allowed to participate?

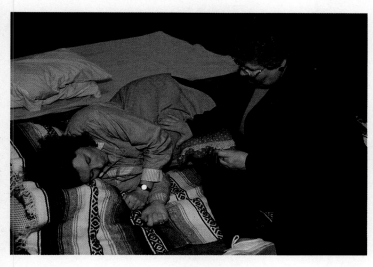

In Lamaze classes, the expectant mother learns special breathing techniques to use during labor. The coach's role will include keeping track of the breathing.

Who Will Deliver the Baby?

Most babies are now delivered either by an obstetrician or by a family doctor. Another option for women who expect a normal, uncomplicated delivery is a nurse-midwife.

- **Obstetricians.** These doctors specialize in prenatal and postnatal care of the mother and baby. They are qualified to handle any emergencies or special situations that may arise.

- **Family doctors.** Some general-practice doctors also deliver babies and provide prenatal and postnatal care. If complications arise during pregnancy or delivery, a family doctor may need to call in an obstetrician.

- **Licensed midwives.** The laws governing the practice of midwifery vary from state to state. There are two types of licensed midwives, each with different educational backgrounds. A certified **nurse-midwife** is *a registered nurse with advanced training in the care of normal, uncomplicated pregnancy and birth*. Nurse-midwives must pass a special licensing exam before they can establish a practice. A **lay midwife** is *a person who has special training in the care of pregnant women and uncomplicated deliveries but does not have a nursing degree*. Like nurse-midwives, lay midwives must pass a special exam before they can be licensed to practice.

How do expectant parents choose their birth attendant? They can get recommendations from their family doctor, the county medical society, or a local hospital. They should visit and talk with each doctor or licensed midwife they are considering. The

---

CLASSROOM MANAGEMENT

Resources Beyond the Classroom
To find a top-notch obstetrician, begin by listing the qualities desired. Then call two of the following professionals, describe the type of physician desired, and ask them for recommendations: head nurse of the labor and delivery ward, chief resident in obstetrics (if it is a teaching hospital), head nurse of the newborn intensive care unit, head nurse of the well-baby nursery.

To locate nurse-midwives in the area or to check certification, contact the American College of Nurse-Midwives (1522 K Street NW, Suite 1000, Washington, DC 20005).

TEACH
Pages 182-187

- **What Is Prepared Childbirth?**
- **Who Will Deliver the Baby?**
- **Where Will the Baby Be Born?**

GUIDED PRACTICE

Promoting Discussion
Let students share and discuss their responses to these questions: What kinds of fears about childbirth might a woman have? How are such fears likely to affect the process of childbirth? How can eliminating fear reduce the need for pain-relieving drugs?

Using the Photograph
Have students describe the scene shown in the photograph on this page. What is the couple doing? Why? How do you imagine they feel about this activity? How important do you think this kind of preparation for childbirth really is?

Critical Thinking
Encourage students to share their ideas in response to these questions: Why might a pregnant woman choose a childbirth partner other than the baby's father? When a woman chooses someone other than the father, what qualities do you think she looks for in a childbirth partner? Why?

Promoting Discussion
Ask students to suggest factors they think a woman should take into account when she decides whether to have an obstetrician, a family doctor, or a licensed midwife deliver her baby.

Family Focus
Many families choose childbirth methods that increase family participation. Discuss with students ways that fathers and siblings can be involved in preparing for childbirth and in the birth itself. What are the advantages of such participation?

GUIDED PRACTICE (continued)

Cooperative Learning
Have students work in groups to prepare a list of questions that a couple would want answered when choosing a birth attendant.

Promoting Discussion
Although most pregnancies are safe and uncomplicated, some women face potential problems with birth and pregnancy because of age, existing medical conditions, lifestyle problems, or genetic problems, such as Down syndrome, Tay-Sachs disease, and hemophilia. Discuss why these women should choose an obstetrician and a hospital delivery.

Practicing Decision Making
Discuss the following case study: Lorena and Jerry are expecting their second child. Lorena used prepared childbirth methods when 5-year-old Beth was born. After the delivery, she had some unexpected bleeding. For this birth, she does not want any medications that would affect the new baby. She wants to have Jerry and Beth with her during the labor and delivery. Where would students recommend that she have her baby? Why?

Promoting Discussion
Sometimes babies arrive before the mother reaches the planned birth location. Ask if students have heard of such situations. What hazards are involved? What do people then do?

Critical Thinking
Ask students to give responses to these questions: Why do alternative birth centers accept only low-risk mothers? What conditions might disqualify a woman from using an alternative birth center?

A licensed midwife is qualified to give prenatal care and to supervise routine, normal births. If complications arise during pregnancy or delivery, an obstetrician will be called in.

parents will want to be sure the person they choose is not only well qualified, but also makes them feel comfortable and can answer their questions clearly.

The parents should find out how emergency calls will be handled at night and on weekends. Another consideration is whether the doctor or licensed midwife is affiliated with a particular hospital or medical center, as most are. The parents should find out what programs and facilities that hospital has. They will also want to know whether the birth attendant's preferences toward delivery procedures agree with their own.

Although the mother-to-be should get medical care as soon as she is pregnant, she may not feel ready to make a decision about the delivery at that time. There is no reason she cannot switch to a different doctor or nurse-midwife during pregnancy if she wishes. The sooner a final decision is made, however, the better prepared both the parents and the birth attendant will be.

Where Will the Baby Be Born?

Until this century, almost all babies were born at home. Today, most American births occur in hospitals. There, sanitary conditions, trained personnel, and special equipment help make the birth process as safe as possible.

In recent years, hospitals have begun to offer a variety of services designed to meet the various needs and preferences of expectant mothers and their families. These services, often referred to as family-centered maternity care, include:
- Childbirth and parenting classes help the parents prepare for delivery and for caring for an infant.
- Special programs help young children prepare for their new baby brother or sister.
- Fathers and other family members are encouraged to help the mother through labor and to be present during delivery.
- "Birthing rooms" provide a homelike atmosphere for both labor and birth. The need to move from a labor room to a separate delivery room is eliminated. Medical equipment is kept out of sight, but is ready for use at a moment's notice.
- Mothers may be able to choose their preferred position for labor and delivery. Instead of lying flat, a woman may be encouraged to walk, rock in a chair, lie on her side, sit propped up, or even shower or soak in a tub. Many women find that these positions are more comfortable and make labor easier.
- Special procedures are often allowed to make the birth special for the family. For example, the lights in the delivery room may be dimmed so that the newborn can open his or her eyes without discomfort.

Did You Know?

President Jimmy Carter was the first American president to be born in a hospital.

MORE ABOUT

Birth Attendants
An important factor in choosing a birth attendant is his or her attitude toward pregnancy and childbirth. Some attendants leave many decisions to the family, seeing birth as a family-centered event. Others feel their medical training should be used to make decisions. Some physicians rely on technology, such as electronic fetal monitoring and certain medications. Other caregivers prefer to use technology only in emergencies. Matching the philosophy of the attendant with that of the family is apt to make the childbirth experience a better one.

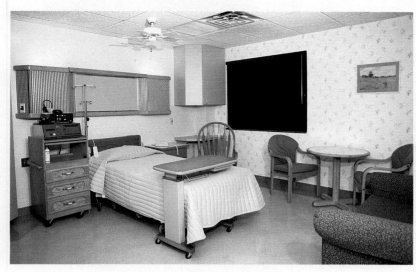

Many hospitals offer birthing rooms that combine a comfortable, homelike setting with full medical facilities. Both labor and delivery take place in the same room, and mother and baby can stay there together.

- The mother and her baby remain together for all or most of the hospital stay, instead of being kept in separate rooms.
- Some hospitals offer the new LDRP concept. In this special unit, the woman labors, delivers, recovers, and spends her postpartum stay all in the same room. The baby stays with the mother; often the father is invited to stay, too.

Expectant parents should take the time to explore the various services offered by local hospitals. Many offer tours of their maternity department, which can be both informative and reassuring. After gathering information, the couple should discuss which services seem most appropriate for their needs.

Some couples choose not to use a hospital at all, but instead go to an **alternative birth center**, *a homelike facility, separate from any hospital, for giving birth.* Alternative birth centers emphasize prepared childbirth and offer many of the nontraditional approaches that are part of family-centered maternity care. Mothers are often assisted during labor and delivery by licensed midwives. Most alternative birth centers accept only low-risk mothers. However, a hospital is usually nearby, and mother and baby can be transferred there if necessary.

The costs of family-centered hospital maternity care or alternative birth centers are usually less than those of traditional hospital maternity care. The time spent at the facility is also usually much less. If there are no complications, parents usually leave the hospital or birth center within 24 hours of delivery, compared with the two- to three-day stay for traditional births.

MORE ABOUT

Hospital Birthing Rooms

In-hospital birthing rooms have been found to be a safe alternative to conventional care. The importance, however, of having back-up hospital facilities has also been demonstrated. For example, one study of an in-hospital birthing center revealed these statistics: 24 percent of the carefully screened women developed complications and were transferred to the conventional labor and delivery suite; 9 percent of the original group, which was considered low risk, had cesarean sections; and 5 percent remained in the hospital for more observation and care after delivery.

INDEPENDENT PRACTICE

Journal Writing

Ask students to write journal entries exploring their own ideas and feelings about childbirth choices. You may want to spark their thinking by asking questions such as these: Childbirth is simply one event in the lives of parents and their children—does it really matter where and how the delivery takes place? If so, how and why does it matter? If not, why not? Which approach to childbirth do you find most appealing? Why?

Student Workbook

Have students complete "It's Your Decision" in the student Workbook.

Extension

Let students work independently or in small groups to complete one or more of these extension activities:

- Read about and practice several breathing exercises used as part of childbirth preparation courses. What is the purpose of each kind of breathing exercise? Demonstrate the exercises to the rest of the class, and explain their uses.
- Investigate the status of medical malpractice insurance as it relates to delivering babies. Have any physicians in your community stopped delivering babies because they are unwilling to pay the high cost of malpractice insurance? Report your findings to the rest of the class.
- Research the philosophy behind alternative birth centers. What led to their establishment? What types of clients are they most apt to have? Write a brief report summarizing your findings.
- Survey the community to find out the numbers of obstetricians, family doctors, and licensed midwives who deliver babies. Which type of birth attendant is most commonly used? Least commonly used? Why? Prepare and present an oral report summarizing your findings.

PARENTING IN ACTION

Promoting Discussion

Encourage students to describe and discuss the photograph before reading this selection. Who is shown in the photo? What are they doing? How do they appear to be reacting? How do you think they feel about what has already happened? About what is going to happen?

Consider the selection title, "Choosing an Appropriate Birth Setting." What choices do expectant parents have in choosing a birth setting? Why is the choice of setting important? What makes one birth setting right for one family but not for another? What might expectant parents gain by exploring choices thoroughly? Which birth setting appeals to you?

After a discussion, have students read the selection.

Thinking Critically

After reading the selection, encourage students to consider the decision the expectant parents made. Why did Ashley and Phil not select an alternative birth center? Would they have been as pleased with their experience at one? Why or why not? Why did they choose the hospital's birthing room? How would a traditional hospital birth have been different from the experience they had in the birthing room? How would those differences have affected Ashley and Phil's attitudes toward their new baby and themselves as parents?

Answers to Think and Discuss

1. Parents and baby can get to know each other right away; feel comfortable and close together. This helps parents feel capable and confident.

2. Encourage students to express and support various opinions.

PARENTING IN ACTION

Choosing an Appropriate Birth Setting

Ashley and Phil were surprised when they visited the new birthing rooms at a local hospital. They liked the setting—a place that looked and felt like home but could handle any emergency. The room was a large lounge with comfortable furniture, lamps, TV, and a stereo.

It was more than the atmosphere, however, that drew them to this kind of birth experience. As Phil explained, "We wanted to have our baby right there with us. We didn't want to be separated."

Ashley and Phil chose that hospital's birthing room setting for the delivery of their daughter, Megan. They were especially pleased because the nursing staff helped them learn to take care of Megan. After less than two days in the hospital, Ashley and Phil took Megan home, feeling very satisfied with their birth experience and increasingly confident in themselves as parents.

THINK AND DISCUSS

1. Why do you think staying with the baby after birth helps new parents feel more confident?

2. What might be some other effects of this kind of birth experience?

Couples have many decisions to make as they prepare for the birth of their child. Where to have the baby is one of these major decisions. Whether the couple decides to have the baby delivered in a hospital, alternative birth center, or at home, safety for both the mother and the baby is the primary concern. Couples should discuss the advantages and disadvantages of each delivery option with their health care provider. Then they should make the decision that is best for them and their baby.

Some women may choose a health care provider who is willing to deliver their baby at home. This setting for delivery has gained popularity during recent years. The family that chooses a home delivery must carefully weigh the benefits and risks. This option is generally possible only for women with uncomplicated pregnancies. A special transport system should be available in case of an emergency.

CLASSROOM MANAGEMENT

Resources Beyond the Classroom

A 1989 survey showed that birth centers offer a 35 percent to 47 percent savings over hospital birth. A nationwide study completed in 1989 concluded that birth centers are a safe alternative for healthy women with normal pregnancies. The study found that in over 11,000 births at birth centers, there were no maternal deaths. The rate of infant mortality was similar to that at university and community hospitals. The same study showed that about one in six women admitted to a birth center was transferred to a hospital. The most common reason was slow or stalled labor. For more information, contact the National Association of Childbearing Centers, RD1, Box 1, Perkiomenville, PA 18074.

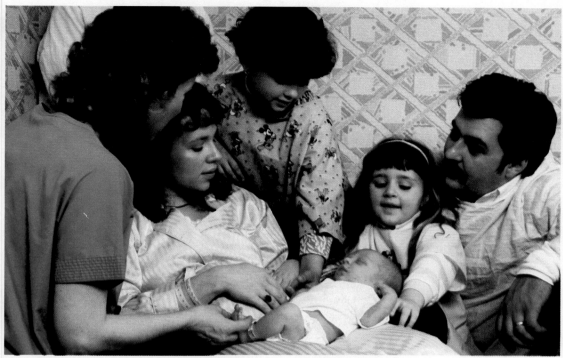

Alternative birth centers emphasize family participation and a relaxed atmosphere.

SECTION 3 REVIEW

CHECK YOUR UNDERSTANDING

1. What is prepared childbirth? List three main points emphasized by most prepared childbirth courses.

2. What is labor? What is delivery?

3. What are the differences between an obstetrician and a licensed midwife?

4. List two questions an expectant couple might ask a doctor or licensed midwife they are considering choosing as their birth attendant.

5. List three services that are often part of family-centered maternity care in a hospital.

6. What is an alternative birth center?

DISCUSS AND DISCOVER

1. Why do you think women might prefer traditional maternity services to family-centered maternity care? What pressures do you think these expectant mothers might feel to use the current, more popular procedures of family-centered care?

Observing & Participating

If possible, arrange to visit either a prepared childbirth class or a hospital tour for maternity patients. Listen carefully to the teacher or the tour guide, and observe the reactions of the prospective parents to what is being said. Besides anticipation, what feelings do the parents express about pregnancy and birth? Describe your impressions of the facilities and of the prospective parents. Also indicate any special services for maternity patients provided by the class or hospital.

SECTION 3 REVIEW

1. A method of giving birth in which pain is reduced through the elimination of fear and the use of special conditioning exercises.

2. Process of the baby moving out of the uterus into the vagina to be born; the birth itself.

3. An obstetrician is a doctor specializing in pre-natal and postnatal care of mother and baby; a licensed midwife is not a doctor, but may be a nurse who is trained in care of pregnant women and in uncomplicated deliveries.

4. Any two: How will you handle emergency calls? With what hospital or medical center are you affiliated? What are your attitudes toward delivery? (Other questions are also acceptable.)

5. Sample: childbirth and parenting classes; birthing rooms. (Other answers are also possible.)

6. A homelike facility for giving birth that is separate from a hospital.

ASSESS

CHECKING COMPREHENSION

Assign students to write their responses to the Check Your Understanding questions in the Section 3 Review. Answers to the questions are given at the bottom of this page.

EVALUATE

Have students complete the Chapter 6, Section 3 quiz in the TCR.

Reteaching

Help groups of students review the options parents have when choosing a birth attendant. What are the particular advantages of each? For which kind of pregnancy is each best suited? Why? Then let students work with partners to plan and make posters illustrating and briefly describing the qualifications and advantages of different kinds of birth attendants.

Enrichment

Have students investigate the philosophy and techniques of the Lamaze and Bradley methods. How are they similar? What are the most important differences? What are the particular advantages of each? To whom is each likely to be especially appealing? Why? Have students write a report summarizing their findings.

Extension

Invite a licensed midwife to speak to students about his or her work. What training is required? Where and how can one receive that training? How has the midwife developed his or her practice, and how does the work coordinate with that of obstetricians? After the midwife has spoken to the class, encourage students to ask follow-up questions.

CLOSE

Have each student complete the following sentence, either orally or in writing:

Childbirth choices are important because ...

Positive Parenting Skills

MOTIVATOR

Ask students to think about why the car safety restraint and the crib are considered the two most important pieces of baby equipment. Ask them to volunteer any knowledge about accidents or injuries caused by unsafe equipment or practices.

Promoting Discussion

1. Why do children need a special type of car restraint?
2. Why does the back seat of a car provide better protection for a child?
3. What are the benefits of using bumper pads inside a crib?

Using Management Skills

Have students use a consumer publication or their own research to learn more about the features of car safety restraints. Have them work in small groups to compile their findings. Then have them make a poster called "Keeping Children Safe" that can be donated to a local child care center or school.

Practicing Decision Making

Point out to students that 80 percent of children who die in car accidents could have been saved by safety seats and belts. Discuss reasons why some people allow children to ride without being strapped in. Ask: What would you do if your child was to be picked up by a another person whose car was not adequately equipped with safety belts?

Extension

Have students brainstorm a list of ideas for entertaining an infant or toddler who is in a car seat during a long trip.

Enrichment

Have students investigate the laws in your state concerning the use of safety restraints for infants and children. What ages are included? How do the laws vary according to a child's age? What are the penalties for violations of these laws?

SAFETY GUIDELINES FOR BABY EQUIPMENT

Two of the most important pieces of baby equipment are the car safety restraint, which is needed immediately, and the crib, which many parents acquire weeks or even months after the baby has been born. Whether these pieces of equipment are purchased new or used, borrowed or handed down, each should be carefully checked for safety.

Car Safety Restraints

Everyone needs to be buckled up in a moving vehicle. Because of their size, children under the age of four need special safety restraints. Regular adult seat belts do not fit or restrain young children properly. There are two types of safety restraints

for young children in cars: rear-facing restraints and forward-facing restraints.

Rear-Facing Safety Restraints

Rear-facing safety restraints are specially designed to keep infants safe. Any baby who weighs less than 20 pounds (9.1 kg) or is less than 26 inches (66 cm) long should ride in one of these bucket-type carriers. The infant should face backwards in a reclining position. A harness in the carrier holds the baby in position, and the carrier is secured with a car seat belt.

Forward-Facing Safety Restraints

Around the age of nine months, most children are ready to sit up and face forward in a safety seat. Some rear-facing safety restraints can be converted to forward-facing seats, but a variety of other types are available.

- **Seat with harness.** A harness comes over the child's shoulders and up between the child's legs. The seat is secured by the car seat belt.

- **Seat with protective shield.** A padded surface protects the child if he or she is thrown forward by an impact or by sudden braking. Look for seats with extended, padded shields around the head. The child is held in place by the car seat belt and sometimes by a harness as well.

- **Booster seat.** This is a strong seat without a back. It is used with the car seat belt and a special harness fastened permanently to the car. Booster seats are designed for young children who have already reached a weight of 40 pounds (18.2 kg) or a height of 40 inches (102 cm). When a child wears a

COOPERATIVE LEARNING

Safety in Child Care Centers

Remind students that safety guidelines are only as effective as the people who follow them. As a class project, have students visit several local child care centers and observe how the centers provide for the safety of the children they serve. Instruct students to write an assessment of the level of safety they observe. When everyone in the class has made such a visit, put students into small groups and have them compare findings. Then instruct them to make a list of both their positive and negative observations. Have a spokesperson from each group summarize the list to the class; then begin a discussion about the results.

seat belt, either with or without a booster seat, it is important to check the fit of the belt. The lap belt should fit snugly over the child's hip bones, not across the stomach. The shoulder belt should be used only if it does not cross the child's neck or face.

Crib

When choosing a crib, parents should consider the safety and comfort of the baby, as well as conveniences for themselves. These are some important points to use in evaluating and selecting a crib:

- Adjustable sides and adjustable mattress height eliminate unnecessary bending for the baby's parents or caregiver. Some cribs have sides that can be dropped or removed when the child is old enough to get in and out of bed alone. This is a good feature to look for when considering cribs.

- A baby's crib should have a firm spring and mattress. Doctors advise against using a pillow in the crib. A pillow is bad for the baby's posture and creates a risk of suffocation.

- The bars or slats of the crib must be no more than 2 ⅜ inches (6.0 cm) apart.

- Corner posts should be no higher than ⅓ inch (8.5 mm) above end panels or side panels. (Canopy cribs are an exception.)

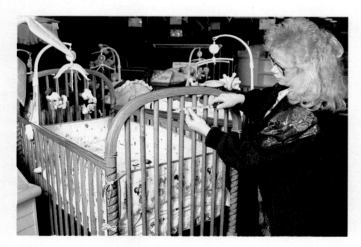

- The top of the crib sides should have a plastic covering, sometimes called a teething rail.

- If the crib has drop sides, check to see whether the mechanism is likely to be accidentally released.

- The higher the sides of the crib when raised, the less chance that an older baby can climb out.

- There should be no rough edges or exposed bolts.

- Cribs and mattresses vary in size. Be sure there is no space between the edge of the mattress and the crib.

189

HEALTHY FAMILIES/HEALTHY CHILDREN

Health and Safety

There is more to crib safety than just the structure of the crib. When a baby is placed in the crib, the sides should always be raised and locked. To prevent accidental smothering, follow these precautions:

- Leave pillows and other unneeded items out of the crib.
- Plastic should not be used to protect the crib mattress.
- Do not hang anything over the sides of the crib.

Family Focus

Have students design a bedroom that will be used by both an infant and a four-year-old child. What considerations regarding safety and efficiency of space must be made? What hazards exist for the infant but not the older child, and vice versa?

Practicing Decision Making

Ask students to imagine that they are new parents who are shopping for baby furniture. Although the retail stores have attractive offers, financial constraints force them to look at second hand stores and private advertisements in newspapers. What advantages will they find when shopping for used furniture? What disadvantages? How can they be sure that used furniture meets the same safety requirements as new?

Cooperative Learning

Have students work in pairs or small groups to investigate what makes a crib safe. Have them price and evaluate at least three different cribs as well as mattresses. Ask them to present their findings to the class in the form of a chart that compares the three examples. Ask: If they were parents, would they purchase any of the three? Why or why not?

Critical Thinking

Ask students to discuss why a thin plastic mattress cover should never be used on a baby crib. Also, what precautions should a parent take when purchasing sleepware for the baby and additional bedding for the crib?

Extension

Have students research and write a report on common injuries and accidents associated with infant car restraints and cribs.

CLOSE

Ask students to volunteer what they have learned about safety guidelines for baby equipment.

Use the Summary and the Reviewing the Facts questions to help students go over the most important ideas presented in Chapter 6; encourage students to ask questions and add details, as appropriate.

CHAPTER 6 REVIEW

1. Consult a doctor; to have the pregnancy confirmed and to begin regular prenatal care.

2. Any four: recording blood pressure, pulse, respiration, and initial weight; taking pelvic measurements; analyzing urine; giving blood test; recording history of past illnesses and operations. The last few months; the growing uterus may put pressure on the lungs.

3. The last months; from pressure by the uterus on the lungs.

4. Milk, yogurt, and cheese group; meat, poultry, fish, dry beans, eggs, and nuts group; vegetable group; fruit group; bread, cereal, rice, and pasta group; fats, oils, and sweets group.

5. 24 to 30 pounds (10.9 to 13.6 kg). Any three: placenta; amniotic fluid; increased size of uterus and supporting muscles; increase in breast tissue; increase in blood volume; increase in fat stores; increase in body fluids.

6. Any two: creates bond; provides natural immunity; speeds return of uterus to normal size; causes fewer digestive upsets; conveniently available; reduces risk of allergies. Any two: allows father to participate; allows mother flexible schedule; permits baby to be fed by anyone.

7. To help them prepare for the expenses of having and raising a baby.

8. Elimination of fear and use of special conditioning exercises.

9. Obstetricians; family doctors; licensed midwives.

10. No; they are intended for low-risk pregnancies and deliveries.

CHAPTER 6 REVIEW

SUMMARY

- A woman should visit a doctor as soon as she suspects she might be pregnant, and she should have periodic checkups throughout her pregnancy.

- Good nutrition is very important for both the developing baby and the mother.

- A pregnant woman needs plenty of rest and moderate exercise.

- Expectant parents should prepare by discussing child care and parenting, deciding on a method of feeding, and assembling the basic items needed for the baby.

- Parents-to-be should estimate the expenses of having a baby, look for ways to reduce those expenses, and make a budget to meet their financial needs.

- Prepared childbirth classes help the expectant mother become physically and mentally ready for labor and delivery.

- Expectant parents must choose who will help deliver their baby and in what setting.

REVIEWING THE FACTS

1. What should a woman who notices one of the signs of early pregnancy do? Why?

2. List four steps that are usually part of a doctor's examination of a woman at the beginning of pregnancy.

3. During which part of pregnancy is a woman likely to feel short of breath? Why?

4. What are the basic food groups in the Food Guide Pyramid?

5. How much weight does a woman usually gain during her entire pregnancy? List three factors, other than the weight of the baby, that contribute to the mother's weight gain.

6. List two advantages of breast-feeding. List two advantages of bottle-feeding.

7. Why is it especially important for expectant parents to have a budget?

8. What methods of reducing pain are taught in childbirth preparation classes?

9. List three kinds of health care professionals who help deliver babies.

10. Are alternative birth centers and home births an option for all pregnant women? Why or why not?

EXPLORING FURTHER

1. Prepare two nutritious snacks that might be part of a healthy, balanced diet for a pregnant woman. Serve these snacks to your classmates. Together, evaluate the snacks in terms of nutrition and appeal. (Section 1)

2. Plan a baby shower for a young couple expecting their first child. Make an invitation for the party, and include general gift suggestions on the invitation. Also write a schedule for the party, noting what activities will be included and what foods will be served. (Section 2)

3. Imagine the feelings a young child might have when his or her mother goes to the hospital for several days and then returns home with a new baby—a baby who becomes the center of everyone's attention. Write and illustrate a small book that could help prepare a child for this event. (Section 2)

4. Investigate three childbirth preparation courses offered in your community. Find out who gives each course, where and when it is given, and what fees, if any, are involved. Share your information with a group of classmates. Together, discuss the apparent advantages and disadvantages of the different courses. (Section 3)

THINKING CRITICALLY

1. **Analyze.** How do you think a woman's emotional responses to her own pregnancy might affect her symptoms of physical discomfort? What effect, if any, do you think her physical discomfort may have on her feelings about her pregnancy and her developing child?

2. **Compare.** Why do you think some women might try to gain less than 20 pounds (9.1 kg) during a pregnancy? Why do you think others might gain more than 35 pounds (15.9 kg)? What risks are

---

CLASSROOM MANAGEMENT

FHA/HERO Planning Process

Educational research shows that students learn best when they are actively involved in the teaching-learning process—as they are when using the FHA/HERO Planning Process. By using this process, students have to track down information, test theories, and evaluate results. Using this approach, teachers spend more time facilitating and guiding instruction and less time reiterating facts. The steps of the planning process include: (1) Identify concerns—brainstorm to determine concerns or problems. (2) Set your goal—set realistic goals and consider the resources available to achieve the goal. (3) Form a plan—decide what needs to be done and determine the who, what, when, where and how of the project. (4) Act—carry out the plan. (5) Follow up—decide if your goal was met.

these groups of women running? Do you think the women in either or both of these groups should be helped? If so, how?

3. **Evaluate.** High-risk mothers are not offered the option of a birthing room. Why might mothers be considered high-risk? Why are the birthing rooms not offered to them?

CROSS-CURRICULUM CONNECTIONS

1. **Writing.** Imagine that you have just received a postcard from a friend who is young, newly married, and far from her familiar neighborhood. Your friend writes that she thinks she is pregnant, but she's not positive. She's also not sure how she feels about being pregnant now. Write your friend a letter, expressing your response and giving her some advice.

2. **Math.** Select twelve items from the list of Basic Baby Supplies on pages 175-176. Visit stores, check newspaper ads, or look in catalogs for prices on those twelve items. Record prices from three sources for each item. Then use the lowest price for each item to write a spending plan for purchasing those twelve items.

SCHOOL TO WORK

Applying for a Job Typically, employers will ask you to fill out an application when you inquire about employment. The application gives the employer an opportunity to know more about you and the skills you have for the job. In some situations, you may be asked to take a performance test, prepare a personal inventory, or provide a letter of application. Regardless of how you apply, your responses should be accurate and neat, using correct spelling and good grammar. How you present yourself on paper may influence the employer's decision.

PERFORMANCE ASSESSMENT

Preparing for Birth

Task
Use what you have learned about planning for a baby's arrival to design a newborn baby's living space. The floor plan should include everything needed to provide a safe, clean, stimulating environment for a newborn baby.

Purpose
You will learn that preparing a safe environment for a newborn baby requires considerable planning, creativity, and preparation.

Procedure
1. Begin by making a sketch of a baby's living area. You could use actual dimensions of a room or a portion of a room at your home and make a scale drawing on grid paper.

2. Make a list of items you will need for the baby.
3. Now sketch the furniture in place using the same scale. Revise as necessary to make the arrangement comfortable and safe. Consider such questions as: Where will diapers be changed? Will someone easily hear the baby crying? Is the room a comfortable temperature? What will the baby see while lying in the crib?
4. Exchange floor plans with a partner and evaluate the safety and suitability of the other student's design.
5. Make any alterations and draw your final floor plan. When your drawing is complete, you might review the checklist on pages 175-176 to determine where all the supplies will be stored.

Evaluation
Your design will be evaluated on your ability to use space efficiently as well as creativity, forethought, preparation, and neatness. Demonstration that you know how to recognize and provide a safe and stimulating environment is essential.

Portfolio Idea When your design is complete, protect it by using clear laminating plastic. Then you can decorate, color, change, or add to your design with washable markers. Be sure to label your floor plan carefully with your name, date, and the activity's objective.

Use the reproducible Chapter 6 Test in the TCR, or construct your own test using the Test-maker Software.

EXTENSION

Arrange a class visit from one or more experienced birth attendants (or help students make arrangements for such a visit). Consider having an obstetrician, a family doctor, a nurse-midwife, a lay midwife, and/or a labor and delivery nurse. Ask the visitors to share their own experiences in helping families with childbirth, expressing their own opinions on the importance of preparation during pregnancy and on appropriate choices for delivery.

CLOSE

Show students a life-size baby doll, and ask them to imagine it is a baby who will come home with them tomorrow. Have students list the five most important things they would do to prepare for the baby's arrival.

TECHNOLOGY OPTION

Computers Students may find, among themselves, someone who has a computer program that allows the user to design floor plans for the Performance Assessment activity on this page. With the program, multiple versions of the same space could be designed or students could reproduce custom designs for other students who submit the dimensions of the space they are working with.

Photography Students might take photographs of an existing nursery or infant area and make the pictures the center of a display that illustrates the room's advantages and, if appropriate, its disadvantages.

PERFORMANCE ASSESSMENT

Floor Plans for a Newborn

For continuity, you may want to duplicate and distribute a variety of floor plans to students. Students may also need a lesson on the basics of scale drawings. Students may want to create a 3-dimensional format, such as a model or diorama, for their floor plans. To help students conceptualize this project, have them draw and cut out furniture and other items found in their living area at home. Then they can place the items on the floor diagram, moving them around until they find suitable arrangements. Additional factors for consideration in preparing the floor plans are the needs of a premature baby, twins or other multiple births, and parents (or infants) who are hearing or visually impaired. If possible, invite a parent to review the floor plans and offer ideas and suggestions.

INTRODUCE

CHAPTER OVERVIEW

Students examine the amazing process of childbirth as they study Chapter 7.

In Section 1, students begin by learning about the early signs of labor. They go on to consider the three stages through which labor progresses, during which uterine contractions first open the uterus, then expel the baby, and finally expel the placenta. Students also examine cesarean birth as a possible alternative to vaginal delivery; then they read about the particular physical characteristics most parents should expect to see in their newborn baby.

Section 2 explains the early evaluation and care of newborn babies. Here students learn about the process of bonding and attachment between parents and infants, which can be initiated immediately after birth. They also learn about the typical procedures of care during the hospital stay, and they consider the special care needs—both physical and emotional—of mothers who have recently undergone the radical changes from pregnancy, through labor and birth, to the nonpregnant state. In the final part of Section 2, students examine the special care that is provided for premature infants.

In the third section of Chapter 7, students consider the newborn infant as a new family member, one who usually requires adjustments and accommodations from (continued next page)

CLASSROOM MANAGEMENT

Resources Beyond the Classroom

The excitement of the birth is over, and the new mother is suddenly left alone to cope with a newborn. Complicating this new situation for some mothers is the problem of postpartum depression. In today's society, the support structure that new mothers once relied on is often absent. Although this lack of support can result in an isolating and demanding experience, the new mother need not feel alone. Support groups such as PACE exist to provide the opportunity for the new mother to share and sometimes commiserate about her new role while learning better coping strategies. In PACE, groups of a maximum of ten mothers and infants meet weekly for eight sessions. For more information about PACE, call (292) 983-9133.

CHAPTER 7

The Baby's Arrival

SECTION 1	The Birth Process
SECTION 2	The Postnatal Period
SECTION 3	A New Family Member

THINK ABOUT

Newborn babies are amazing indeed! After having undergone nine months in a womb, the newborn comes into the world prepared to eat, see, hear, and even communicate! A short hospital stay is only the beginning of a relationship between parents and child that grows with each passing day. As parents and caregivers adjust to the new responsibilities of providing a loving and nurturing environment for a child, they lay the foundation for a happy, healthy family.

ASK YOURSELF

The photo on the opposite shows a proud couple holding their newborn daughter. How do their expressions show their love for the child? What do you see in the photo that tells you they prepared for her arrival? Do you feel they will provide a caring environment for this child? Why? If the parents could talk to you, what do you think they would say about their little girl?

NOW TRY THIS

Identify three personal characteristics that you feel are important in a newborn's caregiver. For each characteristic, explain why you think it is important, what impact it has on the child who is being cared for, and how a person cultivates that characteristic in him- or herself.

193

CHAPTER OBJECTIVES

After completing Chapter 7, students will be able to:

- Explain the three stages through which labor progresses.
- Discuss the usual activities and procedures affecting both newborn and mother during the period following a birth.
- Describe the basic needs of a newborn and explain how those needs can best be met.

INTRODUCING THE CHAPTER

- Display items that relate to newborn babies, such as a baby bottle, a pacifier, a small stuffed animal, a diaper, a grocery shopping bill, and a magazine for parents. Show one item at a time to the class and have them identify it. Then encourage a discussion about the item. Ask how it relates to the arrival of a new baby. After students have discussed all the items, remind them that they will learn more about the arrival of a baby—and the changes that arrival necessitates in any family—as they read Chapter 7.

- Use the photo on the opposite page and the three features on this page—Think About, Ask Yourself, and Now Try This—to begin a discussion about a baby's arrival.

HEALTHY FAMILIES/HEALTHY CHILDREN

Building Healthy Families

Almost all parents spend time imagining what the personality and physical characteristics of their new baby will be. They might hope for attractive features and positive attitudes, or they may fear the presence of unpopular family traits. Regardless of the expectations, the baby arrives and sends out the unspoken message, "I am an individual. I am unique." From that moment of arrival, parents find out how challenging their role can be. It is possible for them to feel threatened or cheated by a child who does not live up to their expectations. Parents and caregivers can destroy a child by focusing on their own disappointments, or they can help the child develop pride, adaptability, and self-acceptance.

FOCUS

SECTION 1 RESOURCES

Teacher's Classroom Resources
- Enrichment 17
- Reteaching 17
- Section 1 Quiz

Student Workbook
- Stages of Labor

SECTION OVERVIEW

In Section 1, students consider the amazing process of childbirth. They learn about the signs that indicate the onset of labor. Then, they examine labor itself, in each of its three stages. What happens to the baby during each stage? What does the mother experience? How can the mother best be helped during each?

Students also examine cesarean births. They read about the changes every newborn undergoes to begin life outside the mother's uterus, and consider the special physical characteristics of newborn infants.

MOTIVATOR

Write the word childbirth on the chalkboard, and ask each student to write the first five words that come to mind. Share and compare their response lists. What positive responses are indicated? Negative? What are similarities and differences among the response words? What accounts for the differences?

USING TERMS TO LEARN

Help students pronounce and briefly discuss the meaning of all six terms. Focus attention on the noun contractions, and help students identify contract as the verb from which the noun is formed. Ask students what contracts during a contraction. Which other muscles can contract? When?

SECTION 1 — The Birth Process

OBJECTIVES

- Recognize the ways in which labor may begin.
- Outline the three stages of labor.
- Describe a newborn's physical changes and appearance at birth.

TERMS TO LEARN

cervix
cesarean birth
contractions
dilates
fontanels
forceps

When a woman labors to bring her child into the world, it is an experience like no other. Labor brings powerful sensations and emotions. It is a challenging experience for most women, but it is a challenge with a very special reward.

The Beginning of Labor

During the last weeks of pregnancy, women often become anxious to finally meet the new baby. Time seems to pass slowly as they watch for any sign that labor is about to begin.

There are many changes that occur in the last days of pregnancy. However, these changes may be very subtle, and the timing of the changes varies a great deal from woman to woman. Even when a woman notices some of these signs, it is still difficult to predict when her labor will actually begin.

One sign that labor is approaching occurs when the baby settles deep into the mother's pelvis, preparing for his or her journey into the world. This settling is often called lightening; it may also be referred to as the baby's dropping.

There are some definite signals that the baby is coming. One is commonly called show or bloody show; it may also be referred to as losing the mucus plug. Throughout the pregnancy, the **cervix**, *the lower part of the uterus*, which serves as a kind of door, is closed and sealed with mucus. This mucus helps prevent bacteria from moving up from the vagina into the uterus where it might cause an infection. As the woman's body prepares for birth, this mucus begins to liquefy. The woman may notice a few drops of blood or a slight pinkish vaginal staining.

In some women, the onset of labor is signaled by a trickle—or even a gush—of warm fluid from the vagina. This indicates

---

MORE ABOUT

False Labor

Real labor is often preceded by Braxton-Hicks contractions, which are sometimes known as false labor. Some women first notice these contractions as a slight feeling of tightening in the lower abdomen. The sensation may seem strange because the tightening occurs involuntarily. These contractions come and go without any consistent pattern and may be noticed well before real labor ever begins. They do not usually interfere with normal activity. A pregnant woman needs to pay attention to the pattern of her contractions so that she can help identify when the contractions of real labor begin, as described in the text.

that the membrane holding the amniotic fluid surrounding the baby has broken. In most women, this membrane does not rupture until she is at the hospital or birthing center, in active labor.

When the membrane breaks, the woman should note the time, the amount of fluid, and the color and odor of the fluid, and should report this information to her doctor or midwife. He or she may want to deliver the baby within 24 to 48 hours after the membrane has broken, to protect the baby from infection.

Though researchers still do not know exactly what causes labor to begin, it appears that the mother's hormones, her uterus, the placenta, and the baby all play an important role. During the final days of pregnancy, each system undergoes changes in preparation for the birth.

Though there are many clues that a woman is entering into labor, the only clear sign that labor is underway are **contractions**, *the tightening and releasing of the uterine muscle.* Many women wonder what these contractions will be like: "Will they hurt? How will I know I'm having one?" When the uterus contracts, it—like any other muscle—gets shorter and harder. Bend your right arm toward your shoulder while making a tight fist. Feel the muscle in your upper arm become thick and hard. Now, slowly relax and lower your forearm. Feel the muscle stretch and soften. With each contraction of labor, the uterine muscle shortens and gets harder, holds that hardness for a short time, and then relaxes and rests for a few minutes.

The contractions of true labor have a characteristic pattern. Over time, they get longer, stronger, and closer together. Many women find it helpful to have their partner use a watch or clock to time their contractions for a while to see whether they follow this pattern. If they do, the woman should contact her health care provider, who will want to know how long the contractions are lasting, how frequently they are occurring, and how she is feeling.

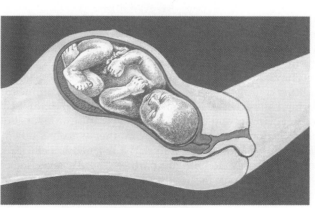

This drawing shows the baby at the end of nine months of pregnancy, before labor begins. The cervix (between the baby's head and the birth canal) is its normal size and shape. On the following pages you will see how the cervix becomes wider and thinner as labor progresses.

HEALTHY FAMILIES/HEALTHY CHILDREN

Fetal Monitoring Devices

Fetal monitoring devices can be used during labor to continuously record the infant's heart rate and the contractions of the uterus. With this information, the medical staff determines the degree of stress on the fetus. Fetal monitoring can be very effective in detecting problems, especially with high-risk births. Some people feel, however, that routine use is unnecessary and interferes with natural childbirth.

TEACH

Pages 194-202

• The Beginning of Labor
• Stages of Labor
• Cesarean Birth
• The Newborn at Birth

GUIDED PRACTICE

Promoting Discussion

Begin by encouraging students to share their own ideas about the emotions and sensations of labor. How do you think first-time parents feel when they recognize the beginnings of labor? What fears and hopes do you imagine they have? Do you think these feelings are different for expectant parents who already have children? If so, how? If not, why not?

Using the Drawing

As students look at the drawing at the bottom of the page, have them describe the position of the baby within the uterus. How does the baby's position conform to the shape and size of the uterus? How has the uterus grown and changed during the pregnancy? How will the uterus change during labor?

Promoting Discussion

Explain to students that, in many cases, the membrane holding the amniotic fluid does not break at the onset of labor, but later during the labor process. One way of referring to the release of amniotic fluid is to say that the mother's water has broken. Encourage students to share information about experiences—either their own or those of women they know—with symptoms that indicate the beginning of labor.

Critical Thinking

Ask students to share their ideas about communication between the pregnant woman and her health care provider. Why is it important for the woman to contact her health care provider when she recognizes the pattern of labor in her contractions? What problems might arise if the woman does not feel comfortable with her health care provider? What other problems might arise if she has not had consistent prenatal care?

GUIDED PRACTICE (continued)

Practicing Decision Making

Present the following situation to the class: Kary has had a healthy pregnancy, with very few discomforts and no complications. She expects her baby to be born in about a week. Today, she is eating lunch with two of her friends. All of a sudden, she feels dampness along her leg. She looks down and sees a small puddle on the floor.

Let students explain what is happening to Kary. What should Kary do? When should she do it? Why?

Critical Thinking

Let students explain why a baby in a breech position may have difficulty moving through the mother's pelvis. Why is it necessary for a birth attendant to continue to monitor the baby and the mother, repeatedly evaluating whether or not a vaginal delivery is safe?

Promoting Discussion

Ask students why, as the text states, the mother can help most by relaxing between and during contractions. What are some ways the labor coach can help her relax?

Cooperative Learning

Let students work in small groups to review prepared childbirth. What is the goal of prepared childbirth? What techniques are usually used? (Refer students to page 182, if necessary.) Then let group members share their ideas in response to these questions: How can a woman use what she learned in childbirth class during the first stage of labor? What difference will this kind of preparation make in the woman's approach and attitude? In her physical condition?

Using the Drawings

Guide students in describing and discussing the drawings on this page and on the next page, showing the first and second stages of labor. How does the cervix change during labor? How does the position of the baby change?

Stages of Labor

When actual labor begins, it progresses through three stages:

- In the first stage, contractions open the cervix.
- In the second stage, the baby is born.
- In the third stage, the placenta is expelled.

The First Stage

Each time the uterus contracts during the first stage of labor, something very special occurs. As the muscles of the uterus shorten and thicken, they gently pull up on the cervix, slowly thinning and opening it until it is wide enough for the baby's head to slip out of the uterus into the birth canal. Ordinarily, the cervix is nearly completely closed. During the first stage of labor, the cervix **dilates**, or *widens*, to form an opening about 4 inches (10 cm) in diameter. Before the cervix can dilate completely, it has to become thinner. It changes from its usual thickness of about ¾ inch (19 mm) to become as thin as a sheet of paper. This process is called effacement.

As labor progresses, the contractions get longer (about 60 seconds), stronger, and closer together (5 to 6 minutes apart). As the contraction pattern intensifies, the woman begins to turn inward, searching for the strength to deal with the sensations of labor. She becomes more serious and focused on the labor, and she needs increasing support from her partner. During this time, the woman usually checks with her doctor or midwife by phone. The birth attendant will tell her when she should go to the hospital or birth center.

As the cervix opens, the baby usually moves down into the lower pelvis, getting ready for birth. In most cases, the baby is head down, but occasionally, babies are in other positions. Some enter the pelvis with their feet, buttocks, or knees first. These positions are called breech presentations. Babies in these positions may have a difficult time moving through the mother's pelvis for birth. An obstetrician will carefully evaluate each situation to determine whether a vaginal delivery is possible or whether a cesarean birth would be safer.

Throughout this first stage of labor, the mother should try to relax as completely as possible, both between contractions and during contractions. Fear and tension cause the muscles of the body to tighten, and tightened muscles can slow labor down and make it more uncomfortable. A mother who has taken a prepared childbirth course may have learned special breathing exercises she can do with her partner. These exercises encourage relaxation, distract the mother from the discomfort of the con-

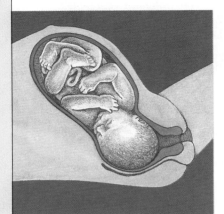

During the first stage of labor, the cervix begins to dilate or widen. The baby's head moves lower in the pelvis.

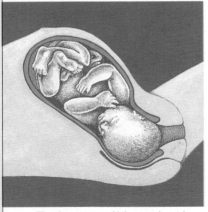

The first stage of labor ends with the cervix fully dilated. The opening of the uterus is now 4 inches (10 cm) wide.

MORE ABOUT

Birth Positions

Years ago, women used an upright position to deliver their babies. Some stood, others squatted, and some used a birth stool. For a while, it was popular to have women lie on their backs in bed during delivery. Then women began giving birth with their knees drawn up. This position is the one used on a delivery table with stirrups. Now many mothers are again using an upright position for giving birth. This position lessens the pressure of the baby and uterus on the mother's veins.

tractions, and help the labor progress. Most mothers may safely assume any positions they find comfortable during the first stage of labor—lying, sitting, standing, walking.

As the first stage of labor comes to an end, the contractions become very strong. They last longer (up to 90 seconds) and come more frequently (2 to 3 minutes apart) than those of early labor. With these last contractions, the cervix stretches and opens until it is fully dilated to 4 inches (10 cm). This part of labor is called transition. It is usually the most difficult part of labor to cope with. A woman's partner needs to be very supportive at this time. The partner can use touch and reassuring words to guide the woman through these last difficult contractions of the first stage.

The Second Stage

Once the cervix is completely dilated and the baby's head has slipped out of the uterus into the vagina, the second stage of labor has begun. The contractions of the second stage are very different from those of the first. They no longer stretch the cervix open. Instead, the contractions work to move the baby down through the pelvis and out the vagina. The second stage of labor may be as short as a few minutes, or it may last up to three hours. It culminates in the event for which the parents have been waiting—the birth of the baby.

You might wonder how a baby could ever fit through what seems to be such a narrow space. Actually, the bones of the pelvis are joined together by ligaments, which are like rubber bands. At the time of delivery, these ligaments are very stretchy, as a result of the influence of a special hormone. The bones of the pelvis gently stretch open as the baby passes through. The vagina is also very stretchy from the effects of the same hormone, so that the baby can safely pass through to be born.

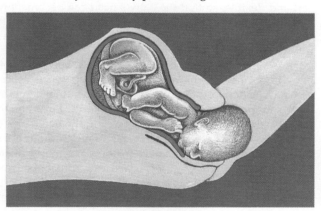

During the second stage of labor, strong contractions push the baby out of the uterus and down the vagina, or birth canal. Notice that the baby begins to rotate to a facedown position.

HEALTH TIP

If the mother finds the first stage of labor very long or difficult, she may choose to use medication to reduce the discomfort. Various kinds of medications are available; their effects vary from changing the woman's perception of pain to completely numbing an area so that no painful sensations are felt. All medications have potential benefits and risks. The possibility of side effects in both the mother and the baby must be considered.

HEALTHY FAMILIES/HEALTHY CHILDREN

Health and Safety

Opinions differ about the use of anesthetics during labor and delivery. Some feel the process is easier and even safer if anesthetics are used. Others feel that medications deprive the mother of the natural experience of childbirth and may even inhibit the process in some way. Some feel that discomforts should be handled in nonmedical ways and are concerned about the effects of drugs on the baby. The important thing for any pregnant woman is to learn about the options and discuss them with the birth attendant ahead of time.

GUIDED PRACTICE (continued)

Promoting Discussion

Discuss with students the transition from the first to the second stage of labor. How does the amount of time spent in each stage compare?

Cooperative Learning

Let students work in groups to discuss this situation: Jerry says, "I almost enjoyed the first stage of labor. Karen was working so hard, and needed me to coach her. Then came the second stage. It was all her show. I felt helpless and useless."

Why do you think Jerry felt that way? How do you imagine Karen felt? Would Karen be in touch with Jerry's feelings during labor? What problems might arise between Jerry and Karen as a result of this situation? Have members of each group brainstorm a list of solutions to Jerry and Karen's problem.

Promoting Discussion

Ask students how a birth attendant might weigh the needs of a mother for pain relief against the probability that it will make the baby sluggish. Who should be the primary concern? Why?

Critical Thinking

Point out to students that some women have very strong feelings—positive or negative—about using medication during labor. Give students an opportunity to explore these feelings and examine possible reasons for them. What would make a woman especially eager to use or avoid pain-relieving medication during labor? With whom should a pregnant woman discuss her preferences? When? What problems might arise if the woman's attitude toward medication differs from that of her care provider? From that of her labor coach?

HEALTH TIP

Regular exercise during pregnancy tones and strengthens the muscles used during labor and lessens some of the discomforts. Less discomfort means less reliance on pain medication.

Using the Drawings
Encourage students to discuss the two drawings on this page. How does the baby's position change during the second stage of labor? What causes that change? How does the baby's head fit through the pelvis and the vaginal canal? How is this passage likely to affect the appearance of the newborn baby?

Promoting Discussion
Ask students to share their own ideas about an episiotomy: Why might a mother want to have an episiotomy or avoid it?

Critical Thinking
Tell students there is some evidence that the use of a birthing chair lessens the need for an episiotomy. What might explain this?

Making Connections: Health
Ask interested students to research recent reasons for using episiotomies? What reasons have been given for avoiding episiotomies or avoiding them? Let students share their findings and encourage a discussion of the advantages and disadvantages.

Cooperative Learning
Let students work in groups to consider the following situations. How would each affect labor—make it easier, make it more difficult, or have no effect? Why? Encourage group members to compare and discuss their ideas.

- A coach is present throughout labor.
- The entire labor, including the birth, takes place at home.
- The mother-to-be has exercised regularly during pregnancy.
- A nurse-midwife, rather than a physician, is the birth attendant.
- The mother-to-be has maintained a healthy diet throughout her pregnancy.
- The mother-to-be lives close to her parents and other family members.
- The mother-to-be has seen a childbirth film.
- The mother-to-be has medical insurance.

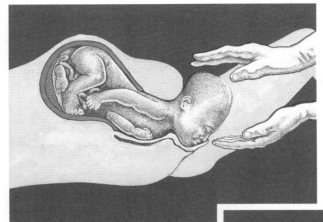

As the head emerges, the baby stretches out. The head may seem "molded" into an odd shape after traveling such a narrow passageway. This is normal and temporary.

Almost there... Getting the head and shoulders out is the "tricky" part of the delivery. After that, the rest of the body slips out easily.

The body of the unborn baby is specially adapted for the journey through the pelvis and the vaginal canal. The skull is soft and flexible, so that the baby's head can become longer and narrower than normal. The skull consists of five separate bones. These bones can overlap each other to allow the baby's head to fit through the pelvis and vagina.

If the birth attendant decides that the fit between mother and baby is not perfect, he or she may use a special procedure to assist in the delivery. One option is to widen the vaginal opening with a surgical incision called an episiotomy. Episiotomy may be used to speed the delivery of the baby in the event of a problem or to prevent tearing of the woman's tissue. Although the procedure was performed routinely in the past, many doctors and midwives now work with women to avoid episiotomy. The woman must be willing to relax the muscles of her bottom and to follow the direction of her birth attendant, so that the vaginal tissues have time to stretch open around the baby's head.

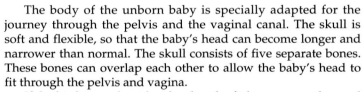

MORE ABOUT

The Baby's Position
The term *station* refers to the location of the baby's head in relation to the three major pelvic bones during second-stage labor. When the baby's head is level with these bones, called the ischial spines, this is zero station. Any position above the bones is a minus station. A plus station is anything below zero station. When the baby's head reaches delivery position, it is at the plus-four station. Sometimes the buttocks or feet, instead of the head, deliver first. Called a *breech birth*, this position puts more pressure on the baby's head during the birth process.

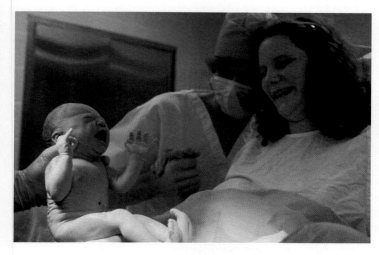

Success! Though she may have felt tired and discouraged earlier in labor, the mother experiences a great surge of energy just before delivery. She is ecstatic and eager to hold her baby.

By bearing down during contractions, the mother begins the delivery of her baby. Women can give birth in a variety of positions. Often women choose a semisitting position in the special birthing bed, with the legs apart and the knees bent. Some women choose squatting, sitting in a birthing chair, lying on the side, or even kneeling on hands and knees for the delivery. If a woman is moved to a traditional delivery table, her legs may be supported by stirrups or foot rests.

As the baby moves down the birth canal, the top of the head appears first. The birth attendant provides gentle support as the head is delivered. The head is followed by one shoulder, and then the other. Then the baby slips out into the world.

Sometimes a doctor uses **forceps**—*specialized tongs made from bands of surgical steel that are molded to fit the shape of a baby's head*—to guide the baby's head during delivery. The forceps enable the doctor to control the movement of the head, helping the baby emerge more quickly—or more slowly—if necessary.

The Third Stage

During the third stage of labor, the uterus gives birth to the placenta. This final stage may be as brief as two minutes, or it may last half an hour. After a period of rest, the mother may again feel some contractions and an urge to push. She usually feels very little discomfort with the contractions of the third stage. These contractions help the placenta separate from the wall of the uterus. The placenta is soft and comes away easily. When the mother pushes and delivers the placenta, the birth process is complete.

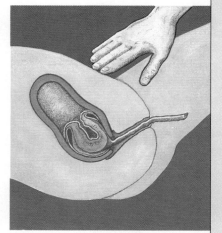

The placenta—no longer needed to nourish the baby—is expelled from the body in the third stage of labor.

HEALTHY FAMILIES/HEALTHY CHILDREN

Fathers and Childbirth

Today, it is common to have the father-to-be present during delivery. Many fathers are eager to share the experience and provide support. Others are not sure about participating or may even be opposed to it. Prepared childbirth classes often help a father gain confidence about participating. Sometimes he quickly forgets his concerns in the excitement of the moment, and the last thing he wants is to be left out. By talking about their feelings ahead of time, a couple can reach a better understanding of what the father's role will be.

GUIDED PRACTICE (continued)

Using the Photograph
Encourage students to describe the photograph at the top of this page and to share their reactions to it.

Using the Drawing
Have students use the drawing to review what happens during the third stage of labor.

Making Connections: Math
Have students investigate the average length of a first labor and compare it with the average length of a second labor. Then ask students to plan and make charts or graphs showing the differences in timing for the three stages of labor.

Cooperative Learning
Let students work in groups to list emotions parents might feel during the birth of their child. Then have them consider and discuss the emotions they have listed. Which emotions would be most likely during each stage of labor? Why?

Family Focus
Have students discuss the benefits of having the baby's father present during labor and delivery. Why would couples want to experience the birth together? How might this strengthen the bond between mother and baby? Between father and baby? Between mother and father?

Promoting Discussion
Explain to students that some people object to the use of forceps because of potential harm to the baby and mother. What dangers might be involved in using forceps? Do you think that the use of forceps has become more—or less—common in recent decades? Why?

Then tell students that, rather than using forceps, some care providers use a vacuum extractor, placed on the baby's head. Why might this technique be safer than using forceps?

GUIDED PRACTICE (continued)

Promoting Discussion

Ask students to consider various reasons for cesarean deliveries. Under what circumstances is a cesarean likely to be planned? What circumstances might lead a care provider to decide on a cesarean close to the time of delivery? Why might a cesarean be performed after labor has started?

Critical Thinking

Ask students to consider the appearance of newborns delivered by cesarean. How would you expect the method of delivery to affect the appearance of the newborn baby? Why?

Promoting Discussion

Ask students why it is a good idea for first-time parents to learn about the appearance of most newborns. When, how, and why would you recommend expectant parents learn this?

Using the Photograph

Encourage students to describe the newborn in the photograph on page 201. How does the infant conform to the text's description of a newborn's unique appearance?

Cooperative Learning

Let students work in groups to examine several photographs of newborn babies and the same babies at one month. Can students match the photos? How have the babies' characteristics changed during the first month of life?

Cultural Exchange

Between 50 and 80 percent of women who have a cesarean delivery are successful in having a vaginal delivery with another child. In 1988, the American College of Obstetricians and Gynecologists began recommending vaginal deliveries after a cesarean birth because of the increased risks of surgery.

Cultural Exchange

THE BIRTH OF CESAREAN

Julius Caesar was one of the most important leaders of ancient Rome. The doctors who attended his birth (probably in 104 B.C.) realized that Caesar's mother was dying in labor. They performed a radical surgery to save her baby— and tiny Julius Caesar was delivered by the procedure that now recalls his name: cesarean birth.

Cesarean Birth

Not all births progress through these three stages of labor. If complications arise during the pregnancy or during labor, a **cesarean birth**—*delivery of a baby through a surgical incision in the mother's abdomen*—may be necessary. Depending on which type of medication is given, the mother may remain awake during cesarean surgery. The father or coach may also be present, with the doctor's permission.

In pregnancies where a cesarean birth is likely, a special cesarean childbirth education class may be recommended to help the parents prepare for the event. After the surgery, the mother and baby usually stay in the hospital for about four days.

The Newborn at Birth

In the hours of labor, the baby undergoes amazing changes. For the first time, the newborn is not completely dependent on the mother's body for life support.

During its development in the uterus, the baby's lungs are filled with fluid. The pressure of being squeezed down the birth canal forces much of the fluid out. When the baby finally emerges, the pressure is released and the baby's lungs automatically expand. The baby takes his or her first breath.

Usually, the breathing reflex continues on its own, and the newborn baby breathes naturally. If the baby needs help, the doctor or nurse-midwife may gently rub the baby's back to get the process started. Any fluid that remains in the airways or mouth is gently suctioned out.

Once the lungs have begun to take in oxygen, the baby's circulatory system changes. A valve in the heart closes and, over the next few days, becomes permanently sealed. Blood now circulates to and from the lungs, rather than bypassing the lungs as before. The umbilical cord, through which the baby has received oxygen and nourishment, is no longer needed. Within a few minutes of birth, the cord stops pulsing and begins to shrink. The cord is clamped, tied, and cut off.

How Does the Newborn Look?

What will our baby look like? When parents imagine their answers to this question, they usually picture a sturdy baby of about six months. They do not often recall that a newborn has a unique appearance.

The newborn's head is wobbly and large; it accounts for one-fourth of the baby's entire length. The head may appear

---

HEALTHY FAMILIES/HEALTHY CHILDREN

Health and Safety

After delivery, the umbilical cord is clamped in two places and cut between the clamps. The remaining stub later dries and falls off, leaving what is know as the belly button, or navel. The timing of this procedure sometimes differs. The placenta contains 25 to 30 percent of a newborn's iron-rich blood, which flows to the infant through the umbilical cord after delivery. Since the iron can help prevent anemia later on, some medical professionals do not clamp the cord until it stops pulsing. Others feel that too much blood can cause problems, so clamping is done immediately or very shortly after delivery.

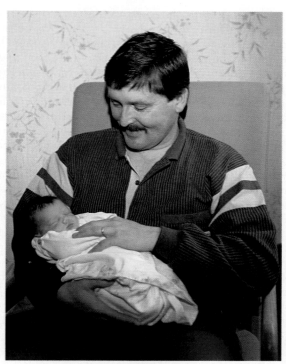

The newborn may have a full head of hair or no hair at all. Red marks on the skin are common. Can you see how the newborn's facial features make sucking easier?

strangely lopsided or pointed from the passage through the birth canal. The bones of the baby's skull are not yet tightly knitted together, so they can be molded together during birth without harm. Any lopsidedness is only temporary.

The baby's head has two **fontanels**, *open spaces where the bones of the baby's skull have not yet permanently joined.* The larger of these "soft spots" is just above the baby's forehead. The other fontanel is toward the back of the skull. These spaces allow the bones of the baby's skull to move together during birth. As the baby grows older, usually between the ages of six and eighteen months, the bone structure comes together to cover the spaces completely. In the meantime, the soft spots are protected by skin that is as tough as heavy canvas.

The newborn typically has fat cheeks; a short, flat nose; and a receding chin. These features make the baby's face well adapted for sucking, because the nose and chin are out of the way.

At birth, a baby's eyes are nearly adult-sized. They are usually dark grayish-blue at birth. The baby's permanent eye color becomes apparent within several months.

MORE ABOUT

Cesarean Births

In the past, a woman who delivered one baby by cesarean birth delivered any later babies by the same method. This was a response to a concern that the scar in the uterine muscle could rupture during the contractions of labor. If it were to rupture, both mother and baby would be in danger.

Improvements in cesarean surgeries, increases the safety and the quality of the birth experience.

In most cases now, the incision into the uterus is made very low in the uterine muscle, where it receives very little stress during labor contractions.

This new incision reduces the risk of uterine rupture, so most physicians encourage women who deliver by cesarean to try vaginal birth for their next baby unless a medical reason prohibits it. Vaginal birth is generally safer and easier to recover from than cesarean birth.

INDEPENDENT PRACTICE

Journal Writing
Ask students to imagine themselves as a mother who has just delivered her first baby, or as a father who has just witnessed birth for the first time. In this role, have students write journal entries, describing what they have experienced and exploring their reactions to it.

Student Workbook
Have students complete "Stages of Labor" in the Student Workbook.

Extension
Let students work independently or in small groups to complete one or more of these:

• Research various pain-reducing medications and/or anesthetics used during labor. Under what circumstances is each likely to be used? What is the effect of each on the mother? On the baby? Write your report.

• Interview three mothers about their experiences with labor. How did each woman realize that labor was beginning? How long did the first stage of labor last? When did she go to the hospital or birthing center? Which part of labor did she find most satisfying? Most difficult? Why? Plan and present an oral report.

• Read books, magazine or journal articles about cesarean births. What percentage of births are cesarean? For what medical conditions might a cesarean be needed? What are the effects of a cesarean birth on mother and baby? Write a short report.

Did You Know?

Hans Christian Anderson, famous Danish writer, popularized the Norse myth that storks deliver babies down the chimney of a house. Storks were known for their gentle, caring nature, and their habit of nesting in the same chimney year after year.

ASSESS

CHECKING COMPREHENSION

Assign students to write their responses to the Check Your Understanding questions in the Section 1 Review. Answers to the questions are given at the bottom of this page.

EVALUATE

Have students complete the Chapter 7, Section 1 quiz in the TCR.

Reteaching

1. Challenge students to complete Enrichment 17 in the TCR.

2. Work with small groups of students to review the three stages of labor. Then let pairs of students plan and make charts identifying the main occurrences during each of the three stages.

Enrichment

1. Have students complete Reteaching 17 in the TCR.

2. Have students interview an obstetrician or read magazine or journal articles written by obstetricians. Ask students to find out about the kinds of pain medication used during childbirth. How do births in which the mother receives pain-relieving medication compare with births in which no pain medications are used? What factors influence the decision to use pain-reducing medication? How and why is a specific kind of medication chosen? Let students present brief oral reports.

Extension

Show the class a videotape or film of an actual delivery, including, if possible, portions of all three stages of labor. Encourage students to discuss the events during each stage of labor and to share their reactions to the birth.

CLOSE

Ask each student to present a fact or a helpful tip about one of the three stages of labor.

At the time of birth, the newborn is often a dusky color. Very quickly after the baby begins to breathe, his or her color improves. It takes some time for the circulatory system to adjust to life outside the womb. As a result, some babies' fingers and toes remain dusky and slightly cooler than the rest of their body for up to 24 hours. Wrapping the baby well and covering his or her head with a cap helps keep the baby warm and comfortable.

Newborns have many unique characteristics that new parents may not be prepared for. Some babies, particularly those born early, have fine, downy hair over their forehead, back, and shoulders. This hair disappears as the baby grows.

While in the uterus, the baby bathes in warm amniotic fluid. To protect their skin from constant exposure to the fluid, babies are covered with a rich, creamy substance called vernix. After the birth, most newborns have some vernix in the folds of their skin, particularly around their ears and neck and under their arms. During the baby's bath, it can be gently removed with warm water and a washcloth.

Many babies have tiny white bumps scattered over their nose and cheeks. These bumps are called milia, or baby acne. They are simply plugged oil ducts, caused by stimulation from the maternal hormones, which remain in the baby's system for a short time after delivery. The milia will disappear in a week or two.

SECTION 1 REVIEW

CHECK YOUR UNDERSTANDING

1. What are contractions?
2. What is the cervix? How does it change during labor?
3. What happens in the second stage of labor?
4. What are forceps? How may they be used?
5. What happens in the third stage of labor?
6. What is a cesarean birth?
7. What causes a newborn to begin breathing?
8. What are fontanels? What purpose do they serve?

DISCUSS AND DISCOVER

1. Why is it important for a mother to relax during labor? What factors can make relaxing especially difficult? What do you think a mother's birthing partner can—and should—do to help her relax?

2. Read more about the experiences of first-time mothers during the three stages of labor. Then draw a time line showing how long each stage typically lasts and what happens during each stage.

Observing & Participating

On the basis of information in this chapter, write a list of the physical characteristics of newborns. Then observe a newborn baby, either in a hospital nursery or at home. Indicate which of the listed physical characteristics you observed. If possible, observe more than one baby and compare findings. Speculate about any differences you notice.

SECTION 1 REVIEW

1. The tightening and releasing of the uterine muscle.

2. The lower part of the uterus; it slowly thins and opens.

3. Contractions move the baby down through the pelvis and out the vagina.

4. Specialized tongs made from bands of surgical steel molded to fit the shape of a baby's head; to guide the baby's head during delivery.

5. The placenta is delivered.

6. Delivery of a baby through a surgical incision in the mother's abdomen.

7. When the baby emerges from the birth canal, pressure on the lungs is released and they automatically expand, the baby's first breath results.

8. Open spaces where the bones of the baby's skull have not yet permanently joined; allow the bones of the skull to move together during birth.

The Postnatal Period

OBJECTIVES

- Describe common hospital procedures following a birth.
- Give recommendations for the postnatal care of the mother.
- Explain the special needs of a premature baby.

The moment of birth signals the end of nine months of preparation and anticipation. Of course, the moment of birth is also a beginning. In a short time, the newborn—also called a neonate—and his or her parents will go home to begin their new life together. First, however, the staff at the hospital or birthing center must make sure the new family gets off to a good start.

TERMS TO LEARN

Apgar scale
bonding
colostrum
incubator
rooming-in

Examining the Newborn

Shortly after delivery, the neonate is usually checked according to the **Apgar scale**, *a method of evaluating a newborn's physical condition*. The infant is given a rating from 0 to 2 in each of these five areas: pulse, breathing, muscle tone, reflex to stimulation, and skin color. A total score of 6 to 10 is considered normal. A lower score is a sign that the baby needs special medical attention. Usually, the Apgar evaluation is given one minute after birth and then again at five minutes after birth. The baby is also given a brief examination to check for any conditions that might require special care.

Within 60 minutes of delivery, drops of silver nitrate or an antiseptic ointment are put into the baby's eyes to guard against infection. The baby is weighed, measured, and, in some cases, cleaned up. A permanent copy of the baby's footprints is made for public record. Two bands giving the baby's family name are clamped to the wrists or ankles. The mother wears a bracelet with the same information. These identification procedures are completed before the baby leaves the delivery room or birthing room to avoid any confusion later.

MORE ABOUT

The Apgar Scale

Because it is normal for white newborns to have blue hands and feet, these babies may not receive perfect scores of 10, either at one or five minutes. The chart on page 135 shows the color scale for a white child. A black newborn who is grayish and pale scores a 0 on the color scale. If the black newborn has a strong body color, but grayish limbs, the score is a 1. A score of 2 is given to a black newborn who has a strong color, pink lips, and pink palms and soles.

SECTION 2
The Postnatal Period
Pages 203-210

FOCUS

SECTION 2 RESOURCES

Teacher's Classroom Resources
- Enrichment 18
- Reteaching 18
- Section 2 Quiz

Student Workbook
- The Postnatal Period

SECTION OVERVIEW

As they read Section 2, students gain important information about the first hours and days in a baby's life. Students begin by considering the appearance and health of the newborn; then they discuss the process of bonding, which can begin as soon as the baby has been delivered. Students also learn about the main events of the hospital stay for both mother and baby, about appropriate postnatal care for mothers, and about the special care needs of premature infants.

MOTIVATOR

Ask students to imagine themselves as newborns, who have just left the dark, warm, confined, and predictable environment of the mother's uterus. Have each student list at least five phrases expressing the newborn's reactions to the "outside world." Then have several volunteers read their lists aloud; encourage students to compare and discuss their ideas.

USING TERMS TO LEARN

Help students pronounce the five vocabulary terms introduced in Section 2, and encourage them to discuss what they already know about the meaning of each. You may want to point out to students that the Apgar scale bears the name of the American physician who designed it—Virginia Apgar 1909-1974.

TEACH

Pages 203-210

- Examining the Newborn
- Bonding and Attachment
- The Hospital Stay
- Postnatal Care of the Mother
- Caring for Premature Babies

GUIDED PRACTICE

Promoting Discussion

Help students consider the word neonate. Have you ever heard parents use this term? Have you heard it used by doctors or other health care professionals? What is the meaning of the prefix neo? What other words can you recall that also begin with the prefix neo? How do you think the root word nate relates to the word natal, with which you are familiar in such words as prenatal and postnatal?

Critical Thinking

Ask students to explain why both the mother and the newborn baby wear identification bands. What problems could arise if the baby were not given an identification band in the delivery room or birthing room? What might be involved in attempts to solve such problems?

Using the Chart

Guide students in reading and discussing the chart, The Apgar Scale, on this page. Explain that the Apgar evaluation is a quick way to assess the newborn's health. A more thorough examination is normally done 12 to 24 hours after the birth. Help students discuss what the Apgar scale evaluates and how the scoring is done.

Family Focus

In many ways, the bonding that takes place in the hours and days following a baby's birth affects the family for years to come. Emphasize to students the importance of bonding as one factor in a strong family life.

Using the Photograph

Encourage students to discuss the family in the photograph on this page. How are the parents and their baby bonding? Why is this process important?

THE APGAR SCALE

	SCORE		
	0	1	2
HEART RATE	Absent	Under 100	Over 100
BREATHING	Absent	Slow, irregular	Good, crying
MUSCLE TONE	Limp	Some movement of extremities	Active motion
RESPONSIVENESS (Baby's reaction when nose is irritated)	No response	Grimace	Cough or sneeze
COLOR	Blue or pale	Body limbs pink, not blue	Completely pink

(The chart above shows the color scale for a white child. An infant of dark-skin color who is grayish and pale scores a 0 on the color scale. If the dark-skinned infant has a strong body color, but grayish limbs, the score is 1. A score of 2 is given to a dark-skinned newborn who has strong color, pink lips, and pink palms and soles.)

Bonding and Attachment

In recent years, researchers have focused increasing attention on the emotional needs of the newborn. Many experts feel that it is natural for lifelong emotional ties to be formed between parents and the newborn soon after birth. Facilitating **bonding**—*the process of forming lifelong emotional ties*—has become a goal in many hospitals and birthing centers. Most facilities now delay such procedures as cutting the umbilical cord, cleaning the infant, and giving eyedrops so that parents have the opportunity to begin bonding with their newborn right away.

Immediately after birth, a healthy baby may be placed in the mother's arms or on her stomach. The baby can feel the mother's skin and hear her familiar heartbeat and voice. The newborn instinctively focuses on the mother's face. In turn, the mother—and the father, if he is present—enjoys stroking and talking to the baby.

If the baby will be breast-fed, the mother may nurse the baby within minutes after birth. The baby knows instinctively what to do. Many hospitals have specially trained professionals who assist the nursing couple at these first feedings to ensure success. The mother's breasts supply *the first breast milk*, called **colostrum**. The colostrum is easy for the newborn to digest and rich in antibodies to protect against disease. It is sometimes thick in consistency; it may be clear or yellow in color.

Bonding takes place as the parents and baby interact through sight, sound, and touch. This process is important for the baby's development. It also brings out the parents' natural desire to love and care for their baby.

HEALTHY FAMILIES/HEALTHY CHILDREN

Health and Safety

Colostrum is a thick, yellowish, milky substance that is present in the breasts even before birth. It is lower in carbohydrates and fat than later breast milk and higher in protein, vitamin A, and minerals. Because of the low fat in colostrum, it is easy for the baby to digest and has a mild laxative effect.

This helps clear the baby's digestive tract of meconium, the greenish-black stools accumulated while the baby was in the uterus. The antibodies in colostrum help prevent infections and illness in the newborn, and the growth hormone it contains promotes healthy growth.

The Hospital Stay

The process of birth is a momentous undertaking for both mother and baby. The newborn must adjust to a whole new world. The mother, too, needs time to adjust. In a matter of hours, her body has gone through many physical changes, from pregnancy to labor and birth and back to the nonpregnant state. Although she probably feels thrilled and excited, she also needs to rest and recuperate.

After delivery, the medical staff monitor the new mother's blood pressure, pulse, and other vital signs until all body functions have stabilized.

Nationally, there are differences in the length of time mother and baby are expected to stay in the hospital. At a minimum, the mother needs a chance to eat, bathe, and rest. She and her infant must also be medically checked, to make sure everything is going well. In some hospitals and birthing centers, a mother and baby who are both healthy may go home if that is where the mother feels she can recuperate best. This may be as soon as 12 hours after the birth. In other hospitals, the average stay for mother and baby following birth is two or three days.

Rooming-In

Many hospitals have a **rooming-in** program, *an arrangement in which the baby stays in the mother's room, rather than in a hospital nursery, after birth.* In most cases, the baby stays at the mother's bedside both day and night.

Rooming-in allows the new family to be together. It is a natural beginning to family unity and warm parent-child relationships. With rooming-in programs, fathers are allowed to visit whenever they wish.

Rooming-in programs have important advantages for all family members. They provide a homelike atmosphere in which grandparents and older brothers and sisters can visit, hold, and get to know the new baby. Couples benefit by having an opportunity to get to know their baby and practice caring for the baby before going home. The baby can be fed whenever he or she is hungry, rather than on a set schedule. In a good rooming-in program, parents enjoy a head start in getting to know their newborn, and babies seem more content.

Birth Certificate

All new parents should make sure their baby has a birth certificate. Usually, the birth certificate is issued free of charge soon after the baby is born.

Getting to know your new baby brother is easier when you can visit Mom in the hospital and even hold the baby yourself.

MORE ABOUT

Leboyer Method

Some health care professionals feel that giving the baby a warm bath right after delivery, as recommended in the Leboyer method is harmful to the baby's respiratory system. The method also suggests late clamping of the umbilical cord, which some doctors feel allows too much blood from the placenta to enter the circulatory system of the newborn. However, one study that measured several factors (including the newborn's temperature, heart rate, and Apgar score) found no evidence of increased danger to the Leboyer babies.

GUIDED PRACTICE (continued)

Practicing Decision Making

Present the following situation to the class: Bob was out of town when Teresa went into labor, two weeks before her due date. He was not able to get home in time for the birth. When he did arrive, he found that, because of her size, the baby had to stay in an incubator; Bob could see his tiny new daughter, but he couldn't hold her.

Then guide students in discussing the situation. What problems might this cause for Bob and the baby? For Bob and Teresa? What suggestions would you make for helping Bob bond with the new baby under these circumstances?

Critical Thinking

Researchers have been able to identify potentially abusive parents by observing the interaction of mothers and fathers with their newborn infants. Have students assume they are doing this kind of research. What specific behaviors do you think would indicate a potential for parental neglect or abuse? What specific behaviors do you think would indicate the beginning of a healthful, nurturing relationship?

Promoting Discussion

Let students share their ideas in response to these questions: What are the advantages of a short hospital stay? What are the advantages of a long hospital stay? Why is there no one best length?

Practicing Decision Making

Describe this situation to students: Latrisha will be giving birth to her third child in the near future. She has two children, ages two and four. Her husband works two jobs in order to make ends meet. Latrisha feels that she will be needed at home soon after the baby is born, but she also remembers how exhausted she was after delivering her last child.

Ask students how soon they think Latrisha should come home from the hospital after giving birth. Why does that seem like a good hospital stay for her? What options might Latrisha have to make this situation easier?

Promoting Discussion

Discuss these questions: Why is a birth certificate the most important piece of personal identification anyone has? What problems can arise for a person who does not have one?

Ask students about their own birth certificates. When did you get one? Where is it kept? Have you ever seen it? Have you ever needed to use it?

Critical Thinking

How might the physical needs of a new mother conflict with the needs of her newborn baby? How should parents respond to these conflicts?

Practicing Decision Making

Ask students to consider this situation: Lisa and the new baby had been home from the hospital for two weeks. The baby seemed to be awake nearly all the time. One night he awoke for feedings at 10:00 p.m., at 1:00 a.m., at 3:00 a.m., and again at 4:30 a.m. When the alarm clock went off at 6:00, Lisa could hardly get out of bed. She felt physically sick, and wished the baby would go away. Lisa thought her baby's not sleeping more meant she was a bad mother. Lisa also felt lonely at home, and missed her friends at work. Worst of all, Lisa felt guilty about her negative feelings. She knew her husband Jim was helping as much as he could, so she kept her feelings to herself and tried to be cheerful. Unfortunately, Lisa's negative feelings just got worse.

Discuss Lisa's feelings. Are they normal? What—if anything—do they indicate about Lisa and her baby? What should Lisa do? Why?

Making Connections: Health

Remind students of the importance of a carefully planned diet for women who are vegetarians and who are breast-feeding their babies. Have students plan a day's menu for a nursing woman who is a vegetarian. It should include combinations of grains and legumes for protein; and large amounts of green leafy vegetables to provide calcium.

Getting a birth certificate when a baby is born is a rather simple process. The parents simply need to fill out a form provided by the hospital or birthing center, at which time a temporary certificate is issued. In many states, the official birth certificate can be applied for by the family or by the hospital on behalf of the family. In our society, a birth certificate is considered the most important piece of personal identification anyone has; it is required for entrance into school.

Postnatal Care of the Mother

After the baby is brought home, it is natural for most of the attention to be focused on the new family member. However, care of the mother is just as important as the baby's care. A new mother has special physical and emotional needs, which continue for several weeks or months after the birth. A doctor or nurse will explain and discuss these needs before the mother and baby go home.

Physical Needs

Physically, the mother needs to recover from pregnancy and childbirth and to regain fitness. She must also take good care of herself so that she is able to care for her child. The best way to accomplish these goals is through rest, exercise, nutrition, and a medical checkup.

Rest and exercise are important to a new mother. A good time to rest is as the baby naps.

- **Rest.** During the first few days and weeks following the birth, the mother is likely to feel tired. She should try to sleep whenever the baby does. This will help her get the rest she needs, even with late-night feedings. Many couples especially appreciate having a relative or friend help with household chores or with baby care during this early period.

- **Exercise.** As soon as the mother feels able and her doctor approves, she should begin mild exercise. At first, this may be just a few simple stretches while lying down. Gradually, the mother can add other exercises to this simple routine. Postnatal exercise helps the woman return to her normal figure and correct posture.

- **Nutrition.** Eating right is just as important after pregnancy as during pregnancy. A mother who breast-feeds her baby should be sure to eat the number of servings recommended by the Food Guide Pyramid for nursing women. She should also drink plenty of water and other liquids. Just as before the birth, the food she eats is supplying the nutrients for the baby as well as for her own needs. Even if the mother is not breast-feeding, good nutrition helps her feel good and regain her energy.

HEALTHY FAMILIES/HEALTHY CHILDREN

Benefits of Breast-feeding

Breast-feeding offers special benefits to a premature infant. Studies show that preterm milk differs in several ways from full-term milk. For one thing, it has about twice as much protein needed for growth. For about a week, it also contains almost double the usual amount of a special nutrient that helps build cell membranes and that aids brain and nervous system development. In addition, preterm milk is easier to digest. If the premature infant cannot be breast-fed right away, the milk can be expressed and frozen for later use.

• **Medical checkup.** About four to six weeks after the birth, the new mother should have a postnatal checkup. At this appointment, the doctor makes sure that the woman's uterus is returning to normal and that there are no unusual problems. This is also an opportunity for the mother to discuss any questions or concerns she has about adjusting to parenthood and about birth control.

Emotional Needs

Having a baby is a joyous event, but also a stressful one. Many new mothers go through a few days of mild depression sometime after the birth. They may have feelings of disappointment, loneliness, or resentment. No one knows for certain why the "baby blues" occur, but they are very common. Actually, new fathers often have these feelings, too.

New parents should expect to experience some unhappy moods after the birth. It helps to talk over their feelings with each other and with empathetic relatives or friends. If possible, the parents should arrange to take some time away from the baby for short periods—even just a few minutes a day. Taking good care of themselves, seeking support, and avoiding isolation helps parents minimize the blues.

The "baby blues" usually clear up in a few days. In the meantime, friends and relatives can help take some of the pressure off the new parents.

HEALTHY FAMILIES/HEALTHY CHILDREN

Health and Safety

The period of depression that some women experience after giving birth is called *postpartum depression.* Generally, the causes are both physical and psychological. A physical change in hormones occurs as the woman's body returns to its non-pregnant state. Psychologically, an emotional let-down may have any of several causes. Sometimes a woman expects automatic maternal feelings and love for the baby. If she doesn't have them, she may feel guilty. Fatigue and anxiety about her ability to care for the child may cause negative feelings. She may even feel unattractive and miss the attention that was focused on her during labor and delivery. A mild depression of short duration is normal. Reassurance and support from those around her will usually see a woman through such times.

GUIDED PRACTICE (continued)

Promoting Discussion
Ask students to identify and discuss the challenges a mother might face in providing for her own physical and emotional needs while, at the same time, caring for her newborn.

Cooperative Learning
Let students work in groups to brainstorm suggestions for relatives and friends who want to help the parents of a newborn baby. Then encourage group members to discuss the suggestions on their lists. Which kinds of help are easiest or most convenient to offer? Which kinds are most appropriate? Why?

Using the Photograph
Encourage students to discuss the couple shown in the photograph on this page. What do you imagine the new mother is feeling? Why? How do you imagine her husband feels? Why? How is he trying to help her? What other kind of help might be appropriate?

Cooperative Learning
Let groups of students work together to develop a list of ways prenatal care can influence the probability of premature birth. Then have each group share its ideas with the rest of the class. Are all premature births caused by poor prenatal care? Why or why not?

Promoting Discussion
Point out to students that the care of premature infants is both costly and risky. Hospital costs may be $1,000 or more per day for weeks or even months. In spite of such efforts and expenditures, some conditions caused by prematurity or its treatment may be permanent. Ask students how these costs, risks, and separations might affect the families of premature newborns.

Also explain that during the 1940s, parents of premature babies were often not allowed to see their babies until they were well enough to take home. (Hospitals feared parents would carry germs and infections.) Ask students how these policies would affect the bonding process.

BUILDING SELF-ESTEEM

Because premature babies are weaker than full-term ones, they are slow to get started with feeding and therefore do not grow as fast, remaining in the lower ranges of growth tables. Yet with excellent care, they catch up to their normal-weight peers by the time they start school.

INDEPENDENT PRACTICE

Journal Writing

Ask students to write journal entries exploring their own feelings about bonding between newborns and their parents. To spark their thinking, pose these questions: What physical conditions might prevent or postpone bonding? What emotional ones? Why? What happens to an infant who fails to bond with a parent or significant caregiver? What can be done to help children who, as infants, were unable to bond?

Student Workbook

Distribute "The Postnatal Period" in the Student Workbook and have students review their answers.

Extension

Working independently or in small groups, complete one or both of these:

- Read about the Kemp Center in Denver, Colorado, known for its research concerning child abuse, bonding, and healthy parenting. Investigate some of the recent research projects at the Kemp Center, write about your findings.

- Interview a physician or other birth attendant who practices the Leboyer method of birth. What procedures are followed during and after the birth? Why has he or she chosen this method? How does he or she feel it affects family bonding? Present your findings in a brief report.

BUILDING SELF-ESTEEM

Meeting the Needs of Premature Babies

Modern medicine is also concerned about the emotional needs of premature babies. In some hospitals, the babies are gently stroked within their incubators. Many hospitals encourage parents to spend time with their babies, touching them within the incubator or holding them outside the incubator for short periods. In one experiment, a tiny, heated waterbed was designed to simulate the warmth and free-floating sensations the baby experiences before birth. In addition, the sounds of the mother's heartbeat, her voice, and soft music were played for the infant. These measures soothed the premature babies, allowing them to save precious energy for growth.

Caring for Premature Babies

Premature babies—those born before prenatal development is complete—require special care. They are smaller than normal at birth. Prematurity can happen for many reasons, not all of which are understood. Any newborn who weighs less than 5 ½ pounds (2.5 kg) or who is born before 36 weeks is considered premature and may need special medical attention. The more the baby weighs at birth and the closer the pregnancy comes to full term, the better the baby's chances of healthy survival.

Premature babies are not ready to live outside the mother's body. Their systems for heat regulation, breathing, and sucking and swallowing are not yet mature. To minimize these problems, a premature baby is usually placed in an **incubator**, *a special enclosed crib in which the oxygen supply, temperature, and humidity can be closely controlled.*

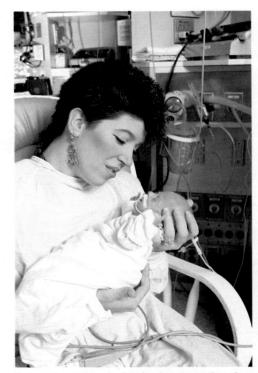

Today, advanced medical technology is combined with a recognition of the premature infant's emotional needs, including close contact with parents when possible.

HEALTHY FAMILIES/HEALTHY CHILDREN

Diabetes and Pregnancy

Pregnant women may develop gestational diabetes. They need to be careful with their diet and how much weight they gain. Otherwise, the baby could develop problems. This condition often goes away after they give birth.

PARENTING
IN ACTION

Caring for Premature Babies

Four-year-old Erica scrambles happily up the climbing equipment in the preschool play yard. She is a sturdy, cheerful child, and she fits in well with her preschool classmates. Looking at her today, you would never guess that Erica was born six weeks early.

Erica weighed only 3½ pounds (1.6 kg) at birth. However, she had no physical problems other than her low birth weight.

As a newborn, Erica became part of a special study. She was one of 79 babies that weighed 2 to 4 pounds (0.9 to 1.8 kg) at birth but were otherwise healthy. Half of the babies in the study were kept in the hospital for standard treatment. The others were sent home 11 days earlier and given intensive nursing services at home.

Erica was one of the babies sent home early. With loving care from both parents and frequent checkups from the medical team, Erica gained weight steadily and developed no health problems.

The medical study was completed when Erica was almost a year old. According to the report, the average costs for the babies discharged early, including home nurses' fees, were almost $20,000 less per infant than the costs of standard hospital treatment. These babies experienced no more medical complications than did the babies kept in the hospital.

THINK AND DISCUSS

1. How do you think Erica's emotional development might have been affected by the kind of care she received?

2. If you were the parent of a premature baby like Erica, would you prefer to have your baby come home early or stay in the hospital? Why?

In the incubator, the baby's heart and lungs are electronically monitored. Special medical procedures and medications may be needed to combat infection, breathing difficulties, and other problems. Advances in medical technology allow many premature infants—even those weighing as little as 1 pound (454 g)—to survive and become healthy.

When they become healthy enough to leave the incubator, premature babies are moved to an open bassinet. Before being allowed to leave the hospital, the baby must achieve the ability to control his or her body temperature and gain weight at the same time.

COOPERATIVE LEARNING

Communication Skills

A critical ingredient in positive group interaction is good communication. To help your students derive maximum benefit from their cooperative endeavors, publish the following list of communication rules, and encourage students to consult the list periodically.

• When working outside the classroom, choose a distraction-free environment, out of earshot of radios, televisions, and loud gatherings.

• In addition to making your own message clear, *listen* to the messages of other group members. Give your undivided attention to the person speaking.

• Never interrupt. When you have finished speaking, yield the floor graciously to the next speaker.

PARENTING
IN ACTION

Promoting Discussion

Introduce this Parenting in Action selection by encouraging students to discuss their ideas about prematurity and its effects. To stimulate the discussion, you might pose questions such as these: How do you react when you see photographs of tiny premature newborns in incubators? How do you imagine they might feel? What future do you imagine they have? How do you think their parents feel? What emotional difficulties do the families of premature infants face? What financial and other problems?

Then ask if any student was born prematurely? What effects—if any—does your prematurity have on you now? Have any of you given birth to premature infants, or have your friends or relatives? What have those experiences been like? How have the premature babies developed?

After this discussion, ask students to read "Caring for Premature Babies."

Thinking Critically

After reading the Parenting in Action selection, ask for reactions to the experiences of Erica and her family. How did going home early benefit Erica? How did it help her parents? Do you imagine Erica's parents still think of her as "our premature baby"? If so, do you think she will always have this status in their family? When might they stop thinking of her as premature? Why?

Answers to Think and Discuss

1. Erica and her parents were probably more easily able to bond than they would have been if she had remained in the hospital.

2. Encourage students to share—and support—various points of view.

ASSESS

CHECKING COMPREHENSION

Assign students to write their responses to the Check Your Understanding questions in the Section 2 Review. Answers to the questions are given below.

EVALUATE

Have students complete the Chapter 7, Section 2 TCR quiz.

Reteaching

1. Ask students to complete Reteaching 18 in the TCR.

2. Show students photographs of babies in a hospital nursery and in various rooming-in settings, and encourage students to share their reactions. In which setting do you think a baby is likely to get the best possible care? Why? In which situation do you think a mother is likely to get the most rest and the best opportunity for recuperation? Why? If given a choice, which situation would you select? Why?

Enrichment

1. Challenge students to complete TCR Enrichment 18.

2. Ask students to research the changes that have taken place in childbirth procedures and in the care of newborns during the last 50 years. What has motivated these changes? What effects have the changes had? Have students write short reports summarizing their findings.

Extension

Invite two or more mothers of young babies to visit the class. Ask them to describe what their babies looked like immediately after birth and to discuss their own emotional responses to their newborn's appearance.

CLOSE

Have each student complete the following sentence, either orally or in writing:

If I were the parent of a newborn, I would want...

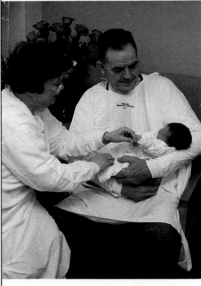

These proud grandparents were able to see and hold the baby just one day after birth.

Medical science continues to work at increasing the survival rate of premature and low birth weight babies. Efforts are also being made to reduce the rate of such births. One way to reach this goal is through educating the public in the importance of good nutrition, good health practices, medical care during pregnancy, and an understanding of the warning signs of premature labor. Helping young people recognize the dangers of teen pregnancy is also important. Researchers continue to explore other factors that increase the risks of prematurity and low birth weight.

If premature labor is recognized soon enough, the mother can be given medication that may stop the contractions before they progress to delivery. A small device that monitors uterine contractions has become available recently. A woman considered at high risk for premature delivery can wear this device for short periods, beginning in about the fifth month of pregnancy. If premature labor begins, the device detects it and the woman's doctor can be quickly alerted.

SECTION 2 REVIEW

CHECK YOUR UNDERSTANDING

1. What is the Apgar scale? When is it used?
2. What is bonding? When does it take place?
3. What is colostrum?
4. List two advantages of rooming-in.
5. How soon after birth should a mother begin to exercise?
6. What are the "baby blues"? Who can suffer from them?
7. What is an incubator? How is it used?

DISCUSS AND DISCOVER

1. Do you think parents and their babies who do not have an opportunity to bond immediately after birth are at a disadvantage? Why or why not? Do you think parents who have cesarean births or who adopt might have trouble bonding with their babies? If so, what kinds of problems could they have? If not, why not?

Observing & Participating

Visit a local hospital and find out if it has any special programs that provide extra handling and attention for premature babies. If so, describe how the program is conducted and who can participate. Share you findings with the rest of the class.

SECTION 2 REVIEW

1. A method of evaluating a newborn's physical condition; one minute and again five minutes after birth.
2. The process of forming lifelong emotional ties. It can begin immediately after the baby's birth.
3. The first breast milk.
4. Any two: allows the new family time together; allows other family members to visit new baby; parents can practice caring for baby before going home; baby can be fed whenever hungry; fosters contentment in baby.
5. When she feels able and her doctor ok's.
6. A mild depression following a baby's birth; mother or father of new baby.
7. A special enclosed crib in which the oxygen supply, temperature, and humidity can be controlled; to minimize problems a premature baby may have with heat regulation and breathing.

A New Family Member

SECTION 3
A New Family Member
Pages 211-219

OBJECTIVES

- Describe babies' basic needs.
- Discuss how babies' needs can best be met.

For the first few months of life, every baby is considered "new." The baby's family, too, is newly expanded, with new relationships to establish. Welcoming this tiny person home and getting to know him or her are exciting aspects of adjusting to life with a new baby.

The Amazing Newborn

Newborn babies are amazing, born with remarkable capabilities. Recent research has shown that newborns can focus their eyes, hear, smell, and vocalize to communicate.

A researcher at Harvard University discovered that babies less than a day old could follow a pattern printed on paper and rolled before their eyes. Other studies show that newborns seem to select certain outlines, such as edges and angles, for attention. Newborns also prefer human faces to other shapes. Hearing is also present at birth, though it takes a few days for the neonate's auditory canals to clear of the amniotic fluid and for the hearing to become fully functional. Infants selectively respond to human sounds, particularly the female human voice—especially the mother's. Newborns can hear many sounds and distinguish between different pitches. Taste, smell, and touch are also present right from birth.

The newborn can breathe independently. The newborn can also cry to signal a variety of needs, such as the need for food, attention, or a dry diaper.

Reflexes

Babies must be able to handle certain of their own needs involuntarily until they learn to do things voluntarily. **Reflexes**—*instinctive, automatic responses, such as sneezing and yawning*—make this possible. These coordinated patterns of

TERMS TO LEARN

grasp reflex
reflexes
rooting reflex
startle reflex
temperament

FOCUS

SECTION 3 RESOURCES

Teacher's Classroom Resources
- Enrichment 19
- Reteaching 19
- Section 3 Quiz

Student Workbook
- Are Baby's Needs Being Met?

SECTION OVERVIEW

Section 3 helps students understand the changes that take place within a family following the birth of a baby. Students begin by examining the abilities and reflexes of newborn babies. Then they consider the special care needs of babies and discuss the adjustments that parents and other caregivers must make in learning to meet the individual needs of a newborn.

MOTIVATOR

Ask students to imagine themselves as newborn infants, entirely dependent on others, as they respond to these questions: What do you require? Whom do you expect to meet your needs? What do you do to communicate your needs? How do you feel when others misunderstand your communication? When they do not respond to your needs? When they keep you waiting? When they do other things while you cry?

After discussion, ask students if adopting the infant's point of view has changed their perception of a newborn's needs.

USING TERMS TO LEARN

Guide students in pronouncing and informally defining all five vocabulary terms. Point out that the root word in temperament comes from a Latin word meaning "to mix properly." What is "mixed properly" in an individual's temperament?

SEE HOW THEY GROW

Sensitivity to Sound

Newborns can tell the difference between two sounds that are only one note apart. They can distinguish sounds that are of different volume, length, and rhythm. Low-pitched, rhythmic sounds are soothing to babies. Babies are frightened and stop moving when they hear sharp, high-pitched sounds. In one study, the sound of a normal heartbeat was played continuously for a group of infants. These newborns cried less, breathed more deeply, and gained more weight than newborns who did not hear the heartbeat. Generally, newborns are more responsive to women's voices than to men's.

TEACH

Pages 211-219

- The Amazing Newborn
- Learning to Care for the Newborn

GUIDED PRACTICE

Promoting Discussion

Encourage students to identify and discuss the many new relationships that are established with the birth of a new baby. How do these new relationships affect the family as a whole? How do they affect existing relationships between husband and wife or between parent and older child?

Critical Thinking

Ask students to consider the sensory abilities of newborns. What sights and sounds are most interesting and appealing? What could parents and other caregivers do to make a newborn's environment especially stimulating? Do you think it is possible to provide too much stimulation in a newborn's environment? If so, what problems might over stimulation cause? If not, why not?

Cooperative Learning

Have students work in groups to develop a list of reflexes they have as teenagers. Then have group members discuss their list. What is the purpose of each of your reflexes? How are your reflexes similar to those you had as infants? How are they different? What accounts for the differences?

Using the Photograph

Let students describe the infant in the photograph at the bottom of this page. How is this baby demonstrating the rooting reflex? How do babies benefit from this reflex? Why does the need for the reflex diminish?

Childhood Reflections

"Who can gaze at a newborn baby, and not wonder again at the miracle?"

Pearl S. Buck

---

behavior help the baby's body function. For example, a sneeze helps clear the baby's nose of lint. Swallowing lets the baby eat without choking.

Some reflex actions, such as sneezing and swallowing, continue throughout life. Others are temporary; they last only until voluntary control develops and takes over. Three of a newborn's temporary reflexes are the rooting reflex, the grasp reflex, and the startle reflex.

- **Rooting reflex.** This is *a newborn's automatic response, when touched on the lips or cheek, of turning toward the touch and beginning to suck*. The rooting reflex, which is completely automatic, helps the baby find his or her food. When babies become aware of their surroundings and use their eyes to search for the bottle or mother's breast, around four months of age, the rooting reflex stops.

- **Grasp reflex.** The **grasp reflex** *is the automatic response of a newborn's hand to close over anything that comes in contact with the palm*. The grip is often so strong that the newborn can be lifted off the bed. However, the baby lets go without warning. When, at about three months of age, the baby begins to reach for objects, the grasp reflex weakens; it disappears by one year of age.

- **Startle reflex.** This is *a newborn's automatic physical response— legs thrown up, fingers spread, arms extended and then brought rapidly back to the midline while the fingers close in a grasping action—to a loud noise or to a touch on the stomach*. The startle reflex disappears when the baby is about five months old.

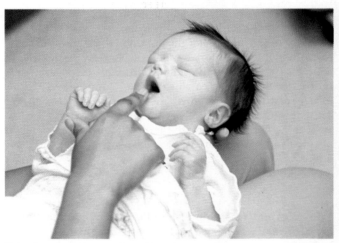

Baby demonstrating rooting reflex.

SEE HOW THEY GROW

Infant Sleep Patterns

The normal sleep of infants includes two distinct patterns, which can be called regular and irregular sleep. When infants are in regular sleep, they have a smooth, even breathing rhythm. Their eyelids are closed, and their eyes do not move. Babies' muscles are very relaxed, and they may show the startle response. During irregular sleep, breathing is alternately slow and rapid. The babies may writhe, gently stir, frown, flutter their eyelids, sigh, grimace, or smile. Rapid eye movement (REM) occurs beneath the closed lids. Scientists believe that the substantial amount of time spent by a newborn in REM sleep is necessary to make the baby better able to process stimulation from outside the body.

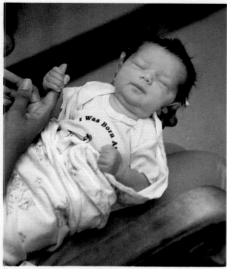

Baby demonstrating startle reflex.

Baby demonstrating grasp reflex.

GUIDED PRACTICE (continued)

Using the Photographs

Encourage students to describe and discuss the infants in the photographs on this page. What reflex is each baby demonstrating? How? How do babies benefit from these two reflexes?

Promoting Discussion

Ask students how parents usually learn to care for newborns. What—or who—are the most easily accessible sources of information? The most reliable sources? How important are books, pamphlets, and magazines in teaching new parents how to care for their infants? How important are television programs and films? To which people do many new parents turn for help and information? Why?

Cooperative Learning

Let students work in small groups to consider the importance of parents' confidence in their own abilities to care for their newborn. How do parents gain confidence? How does a parent's confidence affect his or her handling of the baby? How does a parent's confidence affect the baby's perception of the world? Why? Ask the members of each group to write a list of tips for helping new parents gain confidence in their ability to understand and care for their newborn baby.

Critical Thinking

Let students share their opinions in response to these questions: What are the advantages of establishing a predictable schedule of feeding and sleeping? How does a baby benefit from such a schedule? How do the baby's parents benefit? What are the disadvantages of establishing such a schedule? What problems might it cause for a baby? For the baby's parents?

Learning to Care for the Newborn

At first, it may take some time for new parents to feel comfortable caring for the baby. Soon, they gain confidence and become attuned to the baby's way of communicating. They learn how to recognize the baby's needs and how to adapt their responses to the baby's individual style.

What Do Babies Need?

Adapting to parenting begins with understanding the baby's needs, the needs of parents, and the needs of the entire family. Later chapters in this book present more detailed information about caring for a baby. Here, however, are babies' basic needs:

• **Babies need food.** A hungry newborn is hungry with his or her whole body. The baby squirms about, mouth searching for the mother's breast or a bottle nipple. Crying is the most effective way for a newborn to signal his or her hunger.

Newborns want food immediately when they are hungry, and it is important to give it to them—right away. Having their needs met in this way helps babies learn that they can trust the world.

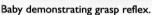

MORE ABOUT

Baby's Skin

Vernix caseosa is a protective covering that keeps the skin from becoming dry. It is most often seen in early or premature babies. *Milia* are pimplelike spots that are common on the baby's nose and face. These are evidence that the baby's oil glands are starting to function, and they should not be picked or scrubbed. Some babies, especially those that are premature, have a downy hair called *lanugo* on their skin. This drops off or is rubbed away quickly.

Promoting Discussion

Guide students in discussing parents' commitment to meeting their infant's needs. Under what circumstances is it relatively easy and especially satisfying to meet the needs of a hungry newborn? What circumstances might make it more difficult for parents to meet a newborn's needs? Do you think parents should expect that the needs of their newborn will be inconvenient—or worse—at times? What conflicts can parents expect between their own needs and the needs of their baby? Is there a right way to resolve such conflicts? If so, what is that way? If not, why not?

Using the Photograph

Let students describe the parent and baby in the photo at the bottom of this page. How does this kind of playing meet a baby's needs? How does it meet a parent's needs?

Promoting Discussion

Ask students to consider the importance of meeting a baby's needs for medical care. When and how should parents find a pediatrician to care for their newborn? How much should parents be expected to know about the signs of good health—and the signs of illness—in an infant? What are the best sources of information on this subject?

Making Connections: Reading

Have students find and read newspaper stories or magazine articles that tell of abandoned newborns. Then let the students summarize and discuss the stories or articles. What happened to the infants? What happened to the parents who abandoned those infants? What do you think would cause a parent to abandon his or her newborn baby?

- **Babies need sleep.** Newborns sleep and wake throughout the day and night. Most young babies take short naps around the clock, waking at night between one and three times for feeding. A newborn sleeps an average of 15 hours a day, typically in six to eight separate sleep periods. However, the level of alertness or drowsiness varies from baby to baby. Every baby is different; what is normal is normal for that individual baby. It is very important for parents to avoid comparisons.

- **Babies need exercise.** In their brief wakeful periods, newborns wave their arms and legs. This activity helps their muscles and nervous system develop. Before a feeding, babies usually become very active, moving all parts of their body. They can kick freely while being diapered, as long as someone watches them closely. Splashing or wiggling during a bath is another good way for small babies to get exercise.

- **Babies need to be kept safe, clean, and warm.** Diapering and bathing soon become a familiar part of the new parent's routine. The parent must also protect the baby from anything that might be harmful. When he or she is awake, a baby should always be under the watchful eye of a responsible person. Anything the baby might come in contact with—a toy, a crib, a garment—should be checked for safety, and any potentially harmful objects should be kept away.

When parents set aside "play time" with their baby, they are helping to fulfill the baby's needs for exercise, stimulation, and close contact.

OBSERVING AND PARTICIPATING

Learning Through Observation

In their eagerness to adjust to a newborn, family members will sometimes make the house totally quiet while baby sleeps. Generally, however, a baby is not disturbed by normal sounds and activities. In fact, parents who insist on quiet might create an unfortunate situation for themselves where baby will not even attempt to sleep unless the house is in absolute silence. Babies are more often affected by internal stimuli, such as hunger, pain, or discomfort, than they are by external stimulation. Their reactions to outer stimulation, such as noise and attention, are a learned response. Careful observance of a baby, rather than an attempt to ensure complete silence, assures parents that baby will be adequately rested and comfortable.

ASK THE EXPERTS

Sudden Infant Death Syndrome

Q. Can you help me understand crib death?

A. What you call crib death is known medically as Sudden Infant Death Syndrome, or SIDS. The loss of a baby to SIDS can be especially difficult to accept, because the death is so sudden and so mysterious. The victims are usually healthy infants between the ages of two weeks and six months. They die in their sleep, with no warning, no cry, and no evidence of pain.

Researchers are continuing to investigate the possible causes of Sudden Infant Death Syndrome; so far, no cause or prevention

has been discovered. However, it is understood that the parents and other caregivers are not at fault when a baby dies of SIDS. Nothing they did—and nothing they failed to do—caused the baby's death.

Parents and other relatives of SIDS victims can often benefit from counseling as they deal with their grief over a baby's death. The baby's pediatrician or another

physician can usually refer families to clinics or to social workers or other therapists who are specially trained in this field.

If you have more questions about SIDS, you can call the SIDS Alliance; the telephone number is 1-800-221-SIDS. This helpful organization has local chapters in cities all over the country; each chapter sponsors group meetings for parents who have gone through the heartbreaking experience of SIDS.

Van D. Stone, MD

Dr. Van Stone
Pediatrician
Tupelo, Mississippi

- **Babies need medical care.** In the first year, an infant will have periodic well-baby checkups to make sure he or she is healthy and developing normally, and to receive immunizations. They may be from a family doctor or a pediatrician, a doctor who specializes in the care of babies and young children.

- **Babies need things to look at, touch, listen to, and play with.** Interesting, stimulating surroundings help babies learn. However, they do not need expensive toys. In fact, an infant's favorite thing to look at is a human face.

Issues and Advice

1. What common characteristics are found among victims of SIDS? (*They are healthy infants between the ages of two weeks and six months.*)
2. What causes and/or preventions are known? (*None.*)
3. What can parents or caretakers do to prevent SIDS? (*Nothing.*)
4. What resources are available for parents of SIDS victims? (*Counseling from social workers or trained therapists.*)

Thinking Like an Expert

Have students form pairs or small groups and discuss the ways in which a person can console parents or caregivers whose child died of SIDS. Ask them to make a skit that uses their ideas. Remind them that the way we comfort people who are grieving can have an effect on the way they perceive themselves and the way they respond to future setbacks. You might suggest that any interested students present their skit from the viewpoint of new parents whose former child was a victim of SIDS. In that way, they can explore the lingering doubts that people have about their parenting abilities.

Interested students might research the various devices available for parents to monitor an infant's functions (e.g., a breathing monitor similar to those used in hospitals). If possible, arrange for a presentation to the class by a representative of SIDS Alliance or a willing adult whose infant died of SIDS. In all cases, stress to your students the importance of genuine compassion and knowledge when dealing with this unfortunate situation.

MORE ABOUT

Sudden Infant Death Syndrome

The statistics associated with Sudden Infant Death Syndrome (SIDS) are sometimes distorted by reports which fail to note that although crib deaths are sudden and unexpected, not all unexpected infant deaths are crib deaths. If the cause of death can be determined to be a congenital disorder, such as heart disease, or a kidney disorder, or

a result of sudden infection, it is not a case of crib death. Therefore, alarming headlines such as "Crib Deaths Caused by Heart Disorder" are false. In instances of unexplained death, an investigation by police and a coroner's inquest are common. Although unpleasant, these investigations might provide parents with an explanation for the cause of death, which, in turn, lessens self-blame.

GUIDED PRACTICE (continued)

Cooperative Learning

Have groups of students work together to develop a list of inexpensive items that would make an infant's environment interesting and stimulating.

Promoting Discussion

Guide students in discussing the universal need for love and acceptance. How do babies express their need for love? How do parents, other family members, and other caregivers express their love to babies? How do appropriate means of expressing love change as a baby grows into childhood, adolescence, early adulthood, middle age, and old age? Do you believe that there is any stage during which individuals no longer need love? During which they no longer need physical contact that expresses affection, caring, and love? If so, what is that stage? If not, why not?

Family Focus

The first weeks after a new infant comes home are often a time of preoccupation with the baby. Each family member is bonding with the infant, and the infant is developing a place in the web of relationships within the family. Discuss with students the importance of these emotional tasks, stressing that family members should not neglect prior relationships in caring for the new baby.

Promoting Discussion

Ask students to name some of the many roles people play in life. How can parents balance these roles? What problems do they often face in trying to achieve a healthy balance?

Cooperative Learning

Divide students into five or ten groups. Assign each group one or two of the needs of parents listed on this page. Have the group members discuss each need, decide why it is important, and devise strategies to help new parents meet the need. Ask the groups to report their ideas to the rest of the class.

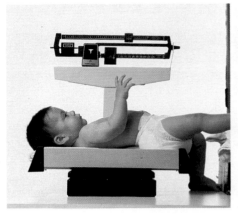

Weighing in to check the baby's physical growth is a routine part of each visit to the doctor.

• **Babies need love.** Just like everyone else, babies want to be near the people who love them. Newborns need close contact with warm, affectionate adults. Love is as important as food and sleep to babies.

There is no one way to love a baby. Every newborn is different—and so is every parent. Each parent should express love for his or her newborn naturally, in the ways that are personally comfortable. Love is one of the strongest forces affecting every person's life. When a healthy baby senses that he or she is loved, the infant is at ease and feels secure.

What Do Parents Need?

Parents of newborns are often so concerned about caring for their babies that they neglect to consider their own needs. New parents have special needs of their own, which—like the baby's needs—must be met for good physical and emotional health. These are some of the things that parents of newborns need:

• Knowledge of how to care for an infant.
• Resources to turn to for answers to their questions.
• Information about normal occurrences and emotions they experience with their newborn.
• Time to fill their many roles—spouse, parent, family member, worker, student, and citizen.
• Emotional support from a network of family and friends.
• Financial planning.
• Reassurance and confidence that both parents are capable and needed.
• Agreement about parenting and household responsibilities.
• Personal health, rest, and nutrition.
• Privacy and time alone.

HEALTHY FAMILIES/HEALTHY CHILDREN

Building Healthy Families

New mothers, preoccupied with the changing routines of the house, have time for two major personal concerns—adequate rest and losing the extra weight they have carried. Getting extra sleep can be tricky since baby's naptime is a tempting opportunity to catch up on other obligations. Whenever possible, mothers should discipline themselves to rest while baby sleeps. As for extra pounds, the combined weight of the fetus, amniotic fluid, and placenta is lost immediately at birth. From that point, it takes about six to eight weeks for the body tissues to shrink back to normal. Any weight-loss program should be started gradually and under a doctor's supervision.

Adjusting to New Routines

During the first few weeks, both parents and babies have to adjust to new patterns of life. A newborn typically needs at least several weeks of trial-and-error before he or she can settle into any predictable pattern of eating and sleeping. Parents must adjust their schedule to the baby's needs. That means feeding the baby whenever hunger strikes, day or night.

Receiving attention and care whenever he or she needs it cannot "spoil" a newborn. At this early stage in life, the baby needs to learn that he or she is important and that his or her needs matter—and will receive attention. Later, when the baby is more mature, he or she can begin to learn other ways to communicate and to get those important needs met.

Of course, every newborn benefits from order in life. Soon certain daily patterns emerge to manage the baby's hunger, sleepiness, and wakefulness. It takes about a month, for example, to establish a fairly predictable feeding and sleeping routine. Meanwhile, the key to the baby's happiness is the parents' flexibility.

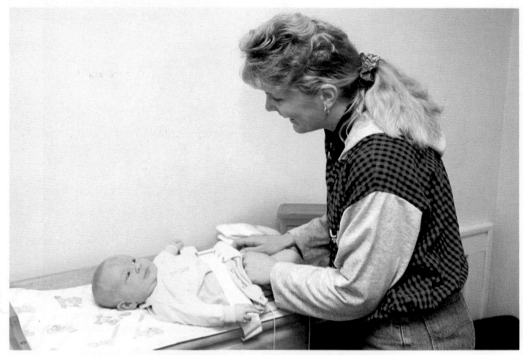

Newborns set their own pace at first, and parents must respond to it. This is how infants learn that their world is safe and dependable. As the baby grows a little older, daily routines will fall into a comfortable pattern.

OBSERVING AND PARTICIPATING

Celebrating Individual Differences

In spite of the common characteristics of all newborns, each is also a unique person. Furthermore, each parent is a unique person. Consequently, not every parent and baby experience the immediate joy of being "natural" with each other; adjustments are often necessary. Some babies are uncuddly and tend to resent, even reject, physical contact. Others are miserable, remaining fretful

and irritable, and taking their time to settle down. Jumpy babies overreact to nearly every kind of stimulus and will quickly break into a crying fit. Sleepy babies demand little and seem unconcerned about their surroundings, unlike wakeful babies who are happy to remain alert and aware of activity. Like those of adults, babies have both temperaments of their positive and negative sides.

GUIDED PRACTICE (continued)

Critical Thinking

Ask students to compare the following situations. Two newborns are cared for by their parents; both are fed when hungry, appropriately clothed, and kept warm and comfortable. In one family, the parents rarely talk or sing to the infant. The other parents often speak directly to their infant; they also sing and chant to the baby frequently.

What effect will this basic difference have on the development of the two babies? What effect will it have on the parents in the two families? Why?

Using Management Skills

Have students work in groups to develop a list of safety precautions to be followed when there is a newborn in the family. Will families find this list relevant when their baby is five months old? A year old? Why or why not?

Promoting Discussion

Ask students to share their ideas about spoiling children. What are the signs of a spoiled child? Who should be held responsible for a child who seems spoiled? At what age can babies or children begin to be spoiled? Are there any advantages to being spoiled? If so, what are those advantages?

Using the Photograph

Encourage students to describe and discuss the mother and infant in the photo on this page. What attitude does the mother appear to have toward her baby? Toward caring for her baby? How does her baby appear to be responding? What is the baby likely to learn from this kind of care?

Promoting Discussion

Ask students to consider the combinations of temperament within a family. Do you think a parent and baby interact more successfully when they have similar temperaments or different temperaments? Why?

GUIDED PRACTICE (continued)

BUILDING SELF-ESTEEM

Touching, holding, and cuddling infants are appropriate acts because they bring the child in close physical contact with others for extended periods of time. This contact builds a foundation of trust and acceptance that later develops into confidence. Gradually, babies will learn to comfort and amuse themselves without relying on another.

INDEPENDENT PRACTICE

Journal Writing

Ask students to consider how their own family lives would be changed by the addition of a newborn baby. What would be the positive aspects of the changes? The negative aspects? Have students write journal entries that explore their reactions.

Student Workbook

Distribute and have students complete "Are Baby's Needs Being Met?" in the Student Workbook.

Extension

Let students work alone or in small groups to complete one or more of these activities:

- Interview a new parent. Ask the parent to discuss how the newborn has changed his or her daily life. Write a short paragraph on the interview.

- Contact the local chapter of the National Sudden Infant Death Syndrome Foundation, and gather information about its work with families. Share the information with the rest of the class.

- In a magazine, journal, or book, read about a research project conducted with infants. What were the researchers trying to find out? What methods did they use? What were the results of the research? Of what use is the knowledge found in the research? Write a brief report.

BUILDING SELF-ESTEEM

Responding to Baby's Needs

*N*ewborn babies often stop crying when they are picked up and held close. The constant reassurance of being picked up by parents and other caregivers comforts the baby and makes him or her feel important. Being held can help relieve the baby of annoying gas. It also provides a chance to hear the comforting sound of a parent's heartbeat.

If a parent or other caring person responds whenever a baby cries, the baby feels secure. He or she soon learns that the person who responds to the crying will help the baby feel better, usually by feeding or comforting the baby. A baby cannot be spoiled by this kind of attention.

Understanding the Baby's Language

Babies have one way to communicate with the world—by crying. Although newborns never cry for fun, their reasons may often be far less serious than the worried new parents imagine. Hunger is usually the reason that newborns cry. Sometimes babies cry because they are too hot or too cold. Sometimes they cry because they are lying in an uncomfortable position and need to be moved. Other reasons for crying are fatigue and loneliness, and sometimes a baby cries for no reason at all. The average amount of crying for a newborn is one hour per day, but individual babies may cry much less or much more than that. A baby's crying seems to have nothing to do with the quality of parenting he or she is receiving. Parents soon learn to recognize their baby's different cries—one for hunger, another for discomfort, and so on.

Every baby has a unique temperament. Parents and other caregivers soon become attuned to these individual differences.

OBSERVING AND PARTICIPATING

Celebrating Individual Differences

Each baby is a unique individual, with identifiable and measurable differences in personality and behavior. The amount of time babies spend sleeping, crying, or being awake and alert can vary tremendously. Some babies are quiet and still, while others are vigorous and active. The amount of movement while asleep also differs among babies. Responses to frustration and stimuli vary, as does a baby's general level of irritability. Babies even differ in how hard they suck for food. In general, babies who are quiet and placid in response to one type of stimulus respond the same way to other stimuli. The same principle applies to babies who respond aggressively.

Early Temperament

Babies differ markedly in their inborn **temperament**, or *style of reacting to the world and of relating to others*. For example, one baby usually moves from sleep to wakefulness with a startled jump and a cry. Another awakens gradually and quietly looks around the room. Some babies may be so easily upset that extra-gentle handling and a smooth routine are necessary to maintain happiness. Others can be handled more playfully without objection. Just as no two babies look exactly alike—even identical twins—no two react in just the same way.

Parents—and others who care for a baby—need to be sensitive to the baby's own style. The baby, too, learns to adapt to the style of his or her parents. Studies have shown that babies as young as two weeks of age adjust their reactions, depending on how parents handle and talk to them. When parents are very gentle and soothing, the baby tends to respond with soft cooing and gentle motions. When parents relate to the baby more playfully, the baby tends to react with excited grunts and active motions. These natural adjustments help parents and babies feel at ease with each other.

SECTION 3 REVIEW

CHECK YOUR UNDERSTANDING

1. What is a reflex? What purpose do a newborn's reflexes serve?
2. What is the rooting reflex? When does this reflex stop?
3. List at least five things newborns need.
4. List at least five things parents of newborns need.
5. How does an infant communicate?
6. What is a person's temperament?

DISCUSS AND DISCOVER

1. How does a baby's temperament affect the baby's parents? How do the parents' temperaments affect the baby? What adjustment problems do you think might be caused by these differences between the temperaments of parents and baby? How do you think parents should try to deal with those problems?
2. Read more about SIDS, sudden infant death syndrome. When and how does it occur? How do families react? Then work with a partner or a small group to plan and perform a short, informative skit about SIDS.

Observing & Participating

Observe parents and small infants in a public place, such as a park or a mall. Record how the parents show their love and affection for their babies. How are the methods of demonstrating love similar? How are they different? Describe how the babies respond to the care and love of the parents.

SECTION 3 REVIEW

1. An instinctive, automatic response; allows baby to handle certain needs involuntarily until he or she learns to do things voluntarily.
2. A newborn's automatic response, when touched on the lips or cheek, of turning toward the touch and beginning to suck; around four months.
3. Any five: food; sleep; exercise; to be kept safe, clean, and warm; medical care; things to look at, touch, listen to, and play with; love.
4. Any five: knowledge to care for an infant; resources to answer questions; information about normal emotions; time to fill roles; emotional support; financial planning; reassurance and confidence; agreement on responsibilities; health, rest, and nutrition; privacy and time alone.
5. By crying.
6. His or her style of reacting to the world and of relating to others.

ASSESS

CHECKING COMPREHENSION

Assign students to write their responses to the Check Your Understanding questions in the Section 3 Review. Answers to the questions are given below.

EVALUATE

Have students complete the Chapter 7, Section 3 TCR quiz.

Reteaching

1. Have students complete Reteaching 19 in the TCR.
2. Working with small groups of students, review the seven basic needs of infants. Why are all seven of these needs important? How should parents and other caregivers try to approach their responsibilities in meeting these needs? Make illustrated charts or posters showing what babies need.

Enrichment

1. Challenge students to complete Enrichment 19 in the TCR.
2. Ask students to plan and write essays on the importance of emotional maturity for successful parenthood. They should respond to these questions: What is maturity? Why do the parents of newborns need to be emotionally mature? What problems can arise when parents are not emotionally mature? Is emotional maturity directly related to age? Why or why not?

Extension

Invite a pediatrician or a pediatric nurse practitioner to speak to the class to discuss the importance of regular well-baby checkups. What happens during these visits? What progress can be monitored, and what problems may be identified? What can parents learn about their babies during these checkups? Encourage questions.

CLOSE

Let each student answer this question, either orally or in writing:

What should parents keep in mind about their newborn babies?

Have a student read the various definitions of the word *bond* from a dictionary. Ask students to identify those definitions that describe human interrelations.

Promoting Discussion

1. Why are family bonds important to an infant?

2. How do parents adjust the methods of strengthening family bonds to the ages and stages of childhood?

3. What social or economic factors restrict the development of family bonds?

Practicing Decision Making

Ask students to discuss the following situation: Sara had been studying methods of responding to children's needs in her child development class. Recently, she took her three-year old brother, Kyle, to the zoo. When the time came to go home, Kyle screamed and cried. Sara said, "Don't have a tantrum, Kyle. You're just tired." Kyle responded by screaming even louder. Why do students think Sara's remark had this effect? What might she have done instead?

Cooperative Learning

Have students work in small groups to prepare a skit that demonstrates a positive and a negative way for parents or caregivers to react to the needs of a child. Be sure that the group defines the age of the child and the circumstances involved. When each group is finished with the skit, ask the students to explain how their reactions, both positive and negative, would change when dealing with a child of a different age.

How do parents prepare themselves for the changing needs of children as they grow and develop?

STRENGTHENING FAMILY BONDS

It is important to remember that bonding is a process, not a moment. The emotional bond between infant and parent continues to grow and strengthen as the parent holds, cuddles, talks to, and cares for the newborn. In fact, the process of bonding is carried out in different ways throughout life; the parent and child revise and solidify their emotional relationship as the child progresses through infancy, childhood, adolescence, and into adulthood.

The following approaches can help parents and other caregivers encourage the bonding process with children of various ages.

Infants

- **Keep the baby close and comforted.** Babies feel warm and secure when they are physically close to a caring parent or caregiver. Look for ways to hold the baby that are comfortable for both of you. Try keeping the young baby close in a sling or front carrier. As the baby grows and becomes more interested in the rest of the world, you may both prefer a backpack-type carrier.

- **Take time to touch the baby.** Touching is a primary key in early bonding; during feeding, changing, and bathing, stroke or pat the baby gently. You may also want to try massaging the baby by gently kneading his or her arms, legs, and back. Notice the baby's response to each kind of touch, and continue with the touching the baby finds most comforting and pleasant.

- **Be responsive to the baby.** Which tone of voice does the baby find most soothing? What music evokes a pleasant response? What colors and shapes does the baby enjoy looking at? How does the baby prefer to be held or cuddled?

Remember that every baby is an individual. Take the time to notice and respond to the baby's individual preferences.

- **Play with the baby.** You can turn routine activities into games for the baby simply by singing, talking, and making caring eye contact. Try making funny faces or imitating the baby's sounds, and see how the baby responds. You might also select toys or other safe objects that catch the baby's attention.

Toddlers and Preschoolers

- Continue to play with the child. Seek out activities that you both enjoy. Sharing a book or a walk can be special for both of you. At least occasionally, join enthusiastically in the child's

220

Building Healthy Families

New parents and caregivers naturally have concerns which range from questions about what the baby will be like to how they will be as parents or caregivers. These questions are important because there are so many decisions that have to be made for or about the baby. As the feature above states, bonding is a result of long-range efforts based on continual attention to the child and his or her needs. However, the ages and stages can shift rapidly and unexpectedly, so that parents may be unable to keep up with the changes. Community support groups offer parents a chance to share their concerns as well as success stories with others. Groups that feature parents whose children range in ages and stages enable everyone to benefit from multiple experiences.

favorite activities, both imaginative and active. Also make a point of finding some regular activity that all the family members can enjoy together.

• **Continue using touch to express your affection and caring.** Most young children enjoy kisses, hugs, and other embraces from parents or other important caregivers.

• **Continue to respond to the child as an individual.** Remember that each child is an individual—and that each child grows and changes. Be thoughtful in noticing the child's development and in responding to the child's changing needs and interests.

School Age Children
• **Continue to be physically affectionate.** Giving and receiving physical signs of affection can strengthen emotional bonds throughout life. However, parents and other important caregivers should be careful to respond to the child's changing needs. For some older children, a pat on the back or an arm around the shoulder is more comforting and acceptable than the familiar hugs that were essential in earlier years.

• **Talk to the child, and encourage the child to talk to you.** Remember that communication involves both talking and listening. Ask the child questions, and listen

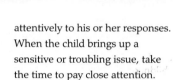

attentively to his or her responses. When the child brings up a sensitive or troubling issue, take the time to pay close attention.

• **Value the child's opinion.** Encourage the child to form and express his or her own opinions, and respect those opinions as fully as possible.

• **Don't stop playing with the child.** Your emotional bond is strengthened whenever you are enjoying one another's company. Seek out games, sports, or other activities that are fun for both of you.

221

COOPERATIVE LEARNING

Preparing for Discussions
Invite several parents or caregivers to class for a forum about family bonds. It would be helpful if the parents represented children of all three age groups mentioned above.

If possible, include teen parents for their unique perspective. Before the day of the discussion, have students work in pairs or small groups to write questions regarding methods of developing and

strengthening family bonds. Questions could range from specific ones (What games pleased your child at the age of six months?) to those of a more general nature. (How do you find time to balance outside obligations with the needs of your child?) Have students take notes and write a summary of what they learned.

Journal Writing
Ask students to respond to these questions in their journals: How do you think family bonds could be strengthened in your own family? What resources are available to you that will help you learn new ways to improve family interactions, which, in turn, will create stronger bonds?

Using Management Skills
In lieu of direct response to the needs of an infant or child, some parents might purchase toys or games designed to amuse and entertain a child. Examples are crib mobiles, plush toys, mechanical devises that gently rock a crib, televisions or video shows for older children, and hand-held computer games. Have students investigate the costs of these items or any others they can think of. When they report their findings to the class, ask them to evaluate the impact, both positive and negative, that these items have on the bonds between family members.

Enrichment
Invite a panel of professionals from the fields of family counseling, health, law enforcement, and education to discuss their views on the effect that strong family bonds have in shaping and preparing a child for future responsibilities.

Family Focus
Have students interview parents and caregivers to learn about their perceptions of family bonds and how they make decisions that are designed to strengthen those bonds. Encourage students to write a summary of their interviews and, wherever possible, compare the situations that arise in different families and how family members adjust to them.

CLOSE

Ask students to summarize the main points they have learned about family bonds.

ASSESS

CHECKING COMPREHENSION

Use the Summary and the Reviewing the Facts questions to help students go over the most important ideas presented in Chapter 7; encourage students to ask questions and add details, as appropriate.

CHAPTER 7 REVIEW

1. Loss of the mucus plug; rupturing of membrane and release of amniotic fluid; contractions.

2. Contractions open the cervix, expel the baby, and then expel the placenta.

3. A valve in the heart closes; blood begins to circulate to and from the lungs.

4. Fat cheeks; a short, flat nose; a receding chin. The nose and chin are out of the way, so they do not interfere with sucking.

5. Heart rate; breathing; muscle tone; responsiveness; color.

6. An arrangement in which the baby stays in the mother's hospital room, rather than in a hospital nursery, after birth. All family members.

7. To help her feel good and regain energy. If she is breast-feeding, to provide nutrients for the baby as well as for herself.

8. About four to six weeks after the birth. To be sure the uterus is returning to normal and there are no unusual problems; to discuss questions about parenthood and about birth control.

9. Rooting reflex; grasp reflex; startle reflex.

10. Crying is a baby's only method of communicating.

CHAPTER 7 REVIEW

SUMMARY

- Labor is the process by which the baby is expelled from the mother's body. A normal birth includes three stages of labor.
- A cesarean birth is performed when medically necessary.
- Physical adjustments in the newborn's body make life outside the uterus possible.
- Bonding is the formation of emotional ties between parent and child.
- To recover from childbirth, a woman needs rest, exercise, proper nutrition, medical checkups, and attention to her emotional needs.
- Premature babies need special care.
- Reflexes help a newborn's body function until voluntary actions take over.
- Babies need food, sleep, exercise, medical care, safe and interesting surroundings, and love.

REVIEWING THE FACTS

1. List three possible indications that labor is beginning.

2. What purpose do contractions serve in the first stage of labor? In the second stage of labor? In the third stage of labor?

3. How does a baby's circulatory system change once the baby's lungs have begun taking in oxygen?

4. Briefly describe a newborn's facial features. How are these features adapted to sucking?

5. List the five areas of a baby's physical condition that are measured by the Apgar scale.

6. What is rooming-in? Who can benefit from a rooming-in program?

7. Why is good nutrition important for the mother after birth?

8. When and why should a new mother have a postnatal checkup?

9. List three of a newborn's temporary reflexes.

10. Why is it important to respond to a newborn's crying?

222

EXPLORING FURTHER

1. Prepare a small kit of items that an expectant couple might find useful or reassuring during labor. Display your kit, and explain your reasons for choosing those items. (Section 1)

2. Survey three or four mothers who have recently given birth and find out their length of labor. Ask them to talk about their condition after the birth. Does there seem to be a relationship between the length of labor and the mother's condition after birth? (Section 1)

3. How should older children behave around a newborn sibling? Think of two or three guidelines. Then compose a simple song or make up a chant that a three- or four-year-old would enjoy, encouraging the child to follow your guidelines. (Section 2)

4. How often should babies have medical checkups during the first year of life? What immunizations should they be given? What other kinds of medical care should they receive? Make a colorful poster or create a short brochure sharing the responses to these important questions. (Section 3)

THINKING CRITICALLY

1. **Compare and contrast.** With a group of classmates, brainstorm a list of the emotions you think mothers and fathers experience during labor. Then discuss your list. Which of the emotions seem contradictory? How are they contradictory? Is it reasonable to expect that such contradictory emotions will arise during this event? Why or why not?

2. **Analyze.** Why do you think some people feel reluctant to hold a newborn baby? What would you say to help someone overcome this reluctance?

3. **Synthesize.** Why do you think so many parents experience at least some symptoms of mild depression following the birth of their baby? Why do you think mothers' depression is more commonly discussed than fathers'? If you had a close friend who was about to become a parent for the first time, would you discuss the "baby

CLASSROOM MANAGEMENT

Writing Skills

Writing assignments provide students with the opportunity to develop communication skills needed throughout life, to organize their thoughts in a logical manner, and to receive constructive criticism. In addition to the traditional subject-matter reports and term papers, there are many opportunities for students to do written assign-

ments. Some of these include keeping a journal or diary; summarizing a reading assignment; evaluating a lab or project; writing job application letters; developing written directions composing reviews for books of interest to peers; and writing letters to congressional representatives, to the editors of newspapers and magazines, and to retailers, manufacturers, and service organizations.

blues" with your friend? If not, why not? If so, what would you say?

4. **Analyze.** Why do you think parents of newborns need time alone? Do you think it is more important for each parent to spend time independently or for the two parents to spend time together, apart from the baby? Why?

CROSS-CURRICULUM CONNECTIONS

1. **Social Studies.** Research the practices for handling labor and delivery in this country—or in another country of your choice—100 years ago. How were they different from modern practices? How do you think the differences affected babies? Parents? Write a brief report of your findings.

2. **Writing.** Read Frederick Leboyer's book *Birth Without Violence*. Then write an essay expressing your reactions to the philosophy and practices described in the book.

SCHOOL TO WORK

Preparing for an Interview Most employers want to interview, or formally meet, a potential employee before deciding whether or not the person is right for the job. The interview allows the employer to learn more about you. It also gives you a chance to learn more about the company. Some general rules apply to the way you prepare for an interview. Before the interview, learn more about the company. Importantly, prepare yourself for the interview by practicing with a teacher, counselor, or other adult. Arrive early enough to be comfortable and ready for the appointment. Dress as if you are coming to work for the day, and take time with your appearance. Go to the interview alone.

PERFORMANCE ASSESSMENT

The Baby's Arrival

Task
Imagine yourself in the role of a new father or mother. Write journal or diary entries addressing your needs and the needs of the newborn.

Purpose
Although you are going to assume a hypothetical role, the purpose of this activity will be to enable you to express some of the feelings and address some of the tangible concerns that an adult might have about parenthood. You should write at least three journal entries--one for each stage of pregnancy.

Procedure
1. Decide whether you are going to assume the role of new father or mother. Don't let your own gender

determine your choice; this is to be a hypothetical situation, similar to a role in a play or skit.
2. Draft a list of points you want to address. The content of your entries should include your opinions, decisions, or attitudes concerning medical care, nutrition, changes in the family, finances, and birth preparation, plus any other matters of concern to you in your new role.
3. As you draft your list, note corresponding feelings to include in your journal.
4. You may want to review the chapter for issues and responsibilities adults need to address when a baby arrives.
5. Determine the tone and style as you write your journal or diary entries.

Evaluation
Your work will be evaluated on your ability to demonstrate knowledge of content and the effectiveness of your communication. Correct grammar, punctuation, and spelling will be part of the evaluation.

Portfolio Idea Use a folder or notebook to store your journal or diary separately. This will enable you to add to it as you learn more about parenting, or revise it for your final portfolio presentation. Prepare a title page that includes your name, date, and objective.

223

PERFORMANCE ASSESSMENT

Journal or Diary Entries
To encourage creativity, have the class brainstorm concerns that new fathers and mothers might have during the three stages of pregnancy. If you have students who need motivation or help with language skills, let small groups work together

to discuss and exchange ideas. If students work on their project collaboratively, remind them to write their own journal entries. You might extend the discussion to include issues such as coping with premature infants or babies with special needs.

EVALUATE
Use the reproducible Chapter 7 Test in the TCR, or construct your own test using the Test-maker Software.

EXTENSION
Invite a panel of parents and expectant parents to speak to the class. If possible, include parents who are expecting a first baby within the next month, parents of one child recently born, and parents of two or more children. When the panel meets, encourage the parents to ask one another questions and to offer one another advice. In addition, encourage students to plan and ask questions of the panel members.

CLOSE

Have each student complete the following sentences in writing:
I think the best part about becoming a new parent is ...
I think the most difficult part about becoming a new parent is ...

SCHOOL TO WORK

Problem-Solving Skills To succeed in the workplace, students must have a command of problem-solving skills rather than a mastery of information. After all, the information they learn today may be obsolete in the near future. To encourage problem-solving skills, engage students in methods of approaching a question or problem in order to isolate possible solutions. One way to begin the process is to pose questions that require critical-thinking skills, not a single answer. Allow students to explore all solutions, even those that they eventually abandon. Your role, as teacher, is as a facilitator in the process of problem-solving, rather than a keeper of knowledge.

INTRODUCE

UNIT 3 RESOURCES

Teacher's Classroom Resources
- Unit 3 Test
- Testmaker Software
- Color Transparency 19

UNIT OVERVIEW

The first year of a baby's life is the subject of Unit 3.

Students begin in Chapter 8 by examining physical growth and development during the first year. They discuss how to handle and feed a baby, as well as how to bathe, dress, and diaper a baby, and how to encourage good sleep habits.

In Chapter 9, students examine the emotional and social development during the first year of life. Students learn to recognize signs of emotional and social development, and they consider the important relationship between the care a baby receives and the emotional and social development of the baby.

Chapter 10 guides students in understanding the intellectual development of babies. Students read about Piaget's stages of learning, and they discuss what parents and other caregivers can do to stimulate a baby's intellectual development.

UNIT OBJECTIVES

After completing Unit 3, students will be able to:

- Describe the physical growth and development during the first year of life and explain the physical care a baby requires.
- Discuss the emotional and social development that takes place during the first year of life.
- Describe the intellectual development of babies and explain how parents and other caregivers can help babies learn.

CLASSROOM MANAGEMENT

Bulletin Board Suggestion

Print the title—"Care Enough to Help a Child Learn"—at the top of the bulletin board, and place several large photographs of parents or other caregivers with infants in the center of the bulletin board. Surround the photos with the following tips for promoting intellectual development:

- Learn about child development.
- Express your love.

- Give time and attention.
- Provide positive feedback.
- Set limits.
- Provide encouragement.
- Be enthusiastic.
- Provide a safe environment.

UNIT 3

The Baby's First Year

THINKING OF BABY

Baby awake is a mischievous elf
Who can keep you busy
In spite of yourself!
A rollicking, frolicking, gurgling sprite
Who may sleep half the day ...
(And cry half the night)!
And yet when you're humming
A last lullaby,
And the sandman has come
And closed each little eye ...
Gone is the elf, and you find out instead
You've just tucked a tired little angel in bed.

Anonymous

CHAPTER 8	Physical Development During the First Year
CHAPTER 9	Emotional and Social Development During the First Year
CHAPTER 10	Intellectual Development During the First Year

MORE ABOUT

Using the Poem
New parents soon discover how physically and emotionally drained they can be when caring for an infant. Parents and caregivers who have other demands such as a job or older children know a greater sense of exhaustion. Yet most parents will have an equal sense of wonder at the preciousness of a baby, especially when he or she is asleep. Ask a student to read the poem aloud, then ask the class to volunteer their thoughts and feelings about watching a baby fall asleep after a hectic day. How accurately has the poet captured the images of life with an infant?

INTRODUCING THE UNIT

- Show a short video of a baby on his or her first birthday (or display several large photos of one-year-olds). Encourage students to identify some of the baby's many skills and abilities. How does this baby move? How does this baby communicate and interact with other people? How does this baby handle toys and other objects? Record students' responses on the chalkboard.
  Then ask students to consider and discuss how the baby has grown and changed in the year since he or she was born. Finally, tell students that they will learn more about this amazing first year of life as they study Unit 3.

- Let a volunteer read aloud the poem "Thinking of Baby," and guide students in sharing their responses. What attitude toward infants does the poem express? Do you think parents of infants can—or should—maintain this kind of attitude most of the time? Why or why not?

ASSESS

EVALUATE

Use the reproducible Unit 3 Test in the TCR, or construct your own test using the Test-maker Software.

EXTENSION

Invite a twelve-month-old baby to visit the class, if possible, accompanied by both parents. Ask the parents to bring along a series of photographs that show how their baby has grown and developed since birth. Encourage students to ask questions about changes in the baby and about the parents' experiences during the past year.

INTRODUCE

CHAPTER OVERVIEW

Chapter 8 helps students understand the patterns of physical growth and development during a baby's first year of life and guides them in providing basic physical care for an infant. In Section 1, students begin by examining patterns of physical development. Then they examine information about average growth in weight and height and about body proportions. They also consider the development of sensory skills and motor skills.

In Section 2, students learn about safe and comfortable ways to hold and feed babies. They also learn about feeding routines and discuss how eating habits change from breast- or bottle-feeding to self-feeding.

Section 3 provides students with information about other aspects of providing physical care for infants. Here students learn about the skills involved in bathing a baby, changing and choosing a baby's clothes, diapering a baby, and helping a baby sleep.

Throughout the chapter, students are encouraged to recognize the important relationship between providing a baby with loving, appropriate physical care and ensuring the baby's healthy growth and development.

CLASSROOM MANAGEMENT

Resources Beyond the Classroom

Many new and expectant mothers are uncertain whether to bottle-feed or breast-feed their babies. One excellent resource to address their breast-feeding concerns is the La Leche League (page 241). By writing their main branch, you can obtain free general information and literature. Additionally, by calling their toll-free number, you or your students may get immediate answers

to questions along with a referral to your local chapter leader who may be willing to give a talk to your class. For further information either call the toll-free number or write their headquarters at:

9616 Minneapolis Ave.
Franklin Pk., IL 60131
or call 1-800-LA LECHE

Physical Development During the First Year

THINK ABOUT

During the first year of life, a baby grows at a rate faster than it will ever grow again. Although each child is unique, three general patterns of development—head to foot, near to far, and simple to complex—organize a baby's physical growth and development. Think about how parents and other caregivers who understand these patterns of development are better prepared to anticipate and respond to a baby's individual needs.

ASK YOURSELF

Look at the baby in the photo on the opposite page. How old do you guess her to be? Why? How does her ability to smile at the photographer indicate improvement in her vision? What other physical developments have taken place since her birth? What kinds of clothing would be more suitable to her level of activity at this age?

NOW TRY THIS

Pretend you are the parent or caregiver of the baby girl in the photo on the opposite page and just walked into her room to find her standing for the first time. How would you greet her? What do you think her response to you would be? Why? What precautions would you take regarding her safety now that she can pull herself upright?

227

CHAPTER OBJECTIVES

After completing Chapter 8, students will be able to:

- Identify the most important milestones in growth and development during a baby's first year of life.
- Describe appropriate methods for handling and feeding an infant.
- Discuss other skills involved in providing physical care for an infant.

INTRODUCING THE CHAPTER

- Using about 2 yards (1.8 m) of butcher paper and pencils, markers, and measuring sticks, have students work in small groups to sketch life-size outlines of a "typical" baby at birth and at age one year. Then encourage students to compare and discuss their sketches. Save the sketches until students have finished the chapter. At that time, have them evaluate their early impressions of infants' sizes.

- Use the photo on the opposite page and the three features on this page—Think About, Ask Yourself, and Now Try This—to begin a discussion about a baby's physical development during the first year.

Childhood Reflections

"… The more people have studied different methods of bringing up children the more they have come to the conclusion that what good mothers and fathers instinctively feel like doing for their babies is usually best after all."

Dr. Benjamin Spock

HEALTHY FAMILIES/HEALTHY CHILDREN

Building Healthy Families

Raising children is an unusually important and time-consuming undertaking—but it is much more, as well. Parents sometimes take their many responsibilities so seriously that they forget to have fun, to be a little silly, and to laugh at life and at themselves.

Humor is an important part of good health for adults, for children, and for families. In one study identifying the characteristics of healthy families, a sense of play and humor ranked as the fifth most important characteristic. Another study showed that humor makes a direct contribution to good physical health.

Parents set the tone for family attitudes and activities. Both for themselves and for their children, parents should keep laughing. Children learn at an early age, through example and participation, to have fun, to laugh, and to enjoy life.

SECTION I RESOURCES

Teacher's Classroom Resources
- Enrichment 20
- Reteaching 20
- Section 1 Quiz

Student Workbook
- Motor Match-ups

SECTION OVERVIEW

Section 1 presents basic information about the growth and development of infants during the first year of life. As they study the section, students learn about patterns of physical development, about babies' growth in weight and height, about babies' changing proportions, and about the development of babies' sensory and motor skills.

MOTIVATOR

Display photographs of the same baby at birth, at the age of six months, and at the age of one year. Guide students in discussing the photographs, focusing on changes in appearance and abilities during the first year of life.

USING TERMS TO LEARN

Guide students in reading and discussing all six terms introduced here. Encourage volunteers to share their knowledge about general definitions of these terms; remind them that more specific definitions of the terms, as they relate to child development, are provided in the text.

To help students understand the word *audiologist*, point out the initial combining form *audio*, meaning "hearing." Ask students to identify and define other words with the same combining form.

SECTION 1

Growth and Development During the First Year

OBJECTIVES

- Explain the three basic patterns that physical development follows.
- Describe physical growth during the first year.
- Describe the development of senses and skills during the first year.

TERMS TO LEARN

audiologist
depth perception
hand-eye coordination
motor skills
primary teeth
proportion

Would you recognize a baby you had seen first as a week-old infant and next on the child's first birthday? If you have ever watched the development of a baby, you know that many changes occur from week to week and from month to month. In the first twelve months, most babies change so much that they would be difficult to match up with pictures taken in the first weeks of life.

Development and growth during the first year are the most rapid of any time in life. In twelve months, the baby who begins as a helpless newborn triples his or her birth weight, learns to stand alone, and may even begin to walk.

Patterns of Physical Development

As you already know, all development follows an orderly sequence. It proceeds step-by-step in about the same order for every baby. Physical development is no exception. You will find it easier to observe physical development if you understand the three basic patterns it follows. Physical development proceeds from head to foot, from near to far, and from simple to complex.

- **Head to foot.** Long before birth, the baby's head takes the lead in development. Two months after conception, the head is about half the size of the entire fetus. The arms and legs do

---

COOPERATIVE LEARNING

Research on cooperative learning has revealed that a system of rewards increases positive interdependence among students. Among techniques for grading cooperative efforts are the following:

- *Awarding individual scores plus group "bonus" points.* Group members study cooperatively to ensure that all have mastered the assignment. Members are then assessed individually

and, in the event all achieve a predetermined score or better, receive bonus test points.

- *Awarding a mean academic score plus a "group performance" score.* Groups jointly master material and are individually assessed. Overall grades consist of the group's average score plus points awarded for collaborative performance skills.

•Patterns of Physical Development

•Growth During the First Year

•Development During the First Year

Both appearance and behavior give clues to a baby's health. A healthy baby is generally happy, active, and curious.

not catch up until later. A newborn's head is still large in proportion to the body. The same head-to-toe pattern continues after birth. First, babies learn to lift their heads to see an interesting object. Later, as the development proceeds down toward their arms and hands in the middle of the body, they will be able to pick that object up. Still later, when development has continued downward to the feet, they can walk to it.

• **Near to far.** Development starts at the trunk of the body and moves outward. First, babies simply wave their arms when they see an object they want. Later, they are able to grab at an object with the palm of the hand. Finally, babies learn to pick up small objects with their thumb and fingers.

• **Simple to complex.** At first, babies' main activities are sleeping and eating. Gradually, they learn more complicated tasks. From being fed, they progress to eating with their fingers. Eventually, they are able to use a spoon and fork for eating.

GUIDED PRACTICE

Promoting Discussion

Encourage students to share and discuss their own experiences with the rapid growth of babies. Ask teen parents to describe the rapid changes they have observed in their own babies; let other students talk about the changes they have seen when visiting a baby at intervals of several weeks or months, for example. Ask questions such as these: What differences does a month make in the size and the skills of a baby? By contrast, what difference does the same period of time make in the growth and development of a teenager?

Using the Photograph

Let students describe and discuss the infant in the picture on this page. What specific indications of good health can you identify in this baby? How old do you think the baby might be? What makes you guess that age?

Cooperative Learning

Have students work in small groups to review the three basic patterns of physical development. Ask group members to select one of those patterns and brainstorm a list of examples demonstrating that pattern. Then students may want to draw pictures or find photographs to illustrate one set of examples. Have the group members work together to create a display of their drawings or photographs and present them to the rest of the class.

SEE HOW THEY GROW

See How They've Grown

Show students pictures of the same baby at birth, six months, nine months, and one year. Discuss the changes in appearance and physical ability in that span of time. Tell students that in this chapter, they will learn about the rapid changes that take place in a baby's development from birth to age one. Remind them that over the course of this time, babies develop more

rapidly than at any other time in their lives. Ask student volunteers to share personal experiences they have had dealing with babies. What can students speculate about the wide range of needs that a baby has when developing this rapidly? What do they feel is the most important need?

GUIDED PRACTICE (continued)

Promoting Discussion

Help students review and discuss the information on growth by asking questions such as these:

- Why do parents and other caregivers refer to growth charts and compare the growth of their infants with that shown on these charts? What problems might arise when parents disregard the information on growth charts? When parents give too much attention to that information?

- Which is more clearly influenced by heredity—weight or height? Why?

- What examples can you cite of biological families in which siblings or other relatives vary widely in their mature height? What do you think accounts for these variations?

- What purpose do fontanels serve? Why do you think they close when they do, rather than when the child is much younger? Much older?

Using the Photograph

Encourage students to describe and discuss the baby in the photograph on this page. How old would you guess this baby is? What reasons can you give for guessing that age? Where do you think this baby probably fits on the chart of average weight and height? On the basis of this photograph, do you think the baby is healthy? Why or why not?

Making Connections: Math

Have students average the weights of these one-year-old babies and then determine whether the group falls within the average weight range for one-year-olds:

- 25 pounds
- 20 pounds
- 18 pounds
- 27 pounds
- 22 pounds
- 17 pounds

(129 ÷ 6 = 21.5. Yes, this average is within the average weight range of 20 to 22 pounds.)

Few babies are precisely average. Unless a child is significantly above or below average, there is no need for concern. All babies grow and develop at their own rate.

Growth During the First Year

You also know that children grow and develop at individual rates. Charts are available that show average weight, height, and abilities at certain ages. These charts help give a general understanding of child growth and development. Remember, that these charts are based on averages.

Weight

In babies, weight gain is one of the best indications of good health. Most babies experience a slight weight loss just after birth. From then on, they gain weight rapidly. For the first six months, a healthy baby gains 1 to 2 pounds (0.45 to 0.9 kg) per month. During the last half of the first year, the average weight gain is 1 pound (0.45 kg) per month. This means that the baby's weight usually doubles within the first few months. By the first birthday, a baby has typically tripled his or her birth weight.

The weight of year-old babies varies widely. The average weight is 20 to 22 pounds (9 to 10 kg). An individual baby's weight and pattern of weight gain may be influenced by heredity, by feeding habits, and by levels of physical activity.

Height

Growth in height is steady during the first year. You know that the average newborn is 20 inches (51 cm) long. By one year of age, the average infant is about 30 inches (76 cm) long.

Heredity has a stronger influence on height than on weight. If both your parents are tall, you are more likely to be tall than is a child of two short parents. This does not mean that tall parents always have tall children. Since human beings carry a mixture of genes, the results of a child's particular mixture cannot be predicted.

Proportion

Proportion is *the size relationship of one thing to another.* In child development, proportion refers to the size relationship between different parts of the body. Compared with adult proportions, a baby's head and abdomen are large. The legs and arms are short and small.

The head grows rapidly during the first year to provide room for the swiftly developing brain. Over half the total growth of the head occurs at this time. The fontanels provide for this growth of the head. The fontanels, which are sometimes visible in the growing infant, close by about age eighteen months.

HEALTHY FAMILIES/HEALTHY CHILDREN

Health and Safety

Careful monitoring of a baby's weight by a pediatrician can give many hints about the infant's health and development. Infants may fail to gain weight if they are sick, fed formula that is mixed incorrectly, or kept to a schedule that is too rigid. Weight loss can also be due to a condition sometimes referred to as failure to thrive. Babies can literally waste away because they are given inadequate love and attention. Too much weight can also be a problem. Overweight babies are sometimes fed too often, given formula that is mixed incorrectly, or given highly sugared beverages. They may also need more physical activity.

Development During the First Year

Although the terms *growth* and *development* are often used to mean the same thing, there is a difference. *Growth* refers to measurable change in size. *Development* refers to an increase in physical, emotional, social, or intellectual skills. Growth and development are both rapid during the first year.

If you observed a group of teens, you could probably tell the older teens from the younger ones, but it would be difficult to identify the exact age of each individual. A fifteen-year-old and a sixteen-year-old look and act much alike. In contrast, it is easy to tell a newborn from a one-year-old. A healthy baby not only grows bigger, but also develops many observable skills during the first year of life.

Sight

Development of sight in the unborn baby is limited by lack of bright light. The fetus's eyes, however, do open and shut before birth.

A newborn's eyes are closed most of the time. When they are open, you may wonder whether the eyes are clearly focused. Uncoordinated muscles cause the eyes to blink separately or to look in different directions. A newborn's eyes may—or may not—produce tears when the baby cries; both conditions are normal.

Eyesight improves rapidly. An infant's vision is blurry at first. Within a week or so, the newborn is increasingly aware of his or her surroundings and can focus on objects that are 7 to 10 inches (17.5 to 25 cm) away. The infant's eyes begin to work together. By about three and one-half months, a baby's vision is almost as good as a young adult's.

Depth perception is *the ability to recognize that an object is three-dimensional, not flat.* Depth perception is not recognizable in babies until the second month. By the third month, babies prefer to look at three-dimensional or real objects rather than flat pictures of objects.

Hand-eye coordination is *the ability to move the hands and fingers precisely in relation to what is seen.* Babies develop this coordination gradually. Around the age of three or four months, babies begin to reach for objects they see; this is an important milestone. Hand-eye coordination continues to develop throughout childhood. It is necessary for many skills, such as eating, catching a ball, coloring, and tying shoes. It continues into adulthood, with the abilities to thread a needle, keyboard, and play sports, for example.

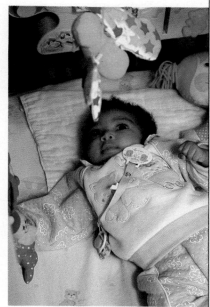

During the first two months this baby will focus on objects 7-10 inches from her nose. By two and one-half months, the baby will be able to follow a moving object with her eyes. By three months she will begin to swipe at it.

SEE HOW THEY GROW

Infants' Vision

Infants have much better vision than we once thought. In two studies, two-day-old and two-month-old infants were shown a series of six disks. Three had plain colors (white, red, and yellow), and three had different patterns (a bull's-eye, newsprint, and a face). In both studies, the infants spent more time looking at each of the patterned disks than at any of the plain ones.

The face pattern was by far the most preferred in the two-month-old group. These studies reinforce the idea that infants prefer complex patterns to plain ones. Infants need lots of opportunities to see things. They like a sitting position and also enjoy moving to different locations for a change of view.

GUIDED PRACTICE (continued)

Critical Thinking

Ask students to imagine themselves as pediatricians. What questions would they ask the parent after examining each of these six-month-old babies?

• Tonya was 6 pounds, 7 ounces (2.9 kg) at birth. Now she is drastically below the weight of an average six-month-old.

• Peter was 6 pounds, 7 ounces (2.9) at birth. Now he is drastically above the weight of an average six-month-old.

Promoting Discussion

Have volunteers review for the class the distinction between growth and development. Ask students to cite examples of growth in infants and development in infants; then ask them to cite examples of growth in older children and adolescents, and development in older children and adolescents.

Using the Photograph

Encourage volunteers to describe the infant in the photograph on this page. What signs indicate that her vision is developing appropriately? What further signs should her parents or caregivers look for as the baby grows older?

Critical Thinking

Encourage students to discuss their ideas in response to these questions:

• How can parents recognize that their baby may have a vision problem?

• What should parents do if they think their baby's vision is not developing appropriately?

• How might parents' own expectations make it difficult for them to recognize a problem with their baby's sight?

• What effect could delaying recognition of a vision problem have on a baby? On the baby's parents?

GUIDED PRACTICE (continued)

Cooperative Learning

Divide students into groups. Give each group several infant toys, including, for example, mobiles, wall hangings, and stuffed animals. Have group members discuss how these toys might help develop an infant's vision. Then have them evaluate the effectiveness—or ineffectiveness—of each toy as an aid to the development of vision.

Critical Thinking

Ask students to consider an infant's sense of smell and compare it with an adult's. How are the abilities different? What do you imagine accounts for those differences? Why, how, and when do you think a baby's sense of smell begins to change?

Promoting Discussion

Encourage students to discuss the importance of early feeding as babies develop a sense of taste. What can parents and other caregivers do during the first year of a child's life to influence the child's later preferences and eating habits?

HEALTH TIP

Have students demonstrate how a baby might react when a parent tests the baby's hearing. As a parent, one student should clap sharply, call out to the child, and make an ordinary sound. Another student might respond as he or she thinks a hearing baby might. Another student could respond as a child with a hearing problem might. (A child who can hear will be startled, turn toward the source of sound, and respond when called. One who does not hear probably will not react in the same alert ways.)

HEALTH TIP

Be alert for these signs of hearing problems:

- A newborn is not startled by a sharp clap.

- A three-month-old never turns toward the source of sounds.

- A baby is not awakened by loud noises, does not respond to familiar voices, and pays no attention to ordinary sounds.

These warning signs should be discussed with the baby's pediatrician. The pediatrician will probably refer the baby to an **audiologist,** *a professional specially trained to test for, diagnose, and help treat hearing problems.*

Hearing

The sense of hearing develops even before birth. In fact, babies still in the uterus often respond to sounds with altered heart rates or with changes in activity levels. At birth, a baby can already tell the general direction a sound comes from.

Newborns respond to the tone of a voice rather than to the words themselves. A soothing, loving voice calms them. A loud or angry voice alarms them. Remember the importance of your tone of voice when you are caring for any child—especially a newborn.

Hearing is essential for normal language development. Listening to words and gradually associating meaning with those words is the first step in learning to speak. Because hearing and listening are so important to a child's development, many physicians recommend that babies have a hearing test by about six months of age. This is especially important if the baby has had frequent ear infections.

Smell and Taste

Since a baby is surrounded by amniotic fluid until birth, the sense of smell does not have much chance to develop. Studies at Brown University have shown, however, that even newborns respond to disagreeable odors. For example, the babies in the study turned away from teddy bears that smelled like vinegar, but responded eagerly to teddy bears with a sweet vanilla scent. During the first few days of life, infants become sensitive to less noticeable smells and adjust quickly to familiar odors. Within ten days they can distinguish by smell their own mother from another person.

The sense of taste develops rapidly. In research studies, two-week-old babies have shown, through their sucking behavior, that they can taste the differences between water, sour liquids, sugar solutions, salt solutions, and milk. Even at this early age, babies show a preference for a sweet taste.

Voice

The newborn's cry, initially quite shrill, becomes softer as the baby's lungs mature and the voice is used. This change in the baby's voice also results from the physical growth of the throat muscles, tongue, lips, teeth, and vocal cords. The tongue and interior of the mouth change in shape and proportion during the first months of life.

These physical changes also affect feeding. At first the infant is able only to suck liquids. Later in the year, when the baby is able to swallow and digest foods more easily, solid foods may be added to the diet.

OBSERVING AND PARTICIPATING

Celebrating Individual Differences

Babies seem to have their own individual levels of irritability from the time of birth. They cry for attention or to communicate various kinds of discomfort. In exploring the reasons for crying, experts do not always find clear-cut answers. Most experts do agree, however, that parents and other caregivers can influence the amount of time and energy a baby expends in crying. Several studies support the theory that when children under six months old cry, they should be responded to quickly. Contrary to the belief that this may spoil a baby, studies show that babies who get quick responses cry less than those whose cries are ignored.

Growth of the mouth, vocal tract, and related areas also affects speech development. Distinct speech depends on that growth. Teeth are necessary to produce some sounds, so even babies who speak early are unable to make certain sounds.

Although young babies cannot speak, they communicate their needs with distinct types of crying. For example, one cry may express a baby's pain and a different cry may express that baby's boredom. Babies also prepare for speech by making word-related sounds. They begin babbling vowel sounds, such as "ooh," "ah," and "au," as early as three months of age.

Many babies are physically ready for speech by the end of the first year. However, children learn to speak at different rates, and many do not say any words until after their first birthday.

Teeth

The development of a baby's teeth actually begins about the sixth week of pregnancy. However, the **primary teeth** or "baby teeth," *the first set of teeth a baby gets,* usually do not appear until six or seven months of age.

At six or seven months, the two lower front teeth are the first to come in. By age two or three, most children have a full set of 20 primary teeth.

BUILDING SELF-ESTEEM

Music to a Baby's Ears

Within hours after birth, babies respond to the sounds around them. Quiet, musical sounds can calm a baby; loud, high-pitched sounds can excite or even frighten a baby.

Within weeks, babies recognize the voices of people in their world, such as, parents, grandparents, siblings, or other caregivers. By three months of age, babies can be observed to awaken from a nap, cry out, and listen for someone to walk toward their room.

Babies also respond with smiles and movement when a parent or other caregiver talks to them, repeats their baby sounds, and stays near them. Apparently, human voices are like music to a baby's ears.

SEE HOW THEY GROW

Babies' Teeth

Teeth develop early, though they do not usually begin to erupt until a baby is about six months old. In some babies, of course, first teeth erupt quite a bit earlier, and a few babies—about 1 in every 2,000—are actually born with at least one tooth already showing. Caring for an infant's teeth, even before those teeth have erupted, is an important responsibility. However, providing dental care should not include using toothpaste with children under the age of two. Very young children are unable to avoid swallowing the toothpaste. As a result, they are likely to ingest too much fluoride, which can cause spotted teeth and can weaken the enamel that protects teeth.

GUIDED PRACTICE (continued)

Promoting Discussion
Encourage students to share their own experiences with and reactions to babies' cries and babbling sounds. How do students usually feel when someone else's baby begins to cry? How are parents and other caregivers likely to feel when newborns cry? When older babies cry? How can parents and other caregivers learn to recognize and respond to a baby's different kinds of crying? Why are family members often especially eager for babies to begin talking? How can parents and other caregivers foster communication and a sense of intimacy with crying babies?

Using the Photograph
Guide students in discussing the infant in the photograph on this page. What does the presence of these first lower teeth indicate about the baby's age? About the baby's ability to speak? About the baby's diet? How are parents and other relatives likely to react to the appearance of a baby's first teeth? Why?

BUILDING SELF-ESTEEM

Making music while interacting with a baby is a valuable part of the bonding process. Have students demonstrate these suggestions for introducing baby to music:

While dressing, changing, or feeding an infant, hum or sing a simple melody that uses the baby's name. Play "listening" games while outside, calling attention to the sounds of nature, then repeating the sounds with their own voices. Remind them to encourage older babies who are beginning to talk to repeat the sounds as well.

While holding an infant, gently dance to music played on a radio or stereo. Infants learn to associate changes in movement with mood and tempo variations in music.

GUIDED PRACTICE (continued)

Practicing Decision Making

Present the following situation to the class: Travis and Jenna have a seven-month-old daughter, Kirsten. For two days, Kirsten has been irritable and has seemed to feel unwell. She has also been drooling a lot and chewing on the front bar of her stroller.

Let students explain what they would do if they were Kirsten's parents.

Critical Thinking

Let students share their responses to these questions:

- How might the teething period produce stress within the family? Who is likely to be affected by that stress?

- What should parents do to relieve or avoid family stress associated with a baby's teething?

Using Management Skills

Have students visit a supermarket, discount store, or pharmacy, and make a list of the medications available for easing teething pain. Ask students to include in their lists the price and size of each product, as well as notes about the directions for using the product. On the basis of price and ease of use, which products, if any, would they try? Why?

HEALTH TIP

Have students research more about caring for an infant's teeth. For a class report, they could find information in baby care books, from parents, and from a pediatric dentist. If possible, have them interview the dentist or arrange for a class visit. Other students might present a demonstration using a doll to show the proper way to clean a baby's teeth.

HEALTH TIP

It's never too early to start caring for a baby's teeth. Even before the first tooth appears, an infant's mouth should be cleaned after each feeding. Just wipe the gums gently with a piece of clean, dampened gauze. This cleaning method can be continued even after early teeth have come in.

Teething is an entirely normal process, but often a painful one for the infant. The teeth must force their way up through the baby's gums. As they do, they stretch and tear the tender gum tissues. This often causes pain and swelling. During teething, a normally contented infant may suddenly become cranky, restless, and wakeful. Some babies refuse food and drool a lot. Teething can also cause other symptoms, including an increased desire for liquid, coughing, and fever.

Discomfort usually lasts from two to ten days for each tooth. You may find these methods helpful for dealing with a teething baby:

- Teething babies like to bite down hard to relieve the pressure on their gums. Offer teething biscuits or teething rings.

- Since cold is a good painkiller, try chilling a liquid-filled teething ring in the refrigerator.

- Rubbing an ice cube on the baby's gums may ease the pain temporarily.

- Commercial medications specifically for teething pain are available. These liquids are rubbed onto the swollen gums to reduce pain. Read and follow all directions.

- If teething pain persists or other serious symptoms develop, consult a doctor.

The teething process continues periodically for about two years, until all 20 primary teeth have come in. The order in which primary teeth appear is fairly predictable. The timing, however, varies widely.

Motor Skills

Much of a baby's development during the first year is in the area of motor skills. **Motor skills** are *abilities that depend on the use and control of muscles.* Although motor skills seem to be signs of physical development, mastering them requires intellectual, social, and emotional development as well. This is because development in each area affects all other areas.

One of the first motor skills infants acquire is control of the head. At birth, the head is large and heavy; the neck muscles are weak. By age one month, babies placed on their stomach can lift their head slightly. By two to three months of age, they can also lift their chest. At this age they can keep their head steady when propped in a sitting position.

The chart on pages 235-236 shows other motor skill accomplishments during the first year.

MORE ABOUT

Teething

The average sequence for the eruption of teeth is central incisors, lateral incisors, first molars, cuspids or canines, and second molars. These sprout four at a time about four months apart. The timing of the first and last teeth varies greatly from baby to baby. Timing seems to be consistent within families, so new parents may wish to find out what their own pattern of teething was in order to look for similarities.

Sometimes serious illnesses may be mistaken for teething. A low-grade fever may be a sign of teething; however, a fever over 100.5° F (38° C) is probably related to illness rather than teething. Diarrhea and vomiting are also symptoms of teething. Diarrhea can be very serious for young children because they can quickly become dehydrated. To be safe, when you are in doubt about the cause of fever, diarrhea, or vomiting, contact a physician.

AVERAGE MOTOR SKILLS DEVELOPMENT

BIRTH TO TWELVE MONTHS

ONE MONTH

* Lifts chin when placed on stomach.

TWO MONTHS

* Lifts chest well above surface when placed on stomach.

THREE TO FOUR MONTHS

* Reaches for objects, but unsteadily.
* Holds up head steadily.
* Rolls from side to back and from back to side.
* Has complete head control when sitting on an adult's lap.
* Holds head erect when carried.

FIVE TO SIX MONTHS

* Sits alone briefly.
* Reaches and grasps successfully, but awkwardly.
* Turns completely over when laid on back or stomach.
* Prefers to sit up with support.
* Uses hands to reach, grasp, crumble, bang, and splash.

(Continued on next page)

OBSERVING AND PARTICIPATING

Learning Through Participation

Many very simple activities can be used to help stimulate a baby's development. What person hasn't watched someone play peek-a-boo with a delighted baby? One variation on this activity is to hold the baby in front of a mirror, moving sideways for repeated peeks. Hiding games are also good. A toy can be pulled in and out from behind a blanket as the caregiver wonders aloud where it has gone. Action rhymes, such as pat-a-cake, can be started early for fun as well as exposure to language. The list of ideas is limited only by a caregiver's creativity. Promoting the child's development and providing feelings of love and happiness are the rewards for the effort.

GUIDED PRACTICE (continued)

Using the Chart

Guide students in discussing the motor skills identified as average for babies of each age range. Encourage volunteers to share their own experiences in observing babies' motor skills; if necessary, emphasize that individual healthy babies may accomplish specific motor skills earlier or later than during the period noted on the chart.

Critical Thinking

Encourage students to refer to the "Average Motor Skills Development" chart as they discuss their responses to these questions: How does the development of motor skills affect the toys that are appropriate for an infant? At what age might a baby begin playing with a squeeze toy? With a toy that makes a sound when struck with a stick?

Using the Photograph

Encourage students to describe the baby shown in the photograph on page 237. What signs indicate that this is a healthy baby? What should parents and other caregivers look for as possible signs that a baby is not healthy?

Practicing Decision Making

Present the following family situation to the class: Darla's sister Kate, who lives in another state, has come home for a two-week visit. Darla is thrilled to be meeting her little nine-month-old nephew Jaramie for the first time. While playing with Jaramie, Darla places him on a blanket on the floor, where he contentedly lies in front of the TV. When Darla props Jaramie up, he quickly falls backwards. He does not reach for the colorful rattle she shakes in front of him, but he does watch it as she moves it from side to side. Darla tries to stand Jaramie on his feet, but his legs fold beneath him.

Encourage students to discuss what they would be likely to conclude if they were in Darla's position? What questions would they ask? Of whom? What actions would they take? Why?

INDEPENDENT PRACTICE

Journal Writing

Ask students to write in their journals about the growth and development of a baby during the first year of life. Suggest that students respond to these questions: What do you consider the most important physical change that takes place during the first year? How does that change affect the baby's life? How does it affect the life of the baby's family members? Why?

Student Workbook

Have students complete "Motor Match-ups" in the Student Workbook.

Extension

Let students work independently or in small groups to complete one or more of these extension activities:

- Have students make a chart or time line showing the physical milestones parents and other caregivers should look for during a baby's first year of life.

- Let students examine a collection of baby photographs. Have them arrange the photographs in order of the babies' ages, from youngest to oldest, and guess the age of each baby. Ask students to explain the reasons for their guesses.

- Provide a stack of photographs of babies clipped from magazines or other sources; include pictures of children with health problems. Have each student select one photograph and, either orally or in writing, describe the baby and evaluate indications of the baby's health.

- Have students plan and make posters that would be visually stimulating to babies. Donate the completed posters to a child care nursery where they can be placed on the walls.

AVERAGE MOTOR SKILLS DEVELOPMENT (cont'd.)

SEVEN TO EIGHT MONTHS

- Reaches for spoon.
- Pulls self up while holding on to furniture.
- Sits up steadily.
- Propels self by arms, knees, or squirming motion.
- Eats with fingers.
- Picks up large objects.

NINE TO TEN MONTHS

- Walks when led.
- Reaches for and manipulates objects with good control.
- Picks up medium-sized objects as well as larger ones.
- Stands holding on to furniture or other supports.
- Is more skillful with spoon.
- Crawls on hands and knees.

ELEVEN TO TWELVE MONTHS

- Stands alone.
- May be walking alone.
- Shows preference for one hand over the other.
- Holds and drinks from a cup.
- Fits blocks, boxes, or nesting toys inside each other.
- Picks up small objects using thumb and forefinger.

TEEN PARENTING

If you have teen parents in your class, you may wish to have them bring their babies to class. Encourage the parents to let their babies "show off" their motor skills; if necessary, remind students that the chart shows averages and that variations in skills development are normal. Then suggest that each teen parent demonstrate a simple game or routine he or she uses with the baby. Sometimes teen parents are not aware of how important such activities are. Help them see that the development of motor skills is related to their activity with the child. Seeing what others do may provide them with new ideas to try.

CHECKING COMPREHENSION

Assign students to write their responses to the "Check Your Understanding" questions in the Section 1 Review. Answers to the questions are given at the bottom of this page.

EVALUATE

Have students complete the Chapter 8, Section 1 quiz in the TCR.

Reteaching

1. Assign Reteaching 20 in the TCR.
2. Guide students in discussing their understanding of the term *motor skill*. Then display pictures of babies, each demonstrating different motor skills. Let students take turns identifying the motor skills each pictured infant has accomplished.

Enrichment

1. Distribute Enrichment 20 in the TCR.
2. Have students investigate and report on methods researchers use to study the sensory development of infants.

Extension

Ask students to bring to class graphs used to record infants' growth in height, weight, and head size during the first year of life. (If necessary, suggest that pediatricians, family practitioners, and parents of young children are good sources of such graphs.) Guide students in examining and discussing the graphs. How do doctors use this kind of graph? What does the information on the graph mean to parents? What is the significance of measurements that vary from the average?

As the baby grows older, the ability to support and control the head improves.

SECTION 1 REVIEW

CHECK YOUR UNDERSTANDING

1. List the three basic patterns that physical development follows.

2. How much weight does an average healthy baby gain each month during the first six months of life?

3. Explain what proportion is. How do a baby's proportions compare with an adult's proportions?

4. What is depth perception? When is it first noticeable in babies?

5. What is hand-eye coordination? When and how does hand-eye coordination develop?

6. What signs would indicate a possible hearing problem in a baby?

7. List at least three motor skills that the average baby develops at seven to eight months.

DISCUSS AND DISCOVER

1. What activities would you suggest parents and caregivers might use to help stimulate hand-eye coordination in their infants?

2. Discuss how speaking—which might be described as a physical ability—requires a combination of physical, emotional, social, and intellectual growth and development.

3. Why may one baby's motor skills develop more slowly or more quickly than average?

Observing & Participating

Observe an infant to identify signs of sensory development. Speculate about whether the baby can hear, see, smell, taste, feel, and make sounds. What signs indicate development in each area? How does the baby's environment help stimulate sensory development? What improvements could be made?

SECTION 1 REVIEW

1. Head to foot; near to far; simple to complex.

2. 1 to 2 pounds (0.45 to 0.9 kg).

3. The size relationship of one thing to another. Compared with adult proportions, a baby has a large head and abdomen, and short, small legs and arms.

4. The ability to recognize that an object is three-dimensional, not flat. Noticeable in babies during the second month.

5. The ability to move the hands and fingers precisely in relation to what is seen. Develops gradually throughout infancy and childhood.

6. Is not startled by a sharp clap; never turns toward the source of sounds; does not awaken to loud noises, respond to familiar voices, or pay attention to sounds.

7. Refer to chart on page 236.

CLOSE

Ask each student to identify one indication of physical growth and development that parents and other caregivers should look for during a baby's first year.

FOCUS

SECTION 2 RESOURCES

Teacher's Classroom Resources
- Enrichment 21
- Reteaching 21
- Section 2 Quiz

Student Workbook
- Advice Column

SECTION OVERVIEW

In Section 2, students learn about the two most basic skills in providing care for infants: handling and feeding. The section provides information on lifting, holding, and carrying babies of various ages, using techniques that provide for both safety and comfort. It also provides information on babies' changing nutritional needs.

MOTIVATOR

Remind students that young children unquestioningly expect their parents to "take care of everything"—to provide for all the child's needs and to solve all the child's problems. Ask students to imagine themselves as new parents who suddenly realize that they have a newborn baby for whom they must provide this kind of care. Let students brainstorm a list of questions and concerns that come to mind.

USING TERMS TO LEARN

Guide students in analyzing the structure of *malnutrition* so that they can better understand its meaning. *Mal* is a prefix meaning "bad" or "wrong." *Nutrition* comes from the Latin word *nutrire*, which means "to nourish." *Malnutrition* is undernourishment resulting from such problems as insufficient food, improper diet, and poor eating habits.

SECTION 2

Providing Care for Infants: Handling and Feeding

OBJECTIVES

- Explain how to hold and feed a baby.
- Identify nutritional needs during infancy.

TERMS TO LEARN

malnutrition
strained foods
weaning

When you take care of an infant, you will spend much of your time responding to the baby's physical needs. Many of your activities will involve lifting, holding, and carrying the baby. Feeding the baby will also be an important concern. With understanding and practice, you will soon develop the skills to handle the baby gently and efficiently, and to recognize and respond to the baby's own special personality and needs.

Handling a Baby

You will find that a baby needs to be lifted and held for all sorts of reasons—to have diapers changed, to be fed, to be dressed, to be bathed, to be moved. There are two more reasons, equally important, for handling a baby—to comfort the baby and to give the baby your attention. When you pick up and hold an infant, for any reason, you have an opportunity to strengthen the bond between you and the baby and to help the baby feel secure and happy.

All babies need to be handled gently and carefully. The lack of head control in younger babies requires more careful handling than is needed by a more mature baby who can support his or her head. You may also find that a baby's temperament influences your handling.

Of all babies, newborns require the greatest care when you are picking them up, carrying them, or holding them. Whenever you handle a newborn, remember that the baby's neck muscles cannot yet support the head. You'll need to keep your hand or arm under the baby's neck and head at all times.

OBSERVING AND PARTICIPATING

Celebrating Individual Differences

In a recent study of the interactions between males and females and their babies, Dr. Jerrold Lee Shapiro found that there are differences in the way women and men hold their babies. A woman more often holds her baby close, with the baby's head toward the mother's chest. In contrast, a man is more likely to hold the baby away from him. Dr. Shapiro feels that the close holding by mothers offers the baby security and lessens the fear of abandonment; the father's holding method allows the baby more freedom and gives the baby and the father an opportunity to gaze at each other. Babies seem to benefit from both holding styles.

To lift a newborn, slide one hand under the baby's buttocks, and slide the other hand under the shoulders and head. Use your forearm to support the neck and head as you raise your hands together to lift the newborn. Remember to move smoothly and gently so that you do not startle the baby.

There are two basic positions for holding a newborn safely and comfortably. You may want to hold the baby upright, cradled in the curve of your arm against your body. In this position, your arm supports the baby's head and neck, and you can easily maintain eye contact with the baby. You may also want to hold the baby against your chest, so that the baby faces—or peeks over—your shoulder. In this position you need to use your hand to support the baby's neck and head.

When you lay a newborn down, continue to support both the neck and head and the body. Bend over, keeping the baby close to your body until the baby comes in contact with his or her next support system. Again, move smoothly and gently so that the baby continues to feel comfortable and secure.

As the baby grows older and stronger, his or her head needs less support. However, it is still important to handle the baby gently and to hold the baby close, to ensure a sense of security.

When you are handling a baby of any age, it is important to avoid shaking and jiggling. These actions can be surprisingly dangerous; they can cause bleeding in the baby's brain and may lead to lasting brain damage.

You can easily have skin-to-skin contact with your cheek and baby's face by holding the baby against your shoulder. Be sure to gently support the neck and head with one hand. Supporting the infant in the curve of your arm lets you stay face-to-face.

SAFETY TIP

With all the stresses involved in caring for a baby, it is sometimes natural to feel anger or frustration—perhaps with the world, perhaps even with the baby. You don't need to worry about feeling angry occasionally, but you *do* need to worry about handling the baby when you are upset. If you feel yourself becoming very angry, try the following:

- Put the baby down in a safe place (the crib, for example) and go into another room.

- Ask a friend or relative to stay with the baby for a while.

- If there is no one available to help, try looking out a window, taking a few deep breaths, slowly drinking a cool glass of water.

SEE HOW THEY GROW

Infants' Comfort

Most infants gain a special sense of comfort and security from being carried and cuddled. Each parent and other caregiver who participates in raising a newborn may develop his or her own style of holding the infant; all, however, should begin by assuming that being held comforts the baby. Some infants have distinct preferences about being held in certain ways, and a very few infants do prefer not to be held too long or too frequently. These babies will soon make their distinct needs known. In general, however, parents and other caregivers should show their love and caring by holding and cuddling the baby as much as possible. They should also be aware that the baby's need to be held and touched continues throughout childhood—and, indeed, throughout life.

TEACH
Pages 238-247

- Handling a Baby
- Feeding a Baby
- Nutritional Concerns

GUIDED PRACTICE
Promoting Discussion

Encourage students to discuss their own experiences in handling babies; if necessary, emphasize that a wide range of experience—or inexperience—is normal in any group. Ask volunteers to describe holding—or declining to hold—other people's babies; if teen parents are present, ask them to describe holding their newborns and their older babies. Encourage students to describe their emotional reactions to holding young babies; again, emphasize that a wide variety of responses is normal.

Using the Photographs

Direct students' attention to the two photographs on this page. Ask volunteers to explain why they think babies like to be held in the two positions pictured. What special benefits does each position offer the baby's caregiver?

Practicing Decision Making

Ask students how they would respond in each situation: You are the parent of a six-week-old infant. Your own father persists in jiggling the baby in a way you consider dangerous. Your father says, "Don't worry—we're just playing."

SAFETY TIP

After students have read the safety tip, ask them to suggest ways to handle this situation: You're visiting a friend and her three-month-old son. Your friend cannot get the baby to stop crying. Finally, in anger, she picks the baby up, shakes him, and screams, "Stop it!"

GUIDED PRACTICE (continued)

Promoting Discussion

Guide students in discussing the probable reactions of an older sibling who sees his or her parents drop everything to cuddle and feed a newborn:

- Should parents moderate their responses to the newborn's needs? If so, how and why? If not, why not?
- How should parents respond to the older sibling? Why?
- Who else might be available to help an older sibling? What suggestions would you make for those people? Why?

Using the Photograph

Encourage students to discuss the two people in the photograph on this page. How do you imagine these two are related to each other? How do they appear to be interacting? What benefits do you imagine each person is getting from this feeding?

Family Focus

Help students discuss how the mood of the family members and the atmosphere of the household may influence the physical development of a baby. How might a baby react when parents or other family members are arguing or yelling? What should be done with a baby when a family disagreement is taking place? If family members argue and yell frequently, what short-term effects are these disagreements likely to have on a baby? What could the long-term effects be?

Promoting Discussion

Encourage students to explore the differences between a feeding schedule and a feeding pattern. Which family members benefit from each? How? Which do students consider more appropriate? Why?

Feeding a Baby

Mealtime provides a baby with much more than physical nourishment. It is also a time for enjoying close contact with other people and for learning more about the world. Especially for a newborn, the cuddling, body contact, and nurturing words that go with feeding are as important as the food.

Feeding Schedules

A newborn's schedule of eating and sleeping is unpredictable at first. Newborns need to eat about as much as they want and as often as they want. In the first few weeks of life, a baby feeds six to eight times—or more—in 24 hours. These frequent feedings are necessary because a newborn's stomach can hold only a small amount at a time.

By the second or third month, a regular pattern generally emerges. The baby may wake for a feeding every three or four hours around the clock. Eventually, the baby will no longer need a late-night feeding. By the time a baby reaches 12 pounds (5.4 kg), he or she can usually sleep through the night, because at that size, the stomach can hold more milk or formula. As the baby grows, the schedule will continue to change. At the end of the first year, most babies eat three meals a day, plus snacks.

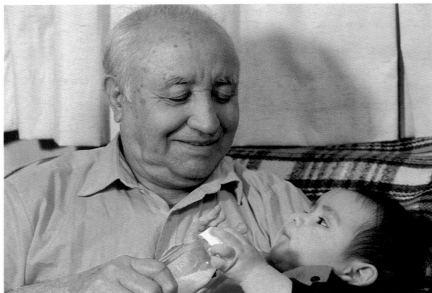

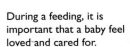
During a feeding, it is important that a baby feel loved and cared for.

OBSERVING AND PARTICIPATING

Learning Through Participation

Occasionally, people take their anger and frustration out on children. Parents and other caregivers have been known to shake a baby simply because the child was crying. This kind of treatment is extremely dangerous to an infant. Severe shaking can cause the membrane connecting the baby's brain to the skull to tear. Such tears can cause blindness, deafness, seizures, mental retardation, and even death. All people need to be able to recognize, accept, and handle their feelings of anger and frustration; this is especially important for those who care for young children. Encourage students to suggest appropriate methods for releasing anger. Then let small groups of students plan and present skits demonstrating safe approaches to recognizing and releasing anger.

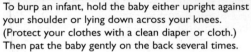

To burp an infant, hold the baby either upright against your shoulder or lying down across your knees. (Protect your clothes with a clean diaper or cloth.) Then pat the baby gently on the back several times.

Mealtime Methods

A mother who breast-feeds can expect to receive feeding instruction and help while she is still in the hospital, or from the midwife if she has delivered her baby at home or at an alternative birth center. Information and assistance are also available from La Leche League, an organization that promotes breast-feeding. Another good source of assistance is a pediatrician or nurse-practitioner, who can offer advice or can help the mother contact a national organization or another nursing mother.

Whenever you feed an infant from a bottle, hold the baby close in a semi-upright position. Remember that the young baby's head and neck need to be supported, and the head should be held well above the level of the baby's stomach. Hold the bottle at an angle, so that the baby can suck comfortably and so that the nipple remains full of milk. If the bottle nipple isn't kept full of milk, the baby will swallow too much air.

Whether you breast-feed or bottle-feed, continue the feeding until the infant seems satisfied. Healthy babies usually eat the amount they need.

Whichever method of feeding you use, you should take time to burp the baby at least twice—once during the feeding and once when the feeding is over. Burping involves holding the baby in a position in which he or she can comfortably expel air swallowed during feeding. Don't be surprised if the baby doesn't actually burp each time; the baby needs the chance to burp but may not always have extra air to expel.

SAFETY TIP

Disease-causing bacteria can grow quickly in a baby's formula. It is important to discard the formula that a baby doesn't drink during a feeding. Trying to save and reuse the formula could lead to illness.

Any bottle from which a baby drinks should be carefully sterilized, either in boiling water or in a dishwasher cycle with very hot water. The nipples, bottle rings, and bottle caps should be sterilized in the same way.

HEALTHY FAMILIES/HEALTHY CHILDREN

Health and Safety

Infants under six months need about 55 calories per pound each day. Most formulas have about 20 calories per ounce. Thus, 3 ounces would supply the calories for 1 pound of an infant's weight (3 ounces x 20 calories = 60 calories). At about 3 ounces of formula per pound of body weight, a 12-pound baby would need about 36 ounces a day. As the young baby grows, the amount of formula he or she needs each day increases. The amount of formula required usually decreases in the second half of the year, since solid foods supply some of the calories formerly provided by formula.

GUIDED PRACTICE (continued)

Using the Photographs

Encourage students to describe and compare the two methods of burping shown in the photographs. Then let volunteers use a life-size baby doll to demonstrate the two methods.

Using Management Skills

Let students prepare bottles of formula using powdered, concentrated, premixed, and ready-to-use varieties. Have them compare the costs and convenience. Why might each type be preferred?

Critical Thinking Skills

Let students share and compare their ideas in response to these questions:

• Why do babies need to be burped?

• How is a baby likely to be affected if a parent or caregiver consistently neglects to burp him or her?

SAFETY TIP

After students have read the safety tip, have small groups or pairs of students conduct a survey of the preparation instruction written on the labels of baby formulas. Ask them to evaluate how clearly the instructions are written and note if warnings about possible dangers of reuse or overheating of formula are included. Ask: Do manufacturers adequately alert consumers to possible dangers? Do they include sufficient instructions to consumers who might not be aware of the harmful effects to an infant if directions are not correctly followed?

Also, ask students to research disposable nursing products (e.g., plastic bottles and liners) that are designed for convenience and safety. What are the advantages of using these products? What are the disadvantages? Remind students to take long-term concerns, such as the environment, into consideration.

GUIDED PRACTICE (continued)

Promoting Discussion

Guide students in discussing bottle-feeding by asking questions such as these: Why do you think parents and other caregivers are tempted to leave a bottle propped so that the baby can drink from it alone? What are the dangers of propping a bottle like this? What does the baby miss? What does the parent or caregiver miss? How is propping a bottle for a young baby different from letting an older baby hold his or her own bottle? Do you think older babies should be allowed to hold their bottles? Why or why not?

Using the Photograph

Use questions such as these to encourage students to describe and discuss the photograph on this page: What is the caregiver here doing? Why? Under what circumstances is this necessary? Why? When isn't it necessary?

Critical Thinking

Encourage discussion by asking students why solid foods become necessary and why they shouldn't be introduced when a baby is under stress. How do students think parents can best determine a good time to introduce new foods?

Cooperative Learning

Have small groups of students work together, tasting one type of baby food in different forms, including dehydrated, junior, and toddler. Have them compare the tastes. Which form of the food do they like best? Would they expect babies to have the same response to the foods? Why or why not?

Using Management Skills

Have students work in groups to demonstrate ways to prepare homemade baby food. Then ask the students in each group to compare their homemade product with a similar commercial baby food, considering the taste, cost, nutrition, equipment needed for preparation, convenience, and safety of each.

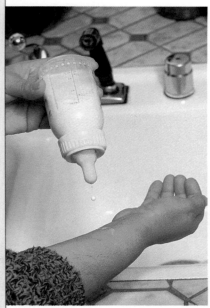

Before you feed the baby, shake a drop of formula onto your wrist or inner arm to check the temperature. The formula should feel lukewarm, not hot.

Many parents prefer to give their baby a warm bottle, although this is not really necessary. If you want to warm the baby's formula, fill the bottle and place it in a pan of water on the stove; heat the water in the pan until it makes the formula lukewarm. You can also use a special bottle warmer. You should not, however, heat the formula in a microwave oven. Microwave heating may create "hot spots," dangerously hot portions in a bottle of formula that seems to be lukewarm. When you are away from home, you can warm the bottle by holding it under hot running water, periodically shaking it and checking to see whether the formula is warm.

No matter how busy or rushed you feel, you should never leave a bottle propped up so that a baby can drink from it without your help. The formula typically gushes from a propped bottle; this can cause digestive problems and ear infections. In addition, the baby misses out on the physical contact and attention you provide when you hold the baby for a feeding.

Introducing New Foods

Around the age of six months, most babies are ready to begin adding other foods to their diet of breast milk or formula. The baby's pediatrician will recommend when these "solids" should be introduced. Maturity, or readiness, is as important in feeding as it is in learning to sit or stand.

With most babies, there is no rush to introduce new foods. Choose a time when the baby and the caregiver are both well, content, and happy. Don't begin solids, for example, if the infant has been sick or the family is moving. You don't need to worry about postponing new foods for a while; breast milk or formula will continue to provide all the nutrition the baby needs.

Usually, a baby's first solid food is cereal—one of several special baby cereals prepared to a smooth and runny consistency. Once the baby has become accustomed to cereal, you can gradually add **strained foods**, *solids processed to make them smooth and runny*. You can prepare strained fruits, vegetables, and meats in small quantities at home or buy them as baby foods in jars or in packages to be mixed for each meal. As you expand the baby's diet, be sure to add only one new food every fourth or fifth day. That way, if a certain food causes a skin rash or digestive trouble, you will be able to identify which food is causing the problem.

Cereal and strained foods present the baby with unfamiliar tastes and textures. Don't be surprised if the baby spits back the first spoonfuls of a new food. Remember to be patient as the baby adjusts to this new experience. Following these feeding tips will help make the experience safe and enjoyable for both the baby and you:

SEE HOW THEY GROW

Feeding Needs

Infants under the age of five or six months thrive on a steady diet of breast milk or formula—or a combination of the two. However, parents are often eager to start babies on "real food," and many mistakenly think that feeding cereal to babies before putting them to bed at night will help them sleep better. A study to test this theory was conducted using 106 babies divided into two groups. The average age of one group was about five weeks, and the other was about four months. The test results indicated that cereal before bed did not alter the amount of time that the babies in either group spent crying, fussing, or sleeping.

- For the first feedings, hold the baby comfortably in a fairly upright position.
- If the baby is used to warm formula, heat solid foods to lukewarm, too. To avoid dangerous hot spots, do not use a microwave to heat a baby's food. Check the temperature of warmed foods by placing a drop on your wrist.
- Be prepared for messy feedings, especially at first. Put a large bib on the baby, and be sure your own clothes are either easily washable or protected.
- Realize that the baby may spit out an unfamiliar food. It may be that the baby dislikes the food. In this case, reintroduce the food later, or try combining it with a favorite food to make it more palatable.
- Especially at first, make the baby's cereal very runny, diluting it with either breast milk or formula. Runny cereal seems more familiar to a young baby—like the breast milk or formula he or she is used to. The cereal should be offered on a spoon, however, not in a bottle, because solid matter in the bottle may cause the baby to choke.
- If you are using baby food from a jar, take out a small portion and place it in a bowl. Then close the jar and refrigerate it immediately. Do not feed the baby directly from the jar. Bacteria from the spoon will multiply rapidly in the food and cause any leftovers to spoil.

Weaning

Sometime around the first birthday, many babies are ready for **weaning**, *a process of changing from drinking from the bottle or breast to drinking from a cup.* Weaning is an important sign of the baby's increasing independence.

There is no precise age at which a baby should be weaned. Nine months is common, but the age varies greatly. The baby usually shows some signs of readiness for weaning, such as playing or looking around while sucking, pushing the nipple away, or preferring to eat from a spoon. It is always best not to force weaning on an unwilling baby; instead, wait until the baby is ready and accepts weaning naturally. Forced weaning may result in other feeding and behavior problems for the child.

Self-Feeding

When babies can sit up steadily, usually around the age of eight or ten months, they start to eat with their fingers and to reach for the spoon. They open their mouth when they see a spoon coming. Before long they want to hold the spoon themselves. These are signs that the infant is ready to begin feeding himself or herself.

GUIDED PRACTICE (continued)

Promoting Discussion

Encourage students to review and discuss the process of introducing solids by asking questions such as these:

- What attitudes do you think parents and other caregivers should demonstrate when introducing new foods to a baby? Why? How can the attitudes of parents and caregivers affect the baby?

- Why do babies spit out foods they don't like? How do you think parents and other caregivers should respond when a baby spits out food? What might make it difficult to respond that way?

- What fruits and vegetables could be mashed and served as one of a baby's first solid foods? What advantages do you see in preparing fruits and vegetables for a baby? What disadvantages?

Cooperative Learning

Have students work in groups to plan skits involving family members who are feeding solid foods to babies. Suggest that students show how a first-time feeding experience might go and that they demonstrate techniques to use to make any feeding experience easier and more fun. Then have the members of each group present their skit to the rest of the class.

Critical Thinking

Let students share and discuss their ideas in response to these questions: Why is it important to encourage a baby's interest in self-feeding? What might make it difficult for parents or other caregivers to let a baby feed himself or herself? How might limiting self-feeding affect a baby's diet? A baby's attitudes and interests?

HEALTHY FAMILIES/HEALTHY CHILDREN

Health and Safety

To prevent burns from hot food, it is recommended that baby's food—like baby's bottles—not be warmed in the microwave oven. Microwave ovens create hot spots because they heat foods unevenly. The hot spots are difficult to detect, and even thorough stirring may not provide complete protection. Another problem with microwaving anything for an infant is that foods continue to cook after they have been removed from a microwave oven. The baby's food or formula may be at a comfortable temperature when it is first removed from the oven. However, when that same food or formula is served several minutes later, it is likely to have become hotter.

GUIDED PRACTICE (continued)

Promoting Discussion

Hold up, one at a time, magazine pictures of different foods. Let students show by raising hands whether or not they think each food is appropriate for a nine-month-old baby. Encourage volunteers to explain their choices and the reasoning behind those choices.

Using the Photograph

Let students describe the baby on this page. How old do you think he is? What motor skills has he already accomplished? What motor skills is he developing as he practices feeding himself? How does he appear to feel about himself and his accomplishments?

Promoting Discussion

Guide students in discussing the responsibilities of parents and other caregivers for meeting the nutritional needs of infants. How does an infant's diet affect his or her early development? How might it affect his or her later development? His or her own attitudes and approaches to nutrition in later life?

Critical Thinking

Point out that as babies begin to feed themselves, some families try to involve the babies in regular family meals; other families encourage babies to eat separately. Ask students to identify the advantages and disadvantages of each approach. Which approach would students choose? Why?

SAFETY TIP

Remind students of the importance of using safety straps when a baby is sitting in a high chair to prevent accidents and injuries.

SAFETY TIP

Finger foods must be chosen carefully. Remember that the baby may have no teeth at all—and cannot be counted on to actually chew with any teeth he or she does have. Avoid giving the baby foods that are difficult to chew or that, without chewing, might block the baby's breathing passage. Avoid giving the baby foods such as cut-up raw vegetables, nuts, whole grapes, candy, chips, pretzels, popcorn, slices of hot dog, chunks of cooked chicken or meat—or any other food that looks to you like it could cause choking. Be sure that the food has been cut into small pieces. Then give the baby just a few pieces at a time. Some babies try to stuff their mouths full of food.

Around the age of eight to ten months, infants show an interest in self-feeding. What developmental skills has this baby mastered in order to feed himself?

To encourage the baby's self-feeding, provide "finger foods," such as strips of dry toast, small pieces of cheese or banana, or small squares of flavored gelatin. Choose nutritious foods that the baby can grasp easily.

The baby's first efforts at self-feeding with a spoon will probably be important and fun for the baby, but they may not result in much actual eating. You can help by using a separate spoon and placing bits of food in the baby's mouth now and then.

You will probably find that it takes patience—and, at least on some occasions, a sense of humor—to encourage a baby's self-feeding. You and the baby will both benefit if you allow plenty of time for each meal. Then encourage the baby's efforts and enjoy the baby's delight in these new accomplishments.

Nutritional Concerns

Feeding a baby involves more than mastering the necessary techniques. Part of the responsibility of parents and caregivers is making sure that babies' nutritional needs are being met. Fortunately, this is usually not difficult if the child receives formula or breast milk until he or she is eating a good variety of

TEEN PARENTING

Meeting the nutritional needs of an infant might be troublesome for teens who are not themselves inclined to have good eating habits. Remind students that as parents or caregivers, they are models to children. If they are careless about good nutrition, they are setting a poor example for children whose growth and development depends on proper nourishment. To make students aware of their own habits, have them keep a record of the foods they eat for two weeks. Besides listing the foods, have them keep a record of calories, fat content, vitamins, and minerals. After the two-week period, ask them to write an evaluation of their eating habits based on the records they kept. What example is set for a child?

cereals, vegetables, fruits, and meats. However, problems can result if the baby is given too much food, too little food, or the wrong kinds of food.

Overfeeding

For years, nutritionists and physicians have been debating the proper weight for babies; they continue trying to determine whether overfeeding in infancy contributes to weight problems in adulthood. There are still no final answers. However, it is clear that eating habits are established very early in life. A baby who is encouraged to overeat is likely to continue overeating during childhood and adulthood. A baby who is frequently given sweet snacks instead of nutritious foods is more than likely to continue choosing sweets later in life. Infancy is the time to begin a lifetime of healthy eating.

Bottle-fed babies have a greater risk of overfeeding than breast-fed babies. Parents and caregivers may be tempted to urge the bottle-fed baby to take any formula left in the bottle. Nursing mothers, on the other hand, can follow their baby's lead when the baby stops sucking.

Malnutrition

Infants have very specific nutritional needs. To be healthy, a baby needs the following:

* Enough calories to provide for rapid growth.
* Food that contains needed nutrients, such as protein, iron, B vitamins, vitamin C, and vitamin D.
* Food that is easy to digest.
* Adequate amounts of liquid.

Until solid foods are well established in the diet of the child, a baby's main source of nutrition is breast milk or formula. Cow's milk alone does not provide the nutrients a baby needs; it is mostly protein and does not contain the carbohydrates a baby requires for energy. However, cow's milk can be added to a baby's diet, usually after the first solid foods have been introduced.

Babies whose diets do not meet the listed requirements may suffer from **malnutrition**, *a lack of enough food or a lack of the proper type of food.* Malnutrition is not a problem faced only by developing countries in other parts of the world. Malnutrition is a problem in this country, as well. Some parents do not have enough money to provide their babies with an adequate diet. Other parents risk infant malnutrition because they do not know about babies' special food needs or because they feed their children high-calorie, low-density foods.

MORE ABOUT

Malnutrition

The symptoms of malnutrition vary depending upon the particular nutrient deficiency. Some possible signs of malnutrition include growth that falls well below average for an age; listlessness; nervous or irritable behavior; scaling around the nose and ears; wounds that are slow to heal; hair that is dull, lifeless, thin, and easy to pull out; swollen and congested eyelids; sensitivity to light; swollen lips; bleeding gums; poor posture and bone deformities; poor coordination; flabby, sore muscles; frequent infections; poor appetite; and diarrhea. The swollen stomach often associated with malnutrition is the result of insufficient protein. This deficiency also causes skin lesions, growth failure, and changes in hair color. Most symptoms of malnutrition can be corrected by improving the child's diet. With protein-calorie malnutrition, however, there is the possibility that mental development may be permanently affected.

INDEPENDENT PRACTICE

Journal Writing
Ask students to record some of their ideas about infant feeding in their journals. Pose these questions to stimulate students' thinking: What should a baby eat during the first year of life? How important is variety in a baby's diet? What does a baby learn about the world from being fed? From beginning to feed himself or herself? How can eating rituals and habits affect the relationship between baby and parent or caregiver?

Student Workbook
Have students complete "Advice Column" in the Student Workbook.

Extension
Let students work independently or in small groups to complete one or more of these extension activities:

* Have students plan, write, and illustrate a simple guide for new parents, explaining how to introduce new foods to their baby.
* Let students use catalogs, newspapers, and magazines to collect pictures of special items available for infant feeding. Guide students in discussing the usefulness of each product.
* Ask students to research the safety of commercial baby food. Have them gather information on possible pesticide contamination, product tampering, and ingredient mislabeling. Let them report their findings to the rest of the class, and encourage a discussion of how parents can know they are using a safe product.
* Have students use food and nutrition reference books to compare the Recommended Dietary Allowances (RDA) for infants with those for teenagers and adults. Ask students to summarize the ways in which nutritional needs change with age.

ASSESS

CHECKING COMPREHENSION

Assign students to write their responses to "Check Your Understanding" in the Section 2 Review.

EVALUATE

Have students complete the Chapter 8, Section 2 quiz in the TCR.

Reteaching

1. Assign Reteaching 21 in the TCR and review key concepts of the section.

2. Work with groups of students to discuss responses to these questions: What is the typical daily diet of a newborn? Of a six-month-old? Of a twelve-month-old? What accounts for the differences?

Enrichment

1. Distribute Enrichment Activity 21 in the TCR.

2. Ask students to read about various aspects of malnutrition. Then have them share and discuss what they have learned, responding to questions such as these: What is malnutrition? How does local malnutrition affect us? How does malnutrition around the world affect us? What can be done about the problems of malnutrition?

Extension

Have students bring to class photos showing caring ways to hold and carry infants. Encourage students to compare and discuss the pictures they have chosen; then suggest that they organize and display their photographs on a school bulletin board.

CLOSE

Give each student an opportunity to use a life-size doll to demonstrate one of these activities: picking up a newborn, putting a newborn down in a crib, comforting a crying newborn, bottle-feeding a newborn.

Some parents, for example, put their infants on diets very low in fat and cholesterol during the first year. They use low-fat milk or skim milk to prepare formula and later for drinking. While cholesterol has been linked to adult heart disease, low-fat and skim milk do not provide enough calories for normal infant growth; in addition, they put a strain on a baby's kidneys. There is also no clear evidence that limiting cholesterol in early childhood prevents adult health problems. Breast milk, considered the ideal food for infants, is itself high in cholesterol.

Malnutrition in infancy can cause lasting physical problems. Severe malnutrition is also linked to poor brain development and learning problems.

Many government and community programs try to eliminate infant and childhood malnutrition. Some of these programs provide food; others teach parents about the nutritional needs of children. The federal government's Women, Infants, and Children Program (WIC) helps meet the special food needs of new mothers and young children. Other programs in your area may be funded by state and local governments.

SECTION 2 REVIEW

CHECK YOUR UNDERSTANDING

1. Which part of a newborn's body do you always need to support when lifting or holding the baby? Why?

2. Describe the position in which a baby should be held for bottle-feeding.

3. Should parents put a bottle in the crib so that the baby can suck and drift off to sleep more comfortably? Why or why not?

4. What are strained foods? When do most babies begin to eat them?

5. What is weaning? What is a common age for weaning?

6. What is the main source of nutrition for babies during most of the first year?

7. What is malnutrition? Who can suffer from infant malnutrition?

DISCUSS AND DISCOVER

1. Discuss the kinds of feeding frustrations that parents of young babies may face. What options do you think frustrated parents have?

Which responses would you recommend? Why?

2. Explain how a newborn's feeding schedule might affect other family members. What problems might arise in a specific family situation, such as a family with a single parent, two employed parents, other small children in the family, or twin newborns? What approaches would you suggest to resolve those problems?

3. Find out which programs in your own community help meet the special food needs of new mothers and young children. How are those programs funded?

Observing & Participating

Feed—or help feed—a baby who has started eating solids. Describe how the baby responds to different foods. How does the baby show his or her interest in self-feeding? Identify methods used by the caregiver to meet the baby's nutritional needs.

SECTION 2 REVIEW

1. The neck and head. The neck muscles cannot yet support the head.

2. Held close in a semiupright position, with the head and neck supported and the head well above the level of the stomach.

3. No. Leaves bacteria in the baby's mouth and increases the risk of tooth decay.

4. Solids processed to make them smooth and runny. Soon after the age of six months.

5. Process of changing from drinking from bottle or breast to drinking from cup. Nine months.

6. Breast milk or formula.

7. A lack of enough food or a lack of the proper type of food. Any baby whose parents do not have enough money to provide adequate nutrition or whose parents do not know about babies' special food needs.

Other Infant-Care Skills

OBJECTIVES

- Demonstrate how to bathe, dress, and diaper a baby.
- Tell how to encourage good sleep habits.

Taking care of a baby can—and should—be fun. A caregiver who is competent and confident in carrying out basic care routines can enjoy the baby and contribute to the baby's appreciation and enjoyment of the world. These routines include bathing, dressing, and diapering. Proper sleep habits are also important for the baby's health.

TERMS TO LEARN

cradle cap
diaper rash
sleeper

Bathing a Baby

A bath helps keep a baby clean and healthy. As is the case when learning other care skills, confidence in bathing a baby comes from knowing what to do and from having a bit of practice. Any time is fine for a bath except right after feeding. Then the baby needs to sleep and digest the meal.

A newborn is given sponge baths until the navel heals. This takes about two weeks. After that, a tub bath—first in a basin of water or a baby bathtub and later in the family tub—may be given. Both require the caregiver's careful attention to ensure safety.

Sponge Baths

Many of the same basic supplies are needed for both sponge baths and tub baths. These include:

- Two soft bath towels.
- A soft washcloth.
- A diaper.
- Mild soap.
- Baby shampoo.
- Cotton balls.

SECTION 3
Other Infant-Care Skills
Pages 247-259

FOCUS

SECTION 3 RESOURCES

Teacher's Classroom Resources
- Enrichment 22
- Reteaching 22
- Section 3 Quiz

Student Workbook
- The Secret Square

SECTION OVERVIEW

Section 3 extends the students' understanding of basic infant-care skills, explaining how parents and other caregivers can bathe, dress, and diaper babies in ways that are both safe and comfortable for the infant. The section also presents information on establishing successful bedtime routines.

MOTIVATOR

Display photographs clipped from catalogs or from magazines, of babies' outfits, or display several different actual outfits. Encourage students to describe the outfits and to discuss their reactions to them. Which outfit would you choose for a baby of your own? How confident do you feel now trying to dress and undress a baby? Why is confidence in this kind of care activity important? At the close of the discussion, explain to students that they will learn more about dressing and other infant-care skills in this section.

USING TERMS TO LEARN

Go over all the items in "Terms to Learn" with the class. If necessary, help students understand the term *cradle cap* by pointing out that it is a condition that may afflict very young babies (during the early months, when they are small enough to sleep in a cradle) on their scalp (the area covered by a cap).

OBSERVING AND PARTICIPATING

Learning Through Participation

Experienced caregivers are comfortable judging safe temperatures for a baby's bath water; students who have never bathed an infant or estimated the temperature of water may benefit from some practice. Encourage students to test the temperature of running water and of standing bath water, using their wrists, fingertips, whole hands, and elbows. Which part is most sensitive to the temperature of the water? Why? If possible, have students use thermometers to check their estimates of water temperature. How do they describe water that measures lukewarm, about 98° F (37° C)? What guidelines can they set for themselves in selecting lukewarm water?

TEACH

Pages 247-259

- Bathing a Baby
- Dressing a Baby
- Choosing Clothes
- Diapering a Baby
- Sleep

GUIDED PRACTICE

Promoting Discussion

Encourage students to discuss the routine of bathing infants. In addition to having physical needs met, what can babies get out of being bathed? What can parents and other caregivers do to encourage their own enjoyment—and the baby's enjoyment—of bath time?

Using the Photograph

Let students describe and discuss the baby in the photograph on page 249. How is the baby being handled? How does the baby seem to be responding? What safety precautions has the caregiver taken?

BUILDING SELF-ESTEEM

Remind students that touch is necessary for a thriving infant. Babies who are held more in infancy show superior cognitive development. Many experts feel that being touched equally influences a baby's physical development. Physical contact suggests to infants that they are safe. Some psychologists believe that physical touch has more emotional importance than any other form of affection. Not only does baby receive the signals of love and security, but parents and caregivers benefit as well!

Encourage interested students to research massaging techniques, or invite to class a knowledgeable person who would demonstrate methods of massaging a baby. Another source of reference about this subject is available in self-help books.

BUILDING SELF-ESTEEM

A Loving Touch

Parents are usually eager to hold and stroke their newborn babies. With these early touches, the process of bonding begins.

Bonding continues as parents and other caregivers hold and touch the baby. Stroking the baby's arm or leg, holding the baby's hand, gently circling the fingertips on the baby's cheek or chest— all these touches send messages of love.

After bathtime, a caregiver can massage baby lotion onto the baby's back, moving the fingertips gently back and forth, up and down, or round and round. After the lotion has been absorbed, turn the baby over and apply a little more lotion to the baby's chest and tummy in the same way.

Before bathing a baby, assemble these articles and the baby's clean clothes in a warm place with no drafts. The temperature of the room should be 70° to 80° F (20° to 26° C). Choose a room with a good work surface—usually the bathroom, kitchen, or baby's room. Place a soft bath towel over the work area for the baby's comfort and safety.

For sponge baths, it is often most convenient to put the bathwater in a basin on the work surface. Test the water with your elbow. (The skin there is more sensitive than that on your hands or wrists.) The water should feel lukewarm, about 98° F (37° C).

Remove the baby's clothes and place the infant on the towel. Lay another towel on top of the baby's body. Begin by washing the baby's face with clear water and a soft washcloth, while supporting the baby with your other hand. Then pat the baby's face dry. A young baby's skin is very tender, so never rub it with a towel.

Wash the rest of the body with baby soap and water, one area at a time. Rinse thoroughly. Pay particular attention to the skin creases. They should be gently separated, washed, and thoroughly dried.

It is not necessary to clean the inside of the baby's mouth, ears, eyes, or nose. Nature takes care of this. Never use cotton swab sticks. Babies move very suddenly and can easily be injured by them. Just wipe the outer ears, and use a clean washcloth to remove any visible mucus from the nose.

Wash the baby's scalp with tear-free baby soap or baby shampoo once or twice a week. On other days, just wipe the scalp with clear water and pat dry.

Sometimes babies develop **cradle cap,** *a skin condition in which the scalp develops patches of yellowish, crusty scales.* To treat cradle cap, apply baby oil or lanolin to the scalp at night. In the morning, gently loosen the scales with a washcloth or a soft hairbrush (not a stiff one!) and shampoo the hair.

You may want to apply baby powder or lotion to the baby after a bath, but neither is really necessary. You must be careful if you choose to use powder. If it accumulates in skin creases, powder can cause irritation. If the powder is inhaled, the baby can develop breathing problems or even suffocate. Never let a baby play with the container of powder. If you do decide to use powder, choose a cornstarch-based product. Apply it by shaking it first into your own hand and then rubbing it onto the baby's skin.

Tub Baths

With proper handling, even a two-week-old baby can be bathed in a tub if the navel has healed. At first the "tub" can be a large dishpan or special baby bathtub. At age six or seven months, the regular tub can be used.

TEEN PARENTING

If you have teen parents in your class, or can find a volunteer teen parent, ask them to lead a demonstration on the proper technique for bathing a child. If possible, have a teen bring an infant to class and, under your supervision, bathe the baby. Ask the parent to display and talk about his or her choices in bath products, equipment, clothing, and bathing methods. Encourage the parent to explain what he or she had to learn about the infant's particular likes and dislikes in order to make the bath a pleasant experience for everyone. Be sure to include a discussion of safety procedures necessary to protect baby.

Bathing a baby can be fun for both parent and baby, but safety is very important. For a young infant, a special baby bathtub placed on the counter allows the baby to lean back and enjoy the experience.

Place a rubber mat or a towel in the bottom of the tub to make the baby comfortable and to prevent falls. Add lukewarm water to a depth of about 2 to 3 inches (5 to 8 cm). Assemble the other equipment and the baby's clean clothes before starting the bath.

Begin by washing the baby's face with clear water and patting it dry. Then lift the baby into the tub with a secure grip. Slide one hand under the baby's shoulders; hold the baby securely under the arm, using your wrist to support the baby's neck and head. Slide your other hand under the baby's thighs, and hold the farther leg securely just above the knee. Be especially careful to hold the baby firmly—yet as gently as possible.

While the baby is in the tub, continue to hold the baby under the arm, with your wrist supporting the baby's back and head. You can use your other hand to wash and rinse the baby. Then lift the baby from the water with the same secure grip. Place the infant on a clean towel, and immediately wrap the towel around the baby to prevent chilling. Then pat the baby dry.

Most older babies enjoy baths, especially when they are able to sit by themselves in the tub. They love to splash and play in the water. A few floating toys add to the fun. Don't forget, however, that safety is the primary concern when bathing a baby of any age.

SAFETY TIP

The bathtub can be a dangerous place for babies, so keep these safety precautions in mind:

- Never leave the baby alone during a bath, even "just for a second." A baby can drown very quickly, even in very shallow water.

- Keep the baby seated in the tub. Standing or climbing can lead to falls.

- Always check the water temperature before you put the baby into the tub.

- Faucets present a double hazard. They are hard, sometimes sharp, surfaces. They may also be hot. Keep the baby away from the faucets.

- Don't let the baby drink the bathwater or suck on the washcloth. Try offering the baby a drink of fresh water instead, or give the baby a teething toy to suck on.

GUIDED PRACTICE (continued)

Promoting Discussion
Let students share and discuss their ideas about cradle cap. What do you think causes this condition? How do you think it feels to the baby? What further problems might develop if cradle cap is not treated? Why might parents or other caregivers ignore or not treat cradle cap? What could be the results?

Using Management Skills
Encourage students to share what they have read and heard about the use of baby powders. What are the advantages of using baby powder on an infant? What are the disadvantages? Which would students choose to do with their own babies? Why?

Cooperative Learning
Let students work in small groups to review the procedures for giving an infant a sponge bath and a tub bath. Then have group members use life-size dolls to practice both procedures. Encourage them to discuss these practice baths, noting the unexpected problems that arise, suggesting solutions, and considering how the baths might be different if a real infant—rather than a doll —were being washed.

SAFETY TIP

Remind students that some babies are so fond of water that a bucket of water, a pool, a toilet, or a wading pool looks inviting! Be careful to keep crawling and walking babies away from standing water, and always keep baby in sight when exploring the house or yard.

HEALTHY FAMILIES/HEALTHY CHILDREN

Health and Safety
Even though the caregiver may test the water before placing the baby in it, a burn can result if a faucet is turned on during the bath. It is not uncommon for this to happen unintentionally; the caregiver might knock his or her elbow against the spigot, for example. To avoid burns from hot tap water, turn down the water heater so that the water temperature is below 130° F (54° C). When the water is about 124° F (51° C), it takes about three minutes for a bad burn to occur. The same burn will occur in five seconds when the water is 140° F (60° C). If the water is 158° F (70° C) or higher, a severe burn will result after only one second of exposure.

Using Management Skills

Let pairs of students work together, experimenting to find the best location for bathing a baby. Using a doll, they may try a basin, a plastic dishpan or washtub, a special baby bathtub, and a regular bathtub. They might also try placing a washtub on the floor, on a table, or on a cabinet. Have students list the pros and cons of each method. Then encourage a general discussion in response to these questions: Which location do you recommend for bathing a baby? Why?

Cooperative Learning

Let students work in small groups to write a list of "do's" and "don'ts" for bathing a baby. Then encourage the groups to share and discuss their completed lists with the rest of the class.

Promoting Discussion

Encourage students to share their ideas and opinions about appropriate clothing for babies. What makes an outfit attractive? Which family member usually chooses the clothing a baby wears? What reasons might that person have for making specific selections?

Did You Know?

Philadelphia was the first city to celebrate Mother's Day on May 10, 1908. In 1914, Congress established the second Sunday in May as Mother's Day, and President Woodrow Wilson proclaimed the date as a national holiday. It was celebrated throughout the nation for the first time on May 10, 1914.

Father's Day was first observed in Spokane, Washington on June 19, 1910. Fathers are now honored across the country on the third Sunday in June.

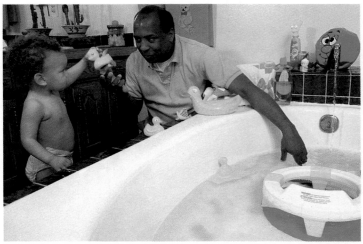

As babies get older, they can sit up in a bathroom tub in a small amount of water. A safety ring in the bathtub and adult supervision helps ensure the baby's safety. Bathtime is a good time for playing and socializing with baby.

Dressing a Baby

When you are choosing the clothes a baby will wear indoors, consider the temperature in the home rather than the season of the year. A good rule of thumb is to check your own clothing needs. An infant does not need to be warmer than you do. Since a newborn's hands and feet often feel cool to the touch, check the baby's body temperature by feeling the arms, legs, or neck. Babies who are too cold usually begin to fuss. Babies who are too warm perspire and become cranky.

The Newborn

A newborn's clothing needs are minimal. Many babies wear a **sleeper**, *a one-piece stretch garment with feet*, for both sleeping and waking, or the baby may be dressed in a cotton undershirt and a gown. In warm or hot weather (if there is no air conditioning), the baby may wear only a diaper and perhaps a short-sleeved undershirt. When taking the baby outdoors in cool weather, add warm outer garments or blankets.

Socks and booties are usually not necessary for everyday wear. They may bind, and babies often get them wet or kick them off. The newborn's feet usually stay covered by a sleeper or blanket. If the baby's feet feel cool to the touch, they should be covered with sleeper feet or with stretchy socks, which stay on the feet better than regular socks or booties.

MORE ABOUT

Infants' Sleepwear

Since 1970, laws have been in effect requiring all children's sleepwear to be "flame-retardant." Parents and other caregivers should be careful to use only those sleeping garments labeled flame-retardant. Parents and others who sew should select fabrics with the flame-retardant label whenever they are making sleepwear. It is also advisable to select flame-retardant fabrics for room accessories and for children's costumes. The safety-enhancing quality of these fabrics is assured at purchase; however, many such fabrics have special care requirements. Parents and other caregivers should be careful to read and follow instructions that will maintain the flame-retardant quality in the fabric.

Older Babies

When babies begin to creep and crawl, they need different kinds of clothing. Overalls, especially those with legs that snap open for easy diaper changes, are good for crawling babies. Very active or determined crawlers may need pants with padded or reinforced knees. Soft, cotton knit shirts are comfortable. For bed, a sleeper keeps the baby covered even if blankets are kicked off.

Shoes are not really necessary until the baby is able to walk outdoors. Many physicians feel the best way to learn to walk is barefooted. This leaves the toes free to grip the floor and gives the ankles flexibility. If the baby is learning to stand and walk indoors on cold floors, slippersocks or nonskid socks will keep the feet warm and the baby safe. Once the baby is ready for shoes, either sneakers or leather shoes are satisfactory.

Dressing Tips

Whenever you dress or undress a baby, take the time to give special attention to the baby—not just to the clothing. Dressing and undressing provide ideal opportunities for extra strokes, pats, hugs, and kisses. This is also a good time for songs, simple rhymes, or "conversations," in which you name the baby's body parts or discuss the clothes you are putting on the baby.

As you dress or undress a baby, do your best to work smoothly and quickly without being rough. Quick, jerking movements often frighten babies. Try following these steps to dress the baby in various kinds of infant garments:

- **Pullover garments.** These garments have a small, but stretchable, neck opening.
  1. Gather the garment into a loop and slip it over the back of the baby's head.
  2. Stretch the garment forward as you bring it down past the forehead and nose. This keeps the face and nose free so that the baby does not feel smothered.
  3. Put the baby's fist into the armhole and pull the arm through with your other hand. Repeat with the other arm.

GUIDED PRACTICE (continued)

Making Connections: Math

Let students use the chart on page 175 (Chapter 6) to make a list of basic clothing needs for a newborn. Then have students use catalogs, newspaper ads, or information from store visits to determine the cost of each item and the total cost of all the clothing items they have listed. Finally, have students compare their totals and calculate an average cost.

Cooperative Learning

Have students work in groups to discuss good sources for buying or borrowing used baby clothes. Then have group members work together to write a checklist for evaluating used clothing for infants.

Critical Thinking

Let students discuss their ideas in response to these questions: Why do you think many physicians feel that babies should learn to walk barefoot? Why do you think parents and other caregivers are often very eager to put shoes on babies, in spite of this advice from physicians? When do you think children should wear shoes? When do you think they should be encouraged to go barefoot? Why?

Using Management Skills

Have students discuss their ideas about sewing garments for an infant. How does the cost of a handmade outfit compare with the cost of a similar ready-made garment? Is it economically reasonable to sew garments for infants? What other factors would you consider when deciding whether or not to sew for your own baby? For friends' babies?

SEE HOW THEY GROW

Babies' Feet

For most infants, shoes aren't necessary until shortly before—or even several months after—the first birthday. When the time does come to buy shoes for a baby, the length and width of both feet should be measured to assure that the new shoes will fit correctly. Each foot should be considered individually, since no one has right and left feet that match exactly in size or shape.

The size and shape of the baby's foot will probably determine some aspects of the shoe style. Beyond choosing the best size, parents should make sure that the baby's shoes are breathable, have a flexible sole, offer arch support, have ample cushioning, and have a rigid support around the heel. Athletic shoes, either high-tops or low-tops, usually meet these requirements.

Using the Photographs

Guide students in describing and discussing the baby in the photographs on this page and on the preceding page. How does the baby appear to feel about being undressed and then dressed? What factors do you think contribute to the baby's feelings? What problems has the caregiver avoided? How?

Cooperative Learning

Have groups of students use a life-size doll to practice dressing and undressing a newborn. Encourage group members to discuss their responses to these questions: Which garment styles are easiest to put on and take off? Why? Which garment styles are most difficult? Why? How would dressing a baby be more difficult than dressing a doll? What might make it easier to work with a baby?

Making Connections: Anthropology

Encourage students to share what they know about infant dress at other times and in other cultures. Let interested volunteers do further research into specific times or cultures, and have them report their findings to the rest of the class.

Promoting Discussion

Let students explain how they think dressing a ten- or twelve-month-old baby would be different from dressing a newborn. In what ways would dressing the newborn be the easier task? What approaches and techniques could a parent or other caregiver use to make the dressing process comfortable for a newborn? In what ways would dressing the older baby be easier? How could a parent or other caregiver make dressing fun for the older baby?

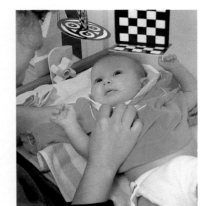

- **Slipover gown or shirt.** If the garment has a larger neck opening than a pullover, use this method.
  1. Gather the garment into a loop, and place it around the baby's face like an oval frame.
  2. Slip the garment down the back of the baby's head.
  3. Put the baby's fist into the armhole and pull it through with your other hand. Repeat with the other arm.
- **Open-front shirt.** The "secret" of this method is first laying the baby facedown. This helps the baby feel secure.
  1. Place the baby on his or her stomach.
  2. Open the shirt and lay it on the infant's back.
  3. Gently turn the baby faceup so that the shirt is underneath.
  4. Put the baby's arms through the sleeves.

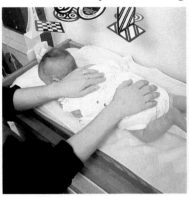

- **One-piece garment with feet.** Putting on this type of garment is easier when the zipper or the snaps go from neck to toes.
  1. Put the bottom part of the garment on first.
  2. Roll the baby onto one side and pull the garment up under the baby's shoulders.
  3. Roll the baby back onto the garment. Then gently pull the sleeves over the baby's arms.

You can follow the same tips for taking each kind of garment off a baby. Just reverse the order of the steps. For example, to remove a pullover top, first take the baby's arms out of the sleeves. Gather the garment into a loop as it lies around the neck. Stretch the garment up and over the baby's face, and slip it off toward the back of the head.

As babies get older, they are better able to help with dressing; for example, they can sit up while you are putting on a shirt, and they can stretch their own arms through short sleeves. However, you may often find that even a capable baby is uncooperative. Sometimes distracting the baby with a toy or a song can help make dressing easier.

MORE ABOUT

Babies' Garments

Particular attention should be paid to the types of fasteners used on baby garments. Although slightly harder to fasten than metal snaps, plastic snaps may be more comfortable on the baby's skin. Buttons may look attractive, but they pose a danger: If the baby chews on the garment, he or she may chew off a button and swallow it. Zippers are quick and easy to close, but the caregiver may pinch the baby's skin unless he or she is extremely careful. Loop and pile fasteners are options for easy dressing as long as they do not come in contact with the baby's skin. The most practical garments may be those with overlapping shoulder flaps or criss-cross wrapping, which require no fasteners at all.

Choosing Clothes

When choosing baby clothes, keep in mind that both comfort and ease in dressing are important. Since clothing is expensive, it is wise to look for clothes with generous hems and extra buttons on shoulder straps and waistbands to allow for rapid growth.

The clothing available today is much better suited to babies' needs than was the case in the past. Clothes are simple and comfortable. Many are made of knit fabrics that contain nonirritating fibers and provide both ease of movement for the baby and ease of care for the parents.

The size of infant wear is indicated by both weight and age of baby. Weight is the more reliable guide. It is usually best to buy nothing smaller than a six-month size for a newborn. At first, the infant will probably "swim" in the shirts and gowns. Babies grow quickly, however, and the tiniest sizes soon become too small. You can simply fold up the hems of large garments for the first few weeks until the baby catches up with the clothes.

Diapering a Baby

Diapers are the most essential part of a baby's wardrobe. Parents have a number of diapering options. Cloth diapers, the traditional favorite, may be the least expensive if home laundry facilities are available. Disposable diapers offer throw-away convenience. They are, however, more expensive than cloth diapers, and they contribute significantly to the country's environmental problems. Commercial diaper services are available in some areas. These services deliver clean cloth diapers and pick up used diapers. These services are convenient and may not be much more expensive than other options.

When you care for a very young baby, you will probably find yourself changing diapers twelve to fifteen times each day. A newborn wets several times an hour, but in small amounts that do not require changing with each wetting. An older baby may need fewer diaper changes each day—and is more likely to let you know when a clean diaper is required.

If you keep your diapering supplies organized and handy, you can turn diaper-changing time into a period of pleasant and interesting interaction with your baby. When the baby seems fussy or sleepy, try singing or humming a soothing tune. When the baby seems alert, talk about what you are doing. A young baby will enjoy listening to your voice—and may even babble an answer to your questions.

Keep your diapering supplies near a sturdy, padded surface (such as the crib or a changing table). Cloth diapers must be folded to the correct size. (The illustration [right] shows a good

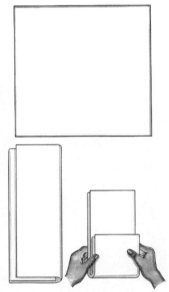

Fold a square diaper in thirds lengthwise so that it is a little wider than the baby's hips. Then turn up one end of the diaper part way.

HEALTHY FAMILIES/HEALTHY CHILDREN

Health and Safety

Loose strings and ties on a baby's garment can be worse than uncomfortable; they can be dangerous. These long ties may get wrapped around the baby's toes or fingers, causing discomfort and even cutting off the baby's circulation. Long strings are especially dangerous when they are out of sight, inside an infant's sacque and footed garment. These hidden ties may get wrapped around a baby's neck and could cause strangulation. If there is any possibility of strangulation, the ties should be completely removed from the infant's garment. In addition, caregivers should carefully inspect garments both before and after putting them on an infant.

GUIDED PRACTICE (continued)

Promoting Discussion

Encourage students to share and discuss their ideas about selecting clothes for infants. How can you identify an outfit that is practical for a baby? Why do parents and other caregivers sometimes choose baby clothes that are not practical? What kinds of problems may arise for parents and other caregivers as a result of these decisions? What kinds of problems may arise for babies and for older children? Why? In what circumstances—if any—are "impractical" clothes an appropriate choice for a baby? Why?

Critical Thinking

Ask students how a baby might be affected if a parent or other caregiver has a difficult time trying to dress the baby. How would the baby be likely to react? How might those reactions affect the parent or caregiver? What can or should be done to avoid a cycle of problems?

Making Connections: Art

Have students describe or bring to class reproductions of paintings that portray infants. Focus students' attention on the clothing of the babies, and ask questions such as these: How does the clothing in this painting differ from the clothing that modern babies wear? How do you think this kind of outfit would affect an infant's comfort and activities? What might be involved in dressing a baby in this kind of outfit? What kind of care do you think this kind of infant clothing must have required?

Using the Illustration

Let students describe the process shown in the illustration on this page, and then give them an opportunity to practice folding diapers. If possible, make prefolded cloth diapers and newborn-size disposable diapers available for comparison. Ask students to identify the advantages of each type of diaper.

GUIDED PRACTICE (continued)

Using the Photograph

Direct students' attention to the photograph on this page; let them describe what appears to make this baby content while having his diaper changed. Then ask students to explain what they would do if, during the diaper changing, the baby suddenly began to squirm and fuss.

Cooperative Learning

Have students work with partners or in small groups to practice all three steps of changing a baby's diaper, using a life-size doll. If possible, include a student with experience in changing diapers in each pair or group of students. Let students practice changing both cloth and disposable diapers, and compare their reactions to each. Ask students how they think this experience compares with changing diapers on an active baby.

Critical Thinking

Ask students to share their ideas in response to these questions: Why shouldn't diapers be washed with the family's other clothing? What problems might arise if the two kinds of laundry were mixed?

Promoting Discussion

Encourage students to describe how babies might react to having diaper rash. How might the baby's mood and activity level be affected? How should parents and other caregivers respond to such changes?

SAFETY TIP

Remind students that babies may well reach for everything in sight but have not yet developed the ability to judge distances. Always keep baby within reach when using a worktable. Also, second hand furniture is often chosen for economical reasons, but caregivers should be concerned that it meets safety standards set by the United States Consumer Product Safety Commission.

SAFETY TIP

Once you have put the baby down on the work surface—whether it is a changing table, a counter, or any other raised area—you must pay constant attention to the baby. Always keep at least one hand firmly on the baby. If you need to leave the work surface, for however short a time, take the baby with you. No one knows when the ability to wriggle, kick, or even roll will develop enough to endanger the baby. Falls from changing tables and other work surfaces cause serious injuries and infant deaths every year.

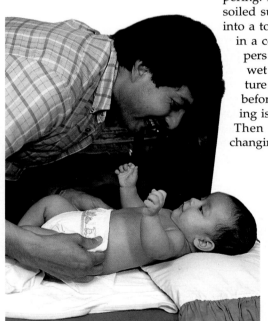

This baby enjoys the attention that comes with changing a diaper. All infant-care routines can be turned into social times by talking or singing to the baby.

method.) Disposable diapers come in several sizes, with thicker diapers available for nighttime wear. In addition to the diaper, you will need a wet washcloth, soft tissues or toilet paper, cotton, and baby oil; or you may choose to use special disposable baby washcloths.

Follow these steps to change a diaper. As you change the diaper and clean up, remember that it is never safe to leave a baby alone on a changing table or other raised surface.

1. **Remove the diaper, and clean the baby.** If the diaper was merely wet, clean the baby with cotton and baby oil. If the baby had a bowel movement, use soft tissue or toilet paper to remove the soil from the baby. Then wash with a washcloth and apply baby oil.

2. **Put on a fresh diaper.** Hold the baby's ankles, and lift the body enough to slide the diaper under. If you are using cloth diapers, place the extra thickness in the back for girls, in the front for boys. If you are using disposable diapers, be sure the adhesive tabs are under the baby. Bring the diaper up between the baby's legs. Use the adhesive tabs to fasten a disposable diaper. Use large safety pins or special diaper pins to fasten a cloth diaper. To protect the baby, place the pins crosswise, keeping your finger between the diaper and the baby's skin as you pin. Waterproof pants may be added over the cloth diaper.

3. **Dispose of used supplies.** Cleanliness is important in diapering. Promptly dispose of used tissues, cotton, and other soiled supplies. Drop solid waste from a disposable diaper into a toilet. Then roll the disposable diaper up and place it in a covered trash container. (Never flush disposable diapers down a toilet. They will clog the plumbing.) Place a wet cloth diaper in a covered container filled with a mixture of water and borax or vinegar. Rinse a soiled diaper before placing it in the container. A good method for rinsing is to hold the diaper firmly in a clean, flushing toilet. Then wash your hands with soap and hot water after changing the diaper.

MORE ABOUT

Disposable Diapers

It is estimated that each baby uses about 7,800 diapers from birth until toilet training. Families that rely on disposable diapers can expect to spend about $1,716 during this period. A wide variety of disposable diapers can be found on the store shelves today. These range from gender-specific diapers to those with popular animated characters across the front. With an increasing concern for the environment, some parents are looking for the new biodegradable, nonchemical diapers. These new diapers are said to break down in the landfills more quickly than nonbiodegradable diapers.

ASK THE EXPERTS

Which Kind of Diapers?

Q. *Can you help us decide which kind of diapers to use?*

A. This is a good question, and I'm glad you're prepared to give it careful consideration. There are some obvious advantages to both cloth and disposable diapers.

Cloth diapers are soft and comfortable against a baby's tender skin. You will have to make an initial investment in cloth diapers, but then your only expenses will be those of running a washing machine and, perhaps, a dryer.

Disposable diapers are also comfortable for most babies, and they are clearly more convenient. However, they are also significantly more expensive than cloth diapers. In addition, disposable diapers contribute to

the growing environmental problems that our country—and our world—must face.

The most important consideration is the comfort and safety of your baby. For that reason, I advise most parents to begin using cloth diapers on their newborn babies. Using cloth diapers for the first few months gives you the chance to see just how sensitive your baby's skin is. It also lets you judge how much extra work may—or may not—be involved in using cloth diapers. After two or three months, parents usually decide to continue using cloth diapers most—but not all—of the time. They often want to use disposable diapers during daytime outings, so they can

change the baby quickly and conveniently. Disposable diapers are also a common choice for traveling with a baby.

If diaper services are available, investigate their prices and compare them to the investment in cloth diapers and in disposable diapers. If you are lucky, friends, relatives, or co-workers may ask you to suggest an appropriate gift for your new baby—a month of diaper service might be just the thing!

Van D. Stone, M.D.

Dr. Van D. Stone
Pediatrician
Tupelo, Mississippi

HEALTHY FAMILIES/HEALTHY CHILDREN

Health and Safety

Occasionally, a baby may develop a diaper-area rash that is somewhat more serious than common diaper rash. A rash that appears blistery is likely to be the result of an infection caused by bacteria; this kind of rash usually requires an antibiotic ointment. If the rash appears as an inflamed area surrounded by tiny pimples, it may be a yeast infection. A red and

raw rash that appears in the creases of the upper thigh may be seborrhea. None of these rashes will respond to the kinds of treatment usually used with simple diaper rash. If any signs of these rashes occur, a pediatrician should be contacted for diagnosis and specific treatment.

GUIDED PRACTICE (continued)

ASK THE EXPERTS

Issues and Advice

1. What is the most important consideration when choosing which kind of diaper to use? (*The comfort and safety of the baby.*)

2. Disposable diapers contribute to which world-wide concern? (*Environmental problems.*)

3. Why does Dr. Stone recommend using cloth diapers for the first few months? (*To see how sensitive the baby's skin is.*)

4. What third option does Dr. Stone remind readers to consider? (*Diaper service.*)

Thinking Like an Expert

Divide students into two teams. One team is assigned to research disposable diapers and the other cloth diapers. Ask the disposable diaper team to calculate the cost of buying disposable diapers for one year. They should compare various brands to determine which is the most and least expensive. Have them read consumer magazines to find out which brands have the best ratings and how price and quality are related. Also have them report on improvements made in biodegradable diapers.

Have the second team find the estimated cost of using cloth diapers and/or a diaper service for the first year. Ask them to find out why vinegar and borax are used for soaking diapers in a diaper pail. Have them research and report on pinless diaper covers that use cloth diapers with the added convenience of disposable diapers. Ask them to demonstrate the correct way to use pinless covers.

GUIDED PRACTICE (continued)

Using the Photograph

Encourage students to describe and discuss the baby in the photograph on page 257. What makes the baby look especially comfortable? How can the bed and the sleeping area affect a baby's sleep patterns? Why does the amount of sleep required vary from baby to baby and from day to day?

Cooperative Learning

Let students work in small groups to examine and discuss this situation: Nick and Ella are the parents of a newborn and a three-year-old. The three-year-old sleeps from 8 p.m. to 6 a.m. and takes a one-hour nap in the afternoon. The newborn is nursed for one-half hour every three to four hours around the clock. Ask group members to plan a possible sleep schedule for Nick and Ella. How many hours of sleep will each parent get every day? How does their sleep schedule compare with students' accustomed sleep schedule?

Family Focus

Present the following situation to the class: When Ray and Beth brought their new baby, Alicia, home from the hospital, she was having some allergy problems. Because they were worried, Ray and Beth hurried to comfort her at every cry during the night. After several months, the allergy problems were solved by a change in formula. Alicia, however, continued to cry frequently through the night until one of her parents came to pick her up and rock her to sleep. A checkup with the doctor showed that Alicia was in good health.

Encourage students to discuss their responses to these questions: Why did Alicia continue to cry, even after her allergy problems had been corrected? How might parents correct a situation like this one?

Washing Cloth Diapers

Washing a baby's cloth diapers requires special care. Washing machines do not always wash out all the bacteria, and bacteria can cause skin problems. It is important always to wash diapers in the hottest water and with a mild soap. (Cold or warm water leaves too many bacteria in the fabric.) You may also want to add special laundry sanitizers to the wash to destroy bacteria. Always wash diapers separately, never with other clothing. Be sure, too, that the diapers are thoroughly rinsed. Soap left in diapers can irritate a baby's skin. Diapers may be dried in a dryer. However, drying them outdoors in the sunshine destroys even more bacteria.

Diaper Rash

Controlling bacteria in diapers is important because babies may develop **diaper rash**, *patches of rough, irritated skin in the diaper area*. Sometimes diaper rash includes painful raw spots. Bacteria from wet or dirty diapers or improperly washed diapers are the usual cause. A sensitivity to disposable diapers can cause similar symptoms.

You can treat a mild case of diaper rash without consulting the baby's pediatrician. Change the baby's diapers more frequently, and clean the baby thoroughly after a bowel movement. Try using one of the products containing zinc oxide and cod liver oil, designed to protect against diaper rash and help it heal more quickly. Also, expose the diaper area to the air as much as possible, and avoid putting waterproof pants on the baby. If the baby's rash continues or gets worse, ask a pediatrician for help.

Sleep

All babies need sleep in order to grow and develop. However, the amount of time an infant spends sleeping decreases considerably during the first year. A newborn may sleep from 12 hours a day to almost continuously. By one year, however, a baby often has as few as two or three sleep periods, including naps.

The amount of sleep needed also depends on the individual baby. An active baby needs more sleep than an inactive one, just as active babies need more food. Babies also require more sleep on some days than on others.

Preparation for Sleep

Putting the baby to bed for the night should be a relaxed and pleasant experience—both for you and for the baby. Begin by

---

OBSERVING AND PARTICIPATING

Celebrating Individual Differences

Like everyone else, infants have individual sleep requirements. However, understanding the average time that babies spend asleep can help parents and caregivers know what to expect. Most one-week-old babies sleep a total of 16 1/2 hours out of every 24 hours. Typically, they sleep 8 1/2 hours at night and 8 hours during the day. (It may be important to remind students

that these sleep periods are not continuous.) A six-month-old baby can be expected to sleep about 11 hours at night and 3 1/4 hours during the day. By twelve months, an average infant sleeps about 13 3/4 hours, with all but 2 of those at night. The total sleeping time decreases by about 3 hours during the first year.

Sleep lets infants regain energy after their brief active periods. During sleep, the body repairs itself and builds new cells for growth.

washing the baby's face and hands and by changing the baby's diaper and clothes. Specific sleeping garments remind the older baby that it is time to go to bed.

Then spend a few minutes rocking the baby or singing a soothing lullaby. This will be comforting and reassuring for the baby. As you put the baby to bed, keep your manner calm and unhurried, even if you don't feel that way. Otherwise, the baby will pick up your feelings and will probably not settle into sleep as well as usual.

Finally, put the baby down in bed with adequate covering. (Never let a baby sleep in a draft, even in very hot weather.) If the infant is too young to roll over independently, you will probably find that the baby sleeps best on his or her back.

Try to follow the same simple routine every night. You will find that the baby soon learns the signals for bedtime and is likely to find comfort in the consistency of the ritual. For example, you and the baby might say "goodnight" to favorite toys in the room, or you might read or tell a simple bedtime story. As the baby grows older, you can change the ritual gradually to suit the baby's age.

Sleep should never be brought about by the use of drugs or sleep medicines of any kind. Consult the baby's pediatrician if sleep problems continue.

Cultural Exchange

THE STORY OF "ROCK-A-BYE-BABY"

It is reported that the author of the well-loved lullaby, "Rock-a-Bye-Baby" was a pilgrim who sailed on the Mayflower. The Wampanoag Indians, who became friends to the pilgrims carried their infants in cradleboards on their backs. In temperate weather, the Indians suspended the cradles from tree limbs so that passing breezes could rock the babies while their mothers tended the maize and beans. Nursery rhymes remain popular in families today. Perhaps the gentle lilt and inflection soothes some children. Perhaps, too, the familiar nursery rhymes reminds youngsters of the cuddling, holding, and reassurance they felt as a young child.

INDEPENDENT PRACTICE

Journal Writing
Ask students to write entries in their journals, discussing how their feelings about caring for an infant have changed. How does knowledge of the skills involved affect your attitude toward taking care of an infant? How does an understanding of the time and effort affect your attitude? Do you feel more or less interested in caring for an infant now than you did before studying Chapter 8? Why?

Student Workbook
Have students complete "The Secret Square" in the Student Workbook.

Extension
Let students work independently or in small groups to complete one or more of these extension activities:

• Have students survey parents of infants, gathering information about clothing sizes. They might ask questions such as these: How old is your baby? How much does he or she weigh? What size clothing does your baby wear now? If you were buying an outfit for your baby now, what size would you buy? Guide students in discussing the results of their surveys, and encourage them to form recommendations for choosing baby clothing in appropriate sizes.

• Ask students to research fiber characteristics and prepare a list of fibers appropriate for use in infant clothing. Have students report on the characteristics of each fiber they select.

SEE HOW THEY GROW

Children and Nursery Rhymes

Nursery rhymes and simple nursery songs have been popular with parents and children for countless generations. They also have real benefits within families. They can strengthen the sense of intimacy between parent and child, and provide a soothing, pleasurable message for a parent to communicate to even the youngest infant. In addition, nursery rhymes and songs stimulate a child's language development.

Unfortunately, the popularity of these old chants and tunes seems to be declining. A recent study of three- to seven-year-olds showed that less than half knew all of "Little Miss Muffet" and only a third of the children could recite "Pat-a-Cake."

Cultural Exchange

Ask students to share other lullabies they know from their own experiences with children or from observing other parents or caregivers. Encourage discussion of lullabies from a variety of countries or cultures.

PARENTING IN ACTION

Promoting Discussion

Introduce this Parenting in Action selection by letting students discuss their reactions to the photograph and to the title, "Who Is Training Whom?" What scenes from their own childhood and from other experiences does that title evoke?

After students have read the selection independently, encourage them to share their initial responses.

Thinking Critically

Ask students what makes this situation so troubling for Laurel and Reggie. What other kinds of issues raise similar concerns for parents of babies? Do these kinds of concerns continue to arise as children grow older?

Answers to "Think and Discuss"

1. Rachel's parents are exhausted and concerned by her behavior; they are also questioning their competence as parents.

2. Her parents' uncertainty and compliance are reinforcing Rachel's bedtime crying.

3. Encourage a variety of responses. Some possible questions: Why does Rachel cry? How soon would she cry herself to sleep? How well would she sleep after crying? Will she feel frightened and abandoned if we don't respond to her crying?

   Some of the people to whom they might turn: doctor, nurse, relatives and friends who are experienced parents, childcare provider.

4. Encourage students to express and support a variety of opinions. If necessary, point out that there is no one "right way" to establish healthy sleep patterns.

PARENTING IN ACTION

Who Is Training Whom?

Rachel's parents are concerned—and exhausted—by her bedtime routine. Laurel and Reggie put Rachel, who has just had her first birthday, down for the night around 7:30. Then the fussing and crying begin. If no one responds, Rachel's cries turn into screams. Eventually, either Laurel or Reggie gets up with a sigh of resignation and goes to Rachel.

Rachel stops crying when one of her parents picks her up and soothes her. As soon as she is put back down in her crib, however, Rachel starts screaming again. This can go on for quite a while, but it always ends the same way. One of her parents brings Rachel out into the living room, where Laurel and Reggie like to relax before going to bed. Rachel finally falls asleep in her parent's arms and is—at last—put back to bed for the night.

Last week Laurel and Reggie mentioned this problem to Rachel's pediatrician. The doctor asked a few questions and then responded, "Rachel's got you trained, not the other way around. You've given in to her crying so long that the habit will only get worse. Bedtime problems usually develop when parents aren't firm enough."

The doctor smiled reassuringly at Laurel and Reggie. "It won't hurt Rachel to cry herself to sleep. If you don't pick her up, she'll soon learn that screams won't help her get her way. It'll be tough for a while—for all of you—but she'll soon learn that when she's put down for the night, she'll stay there. Babies don't keep up behavior that doesn't work."

Laurel and Reggie intend to start following their doctor's advice—soon. For now, however, they both agree that they just can't stand to hear their baby screaming.

THINK AND DISCUSS

1. How is Rachel's bedtime behavior affecting her parents?
2. How is her parents' behavior affecting Rachel?
3. What questions do you think Laurel and Reggie should be asking themselves, and to whom should they turn for answers?
4. If you were in Laurel and Reggie's position, would you follow the doctor's advice? Why or why not? If not, what would you do about Rachel's bedtime routine?

TEEN PARENTING

Adjusting to a lack of time for themselves and their own favorite activities is a problem for almost all new parents. This adjustment can be a particular problem for teen parents. If you have teen parents in your class, encourage them to share their personal responses to this problem: How do they adjust to the lack of time? How do they find time for themselves? To encourage a general discussion of the problem, ask students to consider the situation of Noreen, a fifteen-year-old mother who can hardly wait for her baby to fall asleep so that she can spend some time with her friend across the street. Is Noreen using good judgment? What risks might be involved for Noreen's baby and for Noreen herself? What suggestions would students make to Noreen?

Bedtime Problems

Babies—especially active babies—often become restless while they sleep. During the night, they may waken partially and suck their fingers, cry out, or rock the crib. It is best not to respond to these activities. If you do respond, your presence may become a necessary part of the baby's pattern for getting back to sleep. Infants need to learn to use their own resources for returning to sleep. Of course, this does not mean you should ignore a baby who needs feeding or a diaper change. A baby whose restlessness develops into crying also needs your attention.

SECTION 3 REVIEW

CHECK YOUR UNDERSTANDING

1. What should you do if you have to leave the room while you are giving a baby a sponge bath? Why?
2. Explain what cradle cap is. What should you do to treat cradle cap?
3. List two important considerations in choosing clothes for a baby.
4. List the three main steps in changing a baby's diaper.
5. Explain what diaper rash is. List two things you can do to treat diaper rash.
6. List two things you should do before putting a baby in bed to sleep.

DISCUSS AND DISCOVER

1. Using actual garments or magazine pictures, select four items of children's clothing, ranging in size from newborn to twelve-months. Evaluate each item for comfort, practicality, ease in dressing the baby, and required care. Of all the items you selected, which garment ranks highest on your list?
2. What are some ways to calm a baby down or to help a restless baby fall asleep? Discuss why it is a poor idea to give a baby medicine to cure sleeping problems.
3. Explain why consistent bedtime routines can be beneficial for both the baby and the caregiver. Name three bedtime routines you would suggest for first-time parents.

Observing & Participating

Observe as parents or caregivers undress and dress babies of various ages—one just a month or two old, the other nearly a year old. Decide whether the babies' garments are appropriate to their ages and activities. Describe how the caregivers work with the babies to make dressing easy and fun.

SECTION 3 REVIEW

1. Take the baby with you to prevent a fall.
2. Scalp develops patches of yellowish, crusty scales. Apply baby oil or lanolin; use a washcloth or soft hairbrush to loosen scales; shampoo baby's hair.
3. Any two: comfort, ease in dressing, room to grow.
4. Remove diaper and clean the baby; put on a fresh diaper; dispose of used supplies.
5. Patches of rough, irritated skin in the diaper area. Any two: change diaper more often and clean baby thoroughly after a bowel movement; use a skin-care product with zinc oxide and cod liver oil; expose the diaper area to the air; avoid waterproof pants.
6. Wash baby's face and hands; change diapers and clothes.

ASSESS

CHECKING COMPREHENSION

Assign students to write their responses to the "Check Your Understanding" questions in the Section 3 Review. Answers are given at the bottom of this page.

EVALUATE

Have students complete the Chapter 8, Section 3 quiz in the TCR.

Reteaching
1. Distribute Reteaching 22 in the TCR and have students review key concepts.
2. Let students work with partners to plan and prepare an illustrated poster on one of these topics: How to bathe a baby; Tips for dressing a baby; How to change a diaper.

Enrichment
1. Distribute Enrichment 22 in the TCR.
2. Ask students to research one of the following topics and to summarize their findings in brief oral reports:
   - Special equipment for bathing infants—what is available and how useful is it?
   - Changes in styles of infant clothing during the past 100 years.
   - Current opinions on the ecological impact of disposable diapers.

EXTENSION

Ask a pediatric nurse practitioner, a pediatrician, a childbirth educator, an infant-care provider, or another expert in infancy to visit the class. Have the visitor discuss questions he or she is most often asked by new parents and share the responses he or she gives.

CLOSE

Let each student pull a baby garment from a bag, identify the approximate age of a baby that would wear it, and give a brief evaluation of the garment.

Positive Parenting Skills

Ask students to think about games they have seen played with babies. Next, demonstrate one of the games described in this feature. Ask them if they ever played this game with an infant or saw it being played. How did the baby react?

Promoting Discussion

1. Why is it important that games be fun as well as beneficial to development?

2. What are examples of unsafe games?

3. What games might be fun for the caregiver but not the infant?

4. Why is it important for parents of infants to find time to play with their babies?

Using The Photographs

Direct students' attention to the photos on these pages and ask the following questions: What games are illustrated? How are the baby's senses being stimulated in each situation? What is each baby learning? How do color, texture, sound, and movement help create a stimulating environment for an infant? How does a caregiver know which game is appropriate for a particular age?

Critical Thinking

Ask students to think about the benefits of play on the relationship between the primary caregiver and the baby. What emotional value is the product of such play? Suppose a child receives little playful attention from a caregiver or other family members. What can students speculate about the short- and long-term consequences?

SPENDING QUALITY TIME WITH BABY

Many newborn babies spend most of each day sleeping. When they are awake, they need to be fed, changed, bathed, talked to, rocked, and held. You can turn all these routine activities into "quality time" by focusing on the baby and by doing your best to understand and respond to the baby's signals.

As the baby gets a bit older—and as you become more confident in caring for the baby's daily needs—you will find more and more opportunities to play games with the baby. There are many different games that can both delight and stimulate babies. Here are a few suggestions:

Looking Games

• **Funny Faces.** Shake your head; stick out your tongue; make funny faces. Even babies a few days old often respond to or imitate facial expressions.

• **Light games.** Shine a flashlight on the walls and ceiling of a partially darkened room. Make shadow designs by placing your fingers in front of the beam.

• **Mirrors.** Sit with the baby in front of a mirror. Point to the infant's eyes, nose, mouth, and other features, and name each feature. Do the same with your own features. Eventually, the baby will also point to the features you name.

Listening Games

• **Musical games.** Play or sing music and nursery rhymes. Encourage the older baby (three months and up) to respond by swaying or humming.

• **What's that?** Point out everyday sounds, like running water, the washing machine, and the telephone. Name the sound, and then help the baby see what is making it.

OBSERVING AND PARTICIPATING

Learning Through Observation

The silly little games that parents commonly play with their babies are rooted in sound developmental strategy—which may explain why they've been handed down for generations. In addition to those described above, these old favorites include hugging and stroking, water play during bath time, clapping hands, tossing a ball, and simply rolling around on the floor with the child. All these activities nurture basic skills that set the stage for later learning. Long before scientists discovered developmental sequences, parents seemed intuitively to recognize their existence and incorporate them into games.

tug-of-war. Remember—the baby gets to win. However, if the baby is sitting up, don't let go entirely of the rubber ring, or the baby will tumble backwards.

- **Airplane.** Playing airplane can help strengthen the back and neck muscles of a baby who can already hold his or her head steady. Hold the baby just above the waist, and then slowly lift the baby above your face. Avoid a sudden lift, which could cause the baby's head to wobble. The baby's back will arch and the arms and legs will stretch out. You'll probably want to add some airplane noises, too.

- **Mimic.** Make fun sounds—car noises, animal noises, motorcycle noises, and so on. See whether the baby will imitate you.

Baby Exercises
- **Bicycle.** Lay the baby faceup, and gently hold both his or her ankles. Revolve the baby's legs as if riding a bicycle.

- **Tug-of-war.** Grasp one side of a large rubber ring, and let the baby grasp the other side. Gently play

Old Favorites
- **Peek-a-boo.** Establish eye contact with the baby. Quickly turn your head away, and then turn back again, saying "peek-a-boo." For older babies, cover your eyes and then uncover them. Don't forget to say "peek-a-boo"!

- **Hide and seek.** Make a toy disappear behind your back. Let the baby crawl to find it. Help the baby find toys that you have hidden. Try hiding from the baby yourself—and reappear quickly.

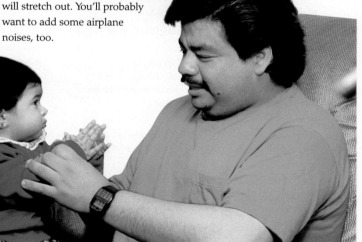

261

OBSERVING AND PARTICIPATING

Celebrating Individual Differences
Parents and other caregivers should be careful to adjust their play activities to suit the baby's temperament and mood. There is an appropriate level of stimulation for every baby—enough to capture the baby's interest and attention, but not so much stimulation that the baby feels overwhelmed and needs to withdraw. The more closely caregivers are attuned to the baby's reac-

tions, the more easily they can make playtime just right for the baby. Does the baby hate loud noises? Then don't provide a metal spoon for banging on the saucepan; give the baby a plastic spatula instead. Is the baby physically tired? Then avoid rough, bouncing games, and play something quiet, like "This Little Piggy Went to Market," instead.

Developing Parenting Skills
On the board, list the areas of development (physical, emotional and social, and intellectual) down the left side and list 1-12 months across the top. Ask students to suggest games for babies, then identify the appropriate age group and the areas of development stimulated by the game. Challenge students to remember games not listed in the text. As each game is classified, have a volunteer write the name on the board in the appropriate area of the chart.

Student Demonstration
Have students work in pairs to demonstrate a baby game they have learned from this lesson or one they learned about from outside reading or observation. Ask them to show how they would adapt the game when playing with two or more infants. Have the students explain how the game is beneficial to the baby and at what age it is appropriate.

Keeping a Journal
Have students observe a parent or caregiver playing games with an infant. In their journals, have them write a description of the game and answer the following questions: How did the infant respond to the game? Was the game appropriate for the baby's age? What areas of development did the game stimulate? Judging from the baby's reactions, did the game continue for an appropriate length of time?

CLOSE

Ask students to summarize the main points they have learned from studying this feature. Discuss how parents can fit baby's games into a busy schedule.

CHECKING COMPREHENSION

Use the "Summary" and the "Reviewing the Facts" questions to help students review the most important ideas.

CHAPTER **8** REVIEW

1. Growth: measurable change in size; development: increase in physical, emotional, social, or intellectual skills. Examples will vary.

2. Sense of hearing is most fully developed. Less fully developed, probably because unpracticed, are the senses of sight, smell, and taste.

3. Cranky, restless, and/or wakeful; may refuse food; and/or may drool a lot. May be helped by a teething biscuit, a teething ring, or commercial medications for teething pain.

4. May cause digestive problems and ear infections.

5. Breast milk or formula, cereal, strained foods, finger foods. Babies should be physically mature enough to eat and digest each kind of food before it is introduced.

6. Playing while sucking; pushing the nipple away; preferring to eat from a spoon. Respond by beginning the process of changing baby from drinking from bottle or breast to drinking from cup.

7. Yes; self-feeding helps baby develop motor skills.

8. Babies are already beginning to form taste preferences and establish eating habits.

9. Sponge bath involves washing baby without immersing in water; tub bath involves putting baby into basin or tub of water. Newborns should have only sponge baths until the navel has healed.

10. Outfits will vary.

CHAPTER **8** REVIEW

SUMMARY

- Development and growth are most rapid during the first year of life.

- Physical development proceeds from head to foot, from near to far, and from simple to complex.

- Development of motor skills depends on physical, intellectual, social, and emotional development.

- Daily care routines include feeding, bathing, dressing, and diapering.

- During the first year, eating habits change from breast- or bottle-feeding to self-feeding a variety of foods.

- Clothing should be easy to put on and take off, should suit the activity of the baby, and should "grow" with the baby.

- Bedtime should be handled with a soothing, familiar routine.

REVIEWING THE FACTS

1. What is the difference between growth and development? Give at least two examples of growth and two examples of development.

2. Which of a baby's senses is most fully developed at birth? Which senses are less developed at birth? Use what you know about prenatal development to account for these differences in development.

3. What are three common symptoms of teething? List at least three things you might do to help a teething baby feel more comfortable.

4. Why shouldn't parents and caregivers prop bottles up for young babies?

5. What are four types of food that might be included in a baby's diet during the first year? List those foods in the order that they should be introduced to the baby. Why is the order important?

6. What are two signs that a baby is ready to be weaned? How should parents respond to these signs?

7. Should parents and caregivers encourage babies over the age of about eight months to feed themselves? Why or why not?

8. Why is infancy the best time to begin learning good eating habits?

9. What is the difference between a sponge bath and a tub bath? Which is safe for newborn babies? Why?

10. Briefly describe an outfit that would be good for an active ten-month-old. Why would that outfit be appropriate for a baby of that age?

EXPLORING FURTHER

1. Take a survey of students in the class. How do their heights compare with the heights of their parents? Give some possible reasons for differences. (Section 1)

2. Hold a 10-pound (4.5-kg) sack of flour in the crook of one arm while you perform various routine activities, such as writing a check, preparing a bottle, opening the mail, opening an umbrella, and tying a shoe. Discuss your experience with classmates. Which activities were easiest for you? Which were the most difficult? How was holding the sack of flour similar to holding a baby? How would your experiences have been different if, instead of the flour, you had been holding a baby? (Section 2)

3. Make a booklet of lullabies to share with others. Perform and teach each one to the class. Try writing a poem that could be used as a lullaby for babies. If possible, set your poem to music, using a guitar, keyboard or piano. (Section 3)

4. Compare the use of cloth diapers, disposable diapers, and a diaper service. Make a chart showing the advantages and disadvantages of each, as well as the costs involved. Calculate the costs per week, per month, and per year. (Section 3)

THINKING CRITICALLY

1. **Analyze.** What do you consider the three most important guidelines for the care of infants? Why?

2. **Synthesize.** What can parents and caregivers learn about infants from growth charts or from lists of average motor skills development? What are the possible dangers in referring to such charts and lists?

OBSERVING AND PARTICIPATING

Learning Through Participation

As students begin studying the growth and development of infants, encourage them to make a regular commitment to helping with the care of a baby, either for a relative or neighbor or at an infant-care center. Ask students to take care of a baby for at least an hour every week, or to help a parent or caregiver at least once a week. Encourage students to share their impressions of the changing infants. What growth and development do they observe? Of course, students who are already parents can contribute regularly, describing how their own infants change from week to week.

3. **Evaluate.** How can a parent's attitudes toward eating and sleeping affect a baby? What do you consider the most helpful attitudes toward eating and sleeping? Why?

CROSS-CURRICULUM CONNECTIONS

1. **Math.** Choose three different types of infant formula—ready-to-use, liquid concentrate, and powdered. Calculate the cost per 4-ounce (118-mL) baby bottle of each kind of formula.

2. **Reading.** Look for ideas on preventing and solving bedtime problems in the book *Solving Your Child's Sleep Problems*, by Richard Ferber, M.D. Share what you learned with the class.

SCHOOL TO WORK

Interview Appearance During a job interview, your appearance will tell the potential employer how you will represent the company. What impression do you think an employer would have of someone with scrubbed and trimmed fingernails, freshly shampooed hair, unwrinkled clothes, and clean teeth? How might an applicant's appearance influence an employer's decision? How might a polished appearance affect an applicant's performance during an interview? Why not organize a class day when everyone dresses as if they are going on an job interview. You could critique each other's appearance and practice interview skills at the same time.

PERFORMANCE ASSESSMENT

Physical Development During the First Year

Task
Prepare guidelines for the appropriate way to hold, feed, bathe, and diaper an infant. Then demonstrate these techniques using your guidelines. Prepare the demonstration for videotape recording or as a photographic essay with step-by-step instructional captions.

Purpose
Your purpose will be to inform prospective parents and caregivers about the safe and appropriate way to handle a baby during routine infant care. In preparation, you will devise a checklist of safety guidelines for this care.

Procedure
1. Use index cards to make notes about each routine you will model: holding, changing diapers, feeding, and bathing an infant. For each behavior, also list key safety guidelines, for example: always support the baby's

neck and head; never leave the baby unattended.
2. Make a draft of your key safety guidelines. Use this list at each rehearsal of your demonstration.
3. Practice your demonstration with a friend or partner. Have your partner use your checklist to assess whether you have accurately used your key safety measures.
4. Make any adjustments and polish your final presentation. If you will be videotaped, rehearse your demonstration and dialogue. If you are making a photographic essay, have a friend or partner take photographs as you demonstrate. Write detailed captions for your photos, making certain to include all of your key safety precautions.
5. Finalize your guidelines. Make them clear, neat, and visually appealing.

Evaluation
Your project will be evaluated on the overall effectiveness of your

demonstration: Was the baby always safe and secure? Were your directions clear and precise? Was the presentation easy to understand and follow? Was it interesting? Your safety guidelines will be evaluated on how accurately they explain safety during infant care.

Portfolio Idea A videotape may be included in your portfolio, although it is not always practical. Therefore, you may want to make a photo essay of your demonstration. Display photographs in sequential order and write clear, succinct captions to accompany each photo. You can mount your photo essay on a small poster board, or place photos in a scrapbook. Include your checklist. Be sure to label each item appropriately.

263

PERFORMANCE ASSESSMENT

Demonstration
To emphasize the importance of safety during routine infant care, suggest that each student act as if he or she were the only person available to teach the prospective audience about the topic. If possible, bring in a variety of life-sized baby dolls for students to handle or to use for their

demonstration. When they are working on the final draft of their safety guidelines, have students work in small groups to evaluate each others' lists. Consider shuffling and redistributing the students' checklists, so each student in the "audience" will use a different set of criteria to assess individual presentations.

EVALUATE

Use the reproducible Chapter 8 Test in the Teacher's Classroom Resources, or construct your own test using the Testmaker Software.

EXTENSION

Invite several new parents to visit the class, bringing their babies, if convenient. Have the parents discuss what they have learned through experience about infant care, noting especially the aspects of infant care they have found most surprising, those they have found most difficult, and those they have found most rewarding.

CLOSE

Go around the class, giving each student an opportunity to present one "tip" that might help parents and other caregivers understand the growth and development of infants or meet the physical care needs of infants.

TECHNOLOGY OPTION

VCR Students who wish to preserve assessment activities, similar to the one on this page, on videotapes may find that they soon accumulate more tapes than can be practically stored. Therefore, you might suggest that they begin with a single tape that eventually includes all activities. The progression would be a visual time line of their accomplishments in the child development class, and simple maintenance problems would be minimal. Encourage them to provide an introduction to each segment, explaining the time and location as well as the objectives of the task. When the tape is full, or the course is over, they can mark the starting times for each segment on the tape's label in order to locate specific segments at a later date.

INTRODUCE

CHAPTER OVERVIEW

As students work through Chapter 9, they gain an essential understanding of the emotional and social development of infants. They learn about the skills and attitudes with which parents and other caregivers can foster healthy emotional and social development.

Students begin Section 1 by learning the definitions of and distinctions between emotional and social development. They then focus on infants' emotional development, including the importance of loving care and a warm, secure home environment. Students also learn about babies' crying and the importance of comforting them; they read about some of the reliable techniques for providing loving comfort. In the final part of Section 1, students examine the various emotions infants experience and learn about the ages at which these emotions are usually first displayed.

In Section 2, students focus on the social development of babies and the signs of healthy social development evident during the first year of life. Students go on to consider attachment and then stranger anxiety, a fear common among healthy infants. Next, students learn about the importance of social influences on what and how babies learn.

(continued next page)

CLASSROOM MANAGEMENT

Resources Beyond the Classroom

During their first year, babies often express their emotions by crying, which can be emotionally draining on young parents. Trying to stop the crying, parents sometimes shake the baby, resulting in Shaken Baby Syndrome (SBS). Many teenagers are unaware of the potentially severe damaging effects of SBS. The Ohio Research Institute on Child Abuse Prevention, a division of the League Against Child Abuse in Ohio, provides literature about SBS as well as a thirty-day free-trial video titled "Don't Shake the Baby." The video presents an authoritative but basic discussion about the dangers of shaking babies and includes various strategies for coping with infants' crying. The literature and/or video can be obtained by calling the Institute at 1-800-858-5222.

Emotional and Social Development During the First Year

SECTION 1   Emotional Development During the First Year

SECTION 2   Social Development and Personality

Finally, students read about the personalities of individuals—what personality is, what influences affect it, and what basic personality patterns they may recognize in young children.

CHAPTER OBJECTIVES

After completing Chapter 9, students will be able to:

- Discuss the signs of healthy emotional development in infants and explain how such development can be fostered.
- Describe the healthy social development of infants and discuss the conditions and attitudes that encourage such development.

INTRODUCING THE CHAPTER

- Display several photographs of infants ranging in age from birth to twelve months. Ask students to describe, if they can, what they think the babies are feeling. Encourage them to explain their responses. Discuss similarities and differences between their interpretations of the babies' emotions. At the end of the discussion, tell students that in Chapter 9 they will learn more about the emotions and social relationships of babies.
- Use the photo on the opposite page and the three features on this page—Think About, Ask Yourself, and Now Try This—to begin a discussion about a baby's emotional and social development during the first year.

THINK ABOUT

While a child's physical growth is obvious during the first year, emotional and social growth is obvious if you think about how two babies might react to the same situation. Where one is content to play alone, another is unhappy if no one is around. Where one squeals in delight while crawling after the pet cat, another retreats in caution. How does knowledge about emotional and social development help you understand these personality differences?

ASK YOURSELF

Study the photo on the opposite page. How does the baby's expression show that he is more aware of his surround-ings than he was at birth? How is the baby's father influencing the child's sense of trust? How would you expect the child to react if you walked up to him while his father held him? Do you think he would come to you if you tried to hold him? Why or why not?

NOW TRY THIS

Imagine you are observing this father and son while they spend time together in a public park. Where would you sit? What general behavior would you look for if you wanted to focus on the social and emotional development of the child? What specific behavior? Write a brief description of your imaginary observation.

265

HEALTHY FAMILIES/HEALTHY CHILDREN

Building Healthy Families

Family mobility has made it difficult for many nuclear families to maintain strong relationships with aunts, uncles, cousins, grandparents, and other relatives. Faced with separations of distance and time, family members often drift apart. Many extended families, however, make the effort to keep in touch with each other and to preserve their emotional ties. They have an advantage over more separated families: family members feel connected to one another, to their past, and to their future.

Alex Haley, the author of *Roots* and *Queen*, encouraged family reunions, saying, "They reaffirm the thread of continuity, establish pride in self and kin, and transmit a family's awareness of itself, from the youngest to the oldest."

FOCUS

SECTION 1 RESOURCES

Teacher's Classroom Resources
- Enrichment 23
- Reteaching 23
- Section 1 Quiz

Student Workbook
- Changing Emotions

SECTION OVERVIEW

Section 1 guides students in understanding the emotional development that takes place during the first year of life. Students explore the importance of parents, other family members, and other caregivers in providing an environment in which infants can flourish. Students also learn about the timing and pattern in which specific emotions develop during infancy.

MOTIVATOR

Choose several specific emotions—anger, fear, hate, joy, sadness, frustration, etc., and write each emotion on a separate card. Ask volunteers to act out the emotion identified on a card. Let other students guess each emotion presented. After emotions have been acted out, encourage students to discuss whether they imagine babies experience those emotions. If so, how do babies express the emotions and how does that differ from how teens express them.

USING TERMS TO LEARN

Go over all three terms with the class, and encourage students to share their current understanding of them. Specific definitions related to child development are in Section 1. Help students recognize the relationship between the verb *pacify* and the noun *pacifier*.

SECTION **1**

TERMS TO LEARN

emotional development
pacifier
social development

Emotional Development During the First Year

OBJECTIVES

- Recognize signs of emotional development in babies.
- Explain how a baby's care affects emotional development.
- Describe how emotions change during infancy.

An infant's physical development is rapid and impressive during the first year. For healthy infants, emotional development and social development are also impressive, but these important kinds of development can be harder to observe and measure.

Distinguishing Between Emotional and Social Development

Emotional development is *the process of learning to recognize and express one's feelings and learning to establish one's identity and individuality*. Healthy emotional development in children is important because it results in an adult who has self-confidence, can handle stressful situations, and displays empathy toward others.

Social development is *the process of learning to interact with others and to express oneself to others*. Healthy social development results in an adult whose actions display a tolerance for others and who has an ability to interact peacefully with others. A socially healthy adult listens to all points of view before acting, communicates accurately with others, and treats both himself or herself and other people with respect and dignity.

Observing and understanding a baby's feelings and relationships with others are important tasks for parents and other caregivers. Succeeding at these tasks requires the ability to recognize and respond to each child's age level and maturity. It is also important to remember that emotional and social development are closely interwoven; a child's feelings about self and a child's behavior toward others are dependent on one another.

COOPERATIVE LEARNING

Family Emotions

Let students work in small groups to discuss various kinds of emotional climates in homes. Ask them to brainstorm specific factors that make the emotional climate positive for a baby's emotional development. What factors make it negative? How can family members identify and change negative factors within their own home? Then ask the group members to work together

to plan and then present a brief skit depicting an approach to improving the emotional climate within a home. After each group presents its skit, ask the remaining students to suggest additional methods of changing a negative emotional environment.

Understanding Emotional Development

Emotional development begins at birth and continues throughout life. Like physical development, emotional development follows predictable patterns but progresses according to each baby's individual timing.

Every baby copes with life in a very personal way. This is because each baby brings his or her own individuality to a situation. For example, all babies react to a sudden shaking of the surface on which they are lying. However, one baby may respond by screaming, while another baby may simply squirm a bit and quickly settle down again.

Emotional development depends on other factors besides the child's individuality. The type of care the baby receives and the atmosphere of the home are two important influences on an infant's emotional development.

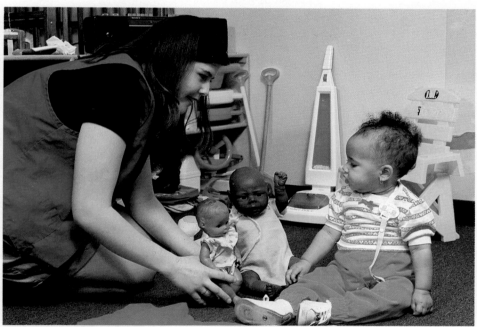

At this age, children can't tell you what they are thinking or feeling. It takes understanding to interpret their moods and the meaning of their behavior.

OBSERVING AND PARTICIPATING

Learning Through Participation

Parents and babies are quick to mimic each other's expressions. One researcher, Jeannette Haviland, Ph.D., used this observation to show how to change a baby's unhappy mood. When the baby is unhappy, the parent matches the child's facial expression for a few seconds to get the child's attention. Next, the parent does something interesting or exciting—raises the eyebrows, makes soothing noises, calls the child's name, gestures, or bounces the child gently. Finally, the parent smiles—and the child usually smiles back. By waiting for the baby to follow his or her lead at each step, the parent can often turn a moody moment into a cheery one.

TEACH

Pages 266-275

- Distinguishing Between Emotional and Social Development
- Understanding Emotional Development
- Crying and Comforting
- Emotions in Infancy

GUIDED PRACTICE

Promoting Discussion

Ask students to explain, in their own words, the differences between emotional development and social development. Then stimulate further discussion with questions such as these:

- What are signs of healthy emotional development in teens and in adults?
- What are signs of healthy social development?
- How are the two kinds of development interwoven? What distinguishes them?
- Do you think healthy emotional development is possible without healthy social development? Why or why not?
- Do you think healthy social development is possible without healthy emotional development? Why or why not?

Critical Thinking

Encourage students to share their ideas about social development. How and why do you think the standards of healthy social development vary in different cultures? Do you think there are several standards of healthy social development within our country? If so, what accounts for the differences? If not, why not?

Using the Photograph

Encourage students to describe and discuss the baby in the photograph on this page. What emotion does the baby appear to be expressing? What might have caused that emotion? How does the baby's mother appear to be responding? What effect do you think this kind of response will have on the baby?

GUIDED PRACTICE (continued)

Promoting Discussion

Guide students in considering the factors that affect an infant's emotional development. How does heredity influence emotional development? How does environment influence emotional development? How do these two influences interact? Which do you consider more important? Why?

Using the Photograph

Guide students in describing and discussing the scene in the photograph on this page. How does the interaction of these two sisters help build a sense of trust in both of them? How do you think the girls' parents have helped make this kind of interaction possible?

Promoting Discussion

Help students consider the problems parents may face in providing the kind of care that promotes the development of trust. How do the emotional ups and downs of daily life affect a parent's ability to provide consistent, loving care for an infant? How is that ability likely to be affected by a parent's responsibilities as an employee, as a marriage partner, and as a parent of older siblings?

Making Connections: Social Studies

Encourage students to share what they know about traditional child care customs in other countries and cultures. How do these customs help babies develop a sense of trust?

BUILDING SELF-ESTEEM

Even adults will attest to the healing power of love and affection. Encourage students to share a time when a caring person listened to their sorrows or hurts and made them feel special, perhaps simply by giving them a hug.

BUILDING SELF-ESTEEM

Holding Baby Can Build Trust

Before birth, a baby has been kept close and secure within the mother's body. After birth, most babies find close, gentle contact very comforting. They feel secure when a caring parent or caregiver holds, strokes, and pats them.

Holding the baby during feedings, rocking the baby when he or she is fussy, and taking the baby for a walk around the house can help the baby develop a sense of comfort and trust. As the baby grows older, he or she begins to count on the presence of parents or caregivers—reliable people who will offer help when the baby needs it, comfort when the baby feels frightened, and companionship when the baby feels lonely.

Building Trust Through Care

The world is a strange new place for newborns. Depending on a baby's early experiences, the world may be a comfortable, secure place—or a confusing, difficult place. The attitudes that newborns develop about their world depend on how well their needs are met.

If the newborn is kept warm and dry, and is fed when hungry, soothed when fussy, and talked to when awake, the infant comes to feel that this world is a comfortable place and develops a sense of security.

On the other hand, if the newborn is made to conform to a rigid schedule of feeding, and crying brings no comfort or adult response, the baby learns that this world is not a very friendly place. The same attitude develops when parents and other caregivers are inconsistent in their care or in their responses to the infant. If schedules are changed often, or if parents and caregivers are sometimes gentle and loving and other times sharp and impatient, the baby has difficulty building trust.

Building trust in infancy is essential for a person's emotional and social development. A baby who learns to trust parents and caregivers will grow into a child who can trust himself or herself and into an adult who can establish and maintain caring relationships with others.

A baby who experiences a world of caring people and interesting things has a good start in life. How do these influences help build trust?

SEE HOW THEY GROW

Developing Empathy

Empathy—the capacity to understand and share the feelings of another person—is one of the indicators of mature, healthy emotional development. Clearly, no infant can display empathy. However, the foundations for empathy may be laid during infancy, when babies sense that parents and other caregivers understand and respond to their needs and feelings. As chil-

dren grow, they can be guided toward empathic behavior. Children benefit from seeing parents and other caregivers behave in empathic ways, both toward the children themselves and toward other people. Children can also be given special opportunities to show that they care for others, including those who are not close relatives.

Establishing a happy, loving home environment is one of the best and most important ways in which parents can provide for their children.

Emotional Climate of the Home

Affection and harmony between parents, caregivers, and all family members are the foundation of successful family life. If the family members and caregivers also love and understand each child as an individual, the conditions are ideal for emotional and social development.

Undoubtedly, you have days when you are grumpy. Have you ever noticed how contagious such feelings are? If you snap at someone, the chances are that person will snap back at you—or at someone else. Babies react the same way. Long before they know the meanings of words, babies catch the tone of adults' feelings. Nervous, worried parents and caregivers are likely to be tense or awkward in handling their baby. They may cuddle the infant in a way that is more anxious than soothing; they may rush the baby through a feeding. The baby senses the person's nervousness and, in turn, becomes irritable and fussy.

Every family has its normal ups and downs, and a baby adapts to these. However, it is essential for the baby to feel that genuine, warm affection and caring are the basis of the family's interactions. Continuing bitterness and mistrust can interfere with the baby's healthy development.

GUIDED PRACTICE (continued)

Using the Photograph
Encourage students to discuss the family scene in the photo on this page and to share their reactions to it. How do you think these parents feel about their baby? What makes you think that? How do you think these parents feel about each other? What makes you think that? How does the baby appear to feel about her parents? How is that likely to affect her feelings about herself? About the world?

Promoting Discussion
Encourage students to share their ideas about the factors that affect parents' capacity to provide a healthy emotional climate for their baby. What particular problems are faced by a single parent? By a teen mother who lives with her own parents? By a couple who married in response to the pregnancy? By a couple who had not intended to have children? By a couple who have recently moved and have no relatives or close friends nearby?

Family Focus
Family structures today are more varied than they have ever been. Because of this, many families are looking for new and different ways to meet the needs of family members. Ask students what families can do to provide the best emotional environment for an infant in each of the situations below. What can be done in each situation when there are other children in the family?

- Couple with one parent employed.
- Dual-worker couple.
- Single parent.
- Divorced parents who have both remarried.

TEEN PARENTING

For teen parents, establishing a good emotional climate for a baby can be challenging. Have students discuss why this is often true, using the following questions to guide the discussion:

- What problems do many teen parents have in knowing the kind of care an infant needs and in providing that care?
- The physical needs of an infant must be met in order to build trust. Why is this a problem for some teen parents?

- What makes stress a problem for many teen parents? How does the parent's stress affect an infant?
- When a teen has become a parent by accident rather than by choice, what special difficulties might the parent face in establishing an emotional bond with the baby?

PARENTING IN ACTION

Adjusting to Parenthood

Jess and Twana were thrilled when they learned they were going to be parents. However, now that the baby, Ashley, is here, they are having difficulty adjusting.

After Ashley was born, Twana quit her job to stay home with the baby. She sometimes feels "trapped" at home and watches sadly as Jess sets off for work every morning. "I miss my job," she explains. "I miss being with my friends at work. Ashley is fun—but I want some time with adults, too."

Jess, on the other hand, feels left out of the life Ashley and Twana share. He also worries because he is now responsible for earning all the money that the family needs.

When Jess comes home from work—often late—he and Twana are both tired. On most nights, they feel angry and end up arguing. Then Ashley wakes up and starts to cry. Her parents, both tense and angry, have trouble comforting her. Last night, when Twana picked her up, Ashley cried even harder. Frustrated, Twana pushed the baby into Jess's arms and shouted, "Here, you take care of her for a change!" Then she ran into the bedroom and slammed the door.

THINK AND DISCUSS

1. How has the emotional climate of Jess and Twana's home changed since Ashley's birth? What are the causes of that change?
2. How do you think Jess feels about Twana? About Ashley?
3. How do you think Twana feels about Jess? About Ashley?
4. What questions do you think Jess and Twana should be asking themselves? What should they be asking each other?
5. If you were in a position to help Jess and Twana, what would you suggest? Why?

Crying and Comforting

The most obvious sign of an infant's emotions is crying. Newborns vary greatly in the amount and the intensity of their crying. Some babies cry infrequently, and they are usually easy to comfort. These are what parents call "easy" or "good" babies. Other babies cry often and loudly, and it is usually hard to comfort them. These babies can be considered "difficult," because being able to comfort and help a crying baby provides a sense of satisfaction—and parents of inconsolable criers often miss out on that satisfaction. Instead, they may develop a sense of frustration at not being able to calm the baby or to remedy the problem.

A young baby who is crying needs attention and care. The first step is to check for any physical problem. Is the baby hun-

---

PARENTING IN ACTION

Promoting Discussion

As an introduction, have students share their ideas about the title, "Adjusting to Parenthood." What adjustments does parenthood require? Are they the same for fathers and for mothers? How might parenthood affect the relationship between a husband and a wife; between friends, or relatives? Encourage students to discuss ideas before they read the selection.

Thinking Critically

After reading the selection, let students compare and discuss ideas about the couple. Do you think either parent is at fault? If so, which parent and why? If not, why not? What could Jess and Twana have done before Ashley was born to prevent these problems? Could they have prevented the problems after Ashley's birth from becoming severe? What do you think will happen to the family if problems are not faced and solved now?

Answers to Think and Discuss

1. The emotional climate is tense and negative as both parents are concerned about—and dissatisfied with—their new roles.

2. Encourage various responses. Example: He loves them both, but also feels jealous and resentful.

3. Encourage various responses. Example: She loves them both, but she also feels jealous and resentful.

4. Encourage various responses. Examples: What can I do to make my responsibilities as a parent easier and more enjoyable? How can we help each other?

5. Encourage a variety of suggestions; remind students to offer reasons to support their suggestions.

OBSERVING AND PARTICIPATING

Learning Through Participation

Parents encounter unexpected challenges and frustrations when a newborn comes into their lives. Often, they turn to experts in the field of child development for help and advice. One of the pioneers in this field was Dr. Benjamin Spock. Since his first book, *Baby and Child Care*, was published in 1946, parents have had access to self-help books that advocate a multitude of philosophies. Ask students to debate the pros and cons of child care theories that have become popular since Dr. Spock's book first appeared.

gry or in need of a diaper change? Is the infant too cold or too hot? Perhaps there's a burp left over from the last feeding. If none of these is the cause of the crying and the baby doesn't seem ill, then you must assume that the baby needs something else—your company, your cuddling, or your comforting. Remember that these are real needs, too. As you and the baby get to know each other, you will probably discover which comforting measures work best. Here are a few to try:

- **Cuddle up with the baby in a rocking chair.** The combination of being held and rocked often soothes a crying baby. You can provide a similar combination by holding the baby close as you walk around. A frontal baby carrier that fits over the shoulders and across the back may assist you in keeping the baby close, comfortable, and soothed by your gently moving.

- **Move the baby to a new position.** Perhaps the baby wants to lie in a different position but isn't yet strong enough to roll over. Perhaps the baby wants to sit in an infant seat and feel involved with the rest of the family.

- **Talk softly to the baby, or sing to the baby.** Don't worry—you don't have to be a great singer. The tone and rhythm of your voice, and the attention they indicate, may comfort the baby.

- **Offer a toy to interest and distract the baby.**

- **Place the baby facedown across your legs as you sit in a sturdy chair.** Support the baby's head with one hand while gently rubbing the baby's back with the other.

Babies also develop their own techniques for comforting themselves. The most common comforting technique is sucking—on a thumb, a fist, or a **pacifier**, *a nipple attached to a plastic ring*.

Many babies also comfort themselves with a soft object such as a certain blanket or stuffed toy. They develop a special attachment to this object and use it for comfort when they are sleepy or anxious. Other babies may comfort themselves by twisting their hair or by rocking themselves back and forth in their crib.

The baby's special self-comforting technique is an indication of his or her individuality and development. Children typically outgrow their need for such techniques and, when they are ready, give up these habits without a problem.

Emotions in Infancy

Think about all the different emotions you experience. You may feel happy, angry, anxious, fearful, or excited. Babies, however, only gradually develop such specific emotions.

SAFETY TIP

During the first few months, a pacifier can help satisfy the baby's need to suck and may even help eliminate some of the air in the stomach. However, in order to be safe for the baby, pacifiers must be used carefully. *Never* tie the pacifier on a string around the baby's neck. To keep the pacifier from falling, use a pacifier ribbon, which snaps on the pacifier at one end and attaches to the baby's clothing at the other end. These ribbons are available in most baby stores. Check the baby's pacifier frequently for cuts and tears in the surface. A pacifier that is old or torn can fall apart and become a health and safety hazard.

GUIDED PRACTICE (continued)

Critical Thinking
Point out to students that when the issue of child abuse is raised, people most often think of physical abuse. Ask students to share their ideas about what constitutes emotional abuse. What effects can it have? Is emotional abuse as dangerous as physical abuse? Why or why not? Who do you think is most likely to abuse a child emotionally? Why? Why is emotional abuse difficult to detect and deal with? What can your community do about emotional abuse? What can and should you do about it?

Promoting Discussion
Encourage students to discuss which comforting measure they find most appealing. How do preferences of caregivers influence effective comforting? How might the individual needs of the baby influence their effectiveness? How should a caregiver judge each technique?

Practicing Decision Making
Would you encourage your baby to use a pacifier if you were a parent? Why or why not?

SAFETY TIP

Caution students that although pacifiers come in attractive designs, consumers should always keep safety in mind. A pacifier should have a large handle or ring that is firmly attached. The mouthguard should be wide, with an inseparable nipple so as to prevent choking. Also, mouthguards must have ventilation holes to prevent obstruction to baby's breathing.

MORE ABOUT

Crying
Researchers are finding that certain characteristics of a newborn's cry, such as pitch and loudness, can be used to predict developmental delays later in childhood. For example, toddlers who as infants had very soft or very high-pitched cries or who had cries that frequently changed in pitch generally scored lower on measurements of certain aspects of mental and physical development at age eighteen months. The same children tended to score lower on scales of general cognitive development at age five. It is not yet possible to predict a baby's exact developmental pattern from cries. Researchers believe that a refined procedure could be used to provide information not available from medical examinations and to identify infants who may be at developmental risk.

GUIDED PRACTICE (continued)

ASK THE EXPERTS

Issues and Advice

1. According to Ms. Clarke, at what age is a daily fussy period common? (*Between three and twelve weeks.*)

2. For what possible reason is the end of the day a fussy period? (*The baby is overloaded and needs to settle down.*)

3. What serious misunderstanding can parents have about crying? (*It is pointless and not necessary to respond to.*)

4. What can a parent do to comfort a fussy baby? (*Possibilities are adding or removing covers, feeding, rocking, singing, talking, bundling, or loosening clothing.*)

5. What should an adult do when a baby cries? (*Try to determine what the baby needs.*)

Thinking Like an Expert

Challenge students to put themselves in the place of a teacher-trainer such as Ms. Clarke. Put students into pairs or small groups and to discuss this question: How would they counsel other adults who are distressed about a fussy baby? Have students list reasons infants cry and suggest solutions to the situations. Then ask volunteers to role-play the parts of counselor and parents. The parents can describe their baby's behavior and their own frustrations. Then the counselor can offer advice and solutions. Encourage the counselor to recommend language that the parents can use in addition to actions. For example, the parents can go to the crying baby and say, "Thanks for calling me; now let's see what you need."

ASK THE EXPERTS

Babies and Crying

Q. Our month-old baby cries and cries each evening, and nothing seems to help. Should we just leave her alone and let her "cry it out"?

A. This is a good question—and a very natural one. Most babies between the ages of three and twelve weeks have a fussy period at the end of the day.

My answer to your question really depends on what you mean by letting your baby cry it out. Some parents let their babies "cry it out" by completely ignoring them. These parents believe— mistakenly—that a baby's crying is pointless and that it is not necessary to respond to an infant's cries.

This approach to crying is never appropriate.

Other parents let their babies "cry it out" during a fussy period by trying various methods of comforting the baby, one method at a time. Then they leave the baby alone for a short period— perhaps five minutes—between attempts to provide comfort. With this approach, the parents might try feeding, rocking, singing, talking, patting, carrying, adding more covers, removing covers, bundling, and loosening clothing all in turn, with short periods in which the baby can cry and can perhaps start learning to comfort himself or herself. This approach to crying it out can help both the baby and the baby's parents.

Crying is a baby's method of letting parents and other caregivers know about his or her needs. When the baby cries, they should be willing to listen, to respond by trying to figure out what the baby needs, and to meet the baby's need as directly as possible.

Jean Illsley Clarke

Jean Illsley Clarke
Director of J.I. Consultants in
Minneapolis, Minnesota

At birth the range of emotions is limited to pleasure or satisfaction, during which the baby is quiet, and pain or discomfort, during which the baby cries. This is why crying does not necessarily indicate pain in a newborn; it may indicate boredom or some other form of discomfort. By the second month, however, babies produce different cries to express different feelings. These more specific responses continue to develop as babies connect their feelings with inner sensations and outer experiences.

MORE ABOUT

Self-Comforting

As babies grow, so does their ability to find ways to comfort themselves instead of expecting comfort from others. Some experts suggest that infants be rocked and held just until they are almost asleep. At this point, they should be placed in the crib so that they can adjust to its comforts and eventually drift off to sleep. A favorite toy, security blanket, or stuffed animal will help the older infant feel secure and comfortable when settling in to sleep. Always be sure that toys and stuffed animals will not endanger the baby. Babies who are accustomed to pacifiers will learn to find one on their own if several are placed around the crib.

HOW EMOTIONS DEVELOP

PLEASANT EMOTIONS

DELIGHT

Beginning at about two months, babies show delight by smiling, perhaps in response to an adult who is making funny faces at them.

ELATION

By seven or eight months, babies show the high spirits of elation.

AFFECTION

At about nine months, babies begin to feel affection for those who provide security and care. Affection for other children comes later.

(Continued on next page)

MORE ABOUT

Emotional Support

Encourage students to share and discuss their ideas in response to these questions: How do you think birth order affects social development? What observations have you made about the influence of older and/or younger siblings on the emotional development of an infant? Students will undoubtedly have a variety of perspectives to offer about their own experiences in a family.

(Be prepared for negative responses as well.) Ask them to suggest ways that a family can work together for the benefit of an infant.

GUIDED PRACTICE (continued)

Promoting Discussion

Encourage students to identify and discuss various techniques that babies use to comfort themselves, as well as commercial devices intended to prevent babies from crying. Which techniques and devices do you consider positive for a baby's emotional development? Why? What problems do you think might be involved in a baby's using the other techniques and devices? Why?

Using the Chart

Guide students in studying and discussing the chart on this page and the next. How soon after birth does the child begin to exhibit both pleasant and unpleasant emotions? By what age are the unpleasant emotions of distress, anger, disgust, and fear all evident? Do babies under the age of twelve months experience feelings of jealousy? At what age does a baby usually develop affection for adults?

Using the Photographs

Have students examine the photographs in the chart on this page and the next. What situation might have triggered the emotion the baby in each photo is expressing? How do you think a parent or caregiver should respond to the baby's expression of emotion? Why?

Critical Thinking

Point out to students that a baby's emotions become more specific and complex as he or she grows older. Then ask how this development might make the job of a parent or caregiver easier. How might it make the job more difficult?

Making Connections: Reading and Writing

Encourage students to find and share with the class poems that illustrate babies' emotions. Then suggest that students write their own poems expressing babies' emotions. Give students an opportunity to read their poems aloud, or post them on a class bulletin board.

INDEPENDENT PRACTICE

INDEPENDENT PRACTICE

Journal Writing

Have students write journal entries describing their reactions to learning about emotional development during infancy. Suggest that they respond to some or all of these questions: Why do you think it is important to understand the emotional development that takes place during the first year of life? How has what you have learned affected your understanding of your own emotional development? How does it help you understand babies for whom you care? What effect, if any, has it had on your interests in becoming a parent or in pursuing a career that involves caring for young children?

Student Workbook

Have students complete "Changing Emotions" in the Student Workbook.

Extension

Let students work independently or in small groups to complete one or more of these extension activities:

- Develop and write a rating scale for evaluating the emotional climate of a home.

- Parents and other caregivers can find a baby's crying so difficult to deal with they respond by becoming physically abusive. With this in mind, identify local resources that are available to help abused women and children, such as hot lines, crisis nurseries, and shelters. In addition, gather information about support groups or hot lines for parents who feel that they are on the verge of committing child abuse. Make the information you have gathered available to others in an interesting and appealing format.

- Act out a conversation between a foster mother and a social worker during which the two discuss the foster mother's new charge, a four-month-old infant who seldom smiles or cries.

HOW EMOTIONS DEVELOP (cont'd.)

UNPLEASANT EMOTIONS

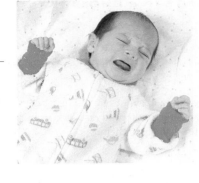

DISTRESS

Very young babies express any discomfort or unhappiness in the same way—by crying.

ANGER

By about four or five months, babies show their anger when they don't get their own way. Older babies show anger at objects as well as at people. They may throw their toys or push something away.

DISGUST

Disgust can also be observed at about four or five months of age. Babies show their dislikes very clearly.

FEAR

Until around the age of six months, babies do not show fear because they cannot recognize threatening situations. Fear of strangers begins at about eight months of age.

OBSERVING AND PARTICIPATING

Learning Through Participation

Make available a collection of photographs of infants, or ask students to cut pictures of babies out of magazines, then work in groups to discuss the emotion the infant in each is displaying.

- What is the emotion?
- What are the indications of that emotion?
- What might have caused that emotion?

- How do you think a parent or caregiver should respond to the baby's emotion? Why?

- How does the baby's age affect the emotion he or she appears to feel? How does the baby's age affect the way he or she displays that emotion?

- Have you experienced a baby expressing that emotion? How did you respond?

ASSESS

CHECKING COMPREHENSION

Assign students to write their responses to the Check Your Understanding questions in the Section 1 Review. Answers to the questions are given at the bottom of this page.

EVALUATE

Have students complete the Chapter 9, Section 1 quiz in the TCR.

Reteaching

Have small groups of students work together to plan and make a chart listing reasons infants cry and noting appropriate responses. Discuss each group's chart , focusing on the ways in which appropriate responses can foster a baby's healthy emotional development.

Enrichment

Ask students to plan and prepare a guide to selecting caregivers and care settings that will foster an infant's healthy emotional development. Encourage students to select a format such as a radio advertisement or a short video.

Extension

Make a tape recording of the different cries of a single baby, or ask a student or a group of students to make the tape recording. Play the tape and encourage students to discuss each cry. What is the baby expressing? How would you respond to this crying? Why? If your first approach was unsuccessful in comforting the baby, what would you try next? How would you feel if the baby continued crying in spite of your attempts to provide comfort? Remind students, if necessary, that there are no "right" answers.

CLOSE

Let each student give one specific suggestion for encouraging the healthy emotional development of an infant.

Building an infant's sense of trust has long-term benefits for all. By the time she is six to nine months old, she will learn to comfort herself with a thumb, a pacifier, a blanket, or a soft toy.

SECTION 1 REVIEW

CHECK YOUR UNDERSTANDING

1. What is emotional development?
2. What is social development?
3. How should parents and caregivers respond to a baby's needs in order to help the baby build a sense of trust?
4. Does it matter to a baby how the adults in the baby's family treat each other? Why or why not?
5. List at least four needs that might cause a baby to cry.
6. What are two measures that might comfort a crying baby?
7. Which of a baby's emotions require attention from a parent or other caregiver? Why?

DISCUSS AND DISCOVER

1. Discuss what parents can do to provide consistency in the care and attention their babies receive. What issues should parents discuss with each other? What issues should they discuss with their baby's other caregivers?
2. Explain how the following factors can affect the emotional climate in a home: the emotional maturity of parents; education; unemployment; substance use and abuse.

Observing & Participating

Visit a center where several infants are cared for. Notice how the caregivers comfort the babies when they cry. Describe how the technique used for each baby seems to suit that baby's particular needs. Speculate about how these techniques will help the infants learn to comfort themselves.

SECTION 1 REVIEW

1. The process of learning to recognize and express one's feelings and of learning to establish one's identity and individuality.
2. The process of learning to interact with others and express oneself to others.
3. Keep baby warm and dry, feed baby when hungry, soothe baby when fussy, and talk to baby.
4. Yes; babies catch the tone of adults' feelings.
5. Any four: hunger, needs diaper changed, burping, company, cuddling, or comforting; hot or cold.
6. Any two: cuddling in rocking chair; moving to a new position; talking softly or singing; offering toy to distract baby; placing baby facedown across lap and gently rubbing baby's back.
7. Crying indicates pain or discomfort and requires attention from a parent or caregiver.

SECTION 2 RESOURCES

Teacher's Classroom Resources
- Enrichment 24
- Reteaching 24
- Section 2 Quiz

Student Workbook
- Hidden Word Puzzle

SECTION OVERVIEW

In Section 2, students explore the social development of infants, noting its close relationship to concurrent emotional development. They examine healthy signs of early social development and explore the meaning and importance of attachment, consider stranger anxiety, patterns of learning behavior, and the influences on individual personalities. Finally, the three general personality patterns—sensitive, placid, and aggressive are presented.

MOTIVATOR

Write on the chalkboard:
Does my baby care who feeds her?
When will my baby start to love me?
These are questions many new parents might ask about their relationships with their newborns. Let students suggest other questions new parents might ask—or want to ask. Add their suggestions to the list on the board, and encourage them to suggest helpful responses.

USING TERMS TO LEARN

Guide students in discussing all nine vocabulary terms. Students may refer to dictionaries to check the definitions of *aggressive*; caution that the definition used to identify one of the three basic personality patterns may differ from the definition with which they are most familiar.

SECTION **2**   Social Development and Personality

TERMS TO LEARN

aggressive
attachment
consistency
failure to thrive
personality
placid
self-concept
sensitive
stranger anxiety

OBJECTIVES

- Recognize signs of social development in babies.
- Explain the importance of attachment to emotional and social development.
- Describe how behavior is learned.
- Define *personality* and describe how it develops.
- Recognize different personality types in babies.

A baby's social development is closely related to his or her physical development and emotional development. Even a newborn responds to other people in ways that encourage those people to satisfy the baby's physical and emotional needs. As the baby develops physically, he or she becomes more capable of involvement and interaction with other people. As the baby develops emotionally, his or her feelings about self become an integral part of the baby's relationships with other people.

Signs of Social Development in Infancy

Like physical and emotional development, social development follows a predictable pattern. The following list shows the common signs of social development for babies during the first year. Like all such lists and charts, this one is designed to indicate typical development for many babies; it should be considered a general guide—not a checklist—for helping you understand individual babies.

- **The first days of life.** From birth onward, babies respond to human voices. A calm, soothing voice will quiet a baby; a harsh or loud voice will upset a baby.

COOPERATIVE LEARNING

Building Cooperation
The need for discipline is essential to any classroom. One way of maintaining the peace, while simultaneously building self-confidence and esteem, is to have students cooperatively assume responsibility for class administration. Begin the process by having the class as a whole jointly draft a set of "rules of order." This step, which should include the teacher as a participant,

should be conducted in a democratic fashion and should entertain as many contingencies as possible. In addition to matters of decorum, the rules may also provide for such issues as arranging for peer teaching. Once rules are in place, they are to be enforced by a student-elected committee.

- **One month.** Most babies stop crying when they are lifted or touched. A baby's face brightens when he or she sees a familiar person—usually a parent.

- **Two months.** Babies begin to smile at people. Now their eyes can follow moving objects, and they especially enjoy watching people move about the room.

- **Three months.** Babies turn their head in response to a voice. Now they want companionship as well as physical care.

- **Four months.** Babies laugh out loud. They look to other people for entertainment.

- **Five months.** Babies show an increased interest in family members other than their parents. They may cry when they are left alone in a room. At this age, babies babble to their toys, dolls, or stuffed animals, or to themselves.

- **Six months.** Babies love company and attention. They delight in playing games such as peek-a-boo.

- **Seven months.** Babies prefer their parents over other family members or strangers.

- **Eight months.** Babies prefer to be in a room with other people. Many babies this age can move from room to room, looking for company.

- **Nine and ten months.** Babies are quite socially involved. They creep after their parents and are often underfoot. At this age, babies love attention. They enjoy being chased; they like to throw toys over and over again—with someone else picking the toys up each time.

- **Eleven and twelve months.** Babies are most often friendly and happy at this age. They are also sensitive to the emotions of others. They know how to influence and adjust to the emotions of the people around them. At one year, babies like to be the center of attention. They like to play games with other family members and are usually tolerant of strangers.

Attachment

Around the age of six months, a baby comes to understand that he or she is a separate person. The baby then works to develop an **attachment**, *a special strong bond between two people,* to parents or other important caregivers. This attachment is a strong emotional bond; it also represents the baby's first real social relationship.

Social development is a natural part of being with parents and other family members.

TEACH
Pages 276-285

- Signs of Social Development in Infancy
- Attachment
- Stranger Anxiety
- How Behavior Is Learned
- Influences on Personality
- Common Personality Traits

GUIDED PRACTICE

Promoting Discussion
Guide students in discussing the typical signs of social development. How are parents and other caregivers likely to respond to these signs of development? How can positive responses from parents and other caregivers encourage further social development? Which specific signs of social development would you, as a parent or caregiver, anticipate most eagerly? Why? Which of these signs—if any—would you find unwelcome? Why?

Using the Photograph
Ask questions such as these to help students discuss the photograph on this page: How are the baby's social needs being met? How are his emotional needs being met? How does the baby appear to feel? How does his father appear to feel? If you were walking toward these people in the park, how would you respond to the baby? Why?

Cooperative Learning
Let students work in groups to discuss their responses to these questions: How does a baby's physical helplessness contribute to his or her social development? As a baby becomes more capable and more independent, how is social development affected? Why?

Critical Thinking
Ask students to share their ideas in response to these questions: Before a baby understands that he or she is a separate person (around the age of six months), how is the baby likely to perceive himself or herself? How is the baby likely to perceive others?

OBSERVING AND PARTICIPATING

Developing Observational Skills
You may want to refer students to Chapter 19, which presents various ways to observe children and techniques for recording their observations. Review with students the differences between an objective and subjective evaluation, and remind them to keep their observations objective. They may find a frequency count or developmental checklist the best method of recording their observations of infants. You may also want to refer them to the Observing and Participating booklet in the TCR.

GUIDED PRACTICE (continued)

Promoting Discussion

Help students consider and discuss attachment. Why is attachment important for an infant? Which aspects of attachment represent emotional development? Which represent social development? When do you think attachment begins to be established between a parent and a baby? In what other kinds of relationships (other than parent and child) does attachment exist?

Critical Thinking

Ask students to identify circumstances that might result in an infant's being left alone much of the time. How would that treatment affect the infant's social development? How would it affect the infant's emotional development?

Promoting Discussion

Guide students in discussing how Harlow's experiments with baby monkeys relate to the problems experienced by children in institutions and in families where they receive little attention.

Using the Photograph

Let students describe the interaction between the gorilla and the kitten in the photograph on this page. What signs of attachment between the two animals can you identify? How is this attachment similar to the attachment between a parent and a child? How is it different?

BUILDING SELF-ESTEEM

Have students discuss the ways in which parents and other caregivers can help babies develop strong emotional attachments. Let each student write a list to share in small groups.

BUILDING SELF-ESTEEM

The Lasting Benefits of Hugs

Infants have a basic need for physical contact—holding, cuddling, rocking, or just being near. Physical contact communicates a clear message to an infant: "You are special to me, and I care about you."

Hugging a baby is one special way to communicate this message. Hugging also shares feelings of excitement, happiness, reassurance, or pleasure with the infant. A hug can be a celebration of happiness after an infant has taken his or her first few steps; or a hug can provide reassurance that you will return after leaving the baby in the crib for his or her nap.

Research studies indicate that physical contact is important for all infants. It helps them develop positive, caring relationships with other people. Hugging does not spoil a child—instead, it shows the child that he or she is loved.

Researchers have discovered that physical contact is an important factor in this attachment. In one famous experiment, an American experimental psychologist, Harry Harlow, used substitute "mothers," monkey-shaped forms in either chicken wire or soft cloth, to raise baby monkeys. All the baby monkeys clung to the soft "mothers," regardless of which kind of "mother" held their feeding bottles. Clearly, the monkeys needed the feeling of physical closeness in addition to the nourishment of their feedings.

However, attachment requires more than physical contact. Once the baby monkeys were grown, it was clear that Harlow's experiment had had a profound effect. These monkeys did not know how to relate to other monkeys; they did not develop normal social relationships. Harlow believed this was caused by the lack of interaction between the babies and their "mothers."

Human babies, of course, are quite different from monkeys, but such research can give us clues to the process of human social development. Interaction with adults seems critical to human development as well.

All babies need lots of love. Even very young babies can experience loneliness. If a baby is left alone most of the time except for physical care, the infant begins to fail to respond to people and objects.

Social relationships are important for many animals as well as for humans. A famous example is Koko the gorilla's attachment to her favorite kitten.

MORE ABOUT

Attachment

The attachment between parent and child is vital to an infant's emotional development. Over weeks and months, this bond grows gradually and deepens with each parent-child interaction. Fostering attachment requires more than providing physical care; it involves making eye contact, smiling, and talking to the infant. Without this attachment, some children may fail to develop normally. As a result of emotional deprivation, these children become listless, show little interest in their surroundings, and appear much younger than they actually are. These emotionally stunted children are often placed in special hospital programs where they are provided with loving care until they begin to thrive and grow.

As babies mature, their attachment to parents, family members, and other caregivers become more recognizable. They respond with smiles and hugs and crawl or walk to parent or caregiver.

This problem is most likely to develop in certain kinds of institutions, where babies may receive physical care but no emotional support or social practice. However, the problem can also develop in families if the parents or caregivers consistently lack the time, energy, or ability to become emotionally and socially involved with the baby. When normal, demanding infants get so little attention and encouragement from parents or caregivers, their cries weaken, their smiles fade, and the babies become withdrawn and unresponsive.

For some babies, a lack of love and attention may result in **failure to thrive**, *a condition in which the baby does not grow and develop properly*. Failure to thrive may be caused by a physical problem, such as heart disease or the lack of proper food. However, failure to thrive can also be a physical symptom of poor emotional and social care. In these cases, parents and caregivers must be given instruction and support so that they can help the baby recover and grow. If these babies are not helped, they become unattached. Throughout development into adulthood, they will be unable to develop caring, meaningful relationships with other people.

Most parents and caregivers, however, can identify signs that the baby is making healthy attachment as he or she matures. Babies who cry to communicate various needs, gaze into the eyes of parents or caregivers, track the movements of parents or caregivers with their eyes, snuggle, cuddle, and become quiet when comforted are showing positive signs of growing attachment. As babies mature and their attachments continue to develop, they vocalize with their parents or caregivers, embrace parents or caregivers, and eventually crawl or walk to parents or caregivers.

HEALTH TIP

Failure to thrive is a specific condition that doctors can—and do—diagnose. It is, in fact, relatively uncommon. Much more common are babies' erratic growth spurts. You may feel that the baby has "stopped growing" or is not growing this month as rapidly as he or she did last month. As a rule, you should not feel worried by such changes. However, if you are concerned that the baby might be suffering from failure to thrive, it is best to take the baby to a pediatrician and discuss all your concerns openly with him or her.

MORE ABOUT

Attachment

A special form of attachment, called imprinting, has been observed in some flock animals. Birds such as swans, ducks, chickens, and geese walk within a short time of hatching. By instinct, they follow the first moving object they see. Usually, this is the parent bird. Researchers have found that the instinct to follow seems to be imprinted in young geese during a specific short period after hatching. During that time, the goslings will imprint with anyone or anything they see. When the mother geese are not there, goslings have been known to imprint with mechanical decoys, other animals, and even the researchers themselves.

GUIDED PRACTICE (continued)

Using the Photograph

Guide students in discussing the photograph on this page. What needs do you think the baby in the picture is expressing? What might have caused those needs? How would you respond to the baby? Why? What might happen to the baby if the needs such as those expressed here are consistently ignored?

Practicing Decision Making

Present students with the following situation: A neighbor has asked you to babysit her daughter, Angelina, every day after school. The neighbor can't pay much, but she assures you that caring for Angelina won't be hard. "Really, you'll find it's very easy. Angelina spends all afternoon in her playpen. As long as the TV is on, she seems pretty content. You'll have plenty of time to study."

Then ask the students to discuss their responses to these questions: What concerns do you have for Angelina's development? Why? Would you discuss your concerns with Angelina's mother? Why or why not? Would you discuss your concerns with anyone else? If so, with whom? If not, why not? Would you accept the job of caring for Angelina every afternoon? Why or why not?

HEALTH TIP

Have students investigate how pediatricians accurately diagnose infants who they suspect are not thriving. What methods of treatment are used? What avenues of counseling are available to parents and caregivers?

Critical Thinking

Let students compare and discuss their responses to this question: What are the relationships between physical health and social and emotional health?

GUIDED PRACTICE (continued)

Making Connections: Psychology

Have students conduct research into the relationship between a parent's behavior toward his or her infant and the parent's own experiences in the first year of life. Have students share and discuss findings.

Promoting Discussion

Ask these questions to help students discuss stranger anxiety: What does stranger anxiety show about a baby's social development? Would you worry about a baby who exhibited no stranger anxiety? Why or why not?

Using the Photograph

Let students describe the individuals and the situation shown in the photograph on this page. How is the baby being given an opportunity to adjust to change? What may happen next? How might the baby respond? Why?

Critical Thinking

Have students discuss responses to this question: How should a parent react if an unfamiliar close relative approaches a ten-month-old baby too quickly or insists that the baby sit on the relative's lap?

Cooperative Learning

Let students work in small groups to practice handling a baby's stranger anxiety. Have group members take turns acting out the role of "parent" to a life-size doll while other group members approach the "baby," who suffers from stranger anxiety. Encourage all the groups to explore a variety of encounters and helpful responses to a baby's fear.

Cultural Exchange

Although stranger anxiety is a universal phenomenon, the reactions of adults might differ according to custom or cultural influences. Ask students to share observations or knowledge of different ways they have seen adults handle an infant's stranger anxiety.

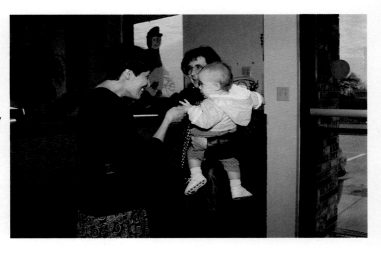

Improved memory allows older babies to realize whether they are in a familiar place with familiar people. Stranger anxiety may be less of a problem if the child is given opportunities to grow use to being around others.

Cultural Exchange

KNOWING A STRANGER

Experiments throughout the world—in American cities, isolated Guatemalan highlands, towns in Israel, and remote areas of the African Kalahari Desert—have shown that all babies experience stranger anxiety. It appears to be universal, regardless of the child's personality or the nature of child-rearing practices.

Stranger Anxiety

Parents and caregivers may recognize and enjoy many signs of a baby's social development. The baby smiles brightly at a familiar face. The baby reaches up to be held. The baby laughs as she drops the ball once more and waits eagerly for her big brother to pick it up again.

Another important sign of social development is not so immediately heartwarming, but it is nonetheless a significant stage for each baby. During the second half of the first year, often around the age of eight months, babies develop **stranger anxiety**, *a fear, usually expressed by crying, of unfamiliar people.* During this period, a baby who used to sit cheerfully on anyone's lap suddenly screams and bursts into tears when an unfamiliar person approaches.

Stranger anxiety is an indicator of the baby's improving memory. At this age, the child is better able to remember the faces of parents and beloved caregivers; these are the people who provide comfort and security. Most other faces suddenly seem strange and make the baby feel fearful.

You can help a baby through this stage by reminding new people to approach the baby slowly and to give the baby time to adjust. You may also want to keep the baby's routine as regular as possible; if you can avoid it, this is not the time to introduce sudden changes in activities or caregivers. If you find the baby's stranger anxiety troubling, you can reassure yourself that this is just a stage for the baby—and it indicates a healthy social development.

OBSERVING AND PARTICIPATING

Celebrating Individual Differences

Although all babies need to be loved, not all babies like to be held. Researchers have demonstrated that infants differ in the amount of physical contact they enjoy. Some are noncuddlers, who unfailingly protest, resist, and avoid any form of close and direct holding. Others love to be held and cuddled. Still others consent to be held, but only when tired or sick and only for a short time. Even noncuddlers, however, enjoy some types of physical contact. They may like to be tickled, kissed, or stroked, as long as they are not picked up and held close. What they don't like is having their movements restricted.

How Behavior Is Learned

An infant learns to behave in certain ways through his or her relationships with other people. What kind of behavior the baby learns depends primarily on the attitudes and expectations of the baby's parents and other caregivers.

Babies learn some behavior through their daily routine. Running water may signal bath time; the rattle of keys may mean a ride in the car. A baby begins to respond to these clues with predictable behavior.

As babies mature, they learn that certain kinds of behavior are rewarded with positive responses, such as smiles, hugs, or praise. Because love is very important to them, they begin to repeat behavior that brings approval. Babies also learn to avoid behavior that provokes negative responses, such as frowns or scoldings.

Babies are more sensitive to attitudes than to words. For example, if a mother says "no" as her ten-month-old blows food all over the high-chair tray, yet laughs at the same time, the baby thinks she approves. This kind of mixed message can be very confusing.

To help a child understand what behavior is expected, parents and caregivers must provide **consistency**, *repeatedly acting the same way*. Their responses, both verbal and nonverbal, should be consistent and should convey the same meaning. A baby will be confused if the same behavior provokes a positive response one time and a negative response the next, or if he or she continually receives mixed messages. Children react best to definite expectations. Parents and caregivers who often change their mind about expectations or who frequently switch moods make learning appropriate behavior difficult for their children.

To a very young child, everything is meant to be explored and played with. Only gradually does the child learn that not all behavior results in praise or approval.

Influences on Personality

As babies develop emotionally and socially, their personalities become increasingly evident. **Personality** is *the total of all the specific traits (such as shyness or cheerfulness) that are consistent in an individual's behavior*. To be consistent, the trait must be present over a period of time and in a variety of activities. For example, babies who always pick themselves up after a tumble and try again can be said to have the personality trait of determination or persistence.

There are many personality traits. Each trait can have many degrees. For example, a person might be described as somewhat shy or very shy. With all the possible traits and all the degrees of each, you can see why no two people are exactly alike!

GUIDED PRACTICE (continued)

Promoting Discussion

Let students share their responses to this statement from the text: "An infant learns to behave in certain ways through his or her relationships with other people." How is this true of infants? To what extent is it true of older children? Do you think it is also true of teens and adults? Encourage students to support and explain their ideas.

Critical Thinking

Ask students to suggest specific behaviors that parents might want to encourage in their eight- to twelve-month-old babies. What specific behaviors might parents want to discourage? What would be the most effective methods of discouraging those behaviors? Why?

Using the Photograph

Have students describe and discuss the situation shown in the photograph on this page. What is the baby doing? Why? How should the baby's parent or other caregiver respond to his behavior? Why?

Promoting Discussion

Ask students how each of the following situations involving an eleven-month-old might be handled inconsistently by a caregiver. Then ask them to suggest a better way of handling each situation.

- The child likes to play with the knobs on the television.
- The child likes to pull the leaves off plants.
- The child is interested in electrical outlets.
- The child often pushes his or her bowl of food onto the floor and laughs as the bowl falls.

Critical Thinking

Ask students how parents can make sure that a baby receives consistent responses to behavior from other family members and from other caregivers.

OBSERVING AND PARTICIPATING

Learning Through Participation

Encourage students to observe infants and notice indications of each baby's personality. If possible, invite several parents to bring their nine- to twelve-month-old babies to visit the class together. Have students observe the babies as they react to each other, to the new surroundings, and to the group of unfamiliar people. Also have them notice how the parents help

their babies feel comfortable. Make several appropriate toys available, and let the babies play with those they find interesting. After the visit, encourage students to discuss what they concluded about each baby's personality.

GUIDED PRACTICE (continued)

Promoting Discussion

Guide students in discussing their ideas about babies' personalities. Which do you think has a stronger influence on a baby's personality—heredity or environment? Why? How do you think a baby's personality is affected by the personality of his or her parents? Does that effect change if the parents are not the baby's primary caregivers? If so, how? If not, why not?

Critical Thinking

Encourage students to share and discuss their opinions in response to these questions: What kinds of expectations do you think parents usually have for their baby's personality? How can those expectations affect the baby? The parents? The relationship between parents and baby?

Using the Photograph

Ask students to describe the twins in the photograph on this page. How do they seem to be reacting to this situation? Would you guess that the twins have the same personality? Similar personalities? What reasons can you give to support your opinion?

Critical Thinking

Ask students what they think accounts for the wide range of personalities within the same family. Does a wide range of personalities usually make family life more or less enjoyable? Why?

Promoting Discussion

Let students suggest traits and behaviors that would typify the "ideal" personality for a baby. Record their suggestions on the chalkboard, and help students recognize that agreement on such a list is unlikely or impossible. Then have students recommend what parents and other caregivers might do to encourage each behavior and personality trait in a child. Which are beyond the control of parents and other caregivers? Why?

Some personality traits seem to be inborn. If you observed a group of newborns for a few weeks, you would see striking differences. One baby, for example, might be very active whenever she is awake; she waves her arms and legs and squirms almost constantly. A second baby might be very different; he lies quietly but cries at the slightest change in his surroundings. A third baby may be different from both of the others; he sleeps quietly, looks around, and rarely cries except when he is hungry.

Family and environment also play an important role in shaping a child's personality. Children tend to pattern themselves after their parents. They adopt some of their parents' likes and dislikes, many of their interests, and some of their ideas. Children may imitate their parents' mannerisms and share many of their attitudes.

In spite of this strong parental influence, a wide range of personalities is possible among children in the same family. Why? Part of the reason is that each child has a unique heredity and so responds in his or her own way to the same environment. Another part of the reason is that the family environment is slightly different for each child. Family experiences for the oldest child are clearly different from those for the youngest child. Middle children, too, have different and unique experiences.

Each child's personality is also influenced by his or her **self-concept,** *a person's feelings about himself or herself.* Self-concept, in turn, is strongly influenced by the way parents and other people regard and treat the child. Babies who are cared for, praised, and admired for their individual strengths are likely to develop positive self-concepts. Babies who are belittled or are often negatively compared with other children risk developing negative self-concepts.

Every baby seems to have a unique way of reacting to the world. Inborn differences may be part of the reason, but environment has a great deal of influence.

CLASSROOM MANAGEMENT

Cross-Reference

- Review pages 267-269 for the influence of heredity and emotional environment on a child's personality.

- See pages 283-285 for more about common personality traits.

Common Personality Traits

Each person has his or her individual personality, composed of a unique set of personality traits. However, it is common for certain clusters of personality traits to occur together. For this reason, people are sometimes considered as belonging to one of three main groups reflecting three general personality patterns. A baby's activity and behavior during the first months of life do not necessarily predict the adult personality that will develop. Still, understanding these personality patterns can help you understand and provide effective care for individual children.

The Sensitive Child

A **sensitive** child is one who, when compared with other babies, is *unusually aware of his or her surroundings and of any changes in those surroundings*. Sensitive children are often quite fussy and irritable as babies; they are more likely to cry and be difficult to comfort than other babies. Babies who cry a great deal, as sensitive babies usually do, need more than the average amount of love and tenderness. Unfortunately, their behavior often causes parents to withdraw rather than to respond with extra attention.

A baby who is easily startled and frightened is likely to become fearful of new experiences. Parents should encourage sensitive babies to explore and try new things. At the same time, parents should be especially patient and understanding with sensitive babies. In these ways, they can help their babies establish self-confidence.

The sensitive child needs more reassurance when introduced to new situations.

OBSERVING AND PARTICIPATING

Learning Through Participation

What can a person do with a newborn who is very sensitive, fussing at almost everything? If basic needs have been met and no physical problem is at fault, the baby may simply need less stimulation. Too many attempts at calming may be hindering rather than helping. For example, smiling at the baby and talking are fine, but together they may be too much. Moving the baby to a quiet room, gently caressing or rocking the baby, or wrapping the baby in a blanket may work. Using soft voices and slow movements may work, too. With a patient and gentle approach, the parent can gradually help the infant learn to handle more stimulation.

GUIDED PRACTICE (continued)

Critical Thinking

Encourage students to share and discuss their opinions about self-concept. How and when does a baby begin to develop a self-concept? How does a baby's self-concept affect his or her later development? Can an individual's self-concept change during childhood? During adolescence? During adulthood? If so, how? If not, why not? Who is responsible for a baby's self-concept? Who is responsible for an adult's self-concept?

Promoting Discussion

Ask students to explain how labeling a child's personality can be helpful. When and how can it be harmful?

Cooperative Learning

Let students work in small groups to list as many synonyms as possible for the words used to label the three basic personality types—*sensitive*, *placid*, and *aggressive*. Then have the groups compare their lists.

Making Connections: Art

Have students draw cartoons of three young children with the three common personality patterns.

Using the Photographs

Encourage students to describe and discuss the babies shown in the photographs on this page and on page 284. What indicators of personality patterns are evident in each photograph? How would you expect the daily activities of these babies to vary? What would you expect them to have in common?

Promoting Discussion

Let students share their ideas about differences in development among children with the three common personality patterns. How are the children likely to differ as preschoolers? Will those differences become more or less evident as the children mature? Why?

INDEPENDENT PRACTICE

Journal Writing

Have students write journal entries exploring their own ideas about personality. Pose the following questions to spark the students' thinking: How do both heredity and environment influence an individual's personality? Given those influences, what kind of control can an individual exert over his or her own personality? By the time an individual becomes a teenager, is his or her personality "set"? If so, why and how? If not, what kinds of changes are possible, and how can those changes be made?

Student Workbook

Have students complete "Hidden Word Puzzle" in the Student Workbook.

Extension

Let students work independently or in small groups to complete one or more of these extension activities:

• On a long sheet of butcher paper or computer paper, create a time line showing social development during the first year of life. Write a brief description of the milestones of social development for each month of the year. Then add drawings or photographs to illustrate those milestones. Display the time line in the classroom or in another part of the school.

• Read more about Harlow's experiments with monkeys, or research the attachments formed by Koko the gorilla. Consider what researchers have learned about social development through the study of animals. Write a brief report, summarizing your findings.

• Prepare and present demonstrations that show how a caregiver can effectively respond to the individual needs of three ten-month-old babies who typify the three basic personality patterns.

The Placid Child

A **placid** child is one who, when compared with other babies, is *remarkably easygoing and accepting of his or her surroundings.* The placid child is, for most families, the easiest personality type to live with. Placid children are less easily upset by changes in schedules and the demands of family life than any other personality type.

When a placid child gets older, he or she is usually cheerful and patient or simply quiet and willing. Placid children adjust easily to new people and situations. They make friends readily and seem to handle life with a minimum of fuss and upset.

Sometimes placid children can be "forgotten." Parents need to remember that these children need as much attention as sensitive and aggressive children.

The Aggressive Child

An **aggressive** child is one who, when compared with other babies, is *unusually strong-willed and determined.* The responses of aggressive babies are extreme. They eat more heartily, cry more

Aggressive babies have a way of reaching out and letting family members and caregivers know exactly what they want. These babies are usually more determined to have their own way.

Ethan seems content to examine a toy while he waits for his snack. How would you describe his personality?

COOPERATIVE LEARNING

Divide students into small groups and have them brainstorm a list of traits that describe each of the three personality patterns discussed on these pages. Challenge the groups to create a skit in which they are in charge of a child care center. They can assume that the infants under their care will exhibit all three personality traits. Ask them to describe how they would manage the infants under their care during different situations, such as feeding, naps, or playtime. What can they speculate about the training of child care specialists that helps them prepare for the demands they will face?

loudly, and kick more strenuously than sensitive or placid babies.

Aggressive babies love activity. They enjoy trying new things and are less likely than other babies to be concerned about failure. They simply pick themselves up and try again.

Aggressive children are especially likely to express anger when they do not get their own way or are frustrated. Parents and caregivers should try to react unemotionally to these outbursts and keep the child from hurting himself or herself and from hurting others. For example, substitute a soft toy for another object the child might want to throw, and keep your voice calm and reassuring. This is when a sense of humor really helps. "Oh my! What a silly clown—angry at everything!" Sometimes the tone of the adult's voice can help calm the child, too.

As time passes, you will want to acknowledge the baby's feelings, rather than discounting them, and help the child express anger and frustration with less extreme behavior.

Parents should remember that aggressive children need love, praise, and immediate attention—usually they can't wait. They also need help in becoming aware of the feelings and interests of other people.

SECTION 2 REVIEW

CHECK YOUR UNDERSTANDING

1. What are two signs of social development that many one-month-old babies exhibit?

2. What is attachment? What kinds of development do early attachments represent?

3. What is failure to thrive? What are two possible causes of failure to thrive?

4. What is stranger anxiety?

5. How do parents' smiles and frowns help babies learn good behavior?

6. What is personality? What are two important influences on personality?

7. What are the three general personality patterns that can be observed in babies? What is one characteristic of each pattern?

DISCUSS AND DISCOVER

1. Collect three photographs (from magazines or other sources) of babies exhibiting various types of social interaction. Write appropriate captions. Then display them, and explain how the caption relates to the infant's social development.

2. Talk with adults who knew you as a baby or a young child. Which type of personality did you have then? What specific behaviors indicated that personality type? Do you think you are still the same? Why or why not?

Observing & Participating

Play a few simple games with a baby who is approaching his or her first birthday. Notice how the baby responds to familiar games and toys and to new games and toys. Describe what the baby's responses indicate about his or her personality type.

SECTION 2 REVIEW

1. Stop crying when lifted or touched; faces brighten on seeing a familiar person.

2. A special strong bond between two people; it represents both emotional development and social development.

3. A condition in which a baby does not grow and develop properly; may be caused by a physical problem or by poor emotional and social care.

4. A baby's fear of unfamiliar people.

5. Babies repeat behaviors rewarded with smiles and avoid behaviors that provoke frowns.

6. The total of all the specific traits that are consistent in an individual's behavior. Any two: heredity, environment, self-concept.

7. Sensitive, placid, and aggressive; identified characteristics will vary.

ASSESS

CHECKING COMPREHENSION

Assign students to write their responses to the Check Your Understanding questions in the Section 2 Review. Answers to the questions are given at the bottom of this page.

EVALUATE

Have students complete the Chapter 9, Section 2 quiz in the TCR.

Reteaching

Work with small groups of students, guiding them in discussing the babies they have cared for, known, or observed. What changes in interactions and behaviors indicate that these babies are developing socially? How does the social development of each baby seem to be related to his or her emotional development? Which babies have exhibited stranger anxiety? How have parents and caregivers responded to signs of stranger anxiety?

Enrichment

Have small groups of students work together to plan and present dramatic sketches about families in which babies are deprived of emotional attachments and social interactions. Encourage the members of each group to explore the effects of these family situations, the causes of the problems, and possible solutions to the problems.

Extension

Invite a psychologist to speak to the class about self-concept. Suggest that he or she discuss questions such as these: Why is it important to foster positive self-concepts in young children? How can parents and other caregivers achieve this goal?

CLOSE

Give each student an opportunity to complete the following statement:

A baby's personality is ...

Encourage a variety of responses.

Positive Parenting Skills

Positive Parenting Skills

MOTIVATOR

Have students give examples of situations in which a teen shows trust, such as confiding a secret, arranging to meet someone at a certain time and place, or making friends in a new school. Ask them to suggest how trust is developed in these situations and why it is important.

Promoting Discussion

1. How does consistent care help build trust in an infant?

2. How does trust contribute to baby's development of a healthy self-concept?

3. Why is a parent or caregiver vitally important to the child's sense of trust?

Critical Thinking

Suppose that a baby receives unresponsive care, lacks familiar routines, and is continually placed in unfamiliar surroundings without sufficient reassurance. Ask students to speculate about the short-term effects of this situation. What would be the long-term effects?

Using the Photographs

Ask students to study the photos in this feature. How is each caregiver helping the infant develop a sense of trust? Ask volunteers to take the part of the adults in the photos and suggest what they might be saying to the infant shown with them.

Family Focus

Ask students to brainstorm a list of ways that a family can work together to develop an infant's sense of trust. What adjustments might family members make to achieve this goal? What resources are available to help a family?

HELPING BABY DEVELOP A SENSE OF TRUST

In the first year, babies are almost entirely dependent on other people. The kind of care they receive determines how babies begin to view themselves and the world around them. For every baby, the foundation of a strong, healthy self-concept is trust.

Responsive Care

A sense of trust begins to develop in newborns when they feel that their needs are being met. One of the most obvious ways to promote trust is to feed a baby who is hungry. Understanding and responding to the baby's emotional needs is just as important.

An infant who is upset or fussy needs to be soothed. However, a baby needs attention when he or she is content, as well. Here are some ways to let a baby know that you are responsive to his or her needs and wants:

- Hold and cuddle the baby often. Carry the baby close to you as you walk, both indoors and outdoors.

- When the baby is able to crawl, don't rely solely on a playpen. Give the baby the freedom to explore independently in a safe, accessible environment.

- Answer the baby's babbles and "funny noises" with your own noises, words, and sentences.

- Let the baby sense your caring and love in your facial expression, your voice, and your touch.

- Learn to read the baby's signals. When the baby smiles and coos, he or she might mean, "Let's play." Turning or looking away may be the baby's way of saying, "That's enough—time to rest."

- Calm an unhappy baby with close contact, rhythmic movement, and soothing sounds.

Your responsive care will help the baby feel secure. It lets the baby know that the world can be a satisfying place.

286

MORE ABOUT

A Sense of Trust

In dysfunctional families, especially families in which one or both parents abuse alcohol or drugs, children are unable to develop a sense of trust. Even babies in such families recognize that their needs are not being met or are being met inconsistently. As these babies grow into childhood and then into adolescence, they lack a reliable, caring adult—and this lack has a disturbing effect on their image of themselves and on their capacity to relate to other people. Children who have been raised in this kind of situation typically have poor self-concepts. Unless they receive special help, they may suffer lifelong difficulties in maintaining close relationships.

Family Routines

Following a consistent schedule is another way to encourage the baby's sense of trust. Babies seem to need a predictable daily routine in order to thrive. Start with the baby's unique pattern of eating, sleeping, and waking. Then you can work out a routine that makes sense for you and for the baby. For example, if you always hold the baby and sing to him or her after a feeding, the baby begins to learn what to expect. He or she will accept and look forward to that pattern of dependable care.

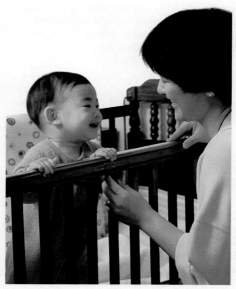

New Faces, New Places

Although it is important for babies to have a consistent routine, they must also learn to accept new situations. A parent or trusted caregiver can soothe away fears and help the baby feel secure in unfamiliar surroundings.

Most babies go through a stage of fearing strangers. During this period, don't force a baby to sit on an unfamiliar lap.

Instead, give the baby some time to get used to the new person's presence. Stay close by and show the baby that you trust this person.

You can help the baby get used to strangers by taking him or her to stores, parks, and other places where young children play. Talk to the baby about what to expect and about what is happening. Speak in a calm, reassuring voice.

Babies who have been helped to develop a sense of trust are happy, loving, and secure. They have the confidence to explore and to learn with enthusiasm.

287

Student Demonstration

Put students into pairs or small groups and have them create skits that portray a parent showing either trust or distrust when caring for an infant. Caution them to keep their choice a secret. When finished, have each group perform the skit in front of the class. Ask other students to indicate what they think the effect on the infant would be. Discuss any differences of opinion.

Journal Writing

Have students write "diary" entries from an infant's viewpoint, describing how the infant might react to caregivers, daily routines, and encounters with strangers. Encourage students to write about both positive and negative experiences an infant might have.

Extension

Have students observe caregivers and infants in various situations. Ask them to give a report to the class based on these questions: In what ways do you observe a sense of trust in the infant? Do you observe any situations in which a caregiver failed to respond in a way that would help the infant develop a sense of trust? If so, what suggestions would you have for alternative responses?

CLOSE

Have students recall the examples of trust they discussed in the motivator on the opposite page. How are these situations similar to that of an infant who is developing basic trust? How are they different?

TEEN PARENTING

Ask students to discuss their ideas in response to these questions: What might be the cause of a teenager's never having developed a sense of trust? What kinds of behavior would you expect from a teen who had never learned to trust others? How would an inferior sense of trust affect the teen's ability to care for a baby? What resources are available to help teens improve their emotional well-being? If possible, ask teen parents to share their experiences with dealing with the emotional demands of an infant. Encourage them to share the negative experiences as well as the positive ones.

CHECKING COMPREHENSION

Use the Summary and the Reviewing the Facts questions to help students go over the most important ideas presented in Chapter 9; encourage students to ask questions and add details, as appropriate.

1. Emotional development involves learning about self and feelings; social development involves interacting with others. Each influences the other.

2. A baby who is fed lovingly and comfortingly whenever he or she is hungry develops a sense of security and trust.

3. Provide an emotional climate at home based on affection and harmony; love and understand each child as an individual.

4. Crying may be caused by hunger, diaper needs, temperature problems, illness, pain, loneliness, or other needs for comforting. Caregivers should try to identify and solve the specific problem.

5. Babies develop specific emotions gradually; by the age of twelve months, they express delight, distress, anger, disgust, fear, elation, and affection. Smiles, other facial expressions, and cries express feelings.

6. Yes; respond to human voices.

7. Physical contact is an important factor in developing attachment.

8. They may suffer from failure to thrive.

9. Shows the baby recognizes and feels attached to familiar people; also indicates improving memory.

10. Repeatedly acting the same way; helps baby understand what behavior is expected.
   (continued next page)

SUMMARY

- Emotional development deals with feelings. Social development deals with relationships.
- The type of care a baby receives and the atmosphere of the home are major influences on emotional development.
- Babies' emotions gradually become more specific and recognizable.
- Babies develop socially to satisfy their physical and emotional needs.
- Physical closeness, interaction, and a strong attachment to parents or other caregivers are necessary for normal social development.
- Behavior is learned through relationships with others. Consistency on the part of caregivers aids this process.
- Each baby has an individual personality, although general personality patterns can be identified.

REVIEWING THE FACTS

1. What is the difference between emotional development and social development? How are the two kinds of development related?

2. How can a baby's feeding schedule affect his or her emotional development?

3. What can parents do to create the best possible climate for their children's emotional and social development?

4. Why do babies cry? How should parents and caregivers respond to a baby's crying?

5. How do babies learn about feelings? What emotions or feelings do they express? How do they express them?

6. Do babies show signs of social development during the first days of life? If so, what are the signs? If not, why not?

7. What did Harry Harlow's experiment with baby monkeys show?

8. How do human babies respond when they are denied emotional support and social interaction?

9. Why is stranger anxiety a sign of a baby's social development? What else does it indicate about the baby?

288

10. What is consistency? Why is it important in helping babies and children learn appropriate behavior?

11. What is self-concept? How can parents and caregivers help a baby develop a positive self-concept?

12. How would you expect a sensitive baby, a placid baby, and an aggressive baby to respond to a new, noisy toy?

EXPLORING FURTHER

1. Work with a partner to write "A Baby's Bill of Rights," a list of everything babies have the right to receive from their parents. Consider making your list into a poster and hanging the poster in a location where parents might see and read it. (Sections 1 and 2)

2. Gather at least five photographs of babies who seem to be expressing various emotions. Mount the photographs on posterboard. Label each picture with the words you think the baby might be saying—if only he or she could talk. (Section 1)

3. Work with a group of classmates to consider and discuss your responses to this question: How can parents select caregivers and child care centers that will encourage babies' emotional and social development? After you have all shared your ideas, work together to write a checklist that parents might use when they are evaluating caregivers and child care centers. (Sections 1 and 2)

THINKING CRITICALLY

1. **Analyze.** What do you think happens to a person who has never learned to build trust? How do you think that lack of trust affects the person's behavior when he or she is a school-aged child? A teenager? An adult? What special problems does he or she face in becoming an effective, loving parent?

2. **Evaluate.** Who do you think is best able to encourage a baby's emotional development—the mother, the father, another relative, or a nonrelated caregiver? Why? What particular advantages do you think each person has in encouraging a baby's emotional development? What disadvantages does each have?

CLASSROOM MANAGEMENT

Resources Beyond the Classroom

Child Development: Birth to One Year is a live-action video that examines the major physical, emotional, and intellectual stages of development for children from birth to elementary school. This program takes a look at the development of a child from birth to the toddler stage, including the five stages of development in an infant and how to recognize the signs which indicate an

infant has entered each new phase. For information contact:
Glencoe/McGraw-Hill
15319 Chatsworth Street
Mission Hills, CA 91345

3. **Interpret.** Why do you think the placid child is usually considered the easiest personality type to live with? What might be the characteristics of parents who would find raising a sensitive child more satisfying? What might be the characteristics of parents who would prefer to raise an aggressive child?

CROSS-CURRICULUM CONNECTIONS

1. **Health.** What happens to babies when their parents abuse alcohol or other drugs? Specifically, what effects does the parents' substance abuse have on babies' emotional and social development? Read at least three articles about substance abuse and its effects. Then consider what impact substance abuse typically has on family life and, in particular, on young children. Give a short oral report on your findings.

2. **Writing.** Write a short essay about your own personality. In the essay, identify the most significant traits within your personality. Also include your responses to these questions: Which of your personality traits do you consider inborn? Why? How do you believe your family influenced your personality? How do you believe other aspects of your environment influenced your personality?

SCHOOL TO WORK

Positive Attitude How well you get along with your employer and other employees will depend on the attitude you bring to the workplace. Think about how these questions apply to you: Do you smile easily? Can you accept responsibility for your mistakes? Are you considerate of other people? Do you complain easily? Are you quick to criticize others? Do you avoid eye contact with people? Often, people with a negative attitude have a difficult time keeping a job. The good news is that with some effort, a negative attitude can be changed to a positive one.

PERFORMANCE ASSESSMENT

Emotional and Social Development During the First Year

Task
Make a collage that illustrates common personality traits and explain how understanding these traits helps you better understand child development.

Purpose
Your collage will show that signs of personality traits are obvious in babies during the first year. Your explanation will show that you know how these traits influence behavior.

Procedure
1. With a partner, brainstorm a list of words that describe the three personality patterns discussed in the chapter.

2. Find pictures of babies or young children that match the words on your list.
3. On your own or with your partner, decide which personality traits you want to portray on your collage.
4. Make labels or headings for each trait.
5. Complete your collage by mounting the pictures under the headings that are appropriate. Give the collage a title, such as *Personality Traits*.
6. Write a description of the traits shown in the collage and explain why it is important to learn about personality patterns.

Evaluation
Your collage will be evaluated on its content, organization, and visual

presentation. Your explanation should demonstrate understanding of the different social and emotional traits that contribute to individual personality development during a baby's first year.

Portfolio Idea If the collage is too large for your portfolio, consider taking a photograph of it and writing a brief summary of your objective and results. You can make a two-sided presentation by mounting the photograph of your collage and the descriptive paragraph on the front and back of stiff cardboard or poster board.

11. A person's feelings about himself or herself; care for, praise, and admire a baby for his or her individual strengths.

12. Sensitive baby would probably be startled and shy away; placid baby would probably explore and then play with the toy; aggressive baby would probably grab it and make as much noise as possible.

EVALUATE

Use the reproducible Chapter 9 Test in the TCR , or construct your own using the Testmaker Software.

EXTENSION

Have students work in groups to make a videotape or a slide show of babies interacting with other people. Instruct the group members to add a narration to the tape or show, describing and discussing indications of the babies' social and emotional development. Give each group an opportunity to share its completed work with the rest of the class.

CLOSE

Go around the class, asking each student to suggest a goal parents might have for the emotional or social development of their infants.

DEVELOPING A PORTFOLIO

Accommodating Work Samples You may want to pre-determine the size of your students' Performance Assessment collages in order to meet size restrictions. Also, it may not be practical or appropriate to ask students to use a camera outside the classroom, and school or classroom finances may not include film and processing costs. A portfolio need not be costly to be well organized and visually appealing.

PERFORMANCE ASSESSMENT

Collage
Since this project will require many pictures, conduct a magazine collection drive prior to the activity. If necessary, brainstorm the list of personality traits with the entire class. Also, a review of the chart on pages 273-274, How Emotions Develop, will help students get started. When the collages are complete, have students present them to the class and read their explanations. Then display them in the classroom or around the school.

INTRODUCE

CHAPTER OVERVIEW

As they study Chapter 10, students gain an understanding of the intellectual development that takes place during the first year of a baby's life. They also explore the relationships between a baby's intellectual development and his or her physical, emotional, and social development, as well as the care and love the baby receives from parents and other caregivers.

Students begin Section 1 by considering the amazing learning that takes place during the first year of life. They go on to explore the basic functions of the brain and the relationship of mind and body in learning. Then students read about the learning theories of Swiss psychologist Jean Piaget and briefly examine the four stages of learning Piaget proposed. In the final part of this section, students consider the ongoing debate over the relative influence of heredity and environment in the development of intelligence.

In Section 2, students explore the important influence of parents and other caregivers on learning during the first year of life. They read about the importance of loving, responsive care in fostering learning, and they (continued next page)

CLASSROOM MANAGEMENT

Resources Beyond the Classroom

When shopping for baby equipment, look for those products that have been certified by the Juvenile Products Manufacturers Association (JPMA). These products have met strict testing standards and will carry a special JPMA certification mark. The safety certification program applies to such products as full-size cribs, strollers and also carriages; high chairs and hook-on chairs; and play yards. Have students evaluate play equipment and report back to the class on which items contained the certification.

Intellectual Development During the First Year

THINK ABOUT

While babies physically grow and develop during the first year, their ability to learn increases as well. Think about how your natural curiosity and the stimulation you receive from your environment help you learn. Then apply that same principle to the intellectual development of a child and think about what you can do to help children learn.

ASK YOURSELF

Look at the photo on the opposite page. How does the child's environment stimulate his senses? What can he learn from this play situation? Notice that he holds a blue ball in his left hand. What does this observation tell you about the connection between his mind and his body? What sounds do you think he is able to make? How would you determine if the child's behavior is considered average for his age?

NOW TRY THIS

Write a short story to read to the boy in the photo. Include the red, yellow, and blue balls as part of the story. Give the child a name and include him too. Remember that your story helps him learn about the relationship between words and objects in his environment. Read your story to a partner and explain how it encourages the child's intellectual development.

291

consider specific suggestions for promoting babies' interest in learning. Then students consider the role of toys in babies' learning and discuss the kinds of toys that are most effective in promoting learning. Finally, students read about babies' development of communication skills, including—but not limited to—the ability to talk.

CHAPTER OBJECTIVES

After completing Chapter 10, students will be able to:

- Describe intellectual development during the first year of life and summarize the learning theories of Jean Piaget.
- Discuss approaches and attitudes parents and other caregivers can use to encourage learning during the first year of life.

INTRODUCING THE CHAPTER

- On a large tray, arrange 12 or more common items. Give students two minutes to study the tray, and then cover it. Instruct them to list the items from memory. Encourage them to compare their lists, then guide them in discussing how they are able to remember facts and concepts in general. Ask them to speculate about how an infant's memory is developed. Explain that in Chapter 10 they will learn more about a child's intellectual development.
- Use the photo on the opposite page and the three features on this page—Think About, Ask Yourself, and Now Try This—to begin a discussion about a baby's intellectual development during the first year.

HEALTHY FAMILIES/HEALTHY CHILDREN

Building Healthy Families

When do couples stop dating—after they become engaged? Once they are married? Wise couples never stop dating and courting each other. Of course, "dating" may take on a different focus for married people raising children, but most happy couples know making time for each other and for themselves as a couple is necessary. Often, couples with young children feel they don't have the time or the money to go out. They can still spend special time together—picnicking in the living room while the baby is asleep, or watching a sunset. Many couples trade nights out with friends; one couple cares for the children from both families while the other couple spends quality time together. Couples who continue "dating" in these ways get extra enjoyment from their marriage and from their family life.

FOCUS

SECTION I RESOURCES

Teacher's Classroom Resources

• Enrichment 25

• Reteaching 25

• Section 1 Quiz

Student Workbook

• Hidden Word Puzzle

• Understanding Intellectual Development

SECTION OVERVIEW

This section presents basic information about the intellectual development of children, especially during the first year of life. Students learn about the mind-body connection and explore the stages of learning theorized by Swiss psychologist Jean Piaget. They consider the signs of intellectual development typical during the first twelve months, and review the influences of both heredity and environment on intelligence.

MOTIVATOR

Write the word *intellectual* on the board, and ask students what it means as an adjective and noun. Encourage a variety of responses.

Identify the definition students are most likely to connect with infancy: What intellectual development might babies experience? What—if anything—might a newborn "know" or "understand"? Does a six-month-old baby "think"? If so, how? Discuss ideas.

USING TERMS TO LEARN

Use all 12 vocabulary terms. Have students consider the two basic parts of egocentric—*ego*, meaning "self," and *centric*, meaning "centered on." Have them identify other words that begin or end with these word parts.

SECTION **1**

Understanding Intellectual Development

TERMS TO LEARN

attention span
cause and effect
central nervous system
concrete operations period
cortex
egocentric
formal operations period
object permanence
perception
preoperational period
sensorimotor period
symbolic thinking

OBJECTIVES

• Give examples of signs of intellectual growth in infants.

• Describe how a baby learns.

• Identify and give examples of Piaget's stages of learning.

Babies grow and develop especially rapidly during the first year of life. Along with his or her physical, emotional, and social development, a young baby experiences rapid intellectual development.

Learning Abilities During the First Year

Right from birth, babies have a number of capabilities. Newborns can hear, see, taste, smell, and feel. They use these abilities as the building blocks of learning.

Researchers still do not fully understand the complex process of learning. They have, however, discovered a great deal about how quickly and efficiently infants learn. Understanding the basics of the learning process will help you care for babies more effectively.

Consider the differences between a newborn and a one-year-old. The newborn knows virtually nothing; the one-year-old has an impressive store of knowledge. By the age of one year, the baby has learned how to:

• Move to a desired location by creeping, crawling, or walking.
• Understand some words and perhaps even say a few words.
• Make his or her wants known, primarily by gestures.
• Play simple games, such as peek-a-boo.
• Handle objects skillfully and manipulate them—put one object inside another, for example.

COOPERATIVE LEARNING

Cooperative Learning Groups

To ensure variety and heterogeneity among cooperative groups, try resorting occasionally to random selection measures. One simple method for randomly constituting a group is to place color-coded cards or stickers in a hat or box, as many color variations as there will be groups. Each student then selects a card or sticker, and students with like colors form a group. (An advan-

tage to using stickers in such a setup is that group members can wear them, at least initially, as group identification tags.) Whether you employ random measures or choose students according to a prearranged plan, try to vary constituency as much as possible over the course of the term.

The Mind-Body Connection

Newborns learn about the world primarily through their senses—sight, hearing, smell, taste, and touch. The blanket feels soft and fuzzy. A fist or a finger tastes different from milk. Mother's heartbeat sounds familiar.

For babies, as for all humans, information is transmitted from the senses through the nerves into the **central nervous system**, which consists of *the spinal cord and the brain*. The sensory information moves through the spinal cord into the brain.

The brain is the key to intellectual development. It receives and interprets the messages from the body. Gradually, the brain also develops the ability to send messages to the body, telling the body what to do. (In general, the responses of a newborn are physical reflexes; they do not originate in these kinds of messages from the brain.)

The brain is divided into distinct sections, each controlling specific functions. The major sections are identified in the diagram below. By the second or third month, the baby's **cortex**, *the outer layer of the brain, which permits more complex learning*, is clearly better developed than it was at birth. **Perception**, or *learning from the senses*, has improved, too.

Memory also begins to develop in the first few months of life. The information from the senses can be crudely interpreted

HEALTH TIP

Most babies love to be rocked, and rocking has a variety of benefits—including a benefit for the baby's brain. Gentle rocking stimulates the cortex of the brain. This stimulation helps the baby gain weight, develops the baby's sight and hearing, and promotes regular sleep habits.

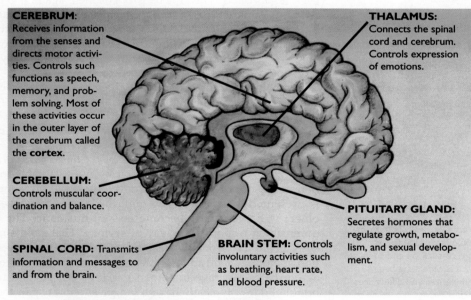

CEREBRUM: Receives information from the senses and directs motor activities. Controls such functions as speech, memory, and problem solving. Most of these activities occur in the outer layer of the cerebrum called the **cortex**.

CEREBELLUM: Controls muscular coordination and balance.

SPINAL CORD: Transmits information and messages to and from the brain.

BRAIN STEM: Controls involuntary activities such as breathing, heart rate, and blood pressure.

THALAMUS: Connects the spinal cord and cerebrum. Controls expression of emotions.

PITUITARY GLAND: Secretes hormones that regulate growth, metabolism, and sexual development.

Each area of the brain has specific functions to perform.

MORE ABOUT

The Brain

The right and left hemispheres of the brain allow it to divide its work. The left brain is responsible for speaking, writing, and understanding language. It excels at math, rhythm, analytical skills, and coordinating complex movements. People with a left-brain preference are likely to favor subjects such as math, management, law, and engineering. The right brain, once thought to be less important than the left, is superior at spacial tasks, perception skills, nonverbal communication, and visualization. Right-brain thinkers tend to favor subjects such as music, art, oral communication, and architecture. Although one hemisphere may dominate, both are necessary for functioning in everyday tasks. The left brain controls sequential thinking, whereas the right brain processes holistically. Each hemisphere does its part and shares information with the other, resulting in a complete pattern of thinking.

TEACH

Pages 292-303

- Learning Abilities During the First Year
- The Mind-Body Connection
- Piaget's Theories
- Heredity Versus Environment

GUIDED PRACTICE

Promoting Discussion

Encourage students to share their own experiences with babies in comparing the abilities of a newborn with those of a baby celebrating his or her first birthday.

Making Connections: Psychology

Ask students to read about methods researchers use to study the learning process. Then let students share their findings with the rest of the class.

Critical Thinking

Point out that according to the text, "the newborn knows virtually nothing." Ask students to explain what they think this means. Is a newborn lacking in intelligence? Why or why not?

Using the Diagram

Go over the diagram with students, reading about the function of each brain area. Encourage students to add to the information there, giving specific examples of activities controlled by each area.

HEALTH TIP

Let students work in small groups to collect pictures that illustrate other activities controlled by different areas of the brain. Encourage them to use the information in the Positive Parenting Skills feature, "Creating a Stimulating Environment," on pages 312-313 as part of this activity. Then have group members work together to plan and carry out an interesting presentation of their pictures.

GUIDED PRACTICE (continued)

Making Connections: Physiology

Have students conduct research on the cerebral cortex and its relationship to cognitive thought. What is the relationship between an animal's intelligence and the complexity of the animal's cortex? How does the complexity of the human cortex compare with that of the cortex of other animals? Give students an opportunity to share and discuss their findings.

Cooperative Learning

Have students work in small groups to identify toys and activities that help infants learn cause-and-effect relationships. Ask group members to list their ideas; then have the groups compare and discuss their lists.

Critical Thinking

Let students share their ideas in response to this question: How would you expect a developing awareness of cause and effect to influence a baby's behavior?

Using the Photograph

Encourage students to describe and discuss the baby in the photograph on this page. What is she doing? What has she already learned in order to be capable of playing with this toy? What is she learning by playing with this toy? Do you consider this an "educational toy"? Why or why not?

Critical Thinking

Encourage students to discuss their ideas in response to these questions: What do you think accounts for the short attention span very bright individuals have during infancy? Why do you think these individuals usually have a longer-than-average attention span after infancy? Do you think an individual can consciously increase his or her attention span? If not, why not? If so, how? Would increasing his or her attention span make the individual more intelligent? Why or why not?

By seven months old, babies have an understanding of cause and effect. They will drop objects and delightfully watch them fall to the ground.

When this little girl was six months old, she would have used these colorful rings to suck on and squeeze. Now that she is older, she begins to recognize similarites and differences and can stack the rings according to size.

in light of past experiences. A two- or three-month-old baby may stop crying when someone enters the room because the baby knows that he or she is now likely to be picked up and comforted. This simple act—the baby's ceasing to cry—also indicates association. The baby associates his or her parent or other caregiver with receiving comfort.

In these first few months, babies also begin to develop an understanding of **cause and effect**, *the concept that one action results in another action or condition.* When a baby closes his or her eyes, it gets dark. When the baby opens them again, it gets light. A baby can reach out a hand and feel a soft, warm surface. Sucking causes milk to flow. If the baby stops sucking, the milk stops. In short, when the infant does something, something else happens, and it happens consistently. Gradually, the baby develops some awareness of such control.

As babies' motor skills develop, cause-and-effect learning changes. By seven or eight months, babies can throw things deliberately. They can pull the string on a toy and make the toy move. At this age, babies have a better understanding of their own power to make certain things happen.

A baby's **attention span**—*the length of time a person can concentrate on a task without getting bored*—gives valuable information about his or her intellectual development. If the same object is presented over and over again, the baby's response to the object will eventually become less enthusiastic. The baby's diminishing response is a way of saying, "That's old stuff. I've seen it before." Generally, very bright babies have a short attention span; they tend to lose interest sooner than babies of average or below-average intelligence. (However, beyond infancy, bright children typically have a longer attention span than others their age.)

HEALTHY FAMILIES/HEALTHY CHILDREN

Building Healthy Families

For many years, the responsibility of understanding and promoting the development of a child, especially an infant, rested primarily with the mother. The father's role was to give the mother support. Today, however, the father's role is changing. Family structures include single fathers, part-time fathers, and dual-career families. Fathers in these situations often share in the care of the children. Some have sole responsibility for children all or part of the time. Even in the more traditional home where the father is employed and the mother is a homemaker, many fathers are taking an active role in child care. To be equipped for their increased involvement with their children, males need to understand how children develop. Only with this information can they make the most of their role as fathers.

AVERAGE INTELLECTUAL DEVELOPMENT

BIRTH TO TWELVE MONTHS

ONE TO TWO MONTHS

- Follows moving objects with eyes.
- Gains information through senses.
- Prefers faces to objects.
- Cries to indicate needs.
- Can distinguish between familiar and unfamiliar voices.

THREE TO FOUR MONTHS

- Recognizes caregivers' faces.
- Can distinguish between familiar and unfamiliar faces.
- Grasps objects that touch hand.
- Tries to swipe at objects.
- Interested in own hands and feet.
- Practices making sounds.
- Responds when caregiver talks.
- Smiles and laughs.

FIVE TO SIX MONTHS

- Is alert for longer periods of time, up to two hours.
- Reaches for objects and grasps them with entire hand.
- Studies objects carefully.
- Looks for objects that are dropped.
- Plays peek-a-boo.
- Recognizes own name.
- Distinguishes between friendly and angry voices.
- Makes sounds to indicate pleasure and displeasure.

(Continued on next page)

OBSERVING AND PARTICIPATING

Developing Observational Skills

As they study the chart above, encourage students to share their own ideas and experiences. Which of these developments have you observed in an infant? How did you respond to the development? Why? Which specific development do you imagine parents find most significant? Why? Which specific developments might make the job of a parent or caregiver easier? More difficult? More rewarding? Under what specific circumstances should parents use the chart as a general guideline only? How should parents make adjustments for babies who are premature or have special needs? What is the significance of the toys pictured on the chart? How do you think each toy relates to a baby's intellectual development during the given age range?

GUIDED PRACTICE (continued)

Using the Chart

With the class, go over each period on the chart. As appropriate, remind students that each sign of development is listed at an average age; this chart is not intended as a checklist for determining how bright a baby might be.

Promoting Discussion

Help students discuss the importance of memory as a prerequisite to developing such concepts as cause and effect. What part does memory play in the development of concepts? Which abilities listed in the Average Intellectual Development chart relate directly to memory?

Cooperative Learning

Let students work in groups to discuss how routine care activities might change in response to a baby's intellectual development. How does the baby's ability to express his or her own needs change? How does the baby's ability to comprehend and respond to the actions and attitudes of the caregiver change? Why is it important for the caregiver to change in response to these developments?

Practicing Decision Making

Ask students to imagine that they have been caring for a baby one afternoon a week for several months. The baby, Ella, is now eleven months old. Ella is unusually quiet, and she does not appear to recognize her own name. She can hold toys, but she does not reach for them or spend time studying new objects. What concerns would you have about Ella's development? Why? Would you discuss your concerns with anyone else? If so, with whom?

Promoting Discussion

Encourage students to consider and discuss the intellectual development typical of a twelve-month-old. How does the rate of development during the first twelve months of life compare with the rate of development during later periods of life? Why? What do you think explains this change in the rate of development? Would it be possible to maintain a child's intellectual development at the same rate at which it progresses during the first year? Why or why not?

Cooperative Learning

Have students work in small groups to compare the intellectual development of a newborn with that of a one-year-old, drawing from their own experiences with babies and from the text. Then have group members work together to plan and present a brief dramatic sketch, illustrating how family life changes in response to an infant's intellectual development.

Making Connections: Psychology

Ask students to theorize how a psychologist might attempt to measure the intelligence of an infant. Then have students investigate actual infant intelligence tests to see what kinds of behaviors are measured. How do the findings relate to the intellectual skills listed in the Average Intellectual Development chart?

Making Connections: Writing

Write the word *intelligence* on the board and circle it. Draw a larger circle around the first circle. Ask students to suggest related words that come to mind when they think of intelligence. Write these words in the larger circle. Then have students use ideas generated in the brainstorming exercise to write a paragraph explaining their own ideas about intelligence.

AVERAGE INTELLECTUAL DEVELOPMENT (cont'd.)

SEVEN TO EIGHT MONTHS

* Imitates the actions of others.
* Begins to understand cause and effect.
* Remembers things that have happened.
* Smiles at self in mirror.
* Sorts objects by size.
* Solves simple problems.
* Recognizes some words.
* Babbling imitates inflections of speech.

NINE TO TEN MONTHS

* Searches for hidden objects.
* Handles medium-sized objects skillfully.
* Takes objects out of containers and puts them back in.
* Plays pat-a-cake.
* Responds to some words.
* May say a few words.
* Obeys simple commands or directions.

ELEVEN TO TWELVE MONTHS

* Manipulates objects skillfully.
* Likes to look at picture books.
* Fits blocks or boxes inside one another.
* Knows parts of body.
* Can pick up small objects with forefinger and thumb.
* Recognizes many words.
* Speaks some words regularly.

MORE ABOUT

Growth and Development

Guide students in discussing the relationship between intellectual development and physical development. Remind them that this relationship might change as a result of both external and internal influences as an individual grows older. For example, a child who becomes seriously ill may not be able to keep up with his or her former pattern of growth and development. Critical injuries affect not only a child's physical growth but also emotional and social development, which, in turn, results in a reluctance, or inability, to grow intellectually. External influences, such as emotional stress in the home, physical or psychological abuse, or the presence of substance abuse in the home, could have an impact on a child's development, either directly or indirectly. Ask students to volunteer additional factors that could influence development, and suggest possible ways to deal with each situation.

Piaget's Theories

Jean Piaget, a Swiss psychologist who died in 1980, had a remarkable influence on what we know about how children learn. His theories of learning and the research they inspired have helped us better understand and appreciate infants and children.

While investigating the development of intelligence, Piaget found that children's responses fell into patterns according to their age. This timetable seemed to control the development of intellectual skills. Piaget believed it suggested that the capacity for logical thought is not learned, but is determined—along with such characteristics as eye color and sex—in the genes. These capacities do not mature, however, until they are used.

Children cannot be forced by parents or teachers to develop understanding any faster than their abilities mature. This is why, in nearly every case, it is a waste of effort to try to teach a two-year-old to read. On the other hand, children who do not get the chance to apply their developing abilities and test their limitations may never reach their full intellectual ability.

According to Piaget, learning stages appear in the same order in all children. What differs is the ages at which the stages develop, although average ages can be given. He identified four major periods of development and gave them these names: sensorimotor period, preoperational period, concrete operations period, and formal operations period.

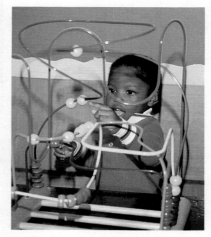

The Sensorimotor Period

The **sensorimotor period** is *Piaget's first stage of learning, lasting from birth until about the age of two, during which babies learn primarily through their senses and their own actions.* During this period, a baby is completely **egocentric**, *thinking only about himself or herself.*

During the sensorimotor period, usually around the age of ten months, a baby develops the concept of **object permanence**, *an understanding of the fact that objects continue to exist even when they are not in sight.* At four months, Maria drops her rubber ring toy and it rolls behind her. She shows no concern; she looks for something else to play with. By eleven months, Maria's memory has improved a great deal. When her ball rolls out of sight, she actively looks for it. She also looks for her favorite stuffed animal when she feels lonely. It is clear that she has learned the concept of object permanence.

The sensorimotor period can be broken down into six shorter stages. At each stage, a baby has specific intellectual abilities. The chart on page 298 explains the stages within the sensorimotor period. It will help you better understand how early learning occurs.

SAFETY TIP

During the later stages of the sensorimotor period, babies' curiosity often leads them to put things into their mouths and to try opening whatever is closed, including doors, drawers, and cabinets. Although curiosity helps the baby learn, safety is of the utmost importance. Anything dangerous must be kept out of a baby's reach. During this period, it is especially important to keep dangerous or poisonous materials locked away; baby-proof locks should be added to most other cabinets.

MORE ABOUT

Jean Piaget

Although Jean Piaget (1896-1980) spent most of his later life researching the mental development of children, his early years were devoted to biology. While studying mollusks, he noted how they changed structurally from one generation to another. This led him to conclude that biological development was a result of environment as well as heredity. He theorized that organisms adapt to the environment as they develop. This idea later carried over into his study of mental development. Human intellectual development, he concluded, is also a process of adaptation. According to Piaget, the mind not only reacts to experiences but also changes accordingly.

GUIDED PRACTICE (continued)

Promoting Discussion

Guide students in discussing Piaget's theories of intellectual development, and help them compare intellectual development to motor skill development. How does the concept of readiness relate to each kind of development? How do encouragement and practice relate to both?

Making Connections: Psychology

Encourage students to do further reading about the work and theories of Jean Piaget. Have them share their findings with the rest of the class.

Promoting Discussion

Help students recognize and define the words *sensory* and *motor* in the term *sensorimotor*. Ask why Piaget used this name for the first period of development.

Then help students consider the egocentricity of infants. Why is a baby egocentric? Is egocentricity in an infant positive or negative? Are older children, teens, and adults also egocentric? To the same degree as infants? Why or why not? Is egocentricity in an adult usually considered positive or negative? Why?

SAFETY TIP

When visiting friends or relatives that do not have babies, parents and caregivers are wise to call ahead and remind others of the particular stage that their child is in. That way, others will have time to adequately prepare a safe and secure place for the baby to play.

GUIDED PRACTICE (continued)

GUIDED PRACTICE (continued)

Promoting Discussion

Guide students in discussing the concept of object permanence. How do you imagine the development of this concept affects a baby? How does it probably affect a baby's parents and other caregivers? Why? What relationship can you identify between the concept of object permanence and the development of stranger anxiety?

Using the Chart

Help students study and discuss the information in the chart on this page. What changes take place during each stage of the sensorimotor period? How do you imagine these changes affect a baby's relationship with his or her parents and other caregivers?

Cooperative Learning

Let students work in groups to find or draw pictures illustrating the activities of children during each of the six stages of the sensorimotor period. Then have group members use their pictures to make a visual display of development during this period.

Critical Thinking

Ask students to identify the approximate age at which children begin to imitate others. Then let them share their ideas in response to these questions: What are some of the positive attitudes and behaviors young children learn through imitation? What are some of the negative attitudes and behaviors they learn that way? How can parents and other caregivers encourage positive learning through imitation?

Making Connections: Reading

Have students analyze children's stories for the behaviors and concepts proposed by Piaget. For example, Winnie-the-Pooh by A. A. Milne is a good example of egocentrism. Give students an opportunity to share their analyses with classmates.

When a toy is out of sight, an infant will simply find a new interest. By four months, however, the memory has improved and the baby will actively look for favorite objects.

THE SENSORIMOTOR PERIOD

BIRTH TO AGE TWO

STAGE	APPROXIMATE AGES	CHARACTERISTICS
Stage 1	Birth to one month	• Practices inborn reflexes. • Does not understand self as separate person.
Stage 2	One to four months	• Combines two or more reflexes. • Develops hand-mouth coordination.
Stage 3	Four to eight months	• Acts intentionally to produce results. • Improves hand-eye coordination.
Stage 4	Eight to twelve months	• Begins to solve problems. • Finds partially hidden objects. • Imitates others.
Stage 5	Twelve to eighteen months	• Finds hidden objects. • Explores and experiments. • Understands that objects exist independently.
Stage 6	Eighteen to twenty-four months	• Solves problems by thinking through sequences. • Can think using symbols. • Begins imaginative thinking.

OBSERVING AND PARTICIPATING

Learning Through Participation

To help a baby learn the concept of object permanence, caregivers can play hiding games. Each game should be played over a period of days or weeks until the baby learns to look for and find the hidden object. First, try placing a special toy (a teddy bear, for example) partway under a small blanket. When the baby learns to find the toy, start putting it completely under the blanket while the baby watches. Once this discovery is mastered, let the baby watch as you hide the toy in ways that are increasingly more complex. The baby may find the toy in an open container, under a box, or in a sack.

The Preoperational Period

The **preoperational period** is *Piaget's second stage of learning, lasting typically from age two to age seven, during which children think about everything in terms of their own activities and in terms of what they perceive at the moment.* Since their intellectual processes are not fully developed, during the preoperational period children may believe that the moon follows them around, or that dreams fly in through the window at night. A child in this stage may think that 8 ounces (237 mL) of water becomes "more to drink" when it is poured from a short, wide glass into a tall, thin glass. The child sees that the water is higher in the second glass and concludes that there must be more of it.

In the preoperational period, children begin to understand abstract terms like *love* and *beauty*. Concentration, though, is limited to one thing at a time. A child cannot think about both pain and the softness of a kitten at the same time, for example. Children this age tend to solve problems by pretending or imitating, rather than by thinking the problems through. You can observe many examples of this "pretending" behavior in children this age. For example, if a toy has been broken or the water has been left running, a young child may blame the mistake on an imaginary friend, saying with complete conviction, "Georgia did it." In many cases, children at this period may not even be aware of what is real and what is make-believe.

Children in the preoperational period love to act out situations like playing firefighter. However, they have trouble thinking about things that they aren't experiencing at the moment.

MORE ABOUT

Intellectual Development

The intellectual development of infants and small children was ignored until the 1920s. Children were considered miniature adults, who were less intelligent simply because they had not yet acquired knowledge. The work of researchers led to the discovery that children think and learn in ways that are distinctly different from adults, and that intelligence develops in a predictable pattern based on age. The stages of intellectual development identified by Piaget are apparently paralleled by the growth of the brain. The brain grows rapidly during the first half of each stage, signaling the appearance of important new functions. During the latter half of each stage, growth levels off until the next stage is reached.

GUIDED PRACTICE (continued)

Promoting Discussion

Encourage students to consider and discuss the learning processes of children in the preoperational period. What are other "misconceptions" children of this age are likely to have? What are some of the other abstract terms they may begin to understand? What are the implications of their limited concentration during this period?

Cooperative Learning

Let students work in groups to identify abstract concepts that would be difficult for young children to understand. Then have group members work together to plan activities that can help children learn these concepts through direct experience. Give the members of each group an opportunity to demonstrate at least one of their activities for the rest of the class.

Promoting Discussion

Let students share and discuss their own ideas about imaginary friends. What do you think having an imaginary friend indicates about a child? Why? If you were the parent of a four-year-old with an imaginary friend, how would you respond? Would your response change if the child still had an imaginary friend at the age of ten? In what way?

Using the Photograph

Let students describe the activities of the children in the photograph on this page. How old do you think these children are? What are they doing? Why? What do you imagine they are learning? Do you think a teacher or caregiver should respond to their activity? If so, how? If not, why not?

Critical Thinking

Why is the distinction between real and make-believe important to older children? To teens? To adults? Do you think this distinction matters to children in the preoperational period? Why or Why not?

GUIDED PRACTICE (continued)

Promoting Discussion

Ask students to summarize the differences between learning during the concrete operations period and during the formal operations period. What are the implications of those differences for parents, teachers, and others who encourage children's learning?

Cooperative Learning

Let students work in groups to list decisions that require abstract thinking; have them focus on decisions, plans, and goals commonly faced by teens. Then have the groups share and discuss their lists.

Promoting Discussion

As students consider symbolic thinking, ask them why it is unfair to expect this kind of thinking from young children. What are the implications for using verbal instructions with young children? What are more effective methods of guiding the learning and behavior of young children?

Using the Photographs

Encourage students to describe and discuss the activities of the children in the pictures on these two pages. In what stage of learning are the children? What are the clues to that stage?

Promoting Discussion

Ask students to review the definitions of *heredity* and *environment*, if necessary. Then encourage them to share their own ideas about the influences of heredity and environment on intelligence. How concerned should parents and teachers be with the influence of heredity on a child's intellectual abilities? With the influence of environment on those abilities?

Critical Thinking

Let students share and discuss their ideas in response to these questions: Why do most people never develop their full potential for learning? Do you think this fact represents "a waste," or do you consider it "just normal"? Why?

Pretending and imitating are the tools that young children use to understand their world.

The Concrete Operations Period

The **concrete operations period** is *Piaget's third stage of learning, lasting usually from seven to eleven years of age, during which children are able to think logically but still learn best from direct experiences.* When problem solving during this stage, children still rely on actually being able to see or experience the problem. However, logical thinking is possible. Children understand that pouring water from one container to another does not change the amount of water. They can also comprehend that operations can be reversed. For example, subtraction will "undo" addition, and division is the reverse of multiplication. During this stage, children also learn to make more complex categories, such as classifying kinds of animals or types of foods.

The Formal Operations Period

The **formal operations period** is *Piaget's fourth stage of learning, lasting from about age eleven through adulthood, during which children become capable of abstract thinking.* In other words, people in this stage are able to think about what might have been the cause of an event without really experiencing that cause. This ability allows problem solving just by thinking. Abstract thinking also allows adolescents to make more realistic future plans and goals. They do not automatically accept everything that they hear or read; instead, they are able to think things through critically and logically. Adolescents can also form ideals and understand deeper, less obvious meanings or subtle messages.

OBSERVING AND PARTICIPATING

Learning Through Participation

Babies in Stages 4 and 5 of the sensorimotor period seem to have a fascination for hinged objects. This makes opening and closing cabinet doors one of their favorite games. In response to this, one understanding mother turned over a low cabinet in the kitchen to her child. The toys kept inside belonged to the child. Even a few plastic kitchen bowls and cups were included in the cabinet's treasures. Eventually, the child learned which cabinet was hers and which ones were to be left alone. For safety reasons, of course, the mother never placed dangerous chemicals or objects in any of the cabinets.

Applying Piaget's Ideas

Although Piaget's theories have been criticized by some for setting boundaries of learning stages too rigidly, his work revolutionized our understanding of child development. He focused attention on the intellectual development of infants, an area of study previously ignored. He drew attention to the importance of developmental steps that researchers continue to study today.

Piaget's work shows that adult intelligence has its origins in infancy. However, his work also shows that attempts to impose adult ideas or understanding on children are bound to fail. Why? Older children can learn through **symbolic thinking**, *the use of words and numbers to represent ideas.* Younger children, who have not yet developed symbolic thinking, rely on concrete experiences. For example, the statement "I have three balls" means nothing to a young child. The child has to see the balls. A further example is the fact that a three-year-old will hold up three fingers when asked how old he or she is, even though the child may say the words, too. The preschool child needs lessons presented with objects or activities, not just symbols. Verbal instruction from a teacher or parent has only a minor role in learning during the early years.

The abstract concept of "three" has no meaning for a young child unless it is associated with something concrete—like three balls or three fingers.

MORE ABOUT

Intelligence and Intelligence Testing

While Piaget was developing his theories on mental development, other researchers were looking for ways to measure infant intelligence. Arnold Gesell and Nancy Bayley, American psychologists, are two of the pioneers in this field. The Bayley Scales of Infant Development is one respected test developed by Bayley and her associates. The use of infant intelligence tests is not without controversy. Studies have indicated that they seem to be more useful in identifying infants with developmental problems than in predicting intelligence in childhood.

INDEPENDENT PRACTICE

Journal Writing

Ask students to write journal entries exploring their own ideas about the periods of learning defined by Piaget. Encourage them to respond to one or more of these questions as they write: Which period of learning do you consider most important? Why? If you are planning a career that involves teaching or working with children in other ways, which learning period would you most like to work with? Why? Which period do you think poses the greatest challenge to parents? Why? How do you imagine the differences in learning periods might affect relationships among siblings? How do you think an understanding of these four learning periods affects you in your understanding of yourself and of other people?

Student Workbook

Have students complete "Hidden Word Puzzle" and "Understanding Intellectual Development" in the Student Workbook.

Extension

Let students work independently or in small groups to complete one or more of these extension activities:

- Find and read at least one magazine or journal article about the study of infant attention spans. Write a one-page summary of the article, and share your summary with the rest of the class.

- Write a letter to (or arrange to interview) a child development specialist. Ask one or two specific questions about the specialist's own experiences as they relate to Piaget's theories. Then report to the rest of the class on what you have learned.

- Read about recent research into the influence of heredity and environment on intellectual development. Summarize your findings in a brief oral report.

Issues and Advice

1. According to Dr. Hilliard, what three capabilities does a newborn have? (*To see, hear, and organize sensory information.*)

2. What pattern of response do infants demonstrate? (*They seek order in their environment.*)

3. When a baby feels comforted and nurtured, what is encouraged? (*Expressiveness and exploration.*)

4. What must parents and caregivers supply to create a sense of trust? (*Enough comfort and stimulation.*)

5. What does Dr. Hilliard advise parents to trust when caring for a baby? (*Their own instincts.*)

Thinking Like an Expert

Dr. Hilliard's recommendation that parents "trust their own instincts" raises an interesting question. What instincts do parents and caregivers have? Self-help books and support groups are available to parents, so we might get the impression that instincts are not as accessible as they should be.

Have students survey parents representing children of various ages and stages in response to these questions: What instincts did you recognize when you first became a parent? What instincts surfaced that you did not realize were present? Where do you think these instincts came from? Did you ever turn to authorities such as doctors or child care experts because you were completely unable to resolve a situation concerning your actions or role as a parent? Did you ever discover that expert advise closely resembled your intuition? How do you use expert advice now as opposed to during your initial parenting experience? Have students discuss their findings.

ASK THE EXPERTS

Infants' Perception

Q. **What can you tell me about how infants perceive their world?**

A. This is an especially interesting question, and our response to it has changed in recent years.

We now recognize that infants come into the world with the ability not only to see and hear what goes on around them, but also with the ability to organize the information they receive from their senses. Young babies are clearly able to select from their environment the things they find interesting; they are further able to operate on those things until they become familiar with them. Infants demonstrate a definite pattern of seeking order in their environment.

Emotionally, infants who are cared for and nurtured apparently feel very comfortable and very free. These feelings encourage the babies' expressiveness and exploration.

Parents and other family members must provide the infant with enough comfort and enough stimulation to allow the baby to feel trusting. When parents allow themselves to respond openly and lovingly to their baby, when they trust their own instincts in caring for their baby, they can provide an incredible push to the infant's awareness and opportunity to learn.

Asa Hilliard, Ph.d.
Fuller E. Callaway Professor of Urban Education at Georgia State University

Heredity Versus Environment

As you know, there is continuing disagreement about the influences of heredity and environment on the development of children. Much of the heredity-environment debate focuses on intelligence. In the past, intellectual ability was thought to be determined mainly by a child's inheritance—bright parents had bright children. However, findings now indicate that a child's environment can actually increase or decrease his or her intelligence.

HEALTHY FAMILIES/HEALTHY CHILDREN

Building Healthy Families

Busy parents often worry about not spending enough time with their children. Since time is often at a premium, it must be used wisely. Here are some suggestions that can help:

• Schedule a little time each day for the child to have the undivided attention of a family member. During this time, turn off the television and remove any other distractions. (Even people who spend large amounts of time around children sometimes give them very little personal attention.)

• Let a household task go undone, if possible, or involve the child. For example, if you must fold clothes, put the baby beside you in a seat and play peek-a-boo with the towels.

• Ask other caregivers to give your child some one-on-one time when you are not around. Child care workers may be doing this already, but it will help if they know you expect it.

It is true, however, that limits for intelligence are present at birth. Even the most stimulating environment cannot raise a person's intelligence beyond that limit. Most people, though, never develop or use their full potential (the highest level of learning possible for an individual). Understanding how intellectual development progresses and how babies learn can help you guide children toward fulfilling their potential.

Both heredity and environment influence intelligence. The influence of heredity is determined before birth. Environmental influences begin before birth, but continue to affect development throughout life.

SECTION 1 REVIEW

CHECK YOUR UNDERSTANDING

1. List at least three things that the average one-year-old child can do because of the learning process.
2. What is the central nervous system? What is its most important function?
3. What is perception? How does a baby's perception change during the first year of life?
4. Explain what an attention span is.
5. What is the name of Piaget's first stage of learning? How do babies learn during this period?
6. What is the name of Piaget's fourth stage of learning? What is the most significant accomplishment during this period?
7. What did Piaget's work show about adult intelligence?

DISCUSS AND DISCOVER

1. Define and then discuss the importance of object permanence. How do you think the development of object permanence affects a baby's behavior? How do you think it affects the baby's parents or caregivers?
2. Explain how Piaget's description of intellectual development can be compared with motor skills.

Observing & Participating

Watch as an infant explores and begins to play with a new toy. Describe how he or she responds to the toy. What does he or she try to do with it? With what results? Use Piaget's theories to determine if the child's behavior is appropriate for his or her age and stage of development.

SECTION 1 REVIEW

1. Any three: move to a desired location by creeping, crawling, or walking; understand some words and perhaps even say a few words; make his or her wants known; play simple games; handle objects skillfully and manipulate them.
2. The spinal cord and the brain; to transmit information to the brain, interpret that information, and send messages to the body.
3. Learning from the senses; improves rapidly.
4. The length of time a person can concentrate on a task without getting bored.
5. Sensorimotor period; babies learn primarily through their senses and their own actions.
6. Formal operations period; development of an ability to think abstractly.
7. That adult intelligence has its origins in infancy.

ASSESS

CHECKING COMPREHENSION

Assign students to write their responses to the Check Your Understanding questions in the Section 1 Review. Answers to the questions are given at the bottom of this page.

EVALUATE

Have students complete the Chapter 10, Section 1 quiz in the TCR.

Reteaching

Work with small groups of students; guide them in collecting, analyzing, and organizing pictures that illustrate intellectual development at various stages, from birth through twelve months.

Enrichment

Have students plan, write, and illustrate a brochure for new parents. The brochure should help parents understand what kinds of learning and intellectual development to expect during their baby's first year; students should select and present the information they consider most important and useful.

Extension

Ask a small panel of experienced parents and/or teachers to speak with the class. Have panel members describe some of their own experiences working with children in the sensorimotor and the preoperational periods (and, if applicable, in the concrete operations and formal operations periods). How has an understanding of these periods of learning affected their ability to work successfully with young children? How has working with young children affected their understanding of Piaget's theories?

CLOSE

Ask each student to complete the following sentence, either orally or in writing:
During the first year of life, a baby learns …

FOCUS

SECTION 2 RESOURCES

Teacher's Classroom Resources
- Enrichment 26
- Reteaching 26
- Section 2 Quiz

Student Workbook
- Toy Evaluation
- Is This Home Safe?

SECTION OVERVIEW

In Section 1, students explored the theories of learning; in this section, they read about practical techniques to encourage learning during the first year of life. Students explore ways in which attentive care and specific forms of interaction can foster learning in babies. They go on to consider toys and their uses in learning, noting which kinds of toys are appropriate for babies of various ages. Finally, students learn about the process by which babies communicate and begin learning to speak.

MOTIVATOR

Prepare a display of infant toys, including perhaps a crib mobile, a wind-up musical toy, a rattle, a set of stacking rings, and a soft stuffed animal. Give students an opportunity to examine and handle the toys. Then guide them in discussing the toys. How would a baby play with each of these toys? At what age do you think a baby would be ready to notice each toy? To handle it? How might the kinds of playing change as the baby grew and developed? What would a baby learn from playing with each toy?

Conclude the discussion by pointing out that these and other baby toys are more than "just fun"—they are tools for helping infants learn.

SECTION 2   Helping Babies Learn

OBJECTIVES

- Discuss ways parents and caregivers can help babies' intellectual growth.
- Identify toys appropriate for a baby's age.
- Explain how babies develop communication skills.

Like physical, emotional, and social development, intellectual development of an infant is closely linked to the responsiveness of others. That is, babies learn more and learn faster when parents and caregivers comfort them, smile at them, talk to them, and play with them. A baby treated this way is likely to be brighter than a similar child who does not receive loving, attentive care. Parents are babies' first and most important teachers.

Providing Care

Even the youngest babies learn about the world from the care they receive. A newborn who feels hungry expresses that feeling by crying. When a parent hears that cry, picks up the baby, speaks soothingly, and feeds the baby, that uncomfortable hunger goes away. If parents and caregivers respond this way whenever the baby feels hungry and cries, the infant learns that all these events are related. There is a consistent pattern— discomfort, crying, parent or caregiver, feeding, and comfort.

If this pattern is not established, the baby senses no relationship between his or her expression of discomfort and the comfort provided by a parent or caregiver. Perhaps the baby's hunger cries are often ignored. Perhaps the baby is fed on a strict schedule decided by someone else and not related to the baby's own sensations. In these cases, there is no predictable pattern for the baby to learn.

OBSERVING AND PARTICIPATING

Celebrating Individual Differences

In an effort to provide a baby with activities that promote development, some parents get carried away. They are so eager to have their babies accomplish new skills that they become almost competitive with other parents and babies. Babies should not be pressured to learn new things. They need to learn at their own pace. Stimulation is important, but simple activities are best. Complex activities can cause confusion and frustration. Eager parents should realize that time spent with their babies will soon be only a memory. It is far better for everyone to enjoy each moment as it comes. Given love and encouragement in a relaxed environment, a normal baby will develop naturally.

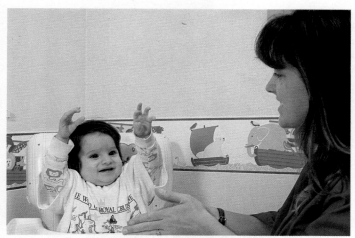

Babies who receive loving care and attention are more likely to approach their full potential, in learning as well as in other areas of development.

When babies receive attentive care in response to their individual needs, they learn that their behavior has consequences, that they can affect and change their environment. This care and learning, in turn, motivates babies to learn more about the world.

Encouraging Learning

Those who care for children have a real influence on the children's intellectual development. Encouraging learning does not require money or special toys. Rather, it depends on the attention, knowledge, and time of parents and other caregivers. Here are some specific suggestions for encouraging learning:

- **Learn about child development.** Understanding how an average child develops can help you provide learning experiences that are appropriate for the age and individual needs of a child.

- **Give your time and attention.** No baby needs attention every waking moment. However, you can help a baby thrive—and learn—just by talking to the baby and playing simple games with him or her.

- **Provide positive feedback.** When the baby demonstrates a new skill or tries out a new activity, show your pleasure and respond with praise. Your reaction will encourage the baby to keep trying new things.

BUILDING SELF-ESTEEM

Encouraging Safe Exploration

Babies need a secure environment in which they can explore freely. Parents and other caregivers should encourage this exploration. However, their first consideration should be that the baby is safe from dangerous situations and materials. You can use the Positive Parenting Skills "Keeping Children Safe and Healthy" on pages 344-345 to make sure that a home or living area is safe for an infant.

TEACH

Pages 304-311

- Providing Care
- Encouraging Learning
- Toys—The Tools of Learning
- Developing Communication Skills

GUIDED PRACTICE

Cooperative Learning

Let students work in small groups to role-play situations that involve providing care for young children. Ask group members to explore attitudes and approaches beneficial to baby development and motivation.

Promoting Discussion

As students consider the specific suggestions for encouraging learning, ask these questions: Which of these suggestions do parents most often neglect? Why? Which suggestion would be easiest for you to follow? Why? What are some games parents and other caregivers can play with four-month-old babies? With ten-month-old babies? What specific things can parents and other caregivers do to provide positive feedback for infants?

Using the Photograph

Encourage students to describe the baby in the photo on this page. What kind of attention is she receiving? What makes this attention appropriate to her age, her development, and her mood? How does she appear to be responding? What is she learning about herself? Her mother? Her world?

BUILDING SELF-ESTEEM

Help students discuss the importance of loving, responsive care for infants. Remind them that often, parents are faced with demands that limit the time they can spend with baby. Ask: How can routine care be turned into a nurturing experience that encourages learning?

COOPERATIVE LEARNING

Remind students that a child will have difficulty learning a language, or learning it properly, if he or she is not exposed to it. To practice ways of improving language stimulation in the home, put students into small groups and have each one demonstrate a way to implement one of the following activities: spending quiet time talking and listening to a child; providing a variety of language types; reading; talking out loud while they perform daily chores, describing their thoughts and actions; repeating the sounds and noises that the baby tries to make; and talking out loud to the child, describing what the child is seeing, doing, or hearing. Encourage the groups to think about and explain how they would vary their activities according to different age groups and different stages of development.

GUIDED PRACTICE (continued)

Promoting Discussion

Encourage students to discuss their responses to these questions: Why should babies be in the same room with other family members as much as possible? What can parents and other family members do to make this easier for everyone involved? Under what circumstances should a television program be substituted for the company of busy family members? Why?

Critical Thinking

Let students share and discuss their opinions. How might trying to keep the home neat stifle a baby's curiosity? Should the baby's needs always take priority over the appearance of the home? Why or why not? If not, under what circumstances should the appearance of the home be given priority?

Using the Photograph

Give students an opportunity to describe and discuss the baby in the photo on this page. What would a child learn from a balloon that floated away? That popped?

Promoting Discussion

Refer students to the statement on page 303 that "most people never develop or use their full potential." What are the implications of this fact for parents and others who want to encourage learning in young children? What is the difference between helping children develop potential and pushing children beyond their limits? How can parents and other caregivers distinguish between the two?

Ask students to share memories about common toys and games when they were young. Have they remained popular today? What variations are noticed across time, cultures, and social groups?

Take a look at everything that is going on in this scene. What sights, sounds, and other sensations does the child experience? How does taking a child to new places enrich learning?

TOYS ACROSS TIME AND CULTURES

Toys are more than "just fun" for children. Throughout time and across cultures, toys have helped children learn and kept them entertained. Even cultural differences can be noted in toys from several hundred years ago. Balls are a good example. Prehistoric children amused themselves with smooth, rounded stones. The Egyptians made balls from painted wood, or colored leather or reeds. The Celts made balls filled with air from bladders of sheep. The Japanese used tissue paper and string to construct their balls. The materials common to the region where the families lived were used to make the toy. In each case, a child's cultural environment influenced the type of ball constructed.

• **Express your love.** Use your personal style to show your love for the baby. You'll be helping the baby grow self-confident and encouraging him or her to try more—and to learn more.

To encourage learning, allow the baby as much freedom of movement at home as possible. In the first few months, this may involve moving the baby from room to room to be with the family. A baby who spends times in different rooms and has the companionship of family members can experience and learn more than a baby who is kept in a crib most of the time. Older babies who can crawl or walk should not be restricted to playpens for long periods of time. It is better to childproof as much of the home as possible and to monitor the child's activities. Learning occurs best when children can explore and try new things.

The Positive Parenting Skills on pages 312-313 presents more ideas for creating a stimulating environment and helping babies learn.

Toys—The Tools of Learning

Ten-month-old Beth sits on the kitchen floor, thumping a spoon against the bottom of a saucepan. She has discovered her own "educational toy." With it, she learns that a certain action will produce a particular sound. She delights in the sound and in her own power to produce it.

OBSERVING AND PARTICIPATING

Learning Through Participation

Of all the toys for babies, one ranks high above the rest. It makes noise and moves. It is creative and fascinating. When baby plays with it, it responds. Best of all, it costs nothing. What is it? A person!

People are like toys to a baby. Notice how babies peer intently at faces, reach for noses, grab at earrings, and laugh at silly faces. Family members can "teach" a baby an imitation game. When baby coughs, sister imitates the sound. Later, baby will learn to cough to start the game. People create all sorts of games to play with babies. They provide the kind of interaction that no real toy can replace.

For children, play is work as well as pleasure. Researchers have found that playtime is not aimless or wasted. Rather, playtime is essential to intellectual development. Toys are the tools with which a child learns.

Play is also a physical necessity through which growth and development take place. When a baby shakes a rattle, stacks blocks, throws a ball, or chews on a teething toy, the activity is not just for amusement. These are serious, absorbing tasks through which babies strengthen their muscles, refine their motor skills, and learn about the world.

Different Toys for Different Ages

Because babies mature and change rapidly during the first year, their toys need to change, too. Here are some ideas about appropriate toys for different stages:

- **Birth to three months.** A baby at this age can do little except look and listen. Bright colors and interesting sounds stimulate development of the senses. A mobile hung above the crib is interesting for the baby to watch. The baby's random arm and leg movements can set the objects in motion and produce sounds. Brightly colored crib liners, wallpaper, and pictures also provide interest.

- **Four to six months.** The sense of touch is important during this period. Babies need things to touch, handle, bang, shake, suck, and chew. Choose toys that are small enough to handle easily but too large to swallow. All items and pieces should be at least 1½ inches (3.8 cm) across. Teething rings, cups, rattles, and plastic toys are good choices. Stuffed toys are fun to touch, and toys that squeak give results for the baby's actions. At this age, babies like simple picture books. Choose washable books with colorful pictures of familiar objects.

- **Seven to nine months.** Babies still need things to handle, throw, pound, bang, and shake. Anything that makes a noise fascinates babies of this age. They enjoy blocks, balls, large plastic beads that pop apart, and roly-poly toys. Safe household items are just as interesting as store-bought toys. Stacking toys, pots and pans with lids, and plastic containers make great playthings.

- **Ten to twelve months.** Babies of this age need things to creep after. Those who are already walking like toys to push or pull. During this period, children especially enjoy toys to manipulate. Baskets, boxes, and other containers are fun. Babies like to put things into them and then dump them out again. Simple books are good for looking at alone or for brief storytimes during the day or before bed.

Infants are just as happy to be playing with simple household objects like these as expensive toys. Be sure, however, that all playthings are safe and suitable for the baby's age.

MORE ABOUT

Toy Selection

Offer the following questions as a basic checklist when shopping for toys:

- Is the toy safe for my child's age?
- Does the toy have lasting play value, or will my child be bored quickly?
- Does the toy stimulate creative involvement from my child?
- Is it well-constructed, or can it be easily destroyed?
- Does it challenge my child's ability, or is it frustrating to use?
- Will the toy grow with my child?
- Can the toy be used in different ways? Can it be used creatively?
- Will the toy expand my child's knowledge beyond the toy itself?

GUIDED PRACTICE (continued)

Critical Thinking

Ask students to express—and support with specific examples—their opinions about the following statement: "For an infant, all toys are educational toys."

Promoting Discussion

As students consider the importance of play in a baby's life, ask these questions: How much should a baby be encouraged to play independently, with a toy or with household objects? How much should a baby be encouraged to play with a parent, caregiver, or sibling? Are the responses to these questions the same for all babies? Why or why not? What different kinds of learning can the baby experience in these two different situations?

Cooperative Learning

Let students work in small groups to list specific kinds of learning that take place while a baby plays.

Using the Photograph

Have students describe the "toys" that have been made available to the baby in the photo on this page. How does she appear to be responding to these toys? What can she learn from looking at these household objects? What can she learn from handling and manipulating them? What can she learn from the response of a parent or caregiver to her chosen form of play?

Using Management Skills

Have students use pictures from magazines and catalogs to make a display of toys intended for babies of various ages, from birth to twelve months. Then guide students in discussing and evaluating the toys. Which of the toys encourage babies to participate and become involved in play? Which provide practice of appropriate skills? Which could be easily replaced by common household objects? After the discussion, ask each student to select the three toys he or she considers worth buying for a baby.

GUIDED PRACTICE (continued)

Promoting Discussion

As students consider communication skills, encourage them to respond to: How are communication skills related to a child's physical, emotional, social, and intellectual development? How do young babies communicate? What do they learn about communication from the way parents and other caregivers respond to their cries? Why is it important to talk to a baby who does not yet understand words?

Cooperative Learning

Let students work in small groups to practice talking to a baby. Have each group member take a turn handling and talking to a life-size doll, using clear words and complete sentences rather than "baby talk." Encourage the other group members to offer suggestions and constructive criticism.

Promoting Discussion

Give volunteers an opportunity to act out gestures that an infant might use to communicate. Let other students guess the intended meaning of each gesture. Help students discuss why nonverbal messages can be misinterpreted. What advantages might a parent or regular caregiver have in interpreting a baby's nonverbal communication?

Making Connections: Music

Discuss what babies might learn from listening to music. How might the kind of music affect a baby's learning? Ask students to suggest musical pieces they would play for infants and to give reasons for their choices.

Choose toys that are appropriate for the child's age and development. Once children start to walk, they enjoy push toys.

SAFETY TIP

Common household objects often make the best toys for babies, but they must be chosen carefully. Never allow a baby or young child to play with plastic bags; small objects that could be swallowed; any objects that might splinter, tear, or break; or any sharp or pointed objects.

When choosing playthings for a young child, look for toys that encourage participation and use. Younger children need simple toys. As a baby's abilities increase, toys can be more complex.

Toys, especially those labeled "educational," can be expensive and may be limited in their function and usefulness. You can provide a baby with as much fun and learning by making common household items available. Try offering the baby items such as these: plastic measuring spoons, a set of plastic or metal measuring cups, a clean bucket, a set of plastic bowls, a metal pan or mixing bowl and a large spoon, a large cardboard box with a "window" cut in it. You may be surprised at the variety of ways young children play with these items.

When you do buy toys, try to choose those that will remain interesting and appropriate for a number of years. A set of blocks is a good example. At the age of six months, Reuben grasped and inspected his blocks. By his first birthday, he could stack several blocks into a tower. At age three, he used the blocks to make roads for his cars. Now, at age six, Reuben creates elaborate houses and castles, using every available block.

Developing Communication Skills

One of the major tasks for infants is to learn to communicate effectively with others. This skill depends on development in all areas—physical, emotional, social, and intellectual. There are wide differences in the rate of development from baby to baby. However, a normal baby should show steady improvement in communication skills.

SAFETY TIP

Parents and caregivers can keep baby preoccupied and safe as they work in the kitchen by filling a floor-level drawer with playthings. Safe household items, such as plastic kitchen objects, and a few favorite toys will make baby feel involved in the daily activities!

HEALTHY FAMILIES/HEALTHY CHILDREN

Health and Safety

Assign small groups of students to investigate safety regulations for infant toys, furniture, equipment, and/or clothing. Look for the answers to one of these specific questions: What agencies are responsible for establishing safety regulations? How do these agencies decide what the regulations should be? What are the current regulations for specific products? How are products tested for safety? What happens when a product fails to meet safety standards? What are the dangers when buying used baby toys, furniture, clothing, and equipment? Have the groups report their findings to the rest of the class. Then have them design and produce a pamphlet, poster, or video about safety regulations. These materials can be made available to local child care facilities and parent groups.

PARENTING IN ACTION

Learning in the Park

Seven-month-old Tina sat in a playpen beside a park bench. Her mother was nearby, helping Tina's four-year-old sister play on the swing and the slide.

Tina watched them from time to time, but she gave most of her attention to a red plastic cup. She turned the cup over and over, staring at it intently. Then she started chewing on the bottom, the rim, and the handle of the cup. Occasionally, she stopped chewing for a minute and banged the cup on the bottom of the playpen.

After a while, Tina grew tired of chewing and banging. She dropped the cup and began pulling herself up to a standing position. When she succeeded, she clung to the edge of the playpen and laughed happily. Tina's mother turned and smiled

appreciatively. "Look at you, Tina," she called.

Tina sat down suddenly. She looked for a moment as if she might cry. Then, she reached up and tried to stand again. Over and over, she pulled herself up, stood for two or three minutes, and then lost her balance.

Finally, Tina sat down with a particularly loud thump. She had had enough of standing, and there was nothing new to play with. Bored, Tina began to cry.

"I'm coming, Tina," answered her mother. A moment later, she was lifting Tina out of the playpen and chatting happily about the swings and slides. "Look, Tina, there goes Laurel down the slide. See what your big

sister learned today? One day you'll learn to go down the slide, too."

THINK AND DISCUSS

1. What were Tina's learning experiences in the park? What stage of the sensorimotor period do her experiences reflect?
2. What toy did Tina play with? How did that toy facilitate her learning?
3. What did Tina's mother do to encourage Tina's learning? What else do you think she should have done? Why?
4. Compare what Tina learned during her time in the park with what her older sister Laurel learned.

Communicating Without Words

Babies communicate long before they are able to talk. By the end of the first year, even without words, they can effectively make most of their needs and wants known.

Crying is a baby's first means of communication. Discomfort automatically causes crying. Someone usually responds to the baby's cries and attempts to relieve the discomfort. Within a month or so, the baby's crying takes on a pattern. A cry is followed by a pause to listen for reactions. If no response is obvious, the baby resumes crying.

OBSERVING AND PARTICIPATING

Learning Through Participation
Few accomplishments are awaited with greater anticipation than a baby's first recognizable word. Caregivers can promote language development in these simple ways:

• Use the baby's name often.
• Point to and name family members and facial features (nose, eyes, mouth). As the baby grows older, identify other parts of the body and ask questions like, "Where is your nose?"

• Play games like "peek-a-boo," "wave bye-bye," and "clap your hands."
• Talk about what is going on around you as though the baby understands.
• Hold and describe safe, interesting, familiar objects.
• Imitate the baby's babble, and encourage the baby to imitate new sounds that you make.

Promoting Discussion
Introduce this selection by encouraging students to discuss the photograph. How old is the baby? What is she doing? Is she learning anything? If so, what? What factors in her environment are encouraging—or discouraging—learning?
Have students read the selection and then share their responses to the people and situations.

Thinking Critically
Many people see children of all ages in the park and think, "It's nice to see children just having a good time. After all, they shouldn't spend all their time learning." Ask students how they would explain to such people that children who are playing are doing more than "just having a good time."

Answers to Think and Discuss
1. She examined and manipulated the cup; banged the cup to make noise; pulled herself up to stand. Tina appears to be in Stage 3 of the sensorimotor period; she is improving hand-eye coordination, and acts intentionally to produce results.
2. A red plastic cup. She explored the cup with her eyes, hands, and mouth, and she used it to make noise.
3. She provided a safe, stimulating setting and an appropriate toy; she responded when Tina cried and talked to her about the events. Encourage various responses to the second question.
4. Ask for discussion of ideas about what each girl learned, who "learned more," and which sister experienced the "more important" kind of learning.

GUIDED PRACTICE (continued)

BUILDING SELF-ESTEEM

Remind students that to infants, what a person says is not as important as how it is said. An animated, loving speaker stimulates language response from the infant, which, in turn, pleases the speaker. Everyone benefits!

INDEPENDENT PRACTICE

Journal Writing

Ask students to complete the following sentence:

In my opinion, helping an infant learn is …

Then have students use their completed sentence to begin a journal entry, expressing their own feelings and ideas about the task of encouraging learning during the first year of life.

Student Workbook

Have students complete "Toy Evaluation" and "Is This Home Safe?" in the Student Workbook.

Extension

Let students work independently or in small groups to complete one or more of these extension activities:

• Read about the research on positive feedback and reinforcement. Report your findings to the class, explaining how these techniques affect intellectual development.

• Evaluate three or more "educational" toys for infants. For what ages is each toy recommended? How developmentally appropriate—or inappropriate—is the toy for babies in that age range? Prepare and share a report of your evaluations.

• Read about the research conducted by B. F. Skinner or by another researcher who has studied children's language development. Plan and present a brief report, summarizing your findings.

BUILDING SELF-ESTEEM

Talking Is Fun!

When parents and caregivers spend time talking with infants, they are helping infants to learn about their environment. Talking together is a wonderful way to build feelings of security, too. During the first few months of life, infants seem to enjoy the attention and close contact involved in having adults talk to them. As they grow older, infants begin to focus more on the words they hear. They may begin to respond to language with their own sounds and babbling. A back-and-forth pattern of talking and listening can develop between a caregiver and an infant. This pattern encourages the baby's language development.

The baby soon develops different cries for different problems. A cry indicating hunger is interrupted by sucking movements. A cry of pain may include groans and whimpers. Those providing care can usually identify the baby's problem by the type of cry.

A baby also communicates by making special sounds. Some noises just provide practice in the use of the voice. The nonsense syllables of babbling, for instance, help the baby learn to make sounds needed for speech. Other sounds, such as giggles, grunts, and shrieks, carry obvious messages.

Babies also communicate effectively with movements and gestures. It's clear a wiggling baby just does not want to get dressed. An eleven-month-old who pushes away a bowl of usually favorite food has had enough to eat. A baby who clings with both arms to a parent's leg is showing a sure sign of fear or shyness. The use of gestures continues into adulthood, but they are used more to reinforce words than as a substitute for words.

Learning to Speak

Before a baby can learn to talk, he or she must learn to associate meanings with words. This is a gradual process. It depends on the parents and other caregivers talking to the baby, even when the baby doesn't appear to respond. For example, when you take a baby for a walk, you can talk about what you see. Use simple words, but not baby talk. Tell the baby the names of

When you talk to an infant and identify names of objects, you are laying a good foundation for the child's speech development.

MORE ABOUT

Communication Skills

Some experts believe that a child's capacity to develop language skills is inborn and genetically determined. These theorists cite research to show that individual children acquire language at different rates and with different levels of skill, regardless of their environments.

Other experts believe that language is acquired by interacting with the environment. Social-learning theorists believe that children learn communication skills by modeling or imitating adults.

These different theories reflect the more general questions regarding the influence of heredity and environment. Although both theories have merit, neither fully explains how children develop language skills.

everyday objects. Although the infant won't understand much of what you say, you are beginning to establish an important habit. Listening to other people talk—especially directly to him or her—is essential for an infant's language development.

A newborn, of course, is physically unable to speak. Over the first year, physical changes take place that allow the baby to make the sounds necessary for speech.

Babies get ready for real speech by babbling—repeating syllables and sounds. You may have heard babies endlessly repeating consonant and vowel sounds such as "mamamamamama" or "gogogogo." This kind of babbling is a baby's preparation for saying recognizable words. Adults can encourage this babbling—and thus encourage language development—by responding to and imitating the baby's sounds.

A child's first real words are usually understandable between the ages of eight and fifteen months. Because the infant typically has been babbling and coming close to real word sounds for some time, it isn't easy to know exactly when a specific word is purposely spoken. First words are usually common, simple words that have special meaning for the baby, such as "mama," "dada," or "bye-bye." Most children don't have a large vocabulary or combine words into simple sentences until after their first birthday.

SECTION 2 REVIEW

CHECK YOUR UNDERSTANDING

1. What do very young babies learn when they receive consistent, attentive care?

2. How does expressing love for a baby help that baby learn?

3. What kinds of toys are appropriate for babies from birth until around the age of three months? Why?

4. What do babies around the ages of ten to twelve months enjoy doing? What kinds of toys are appropriate for them?

5. Before they learn to talk, do babies communicate? If so, how? If not, why not?

6. What is babbling? What is its purpose?

DISCUSS AND DISCOVER

1. Visit toy stores or look through catalogs, and identify six different toys for infants. Evaluate and compare the toys, considering appropriateness, appeal, and price. Which of the toys would you buy for a baby? Why?

2. Why is consistent, attentive care so important for a baby? Do you believe babies who spend time in child care centers or with babysitters can receive that kind of care? If so, how? If not, why not? Discuss with other students.

3. Explain how communication skills are related to a child's physical, social, emotional, and intellectual skills.

Observing & Participating

Observe a parent or caregiver playing with a six- to nine-month old. Describe what the adult does to engage and encourage the baby. How does the baby respond? What do you think the baby is learning through this experience?

SECTION 2 REVIEW

1. That their behavior has consequences, that they can affect and change their environment.

2. Helps a baby grow self-confident and encourages him or her to try more and to learn more.

3. Toys that a baby can watch and hear, without having to manipulate them at all; at this age, babies can do little except look and listen.

4. Enjoy creeping after toys or walking with toys, manipulating toys, and looking at books. Push- or pull-toys; baskets, boxes, and other containers; simple books.

5. Yes; babies communicate by crying, by making special sounds, and by using movements and gestures.

6. Repeating syllables and sounds; to prepare babies for saying recognizable words.

ASSESS

CHECKING COMPREHENSION

Assign students to write their responses to the Check Your Understanding questions in the Section 2 Review. Answers to the questions are given at the bottom of this page.

EVALUATE

Have students complete the Chapter 10, Section 2 quiz in the TCR.

Reteaching

Work with small groups of students and guide group members to discuss specific ways in which parents and other caregivers influence a baby's intellectual development. Then have each student list the ten tips he or she considers most important for parents to keep in mind as they encourage a baby's intellectual development.

Enrichment

Ask students to read about babies who grow up in bilingual homes, learning two languages at once. What advantages do these babies have in the acquisition of communication skills? What disadvantages do they face? Have students summarize their findings in reports to be shared with the class.

Extension

Arrange to have several parents bring babies to class. Ask parents to discuss their babies' means of communicating—crying, other sounds, babbling, and/or words. Encourage parents to explain the processes by which they have learned to understand their babies' messages; also ask them to describe their responses to their babies' communication. If appropriate, let each parent and baby have a "conversation" while students observe.

CLOSE

Let the students suggest sentences they might say to a two-month-old baby during feeding, diapering, or bathing activities.

Positive Parenting Skills

MOTIVATOR

Assemble several objects mentioned on these pages, such as infant toys, plastic containers, a record, and brightly colored pictures. Ask students what these objects and the class members have in common. (*They all can provide an infant with stimulation.*)

Promoting Discussion

1. Why are environment and heredity important influences on a child's development?

2. Why is providing a stimulating environment important?

3. What important safety points should be observed when providing stimulation?

Using the Photographs

Ask students to look at the photos in this feature. How are the baby's senses being stimulated in each case? What is each baby learning? What can students speculate about the appropriateness of the stimulation in each photo? What stimulation can a person provide that a toy cannot?

Childhood Reflections

"A child's world is fresh and new and beautiful, full of wonder and excitement."

Rachel Carson

Critical Thinking

Have students think about the impact of too little stimulation on a baby. What can occur if the baby receives too much stimulation? Ask: How can parents and other caregivers know whether the right amount of stimulations is being given? (*By observing the baby's responses and rate of learning.*)

CREATING A STIMULATING ENVIRONMENT

Babies begin learning the moment they are born. Parents and other caregivers influence both what and how a baby learns. They can offer a variety of appropriate experiences that will help the baby use his or her natural learning abilities fully. Here are some suggestions for helping infants develop their senses and abilities.

Stimulating an Infant's Senses

Establishing a good learning environment is a natural part of providing loving care for an infant. Holding, cuddling, gentle stroking, and soft singing all stimulate an infant's senses. Very young babies should have something interesting to look at, but

just one or two things at a time. Simple shapes and bright or contrasting colors attract babies' interest. If you are decorating a special room or area for a baby, try to use colorful decals, posters, pictures, crib sheets, or wallpaper.

A mobile hung over the crib provides both color and movement for the baby to watch.

You can also hold a bright toy not far from the baby's face and then move the toy slowly, letting the baby's eyes follow it.

Infants like human faces even better than colorful pictures or toys. Let the baby look into your eyes as you hold and play with him or her.

Providing Tactile Objects

You can also stimulate learning by surrounding the baby with interesting things to touch. Offering a variety of textures is more important than providing a great number of toys. Stuffed toys can have different textures, from a furry teddy bear to a simple cotton

312

OBSERVING AND PARTICIPATING

Learning Through Participation

Parents and caregivers who pay close attention to the individual infant find many ways to make a baby's environment stimulating.

• Babies learn with all their senses. Some seem to respond to one sense more than another. If the baby is more excited by music than pictures, caregivers may want to provide more sound stimulation.

• Appeal to a baby's sense of sight by hanging pictures about a foot away. Infants prefer curved and rounded shapes and sharp contrasts to muted colors. Many respond to pictures of faces. Change pictures often to provide visual stimulation.

• Some toys let infants experience results of their actions such as rattles that make noise or mobiles that move when baby pulls a ring.

Using Management Skills

Remind students of the availability of toys, games, and educational programs that claim to provide baby with precisely the right amount of stimulation at the correct stage of development. Ask students to volunteer any experience or knowledge they have about these products and discuss the pros and cons of investment in them.

Practicing Decision Making

Have students plan ways to decorate a baby's room so that a stimulating environment is provided. Set a specific budget limit to encourage low-cost decisions. Have students provide a description or sketch of their plan, an estimate of the cost of each item (in terms of money and/or time), and the total estimated cost.

Extension

Have students try one or more of the suggestions given in this feature when they are interacting with an infant. They might do so with an infant in their own family, one they are babysitting, or one you have arranged to be brought to class by a parent. Have students report on their experiences.

beanbag. Different shapes encourage the baby to touch and explore, too. Small plastic squeeze bottles and empty plastic containers with secured lids are both educational and inexpensive.

Encouraging Listening Experiences

Babies learn from listening, too. The familiar voice of the primary caregiver is the first sound a baby learns to recognize. The different voices of other family members and caregivers provide other listening experiences. Rattles and squeak toys introduce different kinds of sounds.

Babies delight in music, whether it comes from a wind-up toy, a recording, or a caregiver's singing. The rhythm of some music is exciting; so is "dancing" securely in the arms of a caring adult. The rhythm of other music is soothing—especially when a parent or caregiver cuddles the baby and rocks gently in a rocking chair.

As babies begin to experiment with their voice, they soon learn that their own sounds bring responses from an attentive caregiver. When you care for a baby, talk to him or her. Reading to a baby is also a good way to help the infant become familiar with the sounds of words.

Developing Motor Skills

A stimulating environment can help babies learn about their own abilities to move. As the baby starts to reach and grasp, reinforce these skills by encouraging the baby to reach for a special toy. As the baby's large muscle skills develop, gently pull the baby into a sitting or standing position on your lap. Once the baby is ready to take a few steps, be sure your hand is there for the baby to hold—providing both stability and security.

CLOSE

Ask students to summarize the main points they have learned from studying this feature by answering this question: If the parents of an infant asked for advice about creating a stimulating environment, what would you tell them?

313

MORE ABOUT

Language Development

Because infants learn to understand language before they are able to speak it, parents and caregivers are wise to stimulate the child's environment with language-rich experiences. Talk to the infant when performing such ordinary tasks as changing diapers, feeding, bathing, or rocking. The sound of the human voice is comforting, and it encourages a response from the infant. Additionally, proper medical care will diagnose physiological problems that affect a child's ability to hear and speak. A few other factors that are believed to influence an infant's language development are maturation, gender, intelligence level, adult models, amount of affection, the range of experiences offered, and the presence of tension and anxiety.

Use the Summary and the Reviewing the Facts questions to help students go over the most important ideas presented in Chapter 10; encourage students to ask questions and add details, as appropriate.

CHAPTER **10** REVIEW

1. The outer layer of the brain; more complex learning.

2. By repeatedly experiencing the same response to a specific action.

3. Any three: recognizes caregiver's face; distinguishes between familiar and unfamiliar faces; grasps objects that touch hand; tries to swipe at objects; shows interest in own hands and feet; practices making sounds; responds when caregiver talks; smiles and laughs.

4. Sensorimotor period, preoperational period, concrete operations period, formal operations period.

5. During preoperational period; about two to seven years old.

6. During concrete operations period; about seven to eleven years old.

7. The baby's parents; they spend time with baby, create learning environment, and interact with baby.

8. Crying; hunger and pain or discomfort.

9. No; they have not yet had an opportunity to associate meanings with words; also, they are not yet physically capable.

10. Yes, by imitating the sounds and by talking in response to the sounds.

CHAPTER **10** REVIEW

SUMMARY

- Babies first learn through their senses, but they gradually develop memory, learn cause-and-effect relationships, and develop a longer attention span.

- Jean Piaget, a Swiss psychologist, developed important theories of learning; he asserted that all children go through the same four stages of learning.

- Both heredity and environment influence learning.

- An infant's intellectual development is linked to the responsiveness of others, especially of parents and other important caregivers.

- Babies need a safe, stimulating environment for learning. Toys are tools for learning.

- In the first year of life, learning is a combination of intellectual ability and motor skill development.

- Communication skills depend on development in all areas—physical, emotional, social, and intellectual.

REVIEWING THE FACTS

1. What is the cortex? What kinds of learning does it permit?

2. Briefly describe how an infant might begin to develop an understanding of cause and effect.

3. What are three signs of intellectual development that can be observed in most babies three to four months old?

4. What are the four learning periods identified by Piaget?

5. During which learning period do children begin to understand abstract terms? About how old are children during this learning period?

6. During which learning period do children begin to learn through symbolic thinking? About how old are children during this learning period?

7. Who are a baby's most important teachers? Why?

8. What is a baby's first means of communication? What are two messages a baby can communicate this way?

9. Do newborns talk? Why or why not?

10. Should parents and other caregivers respond to babies' babbling? If so, how? If not, why not?

EXPLORING FURTHER

1. Watch an educational television program, such as *Sesame Street*. List the teaching techniques used in the show, and analyze those techniques in terms of Piaget's theories. Discuss your ideas with a group of classmates. (Section 1)

2. Design and make a simple toy for a baby. Present your toy to a group of other students. Let them evaluate the toy in terms of safety, appeal, and appropriateness. (Section 2)

3. Select a specific "educational toy" for infants. Discuss the purpose of the toy. Then explain how babies could use common household objects to achieve the same purpose. (Section 2)

4. Read about a company that provides "learning experiences" for infants. Examine the company's advertising, and, if possible, visit some of its classes. Would you recommend that parents use the services of the company for their babies? Why or why not? (Section 2)

5. Make up at least two songs or chants that would be fun to use in encouraging an infant's babbling. Write your songs or chants and then perform them—if possible, for a baby. Share your experience with the class. (Section 2)

THINKING CRITICALLY

1. **Evaluate.** Why is a short attention span a sign of relatively high intelligence in an infant? What do you think a short attention span indicates about a school-aged child? Why?

2. **Interpret.** Why do you think most people never develop or use their full potential for learning? Do you think people should strive to fulfill their intellectual potential more completely? If so, how? If not, why not?

3. **Synthesize.** Why do you think some parents try to teach their babies to recognize letters and words or to play musical instruments? How would you expect a normally intelligent child to

---

TEEN PARENTING

If you have teen parents in your class, or if you know of any who would be willing to help you, ask them to lead a discussion about their observations and experiences with the intellectual development of the infant prior to the first birthday. Encourage them to tell your students how they learned to adjust to the personality of their child. How did they address the relationship between physical, emotional, and intellectual growth? Other students might benefit from a frank discussion about the challenges and demands that the teens had to face during this introduction to parenting. How did they prepare for the baby's growth, and what incidents or situations were they unable to anticipate? Encourage them also to tell about their success stories, and commend their maturity whenever appropriate.

respond? Would you expect a different response from a child with an unusually high intelligence? Why or why not?

CROSS-CURRICULUM CONNECTIONS

1. **Reading.** Read about the Bayley Scales of Infant Development. What is it? When and by whom was it created? How is it used? Discuss your findings with other students.

2. **Science.** Ask three or more young volunteers (in the range of two to ten years old) to help you with an experiment. Let each child watch as you pour water from a short, wide glass into a tall, narrow glass. Ask the volunteers: "Is there more water in this tall glass than there was in the short glass?" Record the children's responses. Then discuss whether and how your results agree with Piaget's theories.

SCHOOL TO WORK

Getting Along with Others Few people work entirely alone. Therefore, your ability to get along with others will play an important part in your success in a job. Getting along is not always easy, but it isn't that difficult either. The more you learn about individual differences and treat each person with the same respect you ask of yourself, the more successful you will be. Above all, keep a sense of humor. Most people enjoy someone who can laugh at themself!

PERFORMANCE ASSESSMENT

Intellectual Development During the First Year

Task
Design an age-appropriate toy or game for a one-year-old. Evaluate its appropriateness for babies and explain how it promotes learning.

Purpose
Demonstrate understanding of intellectual development during the first year. The toy or game you design must meet safety requirements.

Procedure
1. Use the Average Intellectual Development chart on pages 295-296 to select an age group.
2. Jot down your ideas about toys, games, or other playthings that may be suitable for a child of that age.

3. Draw or sketch an original design and, if possible, make a model of your design. Write a brief description of what it is, what it does, how a baby will play with it, and its safety features.
4. Give your toy or game a name. Then evaluate why and how it encourages learning.

Evaluation
Your toy or game design will be evaluated on suitability for your selected audience, originality of idea, and creativity of design. Your design should demonstrate understanding of the intellectual development of a child during the first year and safety issues relevant to that age and your design.

Portfolio Idea If your toy or game design is on paper and will fit into your portfolio, include it, as well as your description and evaluation. If you make a model, keep it in a box or other suitable package to prevent damage. You might also make a scale drawing or take a photograph of the model to accompany your written work. Be sure to label all items appropriately.

PERFORMANCE ASSESSMENT

Toy or Game Design
You might bring in a sample toy to class or have students study the toy on page 297. Discuss why the sample toy or the one in the picture stimulates intellectual development in a one-year-old. If any of your students have infant siblings, ask them to describe the child's favorite toys. Ask: What characteristics do these toys share? An optional step would have students making a model of their toy or game. Encourage them to use, when possible, recycled materials. Remind them that infants and children should not play with this model, since it may not be safe.

EVALUATE
Use the reproducible Chapter 10 Test in the TCR, or construct your own test using the Testmaker Software.

EXTENSION
Arrange a field trip in which the class visits an infant-care center. Ask students to observe the learning environment that has been established in the center; after the trip, guide students in discussing that environment. How do the caregivers promote learning? How does the setting itself promote learning? How do the toys and other objects promote learning? How do the babies in the center appear to be responding?

CLOSE

Give each student an opportunity to answer this question:
What is the most important thing a parent can do to encourage the intellectual development of his or her infant?

SCHOOL TO WORK

Interpersonal Skills
The diversity of the classroom is representative of the diversity in the workplace. Consequently, getting along with others includes a sensitivity to people with disabilities and diverse cultural backgrounds. Encourage students to invent and role-play situations in a workplace that demonstrate positive behavior between people whose cultures, backgrounds, and ability levels are not similar. Include a discussion of how leadership styles influence the attitudes and behavior of employees. Remind students that interpersonal skills in the workplace apply not only to other employees, but to customers as well.

INTRODUCE

UNIT 4 RESOURCES

Teacher's Classroom Resources

- Unit 4 Test
- Testmaker Software
- Color Transparency 25

UNIT OVERVIEW

In Unit 4, students learn about the growth and development that take place in children aged one, two, and three.

Chapter 11 helps students understand the important milestones in physical growth and development during these early years. Students also consider daily care routines and discuss the importance of encouraging a child's emerging independence in such self-care skills.

In Chapter 12, students consider the general patterns of emotional and social development in young children. Students also learn how to help young children express their emotions appropriately and how to encourage positive self-concepts in young children.

Chapter 13 helps students consider the intellectual development of one-, two-, and three-year-olds. Students examine children's methods of learning and the development of concepts.

UNIT OBJECTIVES

After completing Unit 4, students will be able to:

- Describe the physical growth and development of children from one to three and discuss the physical care they require.
- Discuss the emotional and social development of one-, two-, and three-year-olds.
- Describe the intellectual development of children aged one to three and explain how parents and other caregivers can encourage learning in young children.

CLASSROOM MANAGEMENT

Bulletin Board Suggestions

"From Large to Small—They Learn it All!" Illustrate large and small motor skills by clipping magazine pictures showing children in various activities. Place a placard labeled "Large Motor Skills" on the left side of the board and one labeled "Small Motor Skills" on the right. Place each picture under the correct label.

"Choosing Children's Clothing" Attach an actual article of children's clothing to the center of the bulletin board. (Choose something that could be worn by either a boy or a girl.) Use yarn to identify the characteristics to look for when choosing clothing for children: comfort, durability, care, and economy.

U N I T 4

The Child from One to Three

EVERYBODY SAYS

Everybody says
I look just like my mother.
Everybody says
I'm the image of Aunt Bea.
Everybody says
My nose is like my father's.
But I want to look like ME.

Dorothy Aldis

MORE ABOUT

Using the Poem

As a baby develops from infancy to childhood, family and friends almost cannot resist the temptation to find family resemblance in the child's appearance and behavior. The result can be fun and well-intended, but as indicated above, a child is probably more interested in being a unique individual than a younger version of someone else.

Ask a student to read "Everybody Says" aloud, then have the class discuss the disadvantages of being compared to other family members. Under what circumstances might this comparison be beneficial to a child? How can resemblances set the stage for self-fulfilled prophesies or create pressure for a child to be the same type of person as the one he or she resembles?

INTRODUCING THE UNIT

- Display several toys appropriate for a child about three and one-half years old—paints and a brush, a doll with clothes, a toy train, and a tricycle, for example. Encourage students to describe how a three-year-old would be likely to play with all these toys. Why would the child be likely to enjoy playing with it? Then ask students to describe how a one-year-old would probably react to each toy. What would a younger child try to do with each? How interesting would a one-year-old find these toys? Why?

  Finally, encourage students to draw some conclusions about the growth and development young children experience between their first and fourth birthdays. Explain to students that they will learn more about this growth and development as they study Unit 4.

- Ask one of the students to read "Everybody Says" aloud. Then encourage students to share their responses to the poem. In what ways do teens and adults have feelings similar to those of the speaker?

ASSESS

EVALUATE

Use the reproducible Unit 4 Test in the TCR, or construct your own test using the Testmaker Software.

EXTENSION

Invite a pediatrician, a child psychologist, a child care center teacher or director, and/or two or three parents of young children to share their experiences and opinions with the class. Ask the visitors to discuss the kinds of changes they observe as one-, two-, and three-year-olds grow and develop, emphasizing their own ideas about the importance of those changes.

INTRODUCE

CHAPTER OVERVIEW

Chapter 11 introduces students to the unique physical developments of the toddler. In Section 1, students learn about the changes in height, weight, proportion, posture, and development of motor skills that take place between ages one to three.

In Section 2, they learn about child care skills such as feeding, dressing, toilet training, and handling bedtimes. They explore strategies for helping children learn to feed and dress themselves and practice personal hygiene.

Childhood Reflections

"Children have neither past nor future; they enjoy the present, which very few of us do."

La Bruyère, *Les Caractères*

CLASSROOM MANAGEMENT

Resources Beyond the Classroom

Young teen parents, often a product of an age group and culture that glorifies outdoor activities and tanned bodies, may not be aware of research discussing the harmful effects of unprotected and prolonged exposure to the sun and heat. They may be even less aware that a very young child is even more vulnerable. For valuable information, such as the need to protect the child's head adequately, the required strength of sun block, and other important sunproofing techniques, parents can send for a free brochure. Write to:

The Skin Cancer Foundation
P.O. Box 561, Dept. 5B
New York, NY 10156

Physical Development from One to Three

SECTION 1 Physical Growth and Development from One to Three

SECTION 2 Providing Care for Children from One to Three

CHAPTER OBJECTIVES

After completing Chapter 11, students will be able to:

• Describe the changes in an average child's height, weight, posture, and proportion from age one to three.

• Distinguish between small and large motor skills and give examples of each.

• Plan meals appropriate for small children.

• Identify desirable characteristics in children's clothing.

• Describe common bedtime problems and how they can be minimized.

• Discuss the process of toilet training a child.

INTRODUCING THE CHAPTER

• Read the following statements to students one at a time and ask them to indicate whether they agree, disagree, or are not sure. Discuss each statement as students respond.

— Scribbling is an important skill for children.

— Caregivers will spoil children if they give in to their food likes and dislikes.

— With patience and the right methods, most children can be toilet trained at twelve months or younger.

• Use the photo on the opposite page and the three features on this page—Think About, Ask Yourself, and Now Try This—to begin a discussion about a child's physical development from ages one to three.

THINK ABOUT

Recall an opportunity you had to feed, dress, or bathe a toddler. How old was the child? Think about the challenges you faced, if any, because of the child's level of activity or desire to do things for him- or herself. How did you handle the situation? What could the child accomplish that showed how well his or her hand-eye coordination had improved since infancy?

ASK YOURSELF

Look at the photo on the opposite page. What age do you guess the child to be? Notice how the child is able to hold the spoon in her right hand while she tries to pick up pieces of food with the left. How does this ability show development of the finer muscles in the arm, hand, and wrist? What other skills might you expect her to have at this age? How does her self-feeding influence independence?

NOW TRY THIS

Pretend you are the parent or caregiver of the child in the photo. Plan a meal for her that consists of nutritious foods that she can eat with her fingers as well as with a spoon. Describe how you would make mealtime a controlled, yet relaxed time for both you and the child.

319

HEALTHY FAMILIES/HEALTHY CHILDREN

The Toddler Years

By the time a child reaches the first birthday, little remains of the helpless infant of twelve months before. This new stage finds the child eager to be an independent person; with that search for freedom comes the challenges and struggles of acquiring new skills and obtaining a new understanding of the self and the surrounding world. Toddlers prefer walking to crawling; walking brings new adventures as well as dangers. The increased mobility combined with developing motor skills serves to motivate the toddler to explore and expand territory. Parents and caregivers find their hours filled with a new set of concerns and a vigilance unlike that which was necessary during infancy. During the toddler years, everyone is busy!

FOCUS

SECTION 1 RESOURCES

Teacher's Classroom Resources
- Enrichment 27
- Reteaching 27
- Section 1 Quiz

Student Workbook
- Dictionary of Development

SECTION OVERVIEW

In Section 1, students examine the changes that take place in height and weight between ages one and three. They learn that changes in proportion improve posture, balance, and development of motor skills. In addition to learning about development of primary teeth, students explain factors that determine tooth quality. Finally, students explore the rapid development of large motor skills, such as walking and climbing, and small motor skills, such as manipulation.

MOTIVATOR

Ask volunteers to bring photographs of themselves or siblings taken between the ages of one and three years, or obtain photos of other children at age one and at age three. Show these to the class, and ask them to match each photo of a one-year-old with the correct three-year-old or toddler. Ask students what clues helped them match the photos. What qualities made it difficult?

USING TERMS TO LEARN

Point out that the term *circumference* involves something circular. Circumference means the distance around something circular. (Students may know the term from mathematics.) *Circum* is a prefix meaning "around or on all sides." A similar term is *circumscribe*, meaning "to draw a line around or encircle."

Physical Growth and Development from One to Three

OBJECTIVES

- Describe the changes in an average child's height, weight, proportion, and posture from ages one to three.
- Identify habits that influence tooth development and care.
- Distinguish between large and small motor skills, and give examples of each.

TERMS TO LEARN

circumference
large motor skills
manipulation
small motor skills
toddlers

The time between the first and fourth birthdays is one of many physical changes. During this period, the baby learns to walk, to pick up small objects with thumb and forefinger, and to throw objects. By the age of three, the child is running, jumping, building block towers, and using a fork and spoon. The transition from babyhood to childhood is dramatic!

Toddlers

Actual physical growth slows considerably after the first year. However, the child's physical skills show dramatic improvement. Most children begin to walk a few unsteady steps about the time of their first birthday. In fact, the term **toddlers** is frequently used for *children from the age of first walking, usually about twelve months, until the age of three years*. Their skills develop so remarkably that, by the time children turn four, they not only walk steadily, but also hop, jump, and run. Similar advances are made in most other areas of physical development.

As physical skills develop, toddlers need lots of space to walk and run. They need time set aside each day for active play so they can exercise their muscles and use their stored up energy. Children this age become bored easily, so it may be necessary to change games and activities frequently.

OBSERVING AND PARTICIPATING

Toddlers at Play

Toddlers spend most of their day consumed in play. Although the concept of play seems blissful and carefree, many significant skills are developed. Not only do children acquire physical coordination and motor skills, but they also learn important socialization skills in their playful interaction. A parent or caregiver can promote the benefits of playtime by providing the guidance and materials needed to help make the most of this time. Play in the lives of children helps them enjoy life, learn about the environment, get along with others, and develop their small and large motor skills. Observe toddlers at play and identify the various types of benefits provided by their activities.

Walking is related to growth and changes in posture.

Height and Weight

The toddler's growth in both height and weight is slower than the baby's. A toddler gains only about ½ pound (0.2 kg) per month. That is less than half the average monthly weight gain during the first year of life. Growth in height also slows by about half. The chart on page 322 shows average heights and weights for children one through three.

Hereditary and environmental influences on height and weight are more noticeable during this period. Toddlers show more variation in size than babies usually do. Some toddlers are much larger than average; others are much smaller. Height differences are particularly significant. A tall two-year-old will probably grow to be a tall adult. An unusually short toddler will probably be shorter than average as an adult.

Proportion and Posture

Because of changes in proportion, posture improves during the period from one to three. Until age two, a child's head, chest, and abdomen all have about the same **circumference**, or *measure-*

SEE HOW THEY GROW

Toddlerhood

As a child enters the toddler years, physical growth is slower than during infancy. Instead, the child will increase strength, develop motor skills, and begin the first stages of self-awareness. Toddlers are exhausting! Parents and caregivers find their patience tried in a variety of ways because toddlers are truly busy people. They favor large motor skills, so they are busy running, jumping, climbing, swinging, and bouncing. By the time a toddler has reached the third birthday, he or she will have nearly all 20 baby teeth; will be partially, if not completely, toilet trained; will demonstrate a preference for the right or left hand; and will even dress and undress without help. As toddlers seek independence, they learn quickly from others around them.

TEACH

Pages 320-328

- Toddlers
- Height and Weight
- Proportion and Posture
- Teeth
- Motor Skills

GUIDED PRACTICE

Promoting Discussion

- Have students discuss averages as they pertain to children's growth and development. What is the value of charts that list average heights and weights to parents? What are the possible negative effects of relying on averages? Point out that while such knowledge can let parents know what to expect and alert them to possible problems, it can cause unnecessary worry when a perfectly normal child varies from the average.

- Ask students who have younger siblings, relatives, or friends to describe how these children learned to walk. How old were the children? Did they develop the skill slowly or quickly?

- Ask students to give some examples of hereditary and environmental influences that might affect the physical development of a two-year-old.

Using the Photograph

Refer students to the photograph on this page, and ask them to identify signs that this toddler's walk is unsteady. (Hanging onto adult's hand and placement of feet.)

Did You Know?

Beginning in medieval times and continuing through the eighteenth century, babies wore a "black pudding," a round, thickly wadded cap of black velvet to cushion their heads when they started to walk, protecting them from the inevitable falls.

GUIDED PRACTICE (continued)

Making Connections: Math

Have students use the figures on the Average Heights and Weights chart to figure the average yearly gains in height and in weight.

Critical Thinking

Ask students to consider the following questions:

- What problems would a child experience learning to walk if his or her proportions and posture did not change from those of infancy? What factors would make it difficult for an infant to walk? (An infant lacks the straight spine and upright carriage necessary. The protruding abdomen throws the child off balance. The short limbs are a disadvantage as well.)

- Imagine a child dressing in a pair of pull-on elastic-waist pants and a short-sleeved shirt with buttons. Which activities require large motor skills? Small motor skills? (Stepping into the pants, putting the arms through the holes, and pulling the garments on require large motor skills. Picking up the clothing and buttoning the shirt require small motor skills.)

- How should a parent react to a child who scribbles off the page and onto the table or floor? What suggestion would you make? (Parents should encourage the scribbling, and not force the child to be careful. Perhaps they could place the child's paper over a large newspaper or washable surface to minimize damage.)

?

Did You Know?

In England, members of the upper class found it amusing to dress their children in the clothes of lower-class occupations. In 1876, the most popular costume was the sailor suit.

AVERAGE HEIGHTS AND WEIGHTS

AGES ONE TO THREE

AGE	HEIGHT		WEIGHT	
	Inches	Centimeters	Pounds	Kilograms
One year	29.8	75.7	22.5	10.2
Two years	34.0	86.4	27.7	12.6
Three years	37.7	95.8	32.4	14.7

ment around. All three grow at the same rapid rate. Between ages two and three, however, the chest becomes larger than the head and abdomen. The arms, legs, and trunk grow rapidly during this time. These changes in proportion help improve the toddler's balance and motor skills.

By two years of age, the child stands straighter. The abdomen still protrudes, and the head is somewhat forward. The toddler's knees and elbows are still slightly bent.

By the third birthday, the toddler's posture is more upright. The spine has strengthened, so the back is straighter. The child has lost some—but still not all—baby fat.

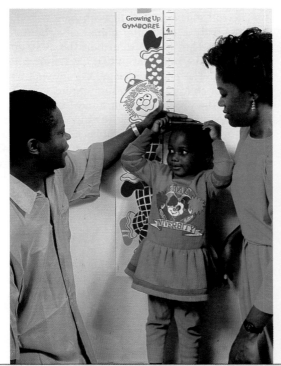

Children undergo dramatic changes in height, weight, and proportion between their first and fourth birthdays. They are proud of "growing up".

MORE ABOUT

Sex Differences in Growing

Differences between the sexes are apparent in the ways children grow. At birth, boys are, on the average, a little longer and heavier. In the first three years, boys gain weight and grow taller at a slightly more rapid rate than girls.

From 3 to 5½ years of age, marked changes occur in body proportion with boys and girls having much the same proportions. From 5½ to 7 years a period of slower growth begins and continues until the second growth spurt.

At 10 years, girls and boys are about the same average height, but girls are growing at a faster rate. Boys by age 10 are not as near their final height as girls are. The second growth spurt for girls is within two years before the first menstruation. Boys gain in height and weight fastest within a few months of puberty, usually shortly before the fourteenth birthday.

Drinking plenty of milk helps build strong teeth that are more resistant to decay. What else influences the health of the teeth?

Teeth

One-year-olds have an average of eight teeth. There is a great deal of variation, however; many children have more than eight or fewer than eight. During the second year, eight more teeth usually come in. For most children, the last four back teeth emerge early in the third year. That makes a complete set of 20 primary teeth.

The quality of a child's teeth is greatly influenced by diet. The diet of the mother during pregnancy and the diet of the child during the first two years lay the foundation for a lifetime of good—or poor—teeth. Dairy products, which are rich in calcium and phosphorus, are especially beneficial. The vitamin D in milk also contributes to the development of strong and healthy teeth and bones.

Heredity also appears to play a role in tooth quality. Dentists have identified a protective mechanism that discourages decay. Some children inherit this mechanism from their parents; others lack this form of natural protection.

Motor Skills

You may recall that physical development proceeds according to these patterns: from head to foot, from near to far, and from simple to complex.

HEALTH TIP

You can help a child build strong teeth not only by providing healthy foods, but also by limiting the foods that promote tooth decay. Avoid giving the child sweet treats, especially candy. Also avoid offering sugar-coated cereals, which often stick between the child's teeth.

GUIDED PRACTICE (continued)

Making Connections: Nutrition
Have students work in groups, reading labels on five popular children's cereals. How many have sugar (or a form of sugar) as one of the top three ingredients? Have students discuss the role these cereals should have in a child's diet. Then have students discuss the following questions:

• What food items are advertised on television during children's programs, such as cartoon shows?

• What effects do these foods have on a child's teeth and general health?

• How are these foods made appealing to young children?

• Are parents likely to be pressured to buy these items?

• How can this kind of pressure be avoided or resisted?

Making Connections: Language Arts
Have students work individually to develop a brochure for parents, explaining the order in which primary teeth appear, factors that affect the quality of teeth, and factors that contribute to tooth decay.

HEALTH TIP

Pediatric dentists witness an alarming number of infants as young as nine months old whose front teeth are so decayed from bottle syndrome that nerve treatment and crowns are required. To avoid this tragedy, parents should never put infants to bed with a bottle containing milk or juice. Apple juice is the most common culprit.

MORE ABOUT

Healthy Teeth
Students may believe that baby teeth are not important because they will be replaced later. Remind them that this is not true. Loss of baby teeth by decay or accident can change the shape of the mouth and cause permanent teeth to come in at an angle. Such problems can affect both the child's comfort and the adult facial structure. They can also affect speech. Students must be aware that they need to monitor a child's oral hygiene habits as soon as the child gets the first tooth. If interested, suggest they consult a pediatric dentist to attend to the child's special dental needs.

GUIDED PRACTICE (continued)

Critical Thinking

Ask students how the habits children develop in early childhood can affect their teeth for the rest of their lives. (Drinking plenty of milk helps ensure that permanent teeth will be strong. Avoiding sweets or eating them with meals or all at once reduces the time teeth are exposed to acid. Frequent brushing destroys the plaque that reacts with food particles and liquids in the mouth to produce the acid that attacks tooth enamel. A child who learns these habits early is more likely to continue them in the future.)

BUILDING SELF-ESTEEM

Affirmations are emotional reinforcements that let children know that they are lovable and capable. If practiced often, affirmations become the foundation for trust and support. Some examples for the one- to three-year-old child are: You belong here; I like to watch you learn and grown; You can ask for help; I love who you are.

Using the Photograph

Have students study the photograph on this page. Then have them read the Building Self-Esteem feature. Ask what opportunities this situation allows for parents to apply the advice in the feature. (The child is being given the opportunity to practice developing motor skills.)

BUILDING SELF-ESTEEM
Praising Children's Accomplishments

As children succeed in developing their large and small motor skills, they need special praise from the important adults in their lives. Simple, sincere praise can help children recognize their accomplishments and feel good about themselves.

Parents and other caregivers who recognize and praise developing skills can help in another way, too. They can be sure the child has a variety of experiences that will allow him or her to practice using and developing that skill. With practice and praise, the child learns this important lesson: I can keep trying, and I can do it!

Both large and small motor skills become increasingly well developed as children grow. What type of motor skills is this little girl using?

When you compare the skills of children at age one and at the end of the third year, these patterns are easy to see. Hand skills are a good example. At thirteen months, a child stacks only two blocks. By the fourth birthday, the same child uses blocks to make high towers, houses, and roads.

Motor skills are often divided into two types. **Large motor skills** are *abilities that depend on the use and control of the large muscles of the back, legs, shoulders, and arms.* Walking, running, and throwing balls are all examples of large motor skills. **Small motor skills** are *abilities that depend on the use and control of the finer muscles of the wrists, fingers, and ankles.* Many small motor skills such as, completing single knob puzzles, grasping colors and paintbrushes, turning pages on cardboard books, and stringing beads, require hand-eye coordination, the ability to move the hands precisely in relation to what is seen.

Children do not acquire physical skills as predictably during the period from one to three as they did during the first year of life. Most toddlers learn some skills earlier than "average" and other skills later than "average." Such variations can be caused by differences in children's physical size, health and diet, interests, temperament, opportunities for physical play, and many other factors. As you learn more about average development for a particular age, remember that many children develop more slowly or more quickly.

SEE HOW THEY GROW

Walking in Their Shoes

Students need to be made aware that a child's footwear needs are different from their own. When a child is learning to walk, he or she is attempting a balancing act that is initially very difficult. What shoes should be worn by a child who is learning to walk? Not all authorities agree on the answer to this question. One study showed that children walked faster and kept their balance better in leather shoes rather than sneakers. Sneakers have a rounded bottom and often do not provide enough room for the wide foot of a toddler. Although most children will learn to walk despite their shoes, a child who has extra trouble with falling might benefit by a switch to leather shoes.

ASK THE EXPERTS

What Does Developmentally Appropriate Mean?

Q. Can you help me understand what the term "developmentally appropriate" means?

A. Since this term has such widespread use and importance for everyone who is involved with children, it is vital to understand the meaning of *developmentally appropriate. Appropriate*, of course, means "suitable" or "right." An activity or behavior that is developmentally appropriate, then, is suitable for the development of an individual child or a group of children.

In considering development to determine developmentally

appropriate behaviors and activities, there are two essential factors. One is the age of the child or children involved. Age alone, however, does not determine developmental appropriateness. The other factor is the individual interest of the child or, in a group setting, of each child. What are the special needs of this child or this group of children? What are

the particular abilities of this child or this group of children? Both these questions must be answered before developmentally appropriate activities can be selected.

A developmentally appropriate approach is relevant to the particular child or group of children. It takes into account both the age of the children and the individual needs, interests, and abilities of the children.

Linda Espinosa

Linda Espinosa
Director of Primary Education for the Redwood City School District in California

Large Motor Skills

Physical exercise and repeated practice of actions are necessary for the development of motor skills. An individual child's improvement in any one skill is typically slow but steady, and follows a predictable pattern.

As you know, most children begin to walk shortly before or after their first birthday. This is an important accomplishment. It gives the child a feeling of pride—and much more mobility for exploration. At first, the toddler walks by holding on to furniture. The child's first steps are wobbly, with toes pointed outward and arms held out for balance. After a few shaky steps, the child collapses into a sitting position. The child's constant

HEALTHY FAMILIES/HEALTHY CHILDREN

Toddler Safety
Anyone who has been in charge of a toddler knows that those exciting early steps are not much fun when a child is injured by a fall. Ask students to explain what could happen and what they would do to prevent accidents when a toddler is walking in a room that contains the following:

• Fireplace.
• Hard floor with loose throw rugs.
• Low table with glass top.
• Table with sharp corners.
• Open stairs to lower level.
• Pedestal table holding a large plant.

GUIDED PRACTICE (continued)

ASK THE EXPERTS

Issues and Advice

1. How can a parent or caregiver determine the appropriateness of an activity or behavior? (*It is suitable for the development of a child or group of children.*)

2. What areas of child rearing should be developmentally appropriate? (*Activities, toys, language and guidance, and behavioral evaluation.*)

3. What two factors are important in determining developmental appropriateness? (*Age of the child and individual interest.*)

4. Who should be concerned with the concept of developmental appropriateness? (*Anyone involved with children.*)

Thinking Like an Expert

Read to your students the following scenario: Kristin is a lively girl of eighteen months. Her favorite meal is dinner when she and her mother, and her three older brothers and sisters are together. She spends much of the mealtime trying to pick up food with a spoon or with her hands, only to throw it onto the floor or, to the delight of her siblings, smear it on her face. Her greatest disappointment is when she runs out of food and no one will give her more.

Ask the students to discuss Kristin's behavior and apply what they know about developmentally appropriate behavior. Guide their discussion with these questions: What reasons can you give for Kristin's behavior? What possible reactions to this conduct might she receive from her parents and family? How can family members minimize mealtime problems? Should her parents worry that she is not eating enough? Why or why not?

GUIDED PRACTICE (continued)

Making Connections: Language Arts

Have students write a description of a toddler, giving information about the child's height, weight, proportion, and posture. How does the child walk? How does the child balance?

Using the Photographs

Refer students to the photographs on pages 324 and 326. Ask students to identify the large and small motor skills illustrated in these pictures.

Cooperative Learning

Have students work in groups and list five large and five small motor skills. Which muscles are involved in each skill? Ask students to make a chart to share with the class.

Critical Thinking

Explain that the next section will cover safety procedures for those caring for children ages one to three. As students study the Average Motor Skills Chart on page 327, have them predict how the safety needs of a three-year-old will be different from those of a one-year-old. In what ways will they be the same? For ideas, refer students to the chart of motor skills. Have them record their predictions and evaluate them after finishing the chapter.

practice of this new skill brings improvement in steadiness, balance, and body control.

Climbing skills follow a similar sequence. Even children who have learned to walk continue to climb stairs on their hands and knees for a while and slide backward when going down the stairs. Then they begin walking up stairs with help, placing both feet on each step. Next, they try walking up and down stairs on their own, holding on to a railing. They continue placing both feet on each step. Most children do not begin alternating feet on stairs until about age three.

Climbing is not limited to stairs. Nothing is safe from the climbing toddler—furniture, counters, ledges, and sometimes even people are conquered like mountains! This activity, of course, makes safety an important concern for parents and other caregivers. The Positive Parenting Skills feature on pages 344-345 gives suggestions for making areas safe for young children's explorations.

Small Motor Skills

Between their first and second birthdays, children learn to feed themselves and to drink from a cup fairly well. At first, poor hand-eye coordination causes many spills. With practice, however, their success and neatness improve. One-year-olds usually enjoy playing with blocks, large pop beads, and pyramids of different-sized rings. They also like jack-in-the-box toys, musical rolling toys, and toy pianos. Activities with these toys help develop small motor skills.

Crayons, large stacking blocks, clay beads to string, blunt scissors, and modeling dough are some of the toys that help toddlers improve their small motor skills. For these young children, how is play like toddler's work?

OBSERVING AND PARTICIPATING

Developing Observational Skills

Ask students to work in pairs or small groups to research the physical development of two or more children between the ages of one and three years. Have them observe and record at least five examples of activities using large motor skills, and the same number of activities using small motor skills. Instruct students to record accurately the kinds of activities the children are involved with,

how proficient they are in performing the activity, and whether the activity presents any challenge to motor skills, both large and small, that the children have not yet mastered. If the activity is challenging, how do the children cope with it? Ask students to prepare a report that summarizes their observations and compares the abilities between different children and, if appropriate, different age groups.

AVERAGE MOTOR SKILLS DEVELOPMENT

AGES ONE TO FOUR

AGE	LARGE MOTOR SKILLS	SMALL MOTOR SKILLS
1 to 1 ½ years	• Improves from walking a few unsteady steps to walking well. • Slides down stairs backwards, one step at a time. • Stoops to pick up toys.	• Turns pages of a book, several pages at a time. • Picks up small objects easily, using thumb and forefinger. • Scribbles.
1 ½ to 2 years	• Runs fairly well. • Stands on one foot. • Learns to walk up and down stairs, holding on, both feet on each step. • Throws objects overhand.	• Buttons large buttons. • Pulls down zippers. • Turns doorknobs. • Stacks several blocks to form a tower.
2 to 2 ½ years	• Walks with more coordination and confidence. • Climbs, even in unsafe places. • Jumps off bottom step. • Pushes self on wheeled toys.	• Turns pages of a book, one at a time. • Strings large beads. • Builds towers of about six blocks.
2 ½ to 3 years	• Runs, but may not be able to stop smoothly. • Alternates feet going up stairs, but not going down. • Throws ball overhand, but inaccurately. • Kicks balls.	• Builds towers of about eight blocks. • Draws horizontal and vertical lines; draws circles. • Screws lids on and off containers.
3 to 4 years	• Jumps up and down in place. • Walks on tiptoe. • Rides a tricycle. • Catches a ball with arms straight.	• Builds towers of about nine or ten blocks. • Makes a bridge from three blocks. • Cuts with scissors. • Draws recognizable pictures. • Uses a fork and spoon with little spilling.

GUIDED PRACTICE (continued)

Using the Chart
Refer students to the chart on this page. Have students suggest an activity parents might provide to develop one of the motor skills for each age group listed. Allow time for students to share and discuss their ideas.

Using the Photograph
Refer students to the photograph on page 328. Ask students to identify the small motor skill illustrated in the picture. (Scribbling) How will the child's ability to draw improve in the next two years? (She will draw recognizable pictures.)

INDEPENDENT PRACTICE
Student Workbook
Have students complete "Dictionary of Development" in the Student Workbook.

Student Demonstration
Have students develop a ten-minute lesson on some element of dental care for a group of three-year-olds. Possible examples could include brushing, flossing, or the role of sweets in tooth decay. If possible, arrange for students to present their lessons to young children. Evaluate the results.

Extension
Have students work independently or in small groups to complete one or more of these extension activities:

• Look through catalogs and magazines to find pictures of toys that promote the development of motor skills. Distinguish between those that use small and large motor skills. Use the pictures to create a bulletin board display or a poster.

MORE ABOUT

Baby's First Steps

The first steps taken by a child are treated as a landmark. Parents and caregivers look forward to them and are almost certain to record them on film or video. Yet this major event will change daily life and has advantages and disadvantages. An obvious advantage is that the child no longer has to be carried everywhere. The child who can walk will interact with people differently as the viewpoint shifts from eye level to a few feet above the ground. The child who is used to seeing a world of human faces now sees a maze of legs. In addition, the toddler is now on the same level as pets and flowers. The mobile toddler requires constant vigilance from caregivers. There are more opportunities for injuries and destruction of property. Just as dangerous is the ease with which a toddler can easily become separated from others on outings.

ASSESS

CHECKING COMPREHENSION

Assign students to write their responses to the Check Your Understanding questions in the Section 1 Review. Answers to the questions are given below.

EVALUATE

Have students complete the Chapter 11, Section 1 TCR quiz.

Reteaching

1. Assign Reteaching 27 in the TCR. Review their responses in class.

2. Conduct a "popcorn" session to review examples of large and small motor skills. The object is for students to pop up and give an example as quickly as possible, identifying the type of skill given.

Enrichment

Have students complete one or more of the following activities:

1. Assign Enrichment Activity 27 in the TCR.

2. Have students respond to this letter in an advice column: Dear Marlene, My one-year-old daughter took her first step today—an exciting moment, I was told. She was at the child care center and I was at work. Now I feel disappointed and guilty. Why? How should I handle my feelings?

3. Have students role-play a conversation between the mother of a healthy, normal boy of thirteen months and a grandmother worried because the child is not yet walking.

Extension

Invite a dentist or a dental hygienist to discuss young children's teeth and the importance of brushing teeth and avoiding sweets. Encourage questions.

CLOSE

Have each student write an ending for this statement:
Between ages 1 and 3, a child …
Then have students read their sentences aloud.

As small motor skills improve, a child's random scribbles gradually become more recognizable lines and shapes.

Two-year-olds show improved **manipulation,** or *skillful use of the hands and fingers*. They can turn the pages of a book one at a time, peel a banana, and turn on a faucet. They enjoy using crayons—typically with a happy abandon that results in marks running haphazardly off the paper and onto the table or floor. They build towers of blocks, which usually reach a maximum height of five or six blocks before the tower topples.

Three-year-olds show considerably more skill. They typically delight in taking things apart and putting them back together again. Children this age can draw circles as well as horizontal and vertical lines.

The chart on pages 327 shows average large and small motor development between the first and fourth birthdays.

SECTION 1 REVIEW

CHECK YOUR UNDERSTANDING

1. What are toddlers?
2. Why does a child's posture improve during the period from one to three?
3. What is the number of primary teeth in a complete set? At about what age do most children have a complete set of primary teeth?
4. Why are milk and milk products especially important for the development of healthy teeth?
5. List at least two large motor skills.
6. List at least two small motor skills.
7. What is manipulation?

DISCUSS AND DISCOVER

1. Cut out at least three pictures of favorite toys for young children, aged one to three. Display the pictures and label each with a list of the motor skills involved in playing with that toy.
2. How do safety concerns in the home change as the baby grows into a one-year-old, a two-year-old, and then a three-year-old? Why do the safety concerns change as the child grows? Discuss with other students.

Observing & Participating

Interact with a group of two or three toddlers to see how each child demonstrates small motor skills. Let the children put puzzles together, string beads, or hammer pegs. Construction paper, crayons, and scissors may also be included on the table. Evaluate each child's hand-eye coordination and his or her small motor development.

SECTION 1 REVIEW

1. Children from the age of first walking, usually about twelve months, until the age of three years.
2. The spine has strengthened, and the child has lost some baby fat.
3. 20 primary teeth; about three years.
4. Provide calcium, phosphorous, and vitamin D.
5. Possible examples: running, climbing. (Other examples are also acceptable.)
6. Possible examples: drinking from a cup, playing with large pop beads. (Other examples are also acceptable.)
7. The skillful use of hands and fingers.

Providing Care for Children from One to Three

OBJECTIVES

- Plan meals appropriate for young children.
- Explain how to help children learn and practice personal hygiene habits.
- Discuss how to encourage children to feed and dress themselves.
- Identify desirable characteristics in children's clothing.
- Describe common bedtime problems, and discuss how they can be minimized.
- Discuss the process of toilet training a child.

TERMS TO LEARN

natural fibers
sphincter muscles
synthetic fibers
training pants

Caring for a one-, two-, or three-year-old is quite different from caring for a baby. By their first birthday, children are already beginning to do things for themselves. If they are encouraged to try out and practice their developing skills, children are capable of a surprising amount of self-care by the time they are three. They may be able to put on their coat, brush their teeth, and butter their toast.

Feeding

Between the first and fourth birthdays, children acquire food habits and attitudes that influence their eating throughout life. They also learn to feed themselves, an activity which both depends on and helps improve their small motor skills.

It is important to understand what toddlers of various ages can—and like to—eat.

- **The one-year-old.** The one-year-old eats a variety of baby foods and many simple foods from the family table. Family foods may include such things as mashed or boiled potatoes,

FOCUS

SECTION 2 RESOURCES

Teacher's Classroom Resources
- Enrichment 28
- Reteaching 28
- Section 2 Quiz

Student Workbook
- Planning Meals for Children
- Handling Sleep Problems
- Clothes Closings

SECTION OVERVIEW

In Section 2, students learn how to provide nutritious and appetizing meals for children and study ways to help toddlers develop good eating and personal hygiene habits. They examine ways to help toddlers feed and dress themselves. They learn to choose appropriate children's clothing, toilet train a child, and minimize bedtime problems.

MOTIVATOR

Encourage students with siblings between ages one and three to describe their activities and abilities. If students have helped care for children of these ages, ask how caring for a young child is different from caring for an infant. Discuss a toddler's increasing desire for independence and the challenges it presents for a caregiver. Explain that this section will provide information about caring for children between one and three years of age.

USING TERMS TO LEARN

Point out that the terms *circumference* (from Section 1) and *sphincter muscles* both involve something circular. Sphincter muscles are circular or ringlike muscles that control elimination. Note the pronunciation of this word (SFINK-tur) and the unusual spelling.

HEALTHY FAMILIES/HEALTHY CHILDREN

Health and Safety

Although nutritional needs are an important food consideration, foods must be chosen carefully for toddlers for another reason. Many hard, round foods cause choking by plugging a child's windpipe. Hot dogs, nuts, raisins, grapes, raw carrots, and hard candies are frequent culprits in this category. Hot dogs that have not been skinned and diced are a common cause of choking in toddlers. Popcorn is dangerous because it can be inhaled into the windpipe. These foods should not be given to a child under the age of four.

TEACH

Pages 329-343

- **Feeding**
- **Bathing**
- **Caring for the Teeth**
- **Dressing**
- **Sleeping**
- **Toilet Training**

GUIDED PRACTICE

Promoting Discussion

- Have students discuss how they would expect caring for a child to be easier as the child develops mobility and the ability to perform more activities independently. Then have them consider the additional challenges the mobility and independence would present. In particular, discuss the balance between nurturing the young child's desire for independence while providing for nutrition and safety.

- Students are not likely to remember what it was like to learn new skills as a toddler. Ask them to recall learning tasks or skills that were difficult for them. For example, have any students ever tried using chopsticks for eating? What was it like? Suggest that students try holding their forks and spoons in the opposite hand at their next meal. Ask how students would feel if nearly everything they wanted to do was a learning experience. Have them consider their answers and the implications for handling of toddlers.

Using the Photograph

Refer students to the photograph on page 330. Ask how the boy feels about dressing himself. What are the challenges in the task the boy is performing? What type of shirt might be easier for him to put on?

As toddlers grow, they become more independent and capable of doing many things for themselves. How do you think this child feels about his new sense of independence?

rice, cooked vegetables, soups, toast, fresh fruit pieces, yogurt, and puddings. In the early months, most foods should be finely chopped. As more teeth come in and the child's ability to chew improves, foods can have a coarser texture.

Finger foods are popular with most young children. For one-year-olds, finger foods improve coordination and encourage self-feeding. Appropriate finger-foods for one-year-olds include cheese chunks, peas, cooked carrot slices, melon or banana pieces, and scrambled eggs.

The transition from being fed to self-feeding is a long process. Babies begin trying to use a spoon before their first birthday. However, most are eighteen months or older before they can use the spoon to feed themselves with little spilling. By the time they are approaching their second birthday, most children can also drink from a cup fairly well.

During the second year, meals can become a battle of wills between parent or caregiver and toddler. One-year-olds want not only to feed themselves, but also to choose what they will eat. They often develop strong food dislikes, though

MORE ABOUT

Promoting Self-Care Skills

Allowing toddlers to practice their self-care skills gives them a sense of confidence and bolsters their self-esteem. You can help them become more independent by following these guidelines:

- Avoid doing things for them that they can do themselves.

- When possible, allow extra time for the children to dress themselves.

- Put cereal, milk, juice, and other foods into small, unbreakable, easy-to-handle containers so that children can serve themselves.

- Put shelves and drawers at the children's level so that they can put away toys, books, and clothes.

By allowing and encouraging such independent activity, the child experiences a sense of self-achievement, and the parent is relieved of some chores.

these usually don't last long. Rather than forcing the child to eat a particular food, it's better to wait until the next meal or snack, when you can offer the child a different food that meets the same nutritional needs. In a few weeks, the sweet potatoes that were rejected so vehemently will probably be a favorite food again.

- **The two-year-old.** Two-year-olds vary greatly in their eating habits. Some are easy to please. Others are very finicky eaters. Most, however, do have specific likes and dislikes; they often refuse to eat certain foods.

  Two-year-olds can usually feed themselves without any help. Some are usually neat eaters; others are usually quite messy. At this age, a child can be taught to use a fork.

  Be patient. It is important to remember that children often take a long time to eat. Eating not only provides nutrition but also allows children to experiment with new textures.

  Conversation during a meal may distract the toddler from eating. For this reason, many families choose to feed the young child before the family meal, but socialization at meals is important. Whenever possible, try to schedule your meals so the young child is able to eat with the rest of the family.

- **The three-year-old.** By three years of age, a child can eat the same foods as the rest of the family. With a full set of primary teeth, chewing foods is not a problem. However, meats and other tough foods should still be served in small pieces.

  Three-year-olds are very active and need food for both growth and energy. They should have three meals a day plus nutritious snacks. The amount that an individual child eats will vary considerably from day to day, depending on the appetite level and the amount of activity he or she has had.

  At this age, it is still best not to make an issue of food likes and dislikes. Children should be encouraged to try new foods, but they should not be forced to eat large amounts of foods they dislike. Substituting foods with similar nutrient value still works at this stage. For example, a child who refuses a cup of plain milk will probably eat milk in cereal, soup, and pudding. If a child is offered nutritious foods, and high fat and sugar foods are not given, most children will eat a well-balanced diet.

Choosing Foods for Children

Parents and other caregivers must consciously choose healthful, nutritious foods for young children. Like adults, children need a variety of nutritious foods daily. The best way to make sure a child gets this variety is to plan meals using the Food

BUILDING SELF-ESTEEM

Responding Positively to Messes

Children from one- to three-years-old are busy little people as they move from one activity to another. At times, they move quickly and do not watch what their hands reach for or where their feet lead them. This is when messes can, and do often happen!

Spilling a glass of milk, dropping a bowl of cereal, or knocking over a plant are common messes that children this age can make. However, the way adults respond to these messes can affect how a child feels about himself. An adult's response can also affect whether a child will try to help with or avoid activities in the future.

Use the incident as a time for teaching. Children can help clean up a mess and can be gently reminded to move the object away from the edge next time, or wait for help.

By responding positively, adults teach children that it is alright to make mistakes or to cause messes. This sends a message to the child that they are OK and still loved.

MORE ABOUT

Food Likes and Dislikes

If a child does not prefer to eat a particular food, be flexible. Try substituting different foods within the same group to provide more variety. For example, if the child prefers sweet potatoes to carrots or peaches to apricots, don't be concerned. All these fruits and vegetables provide vitamins and minerals and are good food choices. Continue to offer different fruits and vegetables,

even if they are rejected at first. Over time, the child may be willing to try them if he or she is not forced to do so.

Encourage the child to experiment with different tastes and textures. Children learn about foods by tasting, touching, and smelling, and through other sensory experiences. Offer the child different shapes, sizes, and textures of foods to stimulate interest.

GUIDED PRACTICE (continued)

Cooperative Learning

Divide the class into groups, and have students discuss their own early childhood memories of mealtime. Do they recall any of their own early food likes and dislikes? Do they remember being asked to eat a disliked food? How do they think spills and dawdling at meals should be handled? On the basis of the discussion, have each group write mealtime guidelines for parents of children between ages one and three. Have a representative from each group share the guidelines with the class.

Christmas Party

Making Connections: Language Arts

Have students write a description of mealtime from a young child's point of view.

BUILDING SELF-ESTEEM

Children imitate others. When you accidentally spill or make a mess, have patience with yourself. Tell yourself (aloud) that it's only an accident and next time you'll be more careful. Let the child hear you forgive and comfort yourself. Set a good example!

Cooperative Learning

In groups, have students discuss how older siblings may, by their example, influence food choices of young children. How, for example, might young children react to seeing older siblings consume sweet snacks or refuse milk? How can potential problems be prevented? Allow time for groups to share their ideas.

Promoting Discussion

Toddlers often enjoy eating food that they have helped prepare. Participation and praise build self-esteem and make them feel more grown up. Have students list kitchen activities that a toddler could perform, such as washing tomatoes, tearing lettuce, peeling a banana, and clearing his or her own place setting.

Critical Thinking

Ask students why some caregivers might not allow toddlers to perform food preparation tasks. (Answers will vary. It may not occur to them. They may believe the children are not ready. They may not want to take the extra time or handle the extra mess involved.)

Promoting Discussion

Have students list foods they dislike the most. Ask whether they can explain why they dislike these foods. (Childhood experiences, texture, etc.) Help students relate their experiences to those of young children, who can't be expected to like every food any more than teens or adults can.

Using the Photograph

Refer students to the photo on this page, and ask them to explain what makes this meal nutritious, appealing, and easy for a youngster to eat.

Cooperative Learning

Ask students to work in small groups to create a dish to be served to a child. Have them use their imaginations to give the food special appeal. For example, they might create a sandwich with a face and ears or a salad that looks like a rabbit. Perhaps they could combine foods to make an object like a flower or a windmill. Have groups present their ideas with drawings or posters. If possible, provide opportunity to prepare the dishes.

Guide Pyramid. The chart on page 164 shows the food groups and the number of servings from each that young children should eat each day.

The primary concern in preparing food for young children is nutrition. It is important to be cautious in serving adult convenience foods to children. Many of these foods are less nutritious than other alternatives. In addition, these foods may contain a great deal of salt and a variety of preservatives, colorings, and artificial flavoring agents. Choose fresh foods when possible. Use the nutrition labels on frozen, canned, and dried foods to help you make nutritious choices.

In addition to considering nutrition, parents and other caregivers should strive to present meals that are appealing in terms of color, texture, shape, temperature, and ease of eating.

- **Color.** A variety of bright colors adds interest to a meal. For example, a meal consisting of cream of chicken soup, applesauce, milk, and vanilla pudding may be nutritious, but it looks boring. Substituting fresh sliced apples for the applesauce would make the meal more visually appealing. Further variety could be added by substituting flavored yogurt topped with granola for the vanilla pudding.

- **Texture.** Think of all the adjectives you might use to describe foods. Applesauce is smooth, a cracker is crunchy, and a strawberry is seedy. Children usually enjoy a meal consisting of foods with a variety of textures.

- **Shape.** Foods with a variety of shapes appeal to young children. For example, you can cut sandwiches into rectangles or squares—or triangles. Then you can help the

Meals need to be nutritious, appealing, and easy for young children to eat. How does this meal satisfy those requirements?

MORE ABOUT

Snack Foods

A child's active body needs energy, and energy is provided by nutrients in foods. Because the time span between meals is often too long for even an adult to endure, snacks may be offered to give the body a lift. As a rule, snacks should be chosen from the four food groups: milk, fruits and vegetables, meat, and breads. Children who are considered overweight should be encouraged to eat more raw fruits and vegetables than foods from the other groups. The American Dietetic Association suggests that picky eaters not be given a snack within half an hour after mealtime, because doing so assures them that the main meal is unnecessary. Another reminder is that snacks should not become a substitute for meals. Above all, make sure that a child is not filling up on empty calories.

child identify the shape before he or she begins to eat. You can even use a cookie cutter to cut special shapes from the bread before you assemble the sandwich.

- **Temperature.** Young children are very conscious of the temperature of food. Check the temperature of all foods before serving them to children. If a food has been cooked or warmed in the microwave, stir it thoroughly to disperse the heat evenly. This stirring prevents "hot spots" that can burn the child's mouth.

- **Ease of eating.** Certain foods are easier than others for young children to eat. For example, ground beef is easier to chew and swallow than steak. Spaghetti is often a favorite, but children can handle it on their own more easily if it is cut into short pieces.

Mealtime Tips

Planning and preparing nutritious, appealing meals for young children is a challenge. However, mealtimes are important events in every toddler's day; they provide a chance to practice skills, experience independence, explore the feel and texture of foods, socialize with others—and have fun. The following guidelines can help you make mealtime enjoyable, both for the child and for yourself:

- Keep the child's mealtimes, including snacks, on a regular schedule. It is difficult for children to wait, especially when they are hungry.
- Keep the atmosphere at meals pleasant. Praise the child, and avoid criticism. Remind yourself that the child's table manners will improve with age.
- Use a sturdy, unbreakable dish or plate with sides for serving the child's food. This will encourage self-feeding; the child can scoop food up against the sides of the plate or dish.
- Choose a cup that the child can hold easily and that does not readily tip.
- Provide child-sized eating utensils. Young children have trouble handling full-sized forks and spoons.
- Let a young toddler sit in a high chair for meals. When the child starts sitting at the family table, use a high stool with a back or a booster seat on a regular chair.
- Never use food as a punishment or a bribe. Eating healthy food should be considered expected behavior. If you say, "You can't have a cookie until you finish your vegetables," you give the impression that vegetables are bad and cookies are good.
- Remember that children imitate others. Set a good example in food choices and in table manners.

By age three, a booster seat makes it easier for children to reach the table.

GUIDED PRACTICE (continued)

Making Connections: Nutrition

Give students a menu that needs improvement in nutrition, color, texture, shape, temperature, and ease of eating. Ask students as a class to identify what is wrong with the menu. Then have them work individually to suggest an improved menu that is suitable for young children.

Using the Photograph

Refer students to the photo on page 333. What item enables this girl to eat at the family table? Why might some children resist using booster seats? What strategies might be used to make a booster seat pleasing to a child? If you did not own a booster seat, what household items might be used instead? Would any of the items suggested be awkward or unsafe to use?

Critical Thinking

Ask students how avoiding distractions during mealtime can help prevent choking. Why is it important to keep an eye on a young child while the child is eating? What should you do if the child chokes on food? (Children are more likely to choke on food than from other causes, especially if they are talking or laughing. If students do not know how to handle choking, refer them to the information about choking on pages 499-501.)

TEEN PARENTING

Nutrition

Teens, especially females, are often the worst offenders when it comes to following the guidelines for good nutrition. Ask students why this is true. Possible responses: Some teens lack the knowledge or the concern for good health. They may be involved with other activities that are more important to them, be overly concerned about weight, or feel that what others are telling them about proper nutrition is not relevant. Getting the right foods may even be a financial problem. If teens become parents, they are responsible for the life of a child. Ask students to discuss the affect a teen's attitude toward nutrition would have on his or her child.

GUIDED PRACTICE (continued)

Practicing Decision Making

Have students work in groups to consider situations that might call for the use of packaged or convenience foods, for example, when traveling by automobile. Provide publications that list nutritional content of common brand-name foods and of items at common fast-food restaurants. Tell groups to list three possible nutritious snacks for traveling and three items at fast-food restaurants that might make acceptable meals for a child of two or three. Have a recorder read the items to the class.

Making Connections: Social Studies

Have students research eating traditions in other cultures and the motor skills toddlers need to acquire in order to eat as adults do. Allow time for students to share their findings in class.

Promoting Discussion

Ask students to name some ways to make bath time fun for toddlers. What household items could toddlers play with in the tub?

SAFETY TIP

As babies grow, they enjoy the play value of a bath more and more. To keep baby safe and ensure pleasure, maintain a water level of 3 inches (7.6 cm) or less. That way there will be plenty of splash without excess worry.

As children grow older, they need less adult help while bathing. However, for safety's sake, a young child should not be left unattended in the bath.

SAFETY TIP

As children become more active and independent in the bath, it is essential to keep the tub a safe place. To prevent dangerous slips, be sure the bottom of the tub has ridges or rough plastic stickers. If the surface is smooth, you can place a rubber mat—or even an old towel—on the bottom of the tub during a child's bath time.

Bathing

During the years from one to three, children establish important attitudes about personal hygiene. Parents and other caregivers need to help young children develop both good attitudes and good hygiene skills.

At this age, most children take baths. Evening baths are usually most practical, and a bath can become an enjoyable part of a child's getting-ready-for-bed routine. Toddlers typically have fun in the bath, which they consider more a place for playing than a place for getting clean.

In the bath, one-year-olds begin to wash themselves. At first, this means merely rubbing the washcloth over the face and stomach. By age two, however, most children can wash, rinse, and dry themselves fairly well, except for the neck and back. By age three, children can bathe themselves with a minimum of supervision.

All young children need attention and supervision while they are in the bath. For children under the age of two and a half, the supervision must be constant. Even a minute away to answer the phone or get clean clothes can have disastrous results. As the mother of a two-year-old relates, "I just left the

---

HEALTHY FAMILIES/HEALTHY CHILDREN

Health and Safety

Manufacturers of infant merchandise offer clever and creative toiletry items that make the bathroom a safe and pleasurable place. Some examples are:

• A step-up toilet seat that fits over the rim of the bowl, allowing toddlers to get on and off by themselves.

• An animal-shaped sleeve of foam that slips over

a tub spout to prevent burns, bruises, and bumps.

• A shield of polyfoam that slips over a child's head to keep shampoo out of the face.

• Bath mitts made of terry cloth in the shape of animals.

• Colorful sponges in geometric and animal shapes.

• Specially formulated soaps and shampoos that do not cause tearing if they get in a child's eyes.

room for a second to get Denny's shoes. He was bathed and fully dressed for the day. When I came back, he was sitting in the tub again—with all his clothes on—playing with his toys in the bath water!" This situation may sound humorous, but the child could have drowned during the short time his mother was away.

Caring for the Teeth

Around the age of eighteen months, most toddlers have several teeth—enough to begin brushing on their own. To encourage independent brushing, give the toddler a small, soft toothbrush and a bit of toothpaste. The child's first attempts will not be very successful, but the opportunity to try is important. Even three-year-olds often only swish the front teeth a few times with the toothbrush. Children of this age still need adult help. In fact, many dentists recommend that parents should also begin flossing the child's teeth and showing the child how to hold and use dental floss.

Dressing

Toddlers are eager to learn dressing skills; adults and other caregivers should encourage self-dressing whenever a child begins to show interest. It is important to remember, however, that dressing involves a number of large and small motor skills, and each of these skills must be learned one step at a time. Patience is important during this long process.

HEALTH TIP

According to many dentists, eighteen months is the recommended age for a child's first dental checkup.

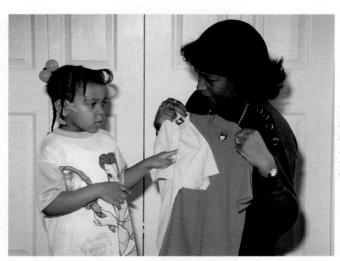

Young children take pride in being able to dress themselves and assist in the clothing decisions. Avoid clothing with fasteners or tight openings. They will only frustrate the child.

GUIDED PRACTICE (continued)

Promoting Discussion
Ask students why early attempts at tooth brushing should be supervised. Why should young children be taught to floss?

Making Connections: Language Arts and Visual Arts
Have students write a story about tooth brushing and draw pictures to illustrate the story. Use the story and pictures to create a children's book. If possible, arrange for students to read the story to a group of young children at a child care center.

Cooperative Learning
Have students work in groups and brainstorm typical mistakes that toddlers make when dressing themselves. Then have them suggest how caregivers should handle specific errors in ways that promote independence and self-esteem. Have a recorder share the group's ideas.

Critical Thinking
Have students attempt to put on one of the following garments while wearing gloves or mittens: sweater with small buttons, jacket with small zipper slide, sweatpants with drawstring, garment with small snaps or hooks and eyes. Ask them to discuss how this activity helps them understand the challenge a child faces when learning self-dressing.

HEALTH TIP

Any child who receives a sharp blow to the teeth should be checked by a dentist. Nerve damage can be present even if there is no bleeding or looseness of the teeth.

MORE ABOUT

Healthy Teeth
Dentists suggest that both adults and children change toothbrushes every three to four months, primarily because wear and tear on the toothbrush makes it less effective. If the bristles on a toothbrush are flattened or if they are falling out, the toothbrush should be replaced sooner. The presence of bacteria is another problem with toothbrushes. Family members should never share a toothbrush. It is a good idea to assign a brush of a specific color to each family member and to buy the same color for that person each time the brush is replaced. Also, if someone in the family has been ill, his or her toothbrush should be disinfected or replaced.

GUIDED PRACTICE (continued)

Critical Thinking

- Ask students why it is important to encourage self-dressing.

- Ask students whether they think a child should be allowed to get his or her clothes dirty when playing outdoors. How might a child who is always warned to stay clean be affected?

- Ask students whether they think a three-year-old should choose the clothes he or she wants to wear on a given day. What happens if the child chooses something inappropriate? What strategy might prevent this inappropriate choice? (Offering the child a choice between two appropriate garments.)

Cooperative Learning

Provide students with references to use in developing a checklist for selecting clothing for young children. Have students work in groups to develop lists of features that ensure comfort, durability, and economy. Combine the groups' lists into one checklist. Reproduce the checklist to share with parents of young children.

Soon after his or her first birthday, a child begins pulling clothing off. At first, it may be just a sock or hat. Between eighteen and twenty-four months, the toddler learns to undress completely, unless his or her clothes have unusually difficult fasteners.

A child usually starts trying to help with dressing around the age of thirteen or fourteen months. He or she may hold out an arm for the sleeve of a shirt, for example. Next, the toddler may learn to actually push his or her own arm through a shirt sleeve. By two years, the child can pull up pants, but putting on shirts continues to be difficult. At this age, children often end up with their garments inside out or backwards. By the age of three, the child can dress independently, except for some help with buttons, other difficult fasteners, and shoe laces.

You can encourage a child's interest in dressing by providing clothing that is easy to put on and take off. Self-dressing helps develop independence, responsibility, cooperation, and self-esteem. This period requires patience on the part of parents and other caregivers. With a relaxed attitude, you can share the child's fun and satisfaction in learning.

Choosing Clothing

Comfort, durability, and economy are the most important characteristics to look for in clothing for young children.

- **Comfort.** Clothes that allow freedom of movement are the most comfortable. Knit clothes that stretch as the child moves are good choices. Fabrics that are stiff or scratchy do not provide comfort, especially for young children.

  Choosing the best clothing size is important in providing comfort. Clothes that are too small restrict movement. Clothes that are too big can also be uncomfortable. Too-long pants can cause a toddler to trip. A shirt with sleeves so long that they cover a child's hands makes it difficult to play. Remember that different articles of clothing labeled with the same size may not fit the same way. Whenever possible, let a child try on clothing before you buy, and remember to allow for some shrinkage.

Clothing labels tell you not only the fiber content of the garment, but how it should be cared for. Why is care an especially important consideration for children's clothing?

- **Durability.** Children's clothes must withstand both hard wear and repeated laundering. Durability is influenced by the quality of the fabric and by the quality of the construction of the clothing. Denim, for example, is a durable fabric; children's jeans and overalls are usually made from denim. In checking the construction of clothing, look for close, even stitching with strong thread. The stitching should be reinforced at points of strain. All fasteners and trims should be firmly attached.

MORE ABOUT

Self-Dressing Features

During the toddler stage, children learn to dress themselves. They will learn faster and more easily if their clothing is chosen with this goal in mind. Front zippers or other front openings allow children to fasten their garments themselves. A garment that has a distinct front and back can help the child know how to put it on. Otherwise, the front and back of the garment should be clearly marked. Big buttons are easier than tiny ones for small hands to handle. Pants and skirts with elastic waistbands and suspenders are also easy for children to master.

Developing Self-Care Skills

Three-year-old Michael cannot dress himself. He wants to dress himself, and he is certainly capable of learning. However, Michael has not had an opportunity to develop and practice dressing skills.

Michael has three older sisters. To make the household run smoothly, each family member has assigned tasks. Dressing Michael is one of twelve-year-old Maria's duties.

Maria took over this job when Michael was still a baby. She learned to dress him quickly and efficiently. Now, when Michael tries to find a shirt in the dresser drawer, Maria invariably pulls out her own choice and says, "Here, Michael, you can wear the red one today. It's all ready for you," and slips it over his head. Maria doesn't let Michael pull up his own pants, button his own shirt, or put on his own shoes. She can do it all much faster herself.

THINK AND DISCUSS

1. What self-dressing skills do other three-year-olds have?
Why hasn't Michael developed those skills?
2. What effect does Maria's help have on Michael? How do you think his inability to dress himself affects the way he feels about himself?
3. If you were Michael's parent, what goals would you establish for Michael? How would you help Michael meet those goals?

Cotton is a good fabric choice, especially for T-shirts and underwear. Cotton wears well, launders well (though some cotton fabrics shrink), and does not irritate the skin. Since it absorbs moisture, cotton is also comfortable to wear. Cotton is one of the **natural fibers**—that is, *fibers that come from plants or animals*—from which clothing is made. Other natural fibers are wool, silk, and linen.

Synthetic fibers, also called manufactured fibers, are *fibers manufactured from chemicals rather than natural sources.* Polyester, nylon, and acrylic are synthetic fibers often used in children's clothes. Fabrics made from synthetic fibers have several advantages. They are durable, wrinkle-resistant, and quick-drying; they require little or no ironing. However, unlike natural fibers, synthetic fibers do not absorb moisture well. They tend to hold heat and perspiration against the body.

OBSERVING AND PARTICIPATING

Learning through Participation

Dressing a two-year-old is much like dressing a bowl of gelatin with arms and legs. Try these techniques to encourage the child's participation rather than resistance:

1. *The Monkey Roundup*: You are Mama Monkey chasing the Baby Monkey. End the game by enticing the Baby Monkey to come to you to get a pretend banana.

2. *The Bunny Hunt*: Quickly pop a shirt onto the child's head and show how the arms of the shirt look like bunny ears. As the child hops around like a bunny, pretend that you are a dog and chase the bunny until you catch it. Then pull the shirt on.

3. *Magic Fingers Show*: Hum a rousing tune, like the theme from *The Lone Ranger*, while magic fingers quickly tie shoes. End with "Ta da!"

PARENTING IN ACTION

Promoting Discussion

Have students discuss the advantages of buying second-hand clothing for children. (Parents can save money; children frequently need new clothing because of their rapid growth. In addition, reuse of any item reduces the negative impact of human activity on the environment.)

Critical Thinking

Have students discuss the cost of clothing a child. To help them understand this concept, ask them to follow up a brief discussion with consumer research.

Have students examine catalogs and advertisements for children's clothing and price the following items for a boy and a girl: a warm jacket, a pair of everyday pants, a T-shirt, a sweater, a pair of socks, and a pair of tennis shoes. They may also call stores for prices. Have them compute the retail cost of a complete outfit. Then have them compute the amount saved by buying on sale, at outlet stores, at thrift stores, or at garage sales.

Answers to "Think and Discuss"

1. Ability to pull clothes on or off. Someone has always done it for him.

2. It denies him the opportunity to learn the necessary skills. He isn't given the chance to test his ability; he may develop a sense of inadequacy; he may learn to depend on others to make choices and supply his needs.

3. Answers may vary, but one possibility is to ask Maria to show Michael how to dress, not just give her the task. Parents could praise Maria's efficiency and encourage her to instruct Michael while she dresses him, gradually allowing him to choose his own clothes and develop the skills needed to dress himself.

GUIDED PRACTICE (continued)

Cooperative Learning

Have students work in small groups to evaluate the fabric, durability, and care of actual garments for young children. Have groups share their findings with the class.

Making Connections: Art

Have students search art history books for paintings showing dress of children in other times and cultures. Have them evaluate the clothing for ease of care and comfort for the child. *The Family of Charles IV*, by Francisco Goya, shows elaborate clothing that would not meet today's standards of comfort or ease of care.

Promoting Discussion

Ask students whether they have experienced any bedtime problems while caring for young children. How did they handle them? Would they do anything differently the next time?

Cultural Exchange

In all likelihood, teens in your class once owned a toy or stuffed animal that comforted them as a child. Many, in fact, might still have that favorite item. Ask students to share and compare their experiences with their version of "Teddy."

Cultural Exchange

SLEEPING WITH TEDDY BEAR

According to a survey cited by Peter Bull in *The Teddy Bear Boo*, 45 percent of British bear-owning children call their bears "Teddy." Prior to 1903, American children referred to their toy bears as "Bruin." Austrian bears are called "Brum" bears, and the French bears go by the name of Martin.

A blend of natural fibers and synthetic fibers is often a good fabric choice. A blend offers the benefits of both kinds of fibers.

By law, all clothing must have a label that identifies the fibers used. Checking clothing labels can also help you determine how to care for each garment.

- **Economy.** Since young children continue to grow rapidly, they outgrow their clothes often. Many parents exchange outgrown clothes to cut costs. Others find good used clothes at yard sales, secondhand clothing stores, and thrift shops.

  Children's clothes are most economical when they can expand a bit to allow for growth. Look for deep hems or cuffs that can be altered after the child has grown. Check that the straps on overalls or jumpers are long enough to allow the buttons to be moved.

  Whenever possible, allow the child some choice in clothing selection. Children usually love brightly colored clothes. In fact, young children choose their clothes more by color than by anything else. Other clothing favorites include "picture clothes"—clothing made from fabrics printed with animals, toys, or story characters, or garments with a picture on the front.

Sleeping

As the second birthday approaches, the sleeping habits of most children undergo a significant change. Children at this age usually require less sleep than before, and they may not sleep as easily or as willingly.

By age two, most children no longer take a morning nap. They do, however, sleep all night and continue to take an afternoon nap. Most three-year-olds require slightly less sleep; many give up regular naps.

Emotionally, a two-year-old appears more dependent on adults than he or she was during the previous year. Typically, the two-year-old calls his or her parents back repeatedly at bedtime. He or she may ask for a drink of water, another story, and one more trip to the bathroom; clearly, what the child really wants is someone near. Children of this age often use self-comforting techniques at bedtime, such as thumb sucking, rocking the crib, or cuddling a favorite blanket or soft toy.

Love and understanding are essential during this period. At bedtime, parents should be sure that the child's physical needs have been fully met. Establishing a consistent bedtime routine and following it will help.

TEEN PARENTING

Creative Economics

Economy is often a concern for teen parents, but they seldom have creative alternatives. Ask students whether they know what the barter system is. How can it help teen parents reduce expenses? You may want to help teen parents in your class set up a system for exchanging clothing, toys, and babysitting services with one another or with other parents. Not only will they save money, but they will have the opportunity to socialize with other young parents.

Forcing a child to sleep in the dark is not likely to eliminate fear. A night-light may be needed, along with the caregiver's patience and reassurance.

It is not unusual for three-year-olds to wake in the middle of the night and even get out of bed. Emotional experiences of the day, excitement at bedtime, or nighttime fears may cause the three-year-old to feel insecure at night.

Fear of the dark is common among two- and three-year-olds. There are many possible causes. For example, the child may have overheard conversations or news reports about prowlers, fires, accidents, or other dangers. The child's fears are very real and usually very troubling. Unfortunately, there is rarely a quick solution. A calm discussion of the problem may help some children. Other children may feel more comforted by a night-light. All children who feel afraid of the dark need patience and understanding. Ridicule or shaming the child only makes the problem worse.

GUIDED PRACTICE (continued)

Using the Photograph
    Refer students to the photo on page 339. Ask students if they had nighttime fears as small children. How were they solved? Have them discuss what fears they have now. Ask whether they can explain their fears. Guide students in recognizing that some fears are not easy for children to overcome.

Making Connections: Language Arts
• Have students consult a children's librarian and examine several children's stories or poems about fear of the dark. Which would be most suitable for reading to a child with nighttime fears?
• Provide copies of cartoon collections such as Bill Watterson's *Something Under the Bed Is Drooling*. Have students discuss how Calvin's humorous fears and fantasies reflect the fears of real-life children.

Critical Thinking
    Pedro is three years old. He is terrified that a lion lives in his closet, waiting to leap out and devour him as soon as he is alone at night. Suggest strategies his parents could use. (Answers will vary. Each night, they could inspect the closet and the room carefully with Pedro. They could provide a night-light and perhaps a baby monitor in case he needs to call for help. They might read aloud stories with likable lions as characters, or natural history books describing the real habitats and lifestyles of lions. They should not ridicule his fear.)

OBSERVING AND PARTICIPATING

Celebrating Individual Differences

Fear of the dark may be the child's response to new things, such as an unfamiliar face or a loud, scary noise on the radio, things that parents or caregivers don't even notice. Sudden fear can also be triggered by toddlers' incomplete understanding of what is going on around them and their inability to put what they are experiencing into words. For example, the child who sees shadows moving on the nursery wall may imagine that the shadows are people because they are moving and that they are dangerous because they are strangers. Parents and other caregivers can help by being patient and reassuring. Fear of the dark usually goes away with time.

GUIDED PRACTICE (continued)

Critical Thinking

Have students share their responses to these questions:

- Ask students what kinds of problems can be caused by starting toilet training before a child is physically ready. Why are parental attitudes toward toilet training important? (Training before physical readiness sets the child up for failure and negative attitudes toward toilet training. Frustration plus an overly strict parental attitude can make toilet training more difficult and cause long-lasting emotional problems.)

- Some parents claim that their children were toilet trained at twelve months, or even younger. Have students explain how children could seem to be trained before they were ready. Ask students whether they think the parents or the children were more trained, and have them support their opinions.

HEALTH TIP

Set a good example for personal hygiene. When you want a child to wash his or her hands, wash your own at a sink with soap and water. Put a stool by the sink, and encourage the child to wash as you are doing. The running water and soapy lather is too much to resist!

HEALTH TIP

Consistent and careful hand-washing is an effective defense against the spread of illnesses. Young children should learn to wash their hands before and after meals, after toileting, and after playing outdoors. By three years of age, most children can handle these tasks independently.

Toilet Training

Most children begin the process of toilet training between the ages of eighteen months and three years. There is no set age at which the process should begin. Rather, each child should start toilet training when he or she is physically mature enough and emotionally ready.

To be physically mature enough for toilet training, a child must be able to control his or her **sphincter muscles**, *the muscles that control elimination.* The child must also be able to recognize the body sensations that precede elimination. Only then is the child ready to start learning to control and release the sphincter muscles.

A child can be considered emotionally ready for toilet training if he or she is happily settled into a familiar daily routine. During a family move or any similar event that requires adjustments, the child should not be expected to deal with the further changes involved in toilet training.

Once the child is physically ready for toilet training and shows an interest in it, the process can usually be accomplished with little trouble.

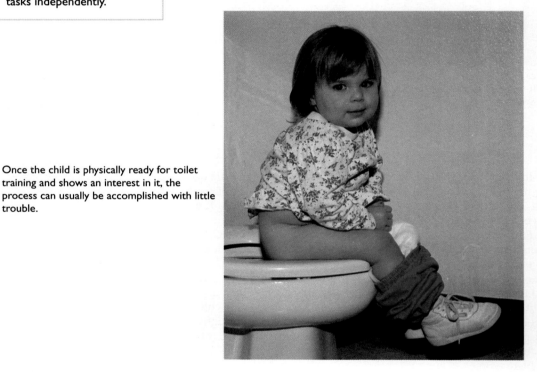

COOPERATIVE LEARNING

Assuming Responsibility

When applied effectively, the cooperative learning method mirrors—and reinforces skills essential to—situations many students will encounter in adult life, such as the need to delegate and accept roles and tasks. You can help students hone such skills by providing your class with an abundant supply of "role" cards. Made by fastening safety pins to 3-x-5-inch index cards that bear one of a variety of labels (e.g., Recorder, Research Coordinator, Search Committee, Think Squad, Publisher), such cards can help group members better keep track of their roles, relationships, and responsibilities over the course of a project.

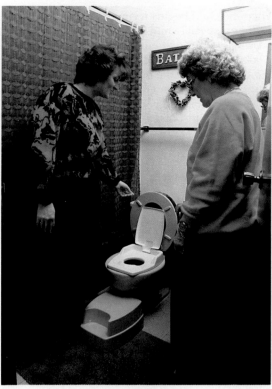

Parents should let other caregivers know about the child's progress so that toilet training is consistent. This mother is explaining the potty chair.

The attitudes of parents and other caregivers toward toilet training are very important. An overly strict approach can make training more difficult and may cause long-lasting emotional problems for the child. Interest and calm encouragement are more effective than rules and punishment. Remember that if the child is physically and emotionally ready for toilet training, he or she genuinely wants to succeed. As is the case with other learning skills, the child needs the chance to practice and to be in charge of his or her progress. It is especially important never to force toilet training. If the child resists, don't insist or even urge. Simply abandon all attempts at toilet training for several weeks; then try again.

GUIDED PRACTICE (continued)

Family Focus

Toilet training can become a battle of wills between a parent and child. Most children are quick to observe that a parent wants certain behavior from them. At the same time, children are usually looking for ways to assert their independence. If the child senses impatience or some other negative attitude, he or she may respond with resistance. Faced with toilet training for the first time, many parents feel lost. How do I start? What do I do? The insecurity alone is sometimes enough to send a child down a resistant path. One mother made the observation that her first child was extremely difficult to train, the second was fairly easy, and she did not remember training the third. Ask students what accounts for this mother's reaction to toilet training. (The mother may have been too eager, anxious, and inexperienced the first time. By the third child, she was probably so busy and calm about training that it simply took place, almost without notice. Children also learn by observing older siblings.)

OBSERVING AND PARTICIPATING

Developing Observational Skills

Most parents and caregivers will attest to the common understanding that children are ready for toilet training when they become aware of bowel or bladder movements. The age a child reaches this awareness is unpredictable and entirely individual. However, people can begin to look for tell-tale signs that a child between the ages of eighteen months and three years is aware of these func-tions. For example, at almost age two, Susie would hide behind a chair for a while or slip into another room alone. Bill, the same age would stop what he was doing, stand still, and look preoccupied. Both children are good candidates for toilet training. Susie's desire for privacy or a change of location would make her more receptive to use of the toi-let sooner. A parent or caregiver should be alert to these changes in a child's behavior.

INDEPENDENT PRACTICE

Student Workbook

Have students complete one or more of the following activities in the Student Workbook: "Planning Meals for Children," "Handling Sleep Problems," and "Clothes Closings."

Student Demonstration

Have students bring children's clothing from home or use pieces of their own clothing to demonstrate the relative advantages of such features as fabrics, fasteners, or front closures, versus back closures.

Extension

Have students work independently or in small groups to complete one or more of these extension activities:

- Cut cheese, carrots, celery, melon, banana, and hard-cooked eggs into sizes and shapes that would encourage self-feeding by a child from one to three.

- Look through catalogs that include furniture, dishes, and utensils for young children's mealtime. Choose one item to evaluate. How would the item encourage self-feeding? How would it reduce mealtime frustration?

- Attempt to eat gelatin squares with a plastic fork, using your nondominant hand. Write a journal entry reflecting on what learning new skills with developing motor skills must be like for a child.

ASSESS

CHECKING COMPREHENSION

Assign students to write their responses to the Check Your Understanding questions in the Section 2 Review. Answers to the questions are given at the bottom of page 343.

EVALUATE

Have students complete the Chapter 11, Section 2 quiz in the TCR.

When the child begins trying to use the toilet, he or she will need either a special child seat on the toilet or a separate potty chair. Using a child seat eliminates the need for another adjustment later, when the child is ready to graduate from a potty chair to the toilet. On the other hand, using a potty chair allows the young child more independence than a special seat on top of the toilet.

Remember that some children are frightened by the flushing of a toilet. Unless the child is particularly interested in the flushing, it may be better to flush the toilet after the child has left the bathroom.

Bowel training usually comes before bladder training. The child is probably ready when he or she shows an awareness that a bowel movement is imminent. When you recognize this awareness in the child's facial expressions or gestures, you can suggest that he or she might try sitting on the special toilet seat or on the potty chair. Be available and encouraging, but remember that being too forceful or demanding will make toilet training more difficult both for the child and for you. Some children seem naturally to follow regular patterns of elimination; these children are more easily trained than those who have irregular bowel movements.

Bladder training typically begins several months after bowel training, although some children learn both at about the same time. The child who is ready for bladder training has a less frequent need to urinate—sometimes as long as from one meal to the next. Other signs that a child is ready include indicating that his or her diapers need changing and expressing a clear understanding that he or she is the cause of that puddle on the floor.

A child's urination habits are often irregular. They are affected by liquid intake, weather, temperament, and excitement. However, the parent or caregiver should take note of the pattern and encourage the youngster to try the toilet or potty for short periods at specific times. These times should include before and after meals, bath, and sleep.

Many young children are encouraged in toilet training by the opportunity to wear **training pants**, *heavy, absorbent underpants*, in place of diapers. Wearing training pants makes it possible for a young child to use a potty independently. Most children also recognize that wearing underpants instead of diapers is a significant sign of maturity.

Even after bowel and bladder training seem to be well established, parents and other caregivers should expect—and accept—accidents. Like other skills, toileting skills develop along a predictable pattern, but at the rate appropriate to the individual child.

MORE ABOUT

Toilet Training

- Forcing a child to sit on the toilet for a specified length of time or getting angry if the child doesn't "perform" when you think he or she should can cause problems. Children do not need this kind of pressure. It may deprive the child of the sense of confidence that comes through learning to use the toilet through his or her own initiative rather than your insistence.

- A first-born child usually takes about two months longer to train than one who has older siblings to imitate.

- Around the age of two, children will have definite opinions and negative moods. Introduce toilet training during a positive mood.

- Some child care programs will not accept children who are not toilet trained. Others charge extra until the child is completely toilet trained.

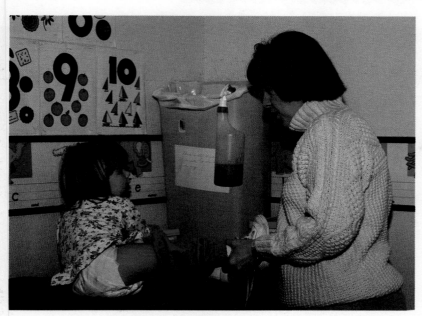

When the child is taking a nap, sleeping at night, or going on a trip, it is best to use diapers. This prevents the child from experiencing too many "discouraging" failures.

SECTION 2 REVIEW

CHECK YOUR UNDERSTANDING

1. List two benefits of providing finger foods for one-year-olds.

2. What is the most important consideration in preparing meals and snacks for young children?

3. How do toddlers usually respond to taking a bath?

4. What should toddlers do to care for their own teeth? What should parents or other caregivers do to care for the toddler's teeth?

5. What is the difference between natural fibers and synthetic fibers?

6. How should parents and caregivers respond to a young child's fear of the dark?

7. At what age should a child begin toilet training?

DISCUSS AND DISCOVER

1. Plan and write out a two-day menu for a young child. Include meals and snacks, and note the quantities of each food taking into account that the child might not eat everything provided. Present your menu to other students, identifying the specific age of the child. Evaluate your plan.

2. With a group of other students, select three or four children's outfits, and evaluate the quality and durability of the garments. What are the advantages of each garment? Are there disadvantages to any of your choices?

Observing & Participating

Spend some time observing a toddler during a meal. Describe what the child eats and how he or she approaches the task of eating. Is the food nutritious and appropriate for a child of this age? If other people are eating at the same time, do they help make the mealtime enjoyable? If so, how?

Reteaching

Choose from the following reteaching activities:

1. Assign Reteaching Activity 28 in the TCR and have students complete the activity and review their responses.

2. Have students write a description of an appropriate bedtime routine for a young child.

3. Have students list ways to encourage self-dressing.

Enrichment

1. Have students interview someone with experience or expertise on toilet training. This might be a pediatrician, pediatric nurse, child care center director, or parent. Ask students to gather information, tips, recommendations, and anecdotes to share with the class.

2. Assign Enrichment 28 in the TCR.

Extension

Have students visit a children's clothing store or department and evaluate the fasteners used on three garments. Ask students to write a description of each garment and its fastener and then describe the appropriateness of the fasteners for a child age one to three.

CLOSE

Have each student write an end for this sentence:
When you are caring for a child between ages one and three, it is important to remember …"
Have students read their sentences aloud.

SECTION 2 REVIEW

1. Finger foods improve coordination and encourage self-feeding.

2. Nutrition.

3. They usually play and have fun.

4. Try brushing on their own. Rebrush child's teeth, begin flossing, and show child how to hold and use dental floss.

5. Natural fibers come from plants and animals, synthetic fibers are manufactured from chemicals rather than natural sources.

6. Discuss the fear calmly; provide a night-light; be patient and understanding.

7. Whenever he or she is physically mature enough and emotionally ready.

Positive Parenting Skills

*Positive
Parenting
Skills*

MOTIVATOR

Ask students to explain how the safety needs of a three-year-old are different from those of a one-year-old. How are they the same?

Promoting Discussion

1. What are common accidents that happen to toddlers?

2. How can parents toddler-proof their homes?

3. How can safety for infants and toddlers be secured when they are away from home?

Using the Photographs

Have students identify the safety precautions illustrated in the photographs on pages 344 and 345. Ask for descriptions of accidents they could prevent.

Critical Thinking

Give each student an object, or a picture of one, that can be used to prevent toddler accidents. Ask students to explain how the item could be used in toddler-proofing a home.

Using Management Skills

Have students look through catalogs and magazines to find pictures of household items and furniture that are commonly found in homes. Have students evaluate the safe and/or unsafe features associated with each item. Ask them to compile a list of alternative choices for those items that would be dangerous to children.

Cooperative Learning

Have students form small groups and collect safety tips for families with toddlers. Advise them to look in books, magazines, pediatrician offices, and social service offices. Then compile the tips by categories, and develop a booklet or poster series that can be donated to child care centers or parents.

KEEPING CHILDREN SAFE AND HEALTHY

As children grow and mature, they are capable of—and interested in—exploring more and more of their home environment. Toddlers walk and climb. They open drawers and cabinets. They turn knobs and stick their fingers into tiny holes. Children try all these things so that they can learn more about the world, but they often put themselves in danger while they're learning.

It's not fair to the child—or to the parents and caregivers—to spend the day saying "no." The best solution is to make the home as safe as possible for the young child. This is called "childproofing" your home. One suggestion is to crawl around

your house at the child's current level, and observe situations that may present a safety hazard. Notice what is accessible to the child. Then use the following tips to help you keep toddlers safe from falls, burns, and other hazards.

Falls
• Keep the floor and all the stairs free of toys and other objects that children—or adults—might trip over.

• Wipe up spills immediately—before someone slips and falls.

• Use a rubber mat or adhesive strips in the tub or shower.

• Use safety gates to block off the top and the bottom of each stairway. Be sure the gates meet current requirements for narrower spaces between the bars.

• Always use the seat belt when the child is in a high chair.

• Be sure that all open windows have secure screens. Windows in high-rise buildings pose a particular danger; they should have special safety latches.

• Once the child begins to walk, remove loose rugs and furniture that might tip easily.

Burns
• As early as possible, teach the child that the stove is hot and must not be touched.

344

Childhood Accidents

More children die or are injured from accidents than from the next five most frequent causes of childhood deaths combined. For babies under one year who were born healthy, accidents are one of the major causes of death.

For children ages one to four, 37 percent of all deaths are caused by accidents. Of these, 34 per-

cent die in cars; 19 percent in fires or of burns; 16 percent from drowning; 6 percent in falls; and 6 percent from poisoning. For children five to fourteen years old, 46 percent of all deaths are due to accidents. Ask your students to speculate on the causes of childhood accidental death and what can be done to prevent it.

to prevent burns. If the water is hotter than that, lower the thermostat on the home water heater.

- Put safety caps on electrical outlets when they are not in use.

- Keep small appliances, such as toasters and irons, unplugged and out of reach when they are not in use.

Other Hazards

- Keep all dangerous materials, such as cleaning supplies, medicines, paints, and insecticides, securely out of the child's reach.

Remember that many toddlers like to climb, so keeping these materials on a high shelf is not enough; they should be stored in locked cabinets or containers.

- Keep sharp knives, razor blades, sharp scissors, and

- Always turn the handles of pots and pans toward the center of the stove.

- Check the temperature of the hot water from the taps. The temperature should be no higher than 120° to 130° F (49°to 54° C)

matches securely out of the child's reach. Many of these items can be conveniently stored in a drawer that has been secured with a sturdy childproof latch. Use "childproof" latches on any cupboard you don't want accessible to the child.

- Lock unused refrigerators and freezers, or remove their doors.

345

Practicing Parenting Skills

Ask students to inspect their yards or the immediate surroundings of their home. Have them make a list of objects or conditions that are potentially dangerous to an infant or small child. For each item on their list, have them suggest a remedy or a precaution that parents or caretakers could make to ensure the safety of a child.

*Visit to Day Care

Cooperative Learning

Have small groups of students visit local child care centers and make a list of safety precautions that are made at the center. In addition to your suggestions, encourage them to check these areas: the materials used to cover floors; the general level of cleanliness; the availability of first aid supplies; the condition of toys and equipment; the ratio of adult supervisors to children; and the well-being and outward health of the children.

Practicing Decision Making

Ask students to imagine they are parents who are planning a visit to another family member who does not have children. How would they ensure the safety of their children at the relative's home? What precautions should be made by all adults involved? How would they react if they arrived at the relative's home and discovered unsafe or unhealthy conditions?

Enrichment

Have each student research one type of accident to learn how many toddlers are injured or die each year.

Extension

Ask students to think about their habits and lifestyles. What modifications would be necessary if they found themselves caring for an infant or a small child?

CLOSE

Ask students to volunteer one way they can make their homes safer for a child.

OBSERVING AND PARTICIPATING

Checking a House for Safety

When parents are in a hurry to leave, they may forget to put something away or lock the medicine cabinet. That is why it is a good idea for a babysitter or child care provider to do a quick safety check of the house no matter how many times he or she has sat for the family.

The sitter should also be aware of the child's stage of development; at certain stages, a child's development can lead to unsafe behavior. For example, a two-year-old has enough hand and finger control to be able to turn a knob. This means he or she can open an unlocked door. Curiosity could then lead the child into the street. Two-year-olds can also turn on a stove and burn themselves. Two-year-olds have enough whole-body coordination to be able to climb. A child can climb up open kitchen drawers and reach an electrical appliance.

Use the Summary and the Reviewing the Facts questions to help students go over the most important ideas presented in Chapter 11. Encourage students to ask questions and add details, as appropriate.

CHAPTER 11 REVIEW

1. Circumference means the measurement around. Until age two, a child's head, chest, and abdomen all have about the same circumference. Between ages two and three, the chest becomes larger than the head and abdomen.

2. Some people have an inherited protective mechanism that discourages decay.

3. Large motor skills are those that use the large muscles of the back, legs, shoulders, and arms. Walking, running, and throwing balls are examples. Small motor skills are those that involve the finer muscles of the wrists, fingers, and ankles. Building with blocks and stringing beads are examples.

4. Large motor skills: runs fairly well, can stand on one foot, can walk up and down stairs, and can throw objects overhand. Small motor skills: buttons large buttons; pulls down zippers, turns doorknobs, and stacks several cubes to form a tower.

5. Because during this time they acquire food habits and attitudes that influence their eating throughout their lives.

6. Do not force the child to eat the food, but wait until the next meal or snack when a different food with the same nutritional value can be offered.

7. Set a good example.

8. Approximately 18 months.

9. A calm discussion of the problem or a night-light.

10. Heavy, absorbent underpants. Children can use the toilet independently and experience the feel of not wearing diapers.

CHAPTER 11 REVIEW

SUMMARY

- For children from one to three years of age, physical growth proceeds more slowly than during the first year of life.
- Posture improves as a child's body proportions change.
- By the age of three, most children have a full set of baby teeth.
- Both large and small motor skills improve greatly during this period.
- Children this age are developing lifetime eating and cleanliness habits.
- Children learn gradually to feed and dress themselves.
- Bedtime problems are common during this stage.
- Toilet training should not be started until a child is physically and emotionally ready.

REVIEWING THE FACTS

1. Define *circumference*. Explain how the circumference of a child's chest changes between the ages of two and three.

2. What role does heredity play in tooth quality?

3. How are large motor skills and small motor skills different?

4. List at least four large and small motor skills that most one-and-one-half- to two-year-olds have.

5. Why are the attitudes that toddlers develop toward food so important?

6. How should parents and other caregivers respond when a toddler refuses to eat a particular food?

7. What is the best way for parents and other caregivers to teach toddlers good table manners?

8. Around what age should children begin having regular dental checkups?

9. What are two approaches that might help a young child who feels afraid of the dark?

10. What are training pants? How can training pants help children during toilet training?

EXPLORING FURTHER

1. Collect several photographs of yourself taken between your first and fourth birthdays. Display the photographs in chronological order and label the physical development noticeable at each stage. (Section 1)

2. Watch at least four different commercial television shows directed at very young children. Notice the food products that are advertised during those shows. Then discuss those ads with other students: What foods do they show young children? How do you think those foods might affect the physical growth and development of young children? (Section 2)

3. Plan and prepare lunch—or another meal—for a two-year-old. Include an appropriate variety of foods; concentrate on including a variety of shapes that would interest and appeal to a young child. (Section 2)

4. Design an article of clothing—or an outfit— for a toddler. Sketch your design, and note the kinds of fabrics and fasteners to be used. Also note the kind of activity for which the clothing is intended. Display your sketch, and invite other students to critique your design. (Section 2)

THINKING CRITICALLY

1. **Synthesize.** Why do you think a toddler typically uses excuses to call his or her parent back at bedtime? Would it be easier for the child if he or she expressed the fear or anxiety directly? Why or why not? Would that be easier for the parent? Why or why not?

2. **Analyze.** Why do you think toilet training is such an important issue in many families? What do you think toilet training represents to a young child? To a child's parents? What attitudes and approaches do you think are most important in dealing with toilet training?

3. **Analyze.** Investigate and evaluate at least four potty chairs and child-sized toilet seats. What special advantages does each offer? What are the disadvantages of each? How much does each cost? If you were preparing to toilet train a toddler, which would you buy? Why?

CLASSROOM MANAGEMENT

Reinforcing Behavior

An instructor's positive approach and reaction to student behavior builds a strong foundation for classroom dynamics. Whether it be through smiles or nods or through words of praise, reinforcement instills a measure of confidence in students. They see that participation is not met with humiliation or rejection. When their thoughts and ideas are valued, they build on this positive response to develop a subject further. They feel complimented, so they learn to compliment others. Reinforcement can be made by rephrasing a statement made by a student. Encouraging a student to explain an idea further uses a student's knowledge and expands his or her communication skills. Most importantly, reinforcement reflects a concern for students' feelings. It tells them that they are important and necessary participants in the learning process.

CROSS-CURRICULUM CONNECTIONS

1. **Math.** Weigh and measure at least ten three-year-olds in a child care center or other group care setting. Calculate the average weight and height of the children in your group. How do the averages for your group compare with the national averages given in the chart on page 322?

2. **Writing.** Plan, write, and illustrate a short story, appropriate for toddlers, about tooth brushing. Read your finished book to a young child or to a small group of children.

SCHOOL TO WORK

Communication Few skills are more valuable in the workplace than communication—speaking, listening, reading, and writing. Since communication involves an exchange of ideas, you should practice both speaking and listening skills. During high school, you can improve your communication skills by taking Language Arts and Speech classes. Also, look for opportunities to lead small groups of peers, where you'll have the chance to see how well your communication skills are developed.

PERFORMANCE ASSESSMENT

Physical Development from One to Three

Task

Evaluate toys and other play objects that encourage motor skills development. Then write a consumer report on one manufactured play item.

Purpose

Learning how to evaluate products is a skill that will be useful to you in all stages of your life. In this activity, you will learn how to assess products designed for toddlers for their developmental appropriateness and safety.

Procedure

1. Visit a park or child care center and observe one- to three-year-olds playing with toys or other play items. Don't overlook the opportunity to evaluate any large play equipment designed for toddlers.

2. Write a description of one toy or object and record how the child plays with or uses it.

3. Refer to the Average Motor Skills Development chart on page 327 to determine the age and stage of motor skills development appropriate for the item you are evaluating.

4. Evaluate why the item is, or is not, developmentally appropriate for toddlers of this age group. Be sure to include safety considerations.

5. Prepare a consumer report on this item. Tell what is good and what is not good about it. Finish by explaining whether or not you would encourage consumers to purchase this item for a toddler.

6. Display your consumer report with a picture or drawing of the item.

Evaluation

Your findings will be evaluated on how well you demonstrate age-appropriateness in toddlers' toys or other play items and your knowledge of motor skills development. Your consumer report will be evaluated for accuracy, clarity of content, and neatness.

 Portfolio Idea For your portfolio, include with your consumer report a statement about your objectives and what you learned. Also include the photograph or drawing of the toy or object you evaluated. To expand your evaluation, apply the same process to other toys or play items manufactured by the same company.

Enrichment

• Have students plan a menu suitable for a young child from one to three. Then have them prepare and serve the meal to a younger relative or friend. Have students write a report on the child's reactions and behavior during the meal.

EVALUATE

Use the reproducible Chapter 11 test in the TCR, or construct your own test using the Testmaker Software.

EXTENSION

Invite a dietician from a children's hospital to speak to the class about the nutritional needs of children from one to three and to suggest appetizing, nutritious foods that toddlers like.

CLOSE

Read aloud the statements made in response to the questions in the Chapter opener. Discuss each statement with the entire class. Then have students review their predictions and verify or modify them.

DEVELOPING A PORTFOLIO

Reviewing Contents Ask students to consider how they will use their portfolio outside the classroom. Tell them to think about what they want to do after high school, or what kinds of education or career they are interested in pursuing. Ask who they think might be interested in looking at their portfolio. Tell them to focus on a target audience, and review their portfolio contents with questions such as: What picture does it paint of me to this audience? What is the overall look of my work samples? How does the portfolio make me appear ambitious? Creative? Well-organized?

PERFORMANCE ASSESSMENT

Consumer Report

Bring a selection of toys or play objects to class. If possible, arrange to take the class to a child care center, where students will have the opportunity to gather the data they need. As an alternative, toddlers could be brought to the classroom by caregivers for observation.

Motivated students might find the toy or item they evaluated at a retail store and read the packaging labels. Encourage them to take notes on the claims made on the package: What is the target age group? What will this item do for the toddler? Is it safe? If so, why? If not, why not? Then have the students evaluate the item again, this time against the claims made on the package.

CHAPTER 12
Emotional
Development from
One to Three

INTRODUCE

CHAPTER OVERVIEW

As students study Chapter 12, they learn about emotional and social development between ages one to three and one-half years. On the basis of that knowledge, they learn to guide toddlers through these stages of development and encourage heathy emotional and social development.

In Section 1, students study the patterns of emotional and social development that take place between ages one through three and one-half years. They examine the emotions of toddlers and how the expression of emotion changes with age.

In Section 2, they explore patterns of social development in children from ages one through three and one-half. They learn the importance of a positive self-concept.

In Section 3, they study the three basic personality types and consider discipline techniques.

CLASSROOM MANAGEMENT

Resources Beyond the Classroom

Quality child care has many benefits, including helping young parents attain success and retain sanity while allowing for early socialization opportunities for the child. However, many young parents are not sure exactly what to look for in child care or how to go about finding it. A valuable school resource is a video produced by The Michigan Child Clearinghouse, which contains a reassuring message about child care. In interviews, real parents share concerns about the process of selecting quality child care while an overview with practical advice is offered by a pediatrician and child care experts. To order this video or to receive more information, call The Michigan Child Clearinghouse at its toll-free number: (800) 421-3225

CHAPTER 12

Emotional and Social Development from One to Three

> **SECTION 1** Emotional Development from One to Three
>
> **SECTION 2** Social Development from One to Three
>
> **SECTION 3** Personality Patterns and Behavior from One to Three

THINK ABOUT

Children begin early to get along with others and communicate effectively. Most of their training comes from watching others—parents, family members, and other caregivers. By watching the people around them and imitating their actions, children start to learn what to expect from others. Therefore, it is important to think about how your behavior encourages children to develop positive social skills.

ASK YOURSELF

Look at the photograph on the opposite page. What age group do the children in

the photograph represent? Do they seem to be playing well with each other? What might they be saying to each other? Besides learning to share and take turns, in what ways might their play be contributing to their social development?

NOW TRY THIS

Think about a playmate you had in your early childhood. What activities do you remember playing together with this child? How old were you? What were some of your favorite toys or games to play with your friend? Explain how this friendship or these activities influenced your social growth and development?

349

CLASSROOM MANAGEMENT

Bulletin Board Suggestions

"Facing Fears" Place illustrations of the following situations on the bulletin board: a child waking from a nightmare, a child's first visit to the dentist, a child's first experience with an unknown babysitter, a child afraid of the dark, and a child afraid of drowning. Use the information on text pages 357-

358 to write cards offering suggestions for each illustrated situation.

"Children Are So Many Things" Make cutouts from poster board of two children playing cheerfully. Using colored construction paper, make descriptive words to place around the children, such as *angry, loving, scared, fun,* etc.

CHAPTER OBJECTIVES

After completing Chapter 12, students will be able to:

- Describe general patterns of emotional and social development in children ages 1 to 3.
- Identify common emotions of young children and changes in how they are expressed.
- Describe how young children gradually learn to play with each other.
- Explain the importance of a positive self-concept and identify ways it can be developed.
- Describe effective discipline techniques.

INTRODUCING THE CHAPTER

- Read the following statements to the class, pausing after each one to discuss students' responses. Encourage them to speculate whether child care professionals would agree or disagree with each statement.
  - With age, toddlers become less fearful, more cooperative, and less prone to tantrums.
  - If parents guide their children properly, they will not have tantrums or display stubbornness or negativity.
  - Parents of children between one and three should always explain the reasons why certain behavior is not appropriate.

Explain to students that in Chapter 12 they will learn more about the emotional and social development of toddlers.

- Use the photo on the opposite page and the three features on this page—Think About, Ask Yourself, and Now Try This—to begin a discussion about a child's emotional and social development from ages one to three.

FOCUS

SECTION 1 RESOURCES

Teacher's Classroom Resources
- Enrichment 29
- Reteaching 29
- Section 1 Quiz

Student Workbook
- Puzzled About Emotional Development?

SECTION OVERVIEW

In Section 1, students study the patterns of emotional development that takes place between ages one and three and one-half years, and how emotional patterns differ in children ages eighteen months, two years, two and one-half years, three years, and three and one-half years. As they study the patterns, they learn how developing skills, increasing desire for independence, emotional development, and behavior are related.

MOTIVATOR

Have students look through Unit 4, examining the photographs of children. Tell them to identify the emotions expressed in each. Ask students whether they have siblings, relatives, or neighbors between 1 and 4 years. Encourage them to discuss these children's emotional behavior at those ages. Which emotions are delightful and which are challenging to handle?

USING TERMS TO LEARN

Many vocabulary terms in this chapter are open or hyphenated compound words. Individual word meanings provide clues to the meaning of the compound word they form. For example, siblings are brothers and sisters and sibling rivalry is competition between brothers and sisters. Ask volunteers to define each term.

SECTION 1

Emotional Development from One to Three

OBJECTIVES

- Describe the general patterns of emotional development in children from ages one to three.
- Identify the common emotions of young children and the changes in how those emotions are expressed.

TERMS TO LEARN

negativism
self-centered
separation anxiety
sibling rivalry
temper tantrums

It is easier to observe emotional development in early childhood than during any other stage in life. During the period from their first to their fourth birthdays, children develop new emotions, such as jealousy, that they did not feel as young babies. Young children display their emotions very clearly, first through their actions and later through their words. At the end of this period, children also begin to control their emotions or to show their emotions in more socially acceptable ways.

General Emotional Patterns

The time between the first and fourth birthdays is one of emotional ups and downs. The child experiences periods of negativism, and rebellion, but also periods of happiness, calmness, stability, and inner peace.

Throughout childhood, emotional development tends to go in cycles. This cyclical pattern can be observed in the predictable emotional stages most children go through. However, it is important to remember that each child is an individual. Jane may not go through the negativism of age two and one-half until she is three years old. Manuel, with his calm and sunny disposition, may not seem to go through it at all. Generally, however, you will find the following characteristics in children at about the ages given.

SEE HOW THEY GROW

Becoming an Individual

Probably the most overwhelming cause of negativism is the toddler's need to become a separate person. Infants do not fully realize that they are distinct from their parents. Toddlers, however, may reject parental suggestions to assure themselves that they are separate individuals. With separateness also comes a feeling of power. Toddlers experiment with their power over others. For example, a toddler may refuse to eat a favorite meal or may hit another child simply to see that child cry. Both of these actions create observable reactions—proof that the toddler is a separate individual who has power over others.

Toddlers show their feelings by their facial expression and their actions. Both smiles and tears are common.

Eighteen Months

Eighteen-month-old children are primarily **self-centered**, that is, *thinking about their own needs and wants, not those of others.* This is not surprising. During infancy, the child's needs and desires are promptly met by parents and other caregivers. At eighteen months, however, parents and caregivers are beginning to teach the child that some desires won't be met immediately and others will never be met. This is a difficult and long-term lesson for a child. An eighteen-month-old is only beginning the process of learning it.

Parents' and caregivers' spoken instructions are usually not very successful at this age. The toddler is likely to do the opposite of what is requested. The child's favorite response—no matter what the question or request—is "no." A request to "give it to me" typically prompts the eighteen-month-old to run off with the object instead.

Negativism, or *doing the opposite of what others want*, is a normal part of development for the toddler. It has a number of causes. One is the child's desire for independence. Saying "no" to parents and other caregivers is merely a way of saying, "Let me decide for myself sometimes." The child may even say "no" to things he or she would really like to do—just for the chance to be in charge of the decision.

Another cause of negativism is simply the frustration that toddlers feel. Their bodies are not developed enough to obey

Being negative is a way for toddlers to prove that they don't always have to follow along with the desires of others.

TEACH

Pages 350-362

- **General Emotional Patterns**
- **Specific Emotions**
- **Evaluating Emotional Adjustment**

GUIDED PRACTICE

Promoting Discussion

Use the following activities and topics to discuss emotional behavior of toddlers.

- Ask students whether they have ever been judgmental about parents whose toddlers are negative, disobedient, or prone to tantrums. Do they talk about parents who "can't control their kids?" Have they ever told themselves their children would never behave in a similar manner? Ask what pressures these prevailing attitudes might place on parents attempting to deal with the difficult emotional stages most children experience as they mature.

- Ask students why the move to independence is a difficult one for both parent and child. Why is it nevertheless important?

- Have students give examples of socially acceptable ways for adults to express emotions; then discuss socially acceptable ways for toddlers to express the same emotions.

- Have students discuss children whose favorite word is "no," and why they often do the opposite of what others want. Encourage them to suggest ways of giving young children more opportunity to be in control.

OBSERVING AND PARTICIPATING

Learning Through Participation

Caregivers should avoid offering choices when:

- The child is tired as he or she may not make a good choice and be unhappy with any.

- The child is in a new situation and unfamiliar with the choices. That can be frustrating.

- The caregiver is not prepared to accept the child's decision. "It's raining. Would you like to wear your raincoat or a sweater?" Both alternatives are often acceptable to the caregiver, but one is preferred. Mention the preferred alternative last. Children often select the last named alternative. Try not to feel disappointment or disapproval if the child's choice is not what is expected. Show no disapproval.

GUIDED PRACTICE (continued)

Critical Thinking

Ask students to consider the following questions:

• Why do children younger and older than toddlers display their emotions less clearly? (Infants experience a more limited range of emotions, and they have fewer ways of expressing them and distinguishing one emotion from the other. Older children quickly become socialized. Their desire for acceptance and their understanding of how to gain it become more pronounced, so they learn to suppress emotions or express them in socially acceptable ways.)

• How does the desire for approval and affection tend to influence children's behavior? (It makes them more cooperative and inclined to behave in ways that please others.) As children mature, can the desire for approval be too strong? (Yes.) Explain. (It can leave an individual's self-esteem at the mercy of others' evaluation and can sometimes lead to wrong behaviors for the wrong reason. Suppose, for example, someone wants them to hide stolen property.)

Making Connections:
Language Arts

Have students write a brief story about the toddler pictured on page 351, explaining what emotions the toddler is experiencing and what happened to evoke them.

BUILDING SELF-ESTEEM

The desire to have choices rather than being told what to do is not foreign to most teens. Ask students to discuss recent experiences in their own lives that point out the emotional value of having choices. Possibilities are their elective classes, the arrangement and condition of their rooms, and compromises about household chores.

BUILDING SELF-ESTEEM

The Game of Offering Choices

*E*ven very young children feel better about themselves when they make their own choices about daily activities. Whenever possible, offer children the opportunity to choose. Cleaning up can become a game when the caregiver asks, "Which should we do first—put these books on the shelf or put these toys into the toy box?" Getting ready for bed is more fun if the child gets to make simple choices—"Do you want to wear your yellow pajamas or the red pajamas tonight?"

However, there are some circumstances under which children should not be asked to make decisions. A child who is very tired or who is in a new situation should not be given choices; the parent or caregiver should guide the child's activities in these situations. Also, parents and caregivers should avoid offering choices if they are unwilling to accept the child's decision.

their wishes, and they don't have sufficient language skills to express their feelings. The result is anger or frustration.

At this age, a child also finally realizes that he or she is a separate person. This realization is both exciting and frightening. The child likes the power of being a separate person but misses the close bond with his or her mother, father, or other primary caregiver.

It is important to remember that negativism is a normal stage in emotional development. Understanding its causes makes it easier to deal with. One of the best ways to combat negativism at this age is simply to eliminate as many restrictions as possible. For example, rather than asking an eighteen-month-old not to touch certain things in the home, remove everything that is dangerous, breakable, or especially valuable. As the child gets older, the objects can gradually be returned.

At this age, distraction can be an effective way of coping with inappropriate behavior. Instead of saying "put that down," for example, you might open a picture book and talk about what you see, or start noisily arranging the child's blocks into an interesting pattern. The child will soon leave the undesirable activity to join you.

It also helps to give the child reasonable choices whenever possible. If the child can choose between a pear and a banana for lunch, it won't matter quite so much that there is no choice about taking a nap. It is best to limit choices to two alternatives, however. Toddlers cannot think about three or four things at the same time.

Around the age of eighteen months, many children start to have **temper tantrums,** *incidents in which children release their anger or frustration by screaming, crying, kicking, pounding, and sometimes even holding their breath.* Children typically have occasional temper tantrums until the age of three or four. At some points, even seemingly minor frustrations can cause temper tantrums.

Two Years

Emotionally, the two-year-old is less at odds with the world than he or she was at eighteen months. The child's speech and motor skills have improved, relieving much of the previous frustration. The child also understands more and is able to wait for longer and longer periods of time for his or her needs to be met.

The two-year-old expresses love and affection freely and actively seeks approval and praise. Though the child still has occasional emotional outbursts, they are fewer and less intense. The child is easier to reason with. Relationships with parents and other children have improved, for the two-year-old tends to be outgoing, friendly, and less self-centered.

TEEN PARENTING

Techniques of Discipline

If appropriate, ask teen parents in the class to share their experiences and concerns about discipline. What approaches have they found work best?

Does discipline ever cause parents to have feelings of guilt or frustration? How can these feelings be minimized? What effect does living in an extended family have on discipline methods?

Two and One-Half Years

Just as parents and caregivers begin to adjust to a smoother, less intense toddler, the child enters a new stage. In some ways, this period is more difficult for parents and other caregivers than the eighteen-month-old stage, because toddlers at two and one-half are not so easily distracted.

At two and one-half, children are learning so much that they often feel overwhelmed. Their comprehension and desires exceed their physical abilities. For example, they may want their blocks and dolls placed just so, but they succeed only partially before accidentally knocking them over. Two-and-one-half-year-olds work hard at talking. They know what they want to say, but they don't always succeed in making themselves understood. If parents or other caregivers answer with an absent-minded "uh-huh" or ignore their efforts to communicate, toddlers at this stage often become even more frustrated.

Toddlers' drive for independence causes them to resist pressures to conform. They are sensitive about being bossed, shown, helped, or directed. Independence and immaturity clash head-on during this stage. At two and one-half, children are sometimes stubborn, demanding, and domineering. However, their moods change rapidly, and within a short time, they can become lovable and completely charming.

One characteristic of this age is the child's desire for consistency; he or she wants the same routines, carried out in just the same way, day after day. This is the child's way of coping with a

At two and one-half, children sometimes want to be grown-up but aren't sure of their ability to do so. At other times, they look for reassurance that they can still be babied when they want.

BUILDING SELF-ESTEEM

Temper Tantrums— Responding Appropriately

In handling a tantrum, there are two main goals. First, you must prevent the child from being hurt or hurting anyone else. Second, you must enforce the limits you have set. If you give in to the child's demands, tantrums are more likely to be repeated.

If a tantrum occurs at home, the behavior sometimes simply can be ignored. Putting the child in his or her room or in a chair away from others often helps.

When a tantrum occurs in a public place, move the child to a quiet spot to cool down, or just go home.

Always remain calm. Acknowledge the child's feelings while reemphasizing the reason his or her demands can't be met. "I know you are upset that you can't go outside and play. It's getting dark now and you can't play in the yard after dark. Tomorrow morning you can go out and play."

GUIDED PRACTICE (continued)

BUILDING SELF-ESTEEM

Perhaps no other negative behavior is more uncomfortable to a parent than a temper tantrum. It pays to remember that the behavior is an indication of the child's search for independence, not a result of a personality flaw. Above all this conduct is not a product of deliberate meanness.

Critical Thinking

Ask students to consider the following questions:

- Why does offering toddlers reasonable choices sometimes avoid negativism? (*It gives the child more control and a feeling of independence.*)

- How, do you think, did the term *terrible twos* originate? Does it refer to children twenty-four months of age? (*It refers to inflexibility, and stubborn, domineering behaviors, but most children go through this stage at two and one-half.*)

- What are some reasons toddlers may have difficulty making themselves understood? (*Their knowledge, thoughts, and desire to communicate outrace their language development. Sometimes busy adults do not take the trouble to understand.*)

Promoting Discussion

Ask students why parents sometimes give in to a child's temper tantrums. Have them give examples of situations where it might be tempting to silence the child quickly or choose the easy option. Why is it better to plan ahead to avoid tantrums rather than handle them as they occur?

MORE ABOUT

Toddler Speech

Speech difficulties during the toddler years are so common that they are considered normal. Speech therapists call these problems "speech disfluencies." Some children stumble over the first letter of words, while others may repeat the first word of a sentence several times. Most speech problems at this age clear up within a few months to a year. One cause of speech problems is stress, which manifests itself in tension in the child's throat area. Some children's minds simply work too fast for their physical speaking skills, so they are not able to articulate clearly. Some therapists believe disfluencies are related to the struggle for power and emotional control. Toddlers may simply be unable to speak about their feelings, causing stuttering and stammering.

GUIDED PRACTICE (continued)

Cooperative Learning

Have students work in pairs or small groups to think of a situation that might cause a toddler to be fearful. Ask the students to act out the situation, with one student playing the part of the child and the other the parent or caregiver. Discuss whether the fears portrayed are realistic ones for the age and how caregivers can help children overcome these fears.

Making Connections:
Language Arts

Read the following to students: Ryan had never sucked his thumb, although as an infant he had briefly used a pacifier. Just about the time he turned three and one-half, Ryan began sucking his thumb before he dropped off to sleep. Then he began sucking it during the day. His parents were puzzled and displeased by his behavior.

Have students write an ending to this story, explaining what they think Ryan's parents should do. Ask for volunteers to read their endings and discuss the pros and cons of each one.

Critical Thinking

Have students give examples of qualities that represent emotional maturity, such as independence, self-discipline, and concern for others. Discuss how the toddler is gradually moving toward theses characteristics at each stage of emotional development. For example, during the sunny, cooperative stage at around age three, the child is learning the pleasure of working with and pleasing others.

Promoting Discussion

What other tensional outlets, besides those mentioned in the text, might be shown by a child of age three and one-half? For comparison, what are some examples of tensional outlets used by teens and adults? How do the outlets of these age groups differ, and how are they the same?

confusing world. The child feels that tasks must be done in exactly the same way and objects must be in exactly the same place. Maintaining a consistent schedule and environment helps build feelings of security and confidence.

At two and one-half, toddlers are part independent, part dependent. Sometimes they seek comfort and help; at other times, they assert their independence and want to do it themselves. Parents and other caregivers can help children of this age most by giving them much love and a great deal of patience—especially when the children are neither lovable nor patient. Two-and-one-half-year-olds need more flexible and adaptable limitations rather than hard-and-fast rules.

Three Years

Most three-year-olds have made remarkable strides in emotional development. They are again generally sunny and cooperative and are learning to be considerate. Since three-year-olds are more physically able to do things, they do not have to deal with as many frustrating situations as the toddler.

Three-year-olds take directions from others with little of their previous resistance. They follow instructions and take pride in the tasks they can perform for others. Three-year-olds are eager for praise and affection, and they are willing to modify their behavior in order to achieve those responses from adults. At three years of age, children generally have fewer and less violent temper tantrums than they may have had earlier.

At three, children love to talk, and they are much better at talking. They talk to their toys, to their playmates, to their imagi-

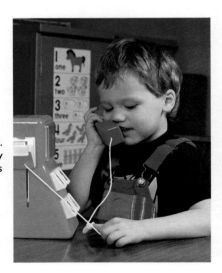

Using a real or toy telephone is a favorite activity for three-year-olds. Children this age are finally able to express themselves clearly by talking.

OBSERVING AND PARTICIPATING

Developing Observational Skills

Have students observe one or more eighteen-month-olds interacting with a caregiver. Afterward, ask students to analyze the behavior they observed, looking for examples of self-centeredness or negativism. Ask them to speculate about what prompted the behavior and how the child showed emotion (e.g., facial expression, running, hitting, or saying "no"). Ask them to describe the reaction of the caregiver. Did students see more or fewer examples of self-centeredness and negativism than they expected? Why do they think this was true? Next, have them observe a group of children around the age of three and one-half, looking for the ways they show emotions. Make comparisons. Do they detect any patterns, similarities or differences? What conclusions can they draw about toddler behavior?

PARENTING IN ACTION

PARENTING IN ACTION

Adapting to Change

Andy, age three and one-half, had been staying with his grandparents while his parents were out of town for a few days. The surroundings were familiar and, aside from an uncharacteristic quietness, Andy seemed to be coping well.

On the third evening, however, just before Andy's bedtime, a neighbor stopped by unexpectedly to visit Andy's grandparents. As soon as the neighbor stepped into the living room, Andy buried his head against his grandmother, covered his eyes, and cried, "I don't want to see anybody!"

THINK AND DISCUSS

1. What particular aspects of the situation influenced Andy's response to the neighbor?

2. How did Andy try to control his environment?

3. Do you think Andy's reaction to the situation—and to the stay at his grandparents' home—would have been different had he been two and one-half? If so, how? If not, why not?

nary companions, and to themselves. They derive emotional pleasure from talking. They also respond to others' talking; they can be reasoned with and controlled with words.

Three and One-Half Years

The self-confident three-year-old is suddenly very insecure at three and one-half. Parents may feel that the child is going backward rather than forward emotionally.

Fears are common at this age. The child may be afraid of the dark, lions and tigers, monsters, strangers, or loud noises—even though none of these were frightening before.

Emotional tension and insecurity often show up in physical ways, too. Some children may exhibit tensional outlets such as thumb sucking, nail biting, or nose picking. Others may stumble or stutter.

At three and one-half, children try to ensure their own security by controlling their environment. They may issue insistent demands, such as "I want to sit on the floor to eat lunch!" and "Talk to me!"

MORE ABOUT

Making Changes

During the toddler years, children experience enormous frustrations while coping with the challenge of growing and developing. In particular, they may react negatively, even defiantly, to changes in a daily routine. Discuss these techniques:

• Give advance warning that you and the child will leave. For a toddler, use ten to fifteen minutes. Repeat a warning five minutes ahead of time.

• Use language that makes sense to a child. For instance, a child understands "We'll leave after lunch," not "We'll leave later on."

• Prepare children for new experiences. Tell them about places they will go to; describe people they will see.

• Always allow extra time when making changes. It's easier on everyone!

PARENTING IN ACTION

Promoting Discussion

Introduce this Parenting in Action feature by allowing students to read the story, "Adapting to Change," independently. Next, encourage them to discuss their reactions to Andy's behavior. Do they identify with his situation and his feelings? Why or why not?

Answers to "Think and Discuss"

1. His age, the time of day (bedtime), and the absence of his parents for three days made him tense and insecure. The neighbor was another change in his life and he finally had enough.

2. By hiding his face and declaring his feelings, Andy finally released his emotions.

3. Probably, at two and one-half he did not have the language skills to clearly state his feelings as well as he can at three and one-half. At both ages, Andy would likely be confused and upset by changes in routines and surroundings.

Thinking Critically

Ask students to discuss their reactions to changes in their lives. How can parents prepare children for predictable changes such as a new sibling or moving to a new residence? How can children be prepared for unexpected changes like illness, death, or natural disasters? What skills help people adapt to change in a positive way?

Cooperative Learning

Have students work in small groups and brainstorm examples of appropriate and inappropriate choices to offer toddlers. Allow time for students to share their ideas.

GUIDED PRACTICE (continued)

Making Connections:
Language Arts

Assign students to write the beginning of a brief story about a child of two and one-half who is being stubborn and demanding. Then have students exchange the stories they have written. Ask them to write endings to their classmates' stories showing how the caregivers dealt with the situations. Share and discuss the solutions.

Promoting Discussion

As a basis for discussion, propose the following situations and have students suggest ways to offer toddlers choices:

- Esperanza wants to wear her new white blouse while she is digging in the yard.
- Huang wants to eat candy for breakfast.
- Bobbie wants the race car that his playmate Masahiko is using.
- Karen wants to take a plastic truck to bed with her.

Using the Photograph

Refer students to the photograph on page 356, and have them identify the emotion the boy is experiencing and the cause of his emotion. At whom or what is his emotion directed? How else might he express this emotion?

Specific Emotions

Children express their emotions openly until the age of two or three. As they mature, they begin to be affected by the cultural demands for more control of emotional expression. The three-year-old begins to learn socially acceptable ways of displaying feelings. For example, three-year-old Jonathan uses words to express his anger. His fifteen-month-old sister, Marta, expresses her anger by kicking and screaming.

Children's emotions become more specific as they grow older. Some of the most common emotions of one- to three-year-olds are anger, fear, jealousy, affection, and sympathy.

Anger

The crying and screaming of temper tantrums are most common at about two to three years; then they begin to decline. When an eighteen-month-old has a tantrum, he or she is not hostile toward any particular person or thing—just easily angered. Between the ages of two and three, the object or person responsible comes under attack. For example, the ten-month-old who is intent on getting a ball is concerned only with that ball. A two-year-old, however, may attack the person who is holding the ball.

Outgoing, confident children tend to display their anger more aggressively, such as by hitting or kicking. Shy, passive children are more likely to cry and seek comfort from an adult.

These primitive expressions of anger gradually disappear if they do not bring the desired results. Children's reactions become less violent and explosive. Physical attacks begin to be replaced by threatening, name-calling, pouting, or scolding.

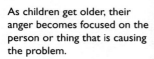

As children get older, their anger becomes focused on the person or thing that is causing the problem.

MORE ABOUT

Anger

The violent expression of anger is generally not acceptable in this culture. Therefore parents sometimes try to make children deny their feelings of anger and hostility. For example, when brothers say to each other, "I hate you!" a parent may say, "Of course you don't hate your brother." At the moment the brothers may well feel hatred for each other. The parent's message simply denies the validity of the children's feelings. Anger that is suppressed or denied can manifest itself in upset stomachs, headaches, tension, nervousness, or anxiety. Rather than teaching children to suppress their anger, parents should help children learn to express their feelings in appropriate ways.

Even though the frequency of anger decreases with age, the intensity of anger changes as the child gets older. Children become capable of lasting hostility. Three-year-olds think about "hitting back" when someone makes them angry.

A number of factors can cause a child to be angry more often than normal. Anger is more frequent in anxious, insecure children. The child who has not learned self-control also tends to have frequent outbursts. Children whose parents are overly critical or inconsistent become frustrated easily and show anger. There are also some common temporary causes of bad temper. When a child is sick, uncomfortable, tired, or hungry, he or she will become angry much more easily than usual.

Frequent, intense outbursts of anger are destructive and disturbing to both parent and child. Parents should recognize and respond to the child's bewilderment and anxiety, rather than reacting angrily themselves. Parents should make sure that the demands on the child are both limited and reasonable as they try to help the child learn self-control.

Fear

Every phase of a child's development has its particular fears. A one-year-old may be frightened of high places, strangers, and loud noises. A three-year-old might be afraid of the dark, animals, and storms. Some fears are actually useful, since they keep the child from dangerous situations. Other fears must be overcome for proper emotional and social development.

Some children have more fears than others. These differences are related to such factors as physical condition, mental development, temperament, feelings of security, and ability to cope with daily life. Thoughtless adults sometimes build fears to ensure obedience. They may say, for example, "Stay on the sidewalk or the police will get you."

Adults often communicate their own fears to children. Even if the fear is never discussed, a child may sense it. For example, a child may pick up fear of dogs simply from the alarmed call of a parent whenever a dog comes near.

At one time or another between the first and fourth birthdays, many children suffer from **separation anxiety**, *a fear of being away from parents, familiar caregivers, or their normal environment.* Nicole cried when her parents left her with a new babysitter; Eli cried when his mother first left him on his own at the child care center; Darnell cried when his father left on the first day of preschool. All these tears are signs of separation anxiety.

A child's separation anxiety can be disturbing for the parents. Parents should be careful to avoid communicating their own concerns to the child; it may be helpful for parents to recall that they have chosen a safe, secure caregiver or care center for

Age three and one-half often brings fears and insecurity, such as a fear of the dark. Parents should be calm and reassuring.

GUIDED PRACTICE (continued)

Cooperative Learning
Remind students that routines are important for the child of two and one-half. Point out that mornings are times when parents may need matters to run smoothly with toddlers. Have students work in small groups to devise an appropriate morning routine for a child of two and one-half. Allow time for groups to share their routines.

Promoting Discussion
Have students discuss fears common to children of three and one-half. Ask students which fears are realistic and how caregivers can help children overcome fears, both realistic and unrealistic.

Making Connections: Careers
Children who need help with emotional problems, such as extreme sibling conflict, usually see child psychologists. Have students research what a child psychologist is, the training involved in becoming one, and what types of work a child psychologist may do. Ask them to write a report on their findings.

SEE HOW THEY GROW

Toddler Fears
Toddlers often fear clowns or puppets that are meant to be entertaining. Since toddlers are just beginning to understand the concept of "real," seeing the "unreal" faces causes alarm. Older children, who have a better sense of the difference between "real" and "unreal," are able to enjoy clowns and puppets.

GUIDED PRACTICE (continued)

Using the Photograph

Refer students to the photo on the right, page 358. Ask why some children might have a fear of dogs while others do not. Discuss how parents could help prevent or reduce fears associated with unfamiliar situations.

Cooperative Learning

Have students collect pictures of children ages one to three showing a variety of emotions. Tell them to compile a scrapbook divided into sections labeled with the emotions the children display.

Critical Thinking

Ask students what problems separation anxiety poses for working parents. (They must leave their children in substitute care.) What could parents do to minimize these problems? (Let the child know what is going to happen. Spend the first day in the situation with the child. Reassure the child that the parent will return each day.)

Making Connections:
Language Arts

Have students locate a book written for toddlers about a child or children with a specific fear. Ask them to write a report about the book, identifying the fear involved, how the characters in the book coped with the fear, and why students feel the book would or would not be a good choice for toddlers.

Did You Know?

The first picture book suitable for children as the Book of Art and Instruction for Young People, *written and published by Sigmund Feyerbend in 1578. The book was a collection of woodcut illustrations of European life, fables, and German folklore.*

Fears depend a great deal on individual experience. A child with a pet dog will probably not be afraid of other dogs. However, unfamiliar situations are likely to prompt fears at first.

the child. Parents can also help both the child and themselves by spending special time with the child at home.

Some of a toddler's generalized fears can be identified as caused by specific incidents. For example, a toddler who is frightened by a loud barking dog may develop a generalized fear of all dogs. Some children may develop fears about sirens, men with beards, or loud noises. When a young child has an experience that seems likely to produce fears, it is best to try to talk with the child about it right away. When the child experiences the "trigger," talk them through it—"See it is just a man with a beard. He is just like your daddy but he has hair on his face." Otherwise, the child's imagination may blow the experience out of proportion.

Parents and other caregivers should be patient in their responses to the fears of young children. The following suggestions will help you deal with the fears of one- to three-year-old children:

- Be careful to avoid shaming a child for his or her fears.
- Encourage the child to talk about his or her fears, and listen seriously and attentively to the child. Recognizing and admitting fears may diminish their impact.
- Offer honest, understandable explanations for events and situations that have frightened the child.
- Nightmares are common at this age; help the child separate reality from fantasy.
- Make unfamiliar situations more secure with your presence. A first visit to the dentist, for example, goes more smoothly in the company of a familiar adult.
- Being unprepared for a situation is one of the chief causes of fear. Discuss new experiences and events in advance; help the child know what to expect.
- Teach the child how to control frightening situations. For example, if the child is afraid of the dark, teach him or her how to turn on the light.
- Be supportive and understanding.

Jealousy

Jealousy becomes a recognizable emotion sometime in the second year. The one-year-old shows no jealous reactions, but by eighteen months, jealousy is very pronounced. It reaches its peak at age three and then declines as outside relationships begin to replace the close ties to home and parents.

Resentment of affection between parents is one of the most common causes of jealousy in early childhood. The very young child may not understand that parents have enough love for everyone.

SEE HOW THEY GROW

Adjusting to Separation

Separation anxiety usually begins sometime in the first year, peaks at fourteen to eighteen months, and then gradually declines. Children are most likely to be upset by separation when they do not understand where parents have gone or when they will come back. Toddlers should be given a brief, reassuring explanation beforehand. Separa-

tion can be difficult for parents as well. Working parents often feel guilty about being away from their children for much of the day. However, research to date has failed to show conclusively that all-day child care has any negative effects on the development of young children. The key, of course, is finding quality child care.

Jealousy of a new baby can lead an older child to return to babyish habits.

Sibling rivalry, or *competition between brothers and/or sisters for their parents' affection and attention*, is another common cause of jealousy. This is often particularly evident when there is a new baby in the family. Suddenly, all the attention is focused on the baby rather than on the older child.

Children between the ages of eighteen months and three and one-half seem to be most jealous of a new baby. They may try to hurt the infant or demand that the baby be "taken back." Some children respond by trying to get attention. They may show off, act inappropriate, or revert to babylike behaviors, such as bed-wetting, thumb sucking, or baby talk.

If parents act shocked or threaten not to love the toddler any-more, they only make the problem worse. The feeling of loss of love caused the negative attention-getting behavior to begin in the first place. Instead of expressing displeasure with the older child's behavior, parents and caregivers need to realize that what the child needs is more affection and reassurance.

The following suggestions are helpful in encouraging a young child to develop a good relationship with his or her new sibling:

- Arrange special time alone with the older child.
- Compliment the youngster on his or her appropriate behavior whenever possible.
- Point out the advantages of not being a baby and all the things he or she can do.
- Acknowledge and label the feelings the child may have—be specific. "It bothers you when he cries." Let the child know that you are trying to understand how he feels and that his feelings are important to you.
- Give the older child extra love and attention.

SAFETY TIP

When a new baby arrives, parents must expect anger, jealousy, and other kinds of upset in a young child who has suddenly been assigned the role of "big brother" or "big sister." For this reason, it is never safe to leave a toddler "in charge" of the baby—even for a few minutes. Many experts recommend not leaving a toddler alone with a baby at all.

MORE ABOUT

Sibling Rivalry

Some child psychologists suggest that it is best if children are spaced at least three years apart. Two-year-olds have not yet learned to share and are still quite dependent on parents for full-time attention. Three-year-olds are better able to understand what is happening and discuss their emotions with parents.

GUIDED PRACTICE (continued)

Critical Thinking

Ask students why an especially imaginative child might have more fears than usual. (In addition to threatening real life situations imagine the child may choose an abundance of situations.)

Making Connections: Social Studies

Have students investigate the ways emotions are expressed or controlled in cultures around the world. Is it considered proper for couples to show affection in pub-lic, and if so, how? What is cus-tomary behavior when mourning the loss of a loved one? Have stu-dents present brief oral reports.

Critical Thinking

Have students consider these questions about the emotional response to the introduction of an infant into the family:

- Have students suggest some possible reasons why children ages eighteen months to three and one-half years tend to have more difficulty coping with a new baby than younger or old-er children do. (*At these ages, children are self-centered. They are adjusting to the fact that they are separate from their parents, balancing the need for a close parental bond with the need for independence, and fighting inse-curities and fears.*)

- The text recommends that a child who must change rooms because of a new sibling should do so months before the birth. Why is this a good idea? (*The child is less likely to connect the move with the baby and feel pushed out or displaced.*)

SAFETY TIP

When a toddler or young child attempts to pick up a baby or play "babysitter" in any way, par-ents and caretakers should act quickly yet calmly to take the baby from the child. Any sud-den rush or scream might star-tle the youngster, who, in turn, might drop the baby or injure it in some way.

Promoting Discussion

Use the following discussion strategies:

• Ask students to react to this situation: One evening, a wife says to her husband, "Dear, I love you so much, I've decided to marry a second husband." What does this suggest about how not to prepare a toddler for a new baby?

• Discuss this statement: "With more maturity, our culture demands more control of direct expression." Do students agree with this statement? Why or why not? How does society influence the way people express emotions?

Practicing Decision Making

Have students imagine they are parents of toddlers and expecting a baby. Tell them to a develop a list of tasks that would allow a toddler to help parents care for a new baby. Have them explain how these tasks could help the toddler feel like a useful part of the family.

BUILDING
SELF-ESTEEM

Learn to support independence. Give a child positive encouragement for his or her efforts whether or not the task performed or choice made measures up to your standards. Praise the efforts and save critiques or reprimands for another time.

BUILDING SELF-ESTEEM

Encouraging Children to Love Themselves

Young children show emotions in simple and direct ways. They may appear to be quite independent one moment, yet quite helpless the next. Though they want to do things for themselves, they have not yet learned to complete all tasks safely or responsibly.

Adults can help young children to handle those times when they are having difficulty. This can be accomplished by helping children to like themselves and realize that they are capable. Children see themselves through the eyes of people around them. When children hear adults say, "David is a happy boy," or "Kristin helps set the table," children see themselves as being happy or helpful. Children who hear these words feel good about themselves and learn to love themselves.

A warm positive relationship between parent and child will foster the child's ability to form good relationships with others.

• If the older child must change bedrooms, make the move months in advance.

• Prepare the child for the baby's coming. Instill the feeling that the new baby is a baby brother or a baby sister and that parents will need the older child's help.

• Ask the child to help with small tasks in caring for the baby. For example, an older child can bring a clean shirt for the baby or help with feeding. Such positive tasks make the child feel like a useful part of the family.

Love and Affection

The relationships that children have with others in their early years form the basis of their capacity for love and affection in later life. Young children must learn, through experience and practice, to love.

First comes "love" of those who satisfy the baby's physical needs. If one person is the baby's primary caregiver, he or she is preferred above all others. Gradually, the baby's affection expands to include other caregivers, siblings, pets, and people outside the home.

Relationships between parents and children should be strong, but not smothering. A child who is overly dependent on his or her parents and other caregivers has difficulty forming other relationships.

HEALTHY FAMILIES/HEALTHY CHILDREN

Building Healthy Families

Infants who have one primary caregiver tend to become most strongly attached to that person. What about infants and toddlers who regularly spend time with different caregivers? Is the attachment to parents weakened? The evidence suggests otherwise. Studies have shown that children who receive quality substitute care have no problems forming secure attachments to their parents. According to experts, even young infants can develop relationships with more than one adult. Studies have also shown that as long as children receive responsive, stable, sensitive care, having a number of different caregivers does not adversely affect development.

Older toddlers may try to comfort someone who appears distressed. However, they don't always know the best way to go about it. Why not?

Sympathy

Most children show little evidence of sympathy until about age two. To feel sympathy, the child must be able to understand that a situation can be upsetting for someone else even though he or she does not feel upset. The child must also be able to relate to other people emotionally. A well-adjusted, happy child is more inclined to be sympathetic than a child whose relationships are less satisfactory.

A child's first sympathetic responses are limited to crying when—and because—another person is crying. Around the age of three, the child first tries to comfort the other person and even tries to remove the cause of that person's distress. A three-year-old may pat and talk to an unhappy baby, or push all his or her own toys into the crib of a crying baby brother or sister. The ability to actually understand the feelings of others develops later.

Evaluating Emotional Adjustment

How can parents tell whether their child is developing well emotionally? Between the first and fourth birthdays, the single most important clue is the harmony of the parent-child relationship. The early pattern established between parents and child is never outgrown. It will have a significant influence on the child's later relationships in life—relationships with his or her spouse, own children, co-workers, and friends.

INDEPENDENT PRACTICE

Student Workbook
Have students complete "Puzzled About Emotional Development?" in the Student Workbook.

Student Demonstration
Have students collect pictures of people of all ages expressing sympathy for others; then show the pictures to the students and have them describe why they think the show of sympathy is appropriate or inappropriate. Discuss how toddlers, teens, and adults differ in expression of sympathy and why it is important to express sympathy for toddlers in appropriate ways.

Extension
Have students conduct research about how suppression of emotion affects adults and how these suppressed emotions may be expressed indirectly. Have them report their findings and include a brief personal essay about the advantages and disadvantages of learning to control direct expression of emotion.

Journal Writing
Have students describe their reactions to what they have learned about patterns of emotional development in toddlers. How might their knowledge help them accept, understand, and guide children of this age? If they have been judgmental about toddlers or their parents in the past, will they reevaluate their judgements?

Childhood Reflections

"Nothing has a stronger influence psychologically on their environment, and especially on their children, than the unlived life of the parents."

Carl Jung

SEE HOW THEY GROW

The Toddler: An Emerging Person
The emotional and social development of the toddler is seen in simple and direct changes. By age fifteen months, a child can express a sense of humor and has an obvious concept of self. By eighteen months, a child uses play to express emotions and resolve minor conflicts and is perfectly happy playing alongside, but not with, another child. At two years, a child makes radical shifts in emotions in a very short time and uses possessive words, such as *I*, *me*, and *mine*. During the third year until the age of thirty-six months, a child will learn to share, take turns, and play cooperatively with others. Socially, the toddler might enjoy the role of authority figure, directing and helping others. Parents and caregivers reinforce the toddler's sense of self by serving as positive role models, demonstrating ways to talk, share, and respect others.

ASSESS

CHECKING COMPREHENSION

Assign students to write their responses to the Check Your Understanding questions in the Section 1 Review. Answers to the questions are given at the bottom of this page.

EVALUATE

Have students complete the Chapter 12, Section 1 quiz in the TCR.

Reteaching

1. Assign Reteaching 29 in the TCR and have students complete the activity and review their responses.

2. Have students make a chart summarizing the emotional characteristics of each age described in the text.

Enrichment

1. Assign Enrichment Activity 29 in the TCR.

2. Have students assume the role of an advice columnist. An expectant parent has written for advice about preparing a three-year-old daughter for the arrival of an infant and minimizing jealousy after the infant's arrival. Have them write an advice column in response to the letter.

Extension

Invite a child psychologist to speak to students about emotional adjustment in toddlers. What is good emotional adjustment? Poor adjustment? Have students prepare questions to ask the speaker.

CLOSE

Have students suggest typical endings for this sentence: My child will never ... Then have them decide whether each ending is realistic in light of section content.

These are important signs of a healthy relationship between parent and child:

- The child seeks approval and praise from parents.
- The child turns to parents for comfort and help.
- The child tells parents about significant events so that they may share in the joy and sorrow.
- The child accepts limits and discipline without unusual resistance.

Another important indicator of emotional adjustment is a child's relationship with his or her siblings. (When the child is slightly older, friends and outside relationships also become important.) Quarreling with brothers and sisters is not always a sign of poor adjustment. Arguing is a normal pattern in some families. However, the child who is continuously and bitterly at odds with brothers and sisters, in spite of parents' efforts to ease the friction, may need professional help.

SECTION 1 REVIEW

CHECK YOUR UNDERSTANDING

1. Explain what it means to be self-centered.

2. What is negativism? What does negativism in a toddler indicate?

3. What kinds of emotions do toddlers release during temper tantrums?

4. Briefly describe the emotional stage typical for a three-year-old.

5. How does a child's expression of emotions change around the age of three?

6. List three factors that may influence the number of fears a young child has.

7. What is the most notable cause of jealousy in children between the ages of eighteen months and three and one-half years?

DISCUSS AND DISCOVER

1. Discuss your own ideas about how parents should deal with sibling rivalry. What goals should parents have in dealing with this kind of jealousy? What are reasonable steps for parents to take toward achieving those goals?

Observing & Participating

Spend some time engaging a three-year-old in a quiet activity, such as reading, painting, or working with play dough. Observe how the child responds to the activity. How does the child respond to your suggestions, instructions, and encouragement? Based on this experience, what can you speculate about the personality of children this age?

SECTION 1 REVIEW

1. To think only about one's own needs and wants, without considering the needs and wants of others.

2. Doing the opposite of what others want; it may indicate a desire for independence and/or frustration.

3. Anger and frustration.

4. Usually sunny and cooperative and learning to be considerate.

5. They enjoy using words to express emotions.

6. Any three: physical condition, mental development, temperament, feelings of security, ability to cope with daily life.

7. A new baby in the family.

Social Development from One to Three

OBJECTIVES

* Describe the general patterns of social development in children from ages one through three.
* Describe how young children gradually learn to play with each other.
* Explain the importance of a positive self-concept, and identify ways it can be developed.

Between the ages of one and four, children develop social attitudes and skills that remain with them throughout their lives. Early experiences in the family must teach a child how to cooperate and adapt to the needs of others.

General Social Patterns

Young children gradually learn to get along with other people, both in their own families and in other groups. This is the beginning of **socialization**, *the process of learning to get along with others*.

Social development is related to emotional, intellectual, and physical development. Certain social characteristics and tasks can be expected at different ages. Remember that individual differences may influence these patterns.

Eighteen Months

The primary socialization goal of children at eighteen months is to begin developing some independence from the family. For most children, the closest relationships are—and will remain—those with family members. However, toddlers need to begin learning about the outside world. This may mean trips to the playground or other opportunities to be with children and adults who are not part of the family.

TERMS TO LEARN

cooperative play
negative self-concept
parallel play
positive self-concept
socialization

SEE HOW THEY GROW

Choosing Playmates

Two-year-olds often play much better with older children than with their peers. When a pair of two-year-olds get together, they are apt to have trouble because they haven't yet learned to share and take turns. However, when playing with older children, two-year-olds are usually so pleased to be included with the "big kids" that they will generally do whatever they are told. For example, they may be the baby or patient in imaginative play. As long as the two-year-old has a chance at the toys and isn't completely ignored, play is apt to be satisfactory to all concerned.

SECTION 2
Social Development from One to Three
Pages 363-369

FOCUS

SECTION 2 RESOURCES

Teacher's Classroom Resources
* Enrichment 30
* Reteaching 30
* Section 2 Quiz

Student Workbook
* Take Your Choice

SECTION OVERVIEW

In Section 2, students examine patterns of social development in children from ages one through three that explain how children gradually learn to play with each other, progressing though parallel play to cooperative play. As part of the process, children begin to take turns and consider the wishes of others in order to gain acceptance. Students learn the importance of developing self-concept.

MOTIVATOR

Remind students that once, like all infants, they were self-involved and concerned with their own desires. Have them list skills, understandings, and attitudes they need now in order to get along with others, including sharing and compromise. How many times in the last 24 hours have they said or done something against their own inclinations in order to be fair, comply with a rule, keep the peace, protect feelings, or maintain a friendship? Then ask students what abilities, qualities, and understandings infants must develop before they can form friendships.

USING TERMS TO LEARN

Have students identify pairs of related words in the list (such as *cooperative play* and *parallel play*). Discuss how understanding the meaning of one term in each pair would make it easier to learn the meaning of the other.

TEACH
Pages 363-369

- General Social Patterns
- Making Friends
- Developing a Good Self-Concept

GUIDED PRACTICE

Promoting Discussion

Have students discuss situations that might require children between two and three to put someone else's wishes ahead of their own in order to get along.

Practicing Decision Making

Have students assume they are parents of an eighteen-month-old. One parent stays home with the child. Have students list ways the child could be given opportunities to develop relationships with people outside the home.

Using the Photograph

Refer students to the photograph on page 364, and have them identify the type of play in which the children are engaged. Have them explain how they identified the type of play. How does it differ from solitary play?

SAFETY TIP

Spanking a child who is aggressive with other children only serves to teach the child that aggressive behavior is condoned; the message is confusing. If children are to learn nonviolent solutions to their anger, use nonviolent methods to teach them.

The younger the children, the less likely they are to interact while playing.

SAFETY TIP

Eighteen-month-olds are usually not ready to share; struggles and even fights over specific toys are not uncommon. It is important that a parent or caregiver resolve such fights for young children. Fighting won't help the children learn about sharing, and one—or both—of the children might be hurt.

At about eighteen months, children begin to notice the presence of other children in play situations. However, there is little real interaction between children at this age.

Parallel play—*playing independently near, but not actually playing with, another child*—is characteristic of this age. The participation between children varies. One child may simply watch another child play with a toy. A different child might grab the toy away. Still another child may seem to pay no attention to the other children at all.

Eighteen-month-olds often seem to treat other people more as objects than as human beings. At this stage, the toddler is intent on satisfying strong desires without regard for anyone who interferes. There may be conflicts over toys that result in screaming, hitting, biting, or hair pulling.

Two Years

By age two, children already have an impressive list of social skills. A two-year-old is especially good at understanding and interacting with his or her primary caregiver. The child can read the caregiver's moods and gauge what kind of behavior he or she will accept. As speech develops, the young child is increasingly able to communicate with others.

Two-year-olds find it is fun to have someone to play with. They enjoy being with other children, although they usually engage only in parallel play.

Most two-year-olds are still not able to share or take turns. However, they like to please other people. Occasionally, they are willing to put the wishes of someone else (usually an adult) above their own wishes.

OBSERVING AND PARTICIPATING

Celebrating Individual Differences

Toddlers often show one of two opposing types of behavior when they are with other children. Some toddlers will give up every toy they have in order to avoid conflict. Others will monop-olize every toy in sight. In each case, caregivers can help children learn appropriate negotiating skills-either to share more willingly or to give up less easily.

Two and One-Half Years

The negativism characteristic at age two and one-half carries over into children's social relationships. During this stage, a child who refuses to do anything for one person may perform tasks willingly for another person. The reasons for these responses are often impossible to understand.

At this age, children are beginning to learn about the rights of others. Social play is still parallel and works best with only two children. Squabbles are frequent, but brief. Children forget about them quickly and resume their play.

Three Years

Most three-year-olds are relatively sunny and agreeable. This shows in their relationships with others. People are important to children of this age. A three-year-old will share, help, or do things another person's way—just to please someone.

Three-year-olds begin **cooperative play**, *actually playing with one another, interacting and cooperating*. They build sand castles together, push toy tractors down the same roads, and park their toy cars side by side in the same garage—all without friction. They can also work together in small groups to build with blocks, act out events for doll families, and fit puzzles together.

Parents, though still very important to three-year-olds, are no longer all-powerful in children's social lives. Most children this age seek friends on their own. They may prefer some companions over others.

At three, children are more sure of themselves, and they are less easily frustrated than at earlier stages. Experience gives them confidence in themselves and in their relationships with others.

By age three, children are able to play together, not just next to each other. This is called cooperative play.

BUILDING SELF-ESTEEM

Helping Toddlers Make Friends

It is not uncommon for toddlers to have difficulty playing with other children. Although they may quickly respond to adults, they may be less inclined to do so with other children. Sometimes they seem more content to watch, rather than play with others. However, you will notice their social skills develop daily.

Toddlers may find it difficult to share playthings, playspace, or people, but as they reach three years old, social changes can be observed. The possessiveness and the grabbing of toys gives way to sharing and playing with other children, at least for short periods of time.

Adults can help toddlers make friends in several ways. First, adults can serve as a positive role models and demonstrate ways to talk, share, and take turns. Next, adults can praise the toddler's attempts of sharing with others. Finally, adults can limit play to short time spans, allowing youngsters to play alone with their toys, though in the presence of another child.

MORE ABOUT

How Toddlers Play

Use these general guidelines to promote discussion of the evolution of toddler play skills:

- One-year-olds: Put a box of toys in the child's play area and let baby reach for one, or put several toys in front of him or her. Chat with the baby about making choices using the names of toys as well as talking about what they do. Introduce a new toy each day, and observe what kinds of choices a child makes.

- Two-year-olds: Provide a child with toys that require some decision making such as plastic shapes to be placed in holes designed to accommodate that shape.

- Three-year-olds: Encourage activities that don't require your participation, such as a tea party, picnic, or "construction" project with other toddler friends.

GUIDED PRACTICE (continued)

Using the Photograph

Refer students to the photograph on page 365, and have them explain how the type of play illustrated differs from that in the photograph on page 364. What qualities must children develop in order to engage successfully in this type of play?

Critical Thinking

Ask students to give examples of adult behavior or activities that are analogous to parallel play. Give one example of behavior on the job, and one that might occur during leisure time. (Answers will vary. Programmers work on different programs and computers side by side. Adults read in each other's company, play games on different machines at an arcade, or swim laps with others in a pool.)

BUILDING SELF-ESTEEM

Direct students to read the Building Self-Esteem feature, "Helping Toddlers Make Friends."

Follow with a discussion of how, by their behavior with other adult friends, they can set examples of positive social behavior. How can they demonstrate these behaviors with family members? Which behaviors are most important for toddlers to observe?

Cooperative Learning

Divide students into groups, and assign each group of students one of the following parenting styles: parents who overprotect, parents who neglect, parents who expect perfection, parents who demand (dictate) and punish, and parents who criticize and disapprove. Ask the groups to discuss why their assigned parenting styles could contribute to negative self-concepts in children. Have group representatives report to the class.

GUIDED PRACTICE (continued)

Cooperative Learning

Have students work in groups to develop a list of toys that would encourage cooperative play in three-year-olds. Have a recorder from each group read and explain the group's list to the rest of the class.

Promoting Discussion

Ask students how brothers and sisters help each other learn social skills. Discuss how the continual interaction and the need to share and focus on each other's needs and wishes prepares them for social relationships with peers.

Cooperative Learning

Have students work in small groups and choose 25 pictures in the text that show children playing. Tell them to list and identify the pictures by page number in three categories: solitary, parallel, and cooperative play. Have a recorder share the photographs and categories with the class.

Three and One-Half Years

By the age of three and one-half, children are experienced in cooperative play; their play becomes more complex and includes more conversation. Disagreements with playmates are less frequent. Because three-and-one-half-year-olds enjoy companionship, they realize that they must share toys and put up with some things they do not like while playing with other children.

There is an increasing ability to evaluate friendships. For example, a three-and-one-half-year-old may say, "I don't like to have Kevin come here. He doesn't play nice." Close friends begin to exclude others, although friendships are not always long-lasting and often change rapidly depending on the needs of the child.

Friendships help young children learn to enjoy companionship, consider other people's desires, and handle disagreements.

OBSERVING AND PARTICIPATING

Learning Through Observation

While watching a group of three-year-olds at play, undoubtedly, the actions of an aggressive child are sure to stand out. Instead of asking to borrow a toy, this child will reach out and grab it in spite of the objections and tears of other children. Whereas a parent or caregiver might perceive this behavior as a problem, the aggressive child sees it merely as a solution. Rather than resort to some form of punishment, teach the child alternative behaviors. For example: "I see you really wanted to play with Jesse's toy, but you cannot just grab it away from her. Next time you want to have someone's toy, ask to borrow it or offer a toy you have in trade for the one you want." Every act of aggressive behavior is an opportunity to teach constructive ways to behave.

Making Friends

Friendships are important to normal social development. They may also be a sign of good social progress. A child who is comfortable and friendly with others and who has at least one friend at a time is usually developing normally. However, if a child is unable or unwilling to make friends, it is important to discover the cause and take steps to help. Remember that this is a crucial stage for developing lifelong social skills.

It is important to expose even very young children to other people. The give-and-take of socializing is needed throughout life. Children who begin to play with others early are not likely to be afraid of other children. They learn to cope with the occasional blows and snatching of other one- and two-year-olds.

Parents often have to make a special effort to arrange play-times with other children for a first or only child in a family. This is important, though, because children who grow up with only adults for companionship may have difficulty interacting with children their own age. Since adults are more polite and considerate than children, a child who does not experience and learn to enjoy the rough-and-tumble companionship of other children until school age may face a difficult adjustment. At five or six, the child's feelings are more easily hurt, and the socialization process takes longer.

What about the child who does not get along with play-mates? Remember that all children sometimes have disagreements and arguments. Whether or not the parent or other caregiver should intervene depends on the situation. Children need to learn how to solve such disagreements. If two children are relatively evenly matched and there is no physical or emotional harm being done, the caregiver can simply observe the situation. If this is not the case, the caregiver will probably need to step in and help the children solve the problem. Talking about the feelings of others, seeking options, and urging compromise helps children learn problem-solving skills that they will need in social situations throughout life.

Enjoying activities with a friend doubles the fun. Children learn social skills that can last a lifetime.

Developing a Good Self-Concept

Your self-concept—the way you feel about yourself—affects your relationships with other people. The formation of self-concept begins at birth and continues throughout life. However, a person's basic attitudes about self are formed in early childhood. In general terms, a person may have a **positive self-concept**—*an inclination to see oneself as good, worthwhile, and capable*—or a **negative self-concept**—*an inclination to see oneself as bad, unimportant, and incapable.*

MORE ABOUT

Self-Concept

Self-concept is closely related to feelings of control. People with a negative self-concept tend to look upon rewards and punishments as being a result of luck or chance rather than their own actions. They see themselves as incapable and helpless. In contrast, people with a positive self-concept tend to have what is called "internal locus of control." They believe that their own characteristics and behavior influence what happens to them. Rewards are seen as achievements rather than random events. Caregivers can help children learn to believe in their own abilities. This will help them develop a positive self-concept.

GUIDED PRACTICE (continued)

Making Connections: Language Arts

Have students locate and read books for toddlers about making, losing, or keeping friends. Have them decide whether or not the book would help a child develop socially, and include that judgment in an oral report to the class.

Critical Thinking

After they have read about self-concept, have students respond to the following:

• How is self-concept apt to be affected if parents' expectations are unrealistically high or too low? How do parents learn what expectations are realistic for children?

• Consider the anecdote about Jackie setting the table. Should a parent compliment a child's efforts even though the child did not do the job the right way? Will this keep the child from learning the right way to do things? What is the parents' goal in this situation?

Making Connections: Language Arts

Have students write four vignettes that describe social behavior at the four ages described in this section. Have students read their vignettes to the class and challenge their classmates to identify the age of the child described in the vignette.

INDEPENDENT PRACTICE

Student Workbook

Have students complete "Take Your Choice" in the Student Workbook.

Student Demonstration

Have students suggest play materials and describe or demonstrate how students might use them at a day care center during the solitary play stage, the parallel play stage, and the cooperative play stage. Examples of play materials might include a set of blocks; a pail, shovel, and sand; puzzles; and several toy automobiles.

Extension

Ask students to write a dialogue in which a parent prepares a three-year-old boy for a visit by a girl of the same age. Have the parent explain, in terms a child can understand, that the boy may have to share his toys, take turns, etc. Then have the parent discuss the advantages of doing so.

Journal Writing

Have students write journal entries reflecting on stages of social development in toddlers. Ask students to consider the following questions: What activities in your life are analogous to solitary play, parallel play, and cooperative play? How does working through these stages prepare children for such activities? What problems of adults and teens are analogous to those children face when they first move into cooperative play?

Ask students to demonstrate nonverbal cues that have a commonly understood meaning to them (e.g., thumbs up or down, crossed arms, or narrowed eyes). Ask them to explain how a small child reaches understanding of body language without having to be told what it means.

Cultural Exchange

UNDERSTANDING NONVERBAL CUES

Raising your eyebrows briefly, called the "the eyebrow flash," indicates friendliness—at least if you are European, Balinese, Papuan, Samoan, or American. However, the Japanese regard the gesture as indecent. Children learn to recognize body language as quickly as spoken language. Most nonverbal communication is not consciously relayed, and, as the examples above demonstrate, may differ from one social group to another. What is common to nonverbal methods is that all cultures teach their members to perceive communications in different ways.

A child forms his or her self-concept in response to the actions and attitudes of other people. Parents usually spend the most time with the young child, so they have the strongest influence on the child's self-concept. A child who is treated with love and respect usually develops a positive self-concept.

Even in the first days of life, a newborn is beginning to form his or her self-concept. If, when the infant cries, the parents respond willingly and quickly with food or comfort, the baby begins to feel like a worthwhile person.

Soon the baby begins to explore his or her surroundings. These explorations give the child a chance to experience different sights, sounds, smells, tastes, and feelings; the child learns about the world and gains a sense of accomplishment.

Parents and other caregivers may—intentionally or unintentionally—discourage the baby's early attempts at exploration. Instead of creating an environment that is safe for exploration, they keep the baby confined to a playpen. This limits the baby's opportunities for successful experiences, and such experiences are essential for developing a positive self-concept.

As children begin to understand language, they are increasingly influenced by what people say to and about them. Children also reveal their image of themselves in their own language and their actions. For example, three young boys were playing together at a neighborhood playground. Two of them scrambled to the top of a log fort. They called to their friend still on the ground, "C'mon up here, Teddy. See how high we are!" Teddy watched them without moving and answered, "I can't. I'm too little. Mommy says I'll fall and get hurt."

Giving children your attention and praise helps them develop a good self-concept.

TEEN PARENTING

Family Interactions

If you have teen parents in your class with children old enough to talk, encourage them to try this activity: During a quiet time at the end of the day, ask the child to talk about his or her activities during the day. Be sure to ask what was good. Guide the teen parent in ways to help the child focus on the successes he or she accomplished and on what was learned. After the teen has tried this activity, open a class discussion about how this daily interaction could help a child develop a positive self-concept. Discuss how this same interaction occurring in an atmosphere of tension, anger, irritability, resentment, or competition can lead to feelings of low self-worth. Ask: How can the general tone of family interaction affect the self-concept of all family members?

Too many "don'ts" hurt a child's self-confidence. Sensible limits protect children, help them learn what they are able to do, and encourage success.

Some parents unintentionally act in ways that hurt a child's self-concept. For example, three-year-old Jackie set the table. Her mother smiled at her and said, "You did a very nice job, Jackie!" Then, however, the mother moved the dishes and silverware to their correct locations. This showed Jackie that her efforts weren't worth much. A better approach would have been for Jackie's mother to avoid making any changes. Then at dinner she might have said, "Jackie set the table tonight. Didn't she do a nice job? She already knows where the knives and spoons go."

Children who have a positive self-concept usually get along well with other people. They don't have to show off or boss other children to prove themselves. They are generally confident and outgoing. When they need help, they can usually ask for it and accept it readily.

Establishing a positive self-concept early in life is essential. Young children accept what others say about them as true. If children believe they are good, they try to act the part. However, if they constantly hear that they are "bad" or "stupid," they will live up to that image. The strong influence of adults' words and actions doesn't diminish until children are older and can judge their own actions. By that time, however, the self-concept and matching behavior are already well established.

SECTION 2 REVIEW

CHECK YOUR UNDERSTANDING

1. What is socialization?
2. What is parallel play? At what age do children typically engage in parallel play?
3. How do two-and-one-half-year-olds often show negativism in their social relationships?
4. What is cooperative play? At what age do children usually begin to engage in cooperative play?
5. Why is it important to give young children opportunities for forming friendships and for playing with friends?
6. What is a positive self-concept? How should parents and other caregivers treat a child to help him or her develop a positive self-concept?

DISCUSS AND DISCOVER

1. Collect at least five toys—or pictures of toys—commonly used by two- and three-year-olds. Explain how each toy could be used in parallel play by younger children and later in cooperative play by older children.

Observing & Participating

Visit a park or a child care center and observe one or more groups of one- to three-year-olds playing. Notice the children who are engaged in parallel play. What are they doing? Which children are engaging in cooperative play? What are they doing together? What type of conversation is taking place?

SECTION 2 REVIEW

1. The process of learning to get along with others.
2. Playing independently near, but not actually playing with, another child; from around eighteen months until about three years.
3. Refusing to do anything for one person, yet willingly performing tasks for another person.
4. Actually playing with one another, interacting and cooperating; around three years.
5. Forming early friendships is a crucial step in developing lifelong social skills.
6. An inclination to see oneself as good, worthwhile, and capable. Treat the child with love and respect; respond willingly to the infant's needs; encourage safe exploration; provide sensible limits.

ASSESS

CHECKING COMPREHENSION

Assign students to write their responses to the Check Your Understanding questions in the Section 2 Review. Answers to the questions are given at the bottom of this page.

EVALUATE

Have students complete the Chapter 12, Section 2 quiz in the TCR.

Reteaching

Assign Reteaching Activity 30 in the TCR and have students complete the activity and review their responses.

Enrichment

1. Assign Enrichment Activity 30 in the TCR.
2. Have students research the importance of a positive self-concept for teenagers. What are some teen problems that have been found to relate to a negative self-concept? Do students think their research findings have any implications for parents of toddlers? Why or why not?

Extension

Invite a child care worker to speak to students about social development in toddlers. In what types of parallel play do students engage at the center? How does the transition from parallel to cooperative play take place? Have students prepare questions to ask the speaker.

CLOSE

Have students suggest endings for this statement:

To develop social relationships, toddlers must learn to …

Encourage a variety of responses.

FOCUS

SECTION 3 RESOURCES

**Teacher's classroom
Resources**

- Enrichment 31
- Reteaching 31
- Section 3 Quiz

Student Workbook

- Being Positive About
  Child Care

SECTION OVERVIEW

In Section 3, students learn that, while each personality is unique, three general personality types can be identified in young children: sensitive, aggressive, and placid. Based on their personality types, toddlers need different types of guidance from caregivers. In the last part of Section 3, students learn how to help toddlers learn to behave in acceptable ways.

MOTIVATOR

Remind students of infant personality types discussed in Chapter 9, Section 2. Encourage them to give examples of how individuals who were sensitive, placid, or aggressive as babies might behave as adolescents. Which types of babies would be adolescent bookworms, bossy, considerate, etc. Have them predict how children at age three might reflect their personality types in social situations. Ask if individuals change their basic personalty type. Suggest they verify or modify their predictions as they read this section.

USING TERMS TO LEARN

Have students define *discipline* as it relates to parenting. Refer them to the text definition on page 373. Have students discuss discipline and punishment. Are they synonomous or interrelated? Would each include the other?

SECTION 3

Personality Patterns and Behavior from One to Three

OBJECTIVES

- Discuss the three basic personality types of young children.
- Describe effective discipline techniques.

An individual's personality is the combination of all the behavior characteristics usually shown by that person. Everyone has a unique personality (unlike that of anyone else), but these three general personality types can be identified in young children: the sensitive child, the placid child, and the aggressive child. An individual's personality type may change from infancy through adulthood.

Respecting Individual Personalities

It is important for parents to recognize and respect their child's individuality. Parents often want their child to be like themselves. Outgoing, assertive parents, for example, may try to make their shy child more outgoing. This doesn't work. Remember that a young child's self-concept depends on how well the child feels accepted—as himself or herself—by other people.

Parents do have a responsibility to guide their children, but this guidance should help each child develop within his or her own personality. For example, a sensitive child needs experiences that will encourage adapting to new people and situations. An aggressive child needs to learn consideration for others.

Descriptions of three basic personality types among one-, two-, and three-year-olds follow. Remember that these descriptions deal with children who are extremely sensitive, placid, or aggressive. The personalities of most children are not so extreme; many children show characteristics of more than one type.

TERMS TO LEARN

discipline
self-discipline

OBSERVING AND PARTICIPATING

Celebrating Individual Differences

Many children have sensitive personalities from birth. If such children have parents who are also quiet and sensitive, these traits are reinforced in the children. When children accept themselves as shy, a self-fulfilling prophecy is set in motion.

How can caregivers help sensitive children achieve better social relationships? A warm and accepting atmosphere is important. Encouraging children to be themselves will help them develop self-confidence. Sensitive children should also be encouraged to develop and master specific skills, such as athletic or musical abilities. When sensitive children make an effort to socialize, caregivers can provide support and praise.

The Sensitive Child

Sensitive, self-restrained toddlers prefer to be alone much of the time. They generally have a longer attention span (the length of time spent without boredom on one activity) than other children. The sensitive child rarely asks, "What can I do now?"

Sensitive children often lack the assertiveness to stand up for their own rights and desires. They tend to be dominated by others. They are less adventurous and often hold back from new experiences, watching until they feel more sure of themselves. They also seem to have less tolerance for conflict than other children do.

Parents and other caregivers must help sensitive children meet new situations with less reluctance. Overprotecting sensitive children makes life easier, but it does not encourage independence. Young children of this personality type should be allowed to explore and achieve slowly. Small tasks that can be successfully achieved help build confidence. Whenever possible, tell the sensitive child what to expect from a new situation. If, for example, the child has learned about the animals and the sounds they make, a trip to the zoo will be more successful and more enjoyable.

New experiences should be presented at a pace appropriate to the individual child. Do not hurry sensitive children into feeding or dressing themselves or into toilet training. Define goals within the individual child's ability. One playmate at a time is best; allow the sensitive child to adjust gradually to groups of children. Sensitive children usually play best with children their own age or younger.

Some sensitive children are especially frightened of strangers. These children need opportunities to learn how to get along without their parents or customary caregivers. The transition should be gradual, not forced. Prepare them for an outsider's care by emphasizing the enjoyment they can expect from the experience. For example, you might say, "Sally's going to help you make soap bubbles while I'm gone," or "Jeff is bringing along a new story about dinosaurs. He's going to read it to you this afternoon."

The Placid Child

Placid toddlers take things as they are. These children are most often at peace with their world. Placid children typically play happily with brothers, sisters, and friends. They are outgoing and respond easily to other people. Placid children usually take guidance well. They often enjoy accepting responsibility for routine tasks; they may make games out of eating, dressing, and bathing.

TEACH

Pages 370-377

- Respecting Individual Personalities
- Discipline

GUIDED PRACTICE

Promoting Discussion

Have students take turns suggesting and discussing situations in which a child of three might react according to personality type. You might describe three children arriving at a child care center where several noisy children are playing in a sandbox without enough shovels and pails to go around.

Critical Thinking

To help students analyze and apply information about personality types, have them consider the following questions:

- In a large family or classroom, which type of child is likely to receive the least amount of attention? (The placid child.) Why? (He or she would create fewer problems.) Would this necessarily mean the other children were more loved or appreciated? (No.) Explain. (Parents and caregivers would appreciate this agreeable child, but be so taxed by the others they may fail to pay attention where it is not demanded.)

- Are placid children apt to go through the same negative stages as other children? (Probably, but the stages will not be as troublesome. Explain your answer. (Placid children may be somewhat more negative. However, sensitive and aggressive types would respond with more hostility, fear, or whining.)

- What are some desirable qualities associated with the aggressive personality? (Children with aggressive personalities are active and energetic. They take initiative and tend to become leaders.) How can parents encourage these qualities? (Praise them for initiative in positive directions. Set positive goals in activities requiring aggression, and praise their achievements.)

COOPERATIVE LEARNING

Child Care Centers

Ask students to collect the names and addresses of child care centers in their communities with programs for two-year-olds. When the information is obtained, put the students into pairs or small groups and assign each group to research at least two centers. Guide them in formulating criteria for an observation. For example: What is the size of the indoor facilities? The outdoor? How many teachers and aids are there per child? What characteristics are observed in the personnel (e.g., patient, concerned, aloof, or ill-tempered)? What qualifications and training are expected of the personnel? Do any restrictions exist concerning eligibility of children to attend the center (e.g., they must be toilet trained)? Have them pool their findings and present pros and cons of sending children to each center.

Promoting Discussion
Explain that a child may have an aggressive personality without necessarily engaging in physical aggression. Then use these strategies to stimulate further discussion:

- Discuss the difference between aggression and assertiveness, which is sometimes used to distinguish positive qualities, such as confidence and leadership, from negative qualities, such as hostility and physical aggression. Have students give examples of assertive behavior and aggressive behavior until they understand the distinction.

- Discuss how the three personality types relate to stereotypical sex roles. Would students expect more girls or boys to have sensitive personalities? Aggressive personalities? Do students think these differences are the result of inborn traits, learned behavior, or their own perceptions and expectations? How is assertive behavior encouraged or discouraged in girls?

Placid children usually play well with others, but are also content to amuse themselves.

Like all other children, placid children need encouragement and praise. Parents and other caregivers should be alert to the needs of these "easy" children and should be careful to offer them plenty of time, attention, and care.

The Aggressive Child

Aggressive toddlers are usually energetic and noisy. They are inclined toward active, physical play. They rarely take time for quiet activities such as coloring or "reading" books.

Aggressive children often simply take the toys they want from other children. If caregivers insist that the toys be returned, the children soon learn to trade toys rather than grab them. Aggressive children often kick, bite, or hit to get their own way. As a last resort, they cry or have a temper tantrum.

Praise is especially useful for guiding aggressive toddlers. When an aggresive child behaves in unacceptable ways, it is best to point out the negative consequences of his or her actions. Physical punishment is not an effective method of discipline and especially ineffective in discouraging excessive aggression; in

OBSERVING AND PARTICIPATING

Celebrating Individual Differences
Children with aggressive personalities are not necessarily overly aggressive. However, they can easily become so if not taught appropriate behavior by caregivers. Aggressive or out-of-control behavior is exhibited by up to one-third of all children referred for mental health services. A pattern of overaggressiveness should be treated early. Long-term studies have found that a large majority

of highly aggressive children are not well adjusted as adults.

How can caregivers help prevent or reduce overly aggressive behavior in children? Suggestions include limiting exposure to TV violence, minimizing arguments between parents, providing opportunities for physical activities, encouraging outdoor play, and providing more adult supervision.

Children with an aggressive personality are even more active and adventurous than most toddlers. They need to be kept within the bounds of safe, acceptable behavior without being punished for their assertiveness.

fact, it generates more hostility and actually encourages further excessively aggressive behavior.

Self-assertive children are usually leaders rather than followers. They set examples—either appropriate or inappropriate—for other children. For this reason, parents and other caregivers should be especially careful to clarify desirable and acceptable behavior goals for aggressive children.

Discipline

Discipline is *the task of helping children learn to behave in acceptable ways* on their own, without the help of the adult. It is a subject that concerns many parents. They realize the need to teach children to control their behavior, but parents worry about how to handle discipline effectively.

Most experts agree that the long-range goal of discipline is to help children develop **self-discipline**, *the ability to control one's own behavior*. There will not always be someone around to tell a child what is right and wrong. Each child must acquire and follow his or her own standards of responsible conduct.

There is no single best approach to discipline. Parents should consider the individual personality of each child, as well as their own personal beliefs, in deciding how to handle discipline. They should also consider each child's age and stage of development,

GUIDED PRACTICE (continued)

Making Connections: Language Arts
Have a group of students present a skit illustrating the characteristics of one of the three personality types. Have the class identify which type of personality was portrayed in the skit.

Cooperative Learning
Have students work in groups to brainstorm and develop a list of toys and play situations that could help aggressive children learn cooperation. Have group representatives share their lists.

Making Connections: Journalism
Have students read magazine and newspaper articles about theories and methods of discipline and describe how the advice given agrees or disagrees with this text. Discuss how students can decide what information is correct and valid among contradictory recommendations.

Family Focus
Ask students to discuss why some experts feel that parents are the most effective disciplinarians for young children. (Children trust their parents and know that their parents love them. Thus they are more willing to follow rules from the parent than from other caregivers.)

Promoting Discussion
Ask student to discuss the following case study: When three-year-old Jimmy spilled his glass of milk on the floor, his mother spanked him, saying, "That will teach you to make a mess in the kitchen." Was Jimmy misbehaving? Do students think this was the most appropriate way to handle the situation? Why or why not? What circumstances might have prompted this mother's response? What recommendations do students have for other ways to handle the situation?

Using Management Skills
Have students survey books available that attempt to explain productive ways to discipline children. Have students present their impressions of those books and methods.

TEEN PARENTING

Coping with Negative Behavior
Teen parents, as well as many older parents, don't always have the emotional maturity to handle a toddler's negativism, tantrums, or stubbornness. They may believe the child is being deliberately naughty or take negativism as a personal rejection. Point out the fallacies of these beliefs. Discuss how

the family interaction is apt to change during the toddler years. How can teens (and all parents) cope with a negative toddler? How might the development of language affect the child's behavior? Would a child's behavior and family interaction be different if the toddler were an only child, an oldest child, or a youngest child?

GUIDED PRACTICE (continued)

Promoting Discussion

Have students suggest possible situations in which a toddler's behavior needs correcting. Then call on volunteers to suggest strategies for handling the situation for each of the age groups listed on pages 374-376. If students have trouble thinking of situations, you might suggest mistreating animals, pulling flowers out of the garden, or taking toys from other children. Some situations may not fit every age group.

Critical Thinking

To stimulate thought about discipline, ask students to consider the following questions:

- What are examples of unsafe objects that should be removed from a one-year-old's reach?

- What are examples of inappropriate threats caregivers might make to toddlers? Why are these inappropriate?

recognizing that different approaches to discipline may be especially effective at various ages.

- **Eight to twelve months.** Children at this age can usually be controlled by distraction. If the baby is chewing on a newspaper, for example, you might jingle a bright rattle in front of the child. As the rattle catches the baby's attention, you will have the chance to remove the newspaper quietly.

- **Twelve to fifteen months.** During this period, remove as many problem or unsafe objects as possible from the baby's reach. Distraction and physically removing the child from forbidden activities or places work best at this age. For example, Jared was fascinated by the lawn mower and tried to follow it around the yard. His older sister picked Jared up and took him into the house, saying, "Let's see if we can find the book about the teddy bear."

- **Fifteen to twenty-four months.** Children this age require distraction, removal, and spoken restrictions. Twenty-month-old Richard started playing with toy cars on the driveway, where a repair truck was parked. Richard's father said, "Let's take your cars into the backyard. You'll have more room there, and maybe we can make another garage for your cars. There are better places to play than our driveway. Driveways are only for big cars and trucks."

Discipline—or establishing some limits on behavior—is often necessary to keep children out of danger. How should you handle this situation?

MORE ABOUT

Handling Tantrums

Dr. T. Barry Brazelton, recognized expert on child care, suggests that discipline be saved for important issues. Too often trivial matters escalate into major confrontations that should be ignored. He suggests these conditions for timeouts:

- Be sure a room is a safe place for isolation.

- Remove breakable, fragile ornaments and plants.

- If a child begins to tease or act up, either ignore the behavior or divert the child's attention.

- If tension escalates, try to hold, soothe, or rock the child. If that does not work, walk away until the child is calmer.

- Compliment the child when he or she regains composure.

ASK THE EXPERTS

Time-Outs

Q. *Can you explain when and how time-outs work best?*

A. A time-out is essentially a cooling-off period during which the child is removed from opportunities for interaction and activity. I believe it is the best way to discipline a child and to encourage the development of that child's self-discipline.

Time-outs should be used when children's behavior is very disruptive, violating a specific set of rules. Both adults and children should always have a clear understanding of the kind of behavior that will result in a time-out. These are two rules commonly used in administering time-outs:

- If you hurt anybody, you will have to go to time-out.
- If you damage or destroy another person's property, you will have to go to time-out.

To ensure that a time-out is effective, it is critical that the adult remain calm and reasonable.

These are the three basic steps of using time-outs:

1. State the rule and the consequences. Remind the child of the rule that he or she has broken but avoid discussing this rule or the child's behavior. Any further talk actually rewards the child with attention.

2. Ignore the child's responses. It is important to show the child, calmly and clearly, that his or her behavior has resulted in

a time-out; no words or actions can change that consequence.

3. Follow through quickly. This helps the child understand that his or her behavior has consistent consequences.

The time-out setting should be an area free of distractions and rewarding activities. The setting should be safe and easy for an adult to monitor. Any dark, enclosed, or especially lonely area is unsuitable; the purpose of a time-out is to discourage inappropriate behavior, not to frighten the child.

Jacqueline L Mault

Jackie Mault
Director of Special Services for the
Toppenish School District in
Toppenish, Washington

COOPERATIVE LEARNING

Sharing Skills

To ensure that your students make the most of your school's and classroom's full complement of resources—and, at the same time, avail yourself of yet another slant on the cooperative learning theme—establish a classroom Barter Board. Having the form of an actual bulletin board (a folder or cordoned-off section of chalkboard will

serve the purpose equally well), the Barter Board is a device by which students can exchange, or barter, skills. Students interested, for example, in acquiring or sharpening their computer skills can write their names and needs on the Barter Board, along with a skill they are looking to swap (e.g., a strategy for mastering the Terms to Learn occurring in each section of the text).

GUIDED PRACTICE (continued)

ASK THE EXPERTS

Issues and Advice

1. What is a time-out? (*A cooling-off period.*)
2. When should a time-out be used? (*With very disruptive behavior.*)
3. What are two common situations that result in a time-out? (*When a child hurts someone and when another's property or person is damaged.*)
4. Briefly describe the three steps of using time-outs. (*State the rule and the consequence; ignore the child's responses; follow through quickly.*)

Thinking Like an Expert

Have students read the feature on this page and discuss their experiences with time-outs. As they respond, list their observations on the chalkboard. Then have them list what more they would like to know about time-outs, recording their questions on the board. Have them list any new information they acquired after reading the feature.

Ask students to list the advantages of time-outs. Stimulate their thinking with questions such as these: What do children want that they are denied by a time-out? (Attention.) What purpose does the time-out have, other than punishment? (Provides a cooling-off period.)

Critical Thinking

Ask students to imagine that a child of two and one-half years has been corrected for pulling the puppy's tail and told not to do it again. An hour later, the same child pulls the cat's tale. Is the child being disobedient? (Probably not.) What could explain the child's behavior? (The child cannot easily transfer the principle from one situation to another.)

INDEPENDENT PRACTICE

Student Workbook

Have students complete "Being Positive About Child Care" in the Student Workbook.

Student Demonstration

Have students demonstrate responding to a three-year-old's misbehavior in a given situation, explaining why the behavior is inappropriate and what the child could do instead.

Extension

Assign students to write a portion of a manual for workers at a child care center for pre-school children. Tell them to describe the three personality types. The manual should explain to workers what types of behavior, positive and negative, to expect of each personality type, and the needs of each. Tell students to provide specific suggestions for handling each.

Journal Writing

Have students write journal entries reflecting on what they have learned about personality types and discipline. Have them consider these questions: Can you identify personality types of close friends and family? What evidence do you see that many people combine features of more than one type? Do you know people who appear to have changed dominant personality types as they matured? How does personality type affect discipline strategies and the child's response to them? What can you learn about yourself from this section?

- **Two to three years.** By the age of two, children have become better at responding to spoken commands and explanations. With their improved knowledge, two-year-olds can more easily understand adults' reasoning. Parents and other caregivers who explain their reasons get better results than those who only issue sharp commands. When she saw that her two-and-one-half-year-old was still not dressed, Kari's mother said, "Kari, you need to get dressed now because Grandma will be here soon to go shopping with us. We can't go unless we are ready."

- **Three to four years.** Three-year-olds take reasonable, loving discipline more readily than children of other ages. They like to please, and they may remind a parent that they were obedient. Three-year-old Marcus came inside on a rainy day and said, "I remembered to wear my boots today, didn't I? See my clean shoes? I'm a good boy, right?"

Discipline Tips

In the long run, desired behavior can best be taught through example. Parents and other caregivers who serve as positive role models in their daily lives have the most lasting influence on young children.

When you are selecting and using specific techniques of discipline, keep these suggestions in mind:

- Make relatively few requests, and be sure those requests are reasonable and age appropriate.

Once children are old enough, simple explanations can help them understand why they must follow rules.

SEE HOW THEY GROW

Toddler Behavior

One of the biggest challenges of parenthood is learning how to deal with the child's disobedience, or noncompliance. There are three types of non-compliance:

- Passive-resistant behavior. The child pouts, whines, or becomes sullen, but eventually complies.

- Openly defiant behavior. The child says, "I won't do it," or has a temper tantrum.

- Spiteful noncompliant behavior. The child does exactly the opposite of the requested behavior.

Noncompliant behavior reaches one peak during the second year of life and another peak during the teen years.

- Be consistent. Don't laugh at the child's behavior one day and punish the child for the same behavior the next day. Parents should discuss their ideas about discipline and agree on methods.
- Let the child know that you mean what you say. Carry out all your promises and/or follow through with the appropriate natural or logical consequence. Use the "when" and "then"approach. For example, *when* your coat is on, *then* you can go outside.
- Look at situations from the child's point of view. When a three-year-old pulls a flower plant out of the garden, he or she may simply be trying to figure out what makes the plant grow or may want to please you by bringing you a flower.
- Respond to misbehavior by telling the child these things:
    This is not a good choice because…
    Why it is not a good choice.
    What he or she should do or try instead.
- Keep explanations simple and brief. Remember that a child's vocabulary and attention span are limited.
- Be prepared to repeat—over and over again. Toddlers have difficulty transferring learning. They don't realize that what applies to one situation also applies to another, similar situation.
- Discipline should not be an outlet for an adult's anger.
- Remember that all children need love and guidance.

SECTION 3 REVIEW

CHECK YOUR UNDERSTANDING

1. What is personality?
2. How should parents or other caregivers prepare a sensitive toddler for a new situation?
3. What general outlook does a placid toddler seem to have?
4. What kinds of activities are typical of aggressive toddlers?
5. What is discipline? What is the long-range goal of discipline?
6. What method of discipline is usually most effective in controlling the behavior of a two-year-old?
7. When responding to a toddler's misbehavior, what three things should you tell the child?

DISCUSS AND DISCOVER

1. Do you think that all children in a family are likely to fit into the same personality pattern? Why or why not? How do you think similarities or differences between siblings might affect parents' responses to the children?

Observing & Participating

Observe two or more children playing under the supervision of a parent or a caregiver. Notice how often the adult intervenes to direct or correct the children's behavior. Discuss whether you would have intervened more often or less often. Why? What guidance techniques does the adult use? With what success?

SECTION 3 REVIEW

1. The combination of all the behavior characteristics usually shown by a person.
2. As far as possible, explain what to expect; encourage child to explore and achieve slowly.
3. Generally seem to feel at peace with the world.
4. Energetic, noisy activities.
5. The task of helping children learn to behave in acceptable ways on their own; self-discipline, the ability to control one's own behavior.
6. Spoken commands and explanations.
7. What specific choice is not appropriate; why it is not a good choice; what the child should do or try instead.

ASSESS

CHECKING COMPREHENSION

Assign students to write their responses to the Check Your Understanding questions in the Section 3 Review. Answers to the questions are given at the bottom of this page.

EVALUATE

Have students complete the Chapter 12, Section 3 quiz in the TCR.

Reteaching

1. Assign Reteaching Activity 31 in the TCR and have students complete the activity and review their responses.
2. Have students work in pairs. One partner should assume the role of a toddler and pose a disciplinary situation, forcing the other partner, as caregiver, to respond. Role-play in front of another pair, and have them evaluate the caregiver's response.

Enrichment

1. Assign Enrichment Activity 31 in the TCR.
2. Have students read a magazine article about discipline and write a report describing how the advice given in the article agrees or disagrees with the information presented in the text. Discuss how students can decide what information is correct when they discover contradictory advice.

Extension

Invite a child psychologist to speak to the class on general personality types and how heredity and environment interact to create a unique individual. Have students discuss the speaker's comments. Did the speaker use the same personality classifications found in the text?

CLOSE

Have each student write an end for this sentence: A child's personality … Then have students read their sentences aloud.

MOTIVATOR

Tie a large towel around a student volunteer's neck. Have the student eat a serving of shaped cereal from a mixing bowl, using a large cooking spoon held in the nondominant hand. When he or she is finished, ask the student to describe the experience.

Promoting Discussion

1. What are the two types of motor skills that children must develop?

2. What is the sequence of motor skills development?

3. How might older siblings help encourage independence?

Using the Photographs

Ask students to look at each photo in this feature. How are these children showing independence? What have caregivers done to encourage independence in each situation?

Critical Thinking

Ask students to recall what self-care skills children can be expected to master at different ages. What is the value of encouraging young children to help others? (It helps the child learn to be a productive member of the family and of society.) Ask students whether they agree with this statement: "Caregivers should take care of children's grooming needs for them because it will go faster with better results." Discuss the differences in opinions.

Family Focus

Ask students who have younger siblings to describe ways they helped their brother or sister learn new skills.

ENCOURAGING INDEPENDENCE

Between the ages of one and three, children long to feel and be more independent. At the same time, they fear independence. Parents and other caregivers must be careful to guide young children in feeling both independent and secure.

SPLAT MAT

378

The following suggestions will help you encourage children to develop self-help skills and to grow, at their own rates, toward independence.

Self-Feeding

• Don't expect a child who is just learning to feed himself or herself to be neat. Minimize the mess with unbreakable dishes and a child-sized spoon and fork and small servings. A cup with a spill-proof lid helps during the learning stage.

• Choose foods that are easy to handle and eat. Cut food into bite-sized pieces before serving. Remember that attractively served food with a variety of colors, shapes, and textures encourages the child's interest.

• Be sure the child is comfortable. For eating at a table, use a high chair with the tray removed or a booster seat to raise the toddler to the right height.

Self-Dressing

• Choose clothes that are easy for the child to put on and take off. Look for roomy shirts that slip on easily. Elastic waistbands make pants, skirts, and shorts easier to handle. Dresses with buttons or zippers in the front are much more convenient than those with back openings.

• Fasteners often cause problems. Velcro fasteners, large buttons, and zippers that don't come apart at the bottom are easiest for toddlers to manage.

OBSERVING AND PARTICIPATING

Celebrating Individual Differences

The right time for a parent or caregiver to release control to a child varies. Independence develops gradually as each child matures physically and emotionally and begins to express a desire to make decisions. The process begins in infancy, but becomes more obvious as children become mobile. The process fosters healthy development of confidence and self-esteem. Parents and caregivers should keep attuned to expressions that indicate a child's desire to accomplish new tasks or learn new skills. Encourage the child and teach techniques to help master skills. Be careful not to push a child before he or she is ready to do things for him- or herself. Above all, be ready to exercise patience during the time it takes for a child to learn each new task or accomplishment.

Put students into small groups. Assign each group a category of products, such as hair care, toiletries, shoes, clothing, or audio-visual material. Ask each group to research products in the category designed specifically to encourage a child's independence and teach self-help skills. Remind students to record the cost of the products and note how safe they are for a child's use.

- If a dressing task is too difficult for the child to do completely, let him or her do at least one part of the task. Pulling up a zipper or slipping a foot into a shoe can be the first step to learning a more complex task.

- Praise the child's efforts as well as his or her accomplishments.

Grooming Skills

- Provide the child with his or her own towel, washcloth, brush, comb, and toothbrush. Be sure that all are within easy reach.

- A small stool can help toddlers cope with adult-sized bathrooms.

- Establish grooming routines, and help the child follow them every day.

- Set a good example yourself. The child is more likely to wash hands before eating if he or she sees you washing your hands, too.

Helping Others

- Putting away toys can start as a game and can be encouraged with praise. Be sure there is adequate storage space within the child's reach.

- Toddlers love to imitate. Let them help with simple chores, such as sweeping, carrying or folding laundry, and setting the table.

- Keep directions short and clear. Younger children can remember only one step at a time.

- Be patient. A child's efforts will always be slower and less efficient than your own, but learning can't take place without practice.

Practicing Parenting Skills

Have pairs of students make a list of additional ways to encourage a child's independence. Then ask the pairs to present a short skit to the class in which they demonstrate a positive approach to helping a child assist an adult with a chore or activity. For example, a child wants to help bathe a newborn, plant flowers, or cook a meal. When the pair is finished, have other students suggest negative ways to assist the child in the same task.

Extension

Have students watch a child's attempts at self-dressing. Have students report their observations to the class. What problems did the child encounter? What might have encouraged the child to be more independent?

CLOSE

Ask students to summarize what they have learned about a child's need for independence. Ask them to explain how a caregiver can respond positively when a child says, "Me do it."

379

MORE ABOUT

Independence at Mealtime

Rather than turn mealtime into a regular battle of will, family members can use these suggestions:

- Let the child decide whether to eat with a spoon or fingers.

- Use toddler-sized portions of foods.

- Don't use desserts as a reward for eating other foods; encourage eating a variety of foods.

- Ask older toddlers to help decide what the family should have for dinner. Provide guiding suggestions about nutrition and a well-balanced diet, but give toddler's menu a try.

- Encourage a child to help in the preparation for meals, such as setting the table or cleaning up, but be alert for safety in the kitchen.

Use the Summary and the Reviewing the Facts questions to help students go over the most important ideas presented in Chapter 12; encourage students to ask questions and add details, as appropriate.

CHAPTER **12** REVIEW

1. Consistency is a child's way of coping with a confusing world. Builds feelings of security and confidence.

2. A child may be anxious or insecure. A child lacks self-control. Parents may be overly critical or inconsistent. A child may be sick, uncomfortable, tired, or hungry.

3. Some fears serve to protect the child from harm in his or her environment. Examples are fear of fire, high places, on-rushing traffic, etc.

4. Primary caregiver first, then siblings, pets, and people outside the home.

5. Sibling rivalry is a competition between brothers and sisters for their parents' affection and attention.

6. Cooperative play actually involves playing with one another, interacting and cooperating, while parallel play is independent.

7. A person with a positive self-concept; gets along with others, doesn't need to show off, accepts help, has confidence, is outgoing.

8. A sensitive child would prefer activities that can be done alone, that avoid conflict, that are not new, and that require a longer attention span.

9. The best way is through example.

10. Reasonable, loving discipline. Because they like to please others.

CHAPTER **12** REVIEW

SUMMARY

- The period between the first and fourth birthdays is a time of emotional ups and downs.
- Negativism is a normal part of toddlers' development.
- Children's emotions become more specific as they grow older.
- The parent-child relationship is an indicator of a child's emotional development.
- Many lifetime social attitudes are developed between the first and fourth birthdays.
- A child needs a positive self-concept in order to develop well emotionally and socially.
- Children with different personality types need different types of guidance.
- The goal of discipline is to help the child develop self-discipline.

REVIEWING THE FACTS

1. Why might a young child insist on unchanging routines?
2. List three reasons a toddler might be angry more often than normal.
3. Why might some fears be helpful? Give an example.
4. Who is the first person a baby loves? What other people gradually are included in a young child's affections?
5. What is sibling rivalry?
6. What is the difference between parallel play and cooperative play? At what ages are children likely to engage in these kinds of play?
7. Identify two ways in which a person with a positive self-concept differs from a person with a negative self-concept.
8. How are the preferred activities of a sensitive child likely to differ from those of an aggressive child and a placid child?
9. What is the best way to teach a child desired behavior?

10. What kind of discipline is especially effective with children between the ages of three and four? Why?

EXPLORING FURTHER

1. Work with several other students to brainstorm a list of childhood fears. Then discuss your experiences with those fears and your ideas about them. Which of those fears did you have as a child? Which have you seen in young children you know or remember? How do you think adults can best help young children deal with each of the fears? (Section 1)

2. Investigate toddler play groups (sometimes called mommy-and-me groups) in your community. Who attends these groups? What kinds of activities are involved? How appropriate do you feel the programs are? Why? Discuss your ideas with other students. (Section 2)

3. Observe parents or caregivers in a store or park. Describe an episode when the adult was required to discipline the child. Was the discipline technique suitable for the inappropriate behavior? Was it a reasonable form of discipline and age-appropriate? (Section 3)

THINKING CRITICALLY

1. **Compare and contrast.** Do you think adolescents and adults ever have temper tantrums? If so, how do they differ from the tantrums of a toddler? If not, why not?

2. **Analyze.** When a child is suffering from separation anxiety, what questions do you think his or her parents ask themselves? What other questions do you think they should ask themselves? What are parents' options in dealing with separation anxiety? What do you think is the best response to this kind of fear? Why?

3. **Analyze.** Why do you think parents often feel so worried about disciplining their children? What could help parents overcome these worries?

CLASSROOM MANAGEMENT

Learning Styles

The circumstance by which a person learns best is called his or her learning style, and it is as unique as the individual. For example, some students learn best by listening to lectures, others do better in collaborative interactions, while still others prefer a trial-and-error method. Teachers are wise to remember that no one way qualifies as better than another; they are just different. Some researchers say that learning styles are indicators of personality traits that relate to learning, such as flexibility, cooperation, and introversion. In order to meet the objectives of a class, a teacher may need to adapt material to present it meaningfully to students according to predominant learning styles. On the other hand, a teacher may wish to expand the scope of an individual's learning style by offering a variety of teaching methods.

CROSS-CURRICULUM CONNECTIONS

1. **Writing.** Should young children be allowed to hear stories and watch television shows that deal with frightening topics? Do you think that kind of exposure can help children deal with their own fears, or do you think such stories and shows only create fears in children? Write a short essay explaining and supporting your ideas.

2. **Social Studies.** What are the acceptable methods of expressing common emotions, such as anger, fear, jealousy, affection, and sympathy, in our culture? In which cultures are acceptable expressions of those emotions different? What are the "right" ways to express those emotions in those cultures? Research some facts on this topic, and present a short oral report on your findings.

SCHOOL TO WORK

Basic Skills You may not realize that in your math classes you are learning a basic skill necessary in the workplace. Math sharpens logical thinking skills and trains your mind to put things in order and follow a sequence of steps. It helps you think through problems and arrive at reasonable conclusions. One point is important—employers expect basic skills to be learned before you apply for a job. If your math skills are weak, take time to sharpen them now.

PERFORMANCE ASSESSMENT

Emotional and Social Development from One to Three

Task
Prepare a poster or chart that illustrates positive ways to encourage appropriate behavior and help children develop self-discipline.

Purpose
To demonstrate positive ways to help infants, toddlers, and preschoolers develop self-discipline, create a poster that illustrates a range of appropriate behaviors for each age group. Include captions that reinforce the caregivers' actions.

Procedure
1. Review what you read in this chapter and devise a list of positive approaches to discipline. For each approach write an example.

2. Find photos, pictures in magazines, or make your own drawings to illustrate your examples.
3. Organize your ideas and plan a layout of text and visual examples on your poster.
4. Before you finalize, review your ideas. Remember the goals for discipline: to help children behave in appropriate ways, and to ensure their safety. Don't overlook the importance of communication skills when using discipline.
5. Complete your poster or chart. Make sure it is neat, readable, and appealing.

Evaluation
Your poster will be evaluated on how clearly and thoroughly you pre-

sent positive methods of teaching discipline to toddlers. Organization, visual appeal, and creativity will be factors in the evaluation.

Portfolio Idea If your poster will physically fit into your portfolio, insert it as is. Attach or include a written paragraph stating the objective, your procedures, and any conclusions you have made about the topic while preparing the poster. If it will not fit, consider reassembling it in a different format, such as a booklet or folder. You might also choose to take a photograph of your poster and insert it into the portfolio with your written statement.

381

PERFORMANCE ASSESSMENT

Poster or Chart

Lead a discussion about misuse of the word *discipline*. It is often used to mean punishment, when it should be thought of as a way of teaching. Ask one student to find the definition of *discipline* in the text (see page 373); ask another to read the dictionary definition, and another to research the word's derivation.

Students who might need help getting started can review the Discipline Tips on pages 376-377. Encourage them to talk about positive and negative examples of discipline. Include discussion about their own self-discipline in doing their school work or participating in organized activities.

EVALUATE
Use the reproducible Chapter 12 Test in the TCR, or construct your own test using the Testmaker Software.

EXTENSION
Have students research several issues of parenting magazines and compile a scrapbook of worthwhile, informative articles and tips for handling toddlers at various stages of emotional development. Include articles about toddlers' social development and the problems and solutions connected with it.

CLOSE

Read aloud the statements in Introducing the Chapter. Discuss each statement again as a class. Then have students review their predictions and verify or modify them. Take a new count of students who believe the authors would agree or disagree with the statements. Have students explain their judgments.

SCHOOL TO WORK

Developing Active Learners Students will carry more with them from the classroom to the workplace if they are actively involved in their own learning process. For example, although your curriculum is probably set, you can offer choices about which activities will be part of a lesson. When you shift the responsibility for planning activities, implementing them, and assessing progress to students themselves, they see learning as a process that offers real-life rewards in the form of improved skills. When they consider how these skills are valued in the workplace, they are willing to invest more of their time and energy.

INTRODUCE

CHAPTER OVERVIEW

As they work through Chapter 13, students study learning theory, ways to encourage learning in toddlers, and language development. In Section 1, students begin with the definitions of *incidental learning, trial-and-error learning, imitation*, and *directed learning*. They explore concept development in toddlers and learn the seven basic elements of intellectual activity.

In Section 2, they study ways to encourage learning in toddlers and how to select age-appropriate toys. They also examine language development, with a focus on development of speech patterns and common speech problems.

CLASSROOM MANAGEMENT

Resources Beyond the Classroom

Toy companies compete vigorously for their share of the growing market for children's toys. They look to toy designers to come up with new ideas—or new variations on traditional ideas—to attract the buyer's attention. The toy designer plays an important part in developing new products. He or she must be a skilled craftsperson, able to work easily with all kinds of materials to develop models of possible new toys. Imagination is also important. A good knowledge of toy construction, production, and marketing, as well as federal safety regulations, is also vital for this career.

The toy designer is challenged to thoroughly understand children's interests, needs, and stages of development to create appropriate toys. Students can research this career in the *Directory of Occupational Handbook* at the library.

Intellectual Development from One to Three

SECTION 1   Understanding Learning and the Mind

SECTION 2   Encouraging Learning from One to Three

CHAPTER OBJECTIVES

After completing Chapter 13, students will be able to:

- Describe various methods of learning.
- Explain how children develop an understanding of concepts.
- Explain the seven basic elements of intellectual activity.
- Suggest ways to encourage young children to learn.
- Select safe, appropriate toys that promote learning as well as physical and social skills.
- Describe how children develop speech patterns and identify common speech problems.

INTRODUCING THE CHAPTER

- Ask students to explain how they acquire skills or knowledge. Examples that you might suggest are learning to in-line skate without falling and memorizing important dates for a history exam. Explain that young children learn by the same processes. Tell students that in this chapter they will study learning processes and how to encourage learning in children from ages one through three.
- Use the photo on the opposite page and the three features on this page—Think About, Ask Yourself, and Now Try This—to begin a discussion about a child's intellectual development from ages one to three.

THINK ABOUT

Try to remember a person who positively influenced you as a child. Think about what that person said or did that made him or her so memorable. Who was the person? What experiences do you remember having together? How did this person contribute to your intellectual development?

ASK YOURSELF

Study the photo on the opposite page. How is the man turning a common event such as potting a plant into a learning experience for the toddler? What could

the child learn? What would they be saying to each other? By allowing the child to help with the task, how does the man contribute to the child's physical development as well? Why might this man become a memorable person to this child?

NOW TRY THIS

Take an imaginary walk with a toddler through your neighborhood or community. Make a list of the people you would meet, the sounds you would hear, and the sights you would see. Describe how you could use the walk to encourage the child's intellectual development.

383

HEALTHY FAMILIES/HEALTHY CHILDREN

Health and Nutrition

In an effort to prove a relationship between diet and intelligence, researchers compared the nonverbal (problem-solving) intelligence levels of 90 British children. All the children were given an intelligence test before beginning the experiment. For the next eight months, one-third of the students were given a multivitamin and mineral sup-

plement; one-third, a placebo; and the other one-third, nothing. When a follow-up test was given, a significant improvement was shown in only the group receiving the multivitamin and mineral supplement. Although the results are preliminary, parents need to be reminded that a good diet is important to a child's learning.

FOCUS

SECTION 1 RESOURCES

Teacher's Classroom Resources

- Enrichment 32
- Reteaching 32
- Section 1 Quiz

Student Workbook

- Secret Square Quiz

SECTION OVERVIEW

In Section 1, students examine intelligence and its role in learning. Next, they study four methods of learning: incidental learning, trial-and-error learning, imitation, and directed learning. Students discover that concept development is essential to learning, and explore it in toddlers. Finally, they learn the seven basic elements of intellectual activity: attention, memory, perception, reasoning, imagination, creativity, and curiosity.

MOTIVATOR

Write on the chalkboard: "I'll never do that again!" Ask for examples of what students would not do again based on past experience. Most incidents will illustrate either trial-and-error learning or incidental learning. Point out examples of these forms of learning. Discuss their advantages and disadvantages as methods of learning.

USING TERMS TO LEARN

Discuss the meaning of the terms *incidental learning* and *directed learning*. *Incidental* is derived from the adjective *incident*, and means "occurring in connection with some other event." Thus, incidental learning is unplanned, happening as a result of something else. In contrast, to direct is to show or point the way. Thus, directed learning involves being shown the way, or taught. Ask for examples of each.

SECTION 1

Understanding Learning and the Mind

SECTION 1 Understanding Learning and the Mind

OBJECTIVES

- Describe various methods of learning.
- Explain how children develop concepts.
- Explain the seven basic elements of intellectual activity.

TERMS TO LEARN

concepts
creativity
directed learning
imitation
incidental learning
intelligence
trial-and-error learning

Learning is a complex and exciting process. This process begins on the first day of life and continues throughout a person's lifetime.

The Role of Intelligence

Intelligence, as you know, is the capacity to learn. However, a more precise definition of intelligence will help you as you read about intellectual development between ages one and three. **Intelligence** is *the ability to interpret or understand everyday situations and to use that experience when faced with new situations or problems.*

A person's intelligence is determined by both heredity and environment. Everyone is born with certain possible limits of intellectual development. Some people have more intellectual potential than others. However, the extent to which an individual's potential is actually developed is greatly influenced by that person's environment.

Environmental experiences, such as interactions with family members, the availability of playthings, and personal encouragement, are especially important during the first years of life. During this early period, the foundation for later learning is formed. During this period, children also establish their attitudes toward learning. If curiosity about everything (a natural toddler's quality) is encouraged and enhanced, the child develops a positive attitude about learning.

MORE ABOUT

Intelligence

In a study of Scholastic Aptitude Test (SAT) scores, one researcher found a correlation between exam scores and family size. In the 1950s, larger families were the trend. As children born during this time grew older, test scores declined (between 1963 and 1980). Family size decreased in the 1960s, however, and the corresponding scores for these children rose in the 1980s. The researcher believes the variation in test scores is due to the time a child spends with adults and recommends having children two years apart in order to give each child adequate adult contact.

Methods of Learning

Children learn in a variety of ways, some of them rather unexpected. Learning doesn't take place just in schools and school-like situations; it is an ongoing process. Children learn on their own through everyday experiences and through play. Researchers have classified children's learning methods into four groups: incidental learning, trial-and-error learning, imitation, and directed learning.

✓**Incidental learning** is *unplanned learning*. A small baby happens to push both feet against the bottom of the crib and discovers that this motion moves his or her body forward. When this happens accidentally a number of times, the baby understands the cause-and-effect situation. After this incidental learning has taken place, the baby may choose to push against the crib on purpose, in order to experience the forward movement. Here's another example of incidental learning: A three-year-old sets an open bottle of bubble liquid down on its side. When she picks the bottle up again to blow some bubbles, she finds all the liquid has poured out. Next time, she will be careful to put the bottle down upright.

Although toys can aid learning, the encouragement of caregivers is far more important.

A close-up view of a fish tank opens the door for learning opportunities.

TEACH

Pages 384-395

• The Role of Intelligence
• Methods of Learning
• Concept Development
• The Mind at Work

GUIDED PRACTICE

Promoting Discussion

On the chalkboard, write the word *intelligence*. Have students list skills and types of knowledge they associate with intelligence. As they respond, list their responses on the chalkboard.

Point out that most people associate intelligence with verbal skills and knowledge of the type they acquire in school. Encourage them to expand their concept of intelligence to conform to the definition in the text and discuss how intelligence would manifest itself in toddlers.

SEE HOW THEY GROW

Preoperational Thought

According to Jean Piaget, children between two and seven years old are in the stage of preoperational thought. Although they can use language and symbols, their thought processes are limited. Their thinking is concrete, and they can't deal with abstractions. Several important concepts that children learn during this stage include conservation of matter, classification of objects, seriation, and an understanding of time, space, and sequence. Children learn these concepts not by direct rote teaching but by interacting with the environment, using their bodies, handling objects, manipulating, watching, and verbalizing.

GUIDED PRACTICE (continued)

Critical Thinking

To help students distinguish among learning methods, ask the following questions:

- In what situations do you learn by incidental learning? Give examples. What knowledge might a toddler acquire by this method?
- In what situations do you learn by trial and error? Compare your examples with knowledge a toddler acquires by trial and error.
- What have you learned by imitation? What evidence shows toddlers learn by imitation?
- What skills described in Chapters 11 and 12 were acquired by directed learning?

Critical Thinking

Have students identify the method by which they would learn each of the following:

- The dog's leg moves when its chest is scratched. (Incidental.)
- Licorice ice cream tastes terrible, but peanut butter and onion sandwiches are delicious. (Trial-and-error.)
- New dance moves. (Imitation, directed learning.)
- Algebra. (Directed learning.)
- How to make pasta. (Directed learning.)

HEALTH TIP

Be cautious of foods labeled "natural." Depending on the content, the food may, or may not, be healthy. A "natural" snack bar containing fruit sugar, honey, and carob is not more healthy than a regular candy bar. For a really good snack, give a child some fruit.

HEALTH TIP

Research shows that good nutrition is essential in helping children develop to their full intellectual potential. Children need protein for building and repairing tissues and cells. They also need carbohydrates for energy.

√**Trial-and-error learning** is *learning in which a child tries several solutions before finding out what works*. Pete, for example, uses trial-and-error learning as he tries to fit four pieces into a new puzzle board. He picks up one puzzle piece and tries fitting it into each hole on the board until he finds the right one. Janet also uses trial-and-error learning when she wants to play with the truck her younger brother is using. First, Janet grabs the truck from her brother, but he screams and her mother makes her give the truck back. Next, she tells her brother to go outside and play, but he doesn't want to. Finally, Janet offers to let her brother use her play dough if she can play with his truck. He agrees, and Janet gets what she wants.

√**Imitation** is *learning by watching and copying others*. Perhaps you have been annoyed by a younger brother or sister who copied everything you did. Did you realize that he or she was trying to learn from you? Children—and adults—often learn by imitating others. Three-year-old Ben gives a doll a bath because that's what his parents do with his baby brother. "There, doesn't that feel good?" Ben asks the doll, using the same tone of voice his mother uses with the baby. Both skills and attitudes are learned by imitation.

It took Colleen many tries before she found where to put the puzzle pieces. What type of learning does this illustrate?

HEALTHY FAMILIES/HEALTHY CHILDREN

Health and Safety

As children use different methods of learning, it is important to think about safety. This is especially true with the trial-and-error and incidental methods. A child should not learn that a stove is hot by burning his or her hand, or that a shock will occur by sticking a paper clip into an electric outlet. Children may also put themselves in unsafe situations when imitating adults. They may try to use curling irons, razors, gardening tools, or other hazardous items. Children need to be provided with their own safe items for imitating adults. The best rule to remember is that supervised learning is safest. Ask students whether they recall incidents when they learned the "hard way."

You might not think pretending is an example of learning, but it is. Much of a child's behavior comes from watching and imitating others.

Directed learning is *learning from being taught, either formally or informally*. His first-grade teacher helps six-year-old Umberto learn to read, step by step. That's directed learning. Her mother shows two-year-old Monica how to point to her eyes, her nose, and her mouth. That's directed learning, too—it's just a less formal process. Directed learning begins in the early years and continues throughout life.

Concept Development

As they learn to think effectively, young children begin to organize the information they receive from their senses. They start to form *concepts*, *general categories of objects and information*. Concepts range from categories for objects such as "fruit," to qualities such as color or shape and to abstract ideas such as time.

As a child matures and learns, concepts become more refined and more accurate. Young babies begin by distinguishing two broad concepts, "me" and "not me." Toddlers and preschoolers make very broad distinctions between people and things. For example, all women are "mama" and all men are "dada." Later, the concepts of "woman," "man," "girl," and "boy" begin to have meaning. Similarly, the child learns that this is a table and that is a chair. Tables have flat surfaces and no backs. They may be small or large, and they vary in color. They are used to eat from or to put things on.

GUIDED PRACTICE (continued)

Using the Photograph
Have students study the photograph on page 386. Discuss the type of learning that is taking place. If Colleen failed to learn by this method, by what method might she learn from an adult?

Cooperative Learning
Divide students into four groups. Give each group a blank transparency and a transparency marker, and assign a type of learning. Have them list as many examples as they can think of for their type of learning. Have the group recorder present the group's list, and encourage classmates to add examples.

Critical Thinking
For exploration of imitative learning, have students consider these questions:
• Why might imitative learning also be called modeling? (Modeling also describes behavior that is learned by watching, and then copying, another person.) Give examples of situations where one individual consciously models for another. (Dance instruction, athletic courses, courses in which teachers model thinking strategies.)
• How might a child's imitative learning be affected if his or her parents or caregivers behave in inconsistent ways? (The child might be confused. An example, would be if the parents expect the child to use good manners but they themselves do not use good manners.)

MORE ABOUT

Children and Learning
Some specialists feel that early educational programs for very young children do not have long-lasting effects. There is even fear that early learning programs may cause stress in young children when rote learning drills and regimented work are emphasized. Instead of these types of activities, specialists feel that children should have experiences they direct themselves. One type of self-directed learning, for example, might be giving children crayons and paper and letting them decide what to do with them instead of instructing the children to write the alphabet.

GUIDED PRACTICE (continued)

**Making Connections:
Language Arts**

Have students choose the type of learning they feel is best for them and explain it in an essay. They should include examples of what they have learned by the method as well as an explanation of why they feel that method is best for them. If students do not believe they learn better by one particular method, have them select a particular area of study and write about how two learning methods apply to that field.

Family Focus

Have students list advantages and disadvantages of toddlers' imitating older siblings. What are some behaviors that toddlers can benefit by learning from older siblings? (Self-dressing, hygiene habits, use of the toilet.) What behaviors may be desirable in older siblings, but undesirable in younger siblings? (Children may put themselves in unsafe situations when imitating older siblings. They may try to climb tall trees, or use curling irons, razors, gardening tools, or other hazardous items.)

This three-year-old can sort objects by colors or shapes. He will also begin to recognize shapes in everyday objects.

Young children also learn to categorize objects by shape, color, and size. Balls are round, and so are biscuits and plates. Grass and trees are both green. When shown balls of three different sizes, most two-year-olds cannot identify the middle-sized ball. By age three, they can do so easily. However, the relationship between two items—"big" and "little"—may be recognized as early as eighteen months. At that time, the larger cat in the picture is called the "mama kitty" and the smaller one, the "baby kitty."

Concepts of life and time are not learned until later. A young child believes that anything that moves or works is alive. This includes clouds, mechanical toys, dolls, and the washing machine. Later, the child will be ready to learn that only plants, animals, and people are alive.

Concepts of time improve slowly during the second and third years. Two-year-olds may be more patient than before because they know that "soon" means something will happen. They know the difference between "before" and "after." However, "today," "tomorrow," and "yesterday" may not be completely grasped until a child is in kindergarten.

The Mind at Work

Intellectual activity is a complex process that coordinates the many elements of the mind. The most basic elements of intellectual activity are attention, memory, perception, reasoning, imagination, creativity, and curiosity. All these elements show remarkable development in children from one to three, but they continue to develop throughout life.

Attention

Every moment, the five senses are bombarded with information. This moment—as you are reading—is a good example. You see the words on the page. At the same time, you are also aware of such things as the size, shape, and color of the book and the amount of light in the room. You can probably hear pages being turned; perhaps you also hear someone walking in the hall or a fly buzzing around the room. You may be able to smell lunch being prepared in the cafeteria, or you might smell fresh wax on the floor. Your skin is telling you that the paper of the book is smooth and cool; it may also be telling you that there is a small rock in your shoe.

Fortunately, you are able to block out most of this sensory information and focus only on the book. You can concentrate. A baby is not able to concentrate. The infant's attention flits from one bit of sensory information to another.

SEE HOW THEY GROW

Concept Development

Between one and one-half years and three years of age, children show tremendous growth in cognitive development. During this age, you can expect them to understand one-step commands (they cannot follow instructions consisting of several steps); identify more and more common objects as they are named; and understand relative size (big and small).

By age two, they know more than 200 words, and by age 3, about 500 words. They can create two-word sentences expressing action ("Baby cry") or possession ("Mommy shoe"); they begin to use three-word sentences, showing sense of word order. They also start to use past tense and plurals and begin to refer to the self by name.

As children mature, they gradually develop the ability to ignore most of the information their senses provide and to concentrate on one item of interest. One- to three-year-olds have short attention spans. However, a three-year-old can focus on one activity for much longer than a one-year-old.

Memory

Without memory, there would be no learning. If an experience left no impression, it would not affect future behavior. A child reacts to a situation by remembering similar experiences in the past. A one-year-old who was frightened by a dog may be afraid of all animals for a time. A three-year-old can remember the particular dog and compare it with others to judge their character.

Memory begins with the routine of a baby's life. The comfortable familiarity of parents is one of a baby's earliest memories.

By age two, a toddler has a fairly good memory. A two-year-old can deliver simple messages. The child can also remember a parent who has been absent for several weeks, repeat bits of favorite stories, and relate experiences after returning from an outing.

Can you explain how playing this "piano" involves attention, memory, perception, and reasoning?

GUIDED PRACTICE (continued)

**Making Connections:
Language Arts**

Have students write definitions for the words *today, tomorrow,* and *yesterday.* Compare the definitions with those given in the dictionary. Ask whether a child of two or three could understand the concepts based on the students' definitions. Discuss the reasons the terms are difficult to define.

Critical Thinking

Use these strategies to encourage students to examine concept development:

• Display a box of crayons, and ask students to list concepts that could be taught with crayons. (Examples include color names, counting, lightness and darkness of colors, shapes, and size.)

• A girl holds up her blue block and says to a younger boy, "Blue." The boy holds up an orange block and says, "Blue." The girl touches her yellow sweater and says, "Yellow." The boy touches his own blue sweater and says, "Yellow." What concept does the boy need to develop before he can learn the words the girl is trying to teach him? (Color.) What could she do to help him develop it? (Point out several objects that are all the same color, such as a yellow banana, dress, piece of chalk, ball, and cap.)

COOPERATIVE LEARNING

Group Cooperation

In order for your students to derive maximum benefit from their cooperative learning experiences, ensure that every group activity is set up so as to:

• Encourage the use of social skills, such as compromise and common courtesy. During organized group discussion, for example, students should be open to the opinions and ideas of other group members and willing to yield the floor when called upon to do so.

• Encourage positive interdependence. The group should see to it that every member has an active role in the project.

• Allow time for postactivity analysis. Groups should be given time to diagnose and reflect on the strengths and weaknesses of the enterprise.

GUIDED PRACTICE (continued)

**Making Connections:
Language Arts**

Have students visit the library to check out a children's book that teaches a concept such as color, shape, texture, or time. Have them read the book to the class and explain how the concept is taught. Would very young children like the book? Why or why not?

Making Connections: Physiology

Have students research brain development to find out why a three-year-old might be better able than a one-year-old to understand the concepts of "Life" and "Time." Have them report their findings in class.

BUILDING SELF-ESTEEM

Don't overlook opportunities to sit quietly and let nature do the entertaining. Depending on a child's age and attention span, make a game of sitting and listening to the sounds of the environment. Encourage a child to imitate the calls of animals; you may be surprised by a response from the animal being imitated!

Childhood Reflections

"The pedagogical method of observation has for its base the liberty of the child; and liberty is activity."

Maria Montessori

BUILDING SELF-ESTEEM

Nature—An Educational Playland!

The outdoors can be an educational playland! Children learn through their senses and nature has different smells, sounds, textures, and tastes.

When children are outdoors, they discover that sticks make wonderful tools for scratching designs or letters in the earth or sand, and rocks come in a variety of sizes and shapes.

When children are surrounded by nature, there are many things to discover, compare, and think about. Flowers have different scents; some birds enjoy the water; the bark of trees can feel rough or smooth. Caregivers can help children in these discoveries by talking about nature and providing opportunities for children to explore and ask questions.

A three-year-old typically remembers simple requests or directions, uses numbers as if counting (although 14 may come directly after 6), and identifies most colors when asked to point to a specific color.

Perception

Perception is the ability to receive and use information from the senses. This ability develops gradually throughout childhood.

A newborn receives a great deal of sensory information but is unable to interpret much of it. Gradually, a baby develops the ability to make broad distinctions between people. These distinctions become more refined with experience.

Parents and caregivers can encourage the development of perception by answering, cheerfully and accurately, the frequent questions common among two- and three-year-olds—"Why?" "What is that?" "How does it work?" They can also encourage learning by making descriptive observations that the child can understand and expand on. For example, when passing a store window, you might say, "Look at the blue coat. Your shirt is blue, too. Let's see what other blue things we can see as we walk." Commenting on the environment and answering questions helps improve a child's perception and aids his or her concept development.

A child whose questions are ignored or brushed aside, on the other hand, loses opportunities for learning. If adults usually respond with an absent-minded "Uh-huh" or "Don't bother me right now—I'm busy," the child eventually stops asking questions.

Reasoning

Reasoning is basic to the ability to solve problems and to make decisions. It is also important in recognizing relationships and forming concepts.

Babies show the beginning of problem-solving ability at about four to six months of age. Around this age, the baby first pushes away one toy in order to get at another.

Later, the child solves problems by actually trying out all possible solutions. For example, young children often enjoy playing with a box in which objects of various shapes can be dropped through matching holes. A fourteen-month-old child will pick up a triangle and try to fit it into all the holes until one works.

By about two or three years of age, problem solving becomes more mental. A child can think through possible solutions to a problem and eliminate those that won't work without actually trying out each possibility.

OBSERVING AND PARTICIPATING

Learning Through Participation

Here are two ways to communicate positive attitudes toward learning:

- Encourage the children's curiosity about the world—and show you're curious, too. Take walks together and wonder aloud at things that fascinate you. Take time to see, listen, smell, feel, even taste (when safe!). Model for the children that there's much to learn about the world when they observe with all their senses.

- Welcome the children's questions—and ask your own. Discuss where you might go to find the answers, such as to the library or to a person who's an "expert" on a particular subject.

- Praise the children's efforts at learning new skills. Help children feel that learning accomplishments are important ones.

Decision making is closely related to problem solving. In fact, a decision can be considered a kind of problem. Gradually, children learn to follow the five basic steps in problem solving by mentally responding to these questions:

1. What is the problem?
2. What do I already know about it?
3. What are the possible solutions?
4. Which is the best solution?
5. Did I make the right choice?

Parents and caregivers can help children learn to make good decisions. One way is to give the child a chance to make real decisions. At first, these decisions should be based on limited choices, and a poor decision should not cause any harm. "Would you rather wear your yellow shirt or your green striped shirt with these brown pants?" "Would you like chicken soup or vegetable soup for lunch?" This kind of practice helps the child avoid making snap decisions. Eventually, the child will learn how to focus on the choices and to make thoughtful decisions on his or her own.

Imagination

Imagination begins to become evident at about two years of age. Actually, babies may also have active imaginations, but there is no way of knowing since they cannot speak. An active imagination is an important part of learning.

Children can be and do almost anything through imagination. An empty box makes a good house. Another day it might become a spaceship or fort.

BUILDING SELF-ESTEEM

Helping Children Make Decisions

If a difficult situation is beyond the toddler, you can give just enough help to prevent discouragement. Show the child a possible solution, and then allow the child to continue. For example, you might say, "Let's see. This piece of the puzzle has green grass on it. Maybe it fits on that side of the picture where everything is green." Remember that children need successful experiences to gain perseverance, self-confidence, and the willingness to test their own reasoning ability.

GUIDED PRACTICE (continued)

Family Focus
Read the following to students: In two-year-old Teresa's house, her parents were always called Carol and Dennis by even Teresa. Often Teresa played with her friend Tammi. At four o'clock each day, Tammi's father arrived home from work. Tammi ran to greet him, calling out, "Daddy!" It wasn't long before Teresa was running to greet him, too, also happily calling out, "Daddy!" Ask students what concept Teresa was learning. Was it accurate?

Promoting Discussion
Have students describe all the sensory information they have around them. What happens when sensory stimuli cannot be blocked? (You cannot concentrate.) What might happen if all sensory stimuli were blocked out? (You might have an accident or get injured.)

Critical Thinking
Ask students to suggest reasons why everyday items might be better than toys for encouraging imaginative play. (Their use as a toy is not immediately obvious, but they lend themselves to imaginative uses.)

Ask students why some parents might stifle creative activities such as finger painting and use of clay. (They are often messy.) What might happen to a child if parents repeatedly stifle imaginative and creative activities? (It might retard the child's intellectual development.)

BUILDING SELF-ESTEEM

Just as important as the encouragement to persevere is the knowledge of when to stop. If a child is overwrought with fatigue or frustration, gently urging the child to stop and set the activity aside until a better time saves wear and tear on everyone's nerves.

OBSERVING AND PARTICIPATING

Learning Through Participation
Young children are usually fascinated with imaginary things. Parents and caregivers can capitalize on this interest in make-believe play by collecting a variety of puppets. Often furry animals and feathery bird puppets are the most appealing. These puppets are helpful in developing a child's imagination, creativity, and vocabulary. Children can use a puppet to express an idea or feeling and to share an experience. They can use the decision-making process as adults pose right and wrong situations. A puppet can become anything a child can imagine. Have your students help preschoolers make and decorate finger puppets, stick puppets, sock puppets, paper plate puppets, or paper bag puppets.

GUIDED PRACTICE (continued)

Promoting Discussion

Have students suggest ways to praise a child's imaginative and creative efforts verbally. Then have them give nonverbal methods that also show praise and recognition.

Making Connections:
Language Arts

Have students collect pictures of children involved in imaginative play. Have them write captions below the pictures indicating what they think the children might be saying.

Practicing Decision Making

Tell students to assume they are parents of a child three years of age. Have students select or design and then describe three activities they would use with the child to promote creativity. Have them explain how they chose the activities and what the child might learn from the activities.

Making Connections:
Language Arts

Have students write a paragraph explaining how imagination and creativity are related. Ask for suggested ways to encourage each.

Critical Thinking

Point out that many parents consciously encourage their children to learn, while others provide encouragement without realizing it. Still others act to discourage learning. Discuss with students what behaviors discourage learning and why parents might act in these ways.

Imagination allows the child to try new things and to be different people—at least in the mind. Chairs become trains, boxes are buildings, and closets are caves. The child becomes a ferocious lion or a busy mail carrier. Many children of this age also have imaginary playmates.

Children use their imaginations to connect what they see and hear with themselves. A child may see an airplane and wonder, "Will I fly in a plane someday?" A child may hear about death and ask, "Will I die, too?"

Unfortunately, adult responses often stifle a child's imagination. When three-year-old Emma makes up a story, she isn't lying—she's using her imagination. In fact, until about the age of five, children are simply not sure where reality ends and imagination begins. However, if Emma's mother says, "Don't be silly. You know that didn't really happen," Emma will be discouraged from using her imagination, and her options for learning will be limited.

Creative activities are a way for children to express themselves. They also help children feel good about their accomplishments.

SEE HOW THEY GROW

Imaginary Friends

While watching her young son play one day, Tyree noticed that he kept talking to someone who was not there. "Who are you talking to?" she asked. "My friend Hoopy," her son replied. Children commonly create companions to fulfill the need for play and fantasy in their lives. Sometimes these imaginary friends are like humans, but they may also be pets or animals. As long as the involvement is not extreme, there should be no concern. Eventually, the friend will disappear. In the meantime, the companion may help the child develop socially and provide an outlet for positive as well as negative emotions.

Creativity

Imagination is closely related to **creativity**, *the use of imagination to produce something*. The product is usually something others can see, such as a finger painting. Daydreams are also products of creativity, as is creative dramatic play where different roles are assumed—mother, baby, firefighter, and so forth.

Creativity, which is an asset throughout life, is most readily developed in early childhood—if children are given opportunities and encouragement. Here are some ways to promote creativity:

- Encourage play activities that depend on exploration, imagination, and creativity. Drawing, playing with clay, building things, dressing up in grown-up clothes or hats, and telling stories are opportunities for creative expression.
- The process of creating is more important than the product. Don't insist on conformity in every aspect of life. The message that being different is always bad stifles creativity. To encourage creativity, you might respond to a child's drawing this way: "Wow, Martin, I've never seen a cat with three eyes before or a purple cat! I wonder what it would be like to have a purple cat, or to have three eyes, or to have a purple cat with three eyes?"
- Praise the child's efforts, with deeds as well as words. Display that new picture of a three-eyed purple cat on the refrigerator and tell other people significant to the child about the picture.

Curiosity

Babies are curious about the world around them. That curiosity is the source of learning and should increase with age. However, parents sometimes stifle a child's curiosity by over-

Learning should be fun. Sharing new experiences with caregivers helps give a child confidence.

SAFETY TIP

Parents and other caregivers need to remember that curiosity stimulates learning, but it can also be dangerous. Young children should be encouraged to explore—once hazards have been removed from their environment and as long as adults check on them frequently. You may want to review the ideas for toddler-proofing presented in Positive Parenting Skills on pages 344-345.

GUIDED PRACTICE (continued)

Critical Thinking

As you read aloud this narrative, have students identify parental behavior that discourages learning: One morning, three-year-old Patti turned her wagon over, sat on it, and laughed as she spun its wheels. Her mother said, "No, Patti, that's not how you use a wagon. Let's turn it over and I'll give you a ride." After the ride, Patti scuffled in some leaves until she found a worm. Her mother cried, "Patti! Put that dirty thing down." Later, at the grocery store, Patti looked at the brightly colored packages. Twice her mother slapped her hand when she reached for a package. Have students explain Patti's behavior and evaluate the way the mother handled Patti. What might be the effect of this treatment? Have students suggest other ways Patti's mother could have responded.

SAFETY TIP

Refer students to the safety tip on this page. Review with them the concept of "childproofing" an area — making it as safe as possible for the young child by removing breakable objects and keeping the child safe from falls, burns, and other hazards. Discuss how a child's curiosity can create hazardous situations and the importance of a caregiver's supervision.

Did You Know?

Children love to be pen pals with celebrities. Big Bird, the lovable character on Sesame Street, receives about 100 letters a month from young fans. His fuzzy green friend, Oscar the Grouch, receives old shoes, bottle caps, and crumpled paper instead of letters!

OBSERVING AND PARTICIPATING

Learning Through Participation

A folding, portable, child-sized puppet stage can be made from a cardboard box. Select a sturdy box that measures 12 to 24 inches (30.5 to 61 cm) on each side. Make an opening in the form by cutting three sides of a square on one side of the box. This will be the armhole for working the puppets. Make an identical opening on the opposite side for the audience to view the puppets. Fold the flaps into the box, and fasten them together to form a stage. Insert a dowel through holes near the top of the box, and hang a curtain from the inside. Decorate the inside and outside of the stage using lead-free paint or self-stick plastic covering. Have students present a puppet show to preschoolers.

PARENTING IN ACTION

Promoting Discussion

To introduce Parenting in Action, have students discuss imaginative stories they have heard from younger children. Ask if they were disturbed by the child's apparent failure to distinguish fact from imagination. Have them read the feature and discuss Jessica's behavior and Jane's handling of it.

Answers to "Think and Discuss"

1. That a trip requires planning and decisions, and she learned the concept of time. By perception, participation, and memory.

2. Imagination, creativity, and reasoning.

3. By including her in the trip to the bus station, and by not discouraging her imaginative play.

4. Answers may vary. Some students will agree with the support and encouragement of imaginative play; others may feel that the parents should acknowledge to Jessica that it would be dangerous for her to think that she could actually take this trip by herself at this time.

INDEPENDENT PRACTICE

Student Workbook

Have students complete "Secret Square Quiz" in the Student Workbook.

Student Demonstration

Have students plan and share a directed learning activity used to teach a concept to a child.

Extension

Make a list of imaginative activities, toys, and games appropriate for one to three-year-olds. Use the list to produce a handout titled "Just Imagine." A brief explanation of each item on the list should be included.

PARENTING IN ACTION

Learning by Pretending

*J*ane Rodriguez was expecting several people for a neighborhood committee meeting. Three-year-old Jessica was underfoot, so her mother suggested she let the neighbors in as they arrived. Jessica greeted each person politely and proceeded to tell about her upcoming trip to visit her grandmother.

"This is my suitcase. I am taking the bus to Nana's. Mommy and Daddy are taking me to the bus. They will put my suitcase on the bus and put me in a bus seat and then go home. I'll go on the bus alone till I get to Grandma's house."

Surprised, each adult asked the same question: "Are you really going alone?"

"Yup. I'm going all by myself. I'm big enough now. I can do things by myself," she answered confidently.

The details were so complete that the adults accepted Jessica's story. As they gathered around the table for their meeting, however, one of them said doubtfully, "Jane, are you sure you want Jessica to go on a bus to Cambria by herself? She's only three! I wouldn't even let my ten-year-old do that!" The other neighbors agreed.

Jessica's mother laughed in surprise. "Oh, you mean Jessie's trip to her grandmother's! Of course, she's not going. She's just pretending she is. Two days ago, we sent Jenny, Jessica's twelve-year-old sister, on the bus to visit her grandmother. It's a nonstop ride, and her grandmother was there to meet her when the bus arrived. Jessie heard all the planning and instructions we gave Jenny. She went with us when we took Jenny to her seat on the bus. Now Jessie is imagining that she's going to make the same trip by herself."

THINK AND DISCUSS

1. What had Jessica learned? By what method had she learned it?

2. Which elements of intellectual activity can you identify in Jessica's "game"?

3. How do you think her parents encouraged those elements of intellectual activity?

4. Do you think there are any potentially harmful elements in Jessica's "game" about going to Grandma's? If so, what? If not, why not?

5. If you had been Jessica's parent, would you have handled the situation differently? Why or why not?

COOPERATIVE LEARNING

Fostering Creativity

Unfortunately, learning and creativity are often more easily discouraged than encouraged. The competition found throughout society means that those children who don't "win" one time may be discouraged from trying the next time. Teachers and parents often emphasize mistakes children make, lowering children's confidence in their ability to do something right or well the next time. The push toward excellence (as illustrated in the old maxim, "It isn't worth doing if it isn't worth doing well") can discourage children from trying if they know their efforts will be criticized. Thus, children are discouraged from learning or showing curiosity.

protecting the child—or by overprotecting the home. Parents and caregivers should remember that children are educating themselves while they are creating clutter.

Young children seem to be into everything. They poke into every corner and closet. They handle and examine everything within reach. It is impossible for caregivers to anticipate what a two- or three-year-old may do next. Surprised parents may find a doll or a truck in the washing machine because "it was dirty." A plastic horse may stand in the center of the mashed potatoes as the child explains, "Horsey eat, too."

It doesn't take much effort to turn everyday activities into learning experiences. This boy is finding out about where the food he eats comes from and how it grows.

SECTION 1 REVIEW

CHECK YOUR UNDERSTANDING

1. What is intelligence?

2. Which method of learning is based on watching and copying others? Who uses this method?

3. What is a concept? List at least three examples of concepts.

4. Why could there be no learning without memory?

5. What is perception? When and how does it develop?

6. What are the five basic steps in problem solving?

7. What is curiosity? Why is it important?

DISCUSS AND DISCOVER

1. Discuss your own responses to the four methods of learning: Which do you find most

useful and enjoyable now? Why? Which do you think you found most useful and enjoyable as a three-year-old? Why?

2. Select a single concept that a three-year-old child might be ready to learn. Devise a simple game or make a simple toy that would help teach that concept to a young child. Share and discuss your game or toy with other students.

Observing & Participating

Observe a toddler and the child's parent or primary caregiver during a play activity. Describe how the play situation provides a relaxed environment in which the child can learn. How is creativity and imagination encouraged? What methods of learning—incidental, trial-and-error, imitation, and directed—do you see?

SECTION 1 REVIEW

1. The ability to interpret and understand everyday situations and to use that experience when faced with new situations or problems.

2. Imitation; both children and adults.

3. General categories of objects and information. Possible examples: fruit, triangle, time, etc.

4. If experience left no impression in the memory, it would not affect future behavior.

5. The ability to receive and use information from the senses; develops gradually throughout childhood.

6. Refer to page 391.

7. The desire to find out about the world and about the things and people in the world; it is the source of learning.

ASSESS

CHECKING COMPREHENSION

Assign students to write their responses to the Check Your Understanding questions in the Section 1 Review. Answers are given at the bottom of this page.

EVALUATE

Have students complete the Chapter 13, Section 1 TCR quiz.

Reteaching

1. Assign Reteaching Activity 32 in the TCR and have students complete the activity and review their responses.

2. List the following words on the chalkboard, and ask students to determine what they all have in common: *color, shape, time,* and *size.* (*They are all concepts.*)

Enrichment

1. Distribute Enrichment 32 in the TCR and challenge students to complete the activity.

2. Have students plan a toddlers' game or activity requiring attention, memory, perception, and reasoning. Tell them to try the activity with a small group of two to three-year-olds and summarize their experience and answer these questions: Could all the children successfully play the game or participate in the activity? Did some children become frustrated? Why?

Extension

Set up a display of brain-teaser puzzles and toys suitable for teenagers and adults. Have students use attention, memory, perception, and reasoning to work the puzzles. Which element did they call on most often? Which method of learning did they use?

CLOSE

Have students brainstorm endings for this:

"To develop intellectually, a child needs ..." Encourage responses that include both intellectual capacity and appropriate experience.

FOCUS

SECTION 2 RESOURCES

Teacher's Classroom Resources
- Enrichment 33
- Reteaching 33
- Section 2 Quiz

Student Workbook
- Using Everyday Objects as Toys

SECTION OVERVIEW

In Section 2, students study ways to encourage learning in toddlers. With readiness and learning in mind, they learn criteria for selecting toys and activities appropriate for the age of the child. They examine language development, with a focus on development of speech patterns and common speech problems.

MOTIVATOR

Refer students to the chapter title and ask how encouraging learning might differ from teaching. Discuss the difference between pushing a child to learn and allowing that child to learn. Remind students of the four methods of learning described in Section 1: incidental, trial-and-error, imitation, and directed learning. Have students discuss what they may be pushed to learn, such as grammar, by directed learning. Then ask them what and how they may be forbidden to learn, such as learning to drive by trial and error. Tell them this section will explain how to encourage learning in young children.

USING TERMS TO LEARN

Pronounce the words listed under "Terms to Learn." Ask students whether they are familiar with any of these. Explain that these terms will be defined in the chapter.

SECTION **2**

Encouraging Learning from One to Three

OBJECTIVES

- Suggest ways to encourage young children to learn.
- Select safe, appropriate toys that promote learning as well as physical and social skills.
- Describe how children develop speech patterns.
- Identify common speech problems.

TERMS TO LEARN

articulation
flammable
speech therapist

P arents and other caregivers inevitably have an effect—either positive or negative—on a child's learning. Adults who provide a relaxed, accepting atmosphere and a variety of experiences encourage young children to learn. On the other hand, adults who are overly harsh, who are too busy with their own lives, or who show children that they do not really care discourage learning.

Readiness for Learning

Children can learn a new skill only when they are physically and intellectually ready. As an extreme example, it would be a waste of time trying to teach a six-month-old to pull a zipper closed—the baby has neither the physical maturity nor the intellectual maturity necessary for that skill. In the same way, nearly all three-year-olds lack the physical and intellectual maturity to learn to print words. When adults push children toward learning for which they are not ready, the children cannot succeed. In such situations, a child's sense of failure often causes him or her to learn more slowly rather than (as the adult intended) more rapidly.

Just as it is important to avoid pushing children into learning skills too early, it is also important to avoid delaying skills that children are ready to learn. For example, Ben's mother put Ben's shoes on for him every time he struggled with the task, but she discovered that this kind of "helping" caused problems later.

HEALTHY FAMILIES/HEALTHY CHILDREN

Families at Play

In a survey of parental attitudes and play, researchers found that 33 percent of the parents surveyed play or take part in recreational activities with their children every day. Several times a week was cited by 39 percent. The other 27 percent ranged from once a week to once a month or less.

Although the daily figure may seem low, 67 percent indicated that they play with their children more than their own parents did with them. This may be a sign that parents are becoming more aware of the fact that play and learning are closely linked.

When Ben was well past the age when he should have succeeded in putting on his own shoes, he continued to bring them to his mother for her to put on.

Guiding Learning

These suggestions will help you as you guide the learning of young children:

- **Give your time and attention.** Children learn best when they are encouraged by someone who cares about them. That doesn't necessarily mean teaching them lessons. Going places together or sharing a game teaches, too. Reading to children can be a very special way of giving your time.

- **Allow time for thinking.** Toddlers need time to consider choices and make decisions. Remember that problem solving and decision making are new experiences for a toddler. When you offer a young child a choice, be prepared to offer time for decision making, too.

- **Give only as much help as the child needs to succeed.** If a toddler is struggling to pull on his or her own socks, don't take over. Instead, just help slip the sock over the child's heel before it gets caught. Then the child learns how to put on socks and enjoys the accomplishment—"I did it myself!" If at all possible, let the child do the final step in any task they may be struggling with.

- **Encourage children to draw their own conclusions.** "Let's find out" is better than an explanation. Seeing and doing helps reinforce learning. For example, let a child help plant a few seeds in a pot of soil. The child can help care for the seeds and watch as they grow into plants.

- **Show how to solve problems.** When a toddler's tower of blocks keeps toppling, demonstrate that stacking one block directly on top of another provides balance. Then remember that building the block tower is the toddler's project—don't try to take it over. Instead of building the tower, you can watch and encourage as the child tries again.

- **Maintain a positive attitude.** Encourage learning by letting the child know that you have confidence in his or her abilities. This may involve offering praise—"What a good try! You really worked hard on that."

- **Keep explanations simple and on the child's level.** When a toddler asks about the fish in the aquarium, you might say, "The fish are in the tank because fish live in the water. People live outside the water. We need air to breathe."

TEACH

Pages 396-405

- **Readiness for Learning**
- **Guiding Learning**
- **Play Activities and Toys**
- **Speech Development**

GUIDED PRACTICE

Promoting Discussion

Have students read the guidelines on pages 396-399. Then share these strategies to stimulate discussion:

- Discuss how each guideline encourages learning.

- Tell students a parent or other caregiver is a child's first reading, art, music, math, science, history, and social studies teacher. Have students discuss what parents and caregivers might do in each of these teaching roles. How do they suggest parents and caregivers prepare to teach children?

Critical Thinking

Suppose a young girl who can unscrew a loose-fitting lid from a jar attempts unsuccessfully to open a new jar of applesauce. What is the best way to help her? (Loosen the lid and give it back to her.) Why? (It allows her to practice and experience success at what she can do, rather than reinforcing complete dependence.)

Cooperative Learning

Divide the class into groups, and have each group write three typical toddlers' questions on separate index cards. Collect and mix the cards. Then redistribute them to the groups. Have each group prepare simple answers, appropriate to the toddlers' level, and report the questions and answers to the class.

COOPERATIVE LEARNING

Setting Realistic Goals

Setting realistic goals is vital to the completion of any project, especially a group effort. Help your students better organize their cooperative enterprises by sharing this model:

1. State your ultimate goal. Although this may seem obvious, concretely verbalizing the end result can help you better channel team efforts.

2. List your intermediate, or short-term, goals. Again, a concrete record of the steps needed to achieve your ultimate plan can be an insurance policy against omitting critical elements in the process.

3. Rank the steps in your list in order of priority. Assigning a numerical value can help you order your short-term goals in the most efficient way.

ASK THE EXPERTS

Issues and Advice

1. According to Dr. Hilliard, what does reading aloud provide for children besides language formation? (*Social involvement and close emotional bonding.*)

2. Why should parents read to a baby before birth? (*It is a natural extension of the human conversation that will take place after birth.*)

3. What is the value of these activities? (*They provide the emotional and social bonds connected with reading, and they show that reading is a pleasurable experience.*)

4. What does Dr. Hilliard recommend to parents with limited reading skills? (*Discuss pictures in a book and enjoy reading-related games.*)

5. What does he feel is the most important aspect of reading to young children? (*Enjoyment.*)

Thinking Like an Expert

Arrange for the class to visit the public library in groups and investigate the types of children's books available. Before the visit, have the class identify questions about books and reading to children that they feel should be investigated. For example, what types of topics do books for each age group focus on? What is the typical ratio of words to pictures? How are rhymes and rhythms used? Do some books seem aimed specifically at only boys or only girls? During the visit, have each group of students survey books for a particular age group. Discuss the results in class.

ASK THE EXPERTS

Reading to Children

Q. *When should I begin reading to my child?*

A. It's never too early to start reading to a child. In fact, I think parents should start reading to their babies even before the babies are born. This kind of reading is an extension of the natural conversing that parents do with their children, both before and after birth.

Reading is much more than a method of communicating information to a young child. Reading is a social event, and reading to a young child can help establish close emotional bonds. When you read to a young child, you have an opportunity for a special kind of personal communication and relationship.

The sense of competency and accomplishment that children gain from reading begins long before they start reading for themselves. They enjoy being part of the close relationship of adult and child.

Parents who especially enjoy reading offer their child another special gift by reading aloud: They have the opportunity to demonstrate and share a valued behavior. Of course, parents who are not themselves avid readers should not feel at a disadvantage in this situation. Whenever they take the time to read to young children and to enjoy sharing books and pictures together, they are also developing both attitudes and skills that will benefit their children. Even parents whose own reading skills are limited can participate in these activities. They can look at books with young children, talk about the pictures and enjoy reading-related games and activities together.

Whatever the age of the child, and whatever the reading skills of the adult, the most important aspect of reading to young children is enjoyment. Don't rush, and don't make reading a daily chore. Instead, enjoy sharing books, and enjoy sharing time together.

Asa Hilliard
Fuller E. Callaway Professor of Urban Education at Georgia State University

• **Allow children to explore and discover.** Recognize the benefits of letting children roll in the grass, climb trees, and squeeze mud through their fingers and toes. Constantly saying "Don't do this" and "Don't touch that" inhibits sensory and motor experiences. Remember, children learn through all their senses and through play.

OBSERVING AND PARTICIPATING

Celebrating Individual Differences

Parents and caregivers should support the child's natural urge to learn by keeping in mind four important ideas:

• **Pay attention to the child's developmental stage.** Remember that children learn at different rates, so stage, not age, is what's important.

• **Follow the child's cues.** Watch for signs of readiness to learn new skills.

• **Don't pressure, and don't compare.** Remember that each child is a unique individual and will learn when ready.

• **Encourage the child's interests.**

- **Help children understand the world and how it works.** Take young children along, even on routine errands, whenever possible. The library, the supermarket, and the gas station can all be places of learning. Wherever you go, talk about what is happening, and why it is happening, in that place. Encourage children to participate at home, too. Let them use small garden tools to help rake fallen leaves; call attention to the different colors and to the crackling sounds, and discuss the changing seasons.

Play Activities and Toys

A child's play can be compared to an adult's work—it is the basic task of that stage of life. Toys are an important part of play. They allow children to experience imaginary situations and act out different roles. They encourage the development of both large and small motor skills. They also help children learn to share and cooperate with others. Today, with thousands of toys to choose from, it is important to know how to choose wisely. When you are selecting a toy, ask yourself these questions:

- Is the toy safe?
- Is it well made and durable?
- Will it be easy to care for?
- Will it encourage the child to use his or her imagination?
- Is it colorful?
- Will it be easy for the child to handle?
- Is it appropriate for the child's age?

A shovel, a pail, and sand are simple toys, yet think of how many areas of development they benefit: creativity, motor skills, cooperative play. What else would you add this list?

SAFETY TIP

Safety should be the most important consideration in choosing toys. This is especially true for toddlers. Remember that toys receive hard use. They should not break easily, have any sharp edges, have small parts that a young child could swallow, or be **flammable**—that is, *easily burned*. Be sure that no lead-based paints are used on the toys, because these paints are poisonous. Read all labels carefully before buying. The Food and Drug Administration and the Consumer Product Safety Commission have the power to recall toys that are unsafe. However, sometimes the danger is not known until a child is seriously injured or even killed by a toy.

GUIDED PRACTICE (continued)

Promoting Discussion

Have students discuss children who tag behind parents or siblings busy at chores. How can parents or siblings encourage learning at these moments? How, for example, can naming items and explaining processes help the child? Which common activities might allow young children to learn by participation? Which are most useful to observe?

Cooperative Learning

Divide students into groups, and give each group several pictures of children involved in various activities. Have students assume they are caring for the children and list suggestions for encouraging the children to learn. Have a representative from each group share the pictures and lists with the class.

Practicing Decision Making

Display toys or pictures of toys in the classroom. Have students choose one that encourages learning and one that does not. Have them explain their selections in writing.

SAFETY TIP

Hand-crafted toys are frequently purchased at craft shows or received as gifts from creative family members and friends. However, with handmade toys, safety codes are more difficult to monitor and enforce. Parents should always question the materials used to make these gifts and check for potential hazards.

COOPERATIVE LEARNING

Working as a Team

Divide students into small groups. Challenge each to create and display in the school a poster emphasizing ways to guide children's learning. Posters could be titled "Direct Children Along the Path of Learning." Place an illustration of a schoolhouse in the upper right corner of the poster board. Then make a road with four intersecting side roads, all leading to the school. Write the following information in the roads leading to the school:

- Give help where needed.
- Show how to solve problems.
- Maintain a positive attitude.
- Allow exploration and discovery.
- Help children understand the world around them.

GUIDED PRACTICE (continued)

Making Connections:
Social Studies

Have students research sex roles and how children learn them. Ask them to write a report on their findings. Have students include examples of what and how parents and society unintentionally teach about sex roles and how toys promote sex roles.

Promoting Discussion

To stimulate discussion, describe the following situation. Jan and Jon want to buy a tricycle for their three-year-old son Eric. Jan wants to buy a tricycle exactly the right size for Eric. Jon wants to buy one a size larger so that Eric can use it longer before they need to replace it. What do you recommend? Why?

Cooperative Learning

In groups, have students create a learning box of items that would safely stimulate curiosity and learning in children. Make the box available for babysitters to check out.

Ask students to volunteer their knowledge of, or experience with, dolls representing different cultures. If possible, have them bring a selection of dolls to class on the day you discuss this section. Ask them to describe the significance of the dolls and discuss the evolution of dolls as toys and as collectors' items.

Cultural Exchange

CULTURALLY DIVERSE DOLLS

Dolls hold a special fascination for children. Today, as distances shrink, dolls are a way for people of one culture to learn about others. Two examples from Africa illustrate this point. A Ndebele mother makes a ceremonial initiation doll for her daughter when the young girl comes of age. The doll symbolizes a new beginning.

During idle winter months, Zulu women make dolls from fabric, discarded clothing, and decorative items that have been collected all year. Culturally diverse dolls give insight into the creative spirit of the individuals who create them and convey a better understanding of diverse cultural backgrounds.

There is nothing more discouraging for a child—or an adult—than having a toy break the first time it is used. When you are buying a toy, think about the child or children who will be using it. How will the toy be used? Is it made of materials that will withstand that kind of use? Are all the parts firmly attached? Choose only toys that will give good value and service for their price.

Many people do not think about care when they are selecting a toy, but it is an important consideration. A stuffed bear that takes a ride through a mud puddle may be ruined unless it can be washed. Similarly, books with wipe-clean covers are the most practical choice for young children.

Many toys for sale today do everything for the child. Although such toys may look inviting, they do not help the child develop an imagination. Simple toys that can be different things or can be used in a variety of ways are better. A child may be able to push a button and make a talking doll say five phrases; that same child can make a nontalking doll say anything he or she wants it to say. Toys that lend themselves to many uses allow toddlers to work out their own ideas and develop self-confidence.

Colorful toys are important. Children—especially young children—respond more readily to colorful objects. Later, bright toys encourage children to learn color names.

When you are buying toys, it is also important to take the size of the child into consideration. A toy that is too large for the youngster to handle alone cannot be played with easily. The excitement of a new tricycle is quickly lost if the child's legs are too short to reach the pedals. A doll that is too big for the toddler to cuddle and carry cannot receive the attention and care the child probably wants to give.

Similar problems can occur when toys are not appropriate for the child's developmental stage. Infant toys are usually not challenging enough for most three-year-olds. Neither will an older child's toys amuse most fourteen-month-olds for long. It is important to know the capacities and interests of children at various ages in order to choose appropriate toys.

- **One to two years.** At this age, a child practices body control and learns through exploration. Many toys can be items found in the home, such as pie tins, wooden spoons, and plastic storage containers. Anything that allows the child to use large muscles is usually popular. This may include swings, small wagons, rocking horses, riding toys with wheels, balls, boxes, and low furniture. Children of this age also enjoy small dolls and animals, sturdy books, and containers of all sorts. Stacking toys, simple puzzles, and toy cars are also popular. Be careful to avoid small toys or toys with small parts that a young child might swallow.

OBSERVING AND PARTICIPATING

Developing Participation Skills

There are five general types of play in which young children participate. *Sensory play* involves experiencing new sounds, tastes, odors, and textures. It teaches children about their bodies, senses, and the environment. *Motion play* includes running, jumping, twirling, and skipping—motion for its own sake. This type of play gives children practice in body coordination. *Play with language* uses sounds, words, syllables, and phrases. Rhymes and rhyming words are an important part of this type of play. *Dramatic play and modeling* allow children to imitate patterns of behavior and indulge in fantasy. As children grow older, they begin to participate in games, rituals, and *competitive play*, which teach cognitive skills, cause and effect, and fitting behavior to rules and patterns.

• **Two to three years.** A child's coordination and understanding improve markedly during this year. In addition, the child wants to do what he or she sees adults doing. This desire to imitate suggests a variety of toys: a child-sized broom, a small shovel, plastic or wooden tools, play dishes, empty food containers, and other similar items. Crayons, clay, large beads to string, books, large blocks, and blunt scissors are popular. A sandbox can provide hours of enjoyment, and some children may be ready for a small tricycle.

• **Three to four years.** At this age, children continue to enjoy many of the same toys they liked as two-year-olds. In addition, their improved motor skills and imagination increase their interest in toys requiring the use of their hands. Dolls to dress, trucks, trains, and similar toys are popular. Children of this age love to color, paint—especially with finger paint, and play with play dough. Three-year-olds also spend longer periods with books and enjoy listening to records or cassettes. They will work and rework simple puzzles, and they are enthusiastic about using playground equipment such as ladders, swings, and slides. Most three-year-olds love the freedom and mobility of a tricycle.

Two-, three-, and four-year-olds need safe opportunities to run, jump, and climb.

GUIDED PRACTICE (continued)

Making Connections: Math
Have students choose a specific age and list toys that would be suitable and safe for a child of that age. Have them price these toys at department stores and total the cost. Ask them to write a report of their findings and to suggest lower-cost substitutes for the recommended toys.

Critical Thinking
Ask students which irregularities in English could present problems for children learning to speak. (Answers will vary. Irregular formation of such features as tense and plurals.)

Cooperative Learning
Divide students into four groups. Assign one group to discuss and list physical problems that could hinder normal speech development. Tell the other groups to discuss social, emotional, and intellectual problems that could affect speech. Have representatives from all groups report the discussions to the class.

MORE ABOUT

The Value of Play
Learning is based on the attitudes and competencies children gain during play. Intellectual development occurs when children throw, run, paste, do puzzles, and place objects in sequential order, such as according to length, height, and width.

Matching games, playing with blocks, balancing toys, and construction activities help children develop mathematical concepts. A base for writing skills is developed through painting, using crayons, pasting, working with clay, and doing puzzles and construction activities.

**Making Connections:
Language Arts**

When an adult adds something to what a child says, this is called elaboration. For example, if the child says, "apple," a caregiver might say, "Yes, that is a bright red apple." Have students work in groups to write ten examples of adult elaboration on children's comments.

Cooperative Learning

Explain that playing conversational games with children not only helps with speech development but also promotes learning and creative thinking. Some parents and caregivers use the "What if?" game for these purposes. Have students work in pairs and take turns making up "What if?" questions appropriate for three-year-olds. The questions may be silly, such as, "What if the bathtub were full of chocolate pudding?" A "What if?" can have a special purpose, for example: "What if you were standing on the sidewalk and someone you didn't know offered you candy?" Have pairs choose their best "What if?" and write it out. Choose a volunteer to compile a class list.

Speech Development

Babies begin learning to say words by repeating sounds. Gradually, they discover that some combinations of sounds—words—have specific meanings. Then, as one-, two-, and three-year-olds, these children acquire speech patterns and learn about grammar simply by listening to other people speaking.

The ability to speak depends on all areas of development—physical, emotional, social, and intellectual. A problem in any one area can slow or even prevent speech development. However, even children without any such problems vary greatly in learning to speak.

Between their first and second birthdays, children work at learning new words. They like to learn the names of everything, and they enjoy listening to the sounds the words make. During this period, most children use one word rather than a whole sentence to express a thought. For example, a child might hold out a cup and say "water"—meaning, quite clearly, "I want a drink of water."

An individual child's language development is strongly influenced by the way adults and older children speak to that child. For example, Jason's mother usually used baby talk with him: "It's time for mommy's itsy-bitsy boy to go night-night. Does little Jason want his ba-ba first?" Not surprisingly, three-and-one-half-year-old Jason still has trouble speaking plainly enough for others to understand him. Amy's parents rarely talked to her when she was a baby. When a neighbor asked them about their silence, Amy's father explained, "I'd feel silly talking to Amy. She can't understand what we're saying." Amy started talking much later than average. Both Jason's and Amy's parents probably contributed to their children's speech difficulties.

You can encourage language development and learning in children aged one to three simply by talking to them, clearly and engagingly, about their daily lives. For example, you can take the time to describe—and guide the child in talking about—whatever he or she is seeing and doing. "My, Cindy! Look at the big bite you've taken out of that shiny red apple. Can you hear the crunch it makes when you put your teeth into it?" "Jake, can you point to the white chicken in the story? Where are the chicken's eggs? Let's count them together. You had an egg for breakfast this morning, didn't you?"

You can see that Cindy and Jake are being encouraged to learn. They hear correctly spoken English that helps them organize and understand what they are experiencing.

At about age two, the child usually starts combining two or three words to make short sentences: "Doggie bark." "Jimmy fall down." At this stage, the child typically calls himself or herself by name.

Developing Participation Skills

Special songs for children offer opportunities for language development as well as dramatic fun. These songs can be found in books and on children's records, which may be borrowed from a library or purchased. Students may already be familiar with some of these, such as "I'm a Little Teapot," "Hokey Pokey," "Itsy Bitsy Spider," and "If You're Happy and You Know It."

Creative Activities for Children in the TCR provides an assortment of finger plays that can be done with children. Finger plays teach children to use their small muscles and to associate words with meaning. They also help children observe, follow, and remember sequences of words and actions.

The sun is in the sky. Can you make a s-s-s sound? Some words and sounds are difficult for young children to articulate. With time and practice, however, most children eventually master them.

Children usually find pronouns (such as *I*, *you*, *me*, and *they*) confusing at first. Two-year-old Katie spent several weeks demanding, "Help you!" and "Change you!" She had been listening to her parents say, "I'll help you," and "I think it's time to change you." She had quite logically concluded that *you* was another word for *Katie*.

At about age two and one-half, children begin to learn some of the rules of grammar. They learn by listening to other people talk rather than by any formal teaching. For example, a child begins to add an *s* to words to make them plural; the child applies this rule to all words. At two and one-half, *foots* and *tooths* make as much sense as *hands* and *eyes*. It is the English language—not the young child—that fails to follow the rules. Gradually, the child will learn the right plural forms by hearing older children and adults speaking correct English.

Speech Difficulties

Many parents are concerned about "late talkers." Delayed speech shouldn't be considered a problem before the age of three if the child understands what others say and if other areas of development are normal. Some parents make the mistake of pressuring the child who talks late or unclearly. Most often, this pressure just makes the child aware of the problem and may result in an exaggeration of the problem.

A child who does not seem to understand what is said and does not speak or speaks very little should have a thorough physical examination. It is important to identify, as soon as

GUIDED PRACTICE (continued)

Using the Photograph
Refer students to the photo on page 403. Have students discuss the reasons a well-meaning parent probably cannot handle a child's speech problems as well as a speech therapist.

Promoting Discussion
Stress that patience and understanding are very important in dealing with a child who stutters or has another speech problem. Ridicule and pressure to improve can make the problem worse. Ask students to suggest ways parents can let a child know that speech problems do not affect the parents love for the child.

Making Connections: Speech
Have students research and report on a historical figure who had a speech impediment. Diogenes, for example, began life as a stutterer, developed techniques for eliminating his stutter, and became an accomplished orator. Students may wish to research the techniques he used.

Making Connections: Music
Bring to class, or have students bring, recorded songs that might be appropriate for helping young children learn language or concepts such as the alphabet or animal noises. Remind them that young children want to hear the same music over and over, so they should select music that would be easy on the parents as well.

OBSERVING AND PARTICIPATING

Celebrating Individual Differences
Many children, especially those whose parents are immigrants, have been raised in homes where English is not the primary language spoken. Bilingualism (the ability to use two languages) can be a valuable skill. However, some of these children speak English poorly or not at all. They may have problems when they enter a preschool or kindergarten where only English is used. Communities with a sizable bilingual population often provide special education programs. In some of these programs, both languages are used in the classroom. English as a Second Language (ESL) programs provide remedial help in English to students who need it.

INDEPENDENT PRACTICE

Student Workbook

Have students complete "Using Everyday Objects as Toys" in the Student Workbook.

Student Demonstration

Have students bring a child's toy or picture of a toy that encourages learning and meets the standards on page 399. Have the students explain the age for which the toy is appropriate, how it encourages learning, and why it meets the standards on the checklist.

Extension

Have students research physical conditions that can interfere with speech development. For example, some children suffer from fluid that collects behind the eardrums, which distorts the sounds these children hear. This condition can be corrected with surgery. Frequent ear infections can also affect a child's hearing. Have students choose a condition and summarize their research in a written report.

Journal Writing

Tell students to write journal entries exploring their thoughts about guiding learning in toddlers. In particular, have them reflect on the multitude of learning opportunities daily life affords.

Most children eventually grow out of their minor speech problems. Sometimes, however, an examination reveals a physical problem affecting speech. The help of a trained professional may be needed.

possible, any physical problem that may be hindering the child's language development. Poor hearing is one physical problem that interferes with speech development. Mental retardation, learning disabilities, and emotional problems may also slow a child's speech.

Many children continue to have problems with **articulation**, or *the ability to use clear, distinct speech,* until they are three or four—or even older. Some children have trouble only with certain sounds. Other children skip syllables or leave off the endings of words. These problems usually correct themselves as the child grows older.

It is best to avoid frequent corrections of a child's pronunciation. Instead, be careful to set a good example with your own speech. If the toddler says "ba" and reaches for a bottle, hand the bottle over, saying, "Bottle. Tommy wants his bottle."

Stuttering is a more serious speech difficulty for young children. However, many adults mistake normal speech hesitations for stuttering. A child may repeat whole words or phrases: "Johnny... Johnny... Johnny. He... he... he hit Collin!" This is not true stuttering. The child's speaking and thinking abilities are still immature. The youngster simply cannot get the words out as rapidly or as smoothly as necessary. The same thing happens when a child who has been offered a choice of colored balloons says, "I ah... ah... ah... I... ah... I want this green one."

OBSERVING AND PARTICIPATING

Developing Participation Skills

One way parents can increase their toddler's verbal skills is to interrupt stories for discussion and to ask open-ended questions. Parents can also praise and expand on their child's answers. These techniques were tested on an experimental group. After one month, the verbal expression and vocabulary skills of the children whose parents used these techniques were tested. These scores were compared with those of a control group whose parents read stories without incorporating the questioning, praise, and expansion. The children in the experimental group scored six months ahead of those in the control group.

The child is thinking and waiting for the right words to come. Some hesitation and repetition are common to all preschool children; they are not a sign of real stuttering.

A true stutter can be identified by the rhythm, pitch, and speed of speech. It is rapid, forced, and short and sharp in sound. Usually, the child repeats only the beginning sound of a word: "I c—c—c—can't g—g—g—go outside." The child usually shows tenseness in some way—gasping, sputtering, or rapid blinking.

The cause of stuttering is still not clearly understood. Most children outgrow it without special help. Some children, however, need the help of a **speech therapist**, *a professional trained to diagnose and help correct speech problems*. Patience and understanding are very important.

No matter what speaking difficulties a child may have, parents must let the child know that it does not affect their love. Such an attitude will help the child cope with—and perhaps even overcome—the problem.

SECTION 2 REVIEW

CHECK YOUR UNDERSTANDING

1. What is required before a child can learn a new skill?

2. Why is it important to give a toddler only as much help as he or she needs in practicing a new skill?

3. Which kinds of development does playing promote?

4. What should be the most important consideration when choosing toys for children? Why?

5. List at least four toys that are appropriate and fun for toddlers between the ages of one and two.

6. What should parents and caregivers do to encourage language development in young children?

7. What is a speech therapist? What kinds of problems might indicate that the help of a speech therapist is needed?

DISCUSS AND DISCOVER

1. Identify at least three local activities or events appropriate for young children. Discuss why you would take one- to three-year olds to these activities or events, what you would expect to do with children there, and what you anticipate children would learn from them.

2. Interview a speech therapist who works with young children, or arrange to have the therapist visit your class. Ask the speech therapist to explain his or her work and to make specific suggestions for parents and caregivers who work with young children.

Observing & Participating

Spend time playing with a one- or two-year-old, or let the child help you with some routine tasks. Make an effort to talk with the child in an appropriate and encouraging way. Notice how much of your language the child seems to understand. How does the child respond to your statements and questions? How comfortable are you in adjusting your language to the child? Why?

SECTION 2 REVIEW

1. Physical and intellectual readiness.

2. To encourage learning and to assure the child enjoys his or her accomplishments.

3. Physical, emotional, social, and intellectual development.

4. Safety; children can be seriously injured or even killed by unsafe toys.

5. Possible toys: wooden spoons, swings, small wagons, sturdy books. (Many other examples are acceptable.)

6. Talk to the children, clearly and engagingly, about their daily lives.

7. A professional trained to diagnose and help correct speech problems. Continued stuttering.

ASSESS

CHECKING COMPREHENSION

Assign students to write their responses to the Check Your Understanding questions in the Section 2 Review. Answers to the questions are given at the bottom of this page.

EVALUATE

Have students complete the Chapter 13, Section 2 quiz in the TCR.

Reteaching

1. Assign Reteaching 33 in the TCR and have students complete the activity and review their responses.

2. Have students choose a specific age child and make a poster showing toys that would be safe and suitable for that age.

Enrichment

1. Assign Enrichment 33 in the TCR.

2. Have students investigate school district programs and personnel that help students with speech problems. Discuss their findings in class.

Extension

Invite a speech therapist to speak to students about how speech problems are diagnosed and treated.

CLOSE

Have students suggest endings for this sentence:

To guide a young child's learning, …

Encourage responses that present both general guidelines and specific strategies.

Positive Parenting Skills

MOTIVATOR

Ask students to think about their favorite children's books. On the board, list the titles as students call them out. Tell them that this feature should help remind them of the lasting value of books.

Promoting Discussion

1. Why is it important to introduce young children to books?

2. At what age can children be given their first books?

3. What types of books are appropriate for infants?

4. What should parents and caregivers consider when selecting books for children of different ages?

Using the Photographs

Have students look at the photos in this feature. How are the books being used in each situation? What are the benefits of using books in these ways? What can storytellers do to make books more interesting?

Critical Thinking

Ask students to think about the advantages of using the library as a source of children's books. How does the library select books? What awards are given to children's books? What might happen to children who have little exposure to books? What secondary benefits come from having an adult read to a child?

READING TO CHILDREN

Sharing a book with a child can be a special experience, both for you and for the child. Books—both fiction and nonfiction—are wonderful learning tools. In addition, reading to a child nourishes close relationships, encourages language and listening skills, and helps the child separate reality from fantasy. Children who learn early in childhood that books are fun are more likely to remain readers throughout life.

Choose Appropriate Books

Children of different ages respond best to different types of books. Understanding their interest will help you choose books they will like.

One-year-olds need short, simple books with large, uncomplicated pictures. They like picture books with objects they can name. Books with rhymes are also popular. Some books have different textures on each page to stimulate the toddler's sense of touch.

Two-year-olds prefer simple stories they can relate to. Books about families and familiar experiences are good choices. Like

one-year-olds, they never tire of hearing their favorite stories again and again.

By age three, children can enjoy longer stories (up to 10 or 15 minutes) with more of a plot. They like realistic stories about children, but also ones that help them use their imagination. Look for books that help them learn how things work and why things happen.

Become a Master Storyteller

Reading a story is much like putting on a play—a play in which you portray all the characters. Vary the tone and rate at which you read

406

MORE ABOUT

Children and Books

One of the best ways for parents to encourage their children to love books is to be readers themselves. Since young children look to their parents as their primary role models, they will imitate their parents' interest in reading. As children grow older, they are more likely to spend time reading if they see that other family members do, too. Parents' enjoyment of books sets the stage for children's lifelong interest in literature and reading.

to create excitement and interest. Give each character a different voice. For example, a bear's voice might be low and growly. A princess's voice might be either shy or commanding. Use your own gestures and facial expressions to reinforce the content of the story.

If you are reading to one or two children, snuggle up close and hold the book so they can see. If you are reading to a group, the children should be in a semicircle facing you. Read loudly enough for everyone to hear. Take time to learn the story beforehand so you can keep the pictures facing the children.

Encourage Participation

Long before they can read, children can participate in stories. Active involvement helps increase learning and fun.

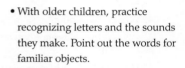

- Even very young children can turn the pages. This gives practice in hand-eye coordination.

- Relate the action and pictures in the book to the child's own life. "You have a red ball, too, don't you?" "In the story, Peter has a baby sister. You have a baby brother."

- Ask questions as you read. "What do you think Melissa will find when she opens the box?" "What color is the dog?" "How would you feel if you were lost in the store? What would you do?"

- With familiar books, let the child play the part of one character. Don't expect word-for-word accuracy. Provide clues, when necessary, to keep the story moving.

- With older children, practice recognizing letters and the sounds they make. Point out the words for familiar objects.

- Encourage children to dramatize a story, either by acting it out of by putting on a puppet show. Let children draw their own pictures to go with favorite stories.

- Remember to keep your focus on the child—not on the story. Reading together should be fun. If the child has stopped enjoying a story, put the book away. It's not necessary to finish every book.

407

Student Demonstration

Have each student select a children's book to read aloud. Ask other students to sit around the reader and play the part of children. Another group of students should observe and evaluate the storyteller's delivery and active involvement with the children.

Enrichment

Have students use the list of favorite children's book to research the current popularity of the same books.

Family Focus

Ask students to remember any traditions or rituals involving reading when they were young. Can they suggest new ideas to establish lasting traditions in modern families?

Extension

Make arrangements for students to observe the story hour at a child care center or library. Assign some students to observe the storyteller and evaluate the techniques used. Ask other students to observe the children. How did they react to the story? Ask students to report their observations to the class.

CLOSE

Ask students to summarize the main points they have learned from studying this feature.

CLASSROOM MANAGEMENT

Resources Beyond the Classroom

Experts agree that young children benefit significantly from being read to at an early age. To supplement reading done by parents at home, many libraries and bookstores have started reading programs for preschoolers. Professional storytellers, whose flair for storytelling enhances the reading experience, often give readings designed especially for the very young. Children have the opportunity to see reading as an enjoyable social activity. Along with this free activity, bookstores often sponsor reading contests and offer reader discounts to help cultivate young readers. For more information on the availability of children's reading programs and events, have your students contact their local bookstores.

CHECKING COMPREHENSION

Use the Summary and the Reviewing the Facts questions to help students go over the most important ideas presented in Chapter 13; encourage students to ask questions and add details, as appropriate.

1. Heredity and environment.

2. Incidental is unplanned.

3. Concepts become more re-fined and more accurate.

4. The basic ability to solve prob-lems and make decisions.

5. Creativity is the use of imagi-nation to produce something.

6. They fail, and this failure causes the child to learn more slowly.

7. Safety.

8. Children respond more read-ily to colorful objects and later it helps them learn color names.

9. Articulation is the ability to use clear, distinct speech. Avoid frequent corrections.

10. A true stutter is forced, short, and sharp in sound. Speech hesitation is a natural part of speech acquisition, whereas stuttering may require spe-cial attention.

SUMMARY

- Intelligence is determined by both heredity and environment.

- Children learn on their own, as well as by being taught.

- Children learn to organize the information they receive from their senses by gradually developing concepts.

- Many elements of the mind are continuously developing.

- Play promotes all aspects of development.

- Toys should be safe, appealing, and appropriate to a child's age.

- The rate of speech development varies greatly.

- The way in which adults and older children speak to a young child greatly influences the child's language development.

- Some young children have difficulties with articulation or stuttering.

REVIEWING THE FACTS

1. What major factors determine an individual's intelligence? How?

2. What is the difference between incidental learning and trial-and-error learning?

3. How do concepts change as a child matures and learns?

4. What is reasoning?

5. What is the difference between imagination and creativity?

6. How do young children usually respond when they are pushed toward learning for which they are not ready?

7. What is the most important consideration in choosing toys for young children?

8. Why should toys for young children be colorful?

9. What is articulation? How should parents and other caregivers respond to a child's problems with articulation?

10. What is the difference between speech hesitations and stuttering? Why is it important to identify the difference?

EXPLORING FURTHER

1. Plan a game or activity for toddlers that requires attention, memory, perception, and reasoning. Discuss the game or activity with other students. Then, if possible, try the game or activity out with a very small group of two- or three-year-olds. (Section 1)

2. Select a simple, appealing food that a three-year-old could help prepare. (Be sure it is a food that a three-year-old might enjoy eating, too.) Write out a recipe for that food, including specific directions that will guide a caregiver in encouraging a child to participate in the preparation. (Section 1)

3. Using a doll to represent a one- or two-year-old, demonstrate how daily routines can be used as language-learning opportunities. For example, you might help or encourage the child to put on a jacket and hat before going outdoors, or you might shop for some fresh vegetables together. As you act out the activity, speak as you would to a young child. Be sure the subject of your conversation and the level of your language are appropriate to the child's experience. (Section 2)

4. Working in small groups, research ideas on ways to store toys. What ideas would be helpful when space is limited? What techniques might help children learn to put away their toys? (Section 2)

THINKING CRITICALLY

1. **Analyze.** Why do some very young children develop poor attitudes toward learning? Do you think such negative attitudes can be overcome? If so, at what age and how? If not, why not?

2. **Synthesize.** What are the most important influences on parents' attitudes toward learning and education? How do parents pass those attitudes on to their children? What is the significance of this transfer of attitudes?

CLASSROOM MANAGEMENT

The Learning Environment

Teachers and students alike will attest to the fact that the classroom develops an atmosphere of tedious boredom over the course of a semester when little is done to break the monotony. To counteract this sense of dullness, institute a few simple changes to stimulate the surroundings, which, in turn, will enhance learning. You can change the appearance of a room by merely rear-ranging the seating. New accessories on shelves or tables, a fresh bulletin board, or a different display creates interest and invites the curiosity of stu-dents. Teachers may solicit the help of student volunteers to design new wall displays.

3. **Analyze.** How do you think a parent or other caregiver can judge how much assistance a child needs in any situation? How could the adult's attitudes and interests interfere with making a good decision? What do you think are the results of giving a young child too much help? Too little help?

CROSS-CURRICULUM CONNECTIONS

1. **Art.** Take a series of photographs or draw a series of pictures expressing a child's actions and feelings as he or she engages in imaginative play.
2. **Writing.** Find out about various local events and activities for young children. Select the events you consider most appropriate in providing fun and learning for one- to three-year-olds. Then make a brochure for parents, describing the events and activities and encouraging families to participate in them.

3. **Math.** Choose a specific age child and make a list of toys that would be sutiable and safe for that age. Price these toys and total the cost. Then make suggestions for lower-cost substitutes for the recommeded toys.

SCHOOL TO WORK

Technology The rise in technology, especially computers, impacts almost every job. It not only changes the way jobs are performed, sometimes replacing human workers with machines, but creates new jobs as well, as in the case of computer engineers. Chances are your future career will somehow involve at least minimal contact with computers. With that in mind, how valuable would a high school course in computer basics be to you right now?

PERFORMANCE ASSESSMENT

Intellectual Development from One to Three

Task
Demonstrate how a common object from nature or an everyday activity can become a learning experience.

Purpose
Show that you recognize how parents and other caregivers can help children learn using objects from nature and everyday activities.

Procedure
1. Review the methods of learning on pages 385-387.
2. Choose as the focus of your demonstration one object from nature such as a flower, or an everyday activity such as cooking.

3. List ways that this object or activity could be used to increase a child's knowledge. Try to find one example for each of the four methods of learning.
4. Prepare a demonstration of your examples using props. Be prepared to explain how a child's age will influence what he or she learns from the object or experience.
5. Present your demonstration to the class.

Evaluation
You will be evaluated on how well you demonstrate that everyday activities and natural objects provide learning opportunities. Clarity of content, accuracy of information, and presentation style will be considered.

Portfolio Idea Have someone videotape your presentation or take a photograph for your portfolio. Write a summary for each activity that explains how it provides a learning opportunity. You might also design a brochure or flyer for parents that promotes awareness of daily learning opportunities.

409

PERFORMANCE ASSESSMENT

Demonstration
If students have trouble generating ideas, use photos in the book to illustrate the concepts. For example, page 382 is an example of directed learning, because the man is teaching or helping the boy. The little girl on page 397 could be learning by trial and error, because some of her objects will go into the clown's mouth and some

won't. Students also might role-play various situations. Prepare by writing some simple activities on flash or note cards, and letting groups or pairs of students select one to act out. Sample activities might include: feeding oneself, building a tower with blocks, and putting on an adult's shoes. Sample objects from nature might include a pet, a rock, and tree bark.

EVALUATE
Use the reproducible Chapter 13 Test in the TCR, or construct your own test using the Test-maker Software.

EXTENSION
Invite a children's librarian to speak to the class about book selections for young children and about reading to them. Have students prepare questions in advance.
Encourage students to volunteer in a storytime program at the local library. If the library does not have a program that includes children younger than four, they may volunteer to help conduct one.

CLOSE

Have students finish the sentence:
Learning is …
Encourage a variety of responses.

TECHNOLOGY OPTION

Computers As mentioned in the School to Work feature on this page, computers are a growing industry. Most recently, the focus in this field is on the electronic technology that makes it possible for users to access information rapidly through on-line services. Why not encourage students to research more about electronic innovations and what the future has in store for computer technology? What more appropriate way to conduct this research than to use the computer itself! Invite a knowledgeable person to speak to the class and, if possible, include a demonstration of the fascinating world that awaits students when they go on-line.

UNIT 5
The Child from Four to Six

INTRODUCE

UNIT 5 RESOURCES

Teacher's Classroom Resources
- Unit 5 Test
- Testmaker Software
- Color Transparency 31

UNIT OVERVIEW

Unit 5 helps students understand the abilities and interests of children aged four, five, and six.

In Chapter 14, students learn about the physical growth and development of four- to six-year-olds. They also examine the special nutritional needs of young children and consider ways in which parents and other caregivers can encourage the development of good self-care habits.

Chapter 15 helps students understand the emotional and social development that takes place in children aged four to six. Students are also guided in understanding moral development, as young children begin to develop a sense of right and wrong.

In Chapter 16, students examine the learning and intellectual development that take place in four-, five-, and six- year-olds. They also examine children's individual learning needs and discuss how schools can meet those needs.

UNIT OBJECTIVES

After completing Unit 5, students will be able to:
- Describe the physical growth and development of children from four to six and discuss the physical care they require.
- Discuss the emotional and social development of four-, five-, and six-year-olds.
- Describe the intellectual development of children aged four to six and discuss school experiences appropriate for young children.

CLASSROOM MANAGEMENT

Bulletin Board Suggestions

"*Signals for Success*" Divide the board in half with a traffic light on each side. Label one light "To Help" and make all three lights green. Label the other light "To Hinder" and make all three lights red. Under the green light list helpful suggestions, such as providing children with books and allowing children to ask questions. Under the red light list items that hinder, such as ignoring a child's questions.

"*Substitute Care Options*" Letter colorful construction paper with the different types of substitute care. Arrange them under the bulletin board title. Under each subheading add a collage of pictures that illustrate the type of substitute care.

UNIT 5

The Child from Four to Six

THE END

When I was One,
I had just begun.

When I was Two,
I was nearly new.

When I was Three,
I was hardly Me.

When I was Four,
I was not much more.

When I was Five,
I was just alive.

But now I am Six, I'm as clever as clever.
So I think I'll be six now for ever and ever.

A.A. Milne

MORE ABOUT

Using the Poem
A. A. Milne has delighted children of all ages with the whimsical stories of Christopher Robin and Winnie-the-Pooh and their adventures in the Hundred Acre Woods. In this poem from *Now We Are Six*, the speaker reflects on his accomplishments from birth to age six. Have a volunteer student read the poem aloud, using the animated voice and tone of an exuberant young boy. How does the speaker's words show his enthusiasm for this new plateau in his life. What does the age represent for the boy? Why would he be content to stay six for ever and ever?

INTRODUCING THE UNIT

- Begin by asking students about their own experiences in preschool and kindergarten. What do you remember about your preschool or kindergarten? How did you feel when you started? Did your feelings change as you became accustomed to school? What do you think you learned during your earliest school experiences? How does recalling your first school experience help you remember what you were like at the age of four or five? How have you changed since then? In what respects are you still the same?

  Conclude the discussion by telling students that they have been recalling an important period in their childhood. They will learn more about this stage of childhood as they study Unit 5.

- Ask students to read "The End," and guide them in discussing the poem. From whose point of view is the poem written? What attitude does it express toward each age of early childhood? Do you agree? Why or why not?

- Ask students to speculate why A.A. Milne's writings are treasured by people of all ages.

ASSESS

EVALUATE
Use the reproducible Unit 5 Test in the TCR, or construct your own test using the Testmaker Software.

EXTENSION
Arrange for the class to visit a kindergarten. Have students spend at least part of the visit observing the kindergarteners at play, noting both similarities among all the children and individual differences. Then allow time for students to interact with the children, participating either in group activities or in individual play.

INTRODUCE

CHAPTER OVERVIEW

Chapter 14 begins tracing the growth and development of the child who is now at the age of four, five, or six. In particular, the chapter concentrates on physical growth.

In Section 1, students learn about the changes in height, weight, proportion, posture, teeth, and development of motor skills that take place between ages four and six.

With this knowledge as a basis, they learn in Section 2 about child care skills such as feeding, dressing, toilet training, and handling bedtimes. They explore strategies for helping children develop good eating, dressing, personal hygiene, and sleep patterns.

Childhood Reflections

"Allow children to be happy in their own way, for what better way will they ever find?"

Dr. Samuel Johnson

CLASSROOM MANAGEMENT

Resources Beyond the Classroom

Considering the diverse fare that television offers for young children, it is particularly important that parents and caregivers monitor their children's viewing habits. One aspect of television that is particularly troublesome is the type of products advertised and aimed at the very young. Your students may be interested in writing for a free publi-

cation titled "Parent's Guide: Advertising and Your Child" or "Self-Regulatory Guidelines for Children's Advertising." To obtain this helpful brochure, have them write to:

Council of Better Business Bureaus
Children's Advertising Review Unit
845 Third Avenue
New York, NY 10022

Physical Development from Four to Six

SECTION 1	Physical Growth and Development from Four to Six
SECTION 2	Providing Care for Children from Four to Six

THINK ABOUT

Have you ever taken care of children between the ages of four and six? If so, how would you describe their level of activity? If not, what differences would you expect to see from the activity level of toddlers? Think about how the physical development at younger stages helped prepare four- to six-year-olds for the rapid development of this stage.

ASK YOURSELF

Look at the photo on the opposite page. How would you describe the emotional atmosphere at this party? What games would you imagine these boys played? How does their physical development at

this age contribute to their ability to play these games? If you were a parent or other caregiver in charge of planning a party for one of the boys in the photo, what activities and foods would you plan? Why?

NOW TRY THIS

Recall a birthday celebration that you attended, particularly as a child. How old were you? Who participated in the celebration? Where was it held? What activities and/or games were part of the festivities? What family or cultural traditions were included? Explain how this birthday was similar to, or different from, birthday celebrations of your own.

413

CHAPTER OBJECTIVES

After completing Chapter 14, students will be able to:

- Describe normal physical growth for children ages four to six.
- Describe motor skill development for this age group.
- Explain the importance of good nutrition for children this age and tell how healthy eating habits can be encouraged.
- Explain how to help children develop good self-care habits.
- Identify the possible causes of enuresis and how the problem should be handled.

INTRODUCING THE CHAPTER

- Have students study the photographs of children ages four to six in this unit and compare them with photos in Unit 4 of toddlers. Ask them to describe the differences in body proportion and shape. Discuss the activities in which the children are engaged and the motor skills these activities require. Tell students that in this chapter they will learn more about the physical growth and development that takes place during the fourth, fifth, and sixth year.
- Use the photo on the opposite page and the three features on this page—Think About, Ask Yourself, and Now Try This— to begin a discussion about a child's physical development from ages four to six.

HEALTHY FAMILIES/HEALTHY CHILDREN

Family Fitness

Since children's early habits are important for healthy adulthood, some researchers have identified the family as the best hope of promoting fitness throughout the country. It is believed that the family can be instrumental in developing a fitness

program that is tailored to meet the interests of its family members. Family members who exercise together as a team and as competitors motivate each other to stick with the plan. As a cohesive unit, the family can bring about positive changes and attitudes in exercise and diet.

FOCUS

SECTION 1 RESOURCES

Teacher's Classroom Resources
- Enrichment 34
- Reteaching 34
- Section 1 Quiz

Student Workbook
- As They Grow

SECTION OVERVIEW

In Section 1, students examine the changes that take place in height and weight between ages four and six. They learn that changes in proportion continue to improve posture, balance, and development of motor skills. Students learn that children begin at age six to lose primary teeth, which are gradually replaced with permanent teeth. Finally, students examine the rapid development of large motor skills and learn that dexterity improves as small motor skills develop.

MOTIVATOR

Have students read the opening vignette. Ask them what evidence reveals Kimberly's pride in her developing small and large motor skills. Have students recall and discuss learning to skip, tie shoes, jump rope, and write letters of the alphabet and how they felt as children if they were ahead or behind most of their peer group in acquiring these skills.

USING TERMS TO LEARN

Discuss the meaning of the terms *dexterity* and *ambidextrous*. Point out that the syllable *dex*, which appears in both words, is a clue that the words are related in meaning. *Dexterity* means "using the hands with skill and ease." The prefix *ambi*, means "both." *Ambidextrous* means "using both hands equally well."

SECTION 1

Physical Growth and Development from Four to Six

OBJECTIVES

- Describe the changes in an average child's height, weight, proportion, and posture from ages four to six.
- Describe motor skill development in children from ages four to six.

TERMS TO LEARN

ambidextrous
dexterity
permanent teeth

Children of four, five, and six are known for their activity. They run instead of walk and they wiggle when they sit, yet there is a purpose behind all this activity. The period between the fourth and seventh birthdays is a time of practicing and refining physical skills.

Height and Weight

The rate of physical growth from ages four to six is only slightly slower than from ages one to three. The average yearly increase in height from four to six is 2½ to 3 inches (6.4 to 7.6 cm). You may remember that, in general, children double their birth length in five years. Thus, a shorter-than-average baby is likely to be shorter than most children at age five. Height and weight charts give average measurements. Many children are smaller or larger than the averages but are still considered to be developing normally.

Differences in height and weight increase as children grow older. You can see this when you look at a group of kindergartners—or even when you consider the students in your own class.

In general, children tend to be taller and heavier than their parents. Improved diet and health habits, enriched foods, and advances in medicine have combined to make children today the largest and healthiest in history.

The chart on page 415 shows average heights and weights for four- to six-year-olds. Most children gain about 4 to 5 pounds (1.8 to 2.3 kg) per year during this period. However, larger or smaller gains are quite common. Boys are often slightly taller and heavier than girls.

OBSERVING AND PARTICIPATING

Learning Through Participation

An active four-year-old can sometimes be wearing on a tired parent. Adults need to remember that perpetual motion is normal for a child this age. Here are some ideas for a resourceful caregiver to reduce the amount of reckless activity:

- Include time for very active play in the yard, at the park, or in any spacious area. Quiet times will be easier after such activity.

- Give the child appropriate tasks and responsibilities. Emptying the wastebaskets, for example, uses up energy, is constructive, and enables a child to feel good about helping.

- Suggest interesting activities even though they are not extremely physical (washing plastic dishes in a sudsy sink, for example). When the mind is focused and interest captured, the body is less likely to get out of control.

AVERAGE HEIGHTS AND WEIGHTS

AGES FOUR TO SIX

AGE	HEIGHT		WEIGHT	
	Inches	Centimeters	Pounds	Kilograms
Four years	40.7	103	36.0	16.3
Five years	43.5	110	40.5	18.4
Six years	46.0	117	45.0	20.4

Proportion and Posture

Between the fourth and seventh birthdays, a child's body becomes straighter and slimmer. The protruding abdomen of babyhood flattens. The shoulders widen and are held more erect. The chest, which was round at birth, remains so until about age three. Then it broadens and flattens. The neck also becomes longer.

The legs lengthen rapidly, growing straighter and firmer. The child's balance and coordination improve, so the arms are held nearer the body when the child walks or runs.

The movements of arms, hands, and fingers become more coordinated, and the ability to do more precise work is seen each year.

At this age, children seem to be always in motion.

TEACH

Pages 414-420

• **Height and Weight**
• **Proportion and Posture**
• **Teeth**
• **Motor Skills**

GUIDED PRACTICE

Promoting Discussion
Ask students to print their names and then switch hands and print their names again. Discuss hand preference and its consequences.

Critical Thinking
Use the following strategies to broaden comprehension of content pertaining to physical growth:

• Have students compare the rate of physical growth in children aged four to six with that of toddlers.

• Ask students what factors might contribute to differences in height and weight among children four to six. Are most children who are smaller or larger than average still developing normally?

• Ask students why children aged four to six often need new clothes. (They outgrow clothes quickly and wear them out because of all their activity.)

❓

Did You Know?

A survey conducted by the Children's Hospital of Philadelphia reports that 67 percent of youngster's falls are a result of untied shoe laces. Shoes with rubber soles and Velcro fasteners are a safer choice.

SEE HOW THEY GROW

Growth and Motor Development
One of the fast-growing parts of the preschooler's body is the brain. At age three, the brain is about 75 percent of its adult weight. Over the next three years, it grows to around 90 percent of its adult weight.

At this age, the shape of the preschooler's body is changing noticeably. The remaining baby fat is quickly being lost. The muscles and skeletal system are becoming much more developed. Overall physical coordination shows marked improvement.

By age five, small and large motor skills are quite advanced. The preschooler can throw well, catch a small ball with arms at the side, and copy a square and a triangle.

GUIDED PRACTICE (continued)

Making Connections: Math

Ask students to convert the average heights shown in the chart on page 415 to feet and inches.

Critical Thinking

Ask students to consider the following questions about physical growth:

• How does physical growth help make a child more independent?

• Can size affect a child's personality? Have them explain their answers. What could a caregiver do to help a child overcome concerns about his or her stature?

• What can happen when a child is younger than his or her size seems to indicate (for example, a two-year-old who is the height of a four-year-old)? (Some people may expect the behavior of a four-year-old from the child.)

Critical Thinking

Have students simulate the process of learning to write by printing with the hand they use the least. Discuss how children might feel as they learn to write.

Did You Know?

In the seventeenth century, the influence of astrology was so strong that the minute and hour of each babies' birth was recorded in the family Bible along with the day, month, and year. When the child was ill, these planetary conjunctions were considered when a remedy was prepared.

Teeth

At about age six, children begin to lose their primary teeth. They are gradually replaced by **permanent teeth**, *the set of 32 teeth that will not be naturally replaced.*

The six-year-old molars, or "first molars," are the first of the secondary teeth to appear. There are four of these molars—two upper and two lower—positioned in back of the 20 primary teeth. These molars appear before the front teeth are replaced and act as a lock to keep all the teeth in position. Later, as the child's front teeth are replaced by larger secondary teeth, the molars prevent the new front teeth from pushing other teeth farther back in the jaw.

In general, the primary teeth are lost in approximately the same order as they came in. The two lower front teeth are usually the first to be replaced, followed by the two upper front teeth.

Thumb sucking

Some four-, five-, and six-year-olds continue to suck their thumb. Like younger children, they use thumb sucking as a self-comforting technique. Most children learn that it is not socially acceptable; they give the habit up entirely or limit it to home.

For children who continue to suck their thumb, the habit may cause other problems. Heavy or strong sucking several times a day or all night can affect the position of the permanent teeth and the shape of the jaw.

Only a professional can diagnose the seriousness of a child's thumb sucking. It is wise to consult a dentist, who can examine the child and make specific recommendations. The dentist may be able to recommend positive methods of stopping the habit. Scolding or punishing the child usually only prolongs the habit.

Motor Skills

During this period, most basic large motor skills, such as walking, running, and climbing, become well developed. Small motor skills, such as drawing, cutting, and stringing beads, also show significant improvement.

Four-, five-, and six-year-olds are very energetic. Their favorite activities are usually physical—jumping, climbing, rapid tricycling, and turning somersaults. At four, children are learning to throw and catch both large and small balls. Five-year-olds show improved speed and coordination in all their activities.

Learning to bat a ball requires large and small motor skills, hand-eye coordination, and lots of practice.

MORE ABOUT

Thumb Sucking

Thumb sucking is a common behavior among small children and occurs even before a child is born. Experts do not agree about whether or not this habit is harmful. Some feel that it gives children a feeling of comfort and security. As children get older, however, many experts believe that thumb sucking can contribute to dental problems. Most agree that the habit should be discouraged after about the age of three or four. Fortunately, children tend to outgrow the habit naturally. When they do not, families can try one technique that has been successful with many children over age three. A liquid medication with a bad taste developed for this purpose is applied to the thumbs. Other materials should not be used. Children are conditioned to dislike thumb sucking because of the taste.

Four- and five-year-olds show improved **dexterity,** *the skilled use of the hands and fingers.* At this age, children have steady hands as they stack blocks to create towers and buildings. Four-year-olds usually learn to lace their shoes, but most children cannot tie shoes until about age five. Five-year-olds pour liquids from a pitcher into a glass, showing improved hand-eye coordination. They like to cut and paste, and can print some letters, but often, not words.

The motor activities and interests of six-year-olds remain much the same, but children of this age show even greater ease and skill. Their movements are smoothly coordinated. Their increased mental abilities lend judgment to throwing, catching, building, and drawing. Six-year-olds enjoy balancing activities, such as walking a curb or riding a two-wheeled bicycle. Rhythm intrigues them. They like to keep time to music and jump rope to chanted jingles.

Children have many opportunities to practice and improve small motor skills when parents, caregivers, and teachers provide activities such as coloring, drawing, painting, tracing, cutting, and writing.

The chart on page 418 summarizes average motor abilities by age. The timing of motor skills development may vary because children have different abilities and interests.

Writing the alphabet is not only an intellectual skill, but a physical one. Can you explain why?

BUILDING SELF-ESTEEM

Encouraging the Development of Skills

From four to six years of age a child loves physical activity, and an increasing skill in motor activities will make the child feel confident about trying new challenges.

During this time children begin comparing themselves with their friends. They may begin to refuse to be involved in activities with other children when they see themselves less competent than their peers.

It's difficult for children to understand that everyone develops skills at different times. However, it is important for caregivers to encourage children in their attempts at activities. Caregivers need to point out those areas in which a child excels, and remind the child that everyone has different skills and interests.

GUIDED PRACTICE (continued)

Family Focus

Read the following to students:

Kari started sucking her thumb as an infant. Even though she is now five years old, she still resorts to the habit at certain times of the day. It comforts her when she is tired or upset. The last time her father saw her sucking her thumb, he reached out and yanked her hand away from her mouth, saying "What do you think you are, a baby?"

Ask half the class to write a paragraph describing Kari's feelings from her point of view. Have the other half assume the father's role and write better responses to Kari's habit. Share these with the class.

Making Connections: Writing

Have students collect chants that children use when jumping rope. They may remember some from their own experience. Others may be collected from friends, relatives, and books. Some students might like to try creating a chant of their own, using the right rhythm for jumping rope. Have them put these together in booklet form and share them with children, parents, and teachers in the community. If possible, they could teach a chant to one or more children.

Critical Thinking

Have students write a sequential list of directions for tying a shoelace. Is it hard to explain how to tie a shoe? Why is this skill difficult for children to learn?

BUILDING SELF-ESTEEM

Exposing a child to a wide range of activities not only gives a child the opportunity to discover his or her area of talent but also makes them aware of a diverse field of knowledge.

OBSERVING AND PARTICIPATING

Learning Through Participation

Dexterity can be encouraged by providing children with appropriate materials and activities. Here are some ideas:

• Make figures and shapes from pipe cleaners.

• Glue ice cream sticks together to make boxes.

• Bring in a tub of snow in the winter, and place it on an old rug. Provide cups and spoons for molding and scooping the snow.

• Let children have small amounts of flour, sugar, salt, and other foods, as well as mixing bowls and utensils, at the table or counter. Let them pretend to make a cake.

• Glue paper strips together to make a paper chain for use as a decoration.

GUIDED PRACTICE (continued)

Making Connections: Art

Show students pictures that children ages four, five, and six have drawn of their families. Have students compare the pictures and suggest the ages of the artists. What specific features of the drawings help indicate the artists' ages?

Refer students to the chart on page 418 for help.

Using the Chart

Have students work in groups and choose one of the age categories from the chart on page 418. Have each group assume that it is in charge of a preschool (or kindergarten) program. The group must plan games and activities that will help develop the motor skills listed for the age selected. Have each group plan three or four specific activities or games for this purpose.

Critical Thinking

Ask students what inconveniences a left-handed person might experience in a predominantly right-handed world.

AVERAGE MOTOR SKILLS DEVELOPMENT

AGES FOUR TO SIX

FOUR YEARS

* Gallops and hops.
* Laces shoes.
* Dresses and undresses self.
* Cuts on line with scissors.
* Jumps forward as well as in place.
* Throws overhand with body control.

FIVE YEARS

* Ties shoelaces.
* Draws recognizable person.
* Skillfully picks up very small items.
* Writes alphabet letters.
* Stands and balances on tiptoe for short period and skips, alternating feet.
* Buttons, snaps, and zips clothes.

SIX YEARS

* Throws and catches ball with more ease and accuracy.
* Builds block towers to shoulder height.
* Cuts, pastes, molds, and colors skillfully.
* Writes entire words.

Hand Preference

By about age five, most children consistently use either the right hand or the left hand for most activities. The hand that is used most often becomes the more skillful. Only a few people are **ambidextrous**, *able to use both hands with equal skill*.

Actually, preference for the right or left hand begins before the second birthday. Researchers are still not certain how hand preference is developed. Some point to heredity as the probable source. Others think it depends on which hand parents usually put objects into during the first several years of a child's life.

OBSERVING AND PARTICIPATING

Developing Participation Skills

Children need opportunities for physical play several times a day. Providing balls, tricycles, large boxes, a small trampoline, and climbing structures encourages lots of physical activity. Children also enjoy obstacle courses to climb over, jump off, crawl through, and balance on. Depending on the facility, these activities can be set up either inside or outside. In addition, children enjoy running games, such as duck-duck-goose. Records and tapes specially designed for children are available and suggest ways to move physically and creatively to music.

**PARENTING
IN ACTION**

PARENTING IN ACTION

Encouraging Motor Skills Development

Joanne Simons teaches kindergarten at Monroe Elementary School. Today, she is the guest speaker on motor skills development in the child development class at a local high school.

"You only have to look at my class of kindergartners," says Ms. Simons, "to realize that motor skill development varies greatly from child to child. The children range in age from four and one-half to five and one-half. However, you can't tell which of the children are older by how well they cut or color or jump.

"One of the youngest children in the class has excellent coordination and concentration. He likes to put together puzzles with 75 or even 100 pieces. Another child in the class is almost a year older but can't put together a 35-piece puzzle or draw a circle that's easy to recognize. There's just a lot of individual variation."

"Try thinking back to your own days in kindergarten," Ms. Simons suggests. "I think you'll remember that many of the class activities are designed to help children improve their small and large motor skills. Painting is fun and creative—but it also helps develop hand-eye coordination. So do cutting and coloring. We play games that involve running and jumping and climbing—all large motor skill activities."

Mario raises his hand and asks, "Why are these skills emphasized so much in school? Don't kids learn them on their own at home? Isn't it the school's job to concentrate on teaching reading and writing and math?"

"That's a good question," replies Ms. Simons. "There are really two reasons for emphasizing motor skills. First, we know that children who have good motor skill development will be more successful learning to read and write. Think about writing for a moment. Forming letters takes the same kind of small muscle control and hand-eye coordination as coloring, doesn't it? The second reason we emphasize these activities is that they provide a transition between home and first grade. They resemble the play activities that children are accustomed to, but they are somewhat more structured or controlled. This emphasis helps children prepare for the more formal learning of first grade."

"Your class will be coming to observe my kindergarten next week," Ms. Simons went on. "I think you'll find the children interesting and see that they're very much individuals. If you look closely, you'll also see lots of learning going on—whether the children are jumping rope or listening to a story. After you've seen the children, I'll come back and answer any more questions you may have."

THINK AND DISCUSS

1. Why do you think Ms. Simons was chosen to speak to this child development class? What do you think the students learned from her that they might have missed otherwise? Do you think all kindergarten teachers would have expressed the same ideas? Why or why not?

2. Which kindergarten activities can you recall that provide practice in small motor skills? In large motor skills?

3. Do you think children who have poor motor skill development should be promoted to first grade or spend another year in kindergarten? Why? What other factors might be considered?

**PARENTING
IN ACTION**

Promoting Discussion

Have students discuss what they remember of kindergarten, centering on the activities that require large and small motor skills. Then have students read Parenting in Action.

Thinking Critically

Ms. Simons points out that children develop at different rates. How might a girl of six feel if most children her age could jump rope, ride two-wheelers, and tie their shoes before she could? (She might feel different and inferior, be left out of some activities, and other children might make fun of her.)

Answers to Think and Discuss

1. She is articulate and knowledgeable; knows how to prepare students for the field trip by explaining how to observe, what to look for, and how to see beyond the obvious. (Answers will vary, based on experience with kindergarten teachers.)

2. Answers will vary.

3. Encourage a variety of responses. If students' parents had to make this decision, ask them to share opinions on the benefits or drawbacks.

INDEPENDENT PRACTICE

Student Workbook

Have students complete "As They Grow" in the Student Workbook.

Extension

Have students work alone or in small groups to complete one or more of these:

- Research the influences of heredity on height and weight. Write a report on it.

- Research and prepare a brochure about care of teeth as baby teeth are being replaced by permanent teeth. Give to parents.

OBSERVING AND PARTICIPATING

Developing Observational Skills

Ask students whether they have ever observed any situations like this one: Six-year-old Damien is standing at the edge of the pool. "Grandma! Grandma! Watch this. Look what I can do." Damien leaps from the side of the pool, arms and legs flying wildly. Damien hits the water and bobs up, looking eagerly for an appreciative smile and applause from his grandmother. She happily complies, and he scrambles from the water to show her again. Ask students why Damien wants his grandmother to watch him. What similar situations have students observed? On the basis of what they have seen, do students think caregivers provide the recognition children need? In what ways?

ASSESS

CHECKING COMPREHENSION

Assign students to write their responses to the Check Your Understanding questions in the Section 1 Review. Answers to the questions are given at the bottom of this page.

EVALUATE

Have students complete the Chapter 14, Section 1 quiz in the TCR.

Reteaching

1. Assign Reteaching 34 in the TCR. Have students complete the activity and review their responses.

2. Have students write a paragraph comparing the physical development of preschoolers and toddlers.

Enrichment

1. Assign Enrichment Activity 34 in the TCR.

2. Have students study the recent research that points to heredity as an influence on hand preference and report to the class.

Extension

• Take students to visit a kindergarten or preschool class to observe differences in height, weight, balance, and coordination. Have them record their observations and discuss them in class.

• Invite a preschool or kindergarten teacher to speak to the class about how parents, teachers, and other caregivers can help promote motor skills development in children. Have students write a summary of suggestions as a follow-up.

CLOSE

Have each student write an end for this sentence:

Between ages four and six, a child …

Then have students read their sentences aloud.

Parents, caregivers, and teachers should not attempt to change a child's hand preference. It doesn't really matter whether a child is right- or left-handed, except for the usually minor inconvenience of being left-handed in a world made for right-handed individuals.

SECTION 1 REVIEW

CHECK YOUR UNDERSTANDING

1. List three changes in physical proportion that take place between the fourth and seventh birthdays.

2. What are permanent teeth? Which are the first secondary teeth to appear?

3. What motivates most children to give up thumb sucking?

4. What is dexterity? Give two examples of a five-year-old's improved dexterity.

5. List at least three motor skills that an average five-year-old develops.

6. What does *ambidextrous* mean?

7. How do children develop hand preference?

DISCUSS AND DISCOVER

1. List at least ten games or activities that four- to six-year-olds enjoy. Which of the games and activities use and help develop large motor skills? Small motor skills? Which of the games and activities would be appropriate for children younger than four? Why?

2. Collect and display pictures that four-, five-, and six-year-olds have drawn of themselves and their families. How are the drawings alike? How are they different? What indications of the artist's age can you identify in each picture?

Observing & Participating

Observe four- to six-year-olds at play in a park or other public area. Notice how the outdoor play equipment is constructed to ensure safety for the children. Which pieces of equipment, if any, could cause injury to the children? Why? Which of the children's activities or behaviors, if any, could cause safety problems?

SECTION 1 REVIEW

1. Any three: body becomes slimmer; abdomen flattens; shoulders widen; chest broadens and flattens; neck and legs become longer.

2. The set of 32 teeth that will not be naturally replaced; the six-year-old molars.

3. Learn thumb sucking is not socially acceptable.

4. The skilled use of hands and fingers; stacking blocks and tying shoes.

5. Any three: ties shoelaces; draws recognizable person; picks up small items; writes alphabet; stands and balances on tiptoe for short periods; skips; buttons, snaps, and zips clothes.

6. Able to use both hands with equal skill.

7. Uncertain. Heredity and parental encouragement to use one hand are probable influences.

Providing Care for Children from Four to Six

OBJECTIVES

- Explain the importance of good nutrition for children from ages four to six, and tell how good nutrition can be encouraged.
- Explain how to help children develop good self-care habits.

Four-, five-, and six-year-olds need less actual physical care than younger children. However, parents and other caregivers must still remind children and guide their self-care efforts. The biggest change in schedule during this period is the addition of school. The term **preschoolers** is often used for *children aged four and five,* but many four-year-olds go to preschool programs, and most five-year-olds go to kindergarten for a half or full day. Six-year-olds are typically in school for a full day.

TERMS TO LEARN

enuresis
group identification
preschoolers

Feeding

Like adults, children get their energy from the food they eat. The amount of food a child needs depends on many factors—activities, height, weight, and temperament of the child. For example, running requires more food energy than watching television. Even the time of year can make a difference. People need more food in cold weather to provide energy for keeping warm.

A child who is overweight is eating more food than his or her body can use. This extra food is stored as fat to meet future energy needs. A child who is underweight is not eating enough food to supply his or her energy needs. Neither of these conditions occurs suddenly (except, perhaps, as a result of illness). Overweight and underweight both result from long-term eating habits that are not right for the individual's needs. With the help of parents and other caregivers, children can learn to balance the amount of food they eat with the specific needs of their body.

HEALTHY FAMILIES/HEALTHY CHILDREN

Health and Safety

According to one researcher, almost one-fourth of school-age children are overweight. The number of obese and superobese children has increased dramatically over the years. Because of increased fat, these children are at greater risk for high blood pressure, respiratory diseases, diabetes, orthopedic disorders, and psychological and social problems. Moreover, the older they are, the more likely they are to become overweight adults.

How can caregivers deal with this problem? They need to realize that nagging does not help an overweight child. Children need input that will raise their self-esteem, not lower it. An overweight child soon realizes there is a problem without being told.

SECTION 2

Providing Care for Children from Four to Six

Pages 421-429

FOCUS

SECTION 2 RESOURCES

Teacher's Classroom Resources

- Enrichment 35
- Reteaching 35
- Section 2 Quiz

Student Workbook

- Children's Clothing—It All Adds Up!
- Reading Nutrition Labels
- TV Ads and Children's Eating Habits

SECTION OVERVIEW

In Section 2, students study nutritional needs of preschoolers, ways to provide nutritious and appetizing meals for children, and ways to help preschoolers develop good eating habits. Then they examine ways to help preschoolers learn self-care habits in personal hygiene and dressing. They learn how to choose appropriate children's clothing and how to encourage good sleep patterns.

MOTIVATOR

Remind students how much physical care children of three and under require. Encourage them to predict how that changes for children between the ages of four and six. Invite them to speculate on the parents' changing roles and responsibilities during this period. How, for example, do parents guide children as they become more independent?

USING TERMS TO LEARN

Pronounce the terms listed under "Terms to Learn." Ask students if they are familiar with any of them. Point out that *group identification*—the need for a feeling of belonging—is very important to children in this age group.

GUIDED PRACTICE

Promoting Discussion

Have students recall and discuss when they first began to bathe and dress themselves and get ready for bed without help. Tell them to discuss the role their parents and other caregivers played in directing these processes.

Using the Photograph

Refer students to the photograph on page 422. Ask them what other foods would make good snacks for a child.

Making Connections: Nutrition and Home Economics

Have students collect nutritious recipe ideas for snacks that children might like. If possible, have students use computer software to create an illustrated booklet of their suggestions. Distribute the booklet to a child care facility for use by parents.

Promoting Discussion

Use these questions to stimulate discussion about food preferences:

- Have you ever sampled unusual foods that you had never had before? How did the foods taste? When children try new foods, are the foods likely to seem just as strange to them?

- Why might a child be willing to taste a vegetable that he or she has helped grow, clean, or prepare?

- How did you learn to like a certain food? Does your experience suggest strategies for introducing children to nutritious foods?

An apple makes a tasty, healthy, and portable snack. Children who learn to enjoy nutritious snack foods when young will still have these habits as adults.

Snacks

Few children grow up without between-meal snacks. Actually, snacks are not bad—if they contribute to the child's daily nutritional needs. Some snacks, such as candy, cake, and soft drinks, provide the body with energy but fail to supply many of the nutrients (such as protein, vitamins, and minerals) necessary to keep the body healthy. Advertising encourages children to ask for snacks like these. Children who are given too many sweets at an early age often develop a "sweet tooth." On the other hand, children who are given nutritious snacks like fresh fruit and raw vegetables continue to enjoy such snacks when they are teenagers and adults.

Poor Nutrition

Poor nutrition has many causes. Though lack of money to buy healthful food is one cause, it is not the most common. Many children in families with sufficient money have poor diets. Parents in these families may not understand good nutrition, or they may not take the time to make sure their children are eating well. In other cases, children are left with the responsibility of choosing and preparing their own meals. The choices these children make are usually not the most healthful.

HEALTHY FAMILIES/HEALTHY CHILDREN

Health and Safety

Dieting is not the answer for an overweight child unless a physician says so. Instead, parents and caregivers should serve low-fat meals and snacks that are appropriate for the whole family. High-calorie foods can be served selectively to everyone so that the child does not feel deprived. Per-

haps the best thing people can do for overweight children, however, is keep them active. A child who regularly participates in sports and other physical activities from a young age is likely to maintain these interests throughout life. For these individuals, weight problems may never occur.

Poor nutrition can have a number of bad effects. Children with inadequate diets have less resistance to colds and infections and may find learning more difficult. Poorly nourished children are easily distracted and often lack motivation to learn.

Teaching Children About Good Nutrition

The best way to make sure children have a proper diet is to teach them about good nutrition early in life. Both home and school are part of this educational process. In our society, many meals are eaten away from the family. That means children regularly choose which foods they will eat—and which foods they won't eat.

One research study showed how four- and five-year-olds can be taught better eating habits. The study focused on helping children eat vegetables, which many youngsters dislike. The researchers began by surveying their young subjects to find out which vegetables the children liked best—and least. Then the researchers selected five of the less popular vegetables—asparagus, broccoli, rutabagas, spinach, and turnips—to use in the experiment. The children helped clean, chop, and cook these vegetables for their own meals. They learned about growing, harvesting, and serving the vegetables. Most importantly, the children learned how each vegetable helped them grow and stay healthy. At the end of the three-month experiment, most children ate the vegetables willingly at school. In addition, their parents reported that they were more willing to try new vegetables and other foods at home.

Shopping for fruits is a good way to learn to enjoy eating them. It also teaches children about nutrition and science, and makes them proud of their ability to help you.

GUIDED PRACTICE (continued)

Critical Thinking
Have students consider these questions about food preferences:

- Do you agree or disagree with this statement: "If parents dislike lima beans, their children will also." Who, besides parents, influences a child's food preferences? (Siblings, peers, television advertisers.)

- What problems might occur if only a few parents are sending children to school with nutritious lunches, while most lunches contain junk food snacks. (Because of the need for group identification, the children will want lunches like most group members, especially if they have already been influenced by television ads.)

Making Connections: Nutrition
Have students read the nutrition labels on foods such as pizza, pasta, canned soups, and TV dinners. Ask them to compare calories and nutritional value and compile the information in chart form. Have them discuss their findings.

Cooperative Learning
Have students work in groups to plan packed lunches for a six-year-old for one week. Have groups exchange plans and evaluate them for nutrition, taste, and variety.

Making Connections: Social Studies
Have students study nutrition problems among children in developing third-world countries and report to the class. Lead a discussion on what is being done to improve child nutrition around the world. What else would students like to see done?

TEEN PARENTING

Community Resources
Teen parents often need support from outside resources. Those who have more than one child may have additional special needs. If you have teen parents in your class, you may want to provide them with a list of agencies in your community that offer legal advice, health care, emergency funds, shelter and protection, substance abuse counseling, and housing. Teen parents also need to know that places like the health department, extension office, police department, hospital, and library are also good resources. Visits to these community resources may be helpful.

GUIDED PRACTICE (continued)

Promoting Discussion

Ask students whether they think children should be allowed to pack their own sack lunches. At what age might this be appropriate?

Family Focus

Ask students to assume they are the adults in a family with two children. Have them suggest ways to handle the following situations:

• Every time your family goes out to eat with friends or relatives, six-year-old Adam sits at the table and announces which foods on the table he does not like.

• Four-year-old Wendy refuses to taste anything that is green.

• Adam wants a peanut butter sandwich for lunch every day.

• Whenever you go the store, Wendy begs for Crispy Crunchies, a sugary cereal she has seen on television.

Similar learning projects can be carried out at home. Four- to six-year-olds love to help in the kitchen, and everyone benefits when they do. The child learns about various foods, improves his or her motor skills, and is usually more willing to try new foods. The parent has a chance to spend time alone with the child, while encouraging the child in improved eating habits and in self-sufficiency.

What can children this age do to help in the kitchen? They can help put food away after a trip to the grocery store, and they can set the table. They love pulling the husks from ears of corn or tearing lettuce for salads. They can use a small egg beater to help prepare pudding, scrambled eggs, or batter. They enjoy rolling and cutting out biscuits or cookies. For an especially fun project, try making mini pizzas—children can flatten biscuit dough, spread on tomato sauce, and sprinkle on cheese and other toppings.

It is important to teach preschoolers good food habits because at this age, children are forming lifetime eating habits. Children learn quickly. As one four-year-old said as he waved his carrot stick during lunch, "This gives me good eyes, Grandma."

Once children start school, many take a packed lunch. Lunches should be nutritious, but there's no need to fall into a boring routine. Consider these tips for keeping packed lunches interesting and fun to eat:

• Let the child choose his or her own lunch box or reusable lunch bag. Encourage the child to add decorations, too.

• Children like finger foods. Cut chicken, cheese, or meat into bite-sized pieces for easier handling.

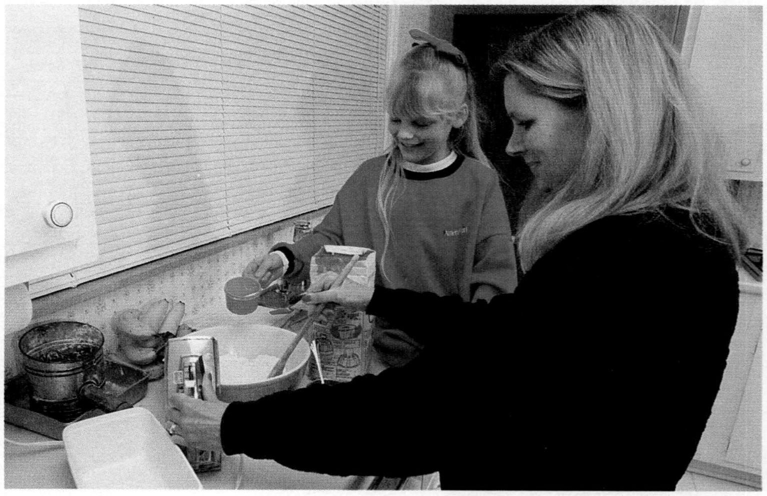

When young and older children help prepare meals, they are more apt to enjoy eating nutritious foods.

MORE ABOUT

Serving Amounts

When serving food to children, remember that they need smaller amounts than adults. A three-year-old eats only half as much as an adult. A six-year-old eats about two-thirds as much. It is better to serve children small amounts that they can handle and let them know that seconds are available. Servings that are too large may cause waste or pressure to overeat. You may want students to review the Food Guide Pyramid on page 164 to review the basic food groups. Remind students that the exact amounts served are less important than maintaining a daily balance of different kinds of nutrients: proteins, fats, carbohydrates, minerals, and vitamins.

ASK THE EXPERTS

Promoting Good Eating Habits

Q. How can I encourage my child to eat a balanced diet now, and how can I help her build healthy eating habits that will last a lifetime?

A. Many parents worry about their children's eating habits. It's a natural concern, but worrying isn't part of the solution. The best approach to helping a child develop good eating habits has three steps:

1. **Understand children's nutritional needs.**
2. **Make nutritious foods available and attractive.**
3. **Set a good example, but don't make eating an issue.**

The first step is easy. Become familiar with the Food Guide Pyramid. The pyramid makes it clear that children—like the rest of us—should be eating more pastas, fruits, and vegetables rather than meat. This usually works well, because most children don't especially like meat.

The second step is easy, too—and it can be fun for both parents and children. Involve the children in selecting, preparing, and serving nutritious foods. Together, find ways to enjoy familiar foods, and experiment with new foods. Try making frozen pops from fruit juice—and slip a piece of fruit into the middle as a special surprise. Let children create—and then

eat—their own necklaces of oat ring cereal. Cut sandwiches or jellied fruit into appealing shapes. Try broccoli "trees" with a cheese dip, or fresh fruit with a yogurt dip.

For many parents, the third step in this approach is the most challenging. Be confident that you are offering your child nutritious, appealing foods; then let go. Treat your child's food preferences— and your child—with respect. Given opportunities, good examples, and respect, children will be inclined to develop healthy, long-lasting eating habits.

Pat Brodeen

Pat Brodeen
Teacher and Teen Parent
Coordinator at Theodore
Roosevelt High School in San
Antonio, Texas

- Sandwiches don't have to be boring. Use a variety of breads and fillings. Cut sandwiches into squares or triangles, or use cookie cutters to cut out fancy shapes.
- Insulated containers make it possible to keep foods hot or cold until lunchtime. Soup, casseroles, and salads are interesting alternatives to sandwiches.
- Muffins, biscuits, rolls, and bread sticks are all good substitutes for slices of bread.

HEALTHY FAMILIES/HEALTHY CHILDREN

Health and Safety

Because they are growing, preschoolers need about 50 percent more protein per pound of body weight than adults do. A diet overly heavy in carbohydrates such as potatoes and noodles does not provide the right nutrients. Preschoolers are active, and their energy requirements are relatively high. Because their capacity for food is small, they cannot afford to eat empty-calorie foods. Empty-calorie foods include pretzels, potato chips, candy, crackers, and so on. These foods are high in calories, low in nutrient density, and many times, contain refined sugar and additives.

GUIDED PRACTICE (continued)

ASK THE EXPERTS

Issues and Advice

1. What are the three steps to help a child develop good eating habits? (*Understand nutritional needs; make healthy food available and attractive; set a good example.*)

2. Why is it possible for a child to eat more vegetables and fruits than meat? (*Children usually don't like meat.*)

3. Why do adults find the third step to be the hardest? (*Because they must let go and trust their child to make good choices.*)

4. How should an adult treat a child's food preferences and choices? (*With respect.*)

Thinking Like an Expert

Ask each student to make a list of ten foods that he or she likes very much and ten foods that are strongly disliked. Next, have students form small groups and compare responses. From their individual lists, have them develop a combined list that represents the most liked and most disliked foods. Combine the group lists to develop a class list, and write the results on the board. Open a discussion of the overall food preferences of the students, and ask them to suggest what the preferences indicate about them.

For a comparison study, have students interview people from another culture or another age group about their food preferences. Have students make inferences about the influence of culture and/or life experiences on eating habits and present them in a written or an oral report.

GUIDED PRACTICE (continued)

Promoting Discussion

Use these strategies to stimulate discussion about clothing choice:

• Ask students how parents can avoid mismatched outfits yet allow their children to make clothing decisions.

• Ask students how they feel when they are appropriately dressed for the occasion. Do they think a six-year-old would have similar feelings?

• Ask students to weigh the pros and cons of hand-me-down clothing. How might a child of this age feel about hand-me-down clothing?

Making Connections: Math

Have students work in groups to plan a wardrobe for a six-year-old child. Ask them to describe the quantity, style, and fabric of the clothing items included. Which items are essential? Which are not? Have students use catalogs to estimate the value of the wardrobe if purchased new. Have them also call thrift shops to estimate what the wardrobe would cost if purchased secondhand.

Practicing Decision Making

Have students work in groups and list the basic cleanliness rules that they believe a person should follow. For example, one guideline might be to wash your hands before eating. What other guidelines would they include? Have group representatives share their lists with the class.

• Pack fruits and vegetables ready to eat. Peel and cut them at home, if necessary. Vegetables can be cut into strips, chunks, or flowers. Try including raw vegetables such as yams, sweet potatoes, broccoli, and cauliflower.

• Lunch "treats" don't have to be cookies or candy. Raisins, peanuts, popcorn, and pumpkin or sunflower seeds are fun to eat and provide more nutrients.

Bathing and Dressing

During this period, children may show a decreased interest in washing, bathing, and dressing. Performing these tasks has already lost its novelty. The three-year-old's satisfaction of accomplishment gives way to boredom and reluctance.

Children need help in maintaining cleanliness habits. Poor habits acquired at this age can continue into adulthood. It is important for the rest of the family to set a good example and provide encouragement.

It is best to set up and maintain routines for bathing, washing hands, and other cleanliness habits. Routines help children accept these tasks as expected behavior, just like bedtime. Praise works better than nagging or scolding. Parents and other caregivers might say, "You always smell so good after your bath!" or "We'll let dinner wait until you've finished washing because it's much nicer when we all sit down together." When the task is done, a comment such as "Terrific—you're nice and clean and ready to eat" helps children feel good about themselves.

Children can be taught at an early age to take pride in their appearance. They will benefit from both good grooming habits and a good self-concept.

OBSERVING AND PARTICIPATING

Developing Observational Skills

Many hours of imaginative play can come from a box of old clothes. Through playing dress-up, children not only test their creativity and imagination but also practice dressing skills, including manipulation of buttons, zippers, and ties. Before throwing away old clothes and accessories, caregivers might want to think twice. These items can turn an afternoon of boredom into one of delight for a child.

Four-, five-, and six-year-olds are usually able to dress themselves independently. Some may need help with complicated fasteners, such as buttons down the back or shoelaces. Many children have difficulty figuring out which clothes match. It's not unusual for preschoolers to choose combinations of prints or colors that clash. In most cases, parents and caregivers should ignore a mismatched outfit and comment instead on how well the child buttoned his or her shirt or how quickly the child was able to get dressed this morning. Parents who are uncomfortable with such outfits should remember that, as a child's matching skills develop, so do his or her skills in selecting clothing.

Choosing Clothes

The guidelines for choosing toddlers' clothes—comfort, durability, and economy—remain important at this age. Knit shirts and jeans are popular and practical for everyday wear.

Four- to six-year-olds have definite likes and dislikes in clothing. Some become as attached to a favorite garment as they do to a particular toy.

Group identification—*the need for a feeling of belonging*—also begins to be important. Wearing the accepted kind of clothing and following clothing fads are an important part of belonging to a group. Within reason, it is important to allow children to make their own clothing choices. Being happy with his or her clothing contributes to a child's self-confidence.

Caring for Clothes

As soon as children begin to care about what they wear, they can begin learning clothing-care habits. This is a long process. Many parents still find it necessary—at least occasionally—to remind ten-year-olds about putting their clothes away.

Children need to be taught that all clothes need care. Parents and other caregivers should show children where and how clean clothing can be hung up or put away, and where dirty clothes belong.

It is important to have adequate storage space that the child can reach, so that putting clothes away is a task the child can accomplish. Hooks just above eye level, low rods, and handy shelves encourage a child to put things where they belong.

Adults should provide consistent guidance, but they should avoid taking over the task. Parents who pick up and put away clothing for their five-year-old should not be surprised when that child expects the same service as a teenager. Parents and other caregivers can best encourage a child to develop good clothing-care habits by offering encouragement, showing patience, and setting a good example.

BUILDING SELF-ESTEEM
Complimenting Children

How do you know when you have completed a task properly? Often, the best indication is that someone tells you so. You are likely to feel especially pleased when someone praises your efforts, skill, or results.

Children feel the same way. However, compliments are even more important for children because they don't yet have the experience to recognize that their efforts are helpful, correct, or even complete.

Compliments can be the reinforcement that helps children feel good about themselves and lets them know that their efforts in attempting or completing a task are appreciated.

Compliments can also encourage children to try more difficult tasks. Compliments are meaningful only when they are sincerely expressed.

GUIDED PRACTICE (continued)

Promoting Discussion

Ask students whether they have ever cared for a child who was reluctant to go to bed. How did they handle the situation? Would they do anything differently if faced with the same situation today?

Making Connections: Language Arts

Have students role-play a conversation between a child of five who has wet his or her pants at school and the child's mother. Assume the child has been teased by the other children and is mortified.

BUILDING SELF-ESTEEM

Compliments do more to stimulate a child's initiative than competition with other children will do. When a child feels a sense of satisfaction and accomplishment, he or she will be motivated to set higher goals. No amount of pushing, coaxing, or comparing will have the same positive effect.

TEEN PARENTING

The Transition to Parenthood

When teens become parents, they must change roles, often very quickly. As teens, they have been cared for by someone else. As parents, they must be the responsible ones, usually with very little preparation for this role. Ask students to make a list of responsibilities associated with caring for a child. (Pages 421-429 offer some ideas about physical care. Students should be able to think of others as well.) Which responsibilities would be the easiest for a new parent to assume? The most difficult? Why? If you have teen parents in your class, ask them how they have handled (or are handling) their transition from child to parent. What methods and resources can be used to help them?

PARENTING IN ACTION

Promoting Discussion

A large percentage of children come from broken marriages and may move from one household to another. Discuss problems that result from varying standards of conduct. Have students read "Dealing With Inconsistencies" to see how they create problems.

Answers to Think and Discuss

1. Sarina has not been given the opportunity to assume responsibility and does not know the sense of satisfaction she would have from doing it herself.

2. Her father and stepmother could gradually come to expect more of her efforts. Her mother could communicate with the father to let him know the problem Sarina faces.

3. All three adults could help her by assessing their expectations and guiding her in understanding that different people will have different ideas about chores.

INDEPENDENT PRACTICE

Student Workbook

Refer students to the following activity sheets that correlate to this section: Children's Clothing—It All Adds Up!, Reading Nutritional Labels, and TV Ads and Children's Eating Habits.

HEALTH TIP

Too often a child is humiliated and embarrassed by parents who are frustrated with bed-wetting. Sadly, this poor treatment only increases anxieties, which, in turn, bring on more incidents of bed-wetting. Discuss positive methods of dealing with bed-wetting, or have interested students find out more about recommended treatment.

PARENTING IN ACTION

Dealing with Inconsistencies

Six-year-old Sarina lives with her father and stepmother. They have never expected Sarina to pick up her own clothes or put them away. Usually, her stepmother hangs up Sarina's jacket after school and sorts out the clothes she takes off at night. She washes the clothes that are dirty and puts everything away for Sarina.

Every other weekend, Sarina goes to stay with her mother. Her mother feels irritated when she sees Sarina's clothes draped over a chair or dropped onto the floor. Her mother reminds Sarina repeatedly to use the laundry hamper and hang up her clothes, but Sarina seems never to remember.

Sarina wants to please her mother, and she feels upset that taking care of her clothes has become such a problem.

THINK AND DISCUSS

1. Why has being responsible for her own clothes become a problem for Sarina?

2. How could this problem have been avoided?

3. Who should help Sarina with this problem? How?

Sleeping

Sleeping arrangements after the third year usually provide separate rooms for boys and girls, if at all possible. An individual bed for each child usually encourages better sleep habits.

Many four-year-olds do not take an afternoon nap. Although, a few continue to do so until they begin a full day of school.

Most four-, five-, and six-year-olds show less reluctance to go to bed. A few children still use delaying tactics, but many children actually ask to go to bed. After saying good night and perhaps looking at a book or listening to soft music for a while, most go to sleep easily. Some children may need conversation, companionship, or a stuffed toy before going to sleep, and many continue to enjoy bedtime stories.

Taking care of clothes, like anything else, can become a habit if parents and caregivers provide praise and encouragement.

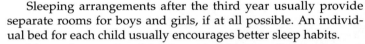

SEE HOW THEY GROW

Taking a "Play Nap"

After age six, most children don't nap. Even at ages three and four, many children don't actually sleep when napping, but read, talk to themselves, or listen to music. A "play nap" is a valuable rest period whether or not the child sleeps. Preschoolers may tire quickly, but they can also recover quickly after only a little rest.

Some preschoolers who may think they are too old to take a nap can be encouraged to lie down for a rest period. Many parents and caregivers discover that the "play nap" turns into a real nap.

Toileting

By the fourth birthday, most children have few toileting accidents. Four- and even five-year-olds may still have occasional accidents when they concentrate so completely on an enjoyable activity that they postpone going to the bathroom. Sickness— even as minor as a cold—is another common cause of accidents.

When they begin school, some children may suffer from constipation or may occasionally wet their pants. These problems can be caused by the tension children feel in their new school surroundings. The length of time for adjustment depends on the individual child. Most children will adjust within a few weeks. For some children, the problem may reoccur at the beginning of school for several years. Adults can help children with these problems by responding with patience and understanding. In addition, parents and other caregivers should develop a morning routine that allows enough time for relaxation and bathroom use before school. A calm, secure home atmosphere is also important.

HEALTH TIP

It is important to treat toileting accidents casually. Shaming or scolding the child cannot help. **Enuresis**, *a lack of bladder control*, is usually not considered a problem until a child is four—and sometimes it should not be treated as a problem even then. About 10 to 15 percent of normal five-year-olds wet the bed at least occasionally. Parents who are concerned about enuresis should consult a pediatrician for help in identifying the cause of the problem and in understanding the most helpful responses.

SECTION 2 REVIEW

CHECK YOUR UNDERSTANDING

1. What is a preschooler? Do any preschoolers go to school?

2. List at least three specific examples of nutritious snacks. What are two reasons young children should be given such nutritious snacks rather than sweet snacks?

3. List two causes of poor nutrition.

4. What is group identification? What is one way for young children to achieve group identification?

5. What clothing-care responsibilities should four- to six-year-olds be given?

6. How should adults respond to four- to six-year-olds who have toileting accidents?

DISCUSS AND DISCOVER

1. Imagine that you are the parent of a six-year-old who wets the bed about once a month. How do you think you would feel about this? How would you try to respond? Why?

Observing & Participating

Work with a four- to six-year-old to prepare a snack or a simple meal (or help a group of children in a preschool program as they prepare a snack or meal). Describe which health habits— such as washing hands before and after preparing food, avoiding contact with pets while handling food, wiping up spills immediately—the child follows independently. About which health habits does the child have to be reminded?

SECTION 2 REVIEW

1. Children aged four and five; many four-year-olds go to preschool programs, and most five-year-olds attend kindergarten.

2. Any three specific fresh fruits and/or raw vegetables. They provide nutrients needed to keep the body healthy; they help the child develop a lifelong preference for healthy snacks.

3. Any two: family's lack of money to buy healthful food; parent's lack of understanding about good nutrition; parent's failure to take time and assume responsibilty for preparing healthy meals.

4. The need for a feeling of belonging; wearing the accepted kind of clothing or following clothing fads.

5. Putting clean clothing away and putting dirty clothes where they belong.

6. With patience and understanding.

Journal Writing

Have students write journal entries reflecting on what they have learned about physical growth, development, and care of children aged four through six. In particular, have then consider how caregivers can provide for their care, health, and safety while fostering self-care.

ASSESS

CHECKING COMPREHENSION

Assign students to write their responses to the Check Your Understanding questions in the Section 2 Review. Answers are given at the bottom of this page.

EVALUATE

Have students complete the Chapter 14, Section 2 TCR quiz.

Reteaching

1. Assign Reteaching 35 in the TCR. Have students complete the activity and review their responses.

2. Ask students to write two or three sentences that summarize the information on bathing and dressing.

Enrichment

1. Have students study fabrics used in children's clothing and evaluate each in terms of comfort, care, durability, and cost. They may use garment labels to obtain some of their information.

2. Have students complete Enrichment 35 in the TCR.

Extension

Have students develop a list of children's books that would be appropriate for bedtime reading. Have them use established criteria to analyze the books.

CLOSE

Have each student write an end for this sentence:
The self-care skills a child needs to learn between ages four and six are …
Then have students read their sentences aloud.

Positive Parenting Skills

MOTIVATOR

Ask students to recall their favorite television shows when they were children. Write the names of the shows on the board. Ask for a show of hands, and record how many students recall watching each show. What types of shows were most popular?

Promoting Discussion

1. What can children learn from watching television?

2. What are some negative effects of watching television?

3. Who should be responsible for decisions regarding children and television viewing?

4. What regulations attempt to control harmful viewing?

Critical Thinking

Remind students that children who watch television without adult supervision are exposed to violence. Ask them to think about how too much violence will affect children. What do students know about the stages of child development that helps them form mature opinions about the dangers of violence on television? To what extent can caregivers control what children watch on television?

Family Focus

Ask students to reflect on their own family's television habits. If they were the parents of the family, how would they change the patterns of television viewing in their family?

MONITORING TELEVISION VIEWING

Should young children watch television? This is a question that evokes strong—and often conflicting— responses. It is, however, probably not the question that parents and other caregivers should be considering. Much more relevant are these questions: Which TV programs should young children watch? How much TV should they watch? With whom should they watch?

Television can help with many types of learning. Shows like Sesame Street, for example, have been specially developed to make learning fun and easy for children. Such shows may teach the alphabet and numbers, help children learn about different cultures, and help them understand

their feelings. Nature shows are both entertaining and educational. Programs on space exploration or other special events can help children develop a sense of history and an interest in the current world.

Certainly, some television shows are both fun and beneficial for children. However, letting the TV serve as a child's "electronic babysitter" is probably not healthy. The more a child watches the TV, the less time he or she has for other activities important to physical, social, and intellectual development. The following are some of the negative effects of television:

• Children learn to expect to be continually entertained. This may make their adjustment to school more difficult.

MORE ABOUT

Television and Violence

Does watching violence on television cause children to be more aggressive? Many different studies have been conducted, and the majority seem to show that the answer is "yes." However, the findings are still controversial. Just as there is a difference between real life and television, there is also a difference between studying aggression in a laboratory, where there is no fear of punishment. But would the same child have hit a sibling at home? If so, can it be proved that television is to blame?

- Children become less active and physically fit.

- Television can stifle imagination and creativity. Children who watch a lot of television may find it difficult to amuse themselves.

- Children who are over dependent on television don't develop the social skills learned through play with other children.

- Children often have trouble distinguishing between reality and fantasy. They can easily be misled into thinking everything they see on TV is true.

It is important to remember that not all TV programs are suitable for children to watch. Some programs frighten or confuse children. Others present topics that are too mature for them to understand or deal with. One particular problem is the amount of violence depicted on television, even in children's

cartoons. Research is still being conducted on the effects of watching TV violence.

Television watching can be an asset or a liability to a child's learning and development. Parents and other caregivers should select shows that are appropriate for the child— musical entertainment, children's stories, or programs that present reassuring images of family life. Whenever possible, adults should watch

along with the child to explain things that may be confusing and to help differentiate between what is real and what is fantasy. If violence or other inappropriate behavior is shown, the caregiver and the child can discuss ways it could have been avoided and better ways of handling the situation. These approaches can make watching TV an enjoyable shared activity.

431

Promoting Discussion
If possible, have each student select a television program and watch the program alongside a child. Encourage students to interact with the child during the viewing, following the suggestions given in this feature. Afterward, ask students to discuss and evaluate their experiences.

Journal Writing
Have each student write a list of suggestions for parents and caregivers regarding television viewing. Then, in small groups, have the students share their lists and develop guidelines for use in selecting and monitoring television viewing. Have each group prepare a brochure explaining their guidelines.

Using Management Skills
Ask interested students to research children's programs available on videotape. If possible, encourage students to view the programs and then evaluate them according to the same criteria used for television shows. What differences and similarities exist between the two categories of programs? What financial considerations must be made when choosing videotapes over television shows?

Practicing Parenting Skills
Have each student observe while a child watches a television program. Ask the student to note the age of the child and record the child's physical reactions and comments during the program and commercials. Ask them to consider this question: If you were this child's parent, what guidelines for television watching would you set for him or her? Why?

CLOSE

Ask students to volunteer any new opinions they might have formed after reading this feature.

SEE HOW THEY GROW

The Effect of Television
Another possible effect of television violence is to influence children's attitudes about aggression. A large number of studies have shown that when children are continuously exposed to television violence, they tend to view others' aggression with

apathy or acceptance. Part of the reason may be children's lack of personal experience and awareness. They may not be able to see the difference between the television world, where violence is usually presented as justified and rewarded, and the real world, where violence is.

Student Demonstration

Present these situations, and have student pairs role-play how they would handle each of them. Discuss their handling with the class.

- Four-year-old Mark keeps coming down the stairs after you put him to bed. He says a monster is hiding in the closet.

- Five-year-old Janet has been told to get ready for bed two times. Both times she has replied, "In a minute."

- It is six-year-old Joel's bedtime. When reminded, he replies, "But I'm not tired!"

ASSESS

CHECKING COMPREHENSION

Use the Summary and the Reviewing the Facts questions to help students go over the most important ideas presented in Chapter 14; encourage students to ask questions and add details.

1. Improved diet and health habits, enriched foods, and advances in medicine.

2. Less reliable—heredity and environment variations.

3. Act as a lock to keep all the teeth in position.

4. Heredity and in which hand the parents usually place objects.

5. Learns about various foods, improves motor skills, tries new foods, spends time with parent, and generally acquires improved eating habits.

6. Maintain routines for bathing, washing, etc.; praise efforts; set a good example.

7. Separate rooms for boys and girls.

8. Give them adequate storage space; avoid taking over the task; set a good example.

9. Tension. Respond with patience and understanding.

10. Enuresis is a lack of bladder control. Parents should consult a pediatrician if they are concerned.

SUMMARY

- Growth in height and weight remains steady from ages four to six.

- Secondary teeth begin to emerge at this age and replace primary teeth.

- Four- to six-year-olds practice and refine their motor skills.

- The amount of food a child needs depends on activities, height, weight, and temperament of the child.

- Establishing good eating habits is an important goal at this age and can influence the child's nutrition habits as an adult.

- Four- to six-year-olds can wash and dress themselves and can help care for their own clothes.

- Enuresis may still be a problem for some children at this age.

REVIEWING THE FACTS

1. Why do children generally tend to be taller than their parents?

2. As a child gets older, do height and weight charts become more or less reliable as guides to healthy growth? Why?

3. What special purpose do six-year-old molars serve?

4. What are two theories about how hand preference is developed?

5. What are four benefits of letting children help prepare meals?

6. What are three ways to help children develop cleanliness habits?

7. What sleeping arrangements should be made, if possible, for children aged four or older?

8. What are three ways to help children become responsible in caring for their own clothes?

9. Why do some children suffer from constipation when they begin attending school? How should parents respond?

10. What is enuresis? How should parents respond to enuresis?

432

EXPLORING FURTHER

1. Think about how you would teach a five-year-old to tie shoelaces. Make a simple chart demonstrating the best teaching steps. Then, if possible, try using your teaching plan with a child who has not yet learned to tie his or her shoelaces. (Section 1)

2. Collect several jump-rope chants that six-year-olds enjoy. Then make up at least one new chant for children to try. Make an illustrated booklet with these chants. Share the booklet with parents, first-grade teachers, or young children. (Section 1)

3. Plan and practice a five- to ten-minute puppet show that teaches young children about good nutrition. If possible, perform your puppet show for a group of preschoolers. (Section 2)

4. Plan and prepare two after-school snacks for six-year-olds. Eat the snacks with the young children. How nutritious are the snacks? How appealing are they? What might make the snacks more nutritious and/or more appealing? (Section 2)

5. Interview three or four parents to determine whether they think it is important for their children to select their clothes for the day. Do the parents think it makes any difference what the children wear? Why or why not? (Section 2)

THINKING CRITICALLY

1. **Synthesize.** What effect, if any, do you think size might have on a child's personality? How do you think parents and other caregivers should help children cope with concerns about their own stature?

CLASSROOM MANAGEMENT

Computers in the Classroom

Good computer programs are available for diet and nutrition analysis. These programs make the laborious calculations of nutrients for diet analysis quick, interesting, and fun. After your students have completed a nutrition analysis of common food items (both nutrient-dense and empty-calorie foods), have them develop a bar chart comparing the nutritional value of those items.

2. **Analyze.** How important do you think it is for families to eat together? Why? What circumstances make such meals difficult for many families? What compromises do you think parents should make? Why?

3. **Synthesize.** How do you think parents should respond to their children's desire to follow clothing fads? Why? What problems might result from allowing children to follow such fads? What problems might result from forbidding children to follow them?

CROSS-CURRICULUM CONNECTIONS

1. **Math.** Help weigh and measure the children in a preschool or kindergarten class. Record all the heights and weights. Then calculate the average height and weight of children in the class. How do the class averages compare with the figures in the Average Heights and Weights chart on page 415?

2. **Computers.** Collect or create recipes for tasty, nutritious snacks for young children. Use computer software to do a nutrient analysis of each recipe. Include serving size, number of calories, and grams of fat, protein, and carbohydrates.

SCHOOL TO WORK

Nutrition and Job Performance You have probably learned by now that what you eat affects how you feel. Can you see how diet affects how you perform on the job as well? Regular, nutritious meals give your body the fuel it needs to get you through routine tasks on the job. Whether your work is physically or mentally demanding, when you apply the basics of a healthy diet to everyday life, your job performance is rewarded.

PERFORMANCE ASSESSMENT

Physical Development from Four to Six

Task
Prepare and present a nutrition lesson designed to teach four- to six-year-olds about the basic food groups and help them prepare a nutritious snack.

Purpose
The purpose of this lesson is to help children understand the basic food groups in the Food Guide Pyramid. Then children will prepare a nutritious snack and identify the food group from which each ingredient comes.

Procedure
1. Review what you learned in this chapter about the value of a healthful diet. You may also want to review the Food Guide Pyramid on pages 163

and 164. Then brainstorm a list of details and examples to include in your lesson.
2. Ask yourself these questions as you prepare your lesson: How will I keep their attention—with puppets, coloring books, or rhymes and jingles? What can I do to involve all children in the cooking experience safely? What supplies will I need? How much time will I have?
3. Prepare your lesson plan and present it to your class or, if possible, to a group of children in this age group.

Evaluation
Your lesson plan will be evaluated by the following criteria: (1) how well you select appropriate lesson materials that demonstrate your knowledge of nutrition; (2) how well

you demonstrate understanding of children's learning levels between the ages of four and six; (3) the organization and presentation of your lesson.

 Portfolio Idea For your portfolio, have another student, friend, or teacher videotape your presentation, and keep the videotape with the lesson plan and your notes in your portfolio. You could also make a visual display from your lesson plan, such as a booklet or poster. Be sure to include the lesson plan, a written description of how you presented the lesson, how your target audience responded, and any anecdotes, notes, or suggestions.

433

PERFORMANCE ASSESSMENT

Nutrition Lesson
It might be helpful if you take your students before they prepare their lesson plans to visit a classroom, child care center, or even a playground. In this way they can familiarize themselves with the language, attention span, interest level, and behavior characteristics of children at this age.

If you have access to a local school or child care center, you could schedule time for your

students to actually present their nutrition lessons. In this case, you could videotape the lessons to review later for evaluation and to observe the children's reactions and responses. You might also have your students prepare an assessment questionnaire in advance of their presentations, so they can evaluate the effects of their lesson plans.

EVALUATE
Use the reproducible Chapter 14 Test in the TCR, or construct your own test using the Test-maker Software.

EXTENSION
Have students contact a recreation supervisor or physical education teacher for his or her opinions and advice on which games and sports are appropriate for children at age four, age five, and age six. Then ask students to include their own ideas on developmentally appropriate activities and compile a master list for each age group.

CLOSE

Have students suggest endings for these sentences:
These changes in growth and development take place between ages four and six: …
Because of these changes, preschoolers can …
Encourage a variety of responses that reflect the development and appropriate self-care skills of preschoolers.

DEVELOPING A PORTFOLIO

Practical Applications The connection between portfolios and future education and/or career goals is important enough that it bears frequent reinforcement. Older students should be impressed by the long-term usefulness of a portfolio. Bring the reality of this usefulness home to them. For example, invite former students who have made practical use of their portfolios as guest speakers to talk to your students. An employer in a child-related profession could also speak to students about the value of portfolios in job interviews. You might even invite professionals or college students who have developed portfolios in child care or other fields to visit the class and describe their experiences.

INTRODUCE

CHAPTER OVERVIEW

In Section 1, students study the patterns of emotional and social development that take place from ages four through six. In particular, they examine how expressions of fear, anger, and jealousy change with age. They focus on cooperation and the influences of competition.

In Section 2, students explore how the patterns studied in Section 1 apply to family and other social relationships. Students learn that a child begins to develop a conscience between ages five and seven.

CHAPTER OBJECTIVES

After completing Chapter 15, students will be able to:

- Describe general patterns of emotional and social development of children ages four, five, and six.
- Give examples of the causes of and responses to anger, fear, and jealousy in children ages four to six.
- Discuss the good and bad effects of competition.
- Tell how school affects a child's emotional and social development.
- Describe a child's relationship to family at ages four, five, and six.
- Explain how children develop a sense of right and wrong.

CLASSROOM MANAGEMENT

Resources Beyond the Classroom

According to recent statistics, reported cases of child abuse have risen in recent years. The increase of economically and emotionally ill-prepared teen parents may be a contributing factor. Fortunately, the National Committee for the Prevention of Child Abuse (NCPCA) is a resource that troubled young parents can turn to. The NCPCA sponsors a nationwide, voluntary home health visitor program for new parents (in conjunction with the Ronald McDonald Children Charities) to help educate parents in health-related issues and coping strategies. For more information, call (213) 663-3250, or write:

National Committee for the Prevention of Child Abuse
332 S. Michigan Avenue, Suite 1600
Chicago, IL 60604

CHAPTER 15

Emotional and Social Development from Four to Six

SECTION 1   Emotional Development from Four to Six

SECTION 2   Social and Moral Development from Four to Six

- Read the following statements to the class. Encourage a discussion of each statement and ask students to speculate about whether they think child care professionals would agree or disagree.

— At age six, a child undergoes some difficult transitions.

— Children at age five are more cooperative and receptive to rules than are children at age four.

— Competition is unhealthy for children.

— A preschooler who says something that is not true is lying.

— When children between ages four and six behave in acceptable ways, they do so only to escape criticism and punishment or to win attention and approval.

Tell students that Chapter 15 will focus on these topics and others that address the emotional and social development of children from four to six.

- Use the photo on the opposite page and the three features on this page—Think About, Ask Yourself, and Now Try This—to begin a discussion about a child's emotional and social development from ages four to six.

THINK ABOUT

Most children between the ages of four and six begin a new adventure—preschool. This setting provides opportunities for children to grow outside the family environment, where values and attitudes were first inspired. Now it's time for the child to learn another role—as part of the human family. Think about the impact that other children will have on the social development of a four- to six-year-old.

ASK YOURSELF

Study the photo on the opposite page. What do you think prompted the imaginary play situation you see in the photo?

Notice the expressions on the children's faces. Are they enjoying themselves? How do you know? What do you imagine them to be saying to each other? How does their play contribute to their emotional and social growth?

NOW TRY THIS

Write a short description of a time when you imagined yourself to be someone you were not. Can you recall the circumstances that prompted your imagination? Did your imaginary play help you deal with a problem or stressful situation? If so, how? Explain how this kind of imaginary role-playing could help a child deal with social situations that would otherwise create anxiety.

435

HEALTHY FAMILIES/HEALTHY CHILDREN

Listening Skills

Reflective listening is a type of listening that involves a special skill that shows people you understand and care. With reflective listening, you reflect, like a mirror, what you see or hear a person saying. One of the easiest ways to make a reflective listening response is to use a phrase based on this model: "You feel [name the feeling—sad, proud, happy] because [name the situation leading to the feeling]." This technique helps the speaker know that you listened and you understand. Here's an example: Speaker 1: "There's no one to play with. Everyone's gone on vacation." Speaker 2: "It must be pretty lonely being by yourself, since all of your friends are away." Reflective listening is a communication skill that families can use and children can learn.

FOCUS

SECTION I RESOURCES

Teacher's Classroom Resources
- Enrichment 36
- Reteaching 36
- Section 1 Quiz

Student Workbook
- Word Jumble

SECTION OVERVIEW

In Section 1, students study the patterns of emotional development that take place between ages four and six, and how emotional patterns differ in children ages four, five, and six. Next, they examine how expressions of fear, anger, and jealousy change with age. They focus on cooperation and the positive and negative effects of competition.

MOTIVATOR

Remind students that play for a toddler is analogous to work for an adult. A toddler's "job" is to learn about the world and develop his or her abilities without accountability. Between ages four and six, however, the child begins to attend school regularly and assume responsibility and accountability for his or her actions. Have students discuss the magnitude of the change from carefree exploration to accountability for behavior within three years. Ask students to predict children's possible reactions to the change.

USING TERMS TO LEARN

Refer students to the term to learn. Have them refer to the Glossary for a preview of the definition and ask them to use the term in the context of a sentence.

SECTION **1**

TERMS TO LEARN

self-esteem

Emotional Development from Four to Six

OBJECTIVES

- Describe general patterns of emotional development in children aged four, five, and six.
- Give examples of the causes of and the responses to anger, fear, and jealousy in children aged four to six.
- Discuss the positive and negative effects of competition.

Four-, five-, and six-year-olds must cope with many changes in their lives. Most begin regular school attendance during this period. School takes children away from their home and into a new environment, to be shared with unfamiliar adults and large groups of other children. In addition, children of this age begin to assume the responsibilities of childhood and become aware that they have left babyhood forever. These major steps require many adjustments for four-, five-, and six-year-olds.

General Emotional Patterns

Like children from one to three, children aged four to six often go through characteristic emotional stages. However, each child differs in some ways from others. Emotional development depends on the individual child's personality, family, and experiences.

Four Years

Most four-year-olds seem intent on asserting their independence. They are more self-centered, impatient, defiant, and boastful than they were as three-year-olds. They often argue and compete, and they are bossier than in the past.

SEE HOW THEY GROW

Building Self-Esteem

Praise is obviously important for preschoolers, who mirror much of their self-image and self-worth through the eyes of parents and other caregivers. Remember to praise children, when appropriate, for their ability to do things like climb on a stool to reach the light switch or fix their own peanut butter and jelly sandwich. Children also burst with pride when their arts and crafts projects are displayed so that everyone can admire them. Giving praise is essential for children this age—it affirms their sense of self, builds confidence, and creates a more independent child.

Four-year-olds can also be unusually loving and affectionate. They need and seek parental approval. A four-year-old may stamp her foot and scream, "I hate you, Mommy!" Three minutes later she may smilingly offer her mother a shiny stone or a flower as a special present.

The independence of four-year-olds has special benefits, too. At this age, children can wash and dress themselves independently. They are typically proud of their accomplishments, abilities, possessions, and creations.

When children of this age make mistakes or disobey rules, they are likely to deny responsibility for their actions. It is common to hear a four-year-old explain, "A big dog came by and knocked it over" or "Joe made me hit her."

Four-year-olds use their language ability with enthusiasm. They enjoy language in part for its sounds. "Antsy-Wantsy-Nancy"—or some similar nonsense—can send them into hysterical laughter. They enjoy trying out bathroom-related words and seeing reactions from other children and adults. They also want to talk the way adults do, though they do not yet have the language skills for mature conversations. They boast, tattle on their friends and siblings, and tell imaginative stories.

Four-year-olds can sometimes be difficult. However, when they are loveable, it's hard to resist them.

TEACH

Pages 436-447

- **General Emotional Patterns**
- **Specific Emotions**
- **Competition—Good or Bad?**
- **Personality and Behavior**

GUIDED PRACTICE

Promoting Discussion

Have students discuss how parents can use a four-year-old's sense of responsibility to help him or her establish good habits and routines.

Critical Thinking

Ask students to consider the following questions about behavior patterns in children of four and five:

- Why do the characteristics of four-year-olds make it important for parents and caregivers to set definite limits on behavior? (Four-year-olds are more mobile and tend to be self-centered, impatient, defiant, competitive, and bossy, which, without limits, can lead to trouble.)

- According to the text, five-year-olds like supervision and obedience to authority, but find adult criticism hard to take. How can a parent or teacher apply this information in guiding children's behavior? (The parent or other caregiver can give positive direction by telling children specifically, in advance, what behaviors are expected and by providing positive reinforcement for compliance and performance.) What is the function of rules? (They let a child know what is expected and how to avoid criticism.)

OBSERVING AND PARTICIPATING

Developing Observational Skills

Have students observe four-year-olds at play, paying special attention to the language used. Ask the students to report on their observations. Did the children use silly names or plays on words? How much boasting or telling of tall tales did students hear? Did the children tell jokes? Have your students prepare objective evaluations of the observations and share their observations with the class.

Promoting Discussion

Use the following strategies to stimulate discussion about truth and fantasy:

- It is not until about age seven that children are really able to separate fantasy from reality. With this in mind, have students discuss how parents should handle standards of honesty.

- Have students discuss the following situation: Four-year-old Jack burst in the door when he came home from preschool. "Dad!" he shouted. "Guess what happened on our nature walk today! First, we saw a giant dog. It was taller than me. The we saw a big bunch of about a million birds. And a big huge rattlesnake bit me!" How do students think Jack's father should respond?

Using the Photograph

Refer students to the photo on page 438. Ask them to relate the emotional characteristics of five-year-olds to their willingness to cooperate with parents and follow reasonable rules.

Making Connections:
Language Arts

Ask students to read a humorous children's book to a two-year-old and a four-year-old. Have the students write reports comparing and contrasting how the two children reacted to the story. Have them include any conclusions about the way the children reacted.

Four-year-olds have trouble separating fact from fantasy. Parents and other caregivers should treat exaggerations with humor, since at this age, children do not tell deliberate lies. It is helpful to let children know what is pretend and what is real. After a wild story about a dinosaur in the backyard, for example, a parent can say, "It's fun pretending there is a dinosaur in our yard."

Four-year-olds enjoy having other people laugh at their jokes, but they are very sensitive about having people laugh at their mistakes. It is important to children this age that they are no longer "babies"—whose mistakes people can laugh at, all in good fun.

Most four-year-olds are in a rather difficult phase of normal emotional development. You can help children of this age by respecting their need to explore and test themselves. Parents and caregivers should make an effort to avoid treating four-year-olds as babies. They should also try to use flexible rules in guiding the behavior of four-year-olds.

Five Years

Five-year-olds enter a quieter period of emotional development, similar to that of age three but at a higher level. Children of five are generally rather practical, sympathetic, and serious. Their improved attention span allows them to finish what they have started, rather than moving from one thing to another. Also, five-year-olds are able to go back and finish uncompleted tasks.

At age five, children are usually willing to cooperate with parents and follow reasonable rules, such as putting away toys. They can stick with a task until it is done.

MORE ABOUT

Children's Humor

Children see humor in repetition. When a preschool child discovers something funny, whether it is an action, joke, or humorous phrase, all the other children want to participate by repeating it themselves. They will still find the joke funny long after adults have become exasperated by the repetition and hilarity.

Five-year-olds have learned that others will not accept tall tales and lies; they are, therefore, increasingly realistic. They are like four-year-olds in their continued enjoyment of slapstick humor. However, their abilities to carry on discussions and ask meaningful questions are noticeably better than those of four-year-olds.

At this age, children conform to rules more easily. They like supervision, accept instruction, and ask permission. They willingly mind their parents and teachers—at least most of the time. However, adult criticism is very hard for five-year-olds to take.

Emotionally, children at age five are more patient, generous, persistent, and conscientious than they were earlier. The occasional anxiety that they feel is usually caused by a desire to achieve acceptable results rather than by general insecurity.

Six Years

Like children of four, six-year-olds are often stubborn and quarrelsome. They resent directions, and they "know everything." They are the center of their own universe—and determined to stay there. Six-year-olds are often at their worst with their own parents.

At six, children have rapidly changing moods. They love and hate, accept and reject, smile and storm—sometimes for no apparent reason. Even a favorite playmate is likely to get a swift whack before being informed, "You bumped into my truck." Of course, a playmate who is also six will probably deliver an immediate blow in return.

Six-year-olds are learning to appreciate humorous situations and jokes. They throw themselves into their fun with the abandon that characterizes all they do.

It is easy to understand why six is a difficult age for children. Many are beginning school full-time; they are faced with the task of developing their status outside the home. This is a time of difficult transitions for most children. It is also a time when children long to feel grown-up—but often feel small and dependent. Six-year-olds crave praise and approval. They are easily hurt, they wilt under criticism, and they are readily discouraged.

Can you interpret the moods this boy is experiencing? Note how the moods change the boy's entire appearance.

Specific Emotions

During the years from four to six, children experience a wider range of emotions—and more intense emotions—than they did when younger. They need guidance in recognizing and expressing all their emotions. Parents and other caregivers of children this age should be careful to accept and help children identify all the emotions they experience.

GUIDED PRACTICE (continued)

Promoting Discussion
Use the following strategies to stimulate discussion about the sense of humor in preschoolers:

• Ask what kinds of things young children find funny. How does this change with age?

• Have students give examples of slapstick humor that appeals to preschoolers.

• As children get older, they begin to use humor to make fun of or hurt others. Have students discuss and give examples of this type of children's humor.

Cooperative Learning
Point out that the average attention span for five-year-olds is less than 15 minutes. Have students work in groups to develop a list of activities suitable for five-year-olds that could be completed within that length of time. Have group representatives read their lists to the class.

Family Focus
Children ages four to six are often bossy in their interactions with others. Sometimes this bossiness results from feelings of powerlessness. Discuss how children can be helped to have feelings of power and importance in the family. How can parents help children overcome the need to be bossy? How might this affect family relationships?

SEE HOW THEY GROW

Five-Year-Olds
When children are about five, the first examples of self-limiting behavior occur. That is, children begin to accurately judge what they are and are not capable of doing. They generally attempt only what they know they can do. In this way, their successes build self-confidence. Have students brainstorm a list of ways or sayings they could use when they are working with children that would promote the children's self-confidence.

GUIDED PRACTICE (continued)

Making Connections:
Language Arts
Have students write vignettes describing either five- or six-year-olds. Tell them to provide details clearly typical of the age they have chosen. Have students exchange papers and read the vignettes to the class. Can students identify the age of the child from the description?

Critical Thinking
Have students consider the following questions about children aged six:

- How can the feeling of being a grown-up affect a six-year-old's emotional development? (Expectations are suddenly much higher as six-year-olds enter school. They establish identities and need acceptance outside the home, which creates additional stress, because they also feel small and dependent.)

- According to the text, children of six wilt under criticism. What age factors might result in children of six being subjected to more criticism than at age five? (Expectations are higher, and they are held accountable for learning as they enter school, and their performance may need correction. The self-centered, stubborn, and quarrelsome stage they are undergoing leads to behavior that invites criticism.)

As children grow older, they find new ways to vent their emotions. Teasing, insulting, and making fun of others are typical of six-year-olds.

Anger

Anger shows more distinct changes during childhood than does any other emotion. Young children show anger freely, without any attempt to restrain themselves. As children grow, they learn to use more subtle means of expressing their anger:

- **Four years.** Four-year-olds may still express their anger by engaging in physical fights. Their anger lasts longer than before. They often threaten and attempt to "get even."

- **Five years.** Five-year-olds often attempt to hurt other children's feelings rather than hurting them physically.

- **Six years.** Six-year-olds are even more stinging with words. They tease, insult, nag, and make fun of others.

The frequency of anger declines during the period from four to six. However, the effects of anger are longer lasting. There are a number of reasons for these changes. A child's tolerance for frustration generally increases as he or she grows older. Also, some sources of earlier frustration are eliminated as the child's motor skills improve. During the period from four to six, a child usually gains a better understanding of the property rights of other people, is able to work well in groups, and begins to learn about and accept the differing personalities of other people.

The most common cause of anger for four- to six-year-olds is disagreements with other children. While quarrels are still loud and verbal, five- and six-year-old children begin to conceal and disguise their feelings. Sometimes their methods of revenge are

HEALTHY FAMILIES/HEALTHY CHILDREN

Emotional Stability
Adults who have not learned to deal with anger in a constructive way offer a poor example to children of the four- to six-year range who are learning to recognize and vent anger. Caregivers who understand the value of positive expressions of anger, then use them when they interact with children, set a good example. Likewise, positive methods of expressing anger in the classroom help reinforce this concept and display additional models on how to cope with negative feelings. As an example, when a teacher becomes angry with a student or with the class, using degrading expressions only fosters resentment and bitterness. Instead, deter inappropriate behavior by saying something like, "It's just not like you to act this way."

indirect. They may pretend indifference, sneer, or make sly remarks. Often they make exaggerated threats. Occasionally, they take their anger out on a scapegoat, such as a younger sibling, a pet, a toy, or the furniture.

School-age children begin to understand that other people sometimes try to provoke their anger. One particularly imaginative five-year-old scored a crushing defeat with this reply to a kick: "Aw, that just felt like a little minnow swimming by me!" The child clearly recognized both his opponent's intent to hurt and the frustration that accompanied the obvious failure to cause pain.

Parents are frequently on the receiving end of a school-age child's anger. To children, parents are the source of rules. Often in their anger, they will "punish" a parent by breaking yet another rule. For example, when six-year-old Hanna was told to go to her room for kicking her brother, she retorted, "Okay, I'm not going to hang my clothes up for a week—or maybe a year!"

Children vary greatly in the amount of anger they show and in the ways in which they show it. Some of these variations depend on each child's personality. However, the way parents express their own anger and the way they respond to the child's anger are also important. All caregivers should set an example by sharing and verbalizing—but not acting out—their own anger and by providing a happy and orderly environment for the child. They should also help teach the child self-control early in life before inappropriate expressions of anger become a habit. Parents and other caregivers can encourage children to use words—not their bodies—in expressing anger. For example, they can teach children to use sentences like these: "It makes me mad when you take my truck!" "It hurts my feelings when you don't want to share with me." "My name is Jason—not Dummy!"

Fear

Children from four to six have well-developed imaginations, and many of their fears center on imaginary dangers. They may be afraid of ghosts, robbers, kidnappers, or vampires. Sensitive and insecure children are especially prone to fears. Many children of this age are afraid of the dark. Some may worry about the possibility of being left alone or abandoned.

Many children fear school, but there can be a number of different causes for this fear. Some children are afraid to be without the security their parents offer. Others may fear a bully at school, a stern teacher, or "hard" school work. Taking the child to school—rather than simply dropping the child off or letting him or her go with another adult—can help. Talking about the problem, acknowledging the fear, and offering an understanding explanation may provide all the reassurance some children need.

GUIDED PRACTICE (continued)

Cooperative Learning
Have students work in groups to take or collect photographs that show the characteristics of six-year-olds. Ask students to use the photos to create a display or a magazine-style photo essay.

Promoting Discussion
How is anger appropriately and inappropriately expressed by teenagers? Compare socially acceptable ways for teenagers to express anger and socially acceptable ways for preschoolers to express anger. How do people learn to express anger?

Making Connections: Psychology and Sociology
Have students read a book or article on child abuse. Discuss with students how child abuse is related to the expression of anger. Why are people who have been abused as children more apt to abuse their own children?

Critical Thinking
Review pages 283-285 for discussion of the three common personality patterns; then ask students how children with different personality types are apt to show anger differently.

Cooperative Learning
Have students work in groups to make a time line indicating how children commonly show anger in infancy, toddlerhood, the preschool years, middle childhood, and the teen years. Display the time lines in the classroom.

MORE ABOUT

Children's Fears

• Most children outgrow their fears when they are in a secure environment and when caregivers discourage their irrational fears.

• Many psychologists believe fears are a child's way of dealing with unacceptable feelings, such as anger and hostility.

• Fears are most common between two and six years of age. In most studies, boys and girls have been found to be equally fearful.

• Childhood fears tend to fall into three categories: (1) fear of physical injury (having an operation, being kidnapped), (2) fear of natural events (storms, darkness, and death), and (3) fears that develop from mental stress (making mistakes, being criticized, and attending school).

GUIDED PRACTICE (continued)

Making Connections: Psychology and Language Arts

Have students watch at least three children's television programs and write reports analyzing these programs in relation to children's fears.

Promoting Discussion

Use these strategies to stimulate discussion about fears in preschoolers:

• Have students discuss their own fears as children or those experienced by children they know. How did students or the other children overcome these fears?

• Ask students to give examples of fears that are useful because they help keep children safe.

Making Connections: Language Arts

Have students look at the children's section of the library and find five books that deal with children's fears. What fears are included in the books? Have students read and report on one book. Do they think the book would help a child overcome fears? Why or why not?

Childhood Reflections

After the birth of his second child, a boy, a father said proudly to his five-year-old little girl, "Well, now we have a son and a daughter." Not about to give up star billing, she politely corrected him. "A daughter and a son," she said.

Anxiety about school is common. Parents or caregivers should be sympathetic, but must help the child understand that going to school is necessary.

As one mother said to her son, "I know you are upset that you have to go to school. Daddy and I go to work. We don't always feel like going, but that's our job. Going to school is your job."

Special fears also arise in four- to six-year-olds. Social acceptance is very important at this age; the threat of its loss is a continual source of anxiety for children.

At this age, children are especially fearful of ridicule. They may not show their other fears openly because they do not want to be ridiculed. Instead, a child may act aggressively, pretend indifference, or deliberately try to distract himself or herself. These kinds of coping are signs of the child's increased maturity.

Parents and other caregivers should not ignore a child's fears. It is usually best to let the child talk about his or her fear. A listening, understanding adult can be especially important to a fearful child. Accept the child's fear by identifying it. Don't tell him or her that the fear does not exist, because it is very real to the child. Guide the child in comfortable actions that will gradually help him or her overcome the fear. Remember that fears won't simply disappear on their own. Unless the child can deal with and overcome the fears, they may pile up and create emotional problems.

Jealousy and Sibling Relationships

Sibling rivalry—jealousy of brothers and sisters—is common during this period. Some parents make the problem of sibling rivalry worse, often without meaning to, by showing favoritism to one child. Another common mistake is trying to improve behavior by comparing one child with another. For example, a father may ask his daughter, "Why can't you be neat and clean

---

SEE HOW THEY GROW

Sibling Rivalry

Children tend to become more rivalrous and competitive with increasing age. Rivalry is most common when siblings are very close in age and of the same sex. Although quarrels among siblings are one of the parents' biggest frustrations, such quarrels have a positive side. They can teach children to express their feelings, stand up for their own rights, defend themselves, and resolve conflicts. Some teasing is simply a way to have fun together. However, when fighting becomes too frequent or too intense, parents should intervene.

PARENTING IN ACTION

Providing Emotional Support

*E*very day when Janie came home from school, she seemed to have a list of complaints. Several times, when her mother asked about her day, Janie burst into tears. "The kids don't play with me." "I can't run fast—I'm always last." "Jimmy calls me 'Freckles,' and now the other kids do, too."

Fortunately, Janie's mother took her child's unhappiness seriously. She didn't simply pass the complaints off with a casual, "Oh, the kids will get over it. They'll like you when they get to know you." Instead, she put aside her work and said soothingly, "I think I'll sit down and have some of this snack with you, and we'll talk about it."

During the snack, Janie's mother learned what was causing the child's complaints. Two friends had indeed rejected Janie's attempts to enter their game that day. Her mother hugged her and said, "Well, honey, maybe they already had enough players. It's not that they don't like you. When it happens

again, ask someone else to play another game. Other kids like to be asked to do things, just like you do."

Janie had complained about not running fast enough because the swings were all taken by the time she got to the playground after lunch. "You run as fast as most of your friends," her mother said reassuringly. "I've seen you do it. Maybe you just don't start out as soon as some of the other children. You can always play on the climbing platform for a while if the swings are all full. Then, pretty soon, a swing will be empty and you can take your turn."

The nickname Freckles prompted this response from Janie's mother: "I think your freckles are beautiful. Your father has freckles, too. That's one of the things I liked first about him. He's so proud that you look like him. And he loves you very much. I wouldn't change one of your cute freckles for the world!"

Janie's unhappiness soon faded, but her mother decided to make the after-school talks a part of their daily routine.

THINK AND DISCUSS

1. What effect do you think these early sessions between Janie and her mother will have on Janie as she grows older?

2. How long do you think Janie and her mother should continue to spend this kind of time together? Why?

3. Why is talking with another person helpful in easing stress? With whom do you talk when you feel you are under a great deal of stress?

PARENTING IN ACTION

Promoting Discussion
Have students recall "bad days" at school, in their experience or that of preschoolers they have known. Did they or the children they know discuss specific problems with parents or other caregivers? Were adults able to help? Have students read "Providing Emotional Support" to analyze the behavior of a child of three and one-half.

Thinking Critically
Guide students in a discussion of these questions:
• Do you think Janie will take her mother's advice? Why or why not?
• What are other possible reasons Janie's friends would not let her join their game?

Answers to Think and Discuss
1. The effect is positive; sessions are the basis for trust, open communication, and respect for feelings.
2. Encourage students to see the long-term value of spending time together at every opportunity; there is no finite age or stage.
3. Emotions are validated and more clearly understood when discussed. Answers to the second part will vary; encourage students to identify as many support resources as possible.

MORE ABOUT

Time Together
Balancing work and family can be a challenge for parents, but they need to plan to spend time with their children. The periods spent together should be void of any distractions, and if possible, all stresses should be left at work.

It is important for families to set time aside every day to simply be a family. Children enjoy these special times. Whether families spend time together watching television, eating dinner, or doing dishes, each activity is important and will add to the security and well-being of family relationships.

BUILDING SELF-ESTEEM

After students read Helping Children Cope with Stress, have them relate the content to the stress they experience and share ways they use for relieving such stress.

Making Connections:
Language Arts

According to Bruno Bettleheim, many common childhood fears are represented in fairy tales. Discuss fairy tales such as Hansel and Gretel and Snow White, and ask what fears they might represent.

Critical Thinking

What benefits might children gain from normal sibling rivalry? (Interpersonal skills such as conflict resolution and assertiveness.) What could be the long-term results if early childhood jealousy is not outgrown? (The child could grow up to be a jealous, immature adult.)

Did You Know?

A sports psychologist from the University of Virginia reports that 80 percent of college women no longer involved in sports were discouraged from athletics because important men in their lives implied that physical activities were not ladylike.

BUILDING SELF-ESTEEM

Helping Children Cope with Stress

Children—like adults—can feel too much stress. This can happen when a child is given too much responsibility, is expected to deal with too many changes, or is overloaded emotionally.

Do the following to help children cope with stress:
- Spending time with the child. Talking and touching or holding the youngster shows the child that he or she has support.
- During private conversations, encourage the child to talk about the changes in his or her life and to examine and express his or her feelings. Reading a story about a character who is experiencing similar disruptions or responses can also be helpful.

like Jeff? I never have to tell him to wash before meals." Such comparisons rarely improve behavior; they are much more likely to damage a child's self-concept and undermine good family relationships.

At this age, jealousy often takes the form of tattling, criticizing, or even lying. Some children react to their own feelings of jealousy by boasting, while others pretend there is no rivalry. Jealousy may also result in tensional outlets such as nail biting, bed-wetting, and tantrums.

Normally, early childhood jealousy fades as the child matures and develops interests outside the family. However, some children never seem to outgrow it and are jealous even as adults. In such cases, jealousy is often a part of deeper emotional problems.

Children and Stress

Stress among teens and adults is a well-recognized problem. Many people, however, fail to realize that children also lead stressful lives. Children may worry about everything from fires to their own popularity, their grades at school, or news about missing children.

As with an adult's stress, a child's emotional stress can lead to physical symptoms. Stomachaches, headaches, moodiness, irritability, and trouble eating or sleeping may be caused by stress, as well as by purely physical ailments.

What should parents and other caregivers do? Hugs help. Other approaches to reducing a child's stress include listening carefully, identifying and showing acceptance of the child's feelings, using a relaxed manner with the child, and building up the child's self-confidence. Talking through problems with the child also helps reduce stress.

Competition—Good or Bad?

People have differing views about the role competition should play in children's lives. Some believe that it helps children excel and prepares them for the competitive world in which adults function. Supporters of competition cite these specific advantages:

- Competition helps a child gain a realistic estimate of his or her own ability in relation to others.
- Competition promotes higher standards.
- Competition stimulates children and adds zest to otherwise dull tasks.
- Competition encourages speed in accomplishment.
- Competition creates an interest in completing tasks.
- Competition stimulates individual effort.

CLASSROOM MANAGEMENT

Cross-Reference

You may wish to refer students to Chapter 18, Section 3, which covers family stresses. This section explores some of the stressful situations that occur in children's lives, including divorce, death, and moving. It gives suggestions of ways to recognize signs that indicate a child may be experiencing

stress. It also presents strategies that caregivers can use to help children cope with their feelings. Students discover that because children are less able to understand and cope with what is happening, they need more help and support in times of stress than do adults. Children should be encouraged to talk about their feelings.

Other people feel that competition discourages cooperation. They believe that, since there are more losers than winners in competitive situations, competition can damage children's **self-esteem**, their *positive sense of self-worth*. These people note the following disadvantages:

- Competition instills in children the idea that success depends on the ability to outdo others.
- Competition leads to hostile relationships with others.
- Defeat in competitive situations may provoke a desire for revenge.
- Those who never win or rarely win may lose interest or quit.
- Competition points out children's inadequacies.
- Competition lowers the status of those who lose.

Sometimes parents' feelings about competition are based on their own desires or experiences. Monica Chavez, for example, wasn't allowed to play on the Little League team as a child, so she pressures her daughter Sara to join the local baseball league. Theo Wills was an "A" student all through school. His son Jess works hard but is an average student. Mr. Wills constantly "encourages" his son to do better. "Don't you want to be at the top of your class?" he asks. Neither parent has really considered the child's interests and abilities.

An added advantage to competitive play is that parents tend to spend time with the child at practice and at their games.

GUIDED PRACTICE (continued)

Promoting Discussion
Use these strategies to stimulate discussion about competition and cooperation:

- Write the word *competition* on the chalkboard. Below it, write the words or phrases that first come to students minds when they think about competition. Do the same with the word *cooperation*. Discuss how the lists are similar or different.

- Have students discuss the advantages and disadvantages of competition; then ask them to suggest activities for four- to six-year-olds that encourage cooperation rather than competition.

Practicing Decision Making
Have students role play a discussion between a parent and child. In this situation, the six-year-old child wants to quit her soccer team because other players make fun of her athletic abilities, and parents of other players criticize her mistakes on the field. Her parent is the coach of the team. Ask students to consider the dynamics of the relationship between parent and child as well as coach and player. How would students resolve this situation?

Did You Know?

In 1560, Flemish painter Peter Brueghel the Elder painted Children's Games, which depicts children of his time at various activities including marbles, hoops, jacks, and making mud pies. Many of these games, including marbles, were enjoyed by children who lived in Egypt 4,500 years before Brueghel.

MORE ABOUT

Competitive Sports
Overly competitive attitudes in sports are learned from others, particularly parents. If parents demonstrate unsportsmanlike behavior—such as losing their temper, breaking the rules of the game, taunting a losing team, or blaming others for their defeats—children learn to do the same. They also learn that the purpose of competition is to triumph over others and avoid losing at all costs.

Poor conduct on the part of other role models, such as athletes in televised sports, can also distort children's attitudes toward competition.

Children may show the following symptoms of overcompetitiveness: prolonged anger or depression over losses; tantrums on the playing field; cheating or attempts to cheat during a sporting event; or extreme nervousness before a sporting event.

Extension
Some youth sports leagues stress competition and winning, while others focus more on teaching the game and having fun with others. Have students investigate the philosophy of youth sports leagues in their community and write a report of their findings.

INDEPENDENT PRACTICE

Student Workbook

Have students complete Word Jumble in the Student Workbook.

Student Demonstration

Assign pairs of students an age from infancy to age six. Ask each pair to make some type of presentation to the class that demonstrates how anger is typically expressed at the assigned age.

Extension

Have students locate and read a children's book that deals with sibling rivalry. How would the book help children deal with feelings of jealousy?

Journal Writing

Have students describe their reactions to what they have learned about patterns of emotional development in children ages four through six. Suggest they write a private journal entry in which they identify some ways their personalities and emotional patterns have changed since they were young children. Tell them to identify the reasons for these changes, if possible.

Cultural Exchange

After students have read "Appreciating Traditions," discuss other holidays and festivals that are important to them. Ask them to speculate about the lasting benefits of traditions.

Cultural Exchange

APPRECIATING TRADITIONS

Holiday traditions are an occasion to understand significant aspects of a culture such as religious rites, the celebration of important people, the changing of seasons, or a great event. December is a month for three holidays important to different groups. Families who celebrate Christmas may attend special church services, decorate a Christmas tree, and hang stockings by their fireplaces. Jewish families celebrate Hanukkah by lighting a candle on a menorah each of the eight nights of the holiday. Children play in a game with a top called a dreidel. African-American families observe Kwanzaa, which lasts for seven days. The holiday celebrates family unity and is a chance for families to join and share baskets of fruit and light candles on a kinara.

Most four-, five-, and six-year-olds prefer cooperative play to competitive games. Older children are more likely to be competitive at play. Parents and caregivers can promote cooperation with group projects and noncompetitive games. "Let's help our friends" can be a key phrase for cooperation.

Competitiveness, often spurred on by sibling rivalry, is likely to show up at home. Children may insist, "Holly gets to stay up until eight o'clock. Why can't I?" or "Why can't I cross the street by myself? You let Dominic!"

Children differ in their responses to competition. Some who constantly lead come to think of themselves as superior. Those who usually lose may develop a harsh, unpleasant attitude to cover their feelings of inferiority. Many, though, find competition a stimulating challenge and suffer no harmful effects.

Personality and Behavior

By age four, many behavior patterns are set; children have many of the characteristics they will exhibit as adults. Other characteristics will change in response to new experiences. For example, children who are shy and withdrawn may become more and more outgoing if they receive positive feedback whenever they exhibit outgoing behavior.

At any age, positive or negative changes in personality can occur. This is one reason that adults should not use labels when discussing a child's behavior. That is, a parents should say, "We

All children need to be encouraged and praised for their own unique abilities.

CLASSROOM MANAGEMENT

Resources Beyond the Classroom

Family Traditions, a book written by Elizabeth Berg, is an appropriate resource for today's child development and family living class. The book presents hundreds of practical and creative ideas, activities, rituals, and special celebrations that can strengthen family ties. It explores creative perspectives on the major holidays: Valentine's Day, Easter, Passover, Mother's Day, Father's Day, Memorial Day, Fourth of July, Halloween, Thanksgiving, Hanukkah, Christmas, New Year's Eve, and New Year's Day. It skillfully combines a sense of tradition with a refreshing blending of new traditions that meet the needs of busy modern families.

expect you to put all your toys back on the shelf when you finish playing," rather than labeling the child by saying, "You're so messy! Why don't you ever put your things where they belong?" Children tend to live up to—or down to—the ideas other people have about them. They may become messy or lazy or unfriendly simply because adults tell them that they are.

A successful business manager recalled that, when he was a child, his father had continually lectured him about his poor management of his paper route. His father said he was "irresponsible and stupid and unable to do anything right!" As an adult, he realized that he had actually handled his responsibilities with better than average efficiency. However, years of hearing about his shortcoming had made him think of himself as a failure. The man developed a realistic view of his abilities when his own judgment and values matured. Many people are not so fortunate; they continue, even as adults, to believe the negative labels they were given as children.

Understanding and guidance from adults is as important for children from four to six as it was in earlier years. Each child— whether sensitive, placid, or aggressive—should be treated as an individual.

SECTION 1 REVIEW

CHECK YOUR UNDERSTANDING

1. What are two important changes that take place for most children between the ages of four and six?

2. Who is more likely to tell tall tales—a four-year-old or a five-year-old? Why?

3. Why is six a difficult age for many children?

4. What is the most common cause of anger in children aged four to six?

5. List at least three fears common among four- to six-year-olds.

6. List at least three things parents can do to help relieve children's stress.

7. List three advantages and three disadvantages of competition among children.

DISCUSS AND DISCOVER

1. How is a child's stress related to the stress his or her parents feel? How can stress build up within a family? What can be the results of family stress? What resources are available to help parents and children dealing with stress?

2. Gather information about local sports programs and other group activities for young children. What official attitude toward competition does each program present? From what you can observe, is that attitude reflected in the children's activities? If not, what accounts for the difference?

Observing & Participating

Observe a four-, five-, or six-year-old playing with one or more siblings. Pay close attention to how the child appears to treat his or her sibling. Notice if the interaction between siblings is affected by the presence—or absence—of a parent or other adult. Describe those values or attitudes being reinforced by the parent or adult.

SECTION 1 REVIEW

1. They begin regular school attendance and begin to assume the responsibilities of childhood.

2. Four-year-olds; five-year-olds have learned that others will not accept tall tales.

3. They are trying to develop status outside the home and long to feel grown-up, but often feel small and dependent.

4. Disagreements with other children.

5. Answers will vary.

6. Any three: hug, listen, identify and show acceptance of child's feelings, be relaxed, build up child's self-confidence, talk through problems with child.

7. Answers will vary. See pages 444-446.

ASSESS

CHECKING COMPREHENSION

Assign students to write their responses to the Check Your Understanding questions in the Section 1 Review. Answers to the questions are given below.

EVALUATE

Have students complete the Chapter 15, Section 1 TCR quiz.

Reteaching

1. Assign Reteaching 36 in the TCR. Have students complete it and review their responses.

2. Have students make a chart that compares and contrasts the emotional characteristics of four-, five-, and six-year-olds.

Enrichment

1. Provide students with examples of cartoons or comic strips that feature children. Have students identify the personality patterns and characteristics of the children in the cartoons.

2. Have students work in groups to design an instructional league for six-year-olds in a sport of the group's choice. How could they encourage cooperation rather than competition? What rules would they change or modify to meet their objectives?

3. Assign Enrichment 36 in the TCR. Have students complete the activity and review their responses.

Extension

Have students research and write a report on the topic of stress in childhood. Have them discuss and share their information in class.

CLOSE

Have students suggest endings for this sentence: Between ages four and six, children's emotions ...

Encourage a variety of responses that reflect the emotional development of children in this age range.

SECTION 2 RESOURCES

Teacher's Classroom Resources
- Enrichment 37
- Reteaching 37
- Section 2 Quiz

Student Workbook
- Teaching by Example

SECTION OVERVIEW

In Section 2, students apply the patterns they have learned to family and social relationships with peers. Students also learn that friends and acceptance become more important to these children. They develop increasing preferences for their own age group and sex, and by age six, they are forming groups that exclude others. Students learn that children begin to develop a conscience between ages five and seven.

MOTIVATOR

Review patterns of behavior in children younger than four. Discuss that as children mature, they will also behave properly in order to avoid the negative consequences of misbehavior. Have students discuss the reasons adults and their own peers choose right or wrong behavior.

USING TERMS TO LEARN

Pronounce the words listed under "Terms to Learn." Ask students if they are familiar with any. Point out to students that the word *conscience* is made up of two syllables, "con" and "science." Although not pronounced the same, the second syllable is spelled the same as the word "science." Remembering this may help students spell "conscience" correctly.

Explain that the word *peer* comes from the Latin term "par," which means "equal." Peers are people one's own age—that is, those who are equal in age.

Social and Moral Development from Four to Six

TERMS TO LEARN

conscience
moral development
peers

OBJECTIVES

- Describe general patterns of social development in children aged four, five, and six.
- Describe a child's relationship to family at ages four, five, and six.
- Explain how children develop a sense of right and wrong.

School brings four-, five-, and six-year-olds into contact with many new people. Children must learn how to meet strangers, make friends, work and play in groups, and accept authority from new people.

General Social Patterns

During the preschool and early school years, social skill development is a major task. As a child moves outside the home, he or she learns to get along with **peers**, *other people of one's own age*. Not all children learn social skills at the same rate, but there are general patterns common at each age.

Four Years

Four-year-olds form friendships with their playmates. At this age, children spend more time in cooperative play than in playing alone. They seem to play best in groups of three or four.

By the age of four, children begin to share their toys and to take turns. However, four-year-olds are still often bossy and inconsiderate, and fighting is common.

Although friends are important to four-year-olds, the family is still more important. Children this age request approval by making frequent remarks such as "I'm a good builder, right?" or "Look how high I can climb!" If things go wrong, they still look to adults for comfort.

HEALTHY FAMILIES/HEALTHY CHILDREN

Social Skills

Children need to learn what makes a valued group member. Children who are popular tend to be considerate, cooperative, generous, sharing, and cheerful. They have a good sense of humor. They ask permission before using other people's possessions and play according to group standards. In contrast, children who are unpopular often tease, insult, tattle, and bully. They are often stingy and bossy. They cry when they lose, gloat when they win, and get their feelings hurt easily. Most children learn social skills by observing the relationships of parents and other adults. Being a good role model in social relationships is an important task for parents.

The preschool years bring more opportunities to develop social relationships outside the home.

Five Years

Most five-year-olds are more outgoing and talkative than they were at age four. They play best in groups of five or six, and their play is more complicated. They prefer friends of their own age. Quarreling is less frequent. When they do quarrel, five-year-olds typically resort to name-calling and to wild threats.

At age five, children have more respect for the belongings of other people. This does not mean that a five-year-old will never snatch a toy from another child. Such behavior, though, is not as common as in earlier years.

As children begin school, social acceptance by peers becomes more important. Children are concerned about what their friends say and do. They don't like to be different.

Six Years

At age six, social relations are often characterized by friction, aggression, threats, and stubbornness. They want everything, and they want to do things their own way. When playing with other children, they may not want to share their own toys; and they are likely to be jealous of other children's toys.

Best friends are usually of the same sex, although six-year-olds play readily in mixed groups. Friendships are closer and longer lasting now than at age five.

At this age, children like the group play and organized teams of school games. As soon as they tire of playing, though, they will drop out of a game with no regard for the team effort.

Cultural Exchange

TREASURES WITHIN A COMMUNITY

Children can be excellent ambassadors of good will. Parents or caregivers know that children quickly become acquainted with adults and other children when they explore their communities.

Regardless of the size of a community, cultural differences within a neighborhood can help children learn about people and appreciate diversity. In some cases, such as gender, race, or language, diversity can be apparent.

Cultural diversity can be appreciated in religious, cultural, and national differences. A simple walk around the neighborhood is a worthwhile experience for all to treasure.

TEACH

Pages 448-453

- **General Social Patterns**
- **Family Relationships**

GUIDED PRACTICE

Promoting Discussion

Have students discuss the groups that form and the social stratification process that occurs within schools and other groups. Encourage them to recall their earliest observations of these processes. When for example, did they first see children their age excluded from a group? When did they become aware of social leaders?

Critical Thinking

As the importance of family diminishes and the influence of teachers and peers increases, what additional challenges face parents in establishing good eating habits, regard for health and safety, and behavior that conforms to family values? (The example provided by peers and the values of peers may conflict with those of the parents, especially with respect to nutrition and safety. Teachers are likely to support most of the parents' values, but where a discrepancy exists, the child is likely to believe that the teacher will be right and the parents are wrong.)

Have students read "Treasures Within a Community." Then have them discuss why children are better able to extend friendship and good will than are some adults.

SEE HOW THEY GROW

Following Rules

By age five, most children are beginning to follow rules and have learned to play simple games. However, almost all preschoolers "cheat" at games. Preschoolers don't fully understand the concept of fairness—they tend to believe that if something benefits them, it's fair. They may understand that games have rules and insist that their opponents follow them; but when their own turn comes, they often want to change the rules to their advantage. This attitude can be frustrating to adults who participate in the game. However, this stage passes. Shortly after children enter first grade, they usually become rigid enforcers of the very rules that they earlier attempted to bend or break.

GUIDED PRACTICE (continued)

Practicing Decision Making

Have students assume they are parents of an only child who is four years old. Have them write a plan that tells how they can provide opportunities for a four-year-old to develop social relationships outside the home. What options are available? How might parental employment influence the choice of options? Have students read their ideas to the class.

Critical Thinking

Ask students what might be the issues in fights between children who are four years old. (Answers will vary. Students might mention taking turns, sharing, choosing an activity.)

BUILDING SELF-ESTEEM

Have students read Manners and the Young Child. Ask them to discuss where manners should fit into caregivers' priorities for children between the ages of four and six.

Making Connections: Social Studies

After a discussion of how important manners can be to adults, both in social and professional situations, have interested students research the importance of manners in present or past monarchies or government circles. For example, Grigori Rasputin might never have gained his fateful influence over the family of Czar Nicholas II had the aristocracy known he never learned to use a knife and fork. A glutton by inclination, he starved at royal banquets. To hide his ignorance and lack of skill, he kept busy talking during courses so that nobody noticed that the servants removed his plate untouched.

Six-year-olds form close friendships, usually with others of the same sex. However, boys and girls still play together in groups.

BUILDING SELF-ESTEEM

Manners and the Young Child

Children learn their manners from the example set by others around them, either in the home or at school.

Young children are capable of practicing some good manners, but the manners should never be given more importance than the activity or than the children themselves. What can be expected? Most children are able to feed themselves fairly well without making a mess; children this age enjoy eating with the family, but usually have trouble sitting through a long meal. Children can learn to say "please" and "thank-you," but they may be inconsistent about using these words on a daily basis. In addition, children this age enjoy helping; they can be encouraged to hold a door open for others, for example, or to answer a telephone politely.

Family Relationships

During the infant and toddler years, children learn to get along with others by forming strong relationships with their parents and other members of their family. They learn cooperation, fair play, and respect for others. In the preschool and early school years, children start putting these social skills to work in social situations outside the home.

Four-year-olds have a strong sense of family and home. They want to feel important in the family. They are proud to perform household chores. However, they are also apt to quarrel and bicker with their brothers and sisters.

In many ways, the family relationships of five-year-olds are similar to those of four-year-olds. They are proud of their parents and delight in helping. At five, though, children play much better with their younger brothers and sisters. They are usually protective, kind, and dependable with younger siblings.

Six-year-olds are less in harmony with their family members. One reason is that children tend to be more self-centered at six. Their own opinions and needs come first. Arguing with parents is common. At six, children are often rough and impatient with younger brothers and sisters, and they may fight with older siblings.

Family, of course, continues to be important to every child. However, once a child begins to attend school, peers, teachers, and other nonfamily influences become increasingly important.

SEE HOW THEY GROW

Role Models

An important social and emotional task for children is learning their male or female (gender) role and related social roles. Children learn these roles from family members, friends, neighbors, and teachers throughout the early years. These significant people are role models for children. These people show through their behavior, attitudes, and activities, and through both informal and formal teaching, how people act, talk, and generally behave. Watching family members who are the same sex helps boys learn about being a boy, a son, and a brother, and helps girls learn about being a girl, a daughter, and a sister. As children mature, they may encounter new role models and modify what they have learned.

Moral Development

Moral development—*the process of gradually learning to base one's behavior on personal beliefs of right and wrong*—begins early in life. Parents have a responsibility to help their children develop a moral sense that will guide their behavior.

As toddlers, children begin to learn the rules their parents and other caregivers set. At this age, though, they can't understand the reasons behind the rules or the difference between right and wrong. They just know that some actions—such as hitting a playmate—make their caregivers unhappy with them. They learn to avoid such behavior because they don't want to lose love and approval.

Between the ages of five and seven, children gradually develop the beginning of a **conscience**, *an inner sense of right and wrong that prompts good behavior and causes feelings of guilt following bad behavior*. The rules learned in early childhood form the basis of the conscience in the early school years.

At this stage, children begin to know the difference between truth and lies. However, that understanding is not always accurate. For example, children may think of a mistake as a lie and expect to be punished for it. Children may also fail to realize that their imaginative stories are fantasy, not reality. Caregivers need to help children separate fact from fiction; they should avoid punishing children for using their imaginations.

At about ages seven to ten, children often don't like or even understand all the rules they are expected to obey, but they don't question the rights of the adults in authority to make and enforce those rules. During this stage, children are still motivated to follow rules primarily by their fear of being punished. They don't yet use their own personal beliefs about right and wrong to control their own behavior.

Guidelines for Moral Development

Most parents take their responsibilities for the moral development of their children seriously. However, it can be difficult to know how to help children learn right from wrong. Here are some guidelines:

- **Consider the child's age and abilities**. For example, a preschooler playing at the sensory table full of rice may start tossing the rice into the air and watching it land on the floor.

Relationships with parents, brothers, and sisters are the foundation for social relationships outside the home.

GUIDED PRACTICE (continued)

Promoting Discussion
Have students discuss the roles of group acceptance and conscience in making and acting on moral choices. Ask them which factor plays a greater role in choices made by their peers. Then have them speculate about the relative importance of acceptance and conscience in the moral choices children make at age six.

Critical Thinking
In Unit 4, students read that toddlers begin to empathize with others' feelings at about age two. How might this help a child develop a conscience later on? (An important element in conscience is the recognition that one's actions have consequences for others. Caring about others' feelings plays an important role.)

Promoting Discussion
What evidence in this section suggests that the need for peer approval and acceptance can influence children's development in negative ways? (The text states that children don't like to be different, positive qualities and exercise of conscience can be "different.") How can this need influence behavior in positive ways? (Encourage sharing, compromise, courtesy, and good grooming.)

Making Connections: Social Studies
Have students research and report on situations in current events or history where otherwise good and moral adults put group acceptance ahead of conscience. Classic historical examples include non-Nazis in Nazi Germany who did not protest Nazi atrocities and people in the South who did not voice their objections to slavery or segregation. Modern examples include people who will not rent or sell homes to minorities for fear of disapproval by neighbors, people who abandon friends who lose their reputations, women who murder their infants rather than admit an out-of-wedlock delivery, people in other cultures who disown their daughters when they are disgraced by rape. Ask what insights this might provide into preschooler priorities.

MORE ABOUT

Moral Development

The moral attitudes and beliefs of parents are generally thought to be the most powerful influences on a child's conscience. The methods parents use in guiding children's behavior may also have an influence. Studies have shown that children with the most highly developed consciences have parents who provide firm but not severe discipline, are consistent in imposing and enforcing rules, and use physical punishment sparingly.

In a sense, a conscience is an internal "code of ethics" that guides behavior. When people violate their internal code, they feel guilty. The unpleasantness of guilt feelings motivates people to do what is right. A person who does not have an effective conscience is inclined to act on impulse, no matter what damage may be done to others.

GUIDED PRACTICE (continued)

ASK THE EXPERTS

Issues and Advice

1. How can tall tales be beneficial to children? (*They promote creativity and help them deal with fears.*)

2. Why might a child tell a lie? (*The child misunderstood; to get a response from an adult; to please others.*)

3. What is the best way to demonstrate conscious, moral behavior to a child? (*Set a good example.*)

Thinking Like an Expert

Have students comment on the following generalities:

• Children are not entirely able to separate fantasy from reality until age seven. How does this affect their concept of what constitutes a lie?

• Preschoolers are just beginning to develop a conscience. Their primary motivation for appropriate behavior is to win approval and avoid disapproval.

INDEPENDENT PRACTICE

Student Workbook

Have students complete Teaching by Example in the Student Workbook.

Student Demonstration

Have students explain the social patterns at age four, five, and six. Have them include information about ideal play group size and how children interact.

Have students work in groups to plan and present skits that show parents setting good moral examples for children.

ASK THE EXPERTS

Children and Lies

Q. *Do young children lie?*

A. Of course children lie. Children learn about their world by exploring it, by trying it out. So we can expect children to learn about lies by lying. However, their lies are often not deliberate attempts to deceive.

Many children, especially four- and five-year-olds, tell tall tales. Telling such tales helps children develop their imagination and creativity; it may also help them deal with their own fears and frustrations.

It's not unusual for young children to mix tall tales with reality. When you need information from a child, you can expect him or her to know the difference. You might explain, "I will listen to your tall tale, and then I need to know what really happened."

Sometimes a statement that sounds like a lie is really the reflection of a child's misunderstanding. For example, a child might feel that he or she has completed a task, but a caregiver is not satisfied. When the child says, "I did what you told me," he or she is not lying. Perhaps the directions were not clear.

Children sometimes tell lies simply to get a response from adults. In these cases, it's usually best to give the child more attention at other times, but to avoid special attention in response to the lying. Remember that all children want—and need—to be noticed.

Children may also lie to protect themselves or to please others. They may not want to risk an adult's anger or disappointment, so they lie about their behavior. Parents and other caregivers can help by encouraging children to accept and deal with their own mistakes or with their own deliberate misbehavior.

As we help children learn when and where and how to tell the truth, we should remember that the development of a conscience as an internal behavior guide takes many years. We should remember, as well, that children learn from our examples.

Jean Illsley Clarke

Jean Illsley Clarke
Director of J.I. Consultants in
Minneapolis, Minnesota

SEE HOW THEY GROW

Children and Moral Development

The first person to study the development of moral behavior in children was Jean Piaget. Piaget asked children of different ages to make moral judgments about a number of different situations. He concluded that moral development was related to intellectual development. Thus, children do not have their own moral philosophies until they can think rationally.

More recently, psychologist Lawrence Kohlberg has taken Piaget's theory and extended it. Both of these psychologists have had a major impact on current thinking and understanding of moral behavior. Have students use the Enrichment activities in the TCR to learn more about theories of moral development.

The teacher will remind the child to keep the rice on the table and then hand the child a broom and dustpan to use in sweeping up the mess. The teacher knows that the child cannot always remember the rules and understands that the child will learn from the consequences of his or her actions.

- **Remember that parents and caregivers teach most effectively by example.** Children receive a mixed message if, for example, they are told that lying is wrong, but they also hear their parents telling lies. If you are around children, you must behave the way you want them to behave.

- **Understand that the process of learning to monitor one's own behavior is a lifelong task.** It is unfair to expect perfection from children. Instead, help children accept and learn from their mistakes.

- **Don't withhold love in response to misbehavior.** It is important for children to know that, although you don't like what they did, you continue to love them.

Both Chapter 3 and the Positive Parenting Skills feature on pages 454-455 present additional suggestions for guiding children effectively.

A developing moral sense helps older children understand the importance of being dependable. Parents can set a good example by the way they approach their own responsibilities.

SECTION 2 REVIEW

CHECK YOUR UNDERSTANDING

1. Who are a person's peers?
2. What kind of play is typical for four-year-olds?
3. Compare the family relationships typical for four-year-olds with those typical for six-year-olds.
4. What is moral development?
5. What is a conscience? What forms the basis of the conscience in children aged four to six?
6. List at least three suggestions for helping children learn right from wrong.

DISCUSS AND DISCOVER

1. What is the difference between a four-year-old's imaginative story and a ten-year-old's lie? Are there stages or circumstances in which it might be difficult to distinguish between an imaginative story and a lie? Why?

Observing & Participating

Ask at least four different four- to six-year-olds this question: What is a friend? Record their responses. If possible, allow the children to draw pictures to go with their responses. From the data you collect, speculate about how children's ideas of friendship vary within this age group.

SECTION 2 REVIEW

1. Other people of one's own age.
2. Cooperative play.
3. Family is especially important to four-year-olds. Six-year-olds' relations with family members may be marked by friction, aggression, threats, and stubbornness.
4. The process of gradually learning to base one's behavior on personal beliefs of right and wrong.
5. The inner sense of right and wrong that prompts appropriate behavior.
6. Any three: consider child's age and abilities; remember that parents and caregivers teach most effectively by example; understand that the process of learning to monitor one's own behavior is a lifelong task; don't withhold love in response to misbehavior.

ASSESS

CHECKING COMPREHENSION

Assign students to write their responses to the Check Your Understanding questions in the Section 2 Review. Answers are given at the bottom of this page.

EVALUATE

Have students complete the Chapter 15, Section 2 quiz in the TCR.

Reteaching

1. Assign Reteaching 37 in the TCR. Have students complete the activity and review their responses.
2. Ask students to consider the following questions: How does this information explain your own social interaction? What role does conscience play in your moral choices relative to group acceptance? How have your priorities changed since age six?

Enrichment

1. Have students bring in examples of cartoons that relate to children's moral development (for example, a cartoon about a child who has misbehaved). Discuss the cartoons in class.
2. Distribute Enrichment 37 in the TCR, and challenge students to complete the activity.

Extension

Have students ask five children, ages three and up, what a friend is and who their friends are. In class, compare and discuss the results. How did the answers vary among the different ages of children? What conclusions can students draw about children's concepts of friendship?

CLOSE

Have students write endings for this sentence:

To develop social relationships and be accepted, preschoolers ...

Ask students to read their endings in class.

Positive Parenting Skills

MOTIVATOR

Have students read the title of the feature, Using Positive Guidance Techniques, and suggest definitions of positive guidance. Remind students that preschool children want attention, approval, acceptance, and praise, and are sensitive to criticism. Have students speculate about how positive guidance techniques can use the desire for approval to their advantage, and minimize the need for criticism.

Promoting Discussion

1. Under what circumstances is physical restraint appropriate? (When a child's behavior is dangerous or seriously inappropriate.)

2. Why should directions to a child be simple and clear? (Complicated, lengthy instructions are confusing to a child.)

3. How does a child benefit when reasons for directions are given? (The child develops a sense of appropriate behavior.)

Using the Photographs

Have students study the photographs in this feature and speculate about what the caregivers are saying to children, and how they are saying it. In the bottom photograph on page 455, have students suggest ways for the person in charge to provide positive guidance for the boy.

Student Demonstration

Have students take turns demonstrating the use of positive direction or correction in situations such as these: preparing a meal with a child; telling a child to get ready for a visit to a relative; cleaning up after an activity. As a point of contrast, you might have students show negative methods of dealing with the same situations above.

USING POSITIVE GUIDANCE TECHNIQUES

One of the most important responsibilities that parents and other caregivers undertake is guiding the behavior of young children. Parents and caregivers serve as role models in the words and actions they use. Occasionally, they may also physically restrain children from dangerous or seriously inappropriate behavior. However, much of the direct guidance that parents and other caregivers provide is verbal.

The following suggestions will help you take a positive and helpful approach to guiding the behavior of young children.

- **Before you give a child directions, be sure you have the child's attention.** You should be close enough to the child to speak in a clear and quiet tone of voice, and you should be on a level that makes eye-contact comfortable for both you and the child. Often, you may need to stoop down or sit beside the child.

- **Use positive statements to give a child directions.** Be sure your directions tell the child what behavior you expect—not the behavior you want the child to avoid. For example, imagine that four-year-old Suki is being too rough with a kitten. The direction "Don't pull the kitten's tail" focuses her attention on only one aspect of her rough handling and fails to tell Suki what she should be doing instead. More helpful would be the direction, "Pet the kitten gently with your whole hand."

- **Begin your direction with an action word that tells the child what to do.** A clear verb should

454

Guidance

Remind students that offering guidance and direction to children while they develop new skills requires time and patience. Throughout the process of guiding and coaching, both the caregivers and the children are susceptible to high levels of stress. Point out that stress is not limited to parenting, but is a normal part of everyday life. Add that, at tense and stressful times, doing the following simple three-step exercise can help drain tension from the body:

1. Close your eyes.

2. Rid your mind of all thoughts—good and bad; concentrate on nothing.

3. Take five deep breaths, letting the air out slowly each time.

be the first word—or at least one of the first words—in a direction to a young child. Beginning with a verb can also help you keep your directions straightforward and simple. For example, the direction "Put your hat back on your head" tells a child just what action is expected. A young child might simply be confused by a direction like this: "I'm afraid that we'll lose your pretty red hat if you keep playing with it, and it's cold out today, so put it back on now."

- **Give a child a direction at the time and in the place you expect the child to carry it out.** When a young child has finished digging in the garden, for example, you might want to give a direction like this: "Put the trowel back on the shelf in the

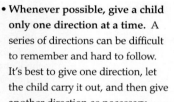

tool closet. That's where we keep it." A very young child—or a child who hasn't used the trowel before— would probably have trouble remembering this direction if it were given while he or she was still busy digging.

- **Whenever possible, give a child only one direction at a time.** A series of directions can be difficult to remember and hard to follow. It's best to give one direction, let the child carry it out, and then give another direction as necessary.

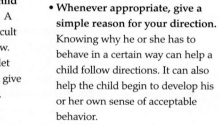

- **Whenever appropriate, give a simple reason for your direction.** Knowing why he or she has to behave in a certain way can help a child follow directions. It can also help the child begin to develop his or her own sense of acceptable behavior.

- **Reward a child for following your direction.** Often, a special smile is enough to show the child that he or she has done a good job. Don't forget, though, to offer more direct praise, too. "That was quick" or "I like the way you listened to my words" or—perhaps best of all—a hug and a kiss can help a child feel proud of following directions.

455

Critical Thinking

Have students rank these factors in order of importance:

- The rules parents set.
- Caregivers' responses to misbehavior.
- Clear, positive directions.
- The examples set by caregivers.
- Explaining the reasons for directions.

After students have ranked the above, ask them to explain their reasons.

Practicing Parenting Skills

Put students into small groups and ask them to compile possible alternative ways for a parent or caregiver to state the following to a child:

- Don't walk on the grass.
- If you leave your toys all over the floor, someone might fall on them.
- You'll get sick with a cold if you don't wear your jacket.

Family Focus

Ask students to agree or disagree with this observation: Child care experts advocate consistency in guidance and discipline techniques; however, the complex factors involved in most family dynamics make consistency difficult to maintain. What examples from their own experiences can they offer to elaborate on this idea? How can each generation strengthen the family units through more positive guidance?

Enrichment

Have students observe a parent or caregiver interacting with a child and write an assessment of the way in which the caregiver offers guidance. Encourage the student to describe the situation from both the child's viewpoint and that of the caregiver.

CLOSE

Ask students to theorize about which of the guidelines presented in the feature are most difficult for adults to follow. Why? What experiences in their lives support or refute the observations of other students?

SEE HOW THEY GROW

Older Children Guiding the Younger

As families increase in size, parents and caregivers often rely on the help of older brothers and sisters. The older siblings, then, find themselves in the position to guide and direct activities such as those described in the Using Positive Guidance Techniques feature. Although the temptation is great to rely on older children, it is important to remember that they are not mature enough to understand the complexities of guidance techniques. These older siblings who are molded into "junior parents" risk sacrificing their own childhood in favor of duty to the family, especially if they are compliant, obedient personalities.

Use the Summary and the Reviewing the Facts questions to help students go over the most important ideas represented in Chapter 15; encourage students to ask questions and add details, as appropriate.

CHAPTER 15 REVIEW

1. Teach children to verbalize their anger and self-control, and to express it appropriately.

2. Possibilities are: Absence of parents, a bully, a teacher, and hard school work.

3. Tattling, criticizing, and lying.

4. A positive sense of self-worth.

5. Those who tend to win think of themselves as superior; those who tend to lose may develop a harsh, unpleasant attitude; others, find it stimulating and suffer no harmful effects.

6. Age four. Encouragement or discouragement of the character.

7. Labelling a child may become a self-fulfilling act.

8. Five-year olds are more outgoing and talkative; prefer groups of five or six; have more respect for others' belongings; have more complicated play; and become more concerned about peer acceptance.

9. Less harmony.

10. Between five and six. Loss of love and approval.

CHAPTER 15 REVIEW

SUMMARY

- Beginning regular school attendance requires many emotional adjustments and brings about rapid social development.

- Although four-, five-, and six-year-olds have better emotional control than younger children, emotional development still alternates between positive and negative stages.

- Expressions of anger become more subtle and less physical at this age.

- An active imagination, school, and the need for social acceptance can lead to a variety of fears.

- Competition can have both positive and negative effects on children.

- As children spend more time with their peers, other factors besides the family influences the child

- Conscience and moral values are developed during this period.

REVIEWING THE FACTS

1. What are two things parents and other caregivers can do to help children learn to channel their expressions of anger?

2. List three possible causes of a child's fear of school.

3. List at least three actions that are often expressions of a child's jealousy.

4. What is self-esteem?

5. What three different responses are various children likely to have to competition?

6. At what age is a child's basic behavior pattern usually clearly established? What might cause some characteristics to change after that age?

7. Why should parents and other caregivers avoid labeling a child when discussing the child's behavior?

8. What differences would you expect to observe between a group of four-year-olds at play and a group of five-year-olds at play?

9. How do six-year-olds typically interact with other members of their families?

10. At what age do children begin to develop their own sense of right and wrong? What motivates children to follow rules before that age?

EXPLORING FURTHER

1. Using magazines, newspapers, or other sources, collect photographs of children and adults expressing anger. Present the photos on a poster or bulletin board display. Encourage other students to describe the pictures and discuss whether each shows an appropriate expression of anger. (Section 1)

2. List eight comments or questions that parents might make, intending to correct or remind their children and unintentionally arousing sibling rivalry. Then rewrite each comment or question so that it presents the same question or reminder without causing jealousy between siblings. (Section 2)

3. Make up a noncompetitive board game or other activity for five- and six-year-olds. Share your game or activity with other students, and encourage them to suggest improvements. Then teach the game or activity to a small group of young children. (Section 2)

4. Interview at least five teachers of kindergarten and first grade. Ask the teachers how they help children make the transition into school and what they do to keep communication open between the school and the family. Discuss your findings with your classmates. (Section 2)

THINKING CRITICALLY

1. **Analyze.** In your opinion, is it possible to raise two or more children without sibling rivalry? Why or why not? What do you think parents can do to reduce or eliminate sibling rivalry among their children? Do you think it is possible to treat all the children in a family in exactly the same way? Do you consider that form of equal treatment desirable? Why or why not?

2. **Analyze.** On the basis of your own experiences and observations, do you think competition is good for children during the early school years?

CLASSROOM MANAGEMENT

Bulletin Boards

When creating bulletin boards, keep in mind that the most effective display is simple and uncluttered, with a clear message. It is better to rotate illustrations than to use too many at once. A bulletin board should provide interesting treatment of space and a variety of materials to attract attention. A variety of textures can also add interest. Background materials may be burlap, felt, or other fabric that will add textural variety without detracting from the primary purpose of the bulletin board. Use real objects, such as small toys or first aid items, to give a three-dimensional look.

Why or why not? If so, what do you think parents can and should do to promote healthy competition for their children? If not, what would you suggest parents do to protect their children from competition?

3. **Analyze.** Why is guiding a child's moral development the responsibility of the parents? What factors might make it difficult—or impossible—for parents to assume this responsibility? How can a lack of such guidance affect a child?

CROSS-CURRICULUM CONNECTIONS

1. **Writing.** Write an original story that begins with the following paragraphs:

> Sandy came home in tears from her first day of kindergarten. Her mother greeted her with a reassuring hug and asked, "Sandy, what's wrong? Didn't you like school?"
> Sandy shook her head and sobbed.
> "What's wrong, honey?" her mother asked. "Did something happen?"

Sandy shook her head again. "I'm not going back there," she told her mother.

2. **Reading.** Read one of these books by Louise Bates Ames and Frances L. Ilg: *Your Four-Year-Old*, *Your Five-Year-Old*, or *Your Six-Year-Old*. Discuss the book and your reactions to it with other students in the class.

SCHOOL TO WORK

Safety on the Job Employers understand the short- and long-term benefits of providing a safe working environment. In return, they expect employees to be equally aware of safety issues. Accidents on the job are often caused by error in judgement, fatigue, lack of skills, an unsafe attitude, and lack of knowledge. Also, employees expose themselves and other to an unsafe environment when they use alcohol or other drugs. What do you know about acting safely that will help you on the job?

PERFORMANCE ASSESSMENT

Emotional and Social Development from Four to Six

Task
Create an activity that will help children recognize their emotions and deal appropriately with emotions such as anger, jealousy, fear, or sadness.

Purpose
As children develop a wider range of emotions, they need direction in recognizing the kinds of emotions they have and how to cope with them. Your activity will help children develop healthy ways to deal with their emotions.

Procedure
1. Brainstorm a list of emotions to include in your activity.

2. Decide the best way to present your activity. Will you use hand puppets or paper plate faces in a skit or have the children play a game of charades about different feelings? What other ideas would accomplish your goal?
3. Determine how much time you need for the activity and how you would involve everyone in the audience.
4. As part of the activity, provide an opportunity for children to talk about the emotions of the puppets or other characters in your activity. Guide them in seeing how they can learn to control their reactions to situations that cause stress, anger, fear, and so on.

5. Present your activity to a group of four- to six-year-olds or to your class.

Portfolio Idea Ask a classmate to photograph or videotape your presentation to include in the portfolio. Write a summary of the activity, including why you chose this activity, what questions you asked yourself when preparing it, and what it taught you about child development. Include any feedback received from your audience, if applicable. Label all items carefully.

457

PERFORMANCE ASSESSMENT

Creative Activity
Encourage students to peruse your classroom resources for activity ideas, or begin a brainstorming session by offering some ideas that you have used. If students create props for children to use during the activity, remind them of relevant safety issues. As part of the activity, students could address environmental factors in your area, such as excessive noise, earthquakes, storms, hurricanes, tornadoes, and so on, that cause stress in children. Remind students that environmental stress might be responsible for some outbursts of negative emotions.

EVALUATE

Use the reproducible Chapter 15 Test in the TCR, or construct your own test using the Test-maker Software.

EXTENSION

Ask a preschool or kindergarten teacher to speak to students about the social characteristics of their students and how these change during preschool years. Allow questions.

Journal Writing

In their journals, have students write entries evaluating what they have learned about emotional development of preschoolers at various ages. In particular, have them relate emotional development at each age with social development and appropriate discipline for the age.

CLOSE

Rediscuss the statements in Introducing the Chapter. Have students review their predictions and verify or modify. Take a new count of students who believe the authors would agree or disagree with the statements. Have students explain their judgments.

SCHOOL TO WORK

Emphasizing Skills Make use of frequent opportunities to remind students that the skills they practice in the classroom have applications to their personal lives as well as future careers. Guide students to understand how and why these skills are important. For example, after a specific activity, have students brainstorm the connection between what they did and how they can use it in real life.

INTRODUCE

CHAPTER OVERVIEW

In Section 1 of Chapter 16, students study the characteristics of the preoperational stage, the relationship between intelligence and learning, intelligence testing, how to encourage learning in preschoolers, and how preschoolers learn to appreciate reading, art, and music.

In Section 2, they learn how schools meet individual learning needs and examine the needs of gifted and talented preschoolers, as well as those with learning disabilities or speech problems.

CHAPTER OBJECTIVES

After completing Chapter 16, students will be able to:

- Describe the characteristics of intellectual development of children aged four to six.
- Explain what IQ tests are and discuss their advantages and disadvantages.
- Give examples of ways children can learn from everyday experiences.
- Explain how parents and caregivers can encourage children's interest in reading, art, and music.
- Identify the effects of learning disabilities and giftedness on school experiences.
- Describe the speech development of children in this age range and identify possible speech problems.

CLASSROOM MANAGEMENT

Resources Beyond the Classroom

As children grow older, they become less self-centered and more interested in the world around them. To help promote or initiate this interest, the U.S. Department of Education publishes a booklet entitled "Helping Your Children Learn From Geography." The publication is aimed at families with elementary school children and is full of fun and informal learning activities designed to stimulate and expand their knowledge of geography. To obtain a copy, have students send a request, along with their name, address, and 50 cents to:

U.S. Department of Education
Geography, Consumer Information Center
Pueblo, CO 81009

Intellectual Development from Four to Six

SECTION 1   Intelligence and Learning from Four to Six

SECTION 2   Schools Meeting Individual Needs

- Read each of the following statements to the class one at a time. Ask students to indicate whether they agree, disagree, or are not sure. Discuss each statement and have students speculate about whether they think child care professionals would agree or disagree.

  — Intelligence tests measure all aspects of intelligence.

  — The more intelligent the child, the more distinct the child's speech.

  — A child who has trouble learning to read is less intelligent than children who learn to read without difficulty.

  — Although gifted children are intelligent, they have special needs.

- Use the photo on the opposite page and the three features on this page—Think About, Ask Yourself, and Now Try This—to begin a discussion about a child's intellectual development from ages four to six.

THINK ABOUT

Was there a time in your life when you enjoyed creating artworks? Perhaps you liked to paint, draw, or make crafts, or maybe you enjoyed other forms of artistic expression such as music and dance. Think about how old you were. What were your favorite activities? Did you share you interest with another person? If so, who? How are your current interests and talents an extension of those early artistic interests?

ASK YOURSELF

Study the photo on the opposite page. Describe what the child is doing. If you asked her to describe her artwork, what do you think she would say? If you were her caregiver, how would you encourage her creativity? What can she learn by painting? How does this activity encourage her intellectual development?

NOW TRY THIS

With a partner, brainstorm a list of themes, such as family, friends, and nature, that would appeal to children ages four to six. Together, identify one creative game or activity for each theme on your list. Then explain how each game or activity stimulates a child's intellectual development.

459

Childhood Reflections

"All of these concepts seemed easy for her to grasp, which surprised me. Where had I been when she was tooling up her brain?"

Phyllis Theroux

HEALTHY FAMILIES/HEALTHY CHILDREN

Strengthening Families

Often we hear the statement "families that play together stay together." Families who work together, however, also build helpful and responsible attitudes. Four-, five-, and six-year-olds can accomplish a great deal in the home and feel a sense of satisfaction, confidence, and importance.

A few examples of household chores that build responsibility and self-esteem include setting the table, putting away groceries, feeding the pet, dusting the furniture, making sandwiches, folding clothes. Have students list other ways to include young children in family household tasks.

SECTION I RESOURCES

Teacher's Classroom Resources

- Enrichment 38
- Reteaching 38
- Section 1 Quiz

Student Workbook

- Deciphering Development
- Understanding Intellectual Development

SECTION OVERVIEW

As they study Section 1, students examine the relationship between intelligence and learning, beginning with the characteristics of the preoperational stage. Next, they study how intelligence is measured, formally and informally, and how it may be misjudged. In addition to school experience, preschoolers continue to learn from everyday experience, and students study ways caregivers can take advantage of the learning opportunities life affords. Finally, students learn to foster appreciation of reading, art, and music in children from ages four through six.

MOTIVATOR

Ask students to recall how they learned to count and recognize colors or letters. Center discussion on out-of-school experiences that allowed learning or application of these concepts. Explain that caregivers have abundant opportunity to help children apply these concepts in everyday life experiences.

USING TERMS TO LEARN

Pronounce the terms under "Terms to Learn." Ask students whether they are familiar with any of these. Explain that these terms will be defined in the chapter.

TERMS TO LEARN

dramatic play
finger plays
intelligence quotient (IQ)

SECTION 1 Intelligence and Learning from Four to Six

- Describe the characteristics of intellectual development in children aged four to six.
- Explain what IQ tests are, and discuss their advantages and disadvantages.
- Give examples of ways children can learn from everyday experiences.
- Explain how parents and caregivers can encourage children's interest in reading, art, and music.

You may recall that Jean Piaget identified the time between ages two and seven as the preoperational period. Four-, five-, and six-year-olds show by their thinking and actions that they are still in this period.

Preoperational Thinking

These are some signs of preoperational thinking observable in children aged four to six:

- **Use of symbols.** Children learn that objects and words can be symbols—that is, they can represent something else. For example, a child hands the teacher an empty cup and instructs, "Drink the hot cocoa. It has marshmallows in it."

- **Make-believe play.** Children continue to learn through fantasy and through creative play. They also learn through **dramatic play**, *imitating real-life situations, such as playing house or playing school.* One four-year-old, for example, builds a coffin in the block area, and he and his friends act out a funeral; the boy's grandfather has recently died.

- **Egocentric viewpoint.** At four, five, and six, children continue to view the world in terms of themselves. Their words and actions show this self-centeredness. For example, when the mother of a five-year-old arrives at the hospital for

SEE HOW THEY GROW

Dramatic Play

From the ages of four to six, children most enjoy dramatic play. It benefits them in the following ways: (1) It provides an outlet for children's inner thoughts and feelings. (2) It helps them solve personal problems. For example, a child who feels left out in other activities may take a leadership role here and make contact with other children.

(3) It teaches children about roles in society. A child can pretend to be a doctor, a teacher, a fire fighter, and so forth. (4) It helps children expand their minds by requiring them to use their imaginations. (5) It provides practice for language skills as children use new words and express ideas. (6) It helps children learn and practice society's rules of courtesy, taking turns, sharing, and cooperating.

surgery, she finds her daughter's "second favorite" blanket stuffed in her suitcase. The child knows that anyone who has to go away from home—especially to the hospital—needs a blanket.

• **Limited focus.** In the preoperational period, children find it difficult to focus on more than one characteristic at a time. For example, you might place 10 tennis balls—3 white and 7 yellow—in front of a four-year-old. If you ask the child whether there are more yellow balls or more tennis balls, he or she will usually say more yellow balls. The child can't focus on both the color and the type of ball at once. An older child, no longer in the preoperational period, would immediately know that all the balls are tennis balls and only some of them are yellow.

Piaget helped adults realize that children this age do not think like adults and should not be treated like adults. They are prelogical in their thinking, and they need to be respected for who and what they are. Between their fourth and seventh birthdays, children make significant gains in their thinking skills; around the age of seven, they enter into the stage Piaget identified as the operational period.

Fantasy play is a way for children to learn. How does the use of these uniforms show symbolic thinking?

BUILDING SELF-ESTEEM

Promoting Pretend Play

Many aspects of children's play involves pretending. Too often, however, people dismiss make-believe play as "a waste of time" or "just pretending—not really doing anything." However, pretend play is an opportunity for young children to control their environment, to examine their own feelings and ideas, and to develop their thinking skills.

Parents and other caregivers can encourage children by allowing them time and freedom to enjoy make-believe play, and by permitting them to use safe household items as props for their games. See Positive Parenting Skills on page 478-479 for other tips on encouraging make-believe play.

TEACH
Pages 460-469

• **Preoperational Thinking**
• **Measuring Intelligence**
• **Everyday Learning Opportunities**
• **Appreciating Reading, Art, and Music**

GUIDED PRACTICE

Using the Photograph
Refer students to the photo on page 461. How do children learn from imaginative play? How can relating the symbols in this photograph—the uniforms—to the professionals develop abilities they will later need in reading and writing?

Critical Thinking
For exploration of learning in the preoperational stage, have students consider these questions:

• Why do children especially enjoy caregivers who will play creatively with them? Should a caregiver's participation in creative play be limited? (Yes, because the child's creativity may be stifled.)

• How do children show their egocentric viewpoint in learning? Give some examples.

Cooperative Learning
Have students work in groups to collect pictures and create posters that illustrate each of the signs of preoperational thinking.

BUILDING SELF-ESTEEM

After students have read "Promoting Pretend Play," open a discussion about the merits of pretend play. Ask them to suggest how an older child, or an adult, might benefit from imaginative play. Also, when buying toys for children, how can students be sure that a child's creative facilities will be stimulated?

COOPERATIVE LEARNING

Promoting Teamwork
It is vital that students in cooperative learning groups of any size share a sense of community. You can help foster this attitude by availing yourself of the following suggestions:

• Use rugs and other classroom fixtures to partition shared spaces.

• Equip groups with the tools necessary to the execution of a given task (e.g., folders, assignment sheets, and progress report forms).

• Provide adequate work space for each group, making allowances for storage space for project-specific materials (e.g., project folders, notebooks, and borrowed library resources).

GUIDED PRACTICE (continued)

Critical Thinking

To help students consider how intelligence is perceived by adults, ask the following questions:

- How do adults judge a child's intelligence?
- Are children treated the same way regardless of perceived intelligence?
- How are children affected by being treated as though they were or were not intelligent?

Promoting Discussion

Have students list and discuss appearance and behavior factors that adults use to label children as "intelligent" or "not intelligent." Do students believe teens are also perceived as intelligent or unintelligent because of appearance? With this perspective as a basis, have students discuss the reason intelligence tests were designed and are administered in schools.

Making Connections: Language Arts

Have students investigate current trends in school use of intelligence testing, both generally and in your district. What tests are used? When are the tests given? How are IQ tests administered to preschool children? How are the test results used? Have them write a brief report of their findings.

Making Connections: Math

Provide students with several raw scores on a group intelligence test. Have them use the table and practice converting raw scores to mental ages and mental ages to IQ. Emphasize that an IQ refers, not to an individual's intelligence, but to the score on an intelligence test.

Measuring Intelligence

When they label children as "intelligent" or "unintelligent," adults are often influenced by observations that have nothing to do with intelligence. Maria is considered bright. She has a dimpled smile, dark curls, and appealing manners; she seems to make a favorable impression on everyone. Zach is considered slow. He is large for his age and is often compared with children several years older. He is actually of average intelligence. Traci is so shy that few people see her true ability. It is difficult to separate a child's intellectual ability from such characteristics as curls, size, and shyness.

Educators use formal intelligence tests to more accurately determine the intellectual abilities of children. The test results can help teachers, principals, and learning specialists understand and meet students' educational needs.

The first intelligence test was developed by a French psychologist, Alfred Binet, in 1905. In 1916, Lewis M. Terman of Stanford University made a major revision of the Binet test. Today the test is commonly called the Stanford-Binet, and it is widely used to test children from ages two to sixteen.

Terman devised a way to give a person's intelligence a numerical score. He did this by having many children take the test. Eventually, he was able to determine how well the average

Before entering kindergarten most children are screened by a teacher to determine their developmental stage. A child who has been led by an older sibling may score high on those screenings.

SEE HOW THEY GROW

Intellectual Development

Intellectual development is not permanently established by the time children reach early childhood. Neither are their IQ scores. A child who has been deprived of stimulation may or may not fully develop intellectually. Some children who start slowly improve their performance later, and some bright preschoolers lose their early advantage during childhood. Intelligence requires continuing nurturing, not simply a dose of stimulation or encouragement here and there.

child of a particular age would do. Then he created a simple mathematical formula to calculate a number representing a child's intelligence. This **intelligence quotient**, or **IQ**, is *a numerical standard that tells whether a person's intelligence is average or above or below average for his or her age.* With this method, the average child of any age has an IQ between 90 and 110.

Intelligence tests are composed of tasks and questions. These correspond to the expected abilities of various age levels. Two-year-olds, for example, cannot read. An IQ test for them might include building a tower of blocks, identifying parts of the body, and fitting simple geometric shapes into corresponding holes.

Disadvantages of IQ Tests

Many types of intelligence tests are used today. However, no one test gives an absolutely accurate estimate of an individual's mental ability. Many things can influence test results. A child's physical or emotional state during the test, limited experiences, or unfamiliarity with the language can all affect the child's score.

Most tests depend a great deal on language ability and the experiences of a particular culture. This may penalize those who speak another language at home or have different cultural traditions.

Another problem with IQ tests is that they do not tell much about specific abilities. Two people with the same IQ may have very different strengths and weaknesses. One person may be unusually good at science and math but poor in language skills. Another may have the opposite strengths and weaknesses.

In addition, IQ test results are not always consistent. The same test administered to the same child at two separate times sometimes show a wide difference in scores.

Unfortunately, some parents and children become too concerned about IQ test scores. The Rockefeller Foundation report on quality in education made a good point: "Tests are effective on a limited front. We cannot measure the rarer qualities of character that are a necessary ingredient of great performance. We cannot measure aspiration, purpose, courage, vitality, determination." Neither do tests measure such positive qualities as originality, creativity, self-confidence, and independence.

More commonly used in preschools and kindergartens today are screening instruments that provide an overview of a child's level of development in all areas, not just thinking skills. If the child falls outside the norms of development for a child of his or her age, then an in-depth assessment of skills can be done. These evaluations help identify problem areas and guide parents, caregivers, and teachers in planning appropriate activities to encourage the child's development.

MORE ABOUT

IQ Tests
One problem with IQ tests is that individual test scores vary over time, especially at young ages. Scores of tests given at age two simply do not predict test scores at age fourteen or eighteen. In fact, test scores at age two are not very good predictors of test scores at age five. At later ages, there is more predictability. Test scores at age fourteen are somewhat accurate predictors of scores at age eighteen. Some experts believe that the variation in individual scores occurs partly because the tests given at various ages have different characteristics. Some also believe that intelligence may change with age.

GUIDED PRACTICE (continued)

Critical Thinking
To help students consider the value of intelligence testing, ask the following questions:
- Intelligence tests are used to determine children's intellectual abilities as well as their educational needs. Which use of such tests is more important? Explain.
- Do you agree or disagree with the following statement? Support your position with information from the text. "All children entering school should take an intelligence test." (Answers will vary. Students agreeing may point out that tests are more precise and objective measures than are other means of evaluating intelligence. The students opposed may cite limitations described in this section and the danger of relying too heavily on such tests in assessing a child's potential.)
- Rubiella is a six-year-old who is learning English as a second language. What might happen when Rubiella takes an IQ test? (She will make mistakes because of failure to understand the questions or directions.) What does the term *culture-free* mean? (Giving no advantage to students with a special language or cultural background.) How does the term relate to intelligence tests? (Some tests are designed to depend less on language and background experience.)

Using the Photograph
Refer students to the photo on page 462. Ask them why students who have been led by older siblings might score higher on such tests.

Practicing Decision Making
Have students take a sample IQ test. Discuss how taking the test made them feel. Can the test measure intelligence accurately? What questions might be a problem for someone from another country? Why? Have each student decide individually if they would use this test at all in an educational setting and explain their answer in writing.

GUIDED PRACTICE (continued)

Critical Thinking

Read the following to students: When Reiko was only three years old, she was placed in an institution for the severely mentally handicapped. Reiko could not speak and had very little control of her muscles. It was not until Reiko was a young woman that a caring worker found a way to communicate with her, only to discover that for many years, a mind with normal intelligence had been trapped inside Reiko's body. Ask students why they think Reiko was institutionalized. How would Reiko have felt over the years? Do students think something like this could happen today? How does this story dramatically illustrate the point made in the text about judging intelligence? (This story, which is based on a similar true one, shows that intelligence cannot be determined by external factors alone.)

Using the Photograph

Refer students to the photo on page 465. Ask them why first-hand experiences are better than reading books or watching television programs.

Promoting Discussion

Have students recall their earliest use of number concepts. Ask them whether the applications were in school or out of school. Encourage them to discuss early recognition of words such as their names, brand names, and names of stores. What helped them learn to recognize these words?

Did You Know?

Research from the University of California at Irvine shows that children who watch two hours of television daily are twice as likely to have high cholesterol as children who watch less. Four hours of daily viewing quadruples the risk.

BUILDING SELF-ESTEEM

Questioning Techniques

Asking questions can be a good way to start conversations with children. Although too many questions discourage most children, parents and other caregivers can use questions to help children think about what they are seeing and to begin talking about their thoughts and feelings.

To encourage thinking and talking, questions should ask for more than "yes" or "no" as a response. Questions beginning with "what," "who," "when," and "how" are especially effective. Questions such as "Where does the rain come from?" and "Why did the rock fall faster than the feather?" encourage learning.

Everyday Learning Opportunities

A four-, five-, or six-year-old learns from a wide variety of experiences. However, these experiences provide more learning if a parent or other important caregiver shares them with the child. You can try techniques like those suggested here whenever you are with children.

Look for opportunities to talk with children about what they are doing. A few positive comments, such as "Wow, the building you are making is so tall—and it has so many windows!" can encourage interest. Questions help children think in new ways about what is happening and encourage them to organize their thoughts into answers.

Explanations and suggestions can also be helpful. You might explain in simple terms why water turns to ice. If a child is trying to lift a heavy box full of toys, you could suggest that pushing the box might be easier.

Asking a child's advice is another effective technique for promoting learning. For example, you might ask how the carrot sticks and radishes should be arranged on the serving plate. Following through on such advice helps the child understand that his or her opinions are valued; it improves the child's self-esteem.

Everyday learning can take place in such simple things as playing a game with parents, friends, or family members.

OBSERVING AND PARTICIPATING

Learning Through Participation

Children are born scientists. It seems to come naturally to children to ask "why?" and "how come?" and "what if?" Libraries have books that describe simple experiments using food, water, and other readily available materials. These resources help caregivers provide experiences that satisfy children's scientific curiosity.

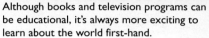
Although books and television programs can be educational, it's always more exciting to learn about the world first-hand.

Recreational activities are important to learning. On short car trips, the child can follow the progress on a clearly marked map. A ride on a bus, or plane can be an exciting adventure; encourage the child to discuss what he or she sees and to ask questions suggested by the trip. Nature walks are fun—and free. Everyone in the family can learn by looking closely at leaves, flowers, and birds.

Children need to be included in household tasks such as shopping, cooking, and keeping the home clean. There is much that children can learn from helping with these routine activities. In addition, sharing these tasks strengthens the bonds between family members, and children develop responsibility, maturity, and independence.

Parents and other caregivers should also take time to help children learn and explore. Even preschoolers can participate in experiments. Finding out what objects magnets attract, determining what floats, and learning why a candle goes out when covered with a jar are just a few possibilities. Other activities can encourage creativity and curiosity. The sound of a watch ticking is magnified when you listen through an empty paper towel tube. Oil floats on top of water, but food coloring mixes with it. Learning should be an everyday, family-centered event.

Children of this age are curious to learn more about their own bodies and about where babies come from. Answer their questions in simple terms they can understand, and help them learn the correct names for body parts. Encourage children to have positive attitudes by answering their questions in an unembarrassed, natural way.

GUIDED PRACTICE (continued)

Critical Thinking
Have students give examples of how helping with the following activities could help students learn or reinforce such concepts as colors, shapes, counting, letters, or written words: shopping, cooking, setting the table. (Shopping: Children can help look for brand names they recognize, the cereal that begins with M, the soup in the red and white can, a square cake. They can read posted numbers, count small amounts of change, or put three apples in the bag.)

Cooperative Learning
Have students work in pairs. Give each pair an index card with the name of a place in your community. Have students find out what opportunities for learning this place can provide for children. You may want to have students assemble the information in booklet form for distribution to the families of young children.

Making Connections: Language Arts
Have students write an answer to a question from a four-year-old about where babies come from. Suggest that they provide only the information necessary to answer the question the child asked and that they use correct terms for body parts.

Critical Thinking
Ask students how children are affected if they are not exposed to reading, art, and music experiences as they grow older. Ask students how a love of reading can boost a child's intelligence. (Books help children learn about and understand the world and the people in it.)

TEEN PARENTING

Time Management
If you have teen parents in your class, ask them to describe how parenting has affected their time. Is it difficult to find time to get everything done? Do they include time in their day for special activities with their children? How can they take every-day activities, such as shopping, cooking, and cleaning, and turn them into learning opportunities for children? Help your students see how time management techniques, such as goal setting, making lists, establishing priorities, using a calendar, and scheduling, can be helpful to them.

GUIDED PRACTICE (continued)

ASK THE EXPERTS

Issues and Advice

1. According to Dr. Espinosa, how do children learn best? (*By experiencing their world.*)

2. At what age are flash cards appropriate for learning? (*After the age of five.*)

3. What concepts are learned through interactions with people and real objects? (*Numbers, series, and categories.*)

4. What are the benefits of computer programs designed for children? (*Possibilities include: they provide immediate feedback, high visual interest, and allow the child to control images on the screen.*)

5. Dr. Espinosa believes that children should be encouraged to learn in what ways? (*Through direct and appropriate ways.*)

Thinking Like an Expert

Have students read the opening question and predict what Ms. Espinosa will advise. Have students read "Flash Cards and Computers" to find out what learning experiences the expert considers valuable, and what place, if any, flash cards and computer learning have in the classroom.

After finishing the feature, ask: What would Dr. Espinosa recommend as an alternative to flash cards or computers for teaching numerals? (*Matching a numeral to a number of objects or simply counting them; or providing a meaningful experience where knowing a number is necessary.*) How does she qualify this recommendation? (*Computers, at most, should have limited use, leaving most instructional time for direct experience.*)

Ask if students support or challenge Dr. Espinosa's advice. Why?

ASK THE EXPERTS

Flash Cards and Computers

Q. When would you recommend introducing flash cards and computers to children?

A. Before you rush them into specific kinds of "learning activities," you should think a bit more about how children learn.

Young children learn by experiencing their world. Every day, in apparently simple activities, children learn about themselves, about other people, about other living things, and about objects.

In my opinion, flash cards are never appropriate for children under the age of five. Young children need interaction with real objects and people. Through these interactions, children can begin to understand concepts, particularly those relating to numbers, series, and categories. Young children need repeated experiences with a variety of objects to begin to internalize such concepts. Flash cards simply cannot provide those kinds of experiences.

A more challenging question is raised regarding the possibilities for learning with new types of interactive computer programs. Many "educational" programs are just a waste of the child's valuable time. For instance, why should a child repeatedly count red dots on a computer screen? The child could learn much more by playing with cubes or small blocks or beads, making counting a natural part of the play.

On the other hand, certain computer programs now allow children to control the images on the screen, to create novel series of events, or to receive immediate feedback to their responses. In these cases, the high visual interest and special quality of a computer-based learning experience may provide some children with an enhanced learning opportunity. Even though these programs may have some usefulness, I feel strongly that they should be given limited use, so that young children are encouraged to learn in the most direct and appropriate ways possible.

Linda Espinosa

Linda Espinosa
Director of Primary Education for the Redwood City School District in California

OBSERVING AND PARTICIPATING

Learning Through Participation

There are plenty of everyday learning opportunities that students can do with children. Suggest the following:

• Have children help make peanut butter by grinding nuts in a blender.

• Have children make placemats for a meal out of paper bags or cardboard and fold napkins in a rectangle or triangle.

• Allow children to tell a story about a jelly bean.

• Have children string cereal or macaroni noodles.

• Have children help cut up fruit and make their own fruit kebabs for lunch.

• Take a tape recorder on a walk with children and record the sounds.

• Make a sand castle in the sandbox.

Appreciating Reading, Art, and Music

Whether or not children enjoy reading, art, and music depends largely on the attitudes of their parents, caregivers, and other important family members. For many people, these are hobbies that provide pleasure throughout their lives. This early school stage is a period in which many children develop an interest in one or more of these areas.

Reading

Young children love books and stories. If this interest is encouraged and adults take time to read to them, children are likely to enjoy reading as they grow older. Developing an interest in reading is important. Books provide an opportunity to learn about and understand the world and the people in it. Children who enjoy reading will find learning easier—and more fun.

Four- to six-year-olds like stories about events that are different from their own experiences. City children can learn about farm life from books. Children who live far from a large city can "experience" buses, apartments, skyscrapers, and other aspects of city life through books.

Children this age also appreciate humor and unusual situations. They giggle over the picture of a horse in the bathtub or a dog wearing a hat. This shows that children are beginning to be able to separate reality from fantasy.

A public library or school library can be a good source of books for children. Most communities have free public libraries that lend children's books. Many of these libraries also offer story hours for young children. Some schools and preschools have books that children and their families may borrow for limited periods of time.

When you are choosing books for children, these questions can help you make appropriate choices:

- Are the pictures colorful, interesting, and easy to understand?
- Will the story appeal to the child's interests?
- Are the situations and settings familiar to the child?
- Does the story include action that will hold the child's interest?
- Will the child understand most of the words?
- Does the book use descriptive language that brings the story alive?
- Is the story short enough to read in one sitting?
- If you are considering buying the book, is it well constructed to stand up under hard use?

THE VALUE OF FAMILY TRADITIONS

Family traditions add order and stability to our lives. Also, they lay a foundation for lifetime spiritual and emotional development. For example, a Jewish parent will encourage a child to study the Old Testament from an early age. A small drop of honey is placed on the page of a Bible, and the child is encourage to pass a finger over the page and lick the honey from the finger. It is believed that this association of honey and sweetness will cause the child to have a sweet experience while studying the Bible. The practice is repeated until the child begins formal Bible study at a later time.

GUIDED PRACTICE (continued)

Practicing Decision Making
Have students read and write a review of a children's book. Ask students to use the checklist on page 467 to evaluate the suitability of the book for a four- to six-year-old.

Promoting Discussion
Ask students what art materials would be appropriate for use by four- to six-year-olds. Have students list throwaway items children could use for projects.

Making Connections: Art
Collect a bag of items from around the house and yard, such as egg cartons, fabric, magazines, yarn, string, cans, pine cones, small stones, pods, etc. Pair students and have each pair draw one item from the bag. Have students plan an art project a four- to six-year-old could make with the item and explain their ideas.

Critical Thinking
Ask students whether or not they think it is important to expose children to all kinds of music. Why or why not?

Making Connections:
Social Studies
Have students research and report on musical instruments children use in other countries.

Making Connections: Music
Have students listen to popular children's music. Discuss what children can learn from it.

Not all family traditions have a religious context. For example, in one family, breakfast is served in bed to each member on his or her birthday. Regardless of other commitments, everyone gets up early enough to treat the celebrant. Another family may go to the ice cream parlor when someone achieves a goal. A tradition guarantees memories and promotes family unity.

SEE HOW THEY GROW

Nurturing Artistic Talent

Caregivers can nurture children's artistic talent in many ways: (1) Point out objects of interest—the big tree, the fuzzy slippers, the black kitten. Use visual—the *tiny* bug, the *hairy* dog. (2) Ask questions: How many blue things do you see in the room? What is the biggest thing you see? The smallest? (3) Show children a group of objects, have them close their eyes and list all the objects they saw. (4) Ask children to point out similarities and differences in objects. (5) Visit galleries and museums. Talk to the children about what they see in each picture or statue. (6) Discuss pictures as you go through art books. (7) Provide art materials and a place for children to work. (8) Display the children's art at home.

INDEPENDENT PRACTICE

Student Workbook

Have students complete "Deciphering Development" and "Understanding Intellectual Development," in the Student Workbook.

Student Demonstration

Have students select a children's story, practice reading or telling the story, and then share it with the class as though their classmates were between the ages of four and six. If possible, have them share it later with a four- to six-year-old child and describe the results to the class.

Extension

Children's literature as such did not exist until recently. In the classic fairy tales, such as those collected by Grimm and Andersen, issues were addressed to adults and children alike. The tales contain many elements that are questionable in stories for young children. Have students examine traditional fairy tales such as "Hansel and Gretel," "Snow White," and "Cinderella." Tell them to consider such elements as beautiful princesses who are prized for their beauty despite appalling character traits, stepparents who plot murder, children abandoned by their parents, witches who eat children, torture and other gruesome punishments for villains, and a girl of seven taking refuge with seven male strangers. Have them write their opinions of such tales. Are they appropriate for young children? If so, what type of discussion should accompany them? Also consider positive elements such as tales in which the small, the young and the weak can vanquish a monstrous or powerful villain that give children hope.

Journal Writing

Have students write journal entries on what they have learned about intellectual development in preschoolers. Include these questions: How is intelligence judged by a casual observer? How should intelligence tests be used and not be used? How can caregivers take advantage of the learning opportunities everyday life affords?

Children love to express their artistic talents on paper—as well as on their fingers, arms, and smocks!

SAFETY TIP

All the materials children use in their art projects should be carefully checked for safety features. For example, paints, pastes, and other supplies must be nontoxic. Sharp objects, including sharply pointed scissors, should not be made available. Also remember that even carefully chosen materials are not safe unless the children know how to use them safely.

Art

Art helps children express their feelings, learn to control their body, and show their creativity. Four- to six-year-olds should have access to a variety of art materials, such as play dough, crayons, paper, paste, paint, and scissors.

Children should be encouraged to experiment with art materials. Don't offer corrections, ridicule, or "lessons." Children need to enjoy the process of creating art; they should not worry about the production.

Instead of guessing what a child's picture represents, ask the child to tell you about it. Then do your best to praise the child's actions rather than the artwork he or she has produced. For example, you might say, "I really like the bright colors you used for the flowers," instead of "That's a good picture."

Music

A baby beats a rhythm with a spoon, enjoying the sound. A boy holds a stick against a fence as he walks, listening to the rhythm. A girl listens to the beat of her footsteps as she runs. All children imitate the sounds they hear around them. They respond naturally to rhythmical sound, which is a part of music.

Singing and rhythm games are fun, especially for four- to six-year-olds. Many children are introduced to singing by **finger plays**, *songs or chants with accompanying hand motions*. Young children usually enjoy singing, especially simple, repetitive songs.

SEE HOW THEY GROW

Something to Sing About

Singing with an adult can help children gain skill in carrying a tune. Children's voices are usually low-pitched, so they often are unable to sing high-pitched songs well. When children sing on their own, they are apt to sing songs in a minor key, although most songs for children are written in major keys.

The opportunity to play simple instruments helps develop children's interest in rhythm. Children enjoy using bells, drums, tambourines, or almost anything that makes a noise. Kitchen pans and mixing spoons provide good substitutes for purchased instruments.

Early, positive experiences with music can lead to a lifetime of enjoyment. Children should have opportunities for creative experiments with sound and rhythm.

SECTION 1 REVIEW

CHECK YOUR UNDERSTANDING

1. List at least three important signs of preoperational thinking.

2. What does an IQ score of 100 tell you about a child? List at least three things the score does not tell you about the child.

3. Why should parents make an effort to spend quality time with their children every day?

4. List at least three questions that will help you select an appropriate book for a child.

5. How should parents and other caregivers respond to a child's artwork?

6. What are finger plays?

DISCUSS AND DISCOVER

1. Early childhood professionals urge that all standardized testing of young children be stopped. Why do you think they are interested in preventing such testing? Do you agree with this position? Why or why not?

Observing & Participating

Observe a small group of four- or five-year-olds in the dramatic play area of a preschool or classroom. Observe how the children begin dramatic play. How do they decide which role each child will have? What do they say to each other? What materials do they use? How long do they sustain their interest in dramatic play?

SECTION 1 REVIEW

1. Any three: use of symbols, make-believe play, egocentric viewpoint, limited focus.

2. That the child has an average intelligence. Any three: aspiration, purpose, courage, vitality, determination, originality, creativity, self-confidence, independence, etc.

3. Children learn from a wide variety of experiences. If a parent or caregiver shares them with the child, more learning takes place.

4. Possible questions: Are the pictures colorful, interesting, and easy to understand? Will the story appeal to the child's interests? Are the situations and settings familiar to the child? (Other questions are also acceptable.)

5. Ask child to tell about artwork; praise child's action rather than the artwork produced.

6. Songs or chants with accompanying hand motions.

ASSESS

CHECKING COMPREHENSION

Assign students to write their responses to the Check Your Understanding questions in the Section 1 Review. Answers to the questions are given at the bottom of this page.

EVALUATE

Have students complete the Chapter 16, Section 1 quiz in the TCR.

Reteach

1. Assign Reteaching 38 in the TCR. Have students complete the activity and discuss their responses.

2. Have students make a chart outlining the advantages and disadvantages of IQ tests.

Enrichment

1. Assign Enrichment 38 in the TCR.

2. Have students make simple rhythm instruments, using inexpensive or throwaway materials. Donate them to a child care program.

Extension

Have students interview a music or kindergarten teacher for music ideas. You may wish to invite such a guest to your class. Tell students to make a list of music activities appropriate for four- to six-year-olds. Next to each activity, they should explain what children can learn from each type of activity.

CLOSE

Have students brainstorm endings for these sentences:

Intelligence testing can …

A preschooler learns best by …

Encourage responses that include both generalities and specifics.

SECTION 2 RESOURCES

Teacher's Classroom Resources
- Enrichment 39
- Reteaching 39
- Section 2 Quiz

Student Workbook
- Learning Disability Simulation

SECTION OVERVIEW

As they complete Section 2, students learn how schools meet the individual learning needs of children from age four through age six. The section opens with a discussion of the school experience and how to prepare the child. Next, students examine the needs of preschoolers with learning disabilities and learn that gifted and talented students also have special needs. Finally, they study the needs of children with language or speech problems.

MOTIVATOR

Encourage students to discuss their memories of the transition from home to a formal learning setting in preschool and school. Have them discuss their reactions to sitting still, listening to the teacher, learning from books, and completing assignments. Point out that the shift from an unstructured to a structured situation, and from a family group to a large group of peers, requires major adjustment on the part of the child. The adjustment is more challenging because a class includes children with differing abilities and needs, and children become aware of how much they differ from other children. Tell students that they will learn how parents can help children make the transition to school and adjust to differences. The section will also identify how schools and caregivers can meet special needs.

SECTION 2

Schools Meeting Individual Needs

TERMS TO LEARN

attention deficit
  hyperactivity disorder
  (ADHD)
dyslexia
gifted children
learning disability
vocabulary

OBJECTIVES

- Explain what learning disabilities are.
- Discuss the effects of learning disabilities and giftedness on school experiences.
- Describe the speech development of children aged four to six, and identify possible speech problems.

Although a child learns from the moment of birth, many people associate learning with school. Most children begin school sometime between the ages of four and six. Some have their first school experience when they go to a child care program or to a preschool program. Others start by attending kindergarten.

The School Experience

Since children will attend school for many years, it is vital that they develop a good attitude at the outset. Children who have a bad experience with classmates or a teacher can develop negative feelings about school. These bad feelings keep them from learning as well as they might.

There are several things parents can do to help make sure a child adjusts well to kindergarten.

- Make sure the child has had complete medical and dental examinations. Vision and hearing tests are especially important since problems with sight or hearing can severely handicap a child's learning.
- Be sure that the child has appropriate self-help skills. He or she should be able to put on and fasten outer garments and shoes. Of course, independence in such tasks as blowing the nose and taking care of toileting needs is essential.
- Be sure the child knows his or her full name, address, and telephone number.

HEALTHY FAMILIES/HEALTHY CHILDREN

Maintaining Health Records

Keeping accurate, up-to-date records of children immunizations and medical treatment is valuable to parents and other caregivers as children enter child care centers and schools. Since most institutions require proof of immunization, a medical history for each child provides instant access to needed dates and relevant information. Most doctors or health clinics provide a form that can be updated at each visit, and are far more convenient to locate than calling a doctor's office or health clinic for information. Families who move, thereby changing the source of medical care, can take the form as reference for the new health caregiver.

How well children do in school depends partly on how well prepared they are for the experience.

- Help the child feel confident about his or her ability to follow simple directions.
- Prepare the child by explaining, as fully as possible, what he or she can expect at school. If possible, visit the school together before the child's first day, or take the child to the school's open house day for new students.

Although most children learn well in school, some have special educational needs. Two common causes of special needs—learning disabilities and unusually high intelligence—are discussed here. Chapter 18 presents information about children with physical, mental, and emotional disabilities.

Learning Disabilities

Not all children learn easily. For some, learning is made more difficult by a **learning disability**, *a disorder in psychological processes that prevents a person from using information received through the senses in a normal way for learning.* The New York Institute of Child Development defines a learning disability as a complicated disorder that generally falls into one or more of these four areas of difficulty:

1. How a child receives information from his or her senses.
2. How the brain puts such information together.
3. How the information is stored in the brain as memory.
4. How the information is expressed as written or spoken language.

MORE ABOUT

Learning Disabilities

Since 1986, a federal law has encouraged states to identify children under age three who may have delayed development. Early Childhood Intervention (ECI) programs can prevent years of frustration and failure for children who might not be diagnosed until much later, if at all.

Parents should be alert to developmental delays that could point to a problem. Language, coordination, and attention span can give clues. Speech should be understandable at least half the time by age three. The chart on page 327 shows what levels of coordination an average toddler usually displays. By age three or four, a child should be able to sit and listen to a story. Problems do not necessarily mean a learning disorder, but a concerned parent should consult a physician. If a learning disability is diagnosed, early help can make a big difference.

USING TERMS TO LEARN

Discuss the meaning of the term *hyperactive*. "Hyper" is a prefix meaning "over, more than normal, or too much." Hyperactive, thus, means "overactive." List and define other words with the prefix "hyper."

Discuss the terms *learning disability* and *dyslexia*. Point out that learning disabilities are communication problems within the brain that prevent people from using information from the senses in a normal way for learning. Dyslexia is a learning disability that occurs when the brain registers letters backwards, upside down, or in reversed order. Note the unusual spelling of dyslexia.

TEACH

Pages 470-477

- The School Experience
- Learning Disabilities
- Gifted and Talented Children
- Speech Development

GUIDED PRACTICE

Promoting Discussion

Have students discuss what parents might explain to children to prepare them for school. In particular, how can they prepare children who have always been in the care of parents? Remind them that these children will need to adjust to being one of many children in the care of a teacher.

Critical Thinking

When teaching children their full names, addresses, and telephone numbers, what cautionary advice should parents give? (Do not give out the information unnecessarily or to anyone not connected with the school.)

Making Connections: Literature

Have students consult with a children's librarian and examine books for young children about the preschool, day care, or school experience. For example, *Jessie's Day Care*, by Amy Valens, illustrates the parallels between Jessie's day at day care and the parents' day at work.

Critical Thinking

To encourage critical examination of issues related to learning disabilities, have students consider the following questions:

- How might parents feel if they suspect or find out their child has a learning disability? What might happen if parents try to ignore their suspicions?

- Some children with learning disabilities are mainstreamed, which means that they go to a regular classroom and are pulled out regularly for special help. Others go to a totally separate program for learning disabled children. Can you identify pros and cons associated with each method. Should the degree of disability be a factor in selecting one program over another? Which would you prefer for your child?

- Read the following to students: In kindergarten, Ty's reading readiness skills were very low. In first grade, Ty made little progress. He often would not pay attention in class. After repeating first grade, Ty was moved on to second grade, where he still could not read and had trouble with math. Through testing in second grade, Ty was finally found to have a high IQ but also a learning disability. Why did Ty have difficulties in school? How might Ty have felt after three years of problems? How does this example support the idea of early intervention?

A severe physical handicap, such as blindness, is not a learning disability. Obviously, lack of sight makes learning more difficult, but blindness is a problem in receiving information through the sense, not a problem in using that information. A person with a learning disability typically can see the writing in a book. However, because of a malfunction in the brain, the person might see every sentence—or perhaps only certain letters—backwards. In this case, the problem is categorized as a learning disability because the brain is not functioning normally to use the information received from the eyes.

In the past, little was known about learning disabilities. Learning-disabled children were simply labeled "dumb" or "lazy," or became "troublemakers" in school. You can imagine the discouragement these children felt. They tried as hard as they could but were still unable to keep up with their classmates.

It is important to note that IQ is unrelated to learning disabilities. Some children with a very low IQ also have one or more learning disabilities. However, so do some children with average or above-average IQs.

There are many types of learning disabilities. Some school children can be diagnosed as having **attention deficit hyperactivity disorder**, or **ADHD**, *a condition involving the inability to control one's activity or to concentrate for a normal length of time*. These children are unusually active and may seem uncontrollable. Some error in their brain may keep them from focusing their attention and controlling their actions.

Other children cannot understand the spatial relationships between objects. They may not understand the difference between "under" and "over" or between "near" and "far," for example. Some children cannot understand what words mean, and others cannot form their own thoughts into speech or cannot write properly. If these and similar problems result from an error in brain processes, they are classified as learning disabilities.

Dyslexia is *a learning disability that prevents a person from handling language in a normal way*. Dyslexia usually causes problems with reading, writing, spelling, and math. Children with dyslexia are often intelligent, but their brains do not process certain kinds of information—especially visual information—normally. Researchers have found that children with dyslexia have difficulty processing series of instructions, such as "Add one to three and then divide by two." They typically have trouble sounding words out and often have a short attention span. Children with dyslexia need special help, particularly during the early school years.

Many of the causes of learning disabilities remain unknown, though research is revealing some answers. Many children with such problems are never identified or helped. Sometimes, too,

MORE ABOUT

Hyperactivity

Most children who are described as hyperactive are simply very active by nature. They are usually not in need of special attention, although they may cause problems for parents and teachers. Most of these children learn to function without difficulty in their daily lives. Only about 3 percent of school-aged children, primarily boys, can be regarded as clinically hyperactive.

the label "learning disabled" can be as harmful as the problem itself. Children who have been diagnosed with learning disabilities risk being treated as if they cannot learn. In fact, they can learn—but somewhat differently from most other children. They need special approaches tailored to their special needs. They also need encouragement and praise for their efforts, because they often have to work especially hard in school.

Gifted and Talented Children

It is estimated that 3 to 10 percent of the nation's students are **gifted children**, *children with an IQ of 130 or above*. Children may also be talented in an area that does not show up well on IQ tests. Ramon, for example, has exceptional musical ability. Jennifer, even as a preschooler, shows remarkable artistic talent. Neither has an IQ over 130; both are talented.

Educators once believed that gifted and talented children would thrive in any environment. It is now known that these children have special needs that must be met. Among these are the needs for recognition and acceptance and for challenging pursuits in which they can be successful. Gifted and talented children need to be free from feelings of inferiority, superiority, or "being different." They benefit from play with a variety of children, but they also need time with other gifted or talented learners.

Children with above-average ability—like all children—need challenging opportunities, but should not feel pressured.

Cultural Exchange

EDUCATION BEGINS WITH ATTITUDE

Research indicates that the cognitive (i.e., learning) abilities of American, Chinese, and Japanese children are similar, but large differences exist in the attitudes and beliefs toward their education. Chinese and Japanese children spend more time at school in academic activities. They also spend more time on homework than do most American children. Contrary to some opinions, the high demands placed on Chinese and Japanese children does not result in a dislike of school. Children in these countries appear happy, enthusiastic, and responsive. Possibly, the reason is that education is highly prized in China and Japan. Homework is assigned in each grade, and parents spend considerable time helping their children with their work. It appears, then, that parental and school attitudes contribute to the overall success of education in China and Japan.

GUIDED PRACTICE (continued)

Using the Photograph
Refer students to the photo on page 473. Why do gifted and talented children need to be challenged? Are they likely to feel pressure? If so, from whom—parents, teachers, or themselves? How can pressure be minimized?

Critical Thinking
To encourage critical examination of issues related to learning disabilities, have students consider the following questions:

• How might gifted children be affected by their desire to be like other children? (They may refuse to display and use their abilities.) How can special programs help them? (In such programs, they are with a peer group where being gifted is the norm.)

• Are most parents good judges of their own children's giftedness? Explain your answers.

Promoting Discussion
Ask students to offer ideas and suggestions for ways that a gifted child's education can be enriched. Why is it important to balance intellectual enrichment with physical, emotional, and social needs?

Cultural Exchange

After students have read "Education Begins with Attitude," ask them to define a positive attitude toward education. What should a parent or caregiver do to instill a sense of value for education and educators? How does our society promote or obstruct advances in education? What can each person do to improve their success in school?

TEEN PARENTING

Prematurity and Learning Disabilities
Point out to students that we do not always know what has caused a learning disability. Severe head injuries and infections such as meningitis may be involved, or the problem may be a genetic one.

Babies who are premature or of low birth weight are at risk for learning disabilities. This is of particular importance to teens, since prematurity and low birth weight are common in teen pregnancies.

GUIDED PRACTICE (continued)

Critical Thinking

To encourage critical examination of issues related to learning disabilities, have students consider the following questions:

• In the past, gifted children often skipped a grade. Why do you think this is less common today?

• Depending on the school district, gifted children are handled in different ways. Some go to a separate school. Others are pulled from the regular classroom to attend special classes. Still others are given extra help within the classroom. What are the pros and cons of these approaches. Which do you think is preferable? Why?

• Do you think a gifted person is more likely to be successful than one who is not? Explain.

Promoting Discussion

Ask students to think about some especially bright children they know. What have these children said or done to show their high levels of thinking and ability? Would students consider any of them to be gifted? Why or why not?

Cooperative Learning

Have students work in pairs to plan activities that would provide gifted children with extra intellectual stimulation. Have each pair report the activities to the class.

Parents, teachers, and other adults should avoid overwhelming gifted and talented children with unrealistic expectations or goals. Instead, these children need encouragement and opportunities for leadership and creativity.

Gifted children can easily become bored and frustrated in school. They risk being labeled "problem children" because they may not conform to classroom procedures and because they often respond with unexpected answers. Some gifted children who are not challenged at school become poor students.

Most bright children exhibit recognizable signs by age two. They may talk early, using complete sentences, and demonstrate an unusually large vocabulary. Many read before school age—some even by age two and one-half. Gifted children are highly curious and ask challenging questions.

Most schools have special educational programs for gifted students. In small schools, enrichment programs within regular classes are often offered. Large school systems usually have special classes or even special schools for gifted children.

Speech Development

By school age, language ability is one of the most dependable indicators of intelligence. What children say tells much about the way they think. Speech also reveals each child's interests and personality. Remember, however, that there are exceptions. Some children who speak poorly or cannot speak at all have above-average intelligence.

A speech teacher works with children by using games or toys that make sounds the child can identify, such as bells, trains, or animal puppets.

OBSERVING AND PARTICIPATING

Celebrating Individual Differences

Gifted and talented children need opportunities to be creative. Some studies show early creativity peaks at about age four, drops at five, develops again from grades one to three, drops again at the beginning of fourth grade. Creative growth declines again at the beginning of seventh grade, and natural curiosity levels off by high school. To encourage creativity at all ages, give children the materials and

freedom to create, and reward persistence. Most important, allow children the freedom to be different. Many programs for gifted children use an Individualized Educational Program (IEP) to plan for their special educational needs. Each plan is developed in a meeting with the parents, the child (if appropriate), and educational personnel and is based on the child's current performance. Goals are set for a year, and methods given for reaching them.

By the time they start school, children have gained an extensive knowledge of language just by listening. They probably do not know what an adjective is, but they can use adjectives confidently and correctly. As children grow older, their **vocabulary**—*the number of words a person uses*—will increase. The sentences they use will become more complex. However, all the basic language forms have already been learned in the preschool period.

Articulation (clear, distinct speech) improves dramatically. At age three, children typically say only about 30 percent of their words correctly. By age six, that has increased to 90 percent.

Much of this improvement depends on physical development. Some sounds are more difficult to make than others. For example, the sounds represented by *b*, *m*, and *p* are produced simply by moving the lips. By three years of age, most children can make these sounds. Sounds such as those represented by *f* and *v* involve both the lips and the teeth. Children may not master these sounds until age five. The most difficult sounds are those represented by *j*, *ch*, *st*, *pl*, and *sl*. They require the smooth coordination and timing of the lips, tongue, and throat muscles. Some children may be six or seven before "pwease" becomes "please" and "shicken" becomes "chicken."

A child's vocabulary should increase rapidly during this period. A normally developing six-year-old knows about two and one-half times the number of words an average three-year-old knows. This means a six-year-old can understand and use approximately 2,500 words!

Some children with hearing loss are taught to communicate using sign language.

Speech Difficulties

When they first send their children to school, parents sometimes worry that the children will talk too much during class. However, many kindergarten and first-grade teachers worry more about the students who don't talk enough. Children who speak very little are not yet comfortable with language. Teachers know that these children will have trouble keeping up with the class. They will not be ready to learn to read until they have more experience with spoken language.

Some children are language-poor in another sense. Although they have plenty of opportunity to listen and speak at home, they hear and use only a limited number of simple words. Children need to hear—and be encouraged to use—language that is specific and rich in detail. For example, rather than using the very general verb *go*, children should be encouraged to use a variety of specific verbs: The cars *roar* up the hill. The boys *race* across the field. The women *jog* every morning. The bugs *creep* down the tree trunk.

Children who speak only a language other than English at home often experience problems when they begin school. They

GUIDED PRACTICE (continued)

Promoting Discussion
Use these strategies to stimulate discussion about speech difficulties:

• Have students list words that they have heard children pronounce incorrectly. As they respond, list the words on the chalkboard. Then ask students to identify the letters and sounds that cause the problems in these words. What other words could caregivers use in conversation that would help children learn these sounds?

• Ask students to recall situations in which a child was treated unkindly by classmates because his or her speech was different. How did the child react? How might this treatment have affected the child?

Cooperative Learning
Have students work in small groups and make up a game for preschoolers to promote speech or vocabulary development. Arrange for students to play their games with a group of preschoolers.

Promoting Discussion
Point out to students the words listed on page 475 that could replace *go*. Ask students to suggest replacements for *big*, *pretty*, *fast*, and *good* when conversing with children.

Making Connections: Language Arts
Read the following to students: Carlin is a six-year-old with a stuttering problem. Sometimes it takes him a long time to complete a sentence. Often people finish his sentences for him. "Sometimes I just want to say it myself," Carlin thinks. Ask students to assume they know Carlin. Have them write a paragraph explaining Carlin's feelings and how they would help him.

OBSERVING AND PARTICIPATING

Celebrating Individual Differences
Children who learn and speak another language at home sometimes have problems learning English language skills. However, learning another language at an early age can also be beneficial. Generally, children find it easier to learn the sound system, vocabulary, and basic structure of a second language than adolescents or adults do. Knowing two languages is a valuable skill in a world where communication among countries is instantaneous and businesses operate globally. In addition, speaking a second language can help children take an interest in and understand a different culture.

PARENTING IN ACTION

Promoting Discussion

Have students discuss the reasons clear speech depends on practice. Have students read "Promoting Language Development" independently and analyze the effects of a child's being deprived of interaction and intellectual stimulation.

Critically Thinking

Does Jill receive intellectual stimulation from the television? If not, why not? If so, why doesn't watching TV help her with her speech?

You have learned that play helps children develop intellectually. Why doesn't Jill develop her language ability playing in her room?

Is it possible that Jill understands language as well as the other children? Explain.

Answers to "Think and Discuss"

1. She has little opportunity to interact vocally; her language skills are unpracticed.

2. Encourage verbal activities such as reading aloud and describing experiences.

3. Responses will vary; encourage students to explain their conclusions.

INDEPENDENT PRACTICE

Student Workbook

Have students complete "Learning Disability Simulation" in the Student Workbook.

Student Demonstration

Have students take turns role-playing interviews with parents, explaining the special needs of a child and what the school can do. Assign several students to explain dyslexia and attention deficit hyperactivity disorder. Have other students explain that a child is gifted or talented, or has speech problems that need attention.

must learn English language skills and, at the same time, keep up with their class. Children who move from one part of the country to another may also have difficulty because of differences in pronunciation.

In all these situations, children may suffer from a communication problem in school. They may not be able to understand the teacher, or they may have difficulty making themselves understood. As a result, learning becomes more difficult for them.

Sometimes these situations can cause emotional difficulties, as well as learning problems, for young children. Classmates are often unkind to a child whose speech is different. The teasing and jokes of other children may add to a child's sense of isolation.

Of course, not all language problems are caused by a child's home environment. Some children have physical problems that prevent normal speech. Some may be mentally deficient. Others may be emotionally immature. These children all require special help, preferably before they begin school.

Most children, however, are able to develop good language skills at home. For these children, parents should remember that they are the child's most influential teacher. Parents who spend time talking with—and listening to—their child are encouraging the child to speak well, and are preparing the child to succeed in school.

Difficulties in school may arise when a child's family speaks a foreign language at home. However, talking with and listening to classmates can help improve the child's English skills.

OBSERVING AND PARTICIPATING

Celebrating Individual Differences

About one-fourth of all children go through a period in which they stutter. Stress may trigger stuttering in a vulnerable child. To avoid creating stress-triggered stuttering, maintain an easy and relaxed environment. Show interest in what the child says by listening carefully and maintaining eye contact. Avoid interrupting when the child is speaking. Avoid asking the child to "perform" verbally for others. By reducing pressure and competition in the child's environment, parents and other caregivers may help stuttering disappear. If not, the child's speech should be evaluated by a speech pathologist with expertise in stuttering.

PARENTING IN ACTION

Promoting Language Development

Jill is an attractive and polite five-year-old. Both her parents work, and Jill spends every weekday with a caregiver, Mrs. Carson. Mrs. Carson is usually busy with household chores, such as cooking and cleaning. She rarely finds time to play or talk with Jill.

When Jill's parents come home from work, they don't seem to have the time or energy to talk with her. Jill usually spends the evening watching television or playing alone in her room.

Recently, Jill started attending a half-day session of kindergarten. Her teacher, Mr. Wiener, is worried about Jill. She is in good physical health and clearly has at least an average IQ. However, Jill speaks only very rarely at school. When she does speak, her pronunciation is noticeably poor.

THINK AND DISCUSS

1. Why does Jill speak so rarely at school? Why is her pronunciation so poor?
2. What do you think Mr. Wiener should do to help Jill at school?
3. Do you think he should also ask Jill's parents for help? If so, what kind of help? If not, why not?

SECTION 2 REVIEW

CHECK YOUR UNDERSTANDING

1. List at least four things parents can do to prepare their children to adjust easily to school.
2. What is a learning disability?
3. What is attention deficit hyperactivity disorder?
4. What is dyslexia?
5. What kind of test can be given to determine whether a child is gifted? What score indicates that a child is gifted?
6. How does an average child's articulation change between the ages of three and six?
7. List three possible causes of a child's speech or language difficulties.

DISCUSS AND DISCOVER

1. When and under what circumstances do you think children should be tested for possible learning disabilities? How does a child benefit when he or she is diagnosed with a learning disability? What problems can such a diagnosis create for the child?

Observing & Participating

Visit an elementary school in your community that has a special program for gifted and talented children. Talk to a representative who can tell you how children are screened for the program. What special learning opportunities are provided? How do the students respond to the programs? If possible, observe a class and record your impressions to share with the class.

ASSESS

CHECKING COMPREHENSION

Assign students to write their responses to the Check Your Understanding questions in the Section 2 Review. Answers to the questions are given at the bottom of this page.

EVALUATE

Have students complete the Chapter 16, Section 2 quiz in the TCR.

Reteaching

Assign Reteaching 39 in the TCR. Have students complete the activity and discuss the results.

Enrichment

• Assign Enrichment 39 in the TCR.
• Have students research non-school programs available in your area for gifted children. Ask them to report to the class.

Extension

Invite a teacher from your school district's gifted and talented program to discuss ways the school district challenges gifted children. How does the district identify gifted and talented children? In what ways are they treated the same as other children? How are they handled differently? Have students prepare a list of questions to ask the speaker.

CLOSE

Have students suggest endings for this sentence:
To meet the individual needs of all students, a school . . .
Encourage responses that present both general guidelines and specific strategies.

SECTION 2 REVIEW

1. Any four: complete medical and dental examinations; appropriate self-help skills; knows full name, address, and phone number; help child feel confident about following directions; explain what to expect at school.
2. A disorder preventing use of information received through senses in a normal way for learning.
3. An inability to control one's activity or concentrate for a normal length of time.
4. A learning disability that prevents a person from handling language in a normal way.
5. IQ test; 130 or above.
6. Improves dramatically.
7. Having little spoken language experience; experience only with very simple spoken language; speaking other than English at home.

Positive Parenting Skills

MOTIVATOR

Ask students to recall what types of make-believe play they enjoyed when they were children. What do they think they gained from make-believe play?

Promoting Discussion

1. How does make-believe play illustrate preoperational thinking?

2. What is the value of make-believe play?

3. How does trying out different roles in pretend play help children understand and prepare for adult roles?

Using the Photographs

Refer students to the photograph on page 478. Have students explain why children like to dress up in adult clothing and what it symbolizes.

Critical Thinking

Ask students to think about the role of adults in a child's fantasy play. Why should a caregiver avoid getting too involved? Why would experts say that, within reason, caregivers should not limit negative fantasy play? How would a caregiver know when negative fantasy play should be stopped?

Review Piaget's concept of the preoperational period (page 299). During this period, from about the age of two to seven, children love to act out situations and think in terms of their own immediate experiences.

ENCOURAGING MAKE-BELIEVE PLAY

Between the ages of two and nine, children often engage in make-believe play. This kind of play is important to a child's development because it helps make the child aware of the adult world.

What Is Fantasy Play?

In fantasy play, children themselves choose what to play, and they create a situation over which they have full control. In their pretend world, children can be successful, feel important, and gain confidence. They can make up their own rules and try out new activities without fear of failure or ridicule.

In make-believe play, children often enact situations they observe in the adult world. After watching an adult bake a cake, a child may pretend to bake a cake for a favorite stuffed animal. Old pots and pans, wooden spoons, toy tools, child-sized benches or chairs and tables, and plastic or toy dishes are good props for make-believe play.

The Benefits of Pretend Play

Pretend play provides endless opportunities for trying out different roles. A chalkboard and some books can turn a room into a school. Old clothes, jewelry, and shoes for dressing up can make playing house more fun.

478

MORE ABOUT

Handling Fears Through Play

Because pretend play is so spontaneous and open, it can help children learn to cope with anxieties and conflicts. In a make-believe situation, a child often feels free to express strong inner feelings—of fear, anger, or loss—that might otherwise become overwhelming. For this reason, play therapy has become a valuable clinical technique for identifying and resolving the emotional problems of young children.

other with pointed fingers or toy guns, a caregiver might explain that he or she doesn't like to shoot people or be shot at. In this way, the caregiver reinforces a set of values without preventing the children from learning about aggressive behavior.

Fantasy play also helps children understand and express their feelings. Stuffed animals, dolls, toy figures, and puppets can all act as good friends—or perhaps enemies to talk to and act out feelings with.

When invited, a parent or other caregiver can take a minor part in fantasy play. As soon as possible, however, the adult should leave the play area, allowing the child to create and control the fantasy.

Guiding Fantasy Play

Within reason, parents and other caregivers should avoid limiting fantasy play. They can, however, let children know how they feel about certain situations. For example, when children are "shooting" each

Family Focus
When confronted with fears, a child might benefit from make-believe play involving the entire family. For example, a child who is afraid to be put in bed might role-play an adult who tucks a parent or older sibling into bed and comforts the pretend child. In this way, the child feels more in control and is better able to work out fears by him- or herself.

Student Demonstration
Ask a student volunteer to explain how to assemble a collection of simple props for a puppet show. Then have the student demonstrate various ways the props can be used in fantasy play.

Journal Writing
On a separate sheet of paper, have students write a short case study describing a specific situation in which a child shows a negative emotion. Then ask students to exchange papers. In their journals, have them write an ending to the story showing how make-believe play helped the child understand and overcome the feeling. Ask for volunteers to read their completed case study to the class. Discuss the solution.

Extension
Ask students to observe children from ages four to six while they are involved in fantasy play. What signs of preoperational thinking can be observed in the children's play? What evidence of imagination and creativity can be seen? What feelings do the children express through their play? Have students report their findings to the class.

CLOSE

Ask students to summarize the caregiver's role in relation to make-believe play.

SEE HOW THEY GROW

The Value of Make-Believe Play

Sometimes parents speak of make-believe play as "a waste of time" or "just playing." They believe their child should be learning more important things, such as reading, writing, and arithmetic.

These parents do not recognize that imaginative play aids the child in developing the ability to conceptualize and to think abstractly. Make-believe play is a vital part of emotional, social, and intellectual development.

CHECKING COMPREHENSION

Use the Summary and the Reviewing the Facts questions to help students go over the most important ideas presented in Chapter 16, encourage students to ask questions and add details, as appropriate.

CHAPTER **16** REVIEW

1. Dramatic play is imitating real-life situations.

2. Intelligence quotient is a numerical standard that tells whether a person's intelligence is average or above average for his or her age.

3. They depend on language ability, are culture-dependent, do not address specific abilities, and are not consistent.

4. Organizational ability, responsibility, maturity, and independence.

5. Because it is an activity they will continue as they grow older and which will provide an opportunity to learn about and understand the world and the people in it.

6. Parents should encourage experiments and ask what the artwork is about. Parents should not ridicule, offer corrections, or guess what the piece represents.

7. To ensure that vision and hearing will not handicap learning.

8. In a learning disability, the brain does not function normally to receive information.

9. They can become easily bored and frustrated and do not conform to classroom procedures.

10. A vocabulary is the number of words a person uses. Between the ages of three and six, correct articulation increases from 30 percent to 90 percent.

SUMMARY

- Children aged four to six are in the preoperational period of thinking.
- Intelligence tests can help determine a child's intellectual abilities.
- Parents and other caregivers who listen, explain, answer questions, and provide learning experiences help children learn better and faster.
- Children should be encouraged to develop an interest in reading, art, and music.
- Children who are properly prepared for school adjust more easily.
- Learning disabilities result from communication problems within the brain.
- Gifted and talented children need opportunities that will challenge, but not overwhelm, them.
- Between the ages of four and six, children show rapid speech development, especially in vocabulary and articulation.
- Some children have speech and language problems that hinder learning.

REVIEWING THE FACTS

1. What is dramatic play?
2. Define the term *intelligence quotient*.
3. List three disadvantages of IQ tests.
4. What are two ways children can benefit from helping with household tasks?
5. Why should children be encouraged to enjoy reading?
6. What should parents do to encourage children's art activities? What should parents avoid doing?
7. Why should children have medical exams before starting school?
8. What is the difference between a learning disability and a physical disability?
9. Why are gifted children sometimes considered problem students?
10. What is a person's vocabulary? How does an average child's vocabulary change between the ages of three and six?

EXPLORING FURTHER

1. Create a personalized book for a child you know. Write a simple story about the child and his or her family. Use photographs, magazine pictures, or your own drawings to illustrate the story. Share your book with the rest of the class, and then give the book to the child for whom you wrote it. (Section 1)

2. Make up an original finger play that you think will appeal to four- to six-year-olds. Teach your finger play to a group of classmates, and encourage them to discuss and evaluate your work. Make any revisions you consider necessary. Then teach your finger play to at least one child or a small group of children. (Section 1)

3. What community resources are available to help learning disabled children and their families? Plan and prepare a flier with basic information about these programs, and make the fliers available to local parents. (Section 2)

THINKING CRITICALLY

1. **Analyze.** What does the term culture-free mean? How is it applied to IQ tests? Do you think IQ tests should be culture-free? Why or why not? Do you believe it is possible to create a truly culture-free IQ test? Why or why not?

2. **Analyze.** What might account for the current trend toward full-day kindergarten programs? What advantages does a full-day program have over a half-day program? What are the disadvantages of full-day kindergartens? Which do you consider better? Why?

3. **Analyze.** Do you think language ability is always an indicator of intelligence? Is it possible that a child who is unusually intelligent and has no physical speech problems might speak very little or even not at all? Why or why not? If so, what might cause the child's speech delay?

CLASSROOM MANAGEMENT

Resources Beyond the Classroom

Child Development: Three to Five is a live-action video program that presents the development of a child during the ages from three to five years, including the cycle of learning and limitations to this learning that children face during these years. Included is an exploration of how children at this age become self-aware and begin socialization. For more information contact:

Glencoe/McGraw-Hill
15319 Chatsworth Street
Mission Hills, CA 91345

CROSS-CURRICULUM CONNECTIONS

1. **Music.** Listen to the recordings of a singer or a group that performs especially for young children. Consider the melodies, harmonies, rhythms, and lyrics the singer or group generally uses. Then compose an original song that would be appropriate for the singer or group to perform. Make your own tape of the song, and play it for your classmates.

2. **Speaking.** Interview an adult who has a learning disability. How did the learning disability affect the person's school experience? When and how was the learning disability diagnosed? How did the diagnosis affect the person's school experience? What effects, if any, does the learning disability have on the adult's daily life? After the interview, plan and present a short oral report of your findings.

SCHOOL TO WORK

Volunteering By definition, volunteers don't get paid for their work, but the work experience they gain may well be worth the time and effort. For example, volunteering a few hours each week at a child care center may show you how the concepts you learn in this classroom are applied to real-life situations. Besides having the experience to add to your résumé, every supervisor is a potential employer who might be looking for someone just like you!

PERFORMANCE ASSESSMENT

Intellectual Development from Four to Six

Task
Create a one-page newsletter for parents and other caregivers of children ages four to six.

Purpose
Show that you recognize the intellectual needs of four- to six-year-olds.

Procedure
1. Decide whether your newsletter will include articles about child development, advertisements for preschools, book reviews, toy reviews, and so on.
2. Write the information needed for each chosen topic. Include your own artwork and clip art if you have access to a computer program.
3. Write short headlines for each item included in the newsletter. Remember that headlines are meant to capture the reader's attention.
4. Arrange columns on a piece of paper the same size that your finished newsletter will be. Print, type, or use a computer to fit the content on the page. Cut where needed to fit, and always have someone check your spelling, punctuation, and grammar. Allow room for the newsletter's title, date, and your name as writer and editor.
5. When you are satisfied with the draft, make a final copy. Proofread again.
6. Copy the finished newsletter and distribute to parents.

Evaluation
The newsletter's content should be appropriate to the intellectual development of the four- to six-year-old. Visual appeal as well as correct spelling, punctuation, and grammar will be evaluated.

Portfolio Idea You could include your rough drafts in your portfolio to show the step-by-step process used to make the newsletter. Another addition to the portfolio would be other newsletters using the same format but focusing on other areas of child development.

481

PERFORMANCE ASSESSMENT

Newsletter
Have samples of newsletters available to serve as models. Encourage students to study the samples for ideas about presentation, length of articles, graphics, and so on. Remind students that the information included in their newsletter should reflect a variety of topics that are relevant to this age group. Have students work in groups to correct each others' work and provide extra support to those whose language skills require more attention. If computer facilities are available, encourage students to use them for a more professional result.

EVALUATE
Use the reproducible Chapter 16 Test in the TCR, or construct your own test using the Testmaker Software.

EXTENSION
Have students research and report on local programs (such as Head Start) that provide language enrichment for children who have limited English-speaking ability or who are from families that do not promote language skills.

Invite a learning disability specialist to speak to the class about the programs provided for children with various learning disabilities. Ask them how caregivers can handle these children's special needs at home. Have students prepare questions to ask the speaker. If possible, arrange for interested students to spend time volunteering in a class for children with learning disabilities.

CLOSE

Reread to the students the statements in Introducing the Chapter. Discuss each statement again as a class. Then have students review their predictions and verify or modify them.

TECHNOLOGY OPTION

Computers While students complete the Performance Assessment activity on this page, you might help them gain access to a computer that provides a program with newsletter templates. Even a basic word processor will allow them to input and manipulate text into columns. Newsletter and newspaper software is available for a more sophisticated presentation; perhaps your school has a journalism department that will help students create a professional-looking newsletter with any available equipment.

INTRODUCE

UNIT 6 RESOURCES

Teacher's Classroom Resources
- Unit 6 Test
- Testmaker Software
- Color Transparency 38

UNIT OVERVIEW

As they study Unit 6, students become acquainted with several areas of study related to young children.

In Chapter 17, students examine important procedures relating to the health and safety of infants and young children.

Chapter 18 helps students consider special challenges that some children face, and such family stresses as divorce and death.

Chapter 19 presents information about the responsibilities child care providers accept when they babysit for children. It also describes techniques students can use in observing young children and in participating in early childhood classrooms.

In Chapter 20, students learn to evaluate their own interests and abilities in light of future career decisions. They examine a number of careers that relate to child development and child care.

UNIT OBJECTIVES

After completing Unit 6, students will be able to:

- Explain procedures for preventing children's accidents, handling emergencies, and caring for sick children.
- Discuss the effects that disabilities, abuse and neglect, and family stresses may have on young children.
- Identify the responsibilities of a child care provider and discuss the skills involved in observing children and participating in early childhood classrooms.
- Discuss various jobs related to child care.

CLASSROOM MANAGEMENT

Bulletin Board Suggestions

"*Handling Special Needs*" Divide the board into three sections: Physical, Mental, and Emotional. Make a collage of children with each type of special need and place it under the appropriate column. In large letters cut out the following words and scatter them on the board: love, acceptance, empathy, understanding, listening, support, and smiles.

"*Close Calls*" Mount ten paper plates face down in a circle to simulate a telephone dial. On each plate apply press-on letters and numbers. In the center of the dial, attach a list of emergency phone numbers.

UNIT 6

Special Areas of Study

THE BIGGEST PROBLEM
(IS IN OTHER PEOPLE'S MINDS)

My brother Bobby never listens when I talk;
Pays close attention though, and watches like a hawk.
Took some time for my hands to learn the signs,
But now the two of us, we get along just fine.

Bobby's biggest problem is in other people's minds;
We do things we like to do and have a great time.
Some kids stay away, but if they knew him they would find
Bobby's biggest problem really is in other people's minds.

Don Haynie

INTRODUCING THE UNIT

- Display several photographs of apparently healthy, happy babies and young children. Let students describe the individual babies and children and briefly discuss what their lives might be like. Then ask how the life of each child might be changed if he or she had a serious accident; had a physical, mental, or emotional disability; became seriously ill; experienced the death of a parent or sibling; experienced the separation and divorce of his or her parents.

At the close of the discussion, explain to students that they have been considering special situations that can arise in any family. They will learn more about such situations as they read Unit 6.

ASSESS

EVALUATION

Use the reproducible Unit 6 Test in the TCR, or construct your own test using the Testmaker Software.

EXTENSION

Arrange to have a panel of speakers visit the class, including a pediatrician, a pediatric nurse specialist, a child psychologist, a child care center worker, an early childhood teacher, and/or others who work in child-related fields. Ask: When and how did you begin learning about child development? What attracted you to working with children? What do you consider the special benefits or problems of your work?

Childhood Reflections

"Children have more need of models than of critics."

John Ray, *English Proverbs*

MORE ABOUT

Using the Poem

As you introduce the study of children with special needs, have students read Don Haynie's poem, "The Biggest Problem (Is in Other People's Minds)." The situation portrayed in the poem identifies the major obstacle facing people whose physical needs are challenging—other people's preconceived ideas. Ask students to describe Bobby's handicap. Apparently, the speaker of the poem (Bobby's brother) has no problem with Bobby's special needs. Why? How does his brother adjust to Bobby's needs? How could both brothers serve as positive role models for other people?

INTRODUCE

CHAPTER OVERVIEW

Chapter 17 discusses the health and safety of children, with specific attention given to accident prevention, emergency procedures, and care for a sick child.

Section 1 deals with rules for safety and with the importance of medical checkups and immunization.

Section 2 treats first aid procedures and guidelines for prompt action in the event of an emergency.

Section 3 details the caregiver's role in the care of a sick or hospitalized child.

CHAPTER OBJECTIVES

After completing Chapter 17, students will be able to:

- Identify safety hazards for children of different ages.
- Explain the role of immunizations and health checkups in preventing illnesses.
- Discuss what allergies are and how they can be treated.
- Recognize emergency situations and plan appropriate responses.
- Demonstrate appropriate first aid for common ailments.
- Identify basic rescue techniques.
- Give basic guidelines for caring for ill children.
- Describe the nutritional needs of sick children.
- Discuss problems involved in the hospitalization of children.

CLASSROOM MANAGEMENT

Resources Beyond the Classroom

A fact of life is that all children become ill at some time during their early years. Fortunately, a wide selection of medication is now available to help alleviate many of the discomforting symptoms of childhood ailments. It is very important, however, for young parents to recognize that young children's medication needs and tolerances are very different from their own. Not following proper medication use can have very serious effects on the health of the child. A free brochure entitled *A Parent's Guide to Medicine Use by Children* contains information on how to talk to your health professional and pharmacist, and more importantly, how to ask the right questions about administering prescribed and over-the-counter medications to your child. For the free brochure, see the address on the next page.

Health and Safety

SECTION 1	Prevention of Accidents and Illness
SECTION 2	Handling Emergencies
SECTION 3	Caring for a Sick Child

THINK ABOUT

Think about the precautions your parents or other caregivers take to keep you healthy and safe. Are they concerned about safety at home, at school, or in the community? Do they remind you about health issues that require your attention? Are these same precautions necessary for a young child? Why or why not? Why is the safety of a child the most important responsibility of parents or caregivers?

ASK YOURSELF

Look at the photo on the opposite page. What concerns about the child's safety is this adult likely to have? What do you

think he is saying to the child? What freedoms and restrictions might be included in the father's instructions? Besides feeling grown-up and independent, how does this activity contribute to the child's growth and development?

NOW TRY THIS

Imagine that you have a sibling who is a toddler. Brainstorm a list of everyday products in your home, such as pencils, vitamins, or cleanser, that would threaten the health and safety of a child who might find them. Next to each item, identify a place to keep it safely out of the child's reach.

485

INTRODUCING THE CHAPTER

- Have each student write a definition of the term *safety*. Allow time for students to compare their definitions before discussing them as a class. Follow up with a discussion about what students think are the safety needs of infants and young children.

- Use the photo on the opposite page and the three features on this page—Think About, Ask Yourself, and Now Try This—to begin a discussion about health and safety concerns when caring for children.

CHAPTER PROJECT

Divide the class into three groups, and ask each to investigate one of the following:

- The most recently available statistics on accidental deaths and injuries and information on particular trouble spots in their own community (e.g., dangerous intersections).

- The existence in their community of a 911 emergency system and typical response times to various emergencies.

- The programs that exist in local hospitals for easing the burden facing children who must undergo hospitalization. Information and relevant charts should be shared in a class forum on health and safety.

HEALTHY FAMILIES/HEALTHY CHILDREN

Building Healthy Families

Although most families work at providing a safe environment for their family members, injuries kill more Americans ages 1 to 34 than all diseases combined, and they're the leading cause of death up to age 44. Frequently people will ask questions concerning the liability when administering first-aid procedures. Assure students that the law will support all Good Samaritans that act in a manner con-

sistent with a reasonably prudent individual. Individuals should do no more, and should do no less, than they have been trained to do.

Tell students that they are members of a larger family group—their community. Explain that their ability to handle emergency situations may someday be beneficial not only to their immediate family, but to someone in the community as well.

Send a self-addressed, stamped envelope to:

National Council on Patient Information and Education
666 11th Street NW, Suite 810
Washington, DC 20001

FOCUS

SECTION I RESOURCES

Teacher's Classroom Resources
- Enrichment 40
- Reteaching 40
- Section 1 Quiz

Student Workbook
- Magic Square

SECTION OVERVIEW

In Section 1, students learn about child safety and the responsibilities of parents and caregivers for the safety of infants and of children ages one to three and four to six. The section also includes information on facets of child health care, including a timetable for immunizations and a brief discussion of allergies.

MOTIVATOR

Provide students with back issues of newspapers covering a period of approximately two months. Working in groups, students are to skim the pages, clipping headlines from stories about accidents in which children were involved. After allowing ample time for groups to gather headlines, have them display and compare their findings. Ask: Which types of accidents most commonly involved babies? Which involved very young children? Then note that, with proper attention to safety, many of the accidents cited might have been prevented. Explain that students will presently be learning specific steps for prevention.

USING TERMS TO LEARN

Ask students to define the terms listed in "Terms to Learn" as best as they are able, recording their responses in their journal. Discuss their definitions and have them make revisions as necessary.

SECTION 1   Prevention of Accidents and Illness

TERMS TO LEARN

allergy
communicable diseases
immunize
infant mortality rate
nontoxic
vaccine

OBJECTIVES

- Identify safety hazards for children of different ages.
- Explain the part immunizations and health checkups play in the prevention of illnesses.
- Discuss what allergies are and how they can be treated.

"**A**n ounce of prevention is worth a pound of cure." That's an old saying that you've probably heard often. The saying is especially true about childhood illnesses and accidents—it's easier to prevent them than to cope with their effects.

Safety

The safety of the child is the most important responsibility of every parent and caregiver. Keeping a child safe requires the following: knowledge of child development; a safe environment; alertness to safety hazards; and, teaching the child safe habits.

Every age has its particular hazards because children of different ages have different abilities and interests. What you know about child development will help you anticipate hazards.

Infants

During the eighteenth century, the American **infant mortality rate**—*the percentage of deaths during the first year of life*—was nearly 40 percent. By the end of the twentieth century, the infant mortality rate in the United States has dropped to about 2 percent. This great improvement is due largely to medical advances. Many infectious diseases that were once life-threatening have now been controlled or even eliminated.

MORE ABOUT

Accidents

Accidents are the greatest single cause of death in children between the ages of one and fifteen. Have students consider the following statistics:

- Almost one-third of home accidents involve children under age four.
- Almost one-fifth of children's accidents take place in the kitchen.

- The second leading cause of child accidents is structural features, such as stairs and windows.
- The third chief cause of accidents is kitchen utensils, such as pans, knives, and cups.

At all ages, more males than females are involved in accidents.

Today, accidents represent the most serious threat to infants. Falls cause the most injuries among babies, and they account for many deaths. Even before an infant can crawl, his or her wiggling can produce enough movement to cause a fall from a bed, a changing table, or an infant seat placed on a table. Such accidents are particularly dangerous because babies tend to fall headfirst. This kind of fall can result in brain damage or other serious injuries. Because of these dangers, no baby should ever be left unattended on any kind of furniture from which a fall is possible.

Babies like to suck and chew on almost anything that comes within reach, so parents and caregivers must be especially careful. Because babies can choke on small objects, anything that could be swallowed—including small toy parts that might be chewed or pulled off—must be kept away from an infant.

Poisoning is another danger for babies. Anything babies could place in the mouth—even the edges of furniture—must be **nontoxic**, or *not poisonous*. Some paints that contain lead are particularly dangerous for children. Plastic bags represent a special hazard. They can cause choking or suffocation. Babies and small children should never be allowed to play with plastic bags. Also, plastic bags should never be used as protective covering for the mattress in a crib or playpen.

A small child should never be left alone near water. Water—indoors in a sink or tub or outdoors in a fish pond, a wading pool, or a swimming pool—can be very dangerous. Drownings happen quickly, even in the time it takes to answer the phone or go to the door.

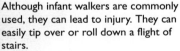

INFANT MORTALITY RATES

According to the Statistical Office of the United Nations, there is a wide range of death rates among infants worldwide. Among their listings are the following number of deaths per 1,000 live births.

Country	
Japan	5.0
Switzerland	6.8
Singapore	7.0
Canada	7.3
France	7.7
United Kingdom	8.8
United States	10.0
Czechoslovakia	11.9
China	12.0
Nigeria	17.6

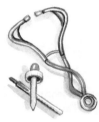

Although infant walkers are commonly used, they can lead to injury. They can easily tip over or roll down a flight of stairs.

TEACH

Pages 486-495

- Safety
- Health Care
- Immunization
- Allergies

GUIDED PRACTICE

Promoting Discussion
Ask students to brainstorm advances in medicine over the past 200 years that have contributed to a drop in the infant mortality rate. Ask: What factors are common to these breakthroughs or areas of research?

Critical Thinking
Direct students' attention to the mention of the fact that toys suitable for older children may contain parts infants and toddlers could swallow. Ask students to discuss what implications this consideration may have for families with more than one child. Ask: What special precautions should such families be urged to take?

Using the Photograph
Have students study the photo on this page. Ask them to discuss the possible advantages, for babies and parents, of infant walkers. Ask: Why are these devices dangerous? How could parents lessen the dangers of a walker's tipping over or rolling down stairs?

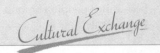

Have students use the figures provided in the Cultural Exchange feature to calculate the percentages for infant mortality rates for each of the countries shown.

OBSERVING AND PARTICIPATING

Developing Observational Skills
Have small groups of students observe young children at play and isolate any possible safety hazards, using information provided on these pages. While still on-site, groups are to complete a safety checklist based on their observation and containing answers to questions such as the following: Were any children hurt during the observation period? Did caregivers use any of the techniques described in the text to maintain the safety of the children? After the observation period, have groups compare experiences and share checklists as a lead-in to a discussion of whether keeping children safe is more difficult than students imagined.

PARENTING IN ACTION

Promoting Discussion

Allow students to independently read "Making Safety Decisions." Discuss their reactions to the story and their familiarity, if any, with similar situations.

Thinking Critically

The following items have been identified by the Consumer Product Safety Commission as commonly involved in injuries to children under age four: built-in fireplaces, irons, oil or kerosene heaters, rocking chairs, television tables or stands, hair curlers, curling irons, Christmas decorations, and tables. Have students discuss injuries that each item might cause and ways to prevent these injuries.

Answers to "Think and Discuss"

1. He might have been shaken up or frightened, but probably not seriously injured; the restraint would have protected him.

2. Encourage a variety of responses: angry (Nina) that she did not insist on the car seat; guilty (both girls) that they put Hector in danger; grateful (both) that the outcome was not fatal.

3. Encourage responses based on students' impressions of how other people respond to accidents.

SAFETY TIP

Remind students that an important part of safety is staying as up-to-date on health information as possible. Tell them, as a case in point, that not too many years ago, it was believed that butter should be rubbed on burns, whereas nowadays it is understood that applying butter to a burn only intensifies the pain and injury.

PARENTING IN ACTION

Making Safety Decisions

Fifteen-year-old Nina was spending the day with her older sister Olivia and Olivia's month-old son, Hector. Just before noon, Nina and Olivia decided to drive to a nearby market to get some milk.

As they were getting into the car, Nina asked, "Where's Hector's car seat?"

"Oh, no," sighed Olivia. "I left it in the apartment. Well, it's only a few blocks. You just hold him. This won't take long."

Both sisters put on their own seat belts, and Nina held Hector carefully while Olivia drove. Just before they reached the store, another car pulled out suddenly, and Olivia had to slam on the brakes. Fortunately, she was able to stop the car in time to avoid a collision. However, the force of the sudden stop was enough to tear Hector from Nina's arms. He was thrown against the dash and seriously injured.

THINK AND DISCUSS

1. What would the result of the sudden stop have been if Hector had been in an infant safety restraint? Why?

2. How do you think Olivia feels about Hector's injuries? How do you think Nina feels?

3. How do you think other family members must feel about the accident and its cause? Why?

SAFETY TIP

Children learn best by example. Parents and caregivers can help children learn about safety restraints by using their own seat belts regularly and by making sure that everyone else in the vehicle—young or old—is securely buckled in for safety.

Automobile accidents cause the most deaths among young children. In spite of that fact, many loving parents allow their children to sit or stand in a moving vehicle without any protection. An accident or even a sudden stop can throw the child against the windshield or instrument panel. Most states now have laws that make child safety restraints mandatory, but the laws alone cannot protect children. Every parent and caregiver must be responsible for putting babies and young children into safe car seats for every trip, short or long.

Car seats and restraints must be carefully chosen and consistently used. Regular adult seat belts cannot keep babies or young children safe. The Positive Parenting Skills on page 188-189 gives information on how to choose and use car seats and restraints.

Ages One to Three

One- to three-year-olds need particularly careful supervision. Any area in which they play or spend time should be carefully checked for safety. In addition, no toddler should be left unat-

SEE HOW THEY GROW

Safety in the Car

Car safety restraints manufactured since 1981 must conform to federal safety standards. There are two basic types of restraints. The type to use depends on the age of the child involved. Infants require a bucket-type carrier. In this type of restraint, the infant is held in a reclining position and faces backward. A harness holds the baby in position, and the carrier is secured with a car seat belt. At about nine months of age, children are ready for a toddler seat. In this type of restraint, the child faces forward and is restrained by shoulder harnesses. Some infant seats, it should be noted, can be converted to toddler seats.

tended for more than a few minutes; even then they should be within hearing distance. Sometimes it is necessary to be in the garage or outside bringing items from a car while the child is sleeping. Under such circumstances, check on the child periodically or carry a child monitor that transmits sounds from the child's room.

Like babies, toddlers must be guarded against choking. Even very young children should be encouraged to follow these safety guidelines:

* Stay seated while eating.
* Always take small bites.
* Swallow what is in the mouth before taking another bite.
* Do not talk or laugh with food in the mouth.
* Chew all food thoroughly.
* Keep small toys and other small objects out of the mouth.

Ages Four to Six

Children aged four to six spend more of their time in unsupervised play. During these years, they need to learn good safety practices. However, you should never rely on young children to remember and follow all the appropriate safety rules. Children need frequent reminders and watchful adults nearby.

Outdoor play equipment, such as a swing set, should be firmly anchored so that there is no danger of its tipping over. When children use this kind of equipment, parents or other caregivers should set and enforce safety rules. One useful rule, for example, is that only one child may be on a swing at a time.

A preschooler should begin learning his or her address and phone number; school-aged children should be able to give this information clearly in an emergency. Children should also be taught how to use a telephone in an emergency, either by calling 911 if it is available in your community or by reaching an operator. Keeping important numbers by the telephone, including the parents' phone numbers at work, can help a child in an emergency.

Children should be taught how to telephone for help before an emergency arises.

SAFETY TIP

Parents and other caregivers can help young children avoid choking by following these safety guidelines:

* Cut foods into small pieces, no more than 1/2 inch (1.3 cm) square.
* Avoid serving peanuts, grapes, popcorn, hard candy, fish with bones, or hot dogs to children under age three.
* Always hold a baby's bottle—don't prop it.
* Always keep an eye on a young child who is eating.
* Keep small objects out of the reach of infants and toddlers.

GUIDED PRACTICE (continued)

Practicing Decision Making

Have students respond to this situation: Keesha and Jamal, who are both in college and struggling to make ends meet, have a ten-month-old son. A relative has offered a ten-year-old car seat for their use. Have students debate whether the couple should accept the gift or wait until they can afford to buy a car seat of their own.

Using the Photograph

Refer students to the photo on this page. Ask them why it is important for children to learn to use the telephone. What happens if a child "practices" calling the police or fire department when unsupervised?

Promoting Discussion

Point out to students that statistics show one of the most dangerous items in the home of one- to three-year-olds to be the telephone. Ask students to discuss why this might be so.

Have students discuss parents' need to be firm in enforcing safety rules even when the child is resistant or unhappy. Ask: What types of rules are most likely to cause children to complain? How should parents handles such complaints when dealing with children ages four to six?

Using Management Skills

Have a group of volunteers investigate the number of injuries sustained annually by children under age four and involving supermarket shopping carts. The volunteers should interview store managers and local safety officials in an effort to determine ways in which such injuries might be prevented. Have the group share its findings with the class.

HEALTHY FAMILIES/HEALTHY CHILDREN

Health and Safety

Parents of children who fly a good deal should consider using a car safety seat for young children during flight. Using such seats protects children during takeoff, landing, and turbulence. When planning to fly, parents should choose an airline that permits the use of such seats. They should also confirm that the seat meets Federal Aviation Administration Safety standards. In general, all seats manufactured after February 26, 1985 have labels stating that they are approved for aircraft use, though some seats manufactured before this date also meet the necessary requirements.

SAFETY TIP

After students have read the Safety Tip, inform them that the most common cause of death in children under the age of one is choking. Discuss how the entire family can learn prevention techniques.

GUIDED PRACTICE (continued)

Using Management Skills

Have students make fire drill plans for their own homes. Ask them to include a main escape route from each room, alternate routes to be used if the main route is blocked, and a meeting place outside the home where family members can be accounted for. If possible, have students conduct fire drills for family members.

Practicing Decision Making

Have each student write a story about a five-year-old who is approached by a stranger asking for directions. Ask students to illustrate their stories and read them to young children. Allow class time for students to share the stories and discuss ways of instructing young children in how to make the appropriate response in such cases.

Cooperative Learning

Have a group of volunteers investigate the phenomenon of latchkey children. The group's research should be guided by questions such as the following: How many latchkey children are estimated to exist in the United States today? What is the age range of such children? What factors have led to the latchkey phenomenon?

SAFETY TIP

One way of helping your students become better acquainted with essentials of fire safety and other safety precautions is by building a classroom library of relevant materials from organizations such as the American Red Cross. You might also try to arrange to have a volunteer from a local chapter of the Red Cross speak to the class about the "stop-drop-roll" method for escaping or minimizing injury in the event of a fire.

Many communities offer safety programs sponsored by the police, fire department, or civic groups. Children can learn traffic rules and other ways to stay safe.

SAFETY TIP

In addition to learning how to get help in an emergency, children must also learn how to recognize a real emergency. One good way to help children with this task is to play the "What If?" game. Ask a child specific questions such as these: What would you do if you woke up at night and smelled smoke? What would you do if you heard a scary noise outside your bedroom window? Use such questions—and the child's responses—to help build an understanding of appropriate behavior in various situations.

Young children are often fascinated by fire. Even those who have been carefully taught that matches are unsafe may sometimes experiment with matches. As the lighted match burns closer to a child's fingers, the child often becomes frightened. He or she may drop the match or even throw it into a wastebasket to hide the evidence. Many fires start this way. Parents and other caregivers should keep all matches locked away and should remain watchful of children's activities.

When young children begin attending school, they should be prepared for several new kinds of dangers. As children approach school age, parents become increasingly concerned about keeping them safe from crime. To help protect their children, parents should discuss crime openly and honestly with them. However, parents should also avoid frightening children unnecessarily. They should avoid discussing terrible things that have happened to children, and they should not introduce the threat of strangers' stealing children away from their parents.

Parents need to set up safety rules for their children. They need to make it clear, for example, that they will never send a stranger to pick the child up. Parents need to teach children never to go anywhere with a stranger and discuss what children should do if they are approached in a threatening way. If the child walks to school, identify the safest route and be sure the child uses that route every day. If possible, arrange for older children to walk with younger ones.

Some families are unable to provide at-home supervision for children after school. Allowing a young child to return to an unsupervised home is never a satisfactory solution to the problem of child care. In these situations, other, more desirable options should be explored: after-school programs either at the school or in the neighborhood, child care programs that provide transportation from school to the child care center, and neighbors or relatives who are willing to care for the child.

If a child must occasionally stay at home alone, the family should establish special rules. These rules should cover contacting a neighbor for help, keeping doors locked, answering the door and the phone, making phone calls, preparing snacks, and deciding whether friends can visit.

Health Care

Everyone should have regular medical checkups. This is especially true for children. A physical can often detect health problems in their early stages. Early treatment can help prevent serious illness or permanent damage to the child's health.

Newborns should be examined frequently during the first year. The baby's physician or clinic will recommend how often.

MORE ABOUT

Safety

Risk taking is directly related to safety. Those who take more risks are apt to have more accidents. People tend to fall into three general categories with regard to risk taking:

- **Overly Cautious.** For these individuals, the concern for safety is paramount; avoiding almost all risks often results in boredom.

- **Reasonable.** These individuals weigh the possible benefits of an action against the probable risks.

- **Reckless.** For these individuals, unreasonable risks often lead to accidents and serious physical or mental harm to themselves and to others.

After the first year, healthy children need checkups less frequently, but at least once a year. Because these checkups are so important, most cities have free or inexpensive clinics that provide good medical care.

Infants can become seriously ill very quickly. If any symptoms of a health problem develop—such as fever, listlessness, prolonged diarrhea, constipation, vomiting, or difficulty in breathing—consult a doctor. In older children, the symptoms of possibly serious illnesses include fever, persistent cough, vomiting, severe headache, and dizziness.

Dental checkups usually begin around three years of age. Fluoride supplementation is often begun at two weeks of age in areas without fluoridated water. Children's secondary teeth can be affected by poor dental care during childhood.

Immunization

To **immunize** is *to protect a person against a particular disease.* People can be protected from many **communicable diseases**— *diseases that are easily passed from one person to another*—by being immunized. Unless people are immunized against them, communicable diseases can easily turn into serious epidemics.

The most common way to immunize people against diseases is with vaccines. A **vaccine** is *a small amount of an antigen introduced to the body, usually by injection, so that the body can build resistance to the disease.* In response to a vaccine, a person's body produces antibodies that fight off the germs for a specific disease. Later, if that person is exposed to the disease, he or she already has antibodies to it. These antibodies ensure that the vaccinated person either will not get the disease at all or will have only a very mild case of the disease.

Every child needs protection from these seven serious diseases: diphtheria, pertussis (whooping cough), and tetanus— often referred to together as DPT; measles, mumps, and rubella (German measles)—often referred to together as MMR; and polio. Many pediatricians also recommend HIB vaccinations, against Haemophilus B, a type of flu associated with ear infections. All these diseases can cause serious illness or even death. The chart on pages 492-494 gives information about the immunizations recommended by the American Academy of Pediatrics and the U.S. Centers for Disease Control. Parents should be sure that their children are immunized according to those schedules and should keep a record of each child's immunizations.

Many states require immunizations for all school children. However, preschool children are most likely to develop complications from the diseases, so parents should not wait until school starts to have their children immunized.

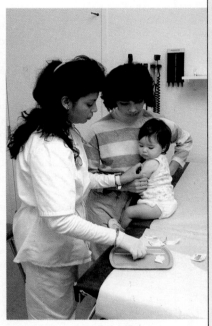

Immunizations have helped many youngsters lead healthier lives.

GUIDED PRACTICE (continued)

Promoting Discussion
Have students discuss why it is especially important for infants to have regular medical examinations during the first year. Ask: Why are such examinations so high a priority for newborns?

Have students review the birth defects that can result if a woman has rubella during pregnancy. Ask: How can having her children immunized against rubella protect a woman of childbearing age?

Have students discuss what an epidemic is and whether there have been any epidemics in their community in recent years. Ask: How can epidemics be halted? What role do immunizations play?

Making Connections: Math
Have students investigate various options for family health coverage, including any low-cost alternatives (e.g., public free clinics) that may exist in their own community. Have students present their findings in a chart that compares the amounts spent on insurance premiums, deductibles, and other cost factors.

Using the Photograph
Direct students' attention to the photograph on this page. Ask: What is happening in this picture? At what age does immunization begin? What are factors that explain why some parents, especially those living below the poverty line, fail to ensure that their children are immunized?

TEEN PARENTING

Health Awareness
Read the following scenario to students: Iris is an eighteen-year-old mother who is working part-time at a department store while trying to finish high school. One day, when her baby, Luis, was about six months old, a co-worker of Iris made a comment about babies and immunizations. Iris responded by saying, "I think taking a baby to the doctor when he or she isn't sick is a waste of time and money—and I don't have a lot of either. Sometime when I have to take him anyway, I'll see about getting his shots." Ask students to discuss what they would say to Iris. Why may teen parents see less need for preventive health care than older parents?

GUIDED PRACTICE (continued)

Using the Chart

Have interested groups of students add a fifth column to the chart on these pages. The column, which is to contain information researched by the students, should be headed "When First Detected" and should briefly review the history of the condition and detail the search for a vaccine.

Practicing Decision Making

Have students consider this situation: Tram is the single parent of a four-year-old girl named Li. For the past two days, Li has been running a fever and having difficulty keeping food down. Tram, who can't afford to take time off from her job, is hoping her daughter just has a touch of the flu. Ask students to discuss what action Tram should take and why.

Making Connections:
Language Arts

Have interested students locate and read books on the following individuals: Louis Pasteur, Edward Jenner, Jonas Salk. In a book report to the class, students are to address the accomplishments of the individual they read about. Students should also state whether they would recommend the book to other students, providing reasons for their view.

Did You Know?

During the Middle Ages, a plague called the Black Death wiped out nearly a quarter of the population of Europe.

DISEASE & IMMUNIZATION

DISEASE	IMMUNIZATION	SYMPTOMS	HOME CARE
CHICKEN POX	Vaccine now available. Check with physician or health care provider.	A rash of tiny red, raised pimples or blisters appears first. In a day or two, scabs form which fall off in 7 to 10 days. The rash affects the whole body. Fever is either absent or no higher than 102° F (39°C). Rash is irritating but child usually does not feel ill otherwise.	Rest in bed during feverish stage. Fever control is recommended but do not use aspirin. Keep the child cool in loose clothing. Apply talcum powder or calamine lotion to relieve the itching. Recovery is usually within 7 days. Once scabs form, and no new pox have appeared for 2 days, the disease is no longer infectious.
DIPHTHERIA	DPT shots against diphtheria, pertussis (whooping cough), and tetanus are given at 2, 4, and 6 months of age. Booster shots at 18 months and between 3 and 6 years. A combined tetanus and diphtheria shot at age 12 and every 10 years thereafter.	Sore throat, pain in limbs, loss of appetite, swollen neck glands, difficulty breathing.	Child should be under close medical supervision. Hospitalization is usually necessary.
HAEMOPHILUS INFLUENZA (HIB)	Vaccinations are given at 2 years of age. Children 18-23 months of age who attend child care facilities should be vaccinated, as the disease is easily spread. Children should be revaccinated 2-12 months later, but not before 24 months of age.	Most common cause of bacterial meningitis. Symptoms include sudden onset of fever, nausea, vomiting, and intense headaches.	A doctor's care is essential. Patient will need immediate hospitalization. Disease is fatal in 5 percent of meningitis cases in children less than 5 years of age. Causes long-term neurological problems in many others.

(Continued on next page)

MORE ABOUT

Immunity and Allergies

Immunization uses the body's natural defensive mechanisms to create artificial protection against communicable diseases. The body protects itself against pathogens (i.e., germs), including bacteria and many viruses, by creating antibodies. The antibodies created remain in the body long after the infection has gone. If the person is exposed to the same pathogen again, the antibodies in the system will fight off the invaders, making the person immune to them. In allergic reactions, the immune mechanism "misfires," creating antibodies against substances that are not normally harmful, such as milk or pollen.

DISEASE & IMMUNIZATION (cont'd.)

DISEASE	IMMUNIZATION	SYMPTOMS	HOME CARE
MEASLES	Vaccination at about 15 months. Combination vacines (a Measles/Rubella and a Measles/Mumps/Rubella are available).	Usually fever, sometimes as high as 105° (41°C). The child may also cough, have a runny nose and inflamed, watery eyes. About 4 days later a blotchy, dusty-red rash appears, often seen first behind the ears or on the forehead and face. On day 6 rash quicky fades and by day 7 all symptoms are gone.	Child should be under a doctor's supervision and kept in bed for the duration of the fever. The disease is most contagious during the few days before and after the rash appears. If patient's eyes are sensitive, the child should be kept in a darkened room and not allowed to read or do other close work.
MUMPS	Vaccine is given at 12 months or thereafter. A parent who has not had mumps may be immunized if his or her child contracts the disease.	Sudden fever, occasional nausea, abdominal pain, and swelling of one or more salivary glands, most commonly those located at the angles of the jaws. Swelling reaches maximum within 24 hours and may last 7-10 days. In boys, infection may also cause painful swelling in the testicles.	A hot-water bottle and analgesics may ease pain. Fluids are easiest to swallow. Mumps is usually a mild disease, leaving no ill effects. However, sometimes deafness occurs.
POLIOMYELITIS	The Sabin vaccine is given orally at 2, 4, and 18 months of age and again at 4 or 5 years.	Sudden fever, headache, vomiting, stiffness of neck. In paralytic cases, the muscles become painful and tender; paralysis follows.	A doctor's care is essential. Patient must be isolated and kept in bed during acute phase. In paralytic cases, even partial recovery takes many months.
RUBELLA (German Measles)	Vaccination between 12 and 15 months of age or thereafter.	Similar to those of a head cold. Mild fever and joint pain are often the first signs, followed by rash on face and head, and later on neck and body. Lymph nodes at back of neck may become tender and swollen.	Child should be kept at home until recovery. The disease is dangerous only for women during pregnancy. It can cause defects in the unborn child.

(Continued on next page)

SEE HOW THEY GROW

Allergies

The greatest single cause of chronic health problems among young children is allergies. Symptoms can range from the mildly annoying to the disabling and even life-threatening. In children, allergies oftentimes go hand in hand with the pulmonary condition known as asthma. As a rule, cases of asthma and asthmatic bronchitis contracted in childhood will lessen or dissipate by the time of adulthood. In some children, a predisposition for asthma exists but remains dormant until adulthood, when it emerges as a condition called late-onset chronic obstructive pulmonary disease (COPD). Although symptoms of COPD are rare in children, they can be quite serious in adults.

GUIDED PRACTICE (continued)

Using the Chart
Have students note the number of illnesses and conditions in the chart that share common symptoms. Have students use the recommended treatment warnings to rank these conditions from 1 to 3, where 1 corresponds to "extremely serious" and 3 corresponds to "less serious."

Using Management Skills
Have an interested volunteer arrange to interview a pediatrician or pediatric nurse about medical care during the first year. In particular, the student should determine how often well-baby visits are scheduled, how much these visits cost, when immunizations are begun, and what advice the health care professional gives parents during well-baby visits.

Promoting Discussion
Have students note that the chart on pages 492-494 contains no mention of an immunization for smallpox. Ask them to discuss why this is so. Are there other diseases that have been similarly controlled or eliminated by medical science?
Ask students what allergies are. What kinds of preventive measures or treatment for allergies are students familiar with? How might allergies affect some children emotionally and socially?

Critical Thinking

Ask students to consider and discuss how travel could present problems for a child who has allergies. (The child might encounter dust and animal hair in other people's homes, be served foods to which he or she is allergic, or come in contact with allergens in household cleaners and bedding.)

INDEPENDENT PRACTICE

Journal Writing

Have students plan and write out a day's balanced menu for a child who is allergic to milk, wheat, eggs, and chocolate. Encourage students to share their menus as a lead-in to a discussion of whether students found it difficult, given the allergy restrictions, to cover the basic food groups.

Student Workbook

Have students complete "Magic Square" in the Student Workbook.

Extension

Let students work independently or in small groups to complete one or more of these extension activities:

• Research and total the number of fatalities in each of the wars the United States has fought. Then research the number of people who have been killed in automobile accidents since the invention of the automobile. Finally, determine the ratio of deaths from all wars combined to those caused by automobiles.

• Research and report on the immune response and how vaccines work. Summarize your findings in a written report.

DISEASE & IMMUNIZATION (cont'd.)

DISEASE	IMMUNIZATION	SYMPTOMS	HOME CARE
SCARLET FEVER and STREPTOCOCCAL SORE THROAT	No prevention. Penicillin or erythromycin helps prevent such complications as rheumatic fever.	Sudden onset, with headache, fever, sore throat. Lymph nodes usually enlarged. In scarlet fever a rash appears, usually within 24 hours, as fine red dots. The rash is seen first on the neck and upper part of the chest, and lasts 24 hours to 10 days. When it fades, skin peels. The rash is the only symptom that differentiates scarlet fever from "strep throat."	Because strep throat and scarlet fever can be followed by or reactivate rheumatic fever, a physician's care is needed. The child should rest in a warm, well-ventilated room. Patient usually recovers in a week's time, but parent should watch for such complications as earache or inflamed neck glands.
WHOOPING COUGH (Pertussis)	See Diphtheria section.	Begins with cough that is worse at night. Symptoms may at first be mild. Characteristic "whooping" cough develops in about 2 weeks, and coughing spasms sometimes end with vomiting.	Child should take antibiotics under a doctor's care. Hospitalization is often required for infants. Rest is important, as is a diet that will not irritate the throat. Keep the child isolated from other children until antibiotics have been taken for at least 5 days.

Allergies

An **allergy** is *an oversensitivity to one or more common substances.* Individuals may have allergic reactions when they eat, breathe in, or touch specific substances, such as grass, molds, milk products, and pollens. Symptoms of allergic reactions may be mild, such as nonitching rash, nasal stuffiness, or a runny nose. Some allergic reactions, however, can be life-threatening and may cause such conditions as constriction of the air sacs in the lungs and severely diminished oxygen intake.

Nearly half of all the children in the United States develop allergies. Specific allergies are not inherited, but the tendency to be allergic is apparently inherited. If both parents have allergies, the chance of their child's developing at least one allergy is about 70 percent.

Although allergies cannot be cured, their effects are often preventable. For example, a child who is allergic to a specific

COOPERATIVE LEARNING

Researching Allergens

Divide the class into small groups, and ask each to research one of the following categories of allergens, noting the specific sources for each, the numbers of individuals it affects, the problems it can lead to, and available remedies or treatment:

• ingestants (foods or oral medicines),

• inhalants (pollens, molds, dust, animal dander),

• contactants (fibers, soaps, dyes, cosmetics, plants such as poison ivy), and

• injectibles (insect stings or medical injections).

Encourage groups to share their results in an illustrated in-class forum.

food can avoid eating that food—even in small amounts. Foods that commonly cause allergies in babies and children include milk, cereal grains, eggs, shellfish, nuts, fresh fruit juices, chocolate, and food additives.

A doctor may prescribe medication to help control an allergy. If the allergy causes severe problems, the child may be given a series of allergy tests to determine which specific substances are causing the problems. Then the child can be gradually desensitized to those substances.

A child who is sensitive to animal hair may still be able to have a pet, as long as it is kept outdoors.

SECTION 1 REVIEW

CHECK YOUR UNDERSTANDING

1. List four things necessary to keep a child safe.
2. Define the term infant mortality rate.
3. When should car safety restraints be used?
4. List four things caregivers should do to reduce the risk of choking for babies and young children.
5. Which telephone numbers should young children learn?
6. List the seven illnesses that children should be immunized against.
7. What is an allergy?

DISCUSS AND DISCOVER

1. Design and make a poster to increase parents' awareness of one aspect of child safety. If possible, display your poster in an area where parents are likely to read it.

Observing & Participating

Visit a local elementary school, and observe a group of kindergartners or first graders as they play outside on the school yard. Describe the playground equipment used by the children. What are the children's other outdoor activities? Are there any apparent safety hazards on the school yard? Who supervises the children's play? How closely?

SECTION 1 REVIEW

1. Knowledge of child development; a safe environment; alertness to safety hazards; teaching the child safe habits.
2. The percentage of deaths during the first year of life.
3. Rear-facing bucket-type carriers; whenever the baby rides in a car.
4. See safety tip on page 489.
5. Their own phone numbers and 911 or 0 for emergency.
6. Diptheria, pertussis, tetanus, measles, mumps, rubella, polio.
7. An oversensitivity to one or more common substances.

ASSESS

CHECKING COMPREHENSION

Assign students to write their responses to the Check Your Understanding questions in the Section 1 Review. Answers to the questions are given at the bottom of this page.

EVALUATE

Have students complete the Chapter 17, Section 1 quiz in the TCR.

Reteaching

1. Assign Reteaching Activity 40 in the TCR and have students complete the activity and review their responses.
2. Have students use the chart on pages 492-494 to make a recommended schedule for immunization of children, listing in chronological order the ages when the various immunizations should be given.

Enrichment

1. Assign Enrichment 40 in the TCR.
2. Have students write to local, state, and national lawmakers, proposing new and more stringent safety laws. For example, students might propose seat belts on public transportation vehicles. Some students may prefer to write to the editor of the local newspaper.

Extension

Have students investigate and report on alternative procedures used by health care providers for determining the presence of an allergic condition. (One example is the use of a blood test rather than the so-called scratch test.)

CLOSE

Have students make posters about car safety restraints with the title "Keeping Children Safe." Posters should include an attention-getting slogan. Display the posters around the classroom.

FOCUS

SECTION 2 RESOURCES

Teacher's Classroom Resources
• Enrichment 41
• Reteaching 41
• Section 2 Quiz

Student Workbook
• Take Action

SECTION OVERVIEW

In Section 2, students learn aspects of handling emergencies involving children, including first aid for animal bites, bleeding, bumps and bruises, burns, choking, convulsions, fainting, fractures and sprains, insect bites and stings, poisoning, shock, and splinters. Coverage of artificial respiration and CPR is also included.

MOTIVATOR

Remind students that children turn to their parents or adult guardians in any emergency, certain that these adults can fix everything. Ask them how they would feel if they suddenly found themselves in charge. On the chalkboard, write the sentence "I am the parent now!" Then have students list the "what if's" that might occur to a new parent. What emergencies might that parent need to face? Explain that this chapter will list the most common emergencies and how to handle them.

USING TERMS TO LEARN

Have students attempt to relate the terms listed in "Terms to Learn" by placing them in a "word tree." Explain that the tree is meant to reveal, among other things, hierarchical relations among words (e.g., in a hypothetical tree, the word *dime* would branch out from the word *coin*). Have students share and compare completed trees.

SECTION **2**

Handling Emergencies

TERMS TO LEARN

artificial respiration
convulsion
CPR (cardiopulmonary
  resuscitation)
fracture
Heimlich maneuver
poison control centers
sprain

OBJECTIVES

• Recognize emergency situations and plan appropriate responses.

• Demonstrate appropriate first aid for common ailments.

• Identify basic rescue techniques.

Someday you may have to take care of a child in an emergency. If that happens, you will have to make decisions and take actions that will affect the child's health and well-being—perhaps even the child's life. You can prepare yourself by learning how to act in an emergency and how to give first aid and use rescue techniques.

Guidelines for Fast Action

Accidents often happen because children fail to recognize danger or to understand their own limitations. If a child in your care does get hurt, these five guidelines will help you make good decisions:

1. **Above all, try to remain calm.** A quiet, soothing approach will help reassure the child and help you think more clearly.
2. **Evaluate the situation.** What seems to be wrong? Is the child burned, bleeding heavily, or unconscious? Does the child have an arm or leg in an awkward position?
3. **Make the victim comfortable.** If the injury is serious, keep the child warm with a blanket, jacket, or other covering.
4. **Call for help, if symptoms indicate a need.** If you are not certain what the problem is or how to care for an injury, call for help. Contact the child's parents, a neighbor, a doctor, or emergency room of a hospital; or call for the paramedics or an ambulance. What you say on the phone is as important as making the call. Give the facts as clearly and concisely as possible. You will be able to save valuable time if you keep near the phone a list of phone numbers you might need and a record of the address where you are.

COOPERATIVE LEARNING

Home Emergency Plans

Have students work in groups to plan an emergency drill that could be used at home to help families practice what to do in case of an accident or other emergency. If possible, arrange to have each student in a group practice the drill at home with his or her family. Groups should then report the results to the class. In particular, students should determine answers to the following questions: Were the drills effective in preparing families for all eventualities? Did each family member know what to do for a given emergency? Was the drill equally effective for large and small families?

5. **Give the minimum necessary first aid treatment.** Knowing what you should *not* do in an emergency is often as important as knowing what you should do. For instance, some injuries can be made worse just by moving the patient. If you are in doubt about how to handle an injured person, give only the most necessary first aid treatment and seek help from someone better trained.

First Aid

It is essential for anyone who takes care of children to be familiar with first aid procedures. The following guidelines are very general. For more information, contact the nearest office of the American Red Cross about first aid training classes.

Animal Bites

Wash the area around the bite with soap and running water. Try to have the animal caught so that it can be tested for rabies. (Wild animals are more likely than pets to have rabies.) The victim should be checked by a doctor. A DPT shot may be necessary.

Bleeding

Stop the bleeding by placing a clean, wet or dry cloth over the wound and pressing hard for about ten minutes without releasing. If the bleeding is severe, send for medical help.

- **Minor cuts or scrapes.** Clean a small cut or a simple scrape with soap and warm water. Apply a mild antiseptic, and cover the wound with a bandage.

- **Deep cuts or wounds.** These may be severe. If the child is pale and bluish and his or her skin is moist, or if the child's breathing is shallow and rapid, send for medical help. Continue to try to stop the bleeding until medical assistance arrives. Elevating the affected area may help. Do not apply a tourniquet. (A tourniquet is a bandage that cuts off the blood supply to a portion of the body.) An improperly applied tourniquet can further harm the victim.

- **Nosebleeds.** A nosebleed may result from an injury, or it may have no apparent cause. Usually, a small blood vessel inside the nose has broken. Have the child sit down and lean slightly forward over a basin or sink. Using the thumb and forefinger, squeeze the child's nose firmly just below the bones in the nose. Continue squeezing for several minutes; then check to see whether the bleeding has stopped. If not,

No one can predict an emergency. However, it is possible to prepare yourself so that you can act quickly if an emergency occurs.

To stop a nosebleed, have the child lean forward slightly. Firmly press above the nostrils and hold for several minutes.

TEACH
Pages 496-506
- Guidelines for Fast Action
- First Aid
- Rescue Techniques
- Allergies

GUIDED PRACTICE
Promoting Discussion
Have students skim headings in the section and discuss which injuries and health emergencies they feel prepared to handle. Then have them identify the emergencies they do not feel prepared to handle and the situations in which these are most likely to occur.
Have students discuss which telephone numbers a parent or caregiver should keep near the telephone in addition to those for police, fire, rescue squad, and poison control center. (The numbers of the nearest emergency rooms, a hospital with a trauma unit, a children's hospital if one is nearby, the family doctor, and the pediatrician.)

Critical Thinking
Have students discuss the responsibilities connected with giving first aid to an accident victim. Ask: What kinds of guidelines would be useful in deciding whether to attempt first aid treatment? Do people ever do the wrong thing when administering first aid? What can happen in these situations? Is this an argument for not giving first aid when needed? How can people feel secure about giving first aid without making mistakes?

Did You Know?
Children who practice the same sport for two hours each day are at a greater risk for developing injuries from the wear and tear on tendons and ligaments, leading to broken bones and torn tissue.

OBSERVING AND PARTICIPATING

Developing Observational Skills
Divide the class into groups of three or four students. Arrange with the school nurse to allow these small groups to observe him or her during the course of a typical day. Instruct group members to carry along pads of paper and pencils, and to make notes about what they see. After allowing ample time for observation, ask groups to use their notes as the starting point for a discussion. Ask: How many patients did the nurse treat? What first aid techniques were administered? Which injuries, if any, were severe enough to require additional medical attention?

Practicing Decision Making

Have students work in pairs to create skits depicting the reactions of children and appropriate steps taken by caregivers in the following situations or others students might create:

• A child deeply gashes a leg in a fall.

• A child is bleeding profusely after a cut with a kitchen knife.

Using the Photograph

Direct students' attention to the bottom photograph on page 497, and ask them to describe what is happening. Ask volunteers who have suffered nosebleeds to describe the first aid that was administered to them. If the treatment was not consistent with that shown here, what conclusions, if any, can students draw about the importance of keeping current on safety procedures?

Using Management Skills

Have students interview an Emergency Medical Technician (EMT) about how emergency service is handled in your community, the types of emergencies EMTs handle, the training needed, and the work schedule and routine of EMTs. Ask students to write a report in the form of a feature article for a newspaper.

Promoting Discussion

Invite a person from the public health department to speak to students about how animal bites are handled. Encourage students to determine answers to questions such as the following: Are most bites from domestic animals or wild animals? What type of confinement facilities does the department have? What procedures are followed when an animal bite is reported? Have students prepare additional questions to ask the speaker.

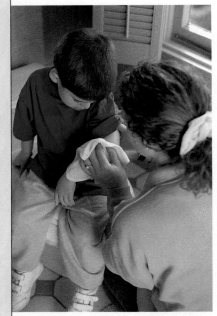

Minor burns should be treated with a cold, wet cloth and covered with a clean, dry cloth. More serious burns require professional medical help.

reapply pressure for five to ten minutes. Sometimes applying cold packs to the nose and forehead also help. If you cannot stop the bleeding, or if the child becomes dizzy or pale, seek medical help.

Bumps and Bruises

Treat bumps and bruises with a cold cloth or ice pack to minimize swelling. An injured arm or leg can be elevated. If the child complains of pain for more than a day, call a physician.

A fall or bump on the head can be serious. Call a doctor if the child loses consciousness, is drowsy or irritable, complains of headache, or vomits.

Burns

How you treat a burn depends on what caused the burn and how bad it is. All but small surface burns are serious because they may cause scarring, infections, or shock. Burns are classified by degree.

• **First-degree burns look red and slightly swollen.** They may be caused by too much sun, hot objects, hot water, or steam. First-degree burns heal rapidly.

• **Second-degree burns are deeper, redder, and blistered.** They remain swollen and somewhat moist for several days. They can have various causes, including very deep sunburn, hot liquids, and flammable products like gasoline. Second-degree burns should be treated by a physician.

• **Third-degree burns destroy the skin.** These burns may look white or charred, or they may resemble second-degree burns at first. There may be little pain at first because the nerve endings have been destroyed. Third-degree burns can be caused by flames, burning clothing, hot water, extremely hot objects, or electricity. The skin is lost and will not grow back. Only scar tissue will cover the area after healing. Third-degree burns are extremely serious and require emergency medical attention. Treat small, surface burns where the skin is not broken with a cold, wet cloth. Apply the cloth several times for short periods to take the heat out of the burn. A burned hand or foot may be placed in a basin of cold water. Then cover the burned area with a clean, loose cloth. Never apply butter or grease to a burn. If the skin has been broken or the burn looks serious, call for medical help. Cover the burn with a clean, dry cloth and keep the patient warm. To help ease the pain, elevate the burned area slightly. The patient should be taken to a hospital as soon as possible.

MORE ABOUT

Bruises

The correct medical name for a bruise is *contusion*. This is an injury to tissues caused by a sudden impact or crushing. In a contusion, tiny blood vessels under the skin are ruptured, causing discoloration (the so-called black and blue marks) although the skin usually remains unbroken. Cold, wet compresses or an ice bag can help reduce pain and swelling from a contusion. Salt-water ice, however, should be avoided. The salt in the water can lower the water's temperature, which, in turn, can result in further tissue damage.

Household products, such as toilet bowl cleaners, drain cleaners, and disinfectants, can cause chemical burns. Using protective gloves or a towel, wash off the affected area immediately and completely with cold water. Remove any clothing with the chemical on it, unless the clothing is stuck to the skin. Apply a clean bandage, and call a doctor.

Electrical burns may be deep, but they often appear minor, leaving only a small black dot on the skin. Cool the burned area with cold water, and cover it with a clean, smooth cloth such as a handkerchief. Then have the patient lie down with legs elevated and head turned to one side. This prevents shock. (See pages 503 and 505 for more information about shock.) Take the child to a hospital emergency room, or call an ambulance.

Choking

Choking occurs when something is caught in a person's throat. With a child, this may be food or a small object. The danger is that choking can cut off the supply of air. When oxygen is restricted, brain damage can occur within a few minutes.

First, recognize the signs of choking: an inability to speak, breathe, or cry; bluish lips, nails, and skin; high-pitched noises or ineffective coughing. If a baby or child is choking, immediately work to help dislodge the object that is blocking the breathing passage. Hold a baby or small child facedown across your lap with the head lowered; for a larger child, kneel on the floor and drape the child facedown over your thighs so that the head is lowered. Use the heel of your hand to give four quick blows between the child's shoulder blades. This often helps get the object out. If this method does not succeed, you can use the **Heimlich maneuver**, a *technique for using pressure on the air within the body to force an object interfering with breathing from the throat.* The diagrams on page 500 show how to administer a rescue maneuver to choking infants and the Heimlich maneuver to older children and adults.

Keep in mind that the amount of pressure to use in the Heimlich maneuver depends on the age and size of the victim. Too much pressure, especially on a young child, can be harmful. It is best to get special training in using the Heimlich maneuver—before you need to use it.

If the baby or child has lost consciousness or stops breathing, begin artificial respiration and call for emergency medical help. (See page 506 for information on artificial respiration.) If the child stops breathing, use your thumb and forefinger to try to locate and remove the object from the child's throat only if you can see the object and remove it safely. Then begin artificial respiration immediately. If you can't remove the object, still try to give air. Continue until help arrives.

GUIDED PRACTICE (continued)

Promoting Discussion
Find pictures of burns of varying severity. Have students identify whether they think the burns are first-degree, second-degree, or third-degree, discussing the reasons for their assumptions.

Using Management Skills
Have students plan and assemble a basic first aid kit. When complete, evaluate the kit. How much did it cost to make? Could it have been done any more cheaply? What other useful items could have been included? How would these additions have affected the cost of the kit?

Critical Thinking
Provide students with empty household cleaner containers that carry warning labels. Have students compare the labels, noting the first aid measures each recommends. Ask: What steps could manufacturers of these products take to further reduce accidents resulting from the products' use?

Cooperative Learning
Have students work in pairs to practice the correct positioning for the Heimlich maneuver. Emphasize that actual abdominal thrusts can cause internal injury and should not be performed unless the person is choking.

HEALTH TIP

When you are assessing a choking situation, it is always best to look for the universal distress signal. This signal consists of clutching the neck between the thumb and index finger. Knowing this signal could save your own life.

TEEN PARENTING

Emergency Preparedness
If you have teenage parents in your class, ask them to share their experiences with illness and emergencies involving their own children. Encourage these students to be prepared for possible problems in the future by having them ask themselves—and find answers to—questions such as the following: Who can I call upon to help out in an emergency? Do I know the location of the nearest telephone at all times? Do I have a list of emergency numbers readily available? Do I know a physician I can call if I need one? How would I go about getting to the hospital in the event of an emergency?

GUIDED PRACTICE (continued)

GUIDED PRACTICE (continued)

Using Management Skills

Ask interested volunteers to prepare a choking safety demonstration for a different class in the school. Students involved in the demonstration should use a mannequin or mock abdominal thrusts to demonstrate the Heimlich maneuver for the audience. Be sure students explain that actual abdominal thrusts should not be performed unless the person is choking.

Cooperative Learning

Have students work in groups to create brochures about the Heimlich maneuver, describing the technique and when to use it. If they wish, students may illustrate their brochures.

Promoting Discussion

Ask students to review the differences between the rescue maneuver used for infants and the Heimlich maneuver used for toddlers, older children, and adults. Ask each student to consider, in terms of his or her own family situation, which of these techniques it would be most valuable for him or her to know.

Making Connections: Health

Ask students to explain why they should use, whenever possible, protective devices when giving emergency assistance. Use the drawings on this page and on page 506 to discuss the use of gloves and masks in a child care setting.

HEALTH TIP

Individuals who know first aid and offer their services in an emergency are protected by a Good Samaritan Law. This law protects individuals from being held accountable for damages to or pain and suffering experienced by the accident victim.

Rescue Maneuver for Choking Infants

1. Turn the infant facedown over your arm.

2. Using the heel of your other hand, give four quick blows between the infant's shoulder blades.

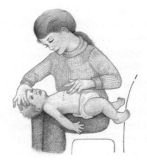

3. Turn the infant over, supporting the head, neck, and back. Position your two middle fingers below the rib cage and above the navel; give four quick thrusts toward the chest. Repeat these three steps, if needed.

Heimlich Maneuver for Children One Year and Older and Adults

If the victim is standing or sitting:

1. Stand behind the victim. Clasp your hands with your fists just below the victim's rib cage.

2. Press your clasped hands into the victim's abdomen with a quick upward thrust. Repeat step 2 if necessary.

If the victim has collapsed:

1. Kneel above the victim's hips. Place both your hands, one over the other, on the victim's abdomen. The heel of your bottom hand should be slightly above the victim's navel and below his or her rib cage.

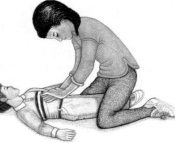

2. Use the force of both hands to press with a quick upward thrust. Repeat step 2 if necessary.

MORE ABOUT

Choking

Each year in the United States, about 3,000 people die from choking. Almost two-thirds of these deaths involve children under age two. Choking occurs most often during eating, with meat being the most common single cause of choking in adults. Other factors that may cause choking include using alcohol, having dentures, and swallowing large, poorly chewed pieces of food.

There are four basic kinds of choking. The first is marked by the sensation of something in the airway; the second, by an obstruction on the mouth side of the epiglottis (the flap guarding the opening to the windpipe); and the third, by an object on the other side of the epiglottis. The fourth type is caused by the presence of a foreign body in the lungs themselves.

Convulsions

A **convulsion** or a seizure is *a period of unconsciousness with uncontrolled jerking or twitching of the muscles.* There are many causes of convulsions. They occur most often in infants, usually as a result of high fever.

If a child of any age, including an infant, has a convulsion, place the child on his or her side on the floor. Move any hard objects out of the way. Don't attempt to hold the child down, and don't force anything between his or her teeth. After the convulsion stops, be sure the child's head is turned to one side to reduce any risk of choking. Check with a doctor for further instructions. If the convulsion lasts more than 15 minutes, take the child to a hospital emergency room or call an ambulance.

Fainting

Fainting is a loss of consciousness. A child may collapse without warning, or he or she may first experience sweating, cold skin, nausea, or dizziness. A child who is about to faint often looks pale or bluish. Anyone who feels faint should lie down or sit with the head between the legs.

If a child has fainted, loosen any tight clothing. Position the child's head to one side. Check to be sure the child is breathing. If breathing has stopped, begin artificial respiration, and have someone call for medical assistance. (See page 506 for information on artificial respiration.) If the child is breathing, expect him or her to revive from the faint within a minute or two. If the child does not gain consciousness within two minutes, call for help. A child who has had a head injury, has experienced seizurelike movements, or has been unconscious for more than two minutes should be seen by a physician immediately.

Fractures and Sprains

A **fracture** is *a break or a crack in a bone.* A **sprain** is *an injury caused by sudden, violent stretching of a joint or muscle.* Both may cause pain, swelling, and bruising. It is often difficult to tell a sprain from a fracture without an X ray.

If you suspect that a child has a fracture or a sprain, do not move the child until you know how serious the injury is. This is especially important for back, rib, neck, or collarbone injuries. You can cause further damage—even paralysis—by moving the child. Call for qualified medical help, and use artificial respiration if necessary.

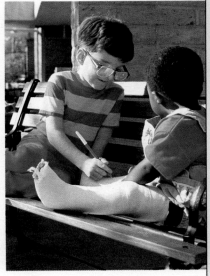

A broken bone must be set by a doctor so that the fracture will heal properly. Children like to have their casts signed by friends.

GUIDED PRACTICE (continued)

Critical Thinking
Ask students why a person suffering a convulsion should be placed on his or her side and why the patient's head is turned to the side after the convulsion.

Promoting Discussion
Have a volunteer read about and report to the class on the subject of epilepsy (a chronic nervous disorder characterized by muscular convulsions with partial or complete loss of consciousness), its symptoms and control. After the report, discuss with students how epilepsy is similar to and different from the convulsion described in the text.

Cooperative Learning
Point out to students that when a child has an accident, such as breaking a leg in a fall, he or she may become excessively fearful as a result of increased feelings of vulnerability. Divide the class into small discussion groups. Ask each group to brainstorm ways in which parents can help alleviate such fears. What coping skills might parents teach the child? Have groups share their responses.

Practicing Decision Making
Have students decide what they would do in the following situation: They are baby-sitting for a neighbor's small child who tends to be very contrary. The child is walking unsteadily along a backyard fence, a fall from which could result in disaster. What measures would students take in dealing with this dangerous situation?

HEALTHY FAMILIES/HEALTHY CHILDREN

Health and Safety
Fainting in young children can be caused by a number of factors that are often radically different from those causing this condition in older children and adults. The causes include anemia, breath-holding, hyperventilation, extreme excitement (hysteria), drug reactions, illness or infection, and poisoning. Discuss with students the steps that need to be taken in the event that a young child faints. Ask: Why would it be important to discover the cause of fainting? Why would an emergency room attendant be interested in the child's medical history?

GUIDED PRACTICE (continued)

Promoting Discussion

Provide students with pamphlets or other handouts on Lyme disease and Rocky Mountain spotted fever. Have them discuss how these diseases, both of which are contracted from insect bites, are different from and similar to the insect-borne diseases mentioned in the text. Ask: What are the symptoms of the two illnesses? What are the treatments?

Critical Thinking

Ask students why it might be difficult to determine whether a child has taken poison and what type of poison he or she has taken. (The child may be unconscious or too young to talk—and, therefore, unable to describe what he or she has done; he or she may be reluctant to admit to breaking rules.)

Using Management Skills

Divide the class into pairs, and provide each pair with a doll. Explain that partners are to take turns practicing what they should do when a child has convulsions, faints, has a fracture, or gets an insect bite.

SAFETY TIP

Most poisonings occur in children under the age of five. According to the Poison Prevention Control Council, one in three poisonings in children occurs when the child is visiting grandparents. Ask students why this might be true. How could grandparents help prevent these poisonings?

You can treat a mild sprain by elevating the injured area. Apply cold packs to help reduce swelling. If the pain persists, check with a doctor.

Insect Stings and Bites

If a child has been stung by a bee, wasp, hornet, or yellow jacket, scrape off any stinger. Apply an ice pack or ice water to the affected area. Then cover the area with a paste made from baking soda and water.

Some people are very allergic to insect stings. For them, a single sting can cause serious illness or even death. Anyone with a known allergy to stings must be taken to a hospital or doctor immediately after being stung. In addition, anyone who becomes dizzy, feels faint, has difficulty breathing, shows signs of generalized swelling, or perspires heavily after a sting needs prompt medical attention.

Ticks are small insects that cling to the skin or scalp. They are dangerous because they carry diseases. If you find a tick on a child, don't try to pull it off. Instead, cover the tick with cooking oil (or a similar heavy oil) until it comes loose. Wash the area well with soap and water.

Mosquito, ant, and chigger bites are annoying, but they are usually not dangerous. A baking soda paste or a coating of witch hazel or rubbing alcohol will give relief.

Poisoning

Poisons are one of the greatest hazards for young children. Too often, parents and other caregivers leave poisonous products within a child's reach around the house. Part of the problem is that so many common household products are poisonous. The chart on page 504 lists common household poisons. These items should be kept out of the reach of children, preferably in a locked cabinet.

Recognizing the fact that a child has been poisoned is not always easy. If a toddler is holding an empty vitamin bottle and has a mouthful of vitamin tablet pieces, the situation is clear. Often, however, it is difficult to tell. Here are some symptoms that may indicate poisoning:

- **Swallowed poisons** can cause difficulty in breathing, unconsciousness, fever, burns in the mouth and throat, and vomiting from swallowed poisons or chemicals.
- **Skin-contact poisons** can cause burns or rash on the skin.
- **Eye-contact poisons** can cause burning or irritation of the eyes, or blindness.
- **Inhaled poisons** can cause choking, coughing, nausea, or dizziness from fumes, sprays, and poisonous gases.

MORE ABOUT

Poisons

Common household poisons are rated according to six toxicity levels, or classes, with each class being progressively more toxic. Class 1 poisons, which are virtually nontoxic, include glues and pastes, soaps, and candles. Class 3—or moderately toxic—substances, by contrast, include fingernail polish, antifreeze, and lighter fluid, while class 6 toxins include insecticides, rodenticides, herbicides, and other "supertoxic" chemicals. A lethal dose of a class 1 poison for a 150-lb (68-kg) person would be in excess of a quart. A lethal dose of a class 6 poison for the same person would consist of less than seven drops!

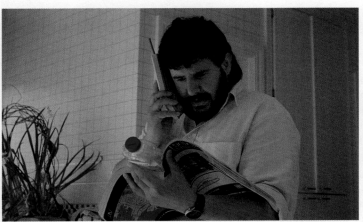

If you suspect poisoning, call for help right away. Be prepared to tell what you think caused the poisoning and how much was involved. Have the container with you when you call.

In case a child is poisoned, you should know what to do:

1. Keep emergency phone numbers and addresses posted by all telephones. Include numbers for the doctor, hospital, police, and poison control center. **Poison control centers** are *special hospital units that are equipped to advise and treat poison victims.* If you care for children in someone else's home, take a copy of your emergency phone number list with you.

2. Determine what has poisoned the child. If the child has swallowed something poisonous, determine about how much he or she swallowed.

3. Phone the poison control center or the child's doctor. Have the container of poison at hand as you call, so that you can give complete, accurate information. (Do not rely on the emergency procedures listed on product labels; they are not always accurate.)

4. Follow the directions you receive from the poison control center or the doctor. Act quickly and calmly.

Anyone who has been poisoned must be checked by a physician, even if emergency treatment has already been given and even if there are no symptoms. Be sure to take the poison container or a sample of the poison substance with you. This information helps the doctor give proper treatment.

Shock

When a person's body is threatened, such as by an injury, by the loss of a great deal of blood, or by poisoning, the body goes into shock. Important body functions, including breathing and heart action, are impaired. The symptoms of shock can include a pale or bluish skin color, rapid pulse, clammy skin, shallow breathing, enlarged pupils, a glassy stare, and nausea. Sometimes a person in shock loses consciousness.

GUIDED PRACTICE (continued)

Promoting Discussion

Ask students why someone who has been poisoned needs to see a physician. What might happen if emergency treatment is given but no medical follow-up occurs?

Have a representative of the nearest poison control center speak to students about the center, where it is located, how it is funded, how citizens can contact the center, the types of calls it gets, and the typical advice given. Have students write questions to ask the speaker.

Using the Photograph

Direct students' attention to the photograph on this page. Ask them why the man in the picture is holding the poison container. What other information should a parent or caretaker have on hand when he or she suspects a child has swallowed poison?

Using Management Skills

Have interested volunteers survey local pharmacies to see whether any carry an antipoison kit. Instruct students to obtain answers to the following questions: How much does a kit cost? What is included in the kit? What types of poisoning would the kit be effective in treating? Discuss with students how such a kit might be used. Could people make such a kit for themselves? Encourage students to share their findings with the class.

HEALTHY FAMILIES/HEALTHY CHILDREN

Treatment for Poisoning

One of the most effective treatments for poisoning in small children and adults alike is vomiting. This process, which empties the stomach, is recommended for all poisons except those that are sufficiently abrasive to cause additional damage on the way back up. Syrup of ipecac is a common emetic, or solution that induces vomiting. This syrup is effective 97 percent of the time. It is,

moreover, inexpensive, easily obtainable (it is available in most drugstores and without a prescription), does not aggravate poisoning, and may be kept in the family medicine cabinet. Before using syrup of ipecac or any other emetic, however, it is vital to contact a poison control center or physician.

Using Management Skills

Have students prepare first aid instruction sheets to be placed inside the door of a kitchen or medicine cabinet. Ask students whether the most needed information might vary according to the ages of the people in the household and, if so, to explain how.

Using the Chart

Have students add a fourth column to the chart on this page, to be titled "Antidotes and Remedies." Have them work in groups to obtain information from outside print resources to fill in the cells in each column.

Critical Thinking

Have students review the emergency situations covered in this section. Ask them to rate each situation from 1 to 5, where 1 denotes "very serious" and 5 denotes "less serious."

Cooperative Learning

Provide pairs of students with a large doll, and instruct partners to take turns practicing artificial respiration. Instruct students that they should refrain from actually making mouth contact with the doll.

Using Management Skills

Have students organize and sponsor a CPR training program. Students can make many of the arrangements, publicize the event, and participate in the program as trainees.

Critical Thinking

Have students obtain literature from the American Red Cross describing the procedure for administering CPR to adults. Ask them to tell in what ways this information is similar to and departs from the procedures for infants and small children.

COMMON HOUSEHOLD POISONS

KINDS OF POISONS	EXAMPLES	TYPE OF CONTACT
MEDICINES	• Sleeping pills • Aspirin • Tranquillizers • Vitamins • Cold preparations	• Swallowing
CLEANING PRODUCTS	• Ammonia • Automatic dishwasher detergent • Laundry detergents • Bleach • Drain and toilet bowl cleaners • Disinfectants • Furniture polish	• Swallowing • Skin • Eyes • Inhaling
PERSONAL CARE PRODUCTS	• Shampoo • Soap • Nail polish remover • Perfumes and after-shave lotions • Mouthwash • Rubbing alcohol	• Swallowing • Skin • Eyes • Inhaling
GARDENING AND GARAGE PRODUCTS	• Insecticides • Fertilizers • Rat and mouse poisons • Acids of all kinds • Gasoline • Paint thinner • Charcoal lighter fluid • Antifreeze	• Swallowing • Skin • Eyes • Inhaling
PLANTS	• Some wild mushrooms • English ivy • Daffodil bulbs • Rhubarb leaves • Holly berries • Poinsettias • Poison ivy and poison oak	• Swallowing • Skin

SEE HOW THEY GROW

Poison Prevention

Have students investigate whether Mr. Yuk symbols are available in your community. Mr. Yuk, a frequently used symbol for poison, was developed at the Children's Hospital in Pittsburgh. The symbol has proved to be more effective in communicating its message to children than the traditional skull and crossbones. Students can determine whether this symbol or some other is used by contacting the poison control center in your area. They can then plan a campaign to publicize the use and recognition of whichever symbol is employed.

Shock can be serious. If you suspect a child is in shock, seek medical help immediately. Until help arrives, be sure the child remains lying down, and keep him or her warm.

Splinters

Although splinters are not dangerous, they do hurt, and they can become infected. Splinters are usually tiny pieces of wood, metal, or glass; thorns may also be treated as splinters.

If part of the splinter is above the surface of the skin, it can be removed with tweezers. Sterilize the tweezers in boiling water or in a flame. If a nonglass splinter is just under the skin surface, it can be carefully taken out with a sterilized needle. Numb the skin over the splinter first with a piece of ice to help dull the pain. After the splinter has been removed, put antiseptic on the wound and cover it with a sterile bandage.

Large or deep splinters and those caused by glass can be more serious. They should be removed by a physician.

Rescue Techniques

When an emergency situation causes the victim to stop breathing and perhaps even causes the victim's heart to stop beating, immediate action is vital. You should become familiar with rescue techniques that enable you to respond quickly to this kind of life-or-death situation.

Artificial Respiration

Artificial respiration is *a procedure for forcing air into the lungs of a person whose own breathing has stopped.* Some emergency situations, including drowning and electrical shock, for example, call for artificial respiration. The technique for giving artificial respiration to infants and small children is slightly different from that for adults. It is shown on page 506. A rescue training class can provide you with more information about the proper way to give artificial respiration and can give you a chance to practice the correct techniques.

CPR

CPR, a short name for **cardiopulmonary resuscitation**, is *a rescue technique used to sustain life when both breathing and heart action have stopped.* Special training from a certified instructor is needed to perform CPR. Many communities offer training programs. To find out where CPR training is offered in your area, call a local chapter of the American Red Cross or the American Heart Association.

GUIDED PRACTICE (continued)

Making Connections: Social Studies
Ask interested students to research and report on the history and original purpose of the American Red Cross. Have them include information about the organization's present range of services.

INDEPENDENT PRACTICE

Journal Writing
Have students write a short first-person narrative in which they are the parent of a small child who falls victim to one of the emergencies described in this section. Have students share their completed stories.

Student Workbook
Have students complete "Take Action" in the Student Workbook.

Extension
Let students work independently or in small groups to complete one or more of these extensions activities:

- Research and write a report on the development of "artificial skin" used in cases of severe disfiguring burns.
- Conduct a poison check of your home, looking for the poisons listed on page 504. Note the following: How many of the products listed did you have at home? Where were the products stored? How easily could a young child be poisoned in your home? What could be done to make your home safer? Write a report summarizing your findings and listing your recommendations.

MORE ABOUT

CPR
It is important to stress to your class at the outset of coverage of rescue techniques that *CPR* should not be performed by anyone who has not taken CPR training and received certification. Emphasize that reading about CPR techniques in books and manuals, no matter how detailed, is no substitute. Incorrectly administering CPR could cause fractured ribs, punctured lungs, and injury to the heart. You may also want to encourage your students to seek approved CPR training, noting that it has been estimated that between 100,000 and 200,000 lives in the United States could be saved each year if more people knew CPR.

Artificial Respiration for Infants and Small Children

1. Turn the child's head to one side. With your finger, carefully clear the child's mouth of any foreign objects or fluid. (However, if the victim is under a year old, do not put your finger into his or her mouth.) If there is an object caught in the child's throat, or to clear the mouth of a young baby, follow the instructions for using the Heimlich maneuver on infants and toddlers, page 500. Be sure that you can see the object and remove it safely.

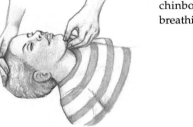

2. Tilt the child's head back slightly. Put two fingers just under the chinbone and lift the jaw into a jutting-out position. Check for breathing.

3. If the child is not breathing, take a deep breath. Seal your lips around the child's mouth and nose. (If you can cover only the mouth, pinch the child's nostrils shut with your fingers.)

4. Blow into the child's mouth and nose. (For an infant, use gentle puffs of air.) When you see the chest lift, remove your mouth and let the air come out. Then blow in again. Repeat 15 to 20 times per minute for a child, or 20 times per minute for an infant. Continue until the child resumes normal breathing or until help arrives.

SECTION 2 REVIEW

CHECK YOUR UNDERSTANDING

1. List the five guidelines for fast action in case of an accident or injury.
2. How should a nosebleed be treated?
3. Briefly describe the three categories of burns.
4. What is the Heimlich maneuver?
5. What is the difference between a fracture and a sprain?
6. What is a poison control center?
7. What symptoms call for artificial respiration? What symptoms call for CPR?

DISCUSS AND DISCOVER

1. Why might it be difficult to remain calm if a child in your care was injured? Why would it be especially important to remain calm? What could you do to help yourself maintain a calm attitude and a clear mind?

Observing & Participating

Visit a child care center at your school site or in your community and find out where first aid supplies are kept. Are the supplies easy to locate? Are they adequate and up-to-date? Are they kept out of the reach of children? Interview a supervisor who can tell you how workers at the facility are trained to handle emergency situations.

ASSESS

CHECKING COMPREHENSION

Assign students to write their responses to the Check Your Understanding questions in the Section 2 Review. Answers to the questions are given at the bottom of this page.

EVALUATE

Have students complete the Chapter 17, Section 2 quiz in the TCR.

Reteaching

1. Assign Reteaching 41 in the TCR and have students complete the activity and review their responses.
2. Divide the students into groups to prepare one-act plays showing how a caregiver should respond if a child has a convulsion, faints, sprains an ankle, breaks an arm, or has a tick on the scalp.

Enrichment

1. Assign Enrichment 41 in the TCR.
2. Have students consult outside sources to find out what a greenstick fracture is. Ask: Who is most likely to have such an injury? How is it treated?

Extension

Have students learn more about signs of shock and how to go about treating this condition.

CLOSE

Have students work jointly on an emergency handbook to be published and distributed to class members. The booklet, which may be mimeographed or photocopied and stapled, is to include names and phone numbers of local hospitals, burn facilities, emergency rooms, poison control center, and other resources in students' own community.

SECTION 2 REVIEW

1. Remain calm; evaluate the situation; make the victim comfortable; call for help, if needed; give the minimum necessary first aid treatment.
2. Have child sit down and lean forward; squeeze child's nose just below bones in nose.
3. First-degree burns look red and slightly swollen; second-degree burns are deeper, redder, and blistered; third-degree burns destroy the skin.
4. A technique for using pressure on the air within the body to force an object interfering with breathing from the throat.
5. A fracture is a break or a crack in a bone; a sprain is an injury caused by sudden, violent stretching of a joint or muscle.
6. Hospital unit for advising and treating poisonings.
7. Breathing has stopped; both breathing and heart action have stopped.

Caring for a Sick Child

OBJECTIVES

- Give basic guidelines for caring for children who are ill.
- Describe the special nutritional needs of sick children.
- Discuss problems involved in the hospitalization of children.

It is never easy caring for a child who is ill. Normal routines are upset. The child may cry often, demand attention, and have a short temper. However, the attitude of the caregiver can be as important as the medical treatment in restoring good health.

The Caregiver's Role

A caregiver should maintain a calm, efficient, confident, and cheerful attitude. It is best to treat the illness matter-of-factly and to discuss it as little as possible.

When a child is ill, the caregiver often has to assume responsibility for entertaining the child. A child who is very ill does not have much energy for play and may spend most of the time sleeping. However, during mild illness or the recovery stage of a serious illness, the child may be easily bored. Reading books, playing with puzzles, and other quiet activities are suitable for the recovering child.

Children of different ages may have different needs during illness.

- **Infants.** Infants who are ill sleep much more than usual. They tend to be cranky and may want a lot of physical comforting. Comforting is important because the baby cannot understand what is wrong. Gently rocking the baby, talking softly, singing, and holding the baby close (perhaps in a cloth carrier) can help the baby feel calm and comforted.

- **Ages one to three.** Young children may need more help than older children in keeping comfortable and occupied during an illness. Young children are usually very physically active, and staying in bed is difficult for them. Doctors often do not

---

HEALTHY FAMILIES/HEALTHY CHILDREN

Health and Safety

Read the following to students: Six-year-old Mattie has lived in three foster homes. She is a very loving child, who always seems to have some physical ailment or problem. Her current foster mother can never tell whether or not a complaint is real. Yesterday morning Mattie fell off the swing in the backyard. She complained, whined, and cried off and on for several hours. It was not until late afternoon that Mattie was taken to the hospital and the doctor discovered that her shoulder bone was broken. Ask students why Mattie was not taken to the hospital right away. Was the foster mother negligent? Why did this happen to Mattie? How can those who take care of Mattie help her?

SECTION 3
Caring for a Sick Child
Pages 507-511

FOCUS

SECTION 3 RESOURCES

Teacher's Classroom Resources
- Enrichment 42
- Reteaching 42
- Section Three Quiz

Student Workbook
- Planning Meals for a Sick Child

SECTION OVERVIEW

Section 3 focuses on illness in children and the responsibilities of the caregiver attending to a sick child. The section also discusses ways to deal with the issue of child hospitalization, including strategies for helping minimize the child's fear and pain.

MOTIVATOR

Encourage students to share their own experiences with illness and the type of care they appreciated. Then ask them to consider the issue of caring for a sick child from a parent's point of view. How would they expect parents' lives and routines to be affected when a child is ill? Have them discuss the special needs of children when they are ill.

HEALTH TIP

There are numerous signs a parent can look for as a means of determining whether a child is sick. Early signs include:
- An oral temperature over 99.4°F (37.4°C).
- An upset stomach or vomiting.
- Diarrhea.
- Unexplained fatigue or irritability.
- Loss of appetite.
- Any undiagnosed rash.
- Any discharge or drainage from eyes, nose, ears.
- Open sores.
- Signs of a developing cold.
- Severe coughing.

GUIDED PRACTICE

Promoting Discussion

Have students work in groups to develop ideas for entertaining sick children. Assign each group a different age child. Have the groups report to the class.

Using Management Skills

Have students interview employed parents who have young children to learn what they do when the children are sick. Which parent stays home from work? What are the arrangements with the children's regular caregiver? How much of a problem are children's illnesses for the family? Have students write a report of the interview.

Critical Thinking

Ask students to consider the risks a caregiver takes when holding a baby who is ill. (The person may expose him- or herself to the illness and perhaps become too ill to care for the infant.) Ask: What steps can caregivers take to protect themselves?

Making Connections: Literature

Have two students volunteer to do a dramatic reading of "A Day's Wait," by Ernest Hemingway. One student will be narrator; the other, the child. In the story, a child believes he is going to die because he confuses the Fahrenheit and Celsius scales. After the reading, ask students how a simple explanation could have spared Schatzy his fear. Ask whether they believe the parent was at fault, and have them explain their answers.

Infants may need to be sung to and rocked to distract them from an illness.

insist on keeping toddlers in bed. A child who is warmly dressed can play quietly around the house. For toddlers, quiet play may include listening to stories, building with blocks, and playing simple games.

• **Ages four to six.** Older children handle ordinary illnesses much better than toddlers usually do. Preschoolers and, especially, school-age children can help care for themselves. Four- to six-year-olds can usually enjoy playing quietly with storybooks, stickers, puzzles, and games.

Because of medical advances, childhood illnesses are viewed differently today. One hundred years ago, people took longer to recover from illness. Today, however, antibiotics and other medical treatments prevent many illnesses from becoming serious. Children are usually up and about in a few days. Often recovery involves no more than keeping the child inside and quiet for a while; it may also be important to keep the child away from other children during the contagious period of an illness.

Of course, serious illnesses or injuries may necessitate additional treatment and a long period of recovery. In these cases, the understanding and cooperation of the entire family are required. The child needs to remain, as much as possible, an active and contributing part of the family.

The chart on pages 492-494 lists the symptoms, immunizations, and care for common childhood illnesses.

Medical treatment keeps many childhood illnesses from becoming serious. Having companionship and fun things to do helps the child feel better, too.

Medicines

The full benefit of medicines is often lost because the patient consumes food or drink that slows the absorption of the medicine or renders it inactive. For example, fruit juices, citrus fruits, tomatoes, vinegar, cola, and pickles will diminish the action of medicines such as penicillin, ampi-cillin, erythromycin, and aspirin, while dairy products reduce the effectiveness of tetracycline. Caregivers should check with pharmacists to learn how prescribed drugs should be taken and what foods, if any, are to be avoided. They must also watch children's diets carefully to ensure the child gets the full benefit of the medication prescribed.

ASK THE EXPERTS

Nutrition During Illness

Q. **Can you give me any tips about feeding children who aren't well?**

A. By providing good nutrition during an illness, you can help a child feel more comfortable and often even encourage the child's recovery.

It's usually important to offer a sick child plenty of water and other liquids. The body needs fluids when fighting a fever, and liquids might be the only food that will stay down. A child with a fever should be encouraged to drink as much as possible.

However, if the child's stomach is upset, even water may cause vomiting. Then it's best to let the stomach rest for at least an hour. After that period, offer the child very small

amounts of water or of clear carbonated soft drinks—just a sip or two at first. You might let him or her suck on chips of crushed ice.

With some illnesses, the child's doctor may recommend a specific diet. In this case, of course, you should follow the doctor's suggestions as closely as possible. In all other cases, it's best simply to offer the sick child small amounts of regular foods. Remember, though, that it is never a good idea to force a child to eat.

In certain cases, a child's doctor may recommend a bland diet or a liquid diet. A bland diet consists of soft, smooth, mild-flavored foods. If recommended, you might offer the child soups, hot cereals, puddings, gelatin desserts, eggs, and mild cooked vegetables. A liquid diet provides foods in liquid form that can be more easily used by the body. If a pediatrician recommends a liquid diet, offer the child fruit juice, carbonated soft drinks, milk, broth, cream soup, ice cream, and pudding.

Van D. Stone, MD

Dr. Van D. Stone
Pediatrician
Tupelo, Mississippi

Hospitalization

A hospital stay is an emotional crisis for almost every child. Child psychologists agree that no experience is more emotionally upsetting to a child than suddenly being separated from home and family. In the hospital, the youngster is surrounded by unfamiliar people, unusual routines, strange noises and smells, and frightening machines.

MORE ABOUT

Hospitalization

Hospitalization can be traumatic for children. Some of the "threats" to the child's emotional health include:

• The illness or injury itself.

• Potential separation from parents.

• Fear of the unknown.

• Lack of knowledge of appropriate behavior.

• Loss of control and autonomy.

• Lack of familiar routine and surroundings.

• Medical and surgical procedures.

Being anxious can interfere with a smooth hospital stay. Children may deny their illness, cry and cling, be uncooperative, be overly aggressive, or regress to earlier stages of development.

GUIDED PRACTICE (continued)

ASK THE EXPERTS

Issues and Advice

1. **Why are water and liquids good for a sick child?** (*The body will crave liquids if fighting a fever, and liquids might be the only food that will stay down during an illness.*)

2. **Describe a bland diet.** (*Consists of soft, smooth, mild flavored foods.*)

3. **Give examples of suitable foods in a bland diet.** (*Soups, gelatin, eggs, canned foods, mild cooked vegetables, hot cereals, and puddings.*)

4. **Give examples of suitable foods in a liquid diet.** (*Fruit juice, carbonated soft drinks, milk, thin cooked cereal, broth, cream soup, ice cream, and pudding.*)

Thinking Like an Expert

Read the following scenario to students: Denise's cold had developed into pneumonia. She was cranky and refused to eat anything but ice cream. She insisted that she couldn't swallow any other food. Ask what students would do if they were caring for Denise. Will Denise become malnourished if she is allowed to eat only ice cream? Have students explain their responses.

Next, remind students that children who are seriously ill might be hospitalized, which adds emotional distress to the physical stress. Have students find children's books that deal with hospitalization. (*Why Am I Going to the Hospital?*, by Claire Ciliotta, is a recommended title.) In small groups, have each student read a book aloud and analyze how the book might help alleviate children's fears.

PARENTING IN ACTION

Promoting Discussion

Ask students to discuss under what circumstances it is or is not possible to prepare a child for a hospital stay. Have students independently read the Parenting in Action story.

Thinking Critically

Instruct students to discuss how a parent reveals to his or her young child that the child is going to have to go into the hospital.

Answers to "Think and Discuss"

1. They explained the situation, took him to see the hospital and meet nurses, role-played with puppets, and brought familiar objects with him to the hospital. His recovery was quick and his attitude was positive.

2. Brother could feel left out or feel jealous of Alex's adventure. Encourage a variety of responses regarding ways to meet his needs.

INDEPENDENT PRACTICE

Student Workbook

Have students complete "Planning Meals for a Sick Child" in the Student Workbook.

Extension

Let students work alone or in small groups to complete one or more of these activities:

- Investigate the proper use of a thermometer orally, rectally, and in the armpit. Discuss the differences in thermometers, the correct procedures, and the ages appropriate for each.

- Interview a hospital dietitian about diets for hospitalized children. How do the meals differ from those served to adults? What kinds of adjustments must be made depending on the particular illness? Prepare a report to present to the class.

PARENTING IN ACTION

Dealing with Hospitalization

When the pediatrician explained that three-year-old Alex would have to be hospitalized for surgery, his parents chose a hospital that encouraged family support.

Ahead of time, Alex went with his parents to see the hospital and to meet several friendly nurses. Later, at home, his parents explained everything that would happen to him, using hand puppets for the doctor-patient stories.

Along with his toothbrush, robe, and pajamas, Alex was allowed to take along several favorite books, small toys, and his cuddly blanket.

After Alex's surgery, his parents took turns staying with him, so one of them was always there. His parents bathed Alex, fed him, and were present during all medical checks. His father slept by his bedside.

Back home, Alex recovered quickly. He told his brother all about his operation and how he got to ride on a bed with wheels.

THINK AND DISCUSS

1. How did Alex's parents prepare him for his experiences in the hospital? What effect do you think those preparations had?

2. What special needs do you think his brother might have had during Alex's hospitalization? How do you think their parents could have helped them?

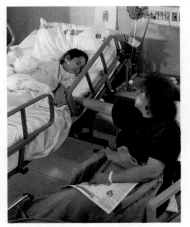

Visits from parents and other family members can help a hospitalized child keep from feeling frightened and alone.

Hospitalized youngsters often fear that their parents have abandoned them. They may be frightened that they will be hurt or mutilated, or that they will die. Some hospitalized children think they are being punished. Children have these fears because they do not understand what is happening to them.

A family who knows in advance that a child will be hospitalized can prepare the child for the event. The parents or doctor should explain to the child in simple words just what to expect. If possible, the parents should take the child to visit the hospital ahead of time. Many hospitals have special tours for children. These tours include a look in the patients' rooms and operating and recovery rooms. They may also include a puppet show or movie. Some hospitals have playrooms where children can play with stethoscopes, masks, identification bracelets, and other equipment. When the child is admitted, these things are already familiar—and less frightening.

Most hospitals realize that children recover better if a parent is allowed to stay in the hospital with them. Some hospitals move a cot into the child's room so that one parent can sleep

---

OBSERVING AND PARTICIPATING

Developing Observational Skills

If possible, arrange with two or more local hospitals to allow a small group of students to come by during visiting hours to observe the goings-on in the children's wing or ward. For a given hospital, have groups note, in particular, the interior decoration of the area and the behavior of the staff in its dealings with the children. Has an effort been made to simulate a child's room at home by the use of bright colors, animal decals, etc.? Do staff members show an understanding of children's apprehensions and fears? When groups return to class, have them compare and contrast their experiences and the amenities they discovered. Ask: Which hospital was best equipped to deal with the trauma of child hospitalization?

A tour of the hospital and its grounds can help eliminate fear for a child scheduled for hospitalization. Do hospitals in your area offer this service?

nearby. Other hospitals have rooms with space for both the child and a parent. Even where this arrangement is not available, visiting hours are usually quite flexible for parents. In addition, many hospitals now perform minor procedures and allow the child to go home that same day.

During hospitalization, a child often undergoes many tests and forms of treatment. When the child asks, "Will this hurt?" the parent should answer truthfully. Parents may be tempted to reassure the child by responding, "Oh, no, this won't hurt." It is actually much more helpful to the child to hear an accurate response, such as, "Yes, it will hurt for a while, but then you will feel much better. It is all right for you to cry when it hurts, if you feel like it."

If emergency hospitalization is necessary, it is important for a parent or other important caregiver to spend as much time as possible with the child. A loving adult can make a difficult situation less frightening by remaining close by, by encouraging communication between the hospital staff and the child, and by offering reassurance and attention. Although it can be agonizing to see a child sick or suffering, it is important for the parent or other caregiver to maintain a calm and encouraging attitude.

SECTION **3** REVIEW

CHECK YOUR UNDERSTANDING

1. Why is physical comforting especially important for an infant who is ill?

2. Why is it particularly difficult to keep toddlers cheerful during illness?

3. List five foods that might be included in a liquid diet.

4. What is the first symptom of chicken pox?

5. What is the recommended treatment for whooping cough?

6. List three fears common among young children who are hospitalized.

DISCUSS AND DISCOVER

1. What would you do while caring for a sick two-year-old during an entire afternoon? What quiet activities would you plan? What else would you expect to do with and for the child? Why?

Observing & Participating

If a local hospital has a volunteer visiting program, arrange to visit at least one pediatric patient there. Before you go, ask a volunteer supervisor to advise you on appropriate activities; then spend time with a young hospital patient. Describe how the patient responds to your visit. What special arrangements are available to the pediatric patient at this hospital?

SECTION **3** REVIEW

1. Baby cannot understand what is wrong.

2. Toddlers are usually very active; staying in bed can be difficult.

3. Any five: fruit juice, carbonated soft drinks, milk, thin cooked cereal, broth, cream soup, ice cream, pudding.

4. A rash of tiny, red, raised pimples or blisters.

5. Antibiotics taken under a doctor's care.

6. Any three: fear of abandonment; fear of pain; fear of mutilation; fear of death.

ASSESS

CHECKING COMPREHENSION

Assign students to write their responses to the Check Your Understanding questions in the Section 3 Review. Answers to the questions are given at the bottom of this page.

EVALUATE

Have students complete the Chapter 17, Section 3 quiz in the TCR.

Reteaching

1. Assign Reteaching 42 in the TCR and have students complete the activity and review their responses.

2. Have students work in pairs to choose a reason for the hospitalization of a child. Have them use information from the text to act out how an adult might explain and describe what will happen to the child during the hospital stay.

Enrichment

1. Assign Enrichment 42 in the TCR.

2. Have students conduct an interview with a parent whose child has been hospitalized, asking about the circumstances surrounding the hospitalization, how the child was prepared, how the child coped, what went well, and what went wrong. Have students write reports of their interviews and share these with the class.

Extension

Have students imagine they are going to babysit for a five-year-old child with chicken pox. Ask them to organize a "fun bag" of games, activities, and other diversions they would plan to take along with them to help entertain the child during the babysitting job.

CLOSE

Have students visit a local hospital and make a list of things they would include in—and omit from—a hospital tour for children.

CHECKING COMPREHENSION

Use the Summary and the Reviewing the Facts questions to help students go over the most important ideas presented in Chapter 17; encourage students to ask questions and add details, as appropriate.

CHAPTER **17** REVIEW

1. Automobile accidents.

2. Health problems can be detected in their early stages, preventing more serious illnesses or permanent damage.

3. Diseases easily passed from one person to another; immunization.

4. See diagrams on page 500.

5. A period of unconsciousness with uncontrolled jerking or twitching of the muscles. Place the person on the floor, lying on his or her side, away from hard objects; when the convulsion is over, turn the head to one side; check with a doctor; call for emergency help if it lasts longer than fifteen minutes.

6. Dizziness, faintness, difficulty breathing, generalized swelling, or heavy perspiration; get medical attention immediately.

7. Possibilities are: difficulty breathing; unconsciousness; fever; burns in the mouth and throat; vomiting; burns or rashes on the skin; burning or irritation of the eyes; blindness; choking; coughing; nausea or dizziness from fumes, sprays, or poisonous gases.

8. Trauma to the body caused by injury, great loss of blood, or poisoning; important body functions are impaired, and a person might lose consciousness.

9. Reading, playing with puzzles, stickers, and games.

10. Truthfully, with comfort and reassurance from the parents; it prepares the child honestly and builds trust.

CHAPTER **17** REVIEW

SUMMARY

- It is easier to prevent illnesses and accidents than to cope with their effects.
- The safety of the child is the most important responsibility of every parent and caregiver.
- Children should have regular medical checkups and should be immunized against childhood diseases.
- Emergencies must be dealt with quickly and calmly.
- Artificial respiration and CPR are rescue techniques used when breathing and heart action have stopped.
- The attitude of the caregiver toward a sick child can be as important as medical treatment to the patient's recovery.
- A hospital stay is usually an emotional crisis for a child.

REVIEWING THE FACTS

1. What is the leading cause of death among young children?

2. Why should children have regular medical checkups?

3. What are communicable diseases? How can they best be controlled?

4. What are the steps in administering the Heimlich maneuver to a child who is standing or sitting?

5. What is a convulsion? What treatment is appropriate for a person having a convulsion?

6. What are the symptoms of an allergic reaction to an insect sting? What is the appropriate response to these symptoms?

7. List four symptoms that may indicate poisoning.

8. What is shock? Why is it dangerous?

9. List three activities appropriate for four- to six-year-olds who are mildly ill.

10. How should parents respond when a child asks whether a medical treatment will hurt? Why?

EXPLORING FURTHER

1. Make up a song, a chant, or a simple game that helps reinforce a safety rule for school-aged children. Teach the song, chant, or game to a group of your classmates, and let them help you evaluate and improve your idea. Then teach your song, chant, or game to a group of five- or six-year-olds. (Section 1)

2. Using a large doll, practice the rescue maneuver as it is used on infants. Then use the doll to teach the rescue maneuver to a friend, family member, or acquaintance who regularly cares for an infant. (Section 2)

3. Investigate the Mr. Yuk poison symbols: How are they used? Why are they effective for alerting young children to poisons? Then design and make your own stickers for labeling poisonous household materials. (Section 2)

4. Plan two days of meals for a four-year-old on a bland diet. Prepare one of your planned meals, and present it in a way that might especially appeal to a sick child. (Section 3)

THINKING CRITICALLY

1. **Analyze.** How can parents and other caregivers encourage children to take responsibility for their own health and safety habits? Who benefits as children accept this responsibility? How do they benefit?

2. **Analyze.** The Poison Prevention Council reports that one in three poisonings among children occurs when the child is visiting his or her grandparents. What do you think accounts for this high rate? What do you think parents should do to help make visits to the grandparents safer for children?

3. **Evaluate.** How do you think parents can tell that a child is too sick to attend school or a child care program? What might motivate a child to pretend to be sick? How do you think parents should respond to a child's invented illness? Why?

CLASSROOM MANAGEMENT

Videotape Presentations

As an alternative to written class assignments and to include greater variety in your instructional techniques, you may want students to act out and videotape presentations. By viewing a videotape of their presentation, students can notice repetitive verbal interactions, annoying facial expressions, or distracting gestures that they may unconsciously do while interacting with children.

After completing this chapter, divide students into groups. Assign various rescue procedures and scenarios to each group. Have students act out the scenario and rescue procedures in front of a video camera. Then have students play the video rescue tape to the entire class and have them critique the way the emergency was handled. This technique gives students the opportunity for self-evaluations and offers them immediate feedback.

CROSS-CURRICULUM CONNECTIONS

1. **Management.** Plan and assemble a basic first aid kit, to be used in your home or to be taken along when you babysit. Calculate how much it costs to make your kit. How much would it cost to buy a prepackaged kit? Does your kit include anything not available in prepackaged kits? Do the prepackaged kits include any first aid supplies you left out of your kit? Could you have assembled your kit any more cheaply? If so, how?

2. **Speaking.** Gather information on Lyme disease: What causes the disease? What are its early symptoms? What other symptoms can develop? How can it be treated? Plan and deliver a short oral presentation based on your findings.

SCHOOL TO WORK

Managing Your Money After you cash your paycheck, you may feel the urge to spend your money, but how you spend it impacts how far it will go. Right now you can practice managing your money. Say no to the impulse to buy something you don't really need. Be patient—maybe the item will be on sale soon, or maybe you'll discover that you don't really need it. Plan your spending, and learn to save for future purchases. Your paycheck will go farther and you will be happier.

PERFORMANCE ASSESSMENT

Health and Safety

Task
Create a list of emergency telephone numbers and community resources to post by each household telephone. The list should include all telephone numbers that might be needed in any kind of emergency.

Purpose
Your emergency telephone list will serve several purposes. First, it becomes a valuable resource in your home. Second, in the process of compiling your list, you will learn the numbers of important emergency contacts.

Procedure
1. Draft a list of emergency contacts, such as doctors, police, poison control, family work numbers, neighbors, and schools. As you organize your list, keep your audience in mind: you and your family members plus any person who might be visiting, babysitting, or managing household responsibilities. Use language that defines each person by the connec-

tion and the name, for example: *Pediatrician—Dr. Marsha Goldberg;* or *Grandfather—Tiquet Wan,* with their phone numbers.
2. Write all of the pertinent information on your draft. Be sure to include all instructions, such as area codes, out-of-the-country dialing instructions, or work or voice mail extensions. Include an out-of-state contact in the event of a major disaster. For services or doctors you do not call frequently, you might want to check to verify the numbers.
3. Show your draft to a friend, classmate, or family member for additional recommendations.
4. Make your final draft of telephone numbers. Be sure your words and numbers are clear and easy to read. Make a list for every telephone you use. Add color or drawings to make your lists attractive. Use clear adhesive shelf paper to protect the lists from wear.
5. Post your lists near each telephone you use.

Evaluation
Your emergency list will be evaluated for the thoroughness of its content and the clarity of your presentation, including its readability and visual appeal. Demonstration that you understand the importance of emergency resources is essential.

Portfolio Idea
For your portfolio, make a blank original of your telephone list, suitable for use in any home, office, or classroom. To do so, delete the specific names and telephone numbers, leaving each title and/or category. Make at least one copy suitable to reproduce. You might want to insert your name and date across the bottom or side, like a copyright line, to remind you of the date you originated your list, in case you want to revise at a later date.

513

PERFORMANCE ASSESSMENT

Emergency Phone List
Remind students to consider the kinds of emergencies that can occur in your geographical area. Then brainstorm a list of community emergency contacts. It might also be appropriate to have students include a person they could reach by foot, in case the telephones are down. Any students with ham radio experience may be encouraged to explain the role they might play in an emergency. Have students who live in homes where more than one language is spoken make their lists in each applicable language. Ask those students to bring in a copy to share with the class for a diverse and interesting cultural display. If you think one or more students may not have a telephone at home, offer the option of writing instructions for using a public telephone to make emergency calls.

EVALUATE
Use the reproducible Chapter 17 Test in the TCR, or construct your own test using the Testmaker Software.

EXTENSION
Invite a health care professional to speak to the class about the personal qualities and training necessary to perform his or her duties. Before the visit, have the class prepare questions and suggest areas of personal interest that they would like to see addressed by the speaker.

CLOSE
Ask students to write and complete the following sentence:
Children are healthier and safer when …

SCHOOL TO WORK
Consumer Credit Eventually, students will want to use credit to make purchases in advance of payment. Yet many may not realize that credit is not simply available for the asking, and it carries a grave responsibility. How they manage their money now and how well they develop wise consumer skills will affect future credit ratings. Take time to discuss the following concerns: Do they take their time when making a purchase? Do they avoid impulse buying? Do they compare prices and services? Do they save money to plan for future expenditures? Encourage them to see how their skill at managing money will benefit them when they are in the workplace.

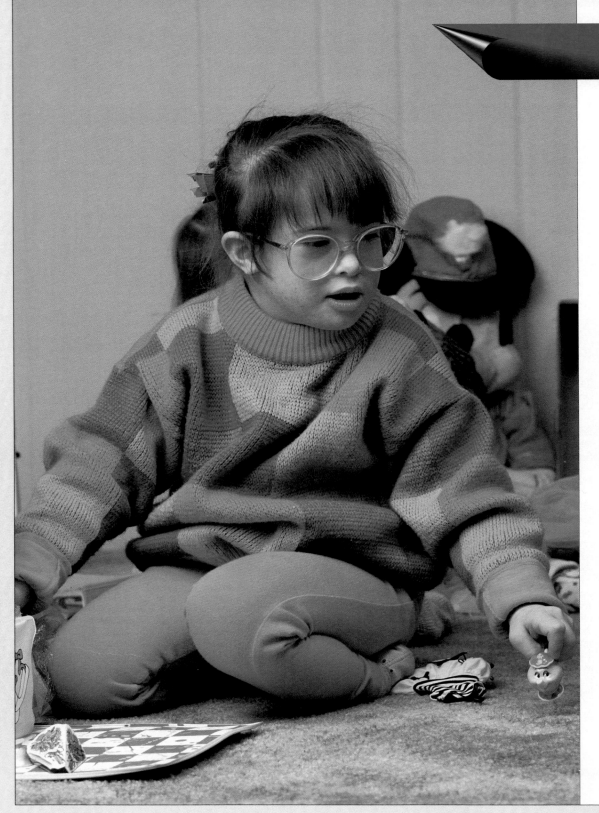

CHAPTER 18
Special Challenges for Children

INTRODUCE

CHAPTER 18 RESOURCES

Teacher's Classroom Resources
- Cooperative Learning 18
- Extension 35, 36
- Observing and Participating 18
- Chapter 18 Test
- Testmaker Software
- Color Transparency 41

Student Workbook
- Chapter 18 Study Guide

CHAPTER OVERVIEW

Chapter 18 helps students understand the special challenges some children face. In Section 1, students examine the physical, mental, and emotional needs of children with disabilities. They learn that whether or not children cope successfully with problems depends largely on the actions and attitudes of their parents and caregivers.

In Section 2, students explore child abuse and neglect. Here, they recognize the severe and long-lasting effects of child abuse and learn that treatment and counseling can help abusive parents learn to cope with their problems and stop the pattern of abuse.

Section 3 provides students with information in how situations such as divorce, death, moving, financial problems, and illness can affect children. This section emphasizes that when children must cope with family stresses, they need special support.

CLASSROOM MANAGEMENT

Resources Beyond the Classroom

The public's attitude toward children with Down syndrome has gradually changed in recent years. The National Down Syndrome Society (NDSS) supports research of Down syndrome and related illnesses, promotes public awareness, and provides services to affected families and individuals. Additionally, the society publishes a fact sheet entitled "Down Syndrome: Facts and Myths."

The group also sponsors a respite program, which provides relief to parents while benefiting the children, who can visit a trained volunteer family. For more information, either call (212) 460-9330, or write:

National Down Syndrome Society
666 Broadway Street, 8th floor
New York, NY 10012

Special Challenges for Children

THINK ABOUT

Think about a person you know who is challenged by a physical, mental, or emotional disability. Can you describe the person's disability? How does the disability pose a challenge to other family members and friends? Is the person involved in a special program that addresses his or her special needs? If so, how does the program benefit the person? How are the person's needs similar to those of all people?

ASK YOURSELF

Look at the photo on the opposite page. What age do you guess the child to be?

How are her needs similar to those of other children the same age? What do you speculate are her special needs? How can these needs be met? What challenges will she face as she grows and develops?

NOW TRY THIS

With a partner, brainstorm a list of challenges that students with physical, mental, or emotional disabilities face in a classroom setting. Then create a second list of how teachers can adapt classroom activities or lessons to accommodate the needs of all students or list special-needs programs available at your school.

515

CHAPTER OBJECTIVES

After completing Chapter 18, students will be able to:

- Describe the needs of children with physical, mental, and emotional handicaps.
- Tell how parents and other caregivers can assist and encourage children with disabilities.
- Explain what is meant by *child abuse*, why it happens, and what can be done about it.
- Describe the emotional effects on children who have to deal with stressful family situations, such as divorce and death, and explain how to minimize the stress.

INTRODUCING THE CHAPTER

- Ask students to identify situations that pose a challenge to students, such as having disabilities, abuse in the home, divorce of parents, and death of someone close. Have students suggest ways that children might be helped to cope with crisis situations. Tell students that when they read Chapter 18, they will learn more about how these situations affect children and what caregivers can do to help children deal with them.
- Use the photo on the opposite page and the three features on this page—Think About, Ask Yourself, and Now Try This—to begin a discussion about special challenges for children.

HEALTHY FAMILIES/HEALTHY CHILDREN

Family Adjustments

The birth of a handicapped child is usually stressful to a family. Parents may find it hard to accept a baby who does not meet family expectations, may be too ill to respond to parents, or who responds in ways the parents see as negative. Parents typically feel guilt, anger, and helplessness. How they resolve these feelings will affect their attitudes toward the child, which, in turn will affect how the child grows and develops.

Handicapped children are overrepresented in the ranks of abused children. Caring for a handicapped child causes stress and problems that build up until some parents simply cannot cope. Abuse of the handicapped child may be one result.

FOCUS

SECTION 1 RESOURCES

Teacher's Classroom Resources
- Enrichment 43
- Reteaching 43
- Section 1 Quiz

Student Workbook
- Coded Messages

SECTION OVERVIEW

Section 1 presents information about the types of disabilities that some exceptional children must face. As they study the section, students learn that children may be physically, mentally, or emotionally handicapped and, therefore, require special individual care.

MOTIVATOR

Ask students whether they have ever been concerned about the appearance of a blemish or a scar. Encourage them to share and discuss their own experiences. Ask: What might a physically disabled person say about such concerns? Tell students that in this section, they are going to learn about children with disabilities. Point out that with proper care and treatment, most handicapped children have the potential to live happy and productive lives.

USING TERMS TO LEARN

Refer students to the vocabulary terms for this section. Explain that the word *empathy* comes from the Greek word *pathos*, which means "feeling." *Empathy* means the ability to share and understand the feelings of another person. Point out that therapy is treatment, especially by methods other than drugs or surgery. A therapist is one who specializes in the treatment of people with mental and physical disabilities.

SECTION 1   Exceptional Children

OBJECTIVES

- Describe the needs of children with physical, mental, and emotional disabilities.
- Explain how parents and other caregivers can assist and encourage disabled children.

TERMS TO LEARN

empathy
therapist

Disabilities—physical, mental, emotional, or any combination of the three—present special challenges for children and their parents.

Children with Disabilities

In the past, babies with severe health or other disabling conditions often died at birth or soon after. If a child with a disability lived, he or she was often hidden away at home or sent to an institution. Fortunately, there is much more awareness of the needs and potential of disabled—also called exceptional—children today. Medical science saves the lives of many infants with physical problems. Doctors are also able to treat many disabilities to make them less severe. Children can often be taught to compensate for their disabilities. With proper care and treatment, disabled children can lead happy, productive lives.

The attitude of parents toward a child with a disability can make an important difference in the child's future. Parents can teach their child to be as independent as possible and to adapt for those limitations that cannot be overcome. Parents who pity, resent, or coddle a child with disabilities hinder the child's healthy emotional development. The child may become angry and self-pitying. Such a child will have difficulty functioning in society. A child with a positive attitude will have a happier life.

Parents of children with disabilities should contact national or community agencies that can offer information and support. Many states now require that public schools provide programs for disabled children and their parents beginning at the time of the child's birth. Many other states provide preschool experiences for children with disabilities beginning at the child's third birthday.

OBSERVING AND PARTICIPATING

Children with Special Needs

Experts have become increasingly wary about telling parents of handicapped children what to expect from their children. The idea of the self-fulfilling prophecy is very critical in dealing with handicapped children. If parents have low expectations and fail to provide stimulation and education, handicapped children will probably fail to develop maximally. On the other hand, parents who believe in their children's potential and work to develop it have had many successes in helping their children live happy, productive lives. Have students interview parents who have children with special needs and find out what they are doing to help their children develop to their full potential.

Special preschool programs give children with disabilities a chance to be like everyone else, enabling all the children to feel empathy.

Not all children with disabilities need to be—or even should be—in special programs. Studies have shown that many children do best when placed in regular preschool programs or mainstreamed in regular classrooms. Both the children with disabilities and those without benefit. This way of providing services, called integration or inclusion, provides an opportunity for all the children to grow intellectually, develop social skills, and learn to feel **empathy**, *a sense of understanding and sharing of another person's feelings.*

Physical Disabilities

Physical disabilities take a wide range of forms and may have widely differing impacts on the lives of children and their parents. A child who must wear leg braces and a child who is missing an arm have obvious physical disabilities, but many disabilities are not so apparent. Such conditions as a hearing loss or a heart defect can also be physical disabilities.

BUILDING SELF-ESTEEM

Meeting the Needs of Exceptional Children

Children with disabilities have the same basic needs as other children. Their most important need is to feel loved and accepted by their families and by society. Like all young children, disabled youngsters need to feel they are actively involved in their family's life. This means doing daily chores and following family rules—as well as going along on special family outings.

TEACH

Pages 516-523

- **Children with Disabilities**
- **Physical Disabilities**
- **Mental Disabilities**
- **Emotional Disabilities**
- **Raising a Disabled Child**

GUIDED PRACTICE

Using the Photograph
Let students analyze and discuss the children at play in the picture on page 517. Discuss what students see as the advantages and disadvantages of mainstreaming exceptional children. Have students discuss their ideas from the point of view of the exceptional child, the rest of the class, and the teacher.

Promoting Discussion
Exceptional children and their families need support from people they know. Have students discuss the right and wrong ways to support exceptional children and their families.

Critical Thinking
What circumstances could cause the family members of an exceptional child to feel guilt? (Answers will vary. One of the family members might have directly caused a birth defect or injury or, by negligence, allowed it to happen. Family members may feel guilt even if they are not responsible in any way. They may also resent the burden at times, and feel guilty about the resentment.) How might this affect their interaction with the child? (Answers will vary. It may make them resentful, cold, overprotective, or overindulgent.)

BUILDING SELF-ESTEEM

Teaching children about disabilities expands their knowledge of themselves as well as others. Being tolerant of others allows them to be more accepting of their own flaws. Correctly guided, children will value how much people are alike, not how much they are different.

COOPERATIVE LEARNING

Strategies for Success
Cooperative learning strategies are limited only by the imagination of the teacher. Following are some of the more fruitful strategies:
- Role-playing.
- Clustering, or having students switch group affiliations in the middle of small-group brainstorming sessions in order to stimulate thinking by introducing, and benefiting from, new ideas.

- Role-playing a panel of experts and audiences.
- Sending small student groups out into the community to conduct research, through surveys and interviews.

For details on these and other strategies, consult "A Guide to Cooperative Learning" in your Cooperative Learning booklet in the Teacher's Classroom Resources.

GUIDED PRACTICE (continued)

Cooperative Learning

Point out to students that one-handed baseball pitcher Jim Abbott was the star of the 1988 U.S. Olympic baseball team, which won the gold medal. He later pitched professionally in the major leagues. Ask students to work in small groups to research and write a report on the lives of handicapped persons who have made important contributions to society. Examples might include Helen Keller and Franklin Delano Roosevelt. Have each group report to the class, describing the disability and the individual's achievements.

Critical Thinking

Ask students to analyze the difference between acquiring a physical handicap at birth and acquiring one later in childhood. How will adjustments be different for the child? For the family?

Promoting Discussion

Have students brainstorm a list of movies they have seen or books they have read about people with disabilities. Ask them to share the premise of the storyline and the way the person overcame adversity.

Using the Photograph

Refer students to the photograph at the top of this page. Why is exercise so important for children with physical disabilities?

Critical Thinking

Ask students whether people should offer their help to a physically disabled child in a specific situation. What about a physically disabled adult? Could some people be insulted by such an offer? How can you know what to do?

Critical Thinking

Ask students to suggest reasons why some people without disabilities use parking places designated for the handicapped. How do they feel about such people?

For a child with a physical handicap, exercise sessions are often part of the daily routine. Though sometimes painful, exercises are necessary to maintain and improve the child's physical abilities.

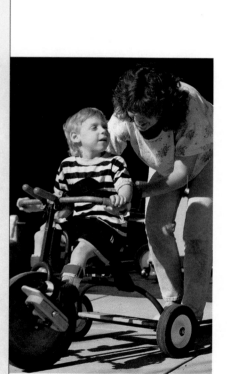

Many fun activities also help develop physical skills. Why might riding a tricycle be good for a handicapped preschooler?

Some physical disabilities are apparent at birth, but others do not become apparent for months—or even years. Parents should seek a complete diagnosis as soon as they suspect their child may have a physical disability. Then the child should begin treatment as soon as possible. Today, through early diagnosis and treatment, many children born with physical disabilities are able to lead fairly normal lives.

Each child with a physical disability has individual care needs. Routines that others take for granted can be difficult or even impossible. For example, a three-year-old with poor coordination may be unable to dress or eat without help.

Special exercises, special equipment, understanding, and patience are the keys to helping children with physical disabilities be as independent as possible. Independence is essential, not only for future living but also for the development of the child's positive self-concept. Self-care skills such as eating, dressing, bathing, and using the toilet are fundamental to this independence.

Bathing is a good example of a daily care skill in which independence can be encouraged. Many disabled children need to be lifted in and out of the tub. Others may need special assistance or supervision. Whatever the limitations a child with a disability must deal with, he or she should be encouraged to handle as much of the bathing routine as possible.

MORE ABOUT

Intervention Programs

Children who are developmentally delayed benefit from early intervention programs. These programs typically enroll children as soon as a developmental delay is diagnosed, which may be as early as one or two months of age. Teaching is usually done by special educators; physical, occupational, and speech therapists; and psychologists. Some programs are home-based. The teacher or therapist visits the family at home and teaches the parents to exercise and stimulate the child. In center-based programs, families go to an outside location for services. Early intervention programs have been shown to reduce the severity of mental retardation and other handicaps. They can also decrease the cost of providing services for handicapped and retarded children later in life.

To encourage independence, the child must feel secure during the bath. This means at least a nonskid mat in the bottom of the tub. It may also mean installing rails on the sides of the tub. Some youngsters may need an inner tube or inflated cushion to keep their head above water. For those who cannot sit independently, the water level must be kept very low for safety.

Most children can perform some aspect of washing themselves. They might use a washcloth made into a mitt, which is easier to handle and less likely to be lost in the water. They can wear a bar of soap on a string around the neck, so that the soap won't slip away. They can dry off using a towel with a hole cut in the middle; this kind of towel can be slipped over the head to simplify the process of drying the whole body. Children who have less functional coordination skills might participate by splashing water on themselves.

Parents and others who care for physically disabled children may need to develop similar adaptations for eating and other routine activities. Some children may need special help with only a few tasks; others may need many adaptations because their physical abilities are limited.

Mental Disabilities

Mentally disabled children grow just as other children do. The major difference is that their mental development is slower and stops at a lower level. There are many degrees of mental retardation. Some disabled children are only a little slow. Other children have the mental ability of babies for life.

Medical professionals can usually diagnose mental retardation early and determine its cause. They can also advise parents about the child's learning potential, but this can be difficult to predict. Education and treatment must begin early to achieve the best possible results. Often doctors recommend special programs for mentally disabled children.

Mentally disabled children learn and respond best when they know what to expect. Directions for these children should be simple and direct. Example and demonstration, along with constant repetition, are usually the most effective teaching methods.

The long-range goal for children with mental disabilities is that they become as independent as possible. Many can learn living and job skills that enable them to live alone, support themselves, and perhaps marry and raise a family. Others need more care and support. Many communities have sheltered care homes that offer supervised group living for those mentally disabled adults who need it. These adults can usually work under supervision. However, some mentally disabled people remain totally dependent on others throughout their life.

Many mentally handicapped children will continue to need special supervised home and work situations as adults.

GUIDED PRACTICE (continued)

Handicap Simulation

Set up several simulations for students that will help them understand what it is like to have a disability. You may wish to have students complete all exercises or have each student complete a different exercise. Possible suggestions:

- Vision. Blindfold students. Have them leave the classroom, walk to another classroom, and then return. After they return, have them pick up certain items and manipulate objects (e.g., unscrew a lid or wrap a present).

- Hearing. Have students put cotton balls or ear plugs in their ears and wear ear muffs over their ears to listen to a song.

- Physical skills. Have students use a wheelchair, crutches, or a walker.

Ask them to participate in a selected everyday activity while simulating the handicap and discuss their experiences. How can disabilities affect a child's learning? Self-concept? Independence? Social acceptance? Then have students explain what they learned from the experience and how it felt to participate in the experience.

Family Focus

When a handicapped baby is born, it is often so ill that it must be separated from the family for special treatment. How might this separation affect the interaction and bonding that takes place between a parent and child? (Often, future parent-child relationships are jeopardized as a result of the strain of a child's illness at birth.) Have students suggest ways parents could work to overcome this separation to establish a positive relationship with their child.

MORE ABOUT

Emotional Handicaps

Emotionally disturbed behavior is characterized as behavior that over a long period of time is inappropriate for the circumstances in which it occurs. It includes a wide range of disorders, the most severe of which are autism (withdrawal and lack of interest in others) and schizophrenia (loss of touch with reality). Emotionally disturbed children may have some of the following characteristics: hostility; hyperactivity; marked and frequent mood changes; withdrawal; pervasive depression; inability to build and maintain relationships; and behavior that is aggressive, disruptive, impulsive, unpredictable, or violent.

GUIDED PRACTICE (continued)

Making Connections: Reading

Have students work in small groups to study a specific physical or mental handicap. Ask each group to report to the class on the limitations and special needs associated with the handicap.

International research involves not only the talents of trained scientists and doctors, but the resources found in various countries as well. Open a class discussion about environmental issues, such as the destruction of the rain forest, and how such issues might have an impact on medical research. Ask students to speculate about future trends and consequences.

Using the Photograph

Refer students to the photo on page 520. Is this child displaying the behavior of an emotionally disturbed child? Under what circumstances might her behavior be quite normal?

Making Connections: Art/Home Economics

Have students examine the work of Henri de Toulouse-Lautrec, who was disabled by a childhood injury to his lower body. Discuss his achievements and contributions.

Some may like to try a recipe from The *Art of Cuisine*, a cookbook by Henri de Toulouse-Lautrec and Maurice Joyant.

Critical Thinking

Tell students that some children are so severely disabled that they must be institutionalized. They must have everything done for them, and they are unable to respond in any way. Ask students whether there is a point at which a person makes no contribution to the world. Could the simple presence of the individual be a contribution for someone? Who should pay for the institutional care of such children?

Cultural Exchange

INTERNATIONAL RESEARCH BENEFITS ALL

Recently, doctors and research scientists from a variety of countries jointly studied victims of autism found in 40 countries. Because this rare disorder affects only about 1 in 3,000 children, international efforts resulted in a more comprehensive study. Then, the results could benefit more children. A similar collaborative effort is found in the study and research of AIDS. Pooling research from many nations results in added understanding and better treatment for all people.

Social acceptance is essential to people with mental retardation—just as it is to everyone else. Children with mental disabilities should be taught grooming, manners, and acceptable social behavior; these skills make social acceptance more likely.

Emotional Disabilities

How can parents know when their child is emotionally troubled and needs professional help? The child's behavior is the best indication. However, there is no clear-cut line between typical behavior and emotionally disturbed behavior. Some troublesome behavior is natural. It may result from the need for a little special attention, or it may just be part of a normal stage of development. Certainly, though, when a child's behavior prevents typical development or disturbs the lives of family members, parents should suspect and explore the possibility of a serious emotional problem.

Nervous habits, loss of appetite, sleeplessness, excessive fear, withdrawal, aggressive or violent behavior, and failing grades

Children with emotional handicaps have difficulty coping with the stresses of life.

HEALTHY FAMILIES/HEALTHY CHILDREN

Emotional Therapy

Studies have shown that having a close relationship with a pet is beneficial for children. Pets may be even more important for children with emotional problems. New research into the bonds between humans and animals has important implications for the treatment of emotionally disturbed children. In one study of children with severe emotional disturbances, half of the children attended standard therapeutic activity groups. The other half played with a dog during therapy sessions. Those who received normal therapy got worse, yet those who had the therapy with a pet increased their ability to control impulses and understand others.

may be signs of emotional disturbance. Keep in mind, however, that other causes for such behavior must be ruled out before emotional disabilities may be cited as their cause.

Behavior that indicates emotional disabilities usually becomes more noticeable and more disturbing over time. For example, at age two, Terry began to rock in his crib and bang his head over and over against the headboard. He resisted toilet training and had frequent toileting accidents, even when he reached school age. His speech was rapid, breathless, and hampered by stuttering. Terry's parents felt concerned, but they didn't know quite what to do. They hoped that once Terry started school, things would get easier.

In school, Terry fought with other children and disrupted classes with his outbursts. He entered the third grade still struggling to gain basic reading and writing skills. At this point, the school recommended that Terry have a psychological evaluation. The evaluation indicated that Terry needed therapy.

Even when a child's behavior shows a pattern that indicates serious emotional problems—as Terry's behavior did—parents may be reluctant to ask for help. They may be ashamed to admit they cannot handle the problem themselves. Parents cannot be expected to have all the answers, however.

When a child does need help, the parents need to find a **therapist** or a **behavior specialist,** *a professional trained in helping people work through emotional problems.* Pediatricians, school counselors, members of the clergy, or a local office of the Mental Health Association can recommend a therapist. Once they have decided to seek professional help, parents should take the time to select a therapist whom they trust and with whom they feel comfortable. Then they can expect the therapist to ask the family for background information on the problem behaviors, get to know the entire family better, observe the child in various situations, and plan treatment for the child. In some cases, the treatment may involve making a few changes in the family's pattern of interactions. For example, the therapist might suggest that the parents spend individual time with the child each day or that the child be introduced to a special activity, such as gymnastics or music, according to his or her interests.

Sometimes the therapist finds that a child's emotional problems have physical causes. If this is the case, the therapist may recommend medical evaluation and treatment.

Often the therapist works directly with the child—and sometimes with other family members—to improve the child's self-image. Skilled emotional therapy can change the way children view themselves and, consequently, the way they behave.

The results of therapy depend to a great extent on the child's parents. They must believe in and support the therapist's work. They must be available to listen and talk when the child is ready.

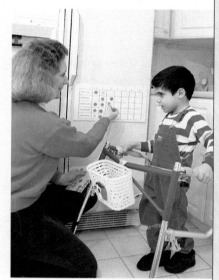

Support groups for parents of special-needs children give parents practical guidance for everyday care. This family uses a sticker award plan for daily tasks the child completes.

GUIDED PRACTICE (continued)

Making Connections: Social Studies

Have students investigate how the treatment of children with disabilities has changed over the years. Have students develop a chart or time line to illustrate these changes.

Critical Thinking

Imagine you are the parent of a six-year-old child. You have invited a family for dinner, and one family member is a mentally disabled six-year-old child. How would you prepare your six-year-old boy to receive the visitor? (Briefly explain that the child will not speak or understand as well as other children his age, and that he may not be able to do things that require complex thought. Also tell the child what he can do or understand. Emphasize that the boy will want friendship, and tell the child to show patience and be willing to listen carefully. Suggest toys and noncompetitive games they can enjoy together.)

Cooperative Learning

Have students work in small groups to write case studies that describe the emotional behavior of children. Each case study should focus on behavior that is either normal or disturbed. Have the groups exchange case studies and then analyze them to determine whether they think the behavior depicted shows normal emotions or signs of disturbed behavior. Have the groups read the case studies to the class and explain their analyses. Do the analyses agree with the intention of the writers of the case studies? Why or why not?

?

Did You Know?

On October 28, 1929, Mrs. T. W. Evans gave birth to a baby girl, the first child born while traveling on an airplane.

MORE ABOUT

Careers as Therapists

Therapists are professionals who are concerned with the treatment of those with physical or mental disabilities. List the following types of therapists on the board: counseling, physical, speech, occupational, respiratory, recreational, music, dance, art. Suggest that students choose one of the careers that interests them and use reference books in the library to further research the requirements of the career. Have students also identify the characteristics, patients purpose of therapy, and different types of therapeutic techniques used.

PARENTING IN ACTION

Promoting Discussion

Introduce this Parenting in Action selection by letting students discuss their reaction to the story "Living with Disabilities." After students have read the selection independently, encourage them to share their response. How does this situation make you feel? With whom do you identify most strongly?

Thinking Critically

Ask students what makes this situation so meaningful for Rosa's parents. How will their support be an important contribution to the other parents?

Answers to Think and Discuss

1. Rosa was born with Down syndrome.

2. They were disappointed, cried, and felt their world was shattered. They were not prepared for having a child with a disability.

3. They attend meetings to learn as much as they can about these disabilities; trained parent-child educators come to their house to work with Rosa; they have set up a program of learning, which includes therapy.

4. Rosa is a happy and lovable child who gives her parents a sense of pride.

INDEPENDENT PRACTICE

Journal Writing

Have students investigate barriers that physically disabled people face in their community. Ask them to write entries in their journals describing some of the improvements that could be made. Ask them to write a "Letter to the Editor" that points out the problems and suggests solutions.

Student Workbook

Have students complete "Coded Messages" in the Student Workbook.

PARENTING IN ACTION

Living with Disabilities

Sylvia and Ed Sanchez hurried to the first meeting of a group of parents of infants with Down syndrome. They were scheduled to talk to the group that evening.

After they had been introduced, Sylvia said, "When I look at all of you, I see Ed and myself sitting there just a few years ago. When you have a baby with Down syndrome, it seems like your world has shattered. I remember that I cried for weeks. I want you to know, though, that your outlook will change—now I laugh much more often than I cry. Our daughter Rosa has made us a happier family."

Ed continued, "Sylvia and I have been actively involved in a local organization for mentally disabled persons. At first, we attended meetings because we needed information, and we needed to talk with other parents in the same boat. We've become more involved because we enjoy it—and because we want to help other parents."

"Rosa's been in a special preschool program since she was two," Sylvia explained. "Before that, trained parent-child educators came into our home on a regular basis. They helped assess Rosa's abilities and set up a program of learning and therapy. They taught us how to teach her most effectively. We also learned exercises to help enhance her physical skills."

"Rosa's such a lovable child! We don't know just how much independence she'll be capable of as an adult. Right now, though, each of her achievements is cause for celebration."

Sylvia paused. "I'm anxious to hear about your own situations," she went on. "Whatever your situation, remember that there are lots of other parents to help and guide you through the network of government and community programs. Give your children a chance to be the best they can be, and give them a chance to enrich your lives."

THINK AND DISCUSS

1. What kinds of disabilities does Rosa have?

2. How did her parents react initially to Rosa's disabilities? How did their reactions change? Why?

3. What are Sylvia and Ed doing to meet Rosa's special needs? What are they doing to help other families with Down's children?

4. How do you think Rosa enriches the lives of her parents?

They need to accept the changes that result from the therapy. Sharing children's personal feelings, learning to understand them, and accepting children for who and what they are—not what parents expect them to be—are actions and attitudes parents can learn to help children overcome their problems.

OBSERVING AND PARTICIPATING

Developing Participation Skills

The following guidelines can help students as they work with special-needs children:

- Consider safety. Keep in mind all the safety guidelines appropriate for the developmental level, not only the age, of the children.

- Be positive. Special-needs children often experience more frustration than their peers, and they are likely to lack confidence in their skills.

- Find ego boosters. Observe each child, and plan activities that build on his or her strengths.

- Avoid pressuring the child. Make your time together enjoyable and tension-free.

- Encourage language skills. Give a special-needs child opportunities to identify familiar objects, answer questions, and predict outcomes.

Raising a Disabled Child

The responsibilities and demands of raising a child with a disability can often seem overwhelming. In acknowledging their child's disabilities, parents may experience a grief process that includes guilt, sadness, anger, and frustration.

Support groups for parents of disabled children serve a valuable function. They help parents explore and accept their feelings. They also help parents meet more successfully the emotional needs of their children. Parents learn to separate the disability from the child and to appreciate the fact that they have a child who happens to have a disability. Children who receive strong emotional support are better able to develop the inner strength, patience, and courage necessary to cope with their disabilities.

Parents can also get together with other parents of disabled children to share comfort, advice, and solutions to everyday problems. In addition, groups can keep members up to date on research and treatment available for children with specific disabilities.

Disabled children can bring as much joy to a family as children without disabilities. Like other children, disabled children give family members a chance to love and be loved, to give, to receive, and to share.

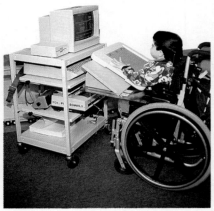

New technologies are giving children with disabilities new tools for learning.

SECTION 1 REVIEW

CHECK YOUR UNDERSTANDING

1. What is the most important need of children with disabilities?

2. Who benefits when children with disabilities are placed in regular preschool programs? How do they benefit?

3. Why is it especially important to encourage independence for children with physical disabilities?

4. Why should children with mental disabilities be trained in grooming, manners, and acceptable social behavior?

5. List five types of behavior that may be signs of emotional disturbance.

6. Who can often make recommendations about finding a therapist?

DISCUSS AND DISCOVER

1. Many children born with disabilities are so ill that they must remain in the hospital for the first weeks—or even months—of their life. How do you think this long period of separation affects the baby? How do you think parents should deal with the problems this kind of separation creates?

Observing & Participating

Visit a preschool class in which some of the students are disabled and others are not. Describe how completely the disabled children appear to be integrated into the classroom activities. What special needs do the disabled children have? How do other children respond to those needs? What evidence do you see that all the children are learning empathy?

SECTION 1 REVIEW

1. To feel loved and accepted by their families and by society.

2. Both; encourages all children to grow intellectually, develop social skills, and learn to feel empathy.

3. To develop both a positive self-concept and life skills.

4. To make social acceptance more likely.

5. Any five: nervous habits, loss of appetite, sleeplessness, excessive fear, withdrawal, aggressive or violent behavior, failing grades.

6. Pediatricians, school counselors, members of the clergy, or a local office of the Mental Health Association.

ASSESS

CHECKING COMPREHENSION

Assign students to write their responses to the Check Your Understanding questions in the Section 1 Review. Answers to the questions are given below.

EVALUATE

Have students complete the Chapter 18, Section 1 TCR quiz.

Reteaching

1. Assign Reteaching 43 in the TCR. Have students complete it and review their responses.

2. Have students complete the following sentence: "If I had a handicapped child, …"

3. Ask students how they would distinguish between normal emotional displays and those requiring outside help.

Enrichment

1. Assign TCR Enrichment 43.

2. Have students read fiction or nonfiction about children or young adults who have met physical challenges. *My Side of the Mountain*, by Jean Craighead George, and *Izzy Willy-Nilly*, by Cynthia Voigt, are familiar favorites. Students may also enjoy reading about families of exceptional children.

Extension

- Invite a special education teacher to speak to the class on the problems children with disabilities face and allow questions.

- Plan a field trip to a sheltered workshop or school for children or adults with disabilities to observe how they learn independent living skills.

CLOSE

Read to students this statement: "Give your children a chance to be the best they can be." Remind students that a family that has this goal for children may not have to alter its goals for disabled children, only its method of achieving them.

FOCUS

SECTION 2 RESOURCES

Teacher's Classroom Resources

Enrichment 44

Reteaching 44

Section 2 Quiz

Student Workbook

•Handle With Care

SECTION OVERVIEW

In Section 2, students learn about the four main categories of child abuse and how child abuse and neglect have reached epidemic proportions. The section provides information on who abuses children and discusses the severity and long-term effects of child abuse, including damage to the physical, emotional, mental, and social health of its victims. Treatment and counseling are two strategies that help abusive parents learn to cope and stop the pattern of abuse.

MOTIVATOR

Write the term *child abuse* on the board. Allow students to give examples, but do not ask for examples from personal experience or you may suggest hypothetical ones. Encourage students to discuss the reasons such incidents occur. Explain that parents may suffer emotional disabilities or be under extreme stress and that child abusers come from all ethnic, religious, cultural, and socioeconomic groups.

USING TERMS TO LEARN

Go over vocabulary words listed in "Terms to Learn." Ask students to define the term crisis. (A personal tragedy, emotional upheaval, or the like.) Tell them that crisis nurseries are child care facilities where troubled parents can leave their children for a short time.

SECTION 2

Child Abuse and Neglect

OBJECTIVES

• Explain what child abuse is and why it happens.

• Discuss what can be done to prevent child abuse.

TERMS TO LEARN

child abuse
crisis nurseries

Child abuse is *the physical and/or emotional mistreatment of a child.* The effects of child abuse, of any type, are long-lasting. Abuse can affect the physical, emotional, mental, and social health of its victims throughout their lifetime.

What Does Abuse Involve?

Most people find it difficult to understand how anyone can abuse children. According to the National Committee for the Prevention of Child Abuse, abuse of children has reached epidemic proportions throughout the world. It is difficult to estimate the total extent because many cases go unreported, but it is believed that abused children number in the millions. Every day an average of five American children are abused so badly that they die.

Child abuse is generally considered in these four categories:

• **Nonaccidental physical injury.** Injury caused by such things as beatings, burns, bites, or scalding water.

• **Neglect.** Failing to provide a child with the basic necessities of life, such as food, clothing, shelter, and medical care.

• **Sexual molestation.** Using a child for the sexual pleasure of an adult.

• **Emotional abuse.** Placing unreasonable, unrealistic, or excessive demands on the child. Examples are constant belittling, teasing, or verbal attacks. Some children never receive the love and affection they need for normal emotional development.

A single incident does not generally indicate child abuse. Abuse involves a pattern of behavior. The longer it continues, the more serious the problem becomes for both child and parent.

MORE ABOUT

Child Abusers

One characteristic observed in families where child abuse occurs is social isolation. Child abusers are often isolated from family, friends, and community support groups. They seldom belong to formal organizations and usually have trouble making and keeping friends. This isolation may prevent them from getting help when stress and problems build up and child abuse occurs. The child abuse may increase the isolation if the parent feels guilty and unworthy of having contact with others.

Who Are Child Abusers?

Contrary to what you might expect, most child abusers are not monsters. They are ordinary people, usually parents or other relatives, caught in emotional situations that they cannot handle. They are often people who feel lonely and can't cope with their own personal problems. Low self-esteem is a common trait among child abusers. In many cases, they were themselves abused as children. Because patterns involving abuse are the only kind of parenting they have known, they repeat the behavior with their own children.

Child abusers come from all income levels, ethnic groups, and religions. Often, only one parent in a family actively abuses the children. However, the other parent may participate in the abuse by refusing to recognize it, by ignoring it, or by refusing to seek help.

Parents who abuse their children are easily provoked and unable to maintain self-control. When they are irritated, they respond quickly and violently, much as a young child does. A three-year-old who is angry responds without thought. The child may kick the cat, smash a toy truck, or throw a doll across the room. An abusive adult displays the same uncontrollable emotions. An argument with a spouse, a car that won't start—almost anything—can trigger an incident of abuse. The child's words or actions are seldom the cause. The child is simply nearby, a defenseless target for violent physical or verbal abuse.

Any type of abuse prevents a child from developing normally. Children who suffer continuing abuse are also more likely to become abusive parents themselves.

Responding to the epidemic proportion of child abuse cases, organizations are sponsoring prevention education as a method to eliminate child abuse.

TEACH

Pages 524-528

• **What Does Abuse Involve?**
• **Who Are Child Abusers?**
• **Are There Any Answers?**

GUIDED PRACTICE

Promoting Discussion

Ask students to identify which type of child abuse might be the hardest to detect. Why? How does child abuse relate to the discussion of emotional handicaps presented in Section 1?

Practicing Decision Making

Have students work in small groups, listing situations that might trigger child abuse (such as a crying child who cannot be quieted). Then have them list nonabusive ways to handle each situation.

Critical Thinking

Ask students to describe the difference between physical punishment and physical abuse. Do all people define these the same way? Do some people cross the line from punishment to abuse too easily? Some people believe that physical punishment is acceptable. Could this belief be contributing to the amount of physical abuse we have in our country?

Critical Thinking

Ask students why many sexual abusers manage to keep their actions a secret. (They threaten the child, make the child feel guilty, and take advantage of the child's trust and innocence.)

Making Connections: Reading

Provide students with newspaper or magazine articles about child abuse. Have each students read an article and summarize the article for the class.

MORE ABOUT

Child Abuse

A majority of abused children are not abused by strangers, but by persons known to them. The abuser is usually a parent or the primary caregiver. Often one child in a family is singled out for abuse. Children with handicaps, especially, and others who require special care and attention are at a high risk for abuse. Infants and toddlers have a greater risk of injury from abuse than do older children. Child abuse is more common in larger families than in smaller ones.

Childhood Reflections

"A torn jacket is soon mended, but hard words bruise the heart of a child."

Henry Wadsworth Longfellow

GUIDED PRACTICE (continued)

Practicing Decision Making

Read the following to students: Beth and Garson had been married for only two months when Gar gave Beth her first black eye. Five years and two children later, he is more abusive than ever. Last week, for the first time, after a night of drinking, Gar shoved two-year-old Natasha into the wall. Beth was gripped by fear. She has no job and no one to turn to. She wonders how much more she can take. Ask students to analyze this situation. Why does Gar act as he does? Why does Beth let this go on? Does Beth have options that she has not considered? What should she do? Who will benefit from any action she takes?

Practicing Decision Making

Have students write suggestions for what they would do in each of the following situations:

• You observe your neighbor in the yard yanking on her child and telling him how stupid and clumsy he is. This is a common scene with them.

• You are the parent of a young child who tells you about some very suspicious things that your stepuncle has said and done to your child.

• Your best friend often wears long sleeves in hot weather and will not explain bruises that she routinely has.

Critical Thinking

Why might a parent fail to take action to protect the children from an abusive spouse? (Answers will vary. The parent may be emotionally or financially dependant on the abusive spouse, or similarly abused and in danger. In the case of sexual abuse, sometimes parents either disbelieve or blame the abused child.)

If abusive parents are criticized by other parents because their children do not behave, could this provoke an incident of abuse? Explain. (Yes. Abusive parents often expect their children to be perfect, and evaluate themselves by their children's behavior. They may be extremely sensitive to criticism.)

Abusive parents generally believe that infants will be spoiled if they are picked up and comforted when they cry. They do not recognize this physical comforting as essential for the development of trust. Abusive parents feel that they must continually show their children "who's boss." They have unrealistic expectations of what children can do. These parents may expect their children to be perfect. For example, they may tell a toddler to "sit up and eat right." They expect the toddler to do just that—promptly—even though the nature of toddlers makes this almost impossible. Abusive parents expect young children to remember commands given only once. Of course, young children learn only after directions have been repeated many times. An abusive parent may see a child's failure to comply as stubbornness, meanness, deliberate disobedience, or revenge—behavior to be severely punished.

Are There Any Answers?

It is against the law in every state to abuse a child. All states also have laws requiring those who work with children, such as doctors, teachers, social workers, and child care workers, to report suspected cases of child abuse. However, many people, even responsible professionals, find it difficult to make such reports. It is essential for the well-being of the children involved that, in spite of personal concerns and hesitations, every case of suspected child abuse be reported to the closest social service agency or child welfare agency.

Once an agency receives a report of suspected child abuse, it begins an investigation into the case. If the child is in immediate danger, the court may place the child in a foster home. If there is a history of past abuse or the child's injuries are severe, uncooperative parents can be charged and tried.

Putting abusive people in jail does not solve the problem of the abuse. It only provides the abused children with temporary protection. In most cases, treatment and counseling are used in an attempt to correct the cause of the abuse—and so bring the abuse to an end.

Most abusive parents can learn to care for their children responsibly. To help parents achieve that goal, there are many types of government, private, and volunteer programs available. Parents Anonymous, one of the best-known groups, is made up of parents who help each other gain self-control.

Some communities have **crisis nurseries**, *child care facilities where troubled parents can leave their children for a short time.* Using a crisis nursery gives parents time to cool off and try to cope with their frustrations and anger away from their children. Volunteers or professionals associated with crisis nurseries usu-

CLASSROOM MANAGEMENT

Resources Beyond the Classroom

In most communities, reports of suspected abuse can be made to the welfare department, the juvenile probation department, or the police department or sheriff's office. A child abuse/neglect hot line can provide information on reporting abuse as well as help those who feel they might commit child abuse. You may wish to contact one of these local organizations to see whether someone from one of these organizations can be a guest speaker for your class.

ASK THE EXPERTS

The Cycle of Abuse

Q. **What is the cycle of child abuse, and how can it be broken?**

A. Child abuse is a cycle in this sense: Once the abusive behavior is begun, a pattern of abusive behavior is established and repeated. A parent who has hit a child for "misbehaving" one day is more likely to hit the child again—probably more severely— the next day. A parent who, as a child, was abused by his or her own parent is very likely to abuse his or her own children; abuse has become part of the parenting style he or she knows best. These cycles of child abuse are understandable. They are not, however, inevitable. The cycle of abuse can— and must—be broken.

Every abuser is caught in the abuse trap, which has four distinct aspects:

- Attitudes and beliefs
- Thoughts
- Actions
- Feelings

In order to avoid getting caught in the abuse trap, an individual must be alert to all four aspects of that trap. It is essential for anyone who is a parent or who comes in contact with children to examine his or her own attitudes, thoughts, actions, and feelings, with special awareness of those that might lead to abuse.

An abuser can be freed from this trap by changing his or her attitudes, thoughts, actions, and feelings. Support groups, counselors, and social workers are good sources of help for abusers.

Since child abuse is not only a personal problem but also a societal problem, each of us can find ways to help. We can support organizations that make life better for children. We can avoid laughing at pain—our own or other people's. We can help create a community that respects all people, that honors children's needs, and that helps all children grow.

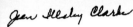

Jean Illsley Clarke

Jean Illsley Clarke
Director of J.I. Consultants in
Minneapolis, Minnesota

ally work with the abusive parents on a one-to-one basis. They help parents understand their frustrations and resolve their problems. They guide parents in learning how to break the cycle of child abuse.

Many family problems, including child abuse, are directly related to poor parenting skills and to a lack of knowledge about

TEEN PARENTING

Teen Parents and Child Abuse

Parents who are involved in child abuse tend to be younger than average. They have their children at younger ages than other parents. Teen parents, therefore, run a high risk of becoming abusive parents. Write the following words on the chalkboard: *isolation, frustration, inadequacy,* and *poverty.* Ask students to explain how these words relate to teen parents. How might these contribute to abu-

sive behavior? To combat the problems teen parents have, many schools and communities provide special programs that teach good parenting skills. The programs also help teens stay in school and maintain the adolescent friendships that are so important to them. Ask students how each of these program components addresses the problems associated with isolation, frustration, inadequacy, and poverty.

GUIDED PRACTICE (continued)

ASK THE EXPERTS

Issues and Advice

1. Why is child abuse a cycle? (*Once it is begun, a pattern of abusive behavior is established and repeated.*)

2. What are four aspects of the abuse trap? (*Attitudes and beliefs, thoughts, actions, and feelings.*)

3. What is the first step toward avoiding the abusive trap? (*Recognize any attitudes, thoughts, actions, and feelings that might lead to abuse.*)

4. Name three sources of help. (*Support groups, counselors, and social workers.*)

5. What can people do to help stop child abuse? (*Support children's organizations, be more compassionate and respectful of all people and their needs.*)

Thinking Like an Expert

As Jean Illsley Clarke points out, child abuse can be prevented by understanding and honoring children's needs. On the chalkboard, write the questions: What are a child's most important physical needs? Emotional needs? Social needs? Intellectual or cognitive needs? Have students copy the questions and interview as many people as possible. Ask students to share their findings and discuss similarities and differences.

INDEPENDENT PRACTICE

Journal Writing

In their journals, ask students to respond to this question: If they were drafting a bill of rights for children, what specific items would be included? Why?

Student Workbook

Have students complete "Handle With Care" in the Student Workbook.

ASSESS

CHECKING COMPREHENSION

Assign students to write their responses to the Check Your Understanding questions in the Section 2 Review. Answers to the questions are given below.

EVALUATE

Have students complete the Chapter 18, Section 2 TCR quiz.

Reteaching

1. Assign Reteaching 44 in the TCR. Have students complete the activity and review their responses.

2. Have students make a poster titled, "Hurting? Where can you call for help?" Have them place a cutout of a telephone receiver in one corner of the poster. Connect this to another telephone receiver in the opposite corner by running a cord along the perimeter of the board. On bright pieces of paper, list people or agencies (and their phone numbers) where students can call for help.

Enrichment

Assign Enrichment 44 in the TCR.

Extension

• Invite a social worker to speak to the class about child abuse, including how to report it and what happens to the child after the abuse is reported. Afterwards, have students write a paragraph explaining how they would report abuse if they saw it.

• Have students investigate the agencies available in the community that provide assistance to abused children and their families and report their findings to the class.

CLOSE

Go around the classroom and have each student give a specific example of how parenting education can help prevent child abuse.

Counselors can help abusive parents understand and change their behavior.

child development. Classes like the one you are taking help give parents—and future parents—realistic ideas about what parenting involves. You know by now that babies are not always clean and happy, and that they don't stay babies forever. You also know what normal behavior is at different ages, so you can make thoughtful decisions about discipline. Preparing people for parenthood before they become parents and providing them with help once they are parents are two basic steps society can take to help eliminate child abuse.

SECTION 2 REVIEW

CHECK YOUR UNDERSTANDING

1. What are the long-term effects of child abuse?
2. List the four general categories of child abuse, and give one example of each.
3. List three traits common among child abusers.
4. Where should child abuse be reported?
5. Who belongs to Parents Anonymous? What do members do?
6. What are two basic steps society can take to help eliminate child abuse?

DISCUSS AND DISCOVER

1. Read about a specific case of child abuse: How was the abuse discovered and reported?

What efforts were made to help the abused child? What happened to the suspected abuser? How does reading about this case make you feel? Share your reactions with your classmates.

Observing & Participating

Talk to a counselor or social worker about why people often find it difficult to report suspected cases of child abuse. What particular problems would a person have in reporting abuse? Describe what you would say and do to encourage a close friend to report his or her suspicions of child abuse.

SECTION 2 REVIEW

1. Abuse can affect the physical, emotional, mental, and social health of its victims throughout their lifetime.

2. Nonaccidental physical injury, such as beatings; neglect, such as failing to provide food; sexual molestation, which involves using a child for sexual pleasure; emotional abuse, such as unreasonable demands. (Other examples are also acceptable.)

3. They are lonely and feel unable to cope with their problems; they have low self-esteem; they were themselves abused as children.

4. The closest social service agency or child welfare agency.

5. Abusive parents; help each other gain self-control.

6. Preparing people for parenthood and providing them with help once they become parents.

Family Stresses

OBJECTIVES

- Describe the emotional effects on children of stressful family situations, such as divorce and death.
- Explain how the emotional effects of family stresses can be minimized.

Every child is exposed to stress at one time or another. The stress may be fairly mild and short-term; for example, the child's family may move from one home to another. Sometimes, however, a child may have to face severe stress, such as when someone close to the child dies.

TERMS TO LEARN

joint custody

Children and Stress

During times of stress, everyone needs support. Children need more help and support than adults because they are less capable of understanding and dealing with the events that cause stress. Children should be encouraged to talk about their feelings, especially during periods of unusual stress. At these times, too, parents must be careful to avoid taking their own stresses out on their children. When parents feel they are faced with more stress than they can handle, they should not hesitate to ask for help. Other family members, members of the clergy, and professional counselors can help parents cope with stressful situations.

Divorce

Child and family experts generally agree that, ideally, children should have the influence of both a mother and a father while growing up. Normal development may be hindered when one parent is absent. On the other hand, experts also know that a home in which parents continually disagree or even fight can be damaging to children. Experts further acknowledge that the divorce of their parents is a fact that nearly 20 percent of children will have to deal with before they turn eighteen.

SECTION 3
Family Stress
Pages 529-537

FOCUS

SECTION 3 RESOURCES

Teacher's Classroom Resources

Enrichment 45

Reteaching 45

Section 3 Quiz

Student Workbook

- Giving Advice

SECTION OVERVIEW

Section 3 explores students' understanding of the stressful situations that can affect children. These situations vary in their severity. Students discover that during times of stress, more help and support is needed. This is especially true for children because they are less able to understand what is happening.

MOTIVATOR

In the last section, students read about possible links between family stress and abuse of children. Lead a discussion about common situations that result in stress on the child or the family. Have students brainstorm situations that might cause stress in families. As they respond, list their suggestions on the chalkboard. Suggest they copy the list, add to it as they read, and take notes on chapter suggestions for helping children cope with stressful situations.

USING TERMS TO LEARN

Have students preview the definition of the term by turning to the glossary and reading the entry.

MORE ABOUT

Children and Stress

Like adults, children are tense and emotionally upset at times. Because they are too young to completely understand these tensions, they resort to ways of expressing their feelings that are physically or socially undesirable. Characteristic behaviors are sucking a thumb or fingers, biting nails, twisting or pulling hair, biting lips, fighting, abusing pets, and acting in a destructive manner. Parents and caregivers are wise to remember that a child's negative behavior is not an indication that he or she is a "bad" person; rather, it indicates that he or she is troubled and cannot yet express feelings in a healthy way. Children taught to handle stress more maturely tend to outgrow undesirable traits.

TEACH

Pages 529-537

- Children and Stress
- Divorce
- Death
- Moving
- Financial Problems
- Illness

GUIDED PRACTICE

Family Focus

- Discuss with students how children are affected by the way parents handle stress. What effect could this have on parent-child relationships? Sibling relationships?

- Ask students to discuss the changes in family relationships that may result from divorce. For example, how might children's relationships with grandparents be different after parents divorce? How do relationships change if parents remarry?

Promoting Discussion

Have students discuss how a divorce might affect celebration of holidays and other special occasions. Ask them to suggest ways of making such occasions happier for children and of minimizing stress or conflict.

Critical Thinking

Suppose one parent is clearly unfit, does not love the children, and intends never to see them again. Should the children be told both parents will always love them? If so, why? If not, how should this situation be handled? (The less said about the absent parent's lack of love, the better. The remaining parent should say, "I will always love you and take care of you.")

When parents divorce, a child's time is often split between two homes. Why should activities with both parents be kept as normal as possible?

If a family is about to break up, the children need to be told about the change in an honest and reassuring way. Experts advise using the following guidelines for helping children deal with separation or divorce:

- **Truth.** The children should be told the truth about the upcoming changes. If possible, both parents should sit down with the children and discuss the situation. All children, even toddlers, should be included in the discussion. Young children often understand much more than parents realize. Parents can say something like this to their children:

  "We're having a hard time right now. We are going to live apart, for a while at least. Still, no matter what happens, we will both always love you and take care of you."

- **Elimination of blame.** Parents should avoid placing blame for the divorce on one another, at least in front of the children. If the parents are not able to discuss the divorce with their children without placing blame, they can ask a counselor or a member of the clergy to help them with this discussion. Each parent should remember that the children will continue to need both their parents, even after a separation or divorce. The children should not be placed in a position where they have to take sides with one parent or the other.

HEALTHY FAMILIES/HEALTHY CHILDREN

Coping with Divorce

Divorce is hard on children, just as it is on adults. However, most child development experts believe that growing up in a family where there is constant bickering and unhappiness is even more damaging to children than divorce. Therefore, in such cases, it is not wise for parents to stay married just "for the sake of the children." By continuing to build healthy relationships with both parents, most children of divorce are able to live happy, well-adjusted lives.

Children must also be reassured that they are in no way responsible for the breakup. Parents should stress that they are separating because of their own differences, not because of anything their children have said or done—or failed to say or do. Most children feel guilty when their parents fail to get along; parents should make a special effort to be reassuring on this point.

- **Reassurance.** The children need reassurance that they will continue to be loved by both parents. After a separation or divorce, the children of a family typically live with only one parent. They need to know that the other parent is still there for emotional support and companionship. Both the parent with whom the children live and the absent parent should reassure children about this kind of continuity.

- **No false hope.** The children should not be encouraged to hope for a reconciliation if their parents are not considering the possibility. After a divorce, children usually hope that their parents will get back together again. This false hope only delays the children's adjustment to their new family situation.

- **Stability and continuity.** The children's lives should be kept as much the same as possible. Siblings should continue living together, if at all possible. Children also feel more comfortable if they do not have to change homes or schools. The absent parent should spend time with the children often and regularly. Frequent contact with relatives from both sides of the family can help retain a sense of belonging.

Emotional Effects of Divorce

Divorce requires many emotional adjustments by everyone in the family—especially children. They have a special need for security, stability, and understanding. The new lifestyle that comes with divorce or separation can cause new problems and require many adjustments.

During a divorce, decisions are made about the custody of the couple's children. Some parents agree to have **joint custody**, *an arrangement in which both parents assume responsibility for the children*. With joint custody, the children usually divide their time between their two parents' homes. More often, one parent is awarded custody of the children. In years past, that parent was almost automatically the mother. Now, most courts base the custody decision on information about which parent can better provide a loving, stable home. When sole custody is awarded, the courts encourage visitation by the other parent so that children can maintain healthy relationships with both parents.

GUIDED PRACTICE (continued)

Critical Thinking
How might custodial parents suffer emotionally if they are resented while the absent parent is idealized? (They might feel hurt, unworthy, unappreciated, resentful of the child, or victimized.) What might help them cope with their feelings? (Studying information such as that in this chapter and attending a divorced parents group, such as Parents Without Partners.)

Critical Thinking
Ask students whether they think divorce is taken too lightly today. Is divorce sometimes preferable to staying together? Under what circumstances?

Practicing Decision Making
Ask students how much time a child should spend living with each parent after a divorce. How many different schedules can they think of that people use for this? What are the pros and cons of each? Should children choose the parent with whom they want to live? Why or why not?

Cooperative Learning
Have students work in small groups to discuss how age affects children's understanding of, and response to, their parents' divorce. Have the groups consider infants and toddlers, preschoolers, school-age children, and teenagers. Which age group would most likely have negative effects from a divorce? Which would be least affected? Why? Have each group report to the class.

MORE ABOUT

Divorce
For children, divorce is a long process that takes place over several years, rather than a single event. Children generally experience divorce in three stages. The initial stage, following the parents' decision to divorce, is very stressful. Children are unhappy and respond aggressively. In about a year, children enter the transition stage, after their strong emotional responses are lessened or gone. This is a period of family restructuring and economic and social change that lasts for two to three years. The restabilized stage occurs when the changes caused by the divorce are incorporated into daily living. Most families reach this stage within five years of the divorce.

GUIDED PRACTICE (continued)

Critical Thinking

Discuss with students how the death of a parent affects relationships among remaining family members. Under what circumstances might family members become closer to each other? More distant from each other? What would the difference be if it were a child who had died rather than a parent?

Critical Thinking

How would you respond to a four-year-old child who asked, "I know Daddy's dead, but when is he coming back?" (Answers will vary. Explain death again, and remind the child that the person does not come back. Religion and belief systems should dictate the explanation of the deceased's present situation.)

Promoting Discussion

Ask students why it might be difficult for a grieving adult to deal with a four-year-old's reaction to death.

Critical Thinking

How could parents use the sight of dead animals or insects as an opportunity to explain death? (They could explain why the animal is not moving and that it won't move, eat, or breathe again. Depending on the age of the child, they can explain decomposition and that the body may nourish other animals and plants. Using an insect or animal that does not evoke much sympathy might allow an explanation of death without emotional upset.) Why might it be a good idea to do so? (The first time the child experiences the death of a pet, friend, or family member, the biological aspects of death may not need to be explained in specific connection with the deceased individual.)

It is not unusual for children to resent the parent they live with and idealize the absent parent. The "home" parent makes and enforces family rules, and often gets the blame for the changed lifestyle. The noncustodial parent, on the other hand, may try to make up for his or her absence by being especially lenient and by buying special gifts. This situation creates conflict for all the family members, and no one benefits.

Parents who are caught up in their own troubles can easily forget that divorce is particularly upsetting for youngsters. Many children, even very young ones, develop behavior problems in response to the family's disruption. Even children who appear to adjust well during the period of their parents' divorce may be hiding their grief and pain. If children have noticeable, continuing adjustment problems, it is wise to seek professional help.

Death

The death of someone close causes special problems for a young child. The age of the child, however, influences the youngster's reaction.

- **Under age three.** Children this young cannot understand anything more than a brief separation. A toddler will react to a parent's death in the same way as to the parent's week-long vacation.

- **Ages three to five.** Children this age think that death is like sleep—you are dead, and then you wake up and are alive again. As a result, children of this age may seem unfeeling about the death of a close relative or family friend. They are worried and concerned for a while, but they do not understand that death is permanent. Some months after her father's death, one four-year-old said, "I know Daddy's dead, but when is he coming home?"

- **Ages five to nine.** As children mature, they accept the idea that a person who has died will not come back. However, they do not view death as something that happens to everyone. They especially do not recognize that they themselves will die. To them, death happens only to other people.

- **Age nine or ten.** At this age, children finally begin to see death as inevitable for everyone. They realize that they, too, will die. This may make them afraid. At this age, children must come to terms with their fear and put it in proper perspective.

MORE ABOUT

Death

Death once took place at home. Most people died in their own beds surrounded by relatives and friends. Children accepted death as a normal part of life because they were exposed to it through epidemics, wars, and childbirth. As dying became a more isolated, private affair, children more often were sheltered from experiencing death. Today, people tend to avoid facing the fact of death, which makes it difficult to explain death to children. When children feel adults are being evasive and withholding information, they become uneasy and worry. Children have the right to participate in the sorrows as well as the joys of life.

Many children first experience death when a pet dies. True understanding and acceptance may not come until much later.

By the time they are five, most children have had some contact with death and are curious about it. Perhaps a pet has died; perhaps they have seen a dead squirrel or bird. Some children will have experienced a death in the extended family. Whatever their experiences, children need an opportunity to discuss their feelings and to ask questions about death.

How Children Cope with Death

Child psychologists believe that children go through a three-step process in accepting death. Parents and other caregivers who understand this process are usually better prepared to help children cope with death and with their feelings about death. These are the three steps:

1. **Disbelief.** In this early stage, children may express anger, hostility, and defiance.
2. **Despair.** Later, children are often withdrawn and depressed. Some children revert to babyish behavior during this stage.
3. **Reorganization.** Finally, children begin to adjust to life without the person who has died.

HEALTHY FAMILIES/HEALTHY CHILDREN

Connecting with the Past

Strong families see themselves as a link between the past and the future. They teach children that "family" does not end with death. They discuss deceased relatives so that memories of the dead are kept alive. They may visit the cemetery where ancestors are buried or look at memorabilia or old pictures of them.

GUIDED PRACTICE (continued)

Making Connections: Drama

Have students work in pairs to act out how they would explain death to a two-year-old, a four-year-old, a six-year-old, and a ten-year-old.

Making Connections: Writing

Have students write two questions that a four-year-old child might ask about the death of a family member. Do the same for a six-year-old and a nine-year-old. The questions should illustrate each child's level of ability to understand death.

PARENTING IN ACTION

PARENTING IN ACTION

Understanding a Child's Fears

Five-year-old Stephen was brought to a mental health clinic by his parents. They were concerned about his sudden, but continuing, bedtime problems. Until recently, they explained, Stephen had not resisted going to bed. Then he suddenly started crying at bedtime and refused to settle down. After Stephen finally fell into an exhausted sleep, he was often awakened in the night by nightmares.

Except for this one problem, Stephen's behavior and emotional adjustment seemed normal. Neither parent was able to offer an explanation.

The therapist used a play session with Stephen to try to find out the cause of his fear. During the session, Stephen told the story of a man who ". . . caught a heart attack. He fell out of bed and died." In response to the therapist's questions, Stephen revealed that he had overheard his mother talking on the telephone, telling someone about a family friend who had suffered a heart attack, fallen out of bed, and died.

Stephen had no idea what a heart attack was or where one came from, but he did understand falling out of bed. If doing that could make you have a heart attack and die, no one was going to get him into a bed again!

With this information, the therapist was able to explain to Stephen why he did not need to worry about going to bed. Then the therapist explained the problem to Stephen's parents and recommended that they try to make bedtime as happy and relaxed as possible.

THINK AND DISCUSS

1. How did Stephen's parents handle his bedtime problem? What might have happened if they had taken a different approach, such as punishing Stephen?

2. Do you think Stephen's parents could have avoided the development of his bedtime problem? If so, how? Do you think they could have solved the problem without a therapist? If so, how?

3. What questions do you think Stephen might have about death? How do you think his parents might help him understand death better?

If a loved one dies, children should be told about the death in an honest way. They may need an explanation of what death is. Children should then be encouraged to talk about their feelings. Parents, in turn, should let children know that they, too, miss the person very much. Sharing memories of the person who has died, looking at photographs, and talking about the special characteristics of the person who has died can help both parents and children deal with the death.

SEE HOW THEY GROW

Children's Fears

Dr. Jean Piaget and other child behavior experts discovered that children evolve through stages of understanding. For example, toddlers between the approximate ages of eighteen to twenty-seven months do not understand relative sizes. They would conceivably fear being pulled down a bathtub drain and disappearing as the water does, because they do not understand that the drain hole is much too small for their size. As impossible as it may sound to adults, to the child, the fear is very real. Although Piaget's theories have been criticized as too rigidly defining, he nevertheless pioneered an understanding of the importance of a child's developmental stages. Parents and caregivers who are patient and knowledgeable with expressed fears will help the child grow and mature smoothly.

PARENTING IN ACTION

Promoting Discussion

Introduce this selection by asking students what fears from their own childhood does the title evoke?

Have students read the selection independently, then encourage them to share their initial response. How does this situation make you feel? With whom do you identify most strongly? What advice would you like to give? Why?

Thinking Critically

Ask students what makes this situation so troubling for Stephen. What other kinds of issues raise similar concerns for parents of preschoolers and school-age children? Do these kinds of concerns continue to arise as children grow older?

Answers to Think and Discuss

1. Stephen admitted that there was a problem, and they brought him to a mental health clinic. It would not have solved Stephen's problems and could have had damaging effects on his personality and behavior.

2. His parents might have observed him closely to gain clues from his actions during his daily activities. They could have tried to talk with him about his reluctance to go to bed. They might even have created a game, such as "animals go to bed," to play with him. This could have helped Stephen talk about what was bothering him in the context of playing a bed-related game.

3. Answers will vary, but may include: What happens when you die? His parents should encourage him to express his fears and feelings about death. Parents should tell children the truth about death as they see it. Children who are given facts simply and honestly can better cope with the stress that death brings.

Children need prompt, direct answers to their questions about the death. A well-intentioned but untrue statement, such as "Grandma went on a long trip," can make the situation more difficult for children to accept. If the children believe the statement, they may be hurt that Grandma went away without saying good-bye. If the children don't believe that explanation, they may conclude that something too awful to discuss has happened to Grandma. Whatever the children think at the time, they will have to face the truth sooner or later. It is important for children to know that they can trust their parents and that their parents, even though they may be sad, are available to discuss the death.

Adults must be very careful about the words they use when discussing death with a child. Especially with very young children, phrases like "passed away" or "gone to sleep" only add to a child's confusion. It is best to use simple, direct references to death and dying. It is also important to remember that children understand most things in terms of themselves. For example, a child who is told that "Grandpa got very sick and died" may worry about dying the next time he or she is sick with a cold. The type of explanation an adult offers must fit the age and understanding of the child, but it should always be honest and direct, no matter how simple.

Some childhood experiences with death are more upsetting than others. A child whose parent dies needs support for an extended period. The death of a parent is the most tragic thing that can happen to a youngster. Many children react to a parent's death with guilt. The child may think, "I wasn't always good when he wanted me to be," or, "I wasn't quiet enough when she was sick." Children need the assurance that nothing they did, said, or even thought caused the death. They also need help coping with their feelings of abandonment.

In most cases, even very young children should be allowed to take part in family funerals or memorial services. Children of any age are capable of mourning. Studies have shown that even infants go through a period of excessive crying and searching for a parent who has died.

Children who are given honest answers about the death of a loved one are more likely to be able to deal with their feelings.

Moving

Moving is stressful for children, because their familiar settings and routines are upset. Often, children don't want to leave their present home, where they feel secure and safe.

Parents can help soothe children's fears by encouraging them to talk about their feelings. Children should also be encouraged to pack their own belongings as much as possible. This activity helps them feel more in control and more involved in the move.

GUIDED PRACTICE (continued)

Practicing Decision Making
Point out to students that parents can make moving less stressful for children by talking about the positive aspects before the move and helping them get settled and adjusted afterwards. Have students assume they are the parents of two children, ages four and seven. They are in the process of moving to a new city. Have students make a list of five specific things they would do for each child to make the move and adjustment easier.

Cooperative Learning
Have students collect information from moving companies and analyze the materials to see what advice is given to help children cope with moving. Have students in small groups write a brochure about moving entitled "Tips for Helping Kids Cope with Moving."

Promoting Discussion
Ask students to name some direct and indirect effects on children when parents have financial problems. How might these affect a child's behavior? Ask students whether they think that financial problems can lead to other problems in a home. Give examples. How are children in the family affected? What can people do to avoid or solve financial problems?

Promoting Discussion
Have students work in small groups to make a list of adjustments that children have to make when a family member is ill. Make a class master list as each group reports its discussion.

MORE ABOUT

Moving
Americans live in a mobile society. Each year, the number of families that move is about one in five. Some families rarely move; for others, moving is a way of life. Military families are moved every two or three years, as are employees of some large corporations. Most family moves are dictated by the husband's job or career. In these cases, the husband typically adjusts more easily to the new location. Moving, however, is one of the most frequent causes of depression in wives. For families that move often, knowing how to integrate themselves into a new community is important for the well-being of parents and children.

INDEPENDENT PRACTICE

Journal Writing

- Have students complete this sentence from the point of view of a seven-year-old: "Every time I have to move to a new town, I feel …" Have students complete the sentence in their journals.

- Ask students to write entries in their journals, discussing ways to entertain sick children to keep them calm and quiet during their illnesses. Include in the entry ways to entertain healthy children that will keep them calm and quiet when others in the household are ill.

Student Workbook

Have students complete "Giving Advice" in the Student Workbook.

Extension

Let students work independently or in small groups to complete one or more of these extension activities:

- Investigate the custody laws in your state and write a one-page analysis of the laws. Do you agree with the preferred legal custody arrangement? Do you think the laws are in the best interests of children? Why or why not?

- Research and write a report on the long-term psychological effects of losing a parent during childhood.

- Research the effects of a serious or long-term illness on a child's development.

Did You Know?

Having a handicapped child can be very costly for parents. Diagnosis and treatment can be expensive, and often treatment extends over many years. Children whose handicaps prevent them from ever living independently will need monetary support their entire lives, creating an enormous financial burden for parents or other family members.

If you moved as a young child, you probably still remember the fear and anxiety you felt. How can talking about these feelings help minimize them?

Parents can also stress aspects of the move that will be positive for the child, such as the opportunity to have his or her own room.

After the move is made, parents should take the time to help the child get settled. To make the adjustment easier, parents can take walks with the child around the new neighborhood, help the child meet nearby children, and take the child to visit his or her new school.

Financial Problems

When a family has financial problems, children sense the tensions even though they may not understand them. The parents may be short-tempered or less attentive then usual. In this situation, children typically believe that they themselves have done something wrong.

Even though children cannot understand complex financial situations, they should be reassured that the problems are not their fault. In addition, parents need to try not to take out their own fears and worries on their children.

Illness

When a family member is ill or hospitalized, the family's routine is disturbed. Parents can help their children cope with this kind of situation by giving a simple, clear explanation of what is happening. If the illness is minor, the child can be reassured that the person will soon be well and everything will return to normal. If the illness is serious or terminal, the child should be told the truth, but in a calm, reassuring way.

When a close relative is ill or injured, it is not unusual for children to worry that they will suffer a similar illness or injury. They may grow afraid of doctors or hospitals. Parents should take the time to explain how the relative's illness or injury differs from any the child is likely to have. As with other situations of family stress, children need their parents' patience and reassurance.

Coping Skills

Healthy families pull together for support when sickness, financial problems, death, or other stressful events occur. They accept and try to solve their problems. They also know that community social service offices offer programs to help them get through their crisis situation.

MORE ABOUT

Financial Problems

When families have money problems, parents worry about current needs, the future, giving their children a good start in life, and whether they are failures. These problems produce tension in parents, which adversely affects the marital relationship as well as parent-child relationships. One of the most destructive outcomes of financial problems is the loss of self-esteem in parents. The end result is often drinking, violence, irritability, increased sensitivity to criticism, and withdrawal. All these factors make the task of being a good parent more difficult.

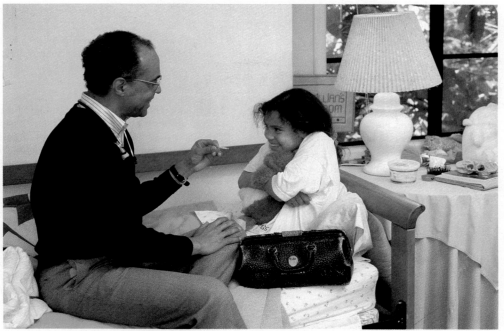
Young children who have long-term illnesses need to understand that doctors and nurses are trying to help them, not hurt them.

SECTION 3 REVIEW

CHECK YOUR UNDERSTANDING

1. List five guidelines for helping children deal with separation and divorce.
2. When sole custody is awarded after a divorce, what kind of relationship should the noncustodial parent establish with the children? Why?
3. What attitude toward death is typical of three- to five-year-olds? At what age do children usually begin to understand that death is inevitable for everyone?
4. List the three stages children often go through in accepting a death.
5. List two things parents can do to help their children feel settled after a move.

DISCUSS AND DISCOVER

1. When divorced parents agree to joint custody, what advantages does the new living arrangement have for the couple's children? For the divorced parents? What are the disadvantages of joint custody for both children and parents?

Observing & Participating

Talk to a professional child care provider to find out how he or she helps children cope with the common stresses discussed in this section. What specific techniques are used? In what ways does the provider adjust his or her techniques according to the age of the child? What resources, if any, does the provider use?

SECTION 3 REVIEW

1. Tell the truth; eliminate blame; reassure the child; don't give false hope; provide stability and continuity.
2. Frequent visits; to provide children with healthy relationships with both parents.
3. They think death is temporary, like being asleep; age nine or ten.
4. Disbelief; despair; reorganization.
5. Any two: take walks with child around new neighborhood; help child meet nearby children; take child to visit new school.

ASSESS

CHECKING COMPREHENSION

Assign students to write their responses to the Check Your Understanding questions in the Section 3 Review. Answers to the questions are given at the bottom of this page.

EVALUATE

Have students complete the Chapter 18, Section 3 quiz in the TCR.

Reteaching

1. Assign Reteaching 45 in the TCR. Have students complete the activity and review their responses.
2. Let students work with partners to plan and prepare an illustrated poster on one of these topics:
   • Helping children cope with divorce.
   • Helping children cope with death.

Enrichment

1. Assign Enrichment 45, in the TCR.
2. Have students study the research related to the effects of divorce and remarriage on children and report their findings to the class.

Extension

Ask for three or four volunteers from the class to form a panel that will discuss the effects of moving. Select students who have experienced this in their lives. Have the panelists explain the circumstances of their moves, what was difficult about leaving, what adjustments they had to make, and what helped them cope. After the presentations, open up the discussion to the class for questions and comments.

CLOSE

Ask students to suggest what they think is the most important idea to remember about dealing with children on the subject of death.

Use the Summary and the Reviewing the Facts questions to help students go over the most important ideas presented in Chapter 18; encourage students to ask questions and add details, as appropriate.

CHAPTER 18 REVIEW

1. Learning good grooming, manners, and socially acceptable behavior.

2. Children receive treatment for a physical disability as early as possible after birth.

3. The ability to understand and share each other's feelings.

4. To help them live independent lives as adults.

5. A professional trained in helping people work through emotional problems.

6. Seek professional help, identify physical causes, support the work of the therapist.

7. Physical or emotional mistreatment of children.

8. Child care facility where parents with problems can temporarily leave their children while they try to cope with their anger and frustration.

9. Both parents should tell children about a decision to divorce. Parents should tell children the truth; avoid blaming each other; provide security, reassurance, stability, and continuity.

10. They can talk about their feelings and share memories of their loved ones.

11. The children sense the tension in the parents, even though they don't understand what is wrong.

12. The children may worry that they will become sick.

Study Guide

You may wish to use Study Guide 18 in the Student Workbook to review key concepts of the chapter.

CHAPTER 18 REVIEW

SUMMARY

- Children may have physical, mental, and/or emotional disabilities. Each child with a disability has individual care needs.

- Child abuse has severe and long-lasting effects.

- Treatment and counseling can help abusive parents learn to cope with their problems and stop the patterns of abuse.

- When a family is divided by separation or divorce, children need to be informed in an honest and reassuring way.

- Children should be told about the death of a loved one in a direct and honest way, appropriate to the child's age and ability to understand.

- Children who must cope with family stresses, including divorce, death, moving, financial problems, and illness, need special support.

REVIEWING THE FACTS

1. List two important things parents should teach their disabled children.

2. At what age should a child begin receiving treatment for a physical disability?

3. What is empathy?

4. What is the long-range goal for children with mental disabilities?

5. What is a therapist? What steps should parents expect a therapist to take in working with a child who has emotional problems?

6. List three important steps parents can take to help children overcome emotional problems.

7. What is child abuse?

8. What are crisis nurseries?

9. Who should tell children about their parents' decision to divorce? How should children be told of the decision?

10. List two things parents and children can do together that will help them deal with the death of a loved one.

11. Why do a family's financial problems create stress for children?

12. What fears are common among children who have a close relative who has been hospitalized?

EXPLORING FURTHER

1. Working with other students, compile a list of local groups for parents of children with various kinds of disabilities. When and where does each group meet? What are the specific interests of the members of each group? How can interested parents contact each group? Publish your list in a format and place that will make it readily available to new parents. (Section 1)

2. Read magazine stories, journal articles, or short books about families with at least one disabled child. Discuss your readings with classmates. How do you think siblings respond to the special needs of the disabled child in a family? How do parents deal with the needs of all their children in such families? (Section 1)

3. Gather information about the work of organizations in your area that provide shelter for families and help with child abuse problems. How can the local office be contacted? What information and help is available through the association's office? Then make a flier or a poster presenting the information you have gathered. (Section 2)

4. Working with one or two other students, plan and present three skits about families in which a death has occurred. In your skits, show how a parent or other adult might explain the death to a three-year-old, a six-year-old, and a nine-year-old. (Section 3)

THINKING CRITICALLY

1. **Analyze.** Disabled children are more likely than nondisabled children to be abused. What factors do you think contribute to this high rate of abuse? What do you think can and should be done to help disabled victims of child abuse? To help those who abuse disabled children?

2. **Synthesize.** Which do you think is more difficult for a child—being raised by a single mother or experiencing the divorce of married parents?

CLASSROOM MANAGEMENT

Discussing Teen Parenting

If you have teen parents in your class, a balance can be found between the reality of their situation and the tendency to pass judgment on them. Use facts to support observations. Point out to students that marriage may not be a good long-term solution to the problem of teen pregnancy. Statistics show that about 60 percent of those who marry before the age of twenty will divorce. Such marriages often aim to provide the child with the influence of two parents, but this reason alone is seldom enough to make the marriage a stable one. If the couple faces additional pressures and stresses, such as financial dependency, substance abuse, and children with disabilities, the prospects for a stable family relationship are greatly diminished.

Why? What advantages can you identify for a child in each situation? On the basis of your opinions about a child's welfare, would you recommend that two people who are expecting a baby should get married, even if they had not considered marriage otherwise? Why or why not?

3. **Compare and contrast.** How do you think the death of a school friend would affect a seven-year-old? Why? How would the effects of the friend's death be similar to the effects of the death of an older relative? How would they be different?

CROSS-CURRICULUM CONNECTIONS

1. **Reading.** Read several current articles about mainstreaming: What attitudes are expressed toward the practice of mainstreaming disabled students in public school classes of mostly nondisabled children? What advantages of mainstreaming are identified? What

disadvantages are discussed? How have attitudes toward mainstreaming changed in recent years? Why? Discuss your reading with other students.

2. **Writing.** Plan and write a short story about moving. Write the story from the point of view of a six-year-old who has had to move several times. Use this sentence beginning to start your story: "Every time my family has to move to a new town, I feel . . ."

SCHOOL TO WORK

Time Management Employees who use their time wisely are an asset to a company. Not only do they contribute to the efficient day-to-day operations, they are better able to control their own work and stress loads. Here are a few suggestions for managing time that you can practice now: set priorities for obligations and activities; make a schedule based on your priorities; and learn to cut back activities when you need to.

PERFORMANCE ASSESSMENT

Special Challenges for Children

Task
Prepare a story book for children that includes characters with disabilities or special needs. Your content should be suitable for and interesting to young children.

Purpose
This assignment challenges you to use your creative writing skills for a different and unique audience—children. The inclusion of characters with special needs or disabilities will be one of the features of your story.

Procedure
1. Think of a story idea and outline your story line. Give your story a beginning, middle, and end.
2. Select the setting and identify human and/or animal characters. Remember

to include one or more characters with special needs or disabilities.
3. Make an informal drawing of your page layouts. Determine the number of pages, place your story text on the pages you select, and note space for your art.
4. Sketch or draw pictures on the pages where you want them to be.
5. Use your imagination to complete your project. Keep your audience in mind as you work, and make your story book one that will appeal to children.
6. As you put your book together, remember to include all parts of a book: cover, copyright page, and title page. Make your book look professional.

Evaluation
Your story will be evaluated on how well you incorporate characters with special needs into a story line that appeals to a young audience. Originality, visual appeal, creativity, and appropriateness of language will be assessed.

Portfolio Idea Make a dedication page such as you find in many books. Write a short introduction to your story book or an evaluation of it, explaining your objectives, your procedures, and telling what you learned.

539

PERFORMANCE ASSESSMENT

Story Book
If possible, bring in examples of magazines and catalogs that feature models with disabilities to show students. Encourage students to go to a library or bookstore to look at the variety of books designed for children. If they are timid about their art, have them note other ways they can illustrate their books: photos, collages, stick figures, or water color drawings. Explain that while their

art will not be evaluated, the effectiveness of communication will. You may want to show them how to draw page layouts by folding a wide piece of paper in half lengthwise to represent the left and right pages, numbering each page, and showing how to indicate placement of text and art. This will enable them to plot their story line ahead of time, and have the appropriate number of pages.

EVALUATE
Use the reproducible Chapter 18 Test in the TCR, or construct your own test using the Test-maker Software.

EXTENSION
Identify local support groups, government agencies, and other groups involved with mental retardation. They can be located through the local or state Association for Retarded Citizens, local mental health agencies, the schools, or the state department of education or child welfare.

CLOSE

Ask each student to write and complete the following sentence:
People should understand and respect the rights of children because …

DEVELOPING A PORTFOLIO

Writing a Preface Remind students that their portfolios should include a Preface or Introduction. Have them think of this Preface as a way of introducing themselves. The Preface should state the intended purpose of the portfolio, some of the processes involved in making selections, and what they feel they have learned and/or accomplished by creating and maintaining a portfolio. Encourage them to include details about their favorite, most difficult, or most informative work samples, or any interesting discoveries about themselves. Direct students to write a rough draft of their Preface. Then, after a few days, they can revise it with a fresh eye.

INTRODUCE

CHAPTER OVERVIEW

Chapter 19 guides students in considering specific ways in which they can provide care for children, both now and in the future, and helps them examine the skills necessary for providing such care.

In Section 1, students discuss work that is already familiar to many of them—that of a babysitter or child care provider. They examine the responsibilities of a child care provider and consider the skills and abilities needed to care for children of different ages. They also review safety tips for child care providers.

Section 2 helps students observe young children, either at home or in group settings. Students begin by considering the benefits of observing young children. Then they examine the specific techniques and approaches that make observations effective. They learn about the various kinds of records that can be kept and how those records can be interpreted and used.

In Section 3, students learn how they can be active and effective participants in an early childhood classroom. They examine the physical organization and furnishings of a classroom, and discuss procedures for protecting the health and safety of the children in the class. Then students read about the importance of planning and learn about kinds of schedules to be used in planning appropriate activities.

CLASSROOM MANAGEMENT

Resources Beyond the Classroom

Now that students have acquired a good deal of information about the issues relating to the needs of children, some resourceful teens might be interested in starting their own child care business. Have them read *The Child Care Notebook* (Cornell University Cooperative Extension). In it, they will learn how to assess the child care needs of their community, what kind of equipment to buy, how to plan age-appropriate activities, as well as strategies for handling licensing, insurance, and food preparation. A valuable discussion of the pros and cons of operating a child care business is also included. To obtain a copy of the publication, send $6 to:

The Media Services Resource Center
Cornell University
7 Cornell Business and Technology Park
Ithaca, NY 14850

Caring for Children

THINK ABOUT

Do you think you are more qualified now to take charge of the health and safety of children than you were one month ago? Three months ago? If so, who or what was influential in guiding your development? If not, what remains to be improved? What differences, if any, do you see between learning about child care and applying the ideas in a child care situation?

ASK YOURSELF

Study the photo on the opposite page. What is the age of the child? What should the caregiver know about a child's growth and development at this age? How does the caregiver show her interest in the child's needs? What personal qualifications do you think this caregiver must have in order be effective as a child care provider? How would the information in this textbook help her enjoy children and be successful as a caregiver at the same time?

NOW TRY THIS

Imagine you are the parent of a child under the age of six years. You need a caregiver to watch your child while you work three days a week. List the personal qualifications you would look for in the caregiver you hire. Then list questions you would ask to determine whether the person has these qualifications.

541

CHAPTER OBJECTIVES

After completing Chapter 19, students will be able to:

- Describe the responsibilities of a child care provider and discuss the skills an effective child care provider should have.

- Explain the importance of observing young children and describe techniques of effective observation.

- Discuss effective methods for organizing early childhood classrooms, for planning early childhood activities, and for promoting positive behavior in the class.

INTRODUCING THE CHAPTER

- Ask volunteer students to describe a time when they had to work with other people to achieve a goal. Examples might be participating on a sports team, being part of a student government committee, or working on a class assignment. Ask them to explain how important cooperation and communication were to the outcome. How important were creativity and leadership skills? Then ask students to discuss how these qualities are related to caring for other people's children, either as a babysitter or as a classroom assistant.

  Then explain that as they study Chapter 19 they will learn more about caring for young children.

- Use the photo on the opposite page and the three features on this page—Think About, Ask Yourself, and Now Try This—to begin a discussion about caring for children.

HEALTHY FAMILIES/HEALTHY CHILDREN

Balancing Work and Family

As more and more women become part of the work force, the need for quality child care increases. Not only must the care provided be good, but it must also be reliable. Have students think about these child care issues: (1) In a dual-earner family, whose responsibility is it to locate good child care? Who should transport the children? (2) What happens when the child is sick? Who stays home? Are there facilities for temporary care of sick children in the community? (3) At what age is a child old enough to be left alone? For how long a period of time? How does this affect children? (4) What can employers do to help working parents solve child care problems?

FOCUS

SECTION 1 RESOURCES

Teacher's Classroom Resources
- Enrichment 46
- Reteaching 46
- Section 1 Quiz

Student Workbook
- Babysitting Safely

SECTION OVERVIEW

Section 1 guides students in considering the activities and attitudes of babysitters, also known as child care providers.

Students begin by examining the responsibilities a child care provider undertakes. They consider the personal characteristics a good child care provider should have, and they discuss preparations and safety guidelines necessary for meeting the specific needs of children in various age groups.

MOTIVATOR

Write the word *babysitter* on the chalkboard, and ask students to jot down the first eight words or phrases that come to mind. Then let volunteers read their lists aloud. What are the most negative responses? The most positive? What accounts for the range of responses?

Next, ask students to consider babysitting from two different points of view: their current perspective, as babysitters or at least potential babysitters; and their former perspective, as children taken care of, at least occasionally, by babysitters. From these two points of view, have students suggest the requirements of a good babysitter. Do the requirements vary according to the point of view? Why or why not?

Finally, ask students to consider the word *babysitter* itself. Explain the term *child care provider* is often used in its place.

SECTION 1 — Being a Babysitter and Child Care Provider

SECTION 1

OBJECTIVES

- List the personal qualities needed for being a good babysitter or child care provider.
- Describe the responsibilities of a child care provider when caring for children of various ages.
- List safety guidelines that are especially important for child care providers.

The most common first child care job is babysitting. Actually, *babysitting* is not a very accurate term. When you undertake this job, you are really providing care for children. The job allows little time for sitting—unless the children are asleep.

Responsibilities

Child care providers have a lot of responsibility. When the parents are gone, they are completely responsible for the safety and welfare of the children. Good caregivers are interested primarily in the children, not just in the money they are earning. They have patience, a sense of humor, and an understanding of children's physical, emotional, social, and intellectual needs. Good caregivers are flexible and can get along well with all types of children. They handle unexpected situations well and make sound judgments in emergencies.

Good Beginnings

When you provide child care, some families may hire you regularly. However, you will probably also receive an occasional call from families you do not know. When you receive such a call, ask how the new family learned about you. If you were recommended by a family you work for regularly, you can ask them about the new family, if necessary. You need to be aware of

---

MORE ABOUT

Keeping References

Most parents will request at least one reference before hiring a babysitter or full-time caregiver. Students interested in pursuing careers in the child care field or in babysitting on a regular basis should try to compile a list of references for future use. Addresses and telephone numbers should be kept up to date.

your own safety, as well as that of the children for whom you provide care. During this first phone call, you will also want to agree on your charges, learn how long the parents intend to be gone, and make arrangements for getting to and from their home. Before you leave for any child care job, be sure your own family knows the name, address, and phone number of the people you will be working for and the approximate time you will return.

The first time you provide child care for a family, make arrangements to arrive about 20 minutes early. This will give the children a chance to get used to you while their parents are still home. It will also allow you enough time to find out any additional information from the parents. When bedtimes are, where the parents will be, how the parents can be reached, and when they will return are obvious questions you will want to ask. Also, learning the family's rules and routines will help you do the job better. For example, knowing that two-year-old Kevin never sleeps without his special blanket might save a lot of problems at bedtime.

When you start a new child care job, the parent should give you a tour of the home and explain the children's routines.

TEACH

Pages 542-547

- **Responsibilities**
- **Caring for Children of Different Ages**
- **Safety Tips for Child Care Providers**
- **How Do You Rate as a Care Provider?**

GUIDED PRACTICE

Promoting Discussion
Encourage students to share and discuss their own experiences as child care providers. In what situations did you especially need patience? A sense of humor? An understanding of children's needs? Flexibility? The ability to get along well with all types of children? The ability to handle unexpected situations? The ability to make sound judgments in emergencies?

Critical Thinking
Let students share their ideas in response to these questions: At what age do you think most people are responsible enough to provide care for a preschooler? A toddler? An infant? Why do you think that age is appropriate? If there are differences in the ages you consider appropriate, what accounts for those differences?

Cooperative Learning
Let students work in groups to write a list of specific questions a child care provider should ask before parents leave. Then let the members of different groups share and compare their lists.

Promoting Discussion
Have students suggest specific questions a child care provider would need to ask parents when he or she was caring for a child with disabilities.

Using the Photograph
Encourage students to describe and discuss the situation shown in the photo on this page. What type of information do you think the parent is sharing with the child care provider?

OBSERVING AND PARTICIPATING

Developing Participation Skills
A babysitter needs to know:
- What the child may eat or drink.
- Hours of bedtime or nap time.
- That doors should not be opened to strangers.
- When to turn off or on certain lights.
- Where the exits to the house are.

- How to lock and unlock doors and windows.
- What play activities the child enjoys.
- What activities are not allowed, inside or out.
- What parts of the house or grounds are off-limits for children or the sitter.
- How baby equipment works.
- What to do in case of an emergency.

Promoting Discussion

Encourage students to share their responses to these questions: What are the advantages of providing child care for the same family regularly? What are the advantages of finding child care jobs with new families?

Practicing Decision Making

Present the following situation to the class: Robin is an experienced child care provider, but this is the first time she has worked for Ms. Watson. Robin arrived early to get to know Ms. Watson and her two-year-old daughter, Renee. Unfortunately, Renee began crying even before her mother left for the evening, and Robin can't find any way to comfort the child. In response to every suggestion Robin makes, Renee screams, "Mommy!" Ms. Watson left half an hour ago and doesn't intend to return for another four hours.

Encourage students to discuss Robin's situation. What are her options? What do you think she should do? Why?

Cooperative Learning

Ask students to form groups in which they can discuss their responses to various child care situations. Have students imagine they are caring for the Conners' two children, aged five and eight. The parents have gone to a movie and plan to return no later than 11:00 p.m. Then ask group members to discuss how they would respond to each of these developments:

- The four-year-old hits the eight-year old on the forehead with a metal toy truck. The cut is bleeding, but it does not seem deep.

- A neighbor phones and asks to borrow the Conners' crock pot.

- A man rings the doorbell and says he accidentally dented the fender of the blue car in front of the house. The blue car is yours.

- It is 12:30 a.m., and you have not heard from Mr. and Mrs. Conners.

Caring for Children of Different Ages

Children of different ages have different needs. When you watch children, you should be prepared to provide different types of care for children in each age group.

Babies

Babies need a great deal of physical care and protection. This means that when you agree to care for an infant, you should have the necessary care skills and understand the characteristics of babies. You may want to review the information on infant care in Chapter 8.

When handling a small baby, be sure to hold the infant firmly, and always support the baby's head and neck. Babies can sense whether their caregiver is confident or nervous, and they will react accordingly.

Never leave a baby on a bed, sofa, or other raised surface. Even a tiny baby can wiggle enough to fall off. Also, be sure to keep harmful objects out of the reach of crawling infants.

When a baby cries, always find out what is troubling him or her. Is the baby too cold or too warm? Perhaps hunger, sickness, or a wet diaper is the trouble. Except for very young infants, babies do cry when they are lonely. If loneliness is the problem, a few minutes of cuddling will help.

Changing diapers is a frequent duty of child care providers. Be sure to gather all the necessary supplies so that they are nearby before you start changing the diaper.

Child care providers are not usually asked to bathe the baby. However, a qualified care provider should be able to undertake this task. Before you agree to do it as part of a child care job, review what is involved and practice bathing a baby under capable supervision.

Toddlers and Preschoolers

Providing care for young children involves giving care different from that required by babies. Young children are more sensitive to their parents' leaving and may need comforting. They like being read to, played with, or talked to.

Because toddlers and preschoolers sleep less and are more adventuresome, they require more watching. Do not leave them alone—even for a minute—while they are awake.

When you are caring for young children, bedtime can be a problem. Toddlers and preschoolers usually don't want to go to bed. Try to follow the child's regular bedtime routine. Undressing, brushing teeth, and going to the bathroom prepare children

MORE ABOUT

Bedtime Routines

Bedtime may be an especially difficult time for babysitters because the parent is not there for the customary bedtime routine. One researcher found seven common features of bedtime routine: stalling, increased use of the child's name by the parents, increased use of the word my by children, increased affection, specific sequence of activities, a bedtime story, and conversation that moves from a past orientation (what happened today) to a future orientation (what will happen tomorrow). Being aware of the difficulties that may arise beforehand can help babysitters know what to expect.

physically and psychologically for bed. Ask the parents in advance about other bedtime activities the child is used to.

A young child may be awakened, frightened or crying, because of a bad dream. Cuddle and comfort the child until he or she can get back to sleep. Later, tell the parents about the bad dream—or about anything else unusual.

Older Children

When you care for older children, you may find some who try to give you a difficult time. Some may feel they are too old for a babysitter. Others are jealous of the time and attention given to younger siblings. Still others try to get away with behavior their parents wouldn't permit.

You can get the relationship off to a good start by making friends with older children. If you show a genuine interest in their possessions, games, or activities, you'll win over even the most independent youngsters.

It helps if the parents establish your authority with the children before they leave. At no time is your maturity as a care provider more important than when a child deliberately misbehaves. You will have better control of the situation if you remain calm. Be fair—but firm.

Children will be fun if you involve yourself with their interests while they are in your care.

GUIDED PRACTICE (continued)

Critical Thinking

Let students share their ideas about the specific types of discipline and of punishment that child care providers should use.

Promoting Discussion

Remind students that the primary responsibility of a child care provider is to keep children healthy and safe. Guide students in discussing what a care provider must do to fulfill this responsibility. What specific precautions should a child care provider take? What should a care provider do in case of an accident? What should parents do to help a child care provider keep everyone in the home safe? What kinds of unsafe situations might a care provider encounter? How should he or she respond to each?

Critical Thinking

Point out to students that friends sometimes stop by to visit a teen who is providing child care. Ask what kinds of problems such visits can cause. What steps can a child care provider take to prevent those problems? To prevent visits at all? To deal with friends who do try to visit?

Cooperative Learning

Let students work in groups to discuss how teenagers who are eager to provide child care can advertise their services. What precautions should be taken to make sure the child care jobs undertaken will be safe for the teen? Have group members summarize their discussion and report to the rest of the class.

Making Connections: Children's Literature

Let interested students select several books appropriate for reading to three-, five-, and seven-year-olds in their care. Encourage students to seek recommendations from experienced adults, including children's librarians and teachers, for example. Ask these students to share their selections with the rest of the class.

OBSERVING AND PARTICIPATING

Developing Participation Skills

Ask students to develop creative projects and games to play while babysitting. These could include rainy-day arts and crafts suggestions, such as collages made from cut-out pictures, fabric scraps, and glue, or active games, such as paper cup bowling or a beanbag toss. Included in the "Babysitter's Bag of Tricks" could be small treats, such as raisins, dried fruit, or sugarless gum; a few inexpensive toys, such as crayons and a coloring book, pipe cleaners, and a deck of cards; a bag of balloons—different colors and shapes; and brown paper lunch bags that can be decorated and used to create a puppet show.

INDEPENDENT PRACTICE

Journal Writing

Let students write journal entries exploring their own ideas about working as a child care provider. Encourage students to respond to some or all of these questions: What are the personal benefits of being a care provider? What makes you well suited to the work? What should you do to improve your skills and abilities as a care provider? With what age group are you most comfortable? How can you find new jobs providing child care for children in that age group?

Student Workbook

Have students complete "Baby-sitting Safely" in the Students Workbook.

Extension

Let students work independently or in small groups to complete one or more of these extension activities:

- Write and illustrate a children's story about a toddler or preschooler who overcomes a dislike of child care providers. If possible, read your story to a young child or to a group of young children. How do they respond to your story?

- Write a public service announcement for radio, presenting a specific tip for child care providers. If possible, work with other students to plan and make an audiotape presenting a series of public service announcements; record appropriate music as transitions between the announcements.

- Write a short essay or a vignette demonstrating how a child care provider can teach an older child an informal lesson about nutrition.

Should you punish children? No matter how a child behaves, avoid using physical punishment, even if the parents have given you permission. Bribery and threats don't work well, either. If you feel you need to punish a child, use a reasonable punishment, such as no TV. You may want to review the information in Chapter 3 on guiding behavior.

Safety Tips for Child Care Providers

Whenever you care for children, you should keep in mind the common causes of childhood accidents, as well as basic first aid procedures. You may want to review the information in Chapter 17.

Caring for children requires your full attention. If you are alert and on the scene when something starts to happen, you can usually succeed in preventing serious problems. You should never let anything distract you from your primary job, which is watching the children

One of the most dangerous situations you might encounter as a child care provider is fire. Fire is fascinating to children, even those old enough to understand its dangers. When you begin a child care job, locate all the outside doors. Note escape routes from various parts of the home. Find out whether the house has smoke detectors and a fire extinguisher. Ask whether the parents have a family escape plan to be used in case of fire; if they do, ask them to review the plan for you.

When you are caring for children, don't let them wander off alone in the home; check on them frequently. Matches, cigarette lighters, candles, fireplaces, gas or electric heaters, and burning trash are all possible sources of fire.

If a fire does break out, remember that the children are your first responsibility. Lead or carry them to safety. Then alert anyone else who may be in danger, and call the fire department. Notify the parents at once.

How Do You Rate as a Care Provider?

As you can see, successful child care requires a careful balance and thoughtful attention to the children. You can raise your rating by learning about the toys, games, and other activities that appeal to children of different ages. Providing purchased toys is surely not the only way—or even the best way—to keep children amused and happy. More important are your interests, imagination, and enthusiasm. An attentive care provider with a headful of stories, rhymes, songs, tricks, and games is more welcome than toys. These kinds of activities can make a child care job a pleasant and worthwhile experience.

Childhood Reflections

"The child is father to the man."
William Wordsworth,
"My Heart Leaps Up"

COOPERATIVE LEARNING

The Value of Cooperative Learning

Cooperative learning need and should not be thought of as an isolated modality or "add-on" to the main body of instruction. Rather, a cooperative approach can help build academic skills in virtually any area. To enhance individuals' reading skills, for example, consider the following:

- Have small groups read aloud selected sections of the student text, after which each member independently paraphrases main and supporting ideas.

- Permit groups to present more technical chapter sections to the class by studying them in advance and preparing visual aids, such as glossary cue cards and pictures culled from external sources.

Admiring Jennifer's rock collection helped Susan start her babysitting job on a positive note.

You will rate well with parents if the children are well cared for, safe, and happy. Parents also want a care provider to arrive on time and to follow the routines or directions provided. In addition, parents appreciate a care provider who straightens up, making sure that toys, books, and games have been put away and any snacks or meals have been cleared away.

SECTION 1 REVIEW

CHECK YOUR UNDERSTANDING

1. What responsibilities does a child care provider undertake?
2. List five qualities of a good care provider.
3. List four questions a care provider who is working for a new family should ask before the parents leave.
4. How should a care provider respond to a crying infant?
5. What should a care provider do to help make bedtime easier for a toddler or preschooler?
6. Why do older children sometimes try to give a care provider a difficult time?

DISCUSS AND DISCOVER

1. Imagine that you are providing care for a family with an eight-year-old, a toddler, and an infant.

The eight-year-old is clearly interested in finding out how much she can get away with. What methods would you use in encouraging appropriate behavior? Under what conditions, if any, would you punish the child? What kinds of punishment would you use?

Observing & Participating

Interview several parents of small children to find out what qualities they consider important in a child care provider. Ask about any responsibilities a provider is expected to have other than caring for children and what the parents feel is an appropriate fee. Record your findings and speculate about the various expectations of parents regarding child care.

ASSESS

CHECKING COMPREHENSION

Assign students to write their responses to the Check Your Understanding questions in the Section 1 Review.

EVALUATE

Have students complete the Chapter 19, Section 1 quiz in the TCR.

Reteaching

1. Have students complete Reteaching 47 in the TCR.
2. Work with small groups of students to review the basic responsibilities of child care providers. Then let students work with partners to plan and make posters describing those responsibilities. Display posters in the classroom or in other areas of the school.

Enrichment

1. Challenge students to complete Enrichment 47 in the TCR.
2. Ask students to plan how they might set up a child care provider service in their own neighborhood. Have them write up their ideas. Plans should include responses to these questions: How would you find child care providers? How would you evaluate their abilities? What kinds of training would you provide? How would you find customers for your service? What financial arrangements would you make?

Extension

Invite several parents with young children to visit the class; ask these parents to discuss what they look for in a child care provider.

CLOSE

Ask each student to complete the following statement, either orally or in writing:

I do/do not want to be a child care provider because ...

SECTION 1 REVIEW

1. Complete responsibility for the safety and welfare of the children.
2. Any five: primary interest in the children; patience; sense of humor; understanding of children's physical, emotional, social, and intellectual needs; flexibility; ability to handle unexpected situations; ability to make sound judgments in emergencies.
3. When is bedtime? Where will parents be, and how can they be reached? When will they return? What are family's rules and routines?
4. Find out what is troubling the baby and take care of it; remember baby may feel lonely and need to be cuddled.
5. Try to follow child's regular bedtime routine.
6. They may feel too old for a babysitter, may be jealous of time and attention given to sibling, may try to get away with inappropriate behavior.

FOCUS

SECTION 2 RESOURCES

Teacher's Classroom Resources
- Enrichment 47
- Reteaching 47
- Section 2 Quiz

Student Workbook
- Developing Observational Skills

SECTION OVERVIEW

In Section 2, students consider the importance of observation skills: Being an effective observer can help parents, teachers, and others who care for children become more attentive and responsive to the needs of children.

They consider specific methods of observing children. They learn about the importance of objectivity, and they compare various types of observation records. They also learn how to conduct themselves during observations and how observation records can be used and interpreted.

MOTIVATOR

Encourage students to discuss their own experiences observing children, in completing Observing and Participating activities for this course or under other circumstances. Whom did you observe? What was your purpose in observing? What did you learn from your observations?

USING TERMS TO LEARN

Have students pronounce all nine vocabulary terms. Let volunteers share their ideas about the definitions of the terms. Help students recognize the relationships between anecdote and anecdotal; *confidential* and *confidentiality*; development and developmental.

SECTION 2   Observing Young Children

OBJECTIVES

- Explain the importance of observing young children.
- Discuss guidelines for observing young children.

Child development really comes to life when you can observe children in action. Learning how to observe young children is an important skill for parents, for teachers, and for others who take care of children.

TERMS TO LEARN

anecdotal record
baseline
confidentiality
developmental checklist
frequency count
interpret
objective
running record
subjective

Why Is Observing Children Important?

One of the most important reasons for observing children is to gain a better understanding of their growth and development. For instance, infants pass through a complex sequence of motor development in learning to walk. Observing infants at various stages of this development makes it easy to see how each motor skill leads to the next. When you understand this sequence, you can appreciate each achievement and provide experiences that will promote each skill as it emerges.

Observing young children also helps you learn about individual children. All children progress through similar stages, but each progresses at his or her individual rate. By observing, you can come to know the skills and needs of individual children, and thus become better able to help develop those skills and meet those needs.

Another reason for observing children is to gain feedback about your own parenting or teaching abilities. For example, you might be trying to develop the guidance technique of using positive reinforcement. By observing how children react to your positive reinforcement, you can determine how effective your methods have been.

Finally, observing children can help you identify those children who might have special needs or disabilities. Once they have been identified, the children can receive the special care and learning opportunities they need to reach their potential.

MORE ABOUT

Research and Observation

Most research on young children is based on observation because children cannot read and answer a questionnaire or explain their feelings and motivations to a researcher. Research can be longitudinal or cross-sectional. In longitudinal research, groups of children are observed over time.

This type of research is especially productive when investigators are trying to observe later effects of an event or action. For example, there has been much research interest in the long-term effects of divorce on young children. Cross-sectional research is discussed at the bottom of page 549.

How to Observe Young Children

Observing children means more than just watching what children do and telling what you think their actions mean. Knowing what you want to observe and understanding how to observe effectively will make your observations more valuable.

Objective Versus Subjective Observations

One of the most difficult aspects of becoming a good observer of young children is learning to separate facts from opinions. Study the following two examples of observations of the same event:

- **Example 1.** Robbie is feeling selfish. He won't let anyone play with the toys in the sandbox. He gets mad at Eric a lot.

- **Example 2.** Robbie is sitting in the sandbox. He reaches out and takes a truck away from Eric. Eric grabs for the truck, but Robbie pulls it away with a jerk. "It's my turn now," says Robbie, looking Eric straight in the face.

Example 1 is a **subjective** observation, an observation *using one's personal opinions and feelings, rather than facts, to judge or describe things*. Notice that, from reading this observation, you cannot tell what really happened between Robbie and Eric. The observer in Example 1 is recording not facts, but his or her opinion about Robbie's feelings.

Example 2 is an **objective** observation, an observation *using facts, not personal feelings or prejudices, to describe things*. The observation is factual. It describes what the observer saw and heard—and nothing more.

Objective observations are much more valuable than subjective observations. One of the main problems with a subjective observation is that it is based on a false assumption—the assumption that the observer knows what is going on inside the child's mind. Because no one, even an experienced observer, can know a child's emotions or motivations, subjective observations are necessarily inaccurate.

The interpretations included in subjective observations present another problem. They add to the potential for inaccuracy. For example, in example 1, the observer interpreted Robbie's actions as signs of selfishness. A teacher who knew that Robbie was generally shy at school would not find example 1 helpful. However, that same teacher, reading example 2, might interpret Robbie's behavior as a sign of emerging self-assertion.

A third problem with subjective observations is that their use is very limited. Because they do not record facts, they are hard for others to use and may be meaningless after time has passed.

Observing children in a class activity period can help you learn how they interact with each other and with teachers.

MORE ABOUT

Cross-Sectional Research

Cross-sectional research consists of observing children of different ages. Researchers have used this approach in studying language development, for example, by observing children's use of vocabulary and sentence structure at various ages. Cross-sectional methods have the advantage of being quicker, cheaper, and more manageable than longitudinal studies. Measurements taken from them, however, may not be valid if subjects differ on important variables other than age—these include health, education, and cultural or socioeconomic background. Both longitudinal and cross-sectional methods have advantages and disadvantages, and both are necessary to any study of human development.

TEACH

Pages 548-554

- **Why Is Observing Children Important?**
- **How to Observe Young Children**

GUIDED PRACTICE

Promoting Discussion

Encourage students to share their responses to these questions: How are the observations of a parent likely to differ from those of a teacher? How are both likely to differ from those of an outside observer? Why is it important for parents and teachers to make a point of observing the children in their care? What special advantages do parents and teachers have in observing children? What disadvantages do they have to overcome?

Critical Thinking

Ask students to cite specific examples in response to this question: What might an observer see that would help identify a child with a special need or disability?

Promoting Discussion

Let several students explain, in their own words, the differences between an objective observation and a subjective observation. Then help students identify and discuss problems that might result from subjective observations of young children.

Cooperative Learning

Have students work in groups to practice making both objective and subjective observations. Give each group a picture of an action scene involving one or more children. Have the group members work together to write up two descriptions of the scene: one objective and the other subjective. Then let the members of each group read their descriptions to the rest of the class. Ask other students to identify each description as objective or subjective and to point out any subjective details that may have been included in the objective description.

GUIDED PRACTICE (continued)

Promoting Discussion

Direct students' attention to this sentence from the text: "When you begin observing, you may find it helpful to imagine yourself as a video camera." Encourage students to share their ideas and opinions in response to that statement. How is being an objective observer similar to functioning as a video camera? How are the two different? Can a video camera be operated in ways that do not serve objective purposes? If so, how? What part should that approach play in making objective observations?

Cooperative Learning

Let students work in groups to write lists of abstract words (such as *happy* and *sad*, *good* and *bad*) that are not appropriate for use in an objective observation. Then have the group members list concrete words that might be used in place of the abstract words in the group's list.

Making Connections: Writing

Show students a short video of one or more young children at play. Assign half the students to write a subjective observation of the play session; assign the other half to write an objective observation of the same session. Then give students an opportunity to compare their completed descriptions. How are all the objective observations similar to one another? Are the same similarities evident among the subjective observations? Why not? What can you conclude about the usefulness and reliability of subjective observations?

Did You Know?

From a poll by Children's Learning Centers: 47 percent of parents spend an average of one to four hours a week reading to their children. Over 33 percent spend that same amount of time watching television with their youngsters.

Objective observations, on the other hand, can be studied at a later date or by another person.

It takes practice and discipline to write good objective observations. When you begin observing, you may find it helpful to imagine yourself as a video camera. You should record (in writing) only what you see and hear. With this guideline in mind, you will avoid abstract words such as *happy* or *sad, good* or *bad*. A video camera cannot see or hear happiness. It may see a smile or hear a laugh. The conclusion that the smiling, laughing person is happy is an interpretation of those actions, and interpretations do not belong in an objective observation. Using only concrete terms to record the actions, language, and physical surroundings you observe can help you make objective observations.

Types of Observation Records

Depending on your purpose, you can choose one of several types of observation recording methods. You will find the running record, the anecdotal record, the frequency count, and the developmental checklist most useful.

- **Running record.** The **running record** is *an observation recording method that involves recording for a set period of time everything observed about a particular child, group, or teacher.* This recording technique is useful if you are just getting to know a child or just learning about what goes on in a group child care setting. A running record can also be used for analyzing a certain area of development, such as social interaction or motor skills.

- **Anecdotal record.** The **anecdotal record** is *a method of recording observations that focus on a particular event or setting.* An anecdotal record is similar to a running record; both involve recording what you observe. However, the anecdotal record focuses on a particular event or setting. For example, you might want to see how a child is adjusting to a new child care setting. You could keep an anecdotal record, observing the child at arrival time each day for several days. If the child is adjusting well, your anecdotal record will show that the child's separation from his or her parent becomes easier during that period.

- **Frequency count.** The **frequency count** is *a tally of how often a certain behavior occurs.* To keep this kind of record, you focus on a specific child and use a tally mark on a record sheet to note how often that child takes a particular action. A frequency count is especially useful when you are trying to change a child's undesirable behavior. For example, you might notice that a particular child seems to hit other

OBSERVING AND PARTICIPATING

Developing Observational Skills

The more specific and focused an observation's purpose is, the more apt observers are to agree on what occurred during an observation. When observers who are watching the same thing agree on what happened, there is high interobserver agreement. However, even when observers are intensively trained, discrepancies in their observation records often occur. An event may look different from opposite sides of the room or may simply be interpreted differently. Many current research efforts videotape data to eliminate problems with interobserver agreement.

children quite often. To be objective, you should make an actual count of how often the child hits in a given period of time. You can begin by taking a **baseline**, *a frequency count taken before efforts are made to correct a particular undesirable behavior.* As you work with the child to change this behavior, you can make periodic frequency counts. When you compare these counts with the baseline, you can see whether the child's behavior is beginning to change.

- **Developmental checklist.** The **developmental checklist** is *a list that identifies a series of specific skills or behaviors that a child of a certain age range should be mastering.* To use the developmental checklist as an observation record, you can check off the specific skills or behaviors you observe in a particular child.

Occasionally, an observer using a developmental checklist must set up certain circumstances in the environment or must interact with the child in some way to ensure that certain behavior occurs. For example, in the sequence of motor development that leads to walking, one skill is pulling up on furniture to a standing position. This behavior could not be observed if furniture were not provided for the infant to use. Another skill is learning to walk while holding an adult's hand. In some cases, the observer may need to be available to provide this support.

Each of these methods of recording your observations of young children will give you valuable information. The method or methods you select will depend on your purpose for observing. Your purpose for observing, in turn, will depend on how you plan to use or interpret the information you gather.

Appropriate Behavior While Observing

While observing young children, you want to be as unnoticed as possible. Your very presence can affect the behavior of the children you are observing and make it difficult for you to gather objective information. There is also the possibility that you might disrupt the teacher or parent who is with the children you are observing. For these reasons, you should position yourself so that once you have responded to the children's initial interest, you can blend into the background.

To accomplish this, choose a spot outside the area in which the children are working or playing. Sit in a comfortable, adult-sized chair, or stand off to one side and use a clipboard. Have your notepad, observation assignment, and pen or pencil ready. Once you are settled, try to remain still. At first, the children may come to you to ask who you are and what you are doing. Answer their questions politely, but briefly. Avoid asking the

One advantage of a developmental checklist is that it is easy to use while observing. Less time is needed to check off items than to write a description of what the child is doing.

OBSERVING AND PARTICIPATING

Developing Observational Skills

Observation Handbook, a separate component for *The Developing Child*, is found in the Teacher's Classroom Resources. This activity booklet contains blackline reproducible masters that help stu-

dents gain skills in observing children, practice providing quality care and education for young children, and enhance their understanding of child growth and development.

GUIDED PRACTICE (continued)

Promoting Discussion

Let students compare and discuss the different types of observation records. How is each used? For what purpose? Under what circumstances does each type have a clear advantage over the others? Why?

Critical Thinking

Ask students to consider the importance of an observer's appropriate behavior. How might other behaviors affect the child or children being observed? How could those changes affect the observations?

Practicing Decision Making

Present the following situation to the class: Matt became interested in Erin's behavior during an observation at the child care center. At first, Erin seemed to wander around the room aimlessly. Matt soon noticed, however, that she was destructive. During the time he observed, Matt saw Erin knock over Hashim's block tower, scatter the dishes Dave and Kristi were using to play house, scribble on Sonya's painting, and throw pieces of the puzzle Jennifer was working.

Let students share their ideas about Matt's observations. How do you think he will interpret Erin's behavior? What do you think Matt should do with his conclusions? Why?

Promoting Discussion

Guide students in discussing how information from observations can be used by parents and teachers. Do members of each group benefit more from the record itself or from an interpretation of the record? Why?

Critical Thinking

Ask students to identify factors that might cause individuals to interpret the same observation differently. Are teachers and parents apt to interpret specific behavior in the same way? Why or why not?

PARENTING IN ACTION

Promoting Discussion

As an introduction to this selection, discuss ideas about the selection title, "Observing and Helping Children." In what ways do observing children and helping them usually go together, yet the goals of each are often considered separately.

Explain to students that this selection describes a situation in which an observer stepped out of her role and intervened to help the children she was observing. Encourage students to suggest situations in which they consider that response appropriate. Why might observers sometimes be tempted to intervene inappropriately? How can they learn to avoid that intervention? After a brief discussion, have students read the selection to determine whether they consider this intervention appropriate.

Thinking Critically

Encourage students to discuss their own responses to Christine's intervention. At what point—if any—would you have first considered intervening to help the boys? Was Christine right to intervene? Did she intervene too soon or too late? What would you have done in Christine's situation? Why?

Answers to "Think and Discuss"

1. She felt worried about the safety of the boys on the climbing structure. Encourage different opinions.

2. Christine was concerned that one of the boys might have fallen on—or from— the structure. Students may think that nothing serious might have happened.

3. Encourage a variety of responses.

4. She should report what happened objectively; she should be sure to include her own role in the incident.

PARENTING IN ACTION

Observing and Helping Children

Christine was observing three active kindergartners chasing each other on the outdoor play equipment. The well-built wooden structure included two ladders, one more difficult than the other. Both ladders led to a wooden platform, from which a suspension bridge led to a tower and two slides. Christine noted that Carl easily took the more difficult route and slid down the higher slide quickly, while Troy and Sean were more cautious; they both moved slowly along the easier route. Carl repeatedly called to his friends, "Come on up here, you guys. It's more fun—don't be a sissy."

After several tries, Troy became more confident. He soon joined Carl on the higher slide, and before long, both boys were yelling at Sean, "Come on! Don't be a baby." Christine saw Carl push Sean once as he hurried past him on the bridge.

Christine felt relieved when she heard Sean say to the other two, "Leave me alone. I'm going somewhere else to play." Before he could get down, however, Carl and Troy began to urge him up to the top of the tower, pushing and pulling and taunting him, "Scaredy-cat! Scaredy-cat!"

Christine knew that the kindergarten teacher was indoors, and she saw the aide on the other side of the playground, helping another group of children. Worried about the boys' safety, she jumped up and ran to the play structure. "Troy! Carl! Sean!" she called up to them. All three boys looked down at her in surprise.

THINK AND DISCUSS

1. What made Christine decide to abandon her role as an observer? Do you agree with her decision? Why or why not?

2. What might have happened if Christine had not intervened?

3. If you had been in Christine's position, what would you have said to the three boys? What response would you have expected?

4. What do you think Christine should tell the kindergarten teacher about this incident? Why?

---

children any questions, which would only encourage further conversation. If the children need to be encouraged to return to their own activities, you might say, "I am writing a story about how children play. If you go back to playing, I can write about you in my story."

A time may arise, however, when you must stop being just an observer and take action. For example, you might see that a

---

CLASSROOM MANAGEMENT

Resources Beyond the Classroom

Building Self-Confidence is a live-action video distributed by Glencoe Publishing Company. This informative program presents ways for parents and caregivers to build the self-confidence of a child. Interviews with parents and child psychologists stress the importance of having high self-con-

fidence and the role that the parent plays in developing the self-confidence of their children and helping them retain it through their formative years. For more information, contact:

Glencoe Publishing Company
15319 Chatsworth Street
Mission Hills, CA 91345

child has been hurt and that the child's teacher or parent is unaware of the problem. In this kind of situation, your concern for the safety of children should override your goal of remaining unnoticed as an observer.

Interpreting and Using Information from Observations

When you set out to observe young children, you decide on your purpose, choose the best method of gathering and recording information, and then gather that information. Once you have the information you need, the next step is to interpret and use it. To **interpret** is *to find meaning in, explain, or make sense of something.* As you gathered information, you made every effort to be objective, to avoid all interpretation. Now, however, it is time for you to express your ideas and opinions about what you observed. An hour's running record of a child's behavior is of little use until you analyze and interpret what you observed.

Objective observations, combined with thoughtful interpretations, can be used in a number of ways. Monitoring a child's pattern of growth and development is one of the most important applications of observation information. A teacher or parent who understands a particular child's stage of development can form appropriate expectations of the child. The parent or teacher can also provide an environment and activities that will help the child reach his or her potential. Children who appear to be far behind in certain areas of development can be referred to specialists, so that any special needs can be identified early.

Information from observations is also useful in solving problems related to children's behavior or to adult-child interaction. When a parent or teacher is having a problem with undesirable child behavior, close observation of the situation can often reveal the underlying cause of the problem and suggest possible solutions. For example, a preschool teacher might be having trouble keeping the noise level down in the classroom. An objective observation by another person might reveal that the teacher uses a very loud voice in speaking to children across the room. This information suggests that the solution might begin with a change in the teacher's behavior; the teacher should use a quieter voice and avoid shouting across the classroom.

Anyone who observes children and interprets information about them should remember and follow the basic rule of **confidentiality**, or *privacy*. In observing young children, confidentiality involves keeping all observations and findings about a child to yourself, sharing them only with the child's parents or with your child development teacher.

Remember that, as part of your course in child development, you will be with the children for only a brief time. What you

INDEPENDENT PRACTICE

Journal Writing

Ask students to write journal entries exploring their feelings about themselves as observers of young children. Pose questions such as these to stimulate students' thinking: How can you benefit now from observing young children? How can you benefit in the future? Which observation skills have you already developed? What should you do to improve your skills as an observer? When and where can you practice observing young children?

Student Workbook

Assign "Developing Observational Skills" in the Student Workbook and have students complete the activity sheet.

Extension

Let students work independently or in small groups to complete one or more of these extension activities:

• Obtain permission to review a file of old observation records from a child care center or from another source. Analyze which types of observation records were kept and what use was made of each type. Summarize your conclusions in a brief oral report.

• Identify magazines and journals published for early childhood teachers or for child care workers. In one of these publications, find an article about observing young children; read the article carefully and write a summary of it.

• Plan and write a developmental checklist that could be used to observe the language skills of children aged two to four. Use this text and other sources to determine which items are appropriate to include in your checklist.

MORE ABOUT

Interpreting Behavior

Interpreting children's behavior is not always easy. One study classified observational records according to the following motivational categories: status recognition—children were concerned with their competence in social, intellectual, or play activities; love and affection—children were concerned with acceptance, warmth, and liking or being liked by others; dominance—children were concerned with control of, or by, others; dependence—children were concerned with having others protect them or make decisions for them; independence—children were concerned with reliance on themselves.

CHECKING COMPREHENSION

Assign students to write their responses to the Check Your Understanding questions in the Section 2 Review.

EVALUATE

Have students complete the Chapter 19, Section 2 quiz in the TCR.

Reteaching

1. Distribute Reteaching 47 in the TCR.

2. Working with small groups of students, review the importance of writing objective observations. Then provide group members with additional examples of objective and subjective observations written on index cards. Ask students to read each observation, discuss it briefly, and identify it as either objective or subjective. Guide students in discussing how each subjective observation might be rewritten as an objective observation.

Enrichment

1. Have students complete Enrichment 47 in the TCR.

2. Ask students to be as creative as possible in writing—or drawing —their own work entitled "Portrait of an Effective Observer."

Extension

Invite to class an educational psychologist, a speech language pathologist, or another professional who regularly observes children to evaluate and diagnose them. Ask this professional to discuss his or her work with the class, emphasizing the observational skills necessary and sharing some experiences in observing young children. Encourage students to ask thoughtful questions.

Go around the room, asking each student to give one tip for observing young children.

---

interpret about a child's behavior during that time may not be accurate, because you may not have all the relevant facts. For this reason, it is especially important to avoid commenting to anyone that, for example, "Devon is spoiled" or "Kendra's child is a slow learner." Any such comments might lead to rumors that could hurt the child and his or her family.

You may, of course, have questions and concerns about a child you observe or about a child care facility you visit. You should discuss those questions and concerns with your teacher—and with no one else.

Becoming a good observer of young children is not easy, but it is a skill worth learning. It will help you become an effective parent or teacher—one who makes a positive difference in the life of a child.

SECTION 2 REVIEW

CHECK YOUR UNDERSTANDING

1. List four reasons for observing children.
2. What is the difference between a subjective observation and an objective observation?
3. List the four types of observation records. What determines which type of record an observer uses?
4. List three things an observer can do to avoid disrupting the children he or she is observing.
5. Which goal should an observer consider more important than the goal of remaining unnoticed?
6. What does it mean to interpret an observation?
7. What is confidentiality? What does confidentiality involve in relation to observing young children?

DISCUSS AND DISCOVER

1. Why do you think confidentiality is considered a basic rule in observing children? Who do you think should follow the rule of confidentiality? What kinds of problems might arise if those people fail to follow it? Are there ever circumstances under which people who work with children should disregard the rule of confidentiality? If so, what are those circumstances?

2. From a magazine, newspaper, or book, choose a photograph showing at least two children; other people may be included in the photo as well. Imagine that you are observing the scene in the photograph, and write two observations of it—one objective and one subjective. Then show the photograph to classmates, and read your observations aloud. Let your classmates help you evaluate and, if necessary, revise your objective observation.

Observing & Participating

Observe a child for a period of ten minutes and keep a running record of your observation. Work with a partner who observes the same child for the same time period. Compare records with your partner and discuss how they are similar and different.

SECTION 2 REVIEW

1. Gain a better understanding of children and their growth and development; gain feedback about one's own parenting abilities; identify children with special needs or disabilities.
2. Subjective: observer uses personal opinions and feelings, rather than facts. Objective: observer uses facts to describe things.
3. Running record, anecdotal record, frequency count, developmental checklist, purpose for observing.
4. Choose spot outside the area children are working or playing; have all tools ready; remain still; don't ask children any questions.
5. The safety of children.
6. To find meaning in, explain, and make sense of the facts recorded.
7. Privacy; keeping all observations confidential.

Participating in Child Care and Education

OBJECTIVES

- Describe effective plans for organizing early childhood classrooms.
- Discuss methods of protecting health and safety in early childhood classrooms.
- Explain how to plan daily schedules and appropriate activities for classes of young children.
- Discuss methods of promoting positive behavior.

TERMS TO LEARN

learning centers
time-out
transitions

A‍s a part of your class in child development, you may have the opportunity to participate in setting up an early childhood classroom. The following guidelines will help you get started and suggest ways that both you and the children can learn together.

The Early Childhood Classroom

Before you can invite young children to your school, you must prepare a place that is designed especially for them. Young children have physical, social, emotional, and intellectual needs different from those of older children and adults. Their environment should be designed to meet those needs and make learning possible.

The first requirement is to make everything possible child-sized. The furniture, including chairs, tables, and shelves, should all be of a size and design that is comfortable for young children. For example, when young children sit in a chair, their feet should easily touch the floor. Shelves should be low so that children can get and return materials independently. A child-sized environment promotes independence. The better the surroundings fit the young children, the more able those children will be to work and play without having to ask adults for help.

MORE ABOUT

Child Care Environments

Minimum standards for child care environments are set and enforced by licensing agencies or other state and local government agencies. Requirements are developed for both indoor and outdoor learning spaces, furnishings, equipment, and supplies. Although these vary from one geographical area to another, some are common to all. These are concerned with personal standards, general facility standards, food preparation and service, sanitation and health standards, fire regulations, construction codes, electrical services, ventilation, water supply and drinking water facilities, space per child, adult/child ratio, records and reports for business and legal purposes, etc. Most states require centers to secure a license to operate which is granted only when certain minimum standards are met.

SECTION 3

Participating in Child Care and Education

Pages 555-567

FOCUS

SECTION 3 RESOURCES

Teacher's Classroom Resources

- Enrichment 48
- Reteaching 48
- Section 3 Quiz

Student Workbook

- Learning Through Participation

SECTION OVERVIEW

Students begin Section 3 by examining the early childhood classroom itself, focusing on the furniture and the organization of the room. Then they discuss the health and safety considerations essential to the classroom itself and to class routines.

Students also examine methods of planning appropriate activities for children and discuss effective methods of promoting appropriate classroom behavior.

MOTIVATOR

Display several large photographs of young children in a variety of activities in a preschool setting, both indoors and outdoors. Ask students to describe the children, activities, and the setting. Why might the parents of these children send them to preschool? What do their parents expect them to learn? From these pictures, what are the children learning? What other learning opportunities will they probably have in preschool?

USING TERMS TO LEARN

Let students read and discuss the three vocabulary terms introduced in this section. Ask whether students are familiar with learning centers in elementary school classes. How would you expect learning centers in a preschool setting to differ from learning centers for older children?

GUIDED PRACTICE

Promoting Discussion

Encourage students who attended preschool to recall and discuss their own experiences. What do you remember most vividly from preschool? What did you especially enjoy? What did you dislike? What do you think you gained from attending preschool?

Critical Thinking

Let students share their ideas in response to these questions: Why do you think it is so important to make everything in an early childhood classroom child-sized? How do child-sized furniture and equipment affect the children's concept of themselves? Of their world?

Making Connections: Management

Have students investigate the cost of child-sized furniture. What would it cost to equip a classroom with 3 large tables, 18 chairs, and 3 sets of shelves? Where is this furniture available at the lowest price? Is that low-priced furniture sturdy and safe? Is it the best buy for an early childhood classroom, or would an investment in more expensive furniture make sense? Why?

Promoting Discussion

Ask students why it is important to mark each learning center off from other areas of an early childhood classroom. How do these demarcations help teachers? How do they help children? In what sense are the demarcations a learning tool?

Learning Centers

Learning centers are *areas of the classroom that are designed for certain types of play, equipment, or learning.* Learning centers vary according to the aims of the program and the space and equipment available. A well-equipped program might have the following centers.

- **Block center.** Small and large blocks, building logs, trucks and cars, people and animal figures, flat boards, shelves or bins for storage.
- **Dramatic play center.** Child-sized play kitchen, table and chairs, dishes, empty food cartons, dress-up clothes, dolls, play money, telephone, mirror.
- **Art center.** Paper, crayons, paints and brushes, markers, easels, clay, paste, yarn, felt, blunt-tip scissors, table and chairs, smocks.
- **Library center.** Books, pictures, puppets, low shelves, rug, large pillows.
- **Discovery center.** Plants, fish, other small animals (such as a hamster), magnets, magnifying glass, shells, thermometers, scale, soil, seeds, plastic tub of water, strainers.
- **Manipulative center.** Puzzles, large beads to string, string, various types of interlocking block or other building sets, board and card games, table and chairs.
- **Music center.** Record player and records or tape recorder and tapes, drums, shakers, tambourines, triangles, bells, piano, rug.

Each learning center should be marked off or distinguished in some way from other centers and from other areas of the room. Low, open shelves work well for defining centers. You might also define centers with pegboard dividers, low book cases, fabric panels suspended securely from the ceiling, different kinds or colors of floor covering, or even colored tape on the floor.

Other guidelines for setting up learning centers include the following:

- Separate noisy centers from quiet centers.
- Place the art center near a sink or other convenient source of water.

A classroom for young children must be designed for their activities and their needs. Discovery centers must have interesting objects to explore. Play equipment and storage areas should be safe, sturdy, and child-sized.

MORE ABOUT

Learning Centers

A classroom for children should be a treasure store of stimulation. Children need to learn to use all their senses: visual, auditory, kinesthetic, tactile, and olfactory. The classroom itself provides visual stimulation. Auditory stimulation is usually planned through music or library center activities. Climbing equipment and materials to manipulate give kinesthetic stimulation. Tactile stimulation can come from the block, dramatic play, art, and discovery centers. Food and special activities can provide olfactory stimulation.

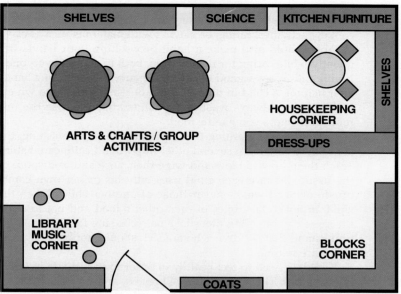

This diagram shows one possible arrangement for an early childhood classroom.

- Keep equipment and supplies neatly organized within easy reach for the children.
- Leave one large, open area for large-group activities.

Learning centers offer children learning choices. Children can select activities, explore different skills and areas of knowledge, and learn through hands-on experiences.

Health and Safety

Protecting the health and safety of the children is the first responsibility of teachers and other staff members in an early childhood classroom. While children are in your care, you must encourage health care routines that will prevent illness, make sure the environment is safe, and supervise their play.

Health Care Routines

Health care routines for young children prevent the spread of illness. They also help make sure the children are well nourished and rested.

The single most important routine for preventing illness is hand washing. The children should be taught to wash their own hands, using a brisk, scrubbing motion, with warm water and soap. They should also be taught to dry their hands completely

---

OBSERVING AND PARTICIPATING

Planning Play Areas

Many child care centers now provide computers, which can be located in one center or set up in different ones. Computer programs can provide children with learning experiences in language arts, math, and science. The difficulty level of the software and the development level of the children should be considered when using computers.

When planning typical outdoor learning centers, include space for wheel toys, sand and water activities, climbing, swinging, and quiet play. Crowding is less likely to occur if there are several interesting play areas. Activities that do not work well together, such as swings and wheeled toys, should be separated. Playground equipment should be sturdy and appropriate.

GUIDED PRACTICE (continued)

Cooperative Learning

Divide students into seven groups, and assign each group one type of learning center listed on page 556. Have group members work together to make complete plans for that center, including a floor plan and a list of specific supplies and equipment. Then ask each group to share and discuss its plans with the rest of the class.

Making Connections: Management

Ask interested students to price the supplies and equipment recommended for one of the learning centers planned in the previous activity (see Cooperative Learning above). Taking into account the cost, safety, durability, and appearance of the supplies and equipment, which do you consider the wisest purchases? Why? Let these students report their results to the rest of the class.

Making Connections: Design

Have each student design a floor plan for a children's classroom that includes at least five learning centers. Then let students share, discuss, and evaluate their floor plans.

Promoting Discussion

Guide students in discussing how the design of a classroom can affect children's safety. For example, what problems might result if the block center were near a major traffic lane? What other potential problems can you identify?

Then ask students to review the health and safety considerations outlined in Chapter 17. Have students use this information to suggest health and safety guidelines for planning and using learning centers in the early childhood classroom. If necessary, emphasize that supplies used in learning centers should be safe and appropriate for the age and development of the children.

GUIDED PRACTICE (continued)

Promoting Discussion

Guide students in discussing the hand-washing habits described here. How faithfully do you follow these habits? When you work with children, why is it important to set a good example? Is it possible to set a good example by following a specific procedure only when the children are paying attention? Why or why not? How can frequent hand-washing help prevent the spread of illness? Why is this form of prevention especially important in a group child care setting?

Making Connections: Art

Ask students to design and make posters reminding children of the importance of hand washing and/or showing children the proper way to wash their hands. Have students create posters that are clear, and colorful, and that include no words, so that the posters are appropriate for use as learning tools for young children. If possible, donate the completed posters to child care centers or other facilities where young children might use them.

Making Connections: Writing

Have students write short rhymes or jingles that could be used to teach health care routines to young children. Let students share their rhymes and jingles with classmates; encourage them to make suggestions for improving one another's work. Then ask students to revise their jingles and, if appropriate, teach them to a group of young children.

with a clean paper towel. All the children should wash their hands after using the toilet or blowing their nose, and before cooking activities, eating, or playing with materials such as clay.

You should also make a habit of washing your hands frequently while caring for the children, both to protect everyone's health and to set a good example. Be sure to wash your hands after helping a child in the rest room or using a tissue to wipe a child's nose. Always wash your hands after you use the rest room and before you handle food.

In addition to learning the importance of hand-washing, the children should learn several other important health care habits. Teach them how to blow and wipe their nose and to dispose of the tissue. Be sure each child uses only his or her own comb, brush, or head wear—never those of another child. Teach the children not to take bites of each other's food and not to share the same cup or eating utensils. Finally, be sure family members understand that children who are sick should not be in a group child care setting.

Children need to feel healthy in order to participate in learning activities. They should be well rested, and they should have had a good breakfast before coming to your early childhood classroom. In some cases, it may be necessary to discuss these needs with family members or others who can help the children. The children will need a nutritious snack about midmorning or midafternoon, if they are staying for a half-day program. You can also help the children feel good and remain healthy by pacing their activities so that they do not become too tired. During the course of each program day, the children need time for both active play and quiet play.

Be sure there is at least one caregiver monitoring each area in which children are playing.

HEALTHY FAMILIES/HEALTHY CHILDREN

Screening Tests

Screening tests, examinations to detect specific health problems, are often provided as part of a child care program. State health rules may require screening tests for specific age groups. Common screening tests that may be given in child care settings are hearing, vision, and physical growth tests.

Some child care programs use other screening tests, such as those to detect lead poisoning, tuberculosis (TB), developmental disorders, and dental problems. Written permission should be secured before screening tests are used at a child care center.

Safety

To keep young children safe, you must check their environment and make sure it is childproof. In addition, you need to supervise the children closely as they work and play.

Check the children's classroom and outdoor play areas for any possible safety hazards. Many of the safety guidelines discussed in Chapter 17 can be applied to child care centers.

Check the classroom thoroughly before each visit from the children. While they are there, the children must be supervised at all times. There should always be an adequate number of teens or adults present to monitor the children playing in each area of the room. If an emergency arises, there should be several teens or adults who can stay with the children in the classroom while someone goes for help. If the rest rooms are located outside the classroom, several teens or adults must accompany children to the rest room while the other children are supervised in the classroom.

Planning Appropriate Activities

Planning also plays an important role in providing appropriate learning experiences for the young children in your care. Much of this planning has already been done by the time you have set up the classroom and equipped the learning centers. Within the framework of this planned environment, the children will learn through play. In addition, you should provide a balanced schedule of activities for individuals and for small and large groups of children. These activities should focus on each important area of development.

Planning activities for each day will help make your experiences with children more successful. What would happen if you didn't plan ahead?

SAFETY TIP

It helps to look at things from a child's point of view. Get down on your knees and look around. What do you see that a child could get into? Be sure to check for these safety precautions:

- There are no sharp edges on furniture or equipment.
- Electrical outlets are covered.
- Electrical cords are all in good condition and are secured to the walls or floor.
- Poisonous substances, such as cleaning supplies, are securely locked away.
- Traffic paths around the room are free of clutter.
- Fire exits are clearly marked, and there is a fire exit plan.
- Dangerous items such as sharp scissors or staplers are locked away.

GUIDED PRACTICE (continued)

Making Connections: Research

Let interested students research local health and safety requirements for child care licensing. What are the specific requirements? How have these requirements changed during the past ten years? What other changes —if any—are expected? To what kinds of facilities do these requirements apply? Which child care facilities—if any—are exempt from these requirements? Have these students report their findings to the rest of the class.

Promoting Discussion

Help students discuss the importance of planning in their own lives. What special events must be planned in order to succeed? How does having a daily plan or schedule help you accomplish more at school? At work? How does following a daily plan give you more free time for relaxing and socializing?

Then guide students in discussing the importance of planning in a child care setting. Why is it necessary to plan children's play activities? How do teachers benefit from careful planning? How do young children benefit from their teachers' planning? How rigid—or flexible— do you think activity plans and schedules should be? Why?

SAFETY TIP

Have students read the safety tip on the page. Emphasize the importance of students being aware of potential dangers for children.

HEALTHY FAMILIES/HEALTHY CHILDREN

Legal Protection

Before you set up an early childhood classroom, it is important to be sure that you and your students are protected in case of litigation. Although there is no foolproof way to avoid a suit should an accident occur, adequate insurance and close attention to accident prevention are necessary defenses.

Depending on state laws, you may need a waiver from parents that allows you to obtain medical treatment for the children in case of an accident. You may also wish to have parents sign a form stating that they will pay any medical expenses arising from the classroom experience.

Promoting Discussion

Ask students to share their own ideas about play. What does the word *play* mean to you? What do you do—and what do you accomplish— when you play? How and why do adults play? How is the concept of play different for young children?

In what sense is playing considered work for young children? How can teachers, parents, and other caregivers help children play?

Critical Thinking

Let students share and discuss their responses to these questions: Which would help you learn more about baking bread— listening to someone explain how to bake bread or actually baking bread yourself? Why? What does this imply about the relationship between active involvement and learning? How would you apply this to planning children's learning activities? To planning children's play?

Promoting Discussion

As students consider play experiences in the child care setting, help them review what they know about parallel play and cooperative play. What is involved in each form of play? When do children typically begin parallel play? When are they usually ready for cooperative play? What use can parents make of this information in planning group experiences for their children? How do you think teachers should use this information in planning classroom activities?

Cooperative Learning

Have students work in groups to list and describe specific play experiences that focus on each of the areas of development listed in the text. Then let the members of each group share their lists with the rest of the class. Which play experiences are appropriate for more than one area of development?

Learning Through Play

For a young child, play means having hands-on experiences that involve the senses and opportunities to talk. It does not mean doing a worksheet or coloring page, and it does not mean listening to an adult lecture. As you plan activities for young children, remember that the more involved they are and the more realistic their experiences are, the more the children learn. For example, a story about a fire truck is not nearly as effective a learning tool as a trip to the fire station and a chance to climb on a real fire truck.

Play experiences for young children can be considered in several ways. One way is to observe how the children are playing in relation to each other. Children may play alone. For example, a child may curl up in a large box with a book and a pillow for some quiet time alone. Children may also play individually but alongside one another, as when several children sit together at a table, each working his or her own puzzle. Children may play in small groups, cooperating in acting out going to the store, for instance. Children may also play in one large group under the guidance of a teacher, as during a music or movement activity.

Another way to consider children's play is by the area of development that is being stimulated. For example, children need many experiences in language. They need opportunities to listen and to speak, to become familiar with written language, and to develop their vocabulary. Learning experiences that stimulate language development include story times, open-ended questions, field trips, games, activity records, and cooking activities, to name but a few of many possibilities.

Play activities can be described according to how children play in relation to each other. Here the children are playing in one large group. Another way to describe play is the area of development being stimulated—in this case, motor skills.

OBSERVING AND PARTICIPATING

Developing Participation Skills

There are many ways to design and implement curriculum for young children. Some centers use themes, or topics of special interest, to carry out the curriculum. A theme is used to link the various activities around a focal point or area of interest. It helps focus the energies and attention of the staff and children. Some themes include family, home, transportation, nature, seasons, animals, plants, and so forth. Have students brainstorm a list of additional themes and develop learning activities around these themes. These activities could be included in their portfolios.

ASK THE EXPERTS

Evaluating Child Care Programs

Q. *How can I know that I'm choosing the best child care program for my child?*

A. Child care is a very important and often a very difficult choice for parents to make. Let me suggest a unique and effective approach to making this decision. Once you have found a program that is convenient and affordable and that offers the hours and services you need, approach that program from your child's point of view.

I want to spend my time with a loving person. Does the caregiver here know how to communicate with me? Will the caregiver give me gentle but firm guidelines for my behavior? Does the caregiver have a high stress tolerance for my noisy activity level? Will he or she love and appreciate me—and all the other children here? If my caregiver's children are also here, will I get the same treatment? Has the caregiver had any educational preparation for dealing with me? Does he or she treat me the way my parents do, so I will have consistency in my day? Do I really like this person?

The facility where I stay is also important to me. Are there few enough children so that I can feel secure in getting plenty of attention? Is the food served nutritious, attractive, and tasty? Will I get regular meals and snacks, so I won't ever feel too hungry? Will I be safe here? Will I be encouraged to explore and

learn, to be creative, to use all my muscles, to pretend, and to laugh—or will I be left in a playpen and expected to watch television most of the time? Is this place clean? Is it attractive, with bright colors and lots of air and light? Will I get to go outside often and play on lots of different kinds of equipment? After I have played and am really tired, will there be a special place for me to rest—a spot with soft, clean sheets that only I use?

Of course, these questions are just a start. You know your own child best, and you are the person who can most fully adopt your child's perspectives and interests in selecting a child care program.

Pat Brodeen

Pat Brodeen
Teacher and Teen Parent
Coordinator at Theodore Roosevelt
High School in San Antonio, Texas

In addition to language, children need play experiences that focus on these areas of development:

- Thinking and problem solving.
- Movement or motor skills for both large and small muscles.
- Creativity, including music, dance, dramatic play, and art.
- Relationships with others in the social world.

GUIDED PRACTICE (continued)

ASK THE EXPERTS

Issues and Advice

1. Whose viewpoint does Ms. Brodeen suggest a parent take when making choices about a child care program? (*The child's.*)
2. What are important qualities to consider about caregivers? (*Possibilities are: communication skills, high stress tolerance, positive guidance techniques, fairness, training, commitment, consistency, personality, awareness of a child's needs.*)
3. What are important factors to look for in a facility? (*Possibilities are: presence of other children, quality of food, safety precautions, amount of stimulation, has a clean and healthy living conditions, an outside play area, and an area for rest and quiet.*)

Thinking Like an Expert

Put students into small groups and tell them that they are about to role-play a child of age three, four, or five years who is in a child care facility for five days each week. Have the students review the recommendations made by Ms. Brodeen in "Evaluating Child Care Programs," then brainstorm specific descriptions of the center where they, as a young child, attend. Then have each student write a journal entry from the viewpoint of a child reflecting his or her thoughts, feelings, and activities during that one day. When the students are finished, have them read their entries to the group.

OBSERVING AND PARTICIPATING

Developing Participation Skills

Programs for young children may be based on instructional or discovery models. With the instructional model, caregivers start the action and children respond. The caregiver decides what materials and experiences to provide. Children follow the directions given. With the discovery model, children initiate activities and caregivers respond. Children explore until they discover how to do a task. They receive minimal help from caregivers. Each child chooses activities from the opportunities available. The caregivers supply materials and help when necessary or when children ask for help. Many child care programs try to reach a balance between instructional and discovery methods.

GUIDED PRACTICE (continued)

Promoting Discussion

Let students discuss the kinds of activities that need to be balanced in a daily schedule. Why is it usually appropriate to schedule teacher-directed activities for shorter periods of time and child-selected activities for longer periods of time? How might these differences change as a group of children matures?

Critical Thinking

Encourage students to share and discuss their responses to these questions: How do teachers and other classroom staff members benefit from following a daily schedule? How do young children benefit from following a daily schedule? What do children learn from following a schedule? How do you think deviations from a regular schedule should be handled? Why?

Practicing Decision Making

Present the following daily schedule for students' consideration:

12:45-1:00   Arrival
1:00-1:15   Snack
1:15-1:45   Outdoor play
1:45-2:30   Learning centers
2:30-3:15   Small-group activities
3:15-3:30   Large-group story
3:30-3:45   Large-group music
             activity
3:45-4:00   Departure

Encourage students to discuss and evaluate the schedule. What problems is it likely to create? How would you alter the schedule? Why?

Making Connections: Health

Let students work with partners to plan a week of nutritious snacks for a group of four-year-olds. Would the snack plan for a morning program differ from the snack plan for an afternoon program? Would children be involved in preparing and/or serving the snack? If so, how? Ask each pair of students to share their plans with the rest of the class.

When planning experiences for young children, keep these types of play in mind. Help the children participate in individual, small-group, and large-group activities each day, and offer experiences that focus on each area of development. Children who are actively involved in the experiences you provide will learn more effectively—and be better behaved—than children who only sit by, watching and waiting.

The Daily Schedule

Planning the daily sequence of events for an early childhood classroom is just as important as planning and preparing the environment. The daily schedule is the master plan for how the children will use their time. Schedules vary greatly from program to program. Study the following schedule for a three-hour session:

8:30-8:45	Arrival and free play
8:45-9:00	Circle time
9:00-9:30	Small-group activities
9:30-9:45	Large-group music activity
9:45-10:00	Toileting and hand-washing
10:00-10:15	Snack
10:15-10:45	Outdoor play
10:45-11:15	Learning centers
11:15-11:30	Large group story time

Good schedules for young children in group settings feature a balance of active and quiet activities, small- and large-group activities, and teacher-directed and child-selected activities. Notice in the sample schedule how these elements are alternated. The small-group activities are learning activities planned and directed by the teaching staff. After these activities, the children move to the large, open area of the classroom for group music experiences. After music, snack time provides the children with an opportunity for relaxed conversations with their friends. Then the children are ready for brisk physical activity, such as outdoor play. If outdoor play is not possible, it is easy to plan an indoor group session for movement or creative dance. After this period of physical activity, the children are ready for the quieter involvement of the learning centers. Here, they can select for themselves the learning centers they want to play in. Finally, the session ends with a story or language activity. This kind of closing allows the children to put away their learning center materials, have quiet time as a group, and be ready to leave on time.

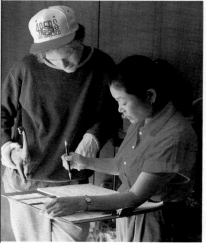

A well-planned schedule ensures that children can participate in a balanced variety of activities.

COOPERATIVE LEARNING

Evaluating Child Care Programs

Have students work in groups of three or four to observe at a preschool or child care center that has an organized educational program. Ask them to identify and analyze the activities in the learning centers. Which ones were designed for intellectual development? Social development? Physical development? Emotional development? Which activities promoted creativity? Were most activities individual, small-group, or large-group? What evidence did students see that planning preceded the activity? Have each group of students prepare a written report and share their observations with the class.

A good daily schedule allows time for **transitions**, *periods during which children move from one scheduled activity to the next.* During a transition, the children need to conclude one activity, put their materials away, and get ready for the next activity. To help the children feel more comfortable during transitions, always let them know a few minutes ahead of time that they will soon have to make a change. Whenever possible, use a song or a game to move the children from one place to another or from one activity to the next. For example, you might sing a special cleanup song as you and the children put away materials after learning centers time. When it is time for the children to go outside, you might make a game of getting ready; name one color at a time, and let all the children wearing that color move to the door.

Whether you are preparing a two-, three-, or four-hour session for the children, plan a schedule carefully to include each of these important features. A well-planned daily schedule will do much to ensure that the children feel involved and interested throughout the session.

Writing Learning Activity Plans

A daily schedule provides an outline for the children's activities each day. With that outline in mind, the coordinator plans the specific activities he or she wants to use during each period of the day.

There are two types of planning forms that can be used to write plans for the children's activities. The first form is based on the daily schedule and on the days or sessions that the children will attend. This planning chart or overview lists the names of the activities that will be provided in each learning center and during each period on the daily schedule. For example, if you are preparing a one-week overview based on the daily schedule shown on page 562, you will record your plans for each day. For each of the music activities, you would note the songs you plan to help the children sing; for each of the story times, you would note the books you want to share.

The second form you might use allows you to record more detailed information about each activity you have planned. On this form, you would include specific information under each of the following headings:

* Title of the activity.
* Objective, or purpose, of the activity.
* Type of activity (for a learning center, small group, or large group).
* Materials needed.
* Procedures to be followed.
* Evaluation—how did the activity go?

A field trip activity to a science exhibit or a museum expands learning and promotes socialization.

MORE ABOUT

Planning Activities

When planners select activities for children, it is important for them to know the characteristics and interests of children at the ages of those in the center. Activities that excite two-year-olds may bore children of four. In addition, planners need to know the attention span of children at particular ages. A half-hour activity for children with an attention span of 15 minutes will not be a success.

Finally, the toys, books, and songs that are selected need to be appropriate for the age group. Age-appropriate materials hold children's interest and promote positive behavior.

Schedule planners should consider these factors: children's abilities, the length of time they are in group care, the types and needs of children, the weather, the arrangement and use of space, and the number of children.

GUIDED PRACTICE (continued)

Making Connections: Music

Have each student identify a music activity appropriate for using with a full class of four-year-olds. Activities might include songs, games, and dances. Let students share their activities with the rest of the class.

Encourage students to share their ideas in response to these questions: Why do you think it is important to include time for transitions in a daily schedule? What would be likely to happen if transition time were not part of a schedule? How would children be affected?

You may want to point out that, in spite of careful planning, transitions can be difficult for many young children. Ask students why this is so. Why is it important to warn young children of approaching transitions? How can teachers help individual children prepare for transition times?

Practicing Decision Making

Present the following situation to the class: Four three-year-olds have been playing in the discovery center. Five minutes ago, the entire class was told that it was time to clean up and get ready for story time. Of the four children, only Mieko has put her materials away and prepared to leave the discovery center. The other three children are still fully involved in their play.

Let students share their ideas about this situation. What would you, as a teacher, do? Why?

Promoting Discussion

Ask students why they think it is important to have both a weekly overview and a daily schedule. In what ways are the two kinds of plans similar? How are they different?

Making Connections: Writing

Have students write a daily schedule for a two-hour program of after-school activities for first-graders. In what ways should this schedule differ from a schedule for preschoolers? Why? Ask students to write two or three paragraphs explaining and justifying their plans.

GUIDED PRACTICE (continued)

Promoting Discussion

Ask students how careful planning encourages appropriate behavior. Then ask how teachers can use activity choices to help promote appropriate behavior and to redirect children whose behavior is inappropriate.

Cooperative Learning

Let students work in groups to discuss methods of presenting rules to young children. Have the members of each group select one of the listed rules and plan an activity that would help teach that rule to a group of preschoolers.

Making Connections: Writing

Have students write a brief opening statement to be made to a preschool class on the first day of school, explaining the kind of behavior expected in the classroom. Remind students to keep in mind that the audience for this statement is a group of young children, who cannot sit still and pay attention for long.

Promoting Discussion

Ask students to suggest specific ways in which teachers can provide positive reinforcement. Do you think material rewards are appropriate forms of positive reinforcement? Why or why not? What problems are likely to arise if candy or other sweets are used as rewards in a classroom?

Did You Know?

In 1827, New York City established the first nursery school "to relieve parents of the laboring classes from the care of their children while engaged in the vocations by which they live, and provide for the children a protection from the weather, from idleness and the contamination of evil example besides affording them the means of early and efficient education."

The type of forms you use is not as important as the fact that you do have written plans. Writing out your plans ahead of time helps you think through the appropriateness of each activity. It also provides a list of everything you need so that the materials can be set up before the children arrive. Also, if you feel nervous or rushed, your written procedures are handy for quick reference when you are presenting the activity.

Following a consistent daily schedule and having written plans for the children's activities will help each session run smoothly—which, in turn, encourages appropriate behavior from the children.

Promoting Positive Behavior

If you have carefully prepared an environment designed for young children, constructed a well-balanced daily schedule, and planned appropriate activities, you have done most of what it takes to promote positive behavior among the children. Most

Children are usually eager to earn the praise of caregivers. By establishing a way to recognize their positive efforts, you can help them behave well and feel good about themselves.

OBSERVING AND PARTICIPATING

Learning Through Participation

When you are working with children and guiding their behavior, imitation can be an effective way to lead the children to the behavior you desire. For example, you begin to pick up toys while instructing the children to do the same. You are demonstrating the desired behavior through your actions.

The imitation approach depends on the children's following the example of the caregiver and other children. If the caregiver encourages children in a firm but kind manner, generally, the children will do the same. Sometimes extra motivation is needed. One way is to mark shelves with color-coded shapes that match the equipment or play material. This helps add interest to the activity.

inappropriate behavior is the result of poor planning on the part of the teacher. However, even the most organized teacher has times when direct guidance of children's behavior becomes necessary. To promote positive behavior, you need to establish classroom rules, use positive reinforcement effectively, be a positive role model, and develop some strategies for dealing with unacceptable behavior.

Establishing Classroom Rules

Young children need classroom rules, but too many rules can overwhelm them. The classroom rules should be stated in positive terms. That is, each rule should instruct the children in what they should do—not what they shouldn't do.

Each classroom rule should also have a clear purpose. The most effective rules are those that deal with protecting the safety of children and property.

The following list shows one possible set of rules for an early childhood classroom:

1. Use your hands gently.
2. Walk inside the classroom.
3. Put materials away when you are finished.
4. Use an inside voice in the classroom.
5. Be a friend to other people.
6. Keep your feet away from others.

Of course, you need to provide activities that help the children understand the meaning of each rule. For example, you might have a collection of pictures showing gentle, friendly touching and aggressive, hurtful touching. Using an open-ended questioning technique, you could explore the pictures with the children and help them understand what each type of touching feels like. Make it very clear that hurtful touching is not allowed in your classroom.

Using Positive Reinforcement

Children enjoy being recognized and rewarded with attention, and they tend to repeat behaviors that are positively reinforced. To make this technique effective, however, you must be sincere in your positive response to a child's behavior. Automatic or inattentive comments and praise do not provide true positive reinforcement.

Being a Good Role Model

Your own behavior in the classroom has a very powerful influence on the children. For this reason, you must be especially careful to be a good role model. Children are more likely to do what you do—not what you say. For example, if you want the

BUILDING SELF-ESTEEM

Using Positive Reinforcement

Probably the most useful direct guidance technique is positive reinforcement. This technique involves giving children recognition or encouragement for appropriate behavior—in other words, a reward. The reward may be very simple. It might be a smile or a hug or a comment such as, "I like the way you wipe your paintbrush on the side of the jar before you paint." Occasionally, when children are just learning a new behavior, the reward might be a small treat, such as a sticker or ribbon.

GUIDED PRACTICE (continued)

Critical Thinking

Ask students to suggest types of behavior that a poor role model might use. Is it acceptable in settings other than a child care center, or would a person benefit by avoiding it completely? Why should caregivers be good role models? Is it necessary for teachers and other care providers to be good role models at all times or only in the classroom?

Practicing Decision Making

Let students suggest how they would respond to two of these instances of unacceptable behavior in a preschool classroom:

- After repeated unsuccessful attempts to cut a piece of paper, Cory throws the scissors across the room.
- In spite of two reminders, Zoe continues to color on the table, not on her sheet of paper.

Promoting Discussion

Guide students in considering specific provisions of an effective time-out. Stress that a time-out should in no way be frightening to a child. Ask students to suggest several acceptable spots for time-outs in a classroom. What areas would not be appropriate as time-out locations? Why? Also, be sure students understand that a time-out should have a clear limit. A good rule of thumb is that the maximum time-out period for a child is one minute for each year of his or her age.

BUILDING SELF-ESTEEM

After reading the suggestions in "Using Positive Reinforcement," remind students that caregivers should remember that some children, out of fear or personal preference, do not like to be hugged. For these, reinforcement comes in alternative forms.

SEE HOW THEY GROW

Guiding Behavior

When children are restless and the potential for misbehavior seems high, caregivers may wish to try the following suggestions to short-circuit misbehavior:

- Play a game of "Say two nice things about each person."
- Change the pace by suggesting a new activity.

- Use a timer to help teach sharing if a squabble over a toy seems imminent.
- Involve children in a "meeting," and ask for ideas of how to solve the current problem.
- Check yourself to be sure that you are not causing the behavior with inattention, irritability, or other inappropriate behavior.

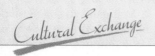

After reading "Promoting Multicultural Awareness," remind students about the child's developing levels of awareness. The questions that a child asks about differences among people are tools by which they learn. Answering honestly and with sensitivity promotes a learning environment that is inclusive, not exclusive.

INDEPENDENT PRACTICE

Journal Writing

Have students write journal entries describing their most satisfying experiences in an early childhood classroom. They might also examine which aspect of working in an early childhood classroom they anticipate will be most satisfying for them.

Student Workbook

Distribute and have students complete "Learning Through Participation" in the Student Workbook.

Extension

Let students work independently or in small groups to complete one or more of these extension activities:

• Plan a learning center for an early childhood classroom, and create a display that describes your learning center. Your display should include a poster with diagrams and explanations, as well as a collection of supplies to be used in the center. Set up your display so that your classmates can examine and discuss it.

• Choose a theme (such as fruits and vegetables) and complete a weekly plan for at least four learning centers based on that theme. Be sure the activities you plan are hands-on, varied, and geared to specific areas of development.

Cultural Exchange

PROMOTING MULTICULTURAL AWARENESS

As infants enter the world, they are alert and aware of their surroundings. As they grow, their perceptions also grow, and even as infants they begin to notice differences in people. For example, four-year-old Sara proudly announces "My new friend has chocolate skin." This awareness is common to the learning process and develops into another natural step—classification. Again, this developmental process is neutral until the child is infected with a prejudiced attitude. Then perceived differences can become an excuse for unfairness and a justification for angry behavior.

Parents, teachers, and caregivers can nurture an appreciation of the inherent values of all cultures. Think about your own attitudes. How do you communicate unbiased feelings toward others?

children to use inside voices, then you, too, must always use a quiet voice indoors. If you want the children to treat each other with kindness, you, too, must deal kindly with everyone. Through your example, the children will learn how to play and use materials properly and how to treat each other with respect.

Dealing with Misbehavior

In spite of careful planning and a clear encouragement of positive behavior, you should be prepared for the fact that children will occasionally behave in unacceptable ways in the classroom. You should know in advance how you will respond. The children should also understand what will happen if they behave in unacceptable ways.

In most cases, a simple statement of what you want the child to do is effective. If a child is using too loud a voice, for example, you might simply say, "Marlie, please use your inside voice. I can't hear well when you are shouting." In other situations, you may offer the child a choice of more acceptable activities. For instance, if a child is not playing well in the block center, you might say, "Heather, you may choose to go to the dramatic play center or the art center now. I can't let you stay in the block center because you are still trying to take Ariel's blocks away from her." Notice that each suggested statement includes an explanation of why the child's behavior was unacceptable.

Some schools provide large indoor areas that allow children to run to use up excess energy that could lead to misbehavior if it were not channeled into play.

MORE ABOUT

Dealing with Inappropriate Behavior

Teach students to use a problem-solving approach to dealing with problem behavior: (1) Identify the problem. What exactly is the child doing? How often does this behavior happen? Why is the behavior a problem? Am I expecting too much? What should the child do instead? (2)

Consider possible solutions and make a plan. What can I do to encourage better behavior? (3) Carry out the plan. (4) Evaluate the results. Did the plan work? Is there less undesirable behavior? Did appropriate behavior replace the undesirable behavior?

For some types of unacceptable behavior, a stronger response is necessary. Behavior that hurts other people or property must not be permitted at any time. Children who break this type of rule should receive an immediate and consistent response. One effective approach is to give the child a **time-out**, *a short period of time spent sitting away from the main activities of the classroom.* See page 77.

Here's how one teacher, Ms. Black, used the time-out technique. After one child hit another child with a block, Ms. Black said, "Don, I can't let you hit Mark. It hurts. Go and sit in time-out for two minutes." After two minutes, Ms. Black went to Don and asked him to choose one of two centers to go to; she did not include the block center in his choices. Using this technique, Ms. Black was able to deal with Don's unacceptable behavior without becoming angry and without raising her voice.

With these basic strategies and skills, you will be able to provide a warm, supportive learning environment for young children. It takes a lot of advance planning, patience, and practice, but you will find that your efforts are worthwhile.

SECTION 3 REVIEW

CHECK YOUR UNDERSTANDING

1. What are learning centers?
2. List seven kinds of learning centers that might be part of a well-equipped preschool program.
3. List three methods that can be used to define a learning center, separating it from other parts of the classroom.
4. How and when should young children wash their hands?
5. List six safety precautions that should be checked for in an early childhood classroom.
6. What are transitions? How can teachers help young children feel comfortable during transition times?
7. What is a time-out? When should it be used?

DISCUSS AND DISCOVER

1. Why do you think it is especially important for early childhood teachers to act as good role models? During what ages are children most attentive to their teachers as role models?
2. Working with several other students, brainstorm a list of possible rules for an early childhood classroom. Then consider and discuss all the rules on your group's list. Select the four most important rules, combining several from your original list. Share your group's rules with the rest of the class.

Observing & Participating

Visit a child care center. Describe the number of children in the center and their ages. How many adults are available to care for the children? How attentive do the adults seem to be? Do you feel the children are receiving personal, loving care? Why or why not? Explain whether the center is appropriate for children of all ages or specific ages only.

SECTION 3 REVIEW

1. Areas designed for certain types of play, equipment, or learning.
2. Block, dramatic play, art, library, discovery, manipulation, and music centers.
3. Any three: low open shelves, pegboard or fabric dividers, low bookcases, tape on floor.
4. Using a brisk, scrubbing motion, using warm water and soap. After using toilet or blowing their nose; before cooking activities or eating.
5. Sample: No sharp edges; covered electrical outlets.
6. Moving from one activity to another. Tell about change in advance, and use a song or game.
7. A short period of time spent sitting away from main activities. When behavior hurts other people or property.

ASSESS

CHECKING COMPREHENSION

Assign students to write their responses to the Check Your Understanding questions in the Section 3 Review. Answers to the questions are given below.

EVALUATE

Have students complete the Chapter 19, Section 3 TCR quiz.

Reteaching

1. Have students complete Reteaching 48 in the TCR.
2. Present a list of activities that might be included in a preschool program. Discuss them, identifying each as active or quiet, small-group or large-group, teacher-directed or child-selected. Have groups work together to arrange the activities in a sequence that provides a balance of activities.

Enrichment

1. Have students complete Enrichment 48 in the TCR.
2. Have students collect daily schedules from at least three local preschools or child care centers. How are they similar? Different? On the basis of these schedules, how would you evaluate the programs? Ask students to write short essays presenting their findings and conclusions.

Extension

Arrange a class visit to a well-equipped early childhood classroom. Have students draw a floor plan of the classroom and label the furnishings in the room; also have them list the supplies and equipment in each learning center. Later, ask students to write an evaluation of the classroom as a learning environment.

CLOSE

Ask each student to complete the following statement, either orally or in writing:

Teachers and assistants in an early childhood classroom can help young children …

CHECKING COMPREHENSION

Use the Summary and the Reviewing the Facts questions to help students go over the most important ideas presented in Chapter 19; encourage students to ask questions and add details, as appropriate.

CHAPTER **19** REVIEW

1. To give children a chance to get adjusted while parents are still at home and to gather additional information from parents.

2. Cuddle and comfort child until he or she gets back to sleep.

3. Parents, teachers, and others who take care of children.

4. Objective observation. Subjective observation is based on false assumption, may be misinterpreted, and has limited use.

5. Frequency count is a tally of how often a certain behavior occurs; developmental checklist is a list that identifies a series of specific skills or behaviors that a child of a given age range should be mastering.

6. Only with the teacher.

7. Any four: washing hands; blowing nose; using only own comb, brush, and head wear; not taking bites of others' food; staying away from group setting when sick.

8. Before each visit from children.

9. Language; thinking and problem solving; movement and motor skills; creativity; relationships with others.

10. Active and quiet activities; small- and large-group activities; teacher-directed and child-selected activities.

11. Gives chance to evaluate appropriateness of each activity; provides list of all materials needed; can be used as handy reference, especially in case of nervousness.

12. In positive terms.

CHAPTER **19** REVIEW

SUMMARY

- A child care provider must be a responsible person who can relate to children of different ages.

- Observing children can help teachers, parents, and other caregivers understand child growth and development, learn about individual children, gain feedback about their teaching or parenting methods, and identify children with special needs.

- Observations, which should be objective, can be recorded using several different recording methods.

- After they have been recorded, observations should be analyzed, interpreted, and used.

- An early childhood classroom should be organized with several different learning centers.

- Encouraging learning through play, following a consistent daily schedule, and writing learning activity plans all help create a comfortable, stimulating classroom environment.

- Early childhood teachers can promote positive behavior by establishing classroom rules, using positive reinforcement, and being good role models.

REVIEWING THE FACTS

1. Why should a child care provider arrange to arrive about 20 minutes early the first time he or she provides care for a family?

2. How should a care provider respond to a toddler who awakens, crying, in the night?

3. Who can benefit from learning how to observe young children?

4. Which is more useful, a subjective observation or an objective observation? Why?

5. What is the difference between a frequency count and a developmental checklist?

6. With whom should you discuss any questions or concerns about a child you observe?

7. List four health care habits that should become routine for children in an early childhood classroom.

8. How often should an early childhood classroom be checked for safety?

9. List the five areas of development on which children's play experiences should focus.

10. What kinds of activities should be balanced in a daily schedule?

11. List three advantages to writing out plans for specific activities in an early childhood classroom.

12. How should classroom rules be stated?

EXPLORING FURTHER

1. Make a "care provider bag" of free or found materials that you could take along on child care jobs and use to help keep the children entertained. Share and discuss your materials with other students. (Section 1)

2. Write your own checklist of behavior that is appropriate for those who are observing young children. Share and discuss your checklist with classmates, and then revise your list as necessary. Finally, observe another student who is observing young children; use your checklist to record your observations of the observer. (Section 2)

3. Make up your own song or game to use during a specific kind of transition in an early childhood classroom. Teach your song or game to a group of other students, and ask them to help you evaluate and improve your work. Make any appropriate improvements to your song or game; then share it with a group of young children in a child care setting. (Section 3)

THINKING CRITICALLY

1. **Analyze.** What factors do you think account for the different interpretations people might make from the same observation records? Is there usually one "right" interpretation of an observation? Why or why not?

2. **Synthesize.** What criteria do you think parents should use in selecting a child care setting for their children? How do you think the information in this chapter might help parents in choosing a child care center? What other factors should parents take into consideration? Why?

CLASSROOM MANAGEMENT

Resources Beyond the Classroom

Child Care Alternatives is a live-action video program that presents an overview of the different types of child care available today: informal arrangements, licensed in-home providers, government-supported child care, and child care services on the work site. With more parents returning to work more quickly after the birth of their children, it is important that possible parents-to-be know all the options that will be available to them. For more information contact:

Glencoe/McGraw-Hill
15319 Chatsworth Street
Mission Hills, CA 91345

3. **Compare and contrast.** Compare the use of time-outs with other methods of dealing with unacceptable behavior. What problems does a time-out solve for the child? For the teacher? What problems, if any, do you think might be associated with using time-outs? How could such problems be avoided?

CROSS-CURRICULUM CONNECTIONS

1. **Writing.** Plan and write your own *Care Provider's Handbook*. Use an appealing format to present guidelines for successfully providing care for children in a particular age range: infants, toddlers and preschoolers, or school-aged children.

2. **Science.** Read about the role of observation in scientific research: How is this kind of observation similar to observations of young children? How are the two kinds of observations different? Share your findings and ideas with your classmates.

SCHOOL TO WORK

Employment Trends In the workplace, obsolete jobs are constantly phased out while new jobs are created. Much of the shift in job descriptions is in reaction to new designs in technology and the ever-changing demands of consumers.

Consequently, you are wise to consider the trends in the job market as you prepare for your career. Talk to a counselor about the types of jobs that are on the rise. Go to a job fair to find out what skills are in demand. Then check your classes and personal involvements to see how they prepare you for future employment.

PERFORMANCE ASSESSMENT

Caring for Children

Task
Create a cartoon-like booklet to be used by preschoolers that will teach them about the importance of good health habits.

Purpose
You will reinforce health habits that are especially critical to children who attend a group child care facility.

Procedure
1. Review pages 557-558 for health issues presented in the chapter. List other possible issues.

2. Plan a method to present each topic—cartoon strips, matching pictures, or coloring, for example. Remember that the words you use and any activities you include must be developmentally appropriate. Use playful visuals that will appeal to children.
3. Create enough activities to fill at least four sides of paper.
4. Make a final copy of the pages, then have them duplicated in separate pages or fastened together as a double-sided booklet.
5. Present your booklet to a group of preschool children and help them complete the activities.

Evaluation
The content of your booklet will be evaluated on the topics included, the appropriateness of the presentation, and visual appeal.

Portfolio Idea Include drafts of your booklet as well as a copy of the final product. If possible, include samples of children's completed activities and your evaluation of how well you anticipated appropriate activities for their age and stage of development.

PERFORMANCE ASSESSMENT

Cartoon Booklet
To help students get started, have them brainstorm ideas in small groups or as a class. For each idea, ask them to suggest ways to present it in a booklet designed for children. Remind them to consider physical and intellectual abilities of the preschool child. Word choice is an important consideration as the audience for the booklet will not have the same vocabulary as an older child or young adult. Any shapes that children will be expected to color or fill in should be large and simple. Also encourage students to offer a creative variety of activities and designs in the booklet to appeal to children.

If you wish, students can work in pairs or small groups to create a booklet. However, each will need a separate booklet for their portfolios.

EVALUATE
Use the reproducible Chapter 19 Test in the TCR, or construct your own test using the Test-maker Software.

EXTENSION
Have students work with partners or in small groups to videotape children at play in a preschool or child care center. (If videotape equipment is not available, ask students to prepare a series of still photographs or drawings showing the children at play.) Ask students to show their videotapes and use them as a basis for discussion, noting opportunities for observation, organization of the classroom or play area, indications of schedule planning, and approaches to promoting positive behavior.

CLOSE

Lead students in a brief discussion of their preferences in providing child care and in observing and participating with children. Which age group do you enjoy most? Why?

TECHNOLOGY OPTION

Computers Students working on the Performance Assessment activity may want to investigate the availability of computer programs with both text and graphic capabilities to generate the pages of their books. Some programs have clip art that can be manipulated on the page, while other programs have drawing programs that allow more creativity in the design. If this technology is not directly available to students, you might seek out parents or community businesses that would donate their time and resources to help students with the task.

INTRODUCE

CHAPTER 20 RESOURCES

Teacher's Classroom Resources

- Cooperative Learning
- Extension 39, 40
- Observing and Participating 20
- Chapter 20 Test
- Testmaker Software
- Color Transparency 44

Student Workbook

- Chapter 20 Study Guide

CHAPTER OVERVIEW

Chapter 20 introduces the students to the many levels of child care careers as well as methods of choosing which career might best suit them.

In Section 1, students are acquainted with interest inventories and aptitude tests designed to suggest career fields. They will also see the importance of education and experience in making those choices.

Section 2 describes the variety of specific jobs in the child care field. This section gives the students an overview of the broad range of child care careers along with the requirements and potential growth and income for each.

CHAPTER OBJECTIVES

After completing Chapter 20, students will be able to:

- Evaluate personal interests and aptitudes in light of future career decisions.
- Explain the importance of education and experience to finding and progressing in a job.
- Describe a number of specific jobs in the child care field.

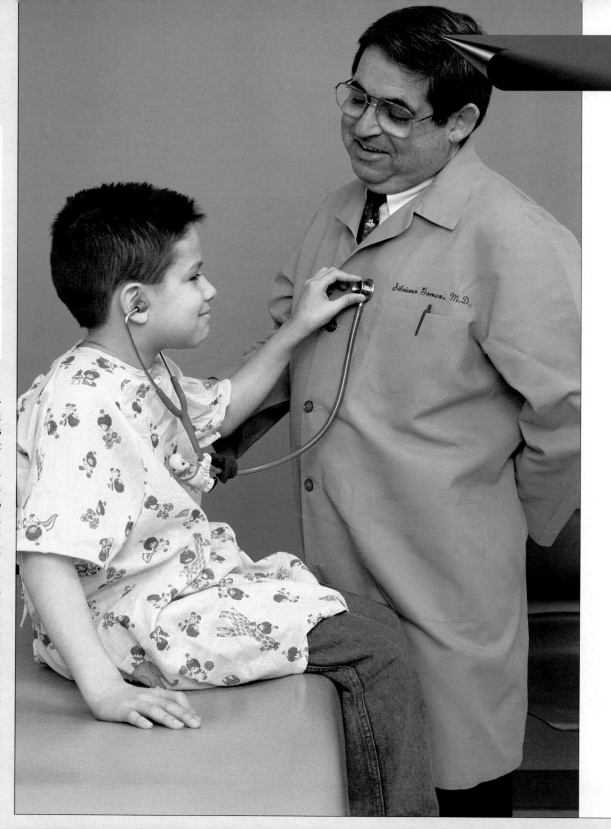

CLASSROOM MANAGEMENT

Resources Beyond the Classroom

Working with children can be an enjoyable and rewarding vocation. To be able to participate in a meaningful way to a young person's developmental years is a significant and lasting contribution, and there are many avenues for an interested teenager to consider. Before deciding on which areas might best suit the student's interests and goals, the stu-

dent should investigate this changing field. For more information on careers in educating children and on issues affecting preschool workers, write to:

National Association for the Education of Young Children
1834 Connecticut Avenue, NW
Wheaton, MD 20009

Careers Relating to Children

SECTION 1   Which Career for You?

SECTION 2   Careers Related to Child Care

INTRODUCING THE CHAPTER

- On slips of paper, have students write a word or phrase that first comes to mind when they hear the words *job* and *career*. Collect the papers and mix them together. Then have each student draw one paper and read it to the others. In general, were the responses more positive or negative? Overall, what conclusions can students draw about their attitudes toward work and careers?

Tell students that in Chapter 20 they will learn more about careers related to the study of child development.

- Write the word *interests* on the board. Have students each identify an interest. Ask: Could any of these interests be used in choosing a career? Why or why not?

- Use the photo on the opposite page and the three features on this page—Think About, Ask Yourself, and Now Try This—to begin a discussion about careers related to children.

THINK ABOUT

Think about the range of interests and talents you have. Have you considered how these interests and talents might influence your choice of career? Has your personal development as a young adult shaped an interest in working in the field of child development? If so, how? If not, how does it make you aware of the need for trained professionals in the child care field?

ASK YOURSELF

Study the photo on the opposite page. What is the doctor's role in the growth and development of this patient? How does the doctor ease any anxieties the boy may have about coming to the doctor's office? What do you imagine the doctor and child are saying to each other? How can the doctor influence other caregivers, such as parents, educators, and social workers?

NOW TRY THIS

Write a list of your interests, abilities, and activities. Next to each item on the list, identify a career related to child care that would benefit from the skills and interests you have. Then write an employment ad for a position in one of the career fields on your list. Include personal qualifications, experience, and skills important to the position.

Childhood Reflections

"Don't limit a child to your own learning, for he was born in another time."

Rabbinic saying

HEALTHY FAMILIES/HEALTHY CHILDREN

Building Healthy Attitudes

Throughout the course of this book, attention has been paid to the idea that a caregiver's attitude is important to the effectiveness of his or her parenting skills. Also, much has been said about a caregiver's serving as a positive role model to a child. As students begin this chapter, remind them that these same human relations skills are vital to career success. A person who really dislikes his or her job but does nothing to reshape the situation not only undermines morale, but also carries over resentment and anger into other areas of life. What a child sees in such a situation is hardly the foundation for a healthy attitude toward life.

FOCUS

SECTION 1 RESOURCES

Teacher's Classroom Resources
- Enrichment 49
- Reteaching 49
- Section 1 Quiz

Student Workbook
- Occupational Interests

SECTION OVERVIEW

Section 1 introduces the students to aptitude tests and interest inventories as tools to help them make an informed career choice. They will see that educational requirements, breadth of experience, and pay range vary significantly when considering an entry-level, paraprofessional, or professional child care career.

MOTIVATOR

Write the word *volunteer* on the board. Ask students how being a volunteer can help them in choosing a job or career. What other ways can they suggest that would give them the experience in choosing a job or career? Have students share experiences they have had working in child related fields.

USING TERMS TO LEARN

Pronounce the words listed under "Terms to Learn." Ask students whether they are familiar with any of these. Explain that these terms will be defined in the chapter.

Point out that a *professional* is a person with specialized knowledge and at least a college degree. The prefix "para" often indicates a helping role. A *paraprofessional* is a trained aide who assists in a certain field. A degree from a two-year college is usually required. Ask students to define "paramedic" and "paralegal."

Which Career for You?

TERMS TO LEARN

aptitude test
entry-level job
interest inventory
paraprofessional
professional
reference

OBJECTIVES

- Evaluate your personal interests and aptitudes in light of future career decisions.
- Explain the importance of education and experience in finding and progressing in a job.

Various people and experiences have influenced you toward particular careers since early childhood. At five, you may have visited a fire station and decided to become a fire fighter. In grade school, liking a certain teacher may have convinced you that you wanted to teach. Parents may also influence you by encouraging some of your interests and discouraging others.

Aptitude Tests

Unfortunately, you cannot try out every job you think might interest you. However, psychologists have developed tests that give insight into people's strengths and weaknesses. These tests, combined with some thoughtful self-appraisal, can help point you in the right direction. Similar tests are also given by employers. These tests help employers know whether prospective employees are suited to the job they are applying for.

An **aptitude test** is *a test that measures a person's abilities and probable success in various skill areas.* A person's scores on an aptitude test can help predict how successful he or she might be in jobs of a particular type. Aptitude tests are often given to students in high school and college to help them plan their careers. Nonstudents can often arrange to take the tests at local colleges or counseling agencies. The following skills are usually checked by aptitude tests:

- **Verbal reasoning.** This is the ability to understand ideas expressed in words and to use words in thinking through your own ideas. Teachers, writers, social workers, and salespeople are among those who should have good scores in verbal reasoning.

MORE ABOUT

Aptitudes

In his book *What Color Is Your Parachute?*, Richard Nelson Bolles says that ultimately, people's skills can be classified in one of these three areas:

- Skills with people, which can include people in general or specific kinds of people, such as those with particular problems.
- Skills with information, also called data, which can be ideas, facts, figures, statistics, etc.

- Skills with things, which can be such physical objects as instruments, tools, machinery, equipment, vehicles, materials, and desktop items.

Suggest that students read the book and analyze their strengths and areas of aptitudes.

- **Abstract reasoning.** Picture in your mind a number of objects with different shapes. Now try to move the objects around to form different patterns. This is an example of thinking logically without using words or numbers—abstract reasoning. Carpenters, scientists, and computer programmers are among those who need to be good at abstract thinking.

- **Numerical ability.** If you are good at solving mathematical problems and working with figures, you may have good numerical ability. This is important in many careers, including engineering, economics, accounting, and banking.

- **Mechanical reasoning.** Those who understand the mechanical principles involved in motors and tools have high scores in this area. Mechanics obviously need these skills, but so do many other workers. They include machinists, medical technicians, technical repairpersons, and engineers.

- **Spatial relationships.** Can you look at a flat drawing of an object and picture in your mind its actual size, shape, and position in relation to other objects? If so, you have an aptitude in spatial relationships, which is important for architects, truckers, interior designers, artists, and laboratory technicians.

- **Clerical speed and accuracy.** A high score in this area indicates good hand-eye coordination, necessary for bookkeepers, bank tellers, and precision assembly workers, among others.

- **Spelling.** Secretaries, editors, writers, and word processors are among those who need to be good spellers.

- **Language usage.** Putting words together correctly and effectively is necessary for many jobs. Careers using these skills include writing, editing, law, teaching, and sales.

Your score in a single aptitude isn't as important as the pattern formed by your three or four highest scores. Most jobs demand a combination of skills. A good aptitude test can guide you in considering career possibilities based on your personal strengths.

Your Interests and Values

Having the ability to master a particular skill doesn't mean that you would be happy spending your life using that skill. In other words, your interests may differ from your aptitudes. Many people aren't sure how their interests fit in with possible

Taking part in an actual child care situation can be a learning experience for both you and the children. It can be fun for all of you, too!

TEACH

Pages 572-577

- Aptitude Tests
- Your Interests and Values
- Education and Experience

GUIDED PRACTICE

Promoting Discussion

Have students list influences on a person's career decision. Do they think the media affects such decisions? Do they think television limits or expands people's views of careers? Why?

Critical Thinking

Read the following to students: Nancy wanted to be a teacher from the time she first started school, but she was very shy and had poor verbal reasoning and language usage skills. When she took an aptitude test before entering college, she was told that teaching would not be right for her, because she did not have the verbal skills to be successful. Nevertheless, Nancy was determined to be a teacher. She took extra courses in speaking and writing and enrolled in a public speaking course one summer. She graduated form college with good grades and excellent references. Now, as a teacher, she is very happy in her job, is loved by her students, is appreciated by their parents, and has the respect of her peers. What do students think might have happened if Nancy had given up her dream of becoming a teacher? What can people do if they want a job or career for which they seem to have little aptitude?

MORE ABOUT

Abraham Maslow

The theories of American psychologist Abraham H. Maslow are widely used today in psychotherapy, education, counseling, business management, and marketing. Maslow believed all human beings are motivated to fulfill certain basic needs, with the highest need being self-actualization, or full use of a person's capabilities. Maslow thought that self-actualized people were better able to receive and express love. He said, "It is ... the ones who have loved and have been well loved, and who have many deep friendships who can hold out against hatred, rejection, or persecution."

GUIDED PRACTICE (continued)

Promoting Discussion

Divide students into small groups. Have them take turns saying to each other, "You are really good at_____." Encourage them to highlight each other's skills and abilities. Then ask them to think of jobs or careers that would take advantage of these skills and abilities.

Family Focus

Although many people consider job and family as two separate spheres of life, they are intricately entwined. Have students work in small groups to list at least ten ways a person's work life can affect family life. What are ten ways family life can affect work life? Have the groups read their lists to the class. How were the lists similar and different? What conclusions can students draw from this activity?

Critical Thinking

Emotional health is as important as physical health in building a happy and satisfying adult life. Discuss with students the relationship between career choice and emotional health. Do they know people whose entire lives have been affected by their job dissatisfaction? What prevents some people from obtaining satisfying careers? What are the emotional benefits of enjoyable, challenging work?

Combining information from an aptitude test will help you make a wise career choice. What aptitudes and interest do you think are needed to work in a child care center?

careers. If you are unsure what jobs might fit your personal interests, you may want to take an **interest inventory**, *a test designed to suggest jobs related to a person's interests.*

Interest inventories vary; most help you examine how you feel about different "themes" related to occupations. For example, if you score highest on the "realistic" theme, you might be interested in work as a mechanic, laboratory technician, farmer, or skilled industrial worker. Other themes suggest different jobs.

Remember, though, that tests are only part of the answer. They cannot measure such things as motivation, personality, or ambition. What's more, career decisions are often influenced by other factors, such as job security and prestige. Tests can show fairly accurately what you could do and what you might like doing, but you have to decide what's most important to you.

Be sure you consider the impact of your career choice on your long-range family values and goals. A career that requires frequent travel, for example, makes close family relationships more difficult. People in high-stress jobs may carry their tensions home with them. These are factors to consider as you evaluate possible careers.

Education and Experience

Having a career is much like climbing a ladder. In every career area, there are many levels of jobs. The more education and work experience you have, the higher you can climb on the career ladder. However, it is essential to remember that jobs at any level are important and worth doing well.

When you read about jobs at various levels, you will probably see words like *entry-level*, *paraprofessional*, and *professional*. Understanding these terms will help you know what qualifications are needed.

An **entry-level job** is *a position for beginners with limited education and training.* As the name indicates, this is the kind of job many people take when they are entering a career area. Most people, however, don't stay at this level. As they become more experienced and perhaps get more education, many people move up to more responsible and better-paying jobs.

A **paraprofessional** is *a person with education beyond high school that trains him or her for a certain field.* Many paraprofessional jobs require a related degree from a two-year college. A paraprofessional typically works in a team with more qualified professionals. For example, a paraprofessional might work in a child care center as an assistant teacher.

A **professional** is *a person employed in a position that requires at least a degree from a four-year college (a bachelor's degree) or technical school in a particular field.* Many professionals have more

MORE ABOUT

Researching Careers

The *Occupational Outlook Handbook (OOH)* is one of the most helpful resources available for career research. Published by the U.S. Department of Labor and updated every two years, the *OOH* discusses more than 200 occupations. It provides

detailed information about the following: (1) How much education and training a job requires. (2) Usual hours of work. (3) Working conditions. (4) Expected earnings. (5) Job outlook. (6) Sources of additional information. Most schools and public libraries will have these references.

advanced degrees—a master's degree or a doctorate—and years of experience. Professionals may be in charge of programs or supervise paraprofessionals and entry-level workers.

Education

Have you thought about getting more education after high school? You may not feel you can afford to go on to college or to a technical school, or you may not want to continue your education. However, you should consider carefully before you make a decision.

If you feel you cannot afford to continue your education after high school, you may find that financial help is available. Government groups, schools, and other institutions offer scholarships and loans. Many schools offer part-time on-campus jobs to students who need money to pay for their education. Most areas have community colleges, where costs are reasonable. These colleges offer academic programs and a variety of training programs that take two years or less to complete. After you graduate from a two-year college, you can transfer to a four-year college or university if you want to continue your studies for a bachelor's degree. Another possibility for financing further education is to work for two or three years after high school, saving enough money to go back to school later.

If you are not interested in education after high school now, you may find that you change your mind after you've been working awhile. You may want a better-paying, more responsible job that requires additional education. You may even become so interested in your work that you want to take classes to learn more about it.

In the years ahead, you may want more education or training so that you can change careers. Experts predict that most people entering the job market now will have several different careers during their working lives. Some jobs will disappear because there will no longer be a need for them. Other jobs may be taken over by machines. Even if your job continues to be available, you may discover that your interests change over time. Perhaps you will find your job boring after several years, or perhaps you will develop an interest in a different field. Any of these developments could motivate you to continue your education in the future.

Experience

If you have ever looked for a job, you know that most employers want to know about your work experience. You may wonder how you can get that experience if you can't get a job. That is a puzzle—but the puzzle has a solution.

GUIDED PRACTICE (continued)

Using the Photograph
Refer students to the photo on page 574. Ask them what aptitudes and interests they think are needed to work in a child care center. Why is it important that this girl enjoy her work?

Promoting Discussion
Ask students to explain the differences among entry-level workers, paraprofessionals, and professionals. Have students list examples of jobs that fall into each category.

Critical Thinking
Ask students why it is important to think beyond an entry-level job when planning for the future.

Divide students into groups and ask each to select a career area. Have them research and design a career ladder for that field.

Using Decision Making
Have students work in small groups to develop lists of personal characteristics they feel are important for success on any job. Ask them to identify and report to the class the five they feel are most important. Discuss the similarities and differences in the "top five" groups reported. Why did different groups choose different characteristics as important?

Did You Know?

Fifty-five percent of children between the ages of two and five years spend at least one day per week with a substitute caregiver.

MORE ABOUT

Financial Aid
Because the cost of higher education has risen faster than the cost of living in recent years, most students who attend college need some form of financial aid. In one midwestern public university, one of every two students receives scholarship or loan assistance from the university. Two of every five students hold part-time jobs while attending the university. To be eligible for scholarships and loans based on financial need, the parents of a student requesting aid must fill out extensive forms about their financial situation. Costs as well as financial aid available vary among public and private schools.

PARENTING
IN ACTION

Discussing Career Choices

Carolyn Dunn is the successful owner of a child care center. When she was asked what led her to that profession, this is what she said:

I think I'm in this career mainly because I've always loved kids. Even when I was a kid myself, I loved playing with babies. At family picnics, I was always carrying someone's baby around.

I started babysitting when I was pretty young. I was a good babysitter, too. Babysitting wasn't work for me—it was fun! To become even better at it, I enrolled in all the free babysitting clinics I could.

When I was in high school, our home economics department had an in-school nursery as part of a child study course. We had about a dozen children at a time, from babies to preschoolers. After school and during the summer, I got a part-time job as an assistant in a real nursery school downtown. I'd dress, feed, and entertain the little ones, help the older ones with their art projects and games, and answer countless questions.

By that time, I knew I wanted-ed to make a career of working with children. I enrolled in our local college and began working toward a degree in early childhood education.

About the time I graduated from college, a computer company in town built a child care center for employees' children. I applied for a job and was hired as assistant to the director. Within four years, I had moved up to the director's position.

During those early years, I'd often hear friends complain about the trouble they had finding good child care for their children. They'd switch from one center to another, trying to find the right one. They complained about poor food, lack of cleanliness, unhappy children, and high prices. I decided that I should start my own child care center, giving customers everything I'd want in a center if I had children of my own. I knew I'd have no trouble getting clients.

I started small, renting space in a church basement. Then we moved to larger quarters in a mall. I remodeled the space, hired the best people I could find, and here we are today—two years later and going strong. We have a waiting list of parents who have heard about us from satisfied customers.

THINK AND DISCUSS

1. How did Carolyn Dunn's love for children develop into her current business? What did she do to gain both the experience and the education she needed?

2. If you were interested in a career in a child-related field, what would you begin doing today? What goals might you set for yourself?

PARENTING IN ACTION

Promoting Discussion

After students have independently read "Discussing Career Choices," ask them to discuss how they might decide if they are interested in a career in child care.

Critical Thinking

Have students describe the attempts they have made to examine their own interests and choose a career direction. How can they prepare now for a future commitment?

Answers to "Think and Discuss"

1. She recognized her pleasure while working with children and improved her skills as she went through school.

2. Answers will vary; encourage long-term awareness of goals and necessary preparation.

INDEPENDENT PRACTICE

Journal Writing

Have students write a brief paper analyzing which of the skills listed on pages 572-573 they do best and why. Point out that an aptitude may be a hidden potential.

Student Workbook

Have students complete "Occupational Interests" in the Student Workbook.

Enrichment

Have students research and write about interest inventories. Can they be taken at your school or must students go elsewhere to take them? Who can take these inventories? Who administers them? What does it cost to take them?

Extension

Have students research a career area that interests them and name one career in it that involves children. (One not already listed in the chapter.) Report on it to the class.

MORE ABOUT

Future Careers

Today, companies spend more than $40 billion yearly on formal training programs. In the future, that price may go higher as new technology makes some jobs obsolete. Because of the importance of ongoing education, companies will look for employees who are flexible and willing to learn. People with broad educational backgrounds will have an advantage over those with narrow ones, *especially* in companies looking for managers. In all areas, higher, paying jobs will go to those who have continued to learn.

Multiskilling—training people in several jobs—will become common. It assures employees of getting jobs for which they are trained if their current jobs become obsolete.

Too often, people think about experience only in terms of a paying job. However, there are many other ways to gain experience. One of the best is through volunteer work. Many programs and agencies depend on volunteer help. In addition to learning the job, volunteers enjoy the satisfaction and pride gained in helping others.

As a volunteer, you will have an opportunity to gain actual experience, build up a good work record, and improve your work skills and attitudes. The people you work with as a volunteer can be good references when you apply for a paying job. (A **reference** is *a person a prospective employer can contact to find out about an applicant's character and skills*.)

Another advantage of volunteering is that it gives you experience you can use in securing a job. As a volunteer, you can learn how important a neat, clean appearance is. You can gain practice in selling your skills and talents to others. Presenting yourself well will be an advantage when you interview for a job.

Another good way to get work-related experience is to create your own job. You can do this by finding a need and filling it. Mowing lawns and shoveling snow are among the more obvious types of "created" jobs. However, other students have become house-sitters, dog-walkers, and even "human alarm clocks" who call to awaken people each morning. Perhaps your area needs someone to repair bicycles—and you know how. Maybe parents in your neighborhood would pay you to entertain and supervise their children on weekend afternoons. These kinds of created jobs can provide good experience in work areas that you find especially appealing.

If you want to be a pediatric nurse, you might consider working as a nurse's aide. It can give you valuable experience and help with the cost of nursing school.

SECTION 1 REVIEW

CHECK YOUR UNDERSTANDING

1. How do parents influence their children's choice of career?
2. List eight types of skills usually checked by an aptitude test.
3. What is an interest inventory?
4. What is an entry-level job?
5. What is the difference between a professional and a paraprofessional?
6. List three benefits of volunteer work.

DISCUSS AND DISCOVER

1. What career choices are you currently considering? Which of the aptitudes listed on pages 572-573 do you think you have? How does your own evaluation of your aptitudes relate to your career interests?

Observing & Participating

Spend at least an hour observing at a child care center, paying particular attention to the employees and their responsibilities. Can you identify which employees have entry-level positions? Which are professionals? What are the indicators of each job level? How much contact do employees at each job level have with the children in the center? Describe your findings.

SECTION 1 REVIEW

1. By encouraging some interests and discouraging others.
2. Verbal reasoning, abstract reasoning, numerical ability, mechanical reasoning, spatial relationships, clerical speed and accuracy, spelling, language use.
3. A test designed to suggest jobs related to a person's interests.
4. A position for beginners with limited education and training.
5. Professional holds a position that requires a four-year-college or technical school degree; paraprofessional holds a position that requires some specialized training beyond high school.
6. Allows you to gain actual experience, build up a good work record, and improve your work skills and attitudes.

ASSESS

CHECKING COMPREHENSION

Assign students to write their responses to "Check Your Understanding" in the Section 1 Review.

EVALUATE

Have students complete the Chapter 20, Section 1 quiz in the TCR.

Reteaching

1. Distribute Reteaching 49 in the TCR and have students share their responses.
2. Have students collect pictures that illustrate different careers associated with the skills measured by aptitude tests.
3. Have students make posters illustrating a career ladder in the field of their choice.

Enrichment

1. Distribute Enrichment 49 in the TCR.
2. Have students research one of the more widely used aptitude tests and write a report explaining how the test is used, the skills it measures, and so on.

Extension

Have students make a list of colleges, universities, and technical schools in your area. Have each student browse a catalog from one of these schools, looking for programs of study that relate to children. Ask them to choose one of the programs and list the courses required. How many required courses actually involve working with children? How many appear to have nothing to do with children? Why do students think these courses are required? Does the course list sound interesting to students? Why or why not?

CLOSE

Have students complete the phrase, "My future career goal is ..."

FOCUS

SECTION 2 RESOURCES

**Teacher's Classroom
Resources**

- Enrichment 50
- Reteaching 50
- Section 2 Quiz

Student Workbook

- Careers Relating to
  Children

SECTION OVERVIEW

Section 2 describes some of
the advantages and disadvantages of the child care field, as
well as the broad spectrum of
career opportunities. These range
from the variety of entrepreneur-
ial options, to the more specific
fields such as special education
teacher, audiologist, social worker,
and pediatric medicine specialties.

MOTIVATOR

Have students work in small
groups to discuss what social
trends have led to the increase in
the number of child care centers.
(Divorce, single parent families,
two-income families, fewer children per family, etc.) How has
each trend affected child care
needs?

USING TERMS TO LEARN

Refer students to the "Terms
to Learn." Explain that the term
entrepreneur comes from the
French language. It is based on
the word "entreprendre," which
means to undertake. In current
English usage, an entrepreneur is
one who creates and markets a
new product or who starts up
and runs a business—in other
words, a person who undertakes
a new business venture.

SECTION 2

Careers Related to Child Care

TERMS TO LEARN

entrepreneur
speech-language pathologist

OBJECTIVE

- Describe a number of specific jobs in the child care field.

Within the area of child care, there is an almost
endless variety of careers. Some careers involve working
with a single child; others, with a group. Some require
extensive study beyond high school; others require only a
high school education. Some jobs, such as teaching in
schools or child care centers, involve working with children
all day. Others, may involve less contact with children.

Child-Related Careers

Brief descriptions of a few child-related careers follow. These
descriptions will give you an idea of the various kinds of jobs that
are available. After reading about these careers, you may have a
clearer idea of whether you are interested in a child-related career.

All jobs have pluses and minuses. You should be aware of
them before you make a final career choice. The chart on page 579
summarizes the advantages and disadvantages of child care
careers.

Child Care Workers

You may have noticed an increasing number of child care centers in your community. There is a growing need for child care
because, in more and more families, there is no parent at home
during the day to care for the children. With this increase in child
care centers, there is an increasing demand for child care workers.

Many child care centers are run by government or community agencies. Some large businesses provide child care centers for
their employees' children. A few child care centers are part of
nationwide or regional chains. However, most centers are run by
entrepreneurs, *people who start up and run their own businesses, or
who create and market new products.*

MORE ABOUT

Careers in Child Care

The following questions will help those considering careers in child care to clarify their goals:

- Why do you want to be involved in influencing
  young children's lives?
- What do you like about young children?
- What do you find challenging and stimulating
  about young children?

- What kinds of interaction do you enjoy with
  children?
- What kinds of communication skills do you
  have for working with children?
- Are you comfortable being responsible for
  events and people?
- What kinds of activities help you feel good
  about yourself?

ADVANTAGES AND DISADVANTAGES OF CHILD CARE CAREERS

ADVANTAGES	DISADVANTAGES
• Job opportunities at all levels of education, experience, and responsibility.	• Salaries vary, but they are often not as high as in other careers with comparable educational requirements.
• Work available in every area of the country.	• Work is often emotionally draining.
• Opportunities for both part-time and full-time work.	• May be necessary to work evenings and weekends.
• Flexible working hours.	• Great responsibility for the health, safety, and development of children.
• Personal satisfaction for those who enjoy helping others.	• Requires exceptional energy and patience.
• Contact with all age groups, from infants to adults.	• Few periods of relaxation during working hours.

Starting and owning a child care center can be an appealing way to enter the business world. In order to succeed, an entrepreneur must have good business management skills, leadership ability, and relationship skills. An entrepreneur must also recognize that there are great risks in owning a business.

Because there are so many different kinds of child care centers, there are many different educational and personal requirements for child care workers. Some states now have regulations and licensing requirements that apply to child care workers.

Jobs in child care, even babysitting, can give you knowledge and experience that will help you be a good parent.

TEACH

Pages 578-585

• Child-Related Careers
• Child Care Workers
• Teachers
• Special Education Teachers
• Speech-Language Pathologists and Audiologists
• Social Workers
• Pediatricians
• Pediatric Dentists
• Physical Therapists
• Creative Artists and Designers

GUIDED PRACTICE

Promoting Discussion

Refer students to the box on page 579. Have them rank the advantages of a child care career in order of importance to them. The #1 item should be the one that they feel is most important. Have them rank the disadvantages in the same way, with the biggest disadvantage receiving a #1. As a class, have students average the rankings for each item. Which advantage was perceived as the most important (the lowest number)? What was the biggest disadvantage? Do students feel the advantages of child care careers outweigh the disadvantages?

MORE ABOUT

Entrepreneurs

As a group, entrepreneurs share certain characteristics. They are risk takers who express self-confidence and show originality. In addition, they are people-oriented, results-oriented, and future-oriented.

Because only one-half of new businesses are in existence longer than 18 months, most entrepre-

neurs need education and training. Poor management is the cause of most business failures. Specific causes include lack of planning, inadequate controls, poor accounting methods, inability to read and understand financial statements, and inability to locate expert advice when needed.

GUIDED PRACTICE (continued)

Making Connections: Writing

Have students choose a career relating to children and interview someone who works in that field. They should ask about job satisfaction, education and training required, special skills needed for the job, possibilities for advancement, physical and mental stresses of the job, relationship skills needed on the job, working conditions, etc. Have students give oral reports of their interviews.

Critical Thinking

Ask students if they think the job of a special education teacher might be frustrating at times. In what ways? In what ways would it be rewarding?

Ask students to read the Cultural Exchange feature "I'm Special" then review ways that their high schools provide for multicultural awareness. Open a discussion on the merits of promoting a variety of ethnic experiences.

Cultural Exchange

I'M SPECIAL

Multicultural activities in the preschool or child care center raise awareness and interest. To emphasize ethnic heritage, children can bring pictures of parents and grandparents for a bulletin board display of families. Pictures of children in everyday settings around the world reinforce appreciation of different lifestyles. An assortment of ethnic foods opens discussion about the value of new and different experiences. As with all child-related efforts, activities should be suitable for the developmental stage of the group of children.

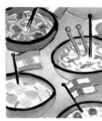

Special education teachers face extra challenges but know they make a difference in children's lives.

Teachers

Teaching is the largest profession in the industrialized world. In many parts of the country, there are more qualified teachers than positions available in elementary and secondary schools. Opportunities for teachers are usually best in preschools, in kindergartens, in grades one to three, and in classrooms for children with mental or physical disabilities.

Teachers are responsible for planning and teaching lessons. The content of those lessons must conform to the guidelines of the state and of the individual school district. In addition, teachers must take the needs and learning abilities of their individual students into consideration.

Most elementary teachers have a class of 20 to 35 students, whom they instruct in several subjects. Some elementary teachers and all secondary teachers specialize in one or two subject areas. They teach their special subjects to the students in several grades or several classes.

In most states, a full-time teacher must have at least a bachelor's degree from a four-year college, usually with an approved teacher education program. Teaching salaries vary with geographic areas, level of education, and experience. The starting salaries for teachers are typically in the low-to-medium range. A common complaint is that, compared with other professionals, teachers do not receive salaries that match the educational requirements and responsibilities of their job. Experience, advanced degrees, and administrative responsibilities can raise teachers' salaries to the middle range and above.

Special Education Teachers

Special education teachers are trained to teach those students with needs beyond the average. This includes students with learning disabilities, mental impairments, social or emotional adjustment problems, and physical disabilities. Sometimes gifted students—those with above-average potential—also receive special education.

Since students vary greatly in the type and degree of their needs, special education teachers must tailor their programs to their individual students.

Special education teachers must complete a four-year program at an approved college or university. Some school districts require special education teachers to have a master's degree, which requires an additional one or two years of study. Special education teachers must be dependable, sensible, patient, and enthusiastic. Their salaries may be somewhat higher than those of regular classroom teachers.

MORE ABOUT

Becoming a Child Care Entrepreneur

The field of child care is a natural one for those who would like to become entrepreneurs. Setting up a home-based care business or owning a child care center are ways to enter the business world.

Becoming an entrepreneur requires good business management skills and leadership ability. Business owners also need good relationship skills. They must work with customers, suppliers, employees, government regulators, and others such as accountants and bankers.

The risk of owning a business is great. Many small businesses fail. While the profits belong to the business owners, so do the losses. Still, many people feel that owning their own business is the best way to participate in our free enterprise system.

Speech-Language Pathologists and Audiologists

About ten percent of all Americans have some communication disorder. Children who have trouble speaking or hearing cannot participate fully with other children in play or in normal classroom activities.

A **speech-language pathologist** is *a professional specially trained to work with people who have speech, language, and voice disorders*. These disorders may be caused by deafness, brain injury, cleft palate, mental retardation, cerebral palsy, or environmental problems. A speech-language pathologist is typically responsible for both diagnosing and treating communication disorders.

An audiologist is a professional specially trained to test for, diagnose, and help treat hearing problems. Because speech and hearing are so closely related, a person trained either as a speech-language pathologist or as an audiologist must be familiar with both fields.

The duties of speech-language pathologists and audiologists vary with their education, experience, and place of employment. Speech and hearing clinics—generally held in schools—use special machines, tests, and diagnostic procedures to identify and evaluate disorders. Then, in cooperation with other health professionals, the speech-language pathologist or audiologist plans and arranges for organized programs of treatment.

A person who chooses either of these professions should approach problems objectively and should have a concern for the needs of others. Both speech-language pathology and audiology require patience, because progress is often slow. Speech-language pathologists and audiologists must accept responsibility, work independently, and be able to instruct others. Working with detail is also important.

Most states require a master's degree or its equivalent for both professions. Some states also require a teaching certificate if work is done in schools. Since the educational requirements for these careers are advanced, starting salaries begin in the above-average range, and later salaries tend to be high.

Social Workers

Social workers help people who have social or emotional problems. There are many different jobs within this broad field. Caseworkers help people on a one-to-one basis; community social workers are involved with groups of people.

The aim of all social service is to strengthen and improve individual and family life and to protect children. Caseworkers

GUIDED PRACTICE (continued)

Have students investigate and prepare a written report on the special education programs offered in your school district. How comprehensive are the programs? How many students are served? Do students think your school district adequately serves those with special needs? Why or Why not?

Making Connections: Writing

Investigate the state and federal laws regulating special education. Have them write a report on their findings in the form of a newspaper feature article. (Reading, Writing)

Making Connections: Careers

Have students locate a catalog for a college that offers a master's degree in audiology or speech therapy. What courses do students in the programs take? How much practical experience is provided in the programs? Does the course of study sound interesting to students?

MORE ABOUT

Speech and Hearing Problems

There is a growing trend today toward earlier recognition and treatment of children with speech and hearing problems. In the past, such children were often thought to have learning disabilities or mental problems. Job opportunities in this field are expected to increase in the coming years.

GUIDED PRACTICE (continued)

Promoting Discussion

Invite a physical therapist who works primarily with children to speak to students. What problems does the therapist see most often? What is the cause of these problems? What led the therapist to specialize in children's problems? Have students prepare questions to ask the speaker.

Critical Thinking

Have students evaluate at least two computer software programs designed for young children. For what age group is each product? Is it educational? What teaching methods are used? Have students rate each product's appeal to children.

Cooperative Learning

Have students work in small groups and develop a survey that can be used in the community to find out what agencies employ social workers. What responsibilities do these social workers have? Is most of their work with children, teens, or adults?

Many different types of community agencies employ social workers. This agency helps young parents and their children get off to a good start.

interview individuals or families who need help. Social workers with this specialty must be skillful at gathering information, getting along with people, and gaining the confidence of their clients. They decide what type of help their clients need—from counseling to medical services—and arrange for the clients to receive that help.

Some social workers place children in foster homes or with adoptive families. School social workers help troubled students adapt to classes, receive tutoring, or benefit from special community services.

A social worker must have a bachelor's degree from a school with an officially recognized social work program. A master's degree is required for some social work jobs.

Social work graduates are qualified for jobs in many government and private agencies. Salaries are in the medium range for entry-level jobs and the high range for administrators. Many social workers find satisfaction in their work because they are helping others. Some, however, find it difficult to cope with the emotional strain of social work.

Pediatricians

A pediatrician's job is the same as your family doctor's, except that all the patients are children. Pediatricians generally examine and treat their patients in their own offices and in hospitals. Some work full-time in hospitals.

Those who want to become pediatricians must have a strong desire to serve the sick and injured. They must be willing to study and keep up with the latest advances in medical science. They will need sincerity and a pleasant personality to help gain the confidence of children. Pediatricians must be able to make quick decisions in an emergency.

OBSERVING AND PARTICIPATING

Developing Participation Skills

Ask students whether they are familiar with the Special Olympics. When and if this program is available in your community, suggest that students who may be interested in special education as a career attend or perhaps even offer their services to the program. Ask them to describe their experience to the class.

All states require a license to practice medicine. To qualify, candidates must graduate from an approved medical school. Most medical schools require applicants to complete at least three years of college before entering; some require four years. Most students receive a bachelor's degree before they enter medical school. After completing medical school, pediatricians must pass a state licensing examination, serve a one- or two-year hospital internship, and usually complete a hospital residency program.

Medical training is very expensive, and it takes a long time to earn a degree. Physicians usually have a high annual income, but most work many hours a week and are often on call day and night for emergencies.

Pediatric Dentists

Dentists are responsible for the health and care of the teeth and gums. They take X rays, fill cavities, straighten teeth, and treat gum disease. Pediatric dentists specialize in the care of children's teeth.

A dentist must be a graduate of an approved dental school and must pass a state examination to receive a license. Dental colleges usually require candidates to have completed four years of college. Then dental training lasts another four years.

Dental education requires an investment of both time and money. Setting up an office and buying equipment are also expensive. However, dentists can expect high earnings after their practice is established. Dentistry, like medicine, is one of the highest paid professions.

Physical Therapists

Physical therapists work with people who have muscle, nerve, joint, or bone diseases or injuries. They help patients cope with or overcome their disabilities.

Physical therapists test patients for muscle strength, motor abilities, and proper body functioning. They develop programs for treatment, and they help patients do exercises to improve their strength and coordination.

Physical therapists must have a license to practice. To earn a license, a candidate must have a degree or certificate and must pass a state examination. Most approved schools of physical therapy offer bachelor's degree programs. A person who already has a bachelor's degree in another field can enroll in a 12- to 16-month course that leads to a certificate in physical therapy.

A master's degree in physical therapy, combined with clinical experience, increases a therapist's opportunities for advancement.

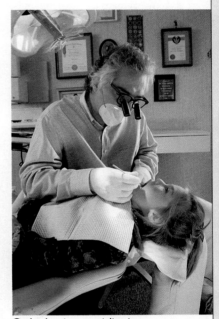

Orthodontists specialize in straightening teeth to improve both health and appearance. Many of their patients are children. The advantages and disadvantages of this career are similar to those of a pediatric dentist.

INDEPENDENT PRACTICE

Journal Writing
Have students research and write reports on leadership, the role of the leader, and why leadership is a valuable trait for an employee to have

Student Workbook
Have students complete "Careers Relating to Children" in the Student Workbook.

Student Demonstration
Have students imagine that they are coming back for a 15-year reunion of their class. Have them also imagine that they have child-related jobs. Ask them to wear nametags with their names and job titles. Serve punch and have students mingle at the "reunion," asking each other questions about their jobs, such as: Why did you select your career? What education or training did you have? What do you do in a typical day at work? What do you like best about your job? Least? Did students have enough information about their chosen jobs to answer questions correctly? Did they need more information about the careers they chose?

Have students locate an article on controlling stress, read the article, and briefly report or demonstrate its contents to the class.

Childhood Reflections

"Backward, turn backward, O Time in thy flight; Make me a child again, just for tonight."

Elizabeth Akers Allen,
"Rock Me to Sleep"

MORE ABOUT

Pediatric Dental Careers
Dental assistants and hygienists may choose to work primarily with children. A pediatric dental assistant might help a pediatric dentist by handing instruments to the dentist or keeping the patient's mouth clear with a suction device. The assistant may also work to make children comfortable and reduce their fears. A pediatric hygienist provides direct patient care under the direction of a dentist. Hygienists clean teeth, take and develop X rays, and provide other preventive services.

ASK THE EXPERTS

ASK THE EXPERTS

Issues and Advice

1. According to Ms. Mault, why are child care opportunities increasing? (*Because more disciplines are addressing children's issues.*)

2. What are examples of professional career opportunities related to child care? (*Possibilities are: professional child care providers such as nurses, educators, and therapists; teachers; social service agents; specialists such as psychologists, speech and language pathologists, physical therapists, occupational therapists, audiologists, and nutritionists.*)

3. What are examples of auxiliary career opportunities? (*Possibilities are: publishers of children's books; designers and manufacturers of children's clothing, toys, and furniture; creators and producers of children's television programs; writers and publishers of parent-education materials; developers and publishers of textbooks and educational software.*)

Thinking Like an Expert

Call students' attention to the observation by Ms. Mault that "more and more disciplines are addressing children's issues." To help students see how this comment might affect their career perspectives, ask them to call out any career that interests them or comes to mind. Have a volunteer student write a list of the careers as they are named. When the possibilities are exhausted, look at each one individually and have the students identify how knowledge of child development would be applied to the career. Which, if any, have no connection? What does this exercise tell them about future career choices? How does it influence their attitudes about careers in child care?

Child Care Careers

Q. *What is the outlook for child care careers in the decades ahead?*

A. Opportunities in child care and education will be increasing in the coming decades. One reason is because more and more disciplines are addressing children's issues.

Perhaps the greatest number of career opportunities will develop in response to the growing demand for quality child care. I anticipate an increasing need for well-trained child care providers with education beyond high school and with special licensing and certification. Nurses, educators, therapists, and other professionals will also find career opportunities in child care settings.

The need for teachers is also increasing again. Many schools are extending their services to include preschool programs, after-school programs, and transition programs for students beyond the twelfth grade.

Social service agencies, both public and private, are expanding their services to children and their families. Health-related fields continue to need pediatricians, pediatric nurses, pediatric dentists, and child psychiatrists.

Specialists who provide specific services to children are always in demand. There are now nationwide shortages of psychologists, speech-language pathologists, physical therapists, occupational therapists, recreational therapists, audiologists, and nutritionists who can address the special needs of children.

There will be special opportunities in creating and publishing children's books; designing and producing children's clothing, toys, and furniture; creating and producing quality television programs for children; writing and publishing parent-education materials; and developing and publishing textbooks and educational software.

Jacqueline S. Mault

Jackie Mault
Director of Special Services for the Toppenish School District in Toppenish, Washington

Creative Artists and Designers

Careers in publishing offer creative opportunities for people who enjoy writing or illustrating books, recording stories or music, or designing computer software.

There may be various education requirements for entering these careers. However, talent, creativity, and an understanding

OBSERVING AND PARTICIPATING

Learning Through Participation

Students interested in a child care career will gain experience by setting up a neighborhood summer camp to keep children busy. All it takes is some empty boxes, plastic bottles, clay, fabric paint, sequins, bags of fancy macaroni, and imagination. Books and magazines at the library give plenty of craft ideas. Plan projects for different ages, and collect supplies from neighbors and family. Decide how often the camp will meet and for how long. Advertise the camp with flyers posted in the neighborhood. Establish a camp fee. Set up tables and chairs in the home or in a spacious back yard.

of what appeals to young children are essential. Those who want to become software designers should have training in computer science and experience with various microcomputer systems.

High school classes can give the basic foundations for these careers, but most people in these fields benefit from a college education. Work experience can sometimes be gained by assisting people already active in the field. The income from this kind of work often takes the form of royalties—a percentage of the profits earned by the book, tape, or software. Only rarely do people in these careers have high earnings.

The work hours can be flexible, but the work involves deadlines that must be met. Some people in these careers work part-time and combine their work with another job.

Illustrating books for children and teens is just one example of a publishing career. Advantages of working in this field include flexibility and the chance to be creative.

SECTION 2 REVIEW

CHECK YOUR UNDERSTANDING

1. List three advantages of having a child care career. Then list three disadvantages.
2. Why is there an increasing demand for child care workers?
3. Which school positions offer the most opportunities for teachers?
4. What are the unique responsibilities of special education teachers?
5. What is the difference between a speech-language pathologist and an audiologist?
6. Why do some people find social work especially rewarding? Why do others find it difficult?
7. Describe the job responsibilities of a physical therapist.

DISCUSS AND DISCOVER

1. Choose and evaluate a software program designed for children: For what age range is the program marketed? Does it suit the needs and interests of children in that age range? Is it intended to be educational? What teaching methods are used? How appealing do you think most children find the program? Why? Share your evaluation with classmates.

Observing & Participating

Volunteer to help with the Special Olympics activities in your community or with a similar local program. Ask for guidance from activity leaders, as necessary. What special needs does each participant have? What can you do to help each participant? What should you allow each participant to do independently? Describe what makes this volunteer work rewarding for you.

SECTION 2 REVIEW

1. Answers will vary.
2. In some families, there is no parent at home during the day to care for children.
3. Preschoolers, kindergartners, grades one through three, and classrooms for children with mental or physical disabilities.
4. Tailor program to meet needs of individual students.
5. Works with people who have speech, language, and voice disorders; audiologist tests for, diagnoses, and helps treat hearing problems.
6. They are helping others; it can be difficult to cope with the emotional strain of social work.
7. Test patients for muscle strength, motor abilities, and proper body functioning; develop programs for treatment; help patients do exercises to improve strength and coordination.

ASSESS

CHECKING COMPREHENSION

Assign students to write their responses to "Check Your Understanding" in the Section 2 Review.

EVALUATE

Have students complete the Chapter 20, Section 2 quiz in the TCR.

Reteach

1. Have students complete Reteaching 50 in the TCR.
2. Have students collect brochures, information, pictures, articles, and other materials to start a permanent reference file on careers related to children.

Enrichment

1. Challenge students to complete Enrichment 50 in the TCR.
2. Invite the director of a child care center to speak to the class about the career ladder in child care occupations. What positions are there in the center the speaker directs? What educational and personal qualifications are needed? How much are workers paid?

Extension

Have students observe in an elementary school classroom. How many students were in the class? What subjects were taught during the observation? What responsibilities did the teacher have? What problems did the teacher encounter? What indications were there that the teacher likes his or her job? What are the negative and positive aspects of this career?

CLOSE

Have students identify one of the child-related careers they would be interested in pursuing and explain reasons why.

CHECKING COMPREHENSION

Use the Summary and the Reviewing the Facts questions to help students review the most important ideas presented in Chapter 20.

CHAPTER 20 REVIEW

1. An aptitude test measures a person's abilities and probable success in skill areas. They can be taken in high school and college. Nonstudents can be tested at colleges or counseling centers.

2. Motivation, personality, or ambition.

3. At least a degree from a four-year college (a bachelor's degree) or technical school in a particular field. Responsibilities may include supervising programs, paraprofessionals, and entry-level workers.

4. A reference is a person a prospective employer can contact to find out about an applicant's character and skills.

5. An entrepreneur is a person who starts up and runs a business, or who creates and markets new products.

6. Must conform to the guidelines of the state and individual school district, and must take the needs and learning abilities of their individual students into consideration.

7. Two major goals are to strengthen and improve individual and family life, and to protect children.

8. Those students with needs beyond average such as learning disabilities, mental impairments, social or emotional adjustment problems, and physical disabilities.

9. Strong desire to serve the sick and injured; willingness to study and learn latest advances in medical science; and sincerity and pleasant personality to help gain the confidence of children.

10. Pediatric dentists specialize in the health and care of children's teeth and gums.

SUMMARY

- Your aptitudes and interests, which may differ, are both important in your choice of careers. Aptitude tests and interest inventories can help you measure each.

- Every career has jobs at different levels. As you climb the career ladder, your responsibilities and salary may grow.

- Additional education and work experience help you advance in a job.

- Many career fields include jobs related to children.

REVIEWING THE FACTS

1. What is an aptitude test? Where can students usually arrange to take aptitude tests? Where can nonstudents take them?

2. List three career-related factors that tests cannot measure.

3. What kind of education does a professional usually have? What kinds of responsibilities does he or she usually have?

4. What is a reference?

5. What is an entrepreneur?

6. List three factors teachers must consider in planning and teaching lessons.

7. What are the two major goals of all social workers?

8. With what kinds of students do special education teachers work?

9. List three characteristics pediatricians should have.

10. What are the responsibilities of pediatric dentists?

EXPLORING FURTHER

1. Find out about the aptitude tests given at your school. Which tests are offered? When are they given? To whom are the tests available? What registration process, if any, is required? With a partner, plan, make, and display posters advertising the available tests. (Section 1)

2. Working with a group of classmates, compile a list of volunteer opportunities in your community. Then prepare an information sheet about those opportunities, giving pertinent information about each. Distribute copies of your information sheet to interested students. (Section 1)

3. Interview a social worker in your community. Who employs the social worker? What are the social worker's responsibilities? With whom does he or she work? What does he or she find most satisfying and most difficult about the position? With a group of other students, discuss what you learned from the interview. (Section 2)

THINKING CRITICALLY

1. **Analyze.** What are ten factors that might influence a person's career decisions? Of those factors, which three do you consider most important? Why? How strong a role do you think television and other media play in influencing career decisions? Do you believe television limits or expands people's views about careers? Why?

2. **Synthesize.** What personal characteristics do you feel are important for success in any job? Why are those characteristics important? What do you think you and other students should be doing to foster these characteristics in yourselves? Why?

Course Evaluation

Have students complete a course evaluation at the end of the semester or year. This will help them think about what they have learned from the course; in addition, their ideas and suggestions can help improve the course the next time you teach it. Some questions to ask include: (1) What are some things you learned from the course? (2)

How has the course changed your ideas about children and about being a parent? (3) Do you plan to have a job working with children? How has this class influenced that decision? (4) What topics studied did you find most interesting? Least interesting? (5) Which class activities did you like best? Least? (6) What do you think should be changed in this course?

grasp reflex. The automatic response of a newborn's hand to close over anything that comes in contact with the baby's palm. (7-3)

group identification. The need for a feeling of belonging. (14-2)

H

hand-eye coordination. The ability to move the hands and fingers precisely in relation to what is seen. (8-1)

Head Start. A program of locally operated child care facilities designed to help lower-income and disadvantaged children function effectively at home, in school, and in the community. (3-3)

Heimlich maneuver. A technique for using pressure on the air within the body to force an object interfering with breathing from the throat. (17-2)

heredity. The passing on of characteristics that are physically inherited from previous generations. (1-2)

hormones. Body chemicals. (4-1)

I

imitation. Method of learning by watching and copying others. (13-1)

immunize. To protect a person against a particular disease, usually by giving a vaccine. (17-1)

incidental learning. Unplanned learning. (13-1)

incubator. A special enclosed crib in which the oxygen supply, temperature, and humidity can be closely controlled. Used for premature infants. (7-2)

infant mortality rate. The percentage of deaths during the first year of life. (17-1)

infertility. Inability to conceive children. (5-2)

intelligence quotient (IQ). A numerical standard that tells whether a person's intelligence is average or above or below average for his or her age. (16-1)

intelligence. The ability to interpret or understand everyday situations and to use that experience when faced with new situations or problems. (13-1)

interest inventory. A test designed to suggest jobs related to a person's interests. (20-1)

interpret. To find meaning in, explain, or make sense of something. (19-2)

J

joint custody. An arrangement in which both divorced parents assume responsibility for the children. (18-3)

K-L

labor. The process by which the baby gradually moves out of the uterus into the vagina to be born. (6-3)

large motor skills. Physical skills that depend on the use and control of the large muscles of the back, legs, shoulders, and arms. (11-1)

latchkey children. Children who are unsupervised from the time they come home from school until their parents return from work. (3-3)

lay midwife. A person who has special training in the care of pregnant women and uncomplicated deliveries but does not have a nursing degree. (6-3)

learning centers. Areas of the classroom that are designed for certain types of play, equipment, or learning. (19-3)

learning disability. A disorder in psychological processes that prevents a person from using information received through the senses in a normal way for learning. (16-2)

M

malnutrition. A health problem resulting from not getting enough food or adequate amounts of needed nutrients. (8-2)

manipulation. Skillful use of the hands and fingers. (11-1)

maternity leave. Time off from a job allowing a woman to give birth, recuperate, and care for her new baby. This time may range from several weeks to several months. (6-2)

miscarriage. The natural ending of a pregnancy before the embryo or fetus could possibly survive. (5-3)

Montessori preschool. An educational facility for three- to six-year-olds that provides special learning materials which children are free to explore on their own. (3-3)

moral development. The process of gradually learning to base one's behavior on personal beliefs of right and wrong. (15-2)

motor skills. Abilities that depend on the use and control of muscles. (8-1)

N

nanny. A specially trained person employed to provide live-in child care services. (3-3)

natural fibers. Fibers that come from plants or animals. (11-2)

negative reinforcement. A response that tends to discourage a particular behavior from being repeated. (3-2)

negative self-concept. An inclination to see oneself as bad, unimportant, and incapable. (12-2)

negativism. Doing the opposite of what others want. (12-1)

nontoxic. Not poisonous. (17-1)

nuclear family. A family group with two generations—a father and mother and at least one child—sharing the same household. (2-1)

nurse-midwife. A registered nurse with advanced training in the care of normal, uncomplicated pregnancy and birth. (6-3)

nurturing. Providing love, support, attention, and encouragement.

nutrition. A balance of all the food substances needed for health and growth. (1-2)

O

object permanence. An understanding of the fact that objects continue to exist even when they are not in sight. (10-1)

objective. Using facts, not personal feelings or prejudices, to describe things. (19-2)

obstetrician. A doctor who specializes in pregnancy and birth. (6-1)

ovum. A female cell or egg. (5-1)

P

pacifier. A nipple attached to a plastic ring. (9-1)

parallel play. Playing independently near, but not actually playing with, another child. (12-2)

paraprofessional. A person with education beyond high school that trains him or her for a certain field. (20-1)

parent cooperative. A child care facility in which part of the supervision is provided by the parents of enrolled children, who take turns donating their services. (3-3)

parenthood. The state of being a parent. (2-2)

parenting. The process of caring for children and helping them grow and learn. (3-1)

paternity leave. Time off from a job allowing a father to care for his new baby. (6-2)

pediatrician. A doctor who specializes in the care of babies and young children.

peer pressure. The influence of people one's own age. (4-1)

peers. Other people of one's own age. (15-2)

perception. Learning from the senses. (10-1)

permanent teeth. The set of 32 teeth that will not be naturally replaced. (14-1)

personality. The total of all the specific traits (such as shyness or cheerfulness) that are consistent in an individual's behavior. (9-2)

placenta. The tissue that connects the sacs around the unborn baby to the mother's uterus. (5-1)

placid. Remarkably easygoing and accepting of one's surroundings. (9-2)

play group. A child care arrangement in which a group of parents take turns caring for each other's children in their own homes. (3-3)

poison control centers. Special hospital units that are equipped to advise and treat poison victims. (17-2)

positive reinforcement. A response that encourages a particular behavior. (3-2)

positive self-concept. An inclination to see oneself as good, worthwhile, and capable. (12-2)

postnatal. After the baby's birth. (6-2)

pregnancy test. A test to determine whether or not a woman is going to have a baby. (6-1)

premature. Born before development is complete. (5-3)

prenatal. During the period before birth. (5-1)

preoperational period. Piaget's second stage of learning, lasting typically from age two to age seven, during which children think about everything in terms of their own activities and in terms of what they can perceive at the moment. (10-1)

prepared childbirth. A method of giving birth in which pain is reduced through the elimination of fear and the use of special conditioning exercises. (6-3)

preschool. A child care center that provides educational programs, usually for children aged three to five. (3-3)

preschoolers. Children aged four and five. (14-2)

primary teeth. The first set of teeth a baby gets. (8-1)

professional. A person employed in a position that requires at least a degree from a four-year college (a bachelor's degree) or technical school in a particular field. (20-1)

proportion. The size relationship of one thing to another. (8-1)

Q-R

recessive. Describes a gene which can determine a particular trait (such as eye color) only when paired with a similar gene. If paired with a stronger, or dominant, gene, the dominant gene will determine the trait, and the characteristic of the recessive gene will not be seen. (5-2)

reference. A person a prospective employer can contact to find out about an applicant's character and skills. (20-1)

reflexes. Instinctive, automatic responses, such as sneezing and yawning. (7-3)

rooming-in. An arrangement in which the baby stays in the mother's room, rather than in a hospital nursery, after birth. (7-2)

rooting reflex. A newborn's automatic response, when touched on the lips or cheek, of turning toward the touch and beginning to suck. (7-3)

running record. An observation recording method that involves recording for a set period of time everything observed about a particular child, group, or teacher. (19-2)

S

self-centered. Constantly thinking of one's own needs and wants, not those of others. (12-1)

self-concept. A person's feelings about himself or herself. (9-2)

self-discipline. The ability to control one's own behavior. (3-2, 12-3)

self-esteem. Positive sense of self-worth. (15-1)

sensitive. Unusually aware of one's surroundings and of any changes in those surroundings. (9-2)

sensorimotor period. Piaget's first stage of learning, lasting from birth until about the age of two, during which babies learn primarily through their senses and their own actions. (10-1)

separation anxiety. A child's fear of being away from parents, familiar caregivers, or the normal environment. (12-1)

sequence. A step-by-step pattern. (1-2)

sexuality. A person's concept of himself or herself as a male or female. (4-1)

sibling rivalry. Competition between brothers and/or sisters for their parents' affection and attention. (12-1)

single-parent family. A family group that consists of one parent and one or more children sharing a household. (2-1)

sleeper. A one-piece stretch garment with feet. (8-3)

small motor skills. Physical skills that depend on the use and control of the finer muscles of the wrists, fingers, and ankles. (11-1)

social development. The process of learning to interact with others and to express oneself to others. (9-1)

socialization. The process of learning to get along with others. (12-2)

speech therapist. A professional trained to diagnose and help correct speech problems. (13-2)

speech-language pathologist. A professional specially trained to work with people who have speech, language, and voice disorders. (20-2)

sperm. A male cell. (5-1)

sphincter muscles (SFINK-tuhr). The muscles that control elimination. (11-2)

sprain. An injury caused by sudden, violent stretching of a joint or muscle. (17-2)

startle reflex. A newborn's automatic physical response—legs thrown up, fingers spread, legs extended and then brought rapidly back to the midline while the fingers close in a grasping action—to a loud noise or to a touch on the stomach. (7-3)

stillbirth. The natural ending of a pregnancy after 20 weeks. (5-3)

strained foods. Solids processed to make them smooth and runny. (8-2)

stranger anxiety. A fear, usually expressed by crying, of unfamiliar people. (9-2)

subjective. Using one's personal opinions and feelings, rather than facts, to judge or describe things. (19-2)

surrogate. A substitute. (5-2)

symbolic thinking. The use of words and numbers to represent ideas. (10-1)

synthetic fibers. Fibers manufactured from chemicals rather than natural sources. (11-2)

T

temper tantrums. Incidents in which children release their anger or frustration by screaming, crying, kicking, pounding, and sometimes even holding their breath. (12-1)

temperament. Style of reacting to the world and of relating to others. (7-3)

therapist (also called a **behavior specialist**). A professional trained in helping people work through emotional problems. (18-1)

time-out. A short period of time spent sitting away from the presence of others or from the center of activity. (3-2, 19-3)

toddlers. Children from the age of first walking, usually about twelve months, until the age of three years. (11-1)

training pants. Heavy, absorbent underpants. (11-2)

transitions. Periods during which children move from one scheduled activity to the next. (19-3)

trial-and-error learning. Learning in which a child tries several solutions before finding out what works. (13-1)

U

ultrasound. A technique of using sound waves to make a video image of an unborn baby to check for specific health problems. (5-3)

umbilical cord. A long tube that connects the placenta to the unborn baby, and through which nourishment and oxygen are carried to the baby. (5-1)

uterus (YOOT-uh-ruhs). The organ in a woman's body in which a baby develops during pregnancy. (5-1)

V

vaccine. A small amount of an antigen introduced to the body, usually by injection, so that the body can build resistance to the disease. (17-1)

values. The principles a person considers important, and uses to guide his or her life. (4-1)

vocabulary. The number of words a person uses. (16-2)

W-X-Y-Z

weaning. A process of changing from drinking from the bottle or breast to drinking from a cup. (8-2)

zygote. Fertilized egg. (5-1)

Glossary/Glosario

A

abstinence/abstinencia. Evitar o abstenerse del coito sexual.

adoption/adopción. Proceso legal en el cual la gente obtiene el derecho permanente para criar a un niño(a) que no es biológicamente propio como si fueran los padres naturales.

aggressive/agresivo(a). Ser de carácter fuerte y determinado.

allergy/alergia. Una sensitividad extrema a una o más sustancias comúnes.

alternative birth center/centro de nacimiento alternativo. Una facilidad tipo hogar, separada de un hospital, donde se da a luz.

ambidextrous/ambidextro. Ser hábil usando ambas manos con la misma facilidad.

amniocentesis/amniocentesis. El proceso de extraer una muestra del fluído amniótico alrededor de un bebé en el vientre de la madre con una aguja especial y examinarlo para buscar indicaciones de defectos de nacimiento u otros problemas de salud.

amniotic fluid/fluido amniótico. Un fluido especial que está alrededor del bebé durante el embarazo y que sirve para proteger su desarrollo.

anecdotal record/expediente anecdótico. Un método para registrar observaciones el cual se enfoca en un evento o un lugar en particular.

anemia/anemia. Una condición causada por la falta de hierro, la cual resulta en falta de apetito, cansancio y debilidad.

Apgar scale/escala Apgar. Un método utilizado para evaluar la condición física de un recién nacido. La criatura es evaluada en una escala de 0 a 2 en 5 cosas: pulso, respiración, tono muscular, sensibilidad y color de piel.

aptitude test/examen de actitud. Un examen que mide las habilidades de una persona y el éxito probable en varias áreas de destreza.

articulation/articulación. La habilidad de hablar clara y precisamente.

artificial respiration/respiración artificial. El procedimiento de forzar aire en los pulmones de una persona que ha dejado de respirar.

attachment/conexión o unión. Un fuerte apego o unión especial entre dos personas.

attention deficit hyperactivity disorder (ADHD)/trastorno de falta de atención e hiperactividad. La condición de la inhabilidad de controlar sus propias actividades o de poder concentrarse por un período de tiempo normal.

attention span/lapso de atención. El período o duración que una persona puede concentrarse en una tarea sin aburrirse.

audiologist/audiólogo. Un profesional entrenado especialmente para examinar, diagnosticar y ayudar a curar los problemas del oído.

B

baseline/línea de referencia. Recuento de frecuencia tomado antes de hacer cualquier esfuerzo para corregir un comportamiento indeseable en particular.

behavior/comportamiento. La manera de actuar y responder.

birth defect/defecto de nacimiento. Una abnormalidad, presente durante el nacimiento, que afecta la estructura o función del cuerpo.

blended family/familia incorporada. Tipo de familia que consiste de una pareja casada y por lo menos un niño(a) del matrimonio o relación anterior de uno de los padres.

bonding/enlace o vínculo. El proceso de formar vínculos emocionales para toda la vida.

budget/presupuesto. Un plan de gastos.

C

cardiopulmonary resuscitation (CPR)/ resucitación cardiopulmonar. Ayuda de emergencia para restaurar la respiración y la circulación.

caregiver/cuidador(a). Cualquier persona que cuide a un niño(a), ya sea a corto o largo plazo.

cause and effect/causa y efecto. El conceptp de que una acción resulta en otra acción o condición.

central nervous system/sistema nervioso central. La parte del sistema nervioso formada por el cerebro y la espina dorsal. Impulsos sensoriales son transmitidos a esta área e impulsos motores pasan de regreso.

cervix/cerviz. El parte posterior del cuello o abertura del útero.

cesarean birth/nacimiento por Cesárea. Alumbramiento de un bebé por medio de una incisión quirúrgica en el abdomen de la madre.

child abuse/abuso infantil. El maltrato físico y/o emocional de un niño(a).

child care aide/ayudante de cuidado de niños. Un asistente para la persona encargada de un programa de cuidado de niños.

child care center/centro de cuidado de niños. Una facilidad diseñada para proveer cuidado para niños de padres que trabajan.

child development/desarrollo infantil. El estudio de como los niños crecen de maneras diferentes—física, mental, emocional, y socialmente.

chorionic villi sampling/muestra de villi coriónico. El proceso de examinar para encontrar defectos de nacimiento específicos, tomando pequeñas cantidades del tejido de la membrana que envuelve el feto.

chromosomes/cromosomas. Estructuras filiformes contenidas en el núcleo de las células que contienen los códigos genéticos de las características hereditarias.

circumference/circunferencia. Medida alrededor de algo apróximadamente de forma circular, como la cabeza de un niño(a).

colostrum/calostro. Leche secretada por las glándulas mamarias poco antes y despúes del parto. Este fluído precede el flujo de la leche y provee al recién nacido alimentación y anticuerpos para protegerlo contra enfermedades.

commitment/compromiso. Una promesa u obligación.

communicable diseases/enfermedades contagiosas. Enfermedades que pueden ser transmitidas de una persona a otra.

conception/concepción. La unión de un óvulo y una esperma, resultando en el comienzo de un embarazo.

concepts/conceptos. Categorías generales de objetos e información.

concrete operations period/período concreto de operaciones. La tercera etapa de aprendizaje de Piaget, que dura usualmente de los siete a los once años, durante la cual los niños pueden pensar lógicamente pero todavía aprenden mejor por medio de experiencias directas.

confidentiality/confidencialidad. Privacidad.

conscience/conciencia. Un sentido interno de lo bueno y lo malo, que induce al buen comportamiento y causa sentimientos de remordimiento después del mal comportamiento.

consequences/consecuencias. Los resultados de una decisión.

consistency/consistencia. Actuar repetidamente de la misma manera.

contraceptives/anticonceptivos. Métodos o dispositivos que previenen contra el embarazo.

contractions/contracciones. Encogimiento fuerte y repentino de los músculos del útero, que ocurre durante el parto.

convulsion/convulsión. Un período de inconciencia con movimientos convulsivos o sacudidas incontrolables de los músculos.

cooperative play/juego cooperativo. Juego entre niños que incluye la interacción y la cooperación.

coping skills/habilidades de adaptación. Técnicas que ayudan a la gente a resolver problemas o a adaptarse a una situación.

cortex/capa cortical. La capa externa del cerebro, la cual permite aprendizaje más complejo.

cradle cap/capa de armazón. Una condición de la piel en la que el cuero cabelludo desarrolla parches de escamas amarillentas y costrosas.

creativity/creatividad. El uso de la imaginación para producir algo.

crisis nursery/guardería de crisis. Facilidades para el cuidado de los niños adonde los padres con problemas pueden dejar a sus niños para que se los cuiden mientras lidian con sus problemas.

D

delivery/parto. Dar a luz.

deprivation/privación. La falta de un medio ambiente sano y de cuidado.

depth perception/percepción de profundidad. La habilidad de reconocer que un objeto es de tres dimensiones, no plano.

developmental checklist/lista para comprobación de desarrollo. Una lista que identifica una serie de habilidades específicas o comportamientos que un niño(a) de cierta edad debe de dominar.

dexterity/destreza. La agilidad del uso de las manos y de los dedos.

diaper rash/salpullido de pañal. Parches de piel irritada en el área del pañal.

dilates/dilata. Ensanchamiento. El cervix se dilata durante el parto.

directed learning/aprendizaje dirigido. Aprender cuando a uno le enseñan, ya sea formal o informalmente.

discipline/disciplina. El deber de enseñarle a los niños a comportarse de maneras aceptables.

dominant/dominante. Describe un gene para un razgo o factor en particular (como el color de los ojos) que es más fuerte e impone el resultado del razgo cuando es emparejado con un gene débil o recesivo.

dramatic play/juego dramático. Imitar situaciones de la vida real, como jugar a la casa o a la escuela.

dyslexia/dislexia. Una incapacidad de aprendizaje que impide que una persona lea bien y que maneje el lenguaje de una manera normal.

E

egocentric/egocéntrico. Pensar sólamente en sí mismo.

embryo/embrión. Un conjunto de células en desarrollo en el útero que dura más o menos de la tercera a la octava semana del embarazo.

emotional development/desarrollo emocional. El proceso de aprender a reconocer y expresar los sentimientos propios y aprender a establecer su propia identidad e individualidad.

empathy/empatía. Una sensación de comprensión y de compartir los sentimientos de otra persona.

entrepeneurs/empresarios. Personas que comienzan y manejan sus propios negiocios, o que crean y mercadean nuevos productos.

entry-level job/trabajo de nível de principiante. Una posición para principiantes con educación y experiencia limitadas.

enuresis/enuresis. La falta de control de la vejiga o vesícula.

environment/medio ambiente. Las personas, lugares, y cosas que rodean e influencian a un individuo.

extended family/familia extendida. Un grupo familiar que incluye a los parientes, aparte de los padres e hijos dentro del mismo hogar.

F

failure to thrive/falta de crecimiento o desarrollo. Una condición en la cual el bebé no crece ni se desarrolla adecuadamente.

family child care/cuidado de niños familiar. Tipo de cuidado de niños en el que un grupo pequeño de niños son cuidados en la casa del cuidador(a).

family life cycle/ciclo de vida familiar. Una serie de etapas en un orden pronosticable.

family/familia. Un grupo de dos o más personas que se interesan y están compremetidos el uno por el otro.

fetal alcohol effects/efectos el alcoholismo fetal. Una condición menos severa que tiene algunos de los síntomas del síndrome de alcoholismo fetal.

fetal alcohol syndrome/síndrome de alcoholismo fetal. Una condición de deformaciones físicas y problemas cognitivos en el feto como resultado del uso excesivo del alcohol por la madre durante el embarazo.

fetus/feto. El embrión o bebé aún no nacido a partir de las ocho semanas de concepción hasta el nacimiento.

finger plays/juegos de dedos. Canciones o salmos que acompañan movimientos de las manos.

fixed expenses/gastos fijos. El costo de cosas que no se pueden cambiar, tales como el pago del alquiler, pagos de propiedad, impuestos, pagos de seguro, y pagos de préstamo.

flammable/inflamable. Que se quema facilmente.

flexible expenses/gastos flexibles. El costo de cosas sobre las cuales la gente tiene cierto control y que pueden ser recortadas o eliminadas si es necesario.

fontanels/fontanelas. Espacios abiertos o huecos adonde los huesos del cráneo de un bebé aún no ha sido permanentemente ligado.

forceps/fórceps. Tenazas o pinzas epeciales hechas de bandas de acero quirúrgico que son moldeadas de la forma de la cabeza de un niño(a).

formal operations period/período formal de operaciones. La cuarta etapa de aprendizaje de Piaget, que dura aproximadamente de los once años hasta la edad adulta, durante el cual los niños son más capaces de pensar abstractamente.

formula/fórmula. Una mezcla de leche o substitutos de leche y nutrientes.

foster child/hijo(a) adoptivo(a). Un niño(a) puesto bajo la responsabilidad legal temporaria de un adulto.

fracture/fractura. Una rajadura o quebradura en un hueso.

frequency count/cómputo o recuento de frecuencia. Una marca de cuantas veces sucede un comportamiento en particular (la frecuencia del comportamiento).

G

genes/genes. Las partes de los cromosomas que determinan las características hereditarias.

gifted children/niños dotados. Niños con un cociente de inteligencia de 130 o más.

grasp reflex/reflejo de empuñar o asir. La reacción automática de la mano de un recién nacido a asir o empuñar cualquier cosa que toque con su palma.

group identification/identificación de grupo. La necesidad de sentir que uno pertenece.

H

hand-eye coordination/coordinación de ojo y mano. La habilidad de mover las manos y los dedos en relación a lo que es visto.

Head Start/programa Head Start. Un programa local de guarderías infantiles diseñado para ayudar a niños de bajos recursos y en desventaja para que funcionen eficazmente en la casa, en la escuela, y en la comunidad.

Heimlich maneuver/maniobra Heimlich. Una técnica para usar presión en el aire dentro del cuerpo para expulsar un objecto de la garganta que interfiere con la respiración.

heredity/herencia. La transferencia de características que son heredadas de las generaciones anteriores.

hormones/hormonas. Sustancias químicas del cuerpo.

I

imitation/imitación. Método de aprendizaje por medio de ver y copiar a los demás.

immunize/inmunizar. Proteger a una persona contra una enfermedad en particular, usualmente por medio de una vacuna.

incidental learning/aprendizaje incidental o accidental. Aprendizaje no planeado.

incubator/incubadora. Una cuna especial cerrada en la cual el oxígeno, la temperatura y la humedad pueden ser controladas. Usada para los bebés prematuros.

infant mortality rate/porcentaje de mortalidad infantil. El porcentaje de muertes infantiles durante el primer año de vida.

infertility/infertilidad. La incapacidad de tener hijos.

intelligence quotient (IQ)/cociente de inteligencia. Un patrón o criterio de números que dicen si la inteligencia de una persona es promedia o superior o inferior que el resto de la gente de su edad.

intelligence/inteligencia. La habilidad de interpretar o entender las situaciones de cada día y de usar esa experiencia cuando se enfrentan nuevas situaciones o problemas.

interest inventory/inventorio de interés. Un examen diseñado para recomendar empleos relacionados a los intereses de la persona.

J

joint custody/custodia en comúm. Un arreglo en el cual ambos padres divorciados asumen responsabilidad por los niños.

K-L

labor/parto. El proceso por el cual el bebé sale del útero a la vagina gradualmente para nacer.

large motor skills/habilidades motoras mayores. Habilidades físicas que dependen del uso y control de los músculos principales de la espalda, de las piernas, de los hombros, y de las manos.

latchey children/niños no supervisados. Niños que no reciben supervisión o cuidado desde la hora que regresan de la escuela hasta la hora que sus padres regresan del trabajo.

lay midwife/partera o comadrona. Una persona que tiene entrenamiento especial en el cuidado de mujeres embarazadas y de partos no complicados pero que no tiene un título de enfermera.

learning centers/centros de aprendizaje. Las áreas de una aula de clases diseñadas para algún tipo de juegos, equipo, o aprendizaje.

learning disability/incapacidad de aprendizaje. Un desorden psicológico que impide que una persona use información recibida por medio de los sentidos en una manera normal de aprendizaje.

M

malnutrition/malnutrición. Un problema de la salud que resulta al no recibir suficiente alimento o las cantidades necesarias de nutrientes.

manipulation/manipulación. Uso hábil de las manos y de los dedos.

maternity leave/ausencia de maternidad. Tiempo libre del trabajo que le permite a una mujer a dar a luz, recuperarse, y cuidar a su nuevo bebé. Este tiempo puede durar de varias semanas a varios meses.

miscarriage/aborto. La terminación natural de un embarazo antes de quel embrión o feto pueda sobrevivir.

Montessori preschool/escuela preescolar Montessori. Una facilidad educacional para niños de tres a seis años que provee materiales de aprendizaje especial que los niños pueden explorar por sí mismos.

moral development/desarrollo moral. El proceso de aprender gradualmente a basar el comportamiento propio en creencias personales de lo que es bueno y malo.

motor skills/habilidades motoras. Habilidades que dependen en el uso y control de los músculos.

N

nanny/niñera. Una persona entrenada especialmente en el cuidado de los niños y que es empleada para proveer estos servicios en casa.

natural fibers/fibras naturales. Fibras que vienen de las plantas o animales.

negative reinforcement/refuerzo negativo. Una reacción que tiende a desalentar un comportamiento en particular para que no sea repetido.

negative self concept/concepto negativo de sí mismo. Una inclinación para verse a sí mismo de una manera mala, sin importancia, e incompetente.

negativism/negativismo. Hacer lo opuesto de lo que los demás quieren.

nontoxic/no tóxico. Que no es venenoso.

nuclear family/familia nuclear. Un grupo familiar con dos generaciones—un padre y una madre y por lo menos un hijo(a)—que comparten el mismo hogar.

nurse-midwife/enfermera-partera. Una enfermera registrada con entrenamiento avanzado en el cuidado de embarazo y nacimientos normales y sin complicaciones.

nurturing/estimulante. Que provee amor, apoyo, atención, y estimulo o incentivo.

nutrition/nutrición. Un balance de todas las sustancias alimenticias necesitadas para la buena salud y el crecimiento.

O

object permanence/permanencia de un objeto. La comprensión de la realidad de que los objetos continuan existiendo aún cuando no están a la vista.

obstetrician/obstetra. Un doctor que se especializa en embarazos y partos.

ovum/óvulo. La célula femenina de la reproducción.

P

pacifier/chupete. Un pezón de biberón ligado a un anillo de plástico.

parallel play/juego paralelo. Jugar independientemente cerca de otro niño(a) pero no con él o ella.

paraprofessional/paraprofesional. Una persona con una educación superior a la escuela secundaria que entrena para algún campo o rama de trabajo.

parent cooperative/cooperativa de los padres. Una facilidad para el cuidado de niños que es en parte supervisada por los padres de los niños que son cuidados en ese lugar, y los padres se turnan donando sus servicios.

parenthood/paternidad y/o maternidad. El estado de ser un padre y/o una madre.

parenting/ser padre y/o madre. El proceso de cuidar de los hijos y ayudarlos a crecer y a aprender.

paternity leave/ausencia de paternidad. Tiempo libre del trabajo que le permite a un padre a cuidar de su nuevo bebé.

pediatrician/pediatra. Un doctor especializado en el cuidado de los bebés y niños pequeños.

peer pressure/presión de contemporáneos. La influencia de la gente de la misma edad.

peers/compañeros o contemporáneos. Otras personas de la misma edad.

perception/percepción. Aprender por medio de los sentidos.

permanent teeth/dientes permanentes. El conjunto de 32 dientes que no pueden ser reemplazados naturalmente.

personality/personalidad. La suma de todas las caraterísticas específicas (como la timidez o la alegría) que son consistentes en el comportamiento de un individuo.

placenta/placenta. El tejido que conecta los sacos alrededor del bebé aún no nacido al útero de la madre.

placid/plácido. Persona muy calmada, que se lleva bien con otros, y que acepta su medio ambiente.

play group/juego en grupo. Un tipo de cuidados de niños en el que los padres toman turnos cuidando otros niños en sus propias casas.

poison control centers/centros de control de envenenamiento. Unidades especiales de un hospital que están equipadas para ayudar y aconsejar a las víctimas de envenenamiento.

positive reinforcement/refuerzo positivo. Una reacción que estimula un comportamiento en particular.

positive self-concept/concepto positivo de sí mismo. Una inclinación a verse a sí mismo de una manera buena, que vale la pena, y capaz.

postnatal/postnatal. Después del nacimiento del bebé.

pregnancy test/examen o prueba de embarazo. Un examen para determinar si una mujer va a tener un bebé.

premature/prematuro. Nacido antes de que el desarrollo se ha completado.

prenatal/prenatal. Durante el período antes del nacimiento.

preoperational period/período preoperacional. La segunda etapa de aprendizaje de Piaget, que dura usualmente de la edad de dos años a los siete años, durante la cual los niños piensan acerca de todas las cosas en términos de sus propias actividades y en términos de los que pueden percibir en ese momento.

prepared childbirth/parto preparado. Un método de dar a luz en el cual el dolor es reducido por medio la eliminación del miedo y del uso de ejercicios especiales.

preschool/escuela preescolar. Un centro de cuidado de niños que provee programas de educación, usualmente para niños de tres a cinco años de edad.

preschoolers/niños de edad preescolar. Niños de cuatro y cinco años.

primary teeth/dientes originales o primarios. El conjunto de dientes de un bebé.

professional/profesional. Una persona empleada en una posición que requiere por lo menos un título universitario de bachiller(a) o un título de una escuela técnica con una especialidad en particular.

proportion/proporción. La relación en tamaño de una cosa a otra.

Q-R

recessive/recesivo. Describe un gene que puede determinar una característica en particular (como el color de ojos) solo cuando es emparejado con un gene similar. Si es emparejado con un gene más fuerte o dominante, el gene dominante determinará la característica , y la característica del gene recesivo no será vista.

reference/referencia. Una persona que un empleador puede contactar para averiguar acerca del carácter del aplicante.

reflexes/reflejos. Reacciones automáticas e instintivas, como estornudar o bostezar.

rooming-in/compartir la habitación. Un arreglo en el cual el bebé se queda en la habitación de la madre, en vez de quedarse en la guardería del hospital, después del nacimiento.

rooting reflex/reflejo radicular. La reacción automática de un bebé, cuando le tocan los labios o las mejillas, de voltearse y comenzar a chupar lo que lo toca.

running record/expediente de funcionamiento. Un método de observación que envuelve tomar apuntes de todo lo observado acerca de un niño(a) en particular, un grupo, o un maestro(a), por un período específico de tiempo.

S

self-centered/egocéntrico(a) o egoísta. Pensar constantemente acerca de las necesidades y deseos propios, y no pensar en las necesidades y deseos de los demás.

self-concept/autoimagen. La imagen que una persona tiene de sí misma.

self-disciplina/autodisciplina. La capacidad de controlar el comportamiento de sí mismo.

self-esteem/autoestima. El sentimiento positivo acerca del valor de sí mismo.

sensitive/sensitivo. Estar muy consciente o al tanto de su medio ambiente y de cualquier cambio que ocurra en él.

sensorimotor period/período sensorimotor. La primera etapa de aprendizaje de Piaget, que dura desde el nacimiento hasta los dos años de edad, durante la cual los bebés aprenden principalmente por medio de sus sentidos y sus propias acciones.

separation anxiety/ansiedad de separación. El miedo de un niño(a) de estar separado de sus padres, cuidadores familiares, o de su medio ambiente normal.

sequence/orden de sucesión. Un modelo de paso por paso.

sexuality/sexualidad. El concepto propio de una persona de ser un hombre o una mujer.

sibling rivalry/rivalidad fraternal. La competencia entre hermanos o hermanas por la atención y afección de sus padres.

single-parent family/familia con sólo la madre o el padre. Un grupo familiar que consite de sólo el padre o la madre y uno o más hijos que comparten un hogar.

sleeper/mameluco para dormir. Un traje de una sola pieza con espacio para los pies, usado para dormir.

small motor skills/habilides motoras menores. Capacidades físicas que dependen del uso y control de los músculos mas finos de las muñecas de las manos, los dedos, y los tobillos.

social development/desarrollo social. El proceso de aprender a obrar recíprocamente con otros y a expresarse con los demás.

socialization/socialización. El proceso de aprender a llevarse bien con los demás.

speech therapist/terapista del habla. Un profesional entrenado a diagnosticar y ayudar a corregir los problemas del habla.

speech-language pathologist/patólogo del habla y el lenguaje. Un profesional entrenado a trabajar con gente que tiene problemas del habla, del lenguaje y de la voz.

sperm/esperma o semen. La cécula masculina de la reproducción.

sphincter muscles/músculos esfínter. Los músculos que controlan la eliminación.

sprain/torcedura. Una lesión causada por un estiraje repentino y violento de una coyuntura o un músculo.

startle reflex/reflejo de respingo o sobresalto. La reacción física automática de un recién nacido—las piernas hacia arriba, los dedos estirados, las piernas extendidas y luego rápidamente encogidas hacia el estómago al mismo tiempo que los dedos se encogen—a un ruido fuerte o a un toque en el estómago.

stillbirth/aborto. La terminación natural de un embarazo de 20 semanas (la muerte del feto).

strained foods/alimentos licuados. Alimento sólido procesado para que este suave y aguado.

stranger anxiety/ansiedad por un extraño. Un miedo, usualmente expresado llorando, de la gente desconocida.

subjective/subjetivo. Usar los sentimientos y opiniones personales, en vez de los hechos, para juzgar o describir las cosas.

surrogate/substituta. Una substituta.

symbolic thinking/pensamiento simbólico. El uso de de palabras y números para representar ideas.

synthetic fibers/fibras sintéticas. Fibras hechas de químicos en vez de recursos naturales.

T

temper tantrums/rabietas o pataletas. Incidentes en los cuales los niños desatan su cólera o frustración gritando, llorando, pateando, golpeando, y algunas veces hasta dejando de respirar momentáneamente.

temperament/temperamento. La manera o estilo de reaccionar hacia el mundo y hacia los demás.

therapist/terapista. Un profesional entrenado para ayudar a que la gente lidie y resuelva sus problemas emocionales.

time-out/tiempo de descanso o interrupción. Un período corto de tiempo aparte de los demás o del centro de una actividad.

toddlers/niños pequeños o que empiezan a caminar. Niños de la edad de cuando empiezan a caminar, como de 12 meses, hasta la edad de tres años.

training pants/calzones o calzoncillos de entrenamiento. Calzones o calzoncillos pesados y que absorben (usados para entrenar a un niño(a) a usar el inodoro).

transitions/trancisiones. Períodos durante los cuales los niños pasan de una actividad planeada a la siguiente.

trial-and-error learning/aprendizaje de prueba y error. Aprendizaje en el cual un niño(a) prueba varias soluciones antes de encontrar lo que funciona bien.

U

ultrasound/ultrasonido. Una técnica que usa ondas de sonido para crear una imagen de video de un bebé aún no nacido para chequear si tiene problemas de salud específicos.

umbilical cord/cordón umbilical. Un tubo largo o cordón que conecta el embrión a la placenta y a través del cual los nutrimientos y el oxígeno son transportados al bebé.

uterus/útero. El órgano en el cuerpo de una mujer en el cual se desarrolla un bebé durante el embarazo.

V

vaccine/vacuna. Una dosis pequeña de patógenos debilitados que es inyectada al cuerpo, usualmente, para que el cuerpo puede hacerse resistente y evitar contraer cierta enfermedad.

values/valores. Los principios que una persona considera importantes, y que usa para guiar su vida.

vocabulary/vocabulario. El número de palabras que una persona usa.

Y-Z

weaning/ablactación o destete. El cambio de beber de un biberón o el pecho de la madre a beber de una taza o vaso.

zygote/cigoto. Una óvulo fertilizado.

Credits

Interior Design: William Seabright & Associates
Cover Photography: Robert F. Kusel
American Red Cross, 148
Arnold & Brown, 39, 52, 77, 78, 108, 122, 126, 195, 363
Jim Ballard, 19, 25, 40, 41, 65, 94, 134, 177, 194, 238, 266, 292, 302, 320, 324, 331, 352, 353, 360, 365, 390, 391, 396, 398, 414, 415, 417, 421, 427, 436, 444, 450, 461, 462, 464, 470, 507, 517, 542, 548, 565, 572
Bassett Furniture Industries, Inc., 174
Roger B. Bean, 7, 18, 27, 33, 49, 66, 69, 87, 104, 138, 142, 144, 150, 151, 158, 167, 169, 170, 173, 177, 185, 188, 201, 206, 210, 212, 213, 217, 218, 311, 329, 370, 384, 385, 388, 460, 464, 475, 486, 516, 521
Marshal Berman Photography/Design Office, 21, 27, 29, 31, 32, 42, 46, 50, 51, 53, 61, 64, 68, 69, 70, 72, 73, 74, 75, 76, 81, 82, 84, 86, 95, 96, 98, 101, 107, 464, 487, 489, 491, 497, 498, 503, 508, 520, 525, 528, 530, 533, 536, 537, 543, 545, 547, 549, 551, 556, 558, 559, 560, 562, 564, 573, 579, 580, 585
Keith Berry, 19, 63, 143, 148, 157, 159, 162, 171, 178, 179, 183, 207, 285, 350, 355, 432, 563
Robert Brisbane, 422
A Child's World/Roger B. Bean, 297, 401
Pete Christie, 321, 335
© Ronald H. Cohn/The Gorilla Foundation, 278
Gail Denham, 214, 399
Laima Druskis, 345
Friendship House/Roger B. Bean, 418
Tim Fuller Photography/Morgan-Cain & Associates, 39, 40, 54, 102, 103, 490, 497, 501, 510, 511, 512, 517, 518, 519, 574, 577, 582, 583
James Gaffney, 206
Bob Gangloff, 117, 118, 119, 120, 122, 137, 195, 196, 197, 198, 199
Ann Garvin, 150, 161, 280, 284, 286, 340, 343, 351, 368, 386, 387, 392, 393, 401, 426, 449, 584, 596
Grand Illusions, 41
Greater Peoria Family YMCA- Child Care Center/Roger B. Bean, 299, 321, 553
Steve Greiner, 450, 453, 478, 479
Hasbro/Playschool, 354
Linda K. Henson, 168, 208, 218, 298, 299, 300, 326, 330, 332, 336, 339, 341, 353, 354, 356, 360, 379, 417, 423, 424, 437, 440, 446, 524
Impact Communications, 163
Johnson & Johnson, 228
Robert F. Kusel, 1, 2, 5, 6, 7, 8, 9, 14-15, 16, 36, 58, 92, 112-113, 114, 154, 192, 224-225, 226, 264, 290, 316-317, 318, 348, 382, 410-411, 412, 434, 458, 482-483, 484, 514, 540, 570
LeLeche League International/D. C. Arendt, 172
McGraw YMCA Evanston, IL?/Mishima, 29
March of Dimes, 131, 139, 578
Mead Johnson Nutritional Group, 80, 116, 124, 130, 182, 203, 211, 216, 344
The Methodist Medical Center of Illinois, 187
Ted Mishima, 6, 8, 22, 23, 24, 38, 45, 47, 55, 62, 67, 79, 83, 97, 100, 151, 156, 160, 161, 247, 255, 272, 276, 325, 356, 362, 367, 371, 372, 439, 448, 452, 465, 473, 496, 509, 527, 531, 532

Chicago Academy for the Arts/Mishima, 105
Murray Language Academy/Mishima, 31, 415, 439, 581
The Child Development Center of the New City
    Y.M.C.A./Mishima, 375, 425, 466
Cristen Nestor Photographers, 367
Leonard Nilsson, Time/Life, 121
PALS Preschool & Kindergarten/Roger B. Bean, 28, 30, 64, 109, 397, 447
Vicki Pedesky, 495
Pegco, 304
PhotoTake, 140
Photo Researchers, Inc.
    Petit Format/Nestle/Science Source, 121
    Porterfield-Chickering, 127
    Will & Deni McIntyre, 159
    Nancy Durrell McKenna, 205
    Lawrence Migdale, 159, 204
    Hank Morgan, Science Source, 208
    Larry Mulvehill, 131
Post Saturday Evening/PhotoTake NYC, 199
Steven Prochnow, 11
Proctor Hospitol New Horizons Employee Child Care
    Center/Roger B. Bean, 175
Liz Purcell, 118, 119, 125, 253, 293
Research Plus, 88
SID's Alliance, Randall Sutter, 215
St. Francis Medical Center, 172
Jeff Stoecker, 557
Linda Sullivan, 20, 26, 44, 71, 88, 106, 128, 145, 171, 180, 186, 200, 209, 257, 258, 270, 280, 306, 309, 322, 337, 338, 355, 368, 394, 400, 419, 428, 443, 446, 449, 467, 473, 477, 487, 488, 500, 506, 510, 520, 522, 534, 552, 566, 576, 580
Superstock, 406
Thomas Jefferson School/Roger B. Bean, 132, 523
Texas Highways, 555
Troll Associates, Inc., 137
USDA, 164
Mary Vogel, 282
WestLight, Julie Houck, 89
Dana C. White, Dana White Productions, 20, 33, 71, 72, 85, 127, 145, 166, 180, 184, 186, 209, 229, 230, 231, 233, 235, 236, 237, 239, 240, 241, 242, 244, 248, 249, 250, 251, 252, 254, 257, 258, 260, 261, 267, 268, 269, 270, 273, 274, 275, 277, 278, 279, 281, 282, 283, 284, 287, 294, 301, 303, 305, 306, 307, 308, 309, 310, 312, 313, 322, 323, 324, 337, 328, 333, 334, 351, 355, 357, 358, 359, 364, 365, 366, 372, 373, 374, 376, 378, 379, 385, 389, 391, 394, 395, 403, 404, 407, 416, 419, 428, 430, 438, 442, 443, 445, 454, 455, 461, 462, 468, 469, 471, 474, 476, 477, 478, 479, 488, 510, 522, 529, 534, 535, 552, 560, 561, 575, 576
Gloria Olsen Williams, 345, 441
Nancy Wood, 125, 220, 221, 315
Duane R. Zehr, 188, 189, 295, 296, 361, 451

Poetry Acknowledgments

"Some Things Don't Make Any Sense At All" by Judith Viorst from IF I WERE IN CHARGE OF THE WORLD AND OTHER WORRIES. Copyright © 1981 by Judith Viorst. Reprinted with permission of Atheneum Publishers, an imprint of Macmillan Publishing Company.

"Thinking About Baby" by Anonymous from A LITTLE BOOK ABOUT BABY. Copyright © 1981 by C. R. Gibson, Norwalk, CT. Used by permission. All rights reserved.

"Everybody Says" by Dorothy Aldis reprinted by permission of G. P. Putnam's Sons from EVERY-THING AND ANYTHING by Dorothy Aldis. Copyright © 1925-1927, copyright renewed 1953-1955 by Dorothy Aldis.

"The End" from NOW WE ARE SIX by A. A. Milne. Copyright 1927 by E.P. Dutton, renewed © 1955 by A. A. Milne. Used by permission of Dutton Children's Books, a division of Penguin Books USA Inc.

"The Biggest Problem" by Don Haynie, from FREE TO BE…A FAMILY by Marlo Thomas & Friends. Copyright © 1987 by Free to Be Foundation, Inc. Used by permission of Bantam Books, a division of Bantam Doubleday Dell Publishing Group, Inc.

Special thanks to the following individuals, schools, businesses, and organizations for their assistance with photographs in this book. **In Peoria, Illinois:** Friendship House, Greater Peoria Family YMCA Childcare Center, PALS Preschool & Kindergarten, Rogy's Gingerbread House, St. Andrew's Day Care Center, St. Francis Medical Center, St. Francis Woods. **In Bloomington/Normal, Illinois:** Mom & Me, Ryan Pharmacy. **In Chicago, Illinois:** Murray Language Academy. **In Oakpark, Illinois:** West Suburban Hospital. **In Southern California:** Lara Belmonte, The Final Frontier, Mt. Olive Pre-School, Santa Monica High School SAPID Program, Consuela Perez, Richland Avenue Children's Center, Jim & Beth Strang, Venice Family Clinic, Westside Women's Health Clinic, Windward School. **In Tuscon, Arizona:** Carondelet, Casita Maria; Carondelet St. Mary's Hospital, Pediatrics Unit; Cerebral Palsy Foundation.

Models and fictional names have been used to portray characters in stories and examples in this text.

Index